FIELD GUIDE TO
NORTH AMERICAN TREES

BY THOMAS S. ELIAS

Drawings by
Ruth T. Brunstetter
Charles Edward Faxon
Mary W. Gill

Cartography by
Delos D. Rowe Associates

Grolier Book Clubs Inc.
Danbury, Connecticut

DEDICATION

To my parents

The publisher is grateful to John T. Sargent for permission to reprint many drawings from *Manual of the Trees of North America*, second edition.

Published by

Grolier Book Clubs Inc.
Sherman Turnpike
Danbury, CT 06816

Produced by Soderstrom Publishing Group Inc.

Library of Congress Cataloging-in-Publication Data

Elias, Thomas S.
  Field guide to North American trees.

  Originally published under title: The complete trees
of North America.
  Includes index.
  1. Trees — North America — Identification.   I. Title.
QK110.E43   1988   582.16097   88-12487
ISBN 1-55654-049-3

Manufactured in the United States of America

Contents

iv / *Contents*

Preface to the Second Edition

I am delighted to see this monumental work going into its second edition. To better convey the book's value as an identification tool, we have altered the book's title from the first edition's *Complete Trees of North America* to the present *Field Guide to North American Trees*. Although still offering the full 948 pages of the original edition, this edition is printed on special paper that reduces the book's former bulk and weight. And the attractive new cover is coated for durability in the field. In addition, I've made some text corrections, and the printer has rephotographed many of the drawings for better reproduction.

Although I have studied trees throughout the world, I am continually impressed with our North American trees. I am thinking now of the stately white pine stands in the Adirondacks and the larch and fir stands in Newfoundland bogs. Of the magnolias and silver bells of the Appalachians. Of the evergreen oaks of the Gulf Coast, warm breezes moving through their draped Spanish moss. Of the bald cypress trees in the old oxbow lake near my hometown in southern Illinois — their bended root "knees" lending an almost eerie beauty.

My first trip to the Rocky Mountains introduced me to the world of ponderosa and jeffery pines and the quaking aspen. But it was the enormously diverse evergreen forests of the Pacific Northwest that lifted my life-long love for trees to new heights. There I stood speechless at the bases of the world's tallest trees — California's coastal redwoods. That speechlessness returned as I hiked among the giant sequoias of California's Sierra Nevada. More recently, I walked among some of the world's oldest trees, the 3,000- to 5,000-year-old bristlecone pines in the White Mountains of eastern California. Standing among those ancient gnarled sentinels, I felt a new reverence for trees and a clearer understanding of man's responsibility to protect them.

For help with the preparation of the first edition of this book, I wish to thank Nancy Cassell; Karin Limburg; Willard Payne; Jay McAninch; John Popenoe; Jane Bock; and my wife Barbara and sons Stephen and Brian. Special thanks goes to Neil Soderstrom, who stuck by me during the preparation of this work, first as editor and then as friend. He worked closely with me through all stages of the first edition and this revision.

The majority of the drawings, done by Charles Edward Faxon, are from the 1905 edition of *Manual of the Trees of North America* by Charles Sargent. Additional drawings by Faxon and Mary W. Gill are here reprinted from the 1922 edition of the Sargent book with permission of John T. Sargent. Several hundred new drawings are by the outstanding botanical illustrator Ruth Brunstetter.

The maps are based largely on the *Atlas of United States Trees*, 1971–1979, published by the U.S. Forest Service.

Finally, I express gratitude for the combined libraries and herbarium of the New York Botanical Garden — among the finest botanical resources in the world. As well, the library and combined herbaria at the Rancho Santa Ana Botanic Garden in Claremont, California, where I am now Director, are outstanding resources for any student of western North American botany. The staffs and students at these gardens have contributed significantly to my knowledge and appreciation of trees.

Thomas S. Elias

THIS BOOK
AND NORTH
AMERICAN TREES

This book is designed to help you quickly and confidently identify any of the over 750 North American trees. These include the 652 native trees occurring north of Mexico, as well as over 100 commonly encountered trees introduced from other countries. Of these introduced trees, most are propagated by man, although many have naturalized, reproducing on their own.

Besides serving for tree identification, this book can add to your appreciation of trees and tree groups you may already be acquainted with. There is information on ranges, favored terrain, and types of trees that often grow in association. I have also noted the ways that the various trees function in their environments. In this regard, you will find the vital factors on seed production, soil types, propagation, and interrelationships with wildlife. I have also mentioned historical and modern commercial uses for individual species as well as many other interesting sidelights.

Whenever useful, I have eliminated technical terms by substituting descriptive phrases and words more familiar to the nonspecialist. For example, the technical phrase "coriaceous, pinnately compound leaves" is rendered here simply as "leathery, feather-like leaves."

How this book is organized. Whenever possible, I have placed closely related trees and groups of trees in an arrangement that reflects their natural relationships. Taxonomists, scientists who specialize in naming, describing, and classifying organisms, have developed convenient categories for the approximately 750,000 different kinds of plants in the world. The two largest categories used here are the conifers (gymnosperms) and the flowering plants (angiosperms). The flowering plants are then subdivided into two main groups that include the hardwoods (dicots) and the palms and yuccas (monocots). The conifers are treated first in this book because they are less specialized and evolved before the flowering plants. Within the flowering plants, the palms and yuccas are generally regarded as being highly specialized and of more recent origin than the hardwoods. The hardwoods, containing the greatest numbers of trees, are arranged here with the less specialized and most primitive groups first.

Tree Names. Both the common name and scientific name are given for each species of tree. An example from the book is shown below:

SCIENTIFIC NAME

COMMON NAME

genus   species   author

Slippery Elm

Ulmus rubra Muhl.

(synonym: *U. fulva Michx.*)

The slippery elm, a medium-size tree, is common in lowland areas from southern Ontario to northwestern Florida. It usually is found from 50–600 m (164–1,970 ft) in elevation on floodplains and flats, along streams and rivers, and on low hillsides.

Common names are useful, but they vary from country to country and even from one North American region to another. To add to the disadvantage of using only common names, several species of trees may be known by the same common name. In most cases, I have used the common names employed by the U.S. Forest Service, since these are the most widely recognized. However, you would be wise to confirm scientific names when consulting other tree books or when talking with people from other regions.

The scientific name, in Latin, is important because it is the universally accepted name. Scientific names for trees, and all other plants and animals, adhere to a binomial (two-word) system. The first word designates the genus, a group of closely related species. The second word is the species. A species is a group or groups of individuals that are similar in appearance and can freely interbreed. Hybrids between plant species do occur.

The scientific name of slippery elm is *Ulmus rubra* Muhl. All true elms belong to the genus *Ulmus*. We distinguish the different kinds of elms by the second name, or species. For example, the American elm is *Ulmus americana*, the September elm is *Ulmus serotina*, the cedar elm, *Ulmus crassifolia*, and so on. The scientific name is always italicized in printed works. The name of a genus always begins with a capital letter—the species name with a small letter.

Each scientific name is followed by a person's name, sometimes abbreviated. This tells you who named the plant. The slippery elm, *Ulmus rubra* Muhl., was named by the botanist Gotthill Muhlenberg. Muhlenberg named many North American plants in the late 1700s and early 1800s. Occasionally, there will be a second scientific name given in parentheses, placed under the first name, and noted in this book as a synonym. The synonym in parentheses in our example, *Ulmus fulva* Michx., was once used for part or all of the slippery elm trees, but that name is no longer correct. Older tree identification guides will use *Ulmus fulva* for the scientific name. Sometimes a tree species with a wide distribution was described by a botanist looking at populations at one end of its range and then described a second time by another botanist from specimens at the other end of its range, not realizing that the two were the same. Whenever this duplication is discovered, the botanist first to describe correctly and publish the name and description of the plant has priority over the second botanist. Synonyms are also generated by people failing to conform to a set of international rules for naming and describing new species of plants.

The species is the basic unit of classification, although sometimes I have noted subspecies, varieties, and forms when significant. There are also categories above the species and genus level. A genus or groups of related genera, genera sharing several important characteristics, are placed in one family. For example, the elms (*Ulmus*), hackberries (*Celtis*), nettle trees (*Trema*), water elm (*Planera*), plus 11 related but non-North American genera comprise the elm family, Ulmaceae. Family names always end in "aceae" with only a few exceptions such as Leguminosae, the bean family, and Compositae, the daisy family, and they are not italicized in print.

How to Identify Trees

Tree identification requires observation and patience. First, collect as much information about the tree as you can. Note the size and shape of the tree, the kind of bark, and details of the twigs. Next observe how the leaves are arranged on the twig; examine several leaves to determine size, shape, color, and degree of hairiness. A single leaf can be misleading. Look carefully for flowers, for on many trees they are small and inconspicuous and sometimes are produced in spring before the leaves have developed fully. If you don't see flowers or fruits on the lower branches, look at the upper branches. Most trees have flowers and fruits on only the uppermost branches. If you don't see any fruits, look on the ground directly beneath the tree. Once you have looked the tree over carefully and have samples in hand, you are ready to proceed with the identification process.

Keys. Throughout this book, you will find keys that can help you determine the identity of any tree. A key is simply an outline that lets you choose between contrasting pairs of features. Making these choices, you actually zero in closer and closer to the characters of the sample in hand and eliminate all others. After making your selections in the series of choices, you will come to a final pair of contrasting choices — one of these naming the sample in hand. Below is a key sample excerpted from the pines.

A. Leaves in clusters of 5; fruits are many-scaled, usually elongated cones.

   1. Cones long-stalked; cone scales thin, flexible, without a spine on the face.

      a. Leaves green, without white bands on the back; cones 10–28 cm (4–11 in) long.

         (1) Leaves slender, flexible, soft to touch; trees of eastern North America
                White pine, p. 37
         (2) Leaves stout, hard, not soft to touch; trees of western North America
              Western white pine, p. 38

      b. Leaves green with conspicuous silvery, narrow bands running lengthwise on the back; cones 27–46 cm (10.6–18 in) long
                Sugar pine, p. 39

   2. Cones short-stalked; cone scales thick, stout, occasionally armed on the face with a short spine.

Western White Pine

Sugar Pine

The keys running through the body of the book are considered summer keys because they show hardwoods and the few deciduous conifers in leaf. Yet most of these summer keys also show flowers occurring from spring through autumn. So these summer keys are useful throughout most of the year—even in winter if some dry leaves still cling to otherwise bare branches. There is also an extensive winter key at the back of the book designed for use when deciduous branches are bare. This winter key covers the important deciduous hardwood genera and the most significant species.

In using the keys, if you have no idea which of the three major groups a specimen belongs to—(1) conifers, (2) hardwoods, (3) yuccas and palms—start with the key on page 26. This will lead you to the appropriate major group. Once there, you will find a key to families which will lead you to the appropriate key to genera and finally to a key to the species in the correct genus. You will soon become familiar with this identification system, enough to skip preliminary keys and turn directly to the appropriate family section before zeroing in on the species.

Illustrations. To aid you in the identification process, you will find over 2,000 labeled illustrations. The more often you use the illustrations on your own, the easier it will be to recognize a family or genus. Then with minimal effort, you can determine the exact species. In fact, after studying the illustrations on trees common in your area, you will often be able to recognize many trees at a distance.

Trees and Their Parts

Trees are woody plants that usually grow to at least 5 m (16 ft) tall and have a single trunk. A shrub, by contrast, is typically a multiple-stemmed woody plant with more than one dominant stem, and shrubs are normally less than 5 m (16 ft) tall. Most woody plants can be identified easily as either a tree or a shrub. Yet some species may have mature members that are shrubby; whereas other members of the same species are clearly tree-like. This book includes those shrubs that occasionally reach tree size.

The tall, unbranched Florida royal palm, the narrow, conical black spruce, and the many-branched, wide-spreading live oak are 3 examples of the diverse shapes and sizes North American trees assume. The basic shape, size, and age are limited by the genetic makeup of each species. But this can be controlled or modified by environmental and physiological conditions. For example, the Engelmann spruce of the Rocky Mountains will grow to 35 m (115 ft) high at 1,800 m (5,900 ft) elevation but usually is only a shrub at tree line, near 3,400 m (11,100 ft).

The shape or form of a tree is determined by the manner in which the terminal shoot (or leader) grows and the formation and growth of lateral buds and branches. Normally, the terminal shoot is more dominant than the lateral buds and branches because it controls the concentrations of growth hormones carried to them. Some trees have strongly dominant terminal shoots, while others show less dominant ones. As a result, the lateral branch of oaks and hickories often will grow as rapidly as the terminal shoot, giving rise to a spreading crown. But in the black spruce, the narrow conical shape results from the strong dominance of the terminal shoot.

Not all North American trees have lateral buds and the capacity to produce branches. Palms usually have a single large terminal bud which produces an unbranched stem topped with big leaves. If this terminal bud is damaged or destroyed by disease, insects, or freezing weather, the entire tree usually dies.

Among the many factors influencing tree growth, water is the most important. Even the slightest difference in moisture content between a mountain slope and an adjacent

Tree Shapes

Black spruce Western redcedar Poplar White spruce Bristlecone pine

Coconut palm Red pine Shagbark hickory Birch Dogwood

Cottonwood Elm White oak

ravine may determine the presence or absence of a tree species. The amount of light and the extent of competition with other plants are also major factors affecting growth and, especially, the establishment of young trees. Both daytime and nighttime temperatures influence the rate of growth.

Trees are long-lived plants, with maximum ages ranging from 40 or 50 years for some smaller deciduous trees of the East to the more than 3,000-year-old bristlecone pines of the high mountains of the West. Yet the life spans vary among individuals in each species. Some of the longest living trees are listed in the accompanying table. Other trees, perhaps more familiar to most people, such as hickories, and many oaks and beeches live 200 to 300 years. Yet they are too short-lived to qualify for inclusion in the list of longest lived trees.

Some of the Oldest Living Species of Trees in North America

	Approximate oldest age	Average height	
	Years	Meters	(Feet)
Great Basin Bristlecone Pine	3,000–4,000	5–15	(16–50)
Giant Sequoia	2,000–3,000	70–100	(230–360)
Rocky Mountain Bristlecone Pine	1,500–2,000	5–15	(16–50)
Coastal Redwood	1,000–1,500	90–110	(295–360)
Western Redcedar	1,000+	50–60	(165–200)
Alaskan Cedar	1,000+	30–40	(100–130)
Sitka Spruce	800+	70–75	(230–250)
Douglas Fir	750+	70–80	(230–265)
Western Larch	700+	50–55	(165–180)
Ponderosa Pine	600+	35–50	(115–165)
Engelmann Spruce	500–600	45–50	(150–165)
Incense Cedar	500+	40–45	(130–150)
Port Orford Cedar	500+	55–60	(180–200)
Oregon White Oak	500+	15–25	(50–85)
White Oak	500+	25–35	(85–115)
Eastern Hemlock	500–600	30–35	(100–115)
Western Hemlock	500+	40–50	(130–165)
Blue Spruce	400–500	35–40	(115–130)

Roots. The root system of a tree serves to anchor the tree, to absorb water and nutrients, and, in many trees, to store food reserves. The larger, more conspicuous roots are the primary anchoring roots, while the very small roots and their microscopic root hairs are the water- and nutrient-absorbing structures. Oaks, hickories, and walnuts are some of the trees in which the root system usually consists of a large, deeply penetrating taproot with a series of smaller, lateral roots. This helps explain why these trees are able to withstand strong winds without being toppled, and why they can grow in drier soils and withstand droughts better than shallow-rooted trees.

Maples, hemlocks, and many other species do not develop a single, large, deep taproot but instead have a series of nearly equal-size roots that spread away from the base of the trunk. The spreading root system of most maples or hemlocks is contained in the top 60 cm (25 in) of soil. These trees cannot withstand strong winds as well as taprooted trees, and are also more susceptible to droughts. Often the much-branched root system extends beyond the spread of the branches above ground. Here the root system will enlarge and extend into areas with favorable water levels.

Roots, like the above-ground parts of a tree, need oxygen to survive. When the ground immediately surrounding a tree becomes compacted or flooded, the amount of oxygen available to the roots may be seriously reduced, causing the death of many roots and ultimately the death of the tree. This is why walkways and roads too near a tree can kill it.

Trunk. Tree trunks range in appearance from the tall straight stem of the Douglas fir to the gnarled and twisted trunk of a bristlecone pine. The trunk supports the crown of leafy branches, and serves to transport water and nutrients from the roots to the crown, as well as from the crown to the root system.

The greatest bulk of the tree trunk is made up of dead cells, although many of these cells still have important functions. The only substantial number of living cells are found just inside the protective layer of bark. Here is a single layer of cells called *cork cambium* which produced the bark, followed by a narrow band of cells called *phloem*, (pronounced FLOW-em) that carries food from the leaves to the rest of the tree. Just inside the band of phloem cells is another cambium. This one produces new phloem cells to the outside and new xylem or wood cells to the inside. This cambial layer is important because it is responsible for wood production and the increase in diameter of the trunk and branches. Inside of that, and comprising 90 percent or more of the trunk, is a series of concentric rings of wood cells called the xylem (pronounced ZIE-lem). Most of these cells are dead at maturity and serve to transport the water and nutrients from the roots to the leaves. The xylem, or wood as it is more commonly known, usually consists of an outer lighter-colored series of rings known as the sapwood. In the center portion of the trunk, the wood is typically darker, due to the filling of the walls of the xylem cells with opaque waste deposits. This darker wood is the heartwood.

Trunk Cross Section

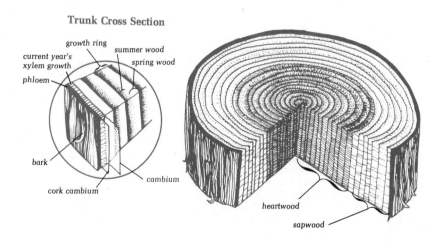

growth ring
current year's xylem growth
summer wood
spring wood
phloem
bark
cork cambium
cambium
heartwood
sapwood

One traditional way of killing a tree is to girdle it. This involves scraping away a complete band of bark around the tree, thereby removing the thin layer of phloem cells that transport food to the roots. As a result, the roots begin to die, followed by the dying of the rest of the tree. Because the tree has a store of food, death may take several months or even years, depending upon the species and the thoroughness of the girdling.

In the temperate climates of North America, a concentric ring of wood is usually produced each year. These growth rings can be used to accurately determine the age of a tree. Occasionally, unusual conditions can interfere with normal growth, producing a double ring. Normally, the springwood cells are larger, less dense, and lighter in color than summerwood cells. The annual growth ring then becomes the contrasting band of small summerwood cells against the larger springwood cells.

Bark. Bark is a multiple layer of cells forming the outer covering of the trunk, branches, and branchlets. It includes thick protective layers of waxy, waterproof cork cells that have the primary function of preventing or deterring entry of disease agents and insects — and preventing the loss of water from the living tissue under the outer layers of bark. Also in the dead layers of bark are bands of dead phloem produced in earlier years. Although new cork cells are produced in the same manner in all trees, the thickness and pattern of the bark are remarkably varied and are often so characteristic that some species can be identified by their bark alone.

American beech trees have thin smooth bark which seldom exceeds 1 cm (0.4 in) in thickness on mature trees when the trunk is more than 60 cm (2 ft) in diameter. Many birches also have a thin bark, but it is marked with numerous, conspicuous, thin pores (lenticels) for gas exchange that are arranged across the trunk. Thin-barked trees are more susceptible to injury by fire than thick-barked trees. The opposite extreme is seen in the giant sequoias of the Sierra Nevada in California. Their deeply furrowed or fissured bark can reach 60 cm (2 ft) in thickness. Forest fires sweeping through a grove of giant sequoias leave the trees unharmed. Also they promote seed germination, and nutrients in the ashes promote the growth of young sequoias.

Each tree species has its own characteristic bark. The bark may be smooth or rough with a series of furrows and ridges. The furrows range from shallow to deep and usually run lengthwise along the trunk, but in some species they can be oblique, or even irregular, as seen in the black locust. Cross furrows also occur, creating a rough checkered bark, as is typical of the tulip tree and most pines. The ridges are composed of layers of bark that become scaly in many species. These ridges range from completely flattened to rounded ones. In the sycamores and a few other species, large flattened scales are produced that slough off occasionally, giving the bark a blotchy appearance. Long, narrow, flattened scales that bend at the ends outward from the trunk distinguish the shagbark hickory from all other hickories.

Mature trees with thick, rough bark may have had thin smooth bark when young. So you should examine only mature trees when attempting to identify trees by the bark characters described in this book. Yet after comparing mature and young bark on various trees you will soon become adept at identifying barks of varied ages.

Branches and Twigs. The crown, or superstructure, of a tree consists of the branches, branchlets, and leaves. Leaves grow on the tips of branchlets, or twigs, with new leaves and leaf stems produced each year. The twigs also increase in diameter, but at a slower rate than the lengthwise growth at the tip. In winter during the dormant season, the embryonic leaves and tissue that produce new plant cells at a twig tip usually are covered with a series of scales that form the bud. Most buds of temperate trees

Bark Types

Shallow lengthwise furrows and flattened ridges

Silver maple

Eastern white pine

Deep lengthwise furrows and flattened ridges

Port Orford cedar

Tulip tree

Deep regular furrows (angled) and flattened ridges

Ponderosa pine

Irregular furrows and short, flattened, scaly ridges

Jeffrey pine

Deep regular lengthwise furrows and pointed to rounded ridges

Black locust

Shallow irregular furrows and broad, flattened plates

Shagbark hickory

Irregular lengthwise furrows, cross furrows forming checkered pattern

Flowering dogwood

Irregular furrows and flat short ridges

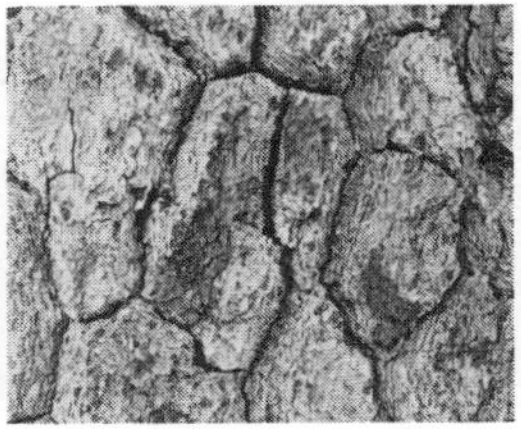

Mountain hemlock

Smooth bark with broad flat plates falling away

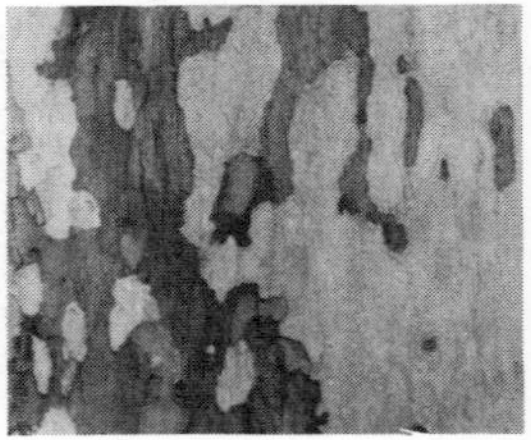

Arizona sycamore

Smooth bark, not peeling

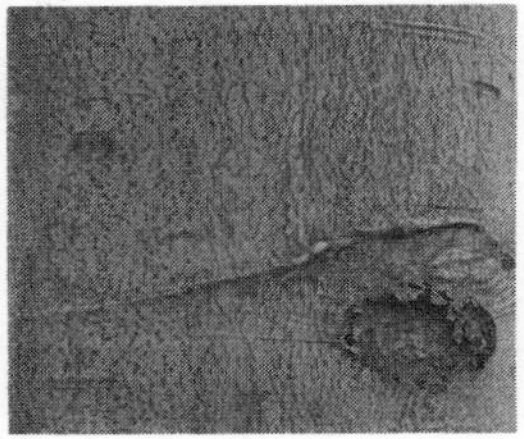

American beech

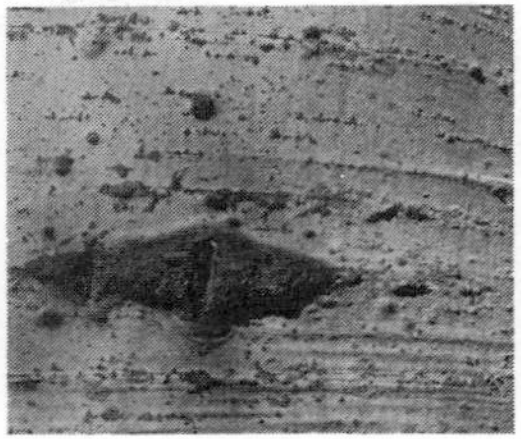

Quaking aspen

Scaly bark with small plates

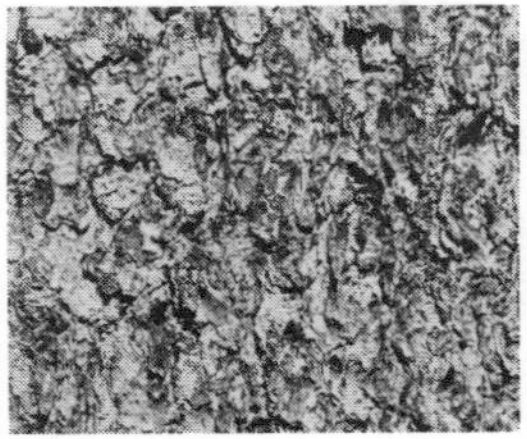

Whitebark pine

Smooth bark, peeling with age

Yellow birch

have tough, waterproof, overlapping scales that protect the tender embryonic tissues from drying out and being injured or destroyed by insects.

In spring when new growth begins, the bud scales fall off, leaving a ring of scars indicating where the scales had been attached. The age of twigs can be determined by starting at the tip and moving back along the stem until the first set of bud scales is encountered. This marks the extent of the previous year's growth. The distance from this set of bud scale scars to the next farther back marks the second year's growth, and so on. Normally, twigs can be aged for 5 to 10 years using this method, but beyond that the scars are obscured by the developing bark.

Leaf scars are left when leaves fall away. The scars may be narrow and slit-like, C-shaped, heart-shaped, or any of a host of other configurations. Each tree species has its own, often distinct, leaf scars which are highly useful for identifying trees in winter. Each leaf scar is marked on its face with 1 to several smaller scars indicating the number and positions of the vascular bundles—the system that transports water and nutrients. The branchlets often are slightly swollen at the point where the leaf or leaves are attached. Just above each leaf scar is a lateral bud that may range from tiny to very

Winter Twigs

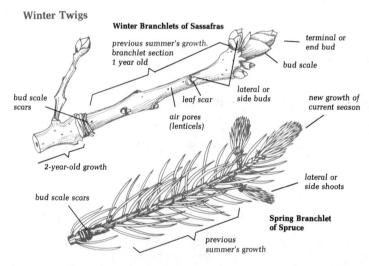

Winter Branchlets of Sassafras

previous summer's growth, branchlet section 1 year old

terminal or end bud

bud scale

bud scale scars

leaf scar

lateral or side buds

new growth of current season

air pores (lenticels)

2-year-old growth

bud scale scars

lateral or side shoots

Spring Branchlet of Spruce

previous summer's growth

conspicuous. The lateral buds form the secondary and succeeding orders of branches. Sometimes you will find lateral flower buds along with buds that will produce branchlets. On certain twigs, you may encounter scars left by the flower stalks.

Often twigs are marked with small, light-colored pores (lenticels). They are responsible for gas exchange between the living tissues in the stems and the air. These pores usually are raised and may give the twigs a roughened appearance. They may be round, elliptical, lens shaped, vertically or horizontally elongated; or they may take on other configurations.

Leaves. Leaves serve primarily to manufacture food. They use energy from sunlight, carbon dioxide from air, and water and nutrients absorbed in the roots to make sugars. A large surface area is needed to carry out this photosynthetic process sufficiently to sustain a large tree. So most leaves are thin, flattened, flexible structures produced in abundance. Leaves are perhaps the most variable organ from one species of tree to an-

Conifer Leaves

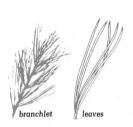

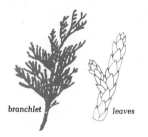

Eastern white pine

Western redcedar

White spruce

Hardwood Leaves

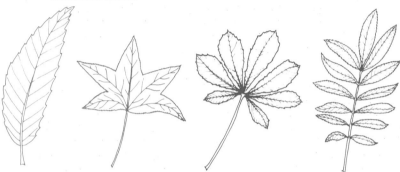

Chestnut oak   **Sweet gum**   **Horsechestnut**   **Pecan**

Leaves of Palms and Yuccas

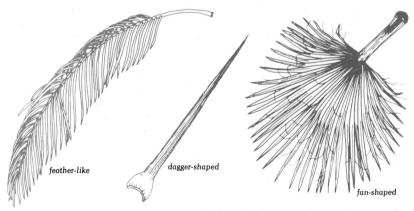

feather-like   *dagger-shaped*   *fan-shaped*

Florida royal palm   **Yucca**   **Washington palm**

other. They range from tiny, scale-like leaves about 1 mm (.05 in) long in the junipers to the enormous feather-like leaves of the Florida royal palm, which reach 4 m (13 ft).

The majority of native North American trees lose their leaves in autumn. These leaves are produced each spring and live for only 1 growing season. Trees losing their leaves in autumn are known as deciduous trees. Other trees, especially the conifers, are clothed in leaves throughout the year and are said to be evergreen. On an evergreen, a particular leaf or set of leaves normally will live from 2 to 5 years before falling. But some trees are exceptions. For example, some of the hardwood trees, such as the bayberries, retain their green leaves until spring and then drop them as the new leaves appear. Still other trees, such as some of the oaks and the American beech, have leaves that turn brown and die in autumn even though many remain on the tree until early spring.

Leaves are produced in a set manner on the branchlets, or twigs. In most tree species the leaves are alternate; that is, there is a single leaf at the point of attachment (node) with the branchlets. The leaves appear to alternate with each other on the twigs. Less common is the opposite leaf arrangement, in which there is a pair of opposing leaves at each node. A few trees have a whorled leaf arrangement with more than 2 leaves present at each node.

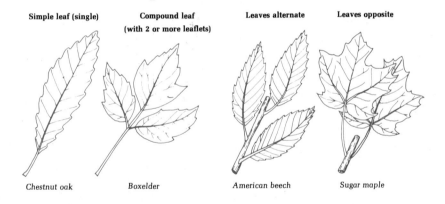

Simple leaf (single)	Compound leaf (with 2 or more leaflets)	Leaves alternate	Leaves opposite
Chestnut oak	*Boxelder*	*American beech*	*Sugar maple*

Each leaf usually is composed of a blade and a supporting leafstalk (petiole). If the blade is all in 1 piece, the leaf is called simple; but, if the leaf is composed of 2 or more separate blades (leaflets) and stalks, then it is called compound.

There is great variety of simple leaves. If the margin of the leaf is smooth and unvaried, the leaf is said to be entire. Often, however, tiny to large coarse teeth are present, so the leaf is said to be toothed. A double row of teeth (double toothed) may be present along the margin, as seen in many elm trees. Other trees have lobed leaves; that is, the blade is divided into lobes by shallow to deep notches, as in the white oak or Oregon white oak. Or a combination of lobes and teeth also occurs, such as in many of the oaks, maples, and sweetgums. Leaves come in a seemingly endless array of shapes. The accompanying drawings show the basic types.

Compound leaves are conveniently divided into 2 basic types: feather-like (pinnate) and hand-like (palmate). Feather-like leaves have a simple axis along which the leaf-

Leaf Margins

entire   finely toothed   toothed   double toothed   wavy margined   deeply lobed

Leaf Tips

notched   broad & notched   long-pointed   tapering   rounded

Leaf Bases

asymmetrical   heart-shaped   squared   rounded   narrow

lets are produced. These feather-like leaves may have a single terminal leaflet (odd pinnately compound) or there may be no terminal leaflet (even pinnately compound). Finally, a rare condition exists, as seen in the Kentucky coffee tree, in which the feather-like leaf is twice or thrice branched to form a bipinnately or tripinnately compound leaf.

Hand-like (palmately compound) leaves have the individual leaflets arising from a central point rather than along an axis. When 3 leaflets are present, as seen in poison ivy, the leaves are commonly referred to as trifoliolate. In horse chestnut trees, there are typically 7 leaflets.

Other characteristics of leaves used in identification include texture and hairiness. Thin, membranous, delicate leaves occur on some trees that grow in warm moist regions of North America. Normally, leaves of North American trees are thicker and somewhat papery in texture. Some trees, especially those growing in more stressful habitats (deserts, semi-deserts, coastal and mountain areas exposed to strong winds) have thick, leathery leaves.

The surface of leaves may be partially or completely covered with hairs. These range from tiny fine hairs, which people often don't notice, to coarse hairs, which can give the leaves a wooly, silky, or rough feel. Many trees have abundant hairs on the young leaves but these leaves become smooth when they reach full size. The lower surface of a leaf often will have hairs, especially near or on the main veins, while the upper surface will be smooth. There are also many types of hairs, with variations, which are noted in the descriptions of tree species throughout this book.

Some North American trees are armed with spines or thorns. These may represent modified leaves or associated leaf parts (stipules) as seen in catclaw acacia, mesquite, or black locust. These spines are usually paired and located on the branchlet at the base of the leafstalks. Large branched spines, that is, modified stems, occur on the branches, branchlets, and even the trunk of the honey locust. Smaller, unbranched spines are present on most species of hawthorns. Other trees armed with unbranched, but usually curved spines (or thorns) include the paloverdes, osage orange, and the gum bumelia. A few trees, especially in the desert Southwest have branchlets which are sharp and spine-like at their tips.

Flowers. All trees have flowers, but many of the flowers go unnoticed because they are small and inconspicuous. Flowers are essential for the production of seeds. In many flowers the reproductive organs are often accompanied by accessory structures such as petals, which do not participate directly in the reproduction process.

Conifer flowers are so different from garden flowers that many people don't think of them as flowers at all. They consist only of the essential reproductive organs enclosed in a cone. The cones are composed of a series of spirally or vertically arranged scales and usually smaller bracts. The scales have reproductive organs that include either male pollen sacs or female ovules that contain the eggs, which are capable of producing seeds. Cones are either male or female. Yet, normally, conifers have both male and female cones on the same tree.

In hardwoods, a typical flower has 4 different kinds of parts: the sepals, petals, stamens, and pistil. The sepals are on the outside near the base of each flower. They are generally green, leaf-like, and may be fused into a cup or tube. In the flowers of palm or yucca trees, there are usually 3 sepals, but in the hardwoods, 4 and 5 sepals are more common.

Petals are the next set of structures inside the sepals. They are usually flattened in shape. In the tulip tree, stewartias, cherries, and others, the petals are large and brightly colored and serve to attract insects and some birds. In many other trees — such as oaks,

Typical Conifer Flowers (Cones)

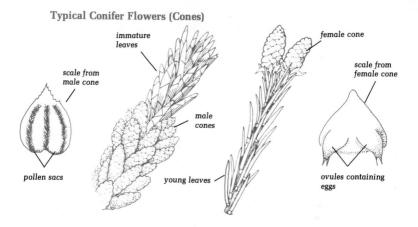

scale from male cone

immature leaves

male cones

female cone

scale from female cone

pollen sacs

young leaves

ovules containing eggs

hickories, and elms—the petals are tiny or even absent. Even though they may aid in promoting reproduction, petals and sepals are considered accessories because they do not participate directly.

Stamens are the male reproductive organs of the flower. Normally there are from 5 to many in every flower. Each usually is composed of a slender stalk with an anther at the tip. An anther contains 1, 2, or 4 pollen sacs in which the pollen grains are produced in great abundance. The stamens may be in a single whorl or in a series of whorls just inside the petals.

The pistil is the female reproductive organ and usually is composed of an ovary, a style, and a stigma. The ovary is an enlarged part at the base which contains the ovules —the seed-producing structures. The style is usually a slender stalk on top of the ovary, while the stigma is an enlarged and specialized part at the tip of the style that receives the pollen. In some flowers only a single pistil is present, as in cherries, while the flowers of other species such as magnolias contain numerous pistils.

The sepals, petals, stamens, and pistil are subject to considerable variation and modification. The majority of tree flowers are bisexual, or perfect, containing both

Bisexual Flower

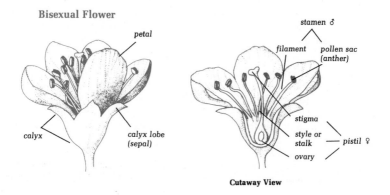

petal

stamen ♂

filament

pollen sac (anther)

calyx

calyx lobe (sepal)

stigma

style or stalk

ovary

pistil ♀

Cutaway View

male (stamens) and female (pistil) reproductive structures. Flowers containing only male or female organs are unisexual, or imperfect, flowers. Trees usually have both sexes present, either as bisexual flowers or as both male and female unisexual flowers. Occasionally, you may encounter trees such as hollies, ginkgos, and date palms which have only male or female flowers. These trees are then said to be male or female. Male trees produce only pollen and are incapable of producing seeds. Female trees can produce seeds but only with pollen from nearby male trees. It is the fusion of the genetic material in the pollen with that of the eggs that results in the development of an embryo tree within the seed.

Flowers commonly are produced on the new growth of the season. In many cases, they occur at the tips of the shoots and are called *terminal*. More frequently though, the flowers develop from lateral buds at the junction of the leaves and the branchlets. The flowers are then called *axillary*. A few species of trees have a flowering pattern known as ramiflory, literally translated "branch flowers." As seen in redbuds, the flowers are produced on the older branchlets, branches, or even with a few on the upper part of the trunk.

In tulip trees, magnolias, and other trees, the flowers are produced singly in a terminal or axillary position. But most tree flowers are small and occur in few to many-flowered clusters (inflorescences). There are technical names for each of the diverse types and variations. But these can be confusing to nonspecialists. The following simple descriptions of the major types serve the purpose of this book.

A *spike* is a simple arrangement in which the unstalked or only slightly stalked flowers occur laterally along an elongated, unbranched axis. This is not common among North American trees, but it occurs on the southwestern mesquite.

A *raceme* is more common than a spike and is identical to it except that each flower has a short to long stalk. Trees producing racemes include pin and black cherries, leatherwood, and locust.

A *catkin*, also called ament, is a specialized spike on which the tiny flowers are either male or female, and on which the petals are absent or hardly noticeable. Male flowers of oaks, hickories, alders, and the male and female flowers of willows and birches are produced in catkins.

In some species, the flowers are densely clustered in a round or nearly round *head*. Flowers may be stalked or not. Heads occur on buttonbush, leadtree, and the female flowers of sycamore and sweetgum.

The *panicle* is common. It is usually longer than broad; has a central axis which is branched once, twice, or many times; and bears stalked flowers. Panicles are produced by horsechestnuts and ashes, among many other trees.

A *corymb* is a broad, flat-topped flower cluster with the outermost flowers opening first and progressing inward. Corymbs occur on trees such as hawthorns, crabapples, and wild plums.

Fruits. Fruits enclose the seeds, protect them from predators, and aid in seed dispersal. Fruits develop from flowers. Once the pistil has received the pollen, and fertilization of the eggs occurs, the base of the pistil (the ovary) begins to enlarge and becomes a fruit. Usually the petals and stamens fall away, leaving the developing ovary or immature fruit. Fruits consist of an outer wall that is often produced in 2 or 3 distinct layers. The outer layer forms the skin of the fruit, while the middle layer, or layers, may become thick and fleshy, fibrous, or even hard and bony. These layers enclose the seeds. If the fruit develops from a single pistil within a flower, it is a simple fruit, as in maples or oaks. More than 1 pistil is often present, and several of

Fruit Types

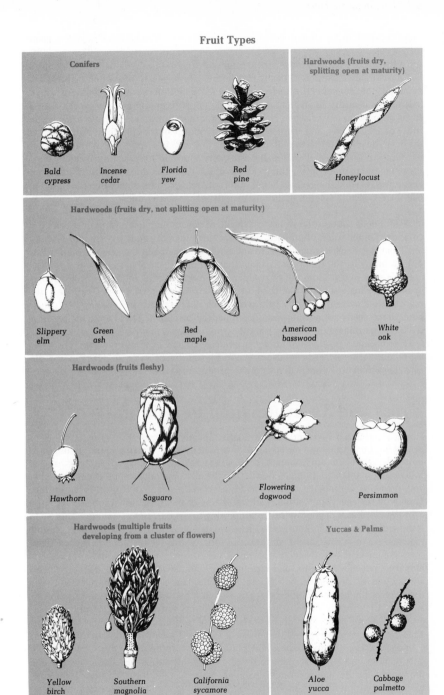

Conifers

Bald cypress | Incense cedar | Florida yew | Red pine

Hardwoods (fruits dry, splitting open at maturity)

Honeylocust

Hardwoods (fruits dry, not splitting open at maturity)

Slippery elm | Green ash | Red maple | American basswood | White oak

Hardwoods (fruits fleshy)

Hawthorn | Saguaro | Flowering dogwood | Persimmon

Hardwoods (multiple fruits developing from a cluster of flowers)

Yellow birch | Southern magnolia | California sycamore

Yuccas & Palms

Aloe yucca | Cabbage palmetto

these may be fertilized and develop into an aggregate fruit, as seen in the magnolias or tulip trees.

Fruits can be divided conveniently into 2 categories—fleshy or dry. Limes, apples, and peaches are examples of fleshy fruits. They are designed to be eaten by birds and mammals that consume the fleshy parts but leave most of the small seeds unharmed. Many trees bear dry fruits. Some of these do not split open to expose or release the seeds but remain closed when ripe. Acorns and hazelnuts are of this type, while the fruits of ashes, elms, and maples represent another variation. In these fruits, part of the ovary develops into a thin, flattened wing that aids in dispersal by wind. Oaks and hazelnuts rely upon small mammals, especially squirrels, to spread the fruits by burying them and then forgetting the locations of some of them. Most dry fruits split open at maturity to shed their seeds. Some fruits split along 1 side, others along 2 sides. Dry fruits are typically smaller and more abundant than fleshy ones.

Seeds. Seeds contain the embryos capable of developing into new plants. A seed is composed of an outer, often hard, coat that surrounds the embryo—the product of a fertilized egg. Food tissue is present and nourishes the plant during germination and until it forms leaves and a root system that can manufacture food.

Seeds vary in size from the tiny, almost microscopic ones produced by rhododendrons to the huge seeds of the coconut. Seeds of most temperate trees require a dormant period, accompanied by cold weather or a dry season, before they will germinate. Some seeds are covered by a thin, papery seed coat. These are usually short-lived and germinate the same season they are shed.

Trees normally produce hundreds, or even thousands, of seeds each year. The greatest number of these seeds are eaten by wildlife and insects or else destroyed by disease. Less than 1 percent will survive to produce new trees.

Trees and Their Relation to Wildlife

North America is a vast land mass primarily covered by conifer or hardwood forests, except for the prairies and desert areas. Trees are the most conspicuous and dominant living element of our environment. Each of the different forest types is a community of interacting plants and animals, partially or wholly dependent upon each other. The very presence, abundance, and health of associated wildlife in a forest is determined largely by the age, composition, and well-being of the trees in that forest.

In the Northeast, a good wildlife-supporting forest consists of a mixed hardwood stand with groups of conifers in the protected valleys or ravines. The conifers provide food and cover during severe winter conditions. Numerous mature, or nearly mature, trees are needed for production of mast (seeds such as acorns and nuts). Oaks, hickories, beeches, walnuts, and hazelnuts are the major hard-mast producing trees; while cherries, dogwoods, hawthorns, and mountain ashes are important soft-mast trees. Associated shrubs and grasses are needed for additional food and cover for the animals. Clearings scattered throughout the forest are needed to permit the best growth of those shrubs and grasses that wildlife uses for food, nesting, and bedding sites. Springs or streams well dispersed in the forest are also essential.

In early spring the expanding buds and the fresh young growth provide food for deer, rabbits, and other browsing animals. During the spring, summer, and early fall, the supply of fruits and seeds sustains many mammals and birds. In the fall, the large trees, often with hollow trunks or limbs, offer nesting sites for bears, raccoons, squirrels, opposums, and many large birds such as owls and woodpeckers.

The production of acorns and nuts comes in fall when summer food sources are disappearing or exhausted for the year. A large crop will attract game birds, deer, and other animals to the drier slopes or ravines containing the oak, hickory, walnut, or beech trees. Mast crops are cyclic, with a large yield followed by 1 to several years of light production. During the years of light or little production, most of the good fruits are eaten by wildlife. Only in the years of heavy production do some of the acorns survive to germinate and produce new trees. These trees then take from 20 to 30 years, depending upon conditions, to reach flowering and fruiting age. The important mast-producing trees are relatively long-lived (200 to 400 years) compared to other hardwoods and need only reproduce themselves once in their 150 to 350 years of fertility in order to maintain their numbers in a forest.

A large oak may produce several thousand acorns in a good year. Some of these acorns will abort due to adverse weather conditions, diseases, or various physiological causes. Several hundred will be partially or wholly destroyed by insect larvae that burrow into the meat of the acorn. The majority will be consumed by wildlife. Squirrels, chipmunks, jays, grouse, and raccoons feed on the ripening acorns still on the trees; while wild turkeys, black bears, whitetail deer, mule deer, blacktail deer, peccaries, and many small rodents eat the fallen acorns. A very small percentage of the acorns will survive in a hidden spot to germinate the following spring, provided weather and soil conditions are suitable, and provided the smaller rodents and insects have overlooked them.

Among birds, the dusky blue grouse illustrates well the interrelationship of a forest

How Conifers Serve Wildlife

	Bark	Twigs	Buds	Leaves	Flowers	Fruits/ Seeds	Cover
High Value							
Pine	M	M	M	B,M,m		b,B,m,M	b,B,m,M
Hemlock	M	M	B,M	b,B,m,M		b,m	b,B,m,M
Cedar		M		M		b,m,	b
Juniper		M		M		b,m	b,B,m,M
Medium Value							
Fir		M	B	B,M		b,m	b,B,m,M
Spruce	m	M		B,M		b,m	b,B,m,M
Douglas Fir	m	M		B,m,M	B	b,B,m	b,B,m,M
Arborvitae, White Cedar		M		M		b	b
Low-Value							
Larch			B	B		b	b
Bald Cypress						B	b

b = small birds   m = small mammals
B = large birds   M = large mammals

How Hardwoods Serve Wildlife

	Bark	Twigs	Buds	Leaves	Flowers	Fruits/Seeds
High Value						
Oak	m	M	b,B	M		b,B,m,M
Hickory						B,m,M
Walnut						m,M
Wild Cherry	m	M	B	M		b,B,m,M
Maple	m	M,B	b,B	M	b	b,B,m
Dogwood	m	M	B	M		b,B,m
Hazelnut		M,m	B	M,m	B	B,m
Serviceberry	m	M,m		M		b,B,m,M
Aspen	m	M	B	M,m	B	
Poplar	m	M	B	M,m	B	
Birch	m	m,M	B	M,m	B	b,B,m
Sumac	m	M		M		b,B,m,M
Willow	m	M,B	b,B,M	M		
Medium Value						
Black Gum		M		M		b,B,m,M
Witch Hazel	m	M		M		B,m
Chestnut		M		M		B,m,M
Holly		M		M		b,B,m
Buckthorn		M		M		b,B,m,M
Mulberry						b,m
Hawthorn	m	M	B	M		b,B,m,M
Hornbeam	m	M	B	M	B	b,B,m
Mountain Ash		M	B	M		b,B,m
Persimmon		M		M		b,B,m,M
Ash		M		M		b,B
Alder	m	M	B	M,m	B	b,B,m
Mesquite	M			m,M		b,B,m,M
Sassafras	M	M		M		b,B,m
Low Value						
Elm		M	b,B,m	M		b,B,m
Magnolia		M		M		b,m
Bayberry						b,m
Osage Orange						b,m
Tulip Tree	m					b,m
Basswood	m	M		M		B,m
Sweetgum	m					b,B,m
Sycamore						b,m
Black Locust				M		B,m

b = small birds   m = small mammals
B = large birds   M = large mammals

and its animals. This grouse is a medium-size forest bird restricted to fir and mixed conifer-and-hardwood forest in the higher mountains of the West, mainly at 2,350–3,350 m (7,700–11,000 ft). The bird depends upon firs and other trees for food and cover. In spring, it descends from the spruce-and-fir forest near timberline to the mixed forest at lower altitudes. Here mating and nesting occur, while the grouse feed on buds, fruits, and seeds of shrubs and herbs, particularly the snowberry, broom grass, groundsel, and vetch. The birds spend the summer and fall in this area, using the trees for roosting. The extent of the fall mast crop of the Gambel oak generally determines whether the dusky blue grouse descend to even lower altitudes to feed on the acorns or whether they ascend. They will feed until the mast crop is largely consumed. Unlike most animals, this grouse moves to higher elevations in late fall and overwinters in the high mountains in the tops of tall fir trees in subalpine forest. During this time, the grouse feed on the buds and leaves of fir, pine, larch, and hemlock. The dense evergreen boughs of the firs provide excellent cover against severe winter conditions.

The Forests of North America

Most of North America is covered by forests. The eastern deciduous forest, the northern coniferous forest, and the western mountain forest are the most extensive in North America. The Pacific coastal forest covers a smaller area than those above but is one of the most valuable. The southeastern coastal plain and subtropical forests are minor elements; yet they possess a fascinating array of trees. The California woodlands are composed of forest types strikingly different from those in the other forests.

Northern Coniferous Forest. This is a broad forest belt lying just south of the tundra and sweeping across Canada from Alaska to Newfoundland and New England. It also extends southward through the higher reaches of the Appalachian Mountains. The climate is typically cold and moist even though the annual precipitation is usually less than 50 cm (20 in) per year. The growing season lasts only 3 to 4 months per year. The most common trees are white spruce and black spruce. In the central and eastern portions of this forest range, balsam fir, tamarack, and jack pine are also common; while in the western and northwestern sections, the alpine fir and lodgepole pine grow in association with the 2 spruces. Although this is clearly an extensive forest of evergreen trees, 3 deciduous trees are common in the central and southeastern portions of the range. These hardy species are the paper birch, quaking aspen, and balsam poplar. Because of the severe climate, poor soils, and limited growing season, many of the trees seldom grow more than 20 m (65 ft) high, but in protected areas or sites with better soils, the trees can be much taller. At high elevations in many parts of the Appalachian Mountains, the forest still is composed primarily of spruce and fir trees, but white spruce is replaced with the red spruce. And in the southern part, Fraser's fir is present instead of the balsam fir.

Pacific Coastal Forest. This coniferous forest is located in an area parallel to the Coast and stretches from southeastern Alaska southward into central California. This

Forests of North America

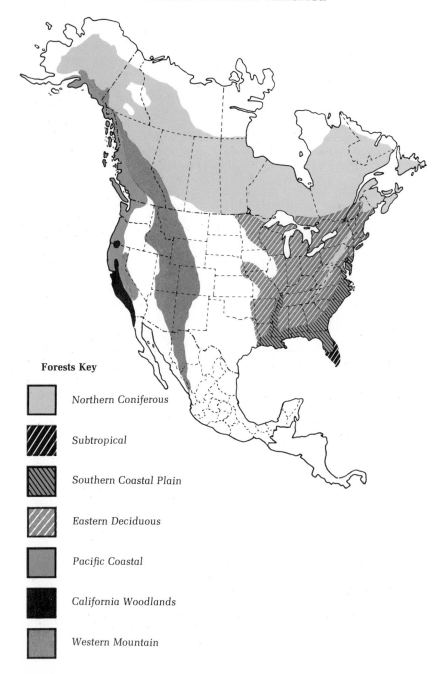

Forests Key

Northern Coniferous

Subtropical

Southern Coastal Plain

Eastern Deciduous

Pacific Coastal

California Woodlands

Western Mountain

region, with its high total precipitation (rain, fog, or snow) and mild winters due to the influence of the warm ocean currents, contains one of the most productive forest stands in the world. Here the amount of living matter, or biomass, produced per hectare (about 2½ acres) is greater than in any other forest in North America. Here are the tallest trees, the most massive trees, and some of the oldest trees in the world.

There are four zones of forest here, based on altitude and proximity to the Coast. In a narrow band along the coastal lowlands, the dominant tree is the sitka spruce, although it becomes less frequent and is replaced eventually by the coastal redwood in southern Oregon and northern California. This zone, which is frequently bathed in low clouds or fog banks, has deep rich soils and the mildest climate. Just inland is an extensive stand of trees dominated by the western hemlock, with western redcedar and Douglas fir also common. Douglas fir is dependent upon fire, and those areas subject to repeated fires are usually nearly pure stands of Douglas fir. At higher elevations of 900–1,500 m (2,900–5,000 ft), cooler weather, and significant winter snow cover, the silver fir becomes the most prevalent large tree. Above this and extending to tree line, the forest community is characterized by the mountain hemlock, and to a lesser extent, the subalpine fir and western white pine. The Pacific coastal forest is rich with species of conifers and hardwoods, but the hardwoods are always a minor component.

Western Mountain Forests. The Rocky Mountains, the major mountain system in western North America, are divided into a series of north-south running ridges. Conifers are the dominant forest trees in this extensive range. Different forest communities develop at different altitudes on the mountains. The basic vegetation zones are the alpine tundra, subalpine, montane, foothills, and mesas. One or more of these zones may be absent on a particular mountain or range, and each of them merges into the next. There is also a rich variety of wild flowers, with many of them restricted to a particular zone.

In Colorado the alpine tundra zone generally occurs at 3,400–4,000 m (11,100–13,100 ft) and is always above tree line. The plants of this zone consist of dwarf willows, numerous deep-rooted, mat-forming, or cushion plants. Below this and at 2,700–3,400 m (8,800 to 11,100 ft) elevation is the subalpine belt. This zone has numerous small- to medium-size narrow trees. Here the most common trees are Engelmann spruce, subalpine fir, and limber pine.

The montane zone, occurring at 2,500–2,700 m (8,200–8,800 ft) elevation, is characterized by lodgepole pine, Engelmann spruce, blue spruce, Douglas fir, and aspen. Ponderosa pine begins to merge with Douglas fir in the foothills zone at 1,800 to 2,500 m (5,900–8,200 ft) elevation. Here scrub oak and mountain mahogany are the characteristic trees. In the lower part of this zone, the ponderosa pines merge with the prairies in the eastern Rockies and with juniper-pinyon scrub forest in the western sections. Below the foothills are the mesas or prairies, which are primarily grasslands. Farther north, in the Canadian Rockies, these zones occur at much lower elevations. In the southern Rockies, these zones occur at higher elevations.

The Sierra Nevada lies in a north-south axis in eastern California and extreme western Nevada. Again, forest belts or zones develop at different altitudes. Alpine tundra is present but is very limited and not as well developed as in the Rockies. The subalpine zone has a forest dominated by the mountain hemlock, alpine larch, subalpine fir, whitebark pine, and foxtail pine. In the middle zone, the Jeffrey pine, red fir, and sometimes sugar pine, are common. In this zone, near 2,000 m (6,500 ft) elevation, the world's largest trees, the giant sequoias, occur. The next, and lowest, zone is that of the ponderosa pine.

California Woodlands. This forest is composed of diverse and complex communities of plants. It extends from northern Baja California through California west of the Sierra Nevada and into southwestern Oregon. Mild winters and warm dry summers, typical of the Mediterranean climate, together with moderate to low annual precipitation, are characteristic. Here occurs a rich flora containing hundreds of plant species found nowhere else in North America. The most apparent vegetation types are the chaparral and the open oak woodlands.

Chaparral is a plant community dominated by small evergreen shrubs with wiry, sometimes spiny, branches and small tough leaves. Manzanita and the scrub oak (*Quercus dumosa*) are 2 typical shrubs. Brush fires occasionally sweep through the chaparral, burning the bushes back to ground level. The roots survive, and the plants soon grow back.

Oak woodlands develop on rolling hills and lower mountain slopes, which are generally cooler and more moist than those supporting chaparral. The small- to medium-size trees are scattered, creating an open forest. Common oaks here are the interior live oak, canyon oak, California black oak, valley oak, and Oregon oak.

The lower mountain ranges along the Coast support other forest types. The lower slopes on the inner side of the coastal ranges are open oak forest, but on the middle and upper slopes open pine forest often develops. Yet on the western side of the coastal ranges, pines and cypresses occur. Monterey pine and Monterey cypress are the conspicuous ones. In northern California, the coastal ranges often support a forest of broad-leafed evergreen trees. The most commonly encountered are the tanbark oak, chinquapin, California laurel, and mandrone.

Eastern Deciduous Forest. The eastern deciduous forest is a complex association of many hardwoods and covers most of the eastern U.S. Most of the original, virgin hardwood forest has been cut and then allowed to regenerate. Since the late 1700s, many of these areas have been cut twice, and even 3 times. This forest type reaches its best development in moist river valleys and on the lower slopes of the southern Appalachian Mountains. In low wet areas, cottonwood, silver maple, sweet gum, and sycamore are often conspicuous. Sugar maple, beech, yellow poplar, and birch are characteristic of lowlands and moist lower mountain slopes. On the drier hillsides, oak and hickory are the most common trees. Conifers intermingle with the hardwoods along the northern edge of the range. They also form pure stands or mix with hardwoods in the higher Appalachians.

The southern Appalachians contain the greatest number of plant species in all of temperate North America, many of which are found only in these mountains. These ancient mountains served as a refuge for many species of plants that were able to survive when glaciers covered much of North America.

Southeastern Coastal Plain Forest. The coastal plain forest occupies a belt along the Atlantic Coast from New Jersey to Florida and continues along the Gulf Coast from Florida to Texas. The land and soil of the coastal plain is of recent geological origin. Much of this area supports extensive pine forests, especially those parts with nutrient deficient soils and those having occasional fires. The pitch pine is the common pine in the north; while loblolly, slash, and longleaf pines are abundant in the southern sections. Hardwood forest develops in the lower wetter parts that are not subject to fires; beech, sweet bay, holly, and live oak are the major trees here. Oaks and hickories dominate the higher and drier sites of the coastal plain unless fires occur, in which case pines replace them. The saw palmetto, cabbage palmetto, and Louisiana palmetto palms are characteristic of the coastal plain in their respective ranges, as shown later in this book.

Subtropical Forests. Subtropical forests are found in southern Florida on the low, flat limestone lands, which are the most recent lands to emerge from the sea. Most of the plants found in southern Florida migrated there from the Caribbean Islands. Others moved in from the southeastern U.S. Many plant communities can be identified easily. The scrub forests on the sandy flatlands are covered by the low-growing sand pines, chapman oaks, myrtle oaks, and live oaks. In the freshwater swamps, bald cypresses, coastal plain willows, and water oaks are the common trees. Pinelands are prevalent in south Florida, with slash pine the conspicuous tree. Here on drier sites persimmon can be found mixed with the pines.

The dense impenetrable thickets of mangrove along the southern and southwestern coastlines make up one of the more conspicuous plant communities in southern Florida. Red mangrove occupies the outer edge of the mangrove where the soils are almost always flooded. Inside of this, and in soils exposed at low tide, the black mangrove replaces the red. White mangrove and buttonwood trees grow in the innermost zone of mangrove and on soils that are not normally flooded at high tide.

Many trees grow along the margins of freshwater ponds and rivers. Common trees of this situation include the water hickory, sugarberry, Carolina ash, southern magnolia, and redbay. Other communities include salt marshes, prairies, coastal strands, and dunes, in all of which trees are a minor component.

Unforested Regions. Of course, not all of North America is covered by trees. The tundra, prairies, and deserts are major vegetation types lacking trees; or at best, trees are a minor element there. Tundra is a rolling, treeless, usually marshy plain which occurs in the northernmost parts of North America. In tundra, in summer, the ground just under the surface remains permanently frozen, and the growing season is often limited to 8 to 12 weeks per year.

Central North America is occupied mainly by grasslands or prairies extending from Indiana and Wisconsin to the Rocky Mountains and from Texas to Manitoba. Densely growing grasses 3–4 m (10–13 ft) high were once typical of the tall grass prairies in the eastern part of the grasslands. In the western part, the grasses are today normally only half as high. Almost all of the tall grass prairies have been converted into farmland, and the short grass prairies serve as grazing land for cattle.

Desert grasslands are present in southeastern Arizona, southern New Mexico, and southwestern Texas. This area primarily lies at 1,000–1,200 m (3,200–3,900 ft) and receives 30–40 cm (12–16 in) of rainfall each year, much less than the prairies receive. Small trees (junipers, pinyon pines, and scrub oaks) along with many shrubs grow here but mainly in gullies and drainages.

North American deserts can be identified as either cool deserts or warm deserts. The Great Basin is a cool desert with an annual precipitation of less than 35 cm (14 in) coming mostly in winter. Dry tough shrubs are the most characteristic plants at lower altitudes, while junipers, single-leaf pines, and scrub oaks are typical trees of the lower mountain slopes and foothills.

Warm desert lands occur in the southwestern U.S. This area receives less rainfall than the cool desert and occurs at lower altitudes, less than 1,000 m (3,200 ft). Trees are infrequent. Joshua trees, yuccas, mesquite, paloverde, and saguaro cacti are characteristic trees here.

Key to Major Subdivisions of Trees

A. Trees resin-bearing, usually evergreen; leaves needle-like, scale-like, lance-shaped, or (rarely) fan-shaped; flowers always unisexual (either male or female); seed producing structures (ovules) exposed on the face of the scales of the cones; fruits usually a leathery to woody cone, rarely a fleshy berry   **Conifers, p. 27**

B. Trees usually not resinous, often deciduous (leaves falling in autumn); leaves usually broad; flowers often bisexual (containing both male and female sex organs); seed-producing structures (ovules) enclosed in an ovary; fruit various; flowering plants.

1. Trees with bark, wood, and central core in stem; leaves with net-like veins; flower parts usually in 4s or 5s; trees temperate to subtropical   **Hardwoods (Dicots), p. 164**

2. Trees with woody fibers scattered throughout stem; leaves with parallel veins; flower parts in 3s; trees mainly subtropical or desert to semi-desert
          Yuccas and Palms (Monocots), p. 904

CONIFERS

(Gymnosperms)

Conifers include hundreds of trees and shrubs worldwide. In North America there are over 90 native species of conifers that grow large enough to be considered trees. These include pines, firs, spruces, cedars, yews, bald cypresses, and related groups. The one unifying feature of all conifers is their naked seeds. That is, the seed-producing structures of the female flowers are not directly enclosed in tissue, as they are in hardwoods and other flowering plants.

Fossil records show that conifers are of earlier origin than hardwoods. Conifers were once more abundant and widespread than they are now. Yet conifers are still the most abundant trees of cold temperate forests and rank among the world's most important natural resources.

Conifers are resin-bearing. Their leaves are needle-like or scale-like, linear, or — with the ginkgo — fan-shaped. Nearly all conifers are evergreen, although a few species — such as ginkgo, bald cypress, and the larches — are deciduous, losing their leaves in autumn. The flowers are produced in spring and are not showy, as is usual among hardwoods. Rather the flowers consist of basic reproductive structures, which are produced in cones. The reproductive structures — the male pollen sacs and the female seed-producing organs — are contained in the spirally arranged scales that make up the cones. The cones are either male or female, and both are usually present on the same tree. But some individual trees may have only male or female cones. The cones are generally leathery to woody, and the number of scales on them may range from a few to over 100. Only one conifer genus — the yews — does not develop cones; instead the fruits are either fleshy or berry-like.

Key to Families of Conifers

A. Leaves fan-shaped, deciduous (the leaves falling in autumn); includes only 1 species, the ginkgo
Ginkgo Family (Ginkgoaceae), p. 30

Ginkgo (fall)

B. Leaves needle-like, scale-like, linear or oblong, persistent, usually evergreen.

  1. Fruits are cones developing from female flowers; cone scales are usually woody, but may be leathery to fleshy; winged seeds on scales.

    a. Leaves flat or needle-like; fruits usually woody cones that are longer than broad, most cone scales having 2 seeds; winter buds covered with scales; genera include pines, larches, spruces, hemlocks, Douglas firs, and firs **Pine Family (Pinaceae), p. 32**

Shortleaf Pine

Eastern Hemlock

    b. Leaves scale-like or narrow and linear; fruits usually cones that are globe-shaped and fleshy or leathery, or at maturity woody; each cone scale with 1–6 seeds; winter buds not covered by scales.

      (1) Leaves are alternate, linear, either spreading or pressed against branchlets; woody cone formed from female flower has numerous spirally arranged scales; genera include sequoias and bald cypresses
Taxodium Family (Taxodiaceae), p. 114

Coastal Redwood

(Key continued on p. 30)

Ginkgo (spring)

Western Larch

Red Spruce

Douglas Fir

Balsam Fir

Giant Sequoia or Sierra Redwood

Bald Cypress

(2) Leaves opposite one another or in 3s, usually scale-like and pressed against the branchlets; small cones formed from female flowers have few scales, the scales opposite one another; genera include incense cedars, arborvitae, white cedars, cypresses, and junipers (including most red cedars)
Cypress Family (Cupressaceae), p. 122

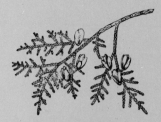

Eastern White Cedar

2. Fruits are berry-like seeds, solitary or few in number, developing from female flowers; seeds wingless; genera include yews and
Yew Family (Taxaceae), p. 156

Pacific Yew

The Ginkgo Family   Ginkgoaceae

This family is represented today by a single surviving species of tree, native to southeastern China, though introduced and planted widely throughout the Northern Hemisphere. It represents an ancient line that is unlike any other living conifer. Many casual observers will not recognize the ginkgo as a conifer. Some botanists believe ginkgos to be a link between the conifers and the more primitive plants: the tree-ferns and cycads. The description of the ginkgo genus (*Ginkgo*) is the same as for the species, below.

Ginkgo, Maidenhair Tree   *Ginkgo biloba* L.

Introduced to North America and planted widely, ginkgos usually display an irregular and unpredictable branching pattern. But, generally, the trees bearing male flowers tend to be more upright in shape, while those bearing female flowers tend to have wider shapes and crowns. The **leaves are usually produced on short, compressed branchlets** that occur on longer, more typical branchlets. The **2-lobed, fan-shaped leaves** with their **conspicuous almost parallel veins** are unlike the leaves of any other conifer and make identification easy. Male and female cones are produced on separate trees. The male cones are small and numerous, and appear in early spring. The small, female cones are solitary or in pairs, on long stalks, and borne at the tips of the short, leaf-bearing branchlets. The **fruits are yellow to orange, circular or globe-**

Common Juniper

One-Seed Juniper

Florida Torreya

Ginkgo

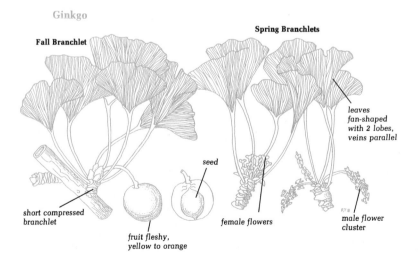

Fall Branchlet

Spring Branchlets

leaves
fan-shaped
with 2 lobes,
veins parallel

seed

short compressed
branchlet

fruit fleshy,
yellow to orange

female flowers

male flower
cluster

shaped, with a thick, fleshy layer surrounding a hard, grayish-white shell that contains the soft, oily, edible kernel of the seed. When mature in the autumn, the **fruits fall and split, giving off a strong unpleasant odor,** often described as putrid.

Ginkgos are often planted in parks, botanical gardens, and arboreta. Male trees are preferred for streetsides because they don't produce foul-smelling fruits as females do and because they can grow in poor, hard-packed soil and polluted air.

In North America, ginkgos may reach 20–30 m (65–100 ft) in height and, if grown in open conditions, they may be wide spreading. They are slow-growing trees and very resistant to insect pests and diseases.

The Pine Family   Pinaceae

This is a medium-size family worldwide, containing about 210 species of trees and shrubs grouped in 9 genera. Members are found primarily in Europe, Asia, and North America. Two genera are found only in China, while a third, the true cedars, are restricted to warm temperate regions of Europe and Asia. The remaining 6 genera have trees in North America. The Douglas firs (*Pseudotsuga*) and hemlocks (*Tsuga*) occur in both North America and eastern Asia. There are about 110 species of pine (*Pinus*) worldwide, with 35 species native to North America. Several pines from Europe are widely planted here. There are 9 species of firs (*Abies*) and 7 spruces (*Picea*) in North America with additional members in Europe and Asia. There are 3 native species of larches (*Larix*) and a fourth species, from Europe, has been widely planted.

The pine family is one of the most valuable and commercially important groups of trees in the world. More lumber, pulp wood, and paper products come from this family than any other family of plants. And they are essential for the survival of many species of wildlife — serving as cover, habitat for nesting, and an important food source.

Members of this family are usually resin-bearing trees, occasionally shrubs with evergreen or deciduous leaves. The winter buds are usually covered with scales. The leaves are needle-like or linear and in cross section they may be either rounded, flattened, or angled. Cones containing the male and female reproductive structures occur on the same tree. The fruits are woody, occasionally leathery, cones with persistent scales (except in firs), each fertile scale containing 2 seeds. The seeds are small and usually winged.

Key to Genera in the Pine Family

A. Leaves needle-like, 2 to many per cluster.

Austrian Pine

1. Leaves evergreen, in clusters of 2 to many, rarely 1, each cluster enclosed at the base by a sheath; cone-like fruits maturing in 2 or rarely 3 seasons   **Pine, p. 34**

2. Leaves deciduous, falling in autumn, appearing in clusters but not enclosed at the base by a sheath; leaves on short, compressed lateral branchlets; cone-like fruits maturing in 1 season **Larch, p. 76**

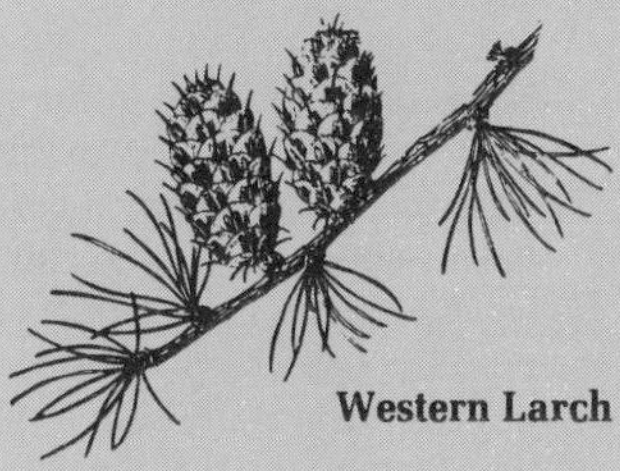

Western Larch

B. Leaves linear, often flattened, occurring singly along the branchlets.

  1. Cones hanging on branchlets, the entire cone falling in 1 unit.

    a. Branchlets rough because scattered peg-like stubs remain on the branchlets after the leaves have fallen.

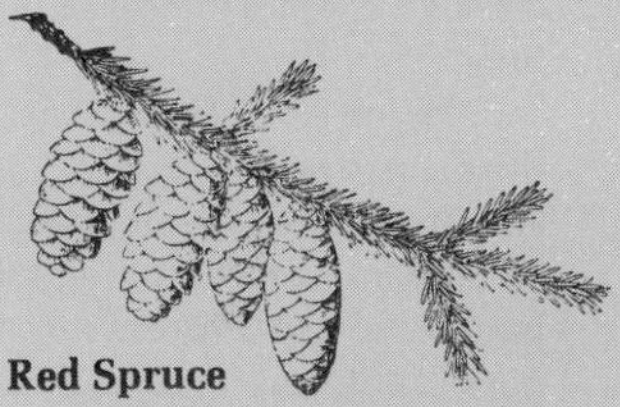

Red Spruce

      (1) Leaves without stalks (sessile), and are 4-sided or flattened **Spruce, p. 80**

      (2) Leaves short-stalked, flattened or slightly rounded **Hemlock, p. 91**

Eastern Hemlock

    b. Branchlets smooth, without peg-like structures; cones with the bracts longer than the scales **Douglas fir, p. 96**

Douglas Fir

  2. Cones upright on the branchlets, the cone scales falling away after the seed is shed, leaving a single, spike-like central axis **Fir, p. 100**

Balsam Fir

The Pine Genus

Pinus L.

Pines are among the most valuable and widely distributed groups of trees in the world. There are approximately 95 species worldwide, with 35 native to North America. They occupy a broad range of habitats from subtropical to north temperate forests and from low, wet swampy sites to bare, rocky outcrops at 4,000 m (13,100 ft) elevation. Pines are of great economic importance because they yield valuable lumber, pulp for paper and woodboard products, tar, turpentine, and edible nuts. Many introduced and some native species are used for ornamental plantings and in reforestation. Two of the introduced species, Scots pine and Austrian pine are included here because they are often encountered in second-growth woodlands and in pine plantations.

Pines are slow- to fast-growing, short- or long-lived evergreen trees with thin to very thick, furrowed, scaly bark. The wood is resinous, soft to hard, coarse- to fine-grained, and sometimes very durable. Winter buds may be moderate to large, and are enclosed by numerous, overlapping scales. The needle-like leaves are produced in clusters or bundles of 2 to 5, rarely 1 or 8, soft to stiff, straight to twisted, with several lines of air pores (stomata), and enclosed at the base by a persistent or a deciduous sheath. Male and female reproductive structures are produced in separate cones but both types of cones occur on the same tree; the oblong male cones are crowded into clusters at the base of the current year's growth; the female cones are usually globe-shaped, composed of numerous, spirally arranged, overlapping scales, each scale containing 2 seed-producing structures, called ovules, and a small bract. The fruits developing from the female flowers are woody cones that are variable in size and shape. They are usually broadest near the base, one-sided or uniformly rounded or tapering, often maturing and opening in 2 seasons or persisting unopened on the branches for several years. They are composed of thin to thickened woody scales. The tip of the scales is thin to thick, often ridged, and usually armed with a spine, each scale with 2 seeds. The seeds have a hard seed coat, are variable in size, shape, and color, and most are winged, but some are not.

Key to Hard and Soft Pine Species

The pines of North America fall into two natural groupings, the soft pines and the hard pines.

A. Soft pines have needle-like leaves enclosed at the base by a sheath, the sheath falling away on mature clusters of leaves; leaves produced in clusters of 5, occasionally 1–4; leaves with 1 vascular bundle in cross section; fruits with the face of the cone scales usually lacking a spine (though present in foxtail and bristlecone pines); wood usually soft, coarse-grained **See key, p. 35**

Limber Pine

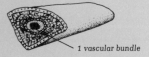

1 vascular bundle

B. Hard pines have needle-like leaves enclosed at the base by a sheath that persists in mature clusters of leaves; leaves produced in clusters of 2–3, occasionally 5; leaves with 2 vascular bundles in cross section; fruits with the face of the cone scales usually armed with a spine; wood usually hard, close-grained **See key, p. 49**

2 vascular bundles

Pitch Pine

Key to Soft Pine Species

A. Leaves in clusters of 5; fruits are many-scaled, usually elongated cones.

   1. Cones long-stalked; cone scales thin, flexible, without a spine on the face.

      a. Leaves green, without white bands on the back; cones 10–28 cm (4–11 in) long.

         (1) Leaves slender, flexible, soft to touch; trees of eastern North America
               White pine, p. 37

         (2) Leaves stout, hard, not soft to touch; trees of western North America
               Western white pine, p. 38

Western White Pine

      b. Leaves green with conspicuous silvery, narrow bands running lengthwise on the back; cones 27–46 cm (10.6–18 in) long
               Sugar pine, p. 39

   2. Cones short-stalked; cone scales thick, stout, occasionally armed on the face with a short spine.

      a. Cones globe-shaped or cylinder-shaped, cone scales without spines on the face, seeds without a wing or if present then very short; leaves 2.5–8.9 cm (1–3.5 in) long.

         (1) Cones almost globe-shaped, 2.5–7.5 cm (1–3 in) long; seeds wingless
               Whitebark pine, p. 40

         (2) Cones almost cylinder-shaped, 10–22 cm (4–8.7 in) long; seeds winged.

Sugar Pine

White Bark Pine

(Continued)

(a) Cone scales spreading at maturity, not strongly bent back at tip
Limber pine, p. 41

(b) Cone scales at maturity strongly bent back at tip
Southwestern white pine, p. 42

b. Cones broadest at the base, cone scales with spines on the face; seeds with long wings; leaves 2.5–3.8 cm (1–1.5 in) long.

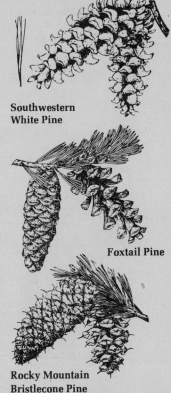

Southwestern White Pine

(1) Leaves uniformly dark green, without conspicuous white spots (resin deposits); individual leaves usually with 2 lengthwise resin ducts; cones rusty reddish-brown.

(a) Cones tapering at the base; trees of the Sierra Nevada, California
Foxtail pine, p. 43

(b) Cones rounded at the base; trees of Utah, Nevada, and western California
Great Basin bristlecone pine, p. 44

Foxtail Pine

(2) Leaves with conspicuous tiny white spots (resin deposits); individual leaves usually with 1 lengthwise resin duct; cones buff to gray-brown; trees of Rocky Mountains
Rocky Mountain bristlecone pine, p. 44

Rocky Mountain Bristlecone Pine

B. Leaves in clusters of 1–4; fruit a few-scaled, short, thickened cone, generally globe-shaped or broadest at the base.

1. Leaves single, 1 per sheath
Singleleaf pinyon, p. 45

2. Leaves 2 to 4 per sheath.

a. Leaves 2 per sheath; trees of Colorado, Utah, Arizona, and New Mexico
Pinyon, p. 46

b. Leaves 3 or 4 per sheath; trees of southern California or southern Arizona, southwestern New Mexico, and western Texas.

(1) Leaves mainly in 3s; trees of southern Arizona, southwestern New Mexico, and western Texas
Mexican pinyon, p. 48

(2) Leaves mainly in 4s; trees of southern California and Baja California
Parry pinyon, p. 48

Singleleaf Pinyon

Parry Pinyon

White Pine

Pinus strobus L.

The white pine is distributed widely in northeastern North America, and it occurs here and there in Mexico and Guatemala. The trees usually grow at low altitudes (up to 1,350 m — 4,500 ft — in the southern Appalachian Mountains). Tolerant of different soils, the white pine grows best on well-drained soil in a cool, humid climate. While this pine will grow in association with many other species, it generally forms stands with southern red oak and white ash, or with eastern hemlock, or with chestnut oak. The white pine blister rust, which lives alternately on currant bushes and white pines, can spread rapidly, killing the infected branches.

These fast-growing, long-lived trees may start producing cones when 5 to 10 years old, but dependable seed production does not begin for another 10 years. Large seed crops are produced every 3 to 5 years, followed by little or no production.

The white pine is very important to birds and to mammals. The black-capped, Carolina, and chestnut-beaked chickadees, red crossbills, and, to a lesser extent, many other birds feed on the soft, evergreen needles and seeds. Beavers, porcupines, and varying hares feed on the bark and twigs; while gray squirrels, chipmunks, and mice eat the seeds. Whitetail deer browse on white pine, and during heavy snows deer often use hemlock and white-pine stands as a yarding area.

This species is one of the most valuable trees in eastern North America. Prior to the arrival of white men, virgin stands contained an estimated 900-billion board feet of

White Pine

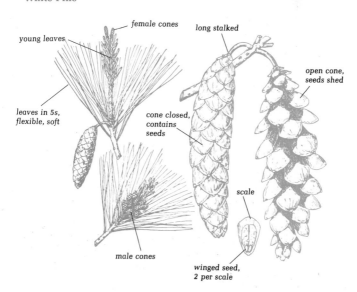

young leaves

female cones

long stalked

leaves in 5s, flexible, soft

cone closed, contains seeds

open cone, seeds shed

scale

male cones

winged seed, 2 per scale

lumber. In the mid to late 1700s and 1800s, these vast stands were cut for the lightweight, straight-grained, light-brown wood. It was used in a variety of ways, including ship masts, bridges, homes, shingles, and inexpensive furniture. Today it is used for cabinets, house interiors, house framing, and for carving. The wood works easily and takes an excellent natural or painted finish.

The white pine is an excellent tree for many planting situations ranging from reforestation projects to landscaping for homes, parks, and highways. It can be pruned to restrict its size and shape and is one of the most important pines in horticulture.

Appearance: medium-size to tall trees 30–70 m (98–230 ft), broadly oval shape with irregular open crown at maturity; trunk usually tall, straight, 1–1.5 m, rarely to 2 (3.2–4.9 ft, rarely to 6.6), in diameter. **Bark:** thin, smooth on young trees but becoming dark, 2.5–5 cm (1–2 in) thick, deeply furrowed with broad ridges composed of closely pressed purple-tinged scales. **Branches:** slender, spreading to ascending, becoming stout and irregular with age; branchlets flexible, green becoming orangish-brown. **Leaves:** *needles, 5 per bundle, 7.5–12.8 cm (3–5 in) long,* slender, *straight, flexible, soft to touch, bluish-green.* **Flowers:** male cones numerous, small, oblong, yellow, on current year's growth; female cones, stalked, light-red, with the scales purple-tipped. **Fruits:** woody, hanging *cones, cylindric, 10–20 cm (4–8 in) long,* green turning light brown, maturing in 2 seasons; scales numerous, not spine-tipped, each scale containing 2 seeds. **Seeds:** 5–8 mm (0.2–0.3 in) long, tapering at both ends, reddish-brown and mottled, winged, the wing 1.5–2 cm (0.6–0.8 in) long.

Western White Pine   *Pinus monticola* Dougl.

An important timber tree of the West, this pine occurs in southern British Columbia, the northwestern states, and the Sierra Nevada of California. In the northern portion of their range, the trees grow from sea level to 750 m (2,500 ft), in the central portion from

750–2,500 m (2,500–8,200 ft), and in the southern part from 2,250–3,850 m (7,400–12,700 ft). Although the larger specimens usually are found on deep, well-drained but moisture-holding soils, the trees grow on a variety of soils on the middle to upper mountain slopes and flats. They may occur in pure stands or grow in association with many other species, including western hemlock, western larch, Douglas fir, grand fir, and western redcedar. Blister rust is a particularly serious disease of western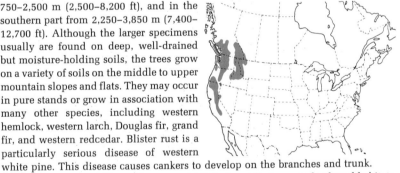

white pine. This disease causes cankers to develop on the branches and trunk.

The trees grow quickly and become established rapidly in severely altered habitats, like those resulting from a forest fire. Normally, the trees require 30 to 40 years before they produce large cone crops, and the cones require 2 growing seasons to mature. Abundant seed production occurs every 3 or 4 years.

The western white pines are important to wildlife. They provide considerable cover, and the seeds are an important food to gray squirrels, Douglas chickarees, white-footed mice, and to various birds, including pine grosbeaks, rosy finches, pygmy and red-breasted nuthatches. Porcupines eat the bark. And bears sometimes claw the trunks in spring to reach the sweet sapwood. These "bear trees" are often so severely damaged that they die.

The western white pine is an important timber tree because of its lightweight,

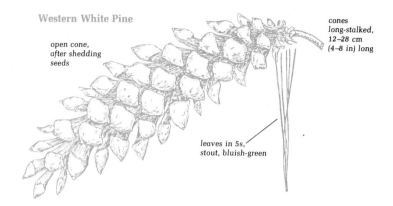

Western White Pine

open cone,
after shedding
seeds

cones
long-stalked,
12–28 cm
(4–8 in) long

leaves in 5s,
stout, bluish-green

soft, straight-grained wood, which is resistant to shrinking and warping. The wood is used for doors, interior finishings, floors, shelves, shutters, and window sashes.

Appearance: tall trees 30–50 m (98–165 ft), pyramid-shaped with a narrow, even crown; trunk tall, straight, 1–2 m, rarely 3 (3.2–6.6 ft, rarely 10) in diameter. **Bark:** on young trees thin, smooth, light gray; on older trees 1.9–3.8 cm (0.8–1.5 in) thick, divided by lengthwise and crosswise fissures to form small, almost square plates, silver-gray and purplish-tinged. **Branches:** slender, spreading; branchlets stout, tough, flexible, dark orangish-brown turning dark reddish-brown to purple with age. **Leaves: *needles, 5 per bundle, 5–10 cm (2–4 in) long, slender, sometimes twisted, stout, bluish-green,*** covered with a whitish bloom. **Flowers:** male cones small, oblong, clustered in small groups near the ends of the upper branchlets; female cones small, 1.2–3.8 cm (0.5–1.5 in) almost globe-shaped, greenish-yellow to pink, stalked, borne at the tips of the upper branchlets. **Fruits:** woody, hanging ***cones, cylindric, long-stalked, 12–28 cm (4–11 in) long,*** bright green, matures in 2 seasons; scales numerous, flexible, not spine-tipped, each scale containing 2 seeds. **Seeds:** 7–9 mm (0.3 in) long, broadest at the middle and tapering at both ends, pale reddish-brown and mottled, winged, the wing about 3 times longer than the body of the seed.

Sugar Pine   *Pinus lambertiana* Dougl.

This species, the titan of North American pines, is the largest and stateliest of all native pines. Found primarily on cool, moist, northern slopes, it ranges from the mountains of southern Oregon to southern California, the Sierra Nevada, and into northern Baja California. The trees occur from 750–3,000 m (2,300–9,200 ft) elevation and reach their greatest size on deep, well-drained soils. A deeply penetrating taproot firmly anchors the trees and prevents their being toppled by high winds. Sugar pines seldom occur in pure stands but usually are found growing with Jeffrey pine, ponderosa pine, incense-cedar, red and white fir, and Douglas fir. Sugar pine is susceptible to the blister rust disease.

Sugar pines are long-lived and may need a century or more before they can be depended upon for seed production. But even then seed production is sparse, with a good cone and seed crop every 4 or 5 years. The cones are the largest of any native pine.

The trees are important to wildlife. Squirrels cut cones, and whiteheaded woodpeckers drill them. The large, edible seeds are sought eagerly by many birds, including pine jays and pygmy nuthatches. Chipmunks and mice compete with the birds for the seeds. Porcupines and bears leave their marks.

The wood of this important timber tree is lightweight, soft, coarse-grained, and used largely for interior finishes such as doors, sashes, shutters, and for woodworking. The name sugar pine is derived from a sweet liquid present in the bark and wood.

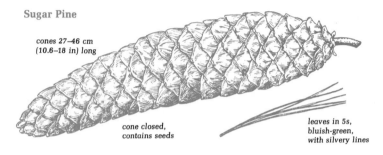

Sugar Pine

cones 27–46 cm
(10.6–18 in) long

cone closed,
contains seeds

leaves in 5s,
bluish-green,
with silvery lines

Appearance: tall trees 55–65 m (180-215 ft), with a pyramid shape and a spreading, flat-topped crown; trunk tall, very straight, 1-2 m (3–6 ft) in diameter. **Bark:** thick, 5–10 cm (2–4 in), cinnamon red to deep purplish-brown (on younger trees thin, gray-green and smooth), deep and irregular furrows separating the long, loosely scaled ridges. **Branches:** spreading, usually stout, often at right angles to the trunk; branchlets slender to stout, turning orange-brown. **Leaves: *needles, 5 per bundle,*** 8.8–10 cm (3.5–4 in) long, stout, stiff, persisting for 2 or 3 years before falling, ***deep bluish-green marked with silvery lines.*** **Flowers:** male cones small, yellow, clustered near the ends of the branchlets; female cones small, pale green, almost globe-shaped, at or near the ends of the upper branchlets. **Fruits:** large, woody cones, upright the first year, hanging by the second year, ***cylindric, 27–46 cm (10.6–18 in) long*** and from 8–12 cm (3.1–4.7 in) in diameter, brown, the scales thickened, rigid, shiny reddish-brown. **Seeds:** broadest near the middle, 1.2–1.5 cm (0.5–0.6 in) long, dark chocolate brown to almost black, winged, the stiff wing about twice as long as the seed.

Whitebark Pine   *Pinus albicaulis* Engelm.

The whitebark pine is a ruggedly handsome tree of the high mountains of western Canada and the U.S. This pine grows at or near timberline from 2,350–3,750 m (7,700–

12,000 ft) elevation. Many trees grow on rocky ridges and bluffs, but the largest trees grow at the lower elevations in protected canyons or ravines. In the exposed areas at timberline, the whitebark pine forms a low, spreading tree, sometimes reduced to a prostrate, gnarled mat. The trees occur in pure stands or grow in association with Engelmann spruce, subalpine larch, or lodgepole pine.

They are slow-growing, long-lived trees

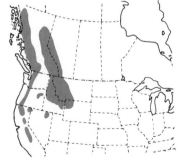

that produce a limited number of cones annually. The cones do not open at maturity; so the Clark's nutcracker and subalpine squirrels have to break apart the hard cones to reach the large, edible seeds. The fallen needles underneath the low, spreading evergreen trees often serve as bedding for deer and wild sheep.

The wood is not important commercially. It is lightweight, soft, and brittle and is used occasionally for fuel. Some people gather the seeds and eat them raw or roasted.

Whitebark Pine

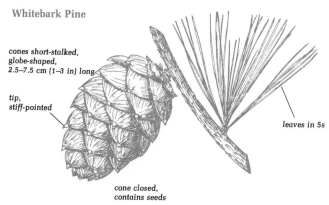

cones short-stalked, globe-shaped, 2.5–7.5 cm (1–3 in) long

tip, stiff-pointed

leaves in 5s

cone closed, contains seeds

Appearance: small, often bushy trees, 2–10 m (6.5–33 ft), rarely to 20 m (66 ft), usually with an irregular spreading shape and broad crown; trunk short, soon branching, 0.6–1.3 m (1.9–4.3 ft) in diameter. **Bark:** thin, 0.6–1.2 cm (0.3–0.5 in) thick, white to whitish gray, furrowed and broken into scaly plates. **Branches:** stout, flexible; branchlets stout, flexible, purplish turning white with age. **Leaves:** *needles, 5 per bundle,* 2.5–6.2 cm (1–2.5 in) long, stiff, slightly incurved, usually clustered near the tip of the branchlets, dark green. **Flowers:** male cones short, 8–10 mm (0.3–0.4 in) long, oval, scarlet; female cones oblong, 0.8–1 cm (0.3–0.4 in) long, bright scarlet. **Fruits:** hard, almost *globe-shaped cones, 2.5–7.5 cm (1–3 in) long, short-stalked,* opens gradually during late fall and early winter, purplish brown, composed of thickened scales, *each scale armed with a stiff, pointed tip.* **Seeds:** broadest near the middle and tapering to a point, slightly flattened, dark brown, *wingless.*

Limber Pine
Pinus flexilis James

The limber pine is distributed widely in the Rocky Mountains from Canada to northern New Mexico. The trees usually are found on dry, rocky ridges and peaks at 2,350–3,600 m (7,700–11,500 ft) altitude. Due to their large taproot that firmly anchors them, they can grow on exposed bluffs, although they may then resemble a large, spreading shrub. In Canada, these pines typically are found at the lower elevations. They are not abundant anywhere in their range and often grow in association with Douglas fir or in spruce-fir forests.

These slow-growing, long-lived trees alternate between a year of heavy seed production and several years of light production. The seeds are consumed by birds and rodents. The wood is light, soft, close-

grained, pale yellow but develops a reddish-tinge upon exposure to air. It has been used for boxes, railroad ties, poles, and mine timbers. It is also used locally for fuel. Generally these trees are harvested along with the more abundant ponderosa pine, with logging companies and mills making no distinction between them.

Limber Pine

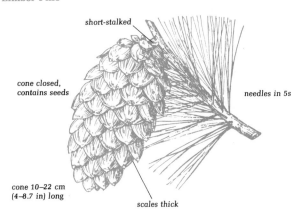

short-stalked

cone closed,
contains seeds

needles in 5s

cone 10–22 cm
(4–8.7 in) long

scales thick

Appearance: small to medium-size trees 10–38 m (32–125 ft), open and with a broadly rounded crown; trunk short, often crooked, 0.6–1.2 m (1.9–3.9 ft) in diameter, soon branching. **Bark:** smooth and light gray to whitish-gray when young, becoming moderately thick, 2.5–5 cm (1–2 in), dark gray, dark brown to almost black, deeply furrowed and with wide, scaly ridges. **Branches:** stout, long-persistent, drooping with age but the tips often upturned; branchlets tough, very flexible. **Leaves:** *needles, 5 per bundle,* 5–8.9 cm (2–3.5 in) long, stout, slender, slightly curved inward, bluish-green. **Flowers:** male cones small, reddish; female cones bright reddish-purple. **Fruits:** hanging, *short-stalked, nearly cylinder-shaped, 10–22 cm (4–8.7 in) long,* green turning yellow-brown in fall, *composed of many thick scales slightly bent back at the tip,* the scales appearing square at the tip, each scale containing 2 seeds. **Seeds:** 0.9–1.3 cm (0.4–0.5 in) long, compressed, dark reddish-brown and black mottled, *winged, each wing about 2 mm (about 0.1 in) wide.*

Southwestern White Pine   *Pinus strobiformis* Engelm.

This pine occurs in the Southwest from southern Colorado through the mountains of Arizona, New Mexico, western Texas, and into northern Mexico. It is related closely to the limber pine and the Mexican white pine. But it can be distinguished from them by its range, a larger trunk, *cone scales with narrow tips bent back* and *needles lacking whitish lines on their backs.* Although the trees are used locally for fuel and for posts, they are not abundant enough to be of commercial value. The seeds are edible, but they are smaller and have a much harder shell than the pinyon pine seeds.

Southwestern White Pine

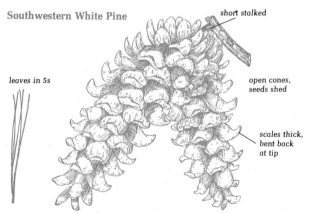

short stalked

leaves in 5s

*open cones,
seeds shed*

*scales thick,
bent back
at tip*

Foxtail Pine — *Pinus balfouriana* Grev. & Balf.

This uncommon pine is restricted to 2 areas of dry, rocky slopes and ridges from 1,650–3,600 m (5,400–11,500 ft) altitude, one in the southern Sierra Nevada and the other in higher mountains in northwestern California. The trees usually have an open, irregular form, giving them a picturesque appearance when they occur on bluffs.

This species is related closely to the bristlecone pine. The trees are from 10–15 m (32–50 ft) high, seldom taller, and the **needles** are **5 per bundle,** stout, rigid, curved, dark green and **2.5–3.8 cm (1–1.5 in) long.** The bundles of needles are clustered at the tips of the branches, giving a tufted or "foxtail" look to them. The distinctive short-stalked, reddish-brown, **oblong cones are 8.8–12.5 cm (3.5–5 in) long** and have scales that are armed with a short spine.

Because of very harsh climate, these long-lived trees may have some dead upper branches, or even the tops may be dead. In spite of this, the lower branches continue

Foxtail Pine

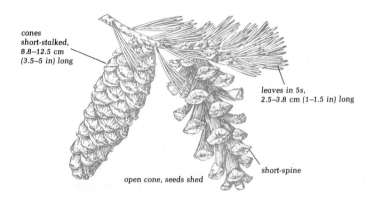

*cones
short-stalked,
8.8–12.5 cm
(3.5–5 in) long*

*leaves in 5s,
2.5–3.8 cm (1–1.5 in) long*

short-spine

open cone, seeds shed

to grow. The soft, yellowish-brown wood is of little value, and the rarity and inaccessibility of the trees renders them of no commercial value.

Great Basin Bristlecone Pine *Pinus longaeva* D. K. Bailey

The Great Basin bristlecone pine and the Rocky Mountain bristlecone pine were recently reclassified as distinct species rather than one. Individual Great Basin Bristlecones may live 3,000 to 5,000 years, making them the oldest living trees known.

This pine occurs in Utah, Nevada, and into western California, primarily on limestone or dolomite soils on dry rocky ridges and slopes from 1,700–3,400 m (5,500–11,000 ft) elevation. The areas the pine grows in typically have low amounts of annual precipitation and long, extended, cold winters.

The trees have an open, irregular crown with characteristic **hanging and twisting branches.** There are **5 needles per bundle** and they have **2 lengthwise resin ducts,** but the **needles lack conspicuous resin deposits** as found in the Rocky Mountain bristlecone pine, described next and which usually has only one lengthwise resin

Great Basin Bristlecone Pine

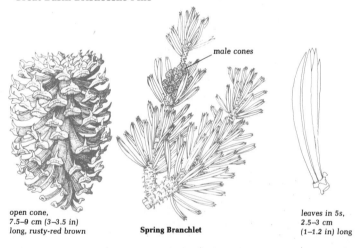

male cones

open cone,
7.5–9 cm (3–3.5 in)
long, rusty-red brown

Spring Branchlet

leaves in 5s,
2.5–3 cm
(1–1.2 in) long

duct per needle. The seed bearing cones are 7.5–9 cm (3–3.5 in) long, broadest near the base, and **rich, rusty red-brown** in color. Other parts of the tree are similar to those in the description of the Rocky Mountain bristlecone pine, covered next.

Rocky Mountain Bristlecone Pine *Pinus aristata* Engelm.

Rocky Mountain bristlecone pines are among the oldest living trees known, with individual trees reaching 1,500 to 2,000 years. The trees are native to high mountain ridges and slopes from 2,500–3,400 m (8,000–11,000 ft) elevation in Colorado, New

Mexico, and Arizona. Often gnarled and twisted by high winds, storms, and deep snows, these trees are often the only ones at treeline. Below treeline, they can grow into attractive, many-branched trees, reaching 20 m (65 ft) in height. Short, 90-day growing seasons, low temperatures, and the possibility of snow on any day of the year contribute to the very slow-growing nature of these trees.

These pines are of limited value to wildlife. White-crowned sparrows, solitaires, and Clark's crows feed on the seeds and occasionally use the trees for cover. The soft, brittle, reddish-brown wood has been used for fuel and for mine timbers.

Rocky Mountain Bristlecone Pine

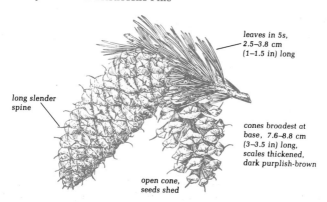

leaves in 5s, 2.5–3.8 cm (1–1.5 in) long

long slender spine

cones broadest at base, 7.6–8.8 cm (3–3.5 in) long, scales thickened, dark purplish-brown

open cone, seeds shed

Appearance: small, often spreading or bushy trees 3–15 m (9–50 ft), often gnarled, with an open, irregular crown; trunk short, thick, soon branching, 0.3–1 m (1–3.3 ft) in diameter. **Bark:** thin, 1.2–1.6 cm (0.5–0.7 in) thick, reddish-brown, irregularly and shallowly fissured with broad, flattened ridges. **Branches:** stout, frequent, becoming contorted with age; branchlets stout, *usually ascending*, light orange turning almost black with age. **Leaves:** *needles, 5 per bundle, 2.5–3.8 cm (1–1.5 in) long*, stiff, usually curved, crowded toward the tips of the branches giving a tufted look, shiny dark green. **Flowers:** male cones short, 1–1.2 cm (0.4–0.5 in) long, oval, dark orangish, often clustered near the tips of the branchlets; female cones, occurring singly or in pairs, near the ends of the branchlets. **Fruits:** hard, oval cones, *7.6–8.8 cm (3–3.5 in) long, dark buff to gray-brown, composed of thick, dark purplish-brown scales, each scale with a slender, bristle-like prickle 1.4–1.8 cm (0.6–0.7 in) long.* **Seeds:** 5–7 mm (0.2–0.3 in) long, oval, flattened, light brown, often mottled, *winged,* the wing terminal, light brown, about 3 times longer than the body of the seed.

Singleleaf Pinyon   *Pinus monophylla* Torr. & Frem.

The singleleaf pinyon is a low, spreading tree of the Great Basin region, principally in Nevada. The trees are a major element of the pinyon-juniper woodland of the lower mountain slopes, foothills, and canyons from 650–2,350 m (2,100–7,800 ft) elevation.

Tolerant of dry, rocky soils, this pine often occurs in pure stands or with juniper trees. It is the easiest species of pine to identify in the field because it is the only one with needles occurring singly or rarely in pairs.

This is a slow-growing tree that normally lives to between 200 and 300 years and produces seed crops almost every year. Heavy crops are borne every 2 or 3 years. The cones take 2 growing seasons to mature, and the seeds usually are shed in August. These large, thin-shelled seeds (referred to locally as pinyon nuts) are eaten readily by birds and squirrels. They have been a staple food for Indians and are still gathered today for home use and for sale. The meat of the seeds is oily and has an agreeable flavor, especially if roasted. The yellowish-brown wood is soft, yet heavy, and is used primarily for fuel and fence posts.

Singleleaf Pinyon

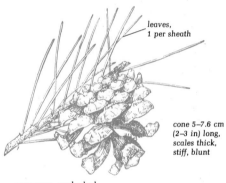

leaves,
1 per sheath

cone 5–7.6 cm
(2–3 in) long,
scales thick,
stiff, blunt

open cone, seeds shed

Appearance: small, low spreading trees 5–10 m (16–33 ft) with a short, flattened crown; trunk short, often branched, 0.3–0.5 m (1–1.6 ft) diameter. **Bark:** smooth when young, becoming irregularly furrowed and rough, dark brown, with thin, scaly ridges. **Branches:** stout, light orange but turning dark brown with age. **Leaves: *needles, 1 per sheath (occurring singly),*** 2.5–5 cm (1–2 in) long, stiff, sharp-pointed, often curved toward the branches, pale yellowish-green to gray green. **Flowers:** male cones small, red, clustered near the tip of the branches; female cones short-stalked, purplish, scattered near the tips of branches. **Fruits:** hard, ***egg-shaped cones, 5–7.6 cm (2–3 in) long, light brown, composed of thick, stiff, blunt scales,*** each scale bearing 2 seeds. **Seeds:** large, egg-shaped, 1.8–2 cm (0.7–0.8 in) long, brown, wingless, thin-shelled.

Pinyon, Colorado Pinyon   *Pinus edulis* Engelm.

The pinyon is a common, widely distributed tree in the southwestern U.S., primarily in Utah, Arizona, New Mexico, and Colorado. This pine is encountered more than any other tree on the south rim of the Grand Canyon National Park. It grows on mesas, plateaus, lower mountain slopes, and foothills from 825–2,350 m (2,700–7,800 ft) elevation. It is drought-resistant and will grow in dry, rocky soils and is a common tree in the Southwest. It may occur in pure stands or with juniper, Gambel oak, and ponderosa pine. Because of the scarcity of water, the trees often form an open woodland composed of scattered individual trees.

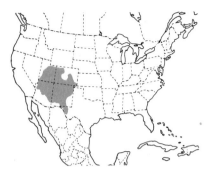

A slow-growing and long-lived tree, the pinyon produces large seed crops every 3 or 4 years. The seeds are very important to wildlife. Pinyon-jays, Mearn's quail, wild turkeys, and other smaller seed-eating birds forage on the seeds in autumn. Squirrels, chipmunks, porcupines, black bears, and mule deer also consume large quantities of the seeds. Because the pinyon nuts (the seeds) are a valuable seed crop, the birds and mammals must compete each fall with the Navajo Indians and other seed collectors. The seeds were a staple in the Indian diet, but the Indians now ship more than 1 million pounds of seeds annually to the East and West coasts. The yellow, soft, heavy wood is used primarily for fuel and fence posts.

Pinyon

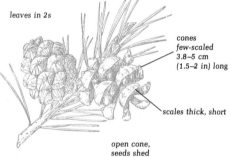

leaves in 2s

cones
few-scaled
3.8–5 cm
(1.5–2 in) long

scales thick, short

open cone,
seeds shed

Appearance: small, spreading, bushy tree 5–14 m (16–46 ft), with a compacted, rounded crown; trunk short, soon branching, 0.3–0.6 m (1–1.9 ft) in diameter. **Bark:** thin, 1.2–1.9 cm (0.5–0.8 in) thick, gray to reddish brown, irregularly furrowed with small, scaly ridges. **Branches:** short, stout, usually erect. **Leaves: *needles, 2 per bundle,*** rarely 1 or 3, 1.2–5 cm (0.5–2 in) long, almost rounded to triangular, stiff, sharp-pointed, incurved toward the branches, bluish-green when young, turning yellowish-green. **Flowers:** male cones small, dark red, clustered near the tips of the branches; female cones short-stalked, purple, also near the ends of the branches. **Fruits:** hard, short, ***egg-shaped cones, 3.8–5 cm (1.5–2 in) long,*** green turning yellowish-brown at maturity, ***composed of thick, blunt scales,*** each scale with 2 seeds. **Seeds:** large, 1.2–1.4 cm (0.5–0.6 in) long, narrowly egg-shaped, pale yellow with reddish-brown markings, wingless, sweet, oily, thin-shelled.

Mexican Pinyon   *Pinus cembroides* Zucc.

This pine is distributed widely in Mexico but extends into North America only in southern Arizona, southwestern New Mexico, and western Texas. These small to medium-size, attractive trees grow in poor, shallow, rocky, or gravelly soils on mountain slopes, canyons, and foothills. They are restricted largely to oak-juniper forest belts from 1,600–2,500 m (5,200–8,200 ft) elevation. This species can be distinguished from the related pinyon pines by its *long, thin, flexible, dark bluish-green needles,* which usually *occur in bundles of 3.* The seeds are a dark chocolate brown and have a heavier shell than other North American pinyons.

Mexican Pinyon

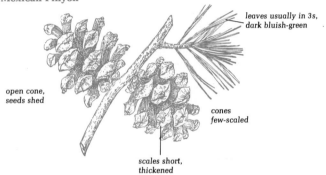

leaves usually in 3s, dark bluish-green

open cone, seeds shed

cones few-scaled

scales short, thickened

The seeds are important to many birds, squirrels, chipmunks, and other small mammals. The sweet seeds are gathered from wild trees and sold in marketplaces throughout Mexico. Roasting improves the flavor. The soft, light yellow wood is of little value except for fuel or fence posts.

Parry Pinyon   *Pinus quadrifolia* Parl.

(synonyms: *P. parryana* Engelm. *P. cembroides* var. *parryana* Voss.)

The Parry pinyon is a rare pine confined to southern California in Riverside and San Diego counties and in northern Baja California. The trees are small, spreading and have a short, rounded crown. The stout, sharp-pointed, pale green leaves are from 3.1–3.8 cm (1.2–1.5 in) long and curved inward toward the branches. The trees grow from 800–1,700 m (2,500–5,400 ft) elevation. This pine, along with the single-leaf pinyon, pinyon, and the Mexican pinyon, comprise the closely related group known as the nut pines. These pines are characterized by large, edible, wingless seeds and needles in bundles of 1 to 4. The Parry pinyon's distinguishing feature is

that its ***needles usually are clustered in bundles of 4.*** As with the other nut pines, the seeds are consumed by wildlife and are gathered by Indians.

Parry Pinyon

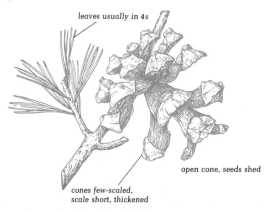

leaves usually in 4s

open cone, seeds shed

cones few-scaled, scale short, thickened

Key to Hard Pine Species

A. Cones near the tips of the branchlets.

    1. Leaves clustered in 2s or 3s.

        a. Leaves clustered in 2s.

            (1) Cone scales unarmed on the face or with a minute prickle that soon falls away.

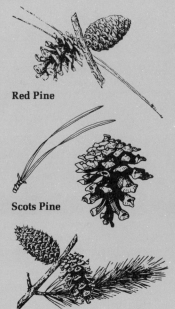

Red Pine

                (a) Leaves 10–15 cm (4–6 in) long, slender; trees of northeastern North America   **Red pine, p. 53**

                (b) Leaves 3.8–7.6 cm (1.5–3 in) long, usually twisted; trees introduced from Europe, and planted widely   **Scots pine, p. 54**

Scots Pine

            (2) Cone scales armed with a small to large conspicuous spine.

                (a) Leaves 2.5–7.6 cm (1–3 in) long, usually twisted; trees of western North America   **Lodgepole pine, p. 55**

                (b) Leaves 9–16 cm (3.5–6.3 in) long, stiff, dark green; trees introduced from Europe, and planted widely   **Austrian pine, p. 56**

Lodgepole Pine

(Continued)

b. Leaves clustered in 3s, rarely 3s and 2s or 3s and 5s.

   (1) Leaves 20–45 cm (8–18 in) long.

      (a) Leaves slender, flexible; cones cylindrical; trees of Coastal Plain of southeastern U.S.
          Longleaf pine, p. 56

      (b) Leaves stout, stiff; cones broadest near the base; trees of southern Arizona, New Mexico, and Mexico
          Apache pine, p. 58

   (2) Leaves 10–28 cm (4–11 in) long.

      (a) Cones 7.6–12.5 cm (3–4.9 in) long, with spines on scales pointed outward; seeds 7–8 mm (0.3 in) long; trees of western North America
          Ponderosa pine, p. 58

      (b) Cones 14–30 cm (5.5–11.8 in) long, with spines on scales curving inward; seeds 1–1.4 cm (0.5 in) long; trees mainly of the California Rockies
          Jeffrey pine, p. 60

2. Leaves clustered in 5s.

   a. Leaves 20–33 cm (8–13 in) long; trees of southern California   **Torrey pine, p. 61**

   b. Leaves 10–20 cm (4–8 in) long; trees of Arizona and New Mexico
          Ponderosa pine, p. 59
          (variety *arizonica*)

B. Cones borne laterally on the branchlets, not clustered near the tips of the branchlets.

1. Leaves clustered in 2s.

   a. Leaves 1.9–9 cm long, rarely to 10 (0.8–3.1 in long, rarely to 4); cones with the scales somewhat thickened on the face and scarcely to well-developed (usually erect) spines; trees of eastern North America.

   (1) Cone scales armed with short spines that soon fall away or are almost totally absent.

      (a) Leaves 4–8 cm (1.6–3.2 in) long, slender, soft; cones usually straight; trees of Coastal Plain of southeastern U.S.   **Spruce pine, p. 62**

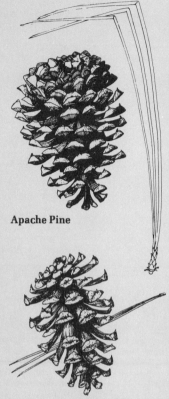

Apache Pine

Ponderosa Pine

Jeffrey Pine

Torrey Pine

(b) Leaves 1.9–3.8 cm (0.8–1.5 in) long, stout, stiff; cones 1-sided, curved; trees of northern North America
Jack pine, p. 62

Jack Pine

(2) Cone scales with well-developed erect to curved spines.

(a) Cones 8–12 cm (3.2–4.7 in) long, cone scales thick, the face of the scales armed with a stout, sharp, curved spine; trees of the Appalachians
Table Mountain pine, p. 63

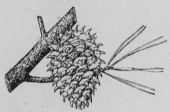

(b) Cones 3.8–8.8 cm (1.5–3.5 in) long, cone scales thin to slightly thickened, the face of the scales armed with a slender or small spine.

Table Mountain Pine

(b1) Cones armed with a slender curved spine on the face of each scale; leaves stout; trees of the east-central states
Virginia pine, p. 64

(b2) Cones armed with a tiny, stout spine on the face of each scale; leaves slender; trees of Florida   **Sand pine, p. 65**

Virginia Pine

b. Leaves 10–15 cm (4–6 in) long; cones with the scales strongly flattened and thickened on the face and armed with a stout, stiff, flattened spine; trees of the California coast   **Bishop pine, p. 66**

Bishop Pine

2. Leaves clustered in 3s.

a. Trees of eastern North America.

(1) Cones globe-shaped or broadest near the base, the cones broader than long.

(a) Leaves slender, flexible, dark yellowish-green, 10–20 cm (4–8 in) long; cone scales armed with a tiny spine that soon falls away; Coastal Plain of southeastern U.S.
Pond pine, p. 67

(b) Leaves stiff, bright green, 7.5–15 cm long, rarely to 20 (3–6 in long, rarely to 8); cone scales armed with a stiff, curved spine; trees of the eastern and northeastern U.S.
Pitch pine, p. 67

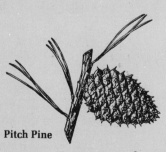

Pitch Pine

(Continued)

mm cm in (ruler)

(2) Cones oblong to cylindrical, the cones always longer than broad.

    (a) Leaves slender, soft, flexible, 7.5–10 cm long, rarely to 12 (3–4 in long, rarely to 4.8); cones 3.8–6.3 cm (1.5–2.5 in) long; trees of southeastern U.S. **Shortleaf pine, p. 68**

    (b) Leaves slender to stout, stiff, rigid, 12–28 cm (4.7–11 in) long; cones 5–15 cm (2–6 in) long.

        (b1) Cones dark brown, cone scales armed with sharp spines curved outward; needles 3 or 2 per cluster; trees of the Southeast

                Slash pine, p. 70

        (b2) Cones light reddish-brown, cone scales armed with short, straight, occasionally curved spines; needles always 3 per cluster; trees of the Southeast **Loblolly pine, p. 71**

b. Trees of western North America.

(1) Leaves 15–43 cm (6–17 in) long; cones large, 15–35 cm (6–13.8 in) long, armed with claw-like spines.

    (a) Cones massive, 25–35 cm (10–14 in) long, 10–12 cm (4–4.7 in) thick, light yellowish-brown; leaves thick, stout, trees of California **Coulter pine, p. 72**

    (b) Cones large, but not massive, 15–25 cm (6–10 in) long, 10–15 cm (4–6 in) thick, light-to-dark brown; leaves, slender, flexible; trees of California **Digger pine, p. 73**

(2) Leaves 7.6–15 cm (3–6 in) long; cones medium-size, 7.5–17.5 cm (3–7 in) long, armed with straight or curved spines.

    (a) Cones strongly 1-sided.

        (a1) Leaves slender, rigid, yellowish-green; cone scales thick, flattened; trees of California and Oregon **Knobcone pine, p. 74**

Shortleaf Pine

Slash Pine

Loblolly Pine

Coulter Pine

Digger Pine

Knobcone Pine

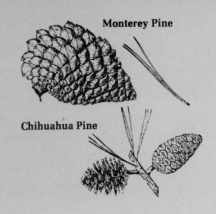

Monterey Pine

Chihuahua Pine

(a2) Leaves slender, flexible, bright green; cone scales thick, tapering to spine; trees of California coast
Monterey pine, p. 74

(b) Cones uniform, egg-shaped, 3.8–7.5 cm (1.5–3 in) long; leaves 6.3–11.5 cm (2.5–4.5 in) long, the sheath soon shedding; trees of Arizona, New Mexico, and Mexico
Chihuahua pine, p. 75

Red Pine, Norway Pine

Pinus resinosa Ait.

The red pine, a tree of northeastern North America, extends from Newfoundland to Manitoba and into the northern portion of the midwestern and northeastern U.S. Red pines occur on rolling hills, ridges, mountain slopes, and plains from sea level to 500 m, or 1,600 ft (900 m, or 3,000 ft, in the Adirondacks). They grow best on light, sandy loam soils that are slightly acidic and where there are mild summers, cold winters, and low to moderate amounts of rainfall. These pines occur in pure stands or mixed with jack pine, white pine, aspen, or some of the oaks.

Growth is slow initially, but the trees soon increase the rate to about 30 cm (1 ft) per year. Reliable seed production begins at 20 to 25 years of age, with heavy seed crops produced every 4 or 5 years. Red squirrels cut the ripening cones. Red crossbills, pine grosbeaks, and pine siskins are more dependent upon pine seeds than many of the other seed-eating northern birds. Chipmunks, mice, and voles consume seeds that have fallen.

The lightweight, pale reddish wood is moderately hard, close-grained and, as such, is an important timber and pulp-wood tree. The lumber is used for structural beams, bridges, piles, and railroad ties. The bark was once used for tanning leather, but synthetic tanning agents have replaced it. Red pine is frequently grown in plantations and reforestation projects, and it is commonly planted along major highways in the northeastern U.S.

Appearance: medium-size trees, 20–30 m (65–100 ft), rarely taller, broadly pyramidal with a broadly rounded crown; trunk tall, straight, 0.5–1.5 m (1.6–4.9 ft) in diameter. **Bark:** thin, 2.5–3.8 cm (1–1.5 in) thick, light reddish-brown, shallow fissures separating the broad, flat, scaly ridges. **Branches:** thick, stout, spreading; branchlets stout, orange-brown turning light reddish-brown. **Leaves:** *needles, 2 per bundle, 10–15 cm (4–6 in) long, slender, straight,* brittle, dark green to dark yellowish-green. **Flowers:** male cones small, clustered near the ends of the growing shoots; female cones small, globe-shaped, at the ends of the upper branches. **Fruits:** woody, hanging cones, broadest near the base and tapering toward the tip, 3.7–5.6 cm (1.5–2.2 in) long, light chestnut brown, matures in 2 seasons; *scales thin, concave, without spine,* each scale

Red Pine

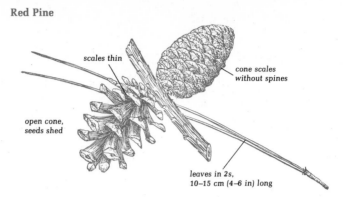

scales thin

cone scales
without spines

open cone,
seeds shed

leaves in 2s,
10–15 cm (4–6 in) long

with 2 seeds. **Seeds:** slightly flattened, broadest near the base, 5–7 mm (0.2–0.3 in) long, dark chestnut brown, mottled, winged, the wing 1.5–1.8 cm (0.6–0.7 in) long.

Scots Pine   *Pinus sylvestris* L.

The Scots pine has been planted widely in temperate and northern North America. It was introduced from Europe long ago, probably in colonial days, as a potential lumber source. Lacking the qualities of some of the native pines, the Scots pine was abandoned for timber, but it is still planted as an ornamental. There are many horticultural forms and selections available. This tree is often incorrectly called the Scotch pine.

It is a medium-size tree, 20–35 m (65–115 ft) tall, usually with an irregular open crown. The spreading upper branches are orange-red in color, and the **bark is distinctly orange and fissured.** The **needles are 2 per bundle, 3.8–7.6 cm (1.5–3 in) long, rigid, twisted, and dark bluish-green.** The yellowish-brown cones are 2.5–6.3 cm (1–2.5 in) long, cone-shaped, **bent back at the tip, and they have flattened scales that are thickened at the tips.**

Scots Pine

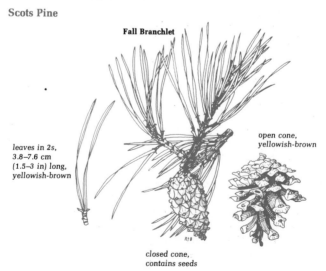

Fall Branchlet

leaves in 2s,
3.8–7.6 cm
(1.5–3 in) long,
yellowish-brown

open cone,
yellowish-brown

closed cone,
contains seeds

Lodgepole Pine

Pinus contorta Dougl.

Although the lodgepole pine extends from Alaska to Baja California, it is more abundant in the northern Rocky Mountains and Pacific Coast region. It is a common tree with 2 intergrading growth forms; 1 form is found in bogs, sand dunes, and on margins of pools and lakes. This form is character-ized by a short, shrubby, and almost contorted appearance. The inland or interior populations are slender, tall, straight trees. These trees generally grow from sea level to 3,600 m (0–11,500 ft) elevation on a variety of soils, including gravelly and rocky ridges, but the best growth occurs in deep, well-drained soils. Large acreages of this pine exist as pure stands, but it also is found in association with the western white pine and ponderosa pine and at higher elevations with Douglas fir, red fir, and subalpine fir. The lodgepole pine is considered an aggressive species that can become established quickly on burned-over sites. It is sometimes seriously damaged by pine beetles. Other insect pests include sawflies and the spruce budworm.

This pine is slow-growing and can live from 400 to 600 years. It reaches cone-bearing age quickly (6 to 10 years) and produces good seed crops every 1 to 3 years. Many of the cones do not open and persist on the trees for many years. Excessively hot days or forest fires usually cause many of the cones to open and shed their seeds.

Lodgepole pine is an important species for wildlife. Lodgepole pine forests are good habitats for spruce grouse. The seeds are a major item in the diet of the pine grosbeak and Clark nutcracker. Squirrels and chipmunks also use the seeds. Porcupines eat the bark and deform young trees. Deer often browse the younger trees.

This pine is a valuable timber tree. The light yellow wood is straight-grained and varies from light and soft to hard and heavy. The wood is worked easily and is used for general construction, poles, fencing, railroad ties, mine timbers, and in the manufacture of pulp. Poles, approximately 3–5 m (9–17 ft) long and 5–6 cm (2–2.4 in) in diameter, were used by the Indians in erecting their tepees or for litters and drag-sleds.

Appearance: small to large trees 10–30 m high, rarely to 50 (33–100 ft, rarely to 165) with a slender, cone shape and a narrow, spire-like crown; trunk short, crooked

Lodgepole Pine

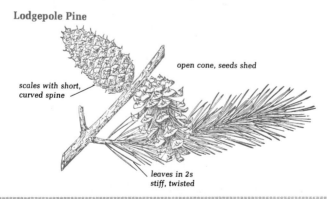

open cone, seeds shed

scales with short,
curved spine

leaves in 2s
stiff, twisted

(coastal trees) or tall, slender, 0.5–1 m in diameter, rarely to 2 (1.6–3.3 ft, rarely to 7). **Bark:** thin, 0.8–1.5 cm (0.3–0.6 in) thick (thicker on Coast), orangish-brown to grayish, forming small, thin, close scales. **Branches:** stout, short, soon branched, the upper ones semi-erect, the lower ones hanging; branchlets stout, orange turning reddish-brown to black. **Leaves:** *needles, 2 per bundle,* 2.5–7.6 cm (1–3 in) long, *stiff, usually twisted,* dark green to yellowish-green. **Flowers:** male cones cylindric, 8–10 mm (0.3–0.4 in) long, at the tip of the branches; female cones short-stalked, globe-like, 8–10 mm (0.3–0.4 in) long cones. **Fruits:** cones, woody, often clustered, usually broadest near the base or the middle, 1-sided, 2.5–5 cm (1–2 in) long, light yellowish-brown; scales thin, concave, *each scale armed with a short, curved spine.* **Seeds:** broadest near the base, 2–3 mm (0.1 in) long, dark reddish-brown to dark brown, usually mottled, winged, the wing usually narrow, 1–1.5 cm (0.4–0.6 in) long.

Austrian Pine, Black Pine *Pinus nigra* Arnold

Native of central and southern Europe and Asia Minor, the Austrian pine was introduced into North America more than 200 years ago. Planted originally as a potential lumber source, this pine is used today mainly for screens, wind breaks, or as an ornamental. It is a handsome tree from 30–50 m (98–165 ft) high, forming a uniform pyramid. On mature trees, the brown to dark-gray bark becomes deeply furrowed, forming irregularly lengthwise scaly plates. The *needles are 2 per bundle, stiff, 9–16 cm*

Austrian Pine, Black Pine

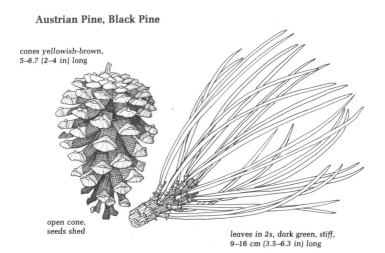

cones yellowish-brown, 5–8.7 (2–4 in) long

open cone, seeds shed

leaves in 2s, dark green, stiff, 9–16 cm (3.5–6.3 in) long

(3.5–6.3 in) long, sharp-pointed, and dark green. The yellowish-brown cones are 5–8.7 cm (2–4 in) long, broadest at the base and taper to a point. *Cone scales* are thickened and ridged on the face and armed *with a short spine.*

Longleaf Pine, Southern Pine *Pinus palustris* Mill.

The longleaf pine is a tall, stately tree of the southeastern Coastal Plain, where it generally occurs on sandhills, flats, and scrub lands from sea level to 650 m (2,200 ft) elevation. The trees grow in poor acid soils that are low in organic material. The growing season is characterized by long, hot summers and mild winters. These pines grow in pure stands or in association with scrub oak, slash pine, and loblolly pine. Longleaf pine shows good resistance to fusiform rust, a serious pine disease.

This pine is usually slow-growing, takes approximately 125 to 150 years to reach full size, and may live from 200 to 300 years. The cones shed their seeds while still on the trees, and the opened cones often persist another year before falling. This pine is important to wildlife, providing cover and food. Squirrels cut the cones for winter stores or feed immediately on the seeds. Birds, especially quail, brown-headed nuthatches, and turkeys, also use them.

The longleaf pine is a valuable species for lumber and for products such as turpentine, rosin, and tar. The light red to reddish-orange wood is strong, tough, hard, heavy, and durable. As a result, it is used in many ways, including posts, masts, structural beams, flooring, and general construction. The oleoresin obtained from the trunk is used to make turpentine.

Longleaf Pine

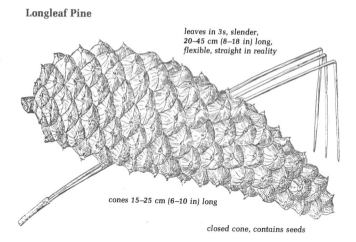

leaves in 3s, slender, 20–45 cm (8–18 in) long, flexible, straight in reality

cones 15–25 cm (6–10 in) long

closed cone, contains seeds

Appearance: medium to tall trees 30–40 m (98–132 ft) with an irregular, open crown; trunk straight, tapering slightly, 0.6–1 m (1.9–3.3 ft) in diameter, older trees free of branches for the lower half to third of trunk. **Bark:** thin, 0.4–1.6 cm (0.2–0.7 in) thick, light orangish-brown to grayish-brown, forming large, thin, irregularly shaped scales. **Branches:** stout, rough, often twisted, dark brown; branchlets stout. **Leaves:** *needles, 3 per bundle, 20–45 cm (8–18 in) long,* crowded towards the ends of the branchlets giving a tufted look, *slender, flexible, usually hanging,* dark green. **Flowers:** male cones short, 5–6 cm (2–2.4 in) long, narrowly cylindric, dark reddish-purple, at the tips of the branchlets; female cones 6–8 mm (0.2–0.3 in) long, oval, dark purple. **Fruits:** *cones,* woody, hanging, *cylinder-shaped* but tapering near the tip, slightly curved, *15–25 cm (6–10 in) long,* dull or pale brown; scales numerous, thin, flattened, rounded, and armed with a small curved spine at the tip, each scale containing 2 seeds. **Seeds:** nearly triangular, 1–1.4 cm (0.4–0.6 in) long, pale brown and mottled, winged, the wing thin, 4–5 cm (1.6–2 in) long, reddish-brown.

Apache Pine, Arizona Longleaf Pine

Pinus engelmannii Carr.
(synonyms: P. *latifolia* Sarg.,
P. *apacheca* Lemm.)

The Apache pine is a medium-size tree, 15–22 m (49–73 ft) high, with few branches and an open, rounded crown. It is an occasional tree of the pine forests in the mountains of southwestern New Mexico and southeastern Arizona and adjacent Mexico, and occurs from 1,650–2,750 m (5,400–9,100 ft) elevation. This pine usually grows with the Arizona and Chihuahua pines and the Arizona and silverleaf oaks. The Apache pine is apparently closely related to the ponderosa pine; but the Apache pine has slightly larger cones, longer needles, fewer and stouter branches. Its restricted range and scattered occurrence renders it of little or no commercial value and of limited use to wildlife.

Apache Pine

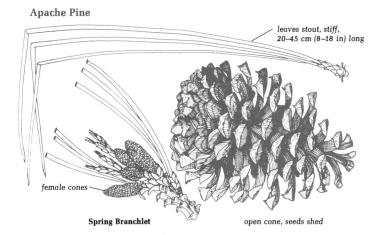

leaves stout, stiff, 20–45 cm (8–18 in) long

female cones

Spring Branchlet

open cone, seeds shed

Ponderosa Pine

Pinus ponderosa Laws

In terms of abundance and range, the ponderosa pine is the dominant tree of western North America. It occurs in Pacific Coast mountain ranges, throughout the Rocky Mountains, and into northern Mexico. It grows from sea level to 2,800 m (9,000 ft) elevation, but the best growth is attained on plateaus from 1,300–2,600 m (4,200–8,600 ft) elevation. Tolerant of a variety of soils, the ponderosa pine reaches its greatest size in deep, well-drained soils. It frequently occurs in pure stands, although it is also found growing with sugar pine, Douglas fir, and larch. Bark beetles can cause severe damage. And the leaves sometimes turn red and die due to the fungus *Elytroderma deformans*.

Because of the wide geographical range of ponderosa pine, several races have developed. One of these usually is treated as the Arizona ponderosa pine (*Pinus ponderosa* variety *arizonica*). This variety has 5 needles per bundle (3 or 2 in the typical form) and a smaller cone.

The trees are very fast-growing and may live from 300 to 600 years. Cone and seed production usually begins near 20 years of age with several years of light to medium production between heavy crops. The ponderosa is an important tree to wildlife. Among birds, spruce grouse, pine jays, and Clark nutcrackers are major seed consumers. Squirrels and chipmunks also use the seeds. Mule deer, porcupines, and some larger rodents feed on the young saplings.

The wood of this important timber tree is light; it varies from soft to hard and from fine to coarse-grained. Its wide use in commerce includes boxes, crates, toys, furniture, construction, mill products, and timbers.

Ponderosa Pine

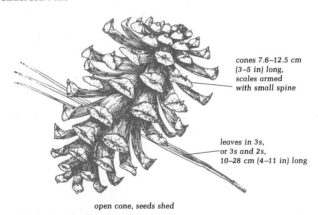

cones 7.6–12.5 cm
(3–5 in) long,
scales armed
with small spine

leaves in 3s,
or 3s and 2s,
10–28 cm (4–11 in) long

open cone, seeds shed

Appearance: medium to tall trees 30–60 m (98–200 ft) with a narrow, conical or almost flat-topped crown; trunk tall, straight, 0.6–1.8 m (1.9–5.9 ft) in diameter, older trees free of branches on lower two-thirds of trunk. **Bark:** medium to thick, 4–10 cm (1.6–4 in), dark brown to black when young to cinnamon red with age, irregularly and deeply furrowed and broken into large, flat plates. **Branches:** short, stout, spreading to slightly drooping; branchlets orangish turning dark brown. **Leaves: *needles 3, or 2s and 3s, occasionally 2, rarely 5, per bundle, 10–28 cm (4–11 in) long,*** stout, clustered near the ends of the branches and appearing tufted, yellowish-green to dark green. **Flowers:** male cones short, 4–5 cm (1.6–2 in) long, cylinder-shaped, at the tip of the branches; female cones nearly globe-shaped, 7–9 mm (about 0.3 in) long, near the tip of the branchlets. **Fruits: *cones,*** woody, sometimes with a short stalk, ***broadest at the base or near the middle, 7.6–12.5 cm (3–5 in) long,*** light reddish-brown; ***scales thin, flexible, narrow, armed with a small spine.*** **Seeds:** broadest near the base, ***7–8 mm (about 0.3 in) long,*** dark brown to brownish-purple, mottled, winged, the wing narrow, 2–2.5 cm (0.8–1 in) long.

Jeffrey Pine

Pinus jeffreyi Grev. & Balf.

(synonyms: *P. ponderosa* var. *jeffreyi* Vasey)

The Jeffrey pine is restricted to mountainous regions of the West from southern Oregon, throughout the Sierra Nevada, to Baja California. The trees normally grow from 1,500–3,000 m (4,800–9,600 ft) elevation, but individuals can be found at lower

points. They are tolerant of a variety of soils but do best in deep, well-drained soils. They are common on the western slopes of the Sierra Nevada and more abundant on the eastern slopes. On flats at lower altitudes, these pines usually occur in pure stands; while at higher elevations, they are found with red fir, western juniper, ponderosa, and sugar pines. They are closely related to and closely resemble the ponderosa pine. The Washoe (*Pinus washoensis*), known only from 3 small popu-

lations in western Nevada and adjacent California, is probably a hybrid between Jeffrey pine and ponderosa pine.

Moderate to rapid-growing, the Jeffrey pine is a long-lived tree, often reaching 400 to 500 years old. It may start producing cones at 10 or 15 years of age, but good production does not begin until twice that age. Animals that are attracted to the ponderosa pine, discussed earlier, also utilize this tree. Lumber companies do not distinguish between this pine and the ponderosa for processing.

Appearance: medium to tall trees 20–60 m (65–100 ft), usually with a long, narrow crown; trunk tall, straight, 0.5–2 m (1.5–6.5 ft) in diameter, older trees free of branches for lower half of trunk. **Bark:** similar to ponderosa pine, dark reddish-brown.

Jeffrey Pine

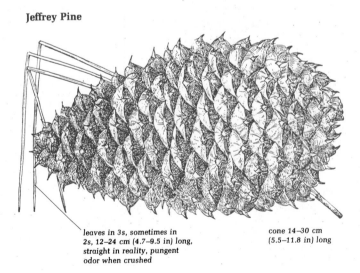

leaves in 3s, sometimes in 2s, 12–24 cm (4.7–9.5 in) long, straight in reality, pungent odor when crushed

cone 14–30 cm (5.5–11.8 in) long

Branches: short, stout, thick; branchlets stout, purplish-tinged, thick, with a distinctive fruity odor when crushed. **Leaves: *needles, 3, occasionally 2, per bundle,*** persisting for many years, giving a dense appearance to the foliage, ***12–24 cm (4.7–9.5 in) long, stiff, with a pungent odor when crushed,*** bluish-green. **Flowers:** male and female cones similar to ponderosa pine. **Fruits: *cones,*** woody, short-stalked, ***broadest near the base,*** tapering to a rounded tip, ***14–30 cm (5.5–11.8 in) long,*** purplish turning russet brown; scales numerous, thin, each scale thickened on the face and armed with a long, slender, ***inwardly curved spine.* Seeds:** broadest near the middle, ***1–1.4 cm (0.5 in) long,*** dark brown and mottled, winged, the wing 2–2.5 cm (0.8–1 in) long.

Torrey Pine   *Pinus torreyana* Parry

The Torrey pine is found only on the low, coastal bluffs of the Soledad Valley north of San Diego and on Santa Rosa Island. This rare pine apparently requires humid air conditions but will tolerate dry soils. It is a small tree, normally from 10–15 m (32–50 ft),

with a short, soon-branching trunk covered with light reddish-brown bark. The stout, ***dark green leaves are 20–33 cm (8–13 in) long, occur in bundles of 5,*** and generally clustered, near the tips of the branches, giving them a tufted appearance. The broad, ***dark chocolate brown cones*** are usually 10–15 cm (4–6 in) long and borne on long stalks. The thick scales are tipped with small spines. The cones will persist for 3 or 4 years before falling. The seeds (1.6–2 cm; 0.6–0.8 in) are edible.

The wood is soft, coarse-grained, and

Torrey Pine

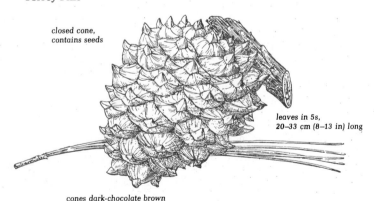

closed cone,
contains seeds

leaves in 5s,
20–33 cm (8–13 in) long

cones dark-chocolate brown

has been used as fuel, but the trees occur in too limited numbers to be of commercial value. The seeds are gathered and eaten, either raw or roasted. The Torrey pine sometimes is planted as an ornamental, but it is not as popular as other pines.

Spruce Pine, Cedar Pine

Pinus glabra Walt.

The spruce pine is a commercially unimportant, medium-size tree that is restricted to the Coastal Plain in the southeastern U.S. It is not abundant anywhere. Swamps, river valleys, river banks, and hammocks are its usual habitats. There are **2 needlelike leaves per bundle, 4–8 cm (1.6–3.2 in) long, slender, soft,** and dark green. The **small, straight cones** are similar to the cones of the shortleaf pine, but the spruce pine cones are smaller and more globeshaped. This species is related closely to the shortleaf pine.

Spruce Pine

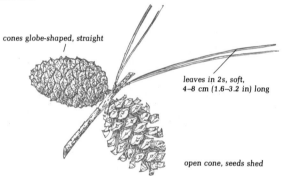

cones globe-shaped, straight

leaves in 2s, soft,
4–8 cm (1.6–3.2 in) long

open cone, seeds shed

Jack Pine

Pinus banksiana Lamb.

The most northern of all pine, jack pine ranges across Canada from the lower Rocky Mountains to northern New England. It normally occurs on rolling or flat sand plains, mainly at 350–500 m (1,100–1,700 ft) elevation, but reaches 850 m (2,790 ft) in the southern part of its range. Jack pine grows in climates with mild to cool summers and

very cold winters with moderate to abundant snowfall. It grows in pure stands or in association with black spruce, paper birch, and quaking aspen. It is considered a pioneer species that readily invades burnedover and exhausted sandy sites. It is related closely to and hybridizes with lodgepole pine in Alberta and the Northwest Territories.

Jack pine is a slow-growing species with a relatively short life. It reaches seed-producing age in 5 to 20 years, with maximum production beginning at 40 or 50 years. Many of the cones remain closed and persist on the trees for many years. They usually do not open until the weather is dry and the air temperature is at least 27° C (80° F) or until after a forest fire. Whitetail deer browse on saplings and young trees. Snowshoe hares and porcupines are considered pests in jack pine forests because hares feed heavily on the seedlings, and porcupines feed on the bark, often causing deformed trees. Red squirrels, chipmunks, and white-footed mice consume large quantities of fallen seeds. Many seed-eating birds, such as goldfinches, bronzed grackles, and robins, feed on the seeds.

The jack pine is of some importance to the forest industry. The wood is moderately hard, heavy, weak, and close-grained. It is used in general construction for timbers, poles, pilings, and for pulp wood.

Jack Pine

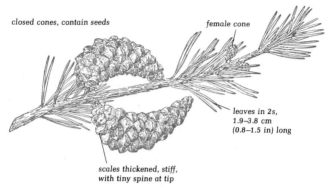

closed cones, contain seeds

female cone

leaves in 2s,
1.9–3.8 cm
(0.8–1.5 in) long

scales thickened, stiff,
with tiny spine at tip

Appearance: small to medium-size trees 10–25 m (32–90 ft) tall with an open, cone-shaped crown; trunk straight, tapering, 0.5–0.8 m (1.6–2.6 ft) in diameter. **Bark:** thin, 1–2.5 cm (0.4–1 in) thick, reddish-brown to dark brown, divided irregularly by furrows, forming narrow, rounded ridges composed of thick, close-pressed scales. **Branches:** slender, spreading and often arching at the tips; branchlets slender, flexible, yellowish-green turning dark purplish-brown with age. **Leaves: *needles, 2 per bundle, 1.9–3.8 cm (0.8–1.5 in) long,*** stout, stiff, straight or slightly twisted, light to dark yellowish-green. **Flowers:** male cones clustered, 8–10 mm (0.3–0.4 in) long, oblong, yellow, at the tips of the branches; female cones clustered, short-stalked, globe-shaped, dark purple, near the tips of the branches. **Fruits: *cones,*** woody, variable in shape but usually oblong to cone-shaped, ***more massive on 1 side,*** curved, 2.5–7.5 cm (1–3 in) long, dark yellowish-brown, shiny; ***scales*** thin, ***stiff, thickened and armed with a tiny spine at the tip.*** **Seeds:** angular, almost triangular, 3–5 mm (0.1–0.2 in) long, black, winged, the wing pale, 8–10 mm (0.3–0.4 in) long.

Table Mountain Pine   *Pinus pungens* Lamb.

A small, rugged tree of the Appalachian Mountains, the table mountain pine usually is found on shale outcrops and dry, rocky or gravelly soils. This pine is normally on or near exposed ridges at elevations up to 1,350 m (4,500 ft). It occurs in pure stands or mixed with spruce or hardwoods. The tough branches often are laden with numerous cones that usually persist on the branches for many years. These cones are armed with stout, hooked spines.

This pine is of limited value to wildlife except for cover. It is slow-growing and produces a soft, weak, brittle wood. It is of no commercial use but occasionally is used locally for firewood or for making low-quality charcoal.

Table Mountain Pine

cones 8–12 cm
(3.2–4.7 in) long

leaves in 2s

scales thickened, hard

closed cone, contains seeds

Appearance: small trees 3–20 m (9–66 ft) with a spreading, irregular shape and a rounded crown; trunk often short, stout, 0.3–1 m (1–3.3 ft) in diameter, soon branching. **Bark:** moderately thick, 1.5–2 cm (0.6–0.8 in), becoming dark reddish-brown, with shallow furrows forming irregular, loosely scaled plates. **Branches:** short, tough, the upper ones upright to spreading, the lower ones hanging; branchlets stout, tough, smooth, becoming dark brown. **Leaves: *needles, 2 per bundle,*** often appearing crowded, 5–10 cm (2–4 in) long, stiff, twisted, light to dark bluish-green. **Flowers:** male cones oblong, loose spike-like, yellow, 1–1.5 cm (0.4–0.6 in) long at the ends of the branchlets; female cones globe-shaped, reddish-purple, borne laterally on the branchlets near the ends. **Fruits: *cones,*** woody, usually clustered in groups of 3 to 5, ***broadest near the base,*** tapering toward the tip, somewhat 1-sided, persistent on the branchlets for many years, ***8–12 cm (3.2–4.7 in) long,*** light brown, shiny, ***the scales strong, heavily thickened at the outer edge and armed with a stout, curved spine.*** **Seeds:** almost triangular, 6–8 mm (0.2–0.3 in) long, light brown, winged, the wing thin, 1.5–2 mm (less than 0.1 in) long, broadest below the middle.

Virginia Pine   *Pinus virginiana* Mill.

The Virginia pine is native to lower elevations, 50–850 m (160–2,800 ft), in the eastern U.S. Specifically, it is common in the Piedmont and foothills of the Appalachian Mountains. Although this pine grows in a variety of soils, it does best in moderate to well-drained clay, loam, or sandy soils. Natively, it is found in pure stands or growing along with shortleaf pine, eastern redcedar, or several of the oaks. It invades old or abandoned fields and is used in reforestation projects aimed at reclaiming exhausted soils.

The Virginia pine is a moderate to slow-growing species, generally short lived. Cone production may start at 5 years of age but usually not until 8 to 10 years. Large crops of cones and seeds are followed by 1 or 2 years of light production. Whitetail deer browse saplings and younger trees; while squirrels, chipmunks, quail, and other seed-eating birds feed on the seeds.

The light orange-colored wood is coarse-grained, light, soft, and brittle. Its main use is for pulp wood, although it also is used as firewood, and occasionally as lumber in rough construction.

Virginia Pine

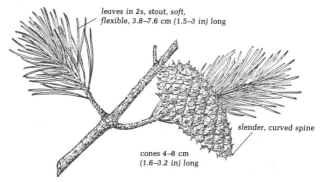

leaves in 2s, stout, soft, flexible, 3.8–7.6 cm (1.5–3 in) long

slender, curved spine

cones 4–8 cm (1.6–3.2 in) long

Appearance: small to medium-size trees 10–15 m tall, rarely to 25 (32–50 ft, rarely to 80), often with an irregular shape and an open, rounded to flat-topped crown; the trunk usually short, 0.3–0.5 m in diameter, rarely 1 (1–1.6 ft, rarely to 3.3). **Bark:** thin, 6–12 cm (2.4–4.8 in) thick, dark brown tinged with red, with shallow furrows separating the flat plates, the plates composed of close scales. **Branches:** spreading to drooping; branchlets slender, tough, green turning grayish-brown with age. **Leaves: needles, 2 per bundle, 3.8–7.6 cm (1.5–3 in) long, stout, soft, flexible,** slightly twisted, fragrant when crushed, grayish-green, shiny. **Flowers:** male cones crowded, oblong, 8–10 mm (0.3–0.4 in) long, orange-brown, at or near the tips of the branchlets; female cones stalked, globe-shaped, 4–6 cm (1.6–2.4 in) long, light green, on lateral shoots of the previous year. **Fruits: cones,** woody, **broadest near the base to cone-shaped,** persistent for several years, **4–8 cm (1.6–3.2 in) long,** dark reddish-brown; **scales thin, flat, slightly thickened and armed with a slender, curved spine at the tip.** **Seeds:** broadest near the base and angular, 5–7 mm (0.2–0.3 in) long, pale brown, winged, the wing broadest above the middle, 7–9 mm (about 0.3 in) long.

Sand Pine

Pinus clausa (Chapm.) Vasey

The sand pine is a small, bushy tree of Florida and the southern tip of Alabama. It grows in poor, sandy soils and is encountered most commonly on sand ridges and sand hills near coastal areas. This pine often grows in open stands in association with the evergreen oaks. The trees are able to establish themselves quickly in burned-over areas. The needles are **2 per bundle, 5–8.8 cm (2–3.5 in) long, slender, flexible, and dark green.** The **cones often are clustered,** broadest near the base, **5–9 cm (2–3.6 in) long,** brown, and the **scales are armed with a short, but stout, spine.** The cones open irregularly from the first through the fourth years and then may persist and eventually become embedded in the branches. The small, triangular seeds are

Sand Pine

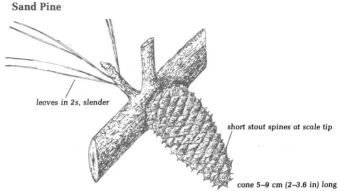

leaves in 2s, slender

short stout spines at scale tip

cone 5–9 cm (2–3.6 in) long

of value as a food source for turkeys, squirrels, and seed-eating birds. The wood is of inferior quality and is not used commercially.

Bishop Pine   *Pinus muricata* D. Don

The Bishop pine grows only in several scattered locations along the coast of California from Humboldt County south to the Pacific shoreline of northern Baja California, and on Cedros Island. The trees are highly variable but are often handsome and round-tipped. The dark, yellowish-green, stiff, thick *leaves are 10–15 cm (4–6 in) long, 2 per bundle,* and crowded together in tight clusters. This species has reliably characteristic cones that may persist on the trees for 15 to 29 years before they open and shed their seeds. These stalked, egg-shaped *cones usually occur in clusters of 3 to 5 and are armed with stout, stiff, flattened spines.*

The heavy, coarse-grained wood is weak and usually contains numerous knots. This, combined with the short and often crooked branches, renders the species of little value commercially. It is of little value to wildlife.

Bishop Pine

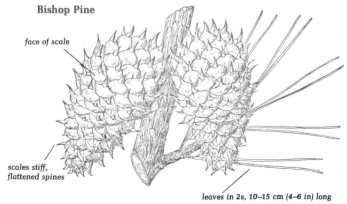

face of scale

scales stiff, flattened spines

leaves in 2s, 10–15 cm (4–6 in) long

Pond Pine, Pocosin Pine
Pinus serotina Michx.

As the name implies, this pine grows on low, wet flatlands or in sandy or peat-laden swamps or bogs along the Coastal Plain of the southeastern U.S. Unlike most pines, the pond pine thrives in soils with a high water table and can tolerate wide fluctuations in water level. The medium-size trees often have an irregular or open, rounded crown and dark gray to reddish-brown bark. The slender, flexible, dark yellowish-green **needles are 3, occasionally 4, per bundle and 10–20 cm (4–8 in) long.** The light yellowish-brown cones are almost globe-shaped to broadest near the base and usually persist on the trees for 1 or 2 years before shedding their seeds. Even then, the open cones remain on the branches for many more years, often be-

coming embedded in the branchlets as they expand in size. This pine is related closely to the pitch pine of the northeastern U.S.

Pond Pine

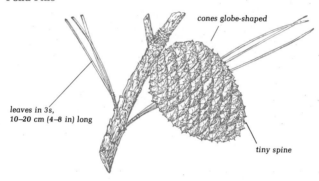

cones globe-shaped

leaves in 3s,
10–20 cm (4–8 in) long

tiny spine

Although this pine is not very important to wildlife, its foliage does provide cover for many birds, and the seeds are eaten by rodents and birds. The pond pine is of little value commercially, except for local use as firewood.

Pitch Pine
Pinus rigida Mill.

Pitch pine is distributed widely in eastern and northeastern North America, usually at low altitudes, but does occur up to 1,500 m (5,000 ft) elevation in the southern part of its range. The trees normally grow in poor, sandy to gravelly soils along river valleys or low coastal areas. The greatest abundance of pitch pine is found in Pennsylvania and in the fascinating pine barrens of New Jersey. There, the pitch pine is the dominant tree species. Throughout most of its range, it grows with red pine, white pine, shortleaf pine, oak, and birch.

During the first 5 years, growth is slow, but then it becomes rapid. Because of their rapid growth and ability to grow on very poor soils, pitch pines are used in reforesting worn-out lands. Fire is responsible for maintaining the large stands of this pine. The cones often persist unopened on the trees until a forest fire; then soon after a fire, many of the cones will open, shedding their seed. This pine is important to wildlife. Whitetail deer and rabbits browse the young sprouts and seedlings. Seed crops are important in the diet of the pine warbler, pine grosbeak, and black-capped chickadee.

Pitch pines have been exploited for many years. The light brown or reddish-brown wood is soft, weak, resinous, and coarse-grained, but it is very resistant to decay. The colonists used this pine in their ship-building industries. This was displaced by the use of the wood to manufacture charcoal for the then active iron ore smelting enterprises. Later, it was used to manufacture turpentine, and some of the lumber was used in rough construction.

Pitch Pine

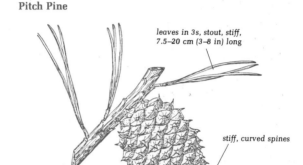

leaves in 3s, stout, stiff,
7.5–20 cm (3–8 in) long

stiff, curved spines

cones 4–8 cm
(1.6–3.2 in) long

Appearance: medium-size trees, 15–30 m (49–100 ft), pyramid-shaped with an irregular, rounded crown; trunk short, thick, soon branching, 0.5–1 m (1.6–3.3 ft) in diameter. **Bark:** moderately thick, 2–4 cm (0.8–1.6 in), reddish-brown with deep furrows forming irregular broad, flat ridges, the ridges composed of loose scales. **Branches:** stiff, spreading to hanging, occasionally contorted. **Leaves: *needles, 3 per bundle, 7.5–20 cm (3–8 in) long, stout, stiff,*** triangular in cross section, bright green, shiny. **Flowers:** male cones clustered, small, cylindrical, 1.5–2 cm (0.6–0.8 in) long, yellowish, at the tips of the branches; female cones globe-shaped, short-stalked, 3–5 mm (0.1–0.2 in) long, light green, on the sides of the branchlets near the tips. **Fruits: *cones,*** woody, usually clustered and persistent for many years, ***almost globe-shaped to broadest near the base, 4–8 cm (1.6–3.2 in) long,*** light brown, the ***scales thin, flattened, ridged on the outer face and armed with a stiff, curved spine.*** **Seeds:** almost triangular, 4–6 mm (0.2 in) long, dark brown, mottled, winged, the wing 6–8 mm (0.2–0.3 in) long.

Shortleaf Pine   *Pinus echinata* Mill.

The shortleaf pine is widespread throughout the southeastern U.S. It usually occurs at low elevations but is known to occur as high as 1,100 m (3,600 ft). The trees grow mainly on old fields and upland woods in a wide range of soils. The greatest size and best growth result from fine, sandy loam or silt loam soils. This pine is found in pure stands or it is mixed with other species, mainly oaks, eastern redcedar, Virginia pine, and loblolly pine. The trees do well on abandoned fields or exhausted farmland. It is sometimes attacked by southern pine beetles and several kinds of weevils. It usually is not seriously affected by fungal diseases.

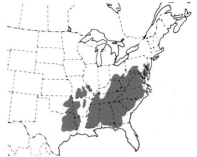

Compared with other pines, shortleaf pine is fast-growing and reaches seed-bearing age after 20 to 25 years. This pine is important to wildlife. Squirrels, chipmunks, mice, and other rodents consume large quantities of the seeds. Many birds forage on fallen seeds.

Because the trees are abundant through most of their range, they are commercially important. The yellow-brown to light orange wood is hard, strong, coarse-grained, and easily worked. It is used for general construction, flooring, interior house trim, plywood, pulp wood, and fuel. Turpentine is made from the wood's oleoresin.

Shortleaf Pine

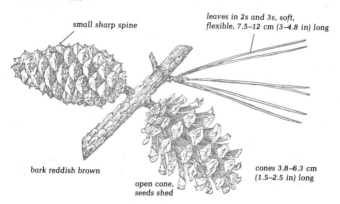

small sharp spine

leaves in 2s and 3s, soft, flexible, 7.5–12 cm (3–4.8 in) long

bark reddish brown

open cone, seeds shed

cones 3.8–6.3 cm (1.5–2.5 in) long

Appearance: medium to tall trees 25–35 m (80–115 ft) tall with short, pyramid-shaped crowns; trunk tall, straight, 0.6–1 m (1.9–3.3 ft) in diameter, older trees free of branches on the lower half of trunk. **Bark:** medium-thick, 2–2.8 cm (0.8–1.1 in), reddish-brown, furrowed, and broken into large, irregular, scaly plates. **Branches:** stout, brittle, becoming dark reddish-brown with age. **Leaves:** *needles, 2, sometimes 3 per bundle, 7.5–12 cm (3–4.8 in) long, slender, soft, flexible,* sharp-pointed, yellowish-green to dark bluish-green. **Flowers:** male cones oblong, 1.5–1.8 cm (0.6–0.7 in) long, pale purple, clustered at the tips; female cones oblong, 7–9 mm (about 0.3 in) long, erect, pale red, single or in small clusters of 2 to 4 near the ends of the branchlets. **Fruits:** *cones,* woody, hanging, *oblong and tapering near the tip, 3.8–6.3 cm (1.5–2.5 in) long,* dull brown; the scales flattened to concave, thin, short, armed with a small, sharp spine. **Seeds:** angular and somewhat irregular in shape, 5–7 mm (0.2–0.3 in) long, brown mottled with black; seeds winged, the wing oblique, 1.5–2 cm (0.6–0.8 in) long, light reddish.

Slash Pine *Pinus elliottii* Engelm.

The slash pine is a common and valuable tree of the Coastal Plain of the southeastern U.S. This pine is restricted to low elevations and normally occurs on wet flatlands, along borders of ponds, streams, rivers, and bays, but also may be found on low, sandy hills. The soils in which it grows are usu-  ally sandy and poor in nutrients. The slash pine almost always is found growing with many different lowland tree species, including longleaf and loblolly pine, swamp tupelo, sweetbay, red maple, and pond cypress. Slash pine is sometimes killed by the fusiform rust disease. This can be serious in large stands. The trees in southern Florida, including the Keys, technically are considered a variety (*densa*) of the typical slash pine.

This is a rapid-growing species and is used frequently in reforestation projects. Cone production may begin at 10 years of age, but 20 years is required for good crops. Large cone and seed crops are produced about once every 3 years.

Slash pine is important to wildlife, providing cover and food for many animals. Slash-pine flatlands or flatwoods are excellent habitats for wild turkey, for the seeds constitute an important component of a turkey's diet. Whitetail deer also use flatwoods for cover and for the associated browse vegetation. Gray and fox squirrels cut the cones just before they open. The seeds are eaten immediately, or entire cones are buried for later use.

This is one of the more important species of pine in the Southeast. The wood is heavy, strong, hard, durable and is used in different kinds of construction. Slash-pine plantations are tapped for the resin, which is manufactured into turpentine.

Slash Pine

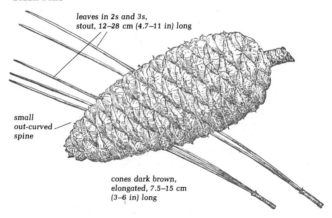

leaves in 2s and 3s, stout, 12–28 cm (4.7–11 in) long

small out-curved spine

cones dark brown, elongated, 7.5–15 cm (3–6 in) long

Appearance: medium-size trees 25–35 m (80–115 ft) with a broadly conical to pyramidal shape and a dense, rounded crown; trunk tall, tapering, 0.5–1 m (1.6–3.3 ft) in diameter, often free of branches on the lower half to two-thirds of mature trees.

Bark: thin, 2–3.2 cm (0.8–1.3 in) thick, light orange to reddish-brown, often tinged with purple, shallowly furrowed and forming large, thin, very loose, scales. **Branches:** stout, spreading; branchlets stout, becoming rough, turning orange-brown with age. **Leaves:** *needles 2, sometimes 3, per bundle, stout, rigid, 12–28 cm (4.7–11 in) long,* dark green, shiny. **Flowers:** male cones clustered, short, 1.2–2.5 cm (0.5–1 in) long, cylindric; female cones stalked, 1–1.5 mm (0.06 in), oval. **Fruits:** *cones,* woody, hanging, *elongated to egg-shaped, 7.5–15 cm (3–6 in) long, dark brown;* scales thin, flexible, ridged on the face and *armed with a small, out-curved spine.* **Seeds:** almost triangular, 6–8 mm (0.2–0.3 in) long, dark gray and black mottled, winged, the wing dark brown, about 2 cm (0.8 in) long.

Loblolly Pine   *Pinus taeda* L.

Loblolly pine is a common tree of the Southeast, in the Coastal Plain, Piedmont, and Mississippi River Valley. It occurs on flatlands or rolling hills from sea level to 700 m (2,300 ft) elevation. This pine grows in different soil types ranging from low, poorly drained areas to well-drained, but often  poor, upland soils. Best growth results from long, hot, and humid summers combined with mild winters and 100–150 cm (39–59 in) of rainfall annually. This species thrives on abandoned, cut-over, or exhausted fields. Loblolly commonly occurs in pure stands but also grows in association with a variety of hardwoods. On low, wet sites sweetgum, water oak, and sweetbay are frequent associates; while on higher ground, shortleaf pine and southern red oak are among many accompanying species. The loblolly pine can be damaged or killed by southern pine beetles. It can also be infected by fusiform rust diseases.

Loblolly pine is fast-growing and may begin to produce seed at 10 years of age, although 30 to 40 years is average. The seeds are released in October. Because of the abundance of this pine and the frequency of large seed crops, it is very important to wildlife. Squirrels, chipmunks, mice, and other rodents consume large quantities of fallen seeds. Many birds also forage on fallen seeds. Both the bobwhite quail and wild turkey favor loblolly seeds.

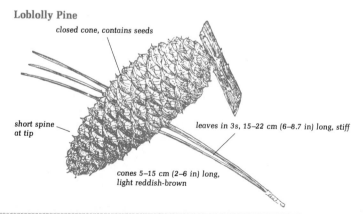

Loblolly Pine

closed cone, contains seeds

short spine at tip

leaves in 3s, 15–22 cm (6–8.7 in) long, stiff

cones 5–15 cm (2–6 in) long, light reddish-brown

The light brown wood is coarse-grained, not very strong, and less durable than the longleaf pine. Yet, commercially, it is an important wood, used in general construction and for pulp.

Appearance: medium to tall trees 25–40 m (80–140 ft) tall with a rounded, compact crown; trunk straight, tall, 0.5–1 m (1.6–3.3 ft) in diameter, older trees free of branches for lower two-thirds of tree. **Bark:** thin, 1.7–2.8 cm (0.7–1.1 in) thick, bright reddish-brown, with shallow furrows separating the irregularly shaped, broad, flattened scales. **Branches:** stout, thick, ascending to spreading; branchlets stout, brownish-yellow turning brown. **Leaves: *needles, 3 per bundle, 15–22 cm (6–8.7 in) long, slender, stiff,*** slightly twisted, pale or light green. **Flowers:** male cones cylindrical, 1.5–3 cm (0.6–1.2 in) long, yellowish, often clustered at the ends of the branchlets; female cones oblong, 1–1.4 cm (0.4–0.6 in) long, yellow, single or in small groups near the ends of the branchlets. **Fruits: *cones,*** woody, ***oblong to cylindric*** and tapering toward the tip, ***5–15 cm (2–6 in) long, light reddish-brown; scales*** thin, flattened, rounded, and ***armed with a short, straight, or curved spine.*** **Seeds:** angular, 4-sided, 2.2–2.6 cm (0.9–1.1 in) long, dark brown and mottled, winged, the wing thin, broadest above the middle, 2–2.5 cm (0.8–1 in) long.

Coulter Pine

Pinus coulteri D. Don

The Coulter pine is found on dry, rocky slopes of the coastal mountains of central and southern California and into northern Baja California. It normally occurs from 380–2,300 m (1,100–7,600 ft) altitude and is scattered in the coniferous forest. This species is related closely to the Jeffrey pine and the Digger pine. The trees are small to medium-size and usually form a loose, but attractive, irregular shape. The long (15–30

Coulter Pine

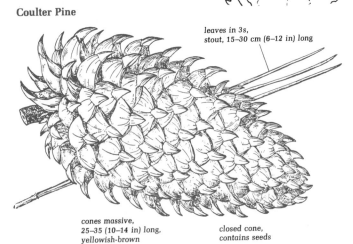

leaves in 3s,
stout, 15–30 cm (6–12 in) long

cones massive,
25–35 (10–14 in) long,
yellowish-brown

closed cone,
contains seeds

cm; 6–12 in), dark blue-green leaves are thick and stout, and occur in bundles of 3 and cluster toward the ends of the branches, giving a tufted appearance. The light yellowish-brown hanging cones are among the largest of any North American pine. These **cones are 25–35 cm (10–14 in) long,** and the thick, broad scales are tipped with flat, incurved claw-like spines. The cones remain on the tree for several years before shedding seeds and then falling.

The wood is soft, lightweight, and coarse-grained and is of limited value except for fuel. The seeds are edible and once were gathered by Indians.

Digger Pine   *Pinus sabiniana* Dougl.

The digger pine is a stout, irregularly shaped, open tree of California's dry foothills and lower mountain slopes from 20–1,000 m (65–3,300 ft) elevation, occasionally higher. It is a common tree of the foothills of the Sierra Nevada where it grows in

small, pure stands or scattered with the blue oak. This is a medium-size pine with a thick trunk and **3 needles per bundle,** which are **17–43 cm (6.7–17 in) long, slender, flexible,** dull blue-green, and usually hanging from the tips of the branchlets. The digger pine also is known as the squaw pine or one of the nut pines because the plump, light-to-dark brown **cones, 15–25 cm (6–10 in) long,** contain large, edible, hard-shelled seeds. These were a favorite food of Indians. Deer, squirrels, other ro-

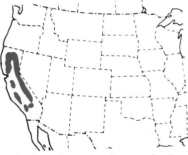

dents, and birds also eat the nuts. The coarse-grained, weak wood makes poor lumber, but it makes good firewood because it generates considerable heat when properly seasoned.

Digger Pine

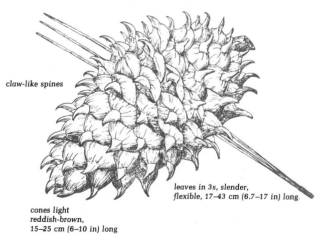

claw-like spines

leaves in 3s, slender, flexible, 17–43 cm (6.7–17 in) long

cones light reddish-brown, 15–25 cm (6–10 in) long

Knobcone Pine

Pinus attenuata Lemm.

Knobcone pines are found on dry, rocky slopes and ridges of the coastal mountain ranges from southern Oregon to Baja California. The trees usually grow at 800–1,350 m (2,600–4,500 ft) elevation, generally on western or southern exposures, and may occur in pure stands, especially in the northern part of their range. They are small to medium-size trees, 3–15 m (9–50 ft) high, rarely more, and the **needles are 3 per bundle, 7.6–15 cm (3–6 in) long**, rigid, **slender,** and **yellowish-green.** The yellowish-brown cones are elongated, broadest near the base, **far more massive on 1 side,** and strongly incurved. They have prominent knobs on the face of each scale; hence the name knobcone. Each of these knobs is armed with a thick, flattened,

Knobcone Pine

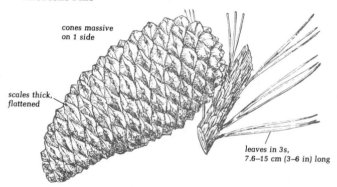

cones massive
on 1 side

scales thick,
flattened

leaves in 3s,
7.6–15 cm (3–6 in) long

curved spine. The cones often persist for several decades and become embedded in the branches. The wood is coarse-grained, light, soft, and weak; thus it is of limited commercial value, except as firewood.

Monterey Pine

Pinus radiata D. Don

This attractive pine is confined to 3 coastal locations in the fog belt of central California and on Santa Cruz and Santa Rosa Islands. The other known native is on Guadalupe Island off the coast of Baja California. The trees are small to medium-size. But on deep, rich soils, they will grow into large trees with a straight trunk. The **bright green leaves are slender, flexible,** and **occur in bundles of 3.** The characteristic **cones are far more massive on 1 side than the other.** They are broadest near the base, **pointed at the tip, 7.6–17.5 cm (3–7 in) long,** and remain closed on the branches for many years. Fire will stimulate them to open, or they eventually will fall to the forest floor, where they may lie for several more years before opening.

The trees are rapid-growing and are used for lumber or for shade. The tough, hard

Monterey Pine

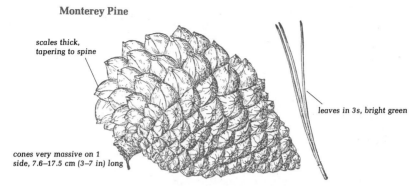

scales thick,
tapering to spine

leaves in 3s, bright green

cones very massive on 1
side, 7.6–17.5 cm (3–7 in) long

wood has been used for flooring, finishings, and fuel. The Monterey pine has been used widely as an ornamental for many years, having been planted in England, southern Europe, the Mediterranean, Africa, and Australia. It is planted in Australia, New Zealand, and southern Africa for timber.

Chihuahua Pine   *Pinus leiophylla* Schiede & Deppe

This Mexican pine extends from Mexico into southwestern New Mexico and southeastern Arizona. The North American populations sometimes are considered a variety (*chihuahuana*) of this species because the northern trees have 3 needles per bundle, while the central and southern Mexican trees have 5 needles per bundle.

The trees occur as scattered individuals in pine forests of 1,650–2,600 m (5,400–8,600 ft) elevation and often grow in association with the Arizona and Apache pines. They are small to medium-size, 10–25 m (32–82 ft) high, open trees with slender, **pale green needles 6.3–11.5 cm (2.5–4.5 in) long. The sheath** (a paper-like wrapping around the base of each bundle of needles) **soon falls away from the needles,** a special feature of this species. The **egg-shaped,** light brown **cones are 3.8–7.5**

Chihuahua Pine

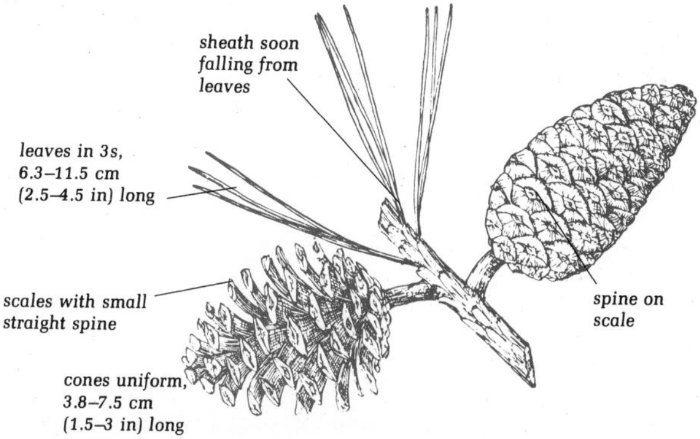

sheath soon
falling from
leaves

leaves in 3s,
6.3–11.5 cm
(2.5–4.5 in) long

scales with small
straight spine

spine on
scale

cones uniform,
3.8–7.5 cm
(1.5–3 in) long

cm (1.5–3 in) long, and grow on stalks. The scales are armed with short spines. This is the only species of pine in North America on which cones must grow for 3 years before they are mature. The small size and limited number of trees make the Chihuahua pine of minor commercial importance.

The Larch Genus   *Larix* Mill.

There are 10 species of larches in the world. All are restricted to the colder regions of the Northern Hemisphere, and most occur in mountainous areas. Three species are native to North America: two are confined to the Northwest, and the third is a widespread species. The European larch, *Larix decidua,* has been planted extensively in northern North America and is the most commonly encountered larch in the northeastern U.S.

Larches are small to large-size, usually irregularly shaped trees with peeling bark. The bark, usually reddish-brown, is rich in tannins and was used for tanning leather. The branches often are slender and droop gracefully with age. The wood is strong, heavy, and durable and is an important timber source in England. The leaves are needle-like and clustered on short, lateral shoots. All larches lose their leaves in fall and remain bare until spring when new growth appears. Male and female cones are produced in separate structures on the same tree. The cones mature in one season but may persist on the trees for another year.

Key to Larch Species

A. Cones with the scales longer than or equal to the narrow bracts; branchlets slender, flexible.

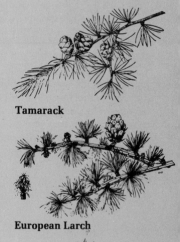

1. Cones 1.2–2 cm (0.5–0.8 in) long, brown, composed of 18–22 scales, not hairy; native to northern and northeastern North America
Tamarack, p. 77

Tamarack

2. Cones 1.9–3.8 cm (0.8–1.5 in) long, bright reddish-brown, composed of 40–50 scales, covered with soft, brown hairs; introduced species planted widely in northern North America   **European larch, p. 78**

European Larch

B. Cones with conspicuous, narrow bracts exceeding the scales; branchlets stout.

1. Branchlets with scattered hairs when young, not densely hairy; leaves triangular in cross section; bark reddish-brown; trees of northwestern U.S. and British Columbia
Western larch, p. 78

Western Larch

2. Branchlets densely hairy; leaves 4-sided in cross section: bark grayish: trees of northwestern U.S., plus British Columbia and Alberta
Subalpine larch, p. 80

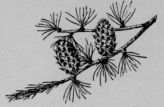

Subalpine Larch

Tamarack

Larix laricina (Du Roi) K. Koch

The tamarack is a northern tree with a natural range larger than most North American conifers. It extends from Newfoundland to Alaska. The trees grow in different habitats including upland stream, river bank, and swampy land. But the best groves occur on

moist, well-drained soils. In low, wet areas the trees may occur in pure stands, but in other areas tamaracks are found in association with several species, including black spruce, balsam fir, white fir, and northern white cedar. Growth is usually slow in wetter sites. Tamarack is relatively free of serious infection by fungal diseases.

Maturity usually is reached in 50 to 75 years with good seed crops every 3 to 6 years. Whitetail deer browse young trees but do not damage them seriously. Porcupines often kill tamaracks by stripping away the outer bark and feeding on the inner bark. Red squirrels snip off the cones and eat the seeds or gather and bury them for later use. Chipmunks and mice are major consumers of the seeds. In early fall red crossbills break apart the cones for the seeds.

Tamarack wood is strong, heavy, and durable, but it is not valued for its lumber. Occasionally the wood is used in rough construction and as poles, piers, and railroad ties.

Tamarack

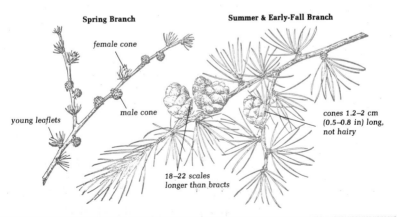

Spring Branch

female cone

young leaflets

male cone

Summer & Early-Fall Branch

cones 1.2–2 cm (0.5–0.8 in) long, not hairy

18–22 scales longer than bracts

Appearance: small to medium-size trees 15–25 m (49–82 ft) tall with an open pyramidal shape and an irregular open crown; trunk usually straight, clear, 0.4–0.6 m (1.3–1.9 ft) in diameter. **Bark:** thin, 1.2–2 cm (0.5–0.8 in) thick, light reddish-brown, peeling in narrow, closely pressed scales. **Branches:** small, slender, spreading, sometimes in graceful down-and-out sweeps when field grown; branchlets slender, light orange-brown turning darker with age. **Leaves:** needle-like, dropping in autumn, spirally arranged and clustered on short, lateral shoots, 2–3.1 cm (0.8–1.2 in) long, triangular in cross section, soft, bluish-green, turning yellow in fall. **Flowers:** male cones small, globe-shaped, light yellow, borne near the tips of the branchlets; female cones small, oblong, light reddish, borne on older branchlets. **Fruits:** *cones,* short-stalked, almost globe-shaped, pointed at the tip, *1.2–2 cm (0.5–0.8 in) long, brown, composed of 18 to 22 scales,* each *scale stiff, longer than broad,* spreading at maturity; bracts on inner face of scale, small, about one-half as long as the scales. **Seeds:** egg-shaped, 2–4 mm (about 0.1–0.2 in) long, light brown, winged, the wing 2 to 3 times longer than the seeds.

European Larch, Common Larch *Larix decidua* Mill.

The European larch is an attractive, irregularly shaped, deciduous tree that is widely planted in northern North America. Native to the Alps of central Europe and the Carpathian Mountains of eastern Europe, it is similar in appearance to the tamarack but grows taller. It can be distinguished from our native larch in that its *cones* are composed of *40 to 50 scales* (native species have fewer). *Its bracts are equal to or shorter than the scales, and its cones are covered with soft, brown hairs.* The European larch has been planted extensively as a timber source throughout Europe. In North America it is used primarily as a decorative planting because of its attractive form, delicate green leaves, and light-green cones turning brown at maturity. Many cultivated forms are available.

European Larch

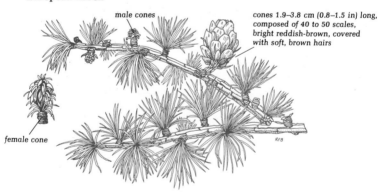

male cones

cones 1.9–3.8 cm (0.8–1.5 in) long,
composed of 40 to 50 scales,
bright reddish-brown, covered
with soft, brown hairs

female cone

Western Larch *Larix occidentalis* Nutt.

The western larch, largest of the North American larches, occurs in the intermountain region of the Northwest. The trees grow in deep to dry, rocky soils, generally at 700–2,350 m (2,300–7,700 ft) elevation. They prefer cool temperatures and moderate amounts of precipitation, often as snow. The largest trees grow on deep, well-drained soils and usually are encountered with ponderosa pine, grand fir, and Douglas fir. Western larch is sometimes attacked by parasitic dwarf mistletoe.

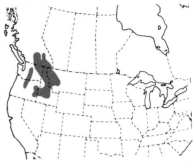

Unlike most conifers, this species loses its leaves in the fall, and the trees remain bare throughout the winter. Western larch is rapid-growing when young but may take 40 to 50 years to produce large quantities of seed. Good cone and seed crops usually are produced every other year. The seeds are consumed by mice, chipmunks, and seed-eating birds (especially the red crossbill). The buds and needles are eaten by spruce and blue grouse. Otherwise these trees are of limited use to wildlife.

This species is the most important timber species of larch. The wood is strong, hard, close-grained, and very durable. It is used for flooring, pilings, fence posts, railroad ties, and interior and exterior finishings.

Western Larch

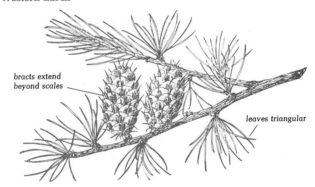

bracts extend beyond scales

leaves triangular

Appearance: medium-size to large trees 30–55 m (98–175 ft), with a narrow pyramidal to almost conical shape and with a sharp-pointed crown; trunk tall, straight to tapering, 1.5–2.6 m (4.9–8.5 ft) in diameter. **Bark:** thick, 12–15 cm (4.7–5.9 in), *light reddish-brown,* forming irregular, flat, scaly plates. **Branches:** short, stout, spreading, dull orange turning dark brown with age; *branchlets stout,* orangish-brown turning dark brown with age. *Leaves:* needle-like, dropping in autumn, spirally arranged in clusters on short, lateral branches, 2.5–4.5 cm (1–1.8 in) long, *almost triangular in cross section,* slender, soft but sharp-pointed, light pale green, turning yellow in autumn. **Flowers:** male cones small, oblong, yellow; female cones larger, short-stalked, oval, composed of almost rounded scales and narrow bracts with a slender point extending beyond the scales. **Fruits:** cones, short-stalked, oval, broadest near the base of the middle, 2.5–3.8 cm (1–1.5 in) long, reddish-brown; scales stiff, almost rounded, widely spreading at maturity; *bracts* with a narrow, slender point *extending beyond the scales.* **Seeds:** egg-shaped, 5–7 mm (0.2–0.3 in) long, pale brown, winged, the wing wedge-shaped, as long as or twice as long as the seed.

mm
cm 1 2 3 4 5 6 7 8 9 10 11
in 1 2 3 4

Subalpine Larch

This species occurs on the high mountain slopes of the northern Rockies at 1,300–2,350 m (4,200–7,700 ft) altitude. The subalpine larch often can be found near timber line. There these trees have a rugged, or even gnarled, appearance. The trees are small to medium-size with an irregular branching pattern. *They can be distinguished easily from the western larch by their densely hairy branchlets*

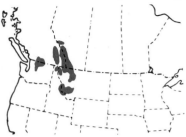

Subalpine Larch

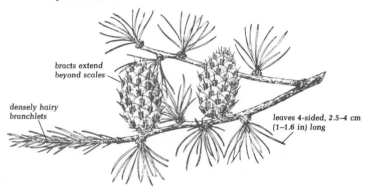

bracts extend beyond scales

densely hairy branchlets

leaves 4-sided, 2.5–4 cm (1–1.6 in) long

and needle-like leaves, which are 2.5–4 cm (1–1.6 in) long and 4-sided in cross section. Because they occur at high altitudes in largely inaccessible areas, the trees are of no commercial value. They are of little to no value to wildlife.

The Spruce Genus

Picea A. Dietr.

The approximately 40 species of spruce in the world occur in the cool and cold temperate regions of the Northern Hemisphere. The trees usually grow in wet sites with poor, shallow soil. There are 7 species native to North America and 1 widely planted European species, the Norway spruce. Four of the spruces are found only in western or northwestern North America; while 2 range across Canada and into the northern U.S., and 1 is restricted to northeastern North America.

Spruces are long-lived, medium to tall, evergreen trees, usually with a tall, tapering trunk, and a cone-shaped outline. The bark is usually thin and scaly. The branches and branchlets are small, slender, and rough due to numerous, small peg-like stalks that bear the leaves. Winter buds are dry, not resinous. The tiny leaves are needle-like, flat, or angled and usually persist for several years. Male and female cones occur on the same tree but on separate branches. The male cones are cylindric or broadest near the base, either upright or hanging, composed of many, spirally arranged pollen sacs (as shown in the book's introduction) and produced in a lateral position on the branchlets. The female cones are usually globe-shaped, violet to purple, and composed of many scales. The fruits are leathery cones, which become dry and papery to woody when ripe and shed their seeds at the end of the first growing season. But the cones may persist on the trees. These cones consist of numerous, thin scales that are smooth, lobed, or round-toothed on the edge and with tiny bracts. There are 2 small, winged seeds for each scale.

Spruces are valuable trees, both to man and to wildlife. Since the spruce grouse is almost entirely dependent upon spruce trees for food and cover, its range is the same as that of the various spruces. The blue grouse also utilizes spruce for food and shelter but to a lesser extent than the spruce grouse. Whitetail deer and rabbits browse twigs and leaves of young plants; while squirrels, chipmunks, and seed-eating birds, especially the white-winged crossbill, consume large quantities of spruce seeds. The soft, odorless wood is used for many purposes. Spruces are probably the most important source of pulp wood in North America. Several species are planted widely for ornamental purposes and for windbreaks. Because of their graceful, almost drooping branches, the Norway spruce and, to a lesser extent, the Serbian and Oriental spruce, have been planted widely throughout temperate North America.

Key to Spruce Species

A. Leaves flattened.

    1. Leaves pointed at the tip; seed-bearing cones narrow, cylindrical, the cone scales broadest near the middle, toothed on the outer edge; branchlets without hairs; lowland trees of the Pacific Coastal area   **Sitka spruce, p. 82**

Sitka Spruce

    2. Leaves rounded at the tip; seed-bearing cones and cone scales broadest near the base, smooth on the outer edge; branchlets with fine hairs; upland trees of southern Oregon and northern California   **Weeping spruce, p. 83**

Weeping Spruce

B. Leaves 4-sided.

    1. Cones with the scales rounded on the outer edge.

        a. Cone scales soft and flexible when mature; branchlets smooth, without hairs; trees of trans Canada   **White spruce, p. 84**

White Spruce

        b. Cone scales tough, stiff, rigid when mature; branchlets with fine hairs.

            (1) Cones persisting for several years, the cones 2–3 cm (1 in) long, purplish-brown to brown; the cone scales wavy or toothed on the outer edge; trees of trans Canada   **Black spruce, p. 85**

            (2) Cones falling after 1 year, the cones 3–5 cm (1.2–2 in) long, brown, the cone scales smooth or only slightly wavy; eastern trees   **Red spruce, p. 87**

Black Spruce

(Continued)

2. Cones with the scales wedge-shaped on the outer edge.

   a. Branchlets with the leaves spreading to semi-erect; cones usually less than 10 cm (4 in) long, native trees.

   (1) Leaves soft, flexible, with a pungent, disagreeable odor when crushed; branchlets with fine, soft hairs; cones 4–8 cm (1.6–3.2 in) long, persisting for 1 year; western trees
   Engelmann spruce, p. 88

Engelmann Spruce

   (2) Leaves stiff, rigid, with a resinous but not disagreeable odor when crushed; branchlets without hairs; cones 5.7–10 cm (2.2–4 in) long, persisting for 2 years; western trees
   Blue spruce, p. 89

Blue Spruce

   b. Branchlets with drooping leaves; cones 10–18 cm (4–7 in) long; introduced species, planted widely   **Norway spruce, p. 90**

Sitka Spruce   *Picea sitchensis* (Bong.) Carr.

The sitka spruce, a tall, massive tree with a buttressed base, grows the largest of all native spruces. It grows in a narrow zone, usually about 80 km (50 miles) wide, along the Pacific Coastal region from southern Alaska to northwestern California. The trees grow at lower elevations, from sea level to 1,000 m (3,300 ft), often in swampy conditions on west-facing slopes, along river valleys, and especially near the mouths of rivers. They require mild temperatures and high, seasonally uniform precipitation, often in the form of dense fog. The inland distribution of the sitka spruce appears to depend upon the inland penetration of fog banks. Sitka spruce frequently grows in

pure stands but also occurs with grand fir, Douglas fir, western redcedar, and red alder. The Engelmann spruce is a close relative, and hybrids of the 2 species occur.

The trees grow very rapidly and are long-lived; ages of 700 to 800 years are not unusual. Best growth and largest size are reached when the trees grow in moist, deep, rich soils. They are prolific seed producers; large seed crops are produced every other year or every third year. These spruce are of some importance to wildlife. Ruffed grouse occasionally feed on the buds and needles. Deer browse the younger trees but usually only when preferred food sources are not available. Squirrels cut the cones — often days before the cones shed their seeds — and feed on the seeds or store the cones for later use. Chipmunks, mice, shrews, and seed-eating birds search the forest floor for fallen seeds.

The wood of the sitka spruce is light brown, lightweight and soft, but strong and resilient. As a result, it has been used in building aircraft. It is used for boxes, crates,

Sitka Spruce

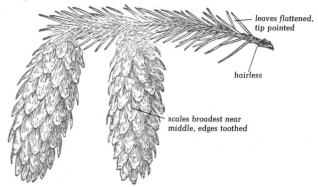

leaves flattened, tip pointed

hairless

scales broadest near middle, edges toothed

sounding boards for musical instruments, plywood, and general construction. This spruce is considered an important North American timber tree. Indians have used the tough, flexible roots for weaving baskets.

Appearance: tall, massive trees 40–60 m, rarely to 70 (130–200 ft, rarely to 230), with a cylindric shape and a short, often open crown; trunk straight, 1–2 m, rarely to 3 (3–6 ft, rarely to 10) in diameter, usually buttressed at the base, older trees free of branches for lower one-third to one-half of tree. **Bark:** thin to moderately thick, 1–2 cm (0.4–0.8 in), reddish-brown, scaly on younger trees, becoming separated into large, loose scales. **Branches:** short, slender, spreading to slightly drooping; ***branchlets*** stout, rigid, light gray to light brown and ***smooth (without fine hairs).*** **Leaves:** linear to broadly needle-shaped, spreading away from branchlets, 1.5–2.5 cm (0.6–1 in) long, stiff, ***flattened,*** straight, ***sharp-pointed at the tip,*** green to yellowish-green, shiny. **Flowers:** male cones numerous, narrow, oblong, reddish, 1.5–2 cm (0.6–0.8 in) long, produced at the tips of the branches; female cones oblong, 2–3 cm (0.8–1.2 in) long, produced on the stiff growing shoots of the branches on the upper part of the trees. **Fruits:** leathery, hanging cones, the cones broadly cylinder-shaped, 6–10 cm (2.4–4 in) long, yellowish-green, turning pale brown at maturity; cone scales numerous, thin, stiff, almost rectangular in shape, ***wavy and irregularly toothed on the outer edge.*** **Seeds:** rounded, pointed at the base, 2–4 mm (about 0.1–0.2 in) long, reddish-brown, winged, the wing narrow, oblique, about 2 to 2½ times as long as the seed.

Weeping Spruce   *Picea breweriana* S. Wats.

The weeping spruce is an attractive subalpine tree found only in the mountains of southern Oregon and northern California, usually at 1,300–2,350 m (4,200–7,700 ft) elevation. This is the only native spruce that has long, hanging branchlets that give it a weeping appearance. The trees grow on mountain slopes and ridges, usually in dry, rocky soils. But the largest of the species grow in deep, moist, well-drained soils. They can be found in pure stands or growing with white fir, incense cedar, mountain hemlock, sugar pine, and western white pine. The light yellowish-brown wood is somewhat heavy but soft and is of little commercial use.

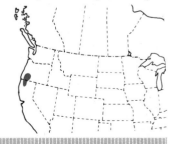

This spruce is a small to medium-size tree, 15–25 m (49–82 ft) high, usually with

Weeping Spruce

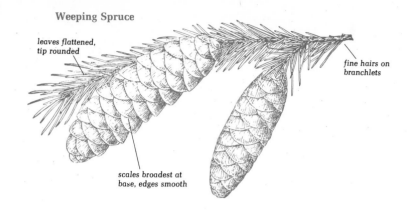

leaves flattened, tip rounded

fine hairs on branchlets

scales broadest at base, edges smooth

branches reaching the ground, and a narrow cone-shaped crown. The branches are numerous, short, and spreading; while the **branchlets are long, thin, hanging,** and are covered with fine hairs. The **leaves** quickly narrow to a **rounded tip** and are flattened, straight or curved, and shiny, dark yellowish-green. The leathery, hanging cones are broadest near the middle or the base, 5–10 cm (2–4 in) long, dull rusty brown, and mature in 1 growing season. The cone scales are thin, widest near the base, but longer than broad, and rounded at the tip. The seeds are pointed at the base, 2–4 mm (about 0.1–0.2 in) long, dark chocolate brown, with a wing about 4 times as long as the seed.

White Spruce   *Picea glauca* (Moench) Voss

White spruce is an extremely hardy tree of the Northern Coniferous Forest, ranging from Alaska to Newfoundland and into the northern northeastern U.S. This spruce grows from sea level to 1,700 m (5,600 ft) elevation along streams and lakes

and along rocky hills and slopes. It can grow in a variety of soil conditions and is often the first tree species that moves into abandoned fields. White spruce seldom occurs in pure stands but grows in association with many trees, including balsam fir, black spruce, eastern hemlock, trembling aspen, white birch, and red maple.

The trees can begin to produce seeds at approximately 20 years of age. But reliable seed production may take twice that long. White spruce are good seed producers, with heavy crops occurring from 2 to 5 years. The leaves of white spruce are often infected by several rust diseases which result in the premature shedding of needles. Serious insect pests include the spruce budworm and spruce sawfly. White spruce are important to grouse and seed-eating birds. Red squirrels cut the cones and young leader shoots. Porcupines are considered pests because they eat the bark, often resulting in a deformed trunk. Black bears may strip the bark for the sweet sapwood.

White spruce produces a light, soft wood that is resilient and straight-grained. In Canada, it is an important timber tree and used extensively for pulp wood. Boxes, shipping crates, and rough lumber for general construction are some of its main uses.

Since its roots are very tough and pliable, the Indians once gathered the smaller ones to lace their birchbark canoes.

White Spruce

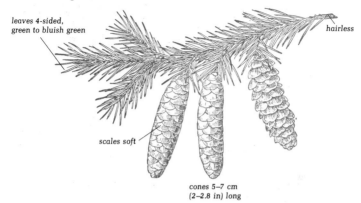

leaves 4-sided, green to bluish green

hairless

scales soft

cones 5–7 cm (2–2.8 in) long

Appearance: medium-size to tall trees, 25–40 m (80–140 ft), with a cone or steeple shape and a cone-shaped crown; trunk tall, tapering, 0.5–1.3 m (1.6–4.3 ft) in diameter, older trees often free of branches for lower half of trunk. **Bark:** thin, 0.6–1.2 cm (0.3–0.5 in), light grayish-brown, produced in irregular, thin, scaly plates. **Branches:** thick, spreading to drooping; ***branchlets*** numerous, stout, ***hairless,*** light gray to orangish-brown. **Leaves:** linear to broadly needle-shaped, crowded on the upper half of the branchlets, often curved inward, 1.8–2.2 cm (0.7–0.9 in) long, ***4-sided,*** blunt at the tip, pungent odor when crushed, green to bluish-green. **Flowers:** male cones numerous, stalked, narrow, cylindric, 1.5–2 cm (0.6–0.8 in) long, yellow; female cones cylindric, 1.4–2 cm (0.6–0.8 in) long, greenish. **Fruits:** leathery, hanging cones, the cones slender, cylindrical, 5–7 cm (2–2.8 in) long, pale green turning light brown at maturity; ***cone scales*** numerous, ***thin, flexible, rounded on the outer edge,*** falling soon after shedding the seeds in fall. **Seeds:** broadest near the middle, 2–4 mm (about 0.1–0.2 in) long, pale brown, winged, the wing about twice as long as the seed and rounded at the tip.

Black Spruce, Bog Spruce   *Picea mariana* (Mill.) B.S.P.

The black spruce, a northern tree, ranges from Alaska across Canada to Newfoundland and into the northeastern U.S. It is one of the most abundant species of conifers in the Northern Coniferous Forest. Its habitat is typically well-drained, but moist, flatlands and lake margins, but in the southern part of its range, it occurs in sphagnum moss bogs. It grows from about 100–850 m (330–2,800 ft) elevation and can tolerate a variety of soil types. The black spruce occurs in pure stands or in mixed stands, primarily with white spruce, balsam fir, jack pine, and aspen. It is closely related to the red spruce, and natural hybrids of the two sometimes occur.

The trees are slow-growing and not very long-lived. They are prolific seed producers, usually beginning to bear cones around 10 years of age. The unopened cones persist on the branches for up to 4 or 5 years. Fire will stimulate the cones, causing them to open and shed their seeds. The trees also can reproduce by a nonsexual method known as layering. This often happens when the lower branches come into contact with, or are slightly buried in, soil or litter. Roots develop at those points and are able to support new shoots that develop from the buried branches.

The black spruce is not an important tree to wildlife. Whitetail deer and moose will not feed on the younger shoots and leaves except as starvation conditions approach. Snowshoe hares feed on younger trees and seedlings, although they too prefer other trees. Squirrels cut the cones for the seeds.

The wood is yellowish-white, soft, relatively lightweight, strong, and somewhat resilient. Because the trees do not reach the size of other spruces, they are not an important lumber source. But they are valuable for pulp wood. They are also used for fuel.

Black Spruce

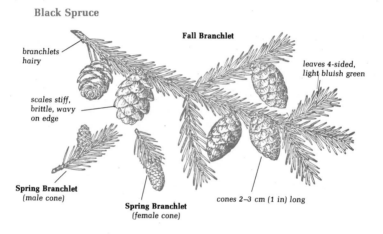

branchlets hairy

Fall Branchlet

leaves 4-sided, light bluish green

scales stiff, brittle, wavy on edge

Spring Branchlet
(male cone)

Spring Branchlet
(female cone)

cones 2–3 cm (1 in) long

Appearance: small to medium-size trees 5–18 m, rarely to 30 (16–60 ft, rarely to 100), with a cone shape and a narrow, pointed crown; trunk straight, 15–30 cm (5.9–11.8 in) in diameter, rarely larger. **Bark:** thin, 6–13 mm (0.2–0.5 in), rusty to grayish-brown, broken into irregular, thin, closely pressed scales. **Branches:** short, slender, spreading to slightly drooping but turning upwards at the tip; branchlets slender, becoming rough due to the formation of numerous peg-like projections on which the leaves are produced; *branchlets covered with many small hairs.* **Leaves:** linear and needle-like, short-stalked, spreading, 0.5–1.5 cm (0.2–0.6 in) long, *4-sided* (cannot be rolled smoothly between fingers), stiff, often slightly curved toward the branchlets, blunt at the tip, light bluish-green. **Flowers:** male cones numerous, cylinder-shaped, small; female cones oblong to cylinder-shaped, produced at or near the ends of the branchlets. **Fruits:** small rigid cones, the cones egg-shaped to broadest near the base, 2–3 cm (1 in) long, dull purplish-brown to brown; *cone scales* nearly circular, *stiff, brittle, wavy on the outer margin.* **Seeds:** broadest near the middle, 2–4 mm (about 0.1–0.2 in) long, dark brown, winged, the wing about twice as long as the seed.

Red Spruce
Picea rubens Sarg.

A medium-size evergreen tree, the red spruce occurs in northeastern North America and in scattered groves along the ridges of the Appalachian Mountains. In the northern part of its range, this spruce grows at or near sea level in swamps, along bogs, or on well-drained slopes. In the southern part of its range, it grows at 1,000–1,500 m (3,300–5,000 ft) elevation, often in thin soils. The trees grow best on well-drained acid soils and can be found in pure stands or mixed with white spruce, balsam fir, eastern white pine, hemlock, and yellow birch. The trees are shallow rooted and are often encountered as windfalls. Eastern spruce beetle and spruce budworm often attack red spruce. At least six species of rust and two needle-cast fungi can seriously infect the leaves.

Where ranges of the red and the black spruce overlap, hybrids occur. Since the hybrids display characteristics of both parents, they sometimes puzzle people attempting to determine species.

Growth rates for red spruce vary from slow to moderately fast, depending upon the amount of light received. Dense shade results in slow growth; while full sun is needed for best growth. Reproduction usually begins at about 15 years of age, but reliable production may take another 5 to 10 years. Large seed crops occur every 4 to 6 years. Red spruce is not a long-lived tree compared with other conifers; its maximum age is generally between 300 and 400 years old.

During the winter months, whitetail deer and rabbits browse red spruces, especially young trees and seedlings. In fall, the ripening, seed-laden cones attract squirrels. Among the seed-eating birds, white-winged crossbills like northeastern spruce forests.

The light-colored wood is very similar to white spruce and is usually sold as white spruce or simply spruce. The lightweight wood is soft, straight-grained, and resilient. Spruce lumber is used in general construction and is commonly used to produce musical string instruments. Red spruce was once abundant on the upper slopes of the Appalachian Mountains. Lumbering and fire have greatly reduced its ranks there.

Red Spruce

branchlets hairy

leaves 4-sided, yellowish-green

scales rounded, stiff, & smooth or slightly toothed on edge

cones 3–5 cm (1.2–2 in) long

Appearance: medium-size trees, 20–30 m (65–100 ft), generally with a column shape and with a short pointed crown; trunk straight, 0.3–1 m (1–3.3 ft) in diameter, on older trees usually free of branches for lower one-third to two-thirds of trunk. **Bark:** thin, 0.6–1.2 cm (0.3–0.5 in) thick, light reddish-brown, forming thin, tight, irregular scales. **Branches:** upper branches upturned, lower ones spreading with the tips upturned; ***branchlets*** slender, becoming rough, turning light brown to orange-brown with age, and ***covered with numerous short hairs.*** **Leaves:** linear and needle-like, spreading, 1.2–2 cm (0.5–0.8 in) long, ***4-sided,*** stiff, usually curved in toward the branchlets, blunt at the tip, bright yellow-green. **Flowers:** male cones numerous yellowish-green, 12–14 mm (0.5 in) long, and broadest near the base; female cones cylinder-shaped, 11–13 cm (4.3–5.1 in) long, produced at the tips of the branchlets. **Fruits:** leathery cones, hanging, the cones cylindrical but tapering to a rounded tip, 3–5 cm (1.2–2 in) long, green turning brown at maturity, ***cone scales rounded, stiff, smooth or slightly toothed on the outer edge.*** **Seeds:** broadest above the middle, 2.4 mm (0.1 in) long, dark brown, winged, the wing broad, about twice as long as the seed.

Engelmann Spruce

Picea engelmannii Parry

Engelmann spruces are medium to large trees in the high elevations of the Rocky Mountains, extending from Canada to Arizona and New Mexico. The northern populations occur from 1,000–2,650 m (3,200–8,700 ft) elevation; while in the central and southern Rockies, they grow from 2,500–3,700 m (8,200–12,000 ft). These spruces grow to timberline, having the ability to thrive in a very cold, humid climate with deep, annual snowfall. Although they can survive on poor, thin, rocky soils, the best growth occurs in deep, well-drained, clay-loam soils. Because of their wide range, they can be found growing in association with many trees. At or below timberline, bristlecone pine, subalpine fir, blue spruce, and mountain hemlock are common companions. In other areas Engelmann spruce may occur in mixed stands

with Douglas fir, limber pine, white fir, and birch. Where its ranges overlap with blue spruce and white spruce, hybrids occur.

Engelmann spruces are moderate to fast-growing trees and often live 500 to 600 years. They are usually able to produce cones at 20 to 25 years of age, with excellent seed production taking place every 2 to 6 years. Their value to wildlife is basically the same as that outlined in the introduction to the spruces earlier.

The yellowish-brown wood is soft, moderately weak, resilient, and is lumped commercially under the general heading of spruce or white spruce. The lumber is used in general construction, although it is of only limited use in the U.S. because of the inaccessibility of its high-elevation habitats. It is also used for fuel and was once used for tanning leather.

Appearance: medium to large trees, 25–35 m, rarely 35 (80–115 ft, rarely 115), with a uniform, narrow, cylinder or cone shape, and a compact, pyramidal crown; trunk straight, slightly tapering, 0.3–1 m (1–3.3 ft) in diameter, rarely larger, older trees usually free of branches for lower half to two-thirds of trunk unless growing in dense forest. **Bark:** thin, 1.2–1.6 cm (0.5–0.7 in) long, reddish-brown, sometimes with a

Engelmann Spruce

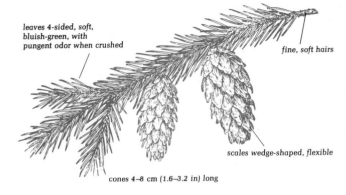

leaves 4-sided, soft,
bluish-green, with
pungent odor when crushed

fine, soft hairs

scales wedge-shaped, flexible

cones 4–8 cm (1.6–3.2 in) long

purplish cast, furrowed and scaly, the scales large, thin, and loose. **Branches:** upper ones spreading with short, hanging, secondary branches; *branchlets* slender, becoming rough, green turning dark yellow-brown, *with fine, soft hairs.* **Leaves:** broadly needle-shaped, *spreading, 2–2.6 cm (0.8–1.1 in) long,* 4-sided, slender, *soft, flexible, with a pungent, disagreeable odor when crushed,* bluish-green. **Flowers:** male cones numerous, cylindrical, 1.2–1.6 cm (0.5–0.7 in) long; female cones very similar to male flowers in size and shape but produced at the tips of the upper branches. **Fruits:** leathery cones, hanging, broadest at the middle to cylinder-shaped and tapering to a rounded tip, 4–8 cm (1.6–3.2 in) long, green turning brown to yellowish-brown at maturity; cone *scales* wide, broadest near the middle, *flexible, irregularly toothed on the outer edge.* **Seeds:** rounded, thickened, 2–4 mm (about 0.1–0.2 in) long, brown to nearly black, winged, the wing wedge-shaped, about twice as long as the seed.

Blue Spruce, Colorado Blue Spruce   *Picea pungens* Engelm.

The blue spruce is an attractive tree native to the higher elevations in the Rocky Mountains. It grows at 1,800–3,400 m (5,750–11,000 ft) altitude, generally along stream banks and other sites with higher moisture levels. It does best in deep, rich, moist gravelly soils. Blue spruce does not occur in large stands; instead it is found as scattered trees, sometimes in small groves, or more commonly with the Engelmann spruce, Douglas fir, lodgepole pine, and ponderosa pine. The western spruce dwarf mistletoe can be a serious parasite. The spruce bark beetle and spruce budworm are major insect pests. Blue spruce are planted extensively in eastern North America and in Europe as ornamentals.

This spruce is slow-growing and long-lived, sometimes reaching 600 to 800 years old. It is a good seed producer, although there are usually 2- or 3-year intervals between large seed crops. Reproduction by seedlings is very low and limited unless the site has been disturbed recently by landslide or fire. A deeply penetrating root system firmly anchors the trees against strong winds. These spruces are of limited value to wildlife, although they do provide cover and seeds for squirrels, rodents, and some birds.

The light to pale brown wood is lightweight, soft, brittle, and often full of knots. Because of this and inaccessible habitats at high elevations, blue spruces are not commercially important as timber.

Blue Spruce

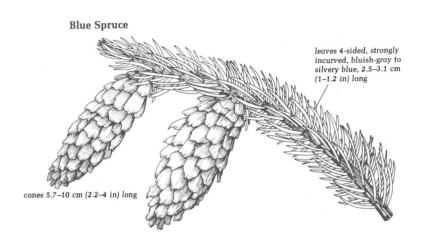

leaves 4-sided, strongly incurved, bluish-gray to silvery blue, 2.5–3.1 cm (1–1.2 in) long

cones 5.7–10 cm (2.2–4 in) long

Appearance: medium-size trees, 20–35 m (65–115 ft), with a narrow pyramidal shape and an open to dense, irregularly cone-shaped crown; trunk straight, tapering, 0.5–1 m (1.6–3.3 ft) in diameter, sometimes forking into 2 or 3 main trunks. **Bark:** thin to moderately thick with age, 1.2–3.2 cm (0.5–1.3 in), pale gray (when young) to reddish-brown, younger trees with small, narrow, flattened scales, later becoming furrowed. **Branches:** short, stout, usually spreading to slightly drooping, the upper ones slightly upturned; *branchlets* short, stout, *smooth (hairless),* turning orangish-brown to grayish-brown with age. **Leaves:** linear and broadly needle-shaped, *spreading away from the branchlets, 2.5–3.1 cm (1–1.2 in) long,* 1.5–2 cm (0.6–0.8 in) long on the upper cone-bearing branches, *4-sided, stiff, strongly incurved,* sharp-pointed at the tip, dull bluish gray to silvery blue. **Flowers:** male cones narrow, cylinder-shaped, 1–1.5 cm (0.4–0.6 in) long, reddish-yellow; female cones similar to male but produced on upper branches. **Fruits:** stiff, leathery to woody *cones,* hanging, cylinder-shaped and tapering slightly toward the tip, *5.7–10 cm (2.2–4 in) long,* rarely longer, green turning shiny chestnut brown at maturity; cone scales flattened, stiff, irregularly toothed on the outer margin. **Seeds:** rounded, 2–4 mm (about 0.1–0.2 in) long, dark brown, winged, the wing wedge-shaped, about twice the length of the seed.

Norway Spruce, Common Spruce   *Picea abies* (L.) Karsten

Native to northern and central Europe, where it becomes large and massive, the Norway spruce is planted widely as an ornamental in temperate and cool regions of North America. More than 100 forms, varieties, or cultivars of this spruce have been named, although only a few of these are seen in cultivation. The trees do best in shady

Norway Spruce

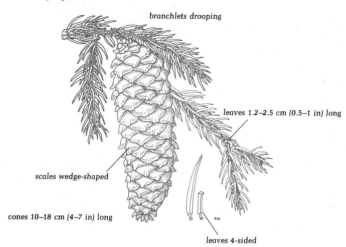

branchlets drooping

leaves 1.2–2.5 cm (0.5–1 in) long

scales wedge-shaped

cones 10–18 cm (4–7 in) long

leaves 4-sided

or partially shaded locations and in deep, rich, moist soils. Larger specimens are often seen on older estates.

In Europe the Norway spruce grows from 40–65 m (130–215 ft) in height. But in North America, it seldom grows beyond 40 m (130 ft).

Unlike all native species of spruce, the Norway spruce has drooping branches and branchlets. The **leaves** are **4-sided,** dark green, broadly needle-shaped, 1.2–2.5 cm (0.5–1 in) long, and blunt at the tip. Branchlets are hairless. The seed-bearing cones are 10–18 cm (4–7 in) long, hanging, and are reddish-brown.

The Hemlock Genus   *Tsuga* (Endl.) Carr.

All hemlocks, a small genus of 10 species, are found in North America, Japan, Taiwan, China, and the Himalayas. Four species occur in North America — 2 in the East, and 2 in the West. The trees usually grow in cool, moist situations, often with some protection from high winds. Although no species are native in Europe today, fossils, reported to be hemlock, have been found there. Hemlocks, especially the eastern hemlock, are used frequently as ornamentals because they are attractive, adaptable to different soils, and responsive to pruning. They make excellent screens and windbreaks.

Hemlocks are evergreens with a characteristic drooping leader shoot and irregular spreading to drooping branches. The bark usually is furrowed deeply and is reddish-brown to cinnamon red. The small, flexible linear leaves are usually flat and are often arranged in 1 plane on the branchlets. Male and female cones occur on the same tree. These small cones are produced in early spring; they mature and shed their seeds in fall or early winter of the same year. The tiny seeds are winged.

Key to Hemlock Species

A. Cones stalked; trees of eastern North America.

    1. Leaves flattened in 1 plane on the branchlets,
toothed; seed-bearing cones 1.2–1.9 cm (0.5–
0.8 in) long, the scales almost as broad as long
Eastern hemlock, p. 92

    2. Leaves spreading in all directions on the
branchlets, not toothed; seed-bearing cones
2.5–3.8 cm (1–1.5 in) long, the scales longer
than wide
Carolina hemlock, p. 94

Eastern Hemlock

B. Cones without stalks (sessile); trees of western
North America.

    1. Leaves flattened, with a groove on the back, ar-
ranged in 1 plane (2-ranked) on the branchlets;
cones 2–2.8 cm (1 in) long, light brown
Western hemlock, p. 94

Western Hemlock

    2. Leaves rounded or ridged on the back, spread-
ing in all directions on the branchlets; cones
usually 4–5 cm (1.6–2 in) long, yellowish-
green to purple   **Mountain hemlock, p. 95**

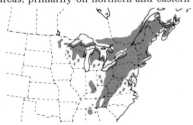

Mountain Hemlock

Eastern Hemlock   *Tsuga canadensis* (L.) Carr.

The eastern hemlock is an attractive tree of the northern Midwest, northeastern
North America, and the Appalachian Mountains. It normally occurs in cool, moist
valleys and ravines and in other protected areas, primarily on northern and eastern
slopes. The trees will grow on different
soil types, but the litter from fallen twigs
and leaves gradually will cause acid soil
conditions, which can discourage competition from some plants. Generally a lowland tree, eastern hemlock can be found up
to 1,700 m (5,600 ft). Unlike many trees,
this hemlock grows best in shade rather
than in full sun. Although stands with

white pine, yellow birch, and red or white spruce are more common, dense pure stands do occur. The leaves of eastern hemlock sometimes turn brown and die due to a needle blight.

The slow-growing and long-lived trees of this species may approach 1,000 years of age. It takes 20 to 40 years for them to begin seed production. Once started, a heavy seed crop usually is followed by 2 or 3 years of light seed crops. The dense evergreen cover provides an excellent habitat for the ruffed grouse, wild turkey, and whitetail deer. Whitetails may browse the trees heavily during periods of heavy snowfall. The black-capped chickadee, pine siskin, and crossbills depend upon this hemlock for protection from the elements and for food (seeds). Snowshoe rabbits browse the seedlings, and porcupines eat the bark.

The moderately lightweight, light reddish-brown wood is coarse-grained and weak, and it splits easily. It is a poor quality wood used only occasionally in rough, general construction. It should not be used in fireplaces or campfires because of its tendency to pop, sending sparks for several feet. The bark once was used widely for tanning leather.

Eastern Hemlock

Spring Branchlet

Fall Branchlet

cones stalked

male cone

Spring Branchlet

leaves in 1 plane, in 2 flattened ranks, toothed

1.2–1.9 cm (0.5–0.8 in) long

female cone

Appearance: medium-size to large trees 20 to 25 m, rarely to 50 (65–82 ft, rarely to 165), pyramid-shaped with pointed and drooping top shoot on younger trees and with rounded top on large, mature trees; trunk tapering, straight, 0.6–1 m (1.9-3.3 ft) in diameter, rarely larger. **Bark:** thin, 1.2–2 cm (0.5–0.8 in) thick, reddish-brown to cinnamon red, with deep furrows separating the broad, flattened scales. **Branches:** slender, spreading to hanging; branchlets slender, flattened, spray-like, yellowish-brown turning grayish-brown. **Leaves:** small, linear, *2-ranked* (arranged in 1 plane horizontal to the ground), 0.7–1.6 cm (0.3–0.7 in) long, 1–2 mm (less than 0.1 in) wide, *flattened,* toothed, rounded to notched at the tip, dark yellowish-green with 2 whitish bands underneath. **Flowers:** male cones small, yellowish, near the tips of the branchlets; female cones small, green, leathery, also near the ends of the branchlets. **Fruits:** *cones* hanging, *short-stalked,* widest at the middle and rounded to pointed at the tip, *1.2–1.9 cm (0.5–0.8 in) long,* light brown, the *scales almost as broad as long,* thin. **Seeds:** egg-shaped, 1–2 mm (less than 0.1 in) long, light brown, winged, the wing 6–8 mm (0.2–0.3 in) long.

Carolina Hemlock

Tsuga caroliniana Engelm.

This seldom seen hemlock is confined to rocky stream beds and lower slopes of the Blue Ridge Mountains, an ancient subunit of the Appalachian Mountains. The trees occur in both North and South Carolina, Tennessee, Virginia, and northern Georgia.

These handsome trees with pyramidal forms, reddish-brown bark, hanging branches, and light green leaves usually are found at 800–1,350 m (2,600–4,500 ft) altitude. Although related to the eastern hemlock, this species can be distinguished from it by the *flattened leaves dispersed uniformly around the branchlets* (the leaves of the eastern hemlock are arranged on 1 plane). Also, *Carolina hemlocks have longer, stalked cones 2.5–3.8 cm (1–1.5 in).*

Carolina Hemlock

leaves spreading in all directions from branchlet, not toothed

cones stalked

2.5–3.8 cm
(1–1.5 in) long

The soft, weak wood is coarse-grained and not commercially valuable. Some of the finest existing groves are protected now in state and federal parks.

Western Hemlock

Tsuga heterophylla (Rafn.) Sarg.

The western hemlock is an attractive tree primarily of the coastal regions of the Pacific Northwest from southeastern Alaska to the southwestern U.S. It occurs from sea level to 2,250 m (7,400 ft) elevation. But at the higher altitudes the trees are smaller. As do most conifers, this hemlock grows best on deep, well-drained soils and in areas with a mild, humid climate. It is particularly abundant along the coasts of Washington and Oregon. It grows in either pure stands or with other evergreens, such as mountain hemlock, western white pine, Douglas fir, silver fir, coastal redwood, and Sitka spruce. Western hemlock is often attacked by the hemlock dwarf mistletoe.

Western hemlocks are moderate to fast-growing trees that may live for several centuries and often produce large quantities of seed. The cones take only 1 growing season to mature, and the seeds are dispersed by wind in early fall. Birds and mice feed on the seed; while rabbits and beavers browse the seedlings. Deer browse hemlocks of all sizes. Snow and wind topple many of these shallow-rooted trees.

The western hemlock has lightweight, hard, tough wood that is commercially superior to the wood from other hemlocks. It is an important tree for building construction and pulp wood. The outer bark has been used for tanning leather.

Western Hemlock

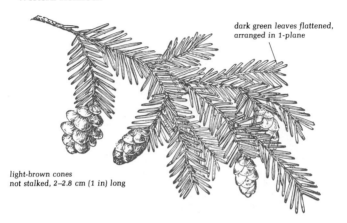

dark green leaves flattened, arranged in 1-plane

light-brown cones not stalked, 2–2.8 cm (1 in) long

Appearance: medium-size to tall trees, 40–65 m (130–215 ft), with a narrow pyramidal crown and *drooping terminal shoot;* trunk straight, tall, 1–3 m (3.2–9.8 ft) in diameter. **Bark:** thin, 2.5–3.3 cm (1–1.3 in) thick, light reddish-brown, with deep fissures dividing the flat ridges composed of closely pressed scales. **Branches:** short, slender, usually hanging; branchlets slender, hanging, yellowish-brown turning dark reddish-brown with age. **Leaves:** small, linear, 2-ranked on the branchlets, 0.6–2 mm (less than 0.1 in) long, 1.2–1.6 mm (less than 0.1 in) wide, *flattened,* rounded at the tip, *grooved on topside;* dark green with 2 broad white bands below. **Flowers:** male cones small, yellow, borne near the tips of the branchlets; female cones small, red or reddish-purple, also near the tips of the branchlets. **Fruits: *cones,*** hanging, oblong to egg-shaped, *without stalks,* pointed at the tip, *2–2.8 cm (1 in) long, light brown,* scales leathery, almost rounded with a wavy edge. **Seeds:** egg-shaped, 2–4 mm (0.1–0.2 in) long, light-brown, winged, the wing 2 to 3 times as long as the body of the seed.

Mountain Hemlock   *Tsuga mertensiana* (Bong.) Carr.

The mountain hemlock grows on exposed ridges and slopes from southeastern Alaska to southern California and in the mountains of British Columbia and Idaho. In Alaska the trees occur at lower altitudes, but farther south they are found at altitudes up to 3,300 m (11,000 ft). The finest stands are in sheltered areas with deep, well-drained, moist soils, high precipitation, and long, cold winters. Mountain hemlocks grow in pure stands or with many other conifers, including Sitka spruce, western hemlock, subalpine fir, red fir, and lodgepole pine.

Tolerant of different soil types, these

slow-growing trees may live 400 to 500 years. Seed production usually begins between 20 and 30 years of age, with heavy crops alternating with years of small seed production. Douglas chickarees eat the bark, buds, and seeds. The dense growth of these evergreens provides ideal cover and food (seeds) for the blue grouse.

The light brown wood is lightweight, soft, weak, and inferior to that of western hemlock. Formerly, it was used in rough construction when other lumber was not readily available.

Mountain Hemlock

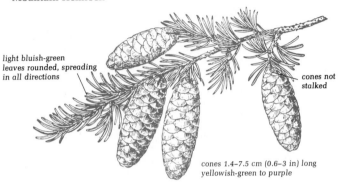

light bluish-green
leaves rounded, spreading
in all directions

cones not
stalked

cones 1.4–7.5 cm (0.6–3 in) long
yellowish-green to purple

Appearance: medium-size trees 25–35 m (80–115 ft), rarely taller, with an open pyramidal shape and an open crown with a long, drooping leader shoot; trunk slightly tapering, 0.8–1.8 m (2.6–5.9 ft) in diameter. **Bark:** thin, 2.5–3.7 cm (1–1.5 in), dark reddish or cinnamon, divided into connected, rounded ridges composed of closely pressed scales. **Branches:** slender, drooping; branchlets drooping, forming delicate sprays, light reddish-brown. **Leaves:** small, linear, *spreading all directions*, 1.2–2.5 cm (0.5–1 in) long, 1.2–1.7 mm (less than 0.1 in) wide, *rounded in cross section*, blunt at the tip, grooved on the top side, light bluish-green. **Flowers:** male cones small, slender, purplish, clustered near the tips of the branchlets; female cones erect, delicate, purplish, near the ends of the branchlets. **Fruits:** *cones,* hanging at maturity, oblong, without stalks, rounded to blunt at the tip, 1.4–7.5 cm (0.6–3 in) long *(usually 4–5 cm; 1.6–2 in), yellowish-green to purple,* the scales leathery, often widest near the tip. **Seeds:** egg-shaped, 2–4 mm (about 0.1–0.2 in) long, light brown, winged, the wing 1–1.3 cm (0.4–0.5 in) long, widest near the tip.

The Douglas Fir Genus *Pseudotsuga* Carr.

The Douglas firs are a small genus of stately evergreen trees ranging in shape from cone to cylinder. They are among the most important timber trees in North America. And they are important as both food source and cover for wildlife. Worldwide, there are 5 species of Douglas firs — 2 in the western U.S., 1 in Japan, and 2 in continental eastern Asia. (Douglas firs have hanging cones; true firs have upright cones.)

They are large, very long-lived trees with thin, smooth, gray, resin-pocked bark when young. But the bark becomes thick, deeply furrowed, and dark reddish-brown with age. The wood is soft and light-colored. Winter buds are long, sharp-pointed, and dry. The soft, evergreen leaves are on short stalks, flattened, persistent for several years and, upon falling, leave an oval scar on the branch. Male and female cones are found on the same tree. The male cones are small and hang along the branches; while the small, hanging, female cones, which mature in one season, are found at or near the ends of the branches. The conspicuous, 3-lobed bracts extend beyond the scales of the cone, and both the scales and the bracts remain in place when the seeds are shed.

Key to Douglas Fir Species

A. Leaves usually blunt or rounded at the tip, dark yellowish-green; cones 5–10 cm (2–4 in) long, the bracts of the cones extending far beyond the scales; western tree **Douglas fir, p. 97**

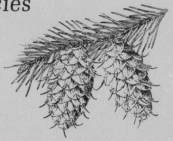

Douglas Fir

B. Leaves pointed at the tip, bluish-gray; cones 10–16 cm (4–6.3 in) long, the bracts of the cones slightly extending beyond the scales; tree of southern California **Bigcone Douglas fir, p. 99**

Bigcone Douglas Fir

Douglas Fir   *Pseudotsuga menziesii* (Mirb.) Franco.

[synonym: *P. taxifolia* (Poir.) Britt.]

The Douglas fir, one of the most abundant and valuable trees in western North America, occurs from British Columbia southward to Mexico. It is found at sea level to 1,650 m (5,500 ft) elevation along the coastal regions, west of the mountain ranges, in British Columbia, Washington, Oregon, and northern California. It also occurs from 630–2,600 m (2,000–8,600 ft) elevation throughout the Rocky Mountains where it is commonly referred to as the Rocky Mountain Douglas fir. This species has its best growth and reaches its largest size on well-drained, deep, loamy soils with goodly amounts of air and soil moisture. It often grows in pure stands or in nearly pure stands. In transitional areas between forest types, it can be found growing in association with many other kinds of conifers. Serious diseases of Douglas fir include a fungus needle disease which causes the premature dropping of leaves and the dwarf mistletoe.

The seed-bearing cones mature in one growing season from August to September, depending upon latitude and, to a lesser extent, altitude. These cones and their seeds are an important food source for small mammals and birds. Both the Douglas squirrel and the Townsend chipmunk break apart the nearly ripe cones for the seeds. Deer mice, meadow mice, and other rodents, as well as seed-eating birds such as wrens, crossbills, and some sparrows, consume the fallen seeds. In the years of light seed production, animal predation may be so extensive that few seeds ever survive to germinate and grow into trees. Grouse, especially the blue grouse, usually are found in older stands of Douglas fir in the northern part of its range, where they feed on the buds and young twigs.

The populations of Douglas fir in the Rocky Mountains are recognized as a distinct variety, the Rocky Mountain Douglas fir [*Pseudotsuga menziesii* variety *glauca* (Beissn.) Franco]. This variant differs in that it has more bluish-colored leaves, smaller cones, and occurs at slightly higher elevations.

Initially, the Douglas fir is a slow-growing species. But it soon becomes a moderately fast-growing tree. Seed production begins at 10 years, but good production usually does not occur until the tree is 25 to 30 years old. The tree reaches maximum production when it is between 200 and 300 years old. This species produces heavy seed crops about every 6 years, followed by light or medium production. The trees are long-lived and may live to be from 800 to 1,000 years old. The soft, light wood is extremely valuable. Large, solid beams are used as structural beams and trusses in buildings, docks, bridges, and as railroad ties. The wood does not warp, takes a beautiful finish, and is suitable for interior finishes and for plywood.

High winds and heavy, wet snows take their toll of trees each year. The Douglas-fir beetle is the principal insect enemy.

The Douglas fir is a good ornamental tree for gardens and parks in northern climates around the world. The Rocky Mountain variety is hardier than typical members of the coastal populations. The trees make excellent windbreaks and wildlife cover.

Douglas Fir

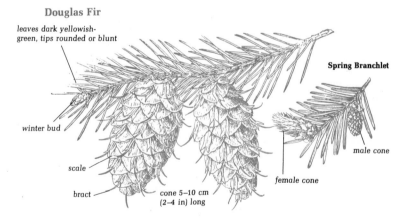

leaves dark yellowish-green, tips rounded or blunt

Spring Branchlet

winter bud

male cone

scale

female cone

bract

cone 5–10 cm (2–4 in) long

Appearance: large, tall trees 50–70 m, rarely to 100 (160–230 ft, rarely to 330), narrow pyramid-shaped (young trees) to cylinder-shaped (older, mature trees) with a short, column-shaped, flat-topped crown; trunk straight or only slightly tapering, 1–3 m, rarely 5 (3–10 ft, rarely 16) in diameter, free of branches for two-thirds of length in forest. **Bark:** on young trees, thin, smooth, gray, with numerous resin pockets; on older trees becoming 10–30 cm (3.9–11.8 in) thick, deeply fissured, with oblong, dark reddish-brown scales. **Branches:** slender, usually crowded, with numerous lateral branches, the upper branches growing slightly upward, the middle and lower ones straight to slightly drooping; branchlets slender, flexible, reddish-brown, often shiny; leaf scars oval. **Winter buds:** broadest at the base, sharp-pointed at the tip, 5–7 mm (0.2–0.3 in) long, shiny brown to reddish-brown. **Leaves:** small, crowded, appearing 2-ranked due to a twisting at the base of the leaves, 1.9–3.2 cm (0.8–1.3 in) long, linear, flat, straight to slightly curved, soft, the upper surface usually deeply grooved lengthwise, usually blunt or rounded at tip, dark yellowish-green to rarely bluish-green. **Flowers:** male cones oblong, orange-red, usually in the juncture of the leaf and the branchlet near the end of the branchlets; female cones oblong, short-stalked, reddish-tinged, usually at or near the ends of the branchlets. **Fruits: *cones, hanging,*** oval, broadest near the base, rounded to pointed at the tip, rounded at the base, ***5–10 cm (2–4 in) long,*** purplish turning yellowish-brown at maturity; scales nearly circular, slightly longer than broad, rounded at the tip, slightly hairy; ***bracts 3-pronged, trident-shaped, exceeding the scales by 1–4 cm (0.4–0.6 in),*** usually sharp-pointed. **Seeds:** oblong-triangular, 5–7 mm (0.2–0.3 in) long, light reddish-brown, shiny, winged, wing dark brown, 5–8 mm (0.2–0.3 in) long, asymmetrically rounded at tip.

Bigcone Douglas Fir *Pseudotsuga macrocarpa* (Vasey) Mayr

The Bigcone Douglas fir grows only in the cool ravines and canyons on the north slopes of the mountains in southern California. The trees often are found at higher elevations, 750–2,350 m (2,400–7,700 ft), growing in association with the Coulter pine and yellow pine. These attractive trees, with graceful, sweeping branches, seldom exceed 20 m (65 ft) in height and about 1 m (3.3 ft) in trunk diameter. A thick (14–16 cm; 5.5–6.3 in), deeply furrowed, dark reddish-brown bark covers the trunk. This species can be distinguished easily from the more widely known Douglas fir by its ***bluish-gray leaves, larger cones*** 10–16 cm (4–6.3 in) long, compared to 5–10 cm (2–4 in) long in the Douglas fir, and ***bracts that extend onlv***

Bigcone Douglas Fir

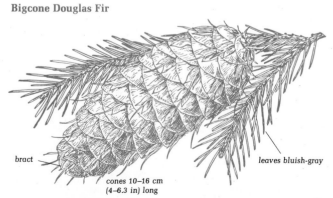

bract

leaves bluish-gray

cones 10–16 cm
(4–6.3 in) long

slightly beyond the scales of the cones. Although this species has a very limited range, it is not endangered because most of the trees are located within the boundaries of national forests.

The Fir Genus   *Abies* Mill.

The firs are stately trees with cone-like to cylinder-like forms. Approximately 40 species occur in the cold and temperate regions of the Northern Hemisphere. Nine species are found in North America: 7 distributed in the western states and provinces, 1 in the higher elevations of the southern Appalachian Mountains, and 1 extending from the northeastern U.S. westward across Canada to Alberta. (These true firs have upright cones, while the related Douglas firs have hanging cones.)

These large, long-lived trees have thin, smooth bark on their trunks, which are marked with blister-like pockets of resin when young but become thick, rough, and furrowed with age. The wood is soft and light-colored. The evergreen leaves are without stalks, usually flattened or in some species 4-sided, persistent for 4 or 5 years and upon falling leave a disc-shaped scar on the branch. Male and female cones are found on the same tree. The male cones are small and hang; while the female cones are erect, cylinder-shaped, and often partially covered with resinous deposits. The female cones mature in 1 season, and the scales and seeds drop away leaving a persistent, upright, stout axis.

Fir trees occur in almost pure stands on the steep slopes at higher elevations and help to protect the forest floor from erosion and to provide suitable habitats for wildlife. They are important trees for pulp and timber. The soft wood, which is easily worked and can be finished with an excellent surface, is best suited for indoor finishes of homes. The resin obtained from the blisters is sold as "Canada balsam," which is used in some medicines and in mounting microscope specimens.

These evergreens are used for both cover and food by wildlife. The twigs and foliage are browsed by moose, whitetail deer, and mule deer. Blue and spruce grouse feed on the leaves. Smaller birds, especially the Hudsonian chickadee and Clark nutcracker, eat the seeds. Red squirrels, porcupines, Douglas chickarees, and chipmunks also incorporate seeds, and to a lesser extent bark, into their diets.

Several species of firs are exceptionally attractive and adapt to planting near homes or other buildings. They are sensitive to industrially produced air pollutants and should not be planted in polluted air. The white fir, Farges fir, nikko fir (introduced from Japan), Spanish fir (introduced from Spain), noble fir, and the California red fir are among the better firs for use as ornamental plantings. They will transplant easily in the spring when young.

Key to Fir Species

A. Cones with short often spoon-shaped, fan-shaped, or 3-pronged bracts; needle-like leaves rounded to pointed but not bristle-tipped; winter buds almost globe-shaped.

Balsam Fir

    1. Leaves flattened, often 2-ranked, spreading and not crowded on the lower branchlets; cones narrow.

a. Cones dark purple, cone scales longer than broad.

    (1) Cone scales approximately twice as long as broad; leaves 2-ranked on the lower branchlets.

Fraser Fir

        (a) Leaves 3–3.4 cm (1.2–1.4 in) long; bracts of the cone scales shorter than the scales and not visible on closed cones; trees of trans Canada and northeastern U.S.
            Balsam fir, p. 102

        (b) Leaves 1.2–2.5 cm (0.5–1 in) long; bracts of the cone scales much longer than the scales and bent over them; trees of the Appalachian Mountains   **Fraser fir, p. 103**

Subalpine Fir

    (2) Cone scales only slightly longer than broad; leaves upright on the lower branchlets; western trees
            Subalpine fir, p. 104

b. Cones yellow to greenish-purple, cone scales broader than long.

    (1) Leaves 3.8–5.8 cm (1.5–2.3 in) long on the lower branchlets, dark green with 2 broad bands on the lower side; cone scales broadly fan-shaped, 2.8–3.2 cm (1.1–1.3 in) wide; western trees
            Grand fir, p. 106

Grand Fir

    (2) Leaves 1.9–3.8 cm (0.8–1.5 in) long on the lower branchlets, dull green above and beneath; cone scales spoon-shaped, 3.5–4 cm (1.4–1.6 in) wide; southwestern trees   **White fir, p. 107**

White Fir

2. Leaves often 4-sided (flattened in silver fir), crowded and curved toward the upper part of the branchlets; cones broad.

    a. Leaves flattened; cones with the bracts half as long as the scales; bark smooth on mature trees, gray to reddish-gray; western trees   **Silver fir, p. 109**

    b. Leaves 4-sided; cones with the bracts as long or slightly longer than scales; bark deeply furrowed on mature trees, reddish-brown.

Silver Fir

(Continued)

(1) Leaves on lower coneless branchlets becoming flattened, distinctly 4-sided on upper cone-bearing branchlets; bracts of the cones longer than the cone scales, papery, bent against cone; trees of Washington, Oregon, and northern California　**Noble fir, p. 110**

Noble Fir

(2) Leaves on all branchlets always 4-sided; bracts of the cones shorter than the cone scales (in the *shatensis* variety, the bracts are longer than the scales); trees of California, Oregon, and Nevada　**California red fir, p. 112**

B. Cones with long, narrow, spine-like bracts extending considerably beyond the scales; needle-like leaves with a bristle-tip; winter buds broadest at the base and tapering to a point; trees of California coast　**Bristlecone fir, p. 114**

Bristlecone Fir

Balsam Fir　　　　　　　　　　*Abies balsamea* (L.) Miller

The balsam fir is a common, yet distinctive, tree of the central and northern Appalachian Mountains, the northeastern U.S., and Canada, extending westward across Canada to Alberta. It is the major component in much of the forests on low, swampy grounds and on well-drained hillsides.

This fir requires considerable moisture in both the soil and air. On hillsides the balsam fir commonly grows in association with white spruce, black spruce, paper bark birch, and trembling aspen. Balsam fir is subject to a variety of leaf and stem diseases, but most are not serious. The balsam wooly aphid and spruce budworm can be serious insect pests.

Moose and whitetail deer browse the foliage, while chickadees, nutcrackers, squirrels, and porcupines eat the oil-rich seeds. The spruce grouse uses the fir forest for cover and the leaves as a food source.

Growth is rapid unless the young trees are in dense shade. Then after their first 6 to 8 years, they require almost full light to continue their rapid growth. In mature fir forests, young trees will grow extremely slowly until a mature tree falls, and then a literal race is on to see which of the numerous young trees will replace the fallen veteran. Good cone and seed production usually begins between 20 and 30 years of age, with heavy seed crops produced every 2 to 4 years.

Balsam fir is important in the pulp-wood industry. The wood is very soft, coarse-grained, light brown, and is not used directly as a lumber source except in the manufacture of some crates and boxes. This fir is commonly used as a Christmas tree.

In addition to human causes, several other factors are responsible for the death of large numbers of mature trees. The shallow root system renders the trees vulnerable to high winds and heavy, wet spring snow storms. Blowdowns are common sights in fir forests. Because their bark is thin, these firs are easily killed by fire. Two serious insect pests—the spruce budworm and the balsam wooly aphid—threaten large stands.

Balsam Fir

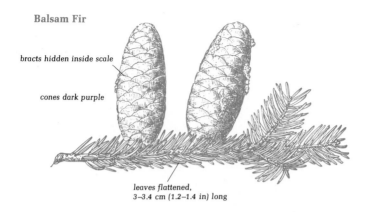

bracts hidden inside scale

cones dark purple

leaves flattened,
3–3.4 cm (1.2–1.4 in) long

Appearance: medium-size trees to 25 m (82 ft), shaped like narrow **pyramids,** and terminated with a **sharp-pointed spire;** the trunk straight, 0.5–1 m (1.6–3.3 ft) in diameter. **Bark:** thin, smooth, grayish, **covered with raised, resin-bearing pockets** when young, becoming fissured with irregular, brownish scales when mature. **Branches:** stout, spreading, lower ones dying in dense forest; branchlets slender, yellow-green, becoming grayish; leaf scars flat, disc-shaped or rounded. **Winter buds: nearly globe-shaped,** 0.3–0.6 cm (0.1–0.3 in) long, scales dark orange-green, lustrous, usually covered with resinous deposits. **Leaves:** small, narrow, without stalks, 2-ranked, on lower branches 3–3.4 cm (1.2–1.4 in) long, flattened, blunt or notched at the tip; on upper branches 1–1.2 cm (0.4–0.5 in) long, pointed at the tip, all leaves dark, shiny green above, with numerous lines of microscopic air pores (stomata) in the silvery white bands beneath. **Flowers:** male cones slender cylinder-shaped, yellow, 4–6 mm (0.2 in) long; female cones cylinder-shaped, purple, 1.8–2.2 cm (0.7–0.9 in) long, borne at the top of the tree. **Fruits:** cones, **upright, cylinder-shaped,** rounded at the top, 5–10 cm (2–4 in) long, **dark purple; scales fan-shaped, 1.8–2.2 cm (0.7–0.9 in) long, usually twice as long as broad; bracts (inside scale) usually 0.9–1.2 cm (0.4–0.5 in) long, broadest and notched near the tip,** with a bristle point. **Seeds:** small, wedge-shaped, 5–7 mm (0.2–0.3 in) long, winged, the wing light, shiny brown, about twice as long as the seed.

Fraser Fir, She Balsam   *Abies fraseri* Poir.

This southern species is related to and closely resembles the northern balsam fir, *Abies balsamea.* The uniformly pyramid-shaped tree reaches a maximum height of 25 m (82 ft) in the high mountains of North Carolina and Tennessee at altitudes of 1,400–2,100 m (4,500–6,900 ft). Fraser's fir extends sporadically along the peaks of the southern Appalachian Mountains to southwestern Virginia and West Virginia. The balsam wooly aphid is a serious pest.

This species, like the balsam fir, has **flattened,** dark green, shiny **leaves 1.2–2.5 cm (0.5–1 in) long** that are grooved on the upper side. Both species have purple-colored, seed-bearing cones. **The bracts of the cone scales in Fraser's fir are longer than their scales and are bent over them;** whereas those of the balsam fir are usually shorter than their scales and are not visible on closed cones.

Fraser Fir

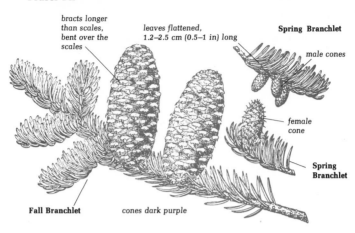

bracts longer
than scales,
bent over the
scales

leaves flattened,
1.2–2.5 cm (0.5–1 in) long

Spring Branchlet

male cones

*female
cone*

**Spring
Branchlet**

Fall Branchlet

cones dark purple

At the higher elevations Fraser's fir and red spruce form a dense forest community, with the forest floor always in deep shade. Ferns, mosses, and the witch hobble shrub (*Viburnum alnifolium*) abound, with an occasional ancient, yellow birch interspersed with the conifers. The mature spruce-fir forest type is as awe-inspiring as the Olympic rain forest in peninsular Washington or the coastal redwoods in northern California. Red squirrels are the primary consumers of the seeds.

Subalpine Fir, Alpine Fir   *Abies lasiocarpa* (Hook.) Nutt.

The subalpine fir is perhaps the smallest of our native firs and, as its common name implies, is usually found at higher elevations than most other firs. In the southern portion of its range, it can be found growing at 3,500 m (11,500 ft) elevation. At the northern end of its range in Alaska, it occurs near sea level. The trees grow to tim-
berline in cold, humid climates extending
from extreme southeastern Alaska, central
Yukon, and British Columbia to the Olympic Mountains of Washington and the Cascade Mountains of Washington and
Oregon. They also occur in the Rocky
Mountains from British Columbia southward to scattered and isolated populations in Arizona and New Mexico. The
subalpine fir will grow in poor soils, in-

cluding rocky ones. It can be found in association with several other conifers in transitional areas between forest types, but it occurs principally with mountain hemlock or
with Engelmann spruce.

The subalpine fir has the greatest range of all North American firs. The southern populations from eastern and northern Arizona and southwestern New Mexico to central Colorado have been described as a separate species, the corkback fir. But they are only a variant—*Abies lasiocarpa* variety *arizonica* (Merriam) Lemm—of the subalpine fir. This variant is distinguished from the typical subalpine fir by its soft, corky, and very light-colored bark; and its seed-bearing cones are longer and narrower.

The seeds are a favorite of red squirrels and form a significant portion of the squirrels' fall and early winter diet. In years of poor seed production, squirrels and other rodents may consume almost all the seeds produced. During these times, there is little or no reproduction of this tree. Spruce and ruffed grouse eat the leaves and buds.

The subalpine fir is a slow-growing tree, with reports of 15-year-old trees of only about ⅓ m (1 ft) or less. Seed production may begin after 20 to 25 years of age; while in other trees this may not begin until nearly 50 years of age. One year of good seed production generally will be followed by 2 years of little or no seed production. The soft, light wood is very weak but is used in making wood pulp and, in limited quantities, boxes and crates.

Fire, the spruce budworm, the black-headed budworm, and the western balsam bark beetle are the main natural enemies of this fir. High winds and heavy, wet snowfalls can result in the uprooting of many trees.

Because of its natural adaptability to high altitudes and cold, moist climates, the subalpine fir is of very limited use as an ornamental tree in lower, drier areas.

Subalpine Fir

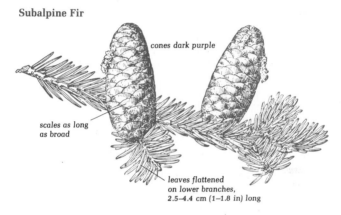

cones dark purple

scales as long
as broad

leaves flattened
on lower branches,
2.5–4.4 cm (1–1.8 in) long

Appearance: small to medium-size trees 20 to 35 m, rarely to 50 (65–115 ft, rarely to 165), extremely narrow and tapering to a dense spire-like crown; trunk tapering slightly, 0.7–1.8 m (2.3–5.9 ft) in diameter, usually with branches near the base; only in dense forest are the lower branches lost. **Bark:** on younger trees thin, smooth, gray, with resin-bearing pockets; on older trees moderately thin, 1.9–3.8 cm (0.8–1.5 in) thick, ash gray to grayish-brown, shallowly fissured, broken into irregular, close scales. **Branches:** stout, short, crowded, slightly hanging in graceful sweeps; branchlets stout, brownish becoming pale orange-brown and ultimately gray to silvery-white with age, hairy becoming smooth after several years; leaf scars circular. **Winter buds:** (not shown) almost globe-shaped, 4–10 mm (about 0.2–0.4 in) in length, scales closely pressed together, light orange-brown, resin covered. **Leaves:** small, narrow, without stalks, *on lower branches flattened,* blunt or notched at the tip, 2.5–4.4 cm (1–1.8 in) long; but on upper cone-bearing branches, thickened, pointed at the tip, 1–1.4 cm (0.4–0.6 in) long, crowded, *nearly erect;* all leaves grayish-blue to deep blue-green. **Flowers:** male cones cylinder-shaped, bluish, 15–20 mm (0.6–0.8 in) long; female cones cylinder-shaped, dark purple, 2–2.5 cm (0.8–1 in) long, borne at the top of the trees. **Fruits:** cones, upright, cylinder-shaped, but tapering slightly towards the tip and base, rounded, flattened or slightly depressed at the tip, 6–10 cm (2.4–4 in) long, dark purple, slightly hairy; *scales* variable, *usually fan-shaped,* 1.8–2.2 cm (0.7–0.9

in) long, ***slightly longer than broad;*** bracts usually broadest near the base, 0.6–0.7 cm (0.2–0.3 in) long, irregularly-toothed, rounded and abruptly long-tipped. **Seeds:** small, wedge-shaped, 7–9 mm (about 0.3 in) long, winged, the wing bluish turning brown, shiny, about twice as long as the seed.

Grand Fir, Lowland Fir   *Abies grandis* (Dougl.) Lindl.

One of the more stately and beautiful fir trees, the grand fir occurs from sea level to altitudes of 1,600 m (5,100 ft) and extends from northwestern California and the coastal regions of Washington and Oregon to western Montana, northern and western Idaho, and southern British Columbia. The grand fir reaches its largest size in the great coniferous rain forest in the Olympic peninsula of Washington. Although it will grow in a variety of soils, the best growth is attained on deep, rich, alluvial soils accompanied by moist, cool air. It usually grows in association with Douglas fir and larch but also occurs with Sitka spruce, silver fir, western hemlock, and western redcedar. In north-

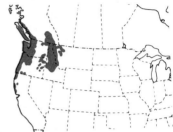

ern California it is found with coastal redwoods. Several needle-cast fungi attack the leaves. The fir dwarf mistletoe is the chief parasite.

Like other firs, the grand fir is an important tree to some small rodents and game birds. The ripe cones frequently are broken apart by the red squirrel in search of the oil-rich seeds. Chickarees feed on the seeds as a minor food source. The blue spruce grouse feeds heavily on the leaves during winter months, and whitetail deer and mule deer forage on the twigs and leaves.

Unlike most conifers, the grand fir is a rapid-growing tree. Yearly height increments of 25–30 cm (12–15 in) are common. Seed production usually does not begin until 20 years of age. Good seed crops are produced on an average of every 3 years. Years of low seed production, especially if accompanied by low production in other forest tree species, can be a limiting factor for winter survival of wildlife dependent on the seeds. The soft, light wood is of little value as lumber. But it is used as pulp wood.

Young trees are particularly susceptible to fire; while the thicker bark on older trees affords a moderate degree of protection against fire injury. As with other firs, certain fungi frequently enter the trees through wounds and grow into the heart of the trunk where extensive rotting can occur. Both the spruce budworm and the Douglas-fir tussock moth have been serious insect pests.

Although this is an exceptionally beautiful tree throughout its natural range, it has not proven to be very satisfactory under cultivation in the eastern U.S. A weeping form of the grand fir, *Abies grandis* Pendula, makes an excellent plant. It does not grow as large as the regular grand fir and thus is better suited for landscaping.

Appearance: tall trees 35–50 m, rarely to 80 (115–165 ft, rarely to 250), cylindrical, with an open, rounded crown; trunk gradually tapering, 0.8–1.2 m (2.6–3.9 ft) in diameter; in the forest, mature trees free of branches on the lower half of trunk; in the open, mature trees' branches also grow near the ground. **Bark:** thin, smooth, blotched with resin-bearing pockets, on older trees becoming moderately thick (5–9 cm; 2–3.6 in), grayish-brown to reddish-brown, with shallow fissures and flat ridges broken into plates of thick scales. **Branches:** stout, long, hanging in graceful sweeping curves; branchlets slender, pale yellow-green becoming reddish-brown to orange-brown with

Grand Fir

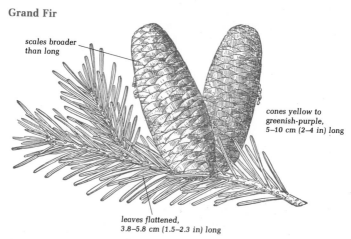

*scales broader
than long*

*cones yellow to
greenish-purple,
5–10 cm (2–4 in) long*

*leaves flattened,
3.8–5.8 cm (1.5–2.3 in) long*

age; leaf scars rounded. **Winter buds:** almost circular, 3–7 mm (0.1–0.3 in) in diameter, with tightly overlapping scales, usually resin-coated. **Leaves:** small, narrow, without stalks, on the lower branches, 2-ranked and scattered, ***3.8–5.8 cm (1.5–2.3 in) long,*** thin, flexible; on the upper cone-bearing branches, the leaves are more crowded, nearly erect, 3.8–5.8 cm (1.5–2.3 in) long; all leaves dark green, shiny above, silvery-white ***with 2 broad bands beneath,*** aromatic when crushed. **Flowers:** male cones oblong, pale yellow, 1.2–2.2 cm (0.5–0.9 in) long; female cones narrow, cylinder-shaped yellow-green, 2.5–3 cm (1–1.2 in) long, borne at the top of the tree. **Fruits:** ***cones, upright, cylinder-shaped,*** rounded to slightly sunken at the tip, ***5–10 cm (2–4 in) long,*** bright green to greenish-purple; ***scales broadly fan-shaped, 2.8–3.2 cm (1.1–1.3 in) wide, broader than long; bracts short, spoon-shaped, 0.7–1.2 cm (0.3–0.5 in) long,*** irregularly-toothed at the tip. **Seeds:** small, wedge-shaped, 0.8–1 cm (0.3–0.4 in) long, light brown, winged, the wing pale, shiny, 1.3–1.5 cm (0.5–0.6 in) long.

White Fir

Abies concolor (Gord. & Glend.) Lindl.

The white fir is an important large tree of higher elevations in the mountains from southern Oregon to southern California and also in the Rocky Mountains from western Wyoming and southern Idaho to southern Arizona and southern New Mexico. The trees will grow on a wide range of soils but prefer areas with moist soils, moderately humid climates, and long winters with moderate to heavy snowfall. In the mountains near the Pacific Ocean, the trees occur as low as 700 m (2,300 ft) but normally are found at 1,000–2,500 m (3,200–8,200 ft) elevation. In the interior mountains, they normally occur at 2,400–3,000 m (7,800–9,900 ft) and occasionally at 3,400 m (11,000 ft). In the southern Cascade Mountains, white fir grows in associ-

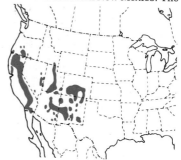

ation with lodgepole pine, sugar pine, grand fir, and the California red fir. But in the Rockies it is usually accompanied by Douglas fir. Bark beetles often attack white fir. Several needle rusts and dwarf mistletoe are the more serious diseases.

White fir is important to many species of wildlife. The leaves and buds are significant in maintaining winter populations of blacktail and mule deer. The bark is a favorite winter food of porcupines. The maturing cones often are harvested in the fall by Douglas pine squirrels, which either eat the seeds promptly or store them for later use. Grouse eat the fallen seeds.

These long-lived trees grow rapidly for the first 50 years or so and then slowly, often to 350 years of age. The oldest trees are 60–70 cm (24–28 in) in diameter. The trees do not begin producing cones and seeds until approximately 40 years old and then do not reach optimum seed production for 10 more years. The flowers appear in spring, and the cones ripen and seeds shed in September or October. On an average, heavy seed crops are produced every fifth year, although this period will vary.

The very soft, coarse-grained wood is used for making paper pulp and in the manufacture of boxes and crates. Some of the timber is used in framing small houses. It is not suitable for larger buildings where greater load-bearing capacities are needed. Prior to the advent and wide use of plastics and stainless steel, white fir was used in the manufacture of tubs for storing butter. The wood lacks a distinctive odor and thus will not affect the taste of the butter.

Both insect pests and diseases will sometimes attack the tree near the top. When this happens, cone production can be seriously affected. The spruce budworm and the Douglas fir tussock moth are two serious insect pests that feed on the leaves. Several different kinds of bark beetles will burrow beneath the bark, weakening the tree or even causing its death. Taller trees often are damaged by high winds. These winds subject the trees to considerable twisting or torque pressures that may result in spiral cracks. Fungal infections often enter the tree through the exposed ends of broken branches and spread into the trunk where extensive heart-rot damage may occur.

The white fir is an excellent ornamental tree for planting near homes and other buildings, in parks and cemeteries. It has proven to be very satisfactory for use in the eastern U.S. and southern Canada. Many selections or cultivars are known, including some fascinating dwarf low-growing forms, such as Globosa, a globe-shaped bush, and Conica, a cone-shaped bush. A weeping white fir is also available under the name *Abies concolor* Pendula.

White Fir

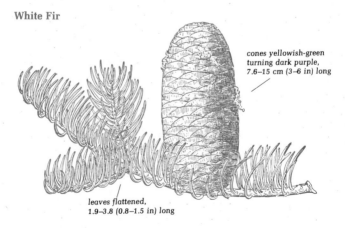

cones yellowish-green turning dark purple, 7.6–15 cm (3–6 in) long

leaves flattened, 1.9–3.8 (0.8–1.5 in) long

Appearance: tall trees 40–50 m, rarely to 70 (130–165 ft, rarely to 230), narrow, with a spire-like crown; trunk straight, 1–1.5 m, rarely 2 (3.2–4.9 ft, rarely 6.6) in diameter, often free of branches for the lower half to third of mature trees. **Bark:** on younger trees thin, smooth, gray, with numerous resin-bearing pockets; on older trees becoming thick, 10–18 cm (4–7.1 in) deep, reddish-brown to light gray, deeply furrowed with broad, rounded ridges broken into irregular, flattened scales. **Branches:** stout, short, usually with longer, persistent lateral branches; branchlets sturdy, dark orange at first, becoming gray-green or gray-brown and then gray; leaf scars circular. **Winter buds:** nearly globe-shaped, 0.3–0.6 cm (0.1–0.3 in) long, scales blunt, closely overlapping, resin-covered. **Leaves:** small, narrow, without stalks, 2-ranked, on lower branches, straight, flat, rounded, or pointed at the tip, 5–7.6 cm (2–3 in) long, on upper cone-bearing branches, curved, thick, and ridged, pointed or notched at the tip, *1.9–3.8 cm (0.8–1.5 in) long,* all leaves pale bluish-green to yellow-green when young, *becoming dull green with age.* **Flowers:** male cones oblong or cylinder-shaped, red to rose, 3–4 cm (1.2–1.6 in) long; female cones narrow, cylinder-shaped, greenish, 3–4 cm (1.2–1.6 in) long, borne at the top of the tree. **Fruits:** cones, *upright, slightly barrel-shaped* (broadest at the middle), rounded to slightly pointed at the tip, *7.6–15 cm (3–6 in) long,* cones yellowish-green (rarely dark purple), slightly hairy; *scales fan-shaped, 3.5–4 cm (1.4–1.6 in) wide, broader than long, rounded at the tip; bracts spoon-shaped, half as long as scales, papery,* notched at the tip. **Seeds:** small, wedge-shaped, 0.8–1.3 cm (0.3–0.5 in) long, winged, the wing rose-colored, almost twice as long as the seed.

Silver Fir, Cascades Fir   *Abies amabilis* (Dougl.) Forb.

The silver fir occurs from sea level in extreme southern Alaska to 350–2,000 m (1,100–6,600 ft) elevation in British Columbia, Washington, and Oregon. It grows on southern and western exposures of canyons and interior valleys, with the best growth attained

in deep, moist soil and cool, wet air conditions as found in fog belts. This is the most common species of fir in the Olympic Mountains of Washington. There the trees reach heights of 70 m (230 ft) and ages exceeding 200 years. Although pure stands of silver fir are known, it usually grows in association with other species. At lower elevations it often grows with white fir, Douglas fir, sitka spruce, and western hemlock. Higher in the mountains, silver fir grows with the noble fir, Engelmann spruce, and the Alaska cedar.

Silver fir communities provide habitat and food for blue grouse and spruce grouse. Both species nest in the brush, often near the base of a spruce or fir and feed on the leaves and especially the seeds. The Clark nutcracker and squirrels also eat the seeds.

These slow-growing trees often take 25 years before they produce cones; then they produce good seed crops every 2 or 3 years. Trees 200 years old will likely be only 60 cm (24 in) in diameter. As with other firs, the silver fir's wood is soft, light, and weak. It is used in limited amounts for framing small houses and in the manufacture of boxes and crates. The wood is also used for paper pulp.

Long thought to be insect and disease free, the silver fir has suffered from attacks of bark beetles and more recently from the balsam wooly aphid. The thin bark renders the trees vulnerable to fire, and the somewhat shallow root system sometimes allows tree falls in heavy winds.

Silver Fir

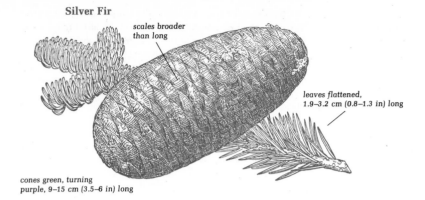

scales broader than long

leaves flattened, 1.9–3.2 cm (0.8–1.3 in) long

cones green, turning purple, 9–15 cm (3.5–6 in) long

Appearance: tall trees to 75 m (246 ft), *slender, with a narrowly cone-shaped crown;* the trunk straight, 1.5–2 m (4.9–6.6 ft) in diameter; mature trees often free of branches on the lower half of the trunk. **Bark:** thin, smooth, pale gray, with slightly *raised, resin-bearing pockets;* older trees with fissured, irregularly divided plates covered with reddish-gray scales. **Branches:** stout, horizontal or drooping in graceful, sweeping arcs; branchlets slender, dark orange-brown, becoming dark purple and ultimately reddish-brown; *leaf scars circular.* **Winter buds:** rounded to globe-shaped, 5–7 mm (0.2–0.3 in) long, scales closely overlapping, dark purple, usually resin-coated. **Leaves:** small, narrow, without stalks, appearing crowded on the upper side of twigs, 1.9–3.2 cm (0.8–1.3 in) long, flattened, deeply grooved, notched or pointed at the tip, shiny, dark green above, silvery white-banded beneath, the bands containing the numerous pores. **Flowers:** male cones cylindrical, bright red, 12–20 mm (0.5–0.8 in) long; female cones narrowly cylindric, dark purple, 3–4 cm (1.2–1.6 in) long, borne at the top of the tree. **Fruits:** cones, *upright,* barrel-shaped (broadest at the middle), rounded at the top, 9–15 cm (3.5–6 in) long, green turning purple; *scales fan-shaped, 3–3.5 cm (1.2–1.4 in) long, as wide as long;* bracts usually half the length of scales, broadest above the middle, slightly toothed and with a slender tip. **Seeds:** small, wedge-shaped, 10–14 mm (0.4–0.6 in) long, winged, the wing shiny, yellowish, twice as long as the seed.

Noble Fir

Abies procera Rehd.

[synonym: *A. nobilis* (Dougl.) Lindl.]

Despite its limited range, the noble fir is one of the more valuable species of native firs because of its excellent timber. It occurs along the Pacific Coast in Washington, Oregon, and northern California. The trees commonly are found at 1,000–1,700 m (3,200–5,600 ft) elevation on the west side of the Cascade Mountains. The noble fir grows best on rich, deep soils with a short, cool growing season and an abundant annual precipitation, mainly in the form of snowfall. The trees also will grow

on thin, poor soils, provided sufficient amounts of moisture are present. This species ordinarily does not grow in pure stands but rather in association with other conifers, such as the Douglas fir, silver fir, western hemlock, mountain hemlock, and western white pine.

The Douglas squirrel or chickaree breaks apart the ripe cones and feeds on the seeds. Mice and other rodents forage for fallen seeds on the forest floor. The spruce-fir forest is a prime habitat for the blue grouse, an upland gamebird that can be seen high in the branches feeding on the leaves and buds.

The noble fir grows slowly for the first 10 to 15 years, then rapidly. Trees 50 cm (20 in) in diameter can be approximately 300 years old. This fir is considered the longest-lived native fir, with some ancient trees estimated at 600 to 700 years old. Normal seed production does not begin until nearly 50 years of age. Good seed crops are sporadic. The wood is hard, heavy, firm, and light brown. Excellent saw timber can be obtained from these trees. The wood works easily and is used in home construction, boats, and boxes.

Although fire is a potentially serious enemy of the noble fir, it enjoys relative freedom from several of the important diseases and insect pests that attack other firs.

The noble fir is an excellent tree for planting in parks or in large yards. Although it can be grown in the eastern U.S., planting is more successful in soil and climate conditions close to those found in the fir's native range.

Noble Fir

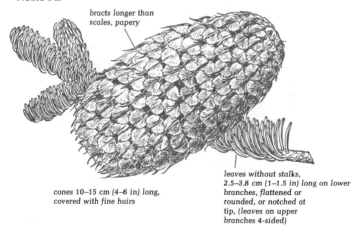

bracts longer than scales, papery

cones 10–15 cm (4–6 in) long, covered with fine hairs

leaves without stalks, 2.5–3.8 cm (1–1.5 in) long on lower branches, flattened or rounded, or notched at tip, (leaves on upper branches 4-sided)

Appearance: tall trees 45–65 m (140–215 ft), rarely taller, narrowly cylinder-shaped with a sharp-pointed spire when young but becoming short and rounded at the top; trunk tapering slightly, 0.7–1.5 m, rarely to 2 (2.3–4.9 ft, rarely to 6.6) in diameter, usually free of branches for two-thirds or more of its height. **Bark:** thin, smooth, gray, and covered with resin-bearing pockets when young, on older trees 2.5–5 cm (1–2 in) thick, bright reddish-brown, with deep lengthwise and diagonal fissures defining the broad, flat ridges, the ridges covered with thick, closely pressed scales. **Branches:** stout, short, lateral branches occasional and at right angles, the upper branches spreading, the lower ones slightly drooping; branchlets slender, reddish-brown, with short hairs for first 4 or 5 years; leaf scars circular. **Winter buds:** broadest near the base, 6–8 mm (0.2–0.3 in) long, scales reddish-brown, resin-covered. **Leaves:** small, linear, without stalks; on lower branches flattened, rounded or notched at the tip, 2.5–3.8 cm (1–1.5 in) long; on upper cone-bearing branches, almost 4-sided, sharp-pointed at the tip, 1.5–1.9 cm (0.6–0.8 in) long, densely crowded, nearly erect, all leaves straight to curved, pale but becoming deep bluish-green, often appearing silvery. **Flowers:** male cones cylinder-shaped, reddish to purple, 1.5–2.5 cm (0.6–1 in) long; female cones cylinder-shaped, greenish-yellow, 2.5–4 cm (1–1.6 in) long, borne at the top of the trees. **Fruits:** cones, upright, cylindric but tapering slightly at the tip and base, rounded at the tip, 10–15 cm (4–6 in) long, 5.7–7.4 cm (2.3–3 in) in diameter, light yellow-green to purplish, covered with fine hairs; scales fan-shaped, 3.2–3.6 cm (1.3–1.4 in) wide, about as long as wide; ***bracts broadest at the tip, very prominent and extending beyond and bent against the cone, 3.8–4.4 cm (1.5–1.8 in) long, papery, the tip slightly fringed and with a long tapering point.*** **Seeds:** medium-size, wedge-shaped, 0.8–1.2 cm (0.3–0.5 in) long, reddish-brown, winged, the wing pale brown, shiny, about twice the length of the seed.

California Red Fir   *Abies magnifica* A. Murr.

The California red fir, with its distinctive red-brown bark, occurs in the southern Cascade Mountains in southern Oregon and into the coastal ranges of northern California. It is more abundant on the high mountain slopes and ridges of the Sierra Nevada of

California and just into the very western tip of Nevada. The trees have their best growth and reach their greatest size on northern or eastern exposures with well-drained, gravelly loam soils and moist, cool air. This species, generally found at 1,600–2,850 m (5,100–9,000 ft) often occurs in pure stands. In some parts of its range, especially near timberline, the California red fir grows in association with the mountain hemlock, lodgepole pine, and western white pine.

An interesting variant of the California red fir with very distinctive seed-bearing cones occasionally grows throughout the range. In these variants the bracts of the mature cones are shorter than the scales and are not visible until the scales are removed. In the variety *shastensis* Lemm. (not shown), the bracts are longer than the scales and extend beyond them. These bracts often are bent backward over their scale.

Several rodents, including different species of mice and the Least chipmunk, gather and eat the seeds of the California red fir. The leaves and twigs serve as a food source for mule deer.

The California red fir is a slow-growing but long-lived species. As in other firs, cone production usually does not begin until the trees approach 25 years old. This fir is a prolific seed producer. Large seed crops are produced every 2 or 3 years, alternating with years of small seed production.

The wood is soft, heavy, brittle, and yellowish-brown. It is more durable than wood of other native firs. So it is used in framing or as facing boards in home construction. It is also used for pulp wood.

All young firs are very susceptible to fire, and this species is no exception. Many of the older trees have heartrot, a fungus-caused disease resulting in the rotting of the center portion of the trunk. If extensive, heartrot can greatly weaken a tree and render much of the wood useless. Dwarf mistletoe, a plant parasite, can cause extensive damage in the upper branches. Injuries caused by this parasite often permit other enemies —fungal disease and insect pests—to penetrate the bark and inflict further damage, causing the death of the tree.

California Red Fir

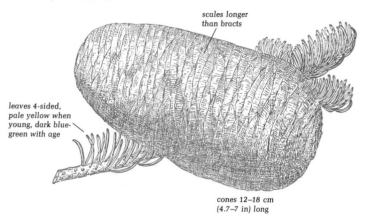

scales longer than bracts

leaves 4-sided, pale yellow when young, dark blue-green with age

cones 12–18 cm (4.7–7 in) long

Appearance: tall trees 30–50 m, rarely to 55 (96–160 ft, rarely to 175) shaped like narrow cylinders and tapering when young to a sharp-pointed crown; on older trees the crown short, narrow, rounded at the top; trunk tapering slightly, 0.8–1.5 m, rarely 2 (2.6–4.9 ft, rarely 6.6) in diameter; usually with branches on the lower half of the trunk. **Bark:** on younger trees thin, smooth, chalky white; on older trees thick, 7–14 cm (2.8–5.5 in) deep, deep reddish-brown, rough, with deep furrows and diagonal or cross fissures and narrow, rounded ridges. **Branches:** small, stout, the upper ones ascending to spreading, the lower ones drooping; branchlets stout, light, yellow-green and slightly hairy the first season, becoming light red-brown and smooth, shiny, ultimately gray or silvery-white; leaf scars circular. **Winter buds:** *broadest at the base and tapering to a sharp point at the tip, 6–10 mm (0.2–0.4 in) long,* scales tightly pressed to the bud, chestnut brown, with a prominent midrib extending to a short point, slightly resinous at the tip or lacking resin. **Leaves:** small, narrow needles without stalks, 4-sided, on lower branches and somewhat flattened, rounded or blunt at the tip, 1.9–3.2 cm (0.8–1.3 in) long, semi-erect; leaves curved on upper branches strongly 4-sided, rounded or blunt at the tip, 1.5–2.8 cm (0.6–1.1 in) long, densely crowded, curved, and erect; all leaves pale yellow-green when young becoming dark blue-green with age. **Flowers:** male cones in cylinder-shaped, deep purplish to dark reddish, 12–20 mm (0.5–0.8 in) long; female cones oblong, reddish-brown, 3–4 cm (1.2–1.6 in) long, the green bracts longer than the rounded scales, borne at the top of the trees. **Fruits:** cones, upright, *cylindric, rounded to slightly depressed at the tip, 12–18 cm long, rarely 20 (4.7–7 in long, rarely 7.9), 6.8–8.8 cm (2.7–3.5 in) in diameter,* purplish to yellow, short, hairy; *scales fan-shaped, 3.8–4.4 cm (1.5–1.8 in) long, slightly longer than broad,* gradually narrowing at base; bracts spoon-shaped, 1.3-1.5 cm (0.5–0.6 in) long (4–4.8 cm—1.6–1.9 in—long in the *shastensis* variety), slightly toothed and sharp-pointed at the tip. **Seeds:** large, wedge-shaped, 15–18 mm (0.6–0.7 in) long, dark brown, winged, wing rose-colored, shiny, about twice as long as seed.

Bristlecone Fir

Abies bracteata D. Don
(synonym: *A. venusta* K. Koch.)

This is a rare fir that occurs in some windswept canyons and high peaks at 625–1,500 m (2,000–4,000 ft) elevation in the Santa Lucia Mountains in Monterey County, California. This unusual fir is easily distinguished in its range by its dense branching pattern that begins near the ground and terminates in a tall, narrow point. The flat leaves are from ***3.8 to 5.7 cm (1.5–2.3 in) long, and longer than other North American firs,*** and are white on the underside. The mature cones are unique too, for they have long (2.5–4.2 cm; 1–1.7 in) needle-like points on the ends of the scale bracts, which give the cones a frilled appearance. The cones are produced every 3 to 5 years and are always at or near the top of the tree. They ripen in late August and shed

Bristlecone Fir

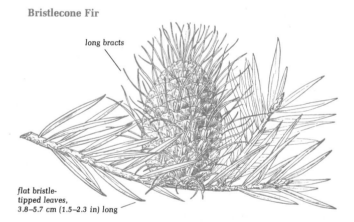

long bracts

flat bristle-
tipped leaves,
3.8–5.7 cm (1.5–2.3 in) long

the bracts and seeds in September. The ***winter buds at the ends of the branches narrow to a point, while all other native firs have a round-tipped winter bud.***

The Taxodium Family   Taxodiaceae

This is a small family of approximately 16 species distributed among 10 genera, many of which are restricted to Japan, China, Taiwan, and Tasmania. Three genera are native to North America: *Sequoia* with 1 species (coastal redwood) in California and southern Oregon, *Giant sequoia* with 1 species (giant sequoia or Sierra redwood) in central California, and *Taxodium* (bald cypresses) with 2 species, 1 in the southeastern U.S. and the other from central Texas into Central America. Fossil remains of these trees indicate that they once occupied a much larger range than they do today. Lumber obtained from this family is very important commercially, largely due to the yield of sizeable knot-free boards and the resistance to decay.

Members of this family are medium- to giant-size trees with narrow, very thin or even bristle-like leaves that are spirally arranged and sometimes opposite one another. Male and female flowers are in separate cones but both kinds occur on the same tree. The fruits are usually globe-shaped cones composed of leathery or woody, spirally arranged scales. There are 2 to 7 seeds per scale and they may or may not be winged.

Key to Taxodium Genera

A. Leaves alternate, persistent, evergreen; trees of California and Oregon.

    1. Leaves linear, mostly spreading and 2-ranked; seed-bearing cones 1.9–2.5 cm (0.8–1 in) long, composed of 12–20 scales, maturing in 1 season; coastal trees of California and southwest Oregon
        Sequoia Genus (species: coastal redwood), p. 115

    2. Leaves egg-shaped to lance-shaped (scale-like), mostly overlapping and closely pressed to the branchlets; seed-bearing cones 3.8–6.3 cm (1.5–2.5 in) long, composed of 25–40 scales, maturing in 2 seasons, with some immature cones visible year-round; trees of central California   **Giant Sequoia Genus (species: giant sequoia or sierra redwood), p. 117**

B. Leaves alternate, deciduous in U.S.; evergreen farther south; cones with 2 seeds per scale; trees of southeastern and southern U.S.
    Bald Cypress Genus, p. 118

Coastal Redwood   **Giant Sequoia or Sierra Redwood**   **Bald Cypress**

The Sequoia Genus   *Sequoia* Endl.

This genus consists of a single species, the coastal redwood. Fossils indicate that other sequoia species once ranged over North America, Europe, Greenland, and China. The coastal redwoods attract high interest because they are the tallest trees in the world and because of public concern for their long-range survival.

Coastal Redwood   *Sequoia sempervirens* (D. Don) Endl.

The redwoods, the world's tallest trees, lie in a narrow, fog-laden belt in the Pacific Coastal region of southwestern Oregon and central to northern California. These towering giants usually grow on low protected flats, along rivers, or in river deltas of the moist coastal plain. Humid conditions, usually caused by frequent fogs sweeping in from the sea, and deep, well-drained soils are essential for maximum development of the trees. When occurring in pure stands, the magnificent groves are awe inspiring. Redwoods also grow in association with western hemlock, Douglas fir, tanbark oak, grand fir, and western red-cedar. Coastal redwoods are relatively free of insect pests and disease, although heart-rot sometimes occurs.

The trees grow well in low light intensities and reach maturity in 400 to 500 years, although most live to twice that age. The oldest tree on record was 2,200 years old. Trees exceeding 65 m (215 ft) in height are common; while the tallest redwoods grow to over 115 m (368 ft) high. Although good production comes much later, seed production may begin after some trees are 20 years old. Redwoods are prolific seed producers but with a higher percentage of bad seed. New sprouts will develop quickly from the stump and root crown of recently cut trees.

The lumber is of high quality because the wood is straight-grained, knot free, durable, termite resistant, and easily worked. Because of the size of these trees, yields of 2½-million board feet of lumber per acre have been obtained. Billions of board feet have been cut to make bridges, piers, caskets, wine casks, outdoor furniture, homes, barns, boxes, shingles, and even railroad ties.

The concerted efforts of a few individuals were responsible for the saving of virgin stands of redwoods from the onslaught of lumbering operations. Some of the finest virgin stands can be seen in the recently established Redwood National Forest in northern California.

Coastal Redwood

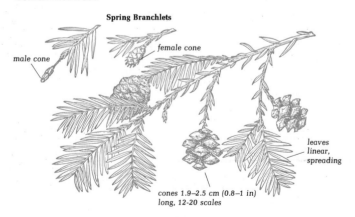

Spring Branchlets

male cone

female cone

leaves
linear,
spreading

cones 1.9–2.5 cm (0.8–1 in)
long, 12-20 scales

Appearance: *tall, narrow trees 65–100 m, rarely to 114 (213–328 ft, rarely to 365),* with a short-pointed to rounded, ragged crown; trunk straight, slightly flaring, but-tressed at the base, 3–5 m (10–16 ft), rarely 10 m (33 ft), in diameter, branchless for lower third of the tree. **Bark:** thick, 15–30 cm (5.9–11.8 in), dark brown, often with grayish tinge, deeply furrowed with rounded ridges of long, fibrous scales. **Branches:** short, upper ones often drooping, lower ones spreading to ascending; branchlets slen-der, 2-ranked. **Leaves:** small, *linear,* 0.6–2 cm (0.2–0.8 in) long, *spreading in 2 ranks,* flat, sharp-pointed, slightly curved, bright deep yellowish-green. **Flowers:** male cones tiny, oblong; female cones tiny, egg-shaped, scattered near the ends of the branchlets. **Fruits:** small, hard *cones, 1.9–2.5 cm (0.8–1 in) long,* oblong, brown, *composed of about 12 to 20 scales.* **Seeds:** tiny, 1.5–2.5 mm (up to 0.1 in) long, broadly egg-shaped, light brown, winged, the wings as broad as the seed.

The Giant Sequoia Genus   *Sequoiadendron* Buchholz

This genus contains a single species, but with many extinct relatives known from fos-sil records. Giant sequoias were once placed in the same genus as the coastal redwood. But they are now placed in their own genus. They can be distinguished from the coastal redwoods by their scale-like leaves and their cones, which take 2 years to mature. Although not as tall as the coastal redwoods, giant sequoias have greater trunk diameter and bulk.

Giant Sequoia, Sierra Redwood   *Sequoiadendron giganteum* (Lindl.) Buchholz

[synonym: *Sequoia gigantea* (Lindl.) Decne]

The giant sequoias, the largest living organisms on earth, grow in isolated groves scat-tered along the western slopes of the Sierra Nevada in central California. The trees generally are found at 1,500–2,500 m (4,900–8,200 ft) on well-drained but moist soils and with 110–155 cm (43–61 in) of annual precipitation per year, principally as snow. They usually occur in groves rather than in association with other species, and it is not unusual for the trees to average 6.5 m (21 ft) in trunk diameter or even larger. The General Sherman tree is the largest liv-ing giant sequoia, measuring 90 m (295 ft) tall and 33.8 m (110 ft) in diameter at 1.3 m (4 ft) from the ground. The giant sequoia is free of serious insect pests and diseases.

These trees are rapid-growing when young but become slow-growing with age. They are one of the longest-lived trees known, with some individuals reaching 2,000 to 3,000 years. They are also massive trees; a single tree 100 m (328 ft) high and 10 m (33 ft) in diameter was estimated to weigh 2,000 tons. The trees produce cones and seeds each year, with heavy seed crops produced every 2 or 3 years. Unlike the coastal redwoods, the giant sequoias cannot produce new sprouts from the stumps or roots.

The trees were logged for the lightweight, soft, coarse-grained wood. This wood was used for shingles, poles, timbers, shakes, flumes, and casks. Many acres of giant sequoias were cut in the mid and late 1800s. Then vast numbers of fallen trees were left to rot on steep hillsides because there were no machines capable of removing the ponderous logs. A bill was passed by the U.S. Congress on October 1, 1890, which created the Yosemite and General Grant national parks and enlarged the Sequoia National Park, thus saving some magnificent virgin stands from plunder.

Giant Sequoia

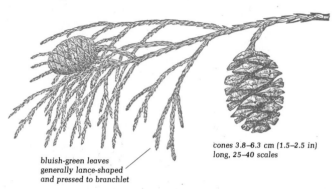

bluish-green leaves
generally lance-shaped
and pressed to branchlet

cones 3.8–6.3 cm (1.5–2.5 in)
long, 25–40 scales

Appearance: tall, *massive trees 60 to 90 m, rarely to 105 (196–295 ft, rarely to 345),* shaped like a narrow cone with a rounded often irregular crown; trunk straight, slightly tapering, fluted, *greatly enlarged and buttressed at the base, 6–15 m (20–50 ft) in diameter,* rarely larger; older trees free of branches for lower half of trunk. **Bark:** thick, 30–60 cm (11.8–24 in), dark reddish or cinnamon brown, often with a slight purplish tinge, deeply furrowed with very large, rounded ridges separating into loose, fibrous scales. **Branches:** short, stout, thick, horizontal, usually becoming irregular and twisted with age; branchlets slender, turning reddish-brown and becoming scaly after the leaves have fallen away. **Leaves:** tiny, egg-shaped to *lance-shaped,* 3–6 mm (0.1–0.2 in) long (on growing shoots to 12 mm – 0.5 in – long), *overlapping and closely pressed* to the branchlets or even somewhat spreading, rounded, and thickened on the lower surface, usually sharp-pointed, bluish-green. **Flowers:** male cones tiny, oblong to egg-shaped, numerous in early spring; female cones small, many-scaled, egg-shaped, the scales yellowish, ridged on the back, scattered near the tips of the upper branchlets. **Fruits:** small, woody *cones, 3.8–6.3 cm (1.5–2.5 in) long,* egg-shaped, dark reddish-brown, *composed of 25 to 40 scales,* each scale thickened near the outer edge, ridged on the back, the cones maturing in 2 years. **Seeds:** tiny, 3–6 mm (0.1–0.2 in) long, linear to lance-shaped, light brown, the 2 wings circling the seed and usually broader than the seed.

The Bald Cypress Genus   *Taxodium* Rich.

There are presently 2 species of bald cypresses in the world. One occurs in the southeastern U.S. and the other from southern Texas to Guatemala. There are fossil records of other species of bald cypresses from temperate parts of the world. The closest living relative of these trees is the dawn redwood (*Metasequoia glyptostroboides*) of central China.

Bald cypresses are large, long-lived, deciduous trees (evergreen in Mexico), usually with a *buttressed trunk covered by light, reddish-brown, furrowed, scaly bark.* The wood is hard, durable, and ranges from light to dark brown. Winter buds are globe-shaped and scaly. The *soft, deciduous leaves are alternate on the twigs, linear, flat-tened, and usually spreading.* Male and female flowers grow on the same tree with the small, male flowers occurring at the ends of the branchlets in long, hanging, flower clusters. The female flowers are scattered on the branchlets and are almost globe-shaped. The hanging, female cones (fruits), that mature in one season are composed of several thick, leathery scales with each scale holding 2 irregularly 3-sided seeds.

Key to Bald Cypress Species

A. Leaves dropping in autumn; branches spreading; trees of the southeastern U.S.
Bald cypress, p. 119
B. Leaves nearly evergreen to evergreen in southern-most part of its range; branches drooping; trees of southern and southwestern Texas, Mexico, and Guatemala
Montezuma bald cypress, p. 121

Bald Cypress

Bald Cypress　　　　　　　　*Taxodium distichum* (L.) Rich.

The bald cypress is a valuable deciduous conifer of low, wet areas, primarily of the coastal regions of the southeastern U.S. It is generally found along streams, rivers, and particularly in swamps where it can occur in almost pure stands. In this situation the

broadly buttressed or flaring trunks, accompanied by several protruding root "knees," totally dominate the swamp setting. Native trees occur on very wet soils, at low elevations (normally less than 200 m or 656 ft), and on relatively flat terrain. The best growth occurs in deep, rich, sandy-loam soils with high moisture levels. The bald cypress grows in association with the water tupelo, black willow, swamp cottonwood, red maple, and water hickory. Bald cypress is relatively free of diseases and serious insect infestations.

Instead of the 2-ranked, spreading leaves of the typical bald cypress, trees in certain bogs and ponds have smaller leaves that are closely pressed against the twigs. These populations were at one time considered a distinct species. But today they are considered to be a variant and are commonly called pond cypresses, *Taxodium distichum* variety *nutans* (Ait.) Sweet.

Large bald cypress swamps are very important to wildlife, especially waterfowl. These shallow swamps, usually rich in aquatic and shoreline vegetation, insects, and crustaceans, are excellent feeding areas. Nuts and acorns from the water hickory and overcup oak also provide wildlife food. These areas provide food and cover for large numbers of ducks and geese, especially Canadian geese. Seeds of the bald cypress are important in the diet of the Florida crane. Whitetail deer often utilize bald cypress swamps as escape routes from hunters. Swamp rabbits feed on the young saplings, while nutria consume the bark and young roots.

These areas are normally moderate to slow-growing and commonly live 500 or 600 years. In second growth conditions, the trees are generally fast-growing. Seed production occurs every year, but good seed crops occur only every third or fourth year. The hard, heavy, straight-grained, light to dark brown wood is very durable, resistant to decay, and easy to work. This wood has been used in the construction of barrels and caskets or as shingles, railroad ties, and bridge beams. Because the trees are slow-growing in virgin stands, reproduction has not kept pace with lumbering operations. This, coupled with the drainage of thousands of acres of swamp habitats, has served to reduce severely the total number of mature bald cypresses. Fortunately, large tracts do occur in state and federal parklands, forests, and preserves.

The bald cypress makes an excellent ornamental tree for parks and large lawns. It is very attractive when planted near a small pond. The trees are hardy when planted as far north as Boston, and they grow well on a variety of upland soils, as well as in wetter locations.

Bald Cypress

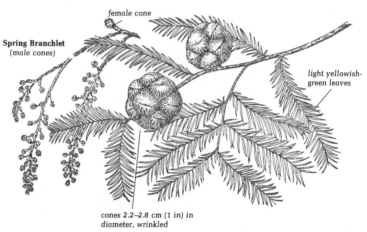

female cone

Spring Branchlet
(*male cones*)

light yellowish-green leaves

cones 2.2–2.8 cm (1 in) in diameter, wrinkled

Appearance: medium to large trees 20–40 m, rarely 45 (65–130 ft, rarely 145), pyramid-shaped when young becoming narrowly pyramidal with age; crown sharp-pointed on young trees but becomes broad and rounded; *trunk* gradually tapering, usually to 1.5 m, rarely to 4 (4.9 ft, rarely to 13) in diameter, often *with a strongly buttressed base;* and if growing in water, the tree will have several *conspicuous, cone-shaped "knees"* produced by the roots and extending above the surface. **Bark:** moderately thin, 2.5–5 cm (1–2 in) thick, light reddish-brown, with shallow furrows dividing the broad, flat ridges that often separate into thin, fibrous scales. **Branches:** short, slender, *often widespreading, slightly drooping;* branchlets slender, flexible, light yellow-green and shiny becoming pale reddish-brown with age; *leaf scars absent* (the lateral twigs fall away with the leaves in autumn). **Winter buds:** rounded, 2–4 mm (about 0.1–0.2 in) diameter, with several closely overlapping, pale brown scales. **Leaves: *deciduous*,** small, appearing **2-ranked,** spreading, giving a **feather-like shape;** leaves are 1.2–1.9 cm (0.5–0.8 in) long, linear, thin, flat, often curved, pointed at the tip, **light yellow-green. Flowers:** male cones hanging, many-flowered, branched, flower clusters, 10–14 cm (3.9–5.5 in) long; female cones few to several near the ends of the branchlets, rounded, composed of several spirally arranged scales. **Fruits: *cones, hanging, often in pairs, rounded to pear-shaped, 2.2–2.8 cm (1 in) in diameter, wrinkled*** and becoming woody, green turning brown at maturity; scales shield-shaped, closely fitting one against another, each scale containing 2 seeds. **Seeds:** irregularly 3-angled, 8–10 mm (0.3–0.4 in) long, brown, with 3 narrow wings.

Montezuma Bald Cypress

Taxodium mucronatum Ten.

This relative of the bald cypress occurs in low, wet, swampy areas from Guatemala to the northeastern state of Coahuila, Mexico. It was not known to occur in the U.S. until 1926 when it was discovered growing in southern and southwestern Texas. The Montezuma bald cypress is a very large, slow-growing, and long-lived tree that can be distinguished easily from the bald cypress by its limited distribution in the U.S. and, in the case of overlapping distribution, by ***its evergreen to nearly evergreen leaves*** and **strongly drooping branchlets.** This tree is not hardy when planted in temperate North America.

Montezuma Bald Cypress

Spring Branchlet

male cones

branchlets
strongly
drooping

female cones

The Cypress Family

Cupressaceae

This is a medium-size family of approximately 140 to 150 species of trees and shrubs unevenly divided into 16 to 18 genera worldwide. They are widespread throughout the world. Five genera are native to North America. A single species of incense cedar (*Calocedrus*) is native and occurs along the Pacific Coast. There are 11 species of cypress (*Cupressus*) that are native to the West. Two native arborvitae (*Thuja*) are found in the North, while 3 species of white cedar (*Chamaecyparis*) are native, 2 in the Pacific Northwest and another in the East. There are 12 tree-size species of juniper dispersed over much of North America. The wood obtained from members of this family is usually easy to work and of some importance commercially. The trees are very important to wildlife for food and cover.

Trees and shrubs in this family have small scale-like leaves that are usually pressed against the branchlets and opposite one another or in 3s. The winter buds are usually not covered with scales. Male and female cones occur in some genera on the same tree; while in other genera, the cones occur on separate trees. The fruits are small, usually globe-shaped or egg-shaped cones composed of scales that are fused with their bracts. The fruits are leathery to fleshy but are usually hard at maturity. Each cone scale has 1 to several small seeds.

Key to Cypress Genera

A. Branches flattened, usually forming flat sprays.

1. Leaves attached to branchlet in 4s and faintly gland-dotted; space on the branchlets between the leaves greater than branchlet's width; trees of California and Oregon
Incense cedars, p. 123

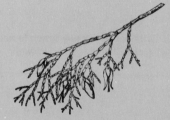

Incense Cedar

2. Leaves usually attached to branchlet in 2s and noticeably gland-dotted; space on the branchlets between the leaves about as long as branchlet's width.

    a. Branchlets considerably flattened into 1 plane; cones oblong, the cone scales thin, flexible, with 2–3 seeds per scale; includes eastern white cedar, western redcedar, Oriental arborvitae   **Arborvitae, p. 125**

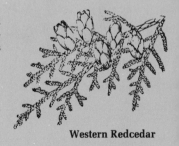

Western Redcedar

b. Branchlets slightly flattened into 1 plane; cones globe-shaped, the scales stiff, hard, with 2 to many seeds per scales; includes Alaska, Atlantic White, Port Orford, Hinoki, Sawara cedars   **White cedars, p. 129**

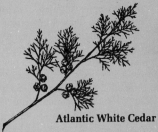

Atlantic White Cedar

B. Branches rounded to 4-sided, usually not forming flat sprays.

1. Fruits leathery or woody, globe-shaped cones; seeds winged; branchlets usually appearing in 1 plane   **Cypresses, p. 135**

Arizona Cypress

2. Fruits fleshy, berry-like cones; seeds wingless; branchlets usually not in 1 plane   **Junipers, p. 141**

Common Juniper

The Incense Cedar Genus   *Calocedrus* Kurz

(synonym: *Libocedrus*, in part)

This is a small genus of only 3 species, the incense cedar of western North America, and 2 other species in China. These species were for many years included in the genus *Libocedrus* with other species native to New Zealand and New Caledonia.

Members of this genus are evergreen trees and shrubs with light brown to reddish-brown, scaly bark, flattened branchlets that branch into fan-like sprays. The mature leaves are small, scale-like, flattened, closely pressed against the branchlets. Male and female cones occur singly on the same tree but on different branchlets. Seed-bearing cones are stalked, woody, narrowly urn-shaped, composed of 4 to 6 opposing scales, the 4 larger scales each bearing 1 or 2 flattened, unequally winged seeds.

Incense Cedar   *Calocedrus decurrens* (Torr.) Florin

(synonym: *Libocedrus decurrens* Torr.)

The incense cedar is native to the Cascade Mountains in Oregon and the Sierra Nevada in California and also extends into Baja California. The trees generally occur on western slopes from 700–2,500 m (2,300–8,200 ft) altitude on a variety of soils with dry, summer climatic conditions. They reach their largest size on deep, well-drained, slightly acidic, sandy loam soils. Seldom found in pure stands, the incense cedars usually grow in association with several species of pine and fir. The leafy mistletoe can be a troublesome parasite.

The small, inconspicuous cones appear in early spring, mature in 1 growing season, and shed their seeds in late August or early September. Growth is normally slow, but the trees may live 500 to 1,000 years.

Although the trees are of limited importance to wildlife, the small seeds are a food source for some birds and small rodents such as the Douglas chickaree. The light weight, close-grained, light reddish-brown, durable wood is used for fences, shingles, interior finishings, doors, and window frames. Because mature trees often are affected by dry rot and usually are scattered throughout the forest, they are not considered a major timber species. The incense cedar is used in the manufacture of wooden pencils. Pencils were made from the eastern redcedar, but the supply of large virgin trees was exhausted and then replaced by the incense cedar, which has the wood-working qualities needed for pencils.

Incense Cedar

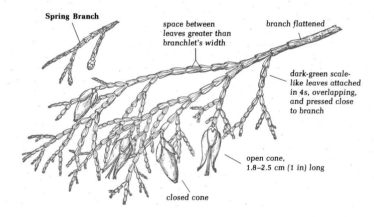

Spring Branch

space between leaves greater than branchlet's width

branch flattened

dark-green scale-like leaves attached in 4s, overlapping, and pressed close to branch

open cone, 1.8–2.5 cm (1 in) long

closed cone

Appearance: medium-size to tall trees 20–50 m (64–164 ft), shaped like columns with a short, open, rounded or flattened crown at maturity; trunk straight, 1–2 m (3.2–6.6 ft) in diameter, rapidly tapering and buttressed at the base, often free of branches on lower half of older trees. **Bark:** moderately thick, 5–7.6 cm (2–3 in), reddish-brown to cinnamon red, deeply furrowed, scaly. **Branches:** short, stout, erect to spreading; branchlets slender, light yellowish-green, turning reddish-brown with age, flattened, branched, forming a fan-shaped spray. **Leaves:** *scale-like,* opposite each other, *overlapping and closely pressed against the branchlets,* on lateral branches 5–7 mm (0.2–0.3 in) long, on growing leader shoots 10–14 mm (0.4–0.5 in) long, oblong to egg-shaped, sharp-pointed at the tip, ridged and faintly gland-dotted on the back, dark green. **Flowers:** male cones numerous, oblong, light yellow, 5–7 mm (0.2–0.3 in) long, borne at the ends of short, lateral branchlets; female cones small, composed of 4 to 12, yellowish-green, spreading scales and occurring at the ends of lateral branchlets. **Fruits:** *hanging cones, urn-shaped, 1.8–2.5 cm (1 in) long,* light reddish-brown. **Seeds:** oblong to lance-shaped, 8–12 mm (0.3–0.5 in) long, with a resin-filled chamber around the seed coat, yellowish to reddish-brown, with a large, papery wing.

The Arborvitae Genus

Thuja L.

There are 6 species of arborvitae known in the world; 2 are native to North America, 1 in the Northeast and the other in the Northwest. The remaining 4 species are native to eastern Asia. One species, the oriental arborvitae, has been introduced into the more temperate regions of North America and is frequently used as an ornamental tree. The different arborvitae will grow in a variety of soils, although preferred sites have well-drained but moist soils. *(Arborvitae have oblong cones with flexible scales, while white cedars have globe-shaped cones with hard scales.)*

Arborvitae are usually slow-growing, long-lived, evergreen trees with a tapering trunk that is generally flaring and buttressed at the base. The thin, shredding, fibrous bark is usually a light reddish-brown. The soft, light wood is not very strong but is resistant to decay. Winter buds are minute and obscured by the leaves. The numerous, tiny, scale-like leaves are closely pressed against the flattened, fan-shaped sprays of the branchlets. The small male and female flowers occur on the same tree and appear in spring near the ends of the branchlets. The seed-bearing cones are small, composed of alternating leathery scales, and mature in 1 growing season. There are usually 2, tiny winged (unwinged in some Asian species) seeds on the middle scales of the cones.

Unfortunately for purists, the native arborvitae are known more commonly as cedars. True cedars, the genus *Cedrus*, are not North American trees.

Key to Arborvitae Species

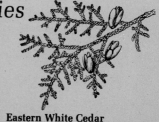

A. Branchlets oriented in horizontal planes; the scales of the seed-bearing cones thin; the seeds thin, winged; native trees.

   1. Trees of northeastern North America; branchlets flattened; leaves gland-dotted, dull yellowish-green   **Eastern white cedar, p. 126**

   2. Trees of northwestern North America; branchlets 4-sided or nearly so; leaves inconspicuously gland-dotted or without gland dots entirely; shiny yellowish-green
        Western redcedar, p. 127

B. Branchlets oriented in vertical planes; the scales of the seed-bearing cones thick, the seeds thick, unwinged; cultivated trees not found wild
        Oriental arborvitae, p. 129

Eastern White Cedar

Oriental Arborvitae

Eastern White Cedar,
Northern White Cedar, Arborvitae   *Thuja occidentalis* L.

The eastern white cedar is a tree of the colder regions of eastern North America. It occurs throughout central and eastern Canada, as well as in northern portions of the midwestern and northeastern U.S., and is scattered in limited numbers along the

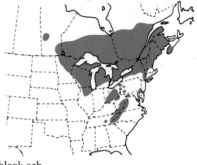

higher elevations of the Appalachian Mountains. This species usually is found at lower elevations in swamps or in low, wet forests. The trees prefer neutral or alkaline soils, especially of limestone origin, along with humid climatic conditions. They grow well in areas of high snowfall and have few serious diseases or insect infestations. In swampy habitats the eastern white cedar, black spruce, and tamarack are the dominant trees. Yet in wet forests, it can be found in association with yellow birch, eastern hemlock, silver maple, and black ash.

Flowers are produced in early spring (late April to early May), and the seed-bearing cones mature in 1 growing season, shedding the seeds in autumn. Although good seed production does not begin until 20 to 25 years, these slow-growing trees can begin to produce seed crops at about 10 years. They produce a large seed crop every 3 to 5 years, and maximum production occurs between 75 and 150 years.

The eastern white cedar is of limited importance to wildlife. Red squirrels eat the buds in spring and cut small, cone-laden branchlets in the fall for their winter caches. Snowshoe hares, whitetail deer, and — to lesser extent — moose browse the trees. The thin-barked trees are sometimes girdled by porcupines. The seeds are an important constituent in the diet of the pine siskin, a small finch of eastern evergreen forests.

The Indians used parts of this tree to treat scurvy. This treatment was passed along to the early French settlers. As a result, the common name arborvitae, translated "tree of life," was given.

The fragrant wood is lightweight, soft, light yellowish-brown, low in strength but high in resistance to decay. It is used where contact with water cannot be avoided. It is commonly used for canoes, boats, fence posts, shingles, and posts for boat docks. It is

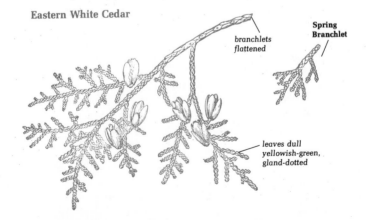

Eastern White Cedar

branchlets
flattened

**Spring
Branchlet**

leaves dull
yellowish-green,
gland-dotted

a good ornamental tree and can be used as a foundation planting, or for hedges and windbreaks, and even in low, wet situations.

Appearance: medium-size trees, 15 to 20 m, rarely to 25 (50–65 ft, rarely to 80), narrowly cone-shaped to pyramid-shaped with a compact, steeple-shaped crown; trunk rapidly tapering, often buttressed and knobby, ½ to 1 m, rarely to 2 (1.6–3.3 ft, rarely to 6.6) in diameter, in open-grown trees the branches occur near to the ground; in forests, trees may be free of branches for lower third of trunk. **Bark:** thin, *light reddish-brown,* 0.6–1.5 cm (0.2–0.6 in) thick, with numerous shallow fissures forming narrow, flat ridges that frequently separate giving a *shredded look.* **Branches:** short, horizontal with some turning upwards; *branchlets flattened* into broad, fan-shaped sprays, light yellowish-green becoming light reddish-brown with age. **Winter buds:** minute, covered by leaves closely pressed to form the bud. **Leaves:** small, scale-like, numerous and lying close to or against the branchlets, 5–7 mm (0.20–0.28 in) long, lance-shaped; on lead branchlets the leaves are thick, sharp-pointed at the tip, *gland-dotted on the back;* on the side branchlets the leaves are smaller, flattened, usually rounded at the tip, not gland-dotted, *all leaves dull yellowish-green.* **Flowers:** male cones tiny, 1–2 mm (less than 0.1 in) long, almost round to egg-shaped; female cones small, 1.5–2.5 mm (to 0.1 in) long, egg-shaped, composed of 4 to 6 pairs of thin scales; both male and female cones occurring singly near the ends of the branchlets. **Fruits:** cones, small, egg-shaped to oblong, rounded to slightly pointed at the tip, 0.7–1.2 cm (0.3–0.5 in) long, green turning pale reddish-brown in the fall; scales in opposing pairs, 10 to 12 per cone, leathery, broadest above the middle, rounded to very slightly pointed at the tip, each scale containing 2 seeds. **Seeds:** narrowly oblong, tapering toward the tip; 2–3 mm (0.1 in) long, light brown, winged, the 2 narrow wings almost encircling the seed and about as wide as the seed.

Western Redcedar   *Thuja plicata* D. Don

The western redcedar is a tall, valuable timber tree of the Pacific Northwest. The trees are restricted largely to areas with abundant rain or snow, high humidity, and cool summers. They grow from sea level to approximately 1,800 m (5,900 ft) elevation, although above 1,500 m (4,900 ft) the western redcedar looks like a low shrub. River bottoms, swamps, moist ravines, and gulches are the favored sites. This tree reaches best growth and largest size on moist bottomland with deep, rich soil. It seldom occurs in pure stands but rather is associated with other conifers, such as the coastal redwood, Sitka spruce, western hemlock, Douglas fir, lowland fir, western larch, or the yellow cedar. Western red-  cedar is relatively free of serious diseases or insect infestations.

The trees produce flowers in mid-April, although this may be delayed at least a month in higher elevations. The fruits or cones begin to mature in late August, and seeds usually are shed from September to early November. The slow-growing trees may begin to produce flowers and fruits about 20 years of age, but the peak seed crops are not produced until 70 to 80 years of age and continue for 100 to 200 years. As with other arborvitae, a heavy seed crop is produced about every 3 years.

The western redcedar is not important to wildlife, except possibly to provide cover for squirrels, grouse, and smaller birds. The smaller seeds of this arborvitae often escape predation because rodents and birds prefer the larger seeds of nearby conifers.

The soft, reddish-brown wood is coarse-grained and very durable and can be used in circumstances where other woods decay rapidly. The lumber is used to make posts, poles, shingles, doors, window sashes and other interior finishings, as well as for boats and greenhouses. The Indians of the Pacific Northwest used the trunk of the western redcedar for totem poles, canoes, and lodges. The strong, tough inner bark is used for baskets.

The trees have excellent value as ornamentals and are better for northern climates than are the eastern white cedars because the foliage of the western species does not turn brown in winter, in the way foliage of eastern cedars does. They can be used in foundation plantings, as windscreens, or as background material for flowering shrubs and flowers.

Western Redcedar

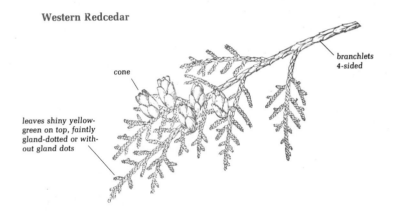

branchlets 4-sided

cone

leaves shiny yellow-green on top, faintly gland-dotted or without gland dots

Appearance: tall trees 30–50 m, rarely to 65 (98–165 ft, rarely to 210), narrowly cone-shaped with irregular or pointed crown; trunk rapidly tapering, flaring and buttressed at the base, 1.2–2.6 m (3.9–8.5 ft) in diameter, rarely larger, in open-grown trees the branches occurring almost to the ground. **Bark:** thin, fibrous, reddish-cinnamon brown, 1.2–1.9 cm (0.5–0.8 in) thick, irregularly divided by shallow fissures into broad ridges, the ridges separating and becoming shreddy looking. **Branches:** horizontal and slightly drooping but usually turned upwards near the tip; *branchlets 4-sided,* flattened into zigzagged, *tapering fan-like sprays,* yellowish-green, often whitish on the underside. **Winter buds:** minute, covered by the numerous closely pressed leaves. **Leaves:** small, scale-like, numerous and lying close to the branchlets, 1.5–3 mm (about 0.1 in) long on branchlets, 3–6 mm (about 0.1–0.2 in) long on vigorous growing leader branchlets, egg-shaped, flattened to slightly thickened, *shiny yellow-green above,* dull green below. **Flowers:** male cones tiny, 1.5–2 mm (less than 0.1 in) long, egg-shaped, dark brown; female cones tiny, 1.8–2.2 mm (about 0.1 in) long, composed of 8 to 12 scales, dark brown; both male and female cones found near tips of branchlets. **Fruits:** cones, small, broadest near the middle, tapering to a point at the tip, 1.2–1.9 cm (0.5–0.8 in) long, light brown, composed of several paired, leathery scales, the *scales with a weak but sharp point near the tip.* **Seeds:** tiny, narrow, elliptic, 4–6 mm (0.2 in) long, light brown, winged, the 2 narrow wings almost encircling the body of the seed.

Oriental Arborvitae

Thuja orientalis L.

The oriental arborvitae, native to northern and western China and Korea, is a commonly planted evergreen, especially in the southern U.S. These symmetrical trees have a graceful appearance with the branchlets usually arranged in horizontal planes,

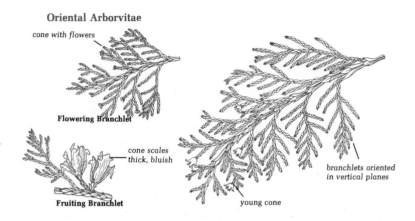

Oriental Arborvitae

cone with flowers

Flowering Branchlet

cone scales thick, bluish

Fruiting Branchlet

branchlets oriented in vertical planes

young cone

so that the edges face away from the tree. *The maturing seed-bearing cones are bluish; the cone scales are thick, and the seeds are wingless. These characteristics distinguish the oriental arborvitae from the native ones.* There are several selections or cultivars of the oriental arborvitae, based largely upon the form and the color of the leaves.

The White Cedar (False Cypress) Genus

Chamaecyparis Spach

The white cedars make up a small group of evergreen trees or shrubs native to North America, Japan, and Taiwan. One species occurs in the eastern U.S. The 2 other species grow in the Pacific Northwest. Three species are native to Japan and Taiwan. There are fossil records of white cedars in southern Europe and Greenland. Two of the Asian members, the Hinoki white cedar and the Sawara white cedar, are important horticulturally and are widely planted ornamentals in North America. (White cedars have globe-shaped cones with hard scales, while arborvitae have oblong cones with flexible scales.)

White cedars are long-lived, evergreen trees or shrubs with aromatic, resin-bearing leaves and wood. The tall trees have a thin, scaly or thick, deeply furrowed bark. The light, whitish wood, usually fine-grained and very durable, makes excellent lumber. Winter buds are inconspicuous. The leaves are numerous, scale-like, opposite one another, sharp-pointed, and usually closely pressed against the flattened, fan-shaped sprays of the branchlets. Male and female cones, both tiny and so easily overlooked, are produced on the same tree and appear in early spring at or near the ends of the upper branchlets. The seed-bearing cones are globe-shaped, hard but slightly fleshy or leathery, and composed of 6 to 8 opposing scales. The fruits mature in 1 or 2 years, producing tiny seeds that are broadly-winged.

The white cedars are closely related to the cypress trees (*Cupressus* species). True cypresses have fruits that mature in 2 growing seasons, usually with many seeds per cone scale and with rounded or 4-sided branchlets. White cedars generally have flattened branchlets. The fruits (cones) generally mature in 1 season (except for the Alaska cedar); and there are usually 2 seeds per cone scale.

Key to White Cedar Species

A. Branchlets arranged in several planes; leaves green above and below; seed-bearing cones composed of 4 or 6 scales.

    1. Leaves 1.5–3 mm (about 0.1 in) long, usually not gland-dotted; seed-bearing cones 0.6–1.2 cm (0.2–0.5 in) long, maturing in 2 years, each scale containing 2–4 seeds; trees of Pacific Northwest   **Alaska cedar, p. 131**

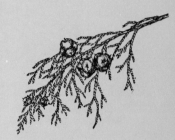

Alaska Cedar

    2. Leaves 1.5–3 mm (about 0.1 in) long, usually gland-dotted; seed-bearing cones 5–8 mm (0.2–0.3 in) long, maturing in 1 year, each scale containing 1–2 seeds; trees of eastern Atlantic Coast   **Atlantic white cedar, p. 132**

B. Branchlets arranged in horizontal planes; leaves green above, paler and usually whitish beneath; seed-bearing cones composed of 6 to 10 scales.

    1. Bark thick, furrowed (mature trees); leaves conspicuously gland-dotted on the back; native trees of Oregon and Washington   **Port Orford cedar, p. 133**

Atlantic White Cedar

    2. Bark thin (mature trees); leaves not gland-dotted or, if present, inconspicuous; introduced trees widely planted in North America.

        a. Leaves closely pressed to the branchlets; seed-bearing cones 0.8–1.2 cm (0.3–0.5 in) in diameter; cultivated   **Hinoki white cedar, p. 134**

        b. Leaves closely pressed to the branchlets; seed-bearing cones 0.5–0.7 cm (0.3 in) in diameter; cultivated   **Sawara white cedar, p. 134**

Hinoki White Cedar

Alaska Cedar, Yellow Cypress
Chamaecyparis nootkatensis (D. Don) Spach

The Alaska cedar is an important timber tree within its range from southeastern Alaska to Oregon. The trees do best in cool, humid climates with a short growing season, and they are commonly found in bottomlands, along streams, or in valleys or basins with moist but well-drained soils.
In Alaska the trees can be found at sea level, but farther south the trees normally are found at 650–2,500 m (1,900–8,200 ft). At the high elevations, the trees are low or even prostrate shrubs. They seldom occur in pure stands but grow with Sitka spruce, western redcedar, western hemlock, and the grand fir. At higher altitudes they grow with western white pine, mountain hemlock, and subalpine fir.

The trees are very slow growing. Some trees measuring only 38–50 cm (15–20 in) in diameter may be 200 to 275 years old; in addition, they are very long-lived, some of them living over 1,000 years. One of these trees is 3,500 years old. Flowering is in April to late May, depending upon longitude, and the fruits usually mature in the next season in late September or early October. Years of heavy seed production generally are followed by 1 to 3 years of light production. This tree is apparently of little value to wildlife.

The pale yellow wood is lightweight, close-grained, and decay-resistant. So it is used in boat construction, greenhouses, and interior finishings, including cabinets. The wood is excellent for pattern-making and for carving. The Indians of the Pacific Northwest carved their ceremonial masks from Alaska cedar, and the wood is used today for canoe paddles. The trees are largely free of insect pests and disease. They have outstanding horticultural value, but they need a cool, moist climate to thrive.

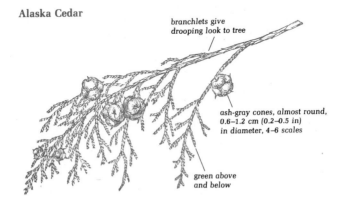

Alaska Cedar

branchlets give drooping look to tree

ash-gray cones, almost round, 0.6–1.2 cm (0.2–0.5 in) in diameter, 4–6 scales

green above and below

Appearance: medium-size to tall trees, 20–30 m (65–100 ft), rarely higher, cone-shaped with a narrow, pyramid-shaped crown; trunk tapering, flaring and broadly buttressed at the base, 1–1.5 m, rarely to 2 (3.2–4.9 ft, rarely to 6.6) in diameter. **Bark:** thin, ash gray to purplish-brown, 1.2–2 cm (0.5–0.8 in) thick, irregularly fissured, shredding by separating into large, thin, loose scales. **Branches:** spreading to slightly drooping; *branchlets loosely hanging giving drooping look to tree, 4-sided* and *slightly flattened into spreading, fan-shaped sprays,* light yellow becoming reddish-brown. **Winter buds:** minute, covered by the evergreen leaves. **Leaves:** small, *scale-like,* numerous, and closely pressed to the branchlets, 1.5-3 mm (about 0.1 in) long on the side branchlets, 4–6 mm (0.2 in) long on the growing shoots, sometimes gland-dotted on the back, pointed at the tip, dark blue-green. **Flowers:** male cones tiny, containing 4 or 5 pollen sacs, scattered on the side branchlets produced in the previous year; female cones tiny, dark reddish, scattered near the ends of the upper branchlets. **Fruits:** *fleshy cones,* hard, *almost round, 0.6–1.2 cm (0.2–0.5 in) in diameter, ash gray* and sometimes covered with a whitish bloom, mature in 2 years (sometimes 1 year in the southern part of the range), composed of 4 to 6 hard, rounded scales, each with a prominent, hard, pointed tip, usually 2 to 4 seeds in each scale. **Seeds:** small, broadest near the base, pointed at the tip, 3–4 mm (0.1–0.2 in) long, brown to dark reddish-brown, slightly flattened, winged, the 2 wings about twice as wide as the body of the seed.

Atlantic White Cedar   *Chamaecyparis thyoides* (L.) B.S.P.

Restricted to a narrow belt along the Atlantic Coastal Plain, the Atlantic white cedar occurs from southern Maine to northern Florida and to southern Mississippi. The trees live in freshwater swamps or wet woods and grow best in acid peat beds where they usually form pure stands. Occasion-ally they can be found growing with red maple, black gum, white pine, swamp tupelo, and bald cypress.

The Atlantic white cedar is a moderate to slow-growing tree that may live for more than 1,000 years. It flowers in early spring, and the fruits mature in 1 growing season. Seed production usually begins when the trees are 5 to 10 years old. Although white-tail deer browse the leaves, the trees are of limited value to wildlife. The light brown, lightweight, soft, close-grained wood is unmatched in its resistance to decay. In the 1700s the wood was used for log cabins, roof shingles, barrels, and boats. But this soon depleted the limited supply. Then it was learned that fallen tree trunks that had been buried for many years could be raised from the peat bogs and used because the wood was still in excellent condition. Other uses have included piers, telephone poles, piling, and ties.

Appearance: medium-size trees 20–28 m (65–92 ft), cylindrical with a narrow, steeple-like crown; trunk straight, 0.6–1.3 m (1.9–4.3 ft) in diameter. **Bark:** thin, 1.8–2.5 cm (0.7–1 in) thick, dark reddish-brown, with shallow furrows and numerous flat, slender ridges. **Branches:** slender, usually spreading to slightly drooping; branchlets 2-ranked, compressed into flat, usually branched, fan-shaped sprays. **Leaves:** tiny, scale-like, numerous, closely pressed and overlapping, *1.5–3 mm (about 0.1 in) long,* broadest near the base, ridged, *gland-dotted,* dull, dark bluish-green, paler beneath. **Flowers:** male cones tiny with 5 or 6 pollen sacs each, dark brown but often black-tipped; female cones small, round, composed of a few broad scales, pale greenish-brown. **Fruits:** rounded, hard, *unstalked cones, 5–8 mm (0.2–0.3 in) in diameter,* green with a bright bluish-white bloom, turning bluish-purple at maturity, *each cone*

Atlantic White Cedar

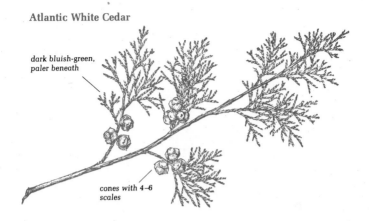

dark bluish-green,
paler beneath

cones with 4–6
scales

scale containing 1 or 2 seeds. **Seeds:** small, 2–4 mm (about 0.1–0.2 in) long, winged, the 2 wings dark brown and as broad as the seed.

Port Orford Cedar, Lawson False-Cypress
Chamaecyparis lawsoniana (A. Murr.) Parl.

This attractive tree has a restricted range extending from Coos Bay in southwestern Oregon southward to the Klamath River in northwestern California. The Port Orford cedar occurs near the coast to about 65 km (40 miles) inland on seaward slopes up to 1,700 m (5,600 ft). But most of the trees occur 5–24 km (3–15 miles) inland. Growth is best on moist, well-drained soils and in moderate climates with high precipitation and humidity. This tree may occur in pure stands, but it is commonly found with western redcedar, Sitka spruce, grand fir, and western hemlock.

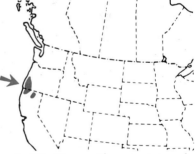

The trees are slow to moderately fast growing and may live for 500 or 600 years. Although dependable production of fruits and flowers usually doesn't begin until the trees are 20 years old, some trees may produce in 10 to 12 years. Flowering is in early spring—fruiting in fall—and the mature seeds shed for several months beginning in the fall. The seeds generally are not eaten by squirrels unless no other food is available. This tree is of little value to other wildlife, except as cover.

The yellowish-white wood is lightweight, fine-grained, hard, and very durable. It has a faint, yet distinct, rose or ginger odor. The wood works easily and takes a fine finish. These qualities make the tree important for timber. But the very limited range and numbers of the trees restrict commercial use. Millions of board feet were harvested for use in boat building, caskets, fences, railroad ties, and interior finishes.

Appearance: tall, narrowly cone-shaped tree 40–65 m (130–215 ft) high, with a spire-like crown; trunk straight, flaring at the base, 1.2–2 m (3.9–6.6 ft) in diameter, rarely larger. **Bark:** *thick,* dark reddish-brown, 15–25 cm (5.9–9.9 in) thick, fibrous,

Port Orford Cedar

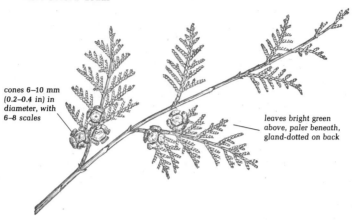

cones 6–10 mm
(0.2–0.4 in) in
diameter, with
6–8 scales

leaves bright green
above, paler beneath,
gland-dotted on back

becoming furrowed and forming round ridges that separate into small, thick scales. **Branches:** short, small, spreading or drooping; branchlets hanging, slender, slightly flattened into spreading, fan-shaped and pale green sprays. **Winter buds:** minute, covered by the evergreen leaves. **Leaves:** tiny, scale-like, numerous, and closely pressed to the branchlets, 1–2 mm (less than 0.1 in) long on side branchlets, 3–6 mm (about 0.1–0.2 in) long on growing leader shoots, broadest near the base, sharp-pointed, ***conspicuously gland-dotted on the back,*** bright green, paler beneath. **Flowers:** male cones small, oblong, containing 10 to 12 pollen sacs each, appearing bright red, scattered on the side branchlets; female cones small, composed of 6 to 8 spreading scales, reddish-brown, scattered near the ends of the upper branchlets. **Fruits:** fleshy, erect ***cones,*** hard, rounded, 6–10 mm (0.2–0.4 in) in diameter, green turning dark rusty brown at maturity, ***composed of 6 or 8 shield-shaped scales,*** the scales overlapping, each scale bearing 2 to 4 seeds. **Seeds:** small, broadest near the base, pointed at the tip, slightly flattened, 2–3 mm (0.1 in) long, light chestnut brown, broadly winged.

Hinoki White Cedar   *Chamaecyparis obtusa* (Sieb. & Zucc.) Endl.

First introduced in 1861, the Hinoki white cedar is a slow-growing shrub or tree. The tree grows to about 14 m (46 ft) high, and has a broad pyramid shape. Its ***leaves are shiny, dark green.*** The reddish-brown bark becomes shreddy and can be peeled in long, thin strips. Several varieties have been developed as ornamental trees, but they all require moist soils and humid air for best growth. This cedar has not been as widely planted as the Sawara white cedar.

Sawara White Cedar   *Chamaecyparis pisifera* (Sieb. & Zucc.) Endl.

Native to Japan, the Sawara white cedar has been cultivated in North America since the 1860s. The trees are narrowly pyramid-shaped with spreading branches that give an open appearance. They are fairly rapid growing and often are used as foundation plantings. Since they can grow to 15 m (50 ft), they commonly outgrow the space allotted for them. The better selections or varieties, of the many known, are: *aurea* with golden yellow leaves and *filifera* with green leaves and very narrow, thread-like branchlets.

Hinoki White Cedar

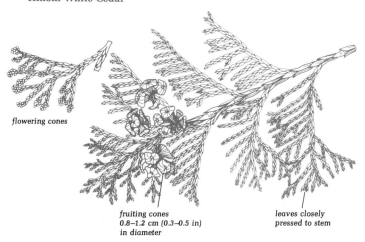

flowering cones

fruiting cones
0.8–1.2 cm (0.3–0.5 in)
in diameter

leaves closely
pressed to stem

Sawara White Cedar

Fruiting Branchlet

Flowering Branchlet

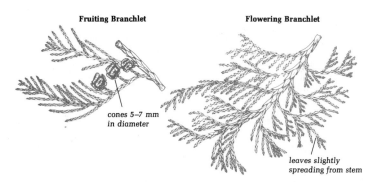

cones 5–7 mm
in diameter

leaves slightly
spreading from stem

The Cypress Genus

Cupressus L.

There are 15 to 20 different cypresses from the warm temperate and subtropical regions of the world. Six tree-size species are native to North America, 5 from California, Oregon, and Baja California, and 1 from the Southwest and adjacent Mexico. [Sargent cypress (Cupressus sargent) is a large bush or, rarely, a small tree of the dry coastal mountain ranges of central California. Because it is rarely tree size, it is not discussed on the following pages. It has thick branchlets and dull-green leaves.] The remaining species are native to the Mediterranean region, the Himalayas, and China. Some of the cypresses are important timber trees. The lightweight, yellowish-brown wood is tough, durable, and easily worked. Its main uses are for fencing, utility poles, and furniture. Because of their ornamental qualities, many cypresses are important cultivated plants. Since they are drought-resistant, they are used as erosion control plants in the southwestern U.S. Cypresses (*Cupressus*) are closely related to the white or false cypress (*Chamaecyparis*). The distinguishing features are given in the discussion of white cedar genus. The species of cypress in North America are closely related and are often difficult to distinguish from one another.

Key to Cypress Species

A. Bark peeling in thin strips, exposing the shiny, reddish-brown inner bark; leaves pale bluish-green; cones 2–3.2 cm (0.8–1.3 in) in diameter.

> **1.** Leaves with or without small glands on the back, pointed at the tip; branchlets grayish
> **Arizona cypress, p. 137**
> **2.** Leaves with small, glandular dots on the back, rounded at the tip; branchlets bright red
> **Tecate cypress, p. 138**

Arizona Cypress

B. Bark with furrows and forming narrow ridges, but not peeling in thin strips; leaves dark or bright green; cones 1.2–2.5 cm (0.5–1 in) in diameter.

> **1.** Leaves conspicuously gland-dotted on the back.
>
> > **a.** Cones reddish or grayish-brown, 1.4–2.1 cm (0.6–0.8 in) in diameter, projections on the face of the cone scales horn-like and prominent   **McNab cypress, p. 138**
> > **b.** Cones silvery or whitish, 1–1.2 cm (0.4–0.5 in) in diameter, projections on face of cone scales short and cone-shaped
> > **Modoc cypress, p. 139**

Modoc Cypress

> **2.** Leaves without obvious glands on the back.
>
> > **a.** Cones 1.2–1.6 cm (0.5–0.7 in) in diameter
> > **Gowen cypress, p. 140**
> > **b.** Cones 2.5–3.8 cm (1–1.5 in) in diameter
> > **Monterey cypress, p. 140**

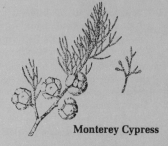

Monterey Cypress

Arizona Cypress
Cupressus arizonica Greene

The Arizona cypress occupies the largest range of all of the North American cypresses. It occurs from the Trans-Pecos region of Texas to southwestern New Mexico, southern Arizona, southern California, and into northern Mexico. This cypress usually grows in rocky or gravelly soils of canyons and ravines from 1,000–2,650 m (3,200–8,700 ft) elevation. As with most trees, the largest ones grow in deeper, well-drained soils. This species forms pure stands or grows in association with ash, willows, alders, or some evergreen oaks.

The trees are rapid-growing, except on poor soils, and long-lived. The small fruits do not mature until the fall of the second year. After the numerous, tiny seeds are shed, the cones may persist for another year or two. The wood is hard, heavy, and durable, which results in its occasional use as fence posts or mine timbers. These trees are very tolerant of drought and are planted on slopes to control erosion. When young, the Arizona cypress has an attractive pyramid shape and is used widely as a Christmas tree in the southwestern U.S., where it is now cultivated for that purpose.

Arizona Cypress

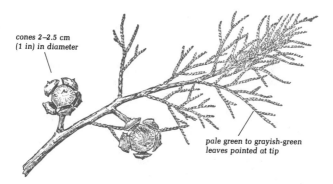

cones 2–2.5 cm (1 in) in diameter

pale green to grayish-green leaves pointed at tip

Appearance: small to medium-size evergreen trees 5–25 m (16–82 ft), steeple shaped with a pointed to broadly flattened crown; trunk straight, 0.3–1 m (1–3.3 ft) in diameter. **Bark:** thin, on young trees *light reddish-brown* and *splitting into thin, narrow, lengthwise strips,* on older trees dark reddish-brown and broken into flat plates. **Branches:** short, stout, upright when young, spreading with age; branchlets slender, becoming stiff, *dark gray.* **Leaves:** tiny, scale-like, numerous, overlapping and closely pressed against the branchlets, about 2 mm (about 0.1 in) long, thick, ridged on the back, sharp-pointed, *pale green* to grayish-green. **Flowers:** male cones tiny, borne at the tips of the branchlets; female cones small, erect, green, borne near the tips of the branchlets. **Fruits:** dry, woody, globe-shaped cones, maturing in 2 years, *2–2.5 cm (1 in) in diameter,* reddish-brown to whitish-gray, composed of 6 to 8 shield-shaped scales. **Seeds:** numerous, oblong, 2–3 mm (0.1 in) long, dark reddish-brown, narrowly winged.

Tecate Cypress
Cupressus guadalupensis S. Wats.
(synonym: C. Forbesii Jepson)

This cypress occurs in ravines, gulches, and ridges in the dry mountain slopes of southern California, Baja California, and on Guadalupe Island. The trees are usually steeple-shaped when young with a few short, upright branches. With age, the branches begin to spread, and the trees may grow from 5–10 m (16–33 ft) tall. Tecate cypresses have a *loosely attached, reddish-brown bark that when partially shed makes the tree look mottled.* The light bluish-green, scale-like leaves are *round tipped* and, as with other cypresses, closely pressed against the branchlets. The fruits are small cones, 2–3.2 cm (0.8–1.3 in) in diameter, composed of 3 or 4 pairs of very

thick scales. These very attractive trees are rapid-growing and drought-resistant. They respond well to pruning or crowding and are used as windbreaks or hedges.

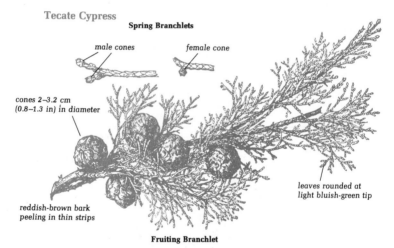

Tecate Cypress

Spring Branchlets

male cones

female cone

cones 2–3.2 cm (0.8–1.3 in) in diameter

leaves rounded at light bluish-green tip

reddish-brown bark peeling in thin strips

Fruiting Branchlet

McNab Cypress
Cupressus macnabiana A. Murr.

This is a small tree 5–13 m (16–43 ft) high. It is bushy or forms a low shrub, and occurs on dry hillsides and flats of the inner, northern coastal mountains in northern California. McNab cypresses are not abundant within their small range. The trees are usually upright when young but develop into an open pyramid shape with spreading branches as they mature. The small, overlapping, scale-like *leaves* are *blue-green,* release a pungent odor when crushed, and *have a conspicuous white resin gland on the back.* The *reddish-brown,* almost round *cones* are composed of only 6 (rarely 8) thickened horned scales, and are *1.4–2.1 cm (0.6–0.8 in) in diameter.*

McNab Cypress

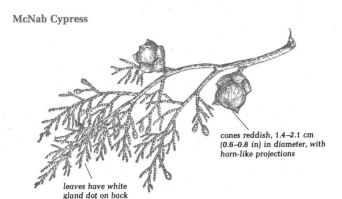

cones reddish, 1.4–2.1 cm
(0.6–0.8 in) in diameter, with
horn-like projections

leaves have white
gland dot on back

Modoc Cypress

The Modoc cypress is a rare species found only in a few isolated groves in the Siskiyou Mountains of northern California and Oregon. In California the trees grow in the barren lava beds. The trees are usually small (12–14 m; 39–46 ft), although larger trees occur in Oregon. The slender branchlets are covered by small, scale-like, **pale green leaves with a narrow ridge on back.** The **small, rounded silvery cones** are composed of 6 or 8 thickened scales and mature in the fall, shedding the numerous, tiny seeds.

Cupressus bakerii Jeps.

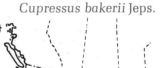

Modoc Cypress

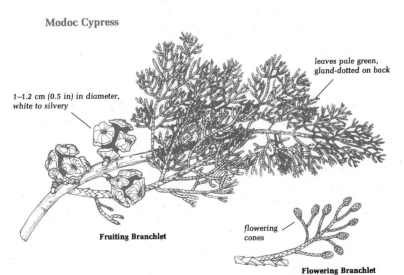

1–1.2 cm (0.5 in) in diameter,
white to silvery

leaves pale green,
gland-dotted on back

Fruiting Branchlet

flowering
cones

Flowering Branchlet

Gowen Cypress

Cupressus goveniana Gord.

The Gowen cypress is a small tree, usually no more than 8 m (26 ft) high, which often grows as a shrub along pine barrens of the coastal ranges of California. The tree is usually compact, the branchlets almost 4-sided. The scale-like *leaves* are light to dark green and *lack a conspicuous gland or pit on the back.* As with the other cypresses, the leaves of this species overlap one another and are pressed closely against the branches. The small, *nearly globe-shaped cones are 1.2–1.6 cm (0.5–0.7 in) in diameter* and are composed of 6 to 10 thickened scales.

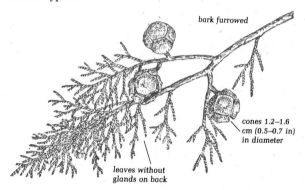

Gowen Cypress

bark furrowed

cones 1.2–1.6 cm (0.5–0.7 in) in diameter

leaves without glands on back

Monterey Cypress

Cupressus macrocarpa Hartw.

This cypress is restricted to a very short and narrow strip along the Pacific Coast of Monterey County, California, from Cypress Point to Point Lobos. The picturesque trees are scattered along the cliffs and low bluffs. In these exposed conditions they are small, contorted, and have a broadly cone-shaped crown. Monterey cypresses are small to medium-size trees, 5–25 m (16–82 ft) tall, with irregular, spreading branches. The small, *scale-like leaves* are pressed closely against the branchlets. The small, *2.5–3.8 cm (1–1.5 in) fruits* are almost *globe-shaped* and are composed of 4 to 6 pairs of scales. This cypress is of little value to wildlife. And because of its limited range and reduced numbers, it is of no importance as lumber. But its striking

Monterey Cypress

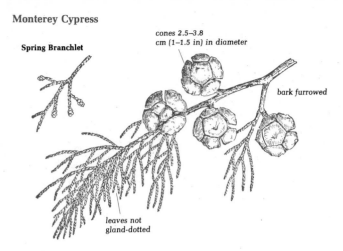

Spring Branchlet

cones 2.5–3.8 cm (1–1.5 in) in diameter

bark furrowed

leaves not gland-dotted

beauty on the bluffs against the background of the sea has brought landscape artists and photographers. It is cultivated for its ornamental value and to serve as windbreaks and hedges.

The Juniper Genus   *Juniperus* L.

There are approximately 45 to 50 different junipers worldwide. They are distributed throughout the Northern Hemisphere from the Arctic Circle to Mexico and the West Indies. Of the 13 species native to North America, one, the creeping juniper (*Juniperus horizontalis* Moench), is a shrub, while the others are large shrubs or small trees. All the junipers are evergreen. Eight of the 13 species occur in western or south-widespread over much of eastern North America. The fourth one, the common southern redcedar is confined to the southeastern U.S., and the Ashe juniper is restricted largely to the southcentral states. A third species, the eastern redcedar, is widespread over much of the eastern North America. The fourth one, the common juniper, is a wide-ranging species of the world.

Junipers are evergreen resinous shrubs or small trees, often shaped like pyramids or cones, and usually with thin, scaly bark that separates in long, loose strips. The branches are often short and stout, while the branchlets are generally slender and may spread or droop. Winter buds are tiny and may or may not be covered with scales. The leaves are either needle-shaped, very sharp-pointed and spreading away from the branchlets, or else they are scale-like, overlapping, and closely pressed against the branchlets. Male and female cones are small and separate, and usually occur on different trees. The male cones are small and cylindric, at the ends of the branchlets, and the female cones are small, leathery, globe-shaped structures, also at the tips of the branchlets. The fruits are fleshy to leathery, berry-like cones that ripen at the end of 1, 2, or 3 growing seasons. They may be sweet and resinous at maturity and contain from 1 to 12 seeds per fruit. The seeds are broadest at the base and taper to a point. They are slightly flattened and grooved on the back, sometimes angled, and light to dark brown.

Key to Juniper Species

A. Leaves needle-shaped, spreading at right angles to the branchlets; cones produced at the junction of the leaves and the branchlets and mature the third season; winter buds scale-covered
Common juniper, p. 143

Common Juniper

B. Leaves scale-like, closely pressed against the branchlets (on vigorous young shoots, sometimes needle-shaped and spreading); cones produced at or near the ends of the branchlets and maturing in 1 or 2 seasons; winter buds not enclosed in scales.

1. Berry-like fruits red to reddish-brown.

a. Bark thick, gray to black, deeply furrowed lengthwise and crosswise to form almost square plates **Alligator juniper, p. 144**

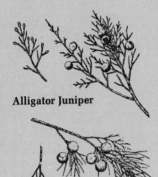

Alligator Juniper

b. Bark thin, reddish-brown to gray, narrowly fissured and forming long, thin, loose, shredding scales.

(1) Fruits bright red
Pinchot juniper, p. 146

(2) Fruits dull reddish-brown.

(a) Scale-like leaves spreading at the tips; branchlets hanging giving trees a weeping appearance; seeds usually 4 to 8 per fruit; trees of extreme southwestern U.S.
Mexican drooping juniper, p. 146

Mexican Drooping Juniper

(b) Scale-like leaves closely pressed against the branchlets; branchlets semi-erect to spreading; seeds 1 to 3 per fruit; trees of western U.S.

(b1) Scale-like leaves in 3s; berry-like fruits 10–16 mm (0.4–0.6 in) in diameter, not resinous; trees of California
California juniper, p. 147

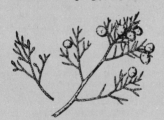

California Juniper

(b2) Scale-like leaves opposite one another; berry-like fruits 6–9 mm (about 0.2–0.4 in) in diameter, resinous; trees of Rocky Mountains
Utah juniper, p. 148

Utah Juniper

2. Berry-like fruits blue to blue-black.

a. Scale-like leaves with minutely toothed margins, opposite one another or in whorls of 3s.

(1) Fruits maturing in 2 seasons, usually with 2 or 3 seeds per fruit
Western juniper, p. 149

(2) Fruits maturing in 1 season, with 1 or 2 seeds per fruit.

   (a) Seeds 1 per fruit, light brown; leaves grayish-green; trees of western U.S. **One-seed juniper, p. 150**

   (b) Seeds 1 or 2 per fruit, light to dark brown; leaves bluish-green; trees of southcentral U.S.
Ashe juniper, p. 151

b. Scale-like leaves smooth on the margins, usually opposite one another.

(1) Fruits maturing in 2 seasons; trees of western U.S.
Rocky Mountain juniper, p. 152

(2) Fruits maturing in 1 season; trees of eastern or southeastern U.S.

   (a) Fruits 5–8 mm (0.2–0.3 in) in diameter, branchlets erect to spreading; trees of eastern U.S.
Eastern redcedar, p. 154

   (b) Fruits 7–10 mm (0.3–0.4 in) in diameter; branchlets sometimes drooping; trees of low wet areas of southeastern U.S.
Southern redcedar, p. 155

Ashe Juniper

Rocky Mountain Juniper

Eastern Redcedar

Common Juniper

Juniperus communis L.

The common juniper is a widespread woody plant in North America, and it is the only species of juniper to occur also in Europe and Asia. The trees (normally bushes) usually grow in poor rocky or gravelly soils, often in disturbed soils. They occur from sea level in the northern part of their range (Canada) to nearly 3,400 m (11,000 ft) in the mountains of northern Arizona. They can be found growing in association with a wide range of trees including other junipers, pines, as well as hardwoods such as oak, hickory, and maple.

These trees are prolific fruit and seed producers with berry-like cones that usually persist for 3 or 4 years. The fruits require 3 years to mature. When mature, many are consumed by cedar waxwings

and quails, as well as by squirrels, chipmunks, and raccoons. The low spreading bushes provide good cover for smaller wildlife and game birds.

The light brown wood is hard, very durable, and close-grained. The trees are seldom large enough to yield any quantity of wood, so they are unimportant commercially. They are occasionally planted as ornamentals, and several cultivated forms have been developed.

Common Juniper

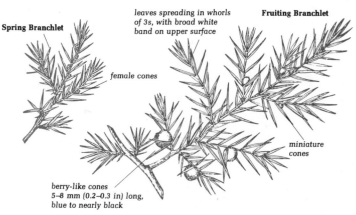

Spring Branchlet

leaves spreading in whorls of 3s, with broad white band on upper surface

Fruiting Branchlet

female cones

miniature cones

berry-like cones 5–8 mm (0.2–0.3 in) long, blue to nearly black

Appearance: usually shrubby or occasionally a small tree, 3–7 m (10–23 ft) tall with a narrow, cone shape and an open irregular crown; trunk short, stout, branching close to the ground, fluted or irregularly lobed, 0.1–0.3 m (0.4–1 ft) in diameter. **Bark:** thin, 1–2 mm (less than 0.1 in) dark reddish-brown, with narrow fissures and separating into long, loose, papery scales. **Branches:** slender, usually erect; branchlets slender, erect to spreading, slightly angled, shiny, greenish-yellow turning reddish-brown with age. **Leaves:** small, *needle-shaped, usually in whorls of 3 and spreading at right angles to the branchlets,* 0.8–1.2 cm (0.3–0.5 in) long, sharp-pointed, keeled on the back, aromatic when crushed, with a broad white band on the upper surface, dark green and shiny beneath. **Flowers:** male and female cones usually on separate trees; male cones solitary between the leaves and the branchlets, broadest near the base, 4–5 mm (about 0.2 in) long; female cones solitary in the junctions of the leaves near the end of the branchlets, almost globe-shaped, composed of 3 or 4 fleshy scales. **Fruits:** berry-like cones, almost globe-shaped to short cylindrical, 5–8 mm (0.2–0.3 in) in diameter or long, with a soft, mealy, sweet, resinous texture, *blue to nearly black, matures in 3 growing seasons.* **Seeds:** 1 to 3 per fruit, broadest near the base and tapering to a pointed tip, 2–3 mm (0.1 in) long, brown, usually 3-angled.

Alligator Juniper

Juniperus deppeana Steud.

(synonym: *J. pachyphloea* Torr.)

This is a relatively common tree of the higher elevations of the southwestern U.S. and adjacent Mexico. The alligator juniper usually is found in open oak or pinyon pine woodlands at 1,400–2,500 m (4,500–8,000 ft) elevation. The trees grow on hillsides or mountain slopes and occasionally will be found in the lower portions of ponderosa pine forests. This tree is recognized easily in the field because of its checkered bark, which resembles an alligator's hide.

The tree is slow-growing, and it is also long-lived. The oldest trees display the effects of centuries of storms, droughts, insects, and diseases. Normally there are large dead branches that add interesting aspects to the tree's gnarled appearance. Fruit and seed production occurs each year, although large seed crops are cyclic. The fruits are a food source for black bears, gray foxes, squirrels, wild turkeys, and many nongame seed-eating birds.

The light reddish wood is soft, lightweight, close-grained, and brittle. Although easily worked, it is of limited value as lumber. Its primary uses are as fence posts and fuel.

Alligator Juniper

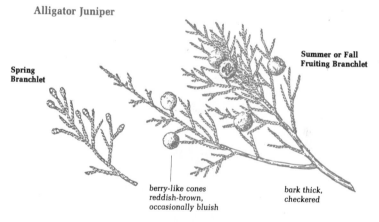

Spring Branchlet

Summer or Fall Fruiting Branchlet

berry-like cones reddish-brown, occasionally bluish

bark thick, checkered

Appearance: medium-size trees 7–15 m, rarely to 20 (23–50 ft, rarely to 65), with a pyramid shape but sometimes spreading and irregular, with a rounded crown; trunk usually short, stout, 0.5–1 m (1.6–3.3 ft) in diameter. **Bark:** *thick, 1.2–2 cm (0.5–0.8 in), gray to black, rough, deeply fissured lengthwise and crosswise to form almost square plates, giving a checkered look.* **Branches:** short, stout, the upper ones semierect, the lower ones spreading; branchlets slender, 4-sided, green turning reddish-brown with age. **Leaves:** tiny, scale-like, opposite one another or in 3s, overlapping, closely pressed against the branchlets, each leaf broadest at the base and tapering to a point, gland-dotted on the back, bluish-green. **Flowers:** male and female cones on separate trees; male cones numerous, small, cylinder-shaped, at the ends of the branchlets; female cones small, almost globe-shaped, composed of several leathery scales. **Fruits:** *leathery berry-like cones,* nearly globe-shaped to almost egg-shaped, *10–12 mm (0.4–0.5 in) long,* hard, *mealy-textured,* resinous, thin-skinned, *reddish-brown* (occasionally bluish) and covered with a whitish cast, *matures in 2 seasons.* **Seeds:** 2 to 4 per fruit, 5–7 mm (0.2–0.3 in) long, broadest near the base and tapering to a slightly rounded tip, brown, shiny, slightly flattened on the back.

Pinchot Juniper, Red-Berry Juniper   *Juniperus pinchotii* Sudw.

This juniper is native to canyons and dry, rocky or gravelly hillsides in western Texas and the Texas Panhandle. It is a small tree, seldom taller than 7 m (23 ft), or sometimes it is an irregularly shaped shrub. The numerous branches often extend to the ground. As with other junipers, the **trees have reddish-brown, shaggy bark.** The tiny

leaves are scale-like, pressed against the branchlets, overlapping, gland-dotted on the back, and yellow-green in color. The flowers are similar to those described for the alligator juniper above. The **cones** are berry-like, nearly **globe-shaped, bright red, 6–7.5 mm (0.2–0.3 in) in diameter,** maturing in 1 growing season. They are red, thin-skinned and mealy-textured. The wood is like that of other junipers, and because of small size and limited occurrence, is used only locally for fence posts and fuel.

Pinchot Juniper

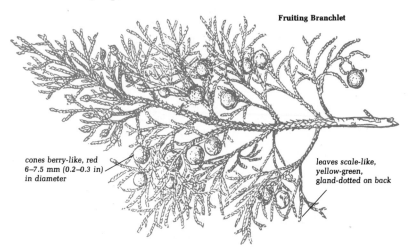

Fruiting Branchlet

cones berry-like, red 6–7.5 mm (0.2–0.3 in) in diameter

leaves scale-like, yellow-green, gland-dotted on back

Mexican Drooping Juniper   *Juniperus flaccida* Schlecht.

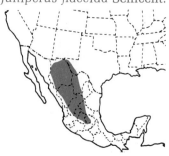

As the name implies, this juniper occurs principally in Mexico and extends into the U.S. only in the Chisos Mountains of southwestern Texas. It inhabits dry, rocky soils in canyons, benches, hillsides, and ridges at elevations of 1,350–2,650 m (4,400–8,700 ft). These junipers are large, spreading bushes or small trees to 10 m (33 ft) and can be distinguished readily from all other junipers by the **pendant, or hanging, branchlets.** This gives the trees a

Mexican Drooping Juniper

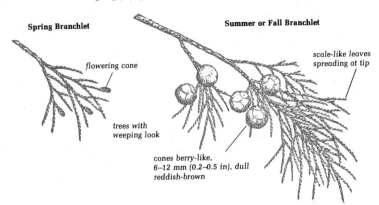

Spring Branchlet

flowering cone

trees with weeping look

Summer or Fall Branchlet

scale-like leaves spreading at tip

cones berry-like, 6–12 mm (0.2–0.5 in), dull reddish-brown

graceful, weeping appearance. The reddish-brown bark separates into long, narrow, loose strips. The tiny, scale-like leaves and flowers are similar to those of the Pinchot juniper. The fruits are globe-shaped, berry-like cones that are 6–12 mm (0.2–0.5 in) in diameter, resinous, mealy-textured, and ***reddish-brown; they mature in 2 seasons.*** There are 4 to 8, sometimes more, seeds per fruit, and fruits are produced each year with large crops every 2 or 3 years.

California Juniper   *Juniperus californica* Carr.

This California juniper is restricted to very dry mountain, canyon, and desert slopes. The trees grow primarily from 125–1,350 m (410–4,500 ft) elevation in dry rocky, gravelly, or sandy soils. They occur in areas with long, dry summers. California junipers are found in almost pure stands or interspersed with pinyon pine, singleleaf pinyon pine, bigcone pine, and yuccas or Spanish bayonet plants. This species is similar to the western juniper but for its lower altitude and its reddish-brown berries, as opposed to the bluish-black berries of the western juniper.

The trees are slow-growing and may be long-lived. They produce large quantities of fruits and seeds, but reproduction is very low. Small mammals and seed-eating birds consume most of the fruits, which are sweet and nonresinous and so can be consumed by man too.

The light brown wood is similar to that of other western junipers. This species seldom occurs in a tree form and thus is commercially unimportant.

Appearance: a small tree 3–10 m (10–33 ft) high, with a cone-shape or a low and spreading shrub with a rounded to cone-shaped crown; ***trunk conspicuously fluted and ridged,*** branching close to ground, 0.3–0.6 m (1–2 ft) in diameter. **Bark:** thin, 2–5 mm (0.1–0.2 in), reddish-brown but ***weathering to an ashy gray,*** with numerous narrow fissures forming long, loose, shredding scales. **Branches:** short, stout, often becoming gnarled in old age; branchlets slender, green turning reddish-brown to ash-gray with age. **Leaves:** tiny, scale-like, arranged in 3s, overlapping and closely pressed against the branchlets, 2–4 mm (about 0.1–0.2 in) long, sharp-pointed, thickened, gland-dotted on the back, light yellowish-green. **Flowers:** male and female cones on separate trees, the cones similar to those of the western juniper. **Fruits:**

California Juniper

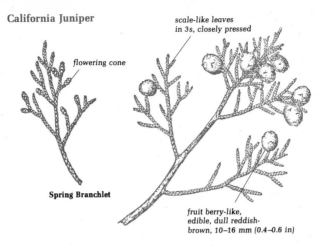

scale-like leaves
in 3s, closely pressed

flowering cone

Spring Branchlet

fruit berry-like,
edible, dull reddish-
brown, 10–16 mm (0.4–0.6 in)

leathery, ***berry-like cones,*** almost globe-shaped to egg-shaped, ***10–16 mm (0.4–0.6 in)*** in diameter, dry, ***fibrous to mealy texture, sweet, not resinous, light reddish-brown,*** mature in 2 seasons. **Seeds:** 1 to 3 per fruit, 5–7 mm (0.2–0.3 in) long, broadest near the base and tapering to a pointed tip, brown, shiny, angled, and ridged on the back.

Utah Juniper
Juniperus osteosperma (Torr.) Little
[synonym: *J. utahensis* (Engelm.) Lemm.]

The Utah juniper is the characteristic tree on the south rim of the Grand Canyon. Its range is largely the Great Basin between the Rocky Mountains and the Sierra Nevada. It is primarily a mountain tree found on mesas, high plains, and mountain slopes from 1,000–2,650 m (3,200–8,700 ft) elevation.  The trees grow in thin, dry, rocky, or gravelly soils. Usually this juniper is found growing in pure stands, although it does occur with the 1-seeded juniper and the singleleaf pinyon pine.

The Utah juniper is a very slow-growing species and can live for several centuries. Nearly all trees bear either male or female flowers, although an occasional tree may bear both. Fruits are produced every year, but large crops occur every other year. The fruits are a popular food for wildlife, with ground squirrels, chipmunks, and seed-eating birds consuming the largest amounts. Deer browse on this juniper. The fruits are edible by man, and were once gathered by Indians.

The light brown wood has properties similar to other juniper woods. It has been used locally for posts, fuel, and—to a minor extent—interior trim.

Appearance: small tree or large shrub to 8 m (26 ft) with a bushy shape and a rounded crown; trunk short, branching close to ground, 0.1–0.3 m (0.4–1 ft) in diameter. **Bark:** thin, 6–10 mm (0.2–0.4 in), weathering to an ashy gray, deeply and irregularly furrowed, with the narrow plates separating into long, loosely attaching scales. **Branches:** numerous, short, stout, spreading; branchlets slender, rounded, pale yellowish-green, turning reddish-brown with age and then weathering to ashy gray. **Leaves:** tiny, ***scale-like, opposite and overlapping one another in 2s*** and ***closely***

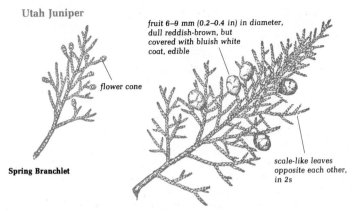

Utah Juniper

fruit 6–9 mm (0.2–0.4 in) in diameter, dull reddish-brown, but covered with bluish white coat, edible

flower cone

Spring Branchlet

scale-like leaves opposite each other, in 2s

pressed against the branchlets, 3–4 mm (about 0.1–0.2 in) long, broadest near the base, usually gland-dotted on the back, with tiny teeth along the margin of the leaves and sharp-pointed at the tip, yellowish-green. **Flowers:** male and female cones usually produced on separate trees; male cones small, cylinder-shaped, borne at the tips of the branchlets; female cones small, almost globe-shaped, also at the tips of the branchlets. **Fruits:** small, leathery, berry-like cones, edible, almost globe-shaped, 6–9 mm (0.2–0.4 in) in diameter, **resinous, sweet, with a mealy texture, reddish-brown** but covered with a bluish-white cast, the skin thin, **matures in 2 seasons. Seeds:** 1 (rarely 2) per fruit, broadest near the base and tapering to a sharp point, 3–4 mm (about 0.1–0.2 in) long, brown, sharply angled on the back.

Western Juniper, Sierra Juniper   *Juniperus occidentalis* Hook.

Western junipers are native to the mountain slopes and high plateaus of Washington, Oregon, western Idaho, and California. They occur from near sea level to approximately 3,100 m (10,000 ft) elevation, where they usually are reduced to gnarled, low trees or shrubs. They grow mainly in areas with long, dry summers and cold winters and thin, rocky, or sandy soils. These junipers usually are found in open woodlands or along margins between grasslands and pine forests. Often occurring in pure stands, western junipers also grow in association with whitebark pine and ponderosa pine.

The trees have a slow to moderate growth rate and are considered long-lived, for they may reach 800 to 1,000 years of age. This juniper is a good seed producer year after year, although some years may be leaner than others. The fruits require 2 growing seasons to mature. They are eaten by mammals, such as mule deer and squirrels, and by several seed-eating birds. In addition, they are edible by man, and have been gathered by Indians. The fruits have served as a survival food for lost travelers.

The light red to reddish-brown wood is lightweight, relatively soft, close-grained, durable, and can be easily worked and exquisitely finished. But because of the western juniper's small size, its branching pattern, and its inaccessible habitats, it is not an important timber tree.

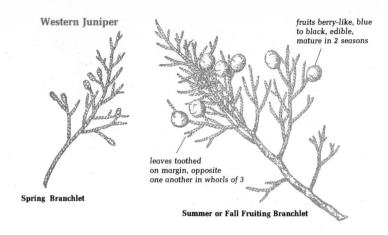

Western Juniper

fruits berry-like, blue
to black, edible,
mature in 2 seasons

leaves toothed
on margin, opposite
one another in whorls of 3

Spring Branchlet

Summer or Fall Fruiting Branchlet

Appearance: large shrub to small tree 5 to 10 m, rarely to 20 (16–33 ft, rarely to 66), variable in shape, often pyramidal or spreading and more shrub-like, with a rounded to flattened crown; trunk straight to thick and very short, 0.4–1 m (1.3–3.3 ft) in diameter, light to bright reddish-brown, with shallow furrows and wide, flattened ridges that become stringy. **Branches:** large, stout, short, spreading; branchlets stout, spreading to sometimes hanging, rounded, green turning reddish-brown with age. **Leaves:** tiny, *scale-like, toothed on margin, opposite one another or in whorls of 3,* overlapping and closely pressed against the branchlets, 2–4 mm (about 0.1–0.2 in) long, broadest at the base and tapering to a point, conspicuously gland-dotted on the back, grayish-green. **Flowers:** male and female cones on separate trees; male cones small, 2–3 mm (0.1 in) long, oblong, produced at the ends of the branchlets; female cones small, ovate, also at the branchlet tips. **Fruits:** small, leathery, berry-like cones, edible, nearly globe-shaped, 6–9 mm (about 0.2–0.3 in) in diameter, *bluish-green* with a whitish cast, thick-skinned, *maturing in 2 seasons.* **Seeds:** *2 or 3 per fruit,* broadest at the base, tapering to a point, 2–4 mm (0.1–0.2 in) long, brown, deeply grooved on back.

One-Seed Juniper,
Cherrystone Juniper *Juniperus monosperma* (Engelm.) Sarg.

The one-seed juniper is a common tree of the plateaus, foothills, and plains of the western U.S., especially on the eastern slopes of the Rocky Mountains. The tree grows in dry, rocky or sandy soils from 1,000–2,300 m (3,200–7,350 ft) elevation. Often it is found with pinyon pines or Utah junipers. It is similar to the Utah juniper, except that it is smaller and bushier.

Like other junipers, this one is also very slow-growing and may live for 500 to 600 years or more under good conditions. Although some fruit is produced each year, fruit and seed production tends to be cyclic, with large crops every 2 or 3 years. The fruits serve as a food source for deer, quail, fox, chipmunks, and squirrels. Indians once gathered and ate these fruits.

The light reddish-brown wood is moderately hard and somewhat heavy. If it is seasoned properly, it is very durable. Its primary use is for posts and fuel. The wood was used by native Indians for prayer sticks, war bows, and other instruments, and Indians also used the bark to obtain a green dye to color their wool.

One-Seed Juniper

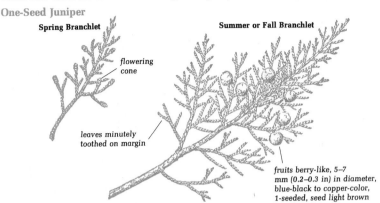

Spring Branchlet

flowering cone

leaves minutely toothed on margin

Summer or Fall Branchlet

fruits berry-like, 5–7 mm (0.2–0.3 in) in diameter, blue-black to copper-color, 1-seeded, seed light brown

Appearance: shrub or small tree to 12 m (40 ft), rarely taller, with a broad shape and a rounded crown; trunk short, branching close to ground, 0.1–0.5 m (0.4–1.6 ft) in diameter. **Bark:** thin, 4–9 mm (0.1–0.4 in) thick, ash gray to gray, soft, with numerous narrow fissures forming ridges composed of long, narrow, shredding scales. **Branches:** numerous, short, stout spreading; branchlets stout, usually 4-sided, green turning reddish-brown with age. **Leaves:** tiny, scale-like, opposite one another or in 3s, overlapping and pressed closely against the branchlets, 1–3.5 mm (about 0.1 in) long, triangular in shape, tapering to a sharp pointed tip, thickened, usually gland-dotted on the back, grayish-green. **Flowers:** male and female cones on separate trees and similar to those of the Utah juniper. **Fruits:** *fleshy, berry-like cones,* almost globe-shaped to egg-shaped, *5–7 mm (0.2–0.3 in) in diameter, dark blue to copper-colored,* thin-skinned, mature in 1 season. **Seeds:** *1 per fruit,* 4–5 mm (0.2 in) long, broadest near the base, light brown, 4-sided and slightly pointed at the tip.

Ashe Juniper

Juniperus ashei Buchholz

[synonyms: *J. mexicana* Spreng., *J. sabinoides* (HBK) Nees]

This juniper is native to the southeastern U.S. and extends from southern Missouri and Arkansas to Texas and adjoining Mexico. The trees occur at lower altitudes and grow mainly on limestone hills or in soils underlain with limestone. They often are found with the scrub oaks. This juniper is related closely to the one-seed juniper and the two are often difficult to distinguish in the field.

The ashe juniper is slow-growing and lives to a moderate age of 200 to 350 years. Fruit and seed production alternate between a year of heavy production and 1 or 2 years of light production. It is important to wildlife. Deer, gray fox, raccoons, squirrels, chipmunks, quail, robins, and cedar waxwings like the berry-like fruit.

The reddish-brown wood is hard, lightweight, close-grained, durable, and easily worked. The trees do not occur in large enough sizes and sufficient quantities to be very important commercially. Their main uses are for posts, railroad ties, and fuel. And they are cultivated as ornamentals.

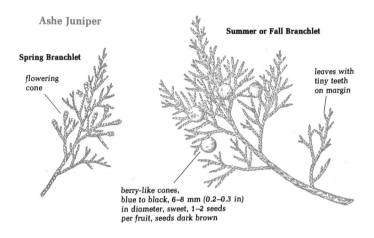

Ashe Juniper

Summer or Fall Branchlet

Spring Branchlet

flowering cone

leaves with tiny teeth on margin

berry-like cones, blue to black, 6–8 mm (0.2–0.3 in) in diameter, sweet, 1–2 seeds per fruit, seeds dark brown

Appearance: large shrub to small tree 10–12 m (32–40 ft), with an irregular shape, often spreading, with a rounded or flattened crown; trunk short, branching close to ground, often ridged. **Bark:** thin, 4–8 mm (about 0.2–0.3 in), gray to reddish-brown, shredding into long, loose scales (normal for most junipers). **Branches:** numerous, short, stout; branchlets slender, rounded, to slightly angled, green turning reddish-brown to gray (in more exposed areas). **Leaves:** tiny, scale-like, opposite one another, overlapping and closely pressed against the branchlets, 1–2 mm (less than 0.1 in) long, broadest at the base and tapering to a point, *not gland-dotted on the back,* bluish-green. **Flowers:** male and female cones on separate trees; male cones numerous, small, oblong, 3–4 mm (about 0.1–0.2 in) long, produced at the tips of the branchlets; female cones almost rounded to egg-shaped, 2–3 mm (0.1 in) long, composed of several leathery scales. **Fruits:** *fleshy, berry-like cones,* broadest near the base to almost globe-shaped, *6–8 mm (0.2–0.3 in) in diameter,* thin-skinned, *resinous, sweet, matures in 1 growing season.* **Seeds:** *1 (rarely 2) per fruit,* 3–4 mm (about 0.1–0.2 in) long, broadest near the base and sharp-pointed at the tip, light to dark brown, slightly flattened, with a shallow groove on the back.

Rocky Mountain Juniper

Juniperus scopulorum Sarg.

The Rocky Mountain juniper is a wide-ranging species, extending from central British Columbia to New Mexico and Arizona. In the northern part of the range, the trees grow near sea level, but in the south they occur up to 3,000 m (9,000 ft) elevation. They grow on bluffs, ridges, cliffs, and dry, rocky hillsides and do best on slightly alkaline/calcium-based soils. They

are not as drought resistant as some of the other western junipers. This juniper sometimes can be found in pure stands but usually is scattered with ponderosa pine, pinyon pine, Douglas fir, one-seeded juniper, or occasionally with other western pines.

A slow growing tree, the Rocky Mountain juniper may live 200 to 300 years. As with other junipers, individual trees are usually male or female. Some fruits are produced every year, with good fruit and seed production every 3 to 5 years. Antelope, mule deer, and bighorn sheep browse it. Turkeys, Bohemian waxwings, and evening grosbeaks feed on the fleshy, sweet tasting fruits.

The Rocky Mountain juniper is closely related to the eastern redcedar, but differs in that it takes 2 years for the fruits to mature rather than 1. Naturally occurring hybrids can be found where the range of the 2 species overlaps. The wood is very similar to that of the eastern redcedar. It is not used as much as its eastern counterpart because the trunks of the trees often branch, making it difficult to obtain good lumber. It is used primarily for posts and fuel.

Rocky Mountain Juniper

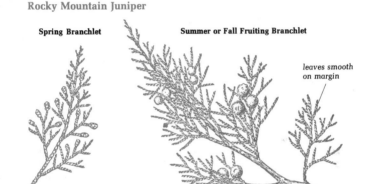

Spring Branchlet

Summer or Fall Fruiting Branchlet

leaves smooth on margin

cones berry-like, sweet, bright blue, often with whitish cast, mature in 2 seasons

Appearance: large shrubs to small trees 5–15 m (16–49 ft), rarely taller, variable in shape but often shaped like pyramids with an irregular to slightly rounded crown; trunk short, stout, soon branching, 0.3–1 m (1–3.3 ft) in diameter. **Bark:** thin, 3–8 mm (0.1–0.3 in), reddish-brown weathering to grayish in exposed areas, scaly, with numerous shallow furrows and long, narrow, loose ridges. **Branches:** stout, thick, spreading to partially upright; branchlets slender, 4-sided and becoming rounded with age, green turning light brown with age. **Leaves:** small, *scale-like, opposite one another, smooth on margin,* and slightly overlapping, closely pressed against the branchlets, 2–4 mm (about 0.1–0.2 in) long, with tiny, inconspicuous glands on the back, pointed at the tip, somewhat thickened, resinous, pale green to dark grayish-green. **Flowers:** male and female cones on separate trees; male cones tiny, 2 mm (about 0.1 in) long, oblong, borne at the tips of the branchlets; female cones tiny, almost globe-shaped, also at the branchlet tips. **Fruits:** small, *fleshy,* sweet berry-like cones, almost globe-shaped, 6–9 mm (about 0.2–0.3 in) in diameter, thin-skinned, *bright blue* and often with a whitish cast, *maturing in 2 seasons.* **Seeds:** *1 or 2 (rarely 3) per fruit,* broadest near the base and tapering to a sharp point, 4–5 mm (about 0.2 in) long, brown, conspicuously grooved and angled.

Eastern Redcedar   *Juniperus virginiana* L.

The eastern redcedar is the most widespread conifer of eastern North America. It is adaptable to many different site conditions and can be found growing in low, wet, swampy areas to dry rocky outcrops containing thin soils. It is most abundant on lands that have been cleared recently and on fields that have been abandoned. This cedar is the most drought resistant conifer in the East. It can be found in loosely assembled groves but is found more commonly as scattered trees. It is often found growing with the hickories, several oaks, and the shortleaf pine.

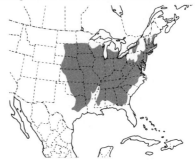

The tree is rather slow-growing and lives to a moderate age of 200 to 350 years. Because male and female flowers usually occur on separate trees, only those bearing female flowers will have the small bluish-colored fruits. Some flowers and fruits are produced each year, but large seed crops occur about every third year. The eastern redcedar is important to both songbirds and game birds for food and cover. Among the game birds eating the fruits are quail, grouse, pheasant, and turkey. Among songbirds the cedar waxwing is the principal customer.

The reddish-colored wood is lightweight and close-grained but brittle and weak. Yet it is easily worked, it takes a fine finish, and it is used for some interior trim, sills, posts, and for chests. The cedar oil in the wood is an effective moth deterrent, and cedar chests were about the only effective way early settlers could protect their woolens. Oil of cedar is distilled from the wood and used as a perfume. The eastern redcedar was the primary source of wood for wooden pencils, but the larger trees have been depleted. The incense cedar (*Calocedrus decurrens*) has replaced the redcedar as the principal pencil wood.

Appearance: small to medium-size trees 10–20 m (32–66 ft), rarely larger, usually with a pyramid shape, sometimes with a low rounded shape and a narrow cone-

Eastern Redcedar

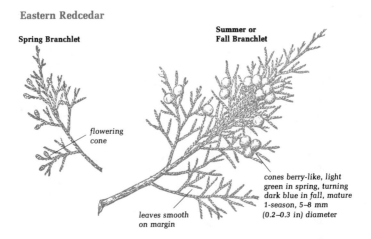

Spring Branchlet

Summer or Fall Branchlet

flowering cone

leaves smooth on margin

cones berry-like, light green in spring, turning dark blue in fall, mature 1-season, 5–8 mm (0.2–0.3 in) diameter

shaped crown; trunk tapering, spreading at the base, often buttressed, 0.2–1 m (0.7–3.3 ft) in diameter. **Bark:** thin, 3–6 mm (about 0.1–0.2 in), light reddish-brown, produced in long, narrow scales that readily separate. **Branches:** short, slender, branching near ground; branchlets slender, fine, light-green turning reddish-brown. **Leaves:** tiny, *scale-like, opposite one another, smooth on margin,* closely pressed against the branchlets and overlapping, 1–1.5 mm (0.06 in) long, broadest at the base and tapering to a point, thick, rigid, resinous, the tip pointed or rounded, dark bluish-green. **Flowers:** Male and female cones usually appearing on separate trees, occasionally both on same tree; male cones small, 2.5–3 mm (0.10–0.12 in) long, cylinder-shaped, each cone with 8 to 12 pollen sacs, the cones produced at the tips of the branchlets; female cones small, 1.2–1.5 mm (less than 0.1 in) in diameter, globe-shaped, the cone scales thick, spreading, the cones produced at the tips of the branchlets. **Fruits:** small, *fleshy, berry-like cones,* almost globe-shaped, *5–8 mm (0.2–0.3 in) in diameter, resinous* (especially evident when crushed), light green turning *dark blue at maturity, mature in 1 season.* **Seeds:** 1 to 4 per fruit, usually broadest at the base and pointed at the tip, 2–4 mm (about 0.1–0.2 in) long, light brown, ridged.

Southern Redcedar   *Juniperus silicicola* (Small) Bailey

The southern redcedar is native to the Coastal Plain region of the southeastern U.S. It inhabits low, wet areas such as swamps, the margins of streams and creeks, and flood-plain woodlands. The trees are able to tolerate varying amounts of soil moisture.

They also are found in open woods and in abandoned fields and generally grow in soils that are limestone in nature.

The southern redcedar is a slow-growing but long-lived tree. Years of large seed crops are cyclic, but some fruits and seeds are produced each year. Seed-eating birds are the primary consumers of the fruits. This juniper is only of slight importance to wildlife.

The dull red wood is soft, weak, light-weight, and straight-grained. It is easily worked and finishes well. Until the larger trees with straight trunks were exhausted, the wood was used extensively for lead pencils. It is a commercially valuable tree, but the now limited supply of better-grade trees severely limits its use. The tree is attractive, and it is used as a cultivated ornamental in the Southeast.

Appearance: small tree to 15 m (50 ft), broadly cone-shaped, and usually with a broad, sometimes flat-topped crown; trunk short, thick, 0.2–0.6 m (0.7–1.9 ft) in diameter, the *lower branches often extending to the ground.* **Bark:** thin, 4–8 mm (0.1–0.3 in) reddish-brown, irregularly furrowed, with the narrow ridges separating into thin, loose shreds. **Branches:** short, numerous, erect near the top to spreading; branchlets slender, numerous, erect, spreading, or slightly drooping, appearing 4-sided, green turning reddish-brown with age. **Leaves:** tiny, *scale-like, opposite one another* and overlapping, smooth on margin, pressed closely against the branchlets, 2–4 mm (about 0.1–0.2 in) long, triangular, gland-dotted on the back, sharp-pointed, light-green; on juvenile or very young branches, the leaves are first very narrow, sharp-pointed

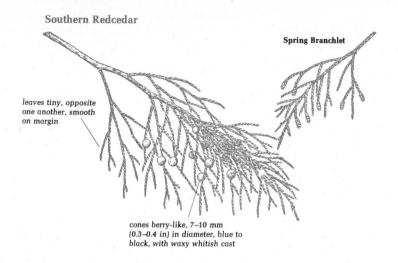

Southern Redcedar

Spring Branchlet

leaves tiny, opposite one another, smooth on margin

cones berry-like, 7–10 mm (0.3–0.4 in) in diameter, blue to black, with waxy whitish cast

and spreading rather than pressed closely against the branchlets. **Flowers:** male and female flowers on separate trees; male flowers in numerous, short, cylindric cones, 5–6 mm (0.2 in) long; female flowers in tiny, egg-shaped or nearly globe-shaped, resinous cones; all cones are produced at the tips of the branchlets. **Fruits:** small, *fleshy, berry-like cones,* nearly globe-shaped to slightly elongated, *7–10 mm (0.3–0.4 in) in diameter,* resinous, thin-skinned, sweet, *dark blue* with a waxy, whitish cast, *matures in 1 season.* **Seeds:** 1 or 2 per fruit, 2–3 mm (0.1 in) long, broadest near the base and tapering to a sharp point, brown, prominently ridged on the back.

The Yew Family

Taxaceae

This is a small family of 14 or 15 species of trees and shrubs divided into 5 genera. Two of them, yews *(Taxus)* and torreyas *(Torreya),* occur in the Northern Hemisphere and in North America. The remaining genera are native to China and New Caledonia, in the South Pacific. Fossils seem to indicate that some members of the yew family once occurred in Greenland.

Generally, the yew family is of minor importance to man and to wildlife. Several species are used widely as ornamentals in the nursery and landscaping industry. And the wood of some species is hard, heavy, durable, and very resilient and is used in limited quantities for hand implements and archery bows.

Members of this family usually flower in the spring. The fruit of yews ripens in late summer of the first year, and the fruit of torreyas ripens in the summer of the second year. Wind transfers the pollen grains from the male to the female flowers. The fruits consist of an edible, fleshy outer covering and a single seed within. The bright color of the mature fruits attracts birds, which distribute the seeds undigested in their droppings. Like flowers of the junipers, male and female flowers of trees in the yew family occur on separate trees, so at least 2 trees, 1 of each sex, are needed in close proximity to produce fruits.

Key to Genera in the Yew Family

A. Fruit a seed partially enclosed in a scarlet or coral red, fleshy cup, maturing in 1 season; leaves 1.2–2.6 cm (0.5–1 in) long   **Yews, p. 157**

Pacific Yew

B. Fruit olive-like, consisting of a seed totally enclosed in a purple-stripped green skin, maturing in 2 seasons; leaves 2.5–8 cm (1–3.2 in) long   **Torreyas, p. 160**

Florida Torreya

The Yew Genus   Taxus L.

Yews make up a small group of 6 to 8 closely related species native to North America, Europe, and Asia. Three species are native to North America, 2 of which are trees and the third a low shrub. The western yew occurs in the Pacific coastal region; while the Florida yew is a rare tree of northwestern Florida. The Canadian yew (*Taxus canadensis*) is a low-growing shrub with leaves and fruits similar to the western yew, but it does not occur as far west as the tree form. Yews are of limited importance as a lumber source, but the hard, heavy, resilient wood is used in hand-tooled implements. As ornamentals, yews are used extensively as foundation plantings and in landscaped entrances to buildings. They are of limited importance to wildlife and even a hazard to domestic animals because of the poisonous leaves. The English yew (*Taxus baccata*) and the Japanese yew (*T. cuspidata*) and the hybrid of these 2 are the most commonly encountered yews in cultivation. These introduced species usually are grown as shrubs in North America.

Yews are evergreen shrubs or small trees with reddish-brown, scaly bark. The bright orange to brown wood is hard, heavy, elastic, and straight-grained. Winter buds are minute, rounded, and covered with thin, closely overlapping scales. The leaves are linear, flattened, often curved, persistent, spirally arranged with 2 light-colored, parallel bands on the underside. The cones occur in the junction of the leaves and the branchlets. Usually the sexes are on separate trees; rarely are both sexes on the same plant, but if they are they are in separate cones. The male cones are globe-shaped, composed of overlapping scales and containing 4 to 8 pollen sacs. The female cones occur individually and are composed of a single ovule (structure containing the egg) with a circular, fleshy disk around the base. The fruit, which ripens in the fall, consists of a small, hard-shelled seed surrounded by a persistent, fleshy, bright red cup.

Key to Yew Species

A. Leaves 1.2–2.5 cm (0.5–1 in) long, yellowish-green; trees of the Pacific Northwest
Pacific yew, p. 158

B. Leaves 2–2.6 cm (0.8–1 in) long, dark green, trees of northwestern Florida   **Florida yew, p. 159**   **Florida Yew**

Pacific Yew   *Taxus brevifolia* Nutt.

Pacific yews are native to the Pacific coastal region from southeastern Alaska southward into California. They occur along stream and river margins, and along moist flats and ravines from 650–2,500 m (2,100–8,000 ft) elevation. They seldom are found in groups and normally occur as scattered understory trees in evergreen forests. Although they can be found growing in association with many trees, these yews occur more commonly with Douglas fir, grand fir, and coastal redwood. They prefer shade, grow slowly, and apparently are long-lived.

The trees produce large quantities of seeds on a regular basis. The bright red, fleshy disk surrounding the seeds attracts birds that unwittingly distribute the undigested seeds in their droppings. Most larger animals avoid this tree because of the poisonous leaves. The light red or rose-colored wood is hard, heavy, strong, durable, fine-grained, and resilient. It is in demand for canoe paddles, archery bows, and other hand- or machine-turned articles. The wood takes a very fine polish.

Appearance: small to medium-size trees 10–18 m tall, rarely to 25 (32–60 ft, rarely to 82) with an open branching pattern and a hard, cone-shaped crown; trunk tall,

Pacific Yew

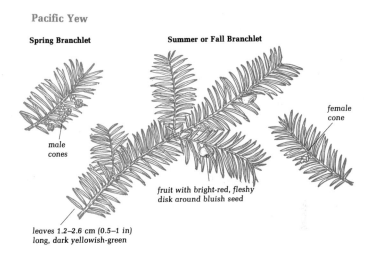

Spring Branchlet   **Summer or Fall Branchlet**

female cone

male cones

fruit with bright-red, fleshy disk around bluish seed

leaves 1.2–2.6 cm (0.5–1 in) long, dark yellowish-green

straight, 0.3–0.6 m (1–1.9 ft) in diameter, rarely larger, conspicuously ridged or fluted. **Bark:** very thin, 0.5–0.7 cm (0.2–0.3 in) thick, dark reddish-brown to purplish-brown, with thin, loose scales. **Branches:** slender, spreading to hanging; branchlets slender, often drooping and giving a weeping look, green turning bright reddish-brown. **Leaves:** small, spirally arranged but spreading and becoming 2-ranked, *1.2–2.6 cm (0.5–1 in) long*, linear, flattened, straight or slightly curved, pointed at the tip, thick, leathery, ***dark yellowish-green.*** **Flowers:** male cones in globe-shaped heads consisting of 6 to 14 yellowish pollen sacs, produced as shown in the drawing; female cones occurring singly, green. **Fruits:** a seed, hard-coated, single, erect, usually broadest near the base, 6–8 mm (0.2–0.3 in) long, pointed near the tip, a bright coral red, fleshy disk nearly enclosing dark bluish seed.

Florida Yew

The Florida yew is a small tree or large shrub that grows in moist, shaded ravines and on protected slopes in Gadsden and Liberty counties in northwestern Florida. The Florida torreya, another rare tree, may grow in association with the Florida yew. Because they are rare trees and have such a restricted range, every effort should be made to preserve their habitat.

Individual plants are less than 10 m (32 ft) in height and have purplish-brown bark that usually separates into thin plates. The

Taxus floridana Nutt.

Florida Yew

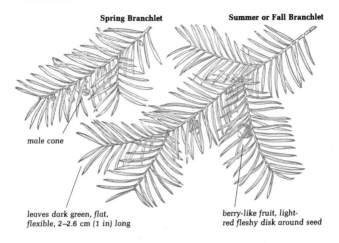

Spring Branchlet

Summer or Fall Branchlet

male cone

leaves dark green, flat, flexible, 2–2.6 cm (1 in) long

berry-like fruit, light-red fleshy disk around seed

flat, linear, ***dark-green leaves, 2.0–2.6 cm (0.8–1 in) long,*** are soft, flexible, and pointed at the tip. Both the leaves and the branchlets have a slight fragrance when crushed. The flowers appear in spring, and the fruits ripen by October. Birds feed on the light-red fruits, digesting the outer part and letting the sticky seeds pass in their droppings. Even though the fleshy outer part of the fruit is edible, the seeds are very poisonous, as is the case with other yews.

The Torreya Genus

Torreya Arn.

Torreyas make up a small group of 6 rare species of evergreen trees and shrubs of North America, Japan, and China. Two species occur in North America, 1 in the mountains of central California and the other in the southeastern U.S. Both are rare trees and resemble yews in appearance. The torreyas can be distinguished from the yews by their longer leaves, the seeds enclosed in a fleshy sac, and the fact that the fruit needs 2 years to mature. They are of minor importance to man and to wildlife. In Asia, oil is pressed from the seeds and used in cooking. In England and Europe, the wood is sometimes used for furniture and cabinets. In suitably warm climates, these trees are planted as ornamentals.

Torreyas are evergreen trees or shrubs with fissured bark and spreading to drooping branches. The yellow wood is strong, straight-grained, durable, and easily worked. Winter buds are small, broadest near the base, and covered by a few, overlapping scales. The leaves are linear and thin; they are thickened and rounded on the upper surface, long-pointed at the tip, dark green, and shiny. Individual trees have either male or female cones. The male cones occur in the junction of the leaves of the previous year's growth and consist of a series of closely whorled pollen sacs. Female cones occur in the junction of the branchlets and the leaves of the current year's growth and consist of an ovule (egg-bearing structure) surrounded by an urn-shaped fleshy sac. Two years are required for the fruit to reach maturity. At that time, the narrow yellowish-brown seed is enclosed in a green and purple-stripped olive-like fruit. When ripe, the fruit splits into 2 parts.

Key to Torreya Species

A. Leaves 3–8 cm (1.2–3.2 in) long, flattened on the upper side, plants with pungent odor when crushed; branchlets reddish-brown; trees of central California **California torreya, p. 161**

B. Leaves 2.5–3.8 cm (1–1.5 in) long, slightly curved and somewhat rounded on the upper side, plants with a foul odor when crushed; branchlets green; trees of northwestern Florida and southeastern Georgia
Florida torreya, p. 162

Florida Torreya

California Torreya, California Nutmeg   *Torreya californica* Torr.

The California torreya, like its southeastern relative, is a rare tree. It grows along mountain streams, protected slopes, and cool, moist canyons of the coastal range and western slopes of the Sierra Nevada in central California. The trees are never abundant and occur scattered in the forest. Normally, they are found from 30–1,200 m (98–4,000 ft) elevation. This torreya resembles the Pacific yew, except that it occurs at a lower altitude and that it has stiff, sharp-pointed leaves with a pungent odor when crushed, as well as fruits that resemble the fruit of the nutmeg tree. Though the fruits are consumed by some birds, the trees are of little importance to wildlife. The soft, yellowish wood is of no commercial value.

California Torreya

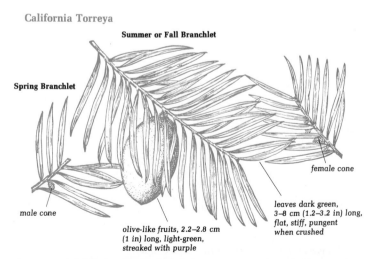

Summer or Fall Branchlet

Spring Branchlet

female cone

male cone

olive-like fruits, 2.2–2.8 cm (1 in) long, light-green, streaked with purple

leaves dark green, 3–8 cm (1.2–3.2 in) long, flat, stiff, pungent when crushed

These torreyas are attractive, medium-size trees 5–20 m (16–66 ft) high with slender, spreading to drooping branches and thin, furrowed bark which forms long, loosely attached, scaly plates. The **leaves** are very narrow, **3–8 cm (1.2–3.2 in) long, flat**, stiff, dark green above, with a spine-like tip and a **pungent odor when crushed**. Although spirally arranged, the leaves are twisted at the base to become flattened or 2-ranked on the branchlets. Flowering cones are similar to those described in the general description of torreyas. The olive-like or nutmeg-like fruits are 2.2–2.8 cm (0.9–1.1 in) long, light green, and streaked with purple.

Florida Torreya, Stinking Cedar   *Torreya taxifolia* Arn.

The Florida torreya or stinking cedar, as it is sometimes called locally, is a rare, small tree that grows in moist, wooded ravines and slopes along the Apalachicola River in northwestern Florida and adjacent southeastern Georgia. This tree occurs in the same

places as the Florida yew does, but it can be distinguished easily because of its very sharp-pointed leaves, the pungent odor of the crushed leaves, and the olive-like fruits. Because of its very limited occurrence, it is of no significant value to wildlife.

This torreya is a small tree with stout, green branchlets and thin, shallowly furrowed bark that peels off in thin, shredding pieces. The leaves are very narrow, lance-shaped, **2.5–3.8 cm (1–1.5 in) long**

and about 2–4 mm (about 0.1–0.2 in) wide, somewhat curved, stout, sharp-pointed at the tip, bright green and shiny on the upper surface, and with a **sharp, disagreeable**

Florida Torreya

Spring Branchlet   **Summer or Fall Branchlet**

female cone

leaves shiny bright green on upper side, 2.5–3.7 cm (1–1.5 in) long, somewhat rounded in cross section, foul odor when crushed

olive-like fruits, dark green, striped with purple, 2.5–3.2 cm (1–1.3 in) long

odor when crushed. They are arranged in 1 plane, usually called 2-ranked, on the branchlets. The cones are described earlier in the general description of the torreya genus. The olive-like fruits are 2.5–3.2 cm (1–1.3 in) long and 1.8–2.5 cm (0.7–1 in) in diameter and dark green, stripped with purple. The hard-coated seed is reddish-brown, and both the fruit and seed ripen in summer.

FLOWERING TREES
(Angiosperms)

Flowering trees are part of a diverse group of a quarter-million flowering plants worldwide that includes herbs, vines, shrubs, and trees. There are about 20,000 flowering plants in North America, of which only about 560 are large enough to be considered trees. The trees include palms, magnolias, cherries, maples, birches, oaks, and some yuccas among many others. The 1 unifying feature of all flowering plants is their enclosed seeds. That is, the seed-producing structures of the female flowers are directly enclosed in 1 or more tissues, whereas the seed-producing structures of conifers (such as pines, larches, and yews) are naked.

Fossil records show that flowering plants are of more recent origin than conifers, and they are structurally more advanced. The greatest diversity and numbers of flowering trees are found in tropical and subtropical climates, although flowering trees are well represented in temperate regions of the world. North American flowering trees have many close relatives in Europe and Asia.

Flowering trees usually do not bear resin, and they almost always have well-developed, flattened leaves. Most of the flowering trees in temperate regions are deciduous (the leaves falling in autumn). In subtropical and tropical regions many of these same trees will have green leaves all year, and thus can be called evergreen in those regions. The flowers contain the reproductive structures, sometimes in separate flowers, plus generally larger, often showy and colorful accessory structures including petals, sepals, and occasionally leaf-like bracts. There are diverse kinds of fruits, all containing anywhere from 1 to many seeds. Seeds have the tiny embryonic plant usually encased in a hard coat.

Flowering trees are grouped either as dicots (including all hardwoods) or monocots (including yuccas and palms).

Monocots show 1 seed leaf at germination. Among North American monocots only the palm and lily families contain tree-size members, and these range only in the South. The palm family has palms and palmettos; the lily family has yuccas. Although there are 60 monocot families containing some 36,000 species worldwide, most monocots are herbs such as lilies, tulips, orchids, and grasses. Among the tree-size monocots, the palms and yuccas have evergreen leaves, with veins arranged in a parallel pattern. Leaf margins of some palms may be toothed. But leaf margins of yuccas and most palms are entire along the margins; that is, they are without teeth or lobes. The sepals, petals, and stamens of the flowers are in 3s or multiples of 3. The trunks do not produce true wood and do not have the annual growth rings present in nearly all North American hardwoods. Information on yuccas and palms begins on page 904.

Dicots, which include the hardwood trees, show 2 seed leaves at germination. Examples are magnolias, cherries, maples, birches, and oaks. Information on the dicots begins on the next page.

Introduction to Keys to Major Groups of Hardwood (Dicot) Families

The majority of North American trees belong to hardwood (dicot) families of flowering plants. There are 78 of these families covered in this book. The keys that follow will help you determine the family a specimen belongs to. On the other hand, if you know that your specimen belongs in, say, the oak genus or the hickory genus, you can skip the keys to families that follow and turn directly to appropriate pages as noted in the book's index. Then you can use keys to species to determine the species.

Below, you will first encounter a short key that divides the hardwood families into 5 major groups based on type of leaf and leaf arrangement. From there, you can decide which of the 5 major-group keys to consult to determine the family of your specimen.

Note: Some families appear several times in the keys, even in different keys. This is because the keys employ identification features that are easiest to use rather than the technical features that botanists use. For example, the legume family contains genera with scale-like leaves (some of the daleas), simple leaves (redbuds), and compound leaves (honeylocust). The citrus family contains some genera with opposite leaves (leaves opposite on the branchlets) while other genera have alternate leaves; and the leaves may be simple (consisting of 1 blade), 3-leafleted, or feather-like (pinnate) compound. Thus, the citrus family occurs in 3 of the 5 major-group keys that follow.

Key to Major Groups of Hardwood (Dicot) Families

A. Leaves scale-like, hardly noticeable or absent, spines sometimes present   **Group A, p. 165**

B. Leaves various shapes, but present and not as above.

  1. Leaves alternate along the branchlets.

    a. Leaves simple (consisting of 1 blade)   **Group B, p. 166**

    b. Leaves consisting of 2 or more leaflets (compound)   **Group C, p. 179**

  2. Leaves opposite along the branchlets.

    a. Leaves simple (1 blade)   **Group D, p. 182**

    b. Leaves consisting of 2 or more leaflets (compound)   **Group E, p. 186**

Key to Hardwood Group A

Leaves scale-like, hardly noticeable or absent, spines sometimes present.

A. Trees with thick juicy stems, without bark and with many clusters of spines
> **Cactus Family (Cactaceae), p. 417**

B. Trees woody, with bark; branches spineless or with single (simple) spines not clustered.

  1. Trees without spines; leaves scale-like.

    a. Flowers male or female, male flowers in terminal spikes, each flower with 1 stamen; female flowers in dense, rounded heads
> **Beefwood Family (Casuarinaceae), p. 413**

    b. Flowers bisexual, with 5 or 10 stamens
> **Tamarisk Family (Tamaricaceae), p. 451**

  2. Trees with spines, leafless or nearly so for most of year (leaves present briefly in spring).

    a. Branchlets flexible, with conspicuous black rings where the branchlets fork; fruit a dry capsule 2 cm (0.8 in) long or longer
> **Spindle Tree Family (Celastraceae), see canotia, p. 718**

    b. Branchlets stout to flexible, lacking conspicuous black rings where the branchlets fork; fruits dry and less than 1.2 cm (0.5 in) long, or a fleshy berry.

      (1) Branchlets covered with dense hairs or hairy only on younger stems; fruits dry capsules or segments.

        (a) Branchlets densely hairy and gland-dotted; fruits pea-like pods (only the dalea genus) **Legume Family (Leguminosae), see desert smoketree, p. 664**

        (b) Branchlets hairy only on younger stems, not gland-dotted; fruits a ring of 5–10 flattened segments (crucifixion-thorn genus) **Quassia Family (Simaroubaceae), p. 811**

      (2) Branchlets lacking hairs or nearly hairless; fruits a shiny, black berry
> **Caper Family (Capparaceae), see allthorn, p. 505**

silhouette

Organ-Pipe Cactus

Desert Tamarisk

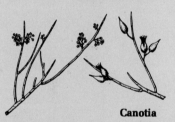

Canotia

Desert Smoketree

Allthorn

Key: Hardwood Group B

Leaves alternate and simple (consisting of 1 blade).

Quaking Aspen

Black Willow

Eastern Hop Hornbeam

American Beech

Oregon White Oak

Pin Oak

A. Leaves deciduous.

  1. Flowers lacking petals.

    a. Flowers male or female.

      (1) Flowers produced in catkins; floral parts attached above the ovary (inferior), except for the corkwood family.

        (a) Leaves with leaf-like growths (stipules) at leafstalk base sometimes falling away; fruits dry capsule, winged, or acorns partly to totally enclosed by a cup or bur.

          (a1) Fruits many seeded, each seed with a tuft of hairs at the end; flowers lacking a calyx; family includes willows and poplars **Willow Family (Salicaceae), p. 456**

          (a2) Fruits 1-seeded, without a tuft of hairs at the end; flowers with a calyx.

            (a2a) Leaves with many, usually fine, teeth; winged seeds or nuts in a catkin, the seeds usually covered by bracts; family includes birches, alders, hornbeams **Birch Family (Betulaceae), p. 385**

            (a2b) Leaves entire, lobed, or coarsely toothed; fruit a nut enclosed in a bur or cup; family includes beeches, oaks, chestnut, chinkapins, tanoak **Beech Family (Fagaceae), p. 298**

        (b) Leaves without stipules; fruits fleshy to leathery, enclosing a hard stone fruit **Corkwood Family (Leitneriaceae), p. 264**

      (2) Flowers produced in dense heads or elongated clusters; flower parts attached at or near the base of the ovary.

(a) Leaves 3–7-lobed.

    (a1) Leaves with many fine teeth along the margin; flowers lacking a calyx and petals; fruits rounded, armed with stout, sharp projections **Witch Hazel Family (Hamamelidaceae), p. 224**

Sweetgum

    (a2) Leaves absent or only with large coarse teeth; flowers with tiny, scale-like calyx lobes and petals; fruits rounded, unarmed, soft to touch **Sycamore Family (Platanaceae), p. 219**

American Sycamore

(b) Leaves entire or toothed, largely or totally unlobed (in the Mulberry family some trees may have both unlobed and lobed leaves).

    (b1) Leaves smooth to hairy; flowers in many-flowered clusters; fruits soft, fleshy; genera include mulberry, fig, and osage-orange **Mulberry Family (Moraceae), p. 251**

Osage-Orange

    (b2) Leaves and branchlets covered with dense silvery scales; flowers in few-flowered clusters; fruits dry, hard **Oleaster Family (Elaeagnaceae), p. 690**

b. Flowers bisexual.

  (1) Leaves toothed along the margin; fruits dry, winged; genera include elm, hackberry, and nettle tree **Elm Family (Ulmaceae), p. 228**

Black Mulberry

  (2) Leaves entire along the margin; fruits leathery to fleshy, not winged.

    (a) Leaves and branchlets smooth or finely hairy; flowers with 4–6 calyx lobes and petals **Olax Family (Olacaceae), p. 709**

Slippery Elm

    (b) Leaves and branchlets covered with dense silvery scales; flowers with 4 calyx lobes and no petals **Oleaster Family (Elaeagnaceae), p. 690**

(Continued)

2. Flowers with petals and calyx lobes.

    a. Petals fused into a tube for part or most of its length.

        (1) Ovary superior (meaning calyx lobes, petals and stamens are attached at or below the base of the pistil).

Sourwood

            (a) Stamens attached near the base of the pistil, free of petals; genera include Elliotta, sourwood, Lyonia, Kalma, rhododendron, blueberry, and madrone
              Heath Family (Ericaceae), p. 511

            (b) Stamens attached to the inner surface of the petals, often on the lower half.

Common Persimmon

                (b1) Stamens opposite the petals; fruits a berry, usually many seeded.

                    (b1a) Flowers 4-lobed; stamens as many or more than the petals; family includes persimmons **Ebony Family (Ebenaceae), p. 538**

Gum Bumelia

                    (b1b) Flowers 5-lobed, rarely 6; stamens as many as the petal lobes; genera include bumelia and others
                        Sapote Family (Sapotaceae), p. 526

                (b2) Stamens alternate with the petals; fruits fleshy to leathery, 1-seeded stone fruits (drupes) **Storax Family (Styracaceae), p. 542**

Little Silverbell

        (2) Ovary inferior or nearly so (meaning calyx lobes, petals, and stamens are attached near or above the ovary, which is the enlarged base of the petal).

            (a) Flowers separate, but in clusters, usually elongated, branched or unbranched; petals 5–10; stamens 15 to many; fruit fleshy, enclosing 1–5 stones, not splitting open
                Sweetleaf Family (Symplocaceae), p. 547

Common Sweetleaf

Big Sagebrush

(b) Flowers grouped into flat or rounded heads; petals 4 or 5; stamens 4 or 5; fruit dry, 1-seeded, often tipped with a dry, needle-shaped scale **Sunflower Family (Compositae), see sagebrush, p. 902**

b. Petals free, the separate lobes not fused into a tube for part or most of its length.

(1) Ovary inferior (meaning calyx lobes, petals and stamens are attached near or above the ovary, the base of the pistil).

(a) Flowers small, inconspicuous, sometimes male or female; stamens usually 5; fruits small, less than 2 cm (1.3 in) long.

(a1) Flowers bisexual, produced in dense, many-flowered clusters at the tip of the branchlet **Dogwood Family (Cornaceae), p. 697**

(a2) Flowers male or female, produced in few-flowered clusters in the junctions of the upper leaves **Tupelo Tree Family (Nyssaceae), p. 705**

(b) Flowers showy, usually large, white, pink, bright-red to orange; stamens 10 to many.

(b1) Flowers white or pink; leaves toothed; includes mountain-ashes, serviceberries, pears, apples, hawthorns **Rose Family (Rosaceae), p. 553**

(b2) Flowers orange to bright red; leaves entire **Pomegranate Family (Punicaceae), p. 683**

(2) Ovary superior (meaning calyx lobes, petals, and stamens are attached near or below the ovary, which is the enlarged base of the pistil).

(a) Flowers with numerous stamens (15 or more).

(Continued)

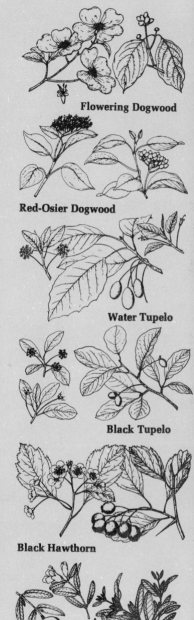

Flowering Dogwood

Red-Osier Dogwood

Water Tupelo

Black Tupelo

Black Hawthorn

Pomegranate

Cucumber Tree

Tulip Tree

Birchleaf Mountain Mahogany

Pawpaw

American Plum

American Basswood

(a1) Flowers with several to many pistils.

(a1a) Leaves with small leaf-like appendages (stipules) at the base of the leafstalk.

*Leaves entire or lobed; flowers with 6–18 petals or petal-like structures (cucumber and tulip trees) **Magnolia Family (Magnoliaceae), p. 188**
Leaves toothed along the margin, unlobed; flowers with 5 petals, rarely without petals; includes mountain mahoganies, and cliffrose **Rose Family (Rosaceae), p. 553

(a1b) Leaves without small leaf-like appendages (stipules) at the base of the leaf-stalk; leaves entire on the margins; flowers with 6 petals; fruits large, fleshy, with the seeds embedded in the pulp; includes pawpaw **Custard Apple Family (Annonaceae), p. 199**

(a2) Flowers with 1 pistil, the pistil 1–5-parted at the base.

(a2a) Leaves with stipules, leaves toothed.

*Leafstalks often with 1 or more conspicuous glands; flowers single or in small clusters from the branchlets; fruits fleshy, 1-seeded, and not splitting open at maturity; includes cherries, plums **Rose Family (Rosaceae), p. 553**
Leafstalks without glands; flowers in elongated clusters on a long stalk attached to a narrow, leaf-like bract **Basswood (Linden) Family (Tiliaceae), p. 435

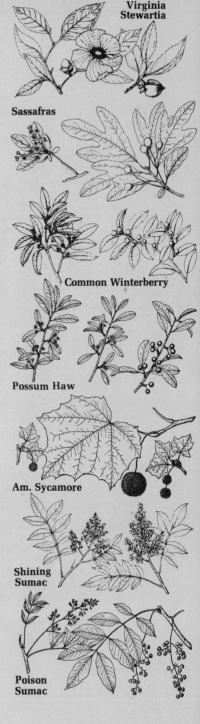

Virginia
Stewartia

Sassafras

Common Winterberry

Possum Haw

Am. Sycamore

Shining
Sumac

Poison
Sumac

(a2b) Leaves without small leaf-like appendages (stipules) at the base of the leafstalk; leaves entire or toothed; includes Stewartias **Tea Family (Theaceae), p. 428**

(b) Flowers with stamens equal to or double the number of petals, though less than 15.

(b1) Flowers male or female or usually so.

(b1a) Male and female flowers on different trees.

Leaves entire, trees with unlobed and 1–3-lobed leaves on the same tree; includes sassafras **Laurel Family (Lauraceae), p. 208**
Leaves finely toothed along the margin, unlobed; fruits orange to bright red (some hollies), includes winterberries and possum haw* **Holly Family (Aquifoliaceae), p. 719

(b1b) Male and female flowers separate but both on same tree; leaves simple or lobed but not on the same tree.

Female flowers in dense, many-flowered, rounded heads; fruits in many-seeded, round heads **Sycamore Family (Platanaceae), p. 219**
Female flowers in tightly to loosely branched, elongated clusters; fruits in elongated, usually branched clusters (some species); includes sumacs* **Cashew Family (Anacardiaceae), p. 796

(b2) Flowers bisexual (in the witch hazel family, female flowers may also be present).

(Continued)

Black Locust

Witch Hazel

Sweet Pepperbush

Cascara Buckthorn

Evergreen Bayberry

Live Oak

Canyon Live Oak

(b2a) Leaves entire; flowers irregular, shaped like peaflowers; 10 stamens
  Legume Family (Leguminosae), p. 658
(b2b) Leaves toothed or entire; with symmetrical flowers, all petals alike; 4–10 stamens.

Fruits capsules, splitting open at maturity.

• Flowers with narrow, ribbon-shaped petals; leaves with large, coarse, often rounded teeth
  Witch Hazel Family (Hamamelidaceae), p. 224
• • Flowers with petals widest near the base and pointed at the tip, not ribbon-shaped; leaves with many, fine, sharp-pointed teeth
  Pepperbush Family (Clethraceae), p. 509

**Fruits fleshy, rounded or nearly so, not splitting open at maturity (some species)
  Buckthorn Family (Rhamnaceae), p. 739

B. Leaves persistent, evergreen.

  1. Flowers without petals, usually reduced and small or in narrow catkins.

    a. Flowers or flower clusters male or female.

      (1) Male flowers in narrow usually hanging catkins.

        (a) Leaves with many tiny resinous glands, fragrant when rubbed; fruits dry, rounded, covered with waxy secretion; includes bayberries
          Wax Myrtle Family (Myricaceae), p. 292
        (b) Leaves without resin glands, not fragrant; fruits are acorns, nut enclosed partly or totally by a spiny bur or scaly cup; includes oaks
          Beech Family (Fagaceae), pp. 312, 351

(2) Male flowers in short branched clusters in the junctions of the leaves and branchlets or on the inside of a closed, nearly round receptacle.

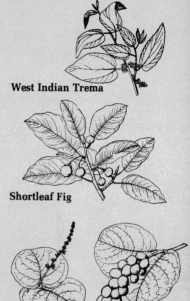

West Indian Trema

(a) Leaves toothed; flowers in short, branched clusters along the branchlets; includes tremas **Elm Family (Ulmaceae), p. 228**

(b) Leaves entire, rarely lobed; flowers on the inside of a closed, nearly round receptacle; includes figs **Mulberry Family (Moraceae), p. 251**

Shortleaf Fig

b. Flowers or flower clusters, bisexual.

(1) Small leaf-like appendages (stipules) present, conspicuous, forming a sheath around the stem at the junction of the leafstalks and branchlet; includes sea grape **Buckwheat Family (Polygonaceae), p. 425**

(2) Small leaf-like appendages (stipules) at the base of the leafstalk usually minute and soon falling away, or if persistent then not forming a sheath around the stem **Buckthorn Family (Rhamnaceae), see Calif. Buckthorn, p. 749**

Sea Grape

2. Flowers with petals.

a. Flowers with the petals free of each other.

(1) Flowers with 12 or more stamens.

(a) Flowers with several to many free pistils.

(a1) Leaves with small leaf-like appendages (stipules) at the base of the leafstalk.

(a1a) Leaves entire; flowers with 9–14 large, showy petals or petal-like structures **Magnolia Family (Magnoliaceae), p. 188**

Southern Magnolia

(a1b) Leaves toothed and/or lobed along the margin; flowers with 5 petals; includes Torrey vauquelinia **Rose Family (Rosaceae), p. 553**

Torrey Vauguelinia

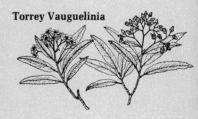

(Continued)

(a2) Leaves without appendages (stipules) at the base of the leafstalk.

(a2a) Flowers with 3 sepals (calyx lobes) and 6 petals in 2 series; fruits large, fleshy, aromatic **Custard Apple Family (Annonaceae), p. 199**

Pond Apple

(a2b) Flowers with numerous petals and petal-like structures, sepals not distinguishable from petals; fruits dry, splitting open at maturity **Anise Tree Family (Illiciaceae), p. 205**

Florida Anise

(b) Flowers with 1 pistil, 1–5-parted at the base.

(b1) Leaves with appendages (stipules) at the base of the leafstalk.

(b1a) Flowers with 4 calyx lobes and petals **Caper Family (Capparaceae), p. 503**

Jamaica Caper

(b1b) Flowers with 5 calyx lobes and petals.

Stamens fused into a tube, appearing to be fused with the stalk (style) of the pistil; includes sea hibiscus **Mallow Family (Malvaceae), p. 445**

Sea Hibiscus

**Stamens free, not appearing to be fused with the stalk (style) of the pistil.*
• Stalk (style) of the pistil emerging from the top of the ovary; includes Christmasberry (photina genus) **Rose Family (Rosaceae), p. 553**

Christmasberry

•• Stalk (style) of the pistil emerging from near the base of the ovary. **Coco-Plum Family (Chrysobalanaceae), p. 621**

Coco-Plum

(b2) Leaves without leaf-like appendages (stipules) at the base of the leafstalk.

Cinnamon Bark

(b2a) Leaves entire, gland-dotted on the surface; fruits soft, fleshy berries
Wild Cinnamon Family (Canellaceae), p. 204
(b2b) Leaves toothed, not gland-dotted; fruits dry capsules, splitting open at maturity; includes loblolly bay
Tea Family (Theaceae), p. 428

Loblolly Bay

(2) Flowers with as many stamens or twice as many stamens as petals (though fewer than 12).

(a) Flowers male or female.

(a1) Trees male or female; branchlets/leaves with clear sap.

(a1a) Flower parts (calyx lobes, petals, and stamens) in 4s (some hollies)
Holly Family (Aquifoliaceae), p. 719
(a1b) Flower parts in 5s.

American Holly

Flowers produced in large, densely-flowered branched, elongated clusters at the tips of the branchlets; includes sumacs **Cashew Family (Anacardiaceae), p. 796**
* * *Flowers produced in few-flowered clusters in the junctions of the upper leaves and branchlets; includes yellow-wood (Schaefferia genus)*
Spindle Tree Family (Celastraceae), p. 712

Lemonade Sumac

(a2) Trees with flowers of both sexes present, branchlets and leaves with a milky sap.

(a2a) Leaves entire; includes oysterwood **Spurge Family (Euphorbiaceae), p. 732**
(a2b) Leaves deeply 5–7-lobed; includes papaya
Carica Family (Caricaceae), p. 454
(Continued)

Oysterwood

Papaya

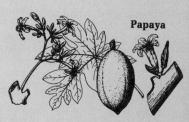

(b) Flowers bisexual.

(b1) Leaves lobed, the lobes radiating like the fingers of a hand; includes fremontias **Sterculia Family (Sterculiaceae), p. 441**

(b2) Leaves entire.

California Fremontia

(b2a) Leaves gland-dotted, strongly aromatic when crushed, without appendages (stipules) at leafstalk base.

California Laurel

Flowers with an outer series of 3 sepals and an inner series of 3 petals (sepals and petals look alike) **Laurel Family (Lauraceae), p. 208**

Flowers with a 3–5-lobed calyx and 3–5 distinct petals (some species)* **Citrus Family (Rutaceae), p. 818

Lime

(b2b) Leaves smooth to hairy, not gland-dotted; not strongly aromatic, with leaf-like appendages (stipules) at the base of the leafstalk.

Flowers produced in densely-flowered, elongated, unbranched spikes, usually at branchlet tips **Titi Family (Cyrillaceae), Buckwheat Genus, p. 508**
**Flowers produced in few-flowered, spreading clusters in the junctions of the upper leaves and the branchlets.*

• Flowers with the stamens opposite the petals.

Buckwheat Tree

Leaves with appendages (stipules) at the base of the leafstalk; stamens shedding pollen by lengthwise slits; includes tallowwood **Olax Family (Olacaceae), p. 709**

Tallowwood

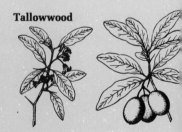

Leaves without appendages (stipules) at the base of the leafstalk; stamens usually shedding pollen through small pores at the tips (some species); includes ceanothus

Buckthorn Family (Rhamnaceae), p. 739

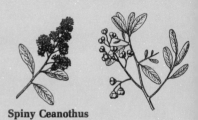

Spiny Ceanothus

• • Flowers with the stamens occurring alternate with the petals, rather than opposite the petals; includes Florida mayten **Spindle Tree Family (Celastraceae), p. 712**

b. Flowers with the petals fused, at least at the lower portions.

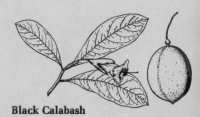

Black Calabash

(1) Flowers irregular, can only be divided into 2 equal halves using the lower petal lobe (bilateral), with 2 or 4 stamens; includes black calabash **Bignonia Family (Bignoniaceae), p. 878**

(2) Flower regular, all petals or lobes similar, can be divided into many equal parts, with 5 or more stamens.

Common Sweetleaf

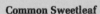

(a) Flowers with numerous stamens, more than twice as many as the lobes of the fused petals

Sweetleaf Family (Symplocaceae), p. 547

(b) Flowers with as many stamens as lobes of the fused petals or twice as many.

(b1) Leaves with many, tiny glands on the surface.

Marbleberry

(b1a) Flowers with 5 fertile (pollen-bearing) stamens and 5 sterile stamens, fertile stamens alternate with (not opposite to) the petal lobes

Joewood Family (Theophrastaceae), p. 549

(b1b) Flowers with 5 fertile (pollen-bearing) stamens, no sterile ones; stamens opposite the petal lobes; includes marbleberry **Myrsine Family (Myrsinaceae), p. 550**

(Continued)

(b2) Leaves smooth to densely hairy, but lacking glands on the surface.

(b2a) Stamens alternate with the lobes of the fused petals, opening to shed pollen by terminal pores
Nightshade Family (Solanaceae), p. 844

Mullein Nightshade

(b2b) Stamens opposite the lobes of the fused petals.

Flowers in small, few-flowered clusters in the junctions of the upper leaves; flowers often with modified sterile stamens (without pollen) alternating with fertile ones; includes willow bustic
Sapote Family (Sapotaceae), p. 526

Willow Bustic

** *Flowers usually in clusters at tips of the branchlets, often showy; flowers with only fertile (pollen-bearing) stamens; includes geiger tree and strongbarks* **Borage Family (Boraginaceae), p. 846**

Geiger Tree

Bahama Strongbark

Key to Hardwood Group C

Leaves alternate on the branchlets and consisting of 2 or more leaflets (compound).

A. Leaves with three leaflets, all originating from one point (trifoliolate).

  1. Branchlets armed with sharp spines; flowers large, showy, red   **Legume Family (Leguminosae), Coral Bean Genus, p. 664**

  2. Branchlets unarmed; flowers small, not showy, greenish-white to white.

    a. Leaves with numerous, tiny glands dotting the surface, deciduous; fruits broadly winged (some species)   **Citrus Family (Rutaceae), p. 818**

    b. Leaves without glands; leaves persistent, evergreen; fruits fleshy, without wings; includes white ironwood **Soapberry Family (Sapindaceae), p. 758**

B. Leaves feather-like (pinnate) or twice feather-like (bipinnate).

  1. Leaves twice feather-like (bipinnate).

    a. Leaflets toothed along the margins.

      (1) Leaves 40–80 cm long; leaves and branchlets armed with spines; includes devil's walking stick **Ginseng Family (Araliaceae), p. 842**

      (2) Leaves 20–40 cm long; leaves and branchlets unarmed **Mahogany Family (Meliaceae), see Chinaberry tree, p. 837**

    b. Leaves usually less than 0.6 m (2 ft) long; leaflets entire along the margins.

      (1) Leaflets usually alternate; flowers male or female; fruits pod-like legumes with 2 valves; includes Kentucky coffee tree **Legume Family (Leguminosae), p. 644**

      (2) Leaflets usually opposite; flowers bisexual, fruits pod-like capsules with 3 valves **Horseradish Tree Family (Moringaceae), p. 506**

  2. Leaves feather-like (pinnate).

    a. Branches and branchlets armed with spines, sometimes paired.

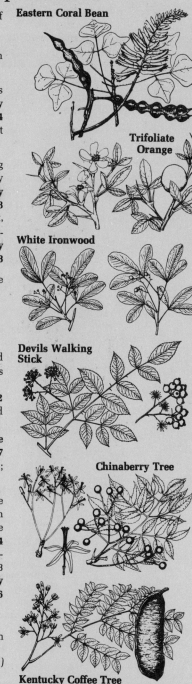

Eastern Coral Bean

Trifoliate Orange

White Ironwood

Devils Walking Stick

Chinaberry Tree

Kentucky Coffee Tree

(Continued)

(1) Leaflets entire along the margin (some species); includes sweet acacia **Legume Family (Leguminosae), p. 624**

(2) Leaflets sharply toothed along the margin; includes Hercules club (prickly ash genus) **Citrus Family (Rutaceae), p. 818**

b. Branches and branchlets without spines (unarmed).

    (1) Leaf-like appendages (stipules) at the base of the leaftstalk.

        (a) Leaves sharply toothed along the margin; winter buds resinous (usually sticky); includes mountain-ashes **Rose Family (Rosaceae), p. 553**

        (b) Leaves entire along the margin; winter buds not sticky (many species, including mimosa tree) **Legume Family (Leguminosae), p. 623**

    (2) Leaf-like appendages (stipules) absent.

        (a) Leaflets deeply dissected or deeply lobed; includes silk oak **Protea Family (Proteaceae), p. 692**

        (b) Leaflets entire or toothed along the margin, not deeply lobed or dissected.

            (b1) Leaves with a single leaflet at the tip and an odd number of leaflets.

            (b1a) Leaflets entire along the margin.

            Flowers with 4 or 5 calyx lobes and petals, 8–10 stamens per flower **Torchwood Family (Burseraceae), p. 792**

            ** *Flowers with 5 calyx lobes and petals, 5 stamens per flower; includes poison sumac* **Cashew Family (Anacardiaceae), p. 796**

Sweet Acacia

Hercules Club

American Mountain-Ash

Mimosa Tree

Silk Oak

Poison Sumac

(b1b) Leaflets toothed along the margin.

Flowers bisexual; produced in elongated, branched or unbranched clusters; fruits dry to fleshy, not splitting open at maturity; includes smooth sumac **Cashew Family (Anacardiaceae), p. 796**
** *Flowers male or female; produced in hanging, unbranched catkins; fruits are nuts enclosed in a husk, sometimes splitting open at maturity; includes walnuts and hickories*
Walnut Family (Juglandaceae), p. 265

Smooth Sumac

Mockernut Hickory

(b2) Leaves without a leaflet at the tip, and having an even number of leaflets.

(b2a) Leaves entire along the margin.

Flowers with the stamens united into a tube
Mahogany Family (Meliaceae), p. 835
** *Flowers with the stamens free (some species, including paradise tree)*
Quassia Family (Simaroubaceae), p. 811

West Indies Mahogany

Paradise Tree

(b2b) Leaves toothed along the margin.

Leaves with numerous, tiny, translucent glands (looking like dots); flowers usually bisexual; includes Biscayne prickly ash **Citrus Family (Rutaceae), p. 818**
** *Leaves without tiny glands; flowers male or female (some species)*
Quassia Family (Simaroubaceae), p. 811
(Continued)

Biscayne Prickly-Ash

Key to Hardwood Group D

Leaves opposite on the branchlets and single (simple).

A. Leaves deciduous, falling in autumn; trees mainly of mild climates.

    1. Leaves toothed along the margin.

        a. Leaves remotely toothed; flowers appearing before the leaves; petals absent; includes ashes **Olive Family (Oleaceae), p. 854**

        b. Leaves closely or regularly toothed; flowers appearing with or after the leaves.

Singleleaf Ash

            (1) Flowers produced in large, many-flowered, compound, rounded, or nearly flat-topped clusters at the tips of the branchlets; fruits fleshy, berry-like (not splitting open at maturity); includes rusty blackhaw **Honeysuckle Family (Caprifoliaceae), p. 892**

Rusty Blackhaw

            (2) Flowers produced in small, few-flowered clusters in the junction of the leaves and branchlets; fruit a nearly fleshy capsule splitting open at maturity (some species) **Spindle Tree Family (Celastraceae), p. 712**

    2. Leaves entire along the margin.

        a. Leaves lobed in hand shape (palmate) **Maple Family (Aceraceae), p. 774**

        b. Leaves not lobed.

Sugar Maple

            (1) Plants either male or female; branchlets and leaves covered with silvery, brown, or golden scales **Oleaster Family (Elaeagnaceae), see silver buffaloberry, p. 690**

            (2) Plants with bisexual flowers; branchlets and leaves smooth to hairy, but not covered with shiny scales.

Silver Buffaloberry

                (a) Leaves with persistent small leaf-like appendages (stipules) at the base of the leafstalk; includes button bush **Madder Family (Rubiaceae), p. 884**

                (b) Leaves without these appendages or with tiny ones falling away early.

Button Bush

(b1) Leaves broadest near base or middle, usually 1–3 times longer than broad **Bignonia Family (Bignoniaceae), see common calabash, p. 882**

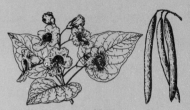

Northern Catalpa

(b1a) Leaves large, usually longer than 12 cm (4.8 in), heart-shaped at the base.

Leaves smooth to slightly hairy beneath, with dark glandular fields at the junction of the main veins (base of leaf); fruits an elongated pod; includes catalpas **Bignonia Family (Bignoniaceae), p. 878**
Leaves densely hairy beneath, without glands in the junction of the main veins; fruits leathery, egg-shaped capsules* **Foxglove Family (Scrophulariaceae), see royal paulownia, p. 877

Flowering Dogwood

(b1b) Leaves usually less than 10 cm (4 in) long.

Flowers in dense, rounded or flat-topped heads **Dogwood Family (Cornaceae), p. 697**
**Flowers in elongated, branched clusters (panicles).*

Red-Osier Dogwood

• Petals often united (free in some species); 4–6 petals; 2 stamens; fruits dry, winged or fleshy and not splitting open **Olive Family (Oleaceae), p. 854**
• • Petals not fused together, usually 6 petals and many stamens; fruits a capsule **Loose Strife Family (Lythraceae), see crape myrtle, p. 672**

Crape Myrtle

(b2) Leaves linear to lance shaped, usually 4–8 times as long as broad **Bignonia Family (Bignoniaceae), see desert willow, p. 881**
(Continued)

Desert Willow

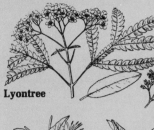

B. Leaves persistent or evergreen; trees mainly of warm climates.

    1. Leaves with persistent small appendages (stipules) at the base of the leafstalk.

Lyontree

        a. Petals and sepals arising from above or on top of the ovary (base of pistil); fruits often tipped with remnants of sepals.

           (1) Petals free; leaves toothed, often feather-like (pinnate); includes lyontree **Rose Family (Rosaceae), p. 553**

           (2) Petals fused into a tube; leaves entire along margin; includes Caribbean princewood **Madder Family (Rubiaceae), p. 884**

Caribbean Princewood

        b. Petals and sepals arising from below the ovary (base of pistil); fruits sometimes with remnants of sepals at base.

           (1) Flowers with twice as many stamens as petals or calyx lobes.

               (a) Flower clusters at the tips of branchlets; 5 petals and sepals, with 2 glands on outer surface of each sepal; petal abruptly contracted at the base into a claw **Malpighia Family (Malpighiaceae), see Key byrsonima, p. 841**

Key Byrsonima

               (b) Flower clusters in the junctions of the upper leaves; 4 petals and sepals, lacking glands; petals not claw-like **Mangrove Family (Rhizophoraceae), p. 694**

Red Mangrove

           (2) Flowers with same number of stamens as petals and calyx lobes.

               (a) Flowers male or female (some species) **Spindle Tree Family (Celastraceae), see falsebox, p. 717**

               (b) Flowers bisexual; includes leadwood **Buckthorn Family (Rhamnaceae), p. 739**

Leadwood

    2. Leaves without appendages (stipules) at the base of the leafstalk.

        a. Leafstalks with two conspicuous glands; includes white mangrove genus **Combretum Family (Combretaceae), p. 685**

White Mangrove

b. Leafstalks lacking glands (glands may be present on the left blade).

(1) Leaves and young branchlets with numerous, small glands (often appearing as dots); includes white stopper eugenia **Myrtle Family (Myrtaceae), p. 673**

White Stopper Eugenia

(2) Leaves and young branchlets smooth to hairy, but not gland-dotted.

    (a) Flowers male or female; plants either male or female.

        (a1) Flowers produced in narrow, elongate, catkin-like clusters; petals absent **Silktassel Family (Garryaceae), p. 696**

Wavyleaf Silktassel

        (a2) Flowers produced singly or in 2s or 3s; petals 6–8, white, fleshy, showy **Garcinia Family (Guttiferae), see balsam apple, p. 433**

    (b) Flowers bisexual.

        (b1) Flowers with a 5-lobed calyx, often petal-like; true petals absent; includes cockspur **Four-O'Clock Family (Nyctaginaceae), p. 415**

Balsam Apple

        (b2) Flowers with a 4- or 5-lobed calyx, petals 4 or 5.

            (b2a) Branchlets, leaves, flowers, and fruits with a milky sap **Dogbane Family (Apocynaceae), p. 843**

            (b2b) Branchlets, leaves, flowers, and fruits with a clear sap.

            Calyx lobes, petals, and stamens arising from above the ovary; fruits often topped with remnants of the calyx; leaves with 3–5 conspicuous main veins, all arising from base of leaf **Melastome Family (Melastomataceae), see Florida tetrazygia, p. 684**

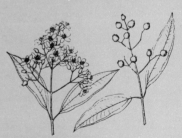

Florida Tetrazygia

**Calyx lobes, petals, and stamens arising from beneath the ovary; leaves with 1 main vein.

• Flowers with 4 stamens per flower; calyx 5-lobed; includes Florida fiddlewood and black mangrove. **Verbena Family (Verbenaceae), p. 851**
•• Flowers with 2 stamens per flower; calyx 4-lobed; includes devilwood **Olive Family (Oleaceae), p. 854**

Florida Fiddlewood

Black Mangrove

Devilwood

Key to Hardwood Group E

Leaves opposite on the branchlets and consisting of 2 or more leaflets (compound).

A. Leaflets 3 per leaf (trifoliolate) or if more than 3, then radiating from a central point (palmate).

  1. Leaves trifoliolate, 3 leaflets per leaf.

    a. Leaves persistent, gland-dotted on lower surface, with a distinct citrus odor when rubbed (some species, including torchwood) **Citrus Family (Rutaceae), p. 818**

    b. Leaves deciduous, falling in autumn, not gland-dotted, lacking a distinct odor when rubbed **Bladdernut Family (Staphyleaceae), p. 757**

  2. Leaves hand-like (palmately compound), with 5–7 leaflets per leaf; includes buckeyes **Horsechestnut Family (Hippocastanaceae), p. 766**

Torchwood

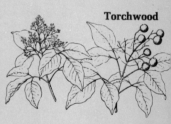

American Bladdernut

Ohio Buckeye

B. Leaves feather-like (pinnate) with more than 3 leaflets along a central axis.

  1. Leaves deciduous, falling in autumn; trees largely of temperate North America.

    a. Flowers with the calyx lobes and petals attached above the ovary (the swollen basal part of the pistil); fruits dry, with conspicuous wings.

Boxelder

      (1) Leaves finely toothed to entire along the margin; calyx lobes and petals of flowers in 4s; fruit with a single large flattened wing; includes ashes   **Olive Family (Oleaceae), p. 854**

      (2) Leaves coarsely toothed along the margin; 5 calyx lobes on flowers, petals absent; fruit with a pair of large flattened wings; includes boxelder   **Maple Family (Aceraceae), p. 774**

    b. Flowers with the calyx lobes and petals attached below the ovary (the swollen basal part of the pistil); fruits fleshy berries; includes elders   **Honeysuckle Family (Caprifoliaceae), p. 892**

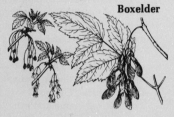

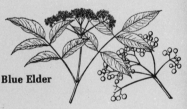

Blue Elder

  2. Leaves persistent, trees with leaves most or all of the year; trees of warm and subtropical regions of North America.

    a. Leaves entire along the margin; flowers with 10 stamens; fruit a 5-parted capsule; trees of Florida; includes holywood lignumvitae   **Caltrop Family (Zygophyllaceae), p. 838**

Holywood Lignumvitae

    b. Leaves toothed along the margin; flowers with 15 stamens; fruits 2-parted, woody; trees of southern California (some species, including lyontree)   **Rose Family (Rosaceae), p. 553**

Lyontree

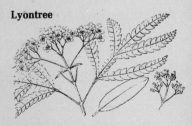

The Magnolia Family

The magnolias are a medium-size family of approximately 180 to 190 species of trees and shrubs of temperate and tropical regions of the world. There are 12 genera worldwide, but only 2 are native to North America: the magnolias, *Magnolia* (6 species), and tulip tree, *Liriodendron* (1 species). Because of its unusual flower and wood characteristics, the magnolia family is considered by most botanists to be the most primitive of the flowering plant families. Fossil records indicate that members of this family were once distributed more widely than they are today.

This family is of economic importance because many of the fragrant, showy, large-flowered magnolias are planted widely, and the tulip tree (also called yellow poplar) is valuable for timber. The family serves as a secondary food source for many birds and small mammals.

Members of this family may be deciduous or evergreen trees or shrubs with simple alternate leaves. The flowers are usually bisexual (include both sexes) and they are often large and showy. Normally the flowers are produced singly at or near the tips of the branchlets. The fruits vary from winged seeds to fleshy berries to being cone-like. The seeds are large and usually are surrounded by a fleshy outer coat.

Key to Magnolia Genera

A. Leaves entire, not lobed; fruit cone-like and composed of many individual compartments that split open to expose the seed
Magnolia, p. 188

Southern Magnolia

B. Leaves 4- or 6-lobed; fruit spindle-shaped, cone-like, composed of dry, winged seeds that fall away leaving a persistent spike-like central axis
Tulip tree, p. 197

Tulip Tree

The Magnolia Genus

There are approximately 70 to 75 species of magnolias distributed primarily in warm temperate to tropical regions of the world. Six species are native to North America, with several others in Central America, the West Indies, and southeastern Venezuela. The 6 native magnolias are found usually in deep, rich woodlands of the southeastern U.S. Because of their large, showy, and often fragrant flowers, magnolias are grown frequently as ornamental trees. Two of the more frequently encountered foreign magnolias are the star magnolia (*Magnolia kobus* variety *stellata*), a low growing shrub with very attractive white flowers, and the hybrid saucer magnolia (*Magnolia X soulangiana*), a large shrub with vase-shaped flowers that are pink to dark purple, and less commonly white. Flowers of both the star magnolia and the saucer magnolia appear before the leaves.

The wood of the magnolia is light-colored, usually soft, and generally brittle. Its use is limited mainly to boxes, crates, and inexpensive furniture. The fleshy outer portion of the seeds is a food source for wildlife, songbirds, and rodents.

Magnolias are deciduous to evergreen trees or shrubs and often have a spreading shape. The bark is usually thin, smooth, and gray to brownish-gray. The branches and branchlets are often stout, erect to spreading, and brittle. The winter buds are large, narrow, and covered by a single scale. The leaves are large, entire, stalked, and sometimes clustered toward the tips of the branchlets. The flowers are usually large, showy, and produced individually at the tips of the branchlets. They consist of 9 to 18 petal-like structures (in magnolias it is impossible to distinguish between actual petals and sepals of a flower); the outer 3 are often smaller and bent back; the inner ones are cream, cream-white, pale yellow, or pale green in color. There are numerous flattened stamens in each flower that surround a central cone-like structure composed of the numerous carpels. The fruit is leathery, cone-like, sometimes hairy, and contains many seeds. When mature, the bright pink to red seeds are suspended on thin, thread-like strands from the fruits. The seeds are composed of a fleshy outer part and a hard-coated seed in the center.

Key to Magnolia Species

A. Leaves evergreen to nearly evergreen.

  1. Leaves evergreen, thick, leathery, 7.5–20 cm (3–8 in) long, covered with reddish rust-colored hairs on the lower surface; petal-like structures of flowers 8–12 cm (3–5 in) long, 5–10 cm (2–4 in) wide
  Southern magnolia, p. 190

  2. Leaves nearly evergreen to evergreen, thin, papery to only slightly leathery, 6.5–12 cm (2.5–5 in) long, covered with silvery hairs on the lower surface; petal-like structures of flowers 4–6 cm (1.6–2.4 in) long, 1.4–2 cm (0.5–0.8 in) wide   **Sweetbay, p. 191**

B. Leaves deciduous, falling in autumn.

  1. Leaves uniformly distributed along the branchlets.

    a. Flowers showy, fragrant, white to cream-white; leaves 6.5–12 cm (2.5–5 in) long, 3.4–5 cm (1.3–2 in) wide, lower surface covered with silvery hairs
    Sweetbay, p. 191

Southern Magnolia

Sweetbay

b. Flowers not very showy, odorless, pale green to greenish-yellow; leaves 12–22 cm (4.7–8.7 in) long, 8-15 cm (3.2–6 in) wide; lower surface pale green and covered with fine hairs   **Cucumber tree, p. 192**

2. Leaves crowded toward the ends of the branchlets.

  a. Leaves uniformly tapering at the base; flowers with a disagreeable odor   **Umbrella magnolia, p. 194**

  b. Leaves with a heart-shaped base or with ear lobe-like projections at the base; flowers fragrant.

    (1) Leaves with whitish to silvery hairs on the lower surface, 20–80 cm (8–32 in) long, 10–25 cm (4–10 in) wide; flowers with the petal-like structures 15–20 cm (6–8 in) long, 5–12 cm (2–4.8 in) wide   **Bigleaf magnolia, p. 195**

    (2) Leaves smooth (without hairs) and pale green on the lower surface; 12–30 cm (4.7–11.8 in) long, 7–20 cm (2.8–8 in) wide; flowers with the petal-like structures 8–13 cm (3–5 in) long, 2.5–4.5 cm (1–1.8 in) wide   **Fraser magnolia, p. 196**

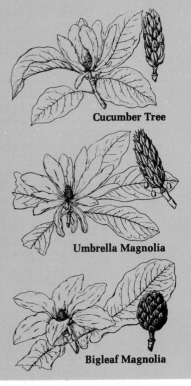

Cucumber Tree

Umbrella Magnolia

Bigleaf Magnolia

Southern Magnolia, Bull Bay   *Magnolia grandiflora* L.

The southern magnolia is a handsome evergreen tree, principally of the Coastal Plain of the southeastern U.S. The trees occur in lowland areas, never above 165 m (540 ft) altitude, along the margins of ponds and swamps, and on hammocks and low rolling hills. When growing in rich, moist, well-drained soil, the trees reach their best growth and greatest size. Southern magnolia does not occur in pure stands but grows in association with other hardwoods, mainly sweetgum, tulip tree, white ash, and American beech.

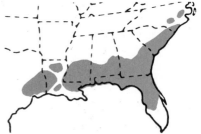

This magnolia is moderately fast-growing and is known to produce flowers as early as 10 years of age. The showy, very fragrant flowers are produced in spring, and the fruits mature and shed their seeds in the fall. Although the seeds are eaten by turkey, quail, other seed-eating birds, squirrels, opposums, mice, and chipmunks, the trees are of limited use to wildlife.

The wood of the southern magnolia is hard, heavy, and white. But it turns brown after exposure to air. It is used in limited amounts for furniture, baskets, and crates. It is a popular ornamental tree and is planted widely throughout the southeastern U.S.

Appearance: large trees 20–30 m (65–100 ft), with a broadly pyramidal to cone shape and a cone-shaped crown; trunk tall, straight, 0.6–1.3 m (1.9–4.3 ft) in diameter.

Southern Magnolia

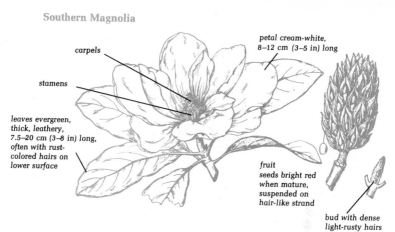

carpels

stamens

leaves evergreen,
thick, leathery,
7.5–20 cm (3–8 in) long,
often with rust-
colored hairs on
lower surface

petal cream-white,
8–12 cm (3–5 in) long

fruit
seeds bright red
when mature,
suspended on
hair-like strand

bud with dense
light-rusty hairs

Bark: thin, 1.2–1.8 cm (0.5–0.7 in) thick, rough, composed of close small plates, brown or gray. **Branches:** stout, covered with dense rust-colored hairs, becoming smooth with age and turning dark brownish-black. **Winter buds:** broadest near the base and tapering to a rounded point, 2.5–3.6 cm (1–1.4 in) long, covered with dense, light, rust-colored hairs. **Leaves:** *evergreen, large,* usually broadest at the middle and tapering to the base and tip, 7.5–20 cm (3–8 in) long, 5–12 cm (2–4.8 in) wide, leathery, *smooth, dark, shiny green above, often covered with reddish rust-colored hairs on the lower surface,* the leafstalks stout, 1–3 cm (0.4–1.2 in) long, usually covered with hairs; stipules free. **Flowers:** large, showy, fragrant, usually with 9 to 14 conspicuous, petal-like structures, thick, fleshy, white to creamy white, broadest at the base to *broadly spoon-shaped* and *rounded at the tip, 8–12 cm (3–5 in) long, 5–10 cm (2–4 in) wide;* stamens numerous, long, narrow, flattened, 12–18 mm (0.5–0.7 in) long; carpels numerous, clustered together to form a central cone-shaped structure, covered with silvery hairs. **Fruits:** dry, cone-like, broadest at the base and tapering to a blunt tip, green turning rusty-brown, hairy, 5–7 cm (2–2.8 in) long. **Seeds:** 9–12 mm (0.4–0.5 in) long, kidney-shaped, covered with a bright red skin.

Sweetbay   *Magnolia virginiana* L.

An attractive tree of the Coastal Plain and Piedmont regions of the eastern U.S., sweetbay grows at low elevations in wet, sandy, often acid soils along streams, swamps, bottom lands, and flatwoods. Largest trees occur in the southern part of the range when growing in deep, rich, moist soils. In the northern part of the range, the trees are deciduous and are often more shrubby in appearance. The trees grow in association with other trees such as the redbay, red maple, holly, and loblolly bay.

Sweetbay is a relatively slow-growing tree that is also spring-flowering. Its value to wildlife is similar to that of the southern magnolia. The pale brown wood is soft, ar-

Sweetbay

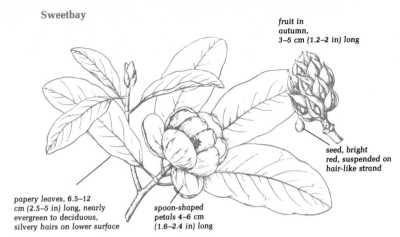

fruit in autumn, 3–5 cm (1.2–2 in) long

seed, bright red, suspended on hair-like strand

papery leaves, 6.5–12 cm (2.5–5 in) long, nearly evergreen to deciduous, silvery hairs on lower surface

spoon-shaped petals 4–6 cm (1.6–2.4 in) long

omatic, straight-grained, easily worked; it finishes well. It is used for furniture, tool handles, boxes, and crates. It is often planted in parks for ornamental purposes.

Appearance: medium-size trees 10–25 m (32–82 ft) with a narrow cone shape or large multi-stemmed shrubs; trunk straight, 0.3–0.5 m (1–1.6 ft) in diameter. **Bark:** thin, 5–9 mm (0.20–0.36 in) thick, smooth, irregularly furrowed and composed of small plates, aromatic when crushed, gray to grayish-brown. **Branches:** usually short, upright to spreading, pale gray; branchlets brittle, covered with tiny hairs, green turning grayish-brown to gray. **Winter buds:** terminal bud broadest at the base and tapering to a rounded point, 1.2–1.8 cm (0.5–0.7 in) long, covered with fine, silky hairs. **Leaves:** *nearly evergreen to evergreen,* variable in shape but usually broadest at the middle or about 3 times longer than broad and with parallel sides, tapering at the base, rounded to pointed at the tip, *6.5–12 cm (2.5–5 in) long, 3.5–5 cm (1.4–2 in) wide,* smooth and shiny dark green on the upper surface, the *lower surface covered with silvery hairs;* the leafstalks stout, 1.5–2.5 cm (0.6–1 in) long, usually smooth. **Flowers:** showy, fragrant, with usually 6 to 14 petal-like structures, the outer 3 curved back away from flowers, white to cream-white, *broadly spoon-shaped to broadest near the tip and rounded at the tip, 4–6 cm (1.6–2.4 in) long, 1.4–2 cm (0.5–0.8 in) wide;* stamens few, long, narrow, flattened, 7–9 mm (0.28–0.36 in) long; carpels numerous, clustered together to form a central cone-shaped structure, smooth, green. **Fruits:** cone-like, egg-shaped to almost globe-shaped, pinkish, 3–5 cm (1.2–2 in) long. **Seeds:** 9–11 cm (3.5–4.4 in) long, variable in shape, covered with a dark red skin.

Cucumber Tree   *Magnolia acuminata* L.

Cucumber trees are the most widespread and hardiest of all native species of magnolias. They occur from western New York to Louisiana and reach their greatest size in the southern Appalachian Mountains. The trees grow on the lower slopes along stream banks and protected valleys usually in deep, rich, moist soils. The trees are found mixed with other hardwoods, such as white oak, white ash, yellow poplar, beech, and sugar maple.

They are rapid-growing trees that often take 25 to 30 years to reach flowering size and may live from 125 to 150 years. The cucumber tree and the southern magnolia are the largest North American magnolias. They produce flowers and some fruits each year and large seed crops every 3 to 5 years. The seeds are consumed by birds and rodents.

The trees are often large enough to be harvested for their timber. The wood is soft, durable, light-grained, and light-colored, but weak. Its main uses are in boxes and crates, with some usage as paneling, inexpensive furniture, and cabinets. Because of its hardiness and ability to tolerate different soil and climatic conditions, the cucumber tree is planted in parks as an ornamental.

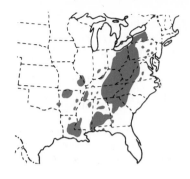

Cucumber Tree

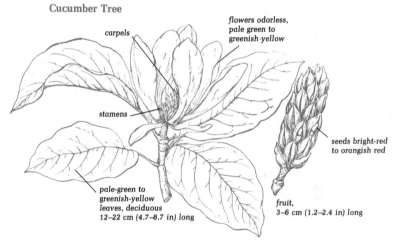

carpels

flowers odorless, pale green to greenish-yellow

stamens

seeds bright-red to orangish red

pale-green to greenish-yellow leaves, deciduous 12–22 cm (4.7–8.7 in) long

fruit, 3–6 cm (1.2–2.4 in) long

Appearance: medium to large trees, 20–30 m (65–100 ft), with a uniform broad pyramid shape and a short pointed crown; trunk straight, often unbranched for lower half, to 1.3 m (4.3 ft) in diameter. **Bark:** moderately thin, 1.2–1.8 cm (0.5–0.7 in) thick, becoming furrowed and scaly, dark brown. **Branches:** slender, spreading to ascending; branchlets brittle, round, reddish-brown, becoming gray with age, usually smooth although some hairs may be present where the leaves are attached. **Winter buds:** terminal buds broadest at the base, slender, 1.2–1.8 cm (0.5–0.7 in) long, covered with numerous, long, silvery hairs. **Leaves: *deciduous,*** usually broadest near the base to broadest near the middle, often uneven and tapering at the base, pointed to long-pointed at the tip, ***12–22 cm (4.7–8.7 in) long, 8–15 cm (3.2–6 in) wide,*** smooth, dark green and shiny on the upper surface, ***pale green and covered with small hairs on the lower surface;*** the leafstalks stout, 2.2–4 cm (0.9–1.6 in) long. **Flowers:** medium-size, ***odorless,*** cup to bell-shaped, upright, with 9 petal-like structures, ***pale green to greenish-yellow,*** the outer 3 bent back, 2–3 cm (0.8–1.2 in) long, the inner 6 upright, 3–8 cm (1.2–3.2 in) long, broadest near the tip; stamens numerous, 8–12 mm (0.3–0.5 in) long; carpels numerous, clustered together to form a central cone. **Fruits:** leathery, cone-like or small cucumber-shape, often irregular-shape, rarely globe-shaped, red, 3–6 cm (1.2–2.4 in) long. **Seeds:** 9–11 mm (0.35–0.44 in) long, almost globe-shaped, compressed, red to reddish-orange.

Umbrella Magnolia

Magnolia tripetala L.

The umbrella magnolia is a small- to medium-size tree of deep rich forests of the southeastern U.S. It occurs in moist soils high in humus and is found mainly in protected ravines, along streams, and on lower mountain slopes to 675 m (2,215 ft) altitude. This magnolia grows in association with many hardwoods, especially sweetgum, yellow poplar, sweet birch, and red maple.

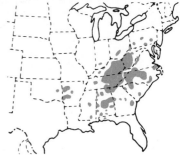

This is a fast-growing tree that flowers in spring. The flowers have a very strong odor that can be disagreeable if too close but delightful from a distance. There is little information about its value to wildlife, but it probably functions in much the same role as the Fraser magnolia. The light-colored wood is soft and weak. It is seldom used because of these qualities and its small size. It is used occasionally as an ornamental.

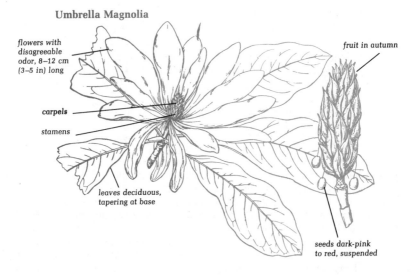

Umbrella Magnolia

flowers with disagreeable odor, 8–12 cm (3–5 in) long

carpels

stamens

leaves deciduous, tapering at base

fruit in autumn

seeds dark-pink to red, suspended

Appearance: small to medium-size trees 10–15 m (32–50 ft), with a spreading open crown, sometimes with several trunks; trunk straight or often leaning when several trunks are present, 15–40 cm (5.9–15.7 in) in diameter. **Bark:** thin, 1–1.4 cm (0.4–0.6 in), smooth, becoming shallowly furrowed with age, light gray. **Branches:** stout, brittle, smooth, green turning light gray, marked with prominent, almost circular scars where prior leaves were attached. **Winter buds:** terminal buds broadest near the base, narrow, long pointed, 3–4 cm (1.2–1.6 in) long, purple. **Leaves:** *deciduous, usually clustered toward the ends of the branchlets,* broadest near the tip, often narrowly so, *tapering at the base.* Pointed at the tip, papery to leathery texture, 20–40 cm (7.9–15.7 in) long, 10–20 cm (3.9–7.9 in) wide, smooth and bright green above, pale green and covered with fine hairs (especially on young leaves) on the underside, the leafstalks stout, 2–4 cm (0.8–1.6 in) long. **Flowers:** large, showy, with a *disagreeable odor close up,* broadly vase-shaped, with 9 or 12 petal-like structures, the outer 3 greenish-white, spoon-shaped and bent backward, 8–12 cm (3–5 in) long, the inner 6 or 9 cream white, broadest above the middle, 8–12 cm (3–5 in) long, 2.5–3.8 cm (1–1.5 in) wide, fleshy; stamens numerous, flattened, 14–20 mm (0.5–0.8 in) long; carpels numerous and grouped into a central cone-shaped mass. **Fruits:** somewhat leathery and cone-like, broadest near the base and tapering to a rounded or slightly pointed tip, green turning pink or red at maturity, 6–19 cm (2.4–7.5 in) long. **Seeds:** 8–11 mm (0.3–0.5 in) long, somewhat compressed, covered with a dark pink to red skin.

Bigleaf Magnolia   *Magnolia macrophylla* Michx.

This handsome, but rare, tree has the largest leaves of any native North American tree. Bigleaf magnolia grows as individual trees or in small groups in sheltered, deep, rich woods, especially in ravines and river valleys of the interior of the southeastern U.S.

Other trees normally found in these areas are yellow poplar, sweetgum, and southern red oak.

This slow-growing magnolia occurs in such limited numbers that it is of no value to wildlife. The brown wood is hard but weak and is not used commercially. The showy fragrant flowers, combined with the intriguing large leaves, have been responsible for its decimation within its range by collectors and would-be gardeners. Although it makes an attractive showpiece in a garden, it is difficult to cultivate and requires complete protection from winds, which can quickly shred the huge leaves.

The Ashe magnolia (*Magnolia ashei*), restricted to the lowlands of northwestern Florida and eastern Texas, is currently recognized as a subspecies of the bigleaf magnolia (*Magnolia macrophylla* subspecies *ashei*) and not distinct enough to be considered a separate species. The Ashe magnolia has a narrower fruit and has slightly smaller flowers.

Appearance: small- to medium-size trees usually 10–15 m (32–50 ft), rarely higher, with a narrow cone shape or widely spreading and rounded top; trunk straight, to 0.5 m (1.6 ft) in diameter. **Bark:** thin, 5–7 mm (0.2–0.3 in) thick, smooth, forming small, inconspicuous plates, pale gray. **Branches:** stout, upright to spreading, gray; branchlets stout, brittle, green and covered with silvery hairs when young and becoming brown to gray and smooth with age, marked with prominent scars where former leaves were attached. **Winter buds:** terminal buds thick, broadest near the base and tapering to a blunt tip, thick, 4–5 cm (1.6–2 in) long, densely covered with long silvery hairs. **Leaves:** *deciduous, usually crowded near the ends of the branchlets,* broadest near the middle to broadest near the tip, *rounded to lobed at the base,* rounded to pointed at the tip, wavy on the edge, very large, *20–80 cm (8–32 in) long, 10–25 cm (4–10 in) broad,* smooth, bright green and shiny above, *the lower surface with whitish to silvery hairs,* especially on the veins, the leaves stalked, the stalks stout, 5–14 cm (2–5.5 in) long, usually hairy. **Flowers:** large, showy, fragrant, cup-shaped, with 9 petal-like structures, the outer 3 greenish, narrowly spoon-shaped, the inner 6 white to cream, broadly spoon-shaped to broadest at the middle or near the base, *15–20 cm (6–8 in) long, 5–12 cm (2–4.8 in) wide;* stamens numerous, 16–18 mm (0.7 in) long;

Bigleaf Magnolia

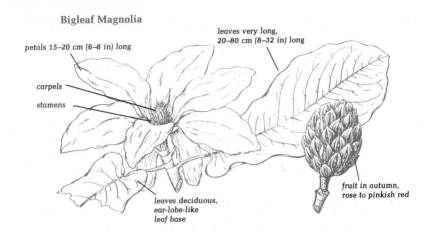

petals 15–20 cm (6–8 in) long

leaves very long,
20–80 cm (8–32 in) long

carpels

stamens

leaves deciduous,
ear-lobe-like
leaf base

fruit in autumn,
rose to pinkish red

carpels numerous, clustered together in a central cone-shaped mass, covered with numerous silvery hairs. **Fruits:** cone-like, almost globe-shaped, rose to pinkish-red, 5–8 cm (2–3.2 in) long. **Seeds:** 10–14 mm (0.4–0.6 in) long, compressed, covered with a dark pink to red skin.

Fraser Magnolia   *Magnolia fraseri* Walt.

The typical Fraser magnolia is an attractive small tree, principally of the lower slopes of the southern Appalachian range. It occurs in deep, rich woods, especially along creeks and stream valleys to altitudes about 1,350 m (4,430 ft). The largest trees are found in moist, well-drained soils. This species commonly occurs with sweetgum, tulip tree, red maple, and sycamore. The variety *pyramidata* was formerly thought to be a separate species, called the pyramid magnolia (*Magnolia pyramidata*) in older texts. This variety occurs farther south, into Florida, and has shorter flower parts and smaller fruits.

Fraser magnolia is a fast-growing magnolia with very fragrant flowers in spring and fruits that mature in the fall. Squirrels, turkeys, quail, and other seed-eating birds feed on the seeds, consuming the outer fleshy portion and depositing the actual seed in their droppings. The wood is white, soft, and weak. Fraser magnolia is occasionally cultivated as an ornamental, although it is often difficult to maintain.

Appearance: small- to medium-size trees 10–15 m (32–50 ft) with a spreading crown; trunk straight, often with multiple stems, usually unbranched for lower half, 20–24 cm (8–9.5 in) in diameter. **Bark:** thin, 4–8 mm (0.1–0.3 in) thick, smooth, forming small, flat plates on older trees, dark brown to grayish brown. **Branches:** spreading, stout, brittle; branchlets stout to slender, brittle, smooth, reddish-brown turning gray with age. **Winter buds:** broadest near the base and tapering to a blunt tip, 2.7–5 cm (1.1–2 in) long, smooth, dark purple to greenish-purple. **Leaves:** *deciduous,* *crowded near the ends of the branchlets,* broadest near the middle, or may be broadly spoon-shaped to broadly lance-shaped, usually with 2 ear-like lobes at the base, rounded to pointed at the tip, *12–30 cm (4.7–11.8 in) long, 7–20 cm (2.8–8 in) wide,* with a papery texture, smooth and bright green above, *duller and smooth beneath,* the veins of the leaves very prominent beneath, the leafstalks slender, 3–8 cm (1.2–3.2 in) long, smooth. **Flowers:** showy, fragrant, cup-shaped to vase-shaped, with 9 petal-like structures, pale yellow to cream white, broadly spoon-shaped to broadest

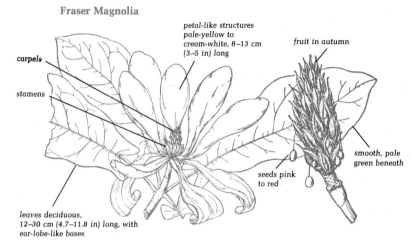

Fraser Magnolia

carpels

stamens

petal-like structures
pale-yellow to
cream-white, 8–13 cm
(3–5 in) long

fruit in autumn

smooth, pale
green beneath

seeds pink
to red

leaves deciduous,
12–30 cm (4.7–11.8 in) long, with
ear-lobe-like bases

near the tip, rounded to pointed at the tip, *8–13 cm (3–5 in) long, 2.5–4.5 cm (1–1.8 in) wide;* stamens numerous, long, narrow, 9–14 mm (0.35–0.55 in) long: carpels numerous, clustered together to form a central cone, smooth, green. **Fruits:** cone-like, broadest near the middle, gradually tapering toward the tip and base, 7–11 cm (2.8–4.3 in) long, bright red. **Seeds:** 9–12 mm (0.4–0.5 in) long, usually broadest near the tip, bright red.

The Tulip Tree Genus   *Liriodendron* L.

There are only 2 species of tulip trees in the world, 1 native to eastern North America (usually called yellow poplar) and the other native to China and Vietnam. The Chinese tulip tree (*Liriodendron chinense*) closely resembles our native tulip but is rarely planted and its flowers are smaller. Both species are important timber trees and are valuable for wildlife.

Tulip trees are large trees with fissured, grayish bark and stout, nearly erect branches and branchlets. Winter buds are flattened and enclosed by 2 scales. The leaves are deciduous, alternate, 2- to 4-lobed, and saddle-shaped. The flowers are tulip-shaped and produced at the ends of the branchlets. The fruits are spindle-shaped cones composed of closely overlapping, winged seeds.

Tulip Tree, Yellow Poplar   *Liriodendron tulipifera* L.

The yellow poplar is an attractive tree of the deciduous forests of the eastern U.S. Although in the southern Appalachian Mountains it occurs at altitudes up to 1,150 m (3,780 ft), yellow poplar normally is found at lower altitudes. The largest trees grow

mm
cm   1   2   3   4   5   6   7   8   9   10   11
in   1   2   3   4

in the Ohio River Valley and the southern Appalachian Mountains. Best growth is obtained in deep, well-drained, but moist, rich soils. Yellow poplars grow in association with many species of trees. But they are found more commonly with hemlock, white oak, red oak, sweetgum, white pine, beech, and maple.

These fast-growing trees are moderately long-lived and may begin to produce flowers, fruits, and seeds at 15 to 20 years of age. The sizeable greenish-orange flowers appear in spring and produce considerable nectar, which often is used by bees. Large quantities of fruits and seeds, which ripen and shed in the autumn, are common. The long-winged seeds serve as food for quail, finches, and cardinals and for such mammals as rabbits, red and gray squirrels, and various mice. Whitetail deer forage on seedlings, saplings, and young trees. Rabbits eat the bark and buds of saplings during the winter months.

The yellow poplar is a very valuable hardwood species. The light yellow to dark brown wood is lightweight, relatively soft, and works easily. Its many uses include interior finishes, furniture, general construction, and plywood. Largely free of insect pests and diseases, this tree is used occasionally as an ornamental or shade tree when there is sufficient room for a large tree.

Tulip Tree, Yellow Poplar

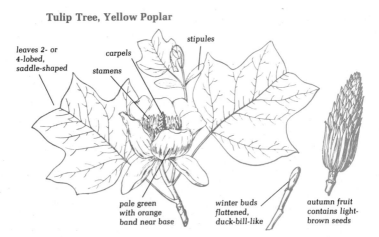

leaves 2- or 4-lobed, saddle-shaped

carpels

stamens

stipules

pale green with orange band near base

winter buds flattened, duck-bill-like

autumn fruit contains light-brown seeds

Appearance: large trees 30–50 m, rarely to 60 (98–165 ft, rarely to 200), with a broadly conical shape, and an open, cone-shaped crown; trunk tall, straight, 1–2 m (3.2–6.6 ft) in diameter. **Bark:** thick, on young trees smooth, dark green, and thin; on older trees becoming rough, irregularly furrowed and forming rounded ridges, ash-gray to brown. **Branches:** stout, usually short; branchlets stout, brittle, reddish-brown to gray. **Winter buds:** *flattened, rounded at the tip (resembles a duck's bill)*, 1.2–1.4 cm (0.5–0.6 in) long, the 2 scales meeting but not overlapping, dark red. **Leaves:** variable in shape but usually broadest at the base and with 2 lobes near the tip and 2 or 4 lobes on the lower sides (often described as saddle-shaped), 7–12 cm (2.8–4.7 in) long, often as broad or broader than long, smooth, bright green above, pale green beneath, the leafstalks, 5–10 cm (2–4 in) long, stipules large, falling away soon after the leaves reach full size. **Flowers: *large, greenish-yellow, tulip-shaped,*** with 3 large, green sepals and 6 erect, broad petals, each petal 4–6 cm (1.6–2.4 in) long, 1.8–3 cm (0.7–1.2 in) wide, blunt at the tip, ***pale green except for an orange band near the base;*** stamens numerous, long, narrow, flattened, short-stalked; carpels numerous, aggregated into a central cone-shaped structure, pale yellow. **Fruits: *dry, oblong cone,*** tapering to a point, 5–7 cm (2–2.8 in) long, ***consisting of numerous winged seeds.*** **Seeds:** 3–4.5 cm (1.2–1.8 in) long, light brown.

The Custard Apple Family
Annonaceae

The custard apple family is made up of approximately 800 species of trees, shrubs, and vines throughout the world. These grow primarily in tropical climates, with a few members in temperate regions. Of the 80 genera, only 2 are found in North America — the pawpaw (*Asimina*) and the custard apple (*Annona*). Each has 1 species of tree native to North America.

The custard apple family is of minor economic importance. Many members of this family have fleshy edible fruits that serve as a supplement to the diet of many people living in tropical countries. Ylang-ylang perfume is obtained from a member of this family. The wood is of poor quality and the trees are too small to be used commercially.

Members of this family are deciduous or evergreen trees, shrubs, or vines with simple, alternate, aromatic leaves. The flowers almost always have both sexes present and are composed of 3 (rarely 2) sepals and 6 petals arranged in an inner and outer series. There are numerous spirally arranged stamens and few to many distinct carpels in the center of the flowers. The fruits are berries or compound fruits (made up of several fused carpels), usually fleshy. Seeds are large and embedded in the fruit.

Key to Custard Apple Genera

A. Flowers green turning deep purple at maturity; trees of eastern North America

Pawpaw, p. 200

B. Flowers cream-white to pale yellow; trees of southern Florida **Custard apple, p. 201**

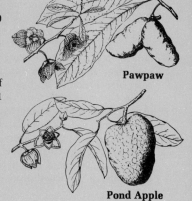

Pawpaw

Pond Apple

The Pawpaw Genus

Asimina Adans.

The pawpaw is a small North American genus of 6 to 8 species; all but one are shrubs of the coastal regions of the southeastern U.S., primarily of pinelands and lowland scrub forests. One species of pawpaw, *Asimina triloba*, is a small tree. The sweet edible fruits are of value to wildlife.

The pawpaws are small trees or shrubs with papery deciduous leaves that emit an unpleasant odor when crushed. The flowers are solitary, stalked, usually hanging, and green turning purple at maturity. They are composed of 3 outer sepals and 2 rows of inner petals. There are numerous, thin, narrow stamens and from 3 to 15 carpels grouped into a central mass. The fruit varies in shape, but is often cylindric and becomes soft, fleshy, and aromatic at maturity. The large seeds are embedded in the fleshy fruit.

Pawpaw

Asimina triloba (L.) Dunal

The pawpaw is an attractive small tree with very large leaves. Primarily a tree of the southeastern U.S., the pawpaw grows in deep, rich, moist soil such as that found in river valleys and bottomlands. When growing in rich soil, it often forms dense

thickets. This understory tree often is found growing in association with sweetgum, swamp chestnut, oak, cherrybark oak, Shumard's oak, and black gum.

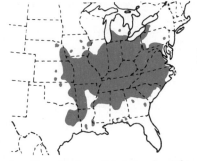

A moderately fast-growing tree, the pawpaw produces its unusual purple flowers in spring, and the large edible fruits mature in late summer or early fall of the same year. The large, fleshy seed fruits are sought eagerly by raccoons, opossums, squirrels, bears, and turkeys. The fruits are delicious to eat, provided one can get to them before the animals do. Early settlers made yellow dye from the ripe pulp of the fruits.

The lightweight wood is soft, weak, light yellow, often streaked with brown or red. Because of these qualities and the tree's small size, pawpaw wood is not used commercially. The trees are planted occasionally for their attractive form and large leaves. They will do well in low, wet sites that usually are unsuited for many other trees.

Appearance: small trees or large shrubs 5–10 m (16–33 ft) with an open form; trunk straight, 10–30 cm (4–11.8 in) in diameter. **Bark:** thin, 2–4 mm (0.1–0.2 in) thick, dark brown, smooth but often spotted with gray blotches and small wart-like projections on older trees. **Branches:** slender, spreading, smooth to covered with fine rust-colored hairs; branchlets slender, light brown tinged with red, covered with rusty hairs when young, becoming smooth with age. **Winter buds:** flattened, pointed at the tip, 2–4 mm (0.08–0.16 in) long, covered with numerous rust-colored hairs. **Leaves:** deciduous, large, simple, usually narrow and broadest near the tip, 18–30 cm (7–11.8 in) long, 8–14 cm (3.2–5.5 in) wide, papery, sharp-pointed at the tip, tapering to the base, light green on the upper surface, pale green beneath, covered with fine, rust-colored hairs when young, becoming smooth above with age. **Flowers:** inconspicuous, *borne along the stems on the wood produced in the previous season,* stalked, broadly bell-

Pawpaw

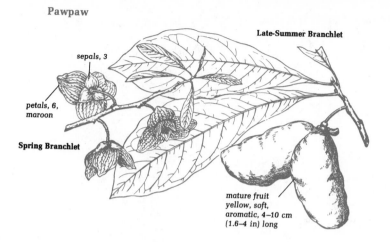

Late-Summer Branchlet

sepals, 3

petals, 6,
maroon

Spring Branchlet

mature fruit
yellow, soft,
aromatic, 4–10 cm
(1.6–4 in) long

shaped, 4–5 cm (1.6–2 in) across, **green turning deep purple,** sepals 3, broadest near the base, hairy, petals 6, thick, almost circular, 2–2.6 cm (0.8–1.1 in) long, the outer 3 often spreading; stamens numerous, linear; carpels 3 to 15. **Fruits:** *irregularly cylinder-shaped, aromatic, green and firm but turning yellow, then black, soft and fleshy at maturity,* 4–10 cm (1.6–4 in) long, 1.5–3.5 cm (0.6–1.4 in) in diameter, the seeds embedded in the fruit. **Seeds:** flattened, 16–20 mm (0.6–0.8 in) long, dark brown.

The Custard Apple Genus

Annona L.

The custard apples are a medium-size genus of 60 to 70 species of trees and shrubs of tropical regions, mainly of the Americas. Only 1 species, pond apple, *Annona glabra,* is native to North America and is confined to southern Florida. Custard apples usually have large, edible fruits and are cultivated widely throughout the tropical world as a food source. In addition to the sugar apple, *Annona squamosa,* 2 other tropical American species are occasionally planted in southern Florida, the soursop, *Annona reticulata,* and the cherimola, *Annona cherimola.* Their fruit has some economic value.

The custard apples are trees or shrubs with persistent, leathery, pungently aromatic leaves. They have thin, usually smooth, bark and spreading to ascending branches. Because they are tropical plants, they do not form winter buds. Flowers contain both sexes, and they occur singly or in clusters on the branchlets that were produced in the previous years. The flowers are cream-white to yellow and composed of 3 small sepals and 6 petals. The petals are arranged in 2 series; the outer series usually is larger than the inner one. There are many narrow stamens in each flower. They surround the numerous carpels, which are on the raised base of the flower (receptacle). The fruit is compound (the result of the fusion of several carpels), large, heart-shaped, globe-shaped, or broadest at the base, fleshy, and usually aromatic at maturity. There are many large seeds embedded in the fleshy fruit.

Key to Custard Apple Species

A. Leaves 7.5–13 cm (3–5 in) long; flower petals wide, broadest near the base; fruits usually with a slightly raised network of veins on the surface
Pond apple, p. 202

B. Leaves 10–16 cm (4–6.3 in) long; flower petals narrow, broadest near the middle to almost lance-shaped; fruits covered with small knobby or raised projections   **Sugar apple, p. 203**

Pond Apple   *Annona glabra* L.

The pond apple is a small to medium-size tree of southern Florida, Central America, the West Indies, and northern South America. In southern Florida, the trees grow along the banks of freshwater streams, ponds, sinkholes, or swampy hammocks. Due to cutting and clearing activities, the trees are no longer as common as they once were. At one time they formed nearly pure stands on the borders of Lake Okeechobee.

The large heart-shaped fruits mature in fall and become fleshy. They are edible and have been used to make jelly and custards. But they are inferior to the fruits of several introduced tropical species of custard apple. As a result, people seldom use them. Wildlife feeds on the aromatic fleshy fruits. The light brown and yellow streaked wood is lightweight, soft, and weak. It is of no commercial importance.

Appearance: small to medium-size trees, 10–16 m (32–53 ft), with a spreading shape and a rounded crown; trunk straight, short, thicker and spreading at the base, 20–45 cm (8–17.7 in) in diameter. **Bark:** thin, 2–4 mm (0.08–0.16 in) thick, dark reddish-brown, smooth but developing shallow fissures and small spreading scales with age. **Branches:** stout, spreading, often contorted; branchlets slender, yellowish-brown turning brown with age, smooth. **Winter buds:** do not form. **Leaves:** simple, broadest near the middle to longer than broad and almost parallel sides, 7.5–13 cm (3–5 in) long, 3.5–5 cm (1.4–2 in) wide, pointed at the tip, tapering to rounded at the base, aromatic, bright green above, pale green beneath, leathery, smooth (without hairs) on both surfaces. **Flowers: *solitary, occurring on wood produced during the previous year,*** hanging or nodding, 2.4–2.6 cm (1 in) in diameter, short-stalked, ***cream-white to pale yellow,*** sepals 3, broadest near the base and tapering to a cone-shaped tip, the

Pond Apple

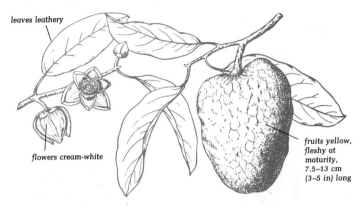

leaves leathery

flowers cream-white

fruits yellow, fleshy at maturity, 7.5–13 cm (3–5 in) long

outer 3, 3–3.5 cm (1.2–1.4 in) long, the inner 3 slightly smaller, the outer ones marked near the base with a red spot; stamens numerous, 3.2–4 mm (0.1–0.2 in) long; carpels numerous. **Fruits:** broadest near the base, almost heart-shaped, depressed at point of attachment and rounded at the tip, 7.5–13 cm (3–5 in) long and up to 9 cm (3.6 in) across, light green and firm turning *yellow, marked with brown spots and becoming aromatic and fleshy when mature.* The seeds numerous, embedded in the fruit, 11–14 mm (0.5 in) long, almost rounded, slightly flattened.

Sugar Apple, Sweetsop   *Annona squamosa* L.

This tropical American tree has been introduced into southern Florida and cultivated for its large, sweet, edible fruits. Unfortunately the ripe fruits are unsuitable for shipping; thus the sugar apple is unknown to most North Americans. Sugar apples have naturalized in the Florida Keys and survive there without cultivation. The trees are *similar* in appearance *to the pond apple, but they have larger leaves, very narrow petals, and a sweet fruit that is covered with small knobby points.*

Sugar Apple

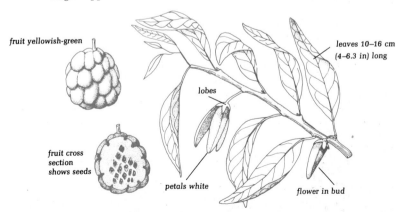

fruit yellowish-green

leaves 10–16 cm (4–6.3 in) long

lobes

fruit cross section shows seeds

petals white

flower in bud

The Wild Cinnamon Family Canallaceae

This is a small family of a dozen species of trees distributed among 5 genera and occurring in tropical America and in Madagascar and tropical Africa. One genus, the cinnamon bark or *Canella*, reaches North America and then only in extreme southern Florida. The family is unimportant economically and of little or no value to wildlife.

The trees in this family have bark that emits a sharp odor when broken or crushed. The evergreen leaves are simple, alternate on the branchlets, entire along the margin, and gland-dotted. Both sexes are present in each flower, which is produced singly or in small clusters. Each flower has 4 or 5 distinct sepals, 4 or 5 free or fused petals, and numerous stamens with a single pistil. The fruit is a berry containing 2 to many seeds.

The Cinnamon Bark Genus *Canella* P. Browne

This genus is generally felt to contain 1 species; therefore, the description of the species will also serve for the genus.

Cinnamon Bark, Canella *Canella winterana* (L.) Gaertn.

The canella is a small tree found only in Florida in the Cape Sable region and the Florida Keys. The rounded crown and shiny dark-green leaves help to identify this tree in the field. Very little is known about its natural history and its role in the plant communities in which it occurs. It is a slow-growing tree that flowers in the fall, and the fruits ripen in the spring. The small, fleshy berries are eaten by birds, which aid in dispersing the seeds.

The dark reddish-brown wood is very hard and heavy, strong, and close-grained. It is not utilized commercially because of its limited range and small size. The inner bark was once stripped and sold as wild cinnamon bark. This bitter but very aromatic property was used in producing tonics and as a spice.

Appearance: small trees 7–10 m (23–33 ft) with an open to compact shape and a round-topped crown; trunk straight, 15–25 cm (6–10 in) in diameter. **Bark:** thin, 2–4 mm (0.1–0.2 in), light gray, on mature trees forming short, thick scales, *aromatic when cut or crushed.* **Branches:** slender, spreading; branchlets stout, rounded, light gray to gray. **Winter buds:** do not form. **Leaves:** alternate on the branchlets, evergreen, narrow but broadest at the tip, 7.5–12.7 cm (3–5 in) long, 3.7–5 cm (1.5–2 in) wide, *leathery,* blunt or rounded at the tip and tapering to a narrow base, *gland-dotted,* dark to bright green, shiny; leafstalks short, grooved on the upper surface. **Flowers:** small, produced in small rounded clusters at or near the tips of the branchlets, the individual *flowers* about 1.1–1.3 cm (0.4–0.5 in) across, upright, *reddish purple,* sepals 4 or 5, almost circular in shape with a rounded tip, upright, leathery; petals 4 or 5, oblong, 4.5–5 mm (0.2 in) long, rounded at the tip, fleshy; stamens numerous, 15 to 20 per flower and fused into a tube and surrounding the single pistil. **Fruits:** *soft, fleshy*

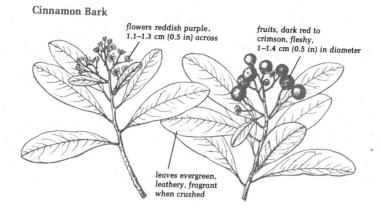

Cinnamon Bark

flowers reddish purple,
1.1–1.3 cm (0.5 in) across

fruits, dark red to
crimson, fleshy,
1–1.4 cm (0.5 in) in diameter

leaves evergreen,
leathery, fragrant
when crushed

berry, globe-shaped or nearly so, ***1–1.4 cm (0.5 in) in diameter, dark red to crimson, ripening in spring.*** **Seeds:** 2 to several per fruit, often broadest near the tip to kidney-shaped, 6–8 mm (0.2–0.3 in) long, black, shiny.

The Anise Tree Family

Illiciaceae

This family is composed of a single genus, the anise tree or *Illicium* with most of the species occurring in southeast Asia. This group of trees was included in the magnolia family for many years; however, studies have shown clearly that it is distinct enough to warrant its own family. Because it contains only 1 genus, the description of the family is the same as the information given for the genus below.

The Anise Tree Genus

Illicium L.

There are approximately 35 species of anise trees, most of which are native to southeastern Asia. However, 5 species are native to the Americas. Of the 5, 2 occur in the southeastern U.S.: the Florida anise tree and the yellow anise tree. The other 3 are restricted to the West Indies and Mexico. Because of their purple to dark-red flowers, members of this genus are grown sometimes as ornamental plants. An oil obtained from one of the Asian species is used in flavorings, medicines, and as a condiment, but it makes the leaves and other plant parts unpalatable for most wildlife.

This genus is made up of small trees or shrubs with evergreen leaves that are alternate on the branchlets, entire on the margin, and slightly leathery. The flowers are solitary, or in 2s or 3s, near the tips of the branchlets. The sepals and petals of the flowers are so similar that they cannot be distinguished. They are numerous, as are the fleshy stamens, and both are arranged in several concentric series. Ten to 15 free carpels are present in the center of the flower and develop into the distinctive fruit. The fruit is dry, flattened on the top, and composed of a series of capsule-like structures, each splitting open at maturity to release the seeds. The seeds are flattened and covered with a hard, shiny coat.

Key to Anise Tree Species

A. Flowers deep red to purple, the petal-like structures 20 to 30, long, narrow
Florida anise tree, p. 206
B. Flowers yellowish, the petal-like structures 5 to 12, broadest near the base to almost circular
Yellow anise tree, p. 207

Florida Anise Tree   *Illicium floridanum* Ellis

The Florida anise tree is a small, often multiple-stemmed, tree or large shrub of the Coastal Plain from northwestern Florida around to southeastern Louisiana. It reappears in northeastern Mexico. The tree grows in lowland wet areas, often in sandy soils along streams, swamps, and at the heads of bays. The interesting star-shaped flowers and fruits that are produced just under the leaves, which are clustered near the tips of the branchlets, are particularly distinguishing features.

This species is slow-growing, and the dark red or purple flowers are produced in spring, with the fruits maturing in summer. The foliage and fruit are of no value to wildlife; in fact, both are poisonous to cattle and probably to other mammals.

Florida Anise

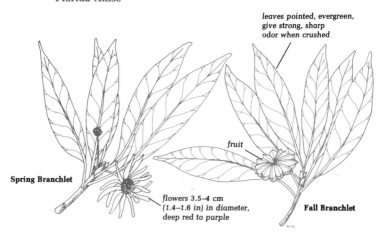

leaves pointed, evergreen, give strong, sharp odor when crushed

fruit

Spring Branchlet

flowers 3.5–4 cm (1.4–1.6 in) in diameter, deep red to purple

Fall Branchlet

Appearance: shrubs or small, usually ***multiple-stemmed, trees to 6–8 m (20–26 ft)*** with an open shape and a rounded crown; trunk often crooked, tall, often leaning, 5–7.6 cm (2–3 in) in diameter. **Bark:** thin, dark brown, smooth but developing narrow shallow fissures with age. **Branches:** slender, upright to spreading, smooth, green turning dark brown with age. **Winter buds:** do not form. **Leaves:** alternate on the branchlets, often clustered near the tips, ***evergreen,*** usually broadest near the middle and tapering toward the tip and base, 6.3–10 cm (2.5–4 in) long, 3–5 cm (1.2–2 in) wide, ***sharp pointed at the tip,*** narrowing at the base, leathery, dark green above, paler beneath, ***with a strong, sharp odor when crushed.*** **Flowers:** produced near the tips of the branchlets, solitary, long-stalked, star-shaped, 3.5–4 cm (1.4–1.6 in) in diameter, deep red to purple, sepals and petals indistinguishable, 20 to 30, long, narrow, sharp-pointed; stamens numerous and surrounding the 10 to 15 free carpels. **Fruits:** ***dry, star-shaped,*** composed of 10 to 15 rays, each splitting open at maturity. **Seeds:** 1 per ray, flattened, broadest near the middle, 5–7 mm (0.2–0.3 in) long, pale to dark brown.

Yellow Anise Tree

Illicium parviflorum Michx.

This is a small tree or shrub that is found only in northeastern Florida, primarily along the headwaters of the St. Johns River. It grows in low, wet sites and, like its relative, is often multi-stemmed. The yellow anise tree is readily distinguished from the other species because this one has ***yellowish flowers with much wider sepals and petals and fewer stamens and leaves with rounded tips;*** while the Florida anise tree has leaves with sharp-pointed tips. Its other qualities are similar to those of the Florida anise tree.

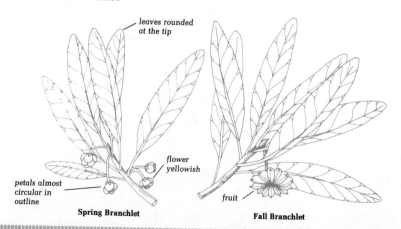

Yellow Anise

leaves rounded at the tip

flower yellowish

petals almost circular in outline

fruit

Spring Branchlet

Fall Branchlet

The Laurel Family

Lauraceae

The laurel family contains 2,400 to 2,500 species of plants distributed among approximately 35 genera. It is essentially a tropical family but has many representatives extending into warm temperate regions of the world. The greatest concentrations of members of the laurel family are in tropical America and southeastern Asia. Eight genera (3 of them contain only shrubs or herbs) are native to North America with a ninth, Cinnamon (*Cinnamomum*), introduced but now naturalized in extreme southeastern U.S. Seven of the 8 native genera are restricted to the eastern and southeastern U.S., while the other, California laurel (*Umbellularia*), has a single species in the mountains of Oregon and California. The sweet bay (*Laurus nobilis*), native to the Mediterranean, has been planted widely in cities in the southeastern, southwestern, and Pacific coastal areas of the U.S.

The laurel family is economically important, although the most valuable members are tropical or subtropical. Cinnamon, the frequently used spice, and camphor, a component of many medicines, are obtained from members of this family. The avocado, a delicious oil-rich fruit, belongs to the laurel family. Many of the tropical species are valuable timber trees because of their hard, fragrant wood, which is suitable for furniture and cabinets. In North America this family is of limited value to wildlife. Birds, especially phoebes and crested flycatchers, feed on the small fruits of sassafras, while thrushes feed on the fleshy fruits of the spice bush (*Lindera benzoin*), a shrubby member of this family.

Members of this family are trees or shrubs with evergreen or rarely deciduous leaves that are usually alternate on the branchlets. The branchlets, roots, leaves, flowers, and fruits contain oils that are responsible for the pleasant odor when the plant parts are broken or crushed. The leaves are simple and usually entire along the margins; rarely are they lobed (sassafras). Flowers usually are grouped in clusters of various shapes and borne in the axils of the leaves. The flowers usually have both sexes present, although some have separate male and female flowers present on the same plant. Each flower is composed of an outer series of 3 sepals and an inner series of 3 petals (both sepals and petals look alike) and 12 stamens arranged in 4 rings. There is a single small pistil in the center of the flower. The fruit is a berry, or berry-like, consisting generally of an outer, fleshy part and a hard, inner seed.

Key to Laurel Genera

A. Trees deciduous, the leaves falling in autumn, leaves entire on the margin, or 2- or 3-lobed; flowers usually either male or female, appearing in spring before or as the new leaves unfold; eastern U.S. **Sassafras, p. 209**

B. Trees evergreen, the leaves persisting throughout the year, leaves always entire (without lobes), flowers with both sexes present in same flower, appearing in spring in the axils of mature leaves.

Sassafras

1. Flowers with 3 fertile stamens; fruits covered at the base by a thick, double-margined, cup-like structure (resembles an acorn); southern tropical Florida **Licaria, p. 211**
2. Flowers with 9 fertile stamens; fruits lacking a thick, cup-like structure at the base of the fruit or, if present, then small and with a single margin.

    a. Flowers with some sterile stamens that are flattened petal-like structures.

        (1) Calyx lobes of the flowers deciduous, not present at the base of the fruit.

            (a) Flowers arranged in many-flowered, flat-topped clusters; California
                California laurel, p. 212
            (b) Flowers arranged in many-flowered, elongated, or pointed clusters.

                (b1) Leaves not strongly spicy when crushed and with feather-like veins; includes red bay, swamp bay, avocado **Persea, p. 213**
                (b2) Leaves with strong spicy or camphor odor when crushed and with 3 main veins all originating at the base of the leaves; includes camphor tree **Cinnamon, p. 217**

        (2) Calyx persistent, present on the base of the fruit; southeastern U.S.
                Persea, p. 213

    b. Flowers with the sterile stamens tiny, reduced, thread-like structures
        Lancewood, p. 218

Gulf Licaria

California Laurel

Red Bay

Camphor Tree

The Sassafras Genus
Sassafras Trew

Sassafras is a small genus of only 3 species: 1 in central mainland China, another in Taiwan, and the third in eastern North America. Neither of the oriental sassafras trees is cultivated in North America.

    Sassafras are small to large trees with thick, furrowed, dark reddish-brown bark at maturity. The bark, roots, branches, branchlets, leaves, flowers, and fruits contain oils that give off a pleasant spicy odor when broken or crushed. Branches and branchlets are usually slender and brittle. Winter buds consist of a few overlapping scales. The leaves are deciduous, simple, alternate on the branchlets, broadest near the middle, entire along margin, and 1-lobed or 3-lobed near the tip. Individual trees usually bear either male or female flowers. Although some flowers appear to have both sexes present in the same flower, they are functionally either male or female. Flowering is in spring, and the flowers usually are grouped in few-flowered, hanging clusters produced at or near the growing tips of the branchlets. The 6 sepals and petals look alike and are small, spreading, yellowish-green lobes. The male flowers contain 9 stamens, whereas the female flowers have 6 sterile stamens and a single central pistil. The fruits are olive-shaped to nearly globe-shaped berries with a dark-colored skin and a thin fleshy layer surrounding a single seed.

Sassafras — *Sassafras albidum* (Nutt.) Nees

Native sassafras are attractive and interesting small to moderately large trees of the eastern deciduous forests of the U.S. The trees generally grow in moist, well-drained soils of open woodlands from sea level to 1,350 m (4,430 ft) elevation in the southern

Appalachian Mountains. In the southeastern U.S., sassafras are among the first tree species to invade abandoned fields. They often appear in clumps or small groves because the parent tree spreads by underground runners. Sassafras do not form pure stands but grow in association with persimmon, bear oak, sweetgum, flowering dogwood, hornbeam, and pawpaw.

The trees are moderately fast-growing and may begin flowering as early as 10 years of age. The sexes are on separate trees. Trees bearing female flowers produce good seed crops every 2 or 3 years. Seed crops are not abundant enough to be of much value to wildlife, although bobwhite quail, wild turkeys, squirrels, foxes, and black bears feed on the fruits. Whitetail deer occasionally forage on the buds and young foliage.

The orange-brown wood is soft, lightweight, brittle, and of little value as timber. Different plant parts, especially the bark on the roots, contain oil of sassafras, which is used to make sassafras tea, perfume, soaps. It was once used in patent medicines.

Sassafras

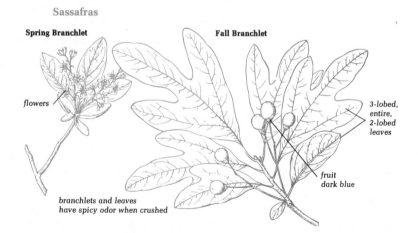

Spring Branchlet

Fall Branchlet

flowers

3-lobed,
entire,
2-lobed
leaves

*fruit
dark blue*

*branchlets and leaves
have spicy odor when crushed*

Appearance: small to medium-size trees, usually 10 to 15 m (32–50 ft), occasionally higher, with an open form and a flat-topped crown; trunk short, thick, to 1 m (3.3 ft) in diameter, rarely larger. **Bark:** thin on young trees, becoming thick, to 3 cm (1.2 in), on older ones, reddish-brown to brown, becoming rough due to deep and irregular furrows separating broad, flattened ridges. **Branches:** short, stout, often irregular, spreading; *branchlets* slender, hairy when young, becoming smooth with age, *yellowish-green, with a spicy odor when broken.* **Winter buds:** broadest near the base and pointed at the tip, 6–8 mm (0.2–0.3 in) long. **Leaves:** deciduous, simple, *in 3 shapes (entire, with a 1-sided lobe, or 3-lobed),* broadest near the base, 10–15 cm (4–6 in) long, 5–10 cm (2–4 in) wide, tapering to a point at the tip and tapering at the base, densely hairy when young, bright green, papery, with a spicy odor when crushed; the leafstalks 2–2.75 cm (0.8–1.1 in) long. **Flowers:** produced in stalked branched clusters at the ends of the twigs in spring, the flowers yellow, small, 5–8 mm (0.2–0.3 in) in diameter, *individual trees and flowers either male or female,* the male flowers with 9 stamens arranged in 3 progressively inward rings, the *inner 3 with stalked glands,* the female flowers with 6 short, sterile stamens and a single central pistil. **Fruits:** an egg-shaped to olive-like fleshy fruit, 1–1.5 cm (0.4–0.6 in) long, dark blue, stalked, the stalk 3.5–4 cm (1.4–1.6 in) long, enclosed at the base by a small, bright red cup (the persistent calyx and corolla).

The Licaria Genus   *Licaria* Aubl.

This assemblage of perhaps 40 species is found in tropical America with 1 of the West Indian species, the Gulf licaria (*Licaria triandra*) extending into south Florida. The genus *Licaria* is not easy to recognize, and only subtle differences of the flowers and fruits distinguish it from other genera in the laurel family.

Licarias are shrubs or trees with simple evergreen leaves. The small flowers usually are produced in few- to many-flowered clusters. They contain both sexes and consist of 6 sepals and petals that are fused near the base into a tube. There are 3 fertile stamens in a ring near the center of the flowers, while the outermost ring of stamens is aborted and modified to resemble a sepal or petal. A tiny single pistil is present in the center of each flower. The fruit is a small berry partly enclosed near the base by a cup.

Gulf Licaria   *Licaria triandra* (Sw.) Kostermans

The Gulf licaria is a very rare tree in North America, being restricted to southern Florida. The greatest concentration of these trees was in an area near Miami. But urban and suburban expansion has reduced the native stands of this species in that area to a few standing trees. It also occurs in the West Indies.

Important identification features of this species are the *large evergreen leaves that are broadest near the middle and have long, pointed tips.* The tiny inconspicuous flowers are overlooked easily. The fruit is dark blue and acorn-shaped but with a fleshy outer layer and enclosed at the base by a bright red cup.

Gulf Licaria

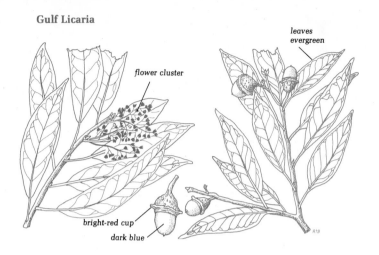

flower cluster

leaves evergreen

bright-red cup

dark blue

The California Laurel Genus   *Umbellularia* (Nees) Nutt.

This genus contains only 1 species, the California laurel, *Umbellularia californica.* As a result, the description for the species also serves as the generic description.

California Laurel, Pacific Myrtle, Pepperwood

Umbellularia californica (Hook. & Arn.) Nutt.

California laurels are valuable hardwood trees of southwestern Oregon, coastal regions of California, and the western slopes of the Sierra Nevada. The trees usually are found at lower altitudes from sea level to 1,000 m (3,280 ft) elevation; in the

Sierras they can reach 2,000 m (6,560 ft) on the mountain slopes. Tolerant of different soil types and conditions, these trees grow in flatlands, lower slopes of hills and mountains, and rock outcroppings; but the largest trees occur in deep, rich soils typical of alluvial sites such as valley bottoms. Unfortunately, many of the larger stands of native California laurels have been cut. They grow in association with many other western tree species including the coastal redwood, sequoia, Port Orford cedar, and the Douglas fir.

These attractive trees are slow-growing and often multi-trunked when growing in poorer soils. The trees begin flowering when very young and flower regularly from December to early spring. Abundant seed crops usually are produced each year. The edible fruits ripen in late summer and early autumn and then fall soon afterward. Gray squirrels, dusky-footed wood rats, other rodents, and some birds feed on the fruits and seeds.

The rich, light brown wood is hard, strong, heavy; and the beautifully grained texture can be finished to a high polish. Although the limited quantity of larger logs and resulting higher costs have limited much of its use today to smaller items, this laurel has been used to make fine cabinets and furniture. Candlesticks, bowls, plates, and an assortment of other specialty products are produced from the wood for the West Coast tourist market.

California Laurel

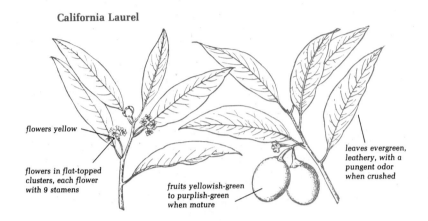

flowers yellow

flowers in flat-topped clusters, each flower with 9 stamens

fruits yellowish-green to purplish-green when mature

leaves evergreen, leathery, with a pungent odor when crushed

Appearance: small to medium-size trees, 7–25 m (23–82 ft), or occasionally shrubby, with broadly rounded, dense crown; trunk straight, often multi-trunked, 0.3–1 m (1–3.3 ft) in diameter, rarely larger. **Bark:** moderately thin, 1.2–2 cm (0.5–0.8 in) thick, dark brown, developing into thin, closely pressed scales. **Branches:** slender, erect, or nearly so; branchlets slender, yellowish-green, smooth, and with a pungent odor when broken. **Winter buds:** tiny, naked (without scales covering the leaf embryos). **Leaves:** simple, alternate on the branchlets, persistent (evergreen), lance-shaped to broadest near the middle, 8.6–13 cm (3.4–5.1 in) long, entire on the margin, pointed to slightly rounded at the tip, tapering at the base, dark green, shiny above, pale beneath, leathery, with a spicy or pungent odor when crushed; leafstalks short, 3–5 mm (0.1–0.2 in) long. **Flowers:** *produced in 4- to 9-flowered, flat-topped clusters* in the axils of the outer leaves, the flowers yellow, small, 10–14 mm (0.4–0.6 in) across, the 6 lobes of the calyx and corolla 7–9 mm (0.3–0.4 in) long, broadest near the tip, spreading, stamens 9, in several series, the inner 3 with tiny stalked glands; pistil 1. **Fruits:** *olive-like, somewhat fleshy,* almost globe-shaped to broadest near the base, *2–2.6 cm (0.8–1 in) long,* green turning yellowish-green or purplish-green, with a thin, fleshy layer surrounding the single seed. **Seed:** broadest at the base, slightly smaller than the fruit, with a hard, light brown outer seed coat.

The Persea Genus

Persea Miller

This is a large, primarily tropical, American genus of approximately 150 members with 3 species extending into North America: the avocado (*Persea americana*) of southern Florida, swamp bay (*P. palustris*), and red bay (*P. borbonia*) of the Gulf and Atlantic Coastal Plain to Virginia. Excluding the avocado, the native species are so closely related that botanists may someday consider them one very variable species.

These are trees or shrubs with evergreen leaves that are alternate on the branchlets. The flowers are produced in branched clusters near the ends of the branchlets at the junction of the leaves with the branchlets. The individual flowers are small, inconspicuous, and bisexual. The calyx and corolla (very similar in appearance) consist of 6 lobes; the outer 3 are hairy and persist on the base of the fruit after flowering. There are 9 fertile anthers and 3 sterile ones arranged in a series of concentric rings. The pistil consists of a tiny centrally located ovary. Fruits may be small and globe-shaped or large and fleshy, and consist of a thick, outer soft layer surrounding a large seed.

Key to Persea Species

Swamp Bay

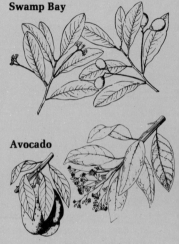

A. Fruits small, 0.7–3 cm (0.3–1.2 in) long, globe-shaped or nearly so; the calyx persisting at the base of the fruit.

    1. Branchlets smooth; leaves smooth beneath; southeastern U.S.   **Red bay, p. 214**
    2. Branchlets hairy; leaves hairy on the lower surface; southeastern U.S.
        Swamp bay, p. 215

Avocado

B. Fruits large, 7–20 cm (3–8 in) long, broadest near the base to pear-shaped; the calyx falling away and not persisting at the base of the fruit; planted widely and now naturalized
        Avocado, p. 216

Red Bay

Persea borbonia (L.) Spreng.

Red bay are attractive trees of the Gulf and Atlantic coastal plains from Texas to Florida to Virginia. The trees grow in sandy to rich, moist soils of low woodlands, coastal forests, along bogs, streams, and swamps. The trees do not form pure stands but rather grow in association with red maple, blackgum, sweetgum, post oak, laurel oak, and bluejack oak. Populations of the red bay occurring in dry sandy areas of Florida may typically have smaller leaves that are densely hairy on the lower surface.

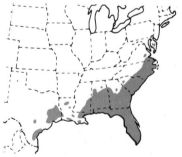

These trees have small, greenish flowers that appear in spring and are followed by the dark blue fruits that ripen in late summer or early fall. The fruits are only slightly fleshy and of limited importance to wildlife. The seeds are eaten by squirrels, quail, and other non-game seed-eating birds. Whitetail deer browse the foliage.

The reddish-colored wood is hard, heavy, close-grained, but brittle. It can be worked and is suitable for interior uses such as cabinets. But trees with large, straight trunks are not sufficiently common to be of commercial importance. The leaves, fresh or dried, can be used as a spice to flavor meats, soups, and other dishes. Because of its attractive evergreen leaves and pest-free nature, the red bay is an excellent tree for cultivation as an ornamental.

Red Bay

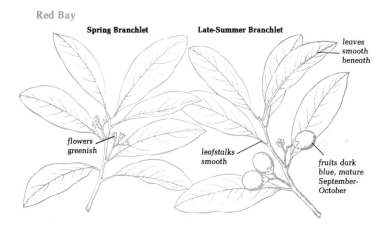

Appearance: large shrubs, small or medium-size trees to 20 m (66 ft), often with a cylinder shape and a dense, rounded crown; trunk straight, often leaning, to 1 m (3.3 ft) in diameter. **Bark:** thick, 1.2–2 cm (0.5–0.8 in), reddish-brown to brownish-purple, irregularly furrowed with shallow interlacing fissures and flattened ridges. **Branches:** stout, upright; branchlets slender, angled, green, *slightly hairy but becoming smooth with age.* **Winter buds:** short, 5–8 mm (0.2–0.3 in) long, covered with dense, rust-colored hairs. **Leaves:** evergreen, simple, lance-shaped, broadest near the middle, or with almost uniformly wide sides, 5–20 cm (2–8 in) long, 2–8 cm (0.8–3.2 in) wide, pointed at the tip, tapering at the base, *sparsely hairy to smooth beneath,* bright, shiny green above, paler beneath, leathery, with a spicy odor when crushed. **Flowers:** produced in few-flowered, compact, branched clusters at the junction of the upper leaves of the branchlets; the flowers small, greenish, composed of 6 tiny lobes surrounding 9 to 12 stamens, the innermost 3 sterile, the single central pistil tiny, inconspicuous. **Fruits:** *almost globe-shaped, 0.7–1.2 cm (0.3–0.5 in) in diameter,* short pointed at the tip, dark blue to almost black, shiny. **Seeds:** 1 per fruit, broadest near the base and tapering to a point.

Swamp Bay

Persea palustris Sarg.

Swamp bay are shrubs or small trees generally growing to 10–12 m (32–40 ft) with leaves, flowers, and fruits that are similar in appearance to red bay. However, *swamp bay are smaller trees with hairy leaves and leafstalks and are more abundant in pine barrens swamps,* especially those near the coasts. Swamp bay will move quickly onto exposed banks or spoilbanks. They are of minor importance as a food source for wildlife. As with the red bay, the leaves of this species are used in flavoring foods.

Swamp Bay

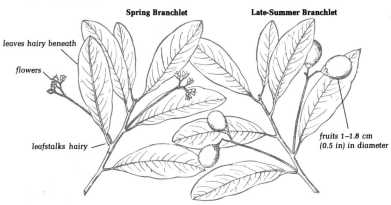

Spring Branchlet

Late-Summer Branchlet

leaves hairy beneath

flowers

leafstalks hairy

fruits 1–1.8 cm
(0.5 in) in diameter

Avocado

Persea americana Mill.

Avocados were introduced into southern Florida by the Spanish and in recent years have become an important fruit crop. The large fleshy fruits are rich in oils and vitamins. Avocados are small to medium-size trees to 20 m (66 ft) and have large, **10–30**

Avocado

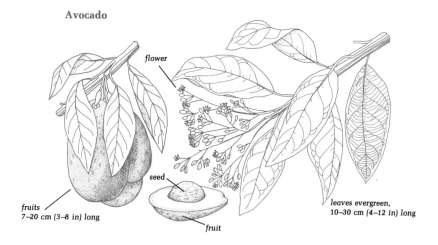

flower

seed

fruit

fruits
7–20 cm (3–8 in) long

leaves evergreen,
10–30 cm (4–12 in) long

cm (4–12 in) long, leathery, evergreen leaves. The flowers are tiny and inconspicuous, but the **fruits** are pear-shaped to globe-shaped and range from **7–20 cm (3–8 in) long or longer.**

They are native to Central America and are planted extensively in tropical and subtropical regions of the world. In southern Florida they have spread from cultivation and have naturalized there. Their large edible fruits distinguish them from the other species of the Persea genus.

The Cinnamon Genus   *Cinnamomum* (L.) Nees & Eberm.

The cinnamon group comprises a large genus of perhaps 200 species of trees and shrubs, all native to eastern Asia or Australia. It contains several economically important tree species, 2 of which are planted in extreme southeastern U.S. These are the camphor tree and the cinnamon tree.

Members of this genus are shrubs or trees with evergreen leaves that are opposite or alternate on the branchlets. The small white to greenish-yellow flowers are assembled together in branched clusters. The calyx or corolla is composed of 6 short lobes and surrounds the 5 to 9 stamens that are arranged in 3 concentric rings. The fruit is an olive-like berry that sits in a cup-shaped structure.

Camphor Tree   *Cinnamomum camphor* (L.) Nees & Eberm.

The camphor tree, the source of the oil of camphora used in medicines, is planted in Florida, southern Georgia, and southeastern Louisiana. It has spread from cultivation and has naturalized in those states. When it does escape, the trees usually are found in drier sites.

They are shrubs or small trees with leathery evergreen leaves that are 5–12 cm (2–5 in) long, broadest near the base or the middle and tapering to a point at the tip. The leaves have a distinct camphor odor when broken or crushed. The tiny yellow flowers are only 1–2 mm (0.1 in) long and are produced in branched clusters in the axils of the leaves. The globe-shaped fruits are 6 to 9 mm (0.4 in) in diameter.

Camphor Tree

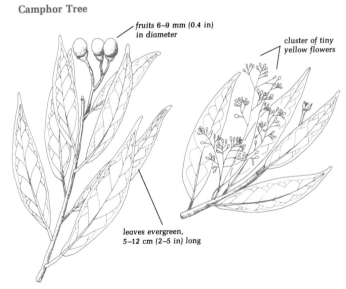

fruits 6–9 mm (0.4 in) in diameter

cluster of tiny yellow flowers

leaves evergreen, 5–12 cm (2–5 in) long

Another species, the cinnamon tree (*Cinnamomum zeylanicum*), the source of the frequently used spice of the same name, grows only in cultivation in extreme southern Florida. The leaves of this species are opposite or nearly so on the branchlets, whereas the leaves of the camphor tree are alternate.

The Lancewood Genus

Nectandra Rolander

There are approximately 165 different species in this tropical American genus. Only 1 member, the Jamaica nectandra (*Nectandra coriacea*), is native to North America in southern Florida. Most of the species occur in South America, with several extending into Central America and the West Indies. The Jamaica nectandra represents the northernmost penetration of this genus. Members of this group are often large with hard, strong, and durable wood, which makes them valuable, tropical-hardwood timber trees.

The genus is composed of trees, rarely shrubs, with leathery leaves that are alternate on the branchlets. The flowers occur in branched clusters that are longer than broad and are found near the tips of the branchlets. Both sexes are present in each of the small flowers. The 6 hairy sepals and petals are similar in size and shape. There are 12 stamens of which 9 are capable of producing pollen; while the other 3 are sterile and smaller. Each stamen has a pair of nectar-secreting glands on the stalk beneath the pollen sacs. A single pistil is present in the middle of each flower. The usually globe-shaped to egg-shaped fruits consist of an outer fleshy coat surrounded by an inner hard seed.

Jamaica Nectandra

Nectandra coriacea (Sw.) Griseb.
(synonym: *Octea coriacea* (Sw.) Britton)

The Jamaica nectandra is generally an attractive, small tree restricted to coastal areas of Florida from Cape Kennedy southward. It often is found growing in moist, sandy soils, with the largest trees occurring in the richer soils of the hammocks. Within its limited range, it is commonly encountered. This species is of limited value to wildlife, and the trees are seldom large enough to warrant cutting for their wood.

Appearance: small trees, 7–14 m (23–46 ft), narrowly rounded at the crown; trunk straight, often angled, 10–14 cm (4–5.5 in) in diameter. **Bark:** thin, 2–4 mm (0.1–0.2 in) thick, dark reddish-brown, rough due

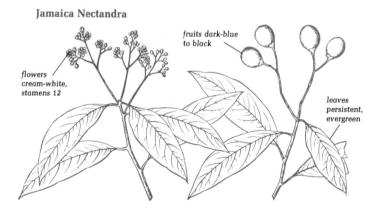

Jamaica Nectandra

flowers cream-white, stamens 12

fruits dark-blue to black

leaves persistent, evergreen

to numerous wart-like projections. **Branches:** slender, spreading, brown; branchlets slender, dark brown becoming lighter and turning almost gray, smooth. **Winter buds:** do not form. **Leaves:** simple, alternate on the branchlets, ***persistent (trees*** appearing ***evergreen),*** usually broadest near the middle and tapering to a pointed to long-pointed tip and tapering toward the base, 7.5–15 cm (3–6 in) long, 2.5–5 cm (1–2 in) wide, ***entire on the margin,*** dark green and shiny above, pale beneath, leathery, with a pleasant, almost sharp, fragrance when crushed; the leaf stalks 8–12 cm (3.1–4.7 in) long, broad, flattened. **Flowers:** produced in ***branched elongated clusters*** near the ends of the branchlets; the flowers 5–7 mm (0.2–0.3 in) in diameter, small, fragrant, cream-white, the 6 lobes of the calyx and corolla 2–3 mm (0.1 in) long, hairy, ***stamens 12, the inner 3 sterile,*** pistil 1. **Fruits:** a slightly fleshy globe-shaped fruit that does not split open, the outer skin dark blue to almost black at maturity, with a thin fleshy layer surrounding the single seed. **Seeds:** near globe-shape, longer than broad, covered with a thin reddish-brown coat.

The Sycamore Family   Platanaceae

The sycamore family contains 10 closely related species, all belonging to a single genus. Three species occur in the U.S., 4 in Mexico and Central America, and the remaining 3 in southeastern Europe and southwestern Asia. Because of its "button ball" flower clusters and fruits, its distinctive large, pointed leaves, and the light-colored, flaking bark, this family is easy to recognize. Fossils indicate that sycamores once covered a much wider range than they do now.

Because of the ornamental qualities of many of the species and their ability to tolerate, and even thrive in, urban environments, this family is of some economic importance. It is of little or no value as a food source for wildlife. Although it is used occasionally for inexpensive furniture and boxes, the wood is of limited use.

Members of this family are large trees with deeply furrowed bark that separates and peels off in large, thin plates that are jigsaw-puzzle-like in shape. The leaves are deciduous, alternate on the branchlets, simple, long-stalked, but large and 3- to 7-lobed. The flowers are minute, and the male and female flowers are produced in separate clusters. The flowers occur in tight, ball-shaped heads that are produced near the tips of the branchlets. Each female flower produces a narrow, elongated, dry, 1-seeded fruit that is packed tightly with numerous other individual fruits to form a single, large, globe-shaped, multiple fruit. These hanging "balls" or multiple fruits are associated commonly with sycamores.

The Sycamore Genus   *Platanus* L.

Since sycamores are the only genus in the family, the features and characteristics of the family also apply here.

Key to Sycamore Species

A. Leaves shallowly 3- to 7-lobed; fruits solitary or in pairs on hanging stalks.

    1. Fruits usually solitary; the lobes of the leaves wider than long; trees of eastern North America   **American sycamore, p. 220**

American Sycamore

2. Fruits usually in pairs; the lobes of the leaves about as wide as long; introduced trees commonly planted along city streets

London plane tree, p. 221

London Plane Tree

B. Leaves deeply 3- to 7-lobed; fruits usually 3 or more per hanging stalk.

1. Leaves usually 3- to 5-lobed, the lobes about half the length of the leaf; trees of California
California sycamore, p. 222
2. Leaves usually 5- to 7-lobed; the lobes greater than half the length of the leaves; trees of Arizona and New Mexico
Arizona sycamore, p. 223

Arizona Sycamore

American Sycamore
Platanus occidentalis L.

The American sycamore is a common tree throughout eastern North America and extends to scattered localities in the mountains of northeastern Mexico. It is a lowland tree, from sea level to 850 m (2,790 ft), ordinarily found along streams, rivers, bottomlands, and flood plains. The trees are tolerant of very wet, poorly drained soils. They also may become established in abandoned fields or spoil banks. But they seldom grow to the size of those in low, wet areas. American sycamores will form small groves along streams and often may be the most abundant tree there, but they usually grow in association with red maple, silver maple, willow, sweetgum, cottonwood, and box elder.

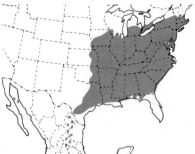

This is a fast-growing, long-lived tree and may reach 20–25 m (65–82 ft) at 20 years old. It is one of the largest trees of the eastern deciduous forest, growing to over 35 m (115 ft) in height and 3.5 m (11.5 ft) in trunk diameter. Flowering is in spring, and the fruits mature by early fall. The fruiting balls slowly begin to break apart, with some of the fruits persisting on the leafless branchlets throughout the winter before falling.

The tree is of little value to wildlife, even for most seed-eating birds, although some of the smaller rodents feed on the fallen seed. The light brown wood is hard, heavy,

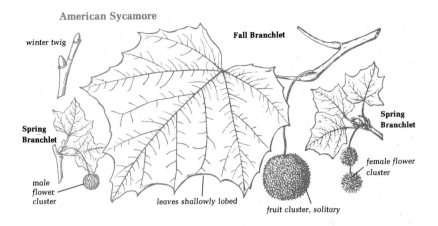

American Sycamore

winter twig

Fall Branchlet

Spring Branchlet

Spring Branchlet

male flower cluster

leaves shallowly lobed

female flower cluster

fruit cluster, solitary

and coarse-grained but not very strong. The lumber is used in manufacturing furniture, boxes, and interior trim.

Appearance: large trees to 35 m (115 ft), occasionally taller, spreading at the top to form a broad, open, irregular crown; trunk straight, tall or soon branching, becoming massive, to 3.5 m (11.5 ft) in diameter. **Bark:** on young trees to 1.5 cm (0.6 in), produced in small, thick scales, dark reddish-brown; on the upper part of the trunk and on older trees, *the bark separating into large, thin, scales that resemble pieces of a jigsaw puzzle and fall away to expose the lighter-colored inner bark.* **Branches:** stout, spreading; branchlets slender, dark green and covered with fine hairs but becoming smooth, orange-brown and shiny. **Winter buds:** end bud usually absent, side buds 6–10 mm (0.2–0.4 in) long, cone-shaped, smooth, shiny, covered by 3 brown scales. **Leaves:** alternate, deciduous, *10–20 cm (4–8 in) long and broad, sometimes larger, broadest near the base and with 3 to 5 broad, shallow lobes along the margin,* with a squared to slightly heart-shaped base, with scattered teeth along the margin, bright green and smooth above (very hairy when young), paler and smooth beneath except for some hairs on the veins; the leafstalks stout, 5–10 cm (2–4 in) long, hairy to smooth. **Flowers:** tiny, male and female flowers produced in dense heads; the male flower clusters 7–10 mm (0.3–0.4 in) in diameter, reddish to yellow, produced on a short stalk on branchlets of the previous year; the female flower clusters 10–14 mm (0.4–0.6 in) in diameter, greenish-red, produced on a short stalk on older branchlets. **Fruits:** *head, rounded, dry, 2–3.5 cm (0.8–1.4 in) in diameter, on a hanging stalk 8–16 cm (3.2–6.3 in) long, the fruiting ball composed of numerous closely packed, long, narrow fruits.*

London Plane Tree   *Platanus* X *acerifolia* (Ait.) Willd.

Planted commonly along city streets, the London plane tree is a familiar sight to people in temperate North America. Although the tree's exact origin is unknown, it is considered to be a hybrid from a natural cross of the American sycamore and the oriental plane tree. First identified in England, the London plane tree has proven to be hardier and more tolerant of urban conditions than either of the parent species. This

mm
cm   1   2   3   4   5   6   7   8   9   10   11
in   1   2   3   4

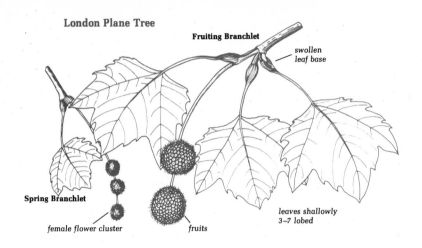

London Plane Tree

Fruiting Branchlet

swollen leaf base

Spring Branchlet

female flower cluster

fruits

leaves shallowly 3–7 lobed

tree also has been planted in cities throughout Europe and parts of western Asia. The trees are medium-size and so closely resemble the American sycamore that the two are often confused. But the London plane usually has *paired fruits rather than solitary ones. And the lobes of its leaves are about as wide as they are long.*

California Sycamore   *Platanus racemosa* Nutt.

The California sycamore grows along stream banks, near occasionally flooded flats, and in moist gullies in central and southern California and adjoining northwestern Mexico. The largest trees occur in the deeper canyons. The trees follow the canyon streams upward to approximately 1,350 m (4,430 ft) elevation. They can grow in a variety of soils ranging from poor and rocky to deep and rich provided the soil has a high moisture level. These trees frequently grow in small, natural groves and also with broadleaf maples, California walnuts, and willows.

This is a rapidly growing, long-lived tree that may begin producing seed at 20 to 25 years of age and continue regular production for the next 200 years. Because it is one of the tallest trees in the canyons, it is used often by birds for nesting sites, but it must be considered a minor food source at best. The fruits often persist on the tree through the winter and then break apart in the spring before the next flowering period. The wood is similar in characteristics and use to the American sycamore.

Appearance: medium-size to tall tree 10–30 m (32–100 ft), spreading above to form an open, generally rounded crown; trunk straight or leaning, tall and unbranched or soon branching, large, to 3.5 m (11.5 ft) in diameter. **Bark:** thick, 2.5–7.5 cm (1–3 in), deeply furrowed and forming broad rounded ridges, dark brown; *on the upper part of the trunk and larger branches, the bark separates and falls away exposing the almost whitish surface of the inner bark.* **Branches:** stout, spreading; branchlets slen-

California Sycamore

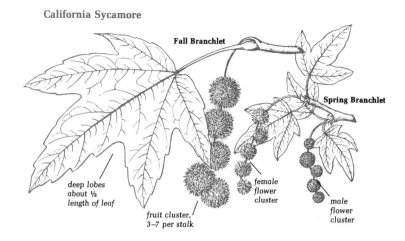

Fall Branchlet

Spring Branchlet

deep lobes
about ½
length of leaf

fruit cluster,
3–7 per stalk

female
flower
cluster

male
flower
cluster

der, covered with numerous, fine hairs when young, becoming smooth and light reddish-brown. **Winter buds:** end buds absent, side buds cone-shaped, 1–1.4 cm (0.4–0.6 in) long, smooth, shiny. **Leaves:** alternate, deciduous, *12–25 cm (4.7–10 in) long and wide,* broadest below the middle, *with 3 to 5 lobes, the lobes about half the length of the leaf,* usually heart-shaped or squared at the base, with coarse, scattered teeth along the margin, light green and hairy on the upper surface when young, paler and more hairy beneath; the leafstalks stout, 2.5–7.5 cm (1–3 in) long, hairy. **Flowers:** tiny, male and female flowers produced in dense heads; the male flowers in 4 or 5 heads per stalk, each stalk produced near the tips of the new branchlets; the female flowers 2 to 7 heads per stalk, produced on older wood. **Fruits:** heads, rounded, dry, 1.8–2.5 cm (0.7–1 in) in diameter, 3 to 7 and appearing zig-zag on a hanging, hairy, or smooth stalk 15–25 cm (5.9–9.9 in) long, the fruiting ball composed of numerous, narrow, closely packed fruits.

Arizona Sycamore

Platanus wrightii S. Wats.

The Arizona sycamore is so closely related to the California sycamore that some authorities consider it to be just a variety of the California species. The Arizona sycamore occurs along streams and in moist gulches in mountains and canyons of southwestern New Mexico, central and southeastern Arizona, and adjacent Mexico. This sycamore usually is found at 1,000–2,000 m (3,200–6,600 ft) elevation. Its size, growth pattern, and general appearance are similar to the other native sycamores. *It can be distinguished by its more frequently and deeply lobed leaves.* Along the streams, the Arizona sycamore is often the largest and most abundant tree of the deciduous trees in the mountain ranges of southeastern Arizona. It is of limited value to wildlife other than birds for nesting and perching.

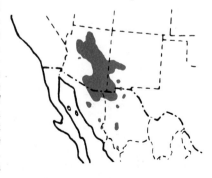

Arizona Sycamore

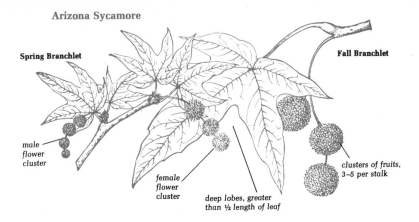

Spring Branchlet

Fall Branchlet

*male
flower
cluster*

*clusters of fruits,
3–5 per stalk*

*female
flower
cluster*

*deep lobes, greater
than ½ length of leaf*

The Witch Hazel Family   Hamamelidaceae

The witch hazel family is a medium-size assemblage of perhaps 24 genera and approximately 110 species of trees and shrubs. The majority of them are native to Asia, with a few in Africa, Australia, and North America. Witch hazels (*Hamamelis*) and sweetgums (*Liquidambar*) have species in both eastern North America and in eastern Asia, while the shrubby genus of witch alders (*Fothergilla*) is restricted to the southeastern U.S. Members of this family in North America are rather distinctive and are not confused easily with other trees or shrubs.

Because of the high quality hardwood lumber that can be obtained from several species, the family is of economic importance. In addition, extracts from witch hazel plants are used in liniments. Several of the sweetgums, witch hazels, and witch alders are cultivated as attractive ornamental shrubs or as shade trees.

Members of this family are trees or shrubs with deciduous simple leaves that are alternate on the branchlets and entire or lobed. The flowers are bisexual or unisexual, tiny and inconspicuous to moderate-size and showy, sometimes clustered together; the calyx and corolla are composed of 4 or 5 lobes; stamens 2 to 8 per flower, tiny; pistil 1, 2-celled at the base, tiny. The fruits are capsules (dried fruits which split open along 1 side) and are usually leathery or woody. The seeds are small, hard, and sometimes winged.

Key to Witch Hazel Genera

1. Leaves star-shaped (5- to 7-lobed); flowers in dense ball-shaped clusters near the tips of the branchlets; flowers lacking petals; medium to tall trees   **Sweetgum, p. 225**

Sweetgum

2. Leaves not lobed; flowers in 2–3 flowered clusters in the axils of the leaves along the branchlets; flowers with narrow, ribbon-like petals; shrubs or small trees

Witch hazel, p. 226

Witch Hazel

The Sweetgum Genus   *Liquidambar* L.

Sweetgums are a small group of 4 or 5 species of trees, with 1 native to North and Central America, another to Asia Minor, and 2 or 3 species in eastern Asia. The Formosa sweetgum (*Liquidambar formosa*) has been introduced into North America but is not as hardy as our native species, so it is seen rarely outside of a few botanical gardens and arboreta. The introduced sweetgum has 3-lobed leaves as opposed to the 5- to 7-lobed leaves of the native species. Fossil records indicate a much greater range than sweetgums presently occupy.

Sweetgums are trees with clear sap, scaly bark, and branchlets that frequently are winged due to corky outgrowths. The leaves are deciduous, alternate, star-shaped or nearly so, toothed along the margin, and long stalked. Male and female flowers are produced almost always in dense clusters on separate, erect or hanging stalks near the end of the branchlets. Fruits are a head composed of numerous dry, hanging, spiny capsules. The seeds are numerous, small, and hard.

Sweetgum   *Liquidambar styraciflua* L.

Sweetgum is native to the southeastern U.S. and extends north along the Mississippi and Ohio River valleys and along the Atlantic Coast to southern New York. It also grows in the mountains in Mexico and Guatemala. It is common in the U.S. on bottomlands or floodplains but may be found in old or abandoned fields. Though tolerant of poorly drained soils and swampy lands, sweetgum does best on rich, moist, alluvial soils. Pure, or nearly pure, stands of sweetgum do occur. But the tree is found more commonly growing in association with tulip tree, pin oak, willow oak, northern red oak, mockernut hickory, and bald cypress.

Sweetgum is a moderate to rapidly growing tree, if in good soil, and usually begins to flower and fruit at 20 to 25 years of age. Flowering is in spring, and the fruits mature by fall when they open and shed their seed. However, many of the empty fruits often persist on the tree throughout the winter. The small seeds are of minor importance to wildlife. They are eaten by eastern goldfinches, purple finches, red and gray squirrels, and chipmunks.

Commercially, this is one of the more important hardwood trees of the southeastern U.S. Although the dark, reddish-brown wood is hard and heavy, it is not very strong. It is a handsome wood that takes an excellent finish; therefore, it is used widely as

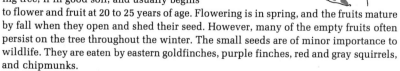

veneer for furniture and plywood panels. A gum can be obtained from the bark and was used during world wars I and II as a base in the manufacture of soaps, drugs, and adhesives. Because of their attractive shape and orange to red color in the fall, the trees sometimes are planted for shade.

Sweetgum

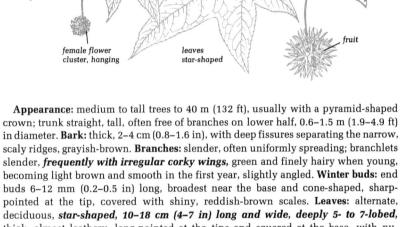

Appearance: medium to tall trees to 40 m (132 ft), usually with a pyramid-shaped crown; trunk straight, tall, often free of branches on lower half, 0.6–1.5 m (1.9–4.9 ft) in diameter. **Bark:** thick, 2–4 cm (0.8–1.6 in), with deep fissures separating the narrow, scaly ridges, grayish-brown. **Branches:** slender, often uniformly spreading; branchlets slender, *frequently with irregular corky wings,* green and finely hairy when young, becoming light brown and smooth in the first year, slightly angled. **Winter buds:** end buds 6–12 mm (0.2–0.5 in) long, broadest near the base and cone-shaped, sharp-pointed at the tip, covered with shiny, reddish-brown scales. **Leaves:** alternate, deciduous, *star-shaped, 10–18 cm (4–7 in) long and wide, deeply 5- to 7-lobed,* thick, almost leathery, long-pointed at the tips and squared at the base, with numerous fine teeth along the margin, bright green and smooth above, paler and smooth beneath except for a few clusters of hairs in the junctions of the main veins; the leaf-stalks slender, 8–16 cm (3.1–6.3 ft) long, smooth. **Flowers:** small, male and female flowers produced in separate stalks, male flowers in several tight clusters on an upright stalk, the stalks 5–9 cm (2–3.6 in) long, produced at the tips of the branchlets; female flowers tightly clustered at the end of a hanging stalk, the stalk 2.5–5 cm (1–2 in) long, the flower cluster 1.2–1.7 cm (0.5–0.7 in) in diameter and produced in the axils of the newer leaves. **Fruits:** *hard, rounded, 2.8–4 cm (1.1–1.6 in) in diameter, light brown, spiny due to numerous woody, horn-like projections,* usually persistent throughout the winter. **Seeds:** 8–12 mm (0.3–0.5 in) long, flattened and angular, with a small wing at the tip.

The Witch Hazel Genus   *Hamamelis* L.

Witch hazels are a small group of 5 or 6 species, with perhaps 4 native to eastern Asia and 2 species in North America. Witch hazel (*Hamamelis virginiana*) is a common fall-flowering shrub or small tree in eastern North America, while the second native witch hazel (*H. vernalis*) is an early, spring-flowering shrub that is restricted to southern Missouri, Arkansas, eastern Oklahoma, Texas, Louisiana, and Alabama.

The trees are of some economic importance owing to their use in lotions and salves. The attractive flowers, leaves, and persistent fruits have resulted in several horticultural selections for use in landscaping. The fruits are of some importance to wildlife, although they are not a major food source.

Witch hazels are usually shrubs or small trees with scaly bark and branchlets that grow in a zig-zag pattern. The winter buds are naked; that is, the outer scales are absent and replaced by numerous hairs. The simple alternate leaves are entire, toothed, uneven at the base. Flowers are bisexual (both sexes present in the same flower), generally 4-parted, with conspicuous, yellow, ribbon-like petals. Fruits are paired, short, stout, and horned on the top.

Witch Hazel

Hamamelis virginiana L.

(synonym: *H. macrophylla* Pursh.)

Witch hazel is a common shrub or small tree native to eastern North America from southeastern Canada to central Florida. It often is found at the edges of forests and woodlands but may also occur along streams or as an understory tree in woodlands.

Although tolerant of a range of soil conditions, including rocky banks, it grows best in deep, rich soils. Witch hazel reaches its greatest size in the Appalachian Mountains in North and South Carolina. A small leafed variety, *H. virginiana* variety *parvifolia*, is recognized as occurring along the Atlantic seaboard.

This slow-growing tree is the last of all trees in eastern North America to flower. The unusual, narrow, ribbon-like petals are produced along the branchlets in October, November, and even into December. The fruits mature about 1 year later and are of minor value to wildlife. Ruffed grouse and squirrels feed on the fruits, and whitetail deer browse the young branchlets and leaves.

The light-brown wood is hard and heavy, but the trees are too small to be a useful lumber source. Experienced water diviners prefer a uniformly branched twig of witch hazel for a divining rod. An oil obtained from the leaves, twigs, and bark is used in limited quantities in liniments and some patent medicines. Witch hazel is cultivated sometimes for its unusual flowers and interesting fruits.

Appearance: large shrubs or small trees to 8 m (26 ft), usually with multiple trunks and a broad, rounded shape; trunk short, soon branching, to 30 cm (11.8 in) in diameter. **Bark:** thin, 3–6 mm (0.1–0.2 in), smooth to slightly scaly, light brown. Branches and branchlets slender, covered with hairs when young and becoming smooth at the end of the growing season, light yellowish-brown turning dark brown. **Winter buds:** end buds 10–14 mm (0.4–0.6 in) long, somewhat flattened and curved, lacking scales but covered with dense, yellowish-brown hairs. **Leaves:** alternate, deciduous, 6–15 cm (2.4–6 in) long, broadest near the base, middle, or tip, and with an ***uneven round to wedge-shaped base,*** entire to toothed and ***somewhat scalloped along the margin,*** dark green and smooth above, paler and hairy only on the veins on the lower surface; the leafstalks short, 7–20 mm (0.3–0.8 in) long, hairy when young but becoming smooth. **Flowers:** ***autumn flowering,*** small but showy, clustered in groups of 3, both sexes present in each flower; calyx 4-parted, the lobes usually bent back, hairy, and

Witch Hazel

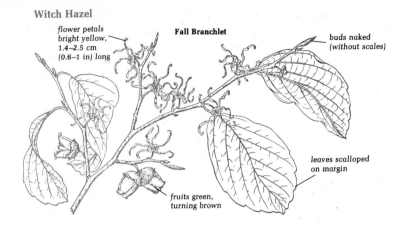

flower petals
bright yellow,
1.4–2.5 cm
(0.6–1 in) long

Fall Branchlet

buds naked
(without scales)

leaves scalloped
on margin

fruits green,
turning brown

orangish-brown, ***petals 4 per flower, strap or ribbon-shaped, bright yellow, 1.4–2.5
cm (0.6–1 in) long, spreading;*** stamens 4, short, inconspicuous; pistil tiny, inconspicuous. **Fruits: *capsule, short, thickened, becoming woody, 2-beaked,*** broadest at or
below the middle, 1–1.6 cm (0.4–0.7 in) long, green turning light brown, splitting
open at the top to expose the seeds, the empty fruits often persisting on the branchlets
for several years. **Seeds:** 7–10 mm (0.3–0.4 in) long, smooth, black, shiny, ejected from
the capsules with considerable force when mature.

The Elm Family   Ulmaceae

This is a medium-size family of 15 genera and approximately 150 species distributed
mainly in temperate regions of the Northern Hemisphere, but with some members extending into subtropical and tropical areas. Four genera are native to North America:
the elms (*Ulmus*) with 6 species, the hackberries (*Celtis*) with 5 species, the nettle
trees (*Trema*) with 2 species, and the water elm (*Planera*) with 1 species. Except for
the water elm, these 3 genera also occur in Europe, Asia, and Africa. There are many
fossil records showing that the elms and hackberries were once more widespread than
today.

The elm family is of some economic importance for its lumber, edible fruits, and ornamental value, and for its food and cover for wildlife. Several of the European and
Asian species have been introduced into North America; they are seldom encountered.

Trees and shrubs of this family have simple leaves that are alternate on the branchlets. The leaves are usually asymmetrical at the base and often toothed on the edges.
Flowers may occur individually or in small branched clusters, usually on the
branchlets produced the previous year. The flowers are small, bisexual, or become
unisexual by aborting one of the male or female reproductive structures. The individual flowers generally have 4 to 8 small lobes with 4 to 8 stamens opposite the lobes
and surrounding the small, central, female reproductive structure. Fruits are small,
dry, thin, often winged or else fleshy and berry-like with a single seed.

Key to Elm Genera

A. Fruits dry, flattened, winged or almost dry and nut-like with small fleshy projections; individual flowers usually with both sexes present.

    1. Leaves with a double row of teeth on the edge (a single row in Siberian elm); fruits flattened, winged; mostly trees of eastern North America   **Elm, p. 229**

    2. Leaves with a single row of teeth on the edge; fruits rounded and broadest near the base, wingless but covered with fleshy projections; trees of southeastern U.S. **Water elm, p. 240**

B. Fruits fleshy, rounded, and juicy, smooth on the outer surface of individual flowers usually either male or female.

    1. Female flowers and fruits occurring singly at the junction of the leaves and the branchlets; branchlets sometimes armed with spines; trees of eastern North America

                    Hackberry, p. 242

    2. Female flowers and fruits occurring in small clusters at the junction of the leaves and the branchlets; branchlets without spines; tropical trees of south Florida   **Nettle tree, p. 249**

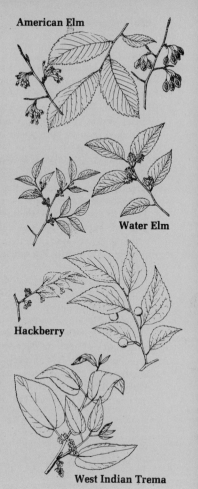

American Elm

Water Elm

Hackberry

West Indian Trema

The Elm Genus
Ulmus L.

There are between 25 and 30 species of elms in the world. They are restricted to temperate regions of the Northern Hemisphere with only 6 species native to North America. These occur in eastern North America, although fossil records indicate that elms once occurred in the West too. Several European and Asian elms that were planted in North America have survived and spread without being cultivated. The English elm (*Ulmus procera*), a tall tree eventually spreading near the top, has broad leaves with a double row of teeth along the edges and smooth young branchlets. The Wych elm (*Ulmus glabra*) also has been planted widely in gardens and parks throughout the northeastern U.S. It is similar to the English elm except that it has short leafstalks and hairy young branchlets. The Siberian elm (*U. pumila*), with small leaves edged with a single row of teeth, has been used in parks and along streets in the East.

Elms are economically important. The yellow to yellowish-brown wood is strong, tough, durable, and heavy. It is sometimes used in furniture, paneling, and ships. The inner bark of the slippery elm contains large quantities of mucilage, which was once used in folk medicines in the southeastern U.S. The trees are not of major importance to wildlife. Seeds, buds, and young twigs do serve as food for songbirds, gamebirds, and browsing animals such as rabbits and whitetail deer. The large quantities of pollen produced in early spring and late summer are major contributors to hayfever (tree fever in this case).

No other tree disease is as well known in North America as the Dutch elm disease. This fungal disease first was detected in North America about 1930 and rapidly spread from east to west, killing hundreds of thousands of American elms. The fungus grows inside the living tissues of the tree and eventually blocks water flow, causing the wilting and death of the infected branches. The disease is spread by bark beetles that fly from tree to tree tunneling beneath the bark. The American elm is particularly vulnerable. Each year millions of dollars are spent removing dead elms. Scientists are attempting to control the spread of the disease and also select and propagate disease-resistant strains.

Elms are small to large trees, usually with deeply furrowed bark and slender branches. Branchlets sometimes have interesting and conspicuous corky wings. Winter buds are small, dark brown, and composed of numerous overlapping scales. The alternate simple leaves are deciduous, and may be lance-shaped to broadest at the base or the middle. These leaves are usually asymmetrical at the base, with a single or double row of teeth on the edges, and they are smooth to hairy on the surfaces. The tiny, bisexual flowers appear either in spring or autumn and are produced in small, few-flowered clusters where the stems of the upper leaves connect to the branchlets. The small flattened fruits that develop soon after flowering usually have wings that may be narrow to broad. The seeds are tiny, flattened, and light to dark brown.

Key to Elm Species

A. Leaves with a double row of teeth along the edges.

    1. Branchlets often with corky wings.

        a. Flowers produced in spring, individual flowers with short unequal lobes.

Rock Elm

            (1) Leaves large, usually 5–10 cm (2–4 in) long, with a distinct leafstalk; fruits broadly winged, egg-shaped; young branchlets hairy; eastern North America   **Rock elm, p. 231**

            (2) Leaves small, usually 3–6 cm (1.2–2.4 in) long, with a short leafstalk; fruits narrowly winged, lance-shaped to narrow but slightly broad near the base; central and southeastern U.S.
                        Winged elm, p. 233

Winged Elm

b. Flowers produced in fall or after leaves have reached full size; individual flowers with uniform, deeply divided lobes.

  (1) Leaves small, 2.5–5 cm (1–2 in) long; flowers not hanging; fruits covered with long white hairs; southeastern U.S. and northeastern Mexico
          Cedar elm, p. 234

  (2) Leaves large, 5–10 cm (2–4 in) long; flowers hanging from slender stalks; fruits with long silvery hairs only on the edges; southern midwest U.S. and western Southeast
          September elm, p. 235

2. Branchlets without corky wings, the bark growing uniformly around the branchlets.

  a. Flowers hanging from long slender stalks; fruits hairy on the edges but smooth on both sides   **American elm, p. 236**

  b. Flowers with little or no stalks; fruits hairless on the edges.

    (1) Leaves with fine hairs along the edges; buds covered with rust-colored hairs, fruits hairy on the sides; eastern U.S.
          Slippery elm, p. 237

    (2) Leaves smooth along the edges; buds smooth or covered with light-colored hairs; fruits smooth on the sides; introduced from Europe.

      (a) Leaves large, 8–16 cm (3.2–6.3 in) long, leafstalks 2–4 mm (0.1–0.2 in) long; seed located in the center of the fruit   **Wych elm, p. 239**

      (b) Leaves small, 5–8 cm (2–3.2 in) long, leafstalks 4–8 mm (0.2–0.3 in) long; seed located near the tip of the fruit   **English elm, p. 239**

B. Leaves with a single row of teeth along the edges; introduced from Asia   **Siberian elm, p. 240**

September Elm

American Elm

Slippery Elm

Wych Elm

Rock Elm

Ulmus thomasii Sarg.

The rock elm occurs principally in the northern part of the midwestern U.S. but extends eastward into southern Canada and the northeastern states. The trees grow from 50–850 m (164–2,790 ft) elevation on hillsides, ridges, limestone outcroppings, and along stream banks. Although tolerant of poor soil conditions, they do best in deep, moist, well-drained sandy-loam soils. Rock elm does not form pure stands but grows in association with other hardwoods such as sugar maple, red maple, yellow birch, and American beech.

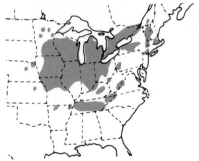

This elm flowers in the spring, with individual trees normally taking 20 to 25 years before flowering. Large seed crops are then produced every 2 or 3 years, and the small seeds are consumed by many birds including pheasants, sharp-tailed grouse, and wood ducks. Beavers and muskrats feed on the bark, while whitetail deer, red squirrels, gray squirrels, and fox squirrels eat the young branchlets, buds, and seeds.

The light-brown wood is relatively heavy, strong, and hard. The close-grained lumber once was used widely in the manufacture of furniture and for the exterior paneling on automobiles. Today it is used in general construction and as a base for veneers.

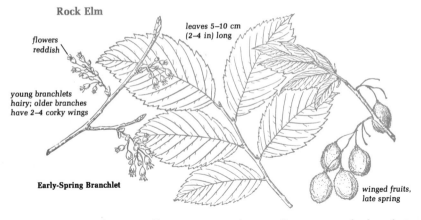

Rock Elm

flowers reddish

leaves 5–10 cm (2–4 in) long

young branchlets hairy; older branches have 2–4 corky wings

Early-Spring Branchlet

winged fruits, late spring

Appearance: medium to tall trees 25–35 m (82–115 ft), narrow at the base but spreading slightly above and forming a narrow rounded crown; trunk tall, straight, to 1 m (3.3 ft) in diameter. **Bark:** moderately thick, 2–2.7 cm (0.8–1.1 in), rough, composed of deep, irregular furrows and broad, flattened ridges, the ridges separating into flat scales, reddish-brown to reddish-gray. **Branches:** stout, often short and spreading, the lower ones strongly drooping; *branchlets* slender, *light brown and finely hairy when young,* becoming reddish-brown and smooth by the second year, *the older branchlets developing 2 to 4 thick corky wings.* **Winter buds:** small, narrow but broadest near the base and pointed at the tip, 5–7 mm (0.2–0.3 in) long, composed of tiny, chestnut-brown, overlapping scales. **Leaves:** alternate, deciduous, *5–10 cm (2–4 in) long, 2–3.2 cm (0.8–1.3 in) wide,* broadest near or above the middle, tapering to a short-pointed tip and unequal but rounded to tapering at the base, with a double row of coarse teeth along the edges, dark green and shiny above, pale and finely hairy on the lower side, the *leafstalks short, 5–7 mm (0.2–0.3 in) long, hairy.* **Flowers:** small, reddish, in hanging, single-branched clusters containing 2 to 4 flowers, each flower consisting of a tiny, bell-shaped calyx with 7 or 8 lobes, 7 or 8 stamens, and a single hairy ovary. **Fruits:** dry, flattened, broadest near the middle or base, 1–1.4 cm (0.4–0.6 in) long, ***broadly winged,*** with a slight notch at the tip, hairy.

Winged Elm   *Ulmus alata* Michx.

The winged elm, or wahoo, is a small- to medium-size tree of the southern Midwest and the southeastern U.S. It grows at lower altitudes and adapts itself to a variety of soil types and conditions. Common sites include dry bluffs, hillsides, flats, aban-

doned fields, and sometimes fence rows and stream sides. As with other elms, this species reaches its greatest size in rich, moist, loamy soils. Winged elm is never a conspicuous tree in a deciduous forest. Rather, it is a minor element of the understory or of a tall shrub forest. It frequently grows in association with post oak, blackjack oak, swamp chestnut oak, red oak, white oak, eastern redcedar, sugarberry, and green ash.

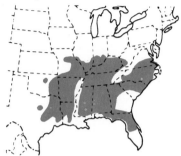

This elm flowers in early spring before the leaves are developed fully. Fruit production usually alternates between years with medium to heavy annual crops and years of light seed production. Although the seeds are eaten by rabbits, opposums, squirrels, other rodents, and larger birds, the winged elm is not very valuable to wildlife.

The light-brown wood is hard and heavy, but it is not strong and tends to be brittle. As a result it is not an important timber tree. In the southeastern U.S. the winged elm is sometimes harvested along with other elm species and lumped in simply as elm. In the South, winged elm is sometimes planted as a street tree.

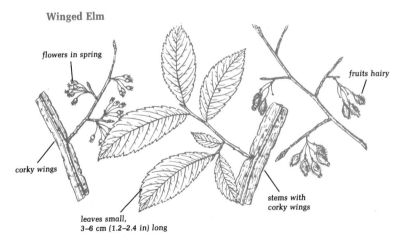

Winged Elm

flowers in spring

fruits hairy

corky wings

stems with corky wings

leaves small, 3–6 cm (1.2–2.4 in) long

Appearance: small- to medium-size trees, 5–20 m (16–66 ft), rarely taller, with a spreading, round-topped crown; trunk usually straight, to 1 m (3.3 ft) in diameter, usually much smaller. **Bark:** becoming thick, to 2 cm (0.8 in), rough, with irregular shallow furrows separating the flat ridges, the ridges composed of closely pressed scales, reddish-brown to gray. **Branches:** stout, often short, spreading; branchlets slender, reddish-brown, hairy when young, becoming smooth with age, ***often with conspicuous, thin, corky wings.*** **Winter buds:** small, broadest near the base and tapering to a point, 3–5 cm (1.2–2 in) long, covered with tiny, overlapping, chestnut-brown scales. **Leaves:** alternate, deciduous, 3–6 cm (1.2–2.4 in) long, 1–3.5 cm (0.4–1.4 in) wide (rarely longer and wider), narrow but usually broadest near the base, sometimes curved, ***with a double row of coarse teeth on the margin,*** dark green and smooth above, pale green and with soft tiny hairs beneath, the leafstalks very short, stout, 2–5 mm (0.1–0.2 in) long, hairy. **Flowers:** small, in short clusters, each flower consisting of a tiny, bell-shaped, 5 to 9 parted calyx; usually 5 stamens; the pollen sacs reddish; 1 tiny pistil. **Fruits:** dry, flattened, broadest at the base or near the middle, long-stalked, 6–9 mm (0.2–0.4 in) long, narrowly winged, hairy, especially along the margin.

Cedar Elm   *Ulmus crassifolia* Nutt.

The cedar elm is a medium-size tree of the southern U.S. and adjacent northeastern Mexico. This elm occurs primarily in bottomlands and along stream and river courses, where it grows most often in limestone soils but adapts also to other soils. Cedar elm is an occasional tree in woodlands and usually grows in association with other bottomland tree species, such as green ash, sweetgum, willow oak, and American elm.

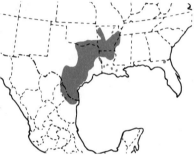

The cedar elm is a fast-growing tree with a short life span. It flowers from August to October, with the small fruits maturing soon afterward. These fruits are of minor importance to grouse, turkeys, and to squirrels and other rodents. The brown wood is close-grained, hard, and heavy. But it is brittle and often contains numerous knots, so it is not an important timber tree. Although they are not the best suited for urban conditions, cedar elms are planted as street trees.

Appearance: small- to medium-size trees to 20 m (66 ft) with a slender base; branches spreading to form a round-topped tree; trunk tall, straight, up to 1 m (3.3 ft)

Cedar Elm

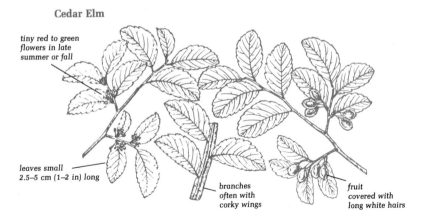

tiny red to green
flowers in late
summer or fall

leaves small
2.5–5 cm (1–2 in) long

branches
often with
corky wings

fruit
covered with
long white hairs

in diameter, usually 0.3–0.6 m (1–1.9 ft). **Bark:** moderately thick, 1.5–2.5 cm (0.6–1 in), light brown to reddish-brown, with deep furrows separating the broad flat ridges. **Branches:** stout, spreading; branchlets slender, long, often hanging, finely hairy when young, becoming smooth with age, reddish-brown. **Winter buds:** small, 2–5 mm (0.1–0.2 in) long, broadest at the base and tapering to a point, covered with tiny, closely pressed, overlapping, dark-brown scales. **Leaves:** simple, alternate, deciduous, *2.5–5 cm (1–2 in) long, 1.9–2.4 cm (0.8–1 in) wide, broadest at the base or near the middle,* tapering to an uneven base, pointed to slightly rounded at the tip, with a *double row of teeth along the margin,* dark green, stiff to almost leathery, hairy beneath; the leafstalks 6–9 mm (0.2–0.4 in) long, hairy. **Flowers:** small, in *short, 3 to 5 flowered clusters,* each flower consisting of a tiny, red to green, bell-shaped, 5 to 9 parted calyx, stamens usually 5 or 6, the pollen sacs reddish-purple, 1 tiny pistil. **Fruits:** dry, flattened, broadest near the middle, *6–12 mm (0.2–0.5 in) long,* deeply notched at the tip, *covered with long white hairs.*

September Elm, Red Elm   *Ulmus serotina* Sarg.

The September elm is a medium-size tree that resembles the American elm but is smaller. It is restricted in the U.S. to an area in the southern Midwest and the western Southeast, where it normally grows in bottomlands, along streams and rivers, and on lower hillsides, especially where limestone is present. This elm can tolerate different soil types, with the best growth occurring in deep, moist, rich soils. It is seldom the dominant tree in woodlands, where it grows in association with sweetgum, silver maple, northern red oak, and beech.

As its name implies, the September elm is a fall-flowering tree, as is the cedar elm. But the flowering of the September elm follows that of the cedar elm by 3 or 4 weeks. The fruits mature in late October or November, and many are eaten by birds,

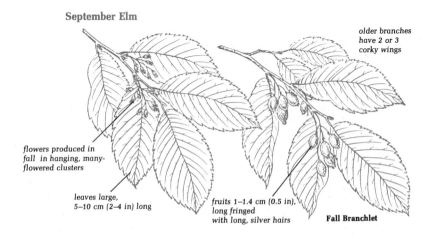

September Elm

older branches
have 2 or 3
corky wings

flowers produced in
fall in hanging, many-
flowered clusters

leaves large,
5–10 cm (2–4 in) long

fruits 1–1.4 cm (0.5 in),
long fringed
with long, silver hairs

Fall Branchlet

including turkeys, grouse, and pheasants, as well as by many rodents. Whitetail deer may browse on young twigs and buds, but elm is not a favored deer food.

Appearance: medium-size trees 10–20 m (32–66 ft), narrow at the base but spreading above to form a broadly-rounded crown; trunk tall, straight, 0.3–0.6 m, rarely to 1 (1–1.9 ft, rarely to 3.3) in diameter. **Bark:** moderately thick, rough, with shallow, slightly irregular furrows separating the broad flat ridges, the ridges consisting of thin, closely pressed scales, brown to reddish-brown. **Branches:** stout, spreading to drooping; branchlets slender, often drooping, sparsely hairy when young, becoming smooth, shiny, brown, *developing 2 or 3 corky wings on older branchlets.* **Winter buds:** small, broadest near the base and pointed at the tip, 5–7 mm (0.2–0.3 in) long, covered with several dark-brown, overlapping scales. **Leaves:** alternate, deciduous, *5–10 cm (2–4 in) long, 2.5–4.5 cm (1–1.8 in) wide, uniformly wide to broadest near the tip,* tapering to a long point, uneven at the base, *with a double row of coarse teeth,* yellowish-green and smooth above, paler and finely hairy beneath, the leafstalks stout, 5–7 mm (0.2–0.3 in) long. **Flowers:** small, *in many-flowered, hanging, branched clusters,* each flower consisting of a tiny, bell-shaped, 5- to 6-parted calyx, 5 to 6 stamens, and 1 tiny pistil. **Fruits:** dry, flattened, shape varies, often broadest near the base or middle, 1–1.4 cm (0.5 in) long, deeply notched at the tip, *the edges fringed with long silvery hairs.*

American Elm   *Ulmus americana* L.

Historically, economically, and aesthetically, the American elm is one of the most important hardwood trees of eastern North America. This large stately tree is found from southern Canada to central Florida. Its native habitats include bottomlands, flats, floodplains, ravines, and protected slopes up to a maximum elevation of about 700 m (2,300 ft). The American elm adapts to a wide variety of soil types, ranging from acidic to mildly alkaline. The largest elms grow in moist, rich, well-drained, loamy soils. They usually are found growing in association with many other trees, including red, silver, and sugar maples, green ash, sycamore, sugarberry, and white and northern red oaks.

American elms are characteristically vase-shaped, usually with a weeping appearance. Indians used the tallest elms as council trees and as meeting places and sites for important events. A variety of the American elm (*Ulmus americana* variety *floridana*) occurs from the Coastal Plain of eastern North Carolina to central Florida. This variety is smaller, and the leaves are more symmetrical at the base.

American elms grow moderately fast and normally do not flower until they are 35 to 40 years old. Flowering is in early spring, with the fruits maturing and falling by late spring. The seeds are an important food source for many game birds, including grouse, partridge, bob white quail, and for rodents, including mice and red and gray squirrels. Whitetail deer and rabbits occasionally browse buds and twigs, especially on saplings.

The yellowish-brown wood is relatively light and soft. When it is properly cut and seasoned, it is tough and resistant to splitting. It is used in the manufacture of furniture, paneling, boxes, and crates and has some exterior uses, such as in boats. American elms once were planted widely along city streets, especially in the northeastern U.S. But the widespread and devastating Dutch elm disease has almost eliminated this grand patriarch of trees. See the introduction to elms, earlier, for details on the disease.

Appearance: medium to tall trees, to 40 m (132 ft), usually 20–30 m (65–100 ft), gently spreading to form a vase-shaped and broadly rounded crown, sometimes with a weeping appearance; trunk usually straight, rarely larger than 1–3 m (3–10 ft) in diameter, often soon branching with sharply rising branches. **Bark:** thick, 2.5–3.8 cm (1–1.5 in), with deep, somewhat irregular and intersecting furrows that separate the

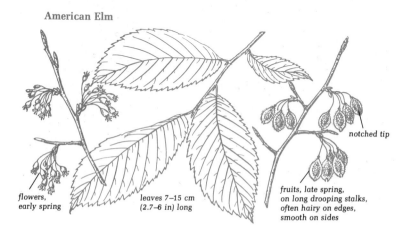

American Elm

flowers,
early spring

leaves 7–15 cm
(2.7–6 in) long

fruits, late spring,
on long drooping stalks,
often hairy on edges,
smooth on sides

notched tip

broad flat ridges, the ridges composed of thin, closely pressed scales, ash-gray to grayish-brown. **Branches:** the lower ones upright, the upper ones spreading, often short; branchlets slender, long, often graceful, reddish-brown turning ash-gray with age, smooth or sparsely hairy. **Winter buds:** small, broadest at the base and tapering to a sharp point, 4–6 mm (0.1–0.3 in) long, covered with tiny, reddish-brown, slightly hairy scales. **Leaves:** alternate, deciduous, *7–15 cm (2.7–6 in) long, 2.4–7.5 cm (1–3 in) wide, often broadest near or above the middle,* tapering abruptly to a point, rounded and uneven at the base, with a double row of coarse teeth on the margin, dark green and smooth or occasionally rough on the upper surface, paler and smooth to softly hairy beneath, the leafstalks 4–8 mm (0.2–0.4 in) long, stout, smooth to slightly hairy. **Flowers:** small, *produced on long, slender, drooping stalks,* usually 3 to 5 clusters, each flower consisting of a tiny, irregularly 6- to 9-lobed calyx, stamens usually 5, the pollen sacs red, 1 tiny pistil. **Fruits:** dry, flattened, broadest near the middle, 0.8–1.2 cm (0.3–0.5 in) long, long-stalked, deeply notched at the tip, *smooth on both sides but often hairy on the edges.*

Slippery Elm
Ulmus rubra Muhl.
(synonym: *U. fulva* Michx.)

The slippery elm, a medium-size tree, is common in lowland areas from southern Ontario to northwestern Florida. It usually is found from 50–600 m (164–1,970 ft) in elevation on floodplains and flats, along streams and rivers, and on low hillsides. Individual trees may reach 40 m (132 ft) in height in the moist, deep, rich, floodplain soils. As do other elms, this species normally grows in association with many

hardwoods, including silver and red maple, white and northern red oak, ash, basswood, and American elm.

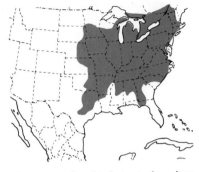

This elm is a moderately fast grower and lives for approximately 150 to 200 years. Flowering and fruiting begin at 15 to 20 years of age, and large seed crops are produced every 2 to 4 years. The seeds are of minor importance to wildlife. Chipmunks, squirrels, finches, grouse, and other large birds and small rodents eat the seeds. Whitetail deer and rabbits occasionally browse young twigs.

The reddish-brown wood is hard and heavy but is considered inferior to American elm. Its commercial uses include furniture and paneling and some boxes and crates. The inner bark contains large quantities of a sticky slime which once was used in powder and liquid form as medicine for fevers and inflammations. Indians used its bark for canoe shells if paper-bark birch was not available.

Slippery Elm

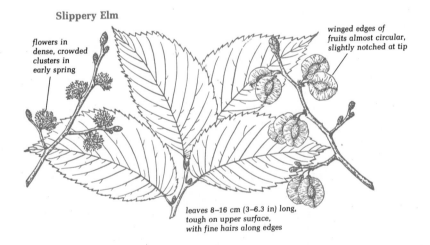

flowers in dense, crowded clusters in early spring

winged edges of fruits almost circular, slightly notched at tip

leaves 8–16 cm (3–6.3 in) long, tough on upper surface, with fine hairs along edges

Appearance: medium-size trees 15–25 m, rarely to 40 (49–82 ft, rarely to 132), narrow at the base but spreading above to form a flat to slightly rounded crown; trunk straight, tall, 0.3–0.6 m (1–1.9 ft) in diameter. **Bark:** moderately thick, 1.8–2.5 cm (0.7–1 in), with shallow, slightly irregular furrows that separate the flattened ridges, the ridges composed of thick plates, dark brown to reddish-brown. **Branches:** stout, spreading; branchlets usually stout, spreading, green to grayish-brown, finely hairy when young, becoming smooth with age. **Winter buds:** small, 5–7 mm (0.2–3 in) long, broadest near the base and tapering to a blunt tip, ***covered with tiny, dark brown scales, rusty, hairy.*** **Leaves:** alternate, deciduous, 8–16 cm (3–6.3 in) long, 5–7.6 cm (2–3 in) wide, usually broadest below or near the middle, tapering abruptly into a long narrow point, rounded and strongly uneven at the base, with a double row of coarse teeth along the margin, ***dark green and roughly hairy beneath,*** the leafstalks 6–9 mm (0.2–0.4 in) long, stout, hairy. **Flowers:** small, ***in short, crowded, few-flowered clusters,*** each flower consisting of a tiny, 5- to 9-lobed calyx, usually 5 stamens, dark red pollen sacs, 1 tiny pistil. **Fruits:** dry, flattened, ***almost circular,*** 1–1.2 cm (0.5 in) across, ***very slightly notched at the tip, hairy.***

Wych Elm   *Ulmus glabra* Huds.

The Wych elm eventually grows into a tall, open, wide-spreading tree suitable for parks and large lawns. This native of northern and central Europe and western Asia was introduced in colonial times and has been planted widely. The reddish-brown

Wych Elm

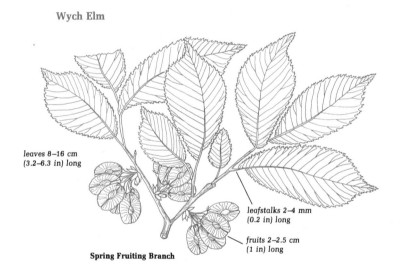

leaves 8–16 cm (3.2–6.3 in) long

leafstalks 2–4 mm (0.2 in) long

fruits 2–2.5 cm (1 in) long

Spring Fruiting Branch

branches bear large leaves that are ***8–16 cm (3.2–6.3 in) long and doubly toothed on the margin.*** Flowers are borne in dense clusters in the spring and soon are followed by the very broad, smooth fruits which reach 2–2.5 cm (1 in) long.

English Elm   *Ulmus procera* Salisb.

The English elm is a native of western and southern Europe and England. It can become a tall stately tree. It was introduced during the colonial days and was subsequently planted in many cities, especially in the northeastern U.S. The ***broad leaves*** are ***5–8 cm (2–3.2 in) long, doubly toothed on the margin, and long-stalked.*** The tightly clustered flowers produced in spring soon give way to the almost circular fruits that are 1–1.3 cm (0.5 in) across.

English Elm

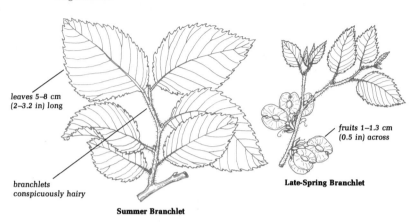

leaves 5–8 cm
(2–3.2 in) long

fruits 1–1.3 cm
(0.5 in) across

branchlets
conspicuously hairy

Late-Spring Branchlet

Summer Branchlet

Siberian Elm
Ulmus pumila L.

The Siberian elm was introduced from northern China and eastern Siberia in the 1860s. This is the hardiest of all elms and does well even when planted in the midwestern states and provinces with cold winters and long periods of summer

Siberian Elm

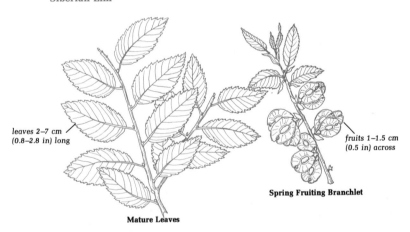

leaves 2–7 cm
(0.8–2.8 in) long

fruits 1–1.5 cm
(0.5 in) across

Spring Fruiting Branchlet

Mature Leaves

droughts. They are small to medium-size trees with generally **small leaves** measuring **2–7 cm (0.8–2.8 in) long, with a single row of teeth along the margin and a short leafstalk.** The flowers are borne in small clusters in the spring, and the fruits are almost circular and 1–1.5 cm (0.5 in) across.

The Water Elm Genus
Planera J.F. Gmelin

This genus contains only a single, little-known species, the water elm, of the southeastern U.S.

Water Elm   *Planera aquatica* J.F. Gmelin

This interesting, but rarely encountered, tree occurs in swamps, floodplains, and along the margin of slow-moving streams. It is found along the eastern Coastal Plain and up the Mississippi River Valley to southern Illinois. The water elm is one of a few trees that can thrive in shallow standing water and areas subject to frequent flooding. It usually grows in association with bald cypress, water oak, and water tupelo.

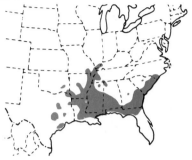

The water elm is a slow-growing tree that flowers in very early spring (February in the southern part of its range), and the fruits mature 4 to 6 weeks later. The seeds are a major food source for waterfowl, especially ducks. Mallard ducks feed heavily on the seeds during the winter months in Louisiana.

The water elm is not a commercial source of lumber. The light brown wood is weak, brittle, poor in fuel value, and subject to decay.

Water Elm

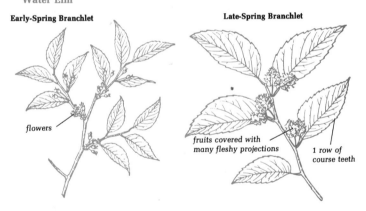

Early-Spring Branchlet

flowers

Late-Spring Branchlet

fruits covered with
many fleshy projections

1 row of
course teeth

Appearance: large shrubs or small trees to 15 m (50 ft) with a slender shape and an open crown; trunk short, to 0.5 m (1.6 ft) in diameter. **Bark:** thin, 5–8 mm (0.2–0.3 in), gray to light brown, eventually separating to form large flattened scales. **Branches:** slender, spreading; branchlets slender, covered with fine hairs when young, becoming smooth with age, reddish-brown to gray. **Winter buds:** small, 6–12 mm (0.2–0.5 in) long, almost globe-shaped, covered with dark brown overlapping scales. **Leaves:** simple, alternate on the branchlets, deciduous, 5–8.5 cm (2–3.4 in) long, 1.9–4 cm (0.8–1.6 in) wide, broadest near the base, usually narrowing to a short pointed tip, tapering to rounded at the base, *with a single row of large coarse teeth along the edge,* dark green and slightly roughened on the upper surface, paler beneath, the leaf-stalks short, 3–6 mm (0.1–0.2 in) long, hairy. **Flowers:** *the flowers bisexual, male and female, grouped together in dense little clusters in the junctions of the leaf stems of 1 year old branches;* the individual flowers with 4 or 5 tiny lobes, 4 or 5 stamens, and/or a tiny pistil. **Fruits:** *broadest at the base, slightly compressed, covered on the surface with many fleshy projections.* **Seeds:** flattened, broadest near the base.

The Hackberry Genus *Celtis L.*

There are approximately 60 species of hackberries widely distributed in both temperate and tropical areas of the world. Six species are native to North America, with a seventh reported but not sufficiently documented to be included here. Numerous fossil remains of hackberries have been discovered in Europe and Asia, signifying their long worldwide presence. Individual trees often display considerable variation in their leaves, flowers, and fruits. Because of this and the presence of individuals with intermediate features, species of hackberries are sometimes difficult to distinguish.

The fleshy fruits of the hackberries are of some importance to wildlife, especially in western North America. The fruit serves as an important food for many winter birds, such as cedar waxwings, mockingbirds, and robins. Mule deer and, to a lesser extent, whitetail deer browse the twigs, buds, and young leaves.

Hackberries are of minor economic importance. Most species, except the sugarberry (*Celtis laevigata*) and the hackberry (*C. occidentalis*), are not large enough to produce logs for the timber industry. The wood of these two species is a clear, light yellow, soft, and weak, limiting their uses to posts, boxes, crates, and inexpensive furniture. Several species of hackberries are used occasionally as street trees.

Hackberries are susceptible to a disease that produces the highly visible "witches broom" effect in the branches. This disease, which is thought to be caused by a fungus, results in an arrangement of numerous short branches that resemble a crudely fashioned, handmade broom.

Members of this genus are shrubs or small, medium, or large trees with smooth, fissured, or warty bark. The branches are sometimes armed with spines. Winter buds are small and are usually covered with tiny scales. The leaves are simple, alternate, deciduous to almost persistent, entire or toothed on the edges, and stalked. Small, stalked flowers are produced in the spring on the young branchlets. The individual flowers are functionally male or female and consist of a 4- or 5-lobed calyx, an equal number of stamens, and a single pistil. The fruits are fleshy, usually rounded, contain a single seed, and mature in the fall.

Key to Hackberry Species

A. Branches without spines; male flowers produced in dense crowded clusters.

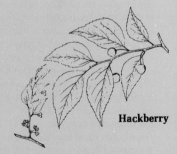

Hackberry

    1. Leaves large, 6.2–8.8 cm (2.4–3.5 in) long, with numerous sharp-pointed teeth along the margin; fruits dark purple at maturity; trees of eastern North America   **Hackberry, p. 243**

    2. Leaves small to large, 3–15 cm (1.2–6 in) long, usually entire or with a few teeth along the margin; fruits orange, red, or yellow.

        a. Leafstalks shorter than the stalks of the fruits; leaves with a prominent network of veins on the lower surface.

(1) Leaves usually less than twice as long
as broad, green and sparsely hairy beneath; western and southwestern U.S.
Netleaf hackberry, p. 244

(2) Leaves usually more than twice as long
as broad, pale beneath due to whitish
hairs; rare; central and southern Texas
Lindheimer hackberry, p. 245

Netleaf Hackberry

b. Leafstalks longer than the stalks of the
fruits; leaves smooth to hairy beneath, lacking a prominent network of veins beneath.

(1) Leaves 6.2–15 cm (2.4–6 in) long,
usually more than twice as long as
wide; trees of southeastern and southcentral U.S.　　**Sugarberry, p. 246**

(2) Leaves 2.5–7 cm (1–2.8 in) long, usually less than twice as long as wide;
trees of eastern U.S.
Georgia hackberry, p. 247

Sugarberry

Spiny Hackberry

B. Branches armed with single or paired spines at
the base of the leaves; male flowers produced in
elongated clusters; trees of southwestern U.S.
Spiny hackberry, p. 248

Hackberry　　　　　　　　　　　*Celtis occidentalis* L.

Hackberry is a small to medium-size tree that is widely distributed in the eastern U.S.
and just into extreme southeastern Canada. It is found on slopes, rocky hills, ridges,
bluffs, and in bottomlands. Adaptable to a variety of soils, hackberry frequently grows
in limestone soils and on limestone out-
crops. Best growth occurs in deep, rich,
alluvial soils. This hackberry normally
does not form pure stands but is often associated with green ash, American elm,
sugarberry, sugar maple, and basswood.

In good soils this tree is fast-growing and
may live up to 200 years. Flowering is in
early spring, and the fruits mature by early
fall. Large fruit crops are produced regularly, and these serve as a moderately important food for wildlife. Quail, pheasants,
turkeys, and grouse are the main game birds that eat them. Squirrels and raccoons a
feed on the fleshy fruits.

The light yellow wood is heavy but soft and weak; thus it is of limited import;
commercially. It is incorporated in inexpensive furniture and fencing and is also
for posts. Because of its drought resistance, it is used as a street tree in many mid·
ern cities.

Hackberry

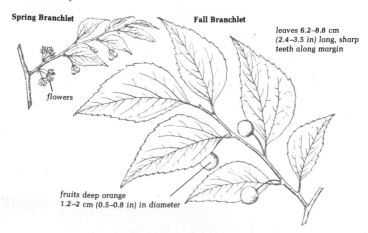

Spring Branchlet

flowers

Fall Branchlet

leaves 6.2–8.8 cm (2.4–3.5 in) long, sharp teeth along margin

fruits deep orange 1.2–2 cm (0.5–0.8 in) in diameter

Appearance: small to medium-size trees 10–18 m (32–60 ft), spreading above to form a rounded crown; trunk straight, 0.2–0.6 m (0.7–1.9 ft) in diameter. **Bark:** moderately thick, 2.5–3.7 cm (1–1.5 in) thick, becoming covered with numerous, irregular, wart-like projections, dark brown to grayish-brown. **Branches:** stout, spreading to hanging; branchlets slender, green turning light brown, smooth. **Winter buds:** small, 6–8 mm (0.2–0.3 in) long, broadest near the base, flattened and tapering to a point, covered by 6 dark-brown scales. **Leaves:** alternate, deciduous, *6.2–8.8 cm (2.4–3.5 in) long, 3.8–5 cm (1.5–2 in) wide,* broadest near the base, tapering to a short point, rounded and uneven at the base, *with sharp-pointed teeth along the margin from midway to the tip,* papery, bluish-green and rough to smooth above, paler and hairy on the veins on the lower surface, the leafstalks slender, short, 6–12 mm (0.2–0.5 in) long, smooth. **Flowers:** small, produced on hanging stalks in dense clusters near the tips of the branchlets, each flower consisting of a 4- or 5-lobed calyx, 4 or 5 stamens, and a single pistil. **Fruits:** fleshy, globe-shaped, 1.2–2 cm (0.5–0.8 in) in diameter, skin tough, *deep orange, turning dark purple,* enclosing a single brown seed.

Netleaf Hackberry

Celtis reticulata Torr.
(synonym: *C. douglasii* Planch.)

The netleaf hackberry is a small, irregularly shaped tree of the western and southwestern U.S. It commonly grows in rocky ravines, canyons, hillsides, and along rocky river banks. This species occurs in drier and higher (300–2,000 m; 985–6,570 ft elevation) habitats than most other hackberries. It can be difficult occasionally to distinguish the netleaf hackberry from the sugarberry, but the main distinguishing features of this

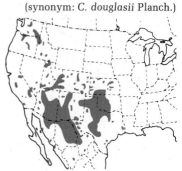

species are the **thick leaves with conspicuous net-like veins on the lower surface, and its habitat.**

The netleaf hackberry is moderate to slow-growing and flowers in early spring as the leaves are unfolding. The female flowers are nearest the tips of the branches and produce the fruits, while the lower ones are the male, or pollen-producing flowers. The edible fruits mature by early fall and are eaten by game birds and song birds and smaller mammals. The light yellow wood is heavy but soft and weak and is not commercially important.

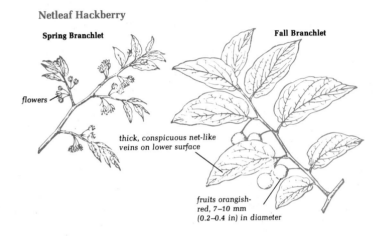

Netleaf Hackberry

Spring Branchlet

Fall Branchlet

flowers

thick, conspicuous net-like
veins on lower surface

fruits orangish-
red, 7–10 mm
(0.2–0.4 in) in diameter

Appearance: small, often irregular, tree to 10 m (33 ft) with an open, irregular crown; trunk often crooked, soon branching, to 0.3 m (1 ft) in diameter. **Bark:** thick, 2–2.5 cm (0.8–1 in) thick, rough, covered with irregular warty projections, gray. **Branches:** stout, upright, often irregular; **branchlets** slender, **reddish-brown and covered with fine hairs when young** but becoming smooth by the second or third year. **Winter buds:** small, broadest near the base and tapering to a point, 3–3.5 mm (0.2 in) long, covered with tiny, overlapping scales, hairy. **Leaves:** alternate, deciduous, 3.5–7.2 cm (1.4–2.8 in) long, 1.8–3.8 cm (0.7–1.5 in) wide, broadest below the middle and tapering to a short pointed tip, strongly rounded and usually uneven at the base, entire or with a few teeth on the edges, **thick, dark green to grayish-green and rough on the upper surface, yellowish-green, hairy,** and **with conspicuous veins on the lower surface,** the leafstalks stout, 3–8 mm (0.1–0.3 in) long, hairy. **Flowers:** small, produced singly or in few-flowered clusters on the young branchlets, stalked, the individual flowers as in other species. **Fruits:** fleshy, globe-shaped, 7–10 mm (0.2–0.4 in) in diameter, hanging on long stalks, **orange-red to reddish-brown,** enclosing a single, globe-shaped seed.

Lindheimer Hackberry   *Celtis lindheimeri* Engl.

This hackberry is little known outside of its restricted range on the Edwards Plateau in central and southern Texas. It is a small tree, growing to 14 m (46 ft) with stout spreading branches that are usually free of spines. The leaves are **broadest beneath the middle, and the upper surfaces are grayish-green and covered with stiff hairs.** The small, greenish-white flowers are produced in the spring in close dense clusters. The fleshy, reddish-brown fruits mature in September. Many are eaten by large birds and small mammals. The wood is of no commercial importance but is used locally for firewood.

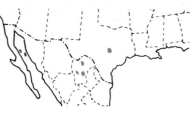

Lindheimer Hackberry

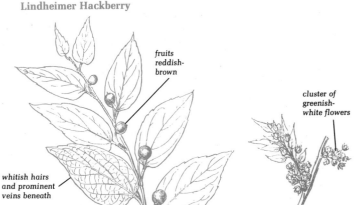

fruits reddish-brown

cluster of greenish-white flowers

whitish hairs and prominent veins beneath

Fall Branchlet

Spring Branchlet

Sugarberry, Hackberry

Celtis laevigata Willd.
(synonym: *C. mississippiensis* Spach)

The sugarberry is a common medium-size tree of the southeastern and southcentral U.S. and northeastern Mexico. It grows in low wet areas such as floodplains, bottomlands, and sloughs, generally in clay soils. Sugarberry occurs in association with

many other trees common to floodplain regions such as sweetgum, sycamore, cottonwood, green ash, willow oak, and American elm. This species usually can be distinguished from the other hackberries by its long leaves, which are entire or only sparsely toothed on the margin. There are variants, with slightly different leaf characters, but they are difficult to distinguish.

Sugarberry is a moderate to fast-growing species that probably does not live more than 125 to 150 years. The tree flowers in spring, and the fleshy fruits mature in fall. Large crops of fruits are produced regularly, and they are of some importance to wildlife, especially birds. Mockingbirds, robins, thrashers, cardinals, and sapsuckers are among the principal consumers.

The light yellow wood is soft and weak and of limited use as a lumber source. The trees are planted in limited numbers as street trees because they are drought resistant. But weak wood breaks under the stresses of snow, ice, and wind.

Sugarberry

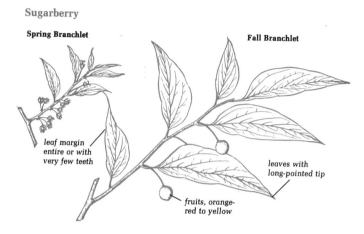

Spring Branchlet | Fall Branchlet

leaf margin entire or with very few teeth

leaves with long-pointed tip

fruits, orange-red to yellow

Appearance: medium-size trees to 28 m (92 ft), with a spreading shape and a broadly rounded crown; trunk straight, 0.3–1 m (1–3.3 ft) in diameter. **Bark:** moderately thick, 1.2–1.8 cm (0.5–0.7 in) thick, covered with wart-like or corky projections, light gray. **Branches:** stout, spreading to almost hanging; branchlets slender, light green, smooth. **Winter buds:** tiny, broadest near the base and tapering to a point, 1.5–3 mm (0.1 in) long, covered with tiny dark-brown scales. **Leaves:** alternate, deciduous, *6.2–15 cm (2.4–6 in) long,* 1.9–3.8 cm (0.7–1.5 in) wide, broadest below the middle, *tapering to a long-pointed tip,* rounded and uneven at the base, often curved, *entire on the edges or with a few small teeth present,* thin, light green and smooth above, paler and smooth beneath, the leafstalk slender, 0.6–1.2 cm (0.2–0.5 in) long, smooth. **Flowers:** small, produced singly or in few-flowered clusters on the younger branchlets at the base of the leaves, each flower consisting of a 4- or 5-lobed calyx, 4 or 5 stamens, and a single pistil. **Fruits:** fleshy, nearly globe shaped, 6–8 mm (0.2–0.3 in) in diameter, thin-skinned, *orange-red to yellow,* enclosing a single seed.

Georgia Hackberry, Dwarf Hackberry

Celtis tenuifolia Nutt.
(synonym: *C. georgiana* Small)

The Georgia hackberry is a shrub or small, often scraggy, tree of eastern, midwestern, and southeastern U.S. It usually grows in dry, rocky or gravelly soils in foothills, bluffs, and commonly in the Piedmont of the Southeast. Some botanists consider this species to be a variety of the common hackberry (*Celtis occidentalis*), and indeed individual trees may be difficult to distinguish with accuracy.

As do other hackberries, this species flowers in early spring as the leaves are un-

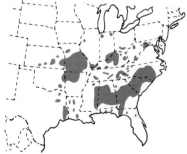

folding, usually in April or early May. The small edible fruits mature by September or October and are eaten by game birds, raccoons, skunks, and squirrels. Although it may be used locally for fence posts, the light yellow wood is of no commercial value.

Georgia Hackberry

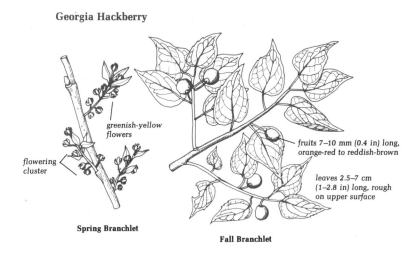

greenish-yellow flowers

flowering cluster

fruits 7–10 mm (0.4 in) long, orange-red to reddish-brown

leaves 2.5–7 cm (1–2.8 in) long, rough on upper surface

Spring Branchlet

Fall Branchlet

Appearance: shrub or small tree to 10 m (33 ft), with an irregular shape and open crown; trunk short, soon branching, to 30 cm (11.8 in) in diameter. **Bark:** thin to moderately thick, to 2 cm (0.8 in) thick, smooth when young but becoming rough due to short, vertical, wart-like ridges, light gray. **Branches:** short, upright to spreading; branchlets slender, green to reddish-brown, hairy when young but becoming smooth with age. **Winter buds:** small, egg-shaped and tapering to a slight to almost rounded point, 2–4 mm (0.1–0.2 in) long, covered with tiny grayish-brown, overlapping, hairy scales. **Leaves:** alternate, deciduous, *2.5–7 cm (1–2.8 in) long,* 1.5–4 cm (0.6–1.6 in) wide, *broadest near the base,* often very broad, tapering to a long pointed tip, rounded to heart-shaped and uneven at the base, entire or with a few large teeth along the upper part of the edges, leathery to thin and papery, light to dark green and rough to the touch above, paler and slightly to conspicuously hairy beneath, the leafstalks slender, 6–11 mm (0.2–0.4 in) long, hairy. **Flowers:** small, produced singly or in few-flowered clusters on the younger branchlets, each flower stalked, greenish-yellow, composed of a 5-lobed calyx, usually 5 stamens, and a single tiny pistil. **Fruits:** fleshy, almost globe-shaped, 7–10 mm (0.3–0.4 in) in diameter, *orange-red to reddish-brown,* sweet, edible, enclosing a single cream-colored seed.

Spiny Hackberry   *Celtis pallida* Torr.

This spiny, densely branched, evergreen shrub is native to the Southwest and adjacent Mexico. The spiny hackberry is distinguished easily from the other hackberries by its *flowers produced in elongated clusters at the base of the younger leaves and the presence of a single or paired spines, also produced where the leaves are attached to the stems.* It is a small tree seldom exceeding 5 m (16 ft) in height with small greenish-white flowers in spring and small, yellow to orange, fleshy, edible fruits maturing in early fall. These fruits are eaten by people, deer, raccoons, rabbits, Gambel's and scaled quail, cardinals, thrashers, and other seed-eating birds. The wood is of little value except for fence posts and firewood.

Spiny Hackberry

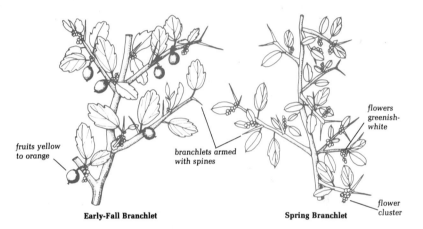

fruits yellow to orange

branchlets armed with spines

flowers greenish-white

flower cluster

Early-Fall Branchlet   **Spring Branchlet**

The Nettle Tree Genus   Trema Lour.

The nettle trees are a fairly small genus of perhaps 30 species distributed in tropical areas of the world. Two tropical American species extend into Florida. Florida trema (*Trema micrantha*) occurs from central Florida southward into the West Indies, Mexico, Central and South America. The West Indian trema (*T. lamarckiana*), native to the West Indies, is restricted to southern Florida and the Florida Keys. The different species of nettle trees are often variable, resulting in great difficulty in distinguishing them.

Nettle trees are generally fast-growing and spring up quickly in disturbed areas along the margins of woodlands, roadways, and stream banks. Unlike most of our native trees, both the Florida and the West Indian tremas flower and fruit throughout most of the year. The small fruits serve as a minor food source for many birds, which, in turn, distribute the seeds. The light-brown wood is soft, and weak, and it lacks durability. So it is not used commercially. It is used locally for fence posts and low-grade firewood.

The genus *Trema* consists of trees or shrubs with smooth to lightly furrowed bark and usually hairy branchlets. The leaves are simple, alternate on the branchlets, variable in shape, usually toothed, and generally with 3 main veins. Both sexes occur on the same tree, and the individual flowers are functionally either male or female. The flowers are tiny and assembled together in small clusters at the junction of the leaves on recent branches. The small, somewhat fleshy, fruits mature a few weeks after flowering and contain a single hard seed.

Key to Nettle Tree Species

West Indian Trema

A. Leaves large, 6–11.5 cm (2.4–4.5 in) long
  Florida trema, p. 250
B. Leaves small, 1–3 cm (0.4–1.2 in) long
  West Indian trema, p. 250

Florida Trema

Trema micrantha (L.) Blume

The Florida trema is usually a short-lived tree that *may grow to 25 m (82 ft)* and have a spreading crown. The tree trunk may approach 1 m (3.3 ft) in diameter. The *bark is dark brown and smooth when young but develops small, wart-like projections with age.* Leaves are often broadly lance-shaped, rounded to slightly lobed at the base, covered on the edges with numerous tiny teeth, and rough to the touch on the upper surface. The small flowers are greenish-yellow and occur in tight clusters in the junctions of the leaf stems. The small *fruits* are 2–3 mm (0.1 in) long, *orange-yellow,* and smooth on the surface.

West Indian Trema

Trema lamarckiana (Roem. & Schult.) Blume

This trema is a much smaller tree (shrub-like) than the Florida trema and has smaller leaves. It *grows to a height of 5–6 m (16–20 ft), and the branchlets are densely hairy.* The leaves vary in shape, but are most often lance-shaped and finely toothed on the edges. The upper surfaces of the leaves are rough to the touch. The flowers are usually white to pink and soon are followed by *pink fruits* that are 2–3 mm (0.1 in) long and smooth on the surface.

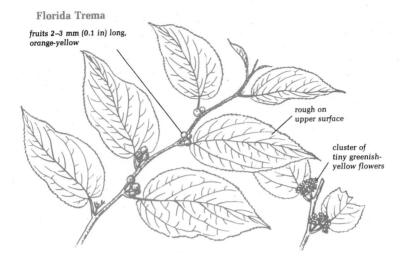

Florida Trema

fruits 2–3 mm (0.1 in) long, orange-yellow

rough on upper surface

cluster of tiny greenish-yellow flowers

The Mulberry Family

Moraceae

The mulberries are a large assemblage of perhaps 75 genera and over 1,000 species, almost exclusively trees and shrubs. They are widespread in tropical and subtropical regions of the world, with 4 genera native to North America: the mulberries, Osage-orange, figs, and hops (a group of vines). Two other genera, paper mulberries and hemp, were introduced into North America and now reproduce on their own.

This is an economically important family because of the edible fruits produced by some members including figs, mulberries, and breadfruit, and the fruits of hops used in flavoring beer. Another member of this family, *Cannabis sativa*, is the source of a tough useful fiber and the drug marijuana. The numerous, often large, edible fruits are an important food source for wildlife throughout the world. The leaves of many species provide excellent browse for deer.

Members of the mulberry family are mainly trees and shrubs, generally with milky sap. The leaves are simple, alternate on the branchlets, entire or lobed, sometimes toothed on the margin. Trees may have both sexes present on the same tree or with male and female trees. Flowers are either male or female, tiny, tightly clustered together, often inside a fleshy, fig-like structure (receptacle). Fruits are fleshy, variable in size and shape, the fruits of a single flower cluster aggregated or fused together into a compound fruit or fig-like fruit.

Key to Mulberry Genera

A. Leaves entire, veins feather-like (pinnate).

  1. Branches without thorns; fruits brown, reddish-brown or purple, small to 3 cm (1.2 in) in diameter; trees of southern Florida
              Figs, p. 252

Shortleaf Fig

2. Branches armed with stout thorns 1–2 cm (0.4–0.8 in) long; fruits green, large, 10–14 cm (4–5.5 in) in diameter; trees of eastern and southern U.S.   **Osage-Orange, p. 257**

Osage-Orange

B. Leaves lobed or toothed, veins radiating from a central basal position (palmate), like fingers from a hand.

1. Flowers in dense, hanging clusters; fruits berry-like.

   a. Fruits short, cylinder-shaped; buds covered with 3–6 scales; leaves always alternate; native trees of the eastern and southwestern U.S.   **Mulberry, p. 258**

   b. Fruits globe-shaped; buds covered with 2–3 scales; leaves sometimes opposite; introduced and naturalized trees   **Paper mulberry, p. 263**

Red Mulberry

2. Flowers produced inside a hollow receptacle; fruits fig-like; leaves very large, deeply 3- to 5-lobed   **Figs, p. 252**

Paper Mulberry

The Fig Genus

Ficus L.

Figs comprise a very large and often difficult to distinguish group of trees of more than 600 species. They are almost exclusively tropical, with a few species extending into subtropical and warm temperate regions of the world. There are only 2 species that are native to North America: the Florida strangler fig (*Ficus aurea*) and the shortleaf fig (*F. laevigata*), both of southern Florida.

Several species have been introduced, including the important common edible fig (*Ficus carica*). Two introductions are often used as houseplants but are grown out-of-doors in Florida; these are the Indian rubber tree (*F. elastica*) and the fiddleleaf fig (*F. lyrata*). The rubber tree has a very smooth uniform leaf that is broadest near the base or the middle, but the fiddleleaf fig has an irregularly margined leaf that is widest near the tip. Several species are grown in southern California as street trees or as specimen trees in parks and yards. The more commonly encountered ones are the rustyleaf fig and the Moreton Bay fig. The rustyleaf fig (*F. rubignosa*) is a large spreading tree with small leaves, 5–10 cm (2–4 in) long, which are covered with rust-colored hairs on the lower surface. The Moreton Bay fig (*F. macrophylla*), native to Australia, is an evergreen with large leaves, 15–25 cm (6–10 in) long, which are brownish beneath.

Economically, figs are of minor importance, considering the vast number of species worldwide. The edible fig is a valuable and nutritious fruit that can be eaten fresh or dried or in a variety of dishes, pastries, and desserts. Several other species of figs are cultivated widely as houseplants, while others are used as street and shade trees in subtropical and tropical cities throughout the world. The wood is generally lightweight, soft, sometimes tough but not durable, and is subject to termite and ant damage. As a result it is not considered a commercially important source of timber.

Figs are small to large massive trees with milky juice and smooth to shallowly fissured bark. The branches are usually short and stout and frequently produce thick roots that grow downward to the ground and eventually develop into additional stems. The buds are often large, pointed, and naked (lacking tough, overlapping bud scales). The leaves are simple, alternate, entire, and usually persistent or evergreen (but deciduous in the edible fig). The flowers are produced inside globe-shaped to pear-shaped receptacles; these can be solitary or in pairs, stalked or unstalked. The fruits are immersed in the thick, fleshy receptacles (the entire receptacle is usually called the fruit). These vary in shape but are typically fig-like fruits. The seeds are tiny, hard, and light to dark brown.

Key to Fig Species

A. Leaves entire, not lobed.

> **1.** Leaves small to medium-size, 5–12 cm (2–4.8 in) long.
>
>> **a.** Fruits without stalks or nearly so; leaves generally tapering at the base; trees native to south Florida
>> **Florida strangler fig, p. 253**
>>
>> **b.** Fruits produced on hanging stalks, 6–12 mm (0.2–0.5 in) long; leaves usually rounded to heart-shaped at the base; trees native to south Florida **Shortleaf fig, p. 255**
>
> **2.** Leaves large, usually 15–30 cm (6–11.8 in) long, cultivated and rarely occurring naturally along highways and disturbed areas
> **Indian rubber tree, p. 256**

B. Leaves 3- to 5-lobed, covered with coarse, rough hairs on the upper surface; introduced and cultivated tree of subtropical, Mediterranean, or warm temperate climates **Common fig, p. 256**

Shortleaf Fig

Indian Rubber Tree

Common Fig

Florida Strangler Fig   *Ficus aurea* Nutt.

The Florida strangler fig, an unusual tree of hammocks and coastal islands of southern Florida and the Bahama Islands, is responsible for the deaths of many other trees. The sticky seeds of this tree often become lodged on the branches of other trees, especially the cabbage palmetto. As the young fig begins to grow from a crotch of the host tree, it forms aerial roots that grow downward and eventually reach the soil. These continue to grow and enlarge and become the trunk of this fig. Meanwhile, the branchlets and leaves rapidly grow over their host and eventually kill the host by shading it out. A single strangler fig can occupy a huge area by the continued production of aerial roots.

This tree flowers almost continuously and produces small globe-shaped fruits that are eaten by birds. These birds then spread the seeds in their droppings. The light brown wood is soft, very weak, coarse-grained, and of no economic importance. It is used occasionally as a shade tree.

Florida Strangler Fig

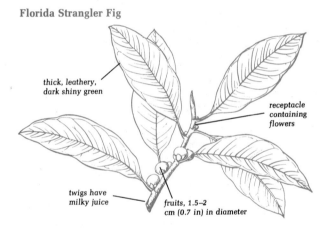

thick, leathery, dark shiny green

receptacle containing flowers

twigs have milky juice

fruits, 1.5–2 cm (0.7 in) in diameter

Appearance: medium-size spreading trees to 20 m (66 ft), ***growing on other trees when young,*** with a broadly rounded crown; multiple trunks, often irregular, to 1 m (3.3 ft) in diameter. **Bark:** thin, to 1 cm (0.4 in) thick, smooth but breaking up into small plates with age, ash gray to almost black. **Branches:** short, stout, spreading, soon branching; often producing numerous, hanging aerial roots; branchlets short, stout, smooth, bright yellow to orange, ***containing milky juice.*** **Leaves:** alternate, ***evergreen,*** 5–12 cm (2–4.8 in) long, 3.6–7.5 cm (1.4–3 in) wide, broadest near the middle to uniformly wide along the sides and tapering to a short broad point at the tip and tapering to rounded at the base, entire along the margin, ***thick and leathery, dark green and shiny above,*** pale beneath, the leafstalks stout, short, 1.2–2.5 cm (0.5–1 in) long, smooth. **Flowers:** small, ***produced inside of a small, globe-shaped, fleshy structure (receptacle),*** each receptacle with a tiny pore, the receptacles and flowers produced near the tips of the branchlets, tiny male and female flowers found within a single receptacle, the receptacles growing to 8 mm (0.32 in) in diameter. **Fruits; *without stalks,*** small, globe-shaped to be broadest near the base, fleshy, 1.5–2 cm (0.7 in) in diameter. **Seeds:** tiny, broadest near the base and rounded at the ends, numerous, light brown.

Shortleaf Fig   *Ficus citrifolia* Mill.

(synonyms: *F. brevifolia* Nutt., *F. laevigata* Vahl)

The shortleaf fig is native to North America only in hammocks of southern Florida and the Florida Keys, but it is not as common as the Florida strangler fig. This fig also occurs in the Bahamas and the West Indies. Its growth habit is similar to that of other strangler figs, and it too may eventually strangle its host tree. As do other wild figs, the shortleaf fig has milky juice in the branchlets, aerial roots, long-pointed buds, and small fig-like fruits.

Flowering and fruiting continue throughout the year, with the flowers being produced near the tips of the young growing branchlets. The tree is of no economic importance. The light brown wood is lightweight, soft, strong, but is susceptible to attack by termites. The fruits do serve as a minor food source for birds and rodents. The Key deer browses the leaves.

Shortleaf Fig

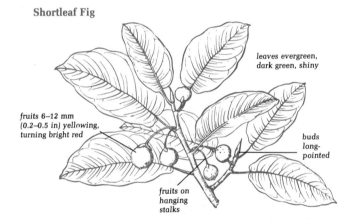

leaves evergreen, dark green, shiny

fruits 6–12 mm (0.2–0.5 in) yellowing, turning bright red

buds long-pointed

fruits on hanging stalks

Appearance: small to medium-size trees to 15 m (50 ft), ***often growing on other trees***, with a spreading and rounded crown; trunk single or multiple, to 0.8 m (2.6 ft) in diameter. **Bark:** thin, 6–10 mm (0.2–0.4 in) thick, smooth but forming small scales with age, light brown to light yellowish-brown. **Branches:** short, stout, spreading, ***often producing numerous hanging aerial roots;*** branchlets short, with a reddish cast and finely hairy when young but turning orangish-brown with age, ***containing milky juice.*** **Leaves:** alternate evergreen, 5–11 cm (2–4.4 in) long, 3.5–9 cm (1.4–3.6 in) wide, broad, broadest near the base or the middle, usually with a broad short point at the tip and rounded to slightly heart-shaped at the base, entire along the margin, thin but leathery, smooth, dark green and shiny above, paler beneath, the leafstalks slender, 1.5–2.5 cm (0.6–1 in) in length. **Flowers:** tiny, produced near the ends of the branchlets in small, globe-shaped structures (receptacles), each receptacle with a tiny pore on the top, the male and female flowers found inside the receptacle. **Fruits:** (receptacle) broadest near the tip, solitary or in pairs, yellow turning bright red when mature, *6–12 mm (0.2–0.5 in) in diameter, produced on hanging stalks 0.6–2.5 cm (0.2–1 in) long.* **Seeds:** tiny, numerous, broadest near the base, light brown.

Indian Rubber Tree *Ficus elastica* Roxbg.

This Asian and East Indian fig is a popular house and conservatory plant and may be seen along roadways in southern Florida. It is the most commonly grown fig and is sold in nurseries, garden centers, and even in supermarkets as a houseplant. In its na-

Indian Rubber Tree

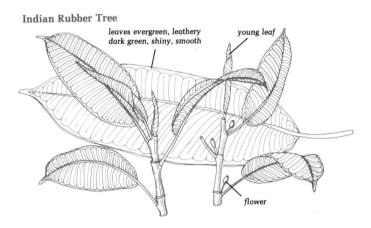

leaves evergreen, leathery dark green, shiny, smooth

young leaf

flower

tive range, the tree grows 30–40 m (98–132 ft) high. But in the subtropical and warm regions of North America, it seldom exceeds 15 m (50 ft). The Indian rubber tree has **large, broad, leathery leaves** that are **dark green, smooth, and shiny on the upper surface.** Greenish-yellow fruits occasionally appear on large older trees.

Common Fig *Ficus carica* L.

The common edible fig is native to the Mediterranean region and has been in cultivation for over 5,000 years. It has been introduced widely into the warm and subtropical

Common Fig

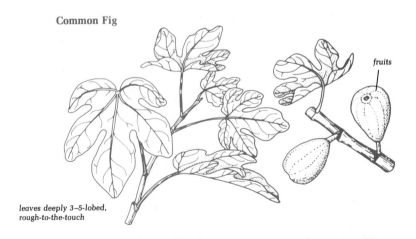

fruits

leaves deeply 3–5-lobed, rough-to-the-touch

areas of North America, especially in Florida and California, where it is grown commercially. The caprifig (*Ficus carica* variety *sylvestris*), a variant of the common fig with inedible fruits, must be planted along with the common fig to ensure the development of mature figs. To carry out adequately the cross pollination process, botanists introduced a tiny fig wasp after many frustrating years of little or no fruit production. It was discovered that only this fig wasp could pollinate this tree. The common fig occasionally establishes itself along roadsides in Florida.

This is a small to medium-size tree or large multi-trunked shrub growing to 8–10 m (26–33 ft). The *leaves,* unlike those of other figs in North America, are *large, broad, deeply 3- to 5-lobed, with stiff, rough-to-the-touch hairs on the upper surface.* The flowers are produced inside a small globe-shaped structure (receptacle) along the branchlets near the growing tips. The fruits vary in size, shape, and color but are still the easily recognizable figs of supermarkets.

The Osage-Orange Genus   *Maclura* Nutt.

This genus contains only a single species, and that one is native to North America. This tree was named in honor of the early American geologist, William Maclure (1763–1840).

Osage-Orange   *Maclura pomifera* (Raf.) Schneid.

The osage-orange is a medium-size, thorny tree native to the southcentral region of the U.S. but is widely planted throughout the East and is occasionally planted in the Northwest. It is a lowland tree that grows best in deep, rich, bottomlands, but it will tolerate a wide range of soils. The osage-orange is an easy tree to recognize in the field due to the bark's orange cast, the spiny branchlets, and the unusual and characteristic large fruits.

Osage-orange flowers in early summer, and the fruits mature by fall. Squirrels may tear apart the messy fruits to eat the small seeds, and blacktail deer may browse the leaves, yet the tree is of little importance to wildlife. The bright orange wood is heavy, very hard, tough, and durable. It is seldom used commercially but makes excellent fuel wood. The Osage Indians used the wood to make bows. A yellow dye can be extracted from the roots and has been used to dye cloth and baskets. Once osage-orange commonly was planted as a windbreak and for hedgerows. But the large heavy fruits are a chore to clean up after they fall.

Appearance: medium-size trees to 20 m (66 ft), usually with a broad shape and a rounded crown; trunk straight, short to 1 m (3.3 ft) in diameter. **Bark:** moderately thick, 1.8–2.5 cm (0.7–1 in), with deep irregular furrows separating the broad ridges, the ridges rounded and composed of tightly pressed scales, orange-brown. **Branches:** stout, erect to spreading; *branchlets* slender, *bearing stout thorns*, green turning light orange-brown, the young branchlets covered with fine hairs but soon becoming smooth. **Winter buds:** end buds usually absent or not evident, lateral buds tiny, partly embedded in branchlets, rounded, covered with 3 to 5 overlapping dark-brown scales. **Leaves:** alternate, deciduous, 7.6–12.5 cm (3–5 in) long, 5–7.5 cm (2–3 in) wide, broadest below the middle and tapering to a long pointed tip, rounded to slightly

Osage-Orange

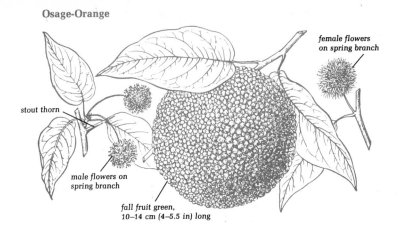

female flowers
on spring branch

stout thorn

male flowers on
spring branch

fall fruit green,
10–14 cm (4–5.5 in) long

heart-shaped at the base, entire along the margin, dark green turning yellow in fall, smooth, paler beneath, the leafstalks slender, 3.5–5 cm (1.4–2 in) long, finely hairy. **Flowers:** small, light green, ***unisexual, trees bearing either male or female flowers;*** male flowers produced in hanging, densely flowered, slightly elongated clusters, about 2.5–3.8 cm (1–1.5 in) long; female flowers produced in hanging, densely flowered, globe-shaped clusters about 1.8–2.5 cm (0.7–1 in) in diameter. **Fruits:** *large, fleshy or pulpy, 10–14 cm (4–5.5 in) in diameter, covered on the surface by numerous, small rounded projections (resembling an orange), containing a milky juice.* **Seeds:** small, compressed, embedded in the fleshy fruit.

The Mulberry Genus   *Morus* L.

Mulberries are a small genus of 8 to 10 species of trees or shrubs of temperate and sub-tropical regions of the northern hemisphere. There are only 2 species native to North America; the majority of species are Asian. The red mulberry is widespread throughout eastern North America, while the lesser known Texas mulberry occurs in southwestern North America. Two Asian species, the white and the black mulberries, were introduced long ago and have become established.

Several species are grown (mainly in Europe and Asia) for their sweet edible fruits, although in North America they are used more as a songbird attractant. Mulberries are an important food source to wildlife, primarily songbirds and smaller mammals such as raccoons and squirrels; and whitetail deer browse mulberries. The light brown to orange wood is soft, usually weak, but is straight-grained and durable; thus it is of some importance as a lumber tree in Asia. A yellow dye can be obtained from the roots and bark of some species.

Mulberries have scaly bark and milky sap. The branches are usually stout, often branched and spreading. The leaves are simple, deciduous, and alternate on the branchlets. The leaves may be 1- or 3-lobed, or they may be undivided. They are toothed along the margin, and have 3 main veins. The trees bear either male or female flowers, or in some species the male and female flowers are produced on different branches of the same tree. The tiny greenish flowers are tightly clustered in hanging cylinder-shaped to almost globe-shaped clusters. The fruits are usually fleshy, cylinder-shaped to broadest near the base, and may range from white to black in color.

Key to Mulberry Species

A. Leaves usually rough on the upper surface and softly hairy beneath.

    1. Leaves tapering to slightly heart-shaped at the base; trees native to eastern North America
                      Red mulberry, p. 259

    2. Leaves deeply heart-shaped at the base; foreign trees, planted or naturalized
                      Black mulberry, p. 260

Black Mulberry

B. Leaves smooth above and usually beneath (the main veins may have scattered hairs).

    1. Leaves 2–5 cm (0.8–2 in) long; fruits red turning black at maturity; trees native to southwestern U.S. and Mexico
                      Texas mulberry, p. 261

    2. Leaves 6–16 cm (2.4–6.3 in) long; fruits white or pink or purple; foreign trees, cultivated or naturalized   **White mulberry, p. 262**

White Mulberry

Red Mulberry

Morus rubra L.

The red mulberry is the most common native mulberry in North America. It occurs occasionally throughout its wide range, extending from southeastern Canada to southern Florida and Bermuda. It is a lowland tree occurring mainly in river valleys and floodplains, and in rich soils of moist low hillsides. The largest red mulberry trees grow in the Ohio River Valley and reach their highest elevation (700 m; 2,300 ft) in the southern Appalachian foothills.

Flowering occurs in early spring as the leaves are developing, and the fruits mature about 2 months later. A red mulberry laden with rip fruits attracts songbirds from a large area. Raccoons and squirrels compete with the birds for the fruits. The dark yellow wood is coarse-grained, soft, weak, but durable; thus it is used locally for fence posts and was once used for barrel making. It is an attractive rapid-growing tree. It should be planted only in parks or in large yards because of its spreading growth form and the fleshy fruits of the female trees.

Appearance: small or medium-size trees to 20 m (66 ft), spreading and developing a broad rounded crown; trunk straight, short, stout, to 1.5 m (4.9 ft) in diameter, soon branching. **Bark:** thin, 1–1.8 cm (0.4–0.7 in) thick, with irregular fissures and long ridges, the ridges composed of close scales, dark reddish-brown. **Branches:** stout, spreading; branchlets slender, smooth, green turning reddish-brown. **Winter buds:** end buds usually absent; lateral buds broadest near the base and pointed to rounded at the base, 5–7 mm (0.2–0.3 in) long, covered with 6 to 8 broad, dark brown overlapping scales, shiny. **Leaves:** alternate, deciduous, *7.5–10 cm (3–4 in) long, 5–5.8 cm (2–2.3*

Red Mulberry

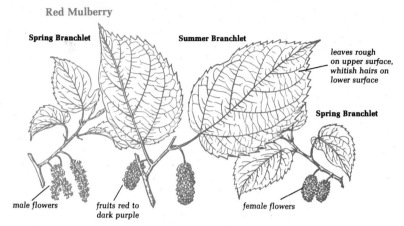

Spring Branchlet **Summer Branchlet**

leaves rough on upper surface, whitish hairs on lower surface

Spring Branchlet

male flowers *fruits red to dark purple* *female flowers*

in) wide, broadest near the base to almost rounded, entire, 1- or 3-lobed, forming a broad point at the tip and *heart-shaped at the base,* with coarse teeth (sometimes a double row) along the margin, thin and papery, dark blue-green, usually rough and slightly hairy when young but becoming smooth at maturity, paler and *covered with whitish hairs on the lower surface;* the leafstalks stout, 1.4–3 cm (0.5–1.2 in) long, hairy when young and becoming smooth at maturity. **Flowers:** small, greenish, trees bearing either male or female flowers, male flowers in stalked, slender, hanging clusters, 2.2–4.8 cm (1–2 in) long; female flowers in broader elongated clusters to 2.6 cm (1.1 in) long. **Fruits:** cylinder-shaped, 2.2–3 cm (1–1.2 in) long, fleshy, *red turning dark purple to almost black,* sweet. **Seeds:** numerous, tiny, broadest near the base and tapering to a point, light brown.

Black Mulberry   *Morus nigra* L.
This native of western Asia was introduced into eastern North America in colonial days and now reproduces on its own, especially in the southeastern U.S. It commonly

Black Mulberry

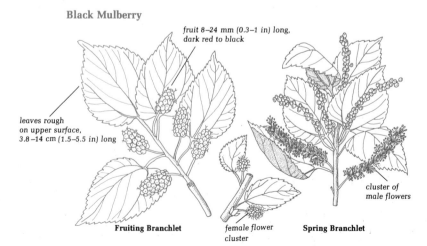

fruit 8–24 mm (0.3–1 in) long, dark red to black

leaves rough on upper surface, 3.8–14 cm (1.5–5.5 in) long

cluster of male flowers

Fruiting Branchlet *female flower cluster* **Spring Branchlet**

is found in older gardens, along roads, and in vacant lands. Black mulberry is usually a short, stout tree with widespreading branches and a rounded crown. The dark green leaves are usually unlobed but may sometimes be 2- or 3-lobed and are 3.8–14 cm (1.5–5.5 in) long. The fruits are often broadest near the base to uniformly wide, 8–24 mm (0.3–1.0 in) long, and dark red to black.

Texas Mulberry
Morus microphylla Buck.

A shrub or small tree of central and western Texas, southern New Mexico, southern Arizona, and adjacent Mexico, the Texas mulberry grows along streamsides, in mountain canyons, and on dry limestone hills at 650–2,000 m (2,100–6,600 ft) elevation. It

is similar to the red mulberry except that its leaves are smooth or finely hairy beneath and the fruits almost globe-shaped.

Texas mulberry flowers in early spring (April), and the fruits mature by late spring. The fleshy fruits are prized by many birds and small mammals. Several species of quail, including the Gambel's and Mearn's, feed on the fruits as do mockingbirds, cardinals, and other songbirds. Raccoons, squirrels, and small rodents also consume ripe berries. The wood is hard, heavy, close-grained, and elastic. But the trees do not reach a large enough size for the wood to be commercially important. Some of the southwestern Indians made bows from the wood.

Texas Mulberry

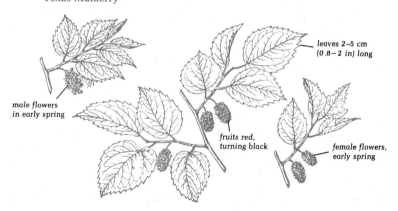

male flowers
in early spring

leaves 2–5 cm
(0.8–2 in) long

fruits red,
turning black

female flowers,
early spring

Appearance: shrubs or small straggly trees to 8 m (26 ft), with an open irregular shape; trunk straight or irregular, to 30 cm (11.8 in) in diameter. **Bark:** thin, rarely to 1.2 cm (0.5 in), smooth but developing deep furrows and scales with age, light gray to reddish-gray. **Branches and branchlets:** slender, with a whitish cast when young, due to fine light-colored hairs, but becoming smooth and reddish-orange. **Winter buds:** broadest near the base and tapering to a sharp point, to 2.2 cm (0.9 in) long, covered with several dark brown, rounded scales. **Leaves:** alternate, deciduous, 2–5 cm (0.8–2 in) long, 1.6–2.5 cm (0.6–1 in) wide, broadest near the base, tapering to a short to long tip, rounded to almost heart-shaped at the base, with large sharp-pointed teeth along the margin, dull green and somewhat rough-to-the-touch on the upper surface, paler and *smooth to somewhat hairy on the lower surface.* **Flowers:** small, green, trees bearing either male or female flowers; male flowers in short, hanging, elongated clusters, usually 1.2–2 cm (0.5–0.8 in) long; female flowers in short, hanging broad clusters, usually 6–12 mm (0.2–0.5 in) long. **Fruits:** *10–14 mm (0.5 in) long, fleshy, elongated to broadest near the base, red turning black at maturity,* sweet to sour, with numerous tiny seeds. **Seeds:** broadest at the base and tapering to a point, light yellow.

White Mulberry *Morus alba* L.

White mulberry is one of the few trees that has been cultivated for several thousand years in China. The leaves are the chief food of the silkworm, which in turn was the basis of the silk industry in China. Silkworms and the white mulberry were introduced into North America in an attempt to establish a silk industry. But the attempt failed. The trees thrived and naturalized in eastern and southern North America. Since the Middle Ages, the southern French have grown the white mulberry for silkworms but with varied success. Around 1600 the English made an attempt to establish the silkworm culture, but the climate proved to be too harsh. For speed in growth and maximum yield from a given plot of land, the trees are started from shoots or root suckers. Then they are cut back at the trunk (pollarded) so that resulting new growth becomes a dense head of foliage. In China and Japan the light yellowish-brown wood is used for decorative carving. In North America it is occasionally used for fence posts and in boat building.

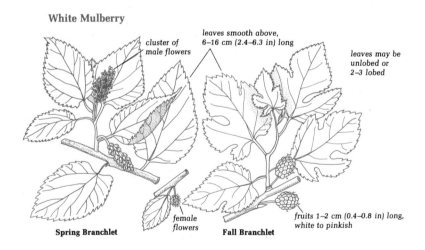

White Mulberry

cluster of male flowers

leaves smooth above, 6–16 cm (2.4–6.3 in) long

leaves may be unlobed or 2–3 lobed

female flowers

fruits 1–2 cm (0.4–0.8 in) long, white to pinkish

Spring Branchlet

Fall Branchlet

White mulberries are medium-size, widespreading trees that may reach 25 m (82 ft). The light green leaves are broadest near the base, 6–16 cm (2.4–6.3 in) long, sharply toothed along the margin, and usually smooth. The small greenish flowers appear in early spring, and the fruits mature in June or July. The nearly globe-shaped, usually fleshy, fruits are generally 1–2 cm (0.4–0.8 in) long and white to pinkish at maturity.

The Paper Mulberry Genus   *Broussonetia* L. Her.

There are 2 to 4 species of paper mulberries in the world, all native to eastern Asia. One species, the paper mulberry (*Broussonetia papyrifera*), was introduced into North America about 1750 and since then has become naturalized throughout much of the eastern U.S. The paper mulberries are trees or shrubs with lobed leaves that are toothed along the margin. Individual trees are either male or female. So only those trees bearing female flowers are capable of producing fruits.

Paper Mulberry   *Broussonetia papyrifera* (L.) Vent.

The paper mulberry was introduced from Asia in about 1750. It is a large shrub or spreading tree to 15 m (50 ft) with new suckers (shoots) emerging freely from the base. It frequently is found growing near homes, along roadways, and on farmlands. The flowers appear in late spring, with the fleshy fruits maturing in summer. The fruits are consumed eagerly by turkeys, quail, grouse, and many songbirds. Squirrels, raccoons, and small rodents compete with the birds for the fruits. The fibrous bark can be used for making a crude paper or cloth, but it is not used in North America for those purposes. The light-colored wood is soft and not very durable; so paper mulberry is not an important timber tree. Paper mulberries are ideal for poor gravelly or nutrient-deficient soils.

The spreading trees or shrubs have a smooth, gray, mottled bark that develops irreg-

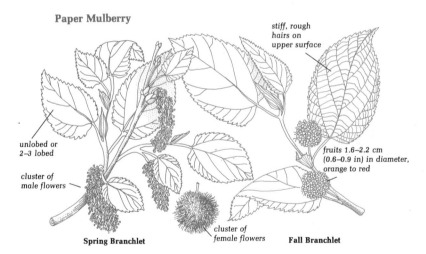

Paper Mulberry

stiff, rough hairs on upper surface

unlobed or 2–3 lobed

cluster of male flowers

fruits 1.6–2.2 cm (0.6–0.9 in) in diameter, orange to red

cluster of female flowers

Spring Branchlet   **Fall Branchlet**

ular patches with age. The **leaves** may be opposite, alternate, or whorled (several connected at one location on the branchlets) and **may be unlobed, 2-lobed, or even 3-lobed.** They **usually** are **covered with stiff or rough hairs on the upper surface** and with **dense soft hairs beneath.** Male flowers are produced in hanging, elongated spikes, while female flowers are borne in globe-shaped, hanging clusters. The **fruits usually are 1.6–2.2 cm (0.6–0.9 in)** in diameter and are orange to red when ripe.

The Corkwood Family
Leitneriaceae

This family contains a single species, the corkwood tree of the southeastern U.S. As a result, the family and genus descriptions are the same as the species description.

Corkwood
Leitneria floridana Chapman

The corkwood is a rare tree found only in swampy areas along the Coastal Plain and parts of the lower Mississippi River Valley. It is a small upright tree that has few side branches. Because of its rarity, it is of no value to wildlife. The pale yellow wood is soft, close-grained, and lightweight. It is one of the lightest of all native North American woods.

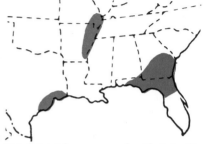

Appearance: shrub or small tree to 8 m (26 ft), with a narrow upright shape; trunk straight, to 15 cm (5.9 in) in diameter. **Bark:** thin, gray to grayish-brown, shallowly fissured on older trees. **Branches:** short, spreading; branchlets slender, reddish-brown turning grayish-brown, hairy when young, becoming smooth with age. **Winter buds:** cone-shaped, 2–5 mm (0.1–0.2 in) long, covered with 8 to 12 overlapping scales, hairy. **Leaves:** simple, alternate on the branchlets, deciduous, lance-shaped to broadest near the middle, *10–15 cm (4–6 in) long, 3.7–6.2 cm (1.5–2.5 in) wide,* short to long-pointed at the tip, tapering at the base, *leathery*, bright green

Corkwood

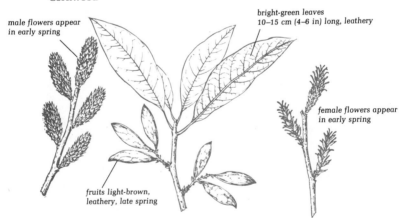

male flowers appear in early spring

bright-green leaves 10–15 cm (4–6 in) long, leathery

female flowers appear in early spring

fruits light-brown, leathery, late spring

and smooth above, pale and softly hairy beneath; leafstalks 3.5–5.5 cm (1.4–2.2 in) long, stout, grooved on the upper surface. **Flowers:** male flowers are tiny and clustered together in cylinder-shaped, light brown catkins, 2.5–4 cm (1–1.6 in) long, produced near the ends of the branchlets at the junction of the leaves and the stem; female flowers are small, clustered together into smaller narrow catkins, 1.5–3 cm (0.6–1.2 in) long, produced on branchlets of the previous year. **Fruits:** *leathery, broadest near the middle to uniformly thick, 1.5–2.5 cm (0.6–1 in) long; rounded on 1 side*

and slightly flattened on the other, rounded at the base and pointed at the tip, brown. **Seeds:** 1 per fruit, flattened, rounded at both ends, marked with a conspicuous black spot.

The Walnut Family   Juglandaceae

The walnut family, a small but economically important group, occurs primarily in temperate regions of the Northern Hemisphere, but extends into the mountains of Central America and Asia. There are 8 genera and about 65 species in this family. Only 2 genera, the walnuts (*Juglans*) and the hickories (*Carya*), occur in North America. These 2 genera are the most important ones in the family worldwide. Walnuts and hickories are prominent components of the eastern and southern deciduous forests. The wood and nuts are exploited commercially.

All species in North America are wind-pollinated. Flowering occurs in early spring before the leaves are fully expanded. The lack of extensive foliage at this time improves the probability that wind will carry the lightweight pollen from the male to female flowers. Following pollination and fertilization, fruits begin to develop and are ripe by autumn. The fruits drop in the fall, usually after a frost in more temperate areas. The nuts serve as forage for many animals including deer, bears, and peccaries. Many birds and smaller mammals, such as turkeys, ground and tree squirrels, and chipmunks, depend upon an annual nut crop. In turn, the walnuts and hickories are largely dependent upon these animals, especially squirrels, to disperse the nuts. Squirrels bury or gather the nuts for winter food stores. The gray squirrel's habit of burying nuts individually and then forgetting their locations, rather than storing them in large caches as the red squirrel does, probably accounts for many of the young trees appearing in the forest. While many of the nuts are consumed by animals, some are not. These overwinter and usually germinate the following spring. Like all native nut trees, individual walnuts and hickories tend to be cyclic in nut production. One or 2 years of lean production often follow a year of heavy nut production. Fortunately, the trees in a particular woods are not synchronized, so different trees fruit heavily each year.

Fossil records of walnuts dating from the Middle to Upper Cretaceous period suggest that the walnut family is an ancient one and that it was once more widespread throughout the temperate world than today.

The family is composed of trees of moderate to large size (to 50 m; 165 ft). The leaves are usually deciduous, alternate on the stems, in a feather-like arrangement with a single end leaflet. The leaves are usually gland-dotted and aromatic. Male and female flowers grow separately, but both occur on each tree. The male flowers are found on hanging, many-flowered catkins on the branches of the previous year's growth or at the base of the current year's growth. Each of the tiny flowers contains from 3 to 100 stamens that produce enormous amounts of pollen. The female flowers are small and inconspicuous and are borne on solitary, usually erect, few-flowered spikes at the tips of the branches of the current year's growth. The female flower is composed of 3 bracts and a 4-parted envelope (the calyx and the corolla) surrounding the reproductive structure, which contains the ovules, or eggs, that can develop into embryos. At the top are feather-like structures (stigmas) that receive male pollen grains. The fruits are usually fleshy or pulpy with a hard, stony, inner portion (the shell) enclosing the kernel. In some tropical members of this family, the fruit is a small nut with a wing or wings to aid in seed dispersal. The seeds are usually large, occasionally sweet, and variously lobed.

Key to Walnut Genera

Walnuts

A. Branches with a chambered pith (core); the male flowers in solitary or paired catkins, each flower with up to 40 stamens; fruit does not split into sections; the nut variously and irregularly furrowed on the outer surface **Walnuts, p. 266**

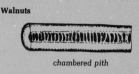

chambered pith

B. Branches with continuous pith; the male flowers in catkins clustered in groups of 3, each flower with usually less than 10 stamens; fruit splitting partially or completely into 4 valves; the nut usually smooth on the outer surface

Hickories, p. 275

Hickories

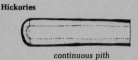

continuous pith

The Walnut Genus

Juglans L.

There are 18 to 20 species of walnuts in temperate and tropical regions of the world. Six species occur in North America: 2 widely distributed in eastern North America, 2 with limited ranges in the southwestern states, and 2 confined to California. Fossils indicate that walnuts once were more widely distributed over the Northern Hemisphere than today.

Walnuts are generally moderate- to large-size trees with hard, durable, dark-colored wood and large, deep taproots. The leaves are alternate, deciduous, arranged in a feather pattern, aromatic. In winter the twigs are recognizable by the 2 pairs of opposite scales on the end bud and the large, elevated, shield-shaped scars left by the fallen leaves. The leaf scars are marked with 3 conspicuous bundle traces, one in each lobe of the scar. (The traces are the sealed ends of the vascular tissue that once supplied the leaves with water and nutrients.) The small and inconspicuous flowers appear in spring, the male flowers in solitary or paired, hanging catkins. The fruits are large, globe-shaped, pear-shaped, to egg-shaped, and covered by a fibrous husk that does not split open at maturity; the nut is usually irregularly furrowed.

The chambering of the pith (core) does not develop until the end of the growing season; thus young twigs do not evidence this chambering.

Walnuts produce some of the world's finest cabinet woods. The hard, durable, dark brown wood has excellent technical properties both for working and for finishing. The nuts are utilized by wildlife, especially squirrels, although beaver and some larger birds eat them.

In addition to the native species of walnuts described here, several European and Asian walnuts have been introduced into North America. Of these, the English walnut and the Japanese walnut are encountered occasionally and deserve mention. The English walnut (*Juglans regia*) has been planted widely in milder regions of North America, especially California. This species yields the walnut sold in packages of mixed nuts in the shell or in packets of shelled and processed walnuts. The Japanese walnut (*Juglans ailantifolia*) is planted occasionally as a shade or ornamental tree and for the nuts, although the nut is inferior in taste to that of the English walnut.

Key to Walnut Species

A. Fruits several, occurring on a long stalk; nuts conspicuously 4-ribbed   **Butternut, p. 268**

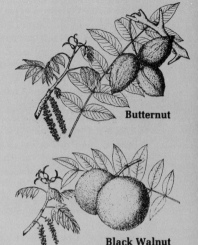

Butternut

B. Fruits solitary or in pairs and then clustered together; nuts not conspicuously ribbed.

  1. Nuts with irregular grooves and ridges; trees of eastern North America   **Black walnut, p. 269**

Black Walnut

  2. Nuts with regular lengthwise grooves and ridges or nuts virtually smooth, grooves obscure; trees of southwestern or western North America.

    a. Nuts with moderate to deep lengthwise grooves.

      (1) Nuts small, globe-shaped, generally 1.5–2.5 cm (0.6–1 in) in diameter.

California Walnut

        (a) Leaves 15–25 cm (6–10 in) long with 9–15 leaflets, the leaflets oblong-lance-shaped; fruits 1–2 cm (0.4–0.8 in) in diameter, nuts with a few shallow grooves
           California walnut, p. 270

        (b) Leaves 20–40 cm (8–16 in) long with 11–25 leaflets; fruits 2–3.5 cm (0.8–1.4 in) in diameter, the nuts with deep, lengthwise, slightly forking ridges
           Texas black walnut, p. 271

Arizona Walnut

Hinds Walnut

      (2) Nuts large, generally 2.5–4 cm (1–1.6 in) in diameter; trees of southwestern U.S. and northern Mexico
         Arizona walnut, p. 273

    b. Nuts virtually smooth, grooves obscure; trees of central coastal California
      Hinds walnut, p. 274

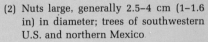

Butternut, White Walnut
Juglans cinerea L.

The fast-growing butternut, or white walnut, thrives on well-drained soils of bottomlands and floodplains in eastern North America. It occurs in forests of mixed hardwoods and is rarely found in pure stands. The butternut is shorter than the black walnut, and its branches spread more. It is a relatively short-lived tree, seldom exceeding 80 to 90 years. As with the black walnut, chemicals produced in the leaves, bark, and fruit have a growth-inhibiting effect on many other plants.

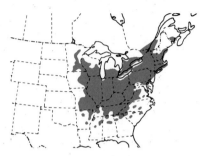

Because the light brown, coarse-grained wood of the butternut is not as strong and durable as wood of the black walnut, it is not as valuable. It is used in limited quantities in cabinet and furniture construction and in the manufacturing of boxes, crates, and some toys. Physicians once used the dried inner bark as a cathartic. A yellow or orange-yellow dye can be obtained from fresh bark and the fruit husks. This dye was widely used by early settlers and during the Civil War when other sources of yellow dye were unavailable. The nuts are sweet and have great potential as a food source for man, as well as being an important food for such animals as squirrels, rabbits, and whitetail deer. Although the trees are grown easily, site selection should be planned carefully because the young trees rapidly produce large, deeply penetrating taproots that soon render them very difficult, if not impossible, to transplant.

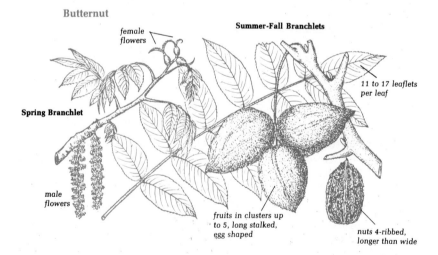

Butternut

female flowers

Summer-Fall Branchlets

Spring Branchlet

11 to 17 leaflets per leaf

male flowers

fruits in clusters up to 5, long stalked, egg shaped

nuts 4-ribbed, longer than wide

Appearance: medium-size tree to 30 m (100 ft); trunk straight, up to 1 m (3.3 ft) in diameter; the crown open, flat to broadly rounded at the top. **Bark:** moderately thick, light gray to light brown, divided by deep furrows into broad, flat-topped, intersecting, scaly ridges forming a rough diamond-shaped pattern. **Branches:** stout, rising and spreading; the branchlets becoming reddish-brown to gray with age, hairy to smooth, often shiny, with conspicuous white pores; leaf scars shield-shaped, elevated, with 3 bundle traces. **Winter buds:** end bud cone-shaped, blunt at the tip, obliquely flattened above, whitish, hairy, 12–18 cm (0.5–0.7 in) long; side buds smaller. **Leaves:** alternate, feather-like arrangement, generally 30–60 cm (11.8–23.6 in) long **with 11 to 17 leaflets, the end leaflet often long-stalked,** the side leaflets up to 5 to 11 cm (2–4.4 in) long and up to 6 cm (2.4 in) wide; **oblong to lance-shaped to broadest above the middle;** pointed at the tip, rounded and uneven at the base, the edge with small teeth, the upper surface yellow-green and slightly wrinkled, paler on the lower surface, with soft hairs, often with glands and sticky when young. **Flowers:** male flowers in cylinder-shaped, hairy, green-yellow catkins, 6–14 cm (2.4–5.5 in) long, each flower with 8–12 stamens; the small female flowers usually 4–7 per spike at the end of the current year's growth. **Fruits:** large, egg-shaped to oblong, tapering to a pointed tip, single or **in clusters up to 5,** the individual fruits 5–8 cm (2–3.2 in) in diameter, green becoming light brown at maturity, often 4-angled, sticky with rust-brown hairs, not splitting open to expose the nut. The **egg-shaped nuts pointed at the tip, 3–6 cm (1.2–2.4 in) in diameter, conspicuously 4-ribbed,** with well-developed wings, the shell deeply furrowed, the kernel oily, sweet.

Black Walnut

Juglans nigra L.

The black walnut grows best at lower altitudes on deep, well-drained soils including suitable bottomlands and floodplains. The trees occur in mixed hardwood stands, rarely in pure stands in the wild. This may be due to a substance called juglone that older established trees leach into the soil; some authorities claim that the juglone inhibits seed germination and the growth of new walnut trees and many other plants. Thus, juglone is believed to limit competition for the soil nutrients.

The beautifully grained, brownish-colored wood of this species makes some of the finest lumber in North America. Many years ago black walnut was so abundant that furniture was made from solid walnut. As the amount of quality black walnut diminishes, the remaining supplies are being used more for the production of veneer for cabinets and furniture than solid walnut items. Most custom-crafted gunstocks are manufactured from select black walnut. The wood's ability to absorb more of the recoil than most other woods and the fact that the wood does not shrink or warp with age make it ideal for gunstocks. As a result of the great demand for the wood, the majority of the larger, naturally occurring black walnuts have been logged. These slow-growing trees are used in selection and hybridization programs in an attempt to find more rapid-growing trees, while retaining the excellent wood qualities. Black walnuts are in demand for use in candies, confections, and ice creams. Efforts are under way to identify strains of the species with larger, but thinner-walled, nuts. The nuts are an important source of food for squirrels.

Appearance: large tree, 30–40 m, rarely to 50 (98–132 ft, rarely to 165); often with a straight trunk for about half its height, to 2 m (6.6 ft) in diameter; the crown open and rounded at the top. **Bark:** in young trees the bark is scaly and light to grayish-brown or even reddish, but with age it becomes thick and deeply furrowed with intersecting ridges and almost black. **Branches:** stout, rising or spreading; the branchlets light brown to orange-brown, hairy but becoming smooth with age; leaf scars shield-

Black Walnut

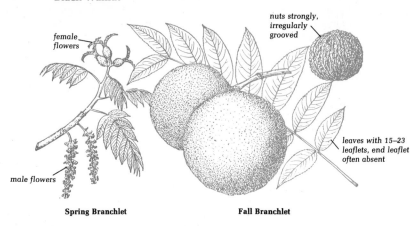

female flowers

nuts strongly, irregularly grooved

male flowers

leaves with 15–23 leaflets, end leaflet often absent

Spring Branchlet   **Fall Branchlet**

shaped, elevated, with 3 bundle traces. **Winter buds:** end buds blunt, broadest at the base and slightly rounded at the top, slightly flattened, pale brown, hairy, about 8–10 mm (0.3–0.4 in) long; side buds smaller. **Leaves:** alternate, feather-like arrangement, from 20–60 cm (8–24 in) long *with 15 to 23 leaflets, the end leaflets smaller than the side ones and often absent,* the side leaflets up to 9 cm (3.6 in) long and to 3.5 cm (1.4 in) broad, *broadest near the base to broadly lance-shaped,* pointed at the tip, rounded and uneven at the base, the edge with sharp-pointed teeth, the upper surface yellow-green and smooth, the lower surface paler and hairy, the leaflets turning yellow in fall. **Flowers:** male flowers single or in clusters of hanging yellow-green (usually hairy) catkins, 5–10 cm (2–4 in) long, each flower with 20 to 30 stamens; the female flowers usually 1 to 4 per short spikes at the end on the new growth. **Fruits:** large, rounded, *usually single or in pairs,* 4–6 cm (1.6–2.4 in) in diameter, the outer husk thick, green to yellow-green, turning dark brown at maturity, slightly hairy, not splitting open to expose the nut. The *globe-shaped nuts are 3–4 cm (1.2–1.6 in) in diameter, the shell irregularly and deeply furrowed,* the kernel 4-lobed at the base, oily, sweet.

California Walnut   *Juglans californica* S. Watson

The California walnut is a rapid-growing tree living to a moderate age of 125 to 150 years. This species is found on moist or dry, gravelly soils along river courses and bottomlands in the coastal region of southern California at elevations up to 1,300 m (4,300 ft). It differs from the other species found in northern California in having smaller nuts with hard, smooth shells.

Although the dark brown wood is attractive, the moderately coarse-grained structure and the short, frequent branching pattern of the trunk limit the use of this species as a lumber source. Besides, commercial and residential developments have eliminated or drastically changed

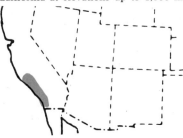

many habitats of the California walnut, resulting in a dwindling population. But where it does occur, it is useful in holding and protecting stream banks. The nuts are gathered and eaten by rodents such as squirrels and rabbits.

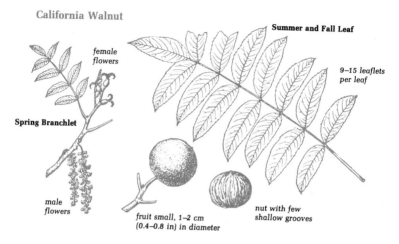

California Walnut

female flowers

Summer and Fall Leaf

9–15 leaflets per leaf

Spring Branchlet

male flowers

fruit small, 1–2 cm (0.4–0.8 in) in diameter

nut with few shallow grooves

Appearance: small to moderate-size tree to 10 m, rarely to 18 (32 ft, rarely to 60), occasionally shrubby; the trunk short, soon branching; the crown open, rounded to broadly rounded at the top. **Bark:** moderately thick, smooth and grayish-white when young, with age becoming deeply furrowed with long ridges broken into dark brown to black scales. **Branches:** stout, spreading, and eventually drooping; the branchlets reddish-brown, with dense rust-colored hairs when young, becoming smooth, with pale pores; leaf scars rounded to triangular, prominent, with 3 bundle scars. **Winter buds:** end buds broadest at the base, somewhat pointed at the tip, compressed along the sides, hairy, approximately 5–7 mm (0.2–0.3 in) long. **Leaves:** alternate, feather-like arrangement, from 15–25 cm (6–10 in) long **with 9 to 15, rarely 17, leaflets,** the leaflets generally **2.5–7.5 cm (1–3 in) long and 1–2 cm (0.4–0.8 in) broad, oblong to lance-shaped, usually curved,** pointed to tapering at the tip, tapering or rounded and uneven at the base, the edge with fine, sharp-pointed teeth, the upper surface yellow-green and smooth above, paler on the lower surface, often with tufts of hairs at the junctions of the main veins. **Flowers:** male flowers in slender, hairy to almost smooth, green-yellow catkins, 5–8 cm (2–3.2 in) long, each flower with 30 to 40 stamens; the small female flowers 1 to 4 per short spike at the tips of new growth. **Fruits: small, globe-shaped, 1–2 cm (0.4–0.8 in) in diameter,** green turning dark brown at maturity, the husk thin, covered with numerous tiny hairs, not splitting open at maturity. The nearly round nuts generally flattened at the base and slightly compressed along the sides, **with few shallow grooves,** the shell thin, light to dark brown, the kernel large, sweet.

Texas Black Walnut, Little Walnut

Juglans microcarpa Berl.
(synonym: *J. rupestris* Engelm.)

The Texas black walnut occurs in valleys, in dry rocky ravines, and along stream banks from southwestern Kansas, western Oklahoma and Texas to New Mexico, Arizona, and northern Mexico. This species thrives in full sun and cannot tolerate shade. The young trees direct most of their energy to the production of a large deep taproot. Then new branches and leaves are produced. The taproot permits the walnut to survive periods of drought that are common within its range. This walnut is a strong-scented tree with delicate, slender leaves resembling pecan leaves; it is closely related to the Arizona black walnut. The two walnuts may hybridize where their ranges overlap.

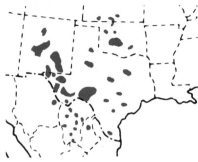

The dark-colored wood is used occasionally in cabinet work, paneling, and veneers. Most of the more attractive, taller growing specimens have been cut for their wood. As a result, only the shorter bushier trees remain. This species is used in the southwestern U.S. in shelterbelts and is planted sometimes outside its natural range as an ornamental. As with other walnuts, this one is an important source of food for rodents.

Texas Black Walnut

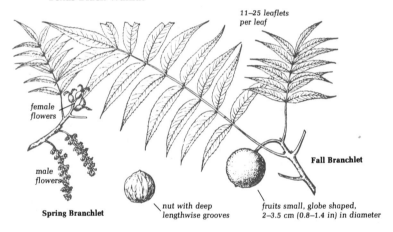

11–25 leaflets per leaf

female flowers

male flowers

Fall Branchlet

Spring Branchlet

nut with deep lengthwise grooves

fruits small, globe shaped, 2–3.5 cm (0.8–1.4 in) in diameter

Appearance: large bush or small to medium-size tree to 15 m (50 ft), sometimes with several trunks, the crown open and usually broadly rounded at the top. **Bark:** smooth and grayish when young becoming thick, deeply furrowed and forming flat-topped ridges, gray to dark brown. **Branches:** stout, often spreading; the branchlets brown to gray-brown, usually hairy when young, becoming smooth with age, with numerous, light-colored pores; leaf scars large, heart-shaped with rounded corners, a dense fringe of long white hairs on the upper margin, with 3 bundle scars. **Winter buds:** end bud widest at the base, compressed at the sides, 6–12 mm (0.2–0.5 in) long, rounded at the tip, gray-brown, very hairy, side buds smaller. **Leaves:** alternate, feather arrangement, from ***20–40 cm (8–16 in) long with 11 to 25 leaflets,*** the side leaflets short-stalked, 9–24 cm (3.5–9.5 in) long and 1–2.7 cm (0.4–1.1 in) wide, ***lance-shaped to narrowly lance-shaped,*** often curved, with a tapering elongated tip and a rounded or tapering, uneven base, the edge usually toothed, the upper surface yellowish-green and smooth, the lower surface paler and usually sparsely hairy, aromatic when crushed. **Flowers:** male flowers in slender, almost smooth, green catkins, 5–10 cm (2–4 in) long, each flower with 20 to 30 stamens; the female flowers usually 1 to 4 per short spike and at the end of the growth. **Fruits:** *small, globe-shaped,* single or in clusters of 2 or 3, *2–3.5 cm (0.8–1.4 in) in diameter,* green turning dark brown, the husk fibrous, with rusty hairs but becoming smooth at maturity. The round nuts generally flattened at the base, **with deep lengthwise, slightly forking ridges,** the shell thick and the kernel small, oily, sweet.

Arizona Walnut

Juglans major (Torr.) Heller

The Arizona black walnut is a rapid-growing tree generally found in dry rocky ravines and stream beds from approximately 700–2,300 m (2,300–7,600 ft). Young seedlings are infrequent since the reproductive rate is low. But the tree's long life, up to 400 years, generally ensures that a healthy mature tree will produce at least a few offspring that will reach maturity. This species is found typically at higher altitudes and is larger than the closely related Texas black walnut. The Spanish name for walnut tree, "nogal," is the source of the name of the Arizona city Nogales.

The dark-colored wood rivals that of the eastern black walnut (*Juglans nigra*). But the limited range and smaller size of this species have restricted the amounts harvested for lumber. The demand for this wood has eliminated the taller trees, leaving only the smaller, poorly shaped ones or those in inaccessible habitats. The tree's spreading branch pattern and its tolerance to drought have resulted in its use as a shade tree in the Southwest. The nuts serve as fall food for squirrels, other rodents, and some of the larger birds.

Arizona Walnut

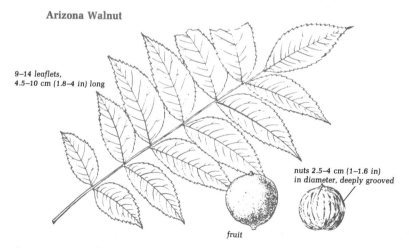

9–14 leaflets, 4.5–10 cm (1.8–4 in) long

nuts 2.5–4 cm (1–1.6 in) in diameter, deeply grooved

fruit

Appearance: small to medium-size tree, 10–18 m (32–60 ft), usually with a straight trunk, up to 1.3 m (4.3 ft) in diameter; the crown open, generally broadly rounded at the top. **Bark:** thin, smooth, and light gray when young, becoming thick, deeply furrowed with ridges, the ridges breaking into irregular, thin scales, dark gray to brownish-black. **Branches:** stout, spreading, and eventually may droop; the branchlets slender, with rust-colored hairs when young, becoming smooth and reddish-brown, pores small, light-colored; leaf scars large, triangular with rounded corners, with 3 bundle scars. **Winter buds:** similar to Texas black walnut. **Leaves:** alternate, feather arrangement (pinnate), from 22–32 cm (8.7–12.6 in) long *with 9 to 14, rarely 19, leaflets,* the leaflets short-stalked, 4.5–10 cm (1.8–4 in) long and 2.5–4 cm (1–1.6 in) wide, *egg-shaped to lance-shaped,* usually curved, tapering to a long point at the tip, tapering to rounded and uneven at the base, the margin coarsely toothed, the upper surface hairy when young but smooth with age, yellow-green, the lower surface paler, smooth except for the slightly hairy main vein. **Flowers:** male flowers in long, slender, hairy, yellowish catkins, 12–20 cm (4.7–8 in) long, each flower with 30 to 40 stamens; the female flowers on short spikes at the tip of the new growth, covered with brown wooly hairs. **Fruits:** *large, globe-shaped to slightly egg-shaped with a small, sharp point at the tip, usually single or in pairs, 2.5–4 cm (1–1.6 in) in diameter,* green turning rusty then dark brown, the husk fibrous, covered with dense hairs. The *round nuts slightly compressed and flattened at the base, 2.5–4 cm (1–1.6 in) in diameter,* brown to black, with deep, broad, lengthwise grooves, the shell thick, the kernel large, sweet.

Hinds Walnut   *Juglans hindsii* Jepson

The Hinds walnut occurs naturally near the coastal region of central California along the banks of the Sacramento River, along streams near the western base of Mt. Diablo, and along the eastern slope of the Napa Range. And it has been introduced and naturalized throughout most of California. The trees are found on rocky and gravelly, well-drained soil. As with other walnuts, the Hinds produces a large, deeply penetrating taproot that gives the tree more tolerance during prolonged dry periods. The smooth nuts readily distinguish the Hinds walnut from the southern California walnut.

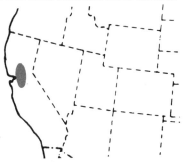

The hard, heavy, dark-brown wood is valuable. Thus, the tree is being planted and cultivated as a timber source in California. Most of the commercial plantations of the English walnut in southern California use the Hinds walnut as rootstock material because the lower stem and root system of the Hinds are much less subject to disease and insect attacks. Young shoots of the English walnut are grafted onto lower stems and roots of the Hinds. Here, the grafted trees have the benefit of the disease, pest, and drought resistance of the Hinds walnut while producing the valuable commercial nuts of the English walnut. The nuts are an important food for squirrels and other rodents.

Appearance: small to moderate-size tree 15–20 m, occasionally to 25 (49–65 ft, occasionally to 82); the trunk straight, to 0.7 m (2.3 ft) in diameter; the crown generally narrowly rounded at the top. **Bark:** smooth but with age becoming cracked along its length, moderately thick, forming narrow, brown-gray plates. **Branches:** stout, spreading, and hanging; the branchlets slender, reddish-brown, covered when young with dense hairs, becoming smooth after 2 or 3 years with scattered pale pores; leaf scars broadly triangular, the corners rounded, elevated, with 3 bundle scars. **Winter buds:**

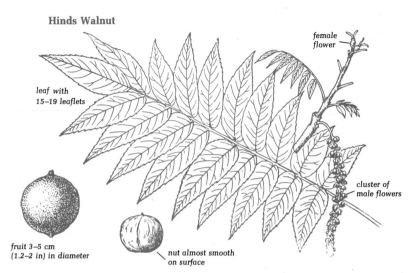

Hinds Walnut

leaf with 15–19 leaflets

female flower

cluster of male flowers

fruit 3–5 cm (1.2–2 in) in diameter

nut almost smooth on surface

end bud nearly globe-shaped, compressed at the sides, rounded at the tip, covered with dense hairs, 6–8 mm (0.3 in) long; side buds smaller. **Leaves:** alternate, feather arrangement, from 22–35 cm (8.6–13.8 in) long *with 15 to 19 leaflets, the leaflets generally 5.5–10 cm (2.2–4 in) long and 1.8–2.6 cm (0.7–1 in) wide, lance-shaped to broadly lance-shaped,* slightly curved, tapering to a long pointed tip, tapering to rounded at the base, the edge with occasional small teeth, bright green and smooth above, paler beneath with tufts of hairs at the junctions of the main veins. **Flowers:** male flowers in slender, hanging, smooth to slightly hairy, green-yellow catkins, 7.5–13 cm (3–5.1 in) long, each flower with 30 to 40 stamens; the female flowers borne on short, generally 1- to 3-flowered spikes at the tip of the new growth. **Fruits:** large, globe-shaped, 3–5 cm (1.2–2 in) in diameter, green turning dark brown, the husk thin, covered with numerous small hairs. The *nuts globe-shaped,* except for the flattened base, *almost smooth, the occasionally lengthwise grooves obscure,* the shell thick, the kernel small and sweet.

The Hickory Genus

Carya Nutt.

There are 15 species of hickories in the world, with 11 species found in the eastern U.S., adjacent Canada, and Mexico. The remaining 4 species occur in southeastern Asia. During the Tertiary Period in geological times, hickories were widespread in favorable temperate climates. Fossils of hickories are known from Alaska, the western and southwestern U.S., Central Europe, the Soviet Union, and China. Hickories no longer occur in western and northwestern North America or in Alaska.

Hickories are moderate to large-size trees with hard, dark-colored wood and taproots. The leaves are alternate, deciduous, pinnately compound (feather-like arrangement), often gland-dotted. In the winter condition, the end bud is large, broadest at the base, covered with large, tight to loosely fitting bud scales; and the leaf scars are large, elevated, shield-shaped, or 3-lobed. The flowers appear in spring, usually in April or May, the male flowers in hanging catkins generally clustered in groups of 3. The fruit has an outer husk that splits into 4 sections (completely or partially) at maturity to expose the nut. The nuts are usually smooth on the surface.

mm
cm   1   2   3   4   5   6   7   8   9   10   11
in   1   2   3   4

It is sometimes difficult to determine hickory species from specimens. But one should not become discouraged after encountering a specimen that appears intermediate between 2 species. The species of hickories exhibit wide variation and are known to hybridize. Thus, offspring display intermediate features.

Hickories produce enormous amounts of pollen in spring and depend upon the wind to carry the male pollen grains to the female flowers. Studies have shown that individual trees are capable of pollinating themselves, but these trees produce fewer fruits and a lower quality nut than trees that are cross-pollinated by other trees. Hickories are partly responsible for many cases of spring hayfever, especially where the trees are abundant. Several species are important sources of lumber. The pecan is the only hickory to be exploited widely for its high-quality, sweet nuts. The nuts of all hickories are important as a food for game animals (black bears, whitetail deer, foxes, rabbits, raccoons, and squirrels), game birds (pheasants, quail, turkeys, ducks), song birds (crows, grosbeaks, and bluejays), and smaller rodents.

Key to Hickory Species

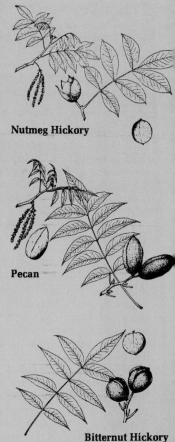

A. Leaves with 7–17, rarely 5 leaflets, usually curved; bud scales 4–6 per bud, the individual scales touching but not overlapping each other; fruit with narrow wings along the seams of the 4-parted husk.

  1. Leaflets slightly curved; nuts rounded, egg-shaped to broadest near the tip, the shell thick **Nutmeg hickory, p. 278**

Nutmeg Hickory

  2. Leaflets curved; nuts flattened or torpedo-shaped (cylinder-shape with a pointed tip), the shell thin.

    a. Leaflets 9–17; fruit rounded, the nut cylindric and usually torpedo-shaped, the kernel sweet   **Pecan, p. 279**

    b. Leaflets 7–13; fruits and nuts flattened to almost globe-shaped, the kernel bitter.

Pecan

      (1) Leaflets 7–13, usually 9–11; the nuts strongly flattened; the end winter buds dark reddish-brown **Water hickory, p. 280**

      (2) Leaflets 7–9, usually 7; the nuts almost globe-shaped; the end winter buds yellow **Bitternut hickory, p. 282**

B. Leaves with 3–9 leaflets, the end one largest; bud scales usually 6 or more, overlapping; fruit usually lacking narrow wings along the seams of the husk.

  1. End buds large, 1.2–3.7 cm (0.5–1.5 in) long;

Bitternut Hickory

branchlets usually stout; fruit large, 2.5–6.5 cm (1–2.6 in) long, the husk splitting open all the way to the base at maturity.

a. Bark of mature trees close pressed, not scaly, leaflets 5–7 per leaf, the leaflets hairy beneath; the branchlets and leafstalks very hairy   **Mockernut hickory, p. 283**

b. Bark of mature trees scaly or shaggy, usually separating in long, loose plates; leaflets 5–9, usually 7; the branchlets and leafstalks smooth to slightly hairy.

    (1) Leaflets usually 5, occasionally 7, the leaflets with sharp-pointed teeth and edged with numerous hairs; branchlets reddish-brown, hairy, the shell of the nut thin   **Shagbark hickory, p. 284**

    (2) Leaflets usually 7; the leaflets with numerous, tiny teeth, not edged with hairs; branchlets orange-brown, becoming smooth, the shell of the nut very thick   **Big shellbark hickory, p. 286**

2. End buds small, 0.6–1.2 cm (0.2–0.5 in) long; branchlets usually slender; fruits usually 2–3.7 cm (0.8–1.5 in) long, the husk splitting only partially to the base at maturity.

a. Branchlets, leaves, and winter buds covered with a dense layer of reddish-brown hairs.

    (1) Fruits globe-shaped to broadest near the tip, 3–5 cm (1.2–2 in) long; leaflets with rust-colored hairs grouped in small clusters on the lower surface; southcentral U.S.
              Black hickory, p. 287

    (2) Fruits globe-shaped to pear-shaped, 2.2–4 cm (0.9–1.6 in) long; leaflets gland-dotted on the lower surface; central to northwestern Florida
              Scrub hickory, p. 288

b. Branchlets, leaves, and winter buds smooth or covered with silvery scales and hairs.

    (1) Leaflets smooth or becoming smooth; leafstalks smooth; fruits broadest near the tip, smooth, dark brown; eastern U.S.   **Pignut hickory, p. 290**

(Continued)

Mockernut Hickory

Shagbark Hickory

Big Shellbark Hickory

Black Hickory

Pignut Hickory

(2) Leaflets covered with tiny silvery scales when young, the lower surface very hairy; leafstalks hairy; winter buds 5–7 mm (0.2–0.3 in) long, hairy and covered with tiny, silvery scales; fruits egg-shaped to globe-shaped, the fruit covered with yellow scales; Atlantic and Gulf Coastal Plain

Sand hickory, p. 291

Sand Hickory

Nutmeg Hickory   *Carya myristiciformis* (Michx. f.) Nutt.

The nutmeg hickory does not occur abundantly within its narrow range. Generally it is found in rich, higher bottomlands and along stream banks. Because of its limited occurrence, this hickory is not a dominant element in forests. Unlike most of the native hickories, relatively little is known about the natural history of this species. The common and scientific name of this species is derived from the fruit, which is approximately the same size and shape as a true nutmeg fruit.

As with other hickories, large nut crops are produced every 2 or 3 years and serve as a valuable source of oil-rich food for larger birds, squirrels, other small rodents, and whitetail deer. Without their caches of nuts, many animals would not be able to survive the winter months. The nutmeg hickory is not sufficiently abundant for the wood to be of economic importance. When it is cut, it is referred to simply as "hickory," with no attempt to distinguish the different types.

Nutmeg Hickory

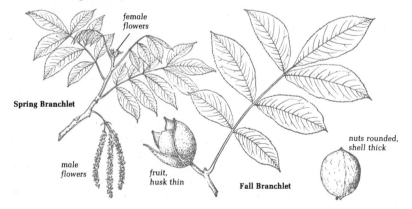

female flowers

Spring Branchlet

male flowers

fruit, husk thin

Fall Branchlet

nuts rounded, shell thick

Appearance: medium to tall narrow trees to 35 m (115 ft), with an open rounded crown; trunk straight, up to 0.7 m (2.3 ft) in diameter. **Bark:** thick, smooth to shaggy, dark reddish-brown, with shallow furrows forming irregular, small, thin scales. **Branches:** stout, slightly spreading to ascending; branchlets slender, covered with brown to yellow scales, light brown to gray and hairy when young, becoming dark reddish-brown with age; the pores small, scattered, leaf scars oval, slightly elevated. **Winter buds:** end buds broadest at the base, blunt at the tip, from 4–6 mm (0.2 in) long, covered by thick, yellowish to brownish hairs, the lateral buds smaller. **Leaves:** alternate on the branchlets, feather-like arrangement, 15–35 cm (6–13.8 in) long, **with 7 to 9 leaflets,** rarely 5, the leaflets 8–12 cm (3.2–4.8 in) long, 2.5–4 cm (1–1.6 in) broad, broadest near the base to broadest near the tip, **slightly curved,** tapering to a sharp point at the tip, tapering to rounded at the uneven base, the edges with many coarse teeth, the upper surface dark green, the lower surface paler, slightly hairy to smooth except for the usually hairy midvein, often shiny. **Flowers:** male flowers in slender, long-stalked catkins, 7.5–10 cm (3–4 in) long, covered with brownish hairs, each flower usually with 6 stamens; the female flowers borne on short, few-flowered spikes at the tip of the new growth, each flower tiny, pear-shaped and 4-angled. **Fruits:** often occurring singly, broadest near the middle and rounded at the ends to broadest near the tip, 2.5–3.5 cm (1–1.4 in) long, with 4 prominent ribs, covered with yellow to brown scaly hairs, the husk very thin, splitting open at maturity to the base of the nut. **Nuts:** *generally broadest near the middle, rounded,* with a small, sharp-pointed tip, smooth, brown to dark brown, *the shell thick,* the kernel sweet.

Pecan — *Carya illinoensis* (Wangenh.) K. Koch

The pecan is native to the rich moist soils of the bottomlands, primarily of the Mississippi River Valley, although its range has been extended greatly by plantings throughout most of the southeastern and southcentral U.S. This species grows best where average summer temperatures are 24–30°C (75–86°F) accompanied by high humidity. The pecan requires a long frost-free period for the nuts to reach maturity and full size in the fall. Native trees, such as sycamore and elm, often are found in association with pecan. The tallest-growing of all native hickories, the pecan begins bearing fruit at approximately 20 years of age, with the best period of production being from 75 to 225 years old.

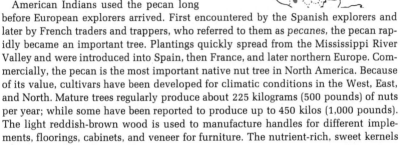

American Indians used the pecan long before European explorers arrived. First encountered by the Spanish explorers and later by French traders and trappers, who referred to them as *pecanes*, the pecan rapidly became an important tree. Plantings quickly spread from the Mississippi River Valley and were introduced into Spain, then France, and later northern Europe. Commercially, the pecan is the most important native nut tree in North America. Because of its value, cultivars have been developed for climatic conditions in the West, East, and North. Mature trees regularly produce about 225 kilograms (500 pounds) of nuts per year; while some have been reported to produce up to 450 kilos (1,000 pounds). The light reddish-brown wood is used to manufacture handles for different implements, floorings, cabinets, and veneer for furniture. The nutrient-rich, sweet kernels

Pecan

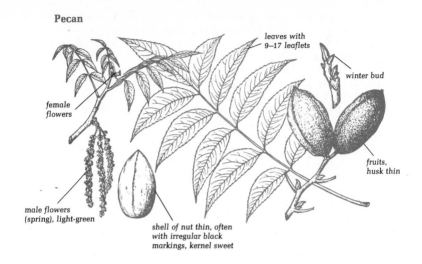

are an excellent food for wildlife, including waterfowl, larger game birds, deer, foxes, and especially squirrels. In fact, squirrels are considered pests in pecan plantations.

Appearance: tall trees to 60 m (200 ft), narrow near the base but spreading at the top, the crown open, usually broadly rounded at the top; trunk straight, large, up to 2.5 m (8.2 ft) in diameter. **Bark:** thick, grayish-brown to light brown when young, becoming dark reddish-brown with age, with deep, narrow furrows irregularly divided to form rough, usually angled ridges or scales. **Branches:** stout, erect to slightly spreading; branchlets stout, often short, light brown and hairy when young, becoming smooth and reddish-brown by the second year, with numerous, elongated orange pores; leaf scars large, elongated, 3-lobed. **Winter buds:** end buds flattened, sharp-pointed at the tip, 10–12 mm (0.4–0.5 in) long, yellow-brown, hairy. **Leaves:** alternate on the branchlets, feather-like arrangement, 32–52 cm (12.5–20.5 in) long *with 9 to 17 leaflets,* the leaflets 8–20 cm (3.2–8 in) long, 2.5–7.5 cm (1–3 in) wide, lance-shaped or nearly so, *curved,* tapering to a long pointed tip, unequally rounded or tapering at the base, the edges coarsely toothed, the upper surface smooth to slightly hairy, dark yellow-green, the lower surface paler, smooth to hairy. **Flowers:** male flowers in slender, usually 3-clustered, slightly hairy, light green catkins, 12–15 cm (4.7–5.9 in) long, each flower with 5 or 6 stamens; the female flowers in few to several-flowered terminal spikes, each flower short, 4-angled, hairy, yellow. **Fruits:** large, oblong to slightly broader near the base, usually clustered in groups of 3 to 6, rarely more, 3.5–5 cm (1.4–2 in) long, pointed at the tip, rounded at the base, the husk thin, narrowly 4-winged and 4-angled, dark brown, hairy, splitting at maturity to expose the nut. **Nuts:** *cylinder-shaped to slightly broadest at the base,* pointed at the tip, light brown to reddish-brown and often with *irregular black markings on the shell, the shell thin, the kernel oily, sweet.*

Water Hickory, Bitter Hickory   *Carya aquatica* (Michx. f.) Nutt.

The water hickory occurs in wet, poorly drained coastal plain flats, river bottoms, and swamps. Although tolerant of poorly drained soils, this species will grow better on well-drained alluvial soils. Within its range, this hickory usually is found in extensive stands with the overcup oak or in stands with American elm, sugarberry, and green ash. The water hickory is a slow-growing tree that generally doesn't begin producing fruits until after age 20.

While the tree trunks may be tall and straight, the heavy, close-grained, light-colored wood is brittle, thus limiting its use. It is used mainly in fencing and as firewood where it yields considerably more heat per cord of wood than many of the lighter, open-grained woods of other trees. The nuts are important to wildlife.

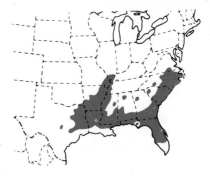

Water Hickory

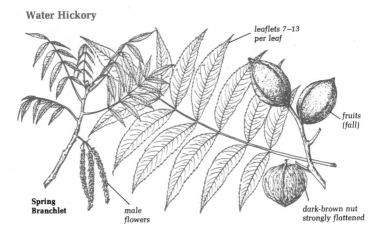

leaflets 7–13 per leaf

fruits (fall)

Spring Branchlet

male flowers

dark-brown nut strongly flattened

Appearance: medium to tall tree to 35 m (115 ft) with a narrowly rounded crown; trunk usually straight, up to 1 m (3.3 ft) in diameter. **Bark:** thick, light brown, sometimes tinged with red, splitting freely into long, loose, plate-like shaggy scales. **Branches:** upright, often slender; the branchlets slender, brown to ash gray, glandular and hairy when young, becoming smooth and lustrous with age; pores pale; leaf scars oval or slightly 3-lobed, slightly raised. **Winter buds:** end buds slightly flattened, pointed at the tip, from 3–5 mm (0.1–0.2 in) long, often dark reddish-brown, covered with yellow scales. **Leaves:** alternate on the branchlets, feather-like arrangement, from 7.2–40 cm (2.8–15.8 in) long *with 7 to 13 leaflets,* leaflets 7.2–10 cm (2.8–4 in) long, 1.2–3.5 cm (0.5–1.4 in) broad, narrowly egg-shaped to lance-shaped, *curved,* tapering to a long point at the tip, rounded to tapering at the base, the margin with fine to coarse teeth, covered with yellow glandular dots, the upper surface smooth, the lower surface hairy, especially along the veins. **Flowers:** male flowers greenish-yellow in stalked catkins 6–7.5 cm (2.4–3 in) long that may be solitary or in groups up to 4, each flower with 5 to 6 stamens and covered with yellow hairs; the female flowers usually 2 to 6 per spike, usually at the tip of the new growth, pear-shaped and usually 4-angled. **Fruits:** usually occurring in clusters of 3 or 4, small, *strongly flattened, 2.5–4 cm (1–1.6 in) long,* pear to egg-shaped, often broadest above the middle, coming to an abrupt tip, with 4 narrow but conspicuous wings along the seams, the husk thin, covered with yellow scales, splitting open for about half its length. **Nuts:** *flattened,* broadest at or above the middle, generally as broad as long, *4-angled,* dark brown, with irregular, lengthwise, shallow furrows, *the shell thin, the kernel very bitter.*

Bitternut Hickory · *Carya cordiformis* (Wangenh.) K. Koch

One of the more commonly occurring species, the bitternut hickory can grow in varied soil conditions. While it is found in swamps and areas subject to frequent flooding, it does best on rich bottomlands and can be found even on drier hillsides. Because of its size and abundance, the bitternut is a major element in many oak-hickory forests encountered in the midwestern, southern, and eastern U.S. Fruit production normally begins at 25 to 30 years of age and then alternates between a year of heavy production and 2 or 3 years of light production. This species occurs in a wide temperature and soil range. Viable nuts are dispersed by water, especially flooding, and by small rodents, especially squirrels.

The heavy, close-grained, hard wood is used for tool handles and formerly was used for wooden wheels. Although the wood has a tendency to be brittle, it has an amazing quality of shock-resistance. The dense heavy wood has high value as a fuel. Oil expressed from the kernels was used by early settlers in oil lamps and in rheumatism medicines. The bitter-tasting nuts are not eaten by man and seem to be less favored by animals than the sweeter-tasting nuts of some other hickories.

Bitternut Hickory

female flowers

male flowers in spring

usually 7–9 leaflets per leaf

nuts nearly globe shaped, kernel bitter

fall fruits

Appearance: tall trees to 35 m (115 ft), narrow but spreading near the top with age, the crown open, rounded at the top; trunk straight, up to 1 m (3.3 ft) in diameter. **Bark:** thin, shallowly fissured and forming flat ridges, light-brown to brownish-red (does not form shaggy bark like the water hickory or shagbark hickory). **Branches:** stout, ascending to spreading; the branchlets slender, greenish, and slightly hairy when young, becoming gray to reddish or yellow-brown by the second or third year, with numerous, small, pale-colored pores; leaf scars small, oval to slightly 3-lobed, somewhat raised. **Winter buds:** end buds *laterally flattened,* with the 2 scales forming an unequal blunt tip, *10–18 mm (0.4–0.7 in) long, yellow, hairy, and scaly.* **Leaves:** alternate on the branchlets, feather-like arrangement, 15–30 cm (5.9–11.8 in) long *with 7 to 9 leaflets,* seldom 5, the leaflets 10–15 cm (4–6 in) long, 2–2.8 cm (0.8–1.1 in) broad, lance-shaped to long lance-shaped, tapering to a long pointed tip, rounded to tapering at the uneven base, the margin with coarse teeth, the upper surface smooth, yellow-green, often shiny, *the lower surface paler, hairy and often gland-dotted.* **Flowers:** male flowers in slender, stalked, clustered, slightly hairy catkins, 7–10 cm (2.8–4 in) long, each flower typically with 4 stamens; the female flowers usually single or in pairs on a short, terminal spike, each flower short, thick, and 4-angled. **Fruits:** *small,* rounded to slightly broader near the tip, *flattened, 2–3.6 cm (0.8–1.4 in) long,* with a short, sharp-pointed tip, with 4 narrow wings from midway to the tip, the husk thin, covered with yellowish, curly hairs. **Nuts:** *generally broadest near the base, laterally compressed,* with a short, sharp-pointed tip, brown to reddish-brown, *the shell thin, the kernel very bitter.*

Mockernut Hickory, White Hickory   Carya tomentosa (Poir.) Nutt.
(synonym: C. *alba* (Mill.) K. Koch)

The mockernut is a common species of hickory and a major component of oak-hickory forests in the eastern U.S. and the most commonly encountered hickory in the southern U.S. The trees occur mainly along ridges, dry hills, and hillsides and grow best in rich, well-drained soils. Trees of this species reach their greatest size on the lower Ohio River Basin and in the Mississippi River Basin in Missouri and Arkansas. These handsome trees have large hairy leaves that do not fall as quickly in autumn as do leaves from other species.

The wood from these tall, straight-growing trees is among the best of the hickories. The tough, hard, strong wood has excellent bending qualities and can withstand compression better than most other woods. It is used for tool handles, wood splints, and for the manufacture of rustic furniture. The early settlers in the vicinity of Niagara Falls extracted a black dye by boiling small pieces of bark in a vinegar solution.

The small nuts generally are not produced until the trees are about 20 years old. The optimum nut-bearing age is between 40 and 150 years of age. These long-lived trees will survive from 300 to 500 years. The sweet kernels are contained in small nuts and enclosed by thick shells that make it difficult to remove the meat. The common name "mockernut" originated as a result of this problem. The nuts are eaten by squirrels, raccoons, chipmunks, and other rodents. Whitetail deer browse on young shoots.

Appearance: large trees to 35 m (115 ft), the crown narrow to broadly rounded; the trunk straight, to 1.5 m (4.9 ft) in diameter, unbranched for about half its height in forest or widely branched and spreading in the open. **Bark:** thin, dark gray, close, with shallow irregular furrows and narrow flat ridges in a criss-cross or net-like pattern, *never shaggy.* **Branches:** stout, upright and rigid, spreading or hanging; the branchlets stout, grayish-brown to reddish-brown and hairy when young, becoming smooth

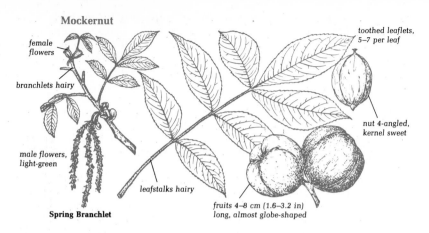

Mockernut

female flowers

branchlets hairy

male flowers, light-green

Spring Branchlet

leafstalks hairy

toothed leaflets, 5–7 per leaf

nut 4-angled, kernel sweet

fruits 4–8 cm (1.6–3.2 in) long, almost globe-shaped

with age, with scattered, conspicuous pale pores; leaf scars large, 3-lobed, the lower most often longer than the others. **Winter buds:** end buds *very broad at the base,* tapering to a pointed or rounded tip, *1.5–2 cm (0.6–0.8 in) long, covered by 3 or 4 overlapping, dark reddish-brown, hairy scales;* lateral buds about half the size of the end bud. **Leaves:** alternate on the branchlets, feather-like arrangement, 14–32 cm (5.5–12.6 in) long, *with 5 or 7 leaflets,* the upper pair of leaflets 12–22 cm (4.7–8.7 in) long and 7.5–12.5 cm (3–4.9 in) wide, the lower pairs about two-thirds as large, fragrant, narrow and widest above the middle, tapering gradually or abruptly to a point, rounded to tapering to an unequal base, the edge with small to large teeth, the upper surface dark yellow-green, shiny, hairy, covered with tiny resinous glands, the lower surface pale, light orange to brown-colored, hairy, with numerous, tiny, resinous glands. **Flowers:** male flowers on stalked, 3-clustered, light green catkins, hairy and covered with yellow-green, loose scales, 10–15 cm (3.9–5.9 in) long, each flower usually with 4 stamens; female flowers 2–5 on short spikes at the ends of new branches, each flower small, pear-shaped, hairy. **Fruits:** *medium-size to large,* occurring singly or in small clusters, nearly globe-shaped to egg-shaped, *4–8 cm (1.6–3.2 in) long* and almost as wide, slightly compressed, 4-angled, pointed at the tip, the husk thick, hairy to almost smooth, splitting to expose the nut. **Nuts:** *nearly rounded to egg-shaped,* slightly compressed laterally, pointed to long-pointed at the tip, rounded at the base, *obscurely to strongly 4-angled,* light reddish-brown, *the shell thick, hard, the kernel sweet.*

Shagbark Hickory, Shellbark Hickory *Carya ovata* (Mill.) K. Koch

[synonym: *C. carolinae-septentrionalis* (Ashe) Engl. & Graebn.]

The shagbark hickory ranges over most of eastern North America and grows on both drier upland slopes to 600 m (2,000 ft) and on deep, well-drained soils in lowlands and valleys. Not as abundant as the bitternut hickory, the shagbark is an occasional member of the oak-hickory hardwood forests of eastern North America.

The nuts of this species were a staple among the fall foods consumed by many

tribes of American Indians. The ground and mashed nuts were mixed with water to extract the oil and make a "hickory milk" that was used in making different types of cakes. Settlers quickly learned of the value and use of these nuts from the Indians. Of all the different hickories, the shagbark is the easiest to distinguish in the field. This aids in collecting only sweet nuts. Like other hickories the shagbark hickory has among the highest fuel values of all American woods. A cord of this hickory is almost equivalent in thermal units to a ton of anthracite coal. It is used frequently to cure hams, sides of bacon, and other meats. The wood of the shagbark hickory is used to produce high-quality charcoal.

The wood is heavy, close-grained, tough, light brown, and is used in the manufacture of handles for axes and other tools, baskets, wagons, and was once used for wooden wheels. The tough resilient qualities of the wood make it suitable for use where wood is subject to impact.

Shagbark Hickory

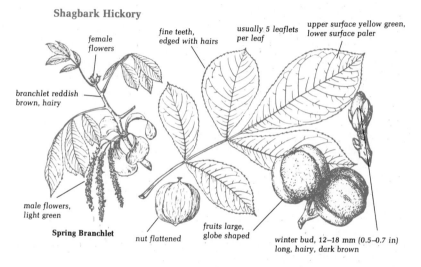

female flowers

fine teeth, edged with hairs

usually 5 leaflets per leaf

upper surface yellow green, lower surface paler

branchlet reddish brown, hairy

male flowers, light green

Spring Branchlet

nut flattened

fruits large, globe shaped

winter bud, 12–18 mm (0.5–0.7 in) long, hairy, dark brown

Appearance: tall trees to 45 m (150 ft), narrow to somewhat spreading, usually broadest above the middle, the crown open, rounded; trunk straight, up to 1.5 m (4.9 ft) in diameter. **Bark:** moderately thick, light to dark gray, *broken into long, loose, flattened plates with the ends curving away from the trunk giving a shaggy appearance.* **Branches:** stout, spreading to sometimes drooping; the branchlets stout, usually angular, reddish-brown and hairy when young but becoming dark gray and smooth with age, with numerous, small, pale pores; leaf scars conspicuous, broadly rounded to slightly 3-lobed, elevated. **Winter buds:** end buds broadest at the base, rounded to blunt at the tip, *12–18 mm (0.5–0.7 in) long, hairy, usually dark brown.* **Leaves:** alternate on the branchlets, feather-like arrangement, 20–36 cm (8–14.2 in) long with *usually 5 leaflets,* sometimes 7, the end leaflets larger than the other leaflets, the leaflets 8–18 cm (3–7 in) long, 1.5–6 cm (0.6–2.4 in) broad, generally broadest near the tip to broadest near the middle, usually tapering to a point at the tip, tapering to rounded at the base, the *margin with fine, sharp-pointed teeth and edged with numerous hairs,* the *upper surface yellow-green and smooth,* the *lower surface paler and occasionally with short, fine hairs,* especially on the primary veins. **Flowers:** male flowers on stalked, clustered, light green, slender catkins, hairy, glandular,

10–13 cm (4–5.1 in) long, each flower usually with 4 stamens; female flowers on few-flowered, short, terminal spikes, each flower short, angled, covered with dense, rust-colored hairs. **Fruits:** large, generally in pairs or solitary, globe-shaped to sometimes longer than broad, 3–5 cm (1.2–2 in) long, depressed or slightly sunken at the tip, the husk moderately thick, dark brown, reddish-brown, or even black at maturity, smooth or hairy, splitting to the base of the nuts. **Nuts:** variable in shape, ***generally longer than broad, flattened, usually 4-angled,*** light-colored, the shell thin, the kernel sweet, aromatic.

Big Shellbark Hickory, King Nut Hickory *Carya laciniosa* (Michx. f.) Loud.

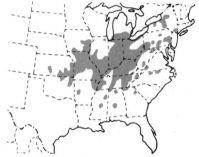

The big shellbark hickory occurs primarily in the Ohio and upper Mississippi River valleys, especially on deep, fertile, moist soils of bottomlands and floodplains. The trees grow best on neutral or slightly alkaline soils and tolerate shallow flooding in early spring. These slow-growing, long-lived trees never occur in pure stands but often are found growing in association with red maple and chestnut oak. Some trees have been shown to gain only 2.5 cm (1 in) in radius in approximately 30 years. Thus, 200- to 300-year-old trees average only 40 cm (16 in) in diameter. One of the largest known big shellbark hickories is found in Big Tree State Park, Missouri. This tree measures about 3.5 m (11.5 ft) in circumference and towers about 45 m (150 ft) high. ***The big shellbark hickory resembles the shagbark hickory in appearance, but the big shellbark generally has 7 leaflets rather than the 5 common to shagbarks. And the big shellbark's leaves do not have hairs at the tip of the teeth.***

The hard, tough, strong, resilient, dark brown wood is used for the same purposes as wood of other hickories. The main uses are tool handles, ladders, baskets, and fuel. The edible nuts are the largest of all hickory nuts and are sought by many mammals,

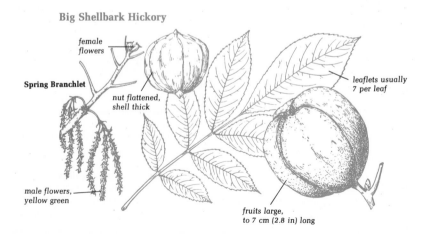

Big Shellbark Hickory

female flowers

Spring Branchlet

nut flattened, shell thick

leaflets usually 7 per leaf

male flowers, yellow green

fruits large, to 7 cm (2.8 in) long

such as black bears, foxes, rabbits, raccoons, tree squirrels, and chipmunks. Whitetail deer feed on the leaves, young shoots, and nuts. Ducks, quail, and wild turkeys also feed upon the nuts.

Appearance: large, generally cylindric trees to 40 m (132 ft); the crown oblong to rounded; the trunk straight, slender, to 1 m (3.3 ft) in diameter, often free of branches for more than half its height. **Bark:** moderately thick, light gray, forming long, thick plates with the ends curving away from the trunk. **Branches:** the lowermost drooping, the others spreading, stout; the branchlets stout, angular and hairy when young, orange-brown, becoming rounded and smooth with age, with scattered, slightly elevated pores; leaf scars conspicuous, 3-lobed. **Winter buds:** end buds broadest near the base, *blunt at the tip, 2.2–2.7 cm (1 in) long,* expanding to 5–6 cm (2–2.4 in) in spring, *with 11 or 12 overlapping, dark-brown scales,* becoming light green or yellow in spring, covered with tiny hairs; side buds about one-fourth size of terminal buds. **Leaves:** alternate, feather-like arrangement, 25–60 cm (10–24 in) long, *with 5–9 leaflets, usually 7,* the upper pair of leaflets from 12–25 cm (4.7–10 in) long, 7.5–12.5 cm (3–5 in) wide, the lower pairs from one-half to one-third as large, lance-shaped to broadest near the base, tapering to sharp-pointed at the tip, tapering to rounded at the nearly symmetrical base, the margin with numerous, tiny teeth, the upper surface dark green, smooth, the lower surface pale, yellow-green, covered with fine, soft hairs. **Flowers:** male flowers on stalked, usually 3-clustered, yellow-green catkins, smooth to covered with rust-colored scales, 12–20 cm (4.7–8 in) long, each flower with 3 to 10 stamens; female flowers 2 to 5 on short spikes at the ends of new branches, each flower small, usually broadest near the base, slightly angled, densely hairy. **Fruits:** large, occurring singly or in pairs, egg-shaped to nearly globe-shaped, to 7 cm (2.8 in) long and 5 cm (2 in) wide, usually depressed at the tip, the husk thick, smooth to downy, brown to yellow-brown, splitting readily to expose the nut. **Nuts:** *egg-shaped to broadest near the tip, flattened, rounded to pointed at the ends,* usually ridged and angled, the *shell very thick, hard,* the *kernel sweet.*

Black Hickory   *Carya texana* Buckl.

The black hickory is found on dry, often rocky, hillsides, on sandy uplands, and along the upper rims of creek banks in rocky soils in the southern midwest and southcentral U.S. Individual trees are scattered throughout its range, occurring at altitudes of 600–700 m (1,900–2,300 ft). Some authorities have recognized 3 varieties of the black hickory, but it is sufficient to consider them all 1 here.

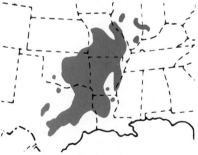

The small to medium-size trees, often with crooked branches, are not important for lumber. The strong hard wood is brittle and is used primarily for fuel. The nut kernels are sweet and are sought after by hogs, but the hard shell limits their availability to small wild mammals and some of the larger birds such as jays.

Appearance: small to medium-size trees to 28 m (92 ft); the crown narrow to spreading; the trunk to approximately 60–70 cm (23.6–27.6 in) in diameter. **Bark:** thick, dark gray to nearly black on older trees, irregularly fissured with shallow to deep furrows forming blocky ridges that separate into thin scales. **Branches:** short, often crooked, the lowermost drooping, the others spreading; the branchlets slender, covered with rust-colored hairs and loose scales when young, becoming dark gray-

Black Hickory

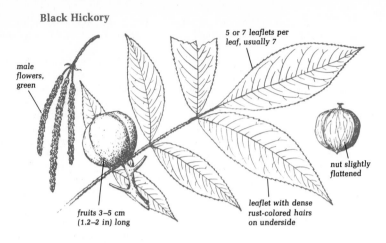

male flowers, green

5 or 7 leaflets per leaf, usually 7

nut slightly flattened

fruits 3–5 cm (1.2–2 in) long

leaflet with dense rust-colored hairs on underside

brown to red-brown and smooth with age, with scattered pale pores; leaf scars large, triangular to 3-lobed. **Winter buds:** end buds *broadest near the base,* rounded to pointed at the tip, *7.5–14 mm (0.3–0.6 in) long* and 3.6–6 mm (0.1–0.2 in) wide, *covered with rusty hairs and yellow-brown, loose scales, the tip with a tuft of white hairs;* lateral buds about half as large. **Leaves:** alternate on the branchlets, feather-like arrangement, 20–30 cm (8–11.8 in) long, *with 5–7 leaflets, usually 7,* the end leaflet usually larger and broadest near the tip, other leaflets 10–15 cm (4–6 in) long, 3–6 cm (1.2–2.4 in) wide, lance-shaped to narrow and broadest near the tip, pointed to tapering at the tip, tapering to a slightly unequal base, the edge with numerous tiny teeth, the upper surface dark green, shiny, smooth, *the lower surface pale, covered with rust-colored hairs grouped in small clusters,* becoming smooth with age, with red or orange-colored tiny glands. **Flowers:** male flowers on stalked, usually 3-clustered, green catkins, hairy, 6–14 cm (2.4–5.5 in) long, each flower with 4 to 6 stamens; female flowers 1 to 2 on short-stalked spikes at the end of new branches, each flower small, pear-shaped, slightly angled, densely hairy. **Fruits:** *medium-size to large,* occurring singly or in small clusters, globe-shaped to broadest near the tip, *3–5 cm (1.2–2 in) long and wide,* slightly depressed at the tip, the husk thin, covered with scattered, rust-colored hairs and yellow or orange-colored tiny glands, splitting along 4 valves to expose the nut. **Nuts:** *globe-shaped to broadest near the tip, slightly flattened,* pointed at the tip, rounded at the base, usually angled, pale brown to reddish-brown, *the shell moderately thick, hard, the kernel sweet.*

Scrub Hickory, Florida Hickory   *Carya floridana* Sarg.

The scrub hickory is confined largely to the scrub vegetation of coastal dunes and dry sand ridges from central to northwestern Florida. This species is adapted to growing on dry sandy soils. The taller-growing trees resemble the pignut hickory; in fact, some authorities question the distinctness of the scrub hickory since it appears to intergrade with the pignut hickory. The scrub hickory generally is associated with evergreen scrub oaks and the sand pines in its native habitat.

    Because of its generally shrubby form and limited range, this species is useless as a timber. Very little is known about this species and about the utilization of the nuts by wildlife, but the sweet kernels undoubtedly are sought by squirrels, other rodents, and larger birds.

Appearance: shrub or small trees to 25 m (82 ft), spreading; the crown usually broad, rounded; the trunk usually straight, up to 0.5 m (1.6 ft) in diameter. **Bark:** moderately thick, pale gray to dark gray-brown or olive-gray, almost smooth when young, close and slightly rough by the shallow, flat-topped, interlacing ridges. **Branches:** stout, usually irregular, slender and spreading; the branchlets slender, often crooked, dark red-brown, with rust-colored hairs when young but becoming

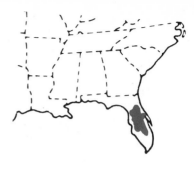

Scrub Hickory

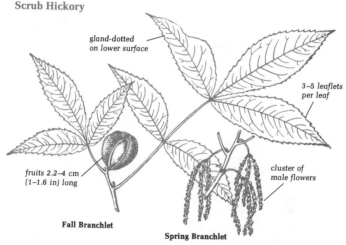

gland-dotted on lower surface

3–5 leaflets per leaf

fruits 2.2–4 cm (1–1.6 in) long

cluster of male flowers

Fall Branchlet

Spring Branchlet

smooth with age, with occasional elongated, raised pores; leaf scars shield-shaped. **Winter buds:** end buds *broadest near the base,* rounded to pointed at the tip, *5–10 mm (0.2–0.4 in) long, covered with rust-colored hairs and yellowish scales,* **Leaves:** alternate, feather-like arrangement, 12–21 cm (4.7–8.3 in) long *with 3 to 5 leaflets,* rarely 7, the leaflets 5–10 cm (2–4 in) long, 2.5–5 cm (1–2 in) wide, the lowest pair of leaflets smaller, lance-shaped to narrow and widest near the tip, tapering to a long pointed tip, rounded to tapering at the uneven base, the edge occasionally toothed, the individual teeth usually with a tough, club-like point, the upper surface yellow-green, hairy when young becoming smooth with age, the lower surface paler and covered with gland-dotted scales. **Flowers:** male flowers on long-stalked, 3-clustered, yellow-green catkins, scruffy, 2.5–4 cm (1–1.6 in) long, each flower with 4 or 5 stamens; female flowers 1 to 3 clustered on short spikes at the ends of new branchlets, each flower small, densely covered with yellow scales. **Fruits:** small to moderate-size, occurring singly or clustered, pear-shaped to globe-shaped, often variable between trees, 2.2–4 cm (1–1.6 in) long, rounded and sometimes slightly depressed at the tip, tapering to a short-stalked base, the husk thin, brown to yellow-brown at maturity, covered with small hairs and small yellow scales, splitting irregularly to the base to expose the nut. **Nuts:** *nearly globe-shaped* to *broadest near the base,* irregularly ridged, the *shell thick,* the *kernel sweet.*

Pignut Hickory

Carya glabra (Mill.) Sweet
(synonym: *C. leiodermis* Sarg.)

The pignut hickory is a common tree of eastern North America, extending from south-western Ontario, Canada, to central Florida. It generally grows in dry woods, primarily on hillsides and along dry ridges. Best growth occurs in deep, moist, well-drained soils. This hickory is a major component of the extensive oak-hickory woodlands in the East. Trees commonly growing in association with pignut hickory include white oak, red oak, black oak, post oak, and blackgum.

The trees are slow to moderately fast growing, depending upon soil conditions. Normally, 25 to 30 years are required before the trees begin to produce fruits and twice that age is needed to reach the peak period of production. The nuts are an important staple in the diet of red, gray, and fox squirrels, chipmunks, and raccoons. The trees are a minor food for the whitetail deer. The light- to dark-brown wood is hard, heavy, and possesses the same qualities of other hickories. It is harvested for lumber.

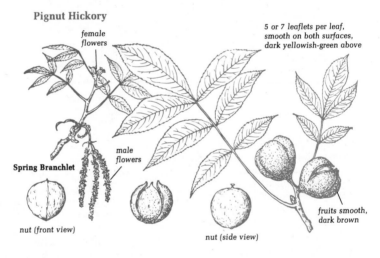

Pignut Hickory

female flowers

5 or 7 leaflets per leaf, smooth on both surfaces, dark yellowish-green above

Spring Branchlet

male flowers

fruits smooth, dark brown

nut (front view)

nut (side view)

Appearance: medium-size to tall trees 25–40 m (82–132 ft), usually with a broad cylinder shape and a rounded crown; trunk straight, to 1.3 m (4.3 ft) in diameter. **Bark:** thin, 1–2 cm (0.4–0.7 in) thick, gray, rough from numerous shallow, criss-crossing fissures forming close, flattened scales. **Branches:** short, stout, spreading; branchlets slender, usually angled, reddish-brown to gray, smooth, with numerous, light-colored pores; leaf scars small, oval to almost 3-lobed. **Winter buds:** end buds broadest at the base to broadest near the middle, 6–9 mm (0.2–0.4 in) long, light brown, smooth. **Leaves:** alternate on the branchlets, feather-like arrangement, 15–30 cm (6–11.8 in) long, **with 5 or 7 leaflets,** the leaflets 8–16 cm (3.1–6.3 in) long, 3–5 cm (1.2–2 in) wide, lance-shaped, narrow but widest at the base or near the middle, the uppermost leaflet largest, usually narrowed at the base and tapering to a long point, the margin with many, sharp-pointed teeth, *dark yellowish-green and smooth above, paler and smooth beneath.* **Flowers:** male flowers in slender, short-stalked, hairy catkins, 5–7 cm (2–2.8 in) long, each flower with 4 stamens; the female flowers in short, few-flowered clusters at the end of the branchlets, each flower short, angled. **Fruits:** medium-size to large, broadest near the tip to almost globe-shaped, 2.5–5 cm (1–2 in) long, rounded at the top, sharply tapering to a narrow base, *smooth, the husk dark brown,* not splitting open uniformly at maturity. **Nuts:** usually broadest near the top, compressed as shown in the drawing, rounded at top and bottom, the shell thick, the kernel usually bitter.

Sand Hickory
Carya pallida (Ashe) Engl. & Graebn.

The sand hickory occurs on dry, sandy, or gravelly soils and is confined largely to the Coastal Plain from southern New Jersey to northwestern Florida and Louisiana to Tennessee. It is relatively common in Alabama, Mississippi, and Louisiana, where it can be found at altitudes up to 700 m (2,300 ft).

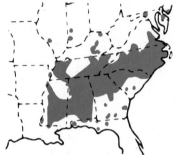

The sand hickory resembles the pignut hickory, but it can be distinguished by its yellowish scales attached to the stalk near the center of the lower surface on the leaves, its yellowish buds and fruits, and its very thin nutshell. The scientific name "pallida" refers to the pale lower surface of the leaves.

This hickory is not abundant enough over most of its range to be of importance as lumber. Some sand hickory undoubtedly is harvested along with other types and sold simply as "hickory." It is used for tool handles and as fuel, since the dense wood has a high heating value. The nuts serve as food for squirrels, other rodents, and larger birds.

Appearance: small to rarely tall trees, 10–15 m, rarely to 35 (32–50 ft, rarely to 115); the crown spreading; the trunk straight, to 1 m (3.3 ft) in diameter. **Bark:** moderately thick, forming lengthwise, usually deep, furrows and rough ridges; the ridges joining and separating to form a rough diamond pattern; the scales gray to nearly black. **Branches:** stout, upright to spreading, the lower branches often hanging; the branchlets slender, reddish-brown, becoming gray to nearly black with age, hairy when young, becoming smooth; covered with silvery to yellowish scales; leaf scars 3-lobed, slightly raised. **Winter buds:** end buds broadest near the base, rounded to pointed at the tip, 5–7 mm (0.2–0.3 in) long, with 5 to 9 overlapping *bud scales, hairy,* and *covered with tiny silvery scales,* reddish-brown to dark brown; side buds small. **Leaves:** alternate, feather-like arrangement, 15–38 cm (6–15 in) long, *with 7 leaflets,* rarely 9, the leaflets 7–15 cm (2.7–6 in) long and 2.5–5 cm (1–2 in) wide, lance-shaped to narrow and broadest at the tip or egg-shaped, rounded to tapering at the uneven base, the margin with tiny teeth, sometimes lacking teeth near the base of the leaflets, the upper surface light green, shiny, *covered with tiny silvery scales when young,* the *lower surface very pale, very hairy,* especially along the veins, gland-dotted. **Flowers:** male flowers on stalked, several clustered, yellow-green catkins, covered with silvery scales, 5–13 cm (2–5.2 in) long, each flower with 4 stamens; female flowers 2 to 6 on short spikes at the ends of new branches, each flower small, oblong, covered with yellow scales. **Fruits:** small, occurring singly or in clusters, egg-shaped, globe-shaped

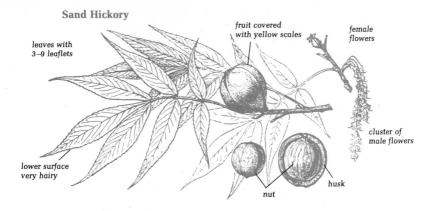

Sand Hickory

leaves with
3–9 leaflets

fruit covered
with yellow scales

female
flowers

cluster of
male flowers

lower surface
very hairy

nut

husk

or egg-shaped with the widest part near the tip, 1.2–4 cm (0.5–1.6 in) long, usually rounded at the tip, the husk thin, turning dark brown at maturity, covered with small hairs and yellowish scales, splitting irregularly to expose the nut. **Nuts: *broadest near the base, laterally flattened,*** ridged to the base, the ***shell very thin,*** the ***kernel*** small, ***sweet.***

The Wax Myrtle Family   Myricaceae

The wax myrtle family is small, with about 50 species of trees and shrubs of temperate to subtropical regions of the Americas, Europe, Africa, and Asia. The wax myrtles or bayberries (*Myrica*), and the sweet fern (*Comptonia*) are native to North America. There are 7 species of wax myrtles in North America — 5 of which may grow into small trees. The other 2 are sweet gale, *Myrica gale*, a shrubby species of northern North America, Europe, and Asia, and the Sierra sweet bay (*M. hartwegii*), a deciduous shrub of the Sierra Nevada in California. Sweet fern (*Comptonia peregrina*) is a low-growing shrub that never reaches tree size. It can be distinguished easily from wax myrtles in that it has pinnatified leaves (with numerous lobes in a feather-like arrangement along a narrow leaf). But wax myrtles have entire to toothed leaves.

This family is important for several reasons. Its species are able to grow in poor soils and to control erosion. The trees also add nitrogen to the soil through nitrogen-fixing nodules on the roots. The numerous fruits are a valuable food source for wildlife, and the wax-like coating on the fruits of wax myrtles is the source of bayberry wax used in scenting candles and soaps.

Members of this family are shrubs or small trees with multiple stems and alternate simple leaves, which are fragrant due to numerous glandular hairs. Individual plants are usually male or female. Male flowers are small, without petals, and densely clustered in elongated catkins. The female flowers are tiny, inconspicuous, usually clustered in groups of 2 to 4 flowers. Fruits are dry, nutlike, or covered with a leathery coat, and they are often covered with numerous bumps and coated with a waxy substance.

The Bayberry or Wax Myrtle Genus

Myrica L.

Bayberries usually are separated into 2 major groups: those with flowers and fruits produced on older branchlets (usually below the leaves) and those with the flowers and fruits produced at or near the tips of the branchlets among the leaves. All the species that can become small trees fall into the first category. The Pacific bayberry is found only in California, and the odorless bayberry is restricted largely to the Gulf Coastal area. The southern bayberry, evergreen bayberry, and northern bayberry are more widespread along the Coastal Plain of the eastern and southeastern U.S.

The fruits and, to a lesser extent, the buds serve as food for wildlife—especially birds, including catbirds, myrtle warblers, tree swallows. Whitetail deer browse the young twigs and leaves. The fruits can be gathered in the fall and placed in boiling water where the wax-like coat will melt and rise to the surface. This can be skimmed off and used in making bayberry candles or soap. Because of their attractive, nearly evergreen leaves, bayberries often are used as landscape plants.

The characteristics of the bayberries are the same as those given for the family, except the fruits always are covered with numerous rounded or irregular projections and usually with a conspicuous, wax-like coating.

Key to Bayberry Species

Southern Bayberry

Odorless Bayberry

Northern Bayberry

A. Trees or shrubs of eastern or southeastern North America; individual trees either male or female.

1. Leaves gland-dotted and frequent on both the upper and lower surfaces, broadest near the tip; fruits small, 2–4 mm (0.1–0.2 in) in diameter; trees of the Southeast
   Southern bayberry, p. 294

2. Leaves smooth above, gland-dotted only on lower surface or glands absent; broader near the middle or the tip; fruits medium-size, 3–8 mm (0.1–0.3 in) in diameter.

   a. Leaves without glands and nonfragrant, usually entire along the margin; trees of Gulf Coastal region
      Odorless bayberry, p. 295

   b. Leaves gland-dotted beneath and fragrant, usually toothed along the margin; trees of northeastern or southeastern Coastal Plain.

      (1) Branches whitish-gray; leaves usually deciduous; fruits very hairy when young; trees of northeastern North America **Northern bayberry, p. 296**

(Continued)

(2) Branches blackish; leaves evergreen; fruits smooth when young; trees primarily of the southeastern Coastal Plain **Evergreen bayberry, p. 296**

B. Trees or shrubs of the Pacific Coast; individual trees containing both male and female flowers **Pacific bayberry, p. 297**

Pacific Bayberry

Southern Bayberry, Wax Myrtle

Myrica cerifera L.

Southern bayberry is native to the Coastal Plain of the southeastern U.S., extending north to New Jersey and west to southwestern Oklahoma. It generally is found growing in sandy wet soils, such as occur in some swamps, pond margins, and pine barrens. This is a common plant in the Everglades, where it often forms large thickets.

The inconspicuous flowers appear in spring, and the fruits mature in late summer or early fall. The fruits are a minor food source for several species of birds. The dark brown wood is soft and brittle and is of no commercial value.

Appearance: large shrub or small tree to 12 m (40 ft), usually forming a narrow, round-topped crown; trunk straight, to 25 cm (9.9 in) in diameter, usually less, often with multiple trunks. **Bark:** thin, 5–7 mm (0.2–0.3 in), smooth, light gray. **Branches:** slender, upright to slightly spreading; branchlets slender, covered with rust-colored hairs and gland-dotted, becoming smooth and dark brown with age. **Winter buds:** narrow, 2–4 mm (0.1–0.2 in) long, pointed at the tip, covered with numerous, dark brown, overlapping scales. **Leaves:**

Southern Bayberry

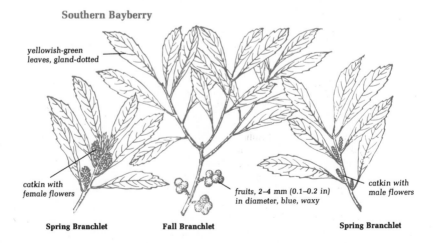

yellowish-green leaves, gland-dotted

catkin with female flowers

fruits, 2–4 mm (0.1–0.2 in) in diameter, blue, waxy

catkin with male flowers

Spring Branchlet   **Fall Branchlet**   **Spring Branchlet**

alternate, persisting until the second year and thus appearing evergreen, **narrow but broadest near the tip**, 3.5–10 cm (1.4–4 in) long, 0.6–1.2 cm (0.2–0.5 in) wide, pointed at the tip and gradually tapering to a long narrow base, with coarse teeth along the margin, **yellowish-green and gland-dotted above, paler and gland-dotted beneath;** the leafstalk short, 4–12 mm (0.2–0.5 in) long. **Flowers:** male and female flowers tiny, appearing in small catkins on separate trees; the male flowers in narrow catkins, 1.2–1.9 cm (0.5–0.8 in) long, produced along the branchlets at the junctions with the leaves; the female flowers in short broader catkins, 0.6–1.2 cm (0.2–0.5 in) long, produced along the branchlets. **Fruits:** 1 to several on a short spike, globe-shaped, 2–4 mm (0.1–0.2 in) in diameter, covered with a thick, light blue, wax-like coating. **Seeds:** light brown, tiny.

Odorless Bayberry
Myrica inodora Bartr.

This bayberry is restricted to the Gulf Coastal Plain of the southeastern U.S. from northwestern Florida to southeastern Louisiana. It usually is found in bogs, along the edges of ponds, and in swamps dominated by pines. Rarely is it found more than 140 km (87 miles) from the ocean. The smooth, odorless, or nonfragrant leaves readily separate this species from all other North American bayberries. Inconspicuous flowers are produced in spring, with the fruits maturing several months later. They are of some value as food for birds.

Appearance: shrubs or small trees to 7 m (23 ft), with a rounded crown; trunk straight, to 24 cm (9.5 in) in diameter, often with multiple trunks. **Bark:** thin, 4–8 mm (0.2–0.3 in) smooth, **light gray to almost white. Branches:** slender, upright, branchlets slender, covered with tiny raised pores (lenticels) and numerous small hairs when young, becoming smooth or almost so and reddish-brown. **Winter buds:** broadest near the base and sharp-pointed at the tip, 4–6 mm (0.1–0.2 in) long, covered with

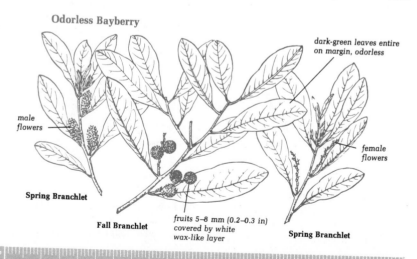

Odorless Bayberry

dark-green leaves entire on margin, odorless

male flowers

female flowers

Spring Branchlet

Fall Branchlet

fruits 5–8 mm (0.2–0.3 in) covered by white wax-like layer

Spring Branchlet

numerous overlapping, reddish-brown scales. **Leaves:** alternate, persisting until the second year and thus appearing evergreen, broadest near the tip and roughly spoon-shaped, 4–9 cm (1.6–3.6 in) long, 1.8–3.8 cm (0.7–1.5 in) wide, rounded at the tip and gradually tapering to a narrow base, *entire (though rarely having a few teeth along the margin)* dark green, *smooth and shiny above, pale green and usually smooth beneath;* the leafstalk very stout. **Flowers:** male and female flowers small, produced in small catkins on separate trees; the male flowers in catkins 1–1.4 cm (0.5 in) long, produced along the upper part of the branchlets at the junctions with the leaves; the female flowers in slender catkins 1.2–2 cm (0.5–0.8 in) long, also produced along the branchlets. **Fruits:** *usually 1 per spike, globe-shaped, 5–8 mm (0.2–0.3 in) in diameter, covered with a thin, white, wax-like layer.* **Seeds:** yellowish-brown, tiny.

Northern Bayberry

Myrica pensylvanica Loisel.

This is a shrub and rarely reaches tree size. It occurs primarily along the coast of northeastern North America. As do other bayberries, this one also grows in or near wet areas, including the shores of Lake Erie. This species is usually a bushy rounded shrub to 2 m (6.6 ft) high and *grows farther north than all the other native bayberries.* It is distinguished by *whitish-gray branches,* usually deciduous *leaves* that are *resin-dotted only on the lower surface,* and *hairy young fruits.* The mature fruits are globe-shaped, 3–4 mm (0.1–0.2 in) in diameter, and covered with a thick, whitish, wax-like layer.

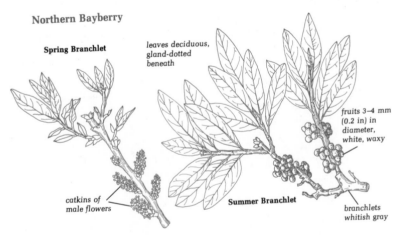

Northern Bayberry

Spring Branchlet

leaves deciduous, gland-dotted beneath

fruits 3–4 mm (0.2 in) in diameter, white, waxy

catkins of male flowers

Summer Branchlet

branchlets whitish gray

Evergreen Bayberry

Myrica heterophylla Raf.

The evergreen bayberry is a Coastal Plain species from southern New Jersey to Florida and west to Louisiana. It normally grows in bogs and low wet sites of the coastal woodlands. The evergreen bayberry is usually a round-topped shrub and rarely reaches tree size. This species is multi-stemmed with **dark, almost blackish branches** and **evergreen leaves** that are **leathery, 6–12 cm (2.4–4.8 in) long** and 3–5 cm (1.2–2 in) wide and **usually smooth above.** The small flowers are produced in spring, and the **fruits** mature in late summer or early fall. They are **smooth, globe-shaped, 3–4.5 mm (0.1–0.2 in) in diameter,** coated with a **whitish, wax-like layer.**

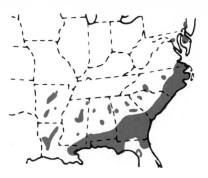

Evergreen Bayberry

leaves leathery, 6–12 cm (2.4–4.8 in) long, 3–5 cm (1.2–2 in) wide, gland-dotted beneath

Spring Branchlet

fruits 3–4.5 mm (0.2 in) in diameter, white waxy, smooth

catkins of female flowers

Fall Branchlet

branchlets dark, almost black

Pacific Bayberry *Myrica californica* Cham.

The Pacific bayberry is **native to the Pacific coastal regions** from western Washington south to southern California. It grows near the coast along streams, wet meadows, flats, sand dunes, or low moist hillsides. The plant is tolerant of poorly drained soils. It can occur as a single bush or tree, in clumps, or even in small pure stands.

Flowering is in spring, with the fruits maturing by late summer or early fall. Many birds eat the fruits, which are a major food of band-tailed pigeons. And an abundant supply of fruits and seeds is produced each year. The tree's only economic value is in its occasional use as an ornamental.

Appearance: shrubs or small trees to 8 m (26 ft), usually with a rounded crown; trunk straight, 7.6–30 cm (3–11.8 in) in diameter, usually with multiple trunks. **Bark:** thin, 2–3 mm (0.1 in) smooth, light gray to brown. **Branches:** short, slender; branchlets: slender to stout, usually upright, covered with tiny hairs and green when young, becoming smooth then roughened and brown to gray with age. **Winter buds:** broadest near the base and pointed at the tip, 7–9 mm (0.3–0.4 in) long, covered with several overlapping, reddish-brown scales. **Leaves:** al-

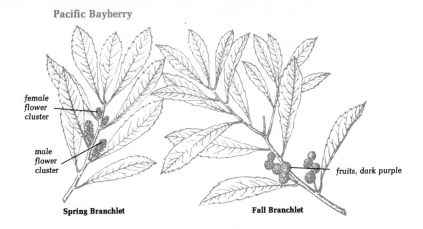

Pacific Bayberry

female flower cluster

male flower cluster

fruits, dark purple

Spring Branchlet

Fall Branchlet

ternate, persisting until the second year and appearing evergreen, *narrow and broadest above the middle,* 5–10 cm (2–4 in) long, 1.2–2.2 cm (0.5–0.9 in) wide, pointed at the tip and gradually narrowing at the base, with occasional teeth along the margin, bright green and shiny above, smooth to slightly hairy and gland-dotted on the lower surface; the leafstalk short, stout, 6–10 mm (0.2–0.4 in) long. **Flowers:** *male and female flowers tiny, appearing in separate flower clusters* (rarely together) *on the same tree;* the male flowers in catkins, 2.2–2.6 cm (0.9–1.1 in) long, produced along the branchlets at the junctions with the leaves; the female flowers in short catkins, 1.2–2 cm (0.5–0.8 in) long, broadest near the base, produced on the branchlets above the male flower clusters. **Fruits:** globe-shaped, occurring in short, crowded clusters, 4–6 mm (0.1–0.2 in) in diameter, covered with numerous small bumps, dark purple. **Seeds:** light reddish-brown, tiny.

The Beech Family   Fagaceae

The beech family is large. It includes 8 genera and about 500 species. It is an economically important group of trees and shrubs distributed throughout the temperate regions of the world and in mountainous tropical areas, except for Africa. Five genera are native to North America: beech (*Fagus*) with 1 species; chestnuts (*Castanea*) with 4 species reaching tree size; oaks (*Quercus*) with over 50 tree members; chinkapin (*Castanopsis*) with 1 member on the Pacific Coast; and the tanoak (*Lithocarpus*), an Asian genus with 1 species primarily on the West Coast. The numerous fossil records of members of the beech family indicate that it is an old group that was once more widespread than now.

Abundance and characteristics of beech family members make them among the most important in the ecosystem, as well as in the hardwood timber industry. The wood is hard, tough, strong, and takes a beautiful finish. Commercial cork is obtained from the bark of the cork oak, a native of the Mediterranean region. Chestnuts, beech-nuts, and some acorns are eaten by people. Wildlife is highly dependent on members of this family for food, nesting, and cover.

Members of this family are deciduous to evergreen trees or shrubs with simple leaves that are alternate on the branchlets. The leaves may be entire, toothed, or variously lobed; they are stalked and have veins in a feather-like arrangement (pinnate). In North America all members have male and female flowers on the same tree or shrub. These male and female flowers are usually produced in separate clusters that may hang or be upright and have few to many flowers. Male flowers are clustered either in small heads or catkins, each flower with 4 to 20 stamens (pollen producing structures). Female flowers are solitary or clustered in either heads or catkins, usually with 1 to 4 flowers in small bracts, the bracts persisting and becoming woody in fruit; there is 1 pistil that is divided into 3 to 6 compartments at the base. The fruit is a 1-seeded nut that occurs singly or in groups of 2 or 3, and enclosed in scaly, bristly, or spiny bracts. The seed is usually large, fleshy, and oily, and fills the cavity of the nut.

Key to Beech Genera

American Beech

Allegheny Chinkapin

Tanoak

Gambel's Oak

Georgia Oak

A. Bark of mature trees smooth; winter buds long, narrow, sharp-pointed; male flowers clustered together in many-flowered, hanging heads; fruits triangular **Beech, p. 300**

B. Bark scaly or furrowed; winter buds usually rounded, egg-shaped, or broadest near the base; male flowers in many-flowered, slender, elongated catkins.

  1. Nut or nuts enclosed in a spiny or prickly burr.

    a. Leaves deciduous, toothed; terminal buds absent; nuts mature in 1 season on current year's branchlets **Chestnut, p. 302**

    b. Leaves evergreen, entire; terminal buds present; nuts mature in 2 seasons on previous year's branchlets **Chinkapin, p. 307**

  2. Nut only partially enclosed by an open scaly cup.

    a. Male flowers produced in many-flowered, narrow, upright catkins; female flowers usually produced at the base of some of the male catkins; trees of southwestern Oregon and California **Tanoak, p. 309**

    b. Male flowers produced in many-flowered, narrow hanging catkins; female flowers always produced in separate catkins; trees common and widespread in North America **Oak, p. 310**

(Continued)

(Continues key on
previous page)

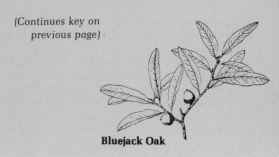

Bluejack Oak

The Beech Genus   *Fagus* L.

The beeches are a small group of 10 species of deciduous trees of north temperate areas of the world. There is 1 species in eastern North America and another very closely related one in the mountains of eastern Mexico. The remaining species are native to Europe, Asia Minor, and eastern Asia. In addition to our native American beech, the European beech has been introduced and is cultivated widely. Records from peat bogs and fossilized leaves indicate that the American beech occurred much farther west than it presently does and that it may have been present in Europe several million years ago.

Beeches are deciduous trees with smooth pale bark and simple leaves that occur alternately on the branches. The winter buds are elongated, narrow, sharp-pointed, and covered with overlapping, dark brown scales. The simple leaves are usually broadest near the middle, toothed on the margin, often leathery, stalked. Male flowers are produced in many-flowered, globe-shaped, hanging heads; while the female flowers are produced in 2- to 4-flowered clusters in the junction of the branchlets and the upper leaves. Fruits are broadest near the base and unequally triangular, chestnut brown, shiny. The 2 triangular fruits are enclosed in almost globe-shaped bracts covered with stout, outcurved prickles.

Key to Beech Species

A. Leaves with 9–14 pairs of veins per leaf, the leaves with numerous small teeth along the margin; trees of eastern North America
American beech, p. 300

B. Leaves with 5–9 pairs of veins per leaf, the leaves with occasional teeth along the margin; European tree introduced, primarily in parks and yards   **European beech, p. 302**

European Beech

American Beech   *Fagus grandifolia* Ehrh.

The American beech is a common forest tree of lower elevations throughout most of eastern North America. It grows best in rich, moist loam soils with high humus content. It reaches its greatest size in the Ohio and Mississippi River Valleys. The tree is encountered more frequently on the cooler and wetter north-facing slopes. In the southern Appalachians, it will occur up to 2,000 m (6,600 ft) elevation. But, farther north it grows at lower altitudes. American beech sometimes forms nearly pure stands but often is found growing in association with sugar maple, yellow birch, black cherry, American basswood, eastern white pine, among others.

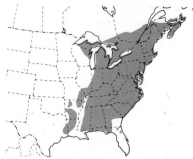

This is a slow-growing tree that often produces sucker shoots, resulting in the formation of clumps or groves of American beech. Flowering is in late April or early May, and the fruits mature and drop by the first heavy frost. Large seed crops generally are produced every 2 or 3 years. The large oily seeds are important to many species of wildlife, especially squirrels and chipmunks; black bears also eat the seeds. The ruffed and spruce grouse, wood duck, and turkey are the principal game birds that consume beech nuts.

The wood ranges in color from light to dark red. It is strong and hard but not durable. It is used for tool handles, flooring, and some furniture. Because of its elastic properties, it was used to make most of the older all-wood clothespins.

American Beech

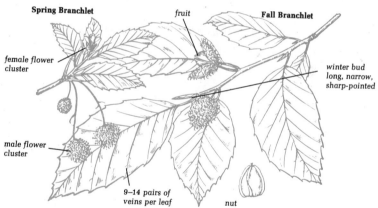

Spring Branchlet   *fruit*   **Fall Branchlet**

female flower cluster

winter bud long, narrow, sharp-pointed

male flower cluster

9–14 pairs of veins per leaf   *nut*

Appearance: medium to large trees to 30 m (100 ft), occasionally taller, with a narrow to spreading rounded crown; trunk tall, straight or short, stout (open grown sites), to 3.5 m (11.5 ft) in diameter. **Bark: thin,** 6–12 mm (0.2–0.5 in), **light gray to blue-gray, smooth,** sometimes mottled. **Branches:** short, upright, spreading; branchlets slender, slightly zig-zag, light green and finely hairy when young, becoming light brown and smooth by the end of the first year. **Winter buds: 2–2.5 cm (0.8–1 in) long,** narrow, **lance-shaped, very sharp-pointed,** covered with overlapping, dark chestnut brown scales. **Leaves:** alternate, simple, deciduous, 6–14 cm (2.4–5.5 in) long, 2.5–7.2 cm (1–2.9 in) wide, usually broadest just below the middle, gradually narrowing at the base short to infrequently long-pointed at the tip, with sharp teeth along the margin, becoming leathery, pale green turning bluish-green and smooth at maturity, paler beneath with tufts of hairs in junctions of the main vein, **9 to 14 pairs of veins per leaf;** the leafstalks slender, 8–16 mm (0.3–0.6 in) long, usually hairy. **Flowers:** male and female flowers produced separately, **male flowers densely clustered in globe-shaped heads, 2.2–2.8 cm (0.9–1.1 in) in diameter, hanging by a slender stalk,** the stalk 4–5 cm (1.6–2 in) long; female flowers usually paired on short stalks 1.2–2 cm (0.5–0.8 in) long, produced at or near the tips of the branchlets. **Fruits:** consisting of 2 nuts, enclosed in 2 spiny bracts, the bracts 1.6–2.2 cm (0.6–0.9 in) long, becoming dark orangish-green, covered with long, slender, curved spines, opening in late summer to expose the nuts; the **nuts unevenly triangular,** 1.8–2.2 cm (0.7–0.9 in) long, **slightly winged on the margins,** yellowish-brown.

European Beech   *Fagus sylvatica* L.

The European beech was introduced into North America in the early colonial days and became a popular tree for use in parks and large yards. It is an important timber tree in its native range of central and southern Europe and was probably brought to

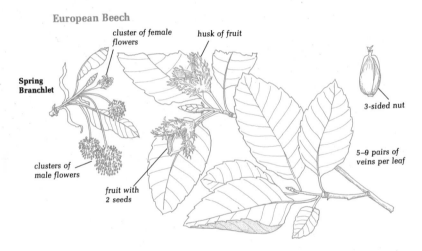

European Beech

cluster of female flowers

husk of fruit

Spring Branchlet

3-sided nut

5–9 pairs of veins per leaf

clusters of male flowers

fruit with 2 seeds

North America by the colonists for that purpose. A slow-growing but very long-lived tree, this beech will reach 30 m (100 ft) in height and have a massive trunk covered with smooth gray bark and a broad, rounded crown. The **leaves are similar to those of the American beech but differ in that they have only 5 to 9 pairs of veins, and fewer and larger teeth along the margins.** This tree has been popular with horticulturists, resulting in the development of many growth forms, leaf shapes, and color forms. The most frequently encountered of these is the purple or copper beech (*Fagus sylvatica* 'atropunicea') with copper or deep purple leaves. The weeping beech (*F. sylvatica* 'pendula'), with hanging branches, is another of the striking cultivated beeches occasionally encountered.

The Chestnut Genus   *Castanea* Miller

This is a small genus of approximately 14 species in temperate regions of eastern North America, southern Europe, northern Africa, and Asia. There are 5 species of chestnuts in North America, 4 largely confined to the southeastern U.S. and the fifth, the American chestnut, once widespread throughout eastern North America but largely eliminated by the chestnut blight. Japanese and Chinese chestnuts have been introduced because of their edible nuts and resistance to the blight.

Chestnuts are economically important because of their durable wood and edible nuts. The American chestnut produced excellent lumber and large sweet nuts, but it was the one most severely infected by the blight and can no longer be grown for lumber and nuts. Commercial chestnut growers in the U.S. have had to rely on Asiatic species and hybrids.

Trees in the chestnut genus may be large at old age or merely small shrubs, all with fissured brown bark. Terminal winter buds are absent, and the lateral buds are small, broadest near the base and tapering to a rounded to slightly pointed tip, covered with 2 or 3 overlapping dark brown scales. The simple, deciduous leaves are alternate, usually broadest near the base, pointed at the tip, with large teeth on the margin; they have a papery texture and are stalked. Male flowers are densely clustered on upright to spreading catkins, white to cream, strong-scented. The female flowers are found scattered at the base of the uppermost catkins on the branchlets. The fruits mature in 1 growing season and thus appear on the current year's branchlets. They are composed of a spiny, 4-parted husk that surrounds the 1 to 3 nuts. The nuts are globe-shaped to somewhat compressed, pointed at the tip, leathery, shiny, bright chestnut brown.

Key to Chestnut Species

A. Leaves smooth on both surfaces; fruit a spiny burr enclosing usually more than 1 nut
American chestnut, p. 303

B. Leaves slightly to very hairy on the lower surface; fruit a spiny burr enclosing usually 1 nut.

  1. Young branchlets covered with wooly hairs; leaves whitish and conspicuously hairy beneath **Allegheny chinkapin, p. 305**

  2. Young branchlets smooth or only finely hairy; leaves pale yellowish-green and with minute or fine hairs beneath.

   a. Leaves 12–22 cm (4.7–8.7 in) long; trees primarily of Ozark Mountains
   Ozark chinkapin, p. 306

   b. Leaves 5–10 cm (2–4 in) long; trees of dry sandy soils of the Coastal Plain
   Florida chinkapin, p. 306

American Chestnut

Allegheny Chinkapin

American Chestnut   *Castanea dentata* (Marsh.) Borkh.

The American chestnut was once a dominant tree in the deciduous forest of eastern North America. It presently persists as stump sprouts or small trees because of the accidental introduction of the virulent chestnut blight, which swept through the entire

range of the chestnut killing every standing tree. It grows in a variety of soils except
in wet, poorly drained types. This chestnut
is common on mountain or hill slopes in
gravelly or rocky, well-drained, glacial
soils. The American chestnut reached its
greatest size in the southern Appalachian
Mountains, where it grew in association
with several species of oaks, hickories,
maples, and birches.

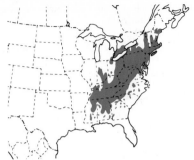

It is a rapid-growing tree that usually
reaches 4–6 m (12–20 ft) in height before it
becomes visibly affected by the chestnut blight, a fungus disease under the bark.
Young saplings arise as sprouts from the old stumps of the original trees. The strong-
scented flowers appear in June or July, and the fruits ripen and drop after the first
frost. The nuts are large, sweet, and highly desired by people, as well as by deer, squirrels, chipmunks, and other animals. Today the young trees rarely survive long enough
to produce flowers and fruits. The reddish-brown wood is lightweight, soft, easy to
split, and very resistant to decay. It was once used in inexpensive furniture, railroad
ties, and split-rail fences. Chestnut split-rail fences can still be found along country
roads throughout the Northeast and the Appalachian chain. Both the bark and wood
are rich in tannins that were used to tan leather.

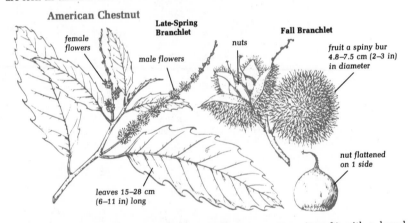

American Chestnut

female flowers

male flowers

Late-Spring Branchlet

nuts

Fall Branchlet

fruit a spiny bur
4.8–7.5 cm (2–3 in)
in diameter

nut flattened
on 1 side

leaves 15–28 cm
(6–11 in) long

Appearance: *formerly medium-size to tall trees* to 35 m (115 ft) with a broad
rounded crown, now persisting mainly as stump sprouts 3–10 m (9–33 ft) high; trunk
straight, tall, 0.6–1.3 m (1.9–4.3 ft) in diameter. **Bark:** thick, 2–5 cm (0.8–2 in), with
shallow irregular furrows separating the broad flat ridges; dark brown. **Branches:**
stout, usually spreading; branchlets slender, yellowish-green and slightly hairy when
young, becoming reddish-brown to dark brown and smooth with age. **Winter buds:**
end buds absent, side buds 5–8 mm (0.2–0.3 in) long, broadest near the base and tapering to a sharp point, covered with thin, overlapping, dark-brown scales. **Leaves:** alternate, deciduous, *15–28 cm (6–11 in) long, 4–8 cm (1.6–3.2 in) wide,* slightly broadest
near the middle to uniformly wide along the side to occasionally broadest near the
base, narrowing to a wedge-shaped base and tapering to a short to long-pointed tip,
with numerous coarse, sharp-pointed teeth along the margin, thin and papery,

yellowish-green, shiny, and *smooth above, paler beneath* and hairy when young but *becoming smooth with age;* the leafstalks stout, slightly angled, 1–1.4 cm (0.4–0.6 in) long. **Flowers:** male flowers densely clustered on semi-erect stalks 12–20 cm (4.7–7.9 in) long, cream-white, strong scented; female flowers inconspicuous, scattered near the base of some of the male-flowered catkins. **Fruits:** large spiny burrs 4.8–7.5 cm (2–3 in) in diameter, *enclosing 1 to 3 nuts,* rarely more; the *nuts* broadest at the base, pointed at the tip, *flattened on 1 side,* brown, shiny; meat sweet, edible.

Allegheny Chinkapin

Castanea pumila Mill.

The Allegheny chinkapin is a small tree or large shrub with a widespread distribution throughout the southeastern U.S. It is a relatively common woody plant and has been separated into 2 varieties: the typical Allegheny chinkapin and the Ashe chinkapin (*Castanea pumila* variety *ashe*). The typi-

cal trees have dense clusters of spines on the fruits or burrs, and are found primarily in dry woodlands, especially in mountains to 1,500 m (5,000 ft). The Ashe chinkapin, which has fruits covered with a few scattered spines, normally grows in dry sandy soils along the coast from Virginia to Florida and along the Gulf Coast.

This chinkapin flowers in July, and the fruits mature in September or October. The sweet nuts are eaten by people and wildlife. In addition to producing edible nuts, the Allegheny chinkapin often forms dense stands providing excellent cover. The brown wood is hard, strong, and easy to split, resulting in its use in fences. The trees are usually too little to make the species a commercially important timber tree.

Allegheny Chinkapin

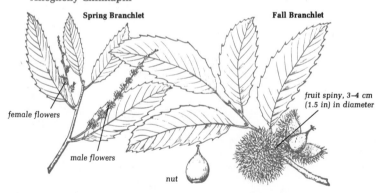

Spring Branchlet

Fall Branchlet

female flowers

male flowers

fruit spiny, 3–4 cm (1.5 in) in diameter

nut

Appearance: shrub or small tree usually to 8 m (26 ft), rarely taller, with rounded crown; trunk 1 to several, short, soon branching, usually less than 25 cm (10 in) in diameter. **Bark:** moderately thick, 1.2–2.5 cm (0.5–1 in), with shallow furrows separating the flattened scales, light reddish-brown. **Branches:** slender, spreading; *branchlets* slender, light reddish-brown and *covered with wooly hairs when young,* becoming dark brown and smooth with age. **Winter buds:** 2–4 mm (about 0.1–0.2 in) long, broadest near the base and tapering to a point, covered with a thick layer of rust-colored hairs. **Leaves:** alternate, deciduous, *6.8–16 cm (2.7–6.3 in) long, 3.8–5 cm (1.5–2 in) wide,* usually broadest near the middle, tapering to an unequally rounded or wedge-shaped base and pointed at the tip, with numerous, large teeth along the margin, becoming leathery, bright green and smooth above, *whitish and hairy beneath;* the leafstalks stout, flattened on the upper surface, 6–12 mm (0.2–0.5 in) long. **Flowers:** male flowers densely clustered on semi-erect to spreading stalks 10–18 cm (4–7.1 in) high; female flowers inconspicuous, scattered near the base of some of the male-flowered catkins. **Fruits:** a *spiny burr 3–4 cm (1.5 in) in diameter, enclosing 1 nut* (rarely 2), the nuts broadest near the base, rounded, tapering to a sharp-pointed tip, 1.8–2.5 cm (0.7–1 in) long, dark brown, shiny, meat sweet, edible.

Ozark Chinkapin
Castanea ozarkensis Ashe

The Ozark chinkapin is a small tree or large, multi-stemmed shrub, primarily of the Ozark Mountains in southern Missouri, Arkansas, and western Oklahoma but also extending into Louisiana and Mississippi. It has gray, finely hairy branchlets and alternate deciduous leaves that are broadly lance-shaped to uniformly wide along the sides, 12–22 cm (4.7–8.7 in) long, coarsely toothed on the margin, and often finely hairy on the lower surface. The spiny burrs or fruits are similar to those of the Allegheny chinkapin (*Castanea pumila*). The seeds, which are rounded and not flattened on 1 side as are the American chestnuts, are of minor importance as a food source to wildlife. Whitetail deer, squirrels, and chipmunks feed on them, but prefer acorns over chinkapin nuts.

Ozark Chinkapin

catkins of flowers

leaves 12–22 cm (4.7–8.7 in) long, hairy on lower surface

spiny burs, each containing 1 seed

Florida Chinkapin
Castanea alnifolia Nutt.

The Florida chinkapin is a large shrub or small tree of the Coastal Plain from North Carolina to northern Florida and southeastern Louisiana. It grows in dry sandy soils to rich upland deciduous woodlands in Florida. The branchlets are smooth, or nearly so, and bear narrow leaves 5–10 cm (2–4 in) long and 3–5 cm (1.2–2 in) wide that are broadest near the tip and usually finely hairy on the lower surface. The flowers and fruits closely resemble the Allegheny chinkapin (*Castanea pumila*). The Florida chinkapin can be distinguished from it by the smooth branchlets. Some members of the Florida chinkapin are a low-growing shrub, frequently forming large clumps but never reaching tree size.

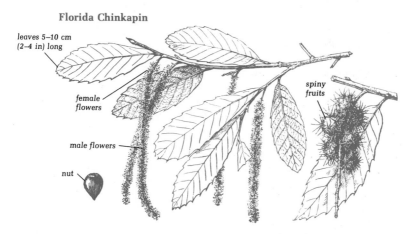

Florida Chinkapin

leaves 5–10 cm (2–4 in) long

female flowers

male flowers

nut

spiny fruits

The Chinkapin Genus   *Castanopsis* (D. Don) Spach

This is a small group of perhaps 30 species of trees and shrubs native to southern and eastern Asia, with 2 members in North America. Both are found in the Pacific coastal mountain ranges. The golden chinkapin is a large tree, while the second species, the bush chinkapin (*Castanopsis sempervirens*), never becomes a tree. The leaves of the chinkapin resemble those of tanoak. But the tanoak nut is covered only at the base by a shallow cup, while the chinkapin nut is enclosed almost entirely within a spiny burr.

Members of this genus are trees or shrubs with scaly bark and alternate evergreen leaves. The leaves are entire or toothed and are usually leathery. Male flowers are densely clustered on upright unbranched or branched spikes. The female flowers are on short, few-flowered stalks or at the base of the stalks bearing the male flowers. The fruits take 2 years to mature, and so mature ones occur on the previous year's branchlets. Fruits consist of 1 to 3 nuts, partially or wholly covered by a spiny bract.

Golden Chinkapin   *Castanopsis chrysophylla* (Dougl.) A. DC.

This tree is native to the mountain slopes of the Pacific Coast region in western Washington, Oregon, and into central California. The golden chinkapin also grows in valleys and sheltered ravines, normally at 1,000–2,000 m (3,200–6,600 ft) but may reach over 3,000 m (9,900 ft) in the San Jacinto Mountains in California. These trees usually occur as individuals scattered in the coastal redwood forest. They do form pure stands but, in addition, are found in association with the western juniper, canyon oak, and scrub oak. Soil conditions vary from dry rocky types to deep rich soils, in which the trees reach their greatest height—over 35 m (115 ft).

Golden chinkapin is a slow to moderate growing species and may live from 400 to 500 years. The trees flower in late spring and often are covered with creamy-white blossoms that emit a strong odor. It is not a prolific nut producer and is cyclic, with years of very little production followed by large nut crops. Black bears, deer, squirrels, and chipmunks eat the nuts, as do jays, thrushes, and small rodents.

The pale reddish-brown wood is soft, brittle, and fine-grained. It is not used commercially, but it is used for wood heating and campfires.

Golden Chinkapin

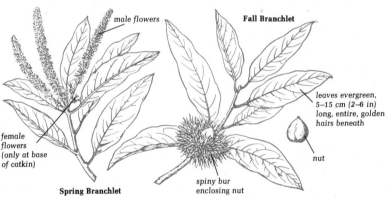

male flowers

Fall Branchlet

leaves evergreen, 5–15 cm (2–6 in) long, entire, golden hairs beneath

female flowers (only at base of catkin)

nut

Spring Branchlet

spiny bur enclosing nut

Appearance: medium to large trees 15–40 m (49–132 ft) with a broad, rounded crown; trunk straight, often fluted, 0.3–1.2 m (1–3.9 ft) in diameter, rarely larger, often unbranched for lower two-thirds of trunk. **Bark:** thick, 2.5–5 cm (1–2 in), dark reddish-brown, with deep fissures dividing the broad, 5–7.5 cm (2–3 in) wide, rounded ridges. **Branches:** stout, spreading; branchlets slender, stiff, light yellow, and covered with numerous scales when young, becoming dark reddish-brown and smooth with age. **Winter buds:** usually crowded near the tip, end bud 5–7 mm (0.2–0.3 in) long, broadest near the base to almost rounded, covered by several overlapping, light-brown scales. **Leaves:** simple, alternate, *evergreen, 5–15 cm (2–6 in) long, 1.2–5 cm (0.5–2 in) wide, broadly lance-shaped to uniformly narrow,* tapering to a narrow base and a long to short-pointed tip, entire and slightly wavy on the margin, leathery, dark green and shiny above, covered with *golden-colored hairs beneath,* the leaf stalks short, 6–12 mm (0.2–0.5 in) long, grooved above. **Flowers:** *male flowers* numerous and clustered *on narrow,* elongated, *nearly erect stalks 5–6.5 cm (2–2.6 in) long,* produced at or near the tips of the branchlets; *female flowers* on short, few-

flowered stalks or **clustered at the base of the stalks bearing the male flowers.**
Fruits: a nut, globe-shaped to broadest near the base, maturing in 2 seasons, with mature nuts occurring on previous year's branchlets; the **nut or nuts** (up to 3) **enclosed in
a spiny, 4-parted, globe-shaped bract** about 2.5–4 cm (1–1.6 in) in diameter.

The Tanoak Genus   *Lithocarpus* Blume

Tanoaks are a moderately large genus of approximately 100 species native to southern
and eastern Asia and Malaysia. A single species, tanoak, is native to Oregon and
California. This group of trees is often considered to be intermediate between the
chestnuts and oaks. The upright male flower clusters are similar to those produced by
chestnuts. But the nuts are hard to distinguish from the acorns produced by oaks.

Trees and shrubs in this genus have deeply furrowed, scaly bark and evergreen
leaves. The winter buds are usually broadest near the base, blunt at the tip, and covered with a few spreading scales. Leaves are stalked and entire or toothed. Flowers are
produced in upright spikes or catkins, the male flowers densely clustered along the
upper three-fourths of the spikes, often with 1 to several female flowers at the base of
the catkins. The fruits are acorns with a cup fringed with slender spreading scales.

Tanoak   *Lithocarpus densiflorus* (Hook. & Arn.) Rehd.

Tanoak grows on the fertile mountain slopes and ridges of the seaward coastal ranges
in southwestern Oregon and California, usually at altitudes of 170–1,000 m (560–
3,300 ft). It is much less common in the Sierra Nevada and usually is found as an
isolated grove. Tanoak requires more mois-
ture than most hardwoods, so it does best
in humid climates, although it can thrive
in a variety of soils. It does form pure
stands but is found more often growing in
association with the coastal redwood, Port
Orford cedar, Douglas fir, bigleaf maple,
and box elder. It also occurs less frequently
with other species.

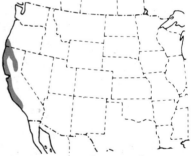

A slow-growing tree, the tanoak may live
to be 300 to 350 years old. Flowering may
commence in the spring, summer, or fall,
yet most flowers are produced in late spring and early summer. The acorns do not mature until the end of the second growing season. Tanoak is a prolific acorn producer,
with large crops produced every other year. The acorns are an important food for
many mammals and birds. Black bears, blacktail deer, squirrels, and chipmunks consume large quantities of the acorns. Many birds feed on them also, including the
California woodpecker, blue-fronted jay, Pacific thrush, and the band-tailed pigeon.

The reddish-brown wood is hard, strong, and close-grained but is not commercially
important. The bark is exceedingly rich in tannins and was used in the tanning of
heavy leathers.

Appearance: moderate to large tree to 30 m (100 ft), rarely higher, with a narrow,
pyramid-shaped crown (in forest) or with a broad, spreading rounded crown (in open
sites); trunk straight, tall to short, to 1.5 m (4.9 ft) in diameter. **Bark:** moderately thick,
1.9–3.8 cm (0.8–1.5 in), reddish-brown, composed of deep narrow fissures dividing
broad rounded, angular to almost square plates. **Branches:** stout, upright to spreading;
branchlets often short, stout, covered with a thick layer of rust-colored hairs when
young and becoming reddish-brown with age. **Winter buds:** small, 6–8 mm (0.2–0.3

Tanoak

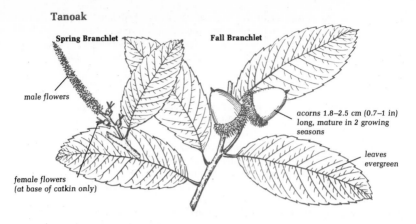

Spring Branchlet

Fall Branchlet

male flowers

acorns 1.8–2.5 cm (0.7–1 in) long, mature in 2 growing seasons

leaves evergreen

female flowers (at base of catkin only)

in) long, broadest near the base and rounded at the tip, covered with loose, overlapping hairy scales. **Leaves:** simple, alternate, ***persisting for 3 or 4 years (evergreen),*** 7–12 cm (2.8–4.8 in) long, 1.9–7.5 cm (0.8–3 in) wide, uniformly wide for most of the length, rounded to quickly tapering at the base and blunt to pointed at the tip, with sharp teeth and somewhat wavy along the margin, light green and hairy above, becoming smooth and shiny with age, hairy beneath, leathery; the leafstalks short, 1–1.5 cm (0.4–0.6 in) long, stout, hairy. **Flowers:** ***produced on stout, upright stalks or catkins 7.5–10 cm (3–4 in) high,*** with male flowers clustered along the upper three-fourths of the spikes and often with 1 to several female flowers at the base of the catkins. **Fruits:** acorns, solitary or in pairs, on a stalk 1.2–2 cm (0.5–0.8 in) long, broadest near the base and gradually narrowing to a pointed or rounded tip, 1.8–2.5 cm (0.7–1 in) long and 1.2–2.2 cm (0.5–0.9 in) thick, light yellowish-brown, the ***cup shallow, hairy, covered with long, spreading or recurved scales;*** matures in 2 growing seasons.

The Oak Genus
Quercus (Tourn.) L.

The oaks are a large genus of about 500 species of trees and shrubs, primarily of the warm temperate regions of the Northern Hemisphere, but with a few species extending into the higher mountains of Central and South America. There are 58 species of oaks native to North America, exclusive of Mexico, which has over 150 species of its own. Oaks are widely distributed in China, southeast Asia, India, western Asia, the Mediterranean, and Europe.

In North America, the distribution of oaks is thought to originate in Mexico. As oaks range northward into colder climates, they change from evergreen trees to deciduous. In addition, for better moisture retention, oak species in drier regions of the southwestern U.S. and Mexico tend to have smaller unlobed or shallowy lobed leaves with thicker waxier surfaces than are found on the more northerly, deeply lobed oak species.

Oaks generally occur in woodlands with moderate precipitation on hillsides and mountain slopes. Yet some oaks grow along the sea coast, in low wet areas, on dry rocky mesas, and in canyons. They prefer well-drained soils where they develop a deeply penetrating taproot. Flowering is in spring shortly before or with the growth of the new leaves. The acorns develop at the end of either 1 or 2 growing seasons. Heavy crops of acorns are produced every 2 to 4 years.

Acorn crops are of considerable value to wildlife. In fact, the success or failure of an annual crop will partly determine how many of the animals will survive the winter. Acorns are an important item in the diet of whitetail and blacktail deer, bears, hogs, peccaries, raccoons, squirrels, and other rodents. Many birds feed on acorns as well; these include wild turkey, wood duck, and some western woodpeckers and jays.

Because of their abundance, coupled with a hard, tough, durable, resilient valuable wood, oaks are extremely important in the hardwood lumber industry. Oak is used for veneer, furniture, flooring, cabinets, shipbuilding, barrels, and many other things. A few species, especially pin oak, are used as street trees. Corks used in wine and champagne bottles come from the thick spongy bark of the European cork oak.

Oaks may be evergreen or deciduous shrubs or trees. Their bark may range from scaly to furrowed. Leaves are alternate on the branches. Winter buds are small, clustered at the ends of the branchlets; each bud is covered by dark to reddish-brown, overlapping scales. The leaves are variable in shape, entire, toothed or variously lobed on the edges, with a papery to tough and leathery texture, and with a stout leafstalk. The tiny male flowers are densely clustered in hanging catkins produced in the junctions of the leafstalks of branchlets of the current season or of the previous season. The tiny female flowers are produced on short, few-flowered spikes in the junction of the leafstalks of branchlets of the season. The fruits are acorns which develop and mature at the end of 1 growing season (white oak group) or at the end of two growing seasons (red-and-black oak group). Thus, ***mature acorns of the white oak group occur on the current year's branchlets. And mature acorns of the red-and-black oak group occur on the previous year's branchlets.*** The acorns are composed of a basal cup that may partially or almost completely enclose the nut. The acorn cup and nut vary in shape and size.

Key to Major Groups of Oaks

A. Leaves entire, toothed or lobed, but not bristle-tipped; acorns maturing at the end of the first season (thus acorns are produced on current year's branchlets); inner surface of acorn shell smooth (lacking hairs)

White Oak Group, p. 312
(Continued)

Gambel's Oak

Chestnut Oak

Live Oak

B. Leaves entire, toothed or lobed, always with bristle-like tips extending beyond the margin of the leaf; acorns maturing at the end of the second year, except for coast live oak (thus acorns are produced on previous year's branchlets); inner surface of acorn shell hairy

Red and Black Oak Group, p. 351

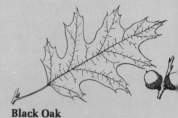

Black Oak

Willow Oak

Interior Live Oak

Key to White Oak Group Species

A. Leaves deciduous, falling away in autumn or turning brown and gradually falling during winter.

   1. Leaves shallowly to deeply lobed or occasionally entire or nearly so, but not resembling a chestnut leaf.

      a. Trees of central and eastern North America, east of the Rocky Mountains, including Texas and Oklahoma.

         (1) Leaves with well-developed lobes along the sides of the leaf, the lobes often deep.

            (a) Acorn cup deeply bowl-shaped, enclosing from half to almost all of the nut, the cup conspicuously fringed on the edge.

               (a1) Leaves 7.5–15 cm (3–6 in) wide, the terminal lobe much larger than the others; acorns 2–5 cm (0.8–2 in) long, the cup enclosing about half to three-fourths of nut; trees of eastern and southcentral U. S.
               Bur oak, p. 319

Bur Oak

(a2) Leaves 2.5–10 cm (1–4 in) wide, the terminal lobes not much larger than the others; acorns 1.5–2.5 cm (0.6–1 in) long, the cup enclosing most or all of nut; trees of southeastern U. S.

Overcup oak, p. 320

Overcup Oak

(b) Acorn cup saucer-shaped, enclosing the lower fourth to third of nut.

(b1) Leaves with 7–10 shallow to deep rounded lobes.

(b1a) Leaves 12–22 cm (4.7–8.7 in) long, bright green above, paler beneath; acorns, 1.2–2 cm (0.5–0.8 in) long, the cup enclosing about one-fourth of the acorn; common woodland tree of eastern U.S.

White oak, p. 321

White Oak

(b1b) Leaves 7.5–12.5 cm (3–5 in) long, dark green above, bluish-green beneath; acorns 2–2.5 cm (0.8–1 in) long, the cup enclosing about one-third of acorn; introduced tree from Europe, cultivated, especially in eastern U.S.

English oak, p. 323

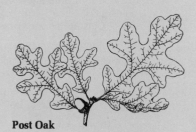

English Oak

(b2) Leaves with 3–5 usually deep lobes.

(b2a) Leaves with 3–5 deep, spreading lobes, the leaves resembling a rough cross, dark green above, hairy beneath; scales of the acrorn cup thin; trees of southeastern and southcentral U.S.

Post oak, p. 323

Post Oak

(b2b) Leaves with 3–5 shallow, ascending lobes, bright green, smooth beneath; scales of the acorn cup thick and rounded; trees of the Coastal Plain in southeastern U.S.

Bastard oak, p. 325

(Continued)

Bastard Oak

(2) Leaves entire, often with a wavy margin, or very shallowly 2–3-lobed near the tip.

    (a) Trees of southern Texas and adjacent Mexico (Edwards Plateau); leaves grayish-green with a smoky cast   **Lacey oak, p. 325**

    (b) Trees of eastern or southeastern U.S.; leaves dark green, shiny to dull.

        (b1) Leaves leathery, broadest near the tip to near the middle.

            (b1a) Acorn cups shallowly saucer-shaped, enclosing just the base of the nut; leaves deciduous; trees of southeastern Coastal Plain   **Durand oak, p. 326**

            (b1b) Acorn cups bowl-shaped, enclosing from one-third to half of the nut; leaves nearly evergreen; trees of southeastern Coastal Plain   **Chapman oak, p. 327**

        (b2) Leaves firm, but not leathery, usually broader below the middle to almost uniformly wide; rare trees, only in western South Carolina and northeastern Georgia.   **Oglethorpe oak, p. 328**

b. Trees of western North America, including the Rocky Mountains, Arizona, and New Mexico.

  (1) Leaves deeply lobed, lobes penetrating to at least half way to middle of leaf.

    (a) Leaves yellowish-green; acorns 2–2.5 cm (0.8–1 in) long; usually shrubby, occasionally 5 m (16 ft); trees of central and southern Rocky Mountains   **Gambel's oak, p. 329**

    (b) Leaves dark green; acorns 2.5–5 cm (1–2 in) long; medium-size to tall trees with rounded crowns; trees of Pacific Northwest or California.

        (b1) Leaves 5–9-lobed, 5–8 cm (2–3.2 in) wide, occasionally

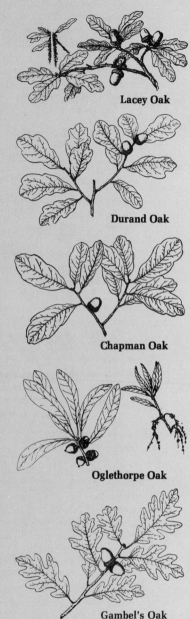

Lacey Oak

Durand Oak

Chapman Oak

Oglethorpe Oak

Gambel's Oak

Oregon White Oak

wider, thick and leathery texture; acorns 2.5–3.2 cm (1–1.3 in) long; trees of Pacific Northwest, including central coast of California

Oregon white oak, p. 330

(b2) Leaves 9–11-lobed, 2.5–5 cm (1.2–2.2 in) wide, thin but firm texture, acorns 3–5.5 cm (1.2–2.2 in) long; trees of California

California white oak, p. 331

California White Oak

(2) Leaves entire to shallowly lobed, the lobes never reaching half way to middle of leaf.

(a) Leaves bluish-green, thin but firm.

(a1) Leaves 3.8–10 cm (1.5–4 in) long, entire, but often shallowly and irregularly lobed; acorn cup very shallow, enclosing only the very base of the nut; trees of California

Blue oak, p. 332

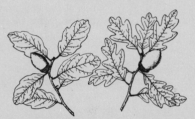

Blue Oak

(a2) Leaves 2.2–5 cm (1–2 in) long, entire; acorn cup top-shaped to bowl-shaped, enclosing one-fourth to one-third of the nut; trees of extreme southwestern U. S. and Mexico

Mexican blue oak, p. 334

(b) Leaves bright green to gray-green, thick and leathery.

(b1) Leaves deciduous, 2–10 cm (0.8–4 in) long, entire, shallowly lobed to coarsely toothed, usually smooth above and hairy beneath; shrub or small tree of Texas and New Mexico

Havard shin oak, p. 334

Mexican Blue Oak

(b2) Leaves nearly evergreen, 1–5 cm (0.4–2 in) long, coarsely toothed along the margin, covered with stiff, rough hairs, shrub or small tree of Texas, New Mexico, Arizona, and Mexico

Sandpaper oak, p. 335

(Continued)

Sandpaper Oak

2. Leaves coarsely toothed, resembling the leaf of a chestnut.

    a. Acorns on long slender stalks 2.5–10 cm (1–4 in) long; the acorn stalks longer than leafstalks   **Swamp white oak, p. 336**

    b. Acorns without stalks or very short-stalked; stalks shorter than leafstalks.

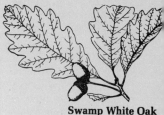

Swamp White Oak

      (1) Acorns large, 2.5–4 cm (1–1.6 in) long, the acorn cups 2.5–3.5 cm (1–1.9 in) across.

        (a) Leaves with regular pointed teeth; acorn cup scales free to the base, often forming a fringe on the edge of the cup; lowland trees of wet sites of southeastern U. S.
          Swamp chestnut oak, p. 337

Chestnut Oak

        (b) Leaves with rounded teeth; acorn cup scales united at the base, the rim of the cup fringeless; trees of dry or rocky bluffs or slopes of northeastern U. S.
          Chestnut oak, p. 338

      (2) Acorns small, 1.5–2.5 cm (0.6–1 in) long, the acorn cups 1–2.5 cm (0.4–1 in) across.

        (a) Medium-size trees to 30 m (100 ft), leaves 10–18 cm (4–7 in) long, with 9–15 pairs of lateral veins; trees of central and eastern U. S.
          Chinkapin oak, p. 339

Chinkapin Oak

        (b) Large shrubs or small trees to 5 m (17 ft); leaves 5–15 cm (2–6 in) long, with 4–8 pairs of lateral veins; trees of central and eastern U. S.
        Dwarf chinkapin oak, p. 340

B. Leaves evergreen or the green leaves persisting into spring when new leaves appear.

    1. Trees of the Coastal Plain of the southeastern U. S.; acorns produced on long stalks
        Live oak, p. 341

    2. Trees of southwestern or western U. S.; acorns usually with short or no stalks, except for Arizona White Oak.

      a. Leaves with a thick coarse network of veins on the lower surface, leaves broadest above the middle.

Dwarf Chinkapin Oak

Live Oak

(1) Acorns several in long-stalked clusters, 1–2.2 cm (0.4–0.9 in) long, acorn cup saucer-shaped, enclosed from one-fourth to half of nut; leaves dark green to grayish-green above; trees of southwestern U. S.   **Netleaf oak, p. 342**

Netleaf Oak

(2) Acorns in 1 to 3s, not on long stalks, 0.8–1.6 cm (0.3–0.7 in) long, acorn cup deeply bowl-shaped, enclosing about half of nut; leaves dull bluish-green above; trees of southwestern U. S.
Arizona white oak, p. 343

Arizona White Oak

b. Leaves with a fine network of veins on the lower surface, leaves often broadest below the middle.

(1) Bark very thick, firm but somewhat spongy when pressed; acorn cup enclosing from half to three-fourths of nut, the cup scales heavy, curled, giving a fringed appearance; introduced trees from Europe   **Cork oak, p. 344**

Cork Oak

(2) Bark thin to moderately thick, often scaly but not spongy; acorn cup enclosing from one-fourth to half of nut, cup scales thin to thickened, but not curling nor fringed.

(a) Trees of the southwestern U. S.

(a1) Mature leaves small, to 3.7 cm (1.5 in) long, rarely longer; acorn cup shallowly saucer-shaped, only enclosing one-fourth or less of the nut.

(a1a) Leaves bluish-green, entire or with a few small teeth along the margin; southeastern Arizona and southwestern New Mexico
Toumey oak, p. 345

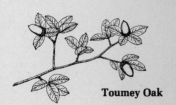

Toumey Oak

(a1b) Leaves green, with 5 or 6 long-pointed teeth along the margin; southern Arizona
Ajo oak, p. 346

(a2) Mature leaves to 10 cm (4 in) long, dark-green to gray-green; acorn cup bowl-
(Continued)

shaped, enclosing one-third to two-thirds of acorn.

(a2a) Acorns broadest near the base; usually rounded at the tip.

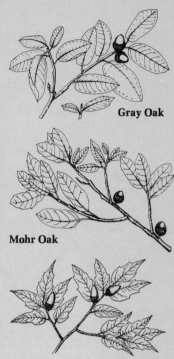

Gray Oak

* *Leaves gray-green, finely hairy on both surfaces; acorn cup enclosing from one-third to half of acorn; shrub or tree of Arizona, New Mexico, western Texas, and adjacent Mexico* **Gray oak, p. 346**

** *Leaves dark shiny green, sparsely hairy on upper surface, more so beneath; acorn cup enclosing from half to three-fourths of acorn; small trees or shrubs of Oklahoma, Texas, eastern New Mexico, and Mexico*

Mohr Oak

Mohr oak, p. 347

(a2b) Acorns cone-shaped, pointed at the tip; common tree of Arizona, New Mexico, western Texas, and northern Mexico **Emory oak, p. 348**

Emory Oak

(b) Trees of California.

(b1) Leaves light to dark green, usually up to 2 times as long as broad.

(b1a) Leaves small 1.6–2.5 cm (0.6–1 in) long, 0.7–1.4 cm (0.3–0.6 in) wide, light green; acorns 1.2–2.6 cm (0.5–1 in) long, broadest near the base to almost cylinder shaped; often shrubby; foothills and chaparral **California scrub oak, p. 349**

California Scrub Oak

(b1b) Leaves medium-size, 2–10 cm (0.8–4 in) long, 1.3–7.5 cm (0.5–3 in) wide, dark green; acorns 2–4 cm (0.8–1.6 in) long, narrowly cone-

shaped; lower slopes of coastal mountains
Coast live oak, p. 380

(b2) Leaves bluish-green to grayish blue-green, variable in shape but usually 2½ to 3 times as long as wide; low hills and mesas of southwestern California
Engelmann oak, p. 350

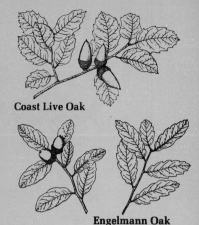

Coast Live Oak

Engelmann Oak

Bur Oak
Quercus macrocarpa Michx.

The bur oak is a medium-size tree of eastern North America with extensions into the southcentral U.S. This drought-resistant oak grows anywhere from moist bottomlands to dry hillsides, mainly in limestone soils. Bur oak is tolerant of varying soil and moisture conditions but reaches its greatest size in the rich bottomlands of the Ohio River Valley. It does occur in pure, or nearly pure, stands but also commonly grows in association with many other hardwoods. In the wetter lowlands, common associates are swamp white oak, American elm, slippery elm, white ash, and hackberry. In the higher drier sites, bur oaks occur commonly with northern red, white, and black oaks, shagbark and bitternut hickories, and green ash.

This slow-growing tree flowers in spring, and the acorns mature by the end of the first growing season. The tree normally does not begin to flower and fruit until it is 30 to 35 years old but then may continue production for the next 200 to 300 years. Large seed crops are produced every 2 or 3 years and are of considerable importance to wildlife. Whitetail deer, squirrels, wood ducks, turkeys, rabbits, mice, and other rodents feed on the acorns.

The wood ranges in color from light to dark brown. Bur oak is very hard, heavy, strong, durable, and of considerable importance as a timber tree. It is usually cut as white oak for furniture, flooring, cabinets, boat decks, and interior finishings.

Appearance: medium to tall tree 20–40 m (65–132 ft), rarely taller, with a broad, spreading, rounded crown; trunk tall, straight, to 2 m (6.6 ft) in diameter, often free of branches for lower two-thirds of trunk. **Bark:** thick, brown, yellowish-brown to reddish-brown, 2.5–5 cm (1–2 in) with deep lengthwise furrows separating the irregular, scaly ridges, similar to white oak. **Branches:** stout, spreading, large, occasionally gnarled; branchlets stout, hairy, and orange to reddish-green turning dark brown and becoming smooth with age, often with corky ridges. **Winter buds:** 3–7 mm (0.1–0.3 in) long, broadest at the base and pointed at the tip, covered with overlapping, reddish-

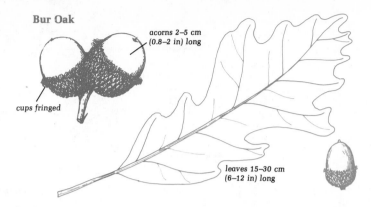

Bur Oak

acorns 2–5 cm
(0.8–2 in) long

cups fringed

leaves 15–30 cm
(6–12 in) long

brown scales. **Leaves:** alternate, deciduous, ***15–30 cm (6–12 in) long, 7.5–15 cm (3–6 in) wide, broadest above the middle, shallowly to deeply lobed, with 5 to 9 lobes, usually with a pair of deep lobes just below the middle,*** the terminal lobe largest, tapering to a narrow base and rounded at the tip, the ***margin edged with large, irregular, rounded teeth,*** leathery, dark green and smooth above, occasionally with a few hairs above, with fine gray to whitish hairs beneath; the leafstalks stout, flattened and grooved above, 8–12 cm (3.2–4.8 in) long. **Flowers:** male and female flowers in separate catkins produced on the current year's branchlets; male flowers in slender, hanging, yellowish-green catkins 9–15 cm (3.5–5.9 in) long; female flowers tiny, reddish, usually in clusters of 1 to 5 on a short, inconspicuous stalk at the junction of the leaves and branchlets. **Fruits:** acorns, maturing in 1 season, usually solitary and stalked, stalkless to long-stalked, 2–5 cm (0.8–2 in) long, 0.8–3.8 cm (0.3–1.5 in) wide, variable in shape, broadest at the base or near the middle, rounded and with a short beak at the tip; cup almost globe-shaped, enclosing usually half to three-fourths of the nut, the cup ***scales*** overlapping, broadest at the base and tapering to a pointed tip, those ***closest to the tip conspicuously fringed.*** **Seeds:** somewhat sweet, edible.

Overcup Oak   *Quercus lyrata* Walt.

The overcup oak is one of several oaks that are primarily lowland or bottomland trees. It is a medium-size tree of the southeastern U.S., especially the Coastal Plain from New Jersey to Florida and Texas and north up the Mississippi River Valley to southern Illinois and Indiana. It grows in heavy, poorly drained soils typical of sloughs, river swamps, floodplains, and other bottomlands. The overcup oak grows in association with lowland trees such as sweetgum, willow oak, Nuttall oak, water hickory, green ash, cedar elm, and sugarberry.

This is a slow-growing tree that does not reach acorn-bearing age until 25 to 30 years old. It flowers in March or April, and the acorns mature by September or October of the same year. Large acorn crops are produced every 3 or 4 years with intervening years of limited seed production. Whitetail deer, hogs, turkeys, squirrels, and smaller rodents eat the acorns.

Overcup Oak

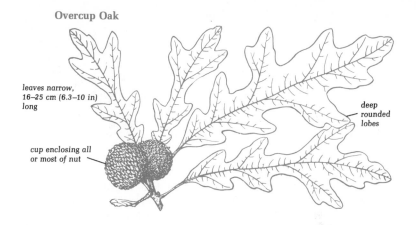

leaves narrow,
16–25 cm (6.3–10 in)
long

deep
rounded
lobes

cup enclosing all
or most of nut

The brown wood is hard, durable, heavy, tough, and strong. It is so similar to white oak that it is usually cut and sold as white oak.

Appearance: medium-size tree, 20–30 m (65–100 ft), with a broad rounded crown; trunk tall and straight or short and often crooked, to 1 m (3.3 ft) in diameter. **Bark:** thin to moderately thick, 1.2–2.5 cm (0.5–1 in), reddish-brown to grayish-brown, divided into flattened, somewhat squarish plates, with fissures separating broad ridges developing on older trees. **Branches:** stout, often short, the lower ones spreading and sometimes hanging near the tips; branchlets slender, hairy when young, becoming smooth with age, green turning reddish-brown or grayish-brown with age. **Winter buds:** 2–4 mm (about 0.1–0.2 in) long, almost rounded, covered with overlapping light-brown scales. **Leaves:** alternate, deciduous, *16–25 cm (6.3–10 in) long, 2.5–10 cm (1–4 in) wide, narrow but broadest above the middle, with several shallow to deeply rounded lobes along the margin,* gradually tapering to a narrow base, rounded at the tip, papery, dark green and smooth above, paler and covered with soft hairs to almost smooth beneath; the leaf stalks stout, hairy to smooth, 0.8–2.5 cm (0.3–1 in) long. **Flowers:** male and female flowers in separate catkins produced on the current year's branchlets; male flowers in slender, hanging, yellow catkins 10–15 cm (4–6 in) long; female flowers tiny, in short, few-flowered spikes near the base of the leafstalks. **Fruits:** acorns maturing in 1 season, solitary or in pairs, with or without a stalk, 1.5–2.5 cm (0.6–1 in) long, *nearly globe-shaped to broadest near the base,* rounded but usually with a short beak at the tip, light brown; *cup deep, nearly globe-shaped, enclosing from two-thirds to nearly all of the nut,* the cup scales broadest near the base and pointed at the tip, thickened, often with a fringe or ragged edge on the rim. **Seeds:** edible.

White Oak   *Quercus alba* L.

The white oak, one of the most important hardwood trees, is widespread across eastern North America from southern Canada to northern Florida. It grows in a variety of soils: sandy, gravelly, loamy, glaciated or nonglaciated but does best in deep, rich, well-drained, loamy soils. White oak usually grows at altitudes under 200 m (660 ft) in the northern part of its range and up to 1,500 m (5,000 ft) in the southern Appalachians. White oak does not occur in pure stands but is found with many other forest trees, usually including other oaks or hickories. In addition, it commonly occurs with sweetgum, blackgum, American basswood, yellow poplar, black cherry, white ash, and American beech.

In spite of its reputation as a slow-grower, white oak can be a moderately fast-growing tree, when provided with good soil and enough water. It flowers in spring and is generally a prolific seed producer, with large seed crops produced every 4 to 6 years. The acorns are important to many species of wildlife, including whitetail deer, raccoons, squirrels, turkeys, and quail.

The light-brown wood is hard, tough, strong, and close-grained. One of the most important woods of North America, it is used in many different ways but is best suited for support timbers, furniture, flooring, and interior finishings. The white oak was the mainstay in North American ships prior to the use of steel.

White Oak

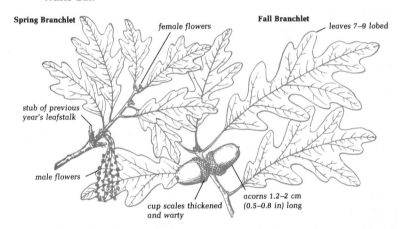

Spring Branchlet

female flowers

Fall Branchlet

leaves 7–9 lobed

stub of previous year's leafstalk

male flowers

cup scales thickened and warty

acorns 1.2–2 cm (0.5–0.8 in) long

Appearance: medium to tall tree to 35 m (115 ft), rarely taller, with broad, rounded crown; trunk tall, straight in forest or short and soon branching in open fields, 0.6–1.5 m (1.9–4.9 ft) in diameter. **Bark:** *thick, 2.5–5 cm (1–2 in), light ash gray,* sometimes with a reddish-brown cast or light gray, with shallow to deep lengthwise fissures separating small scaly blocks or narrow rounded ridges. **Branches:** short to moderate in length, stout, spreading, soon branching; branchlets slender to stout, green to reddish-green and hairy when very young, turning red-brown then ash gray and smooth. **Winter buds:** 3–5 mm (0.1–0.2 in) long, globe-shaped to broadest near the base, covered with several overlapping, smooth, reddish-brown scales. **Leaves:** alternate, deciduous, 12–22 cm (4.7–8.7 in) long, 5–10 cm (2–4 in) wide, usually widest above the middle to almost uniformly wide along the sides, *divided into 7 to 10 shallow to deep rounded lobes,* tapering at the base and rounded at the tip, entire, thin, hairy when young but *bright green, smooth,* and often shiny above, paler beneath; the leafstalks stout, usually grooved above, 1.5–2 cm (0.6–0.8 in) long. **Flowers:** male and female flowers in separate catkins produced on the current year's branchlets; male flowers in hairy to almost smooth, hanging catkins 6.2–7.5 cm (2.4–3 in) long; female flowers usually 2 to 4 on a short stalk in the junctions of the leafstalks, with the branchlets, tiny, inconspicuous. **Fruits:** acorns, maturing in 1 season, solitary or paired, *with or without a short stalk, 1.2–2 cm (0.5–0.8 in) long,* widest near the base or the middle and tapering to a rounded tip, light brown; *cup bowl-like, about 8–12 mm (0.3–0.5 in) deep,* enclosing the lower fourth of the nut, the *scales of the cup thickened and appearing warty.* **Seeds:** somewhat sweet, edible.

English Oak   *Quercus robur* L.

This majestic European species was originally brought over to Colonial America from England. It has been planted in many areas in Canada and the U.S. where occasionally it has escaped from cultivation and reproduced on its own. Individual trees may grow to heights of 45 m (150 ft) or more, surviving for centuries. Many English ships were constructed of sturdy beams from this tree, as were countless interiors of castles and churches. English oak has been honored since ancient times in song and story.

   English oaks have wide-spreading crowns rising from sturdy, fairly short trunks. They are covered with deeply furrowed dark gray bark. The leaves are short-stalked or stalkless, 7.5–12.5 cm (3–5 in) long and half as wide, broadest above the middle, *with 3 to 7 shallow to deep lobes* on each side, dark green above and bluish-green below. The flowers are inconspicuous. The male flowers are in slender hanging catkins, and the female flowers are clustered in small groups of 2 to 5 at the leaf bases. The acorns are *2–2.5 cm (0.8–1 in) long* and *enclosed for one-third of their length by the cup.* The acorns ripen in autumn, the same year as flowering occurs.

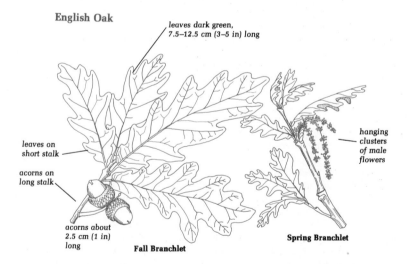

English Oak

leaves dark green,
7.5–12.5 cm (3–5 in) long

leaves on
short stalk

acorns on
long stalk

acorns about
2.5 cm (1 in)
long

Fall Branchlet

hanging
clusters
of male
flowers

Spring Branchlet

Post Oak   *Quercus stellata* Wangenh.

This is a small to medium-size oak that is widespread throughout the southeastern and southcentral U.S. It is a tree of the lower mountain slopes, Piedmont, and Coastal Plain. Post oak grows on rocky or sandy ridges and outcrops, and in dry woodlands in a variety of soils, including gravelly, sandy, poor-upland soils, and heavy, moist, loamy soils where the tree reaches its greatest size. Post oak normally grows in association with blackjack oak, black oak, scarlet oak, hickory, eastern redcedar, shortleaf pine, Virginia pine, and loblolly pine. The shape of the leaves and the presence or absence of hairs on the branchlets is variable; because of this, several varieties are recognized.

Post oak is a slow-growing, drought resistant tree that reaches flowering age between 20 and 30 years. Although variable from tree to tree, this oak usually produces a good crop of acorns every 2 to 4 years. The acorns are an important food source for whitetail deer, turkeys, raccoons, and squirrels. The light-brown to dark-brown wood is hard, very heavy, and durable, and it is often lumped commercially with several other oaks and called white oak. It is used in furniture, interior finishes, fencing, flooring, and is an excellent fuel.

Post Oak

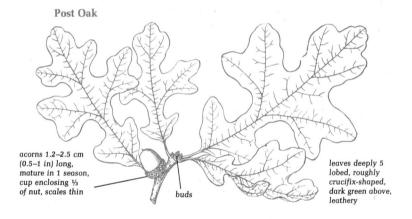

*acorns 1.2–2.5 cm
(0.5–1 in) long,
mature in 1 season,
cup enclosing ⅓
of nut, scales thin*

buds

*leaves deeply 5
lobed, roughly
crucifix-shaped,
dark green above,
leathery*

Appearance: shrubby to small or medium-size tree 10–20 m (32–66 ft), rarely taller, with a broad rounded crown; trunk straight to crooked, 0.3–1 m (1–3.3 ft) in diameter, seldom larger. **Bark:** moderately thick, 1.2–2.5 cm (0.5–1 in), reddish-brown to dark gray, with deep lengthwise furrows separating the rounded, sometimes broad, scaly ridges. **Branches:** stout, spreading; branchlets stout, hairy and orange to reddish-brown when young becoming smooth and gray with age. **Winter buds:** 3–6 mm (about 0.1–0.2 in) long, almost globe-shaped to very broad near the base and usually rounded at the tip, covered with overlapping, dark-brown scales. **Leaves:** alternate, deciduous, *10–15 cm (4–6 in) long, 7.5–10 cm (3–4 in) wide, usually widest above the middle, with 3 to 5 short, wide and deep lobes, giving the leaf the appearance of a rough crucifix*, tapering at the base and rounded at the tip, entire, leathery, hairy when young but becoming dark green and densely to sparingly hairy beneath; the leafstalks stout, often hairy, 1.2–2.4 cm (0.5–1 in) long. **Flowers:** male and female flowers in separate catkins on the current year's branchlets; male flowers clustered on hairy, hanging catkins 7.5–10 cm (3–4 in) long; female flowers tiny, stalkless, hairy, 1–4 on a short cluster in the junction of the leafstalks. **Fruits:** acorns, maturing in 1 season, often 2 to 4 clustered, stalkless or with a short stalk, 1.2–2.5 cm (0.5–1 in) long, 0.7–2 cm (0.3–0.8 in) wide, broadest at the base and tapering to a rounded tip; cup top-shaped, *enclosing about a third of the nut, the outer scales thin, broadest at the base and tapering to a point.*

Bastard Oak, Bluff Oak

Quercus austrina Small

The bastard oak is a medium-size to large tree that occurs infrequently from the Carolinas to Florida and west to Mississippi. It grows in the Coastal Plain along streams and bluffs usually in rich soils. It is closely related to the white oak, and the value of its acorns to wildlife and its wood for timber is similar to that for the white oak. This oak differs from the eastern white oak in that its leaves have fewer lobes and its acorns a thinner cup.

This tree is like the white oak in shape and general appearance. The bark is gray to grayish-brown, furrowed, and scaly. The branchlets are reddish-brown turning gray-brown with age. The leaves are deciduous, **8–16 cm (3.2–6.3 in) long,** 4–8 cm (1.6–3.2 in) wide, broadest above the middle,

Bastard Oak

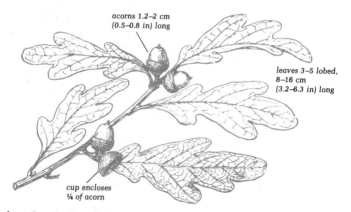

acorns 1.2–2 cm
(0.5–0.8 in) long

leaves 3–5 lobed,
8–16 cm
(3.2–6.3 in) long

cup encloses
¼ of acorn

wedge-shaped at the base and rounded at the tip, with **3 to 5 rounded to somewhat pointed lobes** on the upper half of the leaf along the margin, bright green and shiny above, pale green and smooth beneath. The acorns mature in 1 season and usually occur singly or 2 to 3 per cluster. Like the white oak acorns, these **acorns are 1.2–2 cm (0.5–0.8 in) long,** usually widest near the base, the **cup** bowl-shaped, thin, **enclosing a fourth to a third of the nut.** The scales of the cup are thick and rounded on the back.

Lacey Oak

Quercus glaucoides Mart. & Gal.

(synonym: *Q. laceyi* Small)

Lacey oak is a small tree, which sometimes remains shrubby, and is apparently confined to the Edwards Plateau in Texas, with extensions into northern Mexico. It grows in dry rocky soils on bluffs or along riverbanks where it reaches its greatest size. Although similar to the Durand oak, the Lacey oak can be distinguished from it and other oaks by the smokey cast of its leaves and branches when seen at a distance.

Lacey oak is usually a tree, sometimes to 15 m (50 ft), with spreading branches and a broadly rounded crown. The thick gray bark is divided by deep fissures into flattened narrow ridges. The leaves are *deciduous, leathery, 5–12 cm (2–4.8 in) long, 1.8–5 cm (0.7–2 in) wide,* broadest near the middle or above to uniformly wide, *with a few shallow lobes along the margin, grayish-green* and smooth above, paler and smooth or hairy only along the veins on the lower surface. The acorns ma-

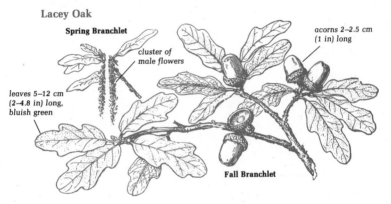

Lacey Oak

Spring Branchlet

cluster of male flowers

acorns 2–2.5 cm (1 in) long

leaves 5–12 cm (2–4.8 in) long, bluish green

Fall Branchlet

ture in 1 season on the current year's branchlets and are usually single or in clusters of 2 to 3 on the branchlets. They are usually broadest near the base to near the middle, shiny reddish-brown, and enclosed for a fourth to half their length by a cup. The cup is saucer-shaped, and its scales are rounded. It is hairy when young but becomes smooth at maturity.

Durand Oak

Quercus durandii Buckl.

This attractive, medium-size tree is native to the southeastern Coastal Plain from North Carolina and west to central Texas. It occurs in river valleys and river bottoms and on dry limestone hills but does best on rich, well-drained soils. This oak is rare in many parts of its range and usually occurs as scattered trees. It is generally encountered growing in association with hackberry, cedar elm, live oak, and Shumard oak.

Durand oak is closely related to the live

oak but differs in that it has smaller acorns and deciduous leaves. Some specialists recognize different varieties of the Durand oak. The trees in Oklahoma, Texas, and Mexico with thicker leaves and rounded acorn cups are often referred to as the short-lobed Durand oak (*Quercus durandii* variety *breviloba*).

Durand oak is a slow to moderately fast growing tree. It flowers in early spring, and the acorns mature by autumn of the same year. Whitetail deer, wild turkeys, squirrels, and smaller rodents eat the acrorns. The reddish-brown wood is hard, heavy, and strong but has little economic value because of its rarity, but it is used as a fuel.

Durand Oak

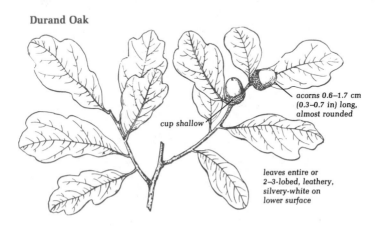

acorns 0.6–1.7 cm
(0.3–0.7 in) long,
almost rounded

cup shallow

leaves entire or
2–3-lobed, leathery,
silvery-white on
lower surface

Appearance: small to medium-size tree 8–30 m (26–100 ft) with an irregular to dense rounded crown; trunk usually straight, 0.3–1 m (1–3.3 ft) in diameter. **Bark:** thin, 4–8 mm (0.1–0.3 in), light gray, breaking into thin scales and becoming furrowed on older trees. **Branches:** small, stout, the lower ones spreading; branchlets slender, pale grayish-brown to brown, hairy when young, becoming smooth with age. **Winter buds:** 2–4 mm (0.1–0.2 in) long, almost globe-shaped to broadest near the base and tapering to a rounded tip, covered with overlapping, reddish-brown hairs or smooth scales. **Leaves:** alternate, deciduous, *6–18 cm (2.4–7.1 in) long, 1.2–8.5 cm (0.5–3.4 in) wide, widest above the middle* to near the middle, *entire to 2 to 3 lobed to irregularly lobed along the margin,* tapering to a narrow base, usually rounded at the tip, leathery, *shiny dark green and smooth above, silvery-white hairs on the lower surface;* the leafstalks stout, smooth, 6–9 mm (0.2–0.3 in) long. **Flowers:** male and female flowers in separate catkins produced on the current year's branchlets; male flowers in slender, hanging, hairy catkins 7.5–10 cm (3–4 in) long; female flowers tiny, usually 1 to 3 on short stalks in the junction of the leafstalks. **Fruits:** *acorns,* maturing in 1 season on current year's branchlets, solitary or in pairs, *0.6–1.7 cm (0.3–0.7 in) long, broadest near the middle to almost rounded, dark brown at maturity; cup saucer-shaped, 6–8 mm (0.2–0.3 in) deep, enclosing just the base of the nut,* the cup scales slightly thickened, silvery, hairy.

Chapman Oak   *Quercus chapmanii* Sarg.

This small, sometimes shrubby, tree is native to the Coastal Plain from southeastern South Carolina to southern Florida. It occurs in sand woods and scrub forest on sandy, well-drained soils and usually grows in association with the sand pine, myrtle oak,

and sand live oak. This oak may reach 8 m
(26 ft) in height and has a broad, spreading,
rounded crown. The leaves are broadest
near the middle or above the middle, the
margin entire, wavy, or shallowly lobed
near the tip. It is related to the Durand oak
and the live oak but can be distinguished
by its nearly evergreen leaves that often
remain into late winter, broad acorns (less
than twice as long as thick), and bowl-
shaped *acorn cups that enclose about
half of the nut.* This oak flowers in early
spring, and the acorns mature by the end of the first season.

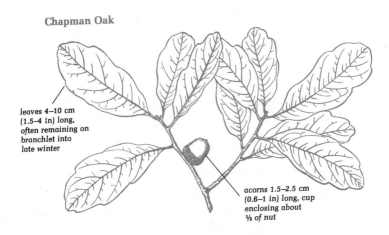

Chapman Oak

leaves 4–10 cm
(1.5–4 in) long,
often remaining on
branchlet into
late winter

acorns 1.5–2.5 cm
(0.6–1 in) long, cup
enclosing about
½ of nut

Oglethorpe Oak   Quercus oglethorpensis Duncan

This medium-size southeastern tree was first described in 1940. It grows only in well-
drained bottomlands in a few counties in western South Carolina and northeastern
Georgia. Its name reflects its place of discovery, Oglethorpe County, Georgia.

Oglethorpe oaks may reach 24 m (80 ft)
in height and the trunk may grow to 60 cm
(23 in) in diameter. The light gray to whitish bark is broken into close-pressed
scales. The branchlets are at first hairy but
eventually lose their hairs. The deciduous
leaves are from *5–12.5 cm (2–5 in) long*
and 1.8 to 3.6 cm (0.7–1.4 in) broad,
broadest near the base, with rounded to
pointed base and tip, *entire margins,* and
coated on the undersides with light yellow
hairs. The gray-brown, egg-shaped acorn is
approximately 1–1.2 cm (0.5 in) long, and is covered for the lower third by a turban-
shaped cup with flat, tan scales.

Oglethorpe Oak

*leaves 5–12.5 cm
(2–5 in) long with
light-yellow hairs
beneath*

*catkins of
male flowers*

*acorns 1–1.2 cm
(0.5 in) long*

Gambel's Oak

Quercus gambelii Nutt.

[synonyms: *Q. novomexicana* (A. DC.) Rydb., *Q. utahensis*
(A. DC.) Rydb., *Q. confusa* Woot. & Standl.]

Gambel's oak is the most common deciduous oak in most of the Rocky Mountains, especially on the eastern slopes. It extends from Utah and Wyoming southward into northern Mexico, and it occurs normally at 1,350–2,800 m (4,400–9,200 ft) but occasionally reaches 3,250 m (10,700 ft) elevation. Gambel's oak grows in dry foothills, canyons, and lower slopes. It is usually a shrub or small tree and often grows in dense colonies, forming thickets that frequently cover entire hillsides. In the canyons of southern Arizona, Gambel's oak occurs with the Arizona sycamore and Arizona cypress. Leaves may vary considerably in size and shape.

This is a slow-growing tree, which flowers in spring. The acorns mature in the autumn of the same year. As with other oaks, acorn production is cyclic, with a year of heavy production followed by several years of light production. Mule deer, wild turkeys, peccaries, goats, squirrels, and jays eat the sweet acorns. Cows, horses, blacktail deer, and porcupines browse the leaves.

The wood is hard, heavy, and close-grained. Although the trees are seldom large enough to be of commercial value, some lumber is produced for local use, but most is used for fuel.

Appearance: thicket-forming shrub, small to medium-size tree to 20 m (65 ft), with a rounded crown; trunk stout, straight, soon-branching in open field trees, to 2 m (6.6 ft) in diameter. **Bark:** thin, light-gray to white, becoming rough and scaly with age. **Branches:** stout, spreading; branchlets stout, reddish-brown and finely hairy when young, becoming darker and smooth with age. **Winter buds:** 6–10 mm (0.2–0.4 in) long, broadest near the base and tapering to a pointed tip, covered with overlapping scales. **Leaves:** alternate, deciduous, 8–16 cm (3.2–6.3 in) long, 4.5–7.6 cm (1.8–3 in) wide, usually broadest above the middle to uniformly wide, moderately to **deeply 5 to 9 lobed,** the lobes rounded, tapering to squared at the base, rounded at the tip, leathery

Gambel's Oak

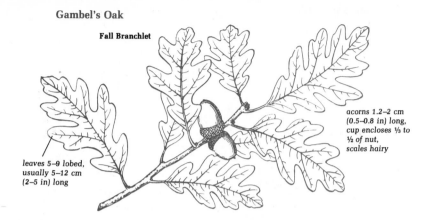

Fall Branchlet

acorns 1.2–2 cm (0.5–0.8 in) long, cup encloses ⅓ to ½ of nut, scales hairy

leaves 5–9 lobed, usually 5–12 cm (2–5 in) long

and shiny *yellowish-green above,* paler and smooth to densely hairy beneath; leaf-stalks slender, 1.4–2.6 cm (0.5–1 in) long, smooth to hairy. **Flowers:** male and female flowers produced in separate catkins on the current year's branchlets; male flowers in slender catkins 2.5–3.5 cm (1–1.4 in) long; female flowers tiny, in few-flowered clusters in the junctions of some of the leaves of current year's branchlets. **Fruits:** acorns maturing in 1 season on current year's branchlets, solitary or in clusters, on short stalks or stalkless, *2–2.5 cm (1.8–1 in) long,* broadest near the base to *nearly globe-shaped,* rounded at the tip, light brown; *cup shallowly to deeply bowl-shaped, enclosing from one-fourth to one-third of the nut,* the scales of the cup broadest at the base and pointed at the tip, thickened, hairy. **Seeds:** edible.

Oregon White Oak — *Quercus garryana* Dougl. ex Hook.

The Oregon white oak is native to the Pacific Northwest from southern British Columbia southward to the central coast of California. It grows on lower mountain slopes, open valleys, and at the margin of the grasslands and forests, normally at lower elevations but reaching up to 1,350 m (4,500 ft) in California. This drought-resistant oak may form pure dense stands in the open valleys; elsewhere it grows in association with the madrone, ponderosa pine, Douglas fir, bigleaf maple, grand fir, and the California black oak.

Oregon white oak is a slow-growing tree that may live to 500 years. The acorns mature in 1 season and usually fall in September and October. As with other oaks, large nut crops are cyclic with a good year followed by 2 or 3 lighter years. The acorns are an important food for blacktail deer, bears, squirrels, woodpeckers, pocket gophers, and other small rodents.

The light-brown to yellowish-brown wood is hard, heavy, and tough. It is used in furniture, cabinets, interior finishes, and general construction.

Appearance: small to medium-size tree 12–20 m (39–66 ft), rarely taller, with a compact rounded crown; trunk short, often crooked, soon branching, to 1 m (3.3 ft) in diameter. **Bark:** thin, becoming moderately thick with age, to 2 cm (0.8 in), light

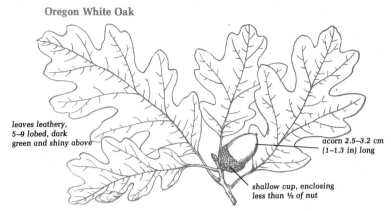

Oregon White Oak

leaves leathery,
5–9 lobed, dark
green and shiny above

acorn 2.5–3.2 cm
(1–1.3 in) long

shallow cup, enclosing
less than ⅓ of nut

brown to gray, sometimes with an orange tinge, with shallow, irregular, lengthwise furrows separating the broad scaly ridges. **Branches:** short, ascending, spreading to upright; branchlets stout, densely hairy and orange-brown becoming smooth and reddish-brown to gray. **Winter buds:** 6–12 mm (0.2–0.5 in) long, broadest near the base and tapering to a pointed tip, covered with densely hairy, overlapping scales. **Leaves:** alternate, deciduous, *7.5–10 cm long, rarely to 15 (3–4 in, rarely to 6), 5–8 cm wide, rarely to 12 (2–3.2 in, rarely to 5),* usually broadest above the middle to uniformly wide, *deeply 5 to 9 lobed, the lobes rounded and unevenly and coarsely toothed,* rounded to wedge-shaped base and rounded to pointed at the tip, *thick and leathery, dark green and shiny above,* paler and finely hairy beneath; the leafstalks stout, flattened, hairy, 12–25 cm (4.7–9.9 in) long. **Flowers:** male and female flowers produced in separate catkins on the current year's branchlets; male flowers in slender, hairy, hanging catkins 4–6 cm (1.6–2.4 in) long; female flowers tiny in few-flowered clusters in the junction of some of the leafstalks with the branchlets. **Fruits:** *acorns,* maturing in 1 season on current year's branchlets, usually solitary or paired, without stalks or with short stalks, *2.5–3.2 cm (1–1.3 in) long, 1.2–2.5 cm (0.5–1 in) thick,* broadest below or above the middle, rounded at the tip, light brown; *cup shallow, bowl-like, enclosing less than a third of the nut,* the *scales* of the cup broadest near the base and pointed at the tip, *thickened, hairy.* **Seeds:** sweet, edible.

California White Oak, Valley Oak *Quercus lobata* Née

The California white oak is the largest of all western oaks and often develops into a massive spreading tree. This oak is restricted to California, occurring in the valleys and foothills of the inner and middle coastal ranges and on the islands of Santa Cruz and Santa Catalina. It grows in the fertile lowlands of the deep rich soils, such as found along river valleys. It is a lowland tree but can be found up to 1,700 m (5,600 ft) elevation. Large numbers of these trees form pure stands of open oak forest, or they may occur with the blue oak and California sycamore. Large tracts have been cleared of this oak for agriculture.

This oak is a slow to moderately fast-growing tree, depending upon soil and moisture conditions. For a deciduous hardwood, it is a long-lived tree, often reaching 300 to 400 years. The tree flowers in March or April, and the acorns mature in 1 season on the current year's branchlets. Every 2 or 3 years, the trees produce a large crop of acorns. The acorns are sweet and once were gathered by Indians for food. The acorns are valuable to wildlife and are eaten by deer, squirrels, California woodpeckers, and small rodents.

The light brown wood is fine-grained, hard, but brittle and weak, rendering it of no commercial value. It is used locally for firewood.

California White Oak

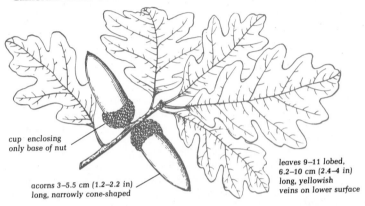

cup enclosing
only base of nut

acorns 3–5.5 cm (1.2–2.2 in)
long, narrowly cone-shaped

leaves 9–11 lobed,
6.2–10 cm (2.4–4 in)
long, yellowish
veins on lower surface

Appearance: medium to tall tree 20–30 m (65–100 ft), rarely taller, with a ***spreading, broadly rounded crown;*** trunk short, thick, soon branching, usually to 1.5 m (4.9 ft) in diameter, rarely to 3.5 m (11.5 ft). **Bark:** ***thick, usually 2–5 cm (0.8–2 in), but reaching 15 cm (6 in) thick on old trees,*** light gray, when young composed of loose scales but developing deep lengthwise fissures and broad flattened ridges with age. **Branches:** stout, often massive, spreading to hanging; branchlets slender, gray-brown to brown and covered with fine hairs when young, becoming paler and smooth by the second season. **Winter buds:** 4–6 mm (0.2 in) long, broadest near the base and sharp-pointed at the tip, covered with overlapping yellowish-brown scales. **Leaves:** alternate, deciduous, ***6.2–10 cm (2.4–4 in) long, 2.5–5 cm (1–2 in) wide, usually broadest above the middle*** to uniformly wide, ***with 9 to 11 deep rounded lobes,*** tapering to rounded at the base, usually rounded at the tip, dull green and finely hairy on the upper surface, becoming smooth with age, paler and hairy and with ***yellowish veins on the lower surface;*** the leafstalks stout, sometimes flattened, 6–12 mm (0.2–0.5 in) long. **Flowers:** male and female flowers in separate catkins produced on the current year's branchlets; male flowers in hanging, hairy, yellowish catkins 5–8 cm (2–3.2 in) long; female flowers tiny, usually solitary or in 2s or 3s, in the junction of the leafstalks. **Fruits:** acorns, maturing in 1 season, solitary or in pairs, ***3–5.5 cm (1.2–2.2 in) long, narrow cone-shaped, tapering to a pointed or rounded tip; cup bowl-shaped to deeply saucer-shaped, enclosing only the base of the nut, the scales of the cup thick, rounded and covered with whitish hairs.***

Blue Oak   *Quercus douglasii* Hook. & Arn.

Blue oak is native from northern to southern California where it occurs on the dry slopes and low hills of the interior valleys. It grows in dry loamy, gravelly, or rocky soils and ascends the mountain slopes to 1,350 m (4,500 ft) elevation. This oak often forms extensive open stands. The digger pine is the tree most commonly encoun-

tered growing in association with the blue oak. Other associates include the California white oak, California live oak, and sabine pine.

This is a slow-growing, long-lived tree that often develops into a rugged pictur-esque specimen. It flowers in April or May, and the acorns mature several months later. Each year of heavy acorn production is followed by 2 to 4 years of light produc-tion. The leaves and acorns are an important food for deer. Wild pigs feed on them during winter and spring. Jays, squirrels, and other rodents also eat the acorns.

The dark brown wood turns nearly black on exposure to air. It is heavy and hard, but brittle, and subject to dry rot, a fungus disease. Because of the strong cross-grain, it is difficult to split. The wood is of little commercial value other than as firewood.

Blue Oak

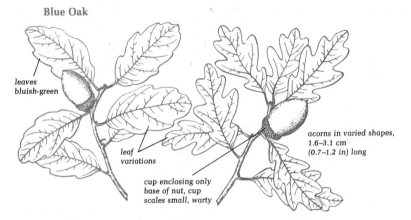

leaves
bluish-green

leaf
variations

cup enclosing only
base of nut, cup
scales small, warty

acorns in varied shapes,
1.6–3.1 cm
(0.7–1.2 in) long

Appearance: small to medium-size tree 7–20 m (23–66 ft) with a rounded crown; trunk stout, usually short and soon branching, to 1.2 m (3.9 ft) in diameter. **Bark:** 1.2–2.5 cm (0.5–1 in) thick, *light gray,* becoming *checkered,* the plates covered with thin scales. **Branches:** stout, short, usually spreading; branchlets stout, brittle, reddish-brown to dark gray and hairy when young and becoming light gray with age. **Winter buds:** 3–7 mm (0.1–0.3 in) long, broadest near the base and rounded at the tip, covered with overlapping, reddish scales. **Leaves:** alternate, *deciduous,* 3.8–10 cm (1.5–4 in) long, 1.9–5 cm (0.8–2 in) wide, uniformly wide to broadest above the middle, rounded to pointed at the tip, rounded to heart-shaped at the base, *entire to shallowly and ir-regularly lobed along the margin, as illustrated in the two branchlets shown,* thin and firm, *bluish-green* and smooth to finely hairy above, paler and finely hairy be-neath; the leafstalks stout, hairy, 0.6–1.2 cm (0.3–0.5 in) long. **Flowers:** male and fe-male flowers in separate catkins on the current year's growth; male flowers in hang-ing, hairy, yellowish-green catkins 2–4 mm (about 0.1–0.2 in) long; female flowers tiny, solitary or in few-flowered clusters at the base of the leaves of the current year's growth. **Fruits:** *acorns,* maturing in 1 season on current year's branchlets, solitary or paired, *usually broadest near the base and rounded at the tip 1.6–3.1 cm (0.7–1.2 in) long,* (but shapes are varied); *cup saucer-shaped,* enclosing *only the base of the acorn,* the *cup scales small, warty,* and finely hairy.

Mexican Blue Oak

Quercus oblongifolia Torr.

The Mexican blue oak is a small spreading tree native to the southwestern corner of New Mexico, extreme southern Arizona, and northern Mexico. This oak is a common tree of the open oak woodland along the Mexican border. It grows in the foothills, on

mountain slopes, and in canyons from 1,500–2,000 m (4,900–6,600 ft) elevation. It flowers in early spring, and the fruits mature later in the season. The acorns are eaten by deer, peccaries, squirrels, and other rodents.

This tree grows to 8 m (26 ft) with a spreading rounded crown and gray checkered bark. The characteristic *leaves are* deciduous, *small, 2.2–5 cm (1–2 in) long,* uniformly wide, *toothless along the margin, blue-green* and smooth. The *acorns* are broadest near the base to near the middle and usually have a rounded tip. They are 1.2–1.8 cm (0.5–0.7 in) long, light to dark brown, and *enclosed from a fourth to a third of their length by a cup.* The cup is shallowly bowl-shaped and covered on the outside by overlapping reddish scales.

Mexican Blue Oak

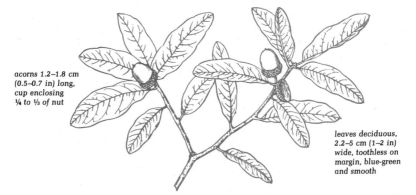

acorns 1.2–1.8 cm (0.5–0.7 in) long, cup enclosing ¼ to ⅓ of nut

leaves deciduous, 2.2–5 cm (1–2 in) wide, toothless on margin, blue-green and smooth

Havard Shin Oak

Quercus havardii Rydb.

Usually a low shrub, Havard shin oak is native to a limited area from the lower part of the Texas Panhandle to eastern New Mexico. It grows in well-drained, sandy soils and forms dense thickets. In poor, deep, sandy soils, it is a small shrub, but in soils with greater humus and moisture-holding capacity, it develops into a small tree. The acorns are eaten by deer, peccaries, quail, and prairie chickens.

Havard shin oak is usually a shrub less than 1 m (3.3 ft) in height and forms a broad round-topped shrub. The leaves are deciduous, 2–10 cm (0.8–4 in) long, 2.3–8 cm (0.9–3.2 in) wide, variable in shape, narrow, and often broadest near or above the middle, ***entire to lobed or coarsely toothed, leathery, bright shiny green*** and usually smooth above, duller and hairy beneath. The acorns mature in 1 season on the current year's branchlets and are usually 1- to 3-clustered on the branchlets. They are variable in shape and size but often broadest near the base, ***1.2–2.5 cm (0.5–1 in) long***, and dark brown at maturity. The ***deep, bowl-shaped cup encloses a third to two-thirds of the nut.*** The cup is covered with reddish-brown, hairy scales.

Havard Shin Oak

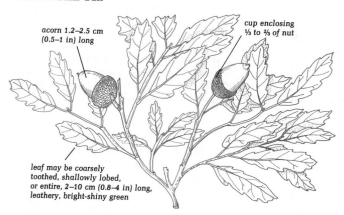

acorn 1.2–2.5 cm (0.5–1 in) long

cup enclosing ⅓ to ⅔ of nut

leaf may be coarsely toothed, shallowly lobed, or entire, 2–10 cm (0.8–4 in) long, leathery, bright-shiny green

Sandpaper Oak

Quercus pungens Liebm.

The sandpaper oak is a large shrub or occasionally a small tree to 8 m (26 ft) high. It is native to western Texas, New Mexico, Arizona, and adjacent northern Mexico. This tree grows on dry limestone hills and in canyons. It is similar to the Mohr oak, but the sandpaper oak is distinguished by its sharply toothed leaves with a rough leaf surface and by saucer-shaped acorn cups.

The Vasey oak (*Quercus pungens* variety *vaseyana*), a variety of the sandpaper oak, also grows on dry limestone hills of central and western Texas and adjacent Mexico. In many areas of its range, the Vasey oak forms dense thickets. It has a slightly larger acorn and fewer teeth along the margin of the leaves than the sandpaper oak.

The sandpaper oak and the Vasey variety are shrubs or small trees with hairy, gray to reddish-brown branchlets. The leaves are evergreen or may persist into late winter. They are broadest near or above the middle to uniformly wide, 1–5 cm (0.4–2 in) long, 1.2–2 cm (0.5–0.8 in) wide, pointed at the tip, and with coarse teeth along the margin.

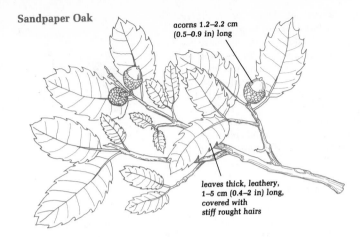

Sandpaper Oak

acorns 1.2–2.2 cm
(0.5–0.9 in) long

leaves thick, leathery,
1–5 cm (0.4–2 in) long,
covered with
stiff rought hairs

The leaves are **thick, leathery, and covered with stiff, rough hairs.** The **acorns** are **broadest near the base or the middle to almost cylinder-shaped, 1.2–2.2 cm (0.5–0.9 in) long,** and light brown. The cup of the acorn is shallowly to **deeply cup-shaped and encloses from one-fifth to one-third of the nut.**

Swamp White Oak   *Quercus bicolor* Willd.

The swamp white oak is a medium-size tree of north central and northeastern U.S. and extends slightly into Canada. This oak grows in lowlands, often at the edges of swamps, in low wet flats or bottomlands and meadows. It is tolerant of poorly drained sites and frequently is found in heavy, mucky soils. While it occasionally occurs in almost pure stands, this oak usually grows with sweetgum, sycamore, silver maple, basswood, willow, and white ash.

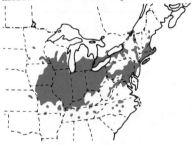

Swamp white oak is a rapid-growing tree that flowers in spring, and the acorns mature and are shed in September or October of the same year. The tree normally is 25 to 30 years old before it begins to flower. Swamp white oak is a moderately long to long-lived tree that may reach 300 to 350 years. As with other oaks, large crops of acorns are produced every 3 to 5 years. The sweet acorns are eaten by whitetail deer, mallards, wood ducks, wild turkeys, squirrels, woodpeckers, and smaller rodents.

The wood is light brown, hard, tough, strong, and close-grained. It is of some importance commercially and usually is cut and sold as white oak. The lumber is used in general construction, furniture, cabinets, veneers, and interior finishes. White oak wood was once widely used in making barrels, but the demand for barrels has dropped sharply since the 1950s.

Appearance: medium-size tree 20–35 m (65–115 ft), with an open, sometimes irregular, round-topped crown; trunk tall, straight, sometimes soon branching, to 1 m (3.3 ft) in diameter. **Bark:** moderately thick, 2.5–5 cm (1–2 in), gray-brown often reddish-tinged, with deep furrows separating the broad flat ridges; bark on upper branches scaly, peeling away. **Branches:** short, stout, the lower ones spreading or even droop-

Swamp White Oak

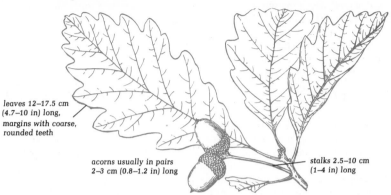

leaves 12–17.5 cm
(4.7–10 in) long,
margins with coarse,
rounded teeth

acorns usually in pairs
2–3 cm (0.8–1.2 in) long

stalks 2.5–10 cm
(1–4 in) long

ing; branchlets short, stout, hairy when young becoming smooth, orange-red turning reddish-brown with age. **Winter buds:** 2–4 mm (about 0.1–0.2 in) long, broadest at the base to almost globe-shaped, rounded at the tip, covered with overlapping, light chestnut-brown scales. **Leaves:** alternate, deciduous, *12–17.5 cm (4.7–10 in) long, 5–11 cm (2–4.4 in) wide, broadest above the middle, with many coarse, rounded teeth along the margin,* tapering to a wedge-shaped base, rounded at the tip, tough, dark green and shiny above, paler and often silvery-white beneath; the leafstalks stout, hairy when young, becoming smooth, 1.2–2.2 cm (0.5–0.9 in) long. **Flowers:** male and female flowers in separate catkins produced on the current year's branchlets; male flowers in slender, hanging, yellowish-green catkins 7.6–10 cm (3–4 in) long; female flowers tiny, usually 2 to 5 on a short stalk near the base of the leafstalks. **Fruits:** acorns maturing in 1 season, *solitary or more commonly in pairs on a long slender stalk, 2.5–10 cm (1–4 in) long, uniformly wide to slightly broadest near the base,* 2–3 cm (0.8–1.2 in) long, short-pointed at the tip, light brown; *cup deeply saucer-shaped, enclosing the lower fourth of the nut,* the cup scales overlapping, broadest near the base and tapering to a point, becoming thickened near the base of the cup, the upper ones sometimes forming a fringe around the rim. **Seeds:** sweet, edible.

Swamp Chestnut Oak   *Quercus michauxii* Nutt.

Swamp chestnut oak is native primarily to the southeastern U.S. where it is found on the Coastal Plain and the Piedmont. Its range extends up the Mississippi River Valley to Illinois and Ohio. It commonly grows in bottomlands, and along streams and borders of swamps and ponds. The large acorns are eaten by whitetail deer, turkey, black bear, squirrels, and chipmunks. The light brown wood is hard, strong, and durable and is often used in flooring and for veneer.

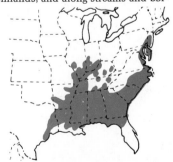

These oaks are medium-size to large trees, to 40 m (130 ft), with a trunk to 2 m (6.5 ft) in diameter, and a thick, scaly, light-gray bark. The leaves are deciduous, 10–22 cm (4–9 in) long, 7–12 cm (2.7–5 in) wide, broadest above the middle, short-pointed at the tip, tapering to rounded at the base, *with numerous shallow lobes or rounded teeth along the margin,* dark green, smooth above and softly hairy beneath, and with leafstalks 2–3 cm (1 in) long. The *acorns* mature in 1 season and are usually produced singly or in clusters of 2 or 3. They are broadest near the base and gradually taper to a rounded tip, *2.5–4 cm (1–1.6 in) long,* and enclosed for one-third to one-half their length by a cup. The cup is 3–3.5 cm (1.3 in) across, bowl-shaped, and *covered with hairy, free scales.*

Chestnut Oak

Quercus prinus L.
(synonym: Q. montana Willd.)

Chestnut oak is native to the eastern U.S. from southern Maine to Georgia and Alabama, excluding the southeastern Coastal Plain. It occurs on dry, sandy, or gravelly soils of wooded slopes but reaches its greatest size in rich, well-drained soils

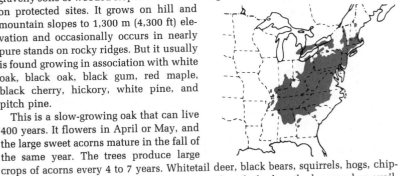

on protected sites. It grows on hill and mountain slopes to 1,300 m (4,300 ft) elevation and occasionally occurs in nearly pure stands on rocky ridges. But it usually is found growing in association with white oak, black oak, black gum, red maple, black cherry, hickory, white pine, and pitch pine.

This is a slow-growing oak that can live 400 years. It flowers in April or May, and the large sweet acorns mature in the fall of the same year. The trees produce large crops of acorns every 4 to 7 years. Whitetail deer, black bears, squirrels, hogs, chipmunks, turkeys, and grouse eat the acorns, and cattle feed on the leaves when available.

The light brown wood, which is heavy, strong, tough, close-grained, and durable, frequently is cut and sold as white oak.

Appearance: medium-size tree 15–30 m (49–100 ft) with a broad, usually open, irregular, rounded crown; trunk tall, straight, or soon branching and spreading if growing in an open area, 0.6–1.3 m (1.9–4.3 ft) in diameter, rarely larger. **Bark:** moderately

Chestnut Oak

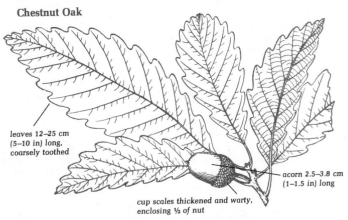

leaves 12–25 cm
(5–10 in) long,
coarsely toothed

acorn 2.5–3.8 cm
(1–1.5 in) long

cup scales thickened and warty,
enclosing ½ of nut

thick, 2–4 cm (0.8–1.6 in) dark brown to reddish-brown, thin and smooth on young branches but developing fissures and broad rounded ridges with age. **Branches:** stout, upright, the lower ones spreading; branchlets stout, reddish-brown, smooth. **Winter buds:** 4–6 mm (0.2 in) long, broadest near the base and tapering to a point, covered with overlapping, shiny, dark-brown scales. **Leaves:** alternate, deciduous, *12–25 cm (5–10 in) long, 3.6–7.5 cm (1.4–3 in) wide, broadest above the middle, coarsely and irregularly toothed along the margin,* gradually narrowing at the base, rounded to pointed at the tip, almost leathery, *yellow-green, shiny and smooth above, paler and finely hairy on the lower surface;* the leafstalks stout to slender, 0.6–1.4 cm (0.2–0.6 in) in length. **Flowers:** male and female flowers in separate catkins produced on the current year's branchlets; male flowers in hanging, hairy, yellowish, slender catkins 5–8 cm (2–3.2 in) long; female flowers tiny, usually 1 to 4 on short stalks at the base of the leaves. **Fruits:** acorns, maturing in 1 season, usually solitary or in pairs, *2.5–3.8 cm (1–1.5 in) long, broadest near the base to almost uniformly broad, rounded to pointed* at the tip, shiny dark brown at maturity; *cup deeply bowl-shaped to top-shaped, enclosing about half the length of the nut, the cup scales thickened and rough or warty, reddish-brown, hairy.* **Seeds:** sweet, edible.

Chinkapin Oak, Yellow Chestnut Oak

Quercus muehlenbergii Engelm.

The chinkapin oak is a medium-size tree of the midwestern and eastern U.S., excluding the Coastal Plain. This oak is not common anywhere in its natural range. It grows in well-drained soils on upland sites, on limestone outcrops and dry bluffs, and on slopes. It requires alkaline, or only slightly acidic, soils. When found, the chinkapin oak is usually growing in association with post oak, white oak, black oak, sugar maple, black walnut, black cherry, or tulip poplar.

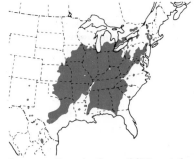

This tree's growth is rapid while the tree is young but slows with age. It flowers in May or June, and the sweet edible acorns mature and drop in September or October of the same year. As with other oaks, large acorn crops are produced every 3 or 4 years. Whitetail deer, raccoons, squirrels, turkeys, quail, and other wildlife eat the nuts.

The brown wood is heavy, strong, close-grained, and durable. Unfortunately, the chinkapin oak is not abundant enough anywhere in North America to be of much commercial importance. Because of its durability, it once was used widely for split-rail fences and railroad ties. It is an excellent fuel; the dense, heavy wood can generate many BTUs of heat per cord.

Appearance: medium-size to occasionally a tall tree, 20–30 m (65–100 ft), rarely taller, with a round-topped crown; trunk tall, straight, to 1.3 m (4.3 ft) in diameter; in fields trunk is soon branching and more spreading. **Bark:** *thin, 5–7 mm (0.2–0.3 in) thick, light gray, broken into thin, narrow scales, seldom with shallow furrows.* **Branches:** short, small, upright, with the lower ones spreading; branchlets slender, green turning yellow-brown to reddish-brown, hairy when young, becoming smooth with age. **Winter buds:** 4–6 mm (0.2 in) long, broadest near the base and tapering to a

Chinkapin Oak

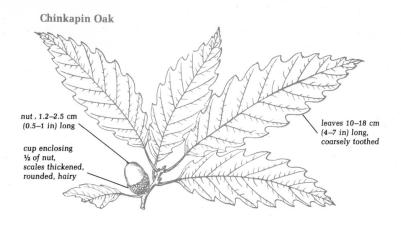

nut , 1.2–2.5 cm
(0.5–1 in) long

cup enclosing
½ of nut,
scales thickened,
rounded, hairy

leaves 10–18 cm
(4–7 in) long,
coarsely toothed

point, covered with overlapping chestnut-brown scales, smooth. **Leaves:** alternate, deciduous, *10–18 cm (4–7 in) long, 3–12.7 cm (1.2–5 in) wide,* narrow but broadest near the base to broadest above the middle, *with numerous coarse teeth along the margin,* tapering to a narrow base and pointed at the tip, tough, yellow-green and smooth on the upper surface, paler and finely hairy on the lower surface; the leaf-stalks slender, 1–3 cm (0.4–1.2 in) long. **Flowers:** male and female flowers in separate catkins produced on the current year's branchlets; male flowers in hairy, hanging, light yellow catkins 7.5–10 cm (3–4 in) long; female flowers tiny, 1 to 5 on a short stalk at the base of the leaves. **Fruits:** acorns, maturing in 1 season, solitary or usually in pairs, stalkless or on a short stalk, *1.2–2.5 cm (0.5–1 in) long, broadest near the base and tapering slightly to a rounded tip, light brown; cup bowl-shaped, enclosing about half of the nut, the cup scales thickened, rounded on the back, hairy, forming a tiny fringe on the margin of the cup.* **Seeds:** sweet, edible.

Dwarf Chinkapin Oak

Quercus prinoides Willd.

The dwarf chinkapin oak is a large shrub, or rarely a small tree, to 5 m (17 ft). It usually forms small thickets and is most frequently found on dry rocky slopes and barrens. This oak is native to a wide portion of the central and eastern U.S. It is similar in appearance to the chinkapin oak and chestnut oak. The shrubby appearance and the sharp teeth along the edge of the leaves are key distinguishing features.

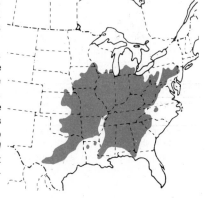

The tree trunks are usually covered with a scaly, light brown bark. The *leaves* are deciduous, narrow, and broadest above the middle and from *5–15 cm (2–6 in) long.* They are *yellowish-green* and have *coarse teeth along the margin.* The *fruit* matures in 1 season, is broadest near the base to uniformly wide, *1.5 to 2.5 cm (0.6–1 in) long,* light brown, and the seed is sweet and edible. Large crops of acorns are produced every year or every other year.

Dwarf Chinkapin

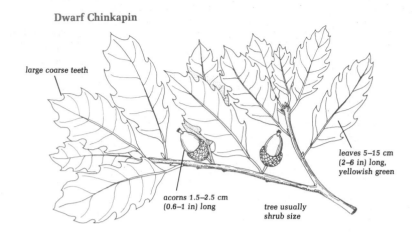

large coarse teeth

leaves 5–15 cm
(2–6 in) long,
yellowish green

acorns 1.5–2.5 cm
(0.6–1 in) long

tree usually
shrub size

Live Oak   *Quercus virginiana* Mill.

Live oak is a large spreading tree of the lower Coastal Plain from southeastern Virginia to southern Florida and to southern Texas. It normally grows in low sandy soils near the Coast but also occurs in moist rich woods and along stream banks. On the Gulf Coast, live oaks often support many types of epiphytic plants, including Spanish moss which hangs in weeping festoons, giving the trees a striking appearance. Live oak is found growing in association with several other hardwoods, including the water oak, laurel oak, sweetgum, southern magnolia, and American holly.

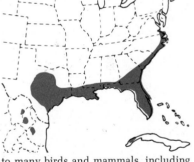

A fast-growing tree, the live oak flowers in early spring (usually in March or April), and the acorns mature by September or October. Sweet edible acorns are usually produced in great abundance and are of value to many birds and mammals, including wild turkeys, wood ducks, jays, quail, whitetail deer, raccoons, and squirrels.

The yellowish-brown wood is hard, heavy, tough, strong, and is used for structural beams, ship building, posts, and in places requiring strength and durability. The trees are planted occasionally in cities but should be restricted to large yards or parks where their spreading form can be accommodated. It ranks as the heaviest native hardwood, weighing 55 pounds per cubic foot when air dry. This weight (density of mass) makes live oak the premier fuel wood.

Appearance: medium-size tree to 20 m (66 ft) with a ***wide-spreading, rounded crown; trunk spreading and buttressed at the base,*** soon branching, 1–2 m (3.2–6.6 ft) in diameter, rarely larger. **Bark:** thick, 1.2–2.5 cm (0.5–1 in), dark brown to dark reddish-brown, shallowly furrowed and forming small, closely pressed scales. **Branches:** stout, spreading; branchlets slender, hairy when young, becoming smooth and gray to brown with age. **Winter buds:** 2–4 mm (about 0.1–0.2 in) long, globe-shaped to widest near the base, covered with overlapping light chestnut-brown scales. **Leaves:** alternate, ***evergreen, 5–12 cm (2–5 in) long, 1.2–6.3 cm (0.5–2.5 in) wide,***

Live Oak

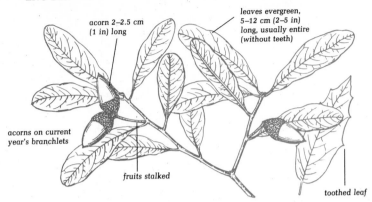

acorn 2–2.5 cm
(1 in) long

leaves evergreen,
5–12 cm (2–5 in)
long, usually entire
(without teeth)

acorns on current
year's branchlets

fruits stalked

toothed leaf

variable in shape, *widest near or above the middle to uniformly broad,* tapering to rounded at the base, rounded to short-pointed at the tip, *usually entire and slightly wavy along the margin,* occasionally with a few teeth, almost leathery, dark green and shiny above, pale and hairy beneath; the leafstalks stout, 5–8 mm (0.2–0.3 in) long. **Flowers:** male and female flowers in separate catkins, produced on branchlets of the current year; male flowers clustered on hanging, hairy catkins 5–7.5 cm (2–3 in) long. **Fruits:** acorns, *maturing in 1 season on current year's branchlets,* solitary to few-clustered, *stalked, 2–2.5 cm (0.8–1 in) long,* broadest at the base to almost uniformly wide, rounded to pointed at the tip, dark brown, shiny; cup enclosing one-fourth of the nut, 1.5–2 cm (0.6–0.8 in) across, the scales thin, broadest at the base and pointed at the tip, overlapping, covered with dense hairs. **Seeds:** sweet, edible.

Netleaf Oak

Quercus rugosa Née

(synonym: *Q. reticulata* H. & B.)

The netleaf oak is native to the wooded slopes and extends near the summits of mountain ranges in Trans-Pecos Texas, New Mexico, Arizona, and adjacent Mexico. In the U.S. this oak is usually a shrub, while in Mexico it is usually a tree. It usually occurs as scattered trees from 1,350–2,000 m (4,400–6,600 ft) elevation and is not abundant anywhere in its range. Cattle, deer, and larger birds eat the young leaves and acorns. *The prominent, coarse, net-like veins of the leathery leaves are a characteristic feature of this southwestern oak.*

The trunk of these small to medium-size trees and shrubs is covered with thin, light to dark brown bark. The **leaves often remain on branchlets into late winter,** broadest above to near the middle, 3.2–6.3 cm (1.3–2.5 in) long, 1.4–3.8 cm (0.6–1.5 in) wide, rounded to pointed at the tip, entire to occasionally toothed on the margin, *leathery,* shiny, and *dark green to grayish-green above,* duller and smooth to hairy on the lower surface. The *acorns* mature at the end of 1 growing season on the current year's branchlets and usually are produced

Netleaf Oak

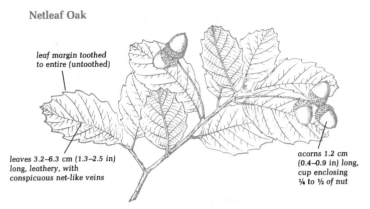

leaf margin toothed
to entire (untoothed)

leaves 3.2–6.3 cm (1.3–2.5 in)
long, leathery, with
conspicuous net-like veins

acorns 1.2 cm
(0.4–0.9 in) long,
cup enclosing
¼ to ½ of nut

singly or in 2s or 3s in long-stalked clusters. They are broadest near the base and the middle and are rounded to pointed at the tip, *1–2.2 cm (0.4–0.9 in) long,* and light brown. The *cup encloses half to one-fourth of the acorn.* The cup is deeply saucer-shaped to cup-shaped, covered with scales that are thickened near the base, dark brown, and usually hairy.

Arizona White Oak   *Quercus arizonica* Sarg.

This is the most abundant oak in southern New Mexico and Arizona and is Arizona's biggest oak. Arizona white oak also occurs in Trans-Pecos Texas and Mexico. It is found in canyons, on rocky outcrops, and mountain slopes from 1,500–3,350 m (4,900–11,000 ft) elevation. At the high elevations, this oak is usually reduced to a shrub. It occurs in the evergreen or oak woodland along with Emory oak, Mexican blue oak, and silverleaf oak. Other trees often found growing in association with this oak are the alligator juniper, chihuahua pine, and Apache pine.

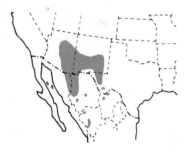

This is a slow-growing tree, which flowers in spring. The acorns mature from September to November of the same year. Acorns are produced in cycles, with large crops alternating with several years of light production. Since the acorns are bitter, wildlife pass them over if acorns of other oaks are available.

The dark brown to black wood is close-grained, very heavy, hard, and strong, but it is difficult to split. Although used for fuel, the trees are seldom large enough or have straight enough trunks to be of much commercial value.

Appearance: shrub to medium-size tree, 5–20 m (16–66 ft), with a spreading rounded crown; trunk often short, soon branching, to 1 m (3.3 ft) in diameter, seldom larger. **Bark:** thin, becoming 2.5 cm (1 in) thick on older trees, pale ashy-gray, scaly, but developing narrow furrows and wide ridges with age. **Branches:** thick, stout, often twisted, spreading; branchlets slender, pale gray to rust-colored and covered with dense hairs at first, becoming reddish-brown and smooth with age. **Winter buds:** 2–4 mm (0.1 in) long, almost globe-shaped, covered with loosely overlapping, hairy to smooth, dark brown scales. **Leaves:** alternate, may be *evergreen to nearly evergreen,*

Arizona White Oak

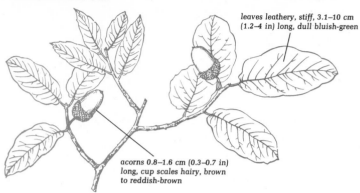

leaves leathery, stiff, 3.1–10 cm
(1.2–4 in) long, dull bluish-green

acorns 0.8–1.6 cm (0.3–0.7 in)
long, cup scales hairy, brown
to reddish-brown

leaves often remaining until late winter, 3.1–10 cm (1.2–4 in) long, 1–5 cm (0.4–2 in) wide, broadest near or above the middle, *entire or with small to large teeth along the margin,* especially near the tip, usually rounded at the base, pointed to rounded at the tip, *leathery and rigid, dull bluish-green and smooth above, duller and hairy on the lower surface;* the leafstalks stout, 2–10 mm (0.1–0.4 in) long, hairy. **Flowers:** male and female flowers in separate catkins on the current year's branchlets; male flowers in hanging, light yellow, densely flowered, hairy catkins 1.6–7.6 cm (0.6–3 in) long; female flowers tiny, in 2- to 6-flowered short stalks at the base of the leaves near the tip of the branchlets. **Fruits:** *acorns,* maturing in 1 season on current year's branchlets, solitary or paired, often on a short stalk, *0.8–1.6 cm (0.3–0.7 in) long, broadest near the base and rounded to pointed at the tip,* shiny brown; *cup deeply bowl-shaped to cup-shaped, enclosing about half of the nut,* the cup scales closely pressed, hairy, brown to reddish-brown, thickened and rounded at the base.

Cork Oak
Quercus suber L.

Like the English oak, the cork oak was introduced to North America in colonial times. These native Mediterranean trees have been planted from Maryland to California, especially in semi-dry conditions. They are of special interest because of their thick, soft bark, which is the source of cork. The cork is stripped every 10 to 20 years from the outer layer of bark along the lower portion of the trunk. The inner living bark is not harmed. One tree yielded over 450 kilos (about 1,000 pounds) of cork in a single crop. Aside from this important product, these trees make excellent ornamentals and grace several California college campuses.

Cork oaks are slow growing and extremely long-lived. Some trees in Europe are over 500 years of age. They may range from 18–30 m (59–100 ft) in height, with massive branches forming a round-topped crown. The *evergreen leaves* are 3.5–7.5 cm (1.4–3 in) long, approximately half as wide, *broadest below the middle, bright green and shiny above, with grayish, veined undersides,* slightly lobed, toothed or entire on the margins, and there are short leafstalks. The male and female flowers appear on the new growth, the male flowers in slender catkins and the females in small, short-stalked clusters. The rounded *acorns* are *2.5–3.5 cm (1–1.4 in) long,* green to brown, and *set deep into fringed cups that have heavy, slightly curled scales.*

Cork Oak

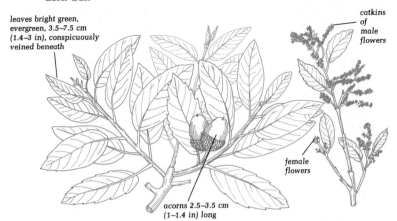

leaves bright green, evergreen, 3.5–7.5 cm (1.4–3 in), conspicuously veined beneath

catkins of male flowers

female flowers

acorns 2.5–3.5 cm (1–1.4 in) long

Toumey Oak

Quercus toumeyi Sarg.

Toumey oak is a poorly known shrub or small tree of southeastern Arizona, the southwestern corner of New Mexico, and northern Mexico. It is found in dry, well-drained soil from 1,150–2,000 m (3,700–6,600 ft) elevation. It flowers in early spring, and the acorns mature in June or July. Deer, rodents, and large birds eat the acorns.

This oak is usually a small shrub to 2 m (6.6 ft) but may become a tree with a broad irregular crown. The trunk soon branches and is covered with scaly brown bark. The leaves are **evergreen**, broadest near the middle to near the base, *1–3.7 cm (0.4–1.5 in) long, 0.7–2 cm (0.3–0.8 in) wide*, pointed at the tip, entire or with a few small teeth, *leathery, smooth, and bluish-green above*, paler and slightly hairy be-

Toumey Oak

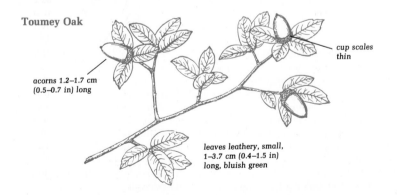

acorns 1.2–1.7 cm (0.5–0.7 in) long

cup scales thin

leaves leathery, small, 1–3.7 cm (0.4–1.5 in) long, bluish green

mm

cm 1 2 3 4 5 6 7 8 9 10 11

in 1 2 3 4

neath. The ***acorns*** are produced singly or in pairs and are broadest near the base, ***1.2–1.7 cm (0.5–0.7 in) long,*** shiny, light brown. The cup is covered with thin, reddish-brown, slightly hairy scales.

Ajo Oak   *Quercus ajoensis* Muller

This small oak from the desert mountains of Arizona and Mexico was recognized as a new species in the 1970s. It grows in canyons, especially on north faces, and in washes in dry rocky soils between 800 and 1,300 m (2,600 and 4,300 ft) elevation. It

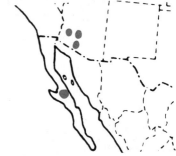

may be a shrub, often forming dense clumps, or a small tree to 10 m (33 ft) in height. It is related to the shrub live oak (*Q. turbinella*), which some botanists consider to be a variety of the Ajo oak. Some trees have intermediate characters, between the two species.

The shrubs or trees have thin, scaly, furrowed, light gray bark and spreading branches. ***Leaves*** are ***evergreen, 1.4–3.5 cm (0.6–1.4 in) long, 0.5–2 cm (0.2–0.8 in) wide,*** rarely longer and wider, broadest near the base, with ***5 or 6 pairs of long-pointed teeth along the margin,*** leathery, with 5 to 8 pairs of prominent veins, green and smooth above, paler and smooth to sparsely hairy below. The acorns mature in 1 growing season on branchlets of the current year, are 1.3–1.5 cm (0.5 in) long, broadest near the base to almost uniformly wide, pointed at the tip. The shallow cup encloses only the base of the nut.

Gray Oak   *Quercus grisea* Liebm.

Gray oak ranges from a shrub to a medium-size tree that may reach a height of 20 m (65 ft). It is native to southern Arizona, New Mexico, the Trans-Pecos region of Texas, and adjacent Mexico. It grows in dry, rocky or gravelly soils and occurs up to 2,600 m (8,530 ft) elevation. Gray oak reaches tree

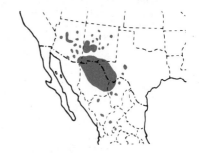

size in canyons with the most moisture and the better soils. Deer and livestock browse the leaves, while squirrels, rodents, and large birds eat the acorns. The wood is of little commercial value, serving primarily as fence posts and firewood. Gray oak is closely related to Mohr oak. But the leaves of the Gray oak are gray-green and hairy on both surfaces, while the leaves of Mohr oak are whitish or silvery and hairy on the lower surface.

This shrub, or tree, has a spreading rounded crown and dark gray, furrowed bark. The leaves are ***evergreen, 2–7.5 cm (0.8–3 in) long,*** 0.8–3.7 cm (0.3–1.5 in) wide, broadest at the base or near the middle, entire or occasionally with a few small teeth along the margin, thick and ***leathery, gray-green and finely hairy on both surfaces.*** The acorns appear on the current year's branchlets, and are usually produced singly or in pairs. They are broadest at the base to near the middle, 1.2–2 cm (0.5–0.8 in) long, and light brown. The bowl-shaped cup encloses a third to a half of the nut. The cup is covered with reddish-brown, hairy, flattened scales.

Gray Oak

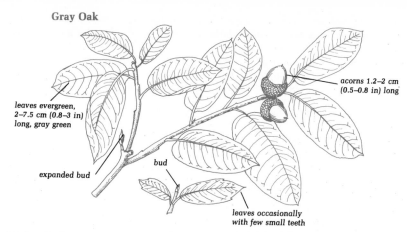

acorns 1.2–2 cm
(0.5–0.8 in) long

leaves evergreen,
2–7.5 cm (0.8–3 in)
long, gray green

expanded bud

bud

leaves occasionally
with few small teeth

Mohr Oak · *Quercus mohriana* Buckl. ex Rydb.

Mohr oak is a small tree and shrub of southwestern Oklahoma, eastern New Mexico, west central Texas, and adjacent Mexico. It grows in dry, well-drained soils on rolling hills, mesas, and canyons. This oak is restricted largely to limestone outcrops or limestone soils. It often forms dense thickets. Mohr oak is related closely to the Gray oak, which occurs primarily on soils or rocks of igneous origin. Deer, peccaries, squirrels, and larger game birds eat the acorns. The wood has no value other than as firewood.

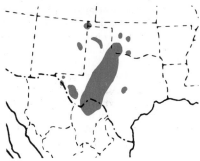

This shrub or tree may grow to 20 m (66 ft) with a rounded crown and furrowed, gray-brown bark. The *leaves* are *evergreen, 1.8–10 cm (0.7–4 in) long,* 1.2–3.8 cm (0.5–1.5 in) wide, narrow and uniformly wide to widest near the base or the middle, en-

Mohr Oak

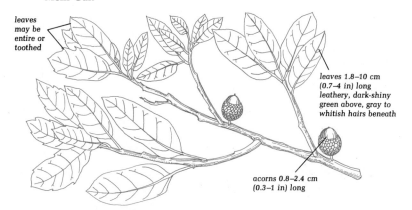

leaves
may be
entire or
toothed

leaves 1.8–10 cm
(0.7–4 in) long
leathery, dark-shiny
green above, gray to
whitish hairs beneath

acorns 0.8–2.4 cm
(0.3–1 in) long

tire or with a few coarse teeth along the upper half of the margin, **leathery, dark shiny green and sparingly hairy above, duller and with gray to whitish hairs on the lower surface.** The acorns mature in 1 season on the current year's branchlets and are produced singly and in clusters of 2 to 3. They are broadest near the base and the middle, 0.8–2.4 cm (0.3–1 in) long. The top- or bowl-shaped cup encloses one-half to two-thirds of the nut. The cup is covered with closely pressed, reddish-brown, hairy scales.

Emory Oak   *Quercus emoryi* Torr.

Emory oak is a common tree of Arizona, New Mexico, Trans-Pecos Texas, and northern Mexico. It occurs in canyons and on dry foothills and mountain slopes at 1,350–2,350 m (4,400–7,700 ft), rarely higher. This oak is found also in the desert

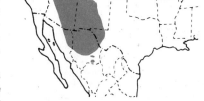

grasslands. Emory oak is often the most common oak in the Mexican oak-pine woodlands, where it occurs along with the silverleaf oak and Arizona oak. It grows in other evergreen woodlands along with the Mexican blue oak, alligator juniper, 1-seeded juniper, and Mexican pinyon pine. Emory oak may be found growing in dense, almost pure, stands.

This is a slow-growing tree that flowers in spring, and the acorns mature from June through September of the same year. The acorns are sweet and are readily consumed by mule deer, whitetail deer, turkeys, quail, squirrels, and chipmunks. Deer also browse the leaves.

The close-grained, dark-brown wood is heavy and strong but brittle on impact. Although of little value as a commercial timber source, it is an important source of firewood in the Southwest.

Appearance: shrub to medium-size tree to 20 m (66 ft) with a spreading rounded crown; trunk short, soon branching, to 1 m (3.3 ft) in diameter. **Bark:** moderately thick, 2.5–5 cm (1–2 in) on older trees, dark brown to black, with deep fissures sepa-

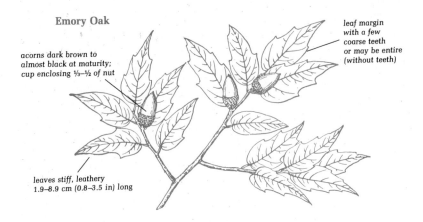

Emory Oak

acorns dark brown to almost black at maturity; cup enclosing ⅓–½ of nut

leaf margin with a few coarse teeth or may be entire (without teeth)

leaves stiff, leathery 1.9–8.9 cm (0.8–3.5 in) long

rating the broad thick plates. **Branches:** stout, spreading to sometimes hanging; branchlets slender, reddish-brown to gray, hairy when young, becoming smooth with age. **Winter buds:** 5–7 mm (0.2–0.3 in) long, broadest near the middle and pointed at the tip, with tightly overlapping reddish-brown scales that are hairy on the margin. **Leaves:** alternate, *nearly evergreen,* falling gradually in spring as new leaves are produced, 1.9–8.9 cm (0.8–3.5 in) long, 0.8–3.3 cm (0.3–1.3 in) wide, *narrow, uniformly wide to broadest near the base* and tapering to a pointed tip, *rounded to almost lobed at the base, entire or with a few coarse teeth along the margin, leathery and stiff, dark green, shiny, and smooth above,* paler and with scattered hairs on the lower surface; the leafstalks stout, 4–12 mm (about 0.2–0.5 in) long, hairy on younger leaves, becoming smooth. **Flowers:** male and female flowers in separate catkins on the current year's branchlets; male flowers in hanging yellow, hairy catkins 2.5–5 cm (1–2 in) long; female flowers tiny, hairy, produced singly or in pairs, at the bases of the leaves near the tips of the branchlets. **Fruits:** *acorns, maturing in 1 season on current year's branchlets,* solitary or paired, sometimes with a short stalk, *cone-shaped,* 1.5–2 cm (0.6–0.8 in) long, rounded to pointed at the tip, *dark brown to almost black; cup deeply bowl-shaped, enclosing one-third to one-half of nut,* the cup scales thin, closely pressed, brown, hairy or with hairs only along the margin of the scales.

California Scrub Oak

Quercus dumosa Nutt.

This shrub or small tree with highly variable leaves and acorns is native to California and Baja California in Mexico. It grows in canyons, on low mountains, and on the slopes of foothills from 350–1,650 m (1,100–5,400 ft) elevation. This oak is a common shrub in the chaparral forest of southern California where it grows in association with Christmas berry, mountain mahogany, manzanita, and ceonothus. It occurs as scattered clumps or forms large low thickets. Owing to considerable variation in size and shape of the leaves and acorns, several varieties of this oak have been named. One of them, MacDonald's California shrub oak (variety *macdonaldii*) is a small tree found only on Santa Cruz, Santa Rosa, and Santa Catalina islands. This variety is considered a distinct species by some authorities.

The California scrub oak is a slow-growing tree that flowers in spring, and the acorns mature later the same year. This tree usually produces acorns abundantly, but individual trees or bushes have intervening years of light production. Deer, jays, and rodents eat the acorns. This oak is one of the most important forage plants for the blacktail deer of the chaparral. It supplies about one-sixth of the deer's annual diet and is especially important to deer during late summer and fall. The light brown wood is hard and brittle and of no value as lumber.

Appearance: shrub or small tree, usually 1–3 m, occasionally to 15 (3–10 ft, occasionally to 50), with a spreading rounded crown; trunk short, stout, soon branching, to 45 cm (17 in) in diameter. **Bark:** thin, brown to light-ash-gray, scaly. **Branches:** stout, stiff, widespreading; *branchlets stiff, often at right angles to the branches,* hairy when young, becoming smooth with age. **Winter buds:** 1.5–4 mm (about 0.1 in) long,

California Scrub Oak

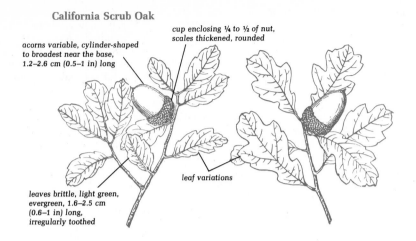

cup enclosing ¼ to ½ of nut,
scales thickened, rounded

acorns variable, cylinder-shaped
to broadest near the base,
1.2–2.6 cm (0.5–1 in) long

leaf variations

leaves brittle, light green,
evergreen, 1.6–2.5 cm
(0.6–1 in) long,
irregularly toothed

broadest near the middle and pointed at the tip, covered with overlapping, thin, reddish-brown, hairy scales. **Leaves:** alternate, *evergreen, 1.6–2.5 cm (0.6–1 in) long, 0.7–1.4 cm (0.3–0.6 in) wide, usually broadest near the middle to uniformly wide or almost rounded, entire or usually irregular spine-like teeth along the margin,* rounded to pointed at the tip, sharply tapering to rounded at the base, brittle, light green and smooth on the upper surface, paler and occasionally hairy beneath; the leafstalks stout, variable, 0.4–2 cm (0.2–0.8 in) long. **Flowers:** male and female flowers in separate catkins on the current year's growth; male flowers in hanging, hairy, yellowish catkins 2–5 cm (0.8–2 in) long; female flowers tiny, in few-flowered, short spikes in the junction of the leafstalks near the tip of the branchlets. **Fruits:** *acorns,* maturing in 1 season, solitary or occasionally paired, the shape variable, *1.2–2.6 cm (0.5–1 in) long, broadest near the base to cylinder-shaped,* rounded to pointed at the tip; *cup saucer-shaped to bowl-shaped, enclosing from one-fourth to one-half of the nut,* the cup scales thickened and rounded on their backs, light rust-colored, forming a fringe of hairs on the margin of the cup.

Engelmann Oak, Mesa Oak   *Quercus engelmannii* Greene

Engelmann oak is a small to medium-size tree of southwestern California. It occurs on low hills and dry rolling mesas in well-drained soils, usually below 1,350 m (4,430 ft) elevation but does not grow along the Coast. Flowering is in April or May, and the acorns mature in 1 season. The dark brown wood is very heavy and dense but is brittle and so is of no commercial value other than as firewood.

This is a tree from 5–18 m (16–60 ft) high with a spreading rounded crown and a grayish-brown bark that has deep fissures separating the broad ridges. The leaves are *evergreen, 2.5–7.5 cm (1–3 in) long* and *1.2–2.5 cm (0.5–1 in) wide,* uniformly wide to broadest above the middle, entire or with a few small teeth, bluish-green to

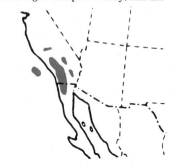

Engelmann Oak

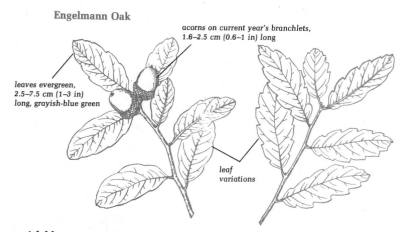

acorns on current year's branchlets,
1.6–2.5 cm (0.6–1 in) long

leaves evergreen,
2.5–7.5 cm (1–3 in)
long, grayish-blue green

leaf
variations

grayish blue-green and smooth above, lighter and usually hairy beneath. The **acorns** mature in 1 season on the current year's branchlets and are usually produced singly or in pairs. They are almost **cylinder-shaped to widest above the middle, 1.6–2.5 cm (0.6–1 in) long,** blunt at the tip. The shallow to deeply bowl-shaped cup encloses half to one-third of the nut and is covered with light brown, thickened scales.

Key to Species in Red and Black Oak Group

California Black Oak

Northern Red Oak

A. Leaves deciduous, falling away in autumn or turning brown and gradually falling during winter.

1. Leaves distinctly lobed.

a. Trees of western U.S., California, and Oregon **California black oak, p. 356**
b. Trees of midwestern and eastern North America and southeastern U.S.

(1) Acorn cups shallowly saucer-shaped, enclosing only the lower fourth or less of the acorn.

(a) Leaves dull green above, 7–9 lobed; acorns 1.2–2.5 cm (0.5–1 in) long; trees of eastern North America
Northern red oak, p. 357
(b) Leaves bright or dark green and shiny above, 3–7 lobed; acorns 1–1.4 cm (0.4–0.6 in) long.

(b1) Leaves dark green, 5–7 lobed;
(Continued)

leafstalks usually 2–5 cm (0.8–2 in) long; acorns without stalks; lowland tree of Middle Atlantic and Central U.S. **Pin oak, p. 358**

(b2) Leaves bright green, 3–5 lobed (rarely 7); leafstalks usually less than 2 cm (0.8 in) long; acorns on short stalks; rare tree of northern Georgia **Georgia oak, p. 360**

Pin Oak

(2) Acorn cups bowl-shaped, often deeply so, enclosing from half to one-third of the acorn.

(a) Leaves with whitish to gray hairs on the lower surface.

Georgia Oak

(a1) Leaves usually 5 lobed, 5–12 cm (2–4.8 in) long; small trees of dry barrens or rocky hillsides of northeastern U.S. **Bear oak, p. 360**

(a2) Leaves with 2 shapes, either 3 lobed near the tip or with 5–11 deep lobes; 12–23 cm (4.7–9.1 in) long; medium-size trees of southern U.S. **Southern red oak, cherrybark oak, p. 362, 363**

Bear Oak

(b) Leaves green below, occasionally with some hairs on veins or with small tufts of hairs in the junctions of the larger veins.

(b1) Leaves tapering to a narrow base.

(b1a) Leaves yellowish-green above; leafstalks 0.6–2 cm (0.2–0.8 in) long; acorns 2.2–2.7 cm (0.9–1.1 in) long; trees of southeastern Coastal Plain. **Turkey oak, p. 364**

Southern Red Oak

Cherrybark Oak

(b1b) Leaves bright green above; leafstalks 3.5–5 cm (1.4–2 in) long; acorns 1.2–2 cm (0.5–0.8 in) long; trees of northern midwest and southern Manitoba

Northern pine oak, p. 365

(b2) Leaves rounded, often broadly so, at the base.

(b2a) Leafstalks 7.5–15 cm (3–6 in) long; leaves yellowish-brown on the lower surface; acorn cup enclosing about half of the acorn; common tree of eastern and midwestern U.S.

Black oak, p. 366

(b2b) Leafstalks to 6.5 cm (2.6 in) long; leaves pale green on the lower surface; acorn cup enclosing from half to one-third of the acorn.

Leaves with 3–7 variable lobes along the margin, 5–10 cm (2–4 in) long; high mountain ranges, Texas

Graves oak, p. 368

**Leaves with 7–11 lobes along the margin, 7.5–20 cm (3–8 in) long; eastern U.S.*

• Leaves dark green above, 12–20 cm (4.7–8 in) long, with 7, 9, or 11 lobes; leafstalks 5–6.5 cm (2–2.5 in) long; large trees of southeastern Atlantic coastal plain **Shumard oak, p. 368**

•• Leaves bright green above, 7.5–15 cm (3–6 in) long, with 7–9 lobes; leafstalks 3.7–6.2 cm (1.5–2.5 in) long; upland trees of eastern U.S. **Scarlet oak, p. 369**
(Continued)

Turkey Oak

Northern Pin Oak

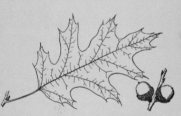

Black Oak

Shumard Oak

Scarlet Oak

2. Leaves entire, not distinctly lobed or somewhat 3–5 lobed near the tip.

   a. Leaves much broader near the tip, occasionally slightly or shallowly 3–5 lobed near the tip.

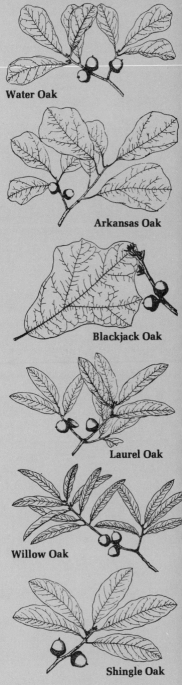

Water Oak

     (1) Mature leaves twice as long as wide; lowland trees of southeastern U.S.
       Water oak, p. 371

     (2) Mature leaves as broad or almost as broad as long.

       (a) Leaves 5–7.5 cm (2–3 in) long; acorns short-stalked, 6–10 mm (0.2–0.4 in) long; acorn cup shallowly saucer-shaped, enclosing only the base of the acorn; woodland tree of southeastern U.S.
        Arkansas oak, p. 372

Arkansas Oak

       (b) Leaves 10–25 cm (4–10 in) long; acorns 1.8–2.4 cm (0.7–1 in) long; acorn cup bowl-shaped, enclosing one-third to one-half of acorn; trees of eastern U.S.
        Blackjack oak, p. 372

Blackjack Oak

   b. Leaves uniformly wide to slightly broader near or below the middle, roughly resembling a willow leaf.

     (1) Leaves smooth on the lower surface, shiny to light green above.

       (a) Leaves thick, leathery, nearly evergreen; often remaining into late winter; acorns 2–2.6 cm (0.8–1 in) long; lowland tree of Coastal Plain
        Laurel oak, p. 374

Laurel Oak

       (b) Leaves thin, papery, deciduous; acorns to 1.2 cm (0.5 in) long; eastern coastal states and southeastern U.S.   **Willow oak, p. 375**

Willow Oak

     (2) Leaves hairy on the lower surface, dark green to bluish-green above.

       (a) Leaves 10–15 cm (4–6 in) long, dark green, finely hairy beneath; acorn cup deeply bowl-shaped, enclosing about one-third of nut; central and eastern U.S.   **Shingle oak, p. 376**

       (b) Leaves 5–12 cm (2–4.8 in) long, bluish-green; distinctly hairy be-

Shingle Oak

neath; acorn cup shallowly saucer-shaped, enclosing only the base of the nut; southcentral and southeastern U.S.   **Bluejack oak, p. 378**

Bluejack Oak

B. Leaves evergreen or nearly so, with the green leaves persisting until the following spring when the new leaves appear.

1. Trees of the Coastal Plain of the southeastern U.S.   **Myrtle oak, p. 379**

2. Trees of western or southwestern U.S.

    a. Leaves smooth to densely hairy, green to yellowish, never white or silvery.

Myrtle Oak

        (1) Leaves small to 3.5 cm (1.4 in) long; acorns 1.8–3.5 cm (0.7–1.4 in) long, almost completely enclosed by the cup; trees of inland California
            Interior live oak, p. 380

        (2) Leaves medium size, 2.5–10 cm (1–4 in) long; acorns 1.2–4 cm (0.5–1.6 in) long, the cup enclosing from one-fourth to one-third of the acorn.

Interior Live Oak

           (a) Acorns narrowly cone-shaped, tapering to a pointed tip.

                (a1) Acorns 2–4 cm (0.8–1.6 in) long, maturing in 1 season on current year's branchlets; California and Mexico
                      Coast live oak, p. 380

                (a2) Acorns 1.5–2 cm (0.5–1 in) long, maturing in 2 seasons on branchlets of previous year; Texas
                      Chisos oak, p. 382

Coast Live Oak

           (b) Acorns egg-shaped, rounded at tip.

                (b1) Leaves without prominent or parallel lateral veins; acorns 1.2–2.5 cm (0.5–1.6 in) long.

                    (b1a) Twigs flexible; leaves wavy-margined or with 1 or 2 spine-like teeth, twice as long as wide; Oregon, California, Arizona and Baja California
                  Canyon live oak, p. 382

Canyon Live Oak

(Continued)

Island Live Oak

Silverleaf Oak

(b1b) Twigs stiff, wide spreading; leaves with several coarse spine-tipped teeth, almost as wide as long; California and Arizona
Dunn oak, p. 383

(b2) Leaves with prominent and parallel lateral veins; acorns 2–3 cm (0.8–1.2 in) long; canyons of some coastal islands of southern California
Island live oak, p. 384

b. Leaves with dense white hairs on the lower surface, giving a silvery appearance to the leaves; southwestern U.S. and Mexico
Silverleaf oak, p. 384

California Black Oak *Quercus kelloggii* Newb.

This western oak is native to western Oregon and California, in both the coastal ranges and the Sierra Nevada. It is usually found on the lower and middle mountain slopes from 350–2,700 m (1,100–8,900 ft) elevation; the higher altitudes are reached in the southern part of the range. California black oak grows in clay or gravelly soils and frequently is found growing in association with yellow or ponderosa pine, Oregon oak, tanoak, and madrone.

This attractive and sometimes graceful oak flowers in April or May, and the acorns mature at the end of the second growing season. The meat of the acorn is bitter, but deer, squirrels, and California woodpeckers eat it. The California woodpecker drills numerous holes in the trunk and then drives acorns into them. These stored acorns are safe from squirrels and serve the woodpeckers as a food reserve. Because the bark is thick the drilling does not damage the tree.

The light reddish-brown wood is coarse-grained, hard, heavy, brittle, not very durable, and of little economic importance. It is used locally for fence posts and for firewood.

Appearance: small to medium-size tree 10–28 m (32–92 ft) with a broad rounded crown; trunk straight, sometimes branching close to the ground, to 1.3 m (4.3 ft) in diameter. **Bark:** smooth when young, becoming 2.5–4 cm (1–1.6 in) thick, developing thick irregular plates, dark reddish-brown to nearly black. **Branches:** stout, spreading; branchlets slender, red or reddish-brown and hairy when young, dark reddish-brown and smooth with age. **Winter buds:** 6–8 mm (0.2–0.3 in) long, broadest near the base and tapering to a pointed tip, covered with closely overlapping, light-chestnut brown scales. **Leaves:** alternate, deciduous, *10–18 cm (4–7 in) long, 5–10 cm (2–4 in) wide, widest above the middle to uniformly wide, usually 7 lobed, rarely 5 lobed,* the lobes shallow to deep, gradually tapering to a broad base and pointed at the tip, thick and firm at maturity, *dark green and smooth above,* paler and hairy to hairy only in

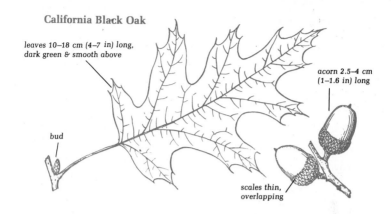

California Black Oak

leaves 10–18 cm (4–7 in) long, dark green & smooth above

acorn 2.5–4 cm (1–1.6 in) long

bud

scales thin, overlapping

the junctions of the veins; the leafstalks slender, 2.5–5 cm (1–2 in) long. **Flowers:** male and female flowers in separate catkins; male flowers in slender, hanging, hairy catkins 10–12 cm (4–4.8 in) long, produced near the tip of the previous year's branchlets; female flowers tiny, inconspicuous, usually in 1- to 3-flowered clusters in the junction of the leaves of the current year's branchlets. **Fruits:** acorns, maturing in 2 seasons, solitary or 2 to 3 per cluster, short stalked, *2.5–4 cm (1–1.6 in) long, cylinder-shaped and tapering to a rounded tip; cup bowl-shaped, enclosing about one-fourth to one-third of the nut* the cup scales thin, overlapping, and light chestnut brown.

Northern Red Oak

Quercus rubra L.
(synonym: *Q. borealis* Michx. f.)

The northern red oak is an attractive tree of the eastern U.S. and extreme southeastern Canada. It is commonly found growing on northern and eastern slopes from the valley floors to the lower and mid slopes of hills and mountains. The largest trees usually occur in protected ravines or on sheltered slopes. This oak can grow in a variety of soils but does best in deep, fine-textured soils. Sometimes it is the most abundant tree species in a particular area, but it often grows in association with many others, such as white pine, white oak, white ash, sweetgum, yellow poplar, mockernut hickory, and basswood. It hybridizes with black oak, willow oak, shingle oak, and bear oak.

This oak is a moderate to fast-growing tree that flowers in early spring as the new leaves begin to unfold. The trees normally require 20 to 25 years to reach flowering age and then may take another 20 years to begin producing abundant acorn crops. Good acorn crops are produced every 2 to 5 years. Animals and insects eat or destroy most of the acorns produced. Whitetail deer, black bears, raccoons, squirrels, turkeys, bluejays, and small rodents eat the fruits. The deer also eat the buds and young twigs during the winter after the acorns are exhausted.

The light reddish-brown wood is hard, strong, coarse-grained, and important as a

Northern Red Oak

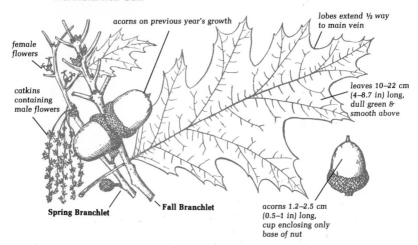

acorns on previous year's growth

lobes extend ½ way
to main vein

female
flowers

catkins
containing
male flowers

leaves 10–22 cm
(4–8.7 in) long,
dull green &
smooth above

Spring Branchlet

Fall Branchlet

acorns 1.2–2.5 cm
(0.5–1 in) long,
cup enclosing only
base of nut

lumber source. It is not as resistant to decay as is the wood of the white oak, but it is used widely for flooring, furniture, veneer, and interior finishing. Because of its ornamental value, this oak has been widely planted in Europe.

Appearance: medium-size tree 18–25 m (59–82 ft) with a narrow to widespreading, often open and irregular rounded crown; trunk tall or short, straight if field grown, to 1.5 m (4.9 ft) in diameter. **Bark:** smooth and slate gray to grayish-brown on young trees, becoming 2.5–4 cm (1–1.6 in) thick on older trees, dark brown to almost black, and developing shallow vertical furrows, low rounded ridges that become checkered with age. **Branches:** stout, few, the lower ones spreading; branchlets stout to slender, covered with fine hairs when young, becoming smooth and reddish-brown. **Winter buds:** 6–8 mm (0.2–0.3 in) long, broadest near the base and narrowing to a pointed tip, covered with thin, overlapping, shiny, smooth, reddish-brown scales. **Leaves:** alternate, deciduous, *10–22 cm (4–8.7 in) long, 6–12 cm (2.4–4.8 in) wide,* often widest above the middle, *usually with 7 to 9 lobes, the lobes extending half way to the main vein, rounded at the bases and tapering toward the tip of the leaf,* tapering at the base and pointed at the tip, with a firm but papery texture, *dull green and smooth above,* paler beneath and smooth except for an occasional tuft of hairs in the junctions of the principal veins; the leafstalks stout, 2.5–5 cm (1–2 in) long. **Flowers:** male and female flowers in separate catkins; male flowers in slender, hanging, hairy catkins 10–13 cm (4–5.2 in) long, produced near the tip of the previous year's branchlets; female flowers tiny, inconspicuous, produced singly or in clusters in the junctions of the leafstalks on the current year's growth. **Fruits:** *maturing in 2 seasons, solitary or in pairs on the previous year's branchlets, 1.2–2.5 cm (0.5–1 in) long,* broadest near the base and gradually tapering to either a rounded to somewhat pointed tip; *cup saucer-shaped, enclosing only the base to the lower fourth of the nut,* the cup scales overlapping, thin, finely hairy, and reddish-brown.

Pin Oak   *Quercus palustris* Muenchh.

Pin oak is a medium-size tree of the middle Atlantic and central states. It is primarily a lowland tree, thriving in wet, poorly drained, claypan soils typical of floodplains and flatlands, where it tolerates short periods of spring flooding. Pin oak occurs also in upland flats and will grow well in deep, well-drained soils. Pin oaks sometimes occur in nearly pure stand᠆ in low flatlands but often grow with bur oak, overcup oak, sweetgum, red maple, green ash, hackberry, and honey locust.

This fast-growing tree, which flowers in the spring as the leaves are beginning to develop, needs 15 to 25 years to reach flowering age. Pin oak is not a long-lived tree and seldom exceeds 150 to 200 years. The acorns do not mature until the end of the second growing season, and large acorn crops alternate with 2 or 3 years of limited production. These crops are of considerable value to wildlife, especially ducks. Whitetail deer, turkeys, squirrels, and small rodents also eat the acorns.

The light brown wood is coarse-grained, hard, and heavy—but not as strong as wood of the red oak. The wood is used occasionally in general construction, as posts, and for firewood.

Pin Oak

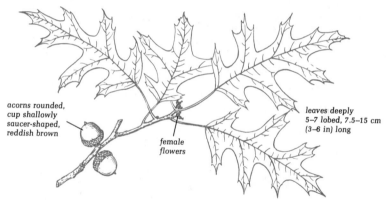

acorns rounded, cup shallowly saucer-shaped, reddish brown

female flowers

leaves deeply 5–7 lobed, 7.5–15 cm (3–6 in) long

Appearance: medium-size tree 15–25 m (49–82 ft), occasionally taller, with a broad, pyramid-shaped crown; trunk tall, straight, usually to 1 m (3.3 ft) in diameter, rarely larger. **Bark:** thin and smooth on young trees, becoming 2–3 cm (0.8–1.2 in) thick on older trees, grayish-brown, smooth or covered with small, closely pressed scales. **Branches:** *slender, spreading, lower ones often drooping;* branchlets slender, short, finely hairy and reddish-brown when young, becoming smooth and grayish with age. **Winter buds:** 2–4 mm (about 0.1–0.2 in) long, broadest near the base and tapering to a pointed tip, covered with overlapping, light reddish-brown scales. **Leaves:** alternate, deciduous, *7.5–15 cm (3–6 in) long, 4–10 cm (1.6–4 in) wide, usually broadest above the middle, with 5 to 7 deep lobes, the lobes rounded at their bases,* tapering, rounded or almost squared at the base, pointed at the tip, with a papery texture, dark green, smooth and shiny above, paler beneath with tufts of hairs in the junctions of the principal veins; the leafstalks slender, 2–5 cm (0.8–2 in) long. **Flowers:** male and female flowers in separate catkins produced on the current year's branchlets; male flowers in hanging, hairy catkins 5–7.5 cm (2–3 in) long; female flowers tiny, occurring singly or in clusters of 2 to 4 on a short stalk, inconspicuous. **Fruits:** *maturing in 2 seasons,* solitary or 2 to 3 clustered *on the previous year's branchlets,* 1–1.4 cm (0.4–0.6 in) long, *almost rounded and short-beaked at the tip;* cup shallowly saucer-shaped, enclosing only the base of the nut, the cup scales overlapping, broadest at the base and tapering to a point, reddish-brown.

Georgia Oak   *Quercus georgiana* M.A. Curtis

Georgia oak is a shrub or small tree found only in a few localities in northern Georgia, one site being the famous Stone Mountain east of Atlanta. It occurs on granite uplifts and is similar to the turkey oak, another southern oak, but may be distinguished from

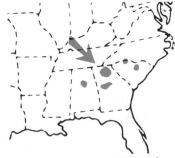

it by its smaller leaves and smaller acorns. This oak is of no commercial value, and its rarity renders it an unimportant food source for wildlife.

Georgia oak is a bushy shrub or tree to 8 m (26 ft) high with a spreading rounded crown and thin, but rough, light-brown bark. The leaves are deciduous, *7–10 cm (2.8–4 in) long and 4–7 cm (1.6–2.8 in) wide,* broadest near or above the middle and *3 to 5, rarely 7 lobed, bright green, shiny,* and smooth. The *acorns* mature in 2 seasons on the previous year's branchlets and are *stalked, 1–1.4 cm (0.5 in) long,* broadest near the base to almost globe shaped. The shallow saucer-shaped cup encloses about one-fourth of the nut.

Georgia Oak

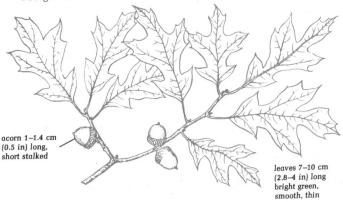

acorn 1–1.4 cm
(0.5 in) long,
short stalked

leaves 7–10 cm
(2.8–4 in) long
bright green,
smooth, thin

Bear Oak   *Quercus ilicifolia* Wangenh.

This small oak occurs in the northeastern U.S., principally in dry sandy barrens and on rocky hillsides. It grows in poor, nutrient-deficient soils and occasionally forms pure, or nearly pure, stands. Dense thickets of bear oak can be encountered, and these are often difficult to penetrate on foot. Bear oak also is found growing in association with black, scarlet, and chinkapin oaks; white, pitch, and shortleaf pines; black locust, sassafras, and red maple.

It flowers in April or May as the leaves are developing, and the fruits mature by the end of the second growing season. The shrubs or small trees often produce large crops of acorns more regularly than do the larger oaks. The dense thickets of bear oak provide cover for wildlife, and the acorns serve as food for whitetail deer, raccoons, turkeys, squirrels, and other rodents. The wood is hard and heavy, but the trees are too small to be of any commercial importance.

Appearance: *shrub or small tree to 8 m (26 ft)*, with an irregular, often open, rounded crown; trunk short, soon branching, 8–15 cm (3.2–5.9 in) in diameter. **Bark:** thin, smooth, developing small scales, dark reddish-brown to dark brown. **Branches:** slender, spreading; branchlets slender, dark green and hairy when young, turning gray then brownish-black and smooth with age. **Winter buds:** 2–4 mm (about 0.1–0.2 in) long, broadest near the base and tapering to a rounded tip, covered with thin, overlapping, dark-brown scales. **Leaves:** alternate, deciduous, *5–12 cm (2–4.8 in) long, 4–7.5*

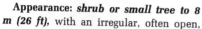

Bear Oak

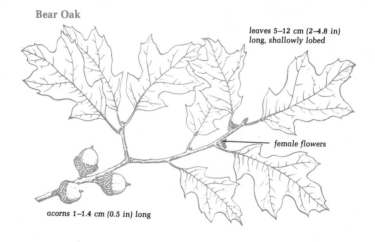

leaves 5–12 cm (2–4.8 in)
long, shallowly lobed

female flowers

acorns 1–1.4 cm (0.5 in) long

cm (1.6–3 in) wide, widest above the middle, ***with 3, 5, or 7 shallow lobes,*** gradually or quickly tapering at the base and pointed and toothed at the tip, firm and almost leathery at maturity, ***dark green and smooth above, paler and covered with fine hairs beneath;*** the leafstalks slender, 2.5–4 cm (1–1.6 in) long. **Flowers:** male and female flowers in separate catkins; male flowers in slender, hanging, hairy catkins 8–12 cm (3.2–4.8 in) long, produced near the tips of the previous year's branchlets; female flowers tiny, inconspicuous, usually in few-flowered clusters in the junctions of the stalks of the current year's leaves. **Fruits: *acorns,*** maturing in 2 seasons, often clustered on the previous year's branchlets, *1–1.4 cm (0.5 in) long and broad, broadest near the base and tapering to a rounded to pointed tip; cup bowl-shaped, enclosing about half to one-third of the nut,* the cup scales thin, overlapping and reddish-brown.

Southern Red Oak   *Quercus falcata* Michx. variety *falcata*

Southern red oak has been divided into two varieties that have enough differences between them to warrant separate discussions. The two are the southern red oak and the cherrybark oak (see Cherrybark Oak next). The typical southern red oak, also

known as Spanish oak, is a medium-large and graceful tree that occurs from Long Island, N.Y., to northern Florida and westward to eastern Texas. It is one of the most commonly encountered upland southern oaks, as well as a familiar sight in many southern towns. Characteristically, southern red oak grows on dry, sandy, or clay upland soils to 600 m (2,000 ft) in elevation and is widely found on a variety of loams. It often occurs on dry ridgetops and on south or westward facing hilltops. Occasionally it will be found in moister, fertile bottomlands, where it achieves its greatest size. This tree is a major component of two forest types. *Virginia pine–southern red oak*, and *shortleaf pine–oak*; it also occurs in a number of other *mixed pine–hardwood* forests. Its associates include several other oak species, hickory, and sweetgum. As well, shortleaf pine in the Piedmont region and loblolly pine in the Coastal Plains region are common companions of southern red oak.

Southern red oaks are moderately fast-growing and live a fairly long life of 100 to 150 years. Seed production begins when the tree is about 25 years old, though the best seed crops are produced between the ages of 50 and 75 years. Flowering begins in April, and goes through May in most of the range. As with other red oaks, the acorns ripen in the fall of the second season after flowering in September and October. Many animals depend on these acorns as a food source; on the other hand, oak trees need the animals to disseminate their seeds. For example, the hoarding of acorns by squirrels protects the nuts from adverse climatic conditions until spring when forgotten nuts germinate. Other wildlife using this oak include deer, turkey, quail, and numerous songbirds.

The wood of southern red oak is light red, coarse-grained, hard and strong, but it cracks badly when left in the sun and rots in contact with soil. It is therefore not prime

Southern Red Oak

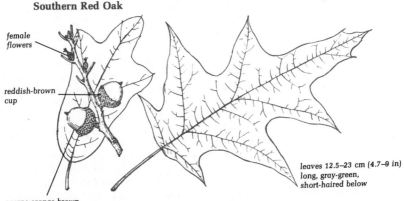

female flowers

reddish-brown cup

leaves 12.5–23 cm (4.7–9 in) long, gray-green, short-haired below

acorns orange-brown, 1.1–1.3 cm (0.5 in) long

timber, although it has many uses: general construction, crates, furniture, and fuel. While this tree is not specifically planted for ornamentation, it is often found gracing the lawns of southern homes and public buildings.

Appearance: a medium-size tree to 30 m (100 ft) in height with a crown that is high and rounded in forests, and much broader and open in clear areas; trunk is also much longer and straighter in forests, up to 1.5 m (4.9 ft) in diameter. **Bark:** dark brown to almost black, broadly ridged and fissured on old trunks, up to 1.9 cm (0.8 in) thick; smoother and lighter on younger growth. **Branches:** widespreading, large, ending in stout, dark-red branchlets that are covered at first by a thick, rust- or orange-colored coating of hairs, becoming dark gray by the second year. **Winter buds:** 3–8 mm (0.1–0.3 in) long, covered with hairy, chestnut-brown scales. **Leaves:** alternate, deciduous, simple, *12–23 cm long, rarely 30 (4.7–9 in, rarely 12)*, 10–12 cm (3.9–4.8 in) wide; with a broadly oval shape to broadest above the middle, and in general highly variable between two types: one is slender, pointed lobes; the other is somewhat bell-shaped, less deeply cut, the lobes notably sharp-tipped; surfaces dark shiny green above, *gray-green and short-haired below.* Flowers: male and female flowers occurring separate on same tree; males in drooping, hairy catkins, 7.5–12.5 cm (3–5 in) long, female flowers tiny, occurring singly or in pairs on short, thick, hairy stems. **Fruits:** orange-brown *acorn,* approximately *1.1–1.3 cm (0.5 in) long,* covered for one-third their length by a thin, shallow, red-brown scaled cup.

Cherrybark Oak, Swamp Red Oak
Quercus falcata variety *pagodifolia* Ell.

The cherrybark oak is actually a large variety of the southern red oak discussed above, but there are a number of important differences between the two. In general, cherrybark oak is limited to the southern portion of the southern red oak range, where it occurs widely on optimal bottomland sites, including well-drained terraces and hill-bottoms where rocks and earth have slid down. Best development is on loamy, well-drained soils. And while these trees do like to "get their feet wet" for part of the year, they do not thrive in wet soils. In forest associations, cherrybark oak is part of the *beech–southern magnolia* type, with sweetgum, magnolia, yellow poplar, and white oak, to name a few. In its other major cover type (*swamp chestnut oak–cherrybark oak*), prominent species include hickories, blackgum as well as white, delta post, and Shumard oaks.

Flowering and seeding habits of the cherrybark oak are similar to those of the southern red oak, except that the blossoms appear a little earlier, in March and April. The acorns, which ripen in the second season, on branchlets of the previous year, are in large part eaten by the domestic hogs that wander through low woodlands in the South. Other acorn consumers include: gray squirrels, turkeys, blue jays, wood ducks, songbirds, raccoons, whitetail deer, and eastern fox squirrels.

This oak is larger (up to 40 m; 132 ft) and better formed than the typical southern red oak, having a straighter branch-free trunk, which makes it ideal for lumber. The wood is harder, heavier, and does not crack when exposed to the sun. The leaves are *more regularly lobed, and each lobe occurs at more of a right angle to the midrib* than do

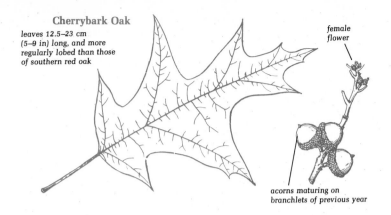

Cherrybark Oak

*leaves 12.5–23 cm
(5–9 in) long, and more
regularly lobed than those
of southern red oak*

*female
flower*

*acorns maturing on
branchlets of previous year*

leaf lobes of southern red oak. Also, the bark is smooth, with narrow, flaky ridges and is tinged red like that of the cherry.

Turkey Oak

Quercus laevis Walt.
(synonym: *Q. catesbaei* Michx.)

Turkey oak is a small tree of the southeastern Coastal Plain. It is common on sand hills and in the poor soils on bluffs and along dry sandy ridges of the coastal area. This oak is one of the few trees that grow well in almost sterile soil. It occurs in association with

many other trees including sassafras, persimmon, laurel oak, bluejack oak, southern red oak, and the sand and longleaf pines. It forms hybrid trees with other species of oak.

Turkey oak is a moderately fast to fast-growing tree with a relatively short life span. Like other oaks, it flowers in early spring as the leaves are unfolding, and the acorns require 2 growing seasons to develop and mature. Turkey oak provides cover for wildlife, and the acorns, produced abundantly every 2 or 3 years, are an important food for whitetail deer, turkeys, raccoons, squirrels, birds, and smaller rodents.

The light brown to light reddish-brown wood is close-grained, hard, and heavy, but the trees do not grow large enough to be of value as timber. The seasoned wood is excellent fuel.

Appearance: small tree, 6–15 m, rarely to 20 (20–50 ft, rarely to 65), with a broad, open or irregular, rounded crown; trunk short, usually soon branching, to 0.6 m (1.9 ft) diameter. **Bark:** 1.2–2.5 cm (0.5–1 in) thick, with deep irregular furrows and scaly rough ridges, dark gray, reddish-gray to nearly black with age. **Branches:** stout, irregular, spreading and soon branching; branchlets stout, covered with fine hairs when young, becoming smooth and dark red, and then dark reddish-brown. **Winter buds:** *1–1.4 cm (0.4–0.6 in) long, elongated* and gradually tapering to a point, covered with thin, rusty, hairy, overlapping, light reddish-brown scales. **Leaves:** alternate, deciduous, *7.5–30 cm (3–12 in) long, 2.5–22 cm (1–8.7 in) wide,* often widest above

Turkey Oak

yellow-green leaves with 3 or 5 (rarely 7) deep, rounded lobes

acorns 2.2–2.7 cm (1 in) long, cup enclosing ⅓ of nut

short stalked

the middle, **with 3, 5, or rarely 7, deep, widely rounded lobes,** gradually narrowing to a tapered base and pointed at the tip, firm to leathery at maturity, **yellow-green,** shiny and smooth (hairy when young), paler and ultimately smooth beneath; the leaf-stalks stout, 0.6–2 cm (0.2–0.8 in) long. **Flowers:** male and female flowers in separate catkins; male flowers in slender, hanging, hairy catkins 8–12 cm (3.2–4.8 in) long, produced near the tips of the previous year's branchlets; female flowers in few-flowered clusters on short stalks in the junctions of the current year's leaves. **Fruits:** **acorns,** maturing in 2 seasons, solitary or in pairs on the previous year's branchlets, **short stalked, 2.2–2.7 cm (1 in) long, broadest near the base** and gradually tapering to a rounded tip; **cup enclosing about one-third of the nut,** the cup scales thin, overlapping, hairy, and reddish-brown.

Northern Pin Oak
Quercus ellipsoidalis E.J. Hill

This is a medium-size tree of the northern midwestern states and southern Manitoba. Northern pin oak occurs not only in dry upland woods but also near ponds or along streams in lowland woods. It does best in rich, well-drained soils, especially those containing clay. This oak grows in associa-tion with white oak, black oak, scarlet oak, northern red oak, red and jack pine, and several species of hickories. It resembles the pin oak but can be distinguished by its more elongated striped acorns.

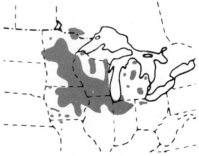

It is a moderately fast-growing tree that flowers in early spring, with the small acorns maturing at the end of 2 growing seasons. Acorn production, as in other oaks, is cyclic, with a year of abundant acorns followed by 2 or 3 sparse years. The acorns are a valuable food for whitetail deer, black bears, turkeys, grouse, many other birds, squirrels, and smaller rodents.

The pale brown wood, which is cut occasionally for lumber, is hard, heavy, and strong. It is used for flooring, furniture, and interior finishings.

Appearance: medium-size tree 15–20 m (49–66 ft) with a narrow cylinder shape and rounded crown; trunk usually short, straight, to 1 m (3.3 ft) in diameter. **Bark:** thin, becoming moderately thick with age, 8–12 mm (0.3–0.5 in) thick, smooth at first but developing shallow furrows and narrow ridges, dark brown to gray-black. **Branches:**

Northern Pin Oak

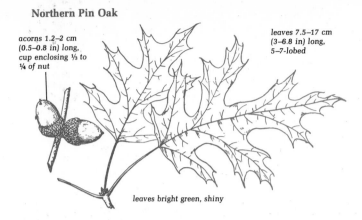

acorns 1.2–2 cm
(0.5–0.8 in) long,
cup enclosing ⅓ to
¼ of nut

leaves 7.5–17 cm
(3–6.8 in) long,
5–7-lobed

leaves bright green, shiny

stout, soon branching, the lower ones spreading; branchlets slender, bright reddish-brown and hairy when young, turning dark grayish-brown and smooth with age. **Winter buds:** 4–7 mm (0.2–0.3 in) long, broadest near the base and tapering to a rounded tip, covered with several thin, overlapping, shiny, reddish-brown scales. **Leaves:** alternate, deciduous, *7.5–17 cm (3–6.8 in) long, 6–15 cm (2.4–6 in) wide, widest above the middle to almost circular in outline, 5 to 7 lobed, the lobes deep, extending three-fourths of the way to the middle vein,* rounded at lobe bases, tapering at the base and pointed at the tip, firm but with a papery texture, bright green, shiny, and smooth above, paler beneath and with tufts of hairs in the junctions of the main veins; the leafstalks slender, 3.5–5 cm (1.4–2 in) long. **Flowers:** male and female flowers in separate catkins; male flowers in slender, hanging, hairy catkins 3.5–5 cm (1.4–2 in) long, produced near the tip of the previous year's branchlets; female flowers tiny, inconspicuous, usually occurring singly or in clusters of 2 to 3 in the junction of the leaves of the current year's branchlets. **Fruits:** *acrons,* maturing in 2 seasons, solitary or in pairs on the previous year's branchlets, short stalked or stalkless, *1.2–2 cm (0.5–0.8 in) long, egg-shaped to nearly globe-shaped; cup top-shaped, enclosing about one-third to one-fourth of the nut,* the cup scales thin, overlapping, hairy, and light brown.

Black Oak   Quercus velutina Lam.

Black oak is a common tree in the eastern and midwestern U.S. and barely extends into Canada along the shore of Lake Erie. It occurs on slopes and upland sites such as rocky or sandy ridges and hillsides. In the Appalachian Mountains, this oak grows to 1,350 m (4,430 ft) elevation. The largest black oaks occur in the Ohio River Valley. Black oak grows in pure stands or, more commonly, in association with post oak, scarlet oak, southern red oak, blackjack oak, and chestnut oak. It usually is found on drier sites than either the white or northern red oak. It often hybridizes with northern red oak.

This is a moderately fast to fast-growing

tree that reaches maturity around 100 years of age and seldom lives over 200 years. It begins to produce acorns between 15 and 20 years of age and produces large crops every 2 or 3 years. The acorns are an important source of food for wildlife: Whitetail deer, turkeys, jays, grouse, squirrels, and other rodents eat the acorns, and deer also browse the buds and young twigs.

The reddish-brown to brown wood is strong, heavy, and coarse-grained. It is of commercial importance as a lumber source, often lumped together with other oaks as "red oak." Before synthetic agents were developed, tannins from the bark were used to tan leather, and the bark also yields a natural yellow dye.

Black Oak

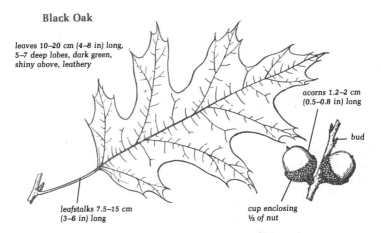

leaves 10–20 cm (4–8 in) long, 5–7 deep lobes, dark green, shiny above, leathery

acorns 1.2–2 cm (0.5–0.8 in) long

bud

leafstalks 7.5–15 cm (3–6 in) long

cup enclosing ½ of nut

Appearance: medium-size tree, usually 18–25 m (59–82 ft), occasionally taller, with an open, sometimes irregular, rounded crown; trunk tall, straight, to 1.3 m (4.3 ft) in diameter, soon branching if growing in open area. **Bark:** 2–4 cm (0.8–1.6 in) thick, smooth and dark brown on young trees, developing deep irregular fissures and broad rounded ridges and becoming dark brown to almost black. **Branches:** stout, the lower ones spreading, the upper ones partly upright; branchlets stout, hairless or covered with fine hairs the first year, then becoming smooth and dark reddish-brown. **Winter buds:** 6–8 mm (0.2–0.3 in) long, broadest near the base, angled, pointed or nearly so at the tip, covered with overlapping, gray, very hairy scales. **Leaves:** alternate, deciduous, *10–20 cm (4–8 in) long* (rarely smaller or larger), *8–12 cm (3.2–4.8 in) wide,* uniformly wide to broadest near or above the middle, *with 5 to 7 large deep lobes, the lobes rounded at their bases,* pointed at the tip, squared to unevenly squared at the base, with a leathery texture, *dark green and shiny above, paler and yellowish-brown below, smooth except along the veins on the lower surface* (young or immature leaves are hairy); the leafstalks stout, 7.5–15 cm (3–6 in) long. **Flowers:** male and female flowers in separate catkins produced on current year's branchlets; male flowers in hanging hairy catkins 10–15 cm (4–6 in) long; female flowers tiny, in few-flowered clusters in the junctions of the short stalks of the current year's leaves. **Fruits:** maturing in 2 seasons, solitary or in pairs on the previous year's branchlets, *1.2–2 cm (0.5–0.8 in) long,* rarely longer, variable in shape, often broadest near the base and gradually tapering to a rounded tip; *cup deeply bowl-shaped, enclosing about half of the nut, the cup scales thin, loosely overlapping, dark brown,* and with a tiny fringe of hairs on their borders.

Graves Oak *Quercus gravesii* Sudw.

Graves oak is native to the high mountain ranges in the Trans-Pecos region of Texas. It is especially common in the Chisos Mountains in moist canyons and is apparently related to Shumard oak whose principal ranges are in the southeastern U.S. Graves oak

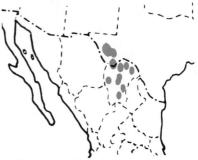

is a tree to 12 m (39 ft) with dark grayish-black bark, which becomes narrowly fissured with age. The alternate leaves are deciduous, broadest near the base or the tip, *5–10 cm (2–4 in) long*, 3.9–8.5 cm (1.5–3.5 in) wide, *with 3 to 7 variable lobes along the margin*, each ending in a bristle-like tip. Leaves are dark green and shiny above, pale and smooth or with scattered hairs on the lower surface. The acorns mature in 2 seasons on branchlets of the previous year, and are 1.2–1.7 cm (0.6 in) long, broadly top-shaped, rounded at the tip. The *saucer-shaped cup encloses one-third to one-half of the nut.*

Shumard Oak *Quercus shumardii* Buckl.

Shumard oak is a large southern oak ranging from the southeastern Atlantic Coastal Plain to Oklahoma and Texas. It is a lowland tree usually found growing in well-drained soils. It often grows along streams, near swamps, or other bodies of water.

This oak does not form pure stands but grows scattered in deciduous hardwood forests along with black oak, swamp chestnut oak, cherrybark oak, post oak, blackgum, white ash, and several hickories. As do many oaks, Shumard oak readily hybridizes with other species including shingle oak, southern red oak, blackjack oak, and water oak. The size and shape of the leaves and acorns are variable; as a result, several varieties of Shumard oak are recognized.

This is a moderately fast-growing tree that flowers in early spring as the leaves are unfolding. The large acorns require 2 seasons to mature. The trees normally reach 25 years before they begin to produce acorns; then large acorn crops can occur every 2 to 4 years. Whitetail deer, black bears, raccoons, turkeys, squirrels, and other rodents relish the acorns.

The light reddish-brown wood is hard, heavy, close-grained, and very valuable. It is cut and marketed as red oak, along with several other species of oaks. Flooring, furniture, and veneer are its main uses, although it is also used in many other ways.

Appearance: medium to tall tree 20–30 m, occasionally to 40 (65–100 ft, occasionally to 132), with a broad, open, rounded crown; trunk tall, straight, to 1.6 m (5.2 ft) in diameter. **Bark:** 2.5–4 cm (1–1.6 in) thick on mature trees, shallowly furrowed and developing small, tight, interlacing ridges. **Branches:** stout, widespreading; branchlets stout to slender, hairy when young, becoming smooth and grayish-brown. **Winter**

Shumard Oak

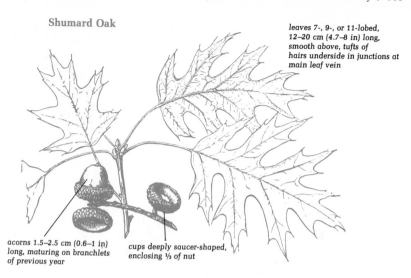

leaves 7-, 9-, or 11-lobed,
12–20 cm (4.7–8 in) long,
smooth above, tufts of
hairs underside in junctions at
main leaf vein

acorns 1.5–2.5 cm (0.6–1 in)
long, maturing on branchlets
of previous year

cups deeply saucer-shaped,
enclosing ⅓ of nut

buds: 3–5 mm (0.1–0.2 in) long, broadest near the base and tapering to a pointed or rounded tip, covered with overlapping, usually smooth, straw-colored scales. **Leaves:** alternate, deciduous, ***12–20 cm (4.7–7.9 in) long, 8–12 cm (3.2–4.8 in) wide, broadest above the middle, with 7, 9, or 11 lobes, the lobes variable, often extending half way to the main vein,*** rounded at their bases and tapering toward the tip, squared to broadly tapering at the base and pointed at the tip, with a firm but papery texture, dark green, shiny, and smooth above, paler beneath and with ***tufts of hairs in junctions at the main vein*** (the young or immature leaves hairy); the leafstalks slender, 5–6.5 cm (2–2.6 in) long. **Flowers:** male and female flowers in separate catkins; male flowers in slender, hanging, hairless catkins 14–18 cm (5.5–7.1 in) long, produced near the tip of the previous year's branchlets; female flowers tiny, inconspicuous, solitary, paired or few-clustered in the junction of the leaves of the current year's branchlets. **Fruits:** ***acorns, maturing in 2 seasons,*** solitary or in pairs on the previous year's branchlets, ***1.5–2.5 cm (0.6–1 in) long,*** broadest near the base and tapering to a rounded tip; ***cup deeply saucer-shaped, enclosing about the lower third of the nut,*** the cup scales overlapping, thin, hairy, and light brown.

Scarlet Oak   *Quercus coccinea* Muench.

Scarlet oak is an attractive tree of the eastern U.S. It occurs on upland sites, such as ridges and middle and upper slopes, in a variety of soils and does well in poor, dry, sandy, or gravelly soils. This tree is common at 800–1,200 m (2,600–4,000 ft) but does grow as high as 1,750 m (5,750 ft) elevation. A component of eastern deciduous forests, scarlet oak grows in association with many other trees including black oak, white oak, chestnut oak, southern oak, post oak, sweetgum, black gum, pitch pine, shortleaf pine, and several of the hickories.

This oak is a rapid-growing tree but does not live as long as the slower growing oaks. It usually flowers in April or May as the leaves are unfolding, and the acorns do not develop and mature until the end of the second growing season. A year of heavy acorn production usually is followed by 3 or 4 years of light production. The acorns are important to wildlife, including whitetail deer, squirrels, turkeys, grouse, and many of the larger songbirds.

The reddish-brown wood is heavy, hard, strong, and coarse-grained, but it is inferior to the wood of white oak. It is cut and marketed intermixed with wood of other species of oak. It is often planted in cities because its leaves turn a bright red or scarlet in autumn.

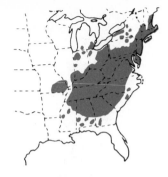

Scarlet Oak

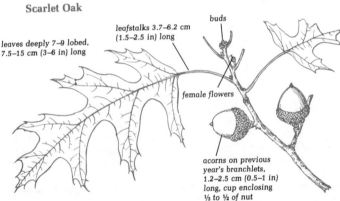

leaves deeply 7–9 lobed, 7.5–15 cm (3–6 in) long

leafstalks 3.7–6.2 cm (1.5–2.5 in) long

buds

female flowers

acorns on previous year's branchlets, 1.2–2.5 cm (0.5–1 in) long, cup enclosing ⅓ to ½ of nut

Appearance: medium-size tree to 20–30 m (65–100 ft) with a narrow open crown; trunk tall, straight, usually to 1 m (3.3 ft) in diameter, rarely larger. **Bark:** thin, smooth, and light brown on young trees, becoming 1.2–2.5 cm (0.5–1 in) thick on older trees, light brown to reddish-brown, with shallow fissures and irregular ridges. **Branches:** medium size to slender and spreading; branchlets slender, covered with fine hairs when young, becoming smooth and pale green, and then light brown with age. **Winter buds:** 3.5–7 mm (0.1–0.3 in) long, broadest near the base or the middle and tapering toward the rounded tip, covered with overlapping, dark reddish-brown scales. **Leaves:** alternate, deciduous, *7.5–15 cm (3–6 in) long, 6.2–10 cm (2.5–4 in) wide, broadest near or above the middle, with 7 to 9 deep lobes along the margin,* the lobes rounded at their bases, pointed and coarsely toothed at the tip, tapering to almost squared at the base, with a firm papery texture, bright green, shiny and smooth above, paler beneath and occasionally with tufts of hairs in the junctions of the main vein; the *leafstalks slender, 3.7–6.2 cm (1.5–2.5 in) long.* **Flowers:** male and female flowers in separate catkins; male flowers in slender, hanging, smooth catkins 7.5–10 cm (3–4 in) long, produced in the junction of the leaves of previous year's branchlets; female flowers tiny, single or in clusters of 2 to 5 on stalks, the stalks to 1.2 cm (0.5 in) long, inconspicuous, produced on current year's branchlets. **Fruits:** *maturing in 2 seasons,* solitary or in pairs on last year's branchlets, *1.2–2.5 cm (0.5–1 in) long, broadest near the base and gradually tapering to a rounded tip; cup deeply saucer-shaped to toy top-shaped, enclosing half to one-third of the nut,* the cup scales overlapping, thin, closely pressed, and light reddish-brown.

Water Oak

Quercus nigra L.

Water oak is a southeastern tree that occurs along the Coastal Plain from southern New Jersey to central Florida and west to eastern Oklahoma. It is a lowland tree that is often common along streams and rivers and in floodplains. This oak also grows in the

southeastern Piedmont along water courses. Best growth and largest size are reached in well-drained, silty clay or loamy soils. Water oak grows in mixed deciduous forests along with slash pine, longleaf pine, loblolly pine, swamp chestnut oak, sugarberry, sycamore, and sweetgum. Water oak and sweetgum commonly occur together in the South.

This oak, which grows rapidly in good soils, needs approximately 20 years to reach flowering age. It usually produces large seed crops every year or two once it begins flowering. Whitetail deer, turkeys, ducks (especially mallards and wood ducks), quail, raccoons, squirrels, and pigs eat the acorns. Deer browse young twigs and buds during late winter.

The light brown wood is close-grained and moderately hard and heavy but inferior to the wood from other species and is sold as red oak or just oak. Water oak is commonly planted along streets and boulevards in southeastern cities.

Appearance: medium-size tree 15–25 m (49–82 ft), occasionally taller, with a broad rounded crown; trunk tall, straight, 0.3–1 m (1–3.3 ft) in diameter, rarely larger. **Bark:** 1–2.5 cm (0.4–1 in) thick, covered with close irregular patches that eventually develop into wide, rough, scaly ridges, grayish-black. **Branches:** numerous, spreading; branchlets slender, smooth, and dull red turning grayish-brown by the second year. **Winter buds:** 4–7 mm (about 0.2–0.3 in) long, broadest near the base and tapering to a pointed tip, strongly angled, covered with overlapping, dark reddish-brown, hairy scales. **Leaves:** alternate, deciduous, *usually 5–10 cm (2–4 in) long and 2.5–5 cm (1–2 in) wide, broadest near the tip, tapering to a long narrow base and pointed at the tip, the margin variable, unlobed, shallowly 3 lobed near the tip or occasionally 5 lobed,* with a papery texture, dull bluish-green and smooth above, paler and with tufts of hairs in the main junctions of the veins on the lower surface; the leafstalks stout,

Water Oak

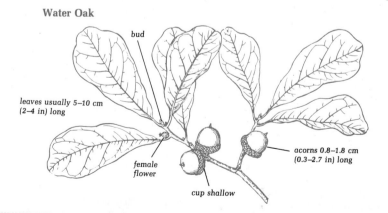

bud

leaves usually 5–10 cm (2–4 in) long

female flower

cup shallow

acorns 0.8–1.8 cm (0.3–2.7 in) long

flattened, 3.5–12 mm (about 0.1–0.5 in) long. **Flowers:** male and female flowers in separate catkins; male flowers in slender, hanging, hairy, reddish catkins 5–7.5 cm (2–3 in) long, produced near the tips of last year's branchlets; female flowers in few-flowered, short-stalked clusters in the junction of the current year's leaves. **Fruits:** *acorns,* maturing in 2 seasons, often solitary, *0.8–1.8 cm (0.3–0.7 in) long,* broadest near the base and broadly rounded at the tip; *cup shallowly saucer-shaped, enclosing the nut only at the base,* the cup scales thin, close-pressed and overlapping, finely hairy, and light reddish-brown.

Arkansas Oak · *Quercus arkansana* Sarg.

This southern oak is a small tree ranging from northern Florida to southwestern Arkansas. It grows in low woods, on bluffs and rolling hills, and usually occurs as scattered trees in deciduous forests. It is similar in appearance and closely related to the water oak and blackjack oak.

Arkansas oak is a medium-size tree 15–25 m (49–82 ft) high. It has a narrow rounded crown and a thick, nearly black bark with deep furrows and long narrow ridges. The *leaves* are *5–7.5 cm (2–3 in) long and broad, broadest above the middle, slightly 3 lobed,* tapering to a narrow base and with a broad rounded tip, light yellow-green above and paler beneath. The acorns mature at the end of 2 growing seasons on branchlets of the previous year. The *acorns* are *short stalked, 0.6–1 cm (0.2–0.4 in) long, very broad near the base and rounded at the tip.* The *shallow saucer-shaped cup encloses only the base of the nut.*

Arkansas Oak

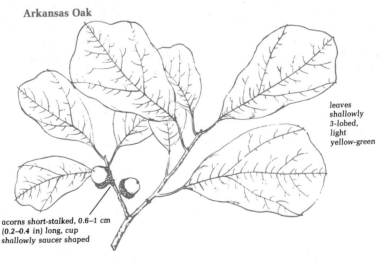

leaves shallowly 3-lobed, light yellow-green

acorns short-stalked, 0.6–1 cm (0.2–0.4 in) long, cup shallowly saucer shaped

Blackjack Oak · *Quercus marilandica* Muenchh.

Blackjack oak is a small scrubby tree of the eastern U.S., but principally in the southeastern region. This oak ranges from Long Island, New York, to northern Florida and west to Iowa and Texas. The club-shaped leaves are responsible for the common name. Blackjack oak grows in poor, barren soils and thus can be used as a field indicator of soil depth and quality.

Blacjack oak grows up to moderate elevations in the southeastern mountains. It is common in open areas and along woodland borders in rocky sandstone areas. This oak can also thrive in dry, sandy, almost sterile soils along with scrub pine. As a pioneer species, blackjack oaks will readily invade barren areas, especially after a fire. Other trees found growing in association with this oak include redcedar, post, black, and red oaks, hickories, longleaf and loblolly pines.

Blackjack oaks are slow-growing and short-lived. When the leaves are about half-unfolded, around mid-April, slender catkins of male flowers and short spikes of females appear. The acorns, which occur singly or in pairs, mature by October of the second season. These, together with the understory built up by young oak trees and other plants, are important to squirrels, turkeys, and deer. Blackjacks are in general too small to be of any commercial value. However, they have been used for railroad ties, fence posts, charcoal, and fuelwood.

Blackjack Oak

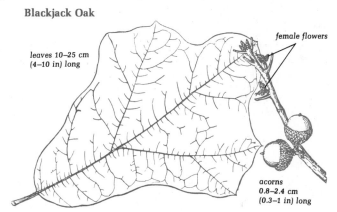

female flowers

leaves 10–25 cm (4–10 in) long

acorns 0.8–2.4 cm (0.3–1 in) long

Appearance: a short tree, seldom exceeding 12 m (40 ft), with a compact, round-topped, or sometimes open, irregular crown; trunk straight or crooked, up to 30 cm (12 in) wide. **Bark:** 2.5–3.7 cm (1–1.5 in) thick on trunk, broken into irregular plates, nearly black; reddish-brown and smoother on younger limbs. **Winter buds:** 6–8 mm (0.2–0.3 in), oval-shaped, set at the bases of leaves, coated with rusty-brown hairs. **Branches:** short, thick, often twisted or slightly drooping; branchlets stout, densely hairy and red-brown at first, becoming brown or ashy-gray. **Leaves:** alternate, deciduous, simple, *10–25 cm (4–10 in) long*, almost as broad as the *abruptly widened tip; 3- or, rarely, 5-lobed, variable, reminiscent of a bird's webbed foot;* mature leaves firm and leathery, dark green, smooth and shiny above, brown-hairy beneath. **Flowers:** male catkins 5–12 cm (2–4.8 in) long, with 30 to 50 flowers on a hairy stalk; 3 to 6 downy, greenish-brown calyx lobes, 2–3 mm (0.1 in) long; 4 to 6 stamens; female clusters at end of new growth, flowers broadly oval-shaped and smaller than males, with brown, pointed hairy base scales, and smooth green ovary with 3 curling styles and bright red stigma. **Fruits:** acorns mature in 2 seasons on previous year's branchlets, on a very short stalk; *nut 1.8–2.4 cm (0.7–1 in) long, 0.9–1.3 cm (0.4–0.6 in) wide, half enclosed in a light yellow-brown cup* with red-brown scales, the upper ones smaller and in several rows, forming a thickened upper edge.

Laurel Oak

Quercus laurifolia Michx.
[synonym: *Q. obtusa* (Willd.) Ashe]

Laurel oak is an attractive tree of the southeastern Coastal Plain from southeastern Virginia to Florida and southern Texas. Laurel oak grows in moist woods, along the edges of streams, rivers, or swamps, and in hammocks. It does best in well-drained soils. Laurel oak does not form pure stands but grows in association with sweetgum, bald cypress, pignut hickory, live oak, longleaf and loblolly pines. It hybridizes with closely related oaks.

Refuting the notion that oaks are slow-growing trees, laurel oak is a rapid-growing, short-lived tree that reaches flowering age in approximately 15 years and maturity at 50 years. It flowers in early spring, and the acorns develop and mature at the end of 2 growing seasons. Large crops of acorns are produced regularly, and they are an important food for wildlife. Whitetail deer, raccoons, squirrels, turkeys, ducks, quail, and smaller birds and rodents readily eat the acorns. The deer browse the buds and young twigs during the winter months after the acorn supply is exhausted.

The dark brown to reddish-brown wood is coarse-grained, hard, heavy, and strong, but it does not make a good grade of lumber. It is used locally for firewood. The trees are sometimes planted as street trees, but their short lives limit their usefulness for that purpose.

Laurel Oak

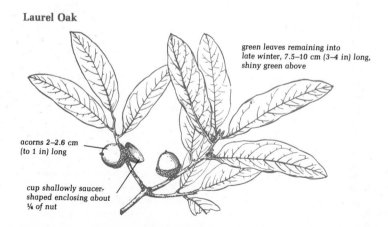

green leaves remaining into late winter, 7.5–10 cm (3–4 in) long, shiny green above

acorns 2–2.6 cm (to 1 in) long

cup shallowly saucer-shaped enclosing about ¼ of nut

Appearance: medium-size tree 20–30 m (65–100 ft), rarely taller, with a full rounded crown; trunk tall, straight, to 1.3 m (4.3 ft) in diameter. **Bark:** 1.2–2.5 cm (0.5–1 in) thick, developing deep furrows that separate the broad flattened ridges, dark brown turning almost black with age. **Branches:** slender, the lower ones spreading; branchlets slender, smooth, and dark red turning reddish-brown to dark gray with age. **Winter buds:** 2–4 mm (about 0.1–0.2 in) long, broadest near the base and tapering to a pointed tip, covered with thin, reddish-brown, overlapping scales. **Leaves:** alternate, *nearly evergreen, gradually falling in late winter or early spring, 7.5–10 cm (3–4 in) long, 1.8–2.2 cm (0.7–0.9 in) wide, narrow but broadest near the middle,* long pointed at the tip and tapering to a narrowed base, *generally entire,* sometimes shallowly 3 lobed near the tip, with a thick leathery texture, *shiny green above,* light green beneath; the leafstalks stout, 4–7 mm (about 0.1–0.3 in) long. **Flowers:** male and female flowers in separate catkins; male flowers in slender, hanging, hairy catkins 5–7.5 cm (2–3 in) long; female flowers tiny, inconspicuous, borne on stout, short stalks in the stem junctions of the current year's leaves. **Fruits:** acorns, maturing in 2 seasons, often solitary, occasionally paired, *2–2.6 cm (0.8–1 in) long,* broadest near the base to globe-shaped, rounded at the tip; *cup shallowly saucer-shaped, enclosing about one-fourth of the nut,* the cup scales thin, overlapping, and reddish-brown.

Willow Oak

Quercus phellos L.

The willow-like leaves of this large, southern member of the oak family give some people the mistaken impression that the willow oak is a hybrid of willow and oak. However, the willow oak is not related to the willow family at all. It occurs in the eastern coastal states from Staten Island to Georgia, and also in the South from southern Kentucky to eastern Texas. The type of site plays an important role in determining growth rate and general quality. Ranging from lowlands to elevations of not more than 500 m (1,640 ft), best sites include low borders of swamps and streams or rich, shady, upland soils. Less suitable sites include hardpan areas or old terraces and hammocks. In some areas, willow oak grows with laurel oak, Nuttall oak and  sweetgum. Elsewhere, it associates with loblolly pine, overcup oak, cherrybark oak, sugarberry, and water hickory.

Willow oak is known for its rapid growth and long life. Seed production begins when the tree reaches about 20 years of age, and good seed crops are normally produced on a yearly basis. A mature tree can produce almost 2 bushels of acorns in a season. Flowering occurs from February to May, just before the leaves emerge. The acorns mature between August and October of the second season. The nuts are an important food source for squirrels, whitetail deer, and turkeys, and to a lesser extent for quail and several kinds of songbirds. When flooding occurs in willow oak sites, mallards and wood ducks feed on the acorns.

Willow oak is sufficiently abundant in parts of the South to merit large-scale lumber operations. The heavy, hard wood is usually marketed simply as "red oak." Its uses include interior finishes, railings, stairs, and furniture. In southern cities, this willow oak is valued as a fast-growing street, ornamental, or shade tree.

Appearance: tall tree, often 20–27 m, occasionally to 35 (65–90 ft, occasionally to

Willow Oak

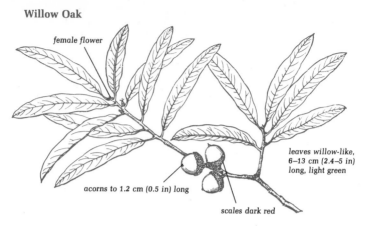

female flower

leaves willow-like,
6–13 cm (2.4–5 in)
long, light green

acorns to 1.2 cm (0.5 in) long

scales dark red

115); with a round top or narrowly open or cone-shaped crown; trunk straight, up to 1.2 m (3.9 ft) wide. **Bark:** 1.2–1.8 cm (0.5–0.7 in) thick, light reddish-brown, smooth on young growth, but roughened into irregular scale-covered plates when older. **Branches:** spreading to slightly drooping at the ends; branchlets smooth, red-brown, becoming dark brown and tinged with red or gray by the second season. **Winter buds:** 3–4 mm (about 0.1–0.2 in) long, egg-shaped, pointed at the tip, covered with chestnut-brown scales that are paler along the margins, the terminal buds larger than the lateral ones. **Leaves:** alternate, ***deciduous, 6–13 cm (2.4–5 in) long, 0.6–2.5 cm (0.2–1 in) wide, willow-like in shape, narrow, entire,*** gradually tapering at both ends, ***light green*** and shiny above, dull and paler below with a conspicuous meshwork of veins; the leafstalks short, stout. **Flowers:** male and female flowers in separate catkins on the same tree; male flowers in slender, hanging, hairy catkins 5–7.5 cm (2–3 in) long; female flowers tiny, in few-flowered clusters in the stem junctions of the leaves. **Fruits:** ***acorns, maturing in 2 seasons on previous year's branchlets,*** borne solitary or in pairs, ***broadly rounded, up to 1.2 cm (0.5 in) long, rounded at the tip; cup saucer-shaped, enclosing about one-fourth of the nut,*** the scales thin, hairy, dark red, and overlapping.

Shingle Oak   *Quercus imbricaria* Michx.

Shingle oak is a handsome, medium-size tree of the central and eastern U.S. This oak occurs from Pennsylvania to northeastern Alabama, and west as far as Kansas. While shingle oak is uncommon in the eastern states, it is one of the most abundant oaks in the lower Ohio River Valley, with best growth in southern Indiana and Illinois. This species may occur on a number of different sites, from dry, upland ridges to rich and moist river bank soils. In the Appalachian foothills the trees grow up to elevations of 660 m (2,200 ft), although these are normally considered to be lowland trees. Shingle oak is never dominant in any forest system, perhaps because it is somewhat intolerant of shading. Oak species such as southern red oak, scarlet oak, and

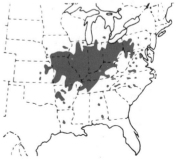

live oak may be found growing with this one, but shingle oak achieves best growth under conditions that also support the pin oak, willow oak, and overcup oak. Shingle oak is characteristic of subclimax forests, rather than fully developed ones.

The shingle oak is a moderately fast-growing tree with a medium life span. Male and female flowers, borne in separate catkins on the same tree, blossom in April and May. The nuts, which are enclosed for one-third of their length by the scaly cups, ripen by the fall of the second growing season. These are an important food source to several kinds of animals, particularly turkeys, deer, and squirrels; quails will often eat pieces left over from squirrel activity because the whole acorns are too large for the quail to consume. When shingle oaks grow along rivers, the nuts are readily taken by mallards, wood ducks, and other waterfowl. Both the common and scientific names of this tree make reference to the once widespread use of the wood in shingle making. Early French pioneers in Illinois lived in cabins that were covered by such shingles. Other timbering uses are limited, though shingle oak may be cut down in mixed stands and is marketed as "red oak." The dark green leaves and regular shape make this tree an attractive ornamental.

Shingle Oak

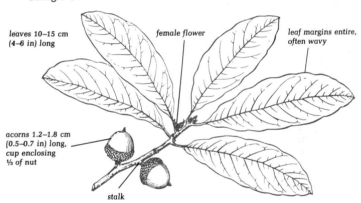

leaves 10–15 cm (4–6 in) long

female flower

leaf margins entire, often wavy

acorns 1.2–1.8 cm (0.5–0.7 in) long, cup enclosing ⅓ of nut

stalk

Appearance: medium-size tree, 15–25 m (49–82 ft) tall, with an open broadly rounded crown, although young trees are pyramid-shaped; trunk very straight, to 1 m (3.3 ft) in diameter, rarely larger. **Bark:** thin, 1.8–3.5 cm (0.7–1.9 in) thick on older trunks, light brown, smooth and shiny on young twigs, becoming ridged, fissured, and scaly when older. **Branches:** slender, tough, spreading to slightly drooping; branchlets slender, dark green and shiny, often reddish when they first appear, later becoming red-brown and darkening after the first year. **Winter buds:** egg-shaped, pointed at the tip, 3–4 mm (about 0.1–0.2 in) long, covered with closely overlapping, light brown scales that are ragged or finely hairy along the margins. **Leaves:** alternate, deciduous, *10–15 cm (4–6 in) long, 2.5–5 cm (1–2 in) wide, uniformly wide to lance-shaped,* broadest near the middle, *slightly wavy-margined,* very shiny above, dark green at maturity, finely hairy on the lower surface; leafstalks stout, 0.8–1.4 cm (0.3–0.6 in) long. **Flowers:** male and female flowers in separate catkins; male flowers in slender, hanging, hairy catkins 5–7.5 cm (2–3 in) long; female flowers tiny, usually in 2s or 3s. **Fruits: acorns,** maturing in 2 seasons on branchlets of the previous year, solitary or in pairs, on stout stalks up to 1.2 cm (0.5 in) long, *nut 1.2–1.8 cm (0.5–0.7 in) long* and nearly as wide, broadest near the base and rounded at the tip; *cup bowl-shaped,* *enclosing about one-third of the nut,* the scales thin, red-brown to dark brown, often with pale stripes.

Bluejack Oak

Quercus incana Bartr.
(synonym: *Q. cinerea* Michx.)

Bluejack oak is a small, often shrubby, tree of the Coastal Plain from southeastern Virginia to southern Florida and central Texas and Oklahoma. This is the common oak of the sandhills. It occurs not only on dry sandy hills and upland ridges but also in richer soils. It grows in pinelands with the longleaf pine and in association with sand post oak, southern red oak, turkey oak, and persimmon. It apparently hybridizes with several other oaks.

It is a moderately fast to fast-growing tree with a short life span, usually less than 100 years. It flowers in early spring, and the acorns require 2 growing seasons to develop and mature. It produces moderate to large crops of acorns each year, and these are valuable to wildlife. Whitetail deer, raccoons, turkeys, quail, squirrels, and other rodents eat the acorns. Besides, bluejack oak often forms dense thickets that provide excellent cover for mammals and birds.

The reddish-brown wood is coarse-grained, hard, and strong, but the trees are too small to be of any use as lumber. The wood is used locally for fuel and occasionally for fence posts.

Bluejack Oak

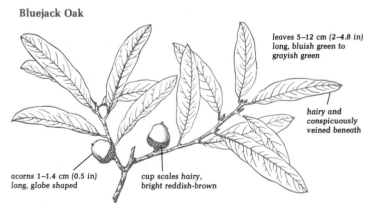

leaves 5–12 cm (2–4.8 in) long, bluish green to grayish green

hairy and conspicuously veined beneath

acorns 1–1.4 cm (0.5 in) long, globe shaped

cup scales hairy, bright reddish-brown

Appearance: large shrub or small tree to 12 m (40 ft), with an open, irregular crown; trunk short, soon branching, to 15 cm (5.9 in) in diameter. **Bark:** becoming thick, 1.2–3.5 cm (0.5–1.4 in), developing into thick, almost square plates, grayish-brown to almost black. **Branches:** stout, spreading; branchlets stout to slender, reddish-brown, hairy when young, becoming smooth and darker with age. **Winter buds:** 5–8 mm (0.2–0.3 in) long, broadest near the base and tapering to a pointed tip, covered with thin, overlapping, bright reddish-brown scales. **Leaves:** alternate, deciduous, *5–12 cm (2–4.8 in) long, 1.2–4 cm (0.5–1.6 in) wide, narrow,* broadest near the base to broadest above the middle, tapering to rounded at the base and rounded to pointed at the tip, **usually entire** or occasionally shallowly 3-lobed near the tip, with a firm texture shiny and **bluish-green to grayish-green, paler, hairy,** and **conspicuously veined beneath;** the leafstalks stout, 6–12 mm (0.2–0.5 in) long. **Flowers:** male and female flowers in separate catkins; male flowers in slender, hanging, hairy catkins 5–7.5 cm (2–3 in) long, produced near the tips of the previous year's branchlets; female flowers in few-flowered clusters on short stalks in stem junctions of the current year's leaves. **Fruits:** acorns, maturing in 2 seasons, often solitary on the previous year's branchlets, short-stalked to stalkless, **1–1.4 cm (0.4–0.6 in) long, globe-shaped to broadest near the base and slightly flattened; cup shallow, saucer-shaped, enclosing the nut only at the base,** the cup scales thin, overlapping, hairy, and bright reddish-brown.

Myrtle Oak   *Quercus myrtifolia* Willd.

Myrtle oak is an evergreen shrub or small tree of the Coastal Plain from southern South Carolina to southern Florida and west to Mississippi. It occurs on dry sandy soils, especially along the coast and on adjacent offshore islands where it often forms

dense thickets. This oak grows in association with the sand pine, longleaf pine, and several of the scrub oaks, including black-jack, live, and laurel. Acorns are produced abundantly each year and are an important food for whitetail deer, turkeys, and squirrels.

This is a bushy shrub or small tree to 12 m (40 ft), rarely taller, with a rounded crown and thin, smooth, dark-brown bark. The leaves are **evergreen, 2–5 cm (0.8–2 in) long, 0.6–3 cm (0.2–1.2 in) wide, broadest above or near the middle, entire on the margin, leathery,** dark green and shiny above, yellowish-green to orangish-brown and smooth to hairy beneath. The **acorns** mature in 2 seasons on the previous year's branchlets, and are **0.6–1.2 cm (0.2–0.5 in) long, almost globe-shaped** to broadest near the base. The **saucer-shaped cup encloses from one-fourth to one-third of the nut.**

Myrtle Oak

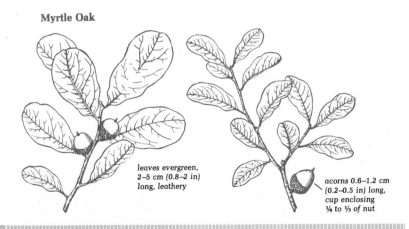

leaves evergreen,
2–5 cm (0.8–2 in)
long, leathery

acorns 0.6–1.2 cm
(0.2–0.5 in) long,
cup enclosing
¼ to ⅓ of nut

Interior Live Oak   Quercus wislizenii A. DC.

Interior live oaks are short to medium-size trees of California. They resemble the coast live oaks of California, but the two are never found together. The interior live oak occurs on desert mountain slopes to altitudes of 1,500 to 2,100 m (4,900–6,900 ft) on inland foothills (especially the foothills of the Sierra Nevada), and in coastal valleys away from the sea in the central part of California. Their most striking feature is their incredibly broad dome-shaped crown, which may be twice as broad as the tree's height, and nearly sweeping the ground. Captain John Fremont, the explorer, was impressed at the sight of these friendly looking trees, which he encountered when descending from the mountains.

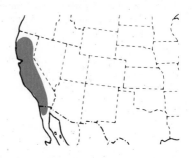

While the wood of interior live oaks is hard, heavy, and sturdy, it is of no commercial value except as fuelwood, for the tree trunks are never tall or clear.

These trees may grow over 9 m (30 ft) but rarely to 20 m (66 ft) tall, with a thick trunk reaching nearly 2 m (6.6 ft) in diameter. On desert canyons these trees are short and scrubby. The bark is thick, ridged, and furrowed. The flat, *evergreen, simple leaves are 2.5–3.5 cm (1–1.4 in) long and 1.5–1.7 cm (0.6–0.7 in) wide,* dark-green, shiny on the upper surface and dull and smooth beneath. The acorns maturing in the fall of the second year are light brown, *1.8–3.5 cm (0.7–1.4 in) long, with minute hairs at the tips,* and nearly encased by the light-brown cup, 1.2–2.5 cm (0.5–1 in) deep.

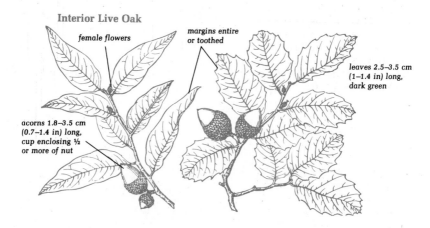

Interior Live Oak

female flowers

margins entire
or toothed

leaves 2.5–3.5 cm
(1–1.4 in) long,
dark green

acorns 1.8–3.5 cm
(0.7–1.4 in) long,
cup enclosing ½
or more of nut

Coast Live Oak   Quercus agrifolia Née

The coast live oak is an attractive evergreen tree ranging from northern California southward to Baja California in Mexico. It is common on the lower mountain slopes, valleys of the coastal mountain ranges, and on some of the nearby islands. This species often forms large, open, pure stands. In the northern part of its range, coast live oak seldom grows at elevations over 1,000 m (3,300 ft). But it can be found growing up to 1,650 m (5,500 ft) in the southern part of its range. This oak hybridizes with the interior live oak. The resulting offspring are difficult to identify because of intermediate characters between the two species. The thick evergreen leaves resemble holly leaves.

This slow-growing, long-lived tree flowers in early spring and the long-pointed acorns mature by the end of the first growing season. It is of limited value to wildlife as a food source.

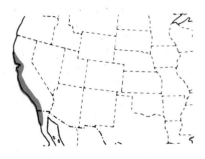

Coast Live Oak

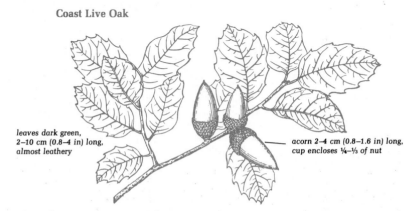

leaves dark green,
2–10 cm (0.8–4 in) long,
almost leathery

acorn 2–4 cm (0.8–1.6 in) long,
cup encloses ¼–⅓ of nut

The reddish-brown wood is hard, heavy, and brittle. It is not used commercially except for firewood. Coast live oak is frequently planted in parks and gardens because of its shape and attractive dark-green leaves. It is sometimes used as a street tree.

Appearance: small to medium-size tree 10–25 m (32–82 ft) with a broad spreading crown; trunk short, soon branching, from 0.3–1.3 m (1–4.3 ft) diameter. **Bark:** thin, becoming very thick (to 7 cm – 2.8 in – thick) with age, smooth and light gray-brown when young, rough, furrowed, and dark brown to almost black with age. **Branches:** stout, wide spreading; branchlets slender, hairy at first but becoming smooth after two years, light brown turning dark gray to reddish-brown with age. **Winter buds:** 6–8 mm (0.2–0.3 in) long, rounded to broadest near the base and tapering to a pointed tip, covered with overlapping, light reddish-brown scales. **Leaves:** alternate, falling gradually in winter and early spring, *2–10 cm (0.8–4 in) long* and *1.3–7.5 cm (0.5–3 in) wide, usually very broad,* often near the base or the middle, rounded to almost heart-shaped at the base and pointed at the tip, *the margin entire or coarsely toothed, almost leathery in texture,* dark green and smooth above at maturity (hairy when young), paler and smooth to thickly hairy beneath, usually with tufts of hairs in the junction at the main vein; the leafstalks stout, 1.2–2.5 cm (0.5–1 in) long, smooth or hairy. **Flowers:** male and female flowers in slender, hanging, hairy, reddish catkins 7.5–10 cm (3–4 in) long; female flowers in few-flowered clusters in the junctions of some of the current year's leaves. **Fruits:** *acorns,* maturing in 1 season on current year's branchlets, solitary or in 2s or 3s, *2–4 cm (0.8–1.6 in) long, about 0.6–2 cm (0.3–0.8 in) thick, elongated into a narrow cone,* gradually narrowing to a pointed tip; *cup top-shaped, enclosing only the lower one-fourth to one-third of the nut,* the cup scales thin, papery, overlapping, and light brown.

Chisos Oak

Quercus graciliformis C.H. Muller

This is a rare oak, occurring in the Chisos Mountains of Brewster County, Texas. Very little is known about it except that it appears to be more closely related to Mexican oaks than to U.S. oaks.

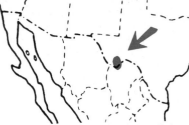

Chisos oak is a *small tree* with *slender graceful branches*. The *leaves* are *nearly evergreen, 7–10 cm (2.8–4 in) long, 2–3 cm (0.8–1.2 in) wide, narrow, with few to 8 or 10 lobes along the margin, long-pointed at the tip*, leathery, shiny green and smooth above, duller beneath. The *acorns* require 2 seasons to mature, so mature ones occur on the previous year's branchlets. The acorns are *1.5–2 cm (0.7 in) long, narrow, elongated,* and *long pointed at the tip.* The shallow, saucer-shaped cup encloses only the base of the nut.

Canyon Live Oak

Quercus chrysolepis Liebm.

Canyon live oak is an evergreen western species whose size and shape vary markedly, depending on conditions of growth. Ranging from Oregon into Baja California in Mexico and into Arizona, canyon live oak grows, in the northern regions, near sea level,

but occurs up to 2,700 m (8,900 ft) in California. This oak prefers deep, cool canyons, where in competition with tall conifers, the tree develops a long straight trunk and reaches its greatest height. Ordinarily the tree grows to lesser heights in more open areas, where the large, wide-spreading branches begin much closer to the ground, almost touching it, and the spreading crown may extend 40 m (131 ft) across. On exposed mountain slopes from 1,200–1,800 m (3,900–5,900 ft) elevation, this same species is a low shrub, 4–6 m (13–20 ft) tall, forming dense thickets. While it occurs at times in small lone stands, canyon live oak more often occurs with such species as California black and live oak, interior live oak, and bigcone spruce.

During the canyon live oak's long life, growth is constant and fairly slow. It is not as good an acorn producer as other oaks; usually scant crops are produced. It does produce large acorn crops at irregular intervals. Flowers are produced from May to June on the same tree and the acorns ripen in the fall of the following year. Trees killed by forest fires will often sprout back from the roots. Like other oaks, canyon live oak is an important source of food to many types of wildlife, including western gray squirrels, gophers, ground squirrels, deer, and several kinds of birds.

The light brown wood is hard, dense, and shock resistant. It is the best western oak timber. Pioneers fashioned it into wedges, which they used for splitting redwood for railroad ties. Young tough trees were fashioned into mauls that were used to drive posts and split logs. Canyon live oak was in high demand among shipbuilders. It also makes an excellent ornamental and shade tree.

Canyon Live Oak

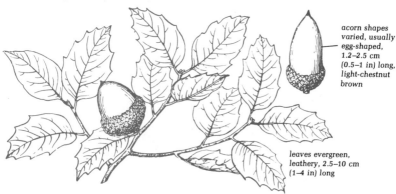

acorn shapes
varied, usually
egg-shaped,
1.2–2.5 cm
(0.5–1 in) long,
light-chestnut
brown

leaves evergreen,
leathery, 2.5–10 cm
(1–4 in) long

Appearance: size and form variable with habitat: shrubby on open montane slopes, but growing 30 m (100 ft) tall in steep upland canyons, with a broad rounded crown, and a trunk diameter up to 2.5 m (8.2 ft). **Bark:** 1.8–3.7 cm (0.7–1.5 in) thick, gray-brown tinged with red, fairly smooth, covered by small, closely pressed scales that eventually flake off. **Branches:** large, spreading to slightly drooping; branchlets slender, flexible or rigid, covered at first with a thick hairy coat of hairs, becoming smooth and light brown to ash-gray. **Winter buds:** broadly egg-shaped, about 3–4 mm (about 0.1–0.2 in) long, sharp pointed at the tip, covered with overlapping dark brown scales. **Leaves:** alternate, *evergreen, 2.5–10 cm (1–4 in) long and 1.2–5 cm (0.5–2 in) wide, broadest near the base,* tapered more gradually at the base than the tip; shape variable; *often toothed or wavy margin,* with 1 or 2 or many spine-like teeth when young; hairy when unfolding, *becoming thick, leathery,* smooth and bright yellowish-green to bluish-green on both surfaces. **Flowers:** male flowers in slender, tawny catkins 5–10 cm (2–4 in) long; female flowers usually solitary, sometimes in short, sparsely flowered spikes. **Fruits:** *acorns, maturing in 1 season, on current year's branchlets,* egg-shaped, 1.2–2.5 cm (0.5–1 in) long, light chestnut brown, the inside of the cup slightly downy; cup thick, covering one-third to one-fourth of the nut, the cup scales thin, triangular, silvery-downy.

Dunn Oak

Quercus dunnii Kellogg

This small, often shrubby, southwestern oak is related to the canyon live oak. Dunn oak occurs as scattered individual trees in the open pinyon-juniper woodland or occasionally along canyon flats from 1,150–2,000 m (3,800–6,600 ft) elevation. Commonly a shrub 2–3 m (7–10 ft) high or sometimes a tree to 7 m (23 ft), Dunn oak has *stiff, wide-spreading branchlets* (twigs of the canyon live oak are not so spreading and are more flexible). Evergreen leaves, closely clustered on the short branchlets, are broad, almost circular in outline to broadest near the base, 2.5–6 cm (1–2.5 in) long, almost as wide, coarsely spine-toothed along the margin, and leathery. The acorns, similar to those of the canyon live oak, have a *bowl-shaped cup.*

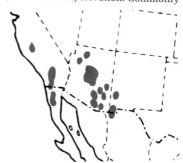

Island Live Oak
Quercus tomentella Engelm.

This relatively small oak is a close relative of the canyon live oak. It is found in deep, narrow canyons and high, windy hillsides of the Channel Islands off the coast of southern California as well as on the Isle of Guadalupe off Baja California in Mexico.

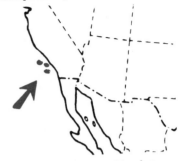

Little information is available on this species. It is too uncommon and isolated to be commercially useful.

Island live oaks are generally shorter than canyon live oaks, reaching only 12 m (40 ft) in height and growing a trunk up to 0.6 m (1.9 ft) in diameter. The form is similar to that of the several live oak species on the mainland. The leaves of the island live oak are broader, being **2.5–10 cm (1–4 in) long and 2.5–5 cm (1–2 in) wide, with either smooth margins or wavy-scalloped lobes** rather than small, sharp-toothed ones. The male flowers are in catkins that vary from 3–35 cm (about 1–14 in) long. The female flowers are similar to those of the canyon live oak. The acorn is 2–3 cm (0.8–1.2 in) long, broadest at the base, full at the tip, covered at the base by a loose-scaled cup often coated with dense, short hairs.

Island Live Oak

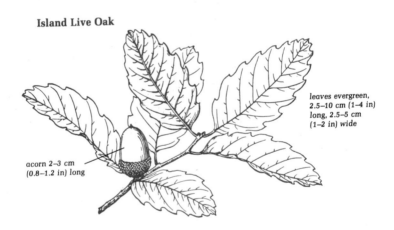

leaves evergreen,
2.5–10 cm (1–4 in)
long, 2.5–5 cm
(1–2 in) wide

acorn 2–3 cm
(0.8–1.2 in) long

Silverleaf Oak
Quercus hypoleucoides A. Camus

Silverleaf oak occurs as a shrub or a medium-size tree in the American southwest and northern Mexico. It grows at 1,500–2,100 m (4,900–6,900 ft) above sea level, often in thick, shrubby clumps and moist, shaded canyons. The tree form may reach up to 18 m (60 ft), with a spreading round-topped crown, although it is usually much smaller (10–12 m; 32–40 ft). It may be found in the mountains, with sycamore and cottonwood, as a component of pine forests. The wood is of no commercial use.

The most striking feature of this species is the leaves, which are thick, leathery, and shiny above, but coated with thick, white wooly hairs on the undersurfaces. They hardly resemble oak leaves at all, **5–10 cm (2–4 in) long and very narrow, unlobed, with smooth margins** and a narrowed tip. The egg-shaped acorns are borne singly or in pairs, sitting directly on the twig or else on a short stalk. They are finely-downy at the tip, dark green and sometimes striped when mature. A thick, **turban-shaped cup covers the lower third of the nut;** the cup scales are round-tipped and often clothed with silver hairs.

Silverleaf Oak

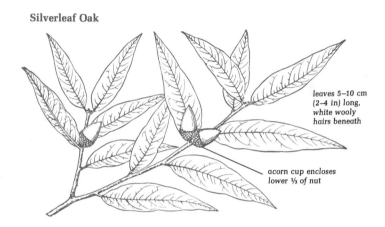

leaves 5–10 cm (2–4 in) long, white wooly hairs beneath

acorn cup encloses lower ⅓ of nut

The Birch Family

Betulaceae

The birch family is a medium-size group of trees and shrubs distributed in 6 genera and about 105 species. They are more common in the Northern Hemisphere, but also occur in parts of the Southern Hemisphere. Five of the 6 genera occur in North America; these are the birches (*Betula*), alders (*Alnus*), hornbeams (*Carpinus*), ironwood (*Ostrya*), and hazel (*Corylus*). Hazels or hazelnuts are the only species that produce large, sweet, edible nuts. The sixth genus occurs only in eastern Asia.

Members of the birch family range in size from dwarf shrubs of the tundra and high mountains to large, lowland trees. Many have little or no economic value, while others are associated with the lumber industry. Several species, including exotic ones imported from Europe, are planted as decorative trees and shrubs. Generally, this family is of limited use to wildlife, although some species, especially birches, are important to many birds and animals.

Members of this family are trees or shrubs, usually with thin, smooth bark. The leaves are simple, alternate, deciduous, and toothed along the margins. The tiny flowers lack the conspicuous showy parts of many other flowers, and they are grouped together in short to elongated clusters commonly called catkins. The flower-containing catkins are either male or female, although both types occur on the same tree.

The fruits are tiny to large, 1-seeded, sometimes winged and covered or enclosed by small to large bracts. In birches and alders the bracts and fruits are grouped into a dry, cone-like structure. In hazelnuts, hornbeams, and ironwood, the small to large nut is enclosed in a pair of larger, green bracts.

Key to Birch Genera

A. Fruits consisting of a small to large wingless nut, partially or completely enclosed in 2 or more leaf-like bracts.

    1. Seeds smooth, enclosed in bladder-like sacs and grouped in clusters on short, drooping stems   **Hop hornbeam, p. 386**

    2. Seeds ribbed, covered by larger, 2- to 3-lobed leaf-like bracts   **Hornbeams, p. 389**

American Hornbeam

B. Fruits consisting of tiny usually winged seeds, not enclosed, although covered by a bract, but grouped with bracts in a cone-like structure.

    1. Female catkins solitary, the scales 3 lobed or unlobed, thin, papery, and falling away at maturity   **Birches, p. 391**

Yellow Bir•

    2. Female catkins usually 3 to 6 clustered, the scales 3–5 lobed, becoming woody at maturity and covering the fruit   **Alders, p. 403**

Mountain Alder

The Hop Hornbeam Genus   *Ostrya* Scop.

The hop hornbeams are a small genus of only 8 species distinct from those in the hornbeam genus. One occurs in Mexico, another in Europe and western Asia, 3 in eastern Asia and Japan, and 3 in the U.S. and Canada. The eastern hop hornbeam is a common, widespread small tree; the Knowlton hop hornbeam occurs in a restricted area in the Southwest. The Chisos hop hornbeam (*Ostrya chisosensis*) is usually a shrub, rarely a tree, of the Trans-Pecos region of Texas.

Hop hornbeams are small, deciduous trees with rough, scaly bark. The winter buds are short, broadest near the base, pointed at the tip, and covered with several overlapping scales. The leaves are alternate on the branchlets, usually broadest below or near the middle, doubly-toothed along the margin, and with a short leafstalk. The male flowers are produced in slender, upright catkins near the tips of the branchlets. Both sexes are found on the same tree. The fruits are grouped in clusters on short, drooping stems. Each seed is enclosed in a bladder-like sac.

Key to Hop Hornbeam Species

A. Leaves twice as long as broad, long-pointed at the tip; fruiting cluster 4–5 cm (1.6–2 in) long; trees of eastern North America
Eastern hop hornbeam, p. 387

Eastern Hop Hornbeam

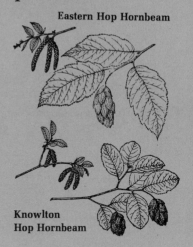

B. Leaves less than twice as long as broad, rounded to short pointed at the tip; fruiting cluster 2.5–4 cm (1–1.6 in) long; trees of southwestern U.S.
Knowlton hop hornbeam, p. 388

Knowlton Hop Hornbeam

Eastern Hop Hornbeam   *Ostrya virginiana* (Mill.) K. Koch

This small, upright tree is widespread in southern Canada, eastern, midwestern, and southeastern U.S., and it extends into northern Mexico. It grows in a variety of areas from moist, fertile soils to sandy sites, doing best on well-drained slopes and ridges. It grows in association with taller-growing sugar maple, beech, yellow birch, basswood, American elm, and several of the hickories. Eastern hop hornbeam is one of the understory trees, along with American hornbeam, redbud, alder, sumac, elder, bittersweet, and grape. The names "ironwood" and "hornbeam" are commonly used for both the eastern hop hornbeam and the American hornbeam.

This tree has a medium rate of growth and is short-lived. Flowers appear in spring, although the clusters of immature male flowers are visible in winter. Fruits mature by fall, and the sacs containing the seeds drop in winter. Eastern hop hornbeam is the only member of this genus that is widespread and of known use to wildlife, though its value to wildlife is limited. Whitetail deer browse on twigs and leaves; various songbirds, grouse, and squirrels eat the seeds, buds, and catkins.

The wood is light brown, tinged with red or white, heavy, and extremely hard. Yet the tree is not large enough for the wood to be of commercial importance. It is used locally for tool handles.

Appearance: small tree reaching 7–12 m (23–40 ft), occasionally taller, with a wide-spreading crown; trunk straight, 13–25 cm (5.1–9.9 in) in diameter. **Bark:** thin, to 4 mm (between 0.1–0.2 in) thick, *developing into narrow, plate-like strips that may peel away from the trunk.* **Branches:** long, slender, often drooping at the ends, light green and covered with fine hairs when young, becoming dark reddish-brown and

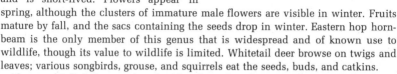

Eastern Hop Hornbeam

leaves dark-yellowish
green, 7–12 cm
(2.8–4.8 in) long,
finely toothed

catkins of
male flowers

Spring Branchlet

fruit cluster, each sac
containing a flattened seed

**Late-Summer or
Fall Branchlet**

smooth. **Winter buds:** 3–4 mm (0.1–0.2 in) long, broadest near the base and tapering to a pointed tip, covered with overlapping, slightly hairy, light reddish-brown scales. **Leaves:** alternate, deciduous, *7–12 cm (2.8–4.8 in) long, 3.8–5 cm (1.5–2 in) wide,* widest near the middle to uniformly wide, tapering to a narrow base and to a long slender point at the tip, *with numerous sharp teeth along the margin,* thin but tough, *dark yellowish-green* above, paler beneath and with tufts of hairs in the junctions of the main veins; the leafstalks 3–4 mm (0.1–0.2 in) long, stout, hairy. **Flowers:** male and female flowers in separate clusters, with both kinds on the same tree; male flowers in slender, cylinder-shaped catkins from 1.5–5 cm (0.6–2 in) long when mature, light reddish-brown; female flowers in slender, light green and often reddish-tinged catkins 5–8 mm (0.2–0.3 in) long; both male and female catkins produced at or near the tips of the branchlets. **Fruits:** *grouped in elongated clusters 4–5 cm (1.6–2 in) long on short drooping stems,* the *seeds flattened, 5–8 mm (0.2–0.3 in) long, each seed enclosed in a papery, sac-like bag,* the bags to 2 cm (0.8 in) long, green turning brown at maturity.

Knowlton Hop Hornbeam — *Ostrya knowltonii* Cov.

Unlike the common and widespread eastern hop hornbeam, Knowlton hop hornbeam is a rare tree. It occurs in canyons at 1,500–2,700 m (4,900–8,900 ft) elevation, 1 population in northern Arizona and southeastern Utah and the other in the Trans Pecos area of Texas and adjoining southeastern New Mexico. It grows in the area known as the pinyon pine belt. This species can be distinguished from its eastern relative in that it has shorter fruit.

Knowlton hop hornbeam is a small tree with a short, soon branching trunk. The *leaves* are *2.5–5 cm (1–2 in) long, 2.5–4 cm (1–1.6 in) wide,* and *rounded to short pointed at the tip.* The catkins bearing the flowers are 1 to 3 clustered at the tips of the branchlets. **Fruits** are an elongated *cluster (2.5–4 cm — 1–1.6 in — long)* of sac-like structures. Each sac encloses a single flattened seed.

Knowlton Hop Hornbeam

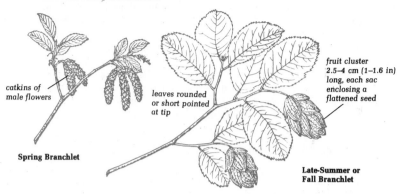

catkins of
male flowers

leaves rounded
or short pointed
at tip

fruit cluster
2.5–4 cm (1–1.6 in)
long, each sac
enclosing a
flattened seed

Spring Branchlet

**Late-Summer or
Fall Branchlet**

The Hornbeam Genus

Carpinus L.

There are perhaps 25 species of hornbeams distributed in Europe, Asia, and in North and Central America. Only 1 species occurs in North America, the common and widespread American hornbeam. Our native species is closely related to the European hornbeam (*Carpinus betulus* L.), which is sometimes planted as a street tree or used in landscaping. The European hornbeam has smooth buds and 3 to 5 veins on the leaflike bracts around the seeds; the American hornbeam has a hairy bud and 5 to 7 veins on the bract.

Hornbeams are small to medium-size deciduous trees or shrubs with smooth to scaly gray bark. Winter buds are small, broadest near the base, tapering to a pointed tip, and are covered with overlapping scales. The leaves are alternate on the branchlets, often egg-shaped, and with numerous fine teeth along the margin. Male and female flowers are in separate catkins on the same tree. The catkins containing the male flowers are slender and hang; while the slender, shorter catkins containing the female flowers are produced at the tips of the branchlets. The fruit is a ribbed nut that is covered by a much larger leaf-like bract.

American Hornbeam

Carpinus caroliniana Walt.

The American hornbeam, also known as ironwood or blue beech, is an attractive small tree in the mixed deciduous forests throughout southern Canada, and eastern and midwestern U.S., and also grows in Mexico, Guatemala, and Belize. It usually occurs in the shade of taller hardwoods in deep, rich, moist soils of bottomlands, swamps, and river margins. It grows in association with northern red oak, sweet gum, mockernut hickory, bur oak, sugar maple, and basswood. American hornbeam also grows with the smaller hop hornbeam, alder, redbud, and sumac.

This tree is slow-growing and short-lived. It flowers in early spring, and the fruits mature by autumn. It produces good seed crops every 3 to 5 years, with lighter crops in intervening years. Male and female flowers are produced in separate catkins, but both occur on the same tree. The seeds, buds, and catkins are of minor importance to the birds, squirrels, and rodents that eat them. Whitetail deer occasionally feed on the young twigs and leaves.

The tree's name, "horn" (meaning tough) and "beam" (similar to the German "baum" for tree), accurately describes the wood, which is close-grained, very hard, and heavy. The pioneers used it to make bowls and dishes because it is not subject to cracking or splitting. It was also used for levers, handles of hammers and other striking tools. It is not important commercially because lumber cannot be obtained in sufficient quantities from such a small tree.

American Hornbeam

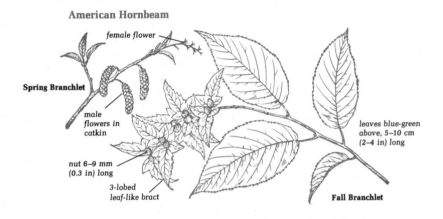

Spring Branchlet — female flower
male flowers in catkin
nut 6–9 mm (0.3 in) long
3-lobed leaf-like bract
leaves blue-green above, 5–10 cm (2–4 in) long
Fall Branchlet

Appearance: small tree 4–8 m, rarely to 12 (13–26 ft, rarely to 40), with a rounded bushy crown; *trunk short, often crooked,* soon branching, *characteristically and irregularly fluted,* the *trunk resembling the muscles in a flexed arm,* 10–30 cm in diameter, rarely to 60 (4–12 in, rarely to 24). **Bark: *thin,*** 2–4 cm (0.8–1.6 in) *slate gray* to light grayish-brown, sometimes marked with wide, dark brown bands around the trunk. **Branches:** short, tough, spreading; branchlets slender, tough, sometimes hanging near the tips, light green and covered with long hairs when young, becoming darker and finally pale gray and smooth with age. **Winter buds:** 2–4 mm (about 0.1–0.2 in) long, broadest near the base, tapering to a point at the tip, covered with reddish-brown, overlapping scales. **Leaves:** alternate, deciduous, *5–10 cm (2–4 in) long, 2.5–4.6 cm (1–1.8 in) wide,* broadest just below the middle, often slightly curved, rounded or wedge-shaped at the base, sometimes unequal, tapering to a long pointed tip, *with a double row of numerous, small, sharp-pointed teeth along the margin, blue-green* and smooth above (hairy on very young leaves), light yellowish-green and smooth beneath except for tufts of white hairs in the junctions of the main vein; the leafstalks slender, 6–9 mm (about 0.2–0.3 in) long. **Flowers:** male and female flowers in separate catkins; male flowers in slender, hanging catkins 2.5–4 cm (1–1.6 in) long, green tinged with red; female flowers in hairy catkins 1–1.5 cm (0.4–0.6 in) long, produced at the tips of the branchlets. **Fruits:** a *small ribbed nut 6–9 mm (about 0.3 in) long,* broadest near the base and pointed at the tip, *lying at the base of a 3-lobed, leaf-like bract,* the *bracts* 2.2–3 cm (0.9–1.2 in) long, *clustered together on a hanging stalk,* the stalks 10–15 cm (4–6 in) long.

The Birch Genus

Betula L.

There are about 50 species of trees and shrubs in the birch genus. They are widely scattered throughout the temperate and subarctic regions of the Northern Hemisphere, and develop into vast forests in the far north. Eight of the 15 species that are native to North America are trees. They range from the Arctic Circle to Texas. The remaining species are shrubs. Occurring from sea level up to elevations of about 1,200 m (3,940 ft) in the southern Appalachian Mountains, birches generally prefer well-drained sandy soils in cool areas, particularly along cold lakes and streams. They establish themselves rapidly on fire-cleared or logged-out lands.

Birches are not of major importance to wildlife, although a considerable number of animals feed on their variable parts. Several species of grouse eat the buds, catkins, and seeds, while a number of songbirds (especially redpoll and pine siskins) eat the seeds. Browsing and bark-eating mammals, including moose, deer, beaver, hare, and porcupine, also feed on birches.

Long before the arrival of western Europeans, birches had been of great use to North American man. Of course, northeastern Indians paddled birchbark canoes. Today three species of birch (yellow, sweet, and paper) are of commercial use; their lumber is mainly used for interior wood finishes and low-grade furniture, although in the past it was also important in shipbuilding and wheel-making, and for log houses. Some species are planted as ornamentals because of their attractive bark and foliage. Two commonly cultivated species, the European birch and the white, have been widely planted in North America.

Most birches are medium-size, fast-growing, relatively short-lived trees, although some may reach 30 m (100 ft) in height and 150 years or more in age. Some species typically grow in clumps, while others are solitary. The branches are slender and lightly drooping, and form a rounded, open crown. The graceful, sometimes curved trunks are covered with a thin bark marked characteristically with lens-shaped pores (lenticels). Some of the species are known for their peeling bark. The leaves are deciduous and simple, usually with a double row of fine teeth along the margins, and vary from oval to triangular in shape. They have pointed tips, rounded or flattened bases, and short leafstalks. The male and female flowers occur separately in hanging clusters or catkins, which are found on the same tree. Large amounts of tiny winged seeds are produced every 1 to 4 years.

Key to Birch Species

A. Bark dark, reddish-brown, yellowish-brown, to almost black.

    1. Bark and twigs with a wintergreen fragrance when cut or broken.

        a. Leaves with 8–12 pairs of veins; medium-size trees to 22 m (72 ft).

            (1) Bark dark red to almost black, turning grayish on old trees; scales of the fruiting cones smooth, 6–12 mm (0.2–0.5 in) long; eastern and northeastern North America   **Sweet birch, p. 393**

                    (Continued)

Sweet Birch

(2) Bark reddish-brown turning dull yellow or yellowish-brown, peeling somewhat in loose, ragged sheets; scales of the fruiting cone hairy, 5–7 mm (0.2–0.3 in) long; northeastern North America **Yellow birch, p. 394**

b. Leaves with 4–6 pairs of veins; small tree or shrub to 8 m (26 ft), very rare, Virginia **Ashe's birch, p. 395**

Yellow Birch

2. Bark and twigs without a wintergreen fragrance when cut or broken.

a. Branchlets covered near the tip with numerous small glands; trees of Rocky Mountains and western Canada **Water birch, p. 396**

b. Branchlets smooth, shiny, no glands present; trees of eastern U.S. **River birch, p. 397**

Water Birch

B. Bark creamy white, pinkish-white or gray.

1. Leaves hairy on the lower surface.

a. Leaves 5–13 cm (2–5.2 in) long, long pointed at the tip; winter buds only slightly or not resinous; native trees of northern North America **Paper birch, p. 398**

b. Leaves 3–7 cm (1.2–2.8 in) long, pointed at the tip; winter buds shiny due to resinous coating; introduced species from Europe **European birch, p. 399**

River Birch

2. Leaves smooth, hairless beneath when mature.

a. Bark dull gray to grayish-white, smooth and not peeling; trees of northeastern North America **Gray birch, p. 400**

b. Bark white to pinkish-white, peeling away.

(1) Leaves 6–10 cm (2.4–4 in) long, rounded at the base; native trees of eastern North America **Blue birch, p. 401**

(2) Leaves 3–5 cm (1.2–2 in) long; squared or truncated at the base; introduced trees from Europe and Asia **European white birch, p. 402**

Paper Birch

Gray Birch

Sweet Birch, Cherry Birch

Betula lenta L.

Sweet birch is a medium-size tree of the eastern woods. It ranges from southern Maine, southern Quebec, and southern Ontario south through the Appalachian Mountains into northern Alabama and Georgia. Sweet birch prefers deep, rich, moist, well-drained soils, although it also grows in rocky soils or even on boulders. It occurs from sea level along the New England coast to upwards of 1,400 m (4,600 ft) in the southern Appalachians. It can be found both in woods and in the open and in uplands on moist, protected, north- or east-facing slopes. This birch is never found in pure stands but is always scattered among such species as white pine, hemlock, yellow birch, sugar maple, beech, black cherry, white oak, basswood, 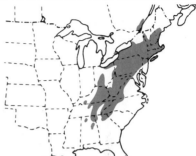 and tulip tree (yellow poplar). Two traits readily distinguish this species: the strong wintergreen aroma of broken twigs or leaves (a feature shared to a lesser degree by the yellow birch) and its close, shiny, mahogany-red bark on young trees, which is similar to that of the cherry tree—hence one of its common names.

Sweet birch is a moderately fast-growing tree, reaching full size in 80 to 100 years. Catkins containing the male flowers develop in late summer and fall and mature by spring; while female flowers are not evident until spring. Both flowers and leaves open in spring, and the seeds, which ripen in late summer and early fall, are spread by the wind. Seed production starts when the tree is about 40 years old, and good crops are produced every year or two. Several animals use sweet birch as a food source: grouse eat the catkins, buds, and seeds; songbirds feed on the seeds; whitetail deer, moose, porcupines, and beavers browse the twigs and young leaves.

Among the birches, sweet birch is second to yellow birch in economic importance as lumber. On exposure to air, the strong, hard wood deepens in color and has been passed off as mahogany. Sweet birch was formerly the source of oil of wintergreen, for which pioneer families would wreak wholesale destruction on young trees and saplings; fortunately, this oil can now be manufactured artificially. A beer can be made from the sap by tapping the trees in late winter and allowing the sap to ferment with corn. Of major birches, sweet birch is the densest, at 40½ pounds per cubic foot air-dry. It is excellent fuel.

Appearance: medium-size trees usually to 18 m (60 ft), occasionally taller with a rounded crown; trunk tall, straight, 0.3–1 m (1–3.3 ft) in diameter, rarely larger. **Bark:** 1.2–2 cm (0.5–0.8 in) thick with age, *smooth and with prominent horizontal branch scars and pores (lenticels),* developing into irregular plates with age, *dark red to almost black on young trees,* becoming grayish on old trees. **Branches:** slender, spreading; *branchlets slender,* slightly hairy when young, light reddish-brown, *with a strong odor and mild taste of wintergreen when broken.* **Winter buds:** 5–7 mm (0.2–0.3 in) long, broadest near the base and tapering to a sharp point, covered with loose, overlapping, chestnut-brown scales. **Leaves:** alternate, deciduous, *6–15 cm (2.4–5.9 in) long, 4–8 cm (1.6–3.2 in) wide,* broadest near the base, gradually narrowing and often heart-shaped at the base, pointed at the tip, *with a double row of fine, sharp-pointed teeth along the margin,* with a thin papery texture, deep green and smooth above, paler and with fine hairs on the veins on the lower surface; the leafstalks stout, deeply grooved on the upper surface, 13–25 mm (0.5–1 in) long. **Flowers:** male and

Sweet Birch

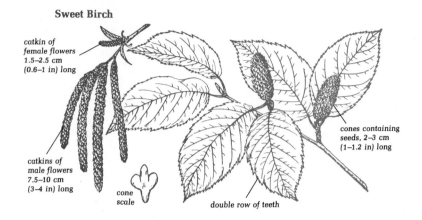

catkin of
female flowers
1.5–2.5 cm
(0.6–1 in) long

cones containing
seeds, 2–3 cm
(1–1.2 in) long

catkins of
male flowers
7.5–10 cm
(3–4 in) long

cone
scale

double row of teeth

female flowers in separate catkins on same tree; male flowers in slender, hanging, bright reddish-brown catkins 7.5–10 cm (3–4 in) long; female flowers in pale green catkins 1.5–2.5 cm (0.6–1 in) long, produced at the tips of the branchlets. **Fruits:** *upright cones 2.5–3 cm (1–1.2 in) long and about 1.2 cm (0.5 in) wide, the cones consisting of numerous scales,* each *enclosing a tiny winged seed.*

Yellow Birch

Betula alleghaniensis Britton
(synonym: *B. lutea* Michx. f.)

Yellow birch is the most important member of the North American birches. It is an attractive northern tree of southeastern Canada, northeastern U.S., and the Lake States and extends southward into the Appalachian Mountains. Basically a tree of lower elevations, this birch can be found above 1,000 m (3,300 ft) elevation only in the southern Appalachians. It is usually found in moist, well-drained soils. But in the southern portion of its range, it can grow in cooler marshlands. Conifers commonly growing in association include eastern hemlock, red spruce, balsam fir, and eastern white pine. Common hardwood associates include sugar maple and American beech.

Growth is slow, and the trees are long-lived for birches — about 200 years. They require 35 to 40 years to reach flowering age, and they usually produce large seed crops annually. Flowering is in spring, and the seeds mature in autumn. Like other birches, yellow birch is of only moderate value to wildlife; small birds and rodents eat the tiny seeds.

Yellow birch is an important source of hardwood lumber. The dark-brown to reddish-brown wood is close-grained, hard, heavy, and strong; thus, tall, straight-trunked trees are in demand. The wood is used for interior finishes, veneers, tool handles, snowshoe frames, and sledges.

Appearance: medium-size tree, 10–22 m (32–72 ft), rarely taller, with a rounded head; trunk tall, straight, 0.6–1.2 m (1.9–3.9 ft) in diameter, rarely larger. **Bark:** to 2 cm

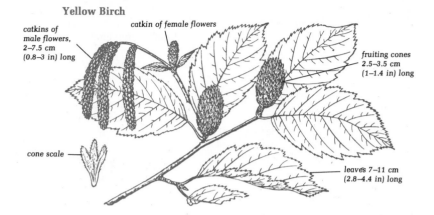

Yellow Birch

catkins of male flowers, 2–7.5 cm (0.8–3 in) long

catkin of female flowers

fruiting cones 2.5–3.5 cm (1–1.4 in) long

cone scale

leaves 7–11 cm (2.8–4.4 in) long

(0.8 in) thick on older trees, peeling into strips on young trees, *but developing ragged-edged, broken plates on older trees, reddish-brown turning dull yellow or yellowish-brown with age.* **Branches:** slender, spreading; branchlets slender, often drooping at the tips, light orange-brown and covered with hairs when young, turning darker and becoming smooth with age. **Winter buds:** end bud absent, side buds 5–7 mm (0.2–0.3 in) long, broadest near the base and tapering to a sharp point, covered with overlapping, somewhat sticky, chestnut-brown scales. **Leaves:** alternate, deciduous, *7–11 cm (2.8–4.4 in) long, 3–5 cm (1.2–2 in) wide, broadest near the base to uniformly wide,* rounded or unevenly heart-shaped at the base and pointed at the tip, with a double row of sharp-pointed teeth along the margin, dull green and smooth above, pale yellowish-green and with fine hairs on the veins on the lower surface; the leafstalks stout, hairy, 1.5–2.5 cm (0.6–1 in) long. **Flowers:** male and female flowers in separate catkins on the same tree; male flowers in slender hanging catkins 2–7.5 cm (0.8–3 in) long; female catkins erect to nearly erect, 1.5–2 cm (0.6–0.8 in) long, produced at or near the tips of the branchlets. **Fruits:** *broad cones 2.5–3.5 cm (1–1.4 in) long, erect,* often persisting into winter, composed of numerous 3-lobed scales, each scale covering a tiny, narrowly winged seed.

Ashe's Birch   *Betula uber* (Ashe) Fern.

This small birch, known only from one county in Virginia, was considered to be extinct until it was rediscovered in 1975. This rediscovery received national attention because of the interest in the Endangered Species Act of 1973, a law that protects threatened and endangered species. Very little is known about this birch, but considerable effort is being made to ensure the survival of the few surviving plants—and the species.

Ashe's birch is a *small tree to 8 m (26 ft) with dark bark.* The bark and branches have a wintergreen fragrance when cut or broken. The deciduous *leaves* are *1.8–2.4 cm (0.7–1 in) long, almost rounded in*

shape, broadly rounded at the base and tip, coarsely toothed along the margin and smooth *(lacking hairs on the blade).* The male and female flowers are produced in separate catkins and are similar in appearance to those of other birches.

Water Birch

Betula occidentalis Hook.
(synonym: *B. fontinalis* Sarg.)

Water birch is a large shrub or small tree of the Rocky Mountains and most of the forested areas of western Canada. It is commonly found along rivers, streams, and springs, but occasionally grows in drier sites. Because of its preference for wetter sites, water birch grows along with many species of alder, willows, and poplars. It does hybridize with the paper birch with the resulting offspring displaying intermediate characters of both parent species.

The trees mature at an early age, usually producing seed by 10 to 12 years. Water birch does not reach sufficient size to be of use as a lumber. Locally it is used for firewood and for fence posts.

Appearance: shrub or small tree to 12 m (40 ft), with an irregular broad, open

Water Birch

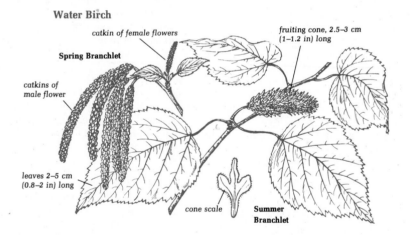

catkin of female flowers

fruiting cone, 2.5–3 cm (1–1.2 in) long

Spring Branchlet

catkins of male flower

leaves 2–5 cm (0.8–2 in) long

cone scale

Summer Branchlet

crown; trunk short, curved, to 35 cm (14 in) in diameter. **Bark:** thin, to 1 cm (0.4 in) thick, smooth, *almost black on young trees, turning reddish-brown,* with conspicuous horizontal pores. **Branches:** slender, upright; *branchlets slender,* reddish-brown, *covered with numerous glands* (appearing as small bumps). **Winter buds:** 6–8 mm (0.2–0.3 in) long, broadest near the base and tapering to a pointed tip, covered with overlapping greenish-brown scales. **Leaves:** alternate, deciduous, *2–5 cm (0.8–2 in) long, 1.5–2.5 cm (0.6–1 in) wide, broadest near the base, with a rounded to wedge-shaped base and a blunt to sharp-pointed tip, with a double row of fine, sharp-pointed teeth* except entire near the base, texture thin and firm, dark greenish-yellow and shiny above, paler and gland-dotted beneath, sometimes with tufts of hairs in the junctions of the veins; the leafstalks stout, hairy, flattened on the upper surface, 0.8–1.2 cm (0.3–0.5 in) long. **Flowers:** male and female flowers in separate catkins on same tree; male flowers in slender catkins 5–6.5 cm (2–2.6 in) long, produced at or near the tips of the branchlets. **Fruits:** hanging or spreading cones 2.5–3 cm (1–1.2 in) long, the cones consisting of numerous 3-lobed scales, each scale enclosing a tiny winged seed.

River Birch

Betula nigra L.

River birch is a medium-size tree of the eastern U.S., extending from southern New Hampshire to northern Florida. It is a lowland species, occurring mainly along streams, rivers, ponds, and swamps. Deep rich soils support the largest trees, but river

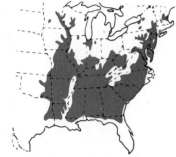

birch also grows in clay soils typical of river bottomlands. This common birch reaches its greatest size in the Mississippi River Valley and its tributaries. It grows in association with other lowland trees such as sycamore, silver maple, red maple, cottonwood, willows, and elms.

The growth rate is moderate to slow, with the tallest trees occurring in the southern part of the range. Male flower clusters appear in mid to late summer but do not open until the following spring. The

fruiting clusters containing the seeds do not mature until fall. River birch is of limited value to wildlife. Whitetail deer browse the young twigs and buds, while grouse, turkeys, many small birds, and rodents eat the abundant, but tiny, seeds.

The brown wood is close-grained, light, strong, and hard but with many knots due to the numerous branches along the trunk. As a result, it is of little value as lumber but is used occasionally for furniture and tool handles. River birch is used as a street tree in the Pacific Northwest and as an ornamental landscape tree in the Northeast.

Appearance: small to medium-size tree 15–25 m (49–82 ft), with a broad spreading

River Birch

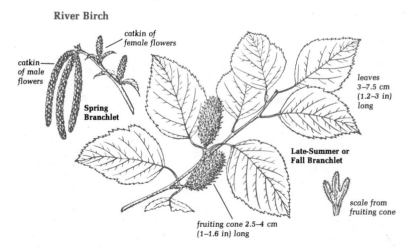

catkin of male flowers

catkin of female flowers

Spring Branchlet

Late-Summer or Fall Branchlet

leaves 3–7.5 cm (1.2–3 in) long

scale from fruiting cone

fruiting cone 2.5–4 cm (1–1.6 in) long

crown; trunk short, thick, soon branching, 0.3–1 m (1–3.3 ft) in diameter, rarely larger. **Bark:** thin on young trees, to 2.5 cm (1 in) thick on older trees, developing coarse scales and marked with narrow, lengthwise pores, *light reddish-brown to silvery gray.* **Branches:** numerous, slender, spreading; *branchlets dark red, shiny, smooth,* with a thin, peeling gray bark produced after the second or third year, no wintergreen odor when broken. **Winter buds:** 5–7 mm (0.2–0.3 in) long, broadest near the base and pointed at the tip, covered with thin, overlapping, downy or slightly sticky scales. **Leaves:** alternate, deciduous, *3–7.5 cm (1.2–3 in) long, 2.5–5 cm (1–2 in) wide, broad and wedge-shaped at the base and elongated at the tip,* with a double row of small, sharp-pointed teeth along the margin, with a thick tough texture, dark green and shiny above, paler and finely hairy to slightly sticky on the lower surface; the leafstalks slender, slightly flattened, hairy, 1–1.5 cm (0.4–0.6 in) long. **Flowers:** male and female flowers in separate catkins on the same tree; male flowers in hanging clusters of slender, shiny, dark brown catkins 5–7.5 cm (2–3 in) long; female flowers in upright, bright green catkins 6–10 mm (0.2–0.4 in) long. **Fruits:** *cylinder-shaped, hanging cones 2.5–4 cm (1–1.6 in) long,* composed of numerous 3-lobed scales, each scale enclosing a single, tiny, winged seed.

Paper Birch

Betula papyrifera Marsh.

This attractive, small to medium-size tree is the most widely distributed birch in North America. It is primarily a Canadian species, extending across Canada and Alaska and southward into the northern U.S. It can be found in a few isolated spots in

the high Appalachian Mountains in West Virginia and North Carolina, and as far south in the West as the Front Range near Boulder, Colorado. Paper birch grows in a wide range of soil and moisture conditions, but it does best on well-drained sandy loam soils. This is one of the first trees to establish itself on areas ravaged by fire. In wetter sites, paper birch may even form pure stands. In the southern parts of its range, paper birch usually occurs in higher and cooler sites, while further north

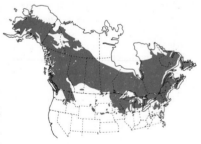

it is found at lower elevations and often on north and east-facing slopes. In eastern North America, it grows in association with many other trees including several species of pine and spruce, aspen, gray and yellow birch, hemlock, sugar maple, northern red oak, and cherry. The commonly associated trees in western North America are white and black spruce and poplar. The shape of the leaf and size and shape of the trees are variable, so several varieties are recognized.

Paper birch is a relatively fast-growing tree that matures and begins to produce seed at about 15 years of age. The flowers in the male and female catkins open in early spring, and the fruits containing the tiny winged seeds mature by late summer or early fall. Seeds are produced every year. The trees are easily killed by fire, but will quickly send up new sprouts from the old root systems.

Paper birch is important to wildlife. The twigs serve as browse for moose and deer in winter, while beaver cut and feed on the inner bark. Grouse eat the buds and small birds and rodents feed on the tiny seeds.

The pale brown wood is strong and hard and is used for veneer and pulpwood, and in making specialty items such as souvenirs. This tree is widely known for its use on birchbark canoes. Here the light but tough bark is stretched over a framework of white cedar, stitched together and sealed with pine or balsam resin. Birch sap can be collected and boiled down for the syrup.

Appearance: small to medium-size trees or shrubs, to 25 m (82 ft), with a rounded to pyramid-shaped crown; trunk straight, to 0.6 m (1.9 ft) in diameter. **Bark:** thin, up to 1.5 cm (0.6 in) thick on older trees, *smooth,* reddish-brown on young trees turning

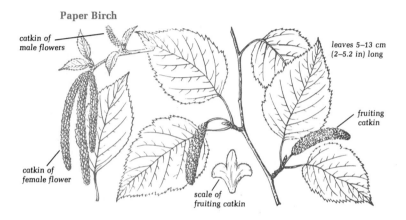

Paper Birch

catkin of
male flowers

leaves 5–13 cm
(2–5.2 in) long

fruiting
catkin

catkin of
female flower

scale of
fruiting catkin

cream-white, readily peeling in large pieces, sometimes exposing a reddish-orange inner bark, marked with prominent branch scars. **Branches:** slender, usually spreading and drooping; branchlets slender, turning dark reddish-brown, smooth or sometimes hairy, *lacking a wintergreen odor when broken.* **Winter buds:** 5–7 mm (0.2–0.3 in) long, narrow, broadest near the base and tapering to a blunt or pointed tip, covered with smooth, dark brown to almost black scales. **Leaves:** alternate, deciduous, *5–13 cm (2–5.2 in) long, 2.5–5 cm (1–2 in) wide, often triangular to egg-shaped, pointed to long pointed at the tip, irregularly toothed along the margin except close to the base of the leaf,* texture thick and firm, dark green and smooth above, pale yellowish-green and smooth or softly downy beneath; the leafstalks stout, smooth or hairy, 1.2–2 cm (0.5–0.8 in) long. **Flowers:** male and female flowers in separate catkins on same tree; male flowers in hanging, brown catkins 7–10 cm (2.8–4 in) long; female flowers in slender, erect greenish catkins 2.5–3 cm (1–1.2 in) long, produced at or near the tips of the branchlets. **Fruits:** drooping or hanging cone-like heads, elongated, 2.5–3.5 cm (1–1.4 in) long, the cones consisting of numerous scales, each enclosing a tiny winged seed.

European Birch
Betula pendula Roth
(synonym: *Betula alba,* in part)

European birch is a common small tree planted in front of homes and businesses in urban and suburban regions, especially in the Eastern U.S. This is the ornamental birch often seen in nurseries and garden centers, usually with multiple trunks. This birch is native to Europe and ranges from Italy and the Balkan Peninsula north beyond the Arctic Circle. It is short-lived and tolerates poor soil conditions typical of many urban and suburban areas. A common insect pest, the bronze birch leaf borer, often disfigures many of the leaves. Other horticultural selections of this birch have also been introduced including the cut-leaved birch and a strongly weeping form.

This birch grows to 15 m (50 ft) and has a rounded crown and spreading to drooping branch system. The slender trunk is covered with a **white, peeling bark.** The deciduous leaves are 3–7 cm (1.2–2.8 in) long, triangular-shaped, pointed at the tip and squared to tapering at the base. The male flowers are produced in long, slender catkins 4–9 cm (1.6–3.6 in) long. The fruits are **cone-like structures 2–4 cm (0.8–1.6 in) long.** They are composed of numerous hairy to smooth 3-lobed bracts, each bract with the lateral lobes larger than the end one. A tiny seed is enclosed by each bract.

European Birch

catkin of female flowers

catkin of male flowers

fruiting cone containing many tiny, winged seeds

leaves 3–7 cm (1.2–2.8 in) long

cone scale

Fall Branchlet

Spring Branchlet

Gray Birch — *Betula populifolia* Marsh.

Gray birch is a small tree, primarily of the Atlantic Seaboard from southeastern Canada to Virginia but also occurring as far west as Indiana. It grows on wet or dry, sandy or gravelly soils. It is a pioneer species that covers large areas of abandoned fields and burned-over lands. The trees do well in poor, almost sterile, soils and even reproduce abundantly and spread in these areas. Gray birch often forms nearly pure stands in cleared areas. It often grows with pitch pine, scrub oak, and white pine.

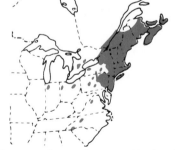

The trees are moderately fast-growing and short-lived, rarely living more than 50 years. They begin flowering at an early age, usually around 10 years, and good seed crops can be produced every year. Like most other birches, gray birch is of limited value to wildlife. Grouse and squirrels eat the young flower clusters and buds, while songbirds and smaller rodents eat the tiny seeds. Whitetail deer browse the young twigs and leaves, especially in late winter and early spring.

This is an economically unimportant tree. The light reddish-brown wood is light, soft, and weak. It has been used locally in turning and as firewood. As the trees reach maturity, they often lean, and many are uprooted when the heavy wet snows of late winter become too much for the shallow roots to withstand.

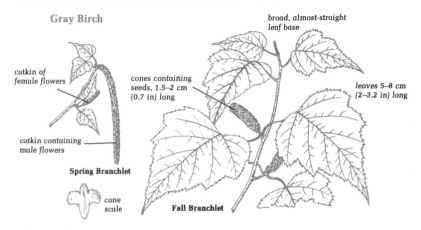

Gray Birch

catkin of
female flowers

cones containing
seeds, 1.5–2 cm
(0.7 in) long

broad, almost-straight
leaf base

leaves 5–8 cm
(2–3.2 in) long

catkin containing
male flowers

Spring Branchlet

cone
scale

Fall Branchlet

Appearance: small tree to 10 m (33 ft), rarely taller, with a narrow, open, irregular cone-shaped crown; trunk straight or curved, often spindly, to 15 cm (5.9 in) in diameter, *often growing in clumps or small groves.* **Bark: thin, smooth** and *not peeling, with black triangular patches below the bases of the branches,* dark brown at first, later turning *dull grayish to almost chalky white.* **Branches:** slender, spreading; branchlets slender, often drooping near the tips, orangish-brown to gray and with scattered, pale, warty glands. **Winter buds:** 6–8 mm (0.2–0.3 in) long, broadest near the base and tapering to a pointed tip, covered with a few overlapping, light grayish-brown, often gummy or hairy scales. **Leaves:** alternate, deciduous, *5–8 cm (2–3.2 in) long, 3–5 cm (1.2–2 in) broad, triangular in shape, with a broad, almost straight base* and a narrow pointed tip (resembling an aspen leaf), with a double row of 2 distinct sizes of teeth along the margin; leaves with a papery texture, dark green, shiny, and somewhat rough on the upper surface, shiny, paler green and smooth on the lower surface; the leafstalks slender, 1.8–2.5 cm (0.7–1 in) long, allowing the leaves to hang and readily tremble in the slightest breeze. **Flowers:** male and female flowers in separate catkins on the same tree; male flowers in slender, hanging, solitary or paired catkins 6–10 cm (2.4–4 in) long; female flowers in erect to almost erect, slender, pale green catkins 1–1.4 cm (0.4–0.6 in) long. **Fruits:** spreading or drooping cones, the *cones 1.5–2 cm (0.7 in) long,* 8–10 mm (0.3–0.4 in) wide, the cones consisting of *numerous 3-lobed hairy scales, each enclosing a tiny, broadly winged seed.*

Blue Birch   *Betula caerulea-grandis* Blanchard

The blue birch is a large tree of northeastern Canada and adjacent U.S., ranging from Labrador, the Gaspé Peninsula, and Nova Scotia south into northern New England and New York. It grows in dry woods and flowers in May and early June.

The true identity of blue birch is debatable. Some botanists considered it closely related to the European birch (*Betula pendula*) and so for awhile, thought them to be the same species. Other botanists now think blue birch may be just a hybrid between paper and gray birch. If opinion gains general acceptance, blue birch will be cited as *Betula* × *caerulea* Blanchard.

Blue birch can grow to 25 m (82 ft) high with a spreading branch system and cream to almost **pink-white bark that peels away on older trees.** The deciduous *leaves* are *6–10 cm (2.4–4 in) long,* broad and widest near the base, pointed at the tip, **rounded and toothed at the base** except near the leafstalk. The fruiting cones

Blue Birch

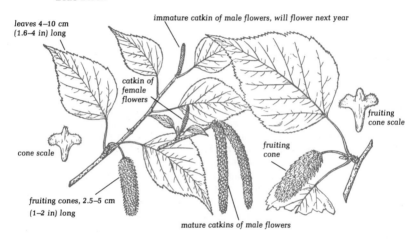

leaves 4–10 cm (1.6–4 in) long

immature catkin of male flowers, will flower next year

catkin of female flowers

fruiting cone scale

cone scale

fruiting cone

fruiting cones, 2.5–5 cm (1–2 in) long

mature catkins of male flowers

are 2.5–5 cm (1–2 in) long, the cones consisting of numerous 3-lobed bracts (the two lateral lobes larger than the end one), each bract enclosing a tiny winged seed.

European White Birch — *Betula pubescens* Ehrh.
(synonym: *Betula alba,* in part)

This medium-size tree, native to Europe and east to Siberia, has been introduced into North America as an ornamental plant for use around homes and commercial buildings. Both this birch and the European birch are often sold in nurseries and garden centers as European white birch (*Betula alba*). The two are similar and both have attractive white, peeling bark. In addition to some technical differences in the fruit, this birch has branches that are erect or spreading and the young branchlets hairy. By contrast, the European birch has spreading and hanging branches and the young branchlets are covered with resinous glands.

The tree may reach 20 m (66 ft) high. The *leaves* are *3–5 cm (1.2–2 in) long,* **broadest near the squared base** and **pointed at the tip,** with a double row of small teeth along the margin, **smooth on the lower surface when mature** (sometimes hairy

European White Birch

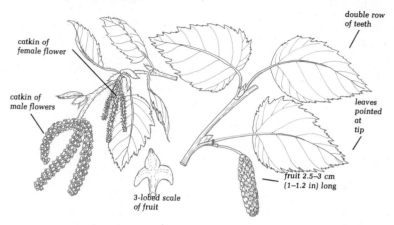

*catkin of
female flower*

*catkin of
male flowers*

*double row
of teeth*

*leaves
pointed
at
tip*

*fruit 2.5–3 cm
(1–1.2 in) long*

*3-lobed scale
of fruit*

when young). The male and female flowers are produced in separate slender catkins. The fruits are **cylinder-shaped, 2.5–3 cm (1–1.2 in) long** and composed of numerous 3-lobed scales, each scale enclosing a tiny winged seed.

The Alder Genus

Alnus B. Ehrh.

There are about 30 species of alders in the world. These small trees or shrubs are distributed primarily in the north temperate regions of the world, but also in higher elevations in Central and South America, northern Africa, and Asia. Eight species native to North America reach tree size, although 7 of them are more often shrubs. The European alder (*Alnus glutinosa*) has been introduced and reproduces on its own in the northeastern U.S. Alders are generally found in moist, cool areas from sea level to 2,400 m (7,900 ft). They often grow along the banks of streams, rivers, ponds, and swamps where they form dense thickets. Because of their dense growth habit and their role in increasing the level of valuable nitrogen to the soil, they are important as erosion-control agents and for the reestablishment of vegetation on burned-out sites.

Alders are of limited value to wildlife. Whitetail deer browse the twigs and leaves, and some birds eat the buds and seeds. The red alder is the only alder large enough to produce lumber on a commercial scale. The remaining species are used for firewood and for smoking fish and meats.

Alders are large shrubs to small trees rarely growing more than 20 m (66 ft) high. The branches often spread into a rounded crown. The leaves are deciduous, simple, usually broadest near the base or the middle and with a single or double row of teeth. The flowers are greatly reduced in size and clustered together in long, narrow, cone-like structures or catkins. Male and female flowers are on separate catkins, but both can be found on the same tree. The fruits are small, leathery to almost woody, cone-like and composed of many scales. Each scale covers a tiny, winged seed.

Key to Alder Species

A. Flowers maturing in spring with the leaves; trees of northwestern North America

Sitka alder, p. 405

B. Flowers maturing and opening before the leaves develop in spring or in autumn.

  1. Flowers opening in spring.

    a. Leaves finely toothed, often in a single row.

      (1) Leaves yellowish-green; trees of western North America.

        (a) Fruits 0.8–1.3 cm (0.3–0.5 in) long; leaves broadest near the middle; trees of the Pacific Northwest and the Sierra Nevada

White alder, p. 406

        (b) Fruits 1.3–2.5 cm (0.5–1 in) long; leaves broadest near the base; trees of Arizona and New Mexico

Arizona alder, p. 407

      (2) Leaves green; trees of eastern U.S.

Hazel alder, p. 408

    b. Leaves coarsely toothed, with a double row of teeth, each large tooth overlapped with a smaller, fine row of teeth.

      (1) Leaves broadest at or above the middle.

        (a) Leaves with 8–15 pairs of veins; leaves yellowish-green; medium to tall trees of the Pacific Northwest

Red alder, p. 408

        (b) Leaves with 5–6 pairs of veins; leaves dark green; small to medium-size trees introduced from Europe, primarily of eastern North America **European alder, p. 409**

      (2) Leaves broadest near the base.

        (a) Fruits 1.3–1.6 cm (0.5–0.7 in) long; leaves with a leathery texture; trees of eastern Canada and northeastern U.S. **Speckled alder, p. 410**

Sitka Alder

White Alder

Red Alder

European Alder

Mountain Alder

(b) Fruits 0.9–1.3 cm (0.4–0.5 in) long;
leaves with a thin but firm texture;
trees of western mountains from
Alaska to New Mexico
Mountain alder, p. 411
2. Flowers opening in autumn; trees of southeastern Coastal Plain and southcentral Oklahoma
Seaside alder, p. 412

Seaside Alder

Sitka Alder
Alnus sinuata (Regel) Rydb.

Sitka alder is a shrub or tree of the Pacific Northwest ranging from northern California through Oregon, Washington, northern Idaho, and Montana to southern Alaska and also in northeastern Asia. It normally occurs from sea level to 1,200 m (3,950 ft) eleva-

tion in rich rocky or gravelly soils. Like other alders, this one quickly invades disturbed areas such as logged and burned sites, and landslides. The nitrogen fixing nodules on the roots add nitrogen to the soil, thus improving soil fertility. Sitka alder grows along streams, rivers, and ponds and in marshy flats and swamps. Trees that grow with Sitka alder include willows, western redcedar, and western hemlock. Sitka alder forms dense thickets in low, wet areas and hybridizes with the green alder, especially in inland Alaska and Canada.

This is a fast-growing plant that lives less than 50 years. Flower buds are first formed in midsummer. They bloom the following summer, and the fruits mature shortly after the flowering. This alder is browsed by deer and moose and its seeds are eaten by small birds. The trees are too small for use as a lumber source, but the wood is excellent for smoking fish and as firewood. They are effective in controlling erosion.

Appearance: shrub or small tree to 10 m (33 ft), with an open, rounded crown; trunk

Sitka Alder

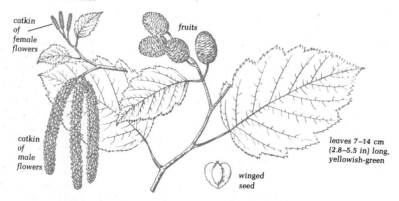

catkin of female flowers

fruits

catkin of male flowers

winged seed

leaves 7–14 cm (2.8–5.5 in) long, yellowish-green

short, soon branching, up to 25 cm (10 in) in diameter, rarely larger, often crooked or leaning. **Bark:** thin, smooth gray to grayish-blue. **Branches:** slender, usually zigzagging, often spreading; branchlets slender, orange-brown, sticky and finely hairy when young, turning gray and becoming smooth with age. **Winter buds:** *1.2–1.4 cm (0.5–0.6 in) long, broadest near the base or middle,* short-stalked or stalkless, tapering to a pointed tip, covered with 3 to 5 dark purple, overlapping scales. **Leaves:** alternate, deciduous, *7–14 cm (2.8–5.5 in) long, 3–10 cm (1.2–4 in) broad, broadest near the base, tapering to a short pointed tip, often uneven and narrowing into a wedge-shaped base, with 2 sets of teeth along the margin,* 1 set of large coarse teeth overlapped by numerous smaller teeth; leaves with a thin papery texture, *yellowish-green and smooth above, paler and shiny below;* leafstalks stout, 1.3–1.9 cm (0.5–0.8 in) long, grooved on the upper surface. **Flowers:** male and female flowers in separate catkins on the same tree; male catkins in spring 10–14 cm (4–5.5 in) long, slender, hanging; female catkins 0.7–1 cm (0.3–0.4 in) long, in long clusters on long stalks. **Fruits:** cone-like, 1.3–1.9 cm (0.5–0.8 in) long, 0.7–0.9 cm (0.3–0.4 in) thick, in small clusters, composed of many scales, the scales leathery and thickened at the tips, each scale enclosing a small, winged seed.

White Alder
Alnus rhombifolia Nutt.

White alder is native to the western mountains ranging from southern British Columbia south across the Cascade Mountains and along the Sierra Nevada in southern California. It grows along streams, in canyon bottomlands, and gulches from near sea level to 2,400 m (7,900 ft). Soils are usually rocky or gravelly. This alder grows in often pure stands or in association with Oregon ash, cottonwood, California sycamore, and western dogwood. It is similar to the more coastal red alder, but their ranges seldom overlap. White alder has unwinged seeds and leaves that are finely toothed on the margin, while red alder has winged seeds and leaves with larger, coarse teeth along the margin.

This is a fairly fast-growing shrub or tree that reaches maximum size in 50 to 60 years. The catkins containing male flowers form in summer, and they mature and open from January to April after the leaves have fallen. The catkins containing female flowers develop in November or December and mature 1 or 2 months later. Large seed crops are produced regularly, sometimes alternating with 1 or 2 years of light production. Wildlife uses are similar to those of other western alders. The wood is of limited value as low-grade lumber, but is used principally for firewood.

Appearance: large shrub to small tree to 20 m (66 ft), rarely larger, with wide rounded crowns; trunks straight, usually 20–60 cm (8–23 in) in diameter, sometimes free of branches for the lower half of the trunk. **Bark:** thin becoming *moderately thick on older trees, to 2.5 cm (1 in) thick,* developing irregular plates and ridges with age, gray or mottled white when young, turning brown with age. **Branches:** slender, upper ones erect, others spreading or even drooping near the tips; branchlets slender, green and hairy when young, turning dark orange-red and smooth with age. **Winter buds:** *1–1.2 cm (0.4–0.5 in) long, slender,* tapering to a rounded or slightly pointed tip, with

White Alder

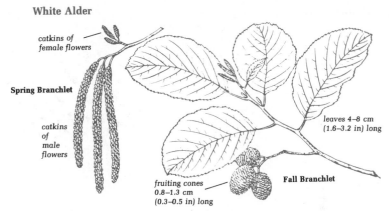

catkins of
female flowers

Spring Branchlet

catkins
of
male
flowers

leaves 4–8 cm
(1.6–3.2 in) long

fruiting cones
0.8–1.3 cm
(0.3–0.5 in) long

Fall Branchlet

overlapping, dark-red scales covered with short hairs. **Leaves:** alternate, deciduous, *4–8 cm (1.6–3.2 in) long, 3–5 cm (1.2–2 in) broad; egg-shaped, broadest near the middle,* tapering at the base and tapering to a pointed tip, *with a double row of either fine or sometimes coarse teeth along the margin,* firm, almost leathery; mature leaves dark green and shiny above, yellowish-green, finely hairy, and with yellowish veins on the lower surface; leafstalks slender, 1.2–1.8 cm (0.5–0.8 in) long, yellowish, hairy, flattened and grooved on the upper surface. **Flowers:** male and female flowers produced in separate catkins on the same tree; male flowers in slender, hanging catkins 10–15 cm (4–6 in) long; female flowers in small stalked clusters, 10–15 mm (0.4–0.6 in) long. **Fruits:** *small, oblong cones, 0.8–1.3 cm (0.3–0.5 in) long,* in clusters of 3 to 6, composed of numerous scales, each scale covering a tiny seed, each with a thin-winged margin.

Arizona Alder

Alnus oblongifolia Torrey

This is a small tree or large shrub of the southwestern U.S. and northern Mexico. It is found in southern and western New Mexico and southeastern Arizona along cool mountain streams and shaded canyons from 1,200–1,900 m (3,900–6,300 ft) elevation.

Arizona alder often grows in forest dominated by ponderosa pine and oak. Little is known about the natural history of this alder and its value to wildlife. Flowering is in late February before the leaves appear.

Arizona alder rarely exceeds 10 m (33 ft) in height. It has a straight trunk with smooth, light brown bark, and an open, rounded crown. The alternate deciduous *leaves* are 5–8 cm (2–3.2 in) long, 3.5–3.9 cm (1.4–1.6 in) broad, *broadest near the base,* tapering to a wedge-shaped base and rounded to pointed at the tip, *dark yellowish-green* and smooth on the upper surface, paler and smooth to finely hairy, especially along the veins, beneath. Male and female flowers are produced in separate slender, hanging catkins on the same tree. The *fruits* are small, *cone-like, 1.3–2.5 cm (0.5–1 in)* long, composed of thin scales, each scale thickened at the tip and enclosing a tiny egg-shaped, winged seed.

Hazel Alder
Alnus serrulata (Ait.) Willd.

This alder is primarily a shrub of the eastern U.S., ranging from Maine to northern Florida, and as far west as Oklahoma. It grows on moist lowlands such as swamps and along ponds and streams. Hazel alder must grow in full sun and will die out if shaded by taller trees. Dense, pure thickets can be found, but this alder more often grows in association with river birch, swamp cottonwood, willows, and red maple.

A fast-growing but short-lived tree or shrub, hazel alder flowers in spring and the fruits and seeds mature by late summer or early fall. Whitetail deer browse the young twigs, and small birds eat the tiny seeds. The wood is of little commercial value.

Appearance: small tree or large shrub to 10 m (33 ft), with a narrow, rounded crown; trunk crooked, often spindly, to 10 cm (4 in) in diameter, usually with multiple trunks. **Bark:** thin, brown, smooth, with numerous, small dark air pores (lenticels). **Branches:** short, soon branching; branchlets slender, smooth, turning brown. **Winter buds:** 0.7–1 cm (0.3–0.4 in) long, broadest near the base or the middle, stalked, rounded at the tip, covered with 2 or 3 reddish scales. **Leaves:** alternate, deciduous, 5–10 cm (2–4 in) long, 3–6 cm (1.2–2.4 in) wide, egg-shaped or broadest at the middle, tapering to a wedge-shaped base, pointed at the tip, *wavy and with a single row of fine teeth along the margin,* green and smooth above, paler and hairy beneath, especially along the veins; leafstalks stout, smooth. **Flowers:** male and female flowers in separate catkins on the same tree; male catkins slender, drooping, 2.5–3.5 cm (1–1.4 in) long, female catkins in shorter, almost rounded catkins, 1.1–1.3 cm (0.4–0.5 in) long, 3 to 6 clustered. **Fruits:** cone-like, 0.7–1.2 cm (0.3–0.5 in) long, in erect clusters supported by a short stalk, composed of numerous scales that are thickened at their tips, each scale enclosing a tiny winged seed.

Red Alder
Alnus rubra Bong.

Red alder is the largest of all of our native alders, reaching to 25 m (82 ft) in height. It occurs in the forested regions of the Pacific Northwest, ranging from southern Alaska to northern California. The trees grow in moist, rich soils, especially bottomlands and along streams. It is a lowland tree seldom growing above 1,000 m (3,300 ft) in elevation, and usually within 80 km (50 miles) of saltwater. Pure stands occur, but red alder more commonly occurs with Douglas fir, Sitka spruce, western redcedar, bigleaf maple, black cottonwood, and Pacific dogwood.

This is a rapid-growing tree. It is an important pioneer tree, seeding-in quickly after a fire or logging operation. The trees are relatively short-lived (60 to 80 years) but they do give shade and protection to other tree species that may eventually replace them. Alders improve the fertility of the soil due to the nitrogen-fixing nodules on their roots. Flowering is in spring with the fruits and seeds maturing by late summer. Large seed crops are produced every 3 to 4 years. Red alder is of limited value to wildlife, though deer and elk browse the leaves and twigs.

It is an important hardwood species in the Northwest due to its straight trunk and light but strong, pale-brown wood. Large quantities are cut each year for use in the manufacture of inexpensive furniture. The wood is also used in smoking meats and for wood carving.

Red Alder

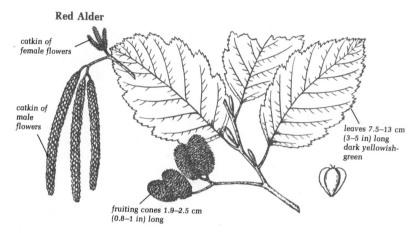

catkin of female flowers

catkin of male flowers

leaves 7.5–13 cm (3–5 in) long dark yellowish-green

fruiting cones 1.9–2.5 cm (0.8–1 in) long

Appearance: *medium-size to large tree, 10–40 m (32–132 ft),* with a narrow to broad rounded crown; trunk straight, tall, the lower half to two-thirds usually free of branches. **Bark:** thin, 1–2 cm (0.4–0.8 in) thick, smooth, developing narrow shallow ridges near the base, *bluish-gray and white mottled when young,* becoming whitish due to heavy covering of lichens. **Branches:** slender, *spreading and often drooping;* branchlets slender, light green and hairy when young, turning bright deep red and smooth with age. **Winter buds:** 0.6–10 mm (to 0.4 in) long, widest near the base but blunt to short pointed at the tip, covered with 2 to 4 *dark red* overlapping scales. **Leaves:** alternate, deciduous, *7.5–13 cm (3–5.1 in) long, 3.5–8 cm (1.4–3.2 in) wide, broadest near the middle or just below,* gradually to sharply narrowing at the base, tapering to a pointed tip, with a double row of irregular large and small teeth along the margin, with a firm almost leathery texture, *dark yellowish-green and smooth above, paler and covered with short rust-colored hairs beneath;* the leafstalks 0.6–1.9 cm (0.3–0.8 in) long, stout, slightly grooved above, orange. **Flowers:** male and female flowers in separate catkins on the same tree; male flowers formed in slender catkins in summer and in spring of the following year expand to 10–15 cm (4–6 in) long; female flowers in short, thickened catkins 0.8–1.2 cm (0.3–0.5 in) long, 0.1–0.2 cm (0.1 in) thick, produced at the tips of the young branchlets. **Fruits:** small, woody cones clustered on erect to spreading stalks, 1.9–2.5 cm (0.8–1 in) long, 0.8–1.2 cm (0.3–0.5 in) thick, composed of many leathery to woody scales; each scale enclosing a tiny winged seed.

European Alder
Alnus glutinosa (L.) Gaertn.

European alder is a medium-size tree or occasionally a large shrub introduced from Europe that is cultivated primarily in eastern Canada and the U.S. It also now

European Alder

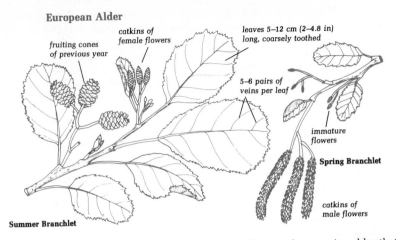

fruiting cones
of previous year

catkins of
female flowers

leaves 5–12 cm (2–4.8 in)
long, coarsely toothed

5–6 pairs of
veins per leaf

immature
flowers

Spring Branchlet

catkins of
male flowers

Summer Branchlet

reproduces naturally in low, wet, or swampy sites. This is a fast growing alder that flowers in early spring before the leaves are fully developed. Fruits mature by late summer or early fall when the seeds are shed. New shoots will develop from the roots, especially if main branches are cut or destroyed.

This tree may reach up to 30 m (100 ft) and may have a straight trunk with lightly furrowed dark brown bark and a rounded crown. The slender branches are often gummy on the new growth. The alternate, deciduous *leaves* are *widest above the middle,* 5–12 cm (2–4.8 in) long, 2–5 cm (0.8–2 in) wide, blunt to almost notched at the tip, with *coarse teeth along the margin, dark green* and smooth above and paler and finely hairy on the lower surface. Flowers and fruits are similar in appearance to those of other alders.

Speckled Alder

Alnus rugosa (Du Roi) Spreng.

This small, spreading tree or, more often, a shrub covers the eastern two-thirds of Canada and the northeastern U S., ranging from north of Hudson's Bay to Virginia. In the northwest, it is replaced by a close relative, the mountain alder. Speckled alder grows in wet sandy or gravelly soils, usually along streams and rivers, but also by ponds and in swamps. This alder occurs in sunny open areas and cannot survive densely shaded spots. Generally it grows in association with hazel alder, dogwood, several willows, and red maple.

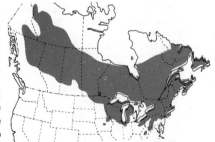

Like other alders, it is fast-growing and short-lived. Flowering is in spring, and the woody fruits open in autumn to shed the tiny seeds. It is of moderate importance to wildlife; ptarmigan and sharptail grouse feed on the buds, and cottontail rabbits, deer, and moose eat the twigs. As a streamside plant it is important because it shades and thus helps keep trout streams cold in summer. Speckled alder's small size renders it of no importance as lumber or fuel.

Appearance: shrub or small tree to 10 m (33 ft), with a broad rounded, irregular crown; often with several crooked trunks. **Bark:** thin, smooth but marked with whitish pores (lenticels) 4–8 mm (0.1–0.3 in) long, dark reddish-brown. **Branches:** slender, usually crooked or twisted, spreading; branchlets slender, nearly smooth, reddish-brown. **Winter buds:** 6–8 mm (0.2–0.3 in) long, *stalked, broadest near the middle, rounded at the tip,* covered with 2 or 3 overlapping, dark reddish-brown scales. **Leaves:** alternate, deciduous, *5-10 cm (2–4 in) long, 2.5–4 cm (1–1.6 in) broad, broadest near the base,* gradually tapering toward the base and pointed at the tip, with a row of 2 distinctly different-size teeth along the margin; leaves with a leathery texture, dull green, lacking hairs, and somewhat wrinkled on the upper surface, paler and covered with rusty-red hairs on the lower surface; the leafstalks short, stout, smooth, white-dotted. **Flowers:** male and female flowers produced in separate catkins on the same tree; male flowers in slender, hanging, solitary or paired catkins 2.5–3.5 cm (1–1.4 in) long; female flowers in catkins that are clustered together on a stalk; catkins short, almost rounded, 1.2–1.4 cm (0.5–0.6 in) long, erect. **Fruits:** hanging cones, often in clusters of 2 to 5, *1.3–1.6 cm (0.5–0.7 in) long,* 0.7–0.9 cm (0.3–0.4 in) broad, on slender stalks, composed of numerous thickened scales, each scale containing a tiny, narrowly winged seed.

Mountain Alder   *Alnus tenuifolia* Nutt.

This is a short western tree or large shrub that ranges from the central Yukon Valley in Alaska south to New Mexico. In Alaska it occurs near sea level but in the southern part of its range, it is found at higher elevations, up to 3,000 m (9,850 ft). It grows in

moist soils along lakes or streams, wet mountain passes, and in swampy sites. Mountain alder is basically a forest tree and together with some willows commonly forms dense thickets along streams. It is closely related to the European speckled alder (*Alnus incana*) and the speckled alder (*Alnus rugosa*) of the eastern U.S.

Mountain alder is a fast-growing, short-lived tree that flowers in early spring. The seeds develop and are shed by the fall of the same year. This is not an important species for wildlife. It is browsed by deer, and rodents and small birds feed on the seeds. It is of no commercial value except as firewood.

Mountain Alder

catkins of female flowers

Spring Branchlet

catkins of male flowers

leaves 5–7.5 cm (2–3 in) long

seed

fruiting cones 0.9–1.3 cm (0.5 in) long

Fall Branchlet

Appearance: large shrub or small tree, to 10 m (33 ft), often forming large spreading clumps with a rounded crown; trunk straight or curved, to 15 cm (6 in) in diameter, rarely larger; reduced to a low shrub in high mountain areas. **Bark:** thin, 0.6–0.8 cm (0.3 in) thick, smooth but becoming scaly when older, gray to dark gray or reddish-gray. **Branches:** slender, spreading; branchlets slender, light green and hairy when young becoming dark orange-red and smooth with age. **Winter buds:** 0.6–0.8 cm (about 0.3 in) long, slender, broadest near the base or the middle, covered with bright red, finely hairy, overlapping scales. **Leaves:** alternate, deciduous, *5–7.5 cm (2–3 in) long, 3–5 cm (1.2–2 in) broad, broadest near the base or the middle,* tapering and usually wedge-shaped at the base, sometimes rounded, tapering to a short pointed tip, *with a double row of teeth,* 1 large and coarse and another of numerous, fine teeth, along the margins, with a thin but firm texture, *dark green and dull at maturity* on the upper surface, *pale yellowish-green and smooth to hairy beneath,* the veins yellowish beneath; leafstalks stout, 1.3–2.5 cm (0.5–1 in) long, orange, slightly grooved on the upper surface. **Flowers:** male and female flowers produced in separate catkins on the same tree; male catkins slender, drooping, usually 3 to 4 clustered, 4–7.5 cm (1.6–3 in) long when mature; female catkins cone-like, clustered on slender, short stalks, 0.7–0.9 cm (0.3–0.4 in) long. **Fruits:** cone-like, *egg-shaped, 0.9–1.3 cm (0.4–0.5 in) long,* grouped in clusters of 2 to 5 on slender stalks, composed of numerous scales, each scale thickened at the tip, leathery, and containing a tiny, almost rounded seed bordered by a thin almost transparent wing.

Seaside Alder   *Alnus maritima* Muhl. ex Nutt.

This small tree occurs in the coastal regions of southern Delaware and southeastern Maryland and then reappears in southcentral Oklahoma. Seaside alder grows in wet soils, primarily along streams and ponds at lower elevations. It does form dense pure stands in swampy areas. Common trees growing in association with this alder include red maple, sweetgum, river birch, and willow.

A moderately fast-growing tree, seaside alder also is a short-lived plant with an approximate life span of 30 to 40 years. The catkins containing the flowers develop in midsummer but do not open until autumn. Fruits and seeds ripen by late summer or fall of the second year. Whitetail deer eat the twigs and leaves, grouse feed on the buds and fruits, and the tiny seeds are eaten by many birds including goldfinch, siskins, and redpolls. This alder is occasionally cultivated as an ornamental. Its small size precludes its use as lumber.

Appearance: small tree or shrub to 10 m (33 ft), *with a narrow, rounded crown;* trunk straight, to 0.1–0.7 m (0.4–2.3 ft) in diameter (rarely larger). **Bark:** thin, 0.2–0.4 cm (0.1–0.2 in), smooth, light brown to brownish-gray. **Branches:** small, usually spreading; branchlets slender, sometimes zigzag, green and hairy when young turning reddish to reddish-orange and becoming smooth, often covered with resinous glands when young. **Winter buds:** small, 0.6–0.8 cm (about 0.3 in) long, broadest near the base and tapering to a pointed tip, covered with a few, dark red, shiny, overlapping scales. **Leaves:** alternate, deciduous, *7.5–10 cm (3–4 in) long,* 3–5 cm (1.2–2 in) wide,

Seaside Alder

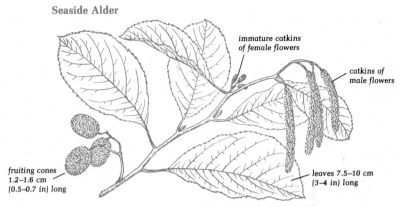

immature catkins
of female flowers

catkins of
male flowers

fruiting cones
1.2–1.6 cm
(0.5–0.7 in) long

leaves 7.5–10 cm
(3–4 in) long

broadest near the base, tapering at the base and rounded to somewhat pointed at the tip, **with a single row of tiny teeth along the margin, very dark green** and shiny above, paler, slightly hairy and with yellowish veins on the lower surface, with tiny glands on both surfaces, the leafstalks stout, 1.3–1.9 cm (0.5–0.8 in) long, yellow, gland-dotted, flattened and grooved on the upper surface. **Flowers:** male and female flowers produced in separate catkins on the same tree; male flowers in hanging, stalked clusters of catkins 4–6 cm (1.6–2.4 in) long, 0.6–1.2 cm (0.2–0.5 in) wide; female flowers in solitary catkins 0.2–0.7 cm (0.1–0.3 in) long, usually produced in the junction of the lower leaves on the branchlet. **Fruits:** spreading or hanging *cones,* usually 2 to 5 clustered, *1.2–1.6 cm (0.5–0.7 in) long,* 1–1.4 cm (0.4–0.6 in) wide, composed of numerous scales, the scales thickened at the edge and each scale covering a small narrow seed, each seed with a thin almost transparent wing.

The Beefwood Family   Casuarinaceae

The beefwood family contains only 1 genus, *Casuarina*, which contains about 45 species of trees. Most are native to Australia, although a few come from Polynesia, Malaysia, and Africa. The most striking feature of this family is the reduction of the leaves to small scales. These scales form toothed "collars" around the jointed branchlets. The trees resemble pines in general appearance. The small branchlets are shed like pine needles, forming thick blankets of mulch beneath the trees.

The small inconspicuous flowers are either male or female, and flowers of both types are found on the same tree. The male flowers are clustered in small cone-like spikes at the tips of the branchlets. Female flowers are grouped in larger, rounded heads. The fruits are small leathery-to-woody cones.

Species of *Casuarina* have been introduced into southern Florida and California. They are used for ornamental plantings along avenues and to create windbreaks. The bark is rich in tannins and can be used to tan leather. In southeast Asia and Australia, the wood is used to make furniture, shingles, and poles.

The 2 species that have been introduced and naturalized in southern Florida are the horsetail casuarina (*Casuarina equisetifolia*) and the Brazilian beefwood (*C. cristata*). Another species, Cunningham's beefwood (*C. cunninghamiana*) from New South Wales, has also been planted in Florida. This species can be distinguished from the 2 more commonly encountered ones by its 8 to 10 scale leaves at each joint of the branchlets.

Key to Beefwood Species

A. Scale leaves 6 to 8 at the junction of the joints of the branchlets; seeds 6–8 mm (0.2–0.3 in) long
Horsetail casuarina, p. 414
B. Scale leaves 12 to 16 at the junction of the joints of the branchlets; seeds 3–5 mm (0.1–0.2 in) long
Brazilian beefwood, p. 415

Horsetail Casuarina   *Casuarina equisetifolia* L. ex J. R. & G. Forst.
This species is a native of Australia, but has naturalized from plantings in southern Florida to the Keys, Bermuda, the West Indies, and Mexico to South America. It is a medium-size to large tree that does well in sandy soils along sea shores, lower montane regions, and tidal estuaries. The trees are often planted along streets and parks because they are unusual and attractive.

Horsetail casuarina is fast growing and yet it is surprisingly long-lived. The tiny separate clusters of male and female flowers bloom in the spring. Following flowering

Horsetail Casuarina

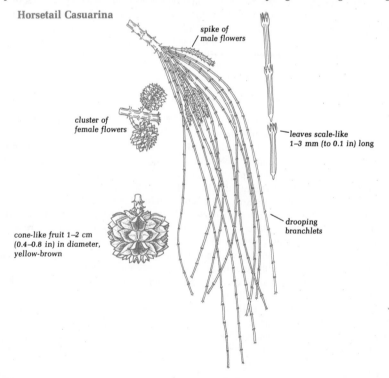

spike of male flowers

cluster of female flowers

leaves scale-like 1–3 mm (to 0.1 in) long

drooping branchlets

cone-like fruit 1–2 cm (0.4–0.8 in) in diameter, yellow-brown

and successful pollination, some of the female flowers develop into fruiting cones that ripen in the fall when the small seeds are shed.

The wood is pinkish-red to brown, very hard, heavy, tough, and strong. It is used for beams, fence posts, fuel, and carts, among other things. In Oceania, Australian aborigines used the wood for war clubs. The bark is used in tanning and dyeing, as well as for making astringent compounds.

Appearance: medium to tall tree to 30 m (100 ft) high, occasionally higher, with a broad cone shape; trunk straight, 30–45 cm (11.8–17.7 in) in diameter. **Bark:** thin and smooth when young, becoming furrowed and splitting into thin strips exposing a reddish-brown layer beneath, dark brown to light gray on the outer parts. **Branches:** slender, long, upper ones erect, lower ones drooping near the tips; branchlets very slender, wiry, green, jointed and grooved, with rings of needle-like leaves appearing at the joints; older branchlets becoming gray-brown and scaly. **Leaves:** *scale-like, 1–3 mm (up to 0.1 in) long,* lance-shaped, broadest at the base and tapering to a long-pointed tip, 6 to 8 per whorl at the joints. **Flowers:** *male and female flowers in separate clusters on the same branchlets; male flowers in slender, tube-like spikes at the tips of the branchlets;* female flowers in almost globe-shaped clusters near the bases of the branchlets. **Fruits:** *cone-like,* rounded to slightly longer than broad, *1–2 cm (0.4–0.8 in) in diameter,* yellowish-brown, with thickened corky scales; seeds small, 6–8 mm (0.2–0.3 in) long, broadest near the middle, pointed at the tip, blunt at the base, brown.

Brazilian Beefwood

Casuarina cristata Miq.
(synonym: *C. lepidophloia* F. Muell.)

This is a smaller tree than the horsetail casuarina that has also been introduced into southern Florida. Unlike the other species, this one does not produce good fruit in Florida, where it is apparently intolerant of salt. The handsome wood is durable and is reportedly used in furniture, fence posts, paneling, and shingling. Beefwood once carried the scientific name (*Casuarina glauco*).

It is a large shrub to medium-size tree to 20 m (66 ft) and with an upright, narrow form. The slender branches are dense and the needle-like *branchlets* are green and *have whorls of 12 to 16 tiny scale-like leaves at their junctions.* The flowers are similar to those of the horsetail casuarina. Brazilian beefwood reproduces by sending sprouts up from the roots, thus producing dense clumps or groves.

The Four O'Clock Family
Nyctaginaceae

This is a primarily tropical or subtropical family of about 30 genera and 275 species of herbs, vines, shrubs, and trees. There are approximately 35 species in this family in the southern and Pacific coastal states, but these are herbs or vines except for 2 species of small trees in southern Florida. Economically unimportant, this family is best known for 2 of its horticulturally useful members, the temperate four o'clock with its bright red, tubular flowers and the colorful tropical vine bougainvillea.

Members of this family typically have simple, generally opposite, persistent leaves. The flowers are in few to many-flowered clusters, and each flower is usually surrounded by large, leaf-like bracts. A flower is composed of 5 sepals, 5 petals (sometimes fused into a tube), and often 5 stamens, although the number of stamens can vary from 1 to 20. Bisexual flowers are the norm for this family; male or female flowers occur in some species. The fruits are either leathery, becoming hardened or fleshy, almost rounded to cylinder-shaped, with lengthwise ribs or angles that may be lined with numerous sticky glandular hairs.

Key to Four O'Clock Genera

A. Fruits dry, enclosing a single seed, the fruits cylinder-shaped, conspicuously angled and with numerous stalked glands on the angles
Cockspur, p. 416

B. Fruits fleshy, enclosing a hard seed, the fruits cylinder-shaped, ribbed but without stalked glands **Blolly, p. 416**

The Cockspur Genus
Pisonia L.

A small genus of about 20 species of vines, shrubs, or trees in the subtropical and tropical region of the Americas. A single species of cockspur occasionally reaches tree size in southern Florida. When mature, the characteristic sticky fruits adhere to the fur of animals or to clothing, thus transporting the seeds to new areas.

Cockspurs often have stiff spines at the base of the usually opposite, entire leaves. Trees or bushes are either male or female, and the flowers are in branched, round to flat-topped groupings. Male flowers are small and usually have 6 to 10 stamens, while the female flowers are tubular and contain a single pistil. Fruits are usually dry, cylinder-shaped to round-shaped, angled, and usually have lengthwise rows of glands on the angles.

Cockspur
Pisonia rotundata Griseb.

Cockspur is a small tree of the Florida Keys, also occurring in the West Indies. It grows at or near sea level in hammocks and pinelands. Little has been written about the life history of this tropical plant or its importance to wildlife and forest ecology. It is of little value to man.

The leaves are opposite, elongated, broadest at the middle, and from 3–9 cm (1.2–3.6 in) in length, with a short stalk. The male and female flowers are produced on separate trees; these are borne in very dense clusters of many *flowers*. The *clusters emerge in groups from the bases of the leaves;* the male flowers are green or whitish, and are downy along the edge. The *sticky fruit is rounded, though slightly elongated, 5–6 mm (about 0.2 in) long.*

The Blolly Genus
Guapira Aubl.
(synonym: *Torrubia* Vell.)

This small genus of approximately 15 species is confined to tropical America. A single species, the blolly tree, extends into southern Florida.

Members of this genus usually have opposite, smooth-margined leaves with short stalks. In the flowers, the 5-lobed calyx is funnel-shaped or tubular; the petals are absent, the stamens are attached beneath the pistil and inserted into the calyx. The fruit is fleshy, cylindrical, and hairless, but has ribs running from base to tip. It contains a single, erect seed.

Blolly

Guapira discolor (Spreng.) Little
(synonym: *Torrubia longifolia* (Heimerl) Britt.

The blolly is a small, spreading tree or large shrub of southern Florida. Best growth is obtained in the southern parts of its range. It is also found on the Bahama Islands and Cuba. Blolly trees are salt-tolerant plants, and grow at sea level along beaches and shores of saltwater lagoons in sandy soils. The thick, firm, and round-tipped leaves and *small, greenish-yellow flowers on stalks that appear at the ends of the branchlets* are primary distinguishing characteristics.

Blolly grows 10–16 m (32–52 ft) in height, with a compact, rounded crown, and a leaning or straight trunk. The bark is thin, light reddish-brown, and breaks up into thin scales. The branches are stout and spreading, and branchlets are marked

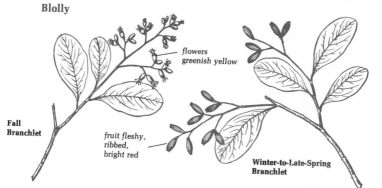

Blolly

flowers greenish yellow

Fall Branchlet

fruit fleshy, ribbed, bright red

Winter-to-Late-Spring Branchlet

with large, raised, crescent-shaped leaf scars. The **greenish-yellow flowers bloom in autumn.** The small calyx lobes partially enclose the stamens and pistil. The **fruit** is **bright red**, and **clusters remain** on the trees during the winter **to mature in late winter or early spring.**

The Cactus Family

Cactaceae

The cactus family is native to North, South, and Central America, and the West Indies, though a number of species have been introduced to parts of the Mediterranean, Africa, and Asia. Because they are so characteristic of the American desert or dry regions, some people are surprised to find cacti in a wide range of other climates and habitats. Some species are found in tropical rainforests, while others occur in temperate areas, ranging as far north as Alberta, Canada.

In North America, cacti are most abundant in Arizona and Texas, and in some parts of California and New Mexico. Here, they can form vast desert forests exhibiting a tremendous variety of sizes and shapes. Even more species occur in Mexico and the drier parts of South America. It should be noted that, in arid regions, cacti have diversified to fill virtually every sort of plant niche. They range from low herbaceous plants to trees. Their capacity to store water during dry spells has made them indispensable to the wildlife they support. Additionally, cacti provide both food and shelter to a large number of animals, including man.

Black marketeers uproot cacti on public lands and sell them to landscapers and individuals desiring drought-resistant plantings. Fines and jail sentences have discouraged some offenders, but high profits and comparatively low risk of detection have resulted in continued illicit traffic. This has taken a heavy toll on cacti communities, where harsh climate and slow growth are standard. The magnificent saguaro cactus, for example, may reach only 1 m (3.3 ft) height at 30 years of age.

The extreme environment in which cacti evolved caused them to develop certain specialized structures to ensure survival. The best-known characteristic separating these plants from others is the lack of leaves and subsequent presence of spines. This adaptation serves a dual purpose: First, spines do not allow water to evaporate as leaves do, and so enhance the cacti's water-storing ability. Second, spines provide protection of the soft, vulnerable parts of the plant from prey.

Spines arise from complex structures, called *areoles*, which are formed from buds on the stem where leaves would otherwise be produced. On cacti with ribbed stems, the *areoles* form along the rib tops or ridges; other cacti with *tubercles* (small, knobby protuberances) produce *areoles* at the tip of these knobs. Additionally, chollas and prickly pear cacti have many small or minute barbed bristles, or *glochids*, along their branches.

The branches of cacti are segmented, and for this reason are often called *joints*. On some plants, the joints are of two distinctly different sizes, which are then referred to as *primary* (larger and older) and *secondary* (smaller and newer) joints.

Many active cacti have bright flowers that appear briefly after the rainy season, which in the desert may only be a few weeks. Some species may not bloom for dozens of years of insufficient rainfall.

The cactus family contains some 11 genera in North America. Of these, 2 genera, *Cereus* and *Opuntia* (prickly pears and chollas), contain members that are trees.

Key to Cacti Genera

A. Branches or stems ribbed, not jointed, but sometimes with large branches; areoles with well-developed spines   **Cereus, p. 419**

Organ-Pipe Cactus

Saguaro

B. Branches not ribbed, composed of a series of cylinder-shaped or flattened joints; areoles with numerous, tiny barbed bristles plus often well-developed spines
Prickly pears and chollas, p. 423

Jumping Cholla

The Cereus Genus

Cereus Mill.

This genus includes a large but as yet undetermined number of species in California, Arizona, New Mexcio, Texas, Florida, Mexico, and South America. There are 16 species in the United States, including both native and introduced ones. While most species are adapted to arid climates, some occur in tropical, humid hammocks in the Caribbean. Like all cacti, cereus members are uniquely adapted to the desert environment, with some wildlife dependent upon them. They provide food, water, and shelter for many animals, and have likewise been used by American Indians since prehistoric times. Four native species—the saguaro, the Deering, and Key West cephalocereus, and the organ-pipe cactus—are considered trees.

Like other genera in the cactus family, the cereus genus contains a large diversity of species. Nevertheless, there are a number of unifying characteristics. For example, all have elongated stems that branch out in varying degrees away from the main stem and are, upon reaching maturity, 15 to 100 times as long as they are wide. Species range from 0.3–15 m (1–50 ft) in height, and from 0.6 cm (0.3 in) to nearly 1 m (3.3 ft) in breadth. Although tiny leaves may form on immature plants, they are indiscernible in mature specimens. Most are armed with clusters of spines. Flowers are generally bright and showy, with many petals and a large central cluster of numerous stamens. Flower widths range from 2.5–25 cm (1–10 in). Both flowers and fruits develop on old growth, rather than on the new tips of the stems and branches. Fruits are fleshy and usually pulpy; many of them are edible. The fruits contain black to dark-brown seeds of diverse textures, which are longer than they are broad.

Key to Cereus Species

A. Large cacti of the desert regions of the southwestern U.S.

  1. Trees to 15.5 m (50 ft) with a main trunk 15–77 cm (6–30 in) in diameter, the thick main trunk usually with 1–5 (up to 20) large branches   **Saguaro, p. 420**

  2. Plants branching at the base, with many erect branches to 6 m (20 ft) in height, branches usu-
(Continued)

Saguaro

ally 10–20 cm (4–8 in) in diameter
Organ-pipe cactus, p.421

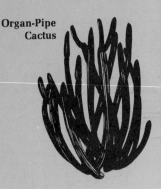

B. Cacti of extreme southern Florida.

    1. Branches nearly upright, pale to dark green; spines in clusters of 25–31; flowers light green; Florida Keys
          Key West cephalocereus, p. 422

    2. Branches nearly upright, blue-green, spines in clusters of 16–20; flowers brownish-purple; rarely, if ever, found wild
          Deering cephalocereus, p. 423

Saguaro, Giant Cactus   *Cereus giganteus* Engelm.

The saguaro (pronounced sa-WAR-o) cactus is perhaps the most famous plant of the American Southwest. With good reason, Arizona has claimed the flower of this towering cactus for its state flower. Saguaros grow from 180–1,100 m (590–3,600 ft) in eleva-
tion, in rocky or gravelly soils that are sturdy enough to anchor their shallow root systems. These trees are characteristic of foothills, canyons, benches, and out-washes of the Arizona and Sonoran deserts. One of the most striking features of the desert scene, saguaros grow on south-facing slopes in the northeastern part of their range, while in drier areas they fol-low drainage patterns. In some areas, this species grows in large forests; the most famous of these is the Saguaro National Monument, near Tucson, Arizona.

Seedling growth in saguaros is very slow; at 8 to 10 years of age, the plants are less than 10 cm (4 in) tall! They may reach 30 years in age before attaining 1 m (3.3 ft) in height. After the initial slow period, however, growth rate accelerates to up to 10 cm (4 in) per year. The largest individuals may be over 200 years in age. In May, large white flowers are produced during the cool of the night, but generally remain fresh throughout the next day. The fleshy, red fruits are ripe a few weeks prior to the sum-mer rainy season. Large seed crops are produced, but birds and ants eat most of the seeds before they can germinate. Once the July rains arrive the surviving seeds sprout rapidly.

Aside from seed-eating birds, many other birds depend on the red pulp of the ma-ture fruit as an important part of their diet. Moreover, an interesting relationship has evolved between elf-owls and woodpeckers through the saguaro. The owls inhabit holes drilled by woodpeckers in their search for insects living in the cactus trunk. Saguaro has few natural enemies or diseases; if a tree is wounded in the rainy season, however, it may die within a week from bacterial infection.

The trunk is a matrix of soft tissue and woody, vertical rods that are like bamboo poles. The average plant is 98 per cent water by weight, though water content varies greatly throughout the seasons. Saguaros have the ability to expand and contract to ac-commodate water gain or loss.

Saguaro

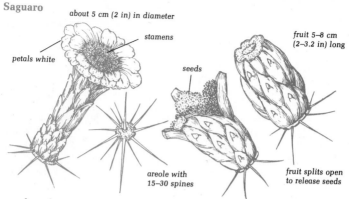

about 5 cm (2 in) in diameter

stamens

petals white

seeds

fruit 5–8 cm
(2–3.2 in) long

areole with
15–30 spines

fruit splits open
to release seeds

Saguaros have been very important to the Papago and Pima Indians, who gather the fruits for sweet food and drink, and use the fatty seeds for chicken feed. The trunks are used for building shelter, light corrals, and novelty furniture and trinkets.

Appearance: saguaros are *column-shaped to 15.5 m (50 ft) tall,* for many years unbranched, but later with 1 to 5 or up to 20 branches; the trunk is straight but bulges slightly about the midsection, with 12 to 30 vertical ribs that stand out 1–3 cm (0.4–1.2 in); trunk is 15–77 cm (6–30 in) in diameter. **Bark:** no true bark, but a tough, leathery, outer skin that is covered with clusters of spines growing in rows along the ribs. **Branches:** seldom as tall as the central trunk, *bending or curving sharply upward,* appearing well above the ground, with little rebranching. **Leaves:** areoles form on saguaros at tops of central spikes and branches, covered with 15 to 30 gray or pink-tinged spines, 2.5–7.5 cm (1–3 in) long, densely brown-felted, their undersurfaces nearly wholly connected to the trunk. **Flowers:** *about 5 cm (2 in) in diameter, with white petals arranged in a crown, up to 2.5 cm (1 in) long,* rounded at the tips and curling; throat about 3 cm (1.2 in) long, and covered with hundreds of white stamens; pistil somewhat tube-like, the pistil wooly at the base. **Fruits:** an elongate berry, broadest near the tip, 5–8 cm (2–3.2 in) long, 2.5–4.5 cm (1–1.8 in) wide; green tinged with red or purple, with a few, scattered oval scales, with or without 1 to 3 short spines; breaks from the plant along 3 symmetrical, vertical lines, exposing the conspicuous red lining; fleshy parts edible; seeds black, 1.2–1.4 mm (0.1 in) long.

Organ-Pipe Cactus

Cereus thurberi Engelm.

Sometimes considered to be a tree, sometimes not, this large plant of the Sonoran desert regions of the American Southwest lives up to its name. *Its many column-like branches sweep up from the desert floor* toward the sky, resembling the pipes of a large church organ. Ranging from Arizona into Mexico, the organ-pipe cactus grows in rocky or sandy soils on hills, mesas, and desert valleys, at elevations of 300–1,050 m (985–3,450 ft).

While little information is available regarding this species' value to wildlife, birds do feed on the tasty fruit. The Papago Indians gather it in great quantity.

In form, *organ-pipe cacti are mostly*

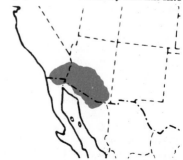

mm

cm 1 2 3 4 5 6 7 8 9 10 11

in 1 2 3 4

Organ-Pipe Cactus

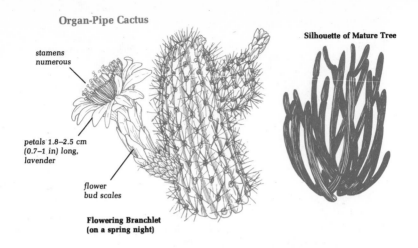

stamens numerous

petals 1.8–2.5 cm (0.7–1 in) long, lavender

flower bud scales

Flowering Branchlet (on a spring night)

Silhouette of Mature Tree

crown and little, if any, trunk. They may reach 6 m (20 ft) in height, with a crown diameter of more than 5 m (16 ft). The branches are as long as the tree itself, **10–20 cm (4–8 in) in diameter,** green, and fairly round; each branch has from 12 to 19 vertical ribs. Although cacti do not have true bark, their skins are tough and leathery; clusters of dark-colored spines run up and down the ribs. Organ-pipes flower at night in the spring, putting forth large, 6–7.5 cm (2.4–3 in) in diameter, lavender flowers that remain open through the following day. The base of the flower is a tube with shingle-like, overlapping scales; the petals are 1.8–2.5 cm (0.7–1 in) long and broadest near the tips, which curl under slightly. The fruit is red, round, and fleshy, and matures in late summer or early fall. It is covered with a dense mass of spines that are easily removable, and it contains numerous, small black seeds.

Key West Cephalocereus *Cereus robinii* (Lem.) L. Benson variety robinii

The Key West cephalocereus is one of two species of cacti reaching tree size in Florida, specifically the Florida Keys. They may be found growing near sea level in hammocks. Little is known about this rarely encountered plant.

This short tree or shrub looks very much like a pole, although it may have a few, nearly upright branches attached to the trunk. All parts are characteristically 9 to 13 ribbed, and **covered with clusters of short spines (25 to 31 to a cluster) along the ribs.** The skin is tough and either **pale or dark green in color.** The **flowers** open in late afternoon and remain open through the night; they are 5–6 cm (2–2.4 in) long, elongated and cup-shaped, and **light green.** The outer flower segments are rounded,  blunt, or notched at the tips, the inner ones are 9–11 cm (3.5–4.4 in) long, rounded at the tip, and narrow at the base. The berry-like fruit is quite flattened, 3.5–4 cm (1.4–1.6 in) wide, and dark red; it contains many small and shiny seeds.

Deering Cephalocereus *Cereus robinii* variety *deeringii* (Small) L. Benson

Like the Key West cephalocereus, this is a rarely encountered tree-size cactus of the hammocks of the Florida Keys. During World War I on Key West, it was largely cleared away by military operations.

This species can be distinguished from the typical variety by the following: It has blue-green skin, which is covered with a whitish bloom; it is 9 or 10 ribbed, the **spines are yellow and occur in clusters of 16 to 20;** the **flowers** are a **brownish-purple,** narrowly goblet-shaped, and have a strong garlic odor when they first open, which fades by the following morning; the petals are pointed at the tips; and the berries are not as dark red.

The Prickly Pear and Cholla Genus   *Opuntia* Mill.

This genus of cacti is widely distributed in the Western Hemisphere. The exact number of species is uncertain. In the U.S., there are approximately 47 species, both native and introduced. Although this genus contains a fair number of tree-cacti, the majority of them grow in South America. Three species are described here for North America.

Opuntia is subdivided into 2 main groups, or subgenera, the prickly pears and the chollas. Prickly pears have flattened branches, and large, well-developed, highly effective barbs. Chollas are characterized by cylinder-shaped joints, and thin, papery sheaths on their spines. These spines are primarily tiny and harmless, except on the underground stems and on the fruits of the low, mat-forming types. Only this genus is characterized by the presence of small barbed bristles (glochids) on the branches. These minute, sharp bristles are produced in the areoles along with the longer spines. Flowers are also produced in the areoles, though only on the growth of the preceding season.

Desert animals eat the fruit and use the plants as water sources. Small birds build homes in the trunks, and many animals use shade afforded by the plants for protection from the desert sun. Man's use of the chollas and prickly pears is rather limited. Many of the fruits are edible, and some of the species are used as garden ornamentals. Moreover, the plants are of special scientific interest because of modifications occurring as they adapt to different desert environments.

Key to Prickly Pear and Cholla Species

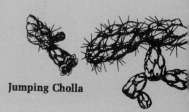

A. Branches composed of cylinder-shaped joints; small trees or bushes of southwestern U.S. desert regions   **Jumping cholla, p. 424**

Jumping Cholla

(Continued)

B. Branches composed of flattened, pad-like joints; small trees or bushes of southern Florida.

   1. First branches from the trunk are flattened and pad-shaped; generally spineless; fruits red

   2. First branches from the trunk are cylinder-shaped and horizontal, secondary branches flattened, pointed at the tip; with spines; fruits yellow

Jumping Cholla   *Opuntia fulgida* Engelm.

Jumping chollas are small trees of the Arizona and Sonoran desert uplands. They are found growing on sandy or gravelly soils from 300–1,370 m (985–4,500 ft) above sea level, on plains, outwashes, mesas, valley slopes, and lower foothills. Two varieties

are known; of these only 1 variety (variety *fulgida*) reaches tree height. Jumping chollas may form forests in the desert, often as the sole species present, or else with other species of cacti, particularly other chollas. Sadly, these striking forests are being diminished by real-estate development in desert areas.

Members of this species are long-lived. Flowering occurs from early spring to September. The fruit is unique in its development: It forms upon old fruits, making chains that may branch out and hang in large clusters. The fruits may remain on the trees up to 25 years in this fashion. The fruits, usually spineless, are juicy and are favored by deer, rodents, and peccaries. Although a prolific seeder, jumping cholla rarely propagates by seed germination. Rather, new plants form when a joint of the plant is blown or knocked off. The joint then produces roots and begins to grow. This process is called asexual, or vegetative, reproduction.

Jumping Cholla

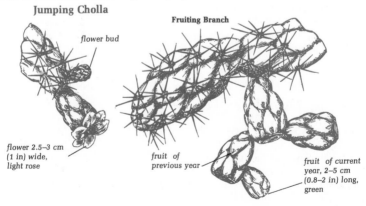

Fruiting Branch

flower bud

flower 2.5–3 cm (1 in) wide, light rose

fruit of previous year

fruit of current year, 2–5 cm (0.8–2 in) long, green

Appearance: small trees or shrubs, up to 3 m (10 ft) or more; with a compact, flattened crown; trunk is woody, 10–20 cm (4–8 in) in diameter; growing in dense clusters. **Bark:** no true bark; covered with yellowish-brown spines that tend to hide the stem. **Branches:** growing along entire length of the trunk, often taller than the trunk itself; curved gently or abruptly upward, terminating in dense clumps of secondary joints; terminal *joints 10–20 cm (4–8 in) long, 3–5 cm (1.2–2 in) in diameter, cylinder-shaped or tube-like,* with succulent prominent tubercles; branches can be easily detached from the main stem. **Leaves:** no true leaves; *spines arising from the areoles, 2 to 12 in number, 2.5–3.5 cm (1–1.4 in) long, needle-like and barbed, spreading in all directions, and covered with loose, papery sheaths.* Flowers: *light rose in color,* 2.5–3 cm (1–1.2 in) wide; petals are 5 to 8 in number, wedge-shaped or elongated and wedge-shaped, rounded at the tip, with tiny teeth along the margins; the stamens very short. **Fruits:** at first knob-like, becoming somewhat pear-shaped at maturity; green, smooth, 2–5 cm (0.8–2 in) long, 2–2.5 cm (0.8–1 in) in diameter, with a shallow cup at the tip, from which successive fruits are produced; *clusters of fruits remain on the trees for many years.*

Indian Fig   *Opuntia ficus-indica* (L.) Mill.

The Indian fig, not a fig but a true cactus, is a small tree or large bush occurring in south Florida and the American tropics. In North America, it ranges only into Florida and Bermuda, and it is cultivated in southern California. This cactus is widely established throughout the world, thus obscuring its native range. Due to its edible fruits and its value as a forage for animals, this species is commonly cultivated in the Middle East, the Mediterranean countries, southern Africa, and Mexico.

The Indian fig is a spreading bush or is straight and tree-like. There is usually a well-defined trunk and a large, spreading crown. The *branches or joints are elongated and flattened, about 30–50 cm (12–20 in) or more long, and grow in dense clusters.* The areoles are small and generally spineless; however, many short barbed bristles are produced in the areoles. These soon drop off. The *flowers are large, up to 7–10 cm (2.8–4 in) broad, and bright yellow.* The fruits are 5–9 cm (2–3.6 in) long, red, and edible.

Brazil Prickly Pear   *Opuntia braziliensis* (Willd.) Haw.

Originating in the drier parts of South America, this short tree-size cactus has naturalized on shell mounds and waste places in southern Florida. It may grow to a height of 4 m (13 ft), attaining a tree-like form with cylinder-shape trunk and a small, rounded crown. One unusual feature of the Brazil prickly pear is its branches, which grow in 2 separate forms. *The primary joints, those coming directly off the main stems, are upright and cylinder-shaped. The secondary ones resemble leaves, because they are flat, pointed at the tips,* and fall off after a time. The flowers are yellow, 5–5.5 cm (2–2.2 in) long, with rather blunt petals. The fruits are yellow, globe-shaped, 3–4 cm (1.2–1.6 in) in diameter. Seeds are usually small, wooly, and covered with a pulp.

The Buckwheat Family   Polygonaceae

This is a large family of about 800 species, mostly soft nonwoody herbs, occurring in temperate zones around the world. Most of the trees and shrubs of this family are native to tropical regions with only 1 tree genus (sea grapes) occurring in North America. Two species of this genus are found in southern Florida.

The buckwheat family is of some importance for food, medicines, and lumber. Buckwheat and rhubarb are 2 edible members of this family, while medicines and astringents are obtained from foreign species. Some species of sea grapes produce a hard, dark, valuable wood.

Members of this family are herbs, shrubs, or trees with simple, alternate leaves that are entire along the margin. Characteristic of this family is the way the stipules (the leaf-like structures at the base of the leafstalk) form a conspicuous sheath around the stem. The flowers are small and contain both sexes and are usually clustered. The fruit may be hard, nut-like, and enclosed by the persistent parts of the flowers, or it may resemble a berry or grape.

The Sea Grape Genus   *Coccoloba* P. Browne

There are perhaps 150 species of sea grapes in the tropical regions of the Americas ranging from Florida and Mexico to South America. Some species are shrubs, others are tall trees, and a few are woody vines.

Sea grapes have simple, evergreen, entire leaves with a conspicuous sheath around the stem where the leafstalk is attached to the stem. The flowers make up branched, elongated clusters (racemes) at or near the ends of the branchlets. There are 5 outer parts (sepals) of the flowers, petals absent, 8 stamens, and 1 pistil. The fruit is egg-shaped or rounded, 3-angled, hard, covered with a thin, acid-tasting flesh. Seeds are rounded at the bottom and pointed at the tip, 3 to 6 lobed, reddish-brown, and shiny.

Key to Sea Grape Species

A. Leaves thick, leathery, almost circular in outline, heart-shaped at the base   **Sea grape, p. 426**

B. Leaves thin, papery, always longer than broad, usually broadest near the base, tapering to a narrowed base   **Dove plum, p. 427**

Sea Grape   *Coccoloba uvifera* (L.) L.

This tree is native to southern Florida, Bermuda, the Bahama Islands, the West Indies, and Central and South America. It is common along the sea shores and beaches but is not found inland. Sea grapes are tolerant of salt sprays and often grow in sandy, rocky, or broken coral soils.

Sea grape flowers almost continuously throughout the year, but more abundantly in spring. The developing fruits look like long drooping clusters of grapes ripening in the fall. While the fruit is sour, it makes a delicious pink jelly. The fruits are of limited value to wildlife.

The dark-brown to violet wood is heavy, hard, and close-grained. It is used for furniture and cabinetmaking.

Appearance: trees or shrubs to 15 m (50

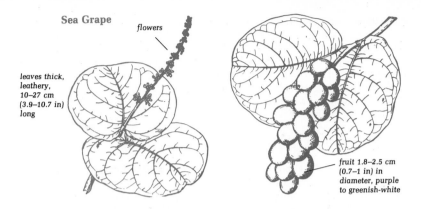

Sea Grape

flowers

leaves thick, leathery, 10–27 cm (3.9–10.7 in) long

fruit 1.8–2.5 cm (0.7–1 in) in diameter, purple to greenish-white

ft) with a compact, rounded crown; trunk short, sometimes gnarled, soon branching. **Bark:** 1–2 mm (less than 0.1 in) thick, smooth, light brown but marked by large, pale, irregular blotches. **Branches:** stout, spreading; branchlets stout, light orange gradually turning darker. **Leaves:** alternate, persistent, and appearing evergreen, 10–27 cm (3.9–10.7 in) long, 12–25 cm (4.7–10 in) wide, *almost circular in outline to very broadly egg-shaped,* rounded to short-pointed at the tip, heart-shaped at the base, *thick and leathery,* dark green and shiny above, paler and hairy beneath; leafstalks short, stout, enlarged at the base, flattened on the upper surface, hairy. **Flowers:** bisexual, appearing almost continuously throughout the year, on slender hairy stalks 3–4 cm (1.2–1.6 in) long, grouped in 1 to 6 flowered clusters in an elongated branch inflorescence, to 30 cm (11.8 in) long. **Fruits:** *egg-shaped to almost rounded, crowded together in long, hanging clusters,* each fruit 1.8–2.5 cm (0.7–1 in) long, purple to greenish-white, covered with a thin, juicy flesh. The seed hard, nut-like, thin-walled, light red.

Dove Plum
Coccoloba diversifolia Jacq.

Dove plum or pigeon plum is a common tree along the seacoast of southern Florida, the Keys, and the West Indies. They may grow to 20 m (66 ft) tall, and they have dense spreading branches that form a rounded crown. The leaves are evergreen, *6–10 cm (2.4–4 in) long, 3.8–5 cm (1.5–2 in) wide, broadest near the base,* sometimes above the middle, and bright green. Flowering is in early spring when the small clusters or

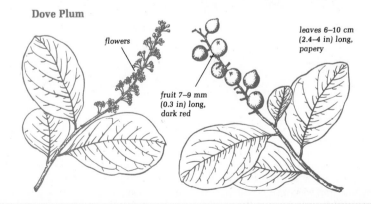

Dove Plum

flowers

fruit 7–9 mm (0.3 in) long, dark red

leaves 6–10 cm (2.4–4 in) long, papery

single flowers are evident. The flowers are produced on branched, elongated clusters (racemes) 5–8 cm (2–3.2 in) long. The *fruits* are broadest near the rounded tip and narrowing to the base, 7–9 mm (about 0.3 in) long, *sparsely grouped on hanging elongated clusters, dark red;* seeds nut-like, thin-walled, light brown.

The Tea Family

Theaceae

The tea family contains about 30 genera and 500 species in tropical and subtropical regions of the world. Three genera containing 4 species are native to the southeastern U.S.; all are small to medium-size trees. All southeastern species are attractive with large, showy white flowers. This is an economically important family because it contains the plant, *Camellia sinensis,* the source of tea. Many members are horticulturally important, including the gardenias and camellias.

Members of this family are trees or shrubs with alternate, simple leaves that are often evergreen and leathery in texture. The flowers are usually bisexual and produced singly or in few-flowered clusters in the junctions of the leaves. Each flower has 5 free calyx lobes, 5 free petals, sometimes united near their bases, many stamens, and a single pistil that is 3- to 5-celled at the base. Fruits are leathery to woody capsules that split open to release the seeds.

Key to Tea Genera

A. Leaves evergreen, leathery; flower stalks long, 3–7 cm (1.2–2.8 in)   **Gordonia, p. 428**

B. Leaves thin, deciduous; flower stalks short, up to 2 cm (0.8 in).

   1. Calyx lobes unequal; fruits splitting open from top and bottom at maturity; trees growing only in cultivation   **Franklinia, p. 430**

   2. Calyx lobes only slightly unequal; fruits splitting open only from top at maturity; trees of southeastern U.S.   **Stewartia, p. 431**

Franklinia

Mt. Stewartia

The Gordonia Genus

Gordonia Ellis

This is a small genus of perhaps 15 species distributed mainly in southeastern Asia and with a single species, the loblolly bay, in the southeastern U.S. The attractive franklinia tree was once considered to be in this genus, but was shown to be sufficiently distinct to warrant its own genus.

Members of this genus are trees or shrubs with simple alternate, almost leathery evergreen leaves. The flowers are produced singly on stalks in the junctions of the leaves. They are usually large, showy, and consist of 5 unequal calyx lobes, 5 free petals, numerous stamens united at their bases to form a cup, and with a single pistil. Fruits are woody 5-celled capsules that contain the flattened winged seeds.

Loblolly Bay — *Gordonia lasianthus* (L.) Ellis

Loblolly bay is an attractive, small to medium-size tree or shrub native to the Coastal Plain from North Carolina to central Florida and southern Mississippi. It is usually found growing in shallow swamps and moist depressions. It grows with slash pine, pond cypress, swamp and black tupelo, red maple, and Atlantic white cedar.

Loblolly bay is a fast-growing, but usually short-lived, shrub or tree. It is sometimes used as an ornamental, but it does not grow well under cultivation. Although the bark was once used for tanning leather, loblolly bay is of little or no commercial use and of little value as a food for wildlife. The reddish wood is light, soft, and fine-grained and is occasionally used in cabinet work.

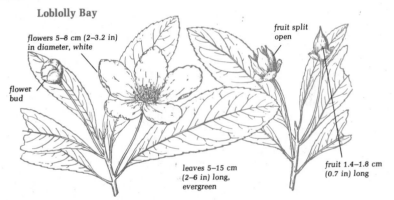

Loblolly Bay

flowers 5–8 cm (2–3.2 in) in diameter, white

fruit split open

flower bud

leaves 5–15 cm (2–6 in) long, evergreen

fruit 1.4–1.8 cm (0.7 in) long

Appearance: small to medium-size tree to 20 m (66 ft) with a tight, compacted crown; trunk straight, to 50 cm (20 in) in diameter. **Bark:** moderately thick, to 2.5 cm (1 in), with shallow to deep furrows separating the narrow flattened ridges, gray to reddish-brown. **Branches:** stout, erect to slightly spreading; branchlets stout, gray turning dark brown, smooth. **Winter buds:** 6–8 mm (0.2–0.3 in) long, broadest near the base and sharp-pointed at the tip, silky hairy. **Leaves:** alternate, simple, *evergreen, 5–15 cm (2–6 in) long, 3–5 cm (1.2–2 in) wide, broadest at or above the middle,* pointed at the tips, tapering to a wedge-shaped base, with fine, blunt teeth along the margin, dark green, shiny, and smooth above, duller and smooth on the lower surface, *leathery,* turning scarlet and dropping at the end of the second year; the leafstalks stout, 1–1.4 cm (0.4–0.6 in) long, slightly winged toward the base of the leaf. **Flowers:** *large, white, showy, fragrant, 5–8 cm (2–3.2 in) in diameter, produced singly at the junctions of the younger leaves,* with 5 calyx lobes, 5 large petals, each broadest above the middle, the margins often fringed, with numerous yellow stamens and a single central pistil. **Fruits: *egg-shaped capsules,*** 1.4–1.8 cm (0.7 in) long, hairy, and ***splitting into 5 sections at maturity; seeds*** 2 to 4 in each section, ***flattened, 6–7 mm (0.2–0.3 in) long, with a papery brown wing.***

The Franklinia Genus

Franklinia Marshall

The genus was established to contain but a single species of small tree from the southeastern U.S. The tree is closely related to the loblolly bay but differs by having deciduous leaves, wingless seeds, the capsules splitting first from the base, and the stamens not fused together. The description of the genus is the same as for the species.

Franklinia

Franklinia altamaha Bartr.

This deciduous small tree or shrub is one of the most historically interesting species in the southeastern U.S. It was originally discovered along the Altamaha River in Georgia in 1765, revisited several times, and then last seen and collected in the wild in 1790. Since that time it has been perpetuated in cultivation because of its attractive flowers and foliage. Franklinia is of special importance in horticulture because it is one of the few trees that flower in summer and continues flowering until the first frost in autumn. Franklinia is of no known value to wildlife.

Appearance: shrub or small tree to 7 m (23 ft) with a tight rounded crown; trunk short, soon branching, to 25 cm (10 in) in diameter. **Bark:** thin, smooth, gray to red-

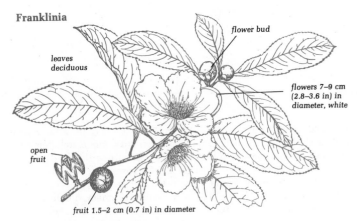

Franklinia

leaves
deciduous

flower bud

flowers 7–9 cm
(2.8–3.6 in) in
diameter, white

open
fruit

fruit 1.5–2 cm (0.7 in) in diameter

dish brown to dark brown. **Branches:** stout, upright to slightly spreading, often angular; branchlets slender, rounded, hairy when young, becoming smooth with age. **Winter buds:** 6–8.5 mm (about 0.2–0.3 in) long, pointed at the tip, hairy, reddish-brown. **Leaves:** alternate, simple, ***deciduous,*** 6–15 cm (2.4–5.9 in) long, 3.8–5 cm (1.5–2 in) wide, broadest above the middle, rounded to pointed at the tip and gradually narrowing at the base, with fine sharp teeth along the margin, especially above the middle, dark green, shiny and smooth except for a slightly hairy main vein, paler and hairy beneath, turning scarlet and falling in the autumn of the second year; leafstalks stout, 0.6–1.3 cm (0.3–0.6 in) long, hairy. **Flowers:** *large, showy, white, fragrant,* produced solitary in the junctions of the upper leaves on the branchlets, stalked, the *flowers 7–9 cm (2.8–3.6 in) in diameter,* with 5 unequal calyx lobes, 5 large petals that are widest above the middle and rounded at the tips, with many stamens and a single central pistil. **Fruits:** woody capsules, almost rounded, 1.5–2 cm (0.7 in) in diameter, *splitting lengthwise from top and bottom starting at the base into 5 sections,* each section with up to 8 seeds, seeds 12–14 cm (4.7–5.5 in) long, angled, *wingless.*

The Stewartia Genus

Stewartia L.

This is a small genus of about 15 species of evergreen or deciduous trees and shrubs. Two of the deciduous species are native to the southeastern U.S. All of the remaining species are native to southeastern Asia. Stewartias are typically understory trees of the deciduous forest belt in warm temperate climates. They are attractive plants often used in ornamental plantings. Their large white flowers bloom in early summer when most trees and shrubs have already finished flowering. In addition, the thin darker bark falls off in irregular, flattened patches, leaving a lighter-colored, handsome mottled bark.

Stewartias are small trees or shrubs with mottled bark and a rounded crown. The simple, alternate leaves are evergreen or deciduous, entire or finely toothed along the margin. Flowers are bisexual, showy, and produced singly in the junctions of the leaflets. They are usually composed of 5 green calyx lobes, 5 large, free petals, many stamens, and a pistil composed of 5 segments. The fruits are woody capsules that split open lengthwise into 5 sections.

Key to Stewartia Species

A. Leafstalks only narrowly winged; the 5 styles of the pistil united; seeds shiny; small trees of Coastal Plain and Piedmont southeastern U.S.
Virginia stewartia, p. 431

B. Leafstalks with a broad wing; the 5 styles of the pistil free; seeds dull; small trees primarily of mountains in southeastern U.S.
Mountain stewartia, p. 432

Virginia Stewartia

Virginia Stewartia

Stewartia malacodendron L.

This member of the tea family is a small deciduous tree or large shrub found along the Coastal Plain and Piedmont from eastern Virginia south to Georgia, western Florida, west to northern Alabama and Mississippi. It grows in fertile, well-drained soils from

sea level to 620 m (about 2,000 ft) elevation, and is usually found near streams in
deciduous forests. Common associated
trees are the American beech, Ashe's magnolia, and the Florida anise tree.

Virginia stewartia is a slow-growing, inconspicuous understory tree, except during early summer when the large attractive
flowers appear. As an ornamental, it is
worthy of cultivation for its large white
flowers and attractive bark. The smooth
mottled bark is silvery, pinkish brown, or

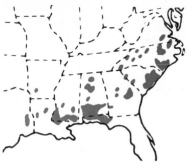

buff colored, which contrasts with the darker reddish-brown, irregular outer patches.
This tree is of little or no value to wildlife and the trees are too small to be of value as a
lumber source.

Virginia Stewartia

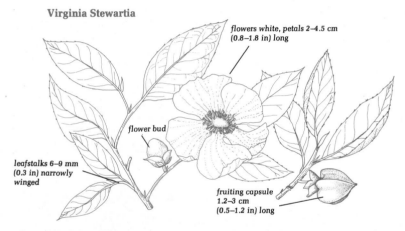

flowers white, petals 2–4.5 cm
(0.8–1.8 in) long

flower bud

leafstalks 6–9 mm
(0.3 in) narrowly
winged

fruiting capsule
1.2–3 cm
(0.5–1.2 in) long

Appearance: small bushy trees or shrubs to 6 m (20 ft) and with a rounded crown;
trunks often multiple, short, irregular, soon branching. **Bark:** thin, 2–6 mm (0.1–0.2 in)
thick, smooth but breaking into thin flat plates giving a mottled appearance, dark
brown with lighter-colored patches underneath. **Branches:** erect, slender; branchlets
slender, light to dark brown to gray, covered with fine straight hairs when young,
becoming smooth with age. **Leaves:** simple, alternate, deciduous, 5–12 cm (2–4.8 in)
long, 2.5–5 cm (1–2 in) wide, broadest near the middle to near the base, tapering to a
narrow base and to a pointed tip, with fine, sharp-pointed teeth along the margin,
bright green and mostly smooth above, lighter green and hairy beneath, with a papery
texture; leafstalks short, stout to 6–9 mm (0.2–0.3 in) long. **Flowers:** *large, showy,
white,* saucer-shaped, *composed of 5 green calyx lobes, 5 petals, 2–4.5 cm (0.8–1.8
in) long and broadest above the middle,* numerous purplish-blue stamens, and a
single central pistil. **Fruits:** dry capsules, 1.2–3 cm (0.5–1.2 in) long, broadest near
the base, weakly angled and pointed at the tip, splitting open into 5 cells; *seeds*
small, dark, *shiny,* reddish-brown, angular, and unwinged.

Mountain Stewartia   *Stewartia ovata* (Cav.) Weatherby

Mountain stewartia is native to the mountains and adjacent Piedmont of the southeastern U.S. It occurs along wooded margins of streams and river bluffs. This is a rare species that may require protection in the future to ensure its survival. The flowers are among the largest of any of the stewartias. Thus, it is of importance as an ornamental.

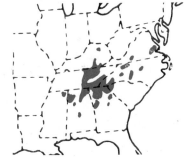

Small trees or bushy shrubs may reach 6 m (20 ft) in height. The bark does not peel away to produce the mottled pattern typical of the Virginia stewartia. The leaves are deciduous, 6–15 cm (2.4–6 in) long, 3–8 cm (1.2–3.2 in) wide, broadest near the middle to near the base; **leafstalks broadly winged.** The flowers have **5 large, spreading petals,** each one 3–4.5 cm (1.2–1.8 in) long and 2–3.5 cm (0.8–1.4 in) wide. The fruits are woody capsules, broadest near the base, angled, pointed at the tip, and 1.5–2 mm (0.1 in) long.

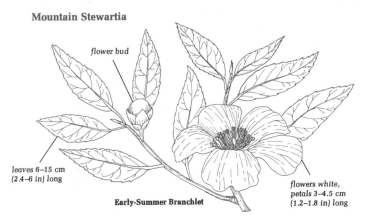

Mountain Stewartia

flower bud

leaves 6–15 cm (2.4–6 in) long

Early-Summer Branchlet

flowers white, petals 3–4.5 cm (1.2–1.8 in) long

The Garcinia Family

Guttiferae

This is a medium-size tropical family of approximately 35 genera and over 400 species. Only 1 species, the balsam apple, grows in North America, in extreme southern Florida. The mangosteen, a delicious tropical fruit, is the best-known member of the family. On the whole, this family is commercially unimportant.

The Clusia Genus

Clusia

This is a large genus of leather-leaved trees and shrubs of the tropics. They have opposite evergreen leaves and usually either male or female flowers. The fruits are usually large capsules. Members of this genus are interesting biologically because of their ability to grow on other trees and eventually kill them.

Balsam Apple

Clusia rosea Jacq.

The balsam apple is a rare evergreen, indigenous tree of scattered places in the Florida Keys. It is also planted as an ornamental in southern Florida. Balsam apple is more common in the West Indies, and also may be found from southern Mexico to French

Guiana. Known also as the copey clusia or wild mammee, this tree is usually found at low elevations along woodland riverbanks and hillsides. The dense, broad crown, the large and showy white flowers, and the yellowish, fleshy seed capsules are major distinguishing features.

The trees usually begin as air-plants (or epiphytes), the young saplings growing from seeds sprouted in the forks of other trees. They send down long aerial roots to the ground. Eventually, the roots thicken into stout vines that cover and encircle the host tree; in time the balsam apple strangles and kills its host. For this reason balsam apple is considered to be a forest pest. When the tree reaches maturity, it flowers and fruits continuously throughout the year. The male and female flowers appear on separate trees, and the fruits they produce are ball-shaped and inedible to humans, although they are eaten by bats.

The reddish-brown wood is hard, heavy, strong, medium to fine-textured, and without growth rings. Its main use in the West Indies is as fuelwood, fence posts, rural construction, and crossties. It is also suitable for light furniture and tool handles. The bark, fruit, and other parts of this tree produce a yellow resinous latex, which is used in caulking boats, in plastering, and even as a medicine. Early Spanish conquistadores used the stout, leathery leaves as playing cards, first drawing figures on them, when their paper cards wore out. Today, balsam apple's salt tolerance makes it popular for planting on exposed ocean-front properties.

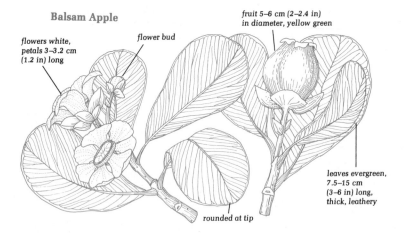

Balsam Apple

flowers white, petals 3–3.2 cm (1.2 in) long

flower bud

fruit 5–6 cm (2–2.4 in) in diameter, yellow green

leaves evergreen, 7.5–15 cm (3–6 in) long, thick, leathery

rounded at tip

Appearance: medium-size tree, up to 18 m (60 ft) in height, with a broad, spreading, dense crown; trunk up to 0.6 m (1.9 ft) in diameter. **Bark:** gray, smooth, slightly cracked and warty; inner bark is pinkish-brown and gritty, with yellow latex. **Branches:** numerous; branchlets are green, stout, and ringed at leaf junctions. **Leaves:** opposite, *evergreen,* simple, *7.5–15 cm (3–6 in) long, 5–12 cm (2–4.8 in) wide; broadest near the rounded or slightly notched tip,* narrowed toward the base; margins smooth and slightly turned under, *thick and leathery,* green to dark-green, slightly shiny above, dull yellow-green beneath; leafstalks 1–2.5 cm (0.4–1 in) long, green, stout, flattened, enlarged at the base. **Flowers:** 7–9 cm (2.8–3.6 in) in diameter, from 1 to 3 at the ends of the branchlets on downward-curving stalks, 1–2 cm (0.4–0.8 in) in length; calyx lobes 4 to 6, rounded, concave, 1.2–1.6 cm (0.5–0.7 in) long, white ringed with pink; petals 6 to 8, white, fleshy, broadest toward the tip, 3–3.2 cm (1.2–1.3 in) long; male flowers have many stamens united by a ring, the inner ones in a resinous mass; female flowers have a brown ring of sterile stamens, and a 7- to 9-celled ovary with a green, resinous mass of 7 to 9 stigmas. **Fruits:** *a nearly round, fleshy seed capsule, 5–6 cm (2–2.4 in) in diameter,* broader than long, *yellow-green,* turning brown at maturity, splitting into 7 to 9 parts, each of which contains many yellow seeds, 0.4–0.6 cm (0.2–0.3 in) long, in an orange-red pulp.

The Basswood, or Linden, Family   Tiliaceae

This is a medium-size family of about 40 genera and over 400 species of trees and shrubs, mainly confined to tropical regions. Several genera have northern distributions. Of the 3 North American genera, only 1, basswood (*Tilia*), contains trees.

Economically, this is a fairly important family because of the diverse products obtained from it. The entire family is noted for the tough, fibrous inner bark. Jute, a coarse fiber used to make burlap, gunny sacks, and cord, is obtained from some of the Asian members of this family. Jute has been under continuous cultivation in India since 800 B.C. Basswood trees yield a valuable lumber and also serve as important shade trees in cities of Europe and Asia.

Members of the family are trees and shrubs with simple alternate, rarely opposite, leaves. The flowers are usually in branched, round to flat-topped, few-flowered clusters. Individual flowers are bisexual, with 5 calyx lobes, 5 corolla lobes, 5 or 10 stamens, and a single pistil. Fruits are small, nut-like, sometimes berry-like and fleshy, or even dry and splitting open at maturity.

The Basswood, or Linden, Genus   *Tilia* L.

The genus *Tilia* is known by 2 common names, in different contexts: in forestry, it is called basswood; in horticulture, it is known as the linden. There are approximately 25 to 30 species that are widely distributed through north temperate regions of the world, extending south to Mexico, southern Europe, and central China. It is absent from western North America.

There are 4 North American species within this genus. These generally prefer moist, but not wet, well-drained sites and often associate with maples, oaks, and ash in the eastern deciduous woodland. Squirrels and birds occasionally feed on the seeds, and deer browse the leaves and twigs.

The basswoods' distinctively long-stalked, large, heart-shaped leaves make them popular as shade and ornamental trees. The European little-leaf linden (*Tilia cordata*) is a commonly planted tree along city streets. It has a dense compact shape and smaller leaves than the American species, and it is an excellent shade tree. The silver linden (*Tilia tomentosa*) from Asia Minor is occasionally encountered, and can be readily distinguished from other lindens by the silvery undersides of its leaves.

Of the native American species, the American basswood (*Tilia americana*) and the white basswood (*T. heterophylla*) are important in the forest industry. The wood is soft, pale, light, and straight-grained. It is widely used in interior finishing, cabinet-making and woodenware, in paper manufacture, and for piano soundboards. All species have a tough, fibrous inner bark that can be made into such diverse items as mats, fishnets, cords, coarse cloths, and shoes. Lime-flower oil is distilled from the flowers of a European species, and is much used in the perfume industry. And, as honey connoisseurs know, basswood flowers produce a honey that is unsurpassed in flavor and delicacy.

Basswoods are deciduous trees, often rising over 30 m (100 ft) in height, with straight trunks and relatively narrow crowns. The bark varies from gray to brown to reddish-brown, becomes up to 2.5 cm (1 in) thick, is very tough, and sometimes broken up into small scales or deep furrows on the surface. The branches are stout and taper into slender, slightly zigzag branchlets. The winter buds are small, flattened, and covered with 2 or 3 scales. The leaves are alternate, long-stemmed, broadly egg-shaped or heart-shaped, with a markedly uneven base and pointed tip. The highly fragrant, cream-colored flowers hang in slender clusters that are borne in late spring or early summer and are attached to the branchlet by a strap-shaped bract. The small, gray fruits, resembling peas, contain 1 to 2 seeds.

Key to Basswood, or Linden, Species

A. Mature leaves smooth (lacking hairs), the young or immature leaves with unbranched hairs.

    1. Trees of northeastern and northcentral U.S.; leafstalks and flower stalks smooth; young leaves with tufts of hairs in the junctions of the main vein, otherwise smooth
                American basswood, p. 436

    2. Trees of southeastern Coastal Plain and Mexico; leafstalks and flower stalks hairy becoming smooth; young leaves hairy but becoming smooth with maturity
                Florida basswood, p. 438

Florida Basswood

B. Mature leaves hairy, the hairs branched and roughly star shaped.

    1. Lower leaf surface pale green, the star-shaped hairs scattered; young branchlets downy the first year; trees of southern and southeastern U.S.
                Carolina basswood, p. 439

    2. Lower leaf surface whitish, the star-shaped hairs densely crowded; young branchlets smooth; trees of eastern U.S.
                White basswood, p. 440

White Basswood

American Basswood   *Tilia americana* L.

The American basswood, a medium-size to large tree of the central and eastern North American woodlands, is the best known of the indigenous basswoods. Ranging from southern Canada to North Carolina, and west to North Dakota, it is found from lowlands up to 1,500 m (4,900 ft). The tree grows on fine-textured, sandy or clay loams, on certain glacial tills, or even on poor sites, such as high, rocky ridges. Best growth is on moist, well-drained sites, such as low woods. This tree is commonly planted in yards, parks, and along streets in eastern towns. In the forest, it is a major component of the sugar maple-basswood and oak-basswood-white ash forest types; in other places it associates with such species as paper and yellow birch, white pine, hemlock, and black cherry.

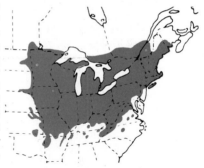

Basswood is a fast-growing, moderately long-lived tree. In early competition for growing space, young trees are often hindered by cropping from rabbits, which are the basswood's chief animal pest. They have been saved on many occasions by their capacity to sprout back from the roots, which they do quite vigorously. Flowering occurs in June or July, some 6 to 8 weeks after the leaves have appeared. The seed crops are usually heavy each year, and ripen in September and October. Trees begin producing viable seed after about 15 years, and their productive lives may span more than 85 years. While less important to wildlife than many other species, basswood seeds are eaten by bobwhite quail, several kinds of squirrel, and other rodents. Rabbits and white-tail deer browse the twigs and foliage. Many insect species trouble the basswood from time to time, though without devastating damage.

American basswood is a tree of major timber importance in portions of the Great Lakes states. The wood is light, soft, and pale-colored, and has been put to many uses — for example, in cabinetmaking and musical instruments, and even in tailors' yard-sticks. It is also cheap and abundant enough to be an important paper-pulp species. Like all members of the linden family, American basswood has a tough inner bark; for centuries this was fashioned by Indians into a tangle-free rope and thread, which was sometimes used to bind up wounds. Iroquois carved masks from the sapwood of the living trees, splitting them off the trunks and hollowing them out from behind.

Appearance: a medium to tall tree, 20–25 m (65–82 ft) tall (maximum 30 m; 100 ft); with a broad form and a large, spreading crown; trunk is straight, usually branchless

American Basswood

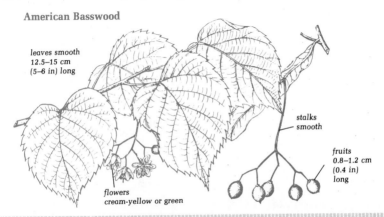

leaves smooth
12.5–15 cm
(5–6 in) long

stalks
smooth

fruits
0.8–1.2 cm
(0.4 in)
long

flowers
cream-yellow or green

up to half its length, up to 1.5 m (4.9 ft) in width. **Bark:** light brown, smooth, deeply furrowed on older trees, up to 2.5 cm (1 in) thick. **Branches:** of varying thickness, ascending or arching upward, or outward-spreading and curling up at the ends to give a manicured impression; branchlets slender, zigzag, yellowish-brown. **Winter buds:** 0.5–0.7 cm (0.2 in) long, broad, often reddish, lopsided, in 2 rows along the twig, with 2 or 3 overlapping scales visible; terminal buds absent. **Leaves:** simple, alternate, deciduous, *12.5–15 cm (5–6 in) long and 7.5–10 cm (3–4 in) across; broadest near the base,* narrowed to an elongated point at the tip, *the base unequally heart-shaped* or sometimes nearly straight across; margins coarsely saw-toothed, curling in; thick and firm-textured; dark, dull green above, paler below. **Flowers:** *creamy yellow or green,* 1.1–1.3 cm (0.5–0.6 in) wide; *on a few-flowered, slender stalk,* which is free for 8–10 cm (3.2–4 in) and *attached midway down to near its base to a leaf-like, narrow bract, 10–12.5 cm (4–5 in) long, 2.5–3 cm (1–1.2 in) wide;* 5 petals lance-shaped, longer than stamens or sepals; pistil covered with long, soft hairs. **Fruits:** nearly round, 0.8–1.2 cm (0.4 in) long, covered with a reddish fuzz; sparse clusters remain on the tree into winter.

Florida Basswood   *Tilia floridana* Small

This is a small to medium-size tree of the southeastern U.S., occurring from Virginia to Texas and in northeastern Mexico. A lowlands tree, the Florida basswood flourishes along coasts or in moist, rich woods and hammocks, and is apparently limited to the longleaf-pine region of the southern coastal states.

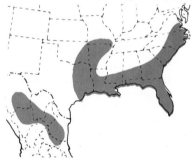

Florida basswoods are fast-growing trees. They flower in early June after their leaves have unfolded; the seeds mature in the early fall. As with other basswoods, sprouting is vigorous. The trees often occur in clumps, the smaller sprouts surrounding a taller, straighter, central trunk. The Florida basswood is of relatively small importance to wildlife, being browsed by the whitetail deer and several species of rodents. Bees gather the nectar, which produces an excellent honey.

The wood is light, pale yellow, and similar to that of its relatives. Many trees have been used for interior finishes, woodworking, and other items requiring lightweight or light-colored wood.

Florida Basswood

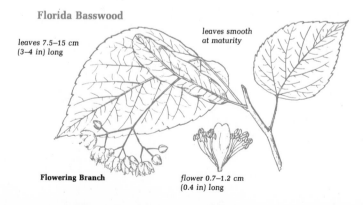

leaves 7.5–15 cm
(3–4 in) long

leaves smooth
at maturity

Flowering Branch

flower 0.7–1.2 cm
(0.4 in) long

Appearance: a small to medium-size tree, 10–20 m (32–66 ft) tall, with an irregularly rounded crown, composed of a few ascending branches; trunk straight, up to 0.6 m (1.9 ft) in diameter; often sprouting many shoots from base. **Bark:** gray, thinnish broken into flat, interlacing ridges that form small scales; somewhat furrowed. **Branches:** few, slender, ascending; ending in reddish-brown to gray, downy, flexible, slightly zigzag branchlets. **Winter buds:** 0.3–0.5 cm (0.1–0.3 in) long, blunt or rounded at the tip, dark reddish-brown, hairless. **Leaves:** simple, alternate, deciduous, *7.5–15 cm (3–4 in) long, 6–10 cm (2.4–4 in) wide; broadest near the base; bases very unequally rounded,* narrowing abruptly at the tip, margins coarsely or shallowly toothed; hairy and red-tinged when they unfold, and at maturity thin, smooth, *dark yellow-green above, paler and smooth beneath or with a few hairs;* leafstalks smooth and slender, 1.9–2.5 cm (0.8–1 in) long. **Flowers:** 0.7–1.2 cm (0.4 in) in diameter, cream to yellow colored, in downy, open clusters of 20 or more, on long, drooping bracts, and attached to them for one-third of their length; sepals and petals usually equal in number, narrow, with many short stamens and a smooth pistil. **Fruits:** round or nearly round, down-coated, woody, 6–12 mm (0.2–0.5 in) in diameter.

Carolina Basswood

Tilia caroliniana Mill.
(synonyms: *T. pubescens* Ait., *T. australis* Small)

The Carolina basswood is a relatively small, southern member of the basswood family. Its range extends from southeastern Virginia to eastcentral Texas; its western component has been classified as a separate variety (*Tilia caroliniana* variety *rhoophila* Sarg.). For best growth, this basswood prefers rich, moist woods or, in Florida, dense hammocks near streams.

A moderately fast-growing tree, this basswood produces clusters of fragrant flowers in early summer. The numerous fruits, which are tiny nutlets, mature in the fall. Basswoods are of minor importance to wildlife: The young shoots, twigs, and foliage are sometimes used for browse by deer and rabbits. The seeds are of no use to songbirds.

The wood is much like that of the American basswood, except that it is lighter in weight. It is likewise suitable for woodwork, cabinetmaking, and interior finishes (though it is not used extensively).

This species is sometimes confused with the Florida basswood, which is a larger tree with a straighter trunk.

Appearance: a small tree, 6–12 m (20–40 ft) in height, with slender form, ending in an irregular crown made up of a few ascending branches; trunk leaning, 30–50 cm (12–20 in) in diameter. **Bark:** dark gray to gray-brown, 12–16 mm (0.5–0.6 in) thick, coarsely furrowed and broken into flat-topped, interlacing ridges. **Branches:** slender, ascending, few in number; branchlets slender, red-brown or gray, downy the first year, curved, somewhat zigzag. **Winter buds:** broadest near the base, pointed at the tip, 0.6–0.7 cm (0.3 in) long, usually smooth but sometimes slightly hairy (variety *rhoophila*). **Leaves:** simple, alternate, deciduous, *8–18 cm (3.2–7 in) long, 6.3–12.5 cm (2.5–4.9 in) wide, broadest near the base, with a lopsided base that is either straight across or slightly lobed,* abruptly long-pointed at the tip, thin but firm in texture, *smooth and dark green above, paler and with light brown, branched hairs underneath;* leafstalks 2.5–3 cm (1–1.2 in) long. **Flowers:** cream-colored, 5–7 mm

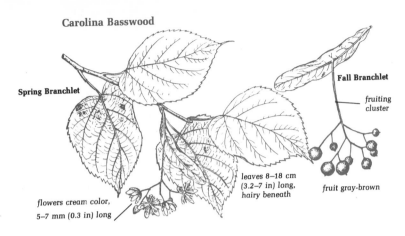

Carolina Basswood

Spring Branchlet

Fall Branchlet

fruiting cluster

leaves 8–18 cm
(3.2–7 in) long,
hairy beneath

fruit gray-brown

flowers cream color,
5–7 mm (0.3 in) long

(0.3 in) long, in clusters of mostly 8 to 15 flowers (up to 50 in the western variety) on a slender, hairy stalk that is 10–12.5 cm (4–5 in) long, attached to a bract, 10–12 cm (4–4.8 in) long and 2 cm (0.8 in) wide from the base up to the middle of the stalk; sepals and petals usually equal in number, sepals downy outside, hairy inside, blunter and shorter than the petals. **Fruits:** gray-brown, downy, woody, round or nearly so, 0.5–0.7 cm (0.3 in) in diameter.

White Basswood   *Tilia heterophylla* Vent.

Although white basswood is a native American tree, it was first identified as a separate species at the end of the 18th century in the gardens of the French emperor Napoleon. These trees are medium in size, and occur throughout the Appalachian region from scattered parts of New York state to northern Florida. White basswood is rare at low elevations, becoming more common in the upper Piedmont region and reaching greatest numbers in the Appalachian Mountains at elevations from 900–1,500 m (2,900–4,900 ft). This species prefers moist, well-drained sites, and is intolerant of extreme wet or dry conditions. Best growth is obtained along mountain streams or coves, in crumbly, deep, humus-rich soils. In the northern part of its

range, white basswood grows with such species as northern red oak, white ash, black cherry, and eastern hemlock. Farther south, its associates are yellow buckeye, yellow and paper birch, sugar maple, and yellow poplar.

These are long-lived and moderately fast-growing trees, when compared to other southern Appalachian species. The fragrant blossoms appear in June or July, well after the leaves are out; often they are hard to spot when standing below the tree. Seeds ripen in September or October and are dispersed in late winter or early spring. The tree can also regenerate from sprouts, though these are less hardy than seedlings. Wildlife use is limited: Whitetail deer occasionally browse the tender twigs and smaller branches. Among insects, bees collect the nectar for a delicate honey; and

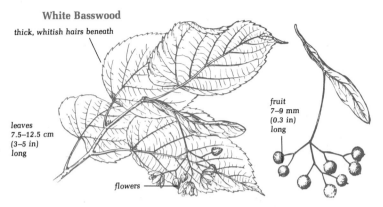

White Basswood

thick, whitish hairs beneath

leaves
7.5–12.5 cm
(3–5 in)
long

fruit
7–9 mm
(0.3 in)
long

flowers

many defoliators, borers, aphids, and gall-midges parasitize the leaves and wood. White basswood is also fairly susceptible to fire damage, due to its thin bark.

The soft, light wood is suitable for cabinetwork and other softwood work, and is used for similar purposes to those noted for the American basswood.

Appearance: a medium-size, well-formed tree, 18–24 m (60–80 ft) in height, with a straight, branch-free trunk ending in a full, spreading crown; maximum trunk diameter, approximately 1 m (3.3 ft). **Bark:** dark gray, thin, deeply furrowed, with broad ridges. **Branchlets:** slender, tapering, smooth, reddish or yellowish brown branchlets. **Winter buds:** slightly flattened, smooth, egg-shaped, 0.5–0.8 cm (about 0.3 in) long. **Leaves:** simple, alternate, deciduous, *7.5–12.5 cm (3–5 in) long, 6.4–7 cm (2.5–2.8 in) wide, broadest near the base, sharply tapering at the tip, unequal and straight to heart-shaped at the base,* margins finely toothed with glandular teeth, dark green and smooth above, *paler below and covered with thick, firmly attached, whitish down;* leafstalks smooth and slender, 3.8–4.4 cm (1.5–1.8 in) long. **Flowers:** 0.6–0.7 cm (about 0.3 in) wide, in clusters of 10 to 20, suspended to a slender stalk that is joined to a narrow, long, leaf-like bract; sepals and petals equal in number, pale, hairy, sharp-tipped. **Fruits:** 7–9 mm (about 0.3 in) long, slightly elongate, ending in a short, pointed tip; woody, covered with short, brownish hairs.

The Sterculia Family   Sterculiaceae

This family is composed of about 50 genera and over 750 species distributed mostly in the tropical and semi-tropical regions of the world. There are 7 genera native to North America, although only 1 contains species reaching tree size. A second genus represented by the southeast Asian species, the Chinese parasol tree, has been introduced throughout southern North America and has naturalized, reproducing on its own. Two tropical members of this family are important commercially, the cocoa tree, the source of chocolate, and species of the *Cola* genus, for flavoring in some soft drinks.

Members of this family have alternate leaves that may be simple or compound, entire, toothed, or lobed, and stalked. The flowers are mainly bisexual and are grouped into clusters, rarely occurring alone. Flowers are composed of 3 to 5 calyx lobes and 5 free small petals, reduced in size or completely absent; stamens are grouped variously into a tube; the pistil is usually composed of 4 or 5 segments. The fruits are leathery to fleshy capsules that may or may not split open at maturity.

Key to Sterculia Genera

Mexican Fremontia

A. Shrubs or small trees to 7 m (23 ft) high; leaves shallowly 3-, 5-, or 7-lobed, 1–7.5 cm (0.4–3 in) wide; flowers yellow, 3–8 cm (1.2–3.2 in) across, showy; native to California, Arizona, and Baja California **Fremontia, p. 442**

B. Small to medium-size trees to 12 m (40 ft) high; leaves distinctly 3 to 5 lobed, 10–30 cm (4–12 in) wide; flowers greenish, 8–12 mm (0.3–0.5 in) across, not showy; introduced from China, usually planted in the southeastern Coastal Plain and in California **Firmiana, p. 444**

Chinese Parasol Tree

The Fremontia Genus

Fremontodendron Cov.
(synonym: *Fremontia* Torr.)

This genus contains only 2 species, both native to southwestern North America, the California fremontia and the Mexican fremontia. Both of these are of some horticultural interest because of their showy flowers. The California fremontia often comes into flower at one time creating great showy masses of flowers. On the other hand, the Mexican fremontia flowers over several months and is not as showy. This genus was named in honor of American western explorer John C. Fremont.

Members of this genus are shrubs or small trees with simple, alternate, evergreen leaves that are almost entire to 3-, 5-, or 7-lobed. The flowers are produced singly at or near the ends of the branchlets. Individual flowers are composed of a bell-shaped, 5-lobed calyx, which is showy and petal-like; true petals are absent. Flowers have 5 stamens, which are alternate with the calyx lobes, and a single 4- or 5-celled pistil. The fruits are dry capsules, broadest near the base and pointed at the tip, splitting lengthwise into 4 or 5 valves when mature, and covered on the outside by long hairs. Seeds are broadest near the base, flattened, hard, and dark.

Key to Fremontia Species

A. Leaves with 1–3 main veins at the base of the leaf blade; flowers 3–6 cm (1.2–2.4 in) across, flattened; occurring on dry granite slopes of California and Arizona at 1,000–2,000 m (3,200–6,600 ft) elevation **California fremontia, p. 443**

B. Leaves with 5–7 main veins at the base of the leaf blade; flowers 6–9 cm (2.4–3.6 in) in diameter, shallowly bowl-shaped; occurring in dry canyons of southern California and adjacent Baja California at 400–600 m (1,300–2,000 ft) elevation **Mexican fremontia, p. 444**

California Fremontia *Fremontodendron californicum* (Torr.) Cov.

(synonym: *Fremontia california* Torr.)

Often called slippery elm by earlier settlers, the California fremontia is native to mountain areas between 1,000–2,000 m (3,200–6,600 ft) elevation of California and central Arizona. It is most abundant on the eastern slopes of the Sierra Nevada, but

reaches its greatest size on the western slopes. This species thrives in poor, dry rocky soils of foothills and slopes where it often forms dense thickets.

Interestingly, the flowers do not have petals. Instead the bright yellow calyx lobes are so large and showy that they can easily be mistaken for petals. The flowers bloom in May and June in beautiful profusion. California fremontia is usually an abundant seed producer. Cattle browse on the nutritious branchlets.

The reddish-brown wood is hard to soft. It is fine grained but is not used commercially because of the small size of the trees. The gummy inner bark resembles that of the eastern slippery elm, and was once used to make poultices.

California Fremontia

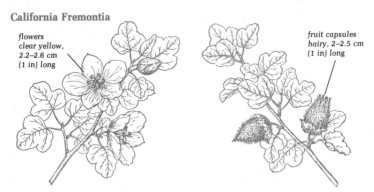

flowers clear yellow, 2.2–2.6 cm (1 in) long

fruit capsules hairy, 2–2.5 cm (1 in) long

Appearance: shrub or small tree to 9 m (30 ft), with a broad, open crown; trunk short, soon branching, to 35 cm (14 in) in diameter. **Branches:** stout, rigid, spreading, sometimes at right angles; branchlets stout, rounded, thickly covered with star-shaped hairs when young, turning light reddish-brown and becoming smooth. **Winter buds:** naked. **Leaves:** alternate, simple, 2.5–3.5 cm (1–1.4 in) long, 1.5–2.5 cm (0.6–1 in) wide, very broad but widest near the base, usually 3 lobed, thick and leathery, light green above, covered with star-shaped whitish to rusty hairs on the lower surface, often falling away after second year; the leafstalks stout, 0.5–1.5 cm (0.2–0.6 in) long.

Flowers: *large, showy,* bisexual, *produced singly on spur-like side branches,* 3 to 5 leaf-like bracts are present around the young flowers but fall away before the flowers open; *calyx bell-shaped, 3–6 cm (1.2–2.4 in) across, deeply 5 lobed, clear yellow; petals absent;* stamens 5, joined half their length into a column; 1 pistil, 4 to 5 parted. **Fruits:** *dry, hairy capsule, 2–2.5 cm (0.8–1 in) long, hairy,* splitting lengthwise into 4 or 5 valves, with soft wooly hairs on the inner surface of the valves; seeds small, 2–4 mm (0.1–0.2 in) long, broadest near the base, flattened, very dark reddish-brown.

Mexican Fremontia	*Fremontodendron mexicanum* A. Davidson

[synonym: *Fremontia mexicana* (Davidson) Macbr.]

This species is native to San Diego County in southern California as well as in northern Baja California, Mexico. It occurs in dry canyons about 400–600 m (1,300–2,000 ft) altitude and is very rare in the U.S. Usually only a shrub in the wild, it becomes a tree in cultivation and in Mexico. The flowers occur among the leaves but are not showy, although they bloom continuously over several months.

The tree grows 2–6 m (6–20 ft) tall, is stiff, and spreads to about as wide as it is tall. The branches are densely covered with star-like hairs that are first yellowish, then become darker. Leaves are thick, rounded, 2.5–7 cm (1–2.8 in) long and

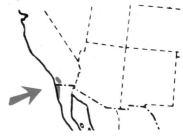

Mexican Fremontia

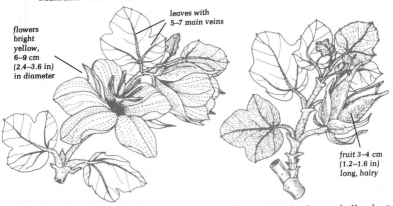

flowers bright yellow, 6–9 cm (2.4–3.6 in) in diameter

leaves with 5–7 main veins

fruit 3–4 cm (1.2–1.6 in) long, hairy

wide, heart-shaped at base, *with 5 to 7 distinct veins from the base,* shallowly 3-lobed, dark green and slightly hairy above, densely brownish hairy beneath; the leaf-stalks are stout, 2–4 cm (0.8–1.6 in) long. The flowers are composed of a slightly *bell-shaped calyx 6–9 cm (2.4–3.6 in) across,* orange, becoming reddish on the outside of the base, *slightly hairy within,* petals absent, with 5 stamens, and a single pistil. The *fruits* are dry capsules, *3–4 cm (1.2–1.6 in) long,* broadest near the base, pointed at the tips before opening, and splitting lengthwise into 4 or 5 sections at maturity.

The Firmiana Genus

Firmiana Marsili

This is a small genus of perhaps as many as 15 species of trees native to southeastern and eastern Asia, Indomalasia, and East Africa. The trees are medium-size to tall and produce large attractive leaves. One species, the Chinese parasol tree, has been introduced in southern regions of North America.

The large, alternately arranged leaves often have up to 7 finger-like lobes radiating outward like the fingers on a hand. The tiny flowers are grouped in large showy clusters. Fruits are capsules splitting open at maturity.

Chinese Parasol Tree

Firmiana simplex (L.) W. F. Wight

[synonym: *F. platanifolia* (L. f.) Schott & Endl.]

This species is native to China and Japan and was introduced into North America in 1757. It has been planted along the Coastal Plain from South Carolina to Florida, west to Texas, and in California. This fast-growing tree has large simple leaves that make it useful as a street or shade tree. It is hardy as far north as Washington, D.C.

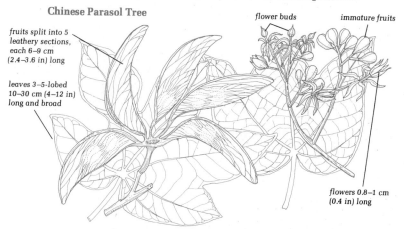

Chinese Parasol Tree

flower buds

immature fruits

fruits split into 5 leathery sections, each 6–9 cm (2.4–3.6 in) long

leaves 3–5-lobed 10–30 cm (4–12 in) long and broad

flowers 0.8–1 cm (0.4 in) long

This is a small to medium-size tree with alternate leaves. The **leaves are almost rounded, with 3 to 5 lobes, 10–30 cm (4–12 in) broad.** The many greenish flowers are produced in long clusters that may be up to 1.2 m (3.9 ft) long. Individual flowers are composed of a 5-parted, bell-shaped calyx, 0.8–1 cm (0.3–0.4 in) long (no petals); there are about 15 stamens and a single pistil. The **fruits are leathery capsules 6–9 cm (2.4–3.6 in) long** that split into 5 sections and contain 1 to 3 large rounded seeds.

The Mallow Family

Malvaceae

The mallow family is a large assemblage of about 40 genera and over 900 species. Members are herbs, shrubs, or small trees distributed in temperate and tropical regions throughout the world. Those native to North America are all herbs, largely confined to the states with mild climates. In North America, the portia tree, upland cotton, and 2 species of hibiscus can reach tree size. These trees have naturalized in the subtropical regions of the U.S.

This is an economically important family of plants because of the fibers and foods obtained from several species. The most valuable is cotton. Okra, a common vegetable in the South, is another member of the mallow family. In Asia, several kinds of hibiscus plants are grown for the long, tough fibers used in making bags and rough fabrics. In North America, the hibiscus is a common showy ornamental most often seen in display greenhouses.

The leaves are alternate, simple, and usually with finger-like lobes and covered with star-shaped hairs. The flowers are produced singly or in various types of clusters. They are sometimes large and showy, always uniform in shape, and usually contain both male and female parts. Often, each flower is enclosed at the base by 2 to many leaf-like bracts. The flowers are composed of 5 calyx lobes that may be joined near the base, 5 petals that can be free or joined at the base. There are many stamens joined into a column that encloses the pistil. The fruit is a dry capsule, composed of 5 segments, each splitting lengthwise upon maturity to free the seeds. The seeds are kidney-shaped, rounded or broadest above the middle, hard, smooth, or rough on the surface, and sometimes hairy.

Key to Mallow Genera

A. Individual flowers enclosed at the base by 5 or more bracts partially fused into a cup
   Hibiscus, p. 446
B. Individual flowers with 2–5 bracts at the base, the bracts free, not fused into a cup.

   1. Leaves largely 3–9 lobed   **Cotton, p. 449**
   2. Leaves entire or wavy on the margin
      Thespesia, p. 450

Upland Cotton

Portia Tree

The Hibiscus Genus   *Hibiscus* L.

This is a large tropical genus of perhaps 200 species of attractive trees, shrubs, and herbs. The species native to North America are all herbs or shrubs. But at least 2 introduced species occasionally reach tree size and now reproduce on their own. Members of the genus are more common in the warmer and most southern regions of North America. They are economically important because of their ornamental, food, and fiber values. The large beautiful hibiscus flowers, mainly *Hibiscus rosa-sinensis*, are often grown in greenhouses, indoors, or out-of-doors in frost-free areas. These showy flowers are usually red, pink, rose, or salmon and last only a single day before wilting. Yet flowering may continue for several months.

Hibiscus are herbs, shrubs, or small trees. The leaves are simple, alternate along the branchlets and entire or shallowly to deeply lobed. The lobes usually radiate like the fingers of a hand. Flowers are produced in the junctions of the leaves; they are medium-size to large, and they are showy. Each flower is partly enclosed at the base by a green cup-shaped bract. The 5 calyx lobes are fused to form a lobed cup, while the 5 large, spreading, brightly colored petals are not fused to one another. There are numerous stamens with their stalks fused into a tube. The pistil is tipped with a conspicuous 5-branched stigma (the structure that receives the pollen grains). Fruits are dry capsules that eventually split lengthwise into 5 valves, exposing the almost globe-shaped to kidney-shaped seeds, which may be smooth to hairy.

Key to Hibiscus Species

A. Plants evergreen; leaves entire, 10–30 cm (4–12 in) long; coastal regions of southern Florida
Sea hibiscus, p. 447
B. Plants deciduous (leaves falling in autumn), leaves 3 lobed, 4–12 cm (1.6–4.7 in) long; eastern North America   **Rose-of-Sharon, p. 448**

Rose-of-Sharon

Sea Hibiscus
Hibiscus tiliaceus L.

This evergreen shrub or small tree with heart-shaped leaves has naturalized along coastal regions of southern Florida and the Florida Keys. It was introduced from Asia as an ornamental plant because of its large showy flowers. Sea hibiscus also occurs in other tropical regions such as the West Indies, Mexico, Central and South America, and Africa.

The sea hibiscus has many uses but is not of significant economic importance. The fibrous bark can be peeled off in strips and made into ropes. It was once used in making fish nets, mats, coarse cloth, and for tying tobacco. In the West Indies it was even eaten in times of famine along with the foliage and roots. Different parts have been used in home remedies. This tree also makes a good honey plant. The wood is me-

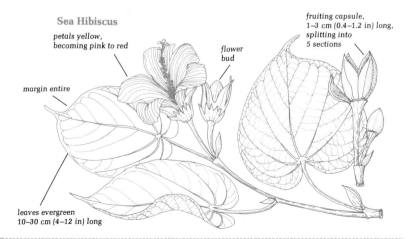

Sea Hibiscus

petals yellow, becoming pink to red

flower bud

fruiting capsule, 1–3 cm (0.4–1.2 in) long, splitting into 5 sections

margin entire

leaves evergreen 10–30 cm (4–12 in) long

dium soft, porous, and moderately heavy. It is used chiefly for fuel, but has been used for floats as a cork substitute.

Appearance: tree to 6 m (20 ft), with a broad, rounded crown; trunk short, crooked, to 15 cm (6 in) in diameter. **Branches:** wide spreading and often crooked, usually bending toward the ground; branchlets slender, becoming brown with age. **Leaves:** alternate, *evergreen, broadest near or just below the middle, 10–30 cm (4–12 in) long,* abruptly short to long pointed at the tip, heart-shaped at the base, *entire along the margin to shallowly toothed;* the leafstalks stout, 5–12 cm (2–4.8 in) long. **Flowers:** each flower produced on a hairy, white stalk and partially enclosed at the base by 9 to 10 narrow bracts fused together to form a cup; petals yellow, becoming pink to red; the calyx tubular with 5 narrow, long pointed lobes, the petals free, rounded but broader on one side, with star-shaped hairs on the outer surface, stamens numerous and fused into a column; there is 1 central pistil. **Fruits:** a dry capsule 1–3 cm (0.4–1.2 in) long, broadest near the base and tapering to a long point, splitting lengthwise at maturity into 5 valves to expose the small, brownish-black seeds.

Rose-of-Sharon *Hibiscus syriacus* L.

This native of Asia has been cultivated in gardens for many years. It has escaped from cultivation in the eastern U.S. from Connecticut to Missouri, south to Texas and Florida. Rose-of-Sharon can often be found growing along roadsides, in vacant lots, or in waste places. This is an old-time favorite of gardeners because of its use as a hedge plant and its late flowering season.

Rose-of-Sharon is a shrub or small tree to 8 m (26 ft). Its young branchlets are hairy. The simple, alternate *leaves* are *4–12 cm (1.6–4.7 in) long,* broadest near the base, *3 lobed,* coarsely toothed along the margin, and with a leafstalk 0.5–1.5 cm (0.2–0.6 in) long. The flowers are single, short-stalked, varying in color from white to red, purple, or violet; they are broadly bell-shaped and 6–10 cm (2.4–4 in) across. The fruiting capsules are 1.5–2 cm (0.6–0.8 in) long, broadest near the base and tapering to a beak. The dark seeds are flattened, 4–6 mm (0.2 in) long and hairy along the margin.

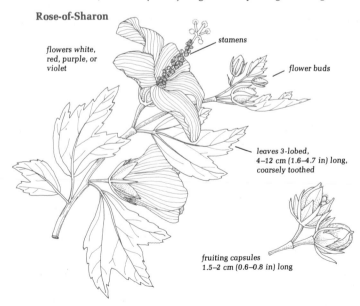

Rose-of-Sharon

flowers white, red, purple, or violet

stamens

flower buds

leaves 3-lobed, 4–12 cm (1.6–4.7 in) long, coarsely toothed

fruiting capsules 1.5–2 cm (0.6–0.8 in) long

The Cotton Genus

Gossypium L.

This is a small genus of perhaps 20 species of herbs, shrubs, or small trees of tropical and subtropical regions of the Americas and Africa. While several species of cotton are cultivated in North America, only 1, wild cotton, reaches tree size and appears to have naturalized.

Millions of acres of land in the southern U.S. are devoted exclusively to the production of cultivated cotton. Cotton, the most important natural plant fiber in the world, is obtained from several species of this genus. The long, tough fibers used to manufacture cotton are found densely covering each seed in the fruiting pods. Once the fibers have been removed from the seeds, the seeds can be pressed to obtain cottonseed oil and cottonseed meal, both important ingredients in foods. Through various processes, cotton lint is treated with nitric and sulphuric acids and made into a powerful explosive called guncotton.

Members of this genus are herbs, shrubs, or small trees that are densely hairy and dotted with small, dark oil glands. The simple, alternate leaves are 3- to 9-lobed, the lobes radiating like the fingers of a hand. The large flowers grow singly in the junctions of the leaves. Each flower consists of a small cup-shaped calyx, 5 petals united near their bases, the petals white or yellow and usually with a large red or purple spot near the base; stamens numerous, stalks fused into a tube; 1 pistil. Fruits are dry capsules, almost globe-shaped, splitting lengthwise to expose the seeds, each seed covered with dense long fibers.

Upland Cotton

Gossypium hirsutum L.

Wild cotton is native to tropical America, but is cultivated in the southern U.S. and widely distributed in tropical countries throughout the world. It occurs as a small tree on sand dunes and coastal hammocks of southern Florida to the Florida Keys, but also occurs along railways. It is distinguished by the large, 3-lobed leaves and large showy, cream-white flowers with purple centers. The seeds are covered with long brownish fibers. The plants will produce flowers and fruits most of the year.

Upland cotton grows as herbs, shrubs, or small trees with wide-spreading branches.

Upland Cotton

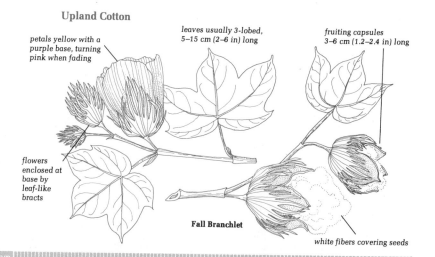

petals yellow with a purple base, turning pink when fading

leaves usually 3-lobed, 5–15 cm (2–6 in) long

fruiting capsules 3–6 cm (1.2–2.4 in) long

flowers enclosed at base by leaf-like bracts

Fall Branchlet

white fibers covering seeds

The branchlets are covered with long, coarse-spreading, simple or star-shaped hairs. The leaves are broadest near the middle, 5–15 cm (2–6 in) long, *usually 3 lobed,* smooth above, with bristly or wooly hairs beneath. The *flowers* are *enclosed at the base by a cup-shaped cluster of leaf-like bracts,* each *bract 3–6 cm (1.2–2.4 in) long, heart-shaped,* and broadest near the base. Each flower consists of a cup-shaped calyx, large petals, fused together only at their bases, yellow with a purple base, turning pink when fading. The fruit is a rough, egg-shaped capsule 3–6 cm (1.2–2.4 in) long and splits lengthwise to expose the white or brownish fiber-covered seeds.

The Thespesia Genus   *Thespesia* Solander ex Correa

This is a small genus of 7 species. They are native to tropical areas of Africa and Asia, but some of them have been introduced widely into tropical and subtropical regions of the Americas.

Members of this genus are shrubs or small trees. The leaves are alternate, simple, entire to 3- to 5-lobed, and long-stalked. The flowers are usually large, showy, and produced singly or in branched clusters. Each flower is partly covered when young by 3 to 5 leaf-like bracts. The 5 calyx lobes are fused to form a cup and the 5 large petals are free and form a bell-shaped flower. Stamens are numerous and united into a tube, while the single pistil is divided into 5 sections (locules) at the base. The fruits are dry to leathery capsules that remain closed at maturity or only partly split open with age. The small seeds are smooth or hairy.

Portia Tree   *Thespesia populnea* (L.) Solander

Introduced as an ornamental shade tree from eastern Asia, the portia tree has natural-ized in southern Florida, the Florida Keys, and also in the West Indies and tropical areas. This tree is considered sacred in Tahiti. Near the sea coast it forms thickets in sand dunes or hammocks or along the edges of swamps. With favorable growing conditions, it may grow to tree size. It is distinguished by rough bark, shiny heart-shaped leaves, pale flowers that cling on the branches for several days and leathery, round capsules.

This tree is often planted as a street tree, or as a living fence post, or just for its or-namental value. The yellow to purplish flowers open one at a time usually in late spring and summer, while the yellow fruits remain on the tree for a short time and then split open.

The wood is rather soft and of medium weight. It is durable and takes a fine polish. The sapwood is light, while the central heartwood is dark brown. The wood is used for furniture, cabinetmaking, boats, houses, and musical instruments. Rope, cof-feebags, and paper have been made from the fibrous inner bark and young shoots. The sap yields a yellow dye.

Appearance: spreading shrub with low branches, or a tree to 15 m (50 ft) with a dense round spreading crown. **Bark:** becoming thick and rough, with light-gray ridges and dark furrows, giving a black and white effect; the inner bark yellowish and fibrous. **Branches:** long, spreading; branchlets, stout, green, covered with small silvery-brown, star-shaped scales, becoming smooth and gray with age, curving

Portia Tree

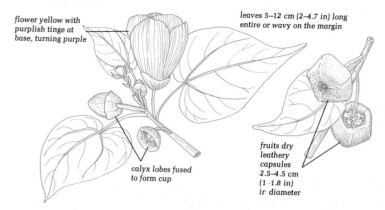

flower yellow with
purplish tinge at
base, turning purple

leaves 5–12 cm (2–4.7 in) long
entire or wavy on the margin

calyx lobes fused
to form cup

fruits dry
leathery
capsules
2.5–4.5 cm
(1–1.8 in)
ir diameter

upward. **Leaves:** alternate, simple, ***broadest near the base, 5–12 cm (2–4.7 in) long, heart-shaped at the base,*** tapering to pointed tip, ***entire or wavy on the margin,*** thin, leathery, dark green becoming glossy above, paler and almost bare beneath; leaf-stalk 5–10 cm (2–4 in) long. **Flowers:** occurring singly at the base of the leafstalks, on stout stalks shorter than leafstalks, ***each flower enclosed (cup-shaped) in a cluster of 3 to 5 leaf-like bracts,*** the bracts shed early, with a cup-shaped calyx, 5 petals, 4–7 cm (1.6–2.8 in) long, large, showy, yellow with purplish tinge at base, changing to purple at day's end; stamens numerous. **Fruits:** firm, leathery, almost globe-shaped, 2.5–4.5 cm (1–1.8 in) in diameter, 5-celled, does not split open or sometimes opens slightly at the tip, each cell containing 2 to 3 hairy seeds, each seed about 1 cm (0.4 in) long.

The Tamarisk Family

Tamaricaceae

The tamarisk family consists of about 100 species primarily from tropical and temperate regions of Europe, the Middle East, Africa, and Asia. The genus is named from an Asiatic river along which many of the plants grow abundantly. Only 1 of the 4 genera in this family is found in North America. There are 3 species of tamarisk reaching tree size that have naturalized in the southern and western U.S.

This family is of minor economic importance and of little value to wildlife. The heath-like shrubs or small trees with feather-like branchlets and leaves are sometimes planted as ornamentals. The pungent bark has been employed in tanning and dyeing.

Members of this family are shrubs or trees, occasionally herbs. The leaves are alternate, entire, often scale-like or needle-shaped, and lack a stalk. The flowers usually have both sexes present and the calyx lobes and petals are often alike in size and shape. The flowers are produced singly or in dense clusters. Each flower has 4 or 5 calyx lobes and petals, and usually 4 or 5 stamens. The fruits are dry capsules with 3 to 5 valves, each valve splitting open lengthwise to expose the small seeds, each seed with a tuft of hairs at one end.

The Tamarisk Genus

Tamarix L.

Tamarisk is a medium-size genus of about 75 species of shrubs and trees from the Mediterranean region and Central Asia to Japan. Perhaps up to 12 species of tamarisk are cultivated in North America, primarily in California but also in the southeastern U.S. They are used as ornamentals and to prevent erosion and stabilize sand dunes. The fine, feather-like foliage and pink to white profusion of tiny flowers make tamarisks especially attractive. Three species of tamarisk are described as trees on upcoming pages, but they all can be found growing as large shrubs as well. Other species are primarily shrubs, which on occasion will grow 5–6 m (16–20 ft) high. This would include the small-flowered tamarisk (*Tamarix parviflora*), which has escaped from cultivation and reproduces on its own along river beds in southern California. The different species of tamarisk are especially difficult to distinguish.

Members of this genus are small trees or shrubs with slender branches and branchlets that often arch near their tips. The small, scale-like leaves clasp the branchlets and often are shed in the autumn in areas subject to frost. The small flowers are produced in dense clusters, usually at the ends of the branchlets, and are very showy.

Key to Tamarisk Species

A. Leaves scale-like, surrounded by a loose sheath, trees 6–10 m (20–33 ft) high; cultivated and naturalized in western U.S. **Desert tamarisk, p. 452**

B. Leaves scale-like, not surrounded by a loose sheath; large shrubs or small trees.

    1. Petals broadest above the middle; cultivated and growing wild in western U.S.
          Five-Stamen tamarisk, p. 453

    2. Petals broadest below the middle; cultivated and naturalized in the eastern U.S. and in California   **French tamarisk, p. 453**

French Tamarisk

Desert Tamarisk   *Tamarix aphylla* (L.) Karst.

This is the largest of the tamarisks cultivated in the warmer regions of the U.S. This

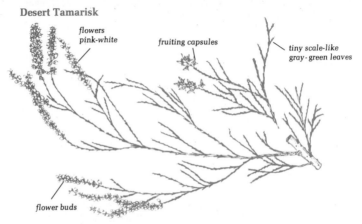

Desert Tamarisk

flowers
pink-white

fruiting capsules

tiny scale-like
gray-green leaves

flower buds

species cannot tolerate freezing. It will grow in poor soils, even saline ones near the sea, and thrives in hot, dry weather. Desert tamarisk are often used as hedges or as windbreaks for orchards in southern California.

This is a small tree to 10 m (33 ft), with an irregular shape. The branches and branchlets are slender, grayish, and noticeably jointed. The ***tiny, gray-green leaves wrap around the branchlets with only the leaf tips free.*** The small, ***pink-white flowers*** are produced in showy elongated clusters. Flowering is in summer followed by the development of the fruits, consisting of small dry capsules that split open to expose the many seeds.

Five-Stamen Tamarisk
Tamarix chinensis Lour.

(synonyms: *T. pentandra* Pall., *T. ramosissima* Ledeb.)

A native of the Mediterranean, this tamarisk occurs in thickets, on waste ground, and along roadsides where it has escaped and naturalized in Oregon and California. Slender clusters of pink flowers usually appear in summer, but sometimes are present most of the year.

The 5-stamen tamarisk is a shrub or small tree to 6 m (20 ft) high. The branches are slender, upright or spreading, while the branchlets are slender, brown to purplish-red, drooping, and covered with thin scale-like leaves. The ***tiny leaves are lance-shaped to broadest at or near the base, covered with a whitish waxy coating.*** They are ***pale***

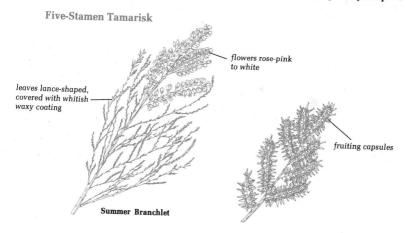

Five-Stamen Tamarisk

leaves lance-shaped, covered with whitish waxy coating

flowers rose-pink to white

fruiting capsules

Summer Branchlet

green, sharp-pointed, and evergreen in mild climates. The tiny, stalked ***rose-pink to white flowers*** are produced in slender, elongated clusters at the ends of the branchlets. Fruits are small dry capsules, splitting open at maturity to release the seeds.

French Tamarisk
Tamarix gallica L.

This native of southern Europe was introduced throughout much of the eastern U.S. and to a lesser extent into the western states. French tamarisk is cultivated as an ornamental and is used for windscreens and erosion control. It reproduces on its own along river banks, bars, salt marshes, thickets, and waste ground. It is one of the more hardy species of tamarisk and the most widespread in North America.

French tamarisks are shrubs or small trees to 10 m (33 ft) high with an irregular spreading shape. The branches and branchlets are slender and arching near the tips.

French Tamarisk

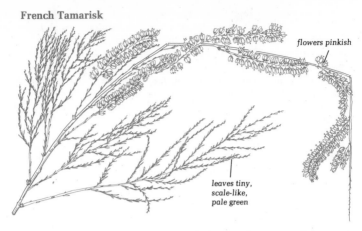

flowers pinkish

leaves tiny,
scale-like,
pale green

The branchlets are covered with tiny, ***scale-like, pale-green, alternate leaves***. Numerous small flowers are crowded together in narrow, elongate clusters at the tips of the branchlets. Individual ***flowers are pinkish***, with 5 calyx lobes, 5 petals, and 5 stamens. Fruits are small dry capsules, 4–5 mm (0.2 in) long, which split open lengthwise to release the tiny seeds.

The Carica Family   Caricaceae

This is a small family of only 4 genera and perhaps 35 species of herbs, shrubs, and small trees primarily of tropical regions of America and Africa. Most of the species belong to the papaya genus. The carica family is economically important because of its delicious, edible fruits. The leaves, young shoots, bark, and green fruit are also of commercial value. Some trees are planted as ornamentals.

Members of this family are herbs and shrubs or small, generally unbranched, trees or large branched trees with milky sap. The leaves are clustered at the top of the plant. They are alternate along the stem, long-stalked, large, simple but with finger-like lobes. Individual plants of some species may have either male or female flowers, while others have both sexes present on the same plant. Individual flowers are either male or female, rarely bisexual. They are usually white and produced in few to many-flowered clusters. The male flowers consist of 5 fused calyx lobes and 5 petals fused into a tube. There are 10 stamens in the male and bisexual flowers. The female flowers have 5 free calyx lobes and petals. The fruit is a large fleshy berry containing many seeds.

The Papaya Genus   *Carica* L.

There are about 30 species of papaya in the tropical region of America. They are cultivated there for their edible fruits, as well as other plant parts that are useful in a variety of ways. The leaves, shoots, and green fruits are cooked as vegetables. As well, the leaves are used as meat tenderizer, and the pulp is used for flavoring and for a soap in face creams and shampoos. The bark fiber is often employed in making ropes. The wood is soft and lightweight, too soft to use as timber. The older trees are sometimes attractive enough to be ornamentals.

Papayas are small trees, shrubs, or large herbs with generally unbranched stems and long-stalked, simple, deeply lobed leaves. Individual trees produce either male or female flowers. The flowers are produced in branched clusters along the upper part of the stem at the junction of the leafstalks. The male flowers have the 5 petals fused into a narrow tube and the 10 stamens arranged in 2 series within the tube. Female flowers have the 5 free petals enclosing a single pistil. The fruit is a small to large, fleshy, many-seeded berry.

Papaya

Carica papaya L.

The papaya is now found in tropical areas all over the world. It is thought to have originated in Mexico. The trees can withstand some frost and have been found growing along roadsides and waste places from Jacksonville, Florida, to Key West. It is not considered a true tree because its stem is mostly soft and nonwoody, and looks somewhat like the palm tree (though unrelated) because of the unbranched stem and very large, lobed leaves.

Papaya is an extremely fast-growing tree, producing many large fruits within 10 to 11 months from seed. The trees can live 15 to 20 years, but are usually cut down after 3 years because the quality of the fruit begins to deteriorate. Leaves, flowers, and fruits are produced along the trunk throughout the year. The tree requires large amounts of water but cannot tolerate standing water around its base for more than 2 days. The fruit of wild plants is often small, sometimes only 8 cm (3.2 in) long, and bitter to taste, while fruit in cultivated plants grows up to 45 cm (18 in) long and weighs up to 8 kilograms (17.5 pounds). Little is known about its value to wildlife, but it is assumed that mammals eat the fruits and birds distribute the seeds in areas away from cultivation.

Papaya

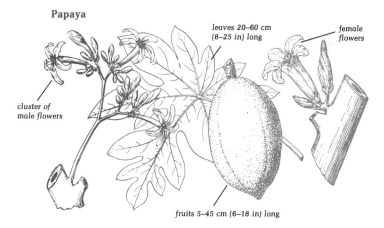

leaves 20–60 cm
(8–25 in) long

female
flowers

cluster of
male flowers

fruits 5–45 cm (6–18 in) long

The melon-like fruit is very nutritious and rich in vitamins. It is served at breakfast or dessert, and is often flavored with lime juice. Delicious preserves and sherbets are also made from the pulp and juice. The juice is extracted and canned, retaining well its flavor and vitamins. Green papayas contain a milky latex that possesses an enzyme, papain, that is absent in mature fruits. Papain aids in the digestion of proteins and curdling milk. The leaves and juice are useful as meat tenderizers and only recently have been marketed commercially. The pulp and juice are used for a soap in face creams and shampoos and for flavoring drinks, ice cream, custards, pastes, jams, preserves, pies, and pickles. The wood is whitish or pale yellow, very soft, and lightweight. The central pith is large, white, and in older trunks is often hollow. The wood is of no commercial value.

Appearance: small, aromatic, evergreen tree to 6 m (20 ft) tall, with a narrow crown; trunk straight, usually less than 20 cm (8 in) in diameter. **Bark:** thin, smooth, green, grayish brown to light gray with broad, nearly horizontal leaf scars; the inner bark is spicy or somewhat bitter tasting. **Leaves:** the upper leaves upright to spreading, the lower ones drooping, alternate, *simple, 7 lobed, the lobes radiating like the fingers on a hand, rounded in outline, 20–60 cm (8–24 in) long,* somewhat thick and fleshy, dull-pale-green above, pale whitish green and covered with a waxy coating beneath; leafstalks 40–60 cm (15–24 in) long, occasionally longer, rounded, hollow. **Flowers:** *male flowers on many-flowered clusters, 15–60 cm (6–25 in) long;* each male flower with a short 5-lobed calyx about 1 mm (about 0.05 in) long, a white tubular corolla consisting of 5 narrow petals, and 10 yellow stamens joined at the base of the corolla tube and enclosing a tiny nonfunctional pistil. *Female flowers produced in few-flowered clusters;* each flower short-stalked, with 5 small, free calyx lobes, 5 free narrow, lance-shaped, fleshy petals, each 3–5 cm (1.2–2 in) long. **Fruits:** *few to many per cluster, clusters near top of tree just below leaves, egg- to pear-shaped, 15–45 cm (6–18 in) long, green turning orange when ripe,* with a soft thick flesh containing milky juice, and a large central area containing many black, rounded seeds.

The Willow Family   Salicaceae

This family of trees and shrubs is widespread throughout the temperate and north temperate regions of the world. Only a few species extend into tropical or subtropical areas. The willow family consists of only 2 genera—the poplars (*Populus*) with about 40 species and the willows (*Salix*) with over 300 species. Hybridization is widespread, making identification of individual plants especially difficult. In North America, about 80 species of willows and 10 poplars occur, not counting hybrids. All of the poplars are trees, and approximately 34 of the willows are trees or reach tree size, although many are typically large shrubs.

Willow and poplar seeds are tiny, viable only for a short time, and require a moist site for germination. Therefore, the trees are usually restricted to moist areas such as stream banks. This family is well known for its capacity to sprout from the roots, and soil conservationists exploit this quick sprouting in fighting soil erosion. Moreover, both genera are important in the natural regeneration of burned-out forests.

Many members of the willow family are important as ornamentals for their graceful forms and handsome, delicate foliage. Some of the species are important in the timber industry. Poplars are used to make paper pulp and many of the pliable willows are used to make baskets. This family is important to wildlife, serving as vital food sources during the winter and early spring.

Members of this family are trees or shrubs with bitter bark, soft, light, usually pale wood, and scaly buds. The leaves are simple, deciduous, and alternately arranged on the branchlets. The leafstalks often have conspicuous glands along their margins. Individual trees will bear either male or female flowers, rarely will both occur on the same tree. The male and female flowers are produced in separate catkins that often appear before or with the developing leaves. The fruiting catkins contain several 2- to 4-valved capsules that contain numerous, small, hairy seeds.

Key to Willow Genera

A. Flowering catkins arching to drooping, the scales surrounding the flowers sharply toothed along the edge; male flowers with 8–30 stamens per flower; winter leaf buds covered with several scales **Poplars, p. 457**

Balsam Poplar

B. Flowering catkins generally upright, the scales surrounding the flowers entire along the margin; male flowers with 1–12 stamens per flower; winter leaf buds covered with only 1 scale **Willows, p. 472**

Black Willow

The Poplar Genus   *Populus* L.

This genus has about 40 species of fast-growing, generally short-lived trees that occur widely throughout the Northern Hemisphere, primarily in North America, Europe, and Asia. They form extensive forests in the northern reaches of their range. Thirteen species, including several hybrids, are native in North America from Alaska to Mexico and Florida. Several species have been introduced from Europe, including the European white poplar and the Lombardy poplar. Positive identification of species may be difficult because the flowers and leaves do not appear at the same time.

Poplars can be divided into 3 major groups: the aspens, the cottonwoods, and the balsam poplars. Aspens have nonsticky buds, male flowers with 12 or fewer stamens, and fruiting capsules that are thin walled. Aspens usually have smooth, green to gray bark and form large second-growth forests in the North. Cottonwoods and balsam poplars have sticky fragrant buds, male flowers with 12 to 60 stamens, and fruiting capsules that are thick walled. They also develop darker-colored, deeply furrowed bark. Cottonwoods are especially common on western prairies, while poplars have a more northern distribution.

All members of this genus have the male and female flowers in separate hanging catkins that bloom in the spring before the leaves unfold. The fruiting capsules are mature by the time the leaves are full grown, generally in late spring. Poplars are important to wildlife, especially as a winter and spring food source. Moose, whitetail deer, and mule deer browse the branchlets and leaves, while beaver and varying hare eat the bark, leaves, and buds. Game birds that feed on the buds and young flower clusters include quail, prairie chickens, and sharp-tailed and ruffed grouse.

The soft wood of many American species is used for paper pulp, crates and boxes, packing material, matchsticks, light construction, and small woodenware. The bark is used in leather tanning, and the balsam resin in the buds of some species has been used in medicine. Rapid growth, ease of propagation by cuttings, and general hardiness once made these trees attractive candidates for street plantings. However, many cities are removing them because the root systems clog up sewers, raise sidewalks, and damage building foundations.

Poplars are pale-barked trees with resinous or nonresinous winter buds along the branchlets; the lowest bud-scale is placed directly above the leaf scar and makes for easy winter identification. The alternate, unlobed leaves (lobed in some European species) are usually broadest near the base, often almost heart-shaped, with glandular-toothed or lobed margins and long, slender leafstalks. Male and female flowers occur in separate catkins. The male flowers, usually more crowded in the catkin than females, have 4 to 12 or 12 to 60 stamens with yellow filaments and red-purple anthers. The females have an oblong to conical, 2-lobed ovary placed at the bottom of the floral disc, with short stigmas and parted style. The fruit capsule varies in color from green to red or brown and separates into 2 to 4 valves. The tiny seeds bear long, white "cotton" hairs, which give them added buoyancy in air dispersal.

Key to Poplar Species

A. Leafstalks distinctly rounded, even at their bases.

  1. Leaves 10–17.5 cm (4–7 in) long, heart-shaped at the base; winter buds small, 6–8 mm (0.2–0.3 in) long and slightly gummy; fruiting capsules 1.1–1.3 cm (0.5 in) long; trees of the Gulf Coastal Plain, Mississippi and Ohio river valleys **Swamp cottonwood, p. 460**

Swamp Cottonwood

  2. Leaves 4.5–12.5 cm (1.8–4.9 in) long, wedge-shaped to rounded at the base; winter buds large, 1.5–2.5 cm (0.6–1 in) long, very gummy and smooth or else not gummy but hairy.

    a. Leaves 7.5–12.5 cm (3–5 in) long, finely toothed but unlobed along the margin; winter buds gummy.

      (1) Leafstalks 7.5–11 cm (3–4.4 in) long; leaves rounded at the base; fruiting capsules 6–7 mm (about 0.3 in) long, broadest near the base and tapering to a point; northern trees from Alaska across Canada to northeastern U.S. and in the Rocky Mountains **Balsam poplar, p. 461**

Balsam Poplar

      (2) Leafstalks 3.7–5 cm (1.5–2 in) long; leaves wedge-shaped to sometimes

rounded at the base; fruiting capsules 3–4 mm (about 0.1–0.2 in) long, rounded; trees of West Coast from Alaska to California
     Black cottonwood, p. 463

b. Leaves 4.5–8.4 cm (1.8–3.3 in) long, 3–5 lobed and finely toothed along the margin; winter buds hairy; trees native to Europe, introduced into North America
     White poplar, p. 464

Black Cottonwood

B. Leafstalks flattened on the sides, at least at their bases.

 1. Leaves lance-shaped; leafstalks rounded, but flattened at their bases; trees of western North America **Narrowleaf cottonwood, p. 464**
 2. Leaves triangular and shield shaped or broadest near the middle or base; leafstalks flattened along their sides for most or all of their length.

  a. Leaves triangular or shield shaped.

Narrowleaf Cottonwood

   (1) Trees with large spreading branches and broad open crowns.

    (a) Leaves 7.5–17.5 cm (3–7 in) long, 10–12 cm (4–4.8 in) broad, shiny green; winter buds 1.7–1.9 cm (0.7–0.8 in) long; trees of eastern North America
     Eastern cottonwood, p. 465

Eastern Cottonwood

    (b) Leaves 5–6.2 cm (2–2.5 in) long, 6.2–7.5 cm (2.5–3 in) wide, light yellowish-green; winter buds 8–12 mm (0.3–0.5 in) long; trees of southwestern U.S.
     Fremont cottonwood, p. 466

   (2) Trees with a tight upright, almost column shape; branches slender, upright; introduced trees often planted as windbreaks or screens; planted throughout North America
     Lombardy poplar, p. 468

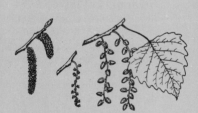

Fremont Cottonwood

  b. Leaves broadest near the middle or near the base and then egg shaped.

   (1) Leaves broadest at the middle, some of the leaves reaching 12.5 cm (5 in) long; trees of southwestern Texas and adjacent areas in Mexico
     Palmer cottonwood, p. 469
      (Continued)

Lombardy Poplar

(2) Leaves broadest near the base, the largest leaves to 8.7 cm (3.5 in) long; trees of northern or mountainous areas of North America.

Quaking Aspen

    (a) Leaves with many fine small teeth along the margin; trees widely occurring in temperate and cold temperate regions of North America
Quaking aspen, p. 469

    (b) Leaves with large blunt or coarse teeth along the margin.

Bigtooth Aspen

        (b1) Leaves 5–7.5 cm (2–3 in) long; leafstalks 3.8–6.3 cm (1.5–2.5 in) long; fruiting capsules narrowly cone shaped, 6–7 mm (0.2–0.3 in) long; winter buds slightly sticky; trees of northeastern North America
Bigtooth aspen, p. 470

        (b2) Leaves 6.2–8.7 cm (2.4–3.5 in) long; leafstalks 6–8.5 cm (2.4–3.4 in) long; fruiting capsules broadest at the base, 9–11 mm (0.4 in) long; winter buds very sticky; trees of the Great Plains
Plains cottonwood, p. 472

Swamp Cottonwood
Populus heterophylla L.

Swampy areas in the Coastal Plain or the Mississippi, Missouri, or Ohio river valleys are the home of this medium-to-tall member of the poplars. Swamp cottonwood occurs mostly on heavy, waterlogged clay soils in sites too wet for eastern cottonwood. It

grows along the edges of muck swamps, sloughs, and wet river bottomlands where the water table remains at ground level most of the year. It is scarce in its range, and it grows in association with such wetland species as bald cypress, water tupelo, black and other willows, green ash, water hickory, red maple, and overcup oak.

Swamp cottonwoods are short-lived, fast-growing trees that start seed production at 10 years of age. Separate male and female flowering catkins dangle from branchlets from March to May before the leaves unfold. Heavy seed crops are produced yearly and distributed by wind and water. Seeds must land on wet, exposed mineral soil, or they will not germinate. Because of its scarcity, swamp cottonwood is of small importance to wildlife. Nevertheless, where it does occur, parts are consumed by songbirds, beaver, squirrel, rabbits, and deer.

Swamp Cottonwood

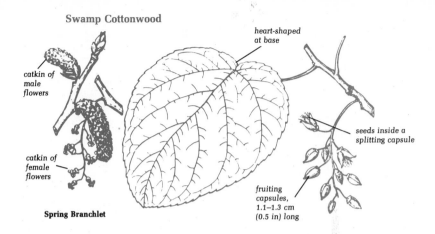

catkin of
male
flowers

catkin of
female
flowers

Spring Branchlet

heart-shaped
at base

seeds inside a
splitting capsule

fruiting
capsules,
1.1–1.3 cm
(0.5 in) long

Swamp cottonwoods grow straight and tall, making them suitable for timber. Like eastern cottonwood, their wood is of second-rate quality and so is used for boxes, crates, and excelsior.

Appearance: medium-size to tall tree, 20–30 m (65–100 ft), with an open irregular crown; trunk straight and branch-free for half its length, 60–90 cm (23–35 in) in diameter. **Bark:** lightly furrowed on young trees, becoming thick, dirty brown, tinged with red, broken into long narrow plates attached at the middle. **Branches:** short, fairly slender, with stout branchlets, at first hairy and marked by long pores, becoming shiny dark brown or ashy-gray, with orange pith; branchlets darker the second season. **Winter buds:** pointed at the tip, *6–8 mm (0.2–0.3 in) long, broadly egg-shaped, with slightly gummy, red-brown scales.* **Leaves:** alternate, deciduous, simple, *10–17.5 cm (4–7 in) long, 7.5–15 cm (3–6 in) wide, broadest near the base,* pointed at the tip, usually heart-shaped at the base, fine or coarsely toothed along the margin, coated when young with white hairs, later becoming smooth and with a papery texture, paler below than above; *leafstalks slender, 6–8.8 cm (2.4–3.5 in) long, rounded.* **Flowers:** sexes on separate trees; male catkins 2.5 cm (1 in) long, and upright, becoming 5–6 cm (2–2.4 in) long and drooping; female catkins few-flowered, larger than males, becoming erect before maturing. **Fruits:** several capsules in a long catkin; capsules 1.1–1.3 cm (0.5 in) long, red-brown, splitting into 2 to 3 parts to release tiny, red-brown seeds.

Balsam Poplar   *Populus balsamifera* L.

Balsam poplar is a hardy species that grows medium-size to tall. It thrives in the cold northern reaches of Alaska and Canada, but it does less well in the southern portion of its range, where it possibly remains left over from the glacial era. It occurs from sea level in Alaska to elevations of 1,650 m (5,415 ft) in the Rocky Mountains. Best growth is reached in northwestern Canada, an area too cold for most trees. Here it prefers the deep, moist, sandy soils of river bottomlands, streambanks, and borders of lakes and swamps. This poplar may grow in pure stands and in association with balsam fir, white spruce, aspens and cottonwoods, and paper birch. It is a pioneer species that cannot tolerate shading; therefore, if forest stands are left uncut, balsam poplar is eventually shaded out by the very trees that grew up under its own protecting cover. Balsam poplar hybridizes with several other poplars.

mm
cm   1   2   3   4   5   6   7   8   9   10   11
in   1   2   3   4

Like other willow family members, these trees are rapid growing and are generally short-lived, although rare 150 to 200 year-old specimens have been found. Catkins of male and female flowers blossom in spring before the leaves unfold, and the fruits develop quickly thereafter. Seeds, ripe before the leaves have even reached full size in June, are dispersed by the wind, and they germinate on suitably bare and wet sites. Propagation also occurs to large extent from suckers produced from the roots. Buds and twigs are fed on by grouse, prairie chicken, and several songbirds. Deer and moose browse the twigs and foliage, while beaver, hare, squirrel, rabbit, and porcupine eat the buds, bark, and leaves.

The light, soft wood is manufactured into paper pulp, excelsior, boxes, and crates. Large logs are cut into thin veneer strips that are used to make fruit baskets.

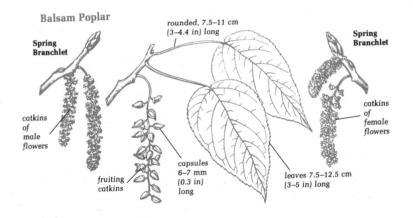

Balsam Poplar

rounded, 7.5–11 cm (3–4.4 in) long

Spring Branchlet

Spring Branchlet

catkins of male flowers

catkins of female flowers

fruiting catkins

capsules 6–7 mm (0.3 in) long

leaves 7.5–12.5 cm (3–5 in) long

Appearance: a medium-size to tall tree to 30 m (100 ft), with a pyramid form and a narrow, irregular, open crown; trunk long, straight, branch-free for much of its length, up to 2 m (6.6 ft) in diameter but usually 30–60 cm (12–24 in). **Bark:** thin, smooth, greenish-brown on young trees, becoming gray, narrowly furrowed with thick, broad ridges and scaly surfaces. **Branches:** few, large, upraised; branchlets shining red-brown, marked by orange pores. **Winter buds:** terminal buds about 2.5 cm (1 in) long, lateral buds 1.5–1.8 cm (0.6–0.7 in) long, long pointed, with 5 scales and covered with a fragrant, gummy balsam. **Leaves:** alternate, deciduous, simple, *7.5–12.5 cm (3–5 in) long, 4–8 cm (1.6–3.2 in) wide, broadest near the rounded base, tapering to a sharp tip,* finely toothed with blunt incurved teeth, dark green above, paler below, often stained by resin blotches; *leafstalk 7.5–11 cm (3–4.4 in) long, thin, rounded, often glandular near the base.* **Flowers:** produced in separate female and male catkins, male catkins 7.5–10 cm (3–4 in) long, female catkins 10–13 cm (4–5.2 in) long when mature. **Fruits:** capsules *broadest near the base and tapering to a point,* 6–7 mm (0.3 in) long, short-stalked, contain many small, brown seeds.

Black Cottonwood   *Populus trichocarpa* Torr. & Gray

The black cottonwood, a majestic West Coast tree occurring from Alaska to California, is largest of all the American poplars. It is able to grow in soils ranging from moist grounds to rich humus, or occasionally dry, sterile sites at elevations from sea level up to 2,700 m (8,900 ft) in California. But best

growth is attained in the Puget Sound area at low elevations on deep river soils. In drier areas these trees grow in protected valleys and canyons, along streams and ponds, meadow borders, and moist foot-hills. Pure stands are sometimes formed, especially on land freshly created from river silting. Trees that commonly grow in association include Douglas fir, western white pine, hemlock, redcedar, alder, spruce, birch, maple, and in California dogwood and live oak.

Black cottonwood grows rapidly and begins to produce flowers at an early age. Male and female flowers bloom on separate trees in April or May, before the leaves unfurl. Large seed crops are produced almost yearly, maturing from late May to mid July. Large and small game mammals browse the young shoots and leaves. Grouse, quail, and songbirds feed on buds, flowers, and seeds.

The light, weak wood is cut on a large scale for timber, going into boxes, crates, pulpwood, packing material, and light woodenware. In Alaska the trees are planted for shade.

The range of this species overlaps slightly with balsam poplar, and hybrids between the 2 occur. The 2 species are similar in appearance, although the seed capsules of balsam poplar are oblong, 2-parted, and smooth, while those of the black cottonwood have a 3-parted capsule. Hybrids have both 2- and 3-parted capsules.

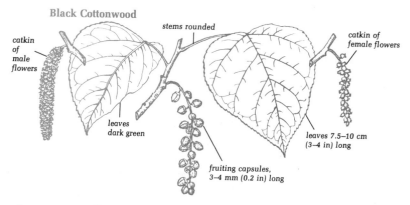

Black Cottonwood

catkin of male flowers

stems rounded

catkin of female flowers

leaves dark green

leaves 7.5–10 cm (3–4 in) long

fruiting capsules, 3–4 mm (0.2 in) long

Appearance: medium-size to tall tree, to 50 m (164 ft), rarely larger, with a narrow and rounded open or pointed crown; trunk straight, tall, branch-free, 0.9–1.5 m (2.9–4.9 ft) in diameter, rarely to 3 m (9.9 ft). **Bark:** smooth, thin, and yellowish-gray at first, turning dark grayish-brown, thick, deeply and sharply furrowed with scaly ridges. **Branches:** erect; branchlets slender, reddish-brown and marked by orange pores the first year, later dark gray and roughened by leaf scars. **Winter buds:** 1.7–1.9

cm (0.7–0.8 in) long, gummy, fragrant, long-pointed with 6 to 7 light orange-brown, fine-haired scales. **Leaves:** alternate, deciduous, simple, *7.5–10 cm (3–4 in) long, 5–6.2 cm (2–2.5 in) wide, broadest near the rounded or abruptly wedge-shaped base,* pointed at the tip, finely toothed along the margin, thick and leathery, dark green and smooth above, silvery white or pale green below with rust-colored spots; *leafstalks 3.7–5 cm (1.5–2 in) long and rounded in cross section.* **Flowers:** sexes on separate trees; male flowers in densely flowered catkins, 3.7–5 cm (1.5–2 in) long, with smooth stems; female catkins loosely flowered, 6.2–7.5 cm (2.5–3 in) long. **Fruits:** many capsules in catkins to 15 cm (6 in); *capsules 3-parted, rounded, 3–4 mm (0.2 in) long,* hairy, and containing numerous tiny hairy seeds.

White Poplar   *Populus alba* L.

This tall, handsome, many-branched import from Europe arrived in early colonial times. White poplar is planted on farms and in cities, as well as along streets. It has proved to be a problem along streets because its water-hungry roots often clog sewers and drainpipes and raise sidewalks. Today it has become naturalized, reproducing on its own in many areas in eastern North America.

These wide-crowned poplars are distinguished by their distinctly *3- to 5-lobed leaves, 4.5–8.4 cm (1.8–3.3 in) long.* The upper surface is deep bluegreen, the lower surface densely coated with white hairs. The bark of young trees is smooth and pale greenish-white. But that of older trees is thick, gray, and furrowed. The catkins appear in early April, before the leaves, while the fruit matures in catkins 5–10 cm (2–4 in) long in May or June.

Narrowleaf Cottonwood   *Populus angustifolia* James

This poplar with narrow, willowy leaves and fragrant buds is found growing on moist, shady or gravelly soils from the upper Sonoran Desert in Mexico northward to southern Alberta in Canada. Narrowleaf cottonwood occurs along mountain streams and moist, upland flats from 1,000–3,000 m (3,200–9,900 ft) elevation. It occurs in pinelands and overlaps on the eastern portion of its range with plains cottonwood (*Populus sargentii*) with which it hybridizes. Such crossings are frequent and make identification difficult.

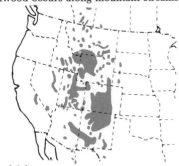

Like other poplars, narrowleaf cottonwood grows quickly and has a short life. The flowers bloom in spring before the leaves appear, and the fruits ripen several weeks later. Songbirds consume the buds. Beaver and other small game eat buds, bark, and foliage.

The wood of narrowleaf cottonwood is soft and weak; this, together with the tree's scarcity and small size, makes this species commercially unimportant. It is used locally for fuelwood and fence posts.

Appearance: small, slender tree to 18 m (60 ft), with a narrowly cone-shaped crown; trunk rarely reaching 0.5 m (1.6 ft) in diameter. **Bark:** on young trees smooth. thin, yellowish-green, becoming thicker at the base of older trees and shallowly fissured with broad, flat ridges. **Branches:** strong, slender, upright; tapering into smooth, slender branchlets, at first yellowish-green, becoming bright or dark orange the first year, then turning to pale gray by the second year. **Winter buds:** terminal buds 6–12

Narrowleaf Cottonwood

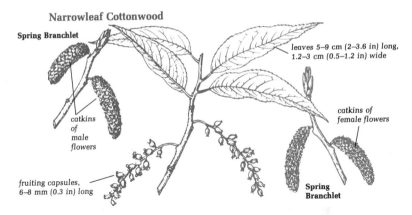

Spring Branchlet

leaves 5–9 cm (2–3.6 in) long,
1.2–3 cm (0.5–1.2 in) wide

catkins
of
male
flowers

catkins of
female flowers

fruiting capsules,
6–8 mm (0.3 in) long

Spring
Branchlet

mm (0.2–0.5 in) long, very sticky, long-pointed, with 5 thin scales. **Leaves:** alternate, deciduous, simple, *5–9 cm (2–3.6 in) long, 1.2–3 cm (0.5–1.2 in) wide, lance-shaped,* broadest near the middle, tapering to a pointed tip, fine-toothed along the margin, *thin and papery, bright yellow-green above,* paler below; *leafstalk short, stout, almost rounded but flattened near the base.* **Flowers:** male and female catkins on separate trees, densely flowered, 2.5–6.3 cm (1–2.5 in) long. **Fruits:** capsules broadly egg-shaped, 6–8 mm (0.3 in) long, splitting into 2 valves to release the hairy, brown seeds, 2–3 mm (0.1 in) long.

Eastern Cottonwood   *Populus deltoides* Bartr.

This species of tall trees is widespread and important in eastern North America. From Minnesota to Texas, and eastward to the Atlantic seaboard, these cottonwoods are found in moist lowlands near rivers, streams, and swamps. Usually cottonwoods do not leave the lowlands, unless to grow on exceedingly moist slopes. While able to survive in various soil types, they grow best on moist, well-drained sands or silts near streams. Cottonwood may form pure stands or grow in moist woods with black willow, sycamore, and several lowland oaks. In the South, old fields are gradually reforested by this species and sweetgum, though sweetgum eventually dominates. Hybrids between this and other cottonwoods are common.

Eastern cottonwood is a remarkably fast-growing tree, often reaching 47 m (120 ft) within 30 years. Seed production begins around 10 years of age, with good crops being the rule rather than the exception. Flowering occurs from February to April throughout its range, prior to the leaves expanding. By May the female catkins will have enlarged to 15 to 25 cm (6–10 in) long, and they will bear fruiting capsules that release the minute, silky-haired seeds. These trees are used by many wildlife species. Small game including beaver, squirrels, and porcupine eat bark, leaves, and buds. Deer and moose consume foliage and tender twigs. Songbirds and grouse consume the buds.

Pioneers brought eastern cottonwood onto the treeless plains with them, and today you can identify small streams from an airplane by following the green, winding

Eastern Cottonwood

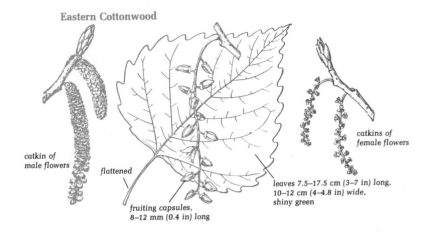

catkin of
male flowers

flattened

fruiting capsules,
8–12 mm (0.4 in) long

catkins of
female flowers

leaves 7.5–17.5 cm (3–7 in) long,
10–12 cm (4–4.8 in) wide,
shiny green

bands of these trees. They have proven unsuitable for city planting, because their extensive root systems in search for moisture raise sidewalks and clog drainpipes. The weak, soft wood tends to warp badly. Nevertheless, it is used for crates and packing material. Open-grown trees have many-forked crowns and are of no timber value.

Appearance: a tall tree, 22–30 m, rarely to 50 (72–100 ft, rarely to 165), in the open, a short, massive trunk supports a broad, irregular, open crown; in forests the crown is short and rounded, trunk straight and tall, 60–120 cm (23–47 in) in diameter (up to 2 m – 6.6 ft – or more). **Bark:** smooth, thin, and yellow-gray when trees are young, becoming dark gray and deeply furrowed. **Branches:** heavy and widespreading or slender and compact; branchlets stout, smooth, angled in cross section, yellowish-brown. **Winter buds:** terminal buds 1.7–1.9 cm (0.7–0.8 in) long, larger than lateral ones, shiny brown, long-pointed, resinous, and fragrant. **Leaves:** alternate, deciduous, simple, *7.5–17.5 cm (3–7 in) long, 10–12 cm (4–4.8 in) broad; triangle-shaped with tapered tip and flat to heart-shaped base,* the margins toothed and wavy, smooth, shiny green above, paler below; *leafstalk slender, flattened,* 3.7–7.5 cm (1.5–3 in) long and glandular. **Flowers:** male and female flowers in separate catkins, on different trees, 5–7.5 cm (2–3 in) long. **Fruits:** several capsules produced on long catkins, each *capsule 8–12 mm (0.4 in) long,* broadest near the base and splitting into 3 to 4 parts to release the finely downy seeds.

Fremont Cottonwood *Populus fremontii* S. Wats.

Fremont cottonwood is a tall southwestern tree that commemorates its discoverer John Charles Fremont, the politician, soldier, and explorer. Found in moist soils near streams and waterholes, Fremont cotton-wood ranges from sea level to altitudes of 2,100 m (6,900 ft). At least 7 varieties have been identified, the best-known of which is the Rio Grande cottonwood (*P. fremontii* variety *wislizenii*).

These short-lived, fast-growing trees are abundant seed-producers. Male and female flowers bloom in separate catkins on different trees in spring before the leaves appear. The cotton-haired seeds, produced in small capsules, are wind dispersed. Mule deer and cattle browse the twigs and foliage.

The weak, light wood is used locally for fuel and fence posts. Mohave Indian women used strips of inner bark in their garments. Indians also ate the raw catkins, used the inner bark to prevent scurvy, and wove baskets of the young twigs. The trees are commonly planted for shade.

Appearance: tall tree to 30 m (100 ft), with a broad, open crown and a short trunk 1 m (3.3 ft) or more in diameter. **Bark:** thick, rough, and splitting, light gray or brownish or whitish; smooth on young trunks. **Branches:** stout and spreading; branchlets light green and smooth, turning yellow-gray by fall, slightly roughened by leaf scars. **Winter buds:** terminal buds 8–12 mm (0.4 in) long, hairless, egg-shaped, pointed at

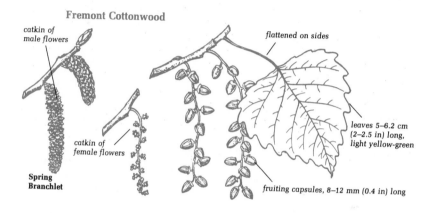

Fremont Cottonwood

catkin of male flowers

flattened on sides

catkin of female flowers

leaves 5–6.2 cm (2–2.5 in) long, light yellow-green

Spring Branchlet

fruiting capsules, 8–12 mm (0.4 in) long

the tip, light-green scales; lateral buds one-third to one-half as long. **Leaves:** alternate, deciduous, simple, *5–6.2 cm (2–2.5 in) long, 6.2–7.5 cm (2.5–3 in) wide, triangular-shaped,* with very broad base and narrow, tapering tip, rarely notched, coarsely and irregularly toothed along the margin, thick and firm, sometimes coated with hairs when new, light yellowish-green; leafstalks yellow, 3.7–5 cm (1.5–3 in) long, flattened. **Flowers:** male catkins densely flowered, 3.7–5 cm (1.5–2 in) long, nearly 12 mm (0.5 in) thick; female flowers in loose-flowered catkins, with stout hairy or smooth stems, becoming 10–13 cm (4–5.1 in) long. **Fruits:** egg-shaped capsules, 8–12 mm (0.4 in) long, thick-walled, blunt, or sharp-tipped, 3- (rarely 4-) valved; seeds 3–4 mm (0.1–0.2 in) long, light brown, covered with silky hairs.

Rio Grande Cottonwood *Populus fremontii* variety *wislizenii* (Torr.) S. Wats.

Long thought to be a separate species, this variety of Fremont cottonwood ranges farther to the east in the Rio Grande Valley. While its leaves are notably tapered at the tips, they are not more so than some of the variable forms of Fremont cottonwood. Distinguishing characters lie in the *catkins,* which *have long, slender stalks, and the fruits, which are more narrowly egg-shaped.*

This tree is favored for nesting by many birds, including the Treganza blue heron, 2 species of oriole, the Gila woodpecker, and the red-shafted flicker. Cattle and horses gnaw at the sweet inner bark. Poles are fashioned from trunks and are used in adobe house frames. The trees are valued for their shade, as well.

Rio Grande Cottonwood

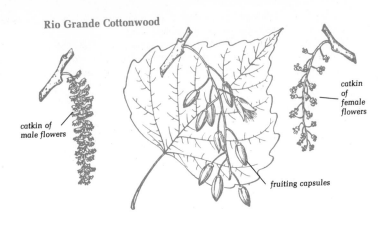

catkin of
male flowers

catkin
of
female
flowers

fruiting capsules

Lombardy Poplar

Populus nigra variety *italica* Muenchh.

The origin of this European import is obscure. It is thought to be a variety of Italian poplar (*Populus nigra*) originating in Lombardy province. However, it may have been brought to that area from western Asia by traders. It is unusual among poplars because of the close, erect branches that form a narrow, spire-like crown instead of the round top characteristic of other poplars. Furthermore, only male trees are known, and these are propagated by cuttings. They are commonly planted as ornamentals in North America, but they are short-lived and begin to become unsightly as large branches begin to die. In North America, they have a much shorter life span than in their native southern Europe. Many were planted by pioneers in the prairies for windbreaks.

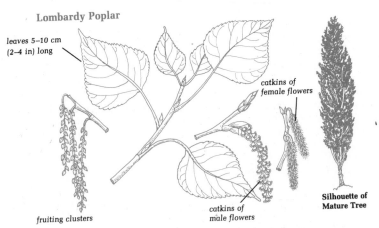

Lombardy Poplar

leaves 5–10 cm
(2–4 in) long

catkins of
female flowers

fruiting clusters

catkins of
male flowers

Silhouette of
Mature Tree

Growing up to 30 m (100 ft) high, Lombardy poplars are covered for most of their length by **upright,** sucker-like **branches.** The young branchlets are olive green, later turning gray; the bark of old trunks is thick, ridged, and furrowed. The **triangular-shaped leaves** are 5–10 cm (2–4 in) long, 4–8 cm (1.6–3.2 in) wide, with flattened or broadly wedge-shaped bases and abruptly tapered tips. They have fine-toothed margins and a papery texture—and are bright green. The **slender leafstalks** are shorter than the blades and *are flattened.* Male flowering catkins are 3.7–6.2 cm (1.5–2.5 in) long.

There is a hybrid of Lombardy poplar and eastern cottonwood called Carolina poplar. It is a large tree with erect, rising branches and may exceed 25 m (82 ft) in height. It spreads easily from cultivation by means of root suckers. Like the Lombardy poplar, Carolina poplar occurs mainly in male form. The leaves and form resemble eastern cottonwood, while twigs and buds are more like those of Lombardy poplar. It is sometimes planted as a street tree.

Palmer Cottonwood   *Populus palmeri* Sarg.

Palmer cottonwood is a small- to medium-size tree native to Texas. It is found in stream canyons of the Chisos Mountains, along the Rio Grande, and in the moist valley of the Nueces River in Trans Pecos Texas. Growing to a height of 18 m (60 ft) with a trunk diameter up to 90 cm (35 in), the tree bears smooth, pale, upright branches that form an open cone-shaped head. The *egg-shaped leaves* with narrowly tapering tips *are 3.7–12.5 cm (1.5–5 in) long* and 5–12 cm (2–4.8 in) wide. The *leafstalks are flattened,* slender, reddish to brown, and 3.7–10 cm (1.5–4 in) long with glands at the top of the stalk. The fruiting catkins are hairless and 7.5–15 cm (3–6 in) in length; the capsules are pitted and split into 3 or 4 valves.

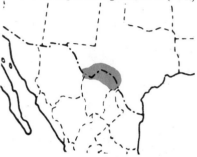

Quaking Aspen   *Populus tremuloides* Michx.

Of all the tree species in North America, quaking aspen has the widest distribution. These rapidly growing trees of medium stature are one of the most aggressive of the pioneer species, moving quickly into bare areas and soon establishing dense stands of young trees by sending suckers from the extensive root systems. From northern Alaska to Labrador, and south into the alpine reaches of Mexico to 3,000 m (9,900 ft) altitude, quaking aspen grows in many diverse soil types, from shallow, rocky, or clay soils to rich, sandy ones. Best growth occurs in rich, porous soils where lime is plentiful. It grows in association with northern pines, spruces, and balsam fir in the North; the Douglas fir, lodgepole pine, and white fir in the West; and also with hemlock, maples, bigtooth aspen, paper birch, and alders. Young stands are often pure, but give way eventually to other, slower-growing species.

Quaking aspens begin to produce seed at around 15 to 20 years of age, and continue for half a century or so. Occasional trees may reach 150 years of age or even 200 in the West, but normally the life expectancy is much shorter. Flowers appear in April and May before the leaves, and the fruits ripen 4 to 6 weeks later. Good seed crops are produced every 4 to 5 years. This species plays an important role in the lives of many organisms. It has been estimated that some 500 species of animals and plants from bear and elk down to lowly fungi, utilize them. Aspens are important browse to many game animals, and are the favorite food of beaver. Many birds, including grouse and quail, devour the buds, catkins, and seeds. They are prone to heart-rot and a number of other parasitic microorganisms.

The light, weak wood does not lend itself to furniture or construction, although it has been used for fences, railings, and barn doors. It is excellent for excelsior, cheap crates, and boxes. Mixed with other wood chips, it makes many paper products.

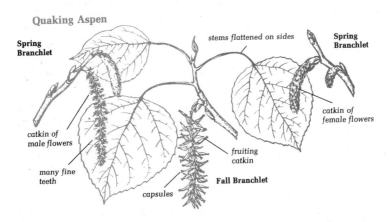

Quaking Aspen

Spring Branchlet

stems flattened on sides

Spring Branchlet

catkin of female flowers

catkin of male flowers

fruiting catkin

many fine teeth

Fall Branchlet

capsules

Appearance: medium-size tree to 12–18 m (39–60 ft), occasionally to 30 m (100 ft) in the West, with a short, rounded crown, trunk straight, 60 cm (23 in) wide or more, branch-free for the lower half of trunk. **Bark:** on young trees thin, pale-green to creamy and powdery; later becoming thick, roughened by warty bands, and divided into flattened ridges. **Branches:** slender, often contorted, slightly drooping; branchlets bright red-brown the first season and covered with light-orange pores, gradually turning gray and roughened by leaf scars. **Winter buds: *6–8 cm (2.4–3.2 in), sharp-tipped, cone-shaped, slightly sticky,*** covered by 6 or 7 shiny red-brown scales. **Leaves:** alternate, deciduous, simple, ***2–8 cm (0.8–3.2 in) long, 1.8–7 cm (0.7–2.8 in) wide, as long or longer than wide, broadest near the base, rounded to heart-shaped at the base,*** with a short pointed tip, ***with fine teeth along the margin,*** smooth, dark green above, paler below; ***leafstalks 2.5–6 cm (1–2.4 in) long, flattened,*** and slender, which make the leaves flutter in the slightest breeze. **Flowers:** separate male and female catkins on different trees, 3.7–6.2 cm (1.5–2.5 in) long, the female catkins becoming 10 cm (4 in) long at maturity. **Fruits:** several in long catkins, each capsule 6–7 mm (0.2–0.3 in) long, light-green, thin-walled, containing many tiny, hairy seeds.

Bigtooth Aspen   *Populus grandidentata* Michx.

Bigtooth aspen is a medium-size tree of northeastern North America, occurring from Nova Scotia to the plains of southeastern Manitoba, and south into the mountains of North Carolina. This tree prefers well-drained sandy soils, and although it is considered an upland tree, it can be found from sea level to 900 m (2,960 ft). Best growth is usually along low-lying streams, lakes, or swamp borders. Bigtooth aspen is a major component of the aspen forest type, usually seen with quaking aspen, red maple, gray and silver birches.

This species is fast-growing and short-lived. Flowering occurs before the leaves unfold in March to May, and the seed matures before the leaves are full grown

(May–June). A second flower crop may follow within 2 weeks of the first. Seed crops are produced when the trees are about 20 years old, and good crops are produced every 4 or 5 years. Seed germination is best on bare ground, such as cut or burned land, for bigtooth aspen is highly intolerant of any shading. After a few seedlings have been established, the stand increases rapidly by means of suckers that shoot up from the root network. So this species is important to forest regeneration, building the soil and protecting slower-

growing species. The buds and catkins are eaten by grouse, quail, prairie chicken, purple finch, and a towhee. Deer, elk, moose, mountain sheep, and smaller mammals such as beaver, muskrat, and rabbit eat the buds, bark, branchlets, and leaves. The soft wood is used mostly for paper pulp.

Bigtooth Aspen

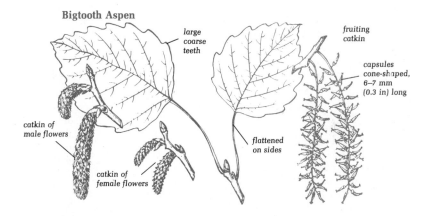

large coarse teeth

fruiting catkin

capsules cone-shaped, 6–7 mm (0.3 in) long

catkin of male flowers

catkin of female flowers

flattened on sides

Appearance: medium-size tree to 20 m (66 ft) or more, with an irregular open crown; trunk straight, up to 60 cm (23 in) in diameter. **Bark:** on younger growth light-gray, tinged with green, later becoming thick, dark brown tinged with red, furrowed with tiny scales. **Branches:** few, coarse, irregular, tapering to stout branchlets marked by orange lenticels, hairy at first, later smooth. **Winter buds:** end buds 8–9 mm (0.3 in) long, lateral buds 3–4 mm (0.1–0.2 in) long, covered with grayish down, slightly sticky, pointed at the tip, oval, with chestnut-brown scales. **Leaves:** alternate, deciduous, simple, *5–7.5 cm (2–3 in) long,* 5–6.2 cm (2–2.5 in) broad, broadest near the base, pointed at the tip, *with large, blunt teeth along the margin,* covered in spring with fine hairs, papery textured, dark green above, paler below; *leafstalks slender, 3.8–6.3 cm (1.5–2.5 in) long, flattened or compressed.* **Flowers:** male and female flowers in separate downy catkins, 2.5–3.7 cm (1–1.5 in) long on different trees; female catkins 10–12 cm (4–4.8 in) long when mature. **Fruits:** in long catkins, with light-green, downy capsules 6–7 mm (0.3 in) long, splitting into 2 parts to release the tiny seeds.

Plains Cottonwood *Populus sargentii* Dode

The plains cottonwood is considered by many botanists to be a smaller, western variety of eastern cottonwood. But in this book it is treated as a separate species. Ranging from Manitoba to the Texas Panhandle, plains cottonwood occurs on various moist, sandy, or river soils at 300–2,100 m (985–6,900 ft) elevation. Best growth is on deep, rich, well-drained loam soils. While the area itself is characterized by dryness punctuated by infrequent, sudden floods, this tree seeks the moisture of river flood plains and bottomlands. Pure stands occur on river sandbars or flood-prone areas in bends of large rivers. Bur oak, black and peach-leaf willows are the most common associates; others include boxelder, elm, and hackberry. The plains cottonwood and

both eastern and western species commonly hybridize.

These quick-growing trees reach maturity in 40 to 50 years and begin to die after that; rarely do they live 100 years. Flowering occurs in spring before the leaves appear, and the fruits mature from June to August. Whitetail and mule deer, songbirds, as well as cottontail and swamp rabbits consume various tender parts of the trees.

The wood has been used for fuel, posts, veneer, and baskets. Pioneers would seek the shade of these trees in the hot summer days, knowing that water was usually nearby. Often cottonwood groves would become crossroads and meeting places where news was exchanged. Large, hollowed-out trunks served as boats for explorers on the Missouri River.

Appearance: medium-size to tall trees, reaching 27 m, rarely to 36 (88 ft, rarely to 120), with a broad, open crown; trunk open, 1.5–2 m (4.9–6.6 ft) in diameter. **Bark:** smooth and pale gray on young trees, becoming thick, deeply cracked with broad, rounded, and scaly ridges. **Branches:** erect and spreading; branchlets stout, smooth, pale yellow, angular to rounded, marked by large leaf scars. **Winter buds:** egg-shaped, sharp-tipped, sticky, with brown, fuzzy scales. **Leaves:** alternate, deciduous, simple, *6.2–8.7 cm (2.4–3.5 in) long,* usually not as wide, *broadest near the base,* tapering to a pointed tip, somewhat coarsely toothed and wavy along the margin, hairy when young, becoming smooth and light-green; *leafstalks slender, 6–8.5 cm (2.4–3.4 in) long, flattened.* **Flowers:** male and female flowers on separate trees, in short-stalked catkins, catkins of male flowers 5–6.2 cm (2–2.5 in) long, female catkins becoming 10–20 cm (4–8 in) long. **Fruits:** capsules in an elongated catkin, each capsule 9–11 mm (about 0.4 in) long, cone-shaped, and containing small brown seeds.

The Willow Genus *Salix* L.

This is a large genus of about 300 species of trees and shrubs. They occur mainly in colder regions of the north-temperate to arctic zones. Willows are one of the few woody plants to survive in the treeless tundra regions of higher elevations in the Rocky Mountains. There are approximately 80 species in North America. Most of these are low shrubs, but many grow into large bushes or small trees, and a few reach moderate to large size. In this book 34 willow species are treated as trees, although many of them are more commonly found as shrubs.

Willow species, more than any other group of trees — except perhaps the hawthorns

—are especially difficult to distinguish from each other. This is due in part to the ready hybridization between many of the species, resulting in trees with intermediate characteristics. Also, some of the willows are highly variable. For example, leaves on rapidly growing new branchlets may be larger than those produced on slower growing stems.

Willows are important trees. They are effective in erosion control because their rapidly spreading and branching root system binds the soil along stream and river banks. To wildlife, they serve as an important source of browse in early spring and as cover. Man uses them for baskets, low-quality fuel, and shade or ornamental trees.

Members of this genus are trees and shrubs with simple, alternate, evergreen leaves that are usually lance-shaped, and entire or toothed along the margins. Male and female flowers are produced separately in densely flowered, elongated clusters or catkins and appear before, with, or immediately after the leaves unfold. The fruits are small, cone to lance-shaped capsules produced on the catkins that bore the female flowers.

Key to Willow Species

A. Leaves smooth at maturity (immature leaves may be hairy at first) and often with a gray to bluish waxy cast on the lower surface.

  1. Leaves 1–4 times as long as broad, usually widest at or above the middle.

    a. Leaf margins entire and wavy or sparsely and irregularly toothed along the margins.

      (1) Leaves 2–10 cm long, rarely to 12 (0.8–4 in, rarely to 4.8); 1–3.5 cm (0.4–1.4 in) wide.

Bebb Willow

        (a) Branchlets reddish-purple to orange-brown; leaves silvery-blue or blue-green beneath.

          (a1) Leaves entire and wavy along the margins; the leafstalks 5–8 mm (0.2–0.3 in) long; widespread in cooler regions of North America
              Bebb willow, p. 480

          (a2) Leaves sparsely toothed along the margins, the leafstalks 1.2–2.5 cm (0.5–1 in) long; widespread in cooler regions of North America
              Pussy willow, p. 481

Pussy Willow

(Continued)

(b) Branchlets gray-yellow; leaves grayish-green beneath; trees of southwestern Oregon and northwestern California
Tracy willow, p. 482

(2) Leaves 12–15 cm (4.7–6 in) long, 4–5 cm (1.6–2 in) broad; trees of northern Florida and southern Georgia
Florida willow, p. 482

b. Leaf margins with many fine teeth.

(1) Leaves broad, only twice as long as broad.

(a) Leaves 5–10 cm (2–4 in) long, 2.5–4 cm (1–1.6 in) wide, teeth with glands, and a papery texture; fruiting capsules 4–5 mm (0.2 in) long; shrubs or small trees, primarily of Canada **Balsam willow, p. 482**

(b) Leaves 4–6.5 cm (1.6–2.6 in) long, 2–3 cm (0.8–1.2 in) wide, fine-toothed, but not with glands, and with a leathery texture; fruiting capsules 7–9 mm (about 0.3 in) long; widespread shrubs or trees of Canada and Rocky Mountains
Missouri willow, p. 483

(2) Leaves narrower, 3–4 times as long as broad.

(a) Leaves conspicuously silvery white beneath; male flowers with 2 stamens; trees of eastern and midwestern North America
Serviceberry willow, p. 483

(b) Leaves pale green beneath, sometimes with a whitish cast.

(b1) Leaves dark to dull green above.

(b1a) Branchlets yellowish, snap or break off easily; leaves dull green; trees of southwestern U.S. and adjacent Mexico
Goodding willow, p. 484

(b1b) Branchlets dark gray or brown to orange or yellowish-brown, tough, do not snap off easily; leaves shiny dark green; trees of western North America from Alaska to California and New Mexico

Pacific willow, p. 484

(b2) Leaves yellowish-green above.
(b2a) Branchlets slender, flexible, drooping, reddish-brown turning gray; leaves light yellow-green; widespread trees of mid-North America

Peachleaf willow, p. 486

(b2b) Branchlets slender but upright to spreading; shiny, dark orange; leaves dark yellow-green; widespread in midwestern to eastern North America

Shining willow, p. 487

Pacific Willow

Peachleaf Willow

Shining Willow

2. Leaves 5–14 times as long as broad, usually lance-shaped, broadest near the base.

   a. Leaves rounded to almost heart-shaped at the base.

     (1) Leaves dark green and shiny above; male flowers with 2 stamens per flower.

       (a) Fruiting capsules smooth, 4–6 mm (about 0.2 in) long; leaves 1.5–3 cm (0.6–1.2 in) broad, sometimes almost entire along the margins; common widespread shrubs or trees

           Heart-leaved willow, p. 488

       (b) Fruiting capsules silky hairy, 2–5 mm (0.1–0.2 in) long; leaves 0.9–1.8 cm (0.4–0.7 in) broad, always with numerous, fine teeth along the margins; shrubs or trees of midwestern and northeastern North America   **Meadow willow, p. 488**

     (2) Leaves light to bright green and sometimes shiny above.

              (Continued)

(a) Mature leaves about 8 times as long as broad; trees of eastern and mid-western North America

Black willow, p. 488

(b) Mature leaves about 5 times as long as broad.

(b1) Branchlets yellow turning reddish to purple; leaves whitish beneath; fruiting capsules 4–6 mm (about 0.2 in) long; trees of southeastern U.S.

Coastal Plain willow, p. 490

(b2) Branchlets light to dark orange-brown; leaves pale green beneath; fruiting capsules 6–8 mm (0.2–0.3 in) long; trees of southwestern U.S. **Red willow, p. 490**

Black Willow

Red Willow

b. Leaves gradually tapering to a narrow base.

(1) Mature leaves 10–14 times as long as broad.

(a) Small tree with erect branches; leaves pale yellowish-green above, irregularly and shallowly toothed along the margin; fruiting capsules 4–6 mm (about 0.2 in) long; trees of the Pacific Northwest

River willow, p. 491

(b) Medium to large spreading tree with drooping branches; leaves bright green above, with many fine teeth along the margins; fruiting capsules 1.5–2.5 cm (0.6–1 in) long; introduced trees commonly planted near ponds or lakes

Weeping willow, p. 492

Weeping Willow

(2) Mature leaves 5–8 times as long as broad.

(a) Leaves entire to occasionally fine-toothed along the margins; trees of western U.S. and northern Mexico

Arroyo willow, p. 492

(b) Leaves uniformly fine-toothed along the margins.

(b1) Fruiting capsules lance-shaped, 6–8 mm (0.2–0.3 m)

Arroyo Willow

long, male flowers with 5–9 stamens per flower; trees of western North America
Pacific willow, p. 484

(b2) Fruiting capsules cone-shaped, 4–6 mm (about 0.2 in) long; male flowers with 2 stamens per flower; introduced trees.

(b2a) Leaves dark green; branchlets only slightly spreading from branches at narrow angles (30–45°), tough, do not break easily
White willow, p. 493
(b2b) Leaves grayish-green; branchlets spreading from branches at wide angles (60–90°), break easily
Crack willow, p. 494

B. Leaves densely hairy at maturity, at least on the lower surface.

1. Leaves broad, widest near or above the middle, 2–4 times as long as broad.

a. Leaves regularly fine to coarse-toothed along the margin.

(1) Branchlets gray to reddish-brown, hairy at first, becoming smooth; leaves finely toothed along the margin; fine silvery hairs beneath; trees of Alaska and extending across Canada
Littletree willow, p. 494
(2) Branchlets dark-brown, densely wooly on older branchlets; leaves coarsely toothed, 5–15 cm (2–6 in) long, 2.5–7.5 cm (1–3 in) wide, densely wooly beneath; trees of coastal Pacific Northwest **Hooker willow, p. 495**

Hooker Willow

b. Leaves entire along the margin, though occasionally with a few sparse teeth, especially near the base.

(1) Leaves smooth on the upper surface, covered with dense wooly hairs on the lower surface; trees of Alaska and northwestern Canada
Feltleaf willow, p. 495
(Continued)

Feltleaf Willow

(2) Leaves hairy on both surfaces, although more densely so beneath.

Sitka Willow

(a) Lower leaf surface covered with straight silky hairs; fruiting capsules 4–6 mm (0.2 in) long, covered with silky hairs; trees of southern Alaska to California
Sitka willow, p. 496

(b) Lower leaf surface covered with short reddish hairs; fruiting capsules 6–9 mm (0.2–0.3 in) long, densely covered with reddish-brown hairs; trees of western North America **Scouler willow, p. 497**

2. Leaves narrow, lance-shaped, broadest near the base or rarely near the middle, 5–15 times as long as broad.

Yew-Leaf Willow

   a. Leaves very small, 0.8–3.3 cm (0.3–1.3 in) long, 2–4 mm (about 0.1–0.2 in) wide; trees of southern Arizona, New Mexico, and southwestern Texas
   Yew-leaf willow, p. 498

   b. Leaves 3.5–15 cm (1.4–6 in) long, 0.3–3.5 cm (0.1–1.4 in) wide.

   (1) Leaves toothed along the margins.

      (a) Leaves with many fine teeth along the margin.

         (a1) Leaves 3.8–12 cm (1.5–4.8 in) long, 3–15 mm (0.1–0.6 in) wide, deciduous, blue-green above; male flowers with 2 stamens per flower; trees widespread in western North America
         Coyote willow, p. 499

Bonpland Willow

         (a2) Leaves 11–15 cm (4.3–6 in) long, 1.2–2.1 cm (0.5–0.8 in) wide, persisting into winter, almost evergreen, bright green above; male flowers with 3 stamens per flower; trees of southwestern U.S. and Mexico
         Bonpland willow, p. 499

      (b) Leaves with few, wide-spaced teeth.

(b1) Leaves long and narrow, 5–15 cm (2–6 in) long, 3–9 mm (0.1–0.3 in) wide, with glandular teeth along the margin, light yellowish-green above; fruiting capsules 7–9 mm (about 0.3 in) long; trees of eastern Canada to interior Alaska
Sandbar willow, p. 500

(b2) Leaves broadest near the middle, 3–7 cm (1.2–2.8 in) long, 1–3.5 cm (0.4–1.5 in) wide, with pointed, nonglandular teeth along the margin, dark bluish-green above; fruiting capsules 3–5 mm (0.1–0.2 in) long; trees of coastal British Columbia to Oregon
Northwest willow, p. 501

Northwest Willow

(2) Leaves entire along the margin.

(a) Leaves blue-green above.

(a1) Leaves 0.3–1 cm (0.1–0.4 in) wide, densely wooly during first season; fruiting capsules 5–6 mm (0.2 in) long; trees of Southern Oregon, California, and Baja California, Mexico
Hinds willow, p. 502

(a2) Leaves 1–3.5 cm (0.4–1.4 in) wide, short, hairy when young; fruiting capsules 3–5 mm (0.1–0.2 in) long; trees of coastal British Columbia to Oregon
Northwest willow, p. 501

(b) Leaves green above.

(b1) Leaves with silky hairs beneath, becoming sparse at maturity; trees of eastern Canada and extreme northeastern U.S. **Satiny willow, p. 502**

(b2) Leaves densely covered with silvery hairs on the lower surface; introduced trees from Europe, sometimes reproducing on their own
Basket willow, p. 502

Bebb Willow

Salix bebbiana Sarg.

This large shrub or small, bushy tree is probably the commonest of all the tree-size willows in Alaska and Canada, stretching from coast to coast and south into New Mexico. It usually occurs on moist, rich soils up to 3,000 m (9,850 ft) in elevation along streams, lakes, and swamps, but may form dense thickets in open meadows. As a pioneer species, Bebb willow readily moves into any cleared-out area where moisture is sufficient. It commonly grows in association with other willows.

Like many other pioneer (or invading) species, it is a fast-grower with a short life span. Flowering begins at an early age. Male and female catkins are produced on separate trees between mid-May and June. The seeds ripen by late June, and in July the catkins, now bearing seed capsules instead of flowers, drop to the ground. Bebb willow is especially important winter forage for moose and snowshoe rabbit in the subarctic zone. Grouse, whitetail deer, hare, and beaver are also dependent on the buds, inner bark, wood, and young shoots.

In Alaska, these trees are the main source of a decorative wood called "diamond willow" because of diamond-shaped depressions on the trunks caused by the attack of a fungus. This wood is carved into canes, lamp posts, and furniture. Bebb willow has been used for baseball bats and wickerwork. Its charcoal was used in gunpowder.

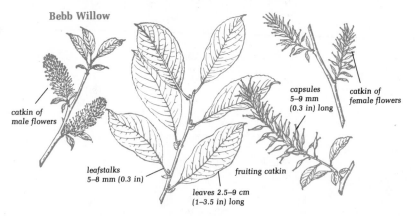

Bebb Willow

catkin of male flowers

leafstalks 5–8 mm (0.3 in)

leaves 2.5–9 cm (1–3.5 in) long

fruiting catkin

capsules 5–9 mm (0.3 in) long

catkin of female flowers

Appearance: a large bush or small tree, 4.5–7.5 m tall, rarely to 10 (14–25 ft, rarely to 33), with a broadly rounded crown; trunk short, 15–30 cm (5.9–11.8 in) in diameter. **Bark:** smooth, gray, becoming rough and furrowed with age. **Branches:** stout, up-turned; branchlets slender, wide-branching, at first downy, later smooth and varying in color from reddish-purple to orange-brown and lightening with age; marked with pale pores. **Winter buds:** oblong, shiny brown, tapering to a blunt point. **Leaves:** alternate, simple, deciduous, *2.5–9 cm (1–3.5 in) long, 1–2.5 cm (0.4–1 in) wide;* broadest at or above the middle, tapered at the ends; *smooth-margined or somewhat wavy;* dull green above, silvery-blue below, *with prominent meshed veins;* somewhat hairy when young; *leafstalks 5–8 mm (0.2–0.3 in) long,* downy, may be slightly grooved.

Flowers: male catkins short cylinder-shaped, densely flowered, with 2 stamens per flower; female catkins up to 7.5 cm (3 in) long, loosely flowered, with ovary densely coated by long, silky white hairs, scales narrow, yellowish with red tips, and hairy. **Fruits:** capsules 5–9 mm (0.2–0.3 in) long, tapered with a long beak and with short hairs, stalks slender up to 1.2 cm (0.5 in) long, seeds 1–2 mm (less than 0.1 in) long, dark purple or green with a ring of fine hairs around the base.

Pussy Willow

Salix discolor Mühl.

In the seemingly lifeless, gray aftermath of winter, the appearance of little "pussyfeet" on the branchlets of this small, often shrubby, tree is a welcome sign of spring. From Newfoundland in the East to central British Columbia in the West, and south into the Smoky Mountains, pussy willow occurs from lowlands to over 1,000 m (3.280 ft) above sea level. While preferring moist soils in meadows and along lakes and streams, it manages to do well in somewhat drier areas than other willows. Normally occurring in pure or nearly pure stands, pussy willow also is seen with other willows, cottonwood, and silver maple.

Flowering of these rapidly growing, short-lived trees occurs from March to May. Pussy willow is familiar even to confirmed "city people" because most florists display the leafless branches bearing the immature catkins. After a week or two, the fuzzy male c tkins mature and are laden with brilliant gold pollen that is sought by early bees. The buds and shoots are food for squirrels, rabbits, and other rodents, while the bark and branchlets are eaten by deer in "hard" winters. Pussy willow is also planted as an ornamental.

Pussy Willow

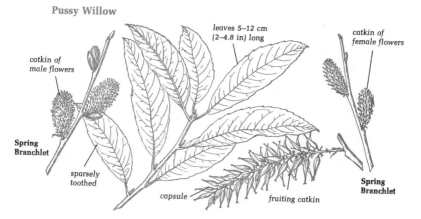

catkin of
male flowers

leaves 5–12 cm
(2–4.8 in) long

catkin of
female flowers

**Spring
Branchlet**

sparsely
toothed

capsule

fruiting catkin

**Spring
Branchlet**

Appearance: small tree, rarely reaching 8 m (26 ft), with an open, rounded crown and trunk diameter of up to 30 cm (11.8 in); or else a shrub with many tall, straggling stems. **Bark:** thin, light brown tinged with red, on old trunks divided into thin, scaly plates. **Branches:** stout, upright; ***branchlets dark reddish-purple and at first downy,***

later smooth, flecked with pale pores. **Winter buds:** 7–9 mm (about 0.3 in) long, flattened and sharp-tipped, shiny, dark reddish-purple. **Leaves:** alternate, deciduous, simple, *5–12 cm (2–4.8 in) long, 1.5–3.5 cm (0.6–1.4 in) broad, lance-shaped to broadest near the middle,* pointed at the tip, wedge-shaped to rounded base, *sparsely toothed along the margin,* thick and firm, *bright green above, silvery or whitish bloom and blue-green below:* leafstalks slender, 1.2–2.5 cm (0.5–1 in) long, stipules 6–7 mm (0.2–0.3 in) long, deciduous. **Flowers:** male catkins densely flowered and fuzzy, 2–4 cm (0.8–1.6 in) long, 1–1.5 cm (0.4–0.6 in) wide, scales dark brown and oval, stamens 2 per flower; female catkins, 1.5–3 cm (0.6–1.2 in) long, densely fuzzy and with brown scales. **Fruits:** capsules in drooping catkins 6–8 cm (2.4–3.2 in) long; capsules cylindric with a long neck, finely hairy.

Tracy Willow · Salix tracyi Ball

Tracy willow occurs only in the Klamath Mountains of southwestern Oregon and northwestern California. It grows on sand and gravel bars of streams and rivers, usually near sea level. This willow is closely related to the arroyo willow and looks similar.

Tracy willows are shrubs or slender trees to 6 m (20 ft) high and have *gray-yellow to brownish branchlets.* The *leaves* are widest above the middle, *2–5 cm (0.8–2 in) long,* 1.4–1.8 cm (0.6–0.8 in) wide, entire to occasionally toothed on the margin, green above and *grayish-green below.* Flowering catkins, appearing before the leaves, are 2–5 cm (0.8–2 in) long. Each male flower has 2 stamens. Fruiting catkins contain several small, lance-shaped capsules, each one 4–6 mm (about 0.2 in) long.

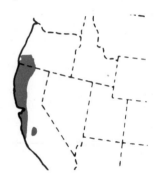

Florida Willow · Salix floridana Chapman

If you chance to encounter this small willow, consider yourself lucky, for it is on the verge of extinction. It has been seen along small streams and in moist woods on limestone soils in Pulaski and Early counties in Georgia, and in Jackson, Columbia, Lake, and Levy counties in Florida. It is distinguished from other willows by its *large, broad leaves, 12–15 cm (4.7–6 in) long, 4–5 cm (1.6–2 in) broad,* that are *usually broadest about the middle.* The tips are pointed, the *bases broadly rounded,* and the *margins irregularly and shallowly toothed* with glands. The upper surfaces are dark green and the lower are whitish and downy.

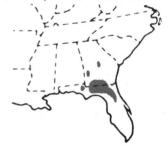

Balsam Willow · Salix pyrifolia Anderss.

The balsam scent of the leaves gives this willow its common name while its scientific name actually means "pear-leaved." Commonly occurring as a shrub less than 3 m (9.9 ft) tall from Newfoundland to British Columbia and south to Michigan, the bal-

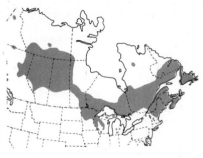

sam willow occasionally reaches a height of 8 m (26 ft) in high parts of Maine. It occurs in moist sites, along mountain streams, lakes, and bogs. It has gray, smooth bark and fuzzy, later smooth, purplish, and shining branchlets; winter buds are small, flattened, pointed, and reddish-purple. The *leaves,* are *5–10 cm (2–4 in) long, 2.5–4 cm (1–1.6 in) wide,* with pointed tips and rounded bases, hairy at first but soon becoming smooth, *with many fine, glandular teeth along the margin,* dark green in the upper surface, paler beneath, offering a sharp contrast when the wind is blowing. The flowering catkins are 3–4 cm (1.2–1.6 in) long and appear when the leaves unfold in May or June. The scales covering most of the flowers are pink and covered with long hairs. Each male flower contains 2 stamens. The fruiting catkins are 5–7.5 cm (2–3 in) long with narrow, smooth capsules 4–5 mm (0.2 in) long (broadest near the base to *cone-shaped*) on slender stalks.

Serviceberry Willow — *Salix monticola* Bebb ex Coult.

(synonym: *S. padophylla* Rydberg)

Serviceberry willow is a shrubby tree, seldom reaching 6 m (20 ft) in height, occurring from central Alaska, across Canada to Quebec and south to Colorado. It occurs scattered along higher mountains and is found along streams, rivers, and wet sites. The

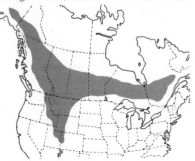

trees are always small and show evidence of heavy browsing by deer. The trees are multi-stemmed with dark, shiny, flexible, yellowish branchlets and yellowish to red-brown buds. The *leaves* are short, broad, widest at or above the middle, *4–6.5 cm (1.6–2.6 in) long, 2–3 cm (0.8–1.2 in) wide, finely toothed along the margins,* dark green above, pale below, and with a leathery texture. The flowering catkins bloom in May before the leaves appear. Catkins containing male flowers are 3–3.5 cm (1.2–1.4 in) long, each male flower with 2 flowers; catkins containing female flowers are 2–2.5 cm (0.8–1 in) long. Fruiting catkins are 6–7 cm (2.4–2.8 in) long, while the individual brown *capsules* are *7–9 mm (0.3 in) long,* egg-shaped, and beaked at the tip.

Missouri Willow — *Salix eriocephala* Michx.

Missouri willow is a small to medium-size tree to 12–15 m (39–50 ft) with a range extending from Newfoundland to Nebraska, and south to Mississippi. It occurs in sandy to rocky soils, near rivers, creeks, and swamps. Usually these willows grow in dense pure stands, but may be intermingled with black willow, peachleaf willow, and sandbar willow, cottonwood, green ash, and red maple. Missouri willows, though fast-growing, tend to live a bit longer and have slightly more durable wood than most other willows. They perform an important ecological function of stabilizing stream banks against spring floods. Whitetail deer and rodents eat the foliage and young shoots. The wood can serve for fence posts.

These trees have slender branches that form a narrow head, and thin, **gray to black, scaly bark.** The new branchlets are green, densely downy, and marked with pale pores; by the second year they become reddish-brown and smooth. Winter buds grow up to 2.5 cm (1 in) long and are red-brown, hairy. The leaves are narrowly lance-shaped, broadest near the base, 10–15 cm (4–6 in) long, 2.5–3.7 cm (1–1.5 in) wide, hairy at first, later smooth, **fine-toothed along the margin,** thick and firm;

the dark green upper surfaces contrast sharply with the **pale often silvery-white lower surfaces.** The densely flowered, wooly, erect catkins bloom in earliest spring before the leaves; the floral scales are light green and silver haired. Each male flower contains 2 stamens. The long-pointed, red-brown seed capsules are 7–9 mm (0.3 in) long.

Goodding Willow *Salix gooddingii* Ball

Goodding willow, a close relative of black willow, occurs in moist soils along streambanks from Utah to Texas and Mexico. It is most abundant on the lower region of the Colorado River, where dense stands form on the nutrient-rich floodplains. It may be

found at 60–1,200 m (200–4,000 ft) elevation in desert, desert grassland, and oak woodland habitats.

This willow was always an important sign to pioneers, for it signaled the presence of water in the arid countryside. Even today, the southwestern Indians collect the slender branchlets, debark them, and use them to weave baskets tight enough to hold water. Deer browse the leaves. Prairie fowl and small mammals eat the buds, catkins, and bark.

This is a medium-size tree, commonly forking at the base to form a loosely spreading, irregular crown. The main distinguishing features are the **yellowish branchlets,** which are narrowed where they join the branch and **snap off easily when pulled.** These may float down river and take root on a sandbar. The long, narrow leaves are 3–14 cm (1.2–5.5 in) long, 0.5–1.5 cm (0.2–0.6 in) wide, broadest near the base, finely toothed along the margins, **dull green and smooth on the upper surfaces, paler and smooth beneath.** The flowering catkins are 2.5–5 cm (1–2 in) long, with hairy, yellow scales. Male flowers bear 5 to 11 stamens. The fruit is a light reddish-brown capsule, 6–8 mm (0.2–0.3 in) long, usually finely hairy.

Pacific Willow *Salix lasiandra* Benth.

[synonym: S. *caudata* (Nutt.) Heller]

Pacific willow, often called yellow or western black willow, grows to medium height in southern California but gradually takes on smaller stature as it ranges northward, becoming a small tree in interior Alaska. These trees occur in well-drained sandy loams to rich, rocky, or gravelly soils from sea level up to 2,550 m (8,400 ft) in the

Sierra Nevada. They are common along banks and sandbars of mountain streams, waterholes, and lakes. They often occur in dense, pure clumps, or else with other willows, red and white alders, black and Fremont cottonwoods, and California sycamore.

The whiplash willow (*Salix caudata*), formerly recognized as a separate species, is considered a variety of the Pacific willow. This variety (*caudata*) has leaves that are green above and below, while typical Pacific willow has leaves that are green above and whitish below.

Like most willows, Pacific willow grows rapidly but has only a short life, during which time it produces abundant seed and many sprouts from its complex root system. Densely flowered catkins are produced at the same time as the leaves. Within a few weeks the female flowers mature into seed-bearing capsules. Deer and moose browse the twigs and foliage, while small game and songbirds consume the catkins, buds, and young tips. Little, if any, commercial use is made of Pacific willow today; in the past, it was a charcoal source, and Spanish Californians used the wood for saddle trees.

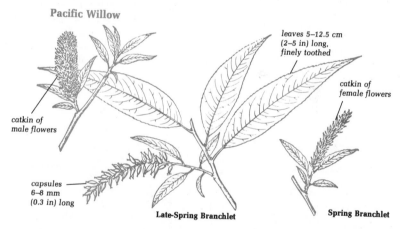

Pacific Willow

leaves 5–12.5 cm
(2–5 in) long,
finely toothed

catkin of
female flowers

catkin of
male flowers

capsules
6–8 mm
(0.3 in) long

Late-Spring Branchlet

Spring Branchlet

Appearance: a tall multistemmed shrub or small to medium-size tree to 18 m (60 ft), with a rounded crown, and trunk up to 90 cm (35 in) in diameter. **Bark:** moderately thick, gray or brown, becoming dark, fissured, with broad, flat, scaly plates. **Branches:** slender, upright, or drooping slightly; branchlets *stout, dark-colored,* and hairy at first, later becoming smooth and varying from *dark purple to bright orange-to-yellow brown.* **Winter buds:** 1–1.3 cm (0.4–0.5 in) long, broadly oval, light chestnut-brown and shiny near the tips, pale at the base. **Leaves:** alternate, deciduous, simple, *5–12.5 cm (2–5 in) long, 1.2–2.5 cm (0.5–1 in) wide,* narrowly elliptic (broadest near the middle), long-pointed, often rounded at the base, *margins finely toothed, shiny dark green above,* paler and with a whitish bloom below; leafstalks short, glandular at the tip. **Flowers:** male and female catkins on separate trees, on leafy stalks, 5–10 cm (2–4 in) long; scales yellowish and hairy at base; *male flowers with 5*

to 9 stamens. Fruits: lance-shaped capsules, 6–8 mm (0.3 in) long, hairless, light red-brown, produced in the female catkins.

Peachleaf Willow   *Salix amygdaloides* Anderss.

Peachleaf willow is a medium-size tree whose geographic range covers much of the U.S. and southern Canada but is most abundant in the Rocky Mountains. From Manitoba to Texas and eastward into central New York, these trees are found along muddy streambanks and low, wet woods bordering on rivers—to elevations of 2,100 m (6,900 ft) in the West. Willows, cot-tonwood, and silver maple are commonly found in the same forests. Peachleaf wil-low is a pioneer species that forms young forests. Second-stage trees such as syca-more, river birch, and green ash may often be seen invading the willow stands.

The flowers of the short-lived, fast-grow-ing peachleaf willow appear in April and May with the leaves. The male and female
flowers are in separate, hairy catkins on different trees. The fruits mature about a month after flowering. This species is moderately important to wildlife. Deer browse the twigs and foliage, and squirrels and rabbits feed on the tender shoots and bark.

The economic uses of the soft, weak wood are limited mainly to charcoal and firewood, although it is sometimes cut for timber. Often the branches droop slightly, giving a weeping effect that has made them popular in landscape plantings.

A variety of peachleaf, known as Wright willow (*Salix amygdaloides* variety *wrightii*) is southernly in distribution and has yellow or yellow-brown, smooth branchlets.

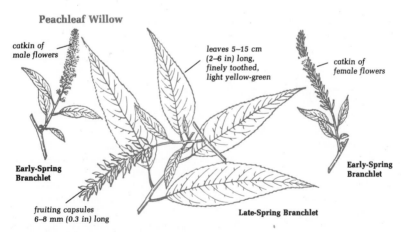

Peachleaf Willow

catkin of male flowers

leaves 5–15 cm (2–6 in) long, finely toothed, light yellow-green

catkin of female flowers

Early-Spring Branchlet

Early-Spring Branchlet

fruiting capsules 6–8 mm (0.3 in) long

Late-Spring Branchlet

Appearance: *a medium-size tree, 15–20 m (49–66 ft) in height,* with an open, irreg-ular head; trunk straight or sometimes leaning, up to 60 cm (23 in) in diameter. **Bark:** thick, brown, irregularly split, with broad, flat, often shaggy ridges. **Branches:** either ascending or ***drooping slightly;*** branchlets range to reddish-brown when young, becoming gray later, ***slender, flexible, drooping,*** with scattered pale lenticels. **Winter**

buds: 2–4 mm (0.1–0.2 in) long, egg-shaped, shiny, brown. **Leaves:** alternate, deciduous, simple, **5–15 cm (2–6 in) long, 1.8–3 cm (0.7–1.2 in) wide; lance-shaped,** broadest below the middle, **fine-toothed,** tapering tip and often uneven at the base, thin, and papery, **light yellow-green;** pale ·with whitish bloom beneath, leafstalks 6–18 mm (0.2–0.7 in) long, often twisted; stipules at base of leafstalk absent or kidney-shaped. **Flowers:** flowering catkins 3.7–5 cm (1.5–2 in) long, slender, scales yellowish-green, hairy, deciduous; **male flowers with 5 to 9 stamens. Fruits:** cone-shaped capsules borne in catkins 6–8 cm (2.8–3.2 in) long; capsules light reddish or yellow, 6–8 mm (0.3 in) long, containing numerous tiny seeds.

Shining Willow

Salix lucida Mühl.

Shining willow is one of the more attractive, smaller eastern willows. It occurs in wet soils along banks, streams, and swamps from Labrador to South Dakota. Often it is a shrub to 4 m (13 ft) high, but occasionally it exceeds 8 m (26 ft) as a small tree. Shining willow commonly appears in small pure stands or else grows in association with other willows, alder, and balsam fir. It is fast-growing, though short-lived, and is recommended for ornamental planting in wet spots. Deer, moose, squirrels, rabbits, and porcupine are among those animals that eat the leaves, buds, flowering catkins, and bark.

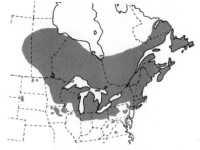

Members of this species have short trunks 15–20 cm (6–8 in) in diameter, upraised **branches** forming a broad, rounded crown, and smooth, **shiny, dark orange branchlets** that darken after their first season. The dark **yellow-green leaves** are **5–13 cm (2–5.1 in) long, 1.2–3.7 cm (0.5–1.5 in) wide,** usually broadest just below the middle, with long-pointed tips, rounded or wedge-shaped bases, **finely toothed margins, smooth,** and shiny. The flowers bloom in catkins in early June, followed by fruiting capsules within the catkins that bore the female flowers. Each of the male flowers contains 5 stamens. The cone-shaped capsules are 5–7 mm (0.2–0.3 in) long.

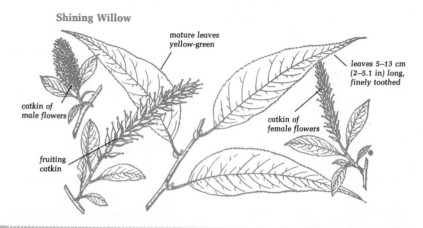

Shining Willow

mature leaves
yellow-green

leaves 5–13 cm
(2–5.1 in) long,
finely toothed

catkin of
male flowers

catkin of
female flowers

fruiting
catkin

Heart-Leaved Willow

Salix rigida Mühl.

[synonyms: S. *lutea* Nutt., S. *mackenziena* Barratt ex Anderss., S. *ligulifolia* (Ball) Ball.]

This is a common shrub or small tree ranging from the Pacific Northwest to Newfoundland and extending southward in the West to California and Arizona and in the East to Virginia. Like other willows, it occurs along streams, rivers, lakes, swamps, and other wet sites up to 2,400 m (7,900 ft) elevation.

Botanists debate whether heart-leaved willow is a highly variable species or an assemblage of closely related ones that are difficult to distinguish. For the purpose of this book, they will be considered a widespread variable species. In eastern North America, the leaves are usually wider than those on the trees in the West.

Heart-leaved willows are multistemmed shrubs or small trees to 9 m (30 ft) with a trunk to 12 cm (4.8 in) in diameter and a wide crown. The young slender branchlets may be hairy or smooth, reddish-brown to yellow. Leaves are lance-shaped to widest near or above the middle, *7–15 cm (2.8–6 in) long, 1.5–3 cm (0.6–1.2 in) wide,* short-pointed at the tip and *rounded to almost heart-shaped at the base, finely toothed to almost entire along the margin,* dark green above, grayish or bluish-green beneath, sometimes with a waxy cast, and smooth at maturity. The flowering catkins appear before or with the leaves and are 2–5 cm (0.8–2 in) long. Male flowers contain 2 stamens. The fruiting catkins contain *smooth, lance-shaped capsules 4–6 mm (about 0.2 in) long.*

Meadow Willow

Salix petiolaris J. E. Smith

From New Brunswick across southern Canada, to Colorado and New Jersey in the U.S., the meadow willow ranges widely across wet meadows and streambanks. Normally it is a clumped shrub with slender upraised stems, growing perhaps to a height of only 3 m (9.9 ft); in its northern reaches it is considered to be a tree, for it sometimes attains 7 m (23 ft). It associates with other willow species, all of them fast-growers but short-lived. It is browsed so heavily by deer that it commonly remains a stubby shrub less than 1 m (3.3 ft) tall.

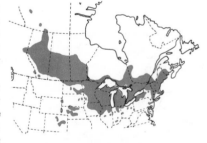

The bark of young trunks is gray-green or red-brown; that of older trunks is darker brown and either smooth or scaly. The leaves, *5–10 cm long,* occasionally to 15 (2–4 in, occasionally to 6) and *0.9–1.8 cm (0.4–0.7 in) wide,* are lance-shaped with tapered ends, *rounded bases* and *finely toothed* margins; young leaves are silky, the mature ones firm, dark green, and fairly glossy. In May and June the flowering catkins appear with the new leaves. Each of the male flowers has 2 stamens. The seed *capsules* are *lance-shaped. 2–5 mm (0.1–0.2 in) long,* blunt or pointed at the tip, and *silky hairy.*

Black Willow

Salix nigra Marsh.

Old black willows rank among the largest willows in the world, reaching great heights in swamps in the deep South; but in the north on poor sites, they are comparatively small trees. Ranging from Maine to Minnesota, and south to Texas, these trees do well on almost any soil, but require a plentiful and constant supply of moisture for their roots during the growing season. They are most common along river margins and in low, wet sites such as swamps and sloughs, and along bayous, gullies, and drainage ditches. These trees are prevalent and attain their best growth along the lower part of the Mississippi River. They form the main component of one wetlands forest type where pure stands are often formed. Black willow is found with such trees as

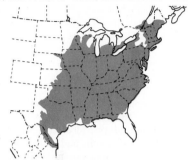

black spruce, cottonwood, river birch, water tupelo, and bald cypress.

Black willow is a fast-growing, relatively short-lived tree averaging 15 m (50 ft) by 10 years of age. Flowering occurs from February to April throughout its range, at about the same time as the leaves unfolding. Seed production begins at age 10, though prime production is from 25 to 75 years. Good crops are borne almost every year. Deer and rodents browse the shoots, and sapsuckers feed on the inner bark.

The bark and roots contain a bitter agent that has been an ingredient in backcountry spring tonics. The light, springy wood is excellent for wickerwork baskets and furniture. The trees are often used in erosion control because their roots form dense networks that stabilize streambanks.

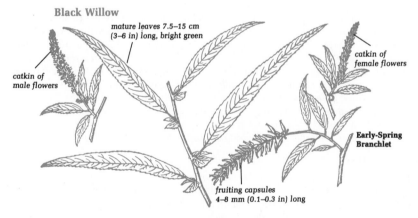

Black Willow

catkin of male flowers

mature leaves 7.5–15 cm (3–6 in) long, bright green

catkin of female flowers

Early-Spring Branchlet

fruiting capsules 4–8 mm (0.1–0.3 in) long

Appearance: in the North, a small to medium-size tree, 9–18 m (30–60 ft) tall; on better sites in the South, a tall tree to 42 m (138 ft), with a tall, straight trunk up to 2 m (6.6 ft) wide supporting a broadly irregular crown. **Bark:** *heavy, black or very dark brown, deeply and narrowly cracked,* becoming shaggy in old age. **Branches:** thick, spreading, upright, and red-brown or grayish branchlets that are downy when they are new, later smooth and breaking easily at the joints. **Winter buds:** pointed, about 3–4 mm (about 0.1–0.2 in) long. **Leaves:** alternate, deciduous, simple, *7.5–15 cm (3–6 in) long, 8–18 mm (0.3–0.7 in) wide, lance-shaped, long-pointed with a wedge-shaped or rounded base, finely toothed,* thin and papery, *bright green above,* paler below; leafstalks short; stipules wing-like at base of leaf. **Flowers:** male and female catkins borne upright on ends of short, leafy branchlets on separate trees, 2.5–7.5 cm (1–3 in) long, scales yellow, broadest near their blunted tips and hairy on the inner surface. Male flowers with 3 to 5 stamens; female flowers with an oval-shaped ovary, short-stalked, dividing slightly into 2 stigma lobes. **Fruits:** capsules egg-shaped, 4–8 mm (0.1–0.3 in) long, light reddish-brown, containing many tiny, silky-haired seeds.

Coastal Plain Willow *Salix caroliniana* Michx.

Coastal plain willow, also called Ward or Carolina willow, is a small slender tree widely distributed in the Southeast, from the mid-Atlantic states to the Rio Grande in Texas. It occurs on sandy or gravelly bars in streams, in swamps, marshy areas, and

other wet areas. It grows in association with black and peachleaf willows, cottonwood, silver maple, and green ash.

This slight, unassuming tree with spreading crown is often mistaken for peachleaf and black willow. Its leaves resemble those of the peachleaf willow and its bark is like that of the black willow. However, its red-brown branchlets do not snap off easily when tugged, as do the peachleaf's, and they are either smooth or finely hairy. The leaves of Coastal Plain willow have a whitish bloom on the undersurfaces; rounded bases; and yellowish glands on the tips of the teeth or in the notches in between. Black willow has reddish glands in those areas.

Appearance: many-branched shrubs or small trees to 10 m (33 ft) with a broad, open crown. **Bark:** becoming thick and deeply checkered, gray. **Branches:** thick, spreading; ***branchlets*** slender, yellowish when young, ***becoming reddish to purple.*** **Winter buds:** as in black willow. **Leaves:** alternate, deciduous, simple, ***lance-shaped, 6–14 cm (2.4–5.5 in) long, 1–3 cm (0.4–1.2 in) wide, long-pointed at the tip, with a rounded or wedge-shaped base, finely toothed along the margin,*** with a firm, papery texture, ***green above,*** whitish below, sparingly hairy; stipules wing-like at the base of the leaves. **Flowers:** male and female catkins borne near the ends of the branchlets, 3–10 cm (1.2–4 in) long; ***male flowers with 4 to 8 stamens.*** **Fruits:** fruiting catkins lax and open, the cone-shaped capsules 4–6 mm (0.2 in) long.

Red Willow *Salix laevigata* Bebb.

Red willow is a small to medium-size western tree. It occurs from Utah to Baja California in Mexico up to 1,350 m (4,500 ft) in elevation. This species prefers well-drained soils as found along the banks of mountain streams and other fast-flowing water-

courses. It often grows with the Pacific willow, Arroyo willow, and white alder, in the oak and pinyon-juniper woodland belts and sometimes in the upper desert in the Southwest. Red willow is so closely related to bonpland willow that some botanists term them both bonpland willows. (See page 499.)

This is a fast-growing, short-lived species. Flowering occurs from March to May, depending on latitude and altitude. The flowers appear simultaneously with the leaves, while the seeds, enclosed in small, elongated capsules, mature several weeks later. Songbirds, such as goldfinches, yellow warblers, and long-tailed chats, use red willow. As well, deer, squirrels, hares, and rabbits browse the leaves. These trees have been spared commercial exploitation because the wood is soft, weak, and brittle.

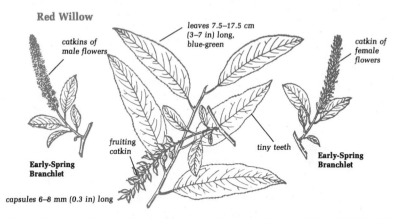

Red Willow

catkins of male flowers

leaves 7.5–17.5 cm (3–7 in) long, blue-green

catkin of female flowers

fruiting catkin

tiny teeth

Early-Spring Branchlet

Early-Spring Branchlet

capsules 6–8 mm (0.3 in) long

Appearance: small to medium-size tree, reaching a maximum of '15 m (50 ft), with greatest trunk diameter of 60 cm (23 in), and with a broadly irregular open crown. **Bark:** dark reddish-brown, deeply and irregularly furrowed with many interconnecting ridges. **Branches:** slender, spreading; *branchlets* slender, *light to dark orange-brown,* and in one variety of red willow hairy. **Winter buds:** oval, pale chestnut-brown, 3–8 cm (1.2–3.2 in) long. **Leaves:** alternate, deciduous, simple, *7.5–17.5 cm (3–7 in) long, 1.8–3.7 cm (0.7–1.5 in) wide; lance-shaped or broadest near the middle, with narrowly rounded, notched, or pointed tips and rounded at the base,* minute teeth along margin, conspicuous yellow mid-rib, blue-green and shiny above, paler and minutely hairy below, leafstalks broad, grooved, up to 1.2 cm (0.5 in) long. **Flowers:** male and female catkins on separate tree, 5–10 cm (2–4 in) long, on leafy branchlets, drooping or upright scales covered with pale hairs; *male flowers with 5 or 6 stamens.* **Fruits:** long, cone-shaped *capsules* produced in the female catkins; each capsule *6–8 mm (0.3 in) long.*

River Willow   *Salix fluviatilis* Nutt.

River willow is a native of the Pacific Northwest and occurs in the drainage basin shared by Washington and Oregon. It forms extensive thickets and rapidly colonizes on sandbars along lowland ponds, lakes, and streams in moist sand or gravel overladen with silt. Because of this colonizing characteristic, river willow is one of the most valuable in its range for natural erosion control. As a pioneer species, it is intolerant of shading. Masses of seedlings quickly sprout new shoots and a network of roots soon holds the streambank securely. Other willows and cottonwoods may be found nearby. The river willow and the northwest willow occur together and hybridize with each other.

mm

cm   1   2   3   4   5   6   7   8   9   10   11

This tree, usually growing to a height of 7 m (23 ft), but occasionally reaching 15 m (50 ft), has a narrow, compact form with slender, upright branches. Often it appears as a short, many-stemmed shrub in dense clumps. The thin, scaly bark is grayish-brown, tinged with red. The long, thin lance-shaped leaves are **7.5–12.5 cm (3–5 in) long, 0.8–1.2 cm (0.3–0.5 in) wide,** pointed at the tip and long-tapering at the base, irregularly and shallowly toothed, ***pale yellow-green*** and smooth above, paler below. The catkins are relatively short and stubby. Each male flower has 2 stamens. The fruiting catkins are 4–10 cm (1.6–4 in) long and the **capsules are 4–6 mm (about 0.2 in) long.**

Weeping Willow
Salix babylonica L.

Weeping willow is a Chinese native and was introduced to North America from Europe in 1730. Growing to 18 m (60 ft), these trees are characterized by long, slender branches gracefully sweeping the ground. Like its relatives, weeping willows prefer moist sites.

Its appearance led Carolus Linnaeus, the originator of the modern system for plant and animal classification, to mistakenly believe that these were the biblical willows of Babylon, and he named them accordingly. The biblical willows were actually poplars. Planted as ornamentals for centuries in North America, Europe, and Asia, weeping willows gained the affection of Napoleon during his banishment. On the island of St. Helena, he would sit beneath one of these trees, thinking of his past glories. Here he died and was buried, and for a long time after, cuttings from it were sought around the world.

Weeping Willow

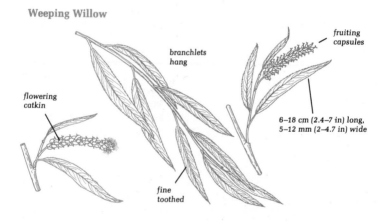

flowering
catkin

branchlets
hang

fruiting
capsules

6–18 cm (2.4–7 in) long,
5–12 mm (2–4.7 in) wide

fine
toothed

These spreading trees have a broadening rounded crown with ***drooping or hanging branches.*** The bark is gray and rough, and the branchlets smooth, yellowish-green to brown, and drooping. The bright-green leaves are **6–18 cm (2.4–7.1 in) long, 5–12 mm (0.2–0.5 in) wide,** broadest near the base, tapered at the tips, and ***finely toothed along the margin,*** silky hairy when young, becoming smooth with age. Flowering catkins are about 2.5 cm (1 in) long, borne on short leafy branchlets in April or May. The fruiting catkins are 1–2.5 cm (0.4–1 in) long and contain many cone-shaped capsules that are 1.5–2.5 cm (0.6–1 in) long.

Arroyo Willow
Salix lasiolepis Benth.

This is another western species, appearing either as a many-stemmed shrub or small tree. Ranging from Washington to northern Mexico, arroyo willow prefers wet, well-drained soils along streams, especially in the narrow gulches and gullies (arroyos) of the southern California hills. It occurs from sea level to 2,250 m (7,400 ft). While it often appears in patches, it grows in association with California sycamore and white alder.

Flowering takes place before the leaves unfold in February or March, with the male and female flowers appearing in separate catkins on different trees. Later, the female catkins elongate as the seed capsules develop. Mule deer occasionally browse the foliage and numerous songbirds nest in the limbs. The light, weak, brown wood has served as fuel, charcoal, and material for basket weaving.

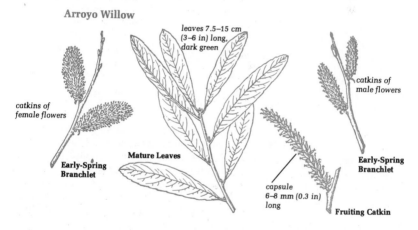

Arroyo Willow

leaves 7.5–15 cm (3–6 in) long, dark green

catkins of male flowers

catkins of female flowers

Early-Spring Branchlet

Mature Leaves

capsule 6–8 mm (0.3 in) long

Early-Spring Branchlet

Fruiting Catkin

Appearance: a shrub with many stems from the base, or a short tree, 5–12 m (16–40 ft) tall, with a slender and upright open form; trunk 7.5–20 cm (3–8 in) in diameter. **Bark:** on younger trees thin, smooth, light pale-green or gray-brown, becoming thick and furrowed, often with nearly white patches. **Branches:** slender, upright, with stout branchlets at first hairy, bright yellow to dark red-brown the first year, becoming dark and smooth the second. **Winter buds:** oval, sharp-tipped, light yellowish-brown, flattened with wing-like edges. **Leaves:** alternate, deciduous, simple, *7.5–15 cm (3–6 in) long, 1.2–2.5 cm (0.5–1 in) wide, broadest about the middle,* tapering at the base and tip; with *entire to occasionally fine-toothed margins that may curl under; at maturity thick and firm, dark green above,* paler below. **Flowers:** produced in catkins about 3.2–3.8 cm (1.3–1.5 in) long, catkins containing the male flowers 1–1.3 cm (0.4–0.5 in) thick, each flower with 2 stamens; catkins of female flowers 2–2.6 cm (0.8–1 in) thick. **Fruits:** a cylinder-shaped capsule 6–8 mm (0.2–0.3 in) long, reddish-brown.

White Willow

Salix alba L.

White willow is native to Europe and central Asia and was brought to North America by European colonists. Today it is widely planted for its ornamental value and reproduces on its own in many areas, preferring moist sites along streams.

In Europe, white willow is fairly important as a source of pliable timber. Its wood is used in basketry and is preferred for cricket bats and balls in England. Many varieties and horticultural strains have been produced. In early Christian Greece, the physician Dioscorides prescribed a tonic of the leaves for curing gout.

White willow trees may reach 25 m (82 ft) in height, with spreading, yellowish-brown branches that form a broad, open crown. They are, like their relatives, fast-growing and short-lived. The **grayish-green, slender, finely toothed leaves** are **4–10 cm (1.6–4 in) long,** long-pointed at the tip, gradually tapering at the base, silky-hairy when young, but later becoming smooth. The leafstalks are quite short and downy. The flowering catkins appear in April or May on short, leafy branchlets. The male flowers are distinguished by 2 stamens. Fruiting catkins, containing many cone-shaped capsules, 4–6 mm (0.2 in) long, appear in May or June.

Crack Willow   *Salix fragilis* L.

Crack willow, a native of Europe, is one of the larger members of this genus, occasion-ally growing over 30 m (100 ft). In much of southeastern Canada and the U.S., it reproduces on its own. In the wild, this species prefers moist soils along streams, swamps, and wet woods, like so many of the native willows. Crack willow cannot grow in deep shade. Rather, it is a pioneer species that tends to move rapidly into bare areas.

The light, reddish wood of crack willow was used during colonial times for char-coal, and in Scotland it was an attractive boat-finishing material. Deer and small rodents feed on the leaves, branchlet tips, and bark.

Crack willow gets its name from its branchlets, which break off easily from the branches. **Branchlets of the crack willow spread at 60 to 90° angles from the branches, whereas those of the white willow spread at 30 to 45° angles.** The trunk of the crack willow may reach 2 m (6.6 ft) in width and supports a spreading crown. The leaves are lance-shaped, **8–15 cm (3.2–6 in) long, 1–2.5 cm (0.4–1 in) wide, finely toothed,** smooth, **dark green above, and pale green below.** Flowering catkins are 2–7 cm (0.8–2.8 in) long and appear in April or May with the leaves. Male flowers have 2 stamens (rarely 1) per flower. The fruiting catkins reach up to 12 cm (4.8 in) in length and bear narrow, short-stalked capsules 4–5 mm (0.2 in) long.

Littletree Willow   *Salix arbusculoides* Anderss.

This shrub or small tree is one of Alaska's commonest willows. Its range extends from Alaska to the west side of Hudson Bay and south to British Columbia, Saskatchewan, and Quebec. Littletree willow grows best in wet sites and is found on gravelly or sandy soils along streams and rivers. This is one of the first tree species to invade recently burned-out woodlots. It is often found in pure, dense thickets or growing with white spruce and birch.

Littletree willow is a multistemmed shrub or small tree to 9 m (30 ft) in height. The bark is smooth and **gray to reddish-brown and hairy when young but becom-ing shiny and reddish-brown with age.** The leaves are usually **broadest near the middle,** 2.5–7.5 cm (1–3 in) long, 1–2 cm

(0.4–0.8 in) wide, tapered at the tip and base, and ***fine-toothed on the margins.*** The upper surface of the leaves is green and smooth, while the lower surface is covered with fine silvery hairs. The flowering catkins are 2.5–5 cm (1–2 in) long at maturity and appear with the leaves from mid-May to early June. The fruits are small, cone-shaped capsules that are covered with silver hairs, and they ripen in late June.

Hooker Willow, Coastal Willow

Salix hookerana Barratt
(synonym: *S. amplifolia* Cov.)

In the Pacific Northwest, the tidewater wanderer may find this small, slender willow growing in streams, ponds, and sloughs near the shore. From Vancouver Island south to northern California, Hooker willow with its broad leaves, white-wooly below, is easy to spot in its habitat of sandy, gravelly, or mucky streamside soil. It occurs in the Yakutat Bay region of Alaska and western Siberia as well.

This fast-growing and short-lived tree flowers in April or May before the leaves unfold. It produces abundant seeds that mature in late May to June. In Alaska, moose browse the twigs and foliage. Deer and small game animals also utilize it. This tree has no commercial uses.

Occasionally, Hooker willow may reach

Hooker Willow

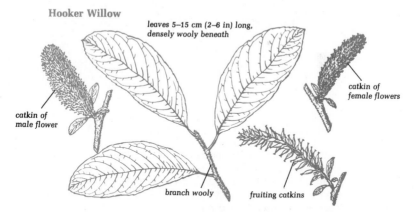

leaves 5–15 cm (2–6 in) long, densely wooly beneath

catkin of female flowers

catkin of male flower

branch wooly

fruiting catkins

9 m (30 ft) in height with a trunk diameter of 30 cm (11.8 in), though normally it appears as a shrub to 6 m (20 ft) and with a trunk 10–20 cm (4–8 in) thick. The ***dark-brown branchlets are densely wooly for 2 or 3 years,*** and the buds reddish-brown and hairy. The leaves distinguish this from other willows in that they are ***half as wide as they are long,*** 5–15 cm (2–6 in) long, 2.5–7.5 cm (1–3 in) wide, coarsely toothed along the margin, and densely wooly beneath. The flowers have yellow, hairy basal scales; ***male flowers have 2 stamens.*** The fruiting capsules are 6–8 mm (0.2–0.3 in) long and hairless.

Feltleaf Willow

Salix alaxensis (Anderss.) Cov.

Feltleaf willows, named for their chief distinguishing feature, are shrubs or small trees to 10 m (33 ft) high of the Northwest Territories, Alaska, and Siberia. Stretching eastward to the western shores of Hudson Bay and south to central British Columbia, they are most abundant along the Arctic coast, where they are often the only trees. They grow in the mixed birch interior forest but often occur with the yakutat willow.

The male and female flowers appear in separate catkins in May and June. Later the female flowers develop into fruiting capsules that mature in June and July. Moose favor the feltleaf willow for browse and avidly pull down branches and young trunks. The inner bark has also served as survival food for humans. In the northern parts of the range, the wood is often the sole source of fuel wood.

Feltleaf Willow

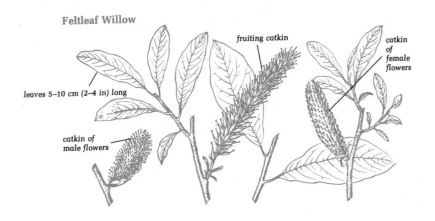

fruiting catkin

catkin of female flowers

leaves 5–10 cm (2–4 in) long

catkin of male flowers

Feltleaf willows are small trees, shrubs, or may even be dwarfed and growing along the ground on exposed sites. The bark is smooth and gray on young trees but becomes furrowed and scaly with age. The first and second year branchlets are often wooly and the winter buds covered with a bluish-white bloom. The leaves, usually **broadest above the middle,** are **5–10 cm (2–4 in) long** and 1.2–4 cm (0.5–1.6 in) wide. They are **usually entire along the margins** and **coated below with thick, white to creamy colored hairs.** The flowering catkins are stout, 5–10 cm (2–4 in) long and appear before the leaves. Male flowers have 2 stamens per flower. The fruiting capsules are cone-shaped, 5–7 mm (0.2–0.3 in) long, and covered with white wooly hairs.

Sitka Willow

Salix sitchensis Sanson ex Bong.
(synonym: *S. coulteri* Anderss.)

Sitka willow is a shrubby or small-tree willow, usually 2–5 m tall, rarely to 10 (6.5–16.4 ft, rarely to 33). It ranges widely from southern Alaska to Montana and California, growing at elevations up to 2,100 m (6,900 ft). It prefers rich, mucky, or other moist soils along borders of streams, meadows, forest openings, or along beaches. The soft,

light wood is not used commercially, although Alaskan Indians burn it to smoke fish. The flexible twigs are used for making handsome baskets or to stretch animal skins; and the bark, when pounded and applied to skin wounds, is reputed to have healing properties.

These willows often have several main trunks, although an occasional tree can be found with a straight upright trunk. The branches are covered with smooth gray bark, and the branchlets snap off neatly when tugged. The leaves are 5–10 cm (2–4 in) long, 1.8–3.7 cm (0.7–1.5 in) broad, widest above the middle, **entire along the margins,** with dark shiny green upper surfaces and **densely satiny short hairs on the lower surface.** Catkins of male flowers are 2–5 cm (0.8–2 in) long (each flower has only 1 stamen). The catkins of female flowers are 3–9 cm (1.2–3.6 in) long. Individual **capsules** produced in the female catkins are **4–6 mm (0.2 in) long, egg-shaped** and **silky.**

Sitka Willow

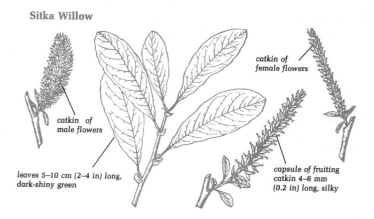

catkin of female flowers

catkin of male flowers

leaves 5–10 cm (2–4 in) long, dark-shiny green

capsule of fruiting catkin 4–6 mm (0.2 in) long, silky

Scouler Willow

Salix scoulerana Barrett ex Hook.

Scouler willow, known also as fire willow for its habit of rapidly colonizing fire-devastated areas, is one of the most common of the Pacific Coast willows, ranging from Alaska to California and New Mexico. It grows on both moist lowland and dry upland soils from sea level to 3,000 m (9,900 ft). These trees occur in a wide range of vegetation and habitats from upland bogs and headwaters or rivers to meadows, roadsides, and clear-cut areas in forests. While often making dense, blue-green thickets in a cleared-out area, scouler willows are also associated with birch, spruce, and aspen to the north. and red alder and bigleaf maple to the south.

Fast-growing in early years, scouler willows differ from others in their family by developing a straight trunk that branches relatively high up into a rounded or narrow crown. In early spring, before the leaves emerge from the bud, fuzzy floral catkins sway in the breeze. The female flowers ripen in a month into downy capsules that disperse the minute seeds. Many species of wildlife depend on these trees, and it is an especially important winter browse for moose, deer, and livestock.

The soft, light wood has no commercial value today, although in the past it was employed for firewood, charcoal, and tool handles. The trees are occasionally planted as ornamentals.

Appearance: a small to medium-size tree, 7.5 m, rarely to 15 (25 ft, rarely to 50), with a **high, rounded or narrow crown; trunk straight,** up to 45 cm (17 in) in diameter. **Bark:** thin, dark brown tinged with red, divided into broad ridges. **Branches:** slender, drooping; branchlets marked by yellow pores, hairy at first, later smooth, changing from yellow-orange to darker hues, eventually dark red-brown and marked by leaf scars. **Winter buds:** red, pointed, with narrow wing-like margins, 6–8 mm (0.2–0.3 in) long. **Leaves:** alternate, deciduous, simple, **broadest above or at the middle, short-pointed at the tip, wedge-shaped at the base,** 5–12.5 cm (2–5 in) long, 1.2–4 cm (0.5–1.6 in) broad, smooth or sparsely wavy-toothed margins, dark green above, **densely covered with reddish hairs beneath.** **Flowers:** male and female flowers produced in catkins on separate trees, very early flowering; catkins of male flowers 2–4 cm (0.8–1.6 in) long, with 2 stamens per flower; catkins of female flowers 3–6 cm (1.2–2.4 in) long, short-stalked. **Fruits:** capsules, **6–9 mm (about 0.2–0.3 in) long,** narrow, beaked, **densely hairy with pale to reddish-brown hairs.**

Yew-Leaf Willow

Salix taxifolia H.B.K.

Yew-leaf willow, a tall shrub or small to medium-size tree, occurs in soils receiving adequate moisture in the region from Trans Pecos Texas to southwestern U.S., and down the mountain regions to Guatemala. It prefers cool streams and canyons at 900–1,800 m (2,900–5,900 ft) elevation and grows in oak woodland, desert grassland, and along streams in desert areas.

Yew-leaf willow may grow up to 15 m (50 ft) in height, the drooping branches swaying to form a broad, open head. The single most readily distinguishing feature is the small leaves, which, as the name implies, bear remarkable resemblance to those of the true yew, described in the Conifer section of this book. The **pale, gray-green** (sage-colored) **leaves** are **0.8–3.3 cm (0.3–1.3 in) long,** and 2–4 mm (about 0.1–0.2 in) wide, **with narrowed, pointed ends,** smooth, thickened margins that slightly curl under, and are finely hairy above, paler and more hairy beneath. Unlike those of most other willows, the **flowers appear well after the leaves have matured;** the floral catkins are small (0.8–1.5 cm; 0.3–0.6 in) and thick; and they are set at the ends of short, leafy branchlets. The male flowers have 2 stamens each. The tiny, bright red-brown, slightly hairy seed capsules are 5–7 mm (0.2–0.3 in) long and can be found releasing seed in November.

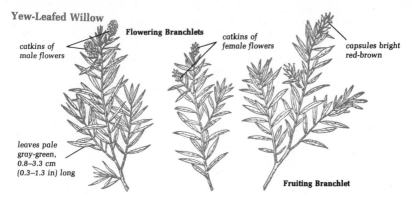

Yew-Leafed Willow

catkins of male flowers

Flowering Branchlets

catkins of female flowers

capsules bright red-brown

leaves pale gray-green, 0.8–3.3 cm (0.3–1.3 in) long

Fruiting Branchlet

Coyote Willow

Salix exigua Nutt.

(synonym: *S. melanopsis* Nutt.)

Also called the basket, sandbar, or narrowleaf willow, coyote willow is variously encountered as a spreading shrub or a small tree to 8 m (26 ft) high. Found mainly in eastern Washington, this willow occurs along streams, lakes, and bottomlands from Alberta, Canada, to Chihuahua, Mexico, at elevations below 2,500 m (8,200 ft). It is a component of desert grasslands, pinyon juniper and oak woodlands, and yellow pine forests in the Southwest. It often hybridizes with other willows growing with it along stream banks. It serves as browse for deer.

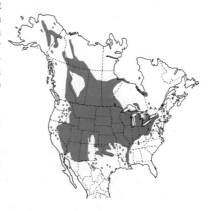

Formerly, coyote willow and dusky willow (*Salix melanopsis*) were considered to be different species, but recently the dusty willow was classed as a subspecies. Plants of the dusty willow have many fine teeth along the leaf margins, while the typical coyote willow has leaves that are mainly entire along the margins.

Members of this species are spreading shrubs or small trees with thin, gray-brown bark and branchlets that turn dark brown to almost black. The **long narrow, lance-shaped leaves are 3.8–12 cm (1.5–4.8 in) long, 3–15 mm (0.1–0.6 in) wide, entire to remotely fine-toothed** (subspecies *exigua*) or **finely toothed** (subspecies *melanopsis*) on the margin, the upper surface blue-green and smooth, the lower surface with a dense covering of silky-white hairs when young, but becoming smooth with age. The flowering catkins appear as the leaves reach full size. Catkins containing male flowers are 3–4 cm (1.2–1.6 in) long, each flower with 2 stamens; catkins of female flowers are 3–4 cm (1.2–1.6 in) long. The fruiting capsules are 3–6 mm (0.1–0.2 in) long and smooth or nearly so at maturity.

Bonpland Willow

Salix bonplandiana H.B.K.

Bonpland willow is a small to medium-size (up to 15 m–50 ft) southwestern and Mexican tree. It is found in well-drained soils along canyon streams and sunny slopes at elevations of 600–1,500 m (1,900–4,900 ft). Desert uplands, grasslands, and oak woodlands are its habitat, but it will be found only where moisture is sufficient. Bonpland willow is so closely related to red willow that some botanists term them both bonpland willow. (See also page 490.)

In Mexico, Bonpland willow has upraised branches that form a narrow crown similar to that of Lombardy poplar. But in the U.S., these trees are more wide-spreading and drooping with age. The main feature distinguishing this willow from other willows is the partially *evergreen leaves,* narrowly lance-shaped, *11–15 cm (4.3–6 in) long, 1.2–2.1 cm (0.5–*

Bonpland Willow

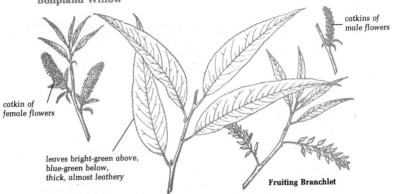

catkins of
male flowers

catkin of
female flowers

leaves bright-green above,
blue-green below,
thick, almost leathery

Fruiting Branchlet

0.8 in) wide, bright green above, blue-green below and softly hairy when young, narrow, tapered and *fine-toothed along the margin.* Its branchlets are reddish or purple, and the long pointed, curved winter buds are a shiny reddish-brown. The flowering catkins stand erect on leafy branchlets. The catkins containing the male flowers are 2.5–3.7 cm (1–1.5 in) long with usually *3 stamens per flower;* the female catkins are somewhat shorter. The egg-shaped to cone-shaped fruiting capsules are light red to yellow.

Sandbar Willow

Salix interior Rowlee

From eastern Canada to interior Alaska, and from New Mexico to Maryland, this wide-ranging little tree receives its common name from its ability to grow on fresh sandbars in rivers and streams. Sandbar willow is perfectly adapted for the sandy, gravelly, or mucky soils in and along watercourses. As soon as the young saplings have established themselves, they begin sending out long, underground shoots—or stolons—from which new branches sprout

up with surprising speed. Soon the sandbars are densely crowded with a thicket of these spindly trunks, and the creek has lost another battle to natural land reclamation. Sandbar willow is closely related to the more western coyote willow and the two are difficult to distinguish where their natural ranges overlap in the eastern base of the Rocky Mountains.

Growing from 5–6 m (16–20 ft) high, sandbar willow has dark red-brown branchlets and smooth, thin bark. The *leaves* are the best recognized feature. They *are 16 to 18 times as long as they are wide [5–15 cm (2–6 in) long, 3–9 mm (0.1–0.3 in) wide*], gradually narrowed at the ends, *with wide-spaced, small, glandular teeth along the margins, light yellow-green, and softly hairy beneath.* The flowering catkins appear after the leaves have matured. Catkins of male flowers are 2–4 cm (0.8–1.6 in) long and each flower has 2 stamens; catkins of female flowers are 4–8 cm (1.6–3.2 in) long. Fruiting capsules are 7–9 mm (about 0.3 in) long, narrowly egg-shaped to cone-shaped and clustered together in the catkins which bore the female flowers.

Northwest Willow
Salix sessilifolia Nutt.

Also known as silverleaf, this is a small northwestern willow that occurs on rivers and streams that range from British Columbia to Oregon. It is closely related to the river willow. These are shrubs or small trees that may grow to 8 m (26 ft) tall, with a trunk up to nearly 1 m (3.3 ft) in diameter and densely short-hairy branchlets. The leaves are *3–10 cm (1.2–4 in) long, 1–3.5 cm (0.4–1.4 in) wide,* usually broadest about the middle, *smooth or sparsely toothed on the edges,* dark bluish-green and coated with silvery hairs, which are thickest on the underside, and with almost no leaf-stalks at all. Flowering catkins appear after the leaves, the male flowers with 2 stamens per flower. Fruiting catkins are 3–5 mm (0.1–0.2 in) long and densely silky hairy.

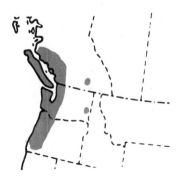

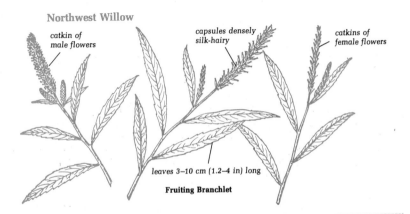

Northwest Willow

catkin of
male flowers

capsules densely
silk-hairy

catkins of
female flowers

leaves 3–10 cm (1.2–4 in) long

Fruiting Branchlet

Hinds Willow

Salix hindsiana Benth.

Hinds willow, a shrubby western species reaching 7.5 m (24.5 ft) under best growth conditions, is common in moist sandy or gravelly soils along the banks of the major streams in the great central valley of California; its range extends from southern Oregon to northern Baja California in Mexico. In the Sierra foothills it is encountered at altitudes up to 900 m (3,000 ft).

Hinds willow is closely related to northwest willow (*Salix sessilifolia*) and both are recognized by the leaves that sit almost directly on the branchlets. The leaves of the northwest willow are densely silverwooly during the first season. The leaves of Hinds willow are **4–8 cm (1.6–3.2 in) long, 0.3–1 cm (0.1–0.4 in) wide, entire** or with very few teeth along the margin, and are **bluish-green under gray,** silky hairs. Flowering catkins appear after the leaves; these, too, are silky haired; the male flowers have 2 stamens. The fruits are small, **cone-shaped capsules 5–6 mm (0.2 in) long** and are produced in catkins and covered with silky hairs.

Satiny Willow

Salix pellita Anderss.

Basically a Canadian species, this large shrub or small tree growing to 5 m (16.4 ft) is widely distributed from Newfoundland and Labrador to Saskatchewan, and just barely dipping into the northern edge of the U.S. It grows in gravelly or floodplain soils along riverbanks and lake shores, and in swamps. The satiny willow trees have brittle yellowish to reddish-brown branchlets. **Leaves** are **narrowly lance-shaped,** sometimes widest above the middle, **5–12 cm (2–4.8 in) long, 8–18 mm (0.3–0.7 in) wide,** long-pointed at the tip and tapering at the base, almost **entire along the margins, green above with silky hairs beneath.** The flowering catkins appear with or before the leaves. The fruits are lance-shaped capsules, 4–6 mm (0.2 in) long and are borne in elongated catkins.

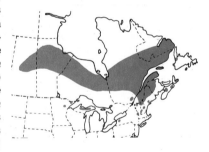

Basket Willow

Salix viminalis L.

This short tree or long-stemmed shrub known in Europe as osier willow is native both to Europe and Asia. It was brought to North America for use in basketmaking, wickerware, and ornamental planting, and has begun reproducing on its own from Newfoundland to Pennsylvania. Basket willow has nearly smooth bark and long, wand-like branches that lend themselves perfectly to the osiers, or withes, which are woven into wicker. The **narrow, straight, lance-like leaves are 7–15 cm (2.8–6 in) long, 4–16 mm (0.1–0.6 in) wide, smooth-margined, dull dark green above and pale below with a dense coat of silvery hairs.** The catkins emerge almost directly sitting upon older branchlets prior to the appearance of leaves in April or May; their floral scales are hairy and darkened at the tips. The male flowers have 2 stamens, the females bearing very wooly ovaries. The fruiting capsules are produced in fuzzy catkins up to 6 cm (2.4 in) long.

The Caper Family   Capparaceae

This family consists of 46 genera and 700 species. The geological record traces the dispersal of this family throughout tropical America, Africa, and Asia. There are 10 or 11 genera in North America, 2 of them with tree-size species. The family is closely related to the mustard family. Like the mustards, this family is best known for the capers used as condiments, such as the pickled flower buds of *Capparis spinosa*. Another species, known as spider flower (*Cleome spinosa*) is a common garden annual.

Members of this family are trees, shrubs, and herbs with alternate, simple or compound hand-like (palmate) leaves. The flowers are produced in simple or multi-branched clusters; each flower has 4 calyx lobes and usually 4 petals. In some species, the petals are absent. There are 6 to numerous stamens, which may be attached to the pistil. The pistil contains a 1-celled ovary. The fruit is a berry or capsule.

Key to Caper Genera

A. Branches without spines; leaves 4–16 cm (1.6–6.3 in) long, present most of the year, fruit a narrow slender pod; Florida   **Capers, p. 503**

Jamaica Caper Tree

B. Branches spiny; leafless most of the year; fruit a globe-shaped berry; Southwest & Mexico   **Allthorn, p. 505**

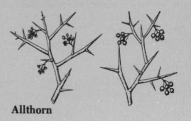

Allthorn

The Caper Genus   *Capparis* L.

This is a genus of up to 350 species of shrubs or small trees throughout tropical and subtropical America, Africa, southeast Asia and Australia. These normally are lowland species, common in coastal regions, but are known to occur to 1,700 m (5,580 ft). Two species occur in North America only in southern Florida.

Capers are either shrubs or trees with hairy, scaly, or smooth branches. The leaves are simple and have smooth margins. The floral clusters contain few to many blossoms. There are 4 free or fused sepals and 4 equal petals; stamens may be few to over 100; the ovary sits on a special structure, called the gynophore, which may be either short or long. The fruit is a long narrow capsule that partly splits open at maturity.

Key to Caper Species

A. Leaves covered with numerous small scurfy, or flaky, scales on the lower surface; buds 4-sided or angular; flowers lavender   **Jamaica caper, p. 504**

B. Leaves smooth on the lower leaf surface; buds rounded; flowers white   **Bay-leaved caper, p. 505**

Jamaica Caper   *Capparis cynophallophora* L.

The Jamaica caper is a small tree that occurs in southern Florida, the West Indies, and Central America. It grows in thickets in drier coastal hammocks, never very high above sea level. It attains tree size in the Florida Keys, but usually is found in Florida as a rangy shrub, growing among other bushes. As such, it is nearly indistinguishable among the general confusion of other branches and leaves.

The major distinguishing features of Jamaica caper are: the **scaly undersides of the leaves,** the **brush-like flowers,** and the **knotty fruits that are vaguely reminiscent of bean pods.** These trees seldom reach 6 m (20 ft) height, with trunks up to 15 cm (6 in) wide. The dark red-brown outer bark is thin and somewhat cracked; the inner bark is light brown and has a spicy flavor like horseradish. The alternate, deciduous **leaves** are 5–10 cm (2–4 in) long and 1.8–3 cm (9.7–1.2 in) wide, generally oval in shape, rounded to pointed at the base and tip, leathery and shiny **yellow-green above, silver-brown below.** The lavender flowers are 2.9–3.1 cm (1.1–1.2 in) wide, with 4 petals, and many purple stamens longer than the flower that forms an obvious tuft. The fruits mature in summer; they are 22–30 cm (8.7–11.8 in) long, long-stalked, slightly swollen over the seeds and covered with tiny, rust-colored scales.

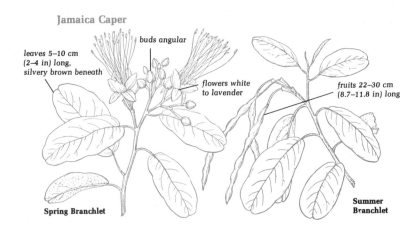

Jamaica Caper

leaves 5–10 cm (2–4 in) long, silvery brown beneath

buds angular

flowers white to lavender

fruits 22–30 cm (8.7–11.8 in) long

Spring Branchlet

Summer Branchlet

Bay-Leaved Caper

Capparis flexuosa L.

The bay-leaved or limber caper is most often seen as a shrub, but it may also reach 8 m (26 ft) in height. It grows in coastal areas, hammocks, and marl flats in south Florida including the Florida Keys, as well as in the West Indies, and from Mexico to South America. The pale-green *leaves,* 4–16 cm (1.6–6.3 in) long, vary greatly in form from willow-like to broadly egg-shaped, and are *smooth on the lower surface.* The loose flower clusters bloom in summer, producing white flowers at the tips of the branchlets. Each flower has 4 petals 1–1.5 cm (0.4–0.6 in) long and sepals half that size. The fruit is an irregularly shaped, fleshy bean-shaped capsule up to 15 cm (6 in) long.

The Allthorn Genus

Koeberlinia Zucc.

This genus contains only 1 species, the allthorn of the southwestern U.S., Mexico, and Bolivia. For many years, it was considered to be its own family, the Koeberlinia-ceae, but now it is considered to be part of the caper family.

Allthorn

Koeberlinia spinosa Zucc.

Allthorn, leafless most of the year, is a spiny shrub or small tree of the Southwest, ranging from New Mexico to southeastern California and into Mexico. It grows on plains, rolling hills, desert grasslands, and even on deserts from 450–1,600 m (1,470–5,200 ft) elevation. There are 2 other thorny, largely leafless trees and shrubs in the Southwest. All 3 are superficially alike but are unrelated. The other 2 are the canotia of the bittersweet family and the smokethorn of the legume family.

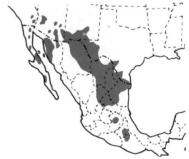

The small greenish-white flowers appear from March to June with fleshy berries maturing by summer. These fruits are eaten by birds and small mammals. The trees are of no economic importance. The dark-brown wood is heavy and very hard, but the trees are seldom large enough to yield useful amounts of wood.

Appearance: shrub or small tree to 4 m (13 ft) with a broad, rounded crown; trunk short, soon branching, growing to 25 cm (10 in) in diameter. **Bark:** thin, dark green becoming rough and scaly with age. **Branches:** stout, spreading, often crooked; *branchlets stout, dark green, ending in sharp, slender spines.* **Winter buds:** tiny, not obvious. **Leaves:** alternate, *scalelike, falling away in spring, the trees leafless most of year.* **Flowers:** produced in small, few-flowered clusters along the branchlets, each flower bisexual, white, composed of 3 to 5 calyx lobes, 4 petals, 8 stamens, and a single pistil. **Fruits:** a berry, almost globe-shaped, 5–7 mm (0.3 in) in diameter, turning shiny black at maturity. *(Note: See art on next page.)*

Allthorn

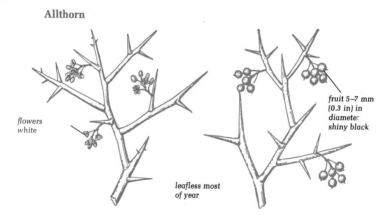

*flowers
white*

*fruit 5–7 mm
(0.3 in) in
diameter
shiny black*

*leafless most
of year*

The Horseradish Tree Family · Moringaceae

This family contains only 1 genus, horseradish trees (*Moringa*), which contain 10 species. They are native to Africa and southeastern Asia but have been planted throughout tropical regions of the world. One species has been introduced into south Florida.

Members of this family have alternate, 2- to 3-branched, feather-like compound deciduous leaves. The flowers, produced in clusters in the junctions of the leaves, have 5 calyx and 5 corolla lobes that are almost indistinguishable, 10 stamens, and a single 3-celled pistil. The fruits are elongated, woody, 3-valved, and contain seeds that are usually winged.

The Horseradish Tree Genus · Moringa Adanson

This is a small genus of perhaps 10 species native to Africa, Malagasy Republic, and the East Indies. At least 1 species has been widely planted for centuries in subtropical and tropical countries of the world. In the Americas, 1 species (*Moringa oleifera*) has been planted in southern Florida, the Bahama Islands, and Central and South America.

The trees are small, growing to about 10 m (33 ft) in height, with a spreading branch system and a thick trunk. The characteristics given in the family description also apply here. In addition to those, the flowers are white, pink, or red. The fruits that hang down split open explosively at maturity dispersing the 3-winged seeds.

Horseradish Tree · Moringa oleifera Lam.

This tree has been introduced into southern Florida and the Florida Keys where it now reproduces on its own, especially along roadsides. The horseradish tree has also been planted in southern California. It has an eye-catching appearance with loose feather-like leaves and showy white flowers. Planted mainly for its ornamental value, the tree is in flower for most of the year. The roots can be used for flavoring of horseradish or made into mustard plasters. The corky bark has been used in India to make mats and coarse paper. The flowers produce large amounts of nectar that bees use for honey making. The fruits are rich in vitamin C and can be eaten fresh or pickled. The soft, weak wood is of little value as timber.

Appearance: small deciduous tree to 9 m (30 ft) and with a trunk to 25 cm (10 in) in diameter. **Bark:** smooth, ***becoming corky, fissured lengthwise, warty,*** and eventually rough and flaking, whitish-gray. **Branches:** stout, spreading, brittle; branchlets dark red and hairy when young, turning brown and becoming smooth with age. **Leaves:** alternate, ***compound and feather-like, 8–15 cm (3.2–6 in) long;*** the central axis slender, hairy, green tinged with red, the ***leaflets in pairs opposite each other, 1–2 cm (0.4–0.8 in) long, broadest near the base,*** rounded to notched at the tip, wedge-shaped to rounded at the base and often uneven at the base, entire along the margin. **Flowers:** produced in spreading or drooping, ***many-flowered clusters*** at the base of the uppermost leaves on the branchlets; individual flowers composed of a 5-lobed calyx, 5 ***white,*** unequal ***petals,*** 5 stamens, and a single, central pistil. **Fruits:** ***long, pointed, pod-like capsules with 3 longitudinal ridges, 30–50 cm (11.8–20 in) long,*** containing many white ***3-winged seeds,*** each seed 2–2.8 cm (0.8–1.1 in) long, including the wings.

The Titi Family   Cyrillaceae

The titi family contains only 3 genera and 13 species of shrubs or small trees that occur along the Coastal Plain of the southeastern U.S., as well as in Central America, the West Indies, and northern South America. Two genera, each with 1 species, occur in North America; these are leatherwood (*Cyrilla*) and buckwheat (*Cliftonia*). Members of this family are not economically important nor is much known about their natural history.

Fossil records—including the remains of leaf fragments, fruits, seeds, wood, and pollen—indicate that members of this family occurred during the Upper Cretaceous age about 90 million years ago. If these fossil records are correct, the family once extended as far north as Vermont.

The family is composed of small trees or shrubs with alternate, simple, entire, leathery leaves. In the southern part of the range, the leaves persist on the trees until the following summer. The flowers are bisexual, short-stalked, and are borne on an elongated flower cluster composed of a single axis. The 5 to 8 calyx lobes overlap one another in the bud, and persist after flowering to surround the fruit; there are 5 to 8 petals arising below the female reproductive structure, each petal appearing free; stamens 5 or 10; pistil 1, divided into 2 to 4 compartments internally. Fruits are a small, dry capsule splitting at maturity, or a leathery to fleshy berry; seeds are tiny.

Key to Titi Genera

A. Flower clusters developing in junction of the leafstalks and the branchlets along the upper part of the stems; leaves not gland-dotted; fruit entire, without wings   **Leatherwood, p. 508**

B. Flower clusters developing at the ends of new branches; leaves gland-dotted; fruit 2- to 4-winged   **Buckwheat, p. 508**

Leatherwood

The Leatherwood Genus *Cyrilla* L.

This genus contains only a single species in the southeastern U.S. As a result, information about the genus will be the same as for the species, as below.

Leatherwood, Ironwood *Cyrilla racemiflora* L.

This species is a small tree or shrub of riverbanks, streamsides, swamps, and wet lowland depressions from Texas eastward along the Gulf Coast to Florida and northward to Virginia. It is often found growing in association with pines. Leatherwood is a good ornamental plant because of its attractive and graceful white flowers produced in the spring, its bright-green leaves, which turn orange and scarlet in late fall, and its ability to tolerate cold temperatures. It is hardy to temperatures of −23°C (−10°F) and can be grown considerably beyond its natural range. The trees are good honey plants because the abundant flowers produce large quantities of nectar favored by honeybees.

Leatherwood grows to 8 m (26 ft) with an open, rounded crown. The leaves, often remaining until summer of the following year, are simple, alternate, 5–10 cm (2–4 in) long, 2–4 cm (0.8–1.6 in) wide, and leathery. The flower clusters are ***elongated, made up of many tiny flowers.*** Each ***flower*** is ***white***, bisexual, composed of 5 free calyx lobes, 5 free petals, 5 stamens, and a single pistil. The fruit, only 2–3 mm (0.1 in) long, consists of 2 thin spongy tissues surrounding single or multiple tiny, hard seeds.

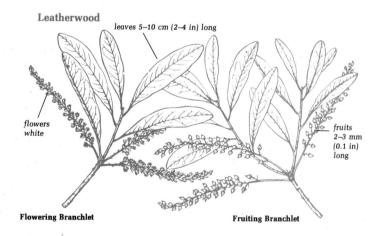

Leatherwood

leaves 5–10 cm (2–4 in) long

flowers white

fruits 2–3 mm (0.1 in) long

Flowering Branchlet   **Fruiting Branchlet**

The Buckwheat Genus *Cliftonia* Banks ex Gaertn.

Like the leatherwood genus, this one also contains only a single species, the buckwheat tree, native to the southeastern U.S.

Buckwheat, Titi Tree *Cliftonia monophylla* (Lam.) Britton ex Sarg.
Buckwheat trees are small trees of the Coastal Plain in Florida, Georgia, and Louisiana. They are common in swampy thickets or along streambanks at low elevations, often in the same habitat as leatherwood. The nectar produced in the flowers is an important source of honey. The brown to reddish-brown wood is hard, close-grained, heavy, but brittle. The trees are too small to be of any use as lumber. Buckwheat trees are shrubs or small trees to 8 m (26 ft) high. The evergreen leaves are narrow but broadest near the base, at the middle, or near the tip, 3–6 cm (1.2–2.4 in) long, **gland-dotted**, and entire along the margin. The **flowers are produced in elongated clusters 2–9 cm (0.8–3.6 in) long at the tips of the new growth.** Individual flowers are fragrant, composed of 4 or 5 small calyx lobes, 5 petals (each about 4–5 mm — 0.2 in — long), and 2 to 5 fused pistils. Fruits are somewhat fleshy, **usually 4-winged,** and from 6–8 mm (0.3 in) long.

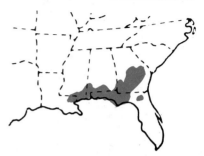

Buckwheat Tree

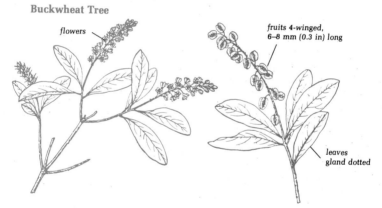

flowers

fruits 4-winged,
6–8 mm (0.3 in) long

leaves
gland dotted

The Pepperbush Family

Clethraceae

This small family consists of only 2 genera, the pepperbushes with about 30 species (distributed mainly in the Americas but also native to Asia and the Pacific islands) and a single little-known relative from Belize. These attractive shrubs or small trees are of limited economic value and of little value to wildlife, except as an excellent source of nectar for bees and other insects. Some species are cultivated for their attractive flowers.

The unifying characteristics of this family are the same as those given in the description of the pepperbushes that follows.

The Pepperbush Genus

Clethra L.

Pepperbushes are shrubs or small trees native to North, Central, and South America, Asia, and the Madeira Islands in the Pacific. Two species are native to the eastern

U.S., the sweet pepperbush (*Clethra acuminata*), a mountainous species, and the alder-leaved pepperbush (*C. alnifolia*), a lowland bush primarily of the Coastal Plain. They and other species of this genus are of little economic importance. Because of their fragrant, showy flowers they are often planted as ornamentals. Some of the Japanese and Chinese species have been introduced into cultivation and are considered to be more attractive than the native species.

They are shrubs or small trees with deciduous or evergreen, simple, alternate leaves. The bisexual flowers are regular, showy, fragrant, and produced in many-flowered, branched or unbranched clusters. There are 5 calyx lobes, 5 free petals, 10 stamens, and a single pistil. The fruits are 3-parted capsules containing numerous, small seeds.

Sweet Pepperbush
Clethra acuminata Michx.

Sweet pepperbush is commonly a shrub, but occasionally it will reach tree size in its native habitat in the southern Appalachian Mountains. It grows in rich, moist deciduous woodlands at higher elevations. This is one of the few North American trees or shrubs that flower in summer, July and August, with the fruits maturing by autumn.

This species is a shrub or rarely a tree to 6 m (20 ft) with spreading to upright branches. The simple, alternate **leaves** are 8–20 cm (3.2–7.9 in) long, 4–10 cm (1.6–4 in) wide, **broadest at or near the middle, long-pointed at the tip, finely toothed along the margins,** light green and smooth above, paler and slightly hairy beneath. The **stalked flowers are densely aggregated on an elongated spike at the tips of the branchlets.** Individual flowers have a 5-lobed calyx, 5 free, oblong petals, each 5–7 mm (0.2–0.3 in) long, 10 stamens in an inner and outer series, and a single pistil. The **fruits** are narrowly **egg-shaped capsules 4–6 mm (0.2 in) long,** 3-lobed, and splitting open to release the flattened seeds that are often winged.

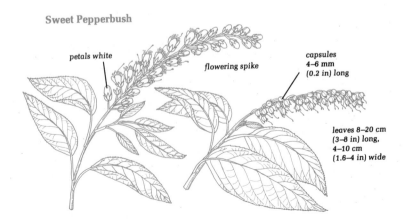

Sweet Pepperbush

petals white

flowering spike

capsules
4–6 mm
(0.2 in) long

leaves 8–20 cm
(3–8 in) long,
4–10 cm
(1.6–4 in) wide

The Heath Family

Ericaceae L.

The heath family is a large assemblage of trees, shrubs, vines, and herbs comprising perhaps 80 genera and 2,000 species. These are widely distributed throughout the cooler regions of both the Northern and Southern hemispheres, though most abundantly in Asia and South Africa. They also occur in the tropical regions, especially at higher elevations. Of the approximately 25 genera in North America, at least 7 contain species that are trees. Some of the Pacific Coast species of manzanita (*Arctostaphylos*) may reach 5 m (16 ft) in height but not with regularity.

This family is well known because of its economic importance for such highly prized ornamentals as rhododendrons, azaleas, and mountain laurel, and for the blueberries, cranberries, and the huckleberries. One of the larger genera (*Erica*), with 650 species, contains the common (sweet-smelling) heaths of northern Europe. Briar pipes are carved from the rootwood of *Erica arborea*, a small Mediterranean tree. The herb wintergreen (*Gaultheria procumbens*) has been so heavily collected for extracting oil of wintergreen that these plants have been threatened with extinction in eastern North America. The fruits and to a lesser extent the leaves are especially important to many species of wildlife.

Members of this family are mainly shrubs or occasionally trees, vines, or herbs with simple alternate, sometimes opposite, or whorled, often leathery and evergreen leaves. The flowers are bisexual and are produced singly or in branched or unbranched clusters at the ends of the branchlets or in the junctions of the leaves. Individual flowers usually have a small calyx of 4 to 7 lobes, 4 to 7 free or united petals, often forming an urn bell, or funnel-shaped flower; 5 to 20 stamens, and a single pistil. The fruits in this family are either capsules that split open at maturity or are berries.

Key to Heath Genera

A. Leaves deciduous, falling in autumn.

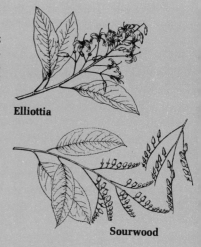

   1. Flowers with 4 calyx lobes and 4 free petals; leaves entire along the margins; bark thin, pale-gray-colored; rare trees of N.E. Georgia and S.W. South Carolina   **Elliottia, p. 512**

   2. Flowers with 5 calyx lobes and 5 fused petals; leaves finely toothed along the margins; bark thick, deeply furrowed, reddish-brown; tree of southeastern U.S.   **Sourwood, p. 513**

Elliottia

B. Leaves evergreen, at least until the new leaves appear the following year.

   1. Fruits dry capsules that split open lengthwise at maturity.

Sourwood

(Continued)

a. Flowers tiny, 3–5 mm (0.1–0.2 in) long, urn-shaped; fruiting capsules with conspicuous lighter colored bands; trees of southeastern U.S.   **Lyonia, p. 514**

b. Flowers large, showy, 2–4 cm (0.8–1.6 in) long, bell-, funnel-, trumpet- or saucer-shape; fruiting capsules uniform in color, no colored bands present.

(1) Stamens fitting into small pouches on the petals of the flower; fruits globe-shaped; shrubs or trees of eastern U.S.; mountain laurel   **Kalmia, p. 516**

(2) Stamens erect, not housed into small pouches; fruits elongated, at least twice as long as broad; shrubs or small trees of eastern or western U.S.
     Rhododendron, p. 517

2. Fruits fleshy, berry-like, not splitting open at maturity.

a. Flowers produced singly or in many-flowered unbranched clusters in the junction of the leaves of the previous year's growth; fruit a smooth-skinned berry containing many tiny seeds; trees of eastern U.S., shrub members also in western North America   **Blueberry, p. 521**

b. Flowers produced in elongated, branched, many-flowered clusters at the ends of the branchlets; fruit with a warty surface, enclosing a hard stone that contains the seeds; trunk and younger branches covered with thin, peeling reddish bark; trees of western and southwestern U.S.
     Madrone, p. 522

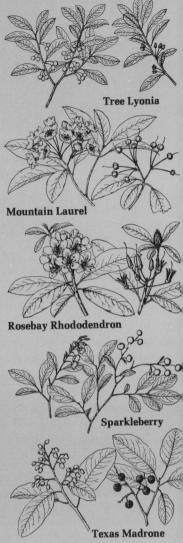

Tree Lyonia

Mountain Laurel

Rosebay Rhododendron

Sparkleberry

Texas Madrone

The Elliottia Genus

Elliottia Mühl. ex Ell.

Elliottia is a genus containing only a single species, which is one of the rarer shrubs or small trees in North America. Since there is but 1 species, the information for the genus is the same as that given for the species.

Elliottia

Elliottia racemosa Mühl. ex Ell.

This shrub or small tree was first discovered in Georgia in the early 1800s and was named after the South Carolina botanist Stephen Elliott. Its range was limited to northeastern Georgia and southwestern South Carolina, but because of habitat destruction, the South Carolina populations are extinct. The plants grow in rich, moist soils, along oak or sand ridges. Flowering occurs in August.

Elliottia grows to 10 m (33 ft) with a pyramid-shaped crown and a short trunk up to 15 cm (6 in) in diameter. The bark is thin and pale-gray colored, while the short, erect branches are light reddish-brown and hairy when young, turning reddish-brown and smooth with age. The alternate, deciduous **leaves** are **3.5–14 cm (1.4–5.5 in) long, broadest near or above the middle,** pointed at the tip, entire along the margin, dark green and smooth above, paler and hairy beneath. The stalked flowers are clustered together on an elongated spike to 25 cm (10 in) long at the ends of the branchlets. An individual **flower** is **1–1.4 cm (0.4–0.6 in) long** and composed of a dark reddish-brown, **4-lobed calyx, 4 white petals, 8 stamens,** a single central pistil. The fruits are small, dried, almost globe-shaped capsules.

Elliottia

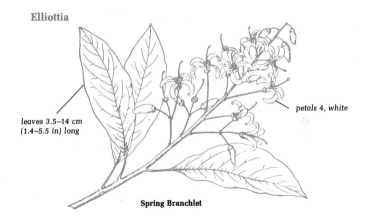

leaves 3.5–14 cm (1.4–5.5 in) long

petals 4, white

Spring Branchlet

The Sourwood Genus   *Oxydendrum* DC.

Sourwood contains only 1 species, which is native to the mid-to-southeastern U.S. The description for the genus is identical to that of its sole representative, the sourwood tree.

Sourwood   *Oxydendrum arboreum* (L.) DC.

True to its name, sourwood is a medium-size tree with sour or acid-tasting sap that ranges throughout woodlands from southern Pennsylvania to northern Florida. It occurs at altitudes up to 1,050 m (3,445 ft), on well-drained, gravelly soils above streams, on bluffs, and in ravines. Never forming pure stands, it is found scattered among oaks, pines, hickories, and sweetgum. And below these grow azalea, mountain laurel, blueberry, and elder.

These slender trees flower in midsummer long after the leaves have matured. The numerous tiny white flowers resemble lily-of-the-valley flowers and they attract thousands of bees. The capsule-shaped fruit ripens in September as the leaves are turning scarlet. Deer browse the twigs and foliage quite heavily; the only insect enemy is the sphinx moth, whose caterpillars also feed on the leaves.

Sourwood is not very important commercially, although sourwood honey is as prized by gourmets as that of its poisonous relatives — the rhododendrons and kalmias — is shunned by beekeepers. The hard, attractive wood is sometimes used in paneling or for tool handles. Sourwood is planted as an ornamental both in the eastern U.S. and in western and central Europe.

Sourwood

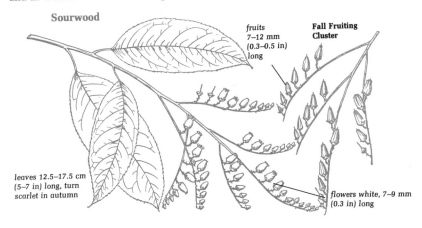

fruits 7–12 mm (0.3–0.5 in) long

Fall Fruiting Cluster

leaves 12.5–17.5 cm (5–7 in) long, turn scarlet in autumn

flowers white, 7–9 mm (0.3 in) long

Appearance: small to medium-size tree, sometimes reaching 18 m (60 ft), with a narrow, oblong crown; trunk tall, straight, 30–50 cm (11.8–20 in) in diameter. **Bark:** thick, deeply furrowed with broad scaly ridges. **Branches:** slender, spreading; branchlets zigzag, angular, green to red, dotted with pores and marked by triangular, elevated leaf scars. **Winter buds:** 1–2 mm (less than 0.1 in) long at first, growing to 2.5 cm (1 in) spoon-shaped, pointed, covered with dark-red scales. **Leaves:** alternate, deciduous, simple, *12.5–17.5 cm (5–7 in) long, 2.5–7.5 cm (1–3 in) wide,* broadest at the middle, *edges finely toothed,* thin and firm, shiny green above, paler below, *turning orange or scarlet in the fall, sour-tasting;* leafstalks 15–17 mm (0.6–0.7 in) long. **Flowers:** in *long, spike-like clusters 17.5–20 cm (6.9–7.9 in) long;* calyx of 5 lobes divided nearly to the base; *corolla 7–9 mm (about 0.3 in) long, cream-white, urn-shaped,* with 5 tiny lobes curling back; stamens 10; with a single pistil. **Fruits:** a tiny 5-valved capsule, 7–12 mm (0.3–0.5 in) long, hanging in spike-like clusters up to 30 cm (12 in) long, persisting on the trees until late fall.

The Lyonia Genus

Lyonia Nutt.

A small genus of perhaps 30 species, Lyonia is native to North America, the West Indies, eastern Asia, and part of the Himalaya Mountains. Four species are native to

North America, but only 1, the tree lyonia or staggerbush, ever grows large enough to be considered a tree. The trees are sometimes planted as ornamentals but are not as attractive as mountain laurel or rhododendrons. Lyonias are of no economic importance in North America and of little value to wildlife.

Members of this genus are evergreen or deciduous shrubs or small trees with alternate, short-stalked leaves that may be entire along the margin to shallowly toothed. The flowers are produced in many-flowered, branched or unbranched elongated clusters or spikes. Individual flowers are usually composed of 5 calyx lobes, an urn- to bell-shaped tube of 5 fused petals, 10 stamens (rarely more), and a single pistil. The fruits are egg-shaped to globe-shaped capsules, which split along 5 valves at maturity.

Tree Lyonia, Staggerbush *Lyonia ferruginea* (Walt.) Nutt.

Tree lyonia, occasionally growing to 9 m (30 ft) high, is native to the Coastal Plain from South Carolina and Georgia to central Florida. It grows in well-drained soils, in hammocks, sandy woods, dunes, and along ridges. Along with other large shrubs, tree

lyonia grows in association with pine and evergreen-oak scrublands. The white flowers appear in April or May, with the fruits maturing by September or October.

Also called staggerbush because of its awkward, sometimes sprawling shape, tree lyonia has rigid twisting branches that form an upright irregular crown. The young branchlets and winter buds are covered with rust-colored scales. The thin, reddish brown bark develops into long, narrow furrows and short, thick scales.

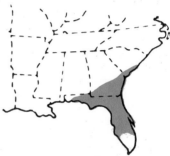

The simple *evergreen leaves* are 2.5–9 cm (1–3.6 in) long, 1.2–5 cm (0.5–2 in) broad, widest at or above the middle, blunt to pointed at the tip, tapering at the base, entire and folded under along the margins, wavy, dark green above, paler and scaly beneath. Flowers 1 to several in the junctions of the leaf stems and branchlets, stalked; each flower with 5 triangular-shaped calyx lobes, 5 fused *white petals forming an urn-shape corolla 3–5 mm (0.1–0.2 in) long;* 10 stamens, and a single pistil. *Fruiting capsules* are broadest at the base and tapering to a point, *3–5 mm (0.1–0.2 in) long,* hairy, splitting open at maturity to shed the tiny, narrow seeds.

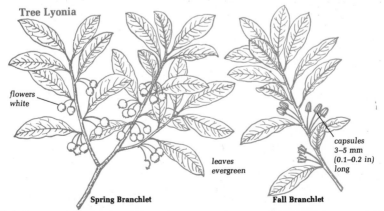

Tree Lyonia

flowers
white

leaves
evergreen

capsules
3–5 mm
(0.1–0.2 in)
long

Spring Branchlet   **Fall Branchlet**

The Kalmia Genus

Kalmia L.

This is a small North American genus of perhaps 8 species, ranging from Alaska and Newfoundland to the West Indies. All of the kalmias are shrubs; however, mountain laurel occasionally reaches tree size in its range in the eastern U.S. The name of the genus honors Peter Kalm, a noted Swedish botanist who traveled extensively in Pennsylvania, New Jersey, New York, and Quebec from 1748 to 1751.

While apparently poisonous to people and livestock, the leaves, buds, flowers, and fruits do not seem harmful to wildlife. Whitetail deer will heavily browse these evergreen plants during the winter. The showy flowers and evergreen leaves of the kalmias, especially the mountain laurel, make them favorite ornamental or landscape plants.

Kalmias are evergreen (rarely deciduous) shrubs or trees with leaves that are alternate, opposite, or in 3s, leathery and stalked. The flowers are produced in umbrella-like clusters at or near the ends of the branchlets. Each flower has a small 5-parted calyx, 5 fused petals forming a bell or saucer shape, 10 stamens, and a single pistil that is 5-celled at the base. The fruits are nearly globe-shaped, 5-valved capsules.

Mountain Laurel

Kalmia latifolia L.

If any mountain spring flower can exceed the beauty of rosebay rhododendron, it is this lovely evergreen shrub, which in some areas reaches tree size. Ranging from New Brunswick to Louisiana, mountain laurel prefers acid soils in a variety of habitats, from northern lowlands to southern mountains 1,200 m (4,000 ft) and more in elevation. To the north it grows in cool bogs, but southward it climbs to higher and drier ground, thriving in the shade of the eastern deciduous forest, or emerging as a tree on rich rocky slopes in the Allegheny and Smoky mountains. Tree associates include several oaks, tulip tree, beech, white pine, sugar maple, and sourwood; understory associates include hydrangea, rosebay, blueberries, and witch hazel.

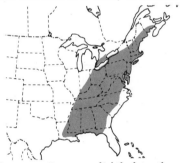

Mountain laurel blooms from April to late June over its range, slightly later than rosebay rhododendron. The stamens bend down and the anthers are tucked into pouches at the bottom of the petals; when a bee, attracted by the flower's color and odor, enters the corolla and touches a stamen, the anther springs up, releasing its pollen over the bee from a small hole at its top. The fruit capsules do not release their seeds until the fall, and still persist on the trees until the following summer. Dense mountain laurel thickets are good escape cover for moulting grouse as well as nesting sites for them and wild turkey. While poisonous to livestock and man, leaves of mountain laurel are eaten by whitetail deer with no ill effect.

Briar or Ivy pipes are sometimes made out of burls (hard tumor-like growths in the wood), although some people claim the pipe-bowls to be inferior to those made from European briar. The chief value of this tree is aesthetic; its beauty and hardiness make it a popular ornamental.

Appearance: a shrub 1–3 m (3.2–9.9 ft) tall, or small tree 6–9 m (20–30 ft) in height, with a bushy form and rounded crown; trunk short, crooked, up to 45–50 cm (17–20 in) broad. **Bark:** very thin, dark red-brown, flaking into long, narrow scales. **Branches:**

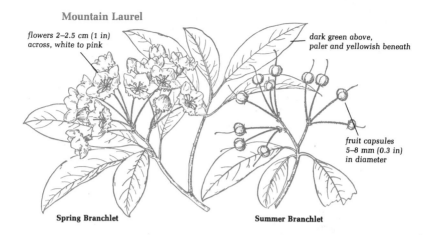

Mountain Laurel

flowers 2–2.5 cm (1 in) across, white to pink

dark green above, paler and yellowish beneath

fruit capsules 5–8 mm (0.3 in) in diameter

Spring Branchlet

Summer Branchlet

stout, forked, and contorted, ending in slender branchlets, green, sticky, and hairy when young, later smooth, darkening to brown tinged with red, marked with deep leaf scars the second year. **Winter buds:** forming before midsummer at leaf bases, growing to 2.5 cm (1 in) long and 1.2 cm (0.5 in) broad, pointed, light green, covered with sticky hairs. **Leaves:** mostly alternate or in groups of 2 or 3, simple, evergreen, 7.5–10 cm (3–4 in) long, 2.5–3.7 cm (1–1.5 in) wide, broadest at the middle, tapered at the ends, entire along the margins, sticky-hairy when they unfold, later thick and firm, dull dark green above, paler and yellow below. **Flowers:** *showy,* produced in many-flowered, rounded, branched clusters 8–14 cm (3.2–5.5 in) across, at or near the tips of the branchlets. Individual flowers are 2–2.5 cm (0.8–1 in) across with a **long, slender, red or green, sticky stalk** with 2 tiny scales at the base, calyx deeply divided into 5 narrow, green lobes, **petals 5, fused to form a saucer-shape, white to deep pink, marked on the inside with purple or rose-colored lines;** stamens 10; pistil 1, central. **Fruits: small dried, globe-shaped capsules 5–8 mm (0.2–0.3 in) in diameter,** usually topped by the persistent stalk of the pistil, splitting into 5 valves at maturity to scatter the numerous, tiny, light-brown seeds.

The Rhododendron Genus   *Rhododendron* L.

Rhododendrons are the best known and most popular of the flowering shrubs or small trees. This is a large genus of roughly 800 species in temperate and colder regions of North America, Europe, and Asia and extending into New Guinea and Australia. The largest concentration of species is in Asia, especially in the higher mountains, including the Himalayas. Of the 24 species in North America, only 3 qualify as trees, the mountain rosebay or catawba, the rosebay, and the Pacific rhododendron.

This genus is subdivided into 2 workable groups: the rhododendrons with leathery, evergreen leaves and flowers with 10 to 20 (rarely 5) stamens, and the azaleas with papery, deciduous leaves and flowers, which bloom before or as the leaves appear, with 5 to 10 stamens. Rhododendrons and azaleas are very popular as ornamental plantings because of their showy flowers and attractive leaves. The propagation, growing, and selling of rhododendrons is a multimillion dollar business. More than 100 species have been introduced into North America, especially in the Pacific Northwest and the southeastern U.S. Also, hundreds of crosses or hybrids have been made, and many of these are sold in nurseries and garden centers. Accurate identification of these hybrids is difficult.

The plants generally prefer well-drained, acid soils rich in organic matter. Flowering is in spring, with the seed capsules maturing in the fall of the same year. Native rhododendrons provide good cover for wildlife, but are not very important as a food source. The wood is dense, hard, and fine-grained, but rarely is used because of its small size. Rhododendrons are evergreen or deciduous shrubs, or rarely trees with twisting stems covered with scaly bark and large flower buds covered with overlapping scales. The simple, alternate leaves are variously shaped, entire or rarely finely toothed along the margins, with a leathery to papery texture, and often crowded at or near the ends of the branchlets. The large attractive flowers are in dense to loose, terminal, elongated to rounded clusters. The small calyx is 5 lobed or toothed and persists on the fruit; the showy, wide-spreading petals form a bell-, funnel-, or trumpet-shaped corolla; stamens 5 or 10 (rarely more); a single pistil. The fruits are elongated capsules that split into 5 sections at maturity to release the tiny, scale-like seeds.

Key to Rhododendron Species

A. Trees of eastern North America.

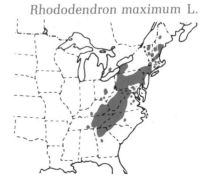

Mountain Rosebay

    1. Leaves 10–30 cm (4–12 in) long, pointed at the tips; flowers with the calyx lobes 4–6 mm (0.2 in) long; mountain slopes usually below 1,000 m (3,280 ft)   **Rosebay rhododendron, p. 518**

    2. Leaves 8–15 cm (3.2–6 in) long, rounded to blunt at the tip; flowers with the calyx lobes 1 mm (0.04 in) long or less; on mountain slopes usually above 1,000 m (3,280 ft)
          Mountain rosebay, p. 520

B. Trees of the Pacific Coastal region; leaves 6–25 cm (2.4–10 in) long, pointed at the tips; flowers with the calyx lobes about 1 mm (about 0.04 in) long; shaded woods below 1,250 m (4,100 ft)
          Pacific rhododendron, p. 520

Rosebay Rhododendron

Rhododendron maximum L.

Rosebay rhododendron, a shrub or bushy small tree, grows rather sparingly in northern swamps and more abundantly on the Appalachian mountain slopes along streams and in cool, shady, moist woods in acid soils up to 1,000 m (3,280 ft) elevation. It is most common in hardwood forests, growing with northern red, white, scarlet, and black oaks, tulip tree, white pine, hemlock, and basswood.

In June, rounded umbrella-shaped clusters of flowers appear on the ends of new growth. The white-to-pink flowers are showy and attract bees; yet honey produced from them is poisonous and so is avoided by beekeepers. The dark-brown, bristle-coated capsules remain on the branches over winter and spring. Ruffed grouse, mice, and rats make minimal use of the buds and leaves, although they are heavily browsed by whitetail deer. The dense growth habit provides year-round protective cover for birds and small game.

Rosebay rhododendron is sometimes planted for its attractive foliage. The flowers are not as attractive as other rhododendrons and the trees do not always flower each year. The light-brown wood is fine-grained, hard, and strong. It has been used in tool handles, as fuel, and as a substitute for boxwood in engraving. And it is still used in the bowls of briar pipes.

Rosebay Rhododendron

leaves evergreen, 10–30 cm (4–12 in) long

flower bud

flowers pale pink, white, or reddish-pink, 2.5–3 cm (1–1.2 in) long

closed capsule

fruit capsule open to shed seeds

calyx lobe

Spring Branchlet

Fall Branchlet

Appearance: a shrub to bushy tree, growing to 12 m (40 ft), with a rounded crown and short, crooked trunk, 25–30 cm (10–12 in) in diameter, sometimes prostrate along the ground. **Bark:** thin, light red-brown, broken into thin, shaggy scales. **Branches:** twisting, often interlocking in the same or adjacent trees; branchlets at first coated with rust-colored, sticky bristles, later smooth and dark green; becoming bright red-brown the second season, finally gray and marked by large scars from bud scales. **Winter buds:** leaf buds cone-shaped, dark green, with many closely overlapping, sticky scales 3.5–3.7 cm (1.4–1.5 in) long and 6–8 mm (0.2–0.3 in) wide at maturity; flower buds slightly larger, surrounded by several loose, narrow, leafy scales, the bud scales themselves contracted at the tips into long, slender points. **Leaves:** alternate, simple, *evergreen, 10–30 cm (4–12 in) long, 3.5–6.5 cm (1.4–2.6 in) wide, broadest at the middle, tapering to a pointed tip,* entire along the margins (when young, coated with sticky, pale, or rusty hairs; at maturity, thick and leathery, dark shiny green above, pale below with a prominent midvein). **Flowers:** in clusters of 12 to 30 flowers at the tips of the branchlets, 10–13 cm (4–5.1 in) across individual flowers with a 5-lobed calyx, the lobes 4–6 mm (0.2 in) long, light green and hairy, 5 showy *petals* united into a tube below their broad lobes, *pale pink, white, or reddish-pink, 2.5–3 cm (1–1.2 in) long,* the upper lobes marked with greenish spots; stamens usually 10, of different lengths; and with a single pistil. **Fruits:** an elongated capsule 1.1–1.3 cm (0.5 in) long, sticky, splitting into 5 sections at maturity to release the tiny, flattened seeds.

Mountain Rosebay — *Rhododendron catawbiense* Michx.

This small tree, or more often a large shrub, is native to the southeastern U.S. and ranges from Virginia to Georgia and northern Alabama. It occurs in the Piedmont and mountains, usually over 1,000 m (3,280 ft) in elevation, along ridges, on bluffs, in woods, or along stream banks. It often grows in association with chestnut oaks, white pine, Fraser fir, and mountain laurel.

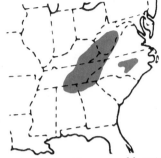

Like its larger relative, the rosebay rhododendron, mountain rosebay may form dense, almost impenetrable thickets that provide excellent escape cover for grouse and other small animals. Flowering occurs from mid-April to mid-May and the fruits mature by autumn. These shrubs or trees or hybrids of the mountain rosebay are hardy to the northeastern U.S., where they are often planted to add grace and beauty to gardens.

The **leaves** of the mountain rosebay are similar to the rosebay rhododendron, but differ by being **smaller, 8–15 cm (3.2–6 in) long, wider, 3–7 cm (1.2–2.8 in) wide, and rounded to blunt at the tip.** The striking lilac-purple or magenta, rarely white, flowers are more showy than the paler flowers of the rosebay. The fruiting capsules are 1–1.8 cm (0.4–0.7 in) long, rusty-brown, and hairy.

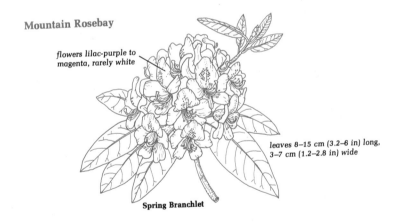

Mountain Rosebay

flowers lilac-purple to magenta, rarely white

leaves 8–15 cm (3.2–6 in) long, 3–7 cm (1.2–2.8 in) wide

Spring Branchlet

Pacific Rhododendron — *Rhododendron macrophyllum* D. Don

Pacific rhododendron occurs in the coastal mountains from southeastern British Columbia to central California. It grows in shaded forest, usually below 1,250 m (4,100 ft), and is often associated with coastal redwoods, Douglas fir, and yellow pine. Flowering occurs from April through July followed by the developing fruits. When in flower, this rhododendron is particularly attractive against the dark background of the coniferous forest. Mountain beaver feed on the branches.

This rhododendron is a shrub or small tree to 7.5 m (25 ft) tall with reddish-brown scaly bark. The simple, alternate *leaves are 6–25 cm (2.4–10 in) long, 3.5–6.5 cm (1.4–2.6 in) wide,* leathery, shiny, *evergreen* and with the margins curling under. The *flowers,* blooming in broad, terminal clusters about 12 cm (4.8 in) across, are *white to pink, trumpet-shaped, and 3.5–4 cm (1.4–1.6 in) long.* The fruits are reddish-brown capsules 1.5–2 cm (0.6–0.8 in) long.

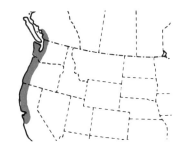

The Blueberry Genus

Vaccinium L.

The blueberries are a moderately large genus of approximately 150 species that are widely distributed throughout the world. They occur within the Arctic Circle and are common in the northern temperate regions of North America, Europe, and Asia. As well, they are native to high mountain areas in tropical countries. Only 1 species, the sparkleberry (*Vaccinium arboreum*), grows to a small tree. The remaining 35 or so species are small to large shrubs.

Domesticated selections of the highbush blueberry (*Vaccinium corymbosum*) are the source of the cultivated blueberries in supermarkets. Wild blueberries are often gathered from the lower-growing, velvet-leaved blueberry (V. *myrtilloides*) or the low, sweet blueberry (V. *angustifolium*); these are then sold in markets or canned. Blueberries are of considerable food value to wildlife. They have also been used in herbal medicines.

Members of this genus are mainly shrubs or rarely small trees with thin, leathery leaves that may be deciduous or evergreen. The flowers are small and occur singly or in many-flowered, unbranched spikes with small, leafy bracts at the base of each flower. The flowers are urn- or bell-shaped. Each has 4 or 5 calyx lobes, 4 or 5 fused petals, and 8 to 10 stamens. There is a single pistil that is 4- or 5-celled at the base. The fruit is a thin-skinned, fleshy berry crowned with the remnants of the calyx, and containing many tiny, hard seeds.

Sparkleberry, Farkleberry

Vaccinium arboreum Marsh.

Sparkleberry or farkleberry is a small slender tree with crooked branches forming an irregular crown. It is usually found in moist, shady, slightly alkaline soils along stream banks, ponds, bluffs, hammocks, and in open woods from Virginia to Florida. It may be found growing underneath white, scarlet, southern red, and post oaks, as well as loblolly and shortleaf pines.

Sparkleberry flowers from late April through June and the fruits mature in September or October. The berries are eaten by black bear, opossum, fox, raccoon, skunk, game birds, and songbirds. Whitetail deer browse the twigs, young leaves, and fruits. The wood, when available in large enough sizes, has been used for tool handles and miscellaneous small articles. The roots, bark, and leaves were once used to treat diarrhea.

These are shrubs or small trees growing to 9 m (28 ft) with bark that flakes off in large scales. The simple, alternate, *evergreen to almost evergreen leaves* are *1.5–7 cm (0.6–2.8 in) long, 0.8–3.5 cm (0.3–1.4 in) wide,* variable in shape but broadest above, below, or at the middle, rounded to pointed at the tip, gradually or abruptly tapering at the base, entire or finely toothed along the margin, dark and shiny above, paler and with conspicuous netted veins beneath. The *bell-shaped, white flowers are 5–8 mm (0.2–0.3 in) long* and produced in slender, drooping clusters 5–8 cm (2–3.2 in) long in the junction of the leaves of the previous year. The *fruits* are *berries 6–8 mm (0.2–0.3 in) in diameter, black, shiny,* edible, and often remaining on the trees through winter.

Sparkleberry

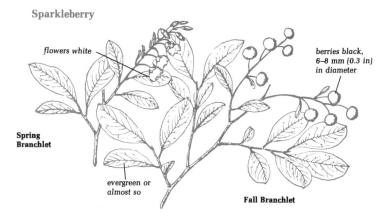

flowers white

berries black,
6–8 mm (0.3 in)
in diameter

**Spring
Branchlet**

evergreen or
almost so

Fall Branchlet

The Madrone Genus

Arbutus L.

This is a small genus of about 20 species of trees or shrubs in western North America, Central America, and southern Europe, including the Mediterranean region. Three species, all trees, occur in our range. These are the Pacific madrone, the Texas madrone, and the Arizona madrone, 3 distinct species occupying 3 different areas.

Madrones are of some economic importance. The attractive bark and evergreen leaves makes them a popular ornamental tree. Unfortunately, none of the species is very hardy. The fleshy fruits serve as a food source for many birds and other animals. Deer feed on the leaves. The wood is hard and close-grained, producing a fine grade of charcoal that was once used in the manufacturing of gunpowder. The bitter principles in the bark and leaves can be used as an astringent.

They are small to medium-size trees with bark that is either smooth, scaly, and peeling away or else furrowed and not peeling. The leaves are simple, alternate, evergreen, entire along the margins or toothed, leathery, and with a conspicuous leaf-stalk. The bisexual flowers are produced in elongated, branched clusters at the ends of the branchlets. Individual flowers are small, urn- or bell-shaped, white or pale pink, and composed of a persistent, 5-lobed calyx, 5 fused petals, 10 stamens, and a single pistil. The fruits are berry-like, rounded, with a warty surface, and a thin, fleshy region surrounding a hard stone that contains the seeds.

Key to Madrone Species

Pacific Madrone

A. Leaves egg-shaped, twice as long as broad; bark on trunk dark reddish-brown.

    1. Leaves 7.5–13 cm (3–5.1 in) long; fruits 1–1.4 cm (0.4–0.6 in) in diameter, bright orange-red; trees of coastal Pacific Northwest
                        Pacific madrone, p. 523

    2. Leaves 2.5–7.5 cm (1–3 in) long; fruits 7–10 mm (0.3–0.4 in) in diameter, dark red; trees of Texas, New Mexico, and Mexico
                        Texas madrone, p. 524

B. Leaves lance-shaped, 3 times as long as broad; bark on trunk pale gray
                        Arizona madrone, p. 525

Arizonia Madrone

Pacific Madrone

Arbutus menziesii Pursh

The small to towering Pacific madrone, a distinctive West Coast species, is the largest of any member of the heath family. It occurs from southwestern British Columbia and southward less commonly into lower California. It can grow in a wide range of soils and climates from sea level to 1,800 m (5,900 ft). It is found in many different habitats, from streambanks, canyons, and valleys to coastal dunes or sunny mountain slopes. But best growth is in rich, well-drained lowlands such as in the redwood or fog belt of northern California. Trees growing in association wth the Pacific madrone include Douglas fir, coastal redwood, several oaks, western hemlock, tanoak, big-leaf maple, and several pines.

Madrones are slow-growing trees that may live to 225 years of age. Their abundant clusters of tiny, urn-shaped flowers bloom from April to June, according to latitude and elevation, attracting honeybees. Later in September and October, clusters of grainy-skinned, red, berry-like fruits mature and are readily devoured by banded pigeons, chats, thrushes, and small mammals. Blacktail and mule deer occasionally browse the leaves and branchlets.

These trees are too scarce to be of commercial importance, although the wood is heavy, fine-grained, and relatively strong. It is used locally for fuel, cabinetwork, and woodturning. Indians used to eat the bland fruits, both raw and cooked.

Appearance: trees 9–12 m (30–40 ft) high in the north but growing 24–40 m (78–131 ft) in redwood forests in northwestern California, with a rounded, irregular crown supported by a normally scraggly, twisty, or sprawling trunk, 60–120 cm (23–47 in) in diameter. **Bark:** *thin, reddish-brown, peeling in papery strips* to reveal smooth, yellowish-green new bark beneath; on old trunks thicker, flaky. **Branches:** upright or spreading, or twisting; branchlets red, green, or orange when young, sometimes pale-hairy, darkening the first winter to reddish-brown. **Winter buds:** 7–9 mm (about 0.3

in) long, broadest near the tip, short pointed, with many overlapping red scales. **Leaves:** alternate, simple, **evergreen**, shed in May or late summer of the second year, **7.5–13 cm (3–5.1 in) long**, 3.7–7.5 cm (1.5–3 in) wide, broadest near the middle or finely toothed along the margin, rounded at the tip, tapering at the base, leathery, dark shiny green above with many fine veins, pale or almost white below; the leafstalks 1–2.5 cm (0.4–1 in) long. **Flowers:** produced in **many-flowered, hairy, branched clusters** 12–15 cm (4.7–5.9 in) long; the individual flowers 7–9 mm (about 0.3 in) long, white to pink, urn-shaped, calyx tiny, the lobes about 1 mm (about 0.04 in) long, petals fused together, 6–8 mm (0.2–0.3 in) long, stamens 10, and with a single pistil. **Fruits:** round, **1–1.4 cm (0.5 in) in diameter, bright orange-red,** with a granular or bumpy surface, a fleshy pulp that contains a 5-celled, thin-walled stone containing several dark-brown seeds.

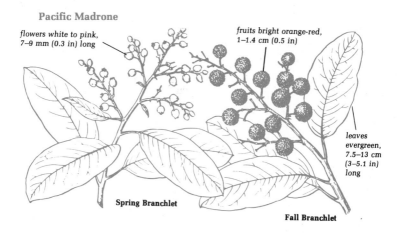

Pacific Madrone

flowers white to pink, 7–9 mm (0.3 in) long

fruits bright orange-red, 1–1.4 cm (0.5 in)

leaves evergreen, 7.5–13 cm (3–5.1 in) long

Spring Branchlet

Fall Branchlet

Texas Madrone

Arbutus texana Buckl.

Texas madrone is a small tree that occurs from the Edwards Plateau in Texas to New Mexico, and south into Nuevo Leon, Mexico. It grows on dry, limestone, or igneous hills and mountainsides. Flowering is in February or March, and the dark red to yellow, berry-like fruits mature in the summer. These are eaten by songbirds, thus helping to disperse the seeds and start new colonies of this plant. The reddish-brown wood is hard and heavy and has been used locally for tool handles, fuel, and charcoal. The bark and leaves have astringent properties that have been used in medicine.

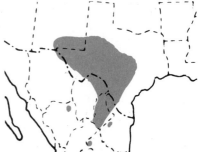

Texas madrone is a small tree to 8 m (26 ft) with a short trunk to 30 cm (12 in) in diameter and stout but crooked branches. In its range, it is easily recognized by the **shaggy thin, reddish bark that peels away in large papery scales** to expose the lighter inner bark. Older trees develop a furrowed, dark reddish-brown bark. The simple, alternate, **evergreen leaves** are **2.5–7.5 cm (1–3 in) long,** 1.7–3.7 cm (0.7–1.5

in) wide, broadest at or below the middle, rounded to pointed at the tip, rounded to tapering at the base, entire to finely toothed along the margin, leathery, dark shiny green above, paler and hairy beneath. The small, white or pink, urn-shaped flowers are produced on stout, hairy stalks in compact, cone-shaped, branched clusters 5–8 cm (2–3.2 in) long. The *fruits* are *round, 7–10 mm (0.4 in) in diameter, dark red,* with a *granular or bumpy surface,* and a thin flesh that surrounds a hard stone containing several small seeds.

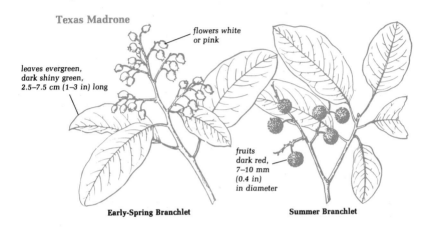

Texas Madrone

flowers white
or pink

leaves evergreen,
dark shiny green,
2.5–7.5 cm (1–3 in) long

fruits
dark red,
7–10 mm
(0.4 in)
in diameter

Early-Spring Branchlet   **Summer Branchlet**

Arizona Madrone   *Arbutus arizonica* (A. Gray) Sarg.

This attractive, medium-size evergreen tree occurs in southeastern New Mexico, southwestern Arizona, and into northern Mexico. There it grows on dry, gravelly benches and mountains at 1,200–2,400 m (3,900–7,900 ft) elevation. Arizona madrone is a slow-growing member of the oak woodland, occurring among the gray and Emory oaks, and Apache pine. It is apparently more closely related to other Mexican species than the North American madrones.

Arizona madrones are trees 6–15 m (20–50 ft) high, with a dense, compact crown. The *bark* is *very pale gray, thick, furrowed, and scaly.* On the spreading branches and twisting branchlets, the bark is thin, smooth, dark red, and peels away in large strips. The leaves are *lance-shaped, 3.7–7.5 cm (1.5–3 in) long, 1.2–2.5 cm (0.5–1 in) broad,* rounded or pointed at the tip, entire or finely toothed along the margins, thick, firm, and pale green. The flowers open from April to September in loose, branched clusters 5–8 cm (2–3.2 in) long. Each flower is white to pink, urn-shaped, 6–8 mm (0.3 in) long; contains 10 stamens and a single pistil. The *round fruits are 7–10 mm (0.4 in) in diameter,* orange-red, and ripen in October or November.

(Note: See art on next page.)

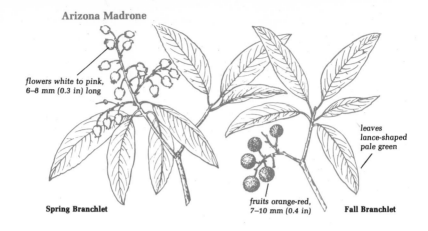

Arizona Madrone

*flowers white to pink,
6–8 mm (0.3 in) long*

*leaves
lance-shaped
pale green*

Spring Branchlet

*fruits orange-red,
7–10 mm (0.4 in)*

Fall Branchlet

The Sapote Family

Sapotaceae

Sapote (pronounced *sa-POTE-ee*) is a moderately large family of close to 600 species distributed among approximately 45 genera. Members occur primarily in tropical and subtropical regions of Africa, Asia, and the Americas. Six genera have members native to or naturalized in North America, mainly in Florida and Texas.

The chiclé that is obtained from the latex of the sapodilla tree is used in chewing gum. Sapodilla and other members bear edible fruits. Another species yields an inelastic rubber called gutta-percha, which is used to insulate sea cables, soles for shoes, and machine belts. Other members are economically important timber trees in tropical countries.

Members of this family are trees and shrubs with mostly alternate, simple, entire, often leathery leaves. The small flowers usually contain both sexes, and are produced in clusters in the junctions of the leaves. Each flower consists of 5 to 8 calyx lobes that persist on the fruit; 5 to 8 petals, usually with additional lobes at their bases. The flower parts are joined below the ovary. The fertile stamens (with pollen) are joined to the base of the petals and alternate with sterile stamens (without pollen). The fruit is a fleshy to dry berry containing several large, shiny seeds.

Key to Sapote Genera

A. Branchlets armed with stout spines
   Bumelia, p. 527
B. Branchlets unarmed, not bearing stout spines.

   1. Flowers with 5 fertile stamens (with pollen); leaves reddish-brown to copper colored beneath; includes satinleaf **Goldenleaf, p. 532**
   2. Flowers with 5 fertile stamens (with pollen) and 5 sterile stamens (without pollen); usually

Satinleaf

modified into a flattened structure; leaves pale green to yellowish-green beneath.

- **a.** Flower petals without a lobed appendage on each side; includes false mastic
  Jungle plum, p. 533
- **b.** Flower petals with a lobed appendage on each side.
    - (1) Flowers in dense, many-flowered clusters in the junctions of the leaves; fruits black **Bustic, p. 534**
    - (2) Flowers in loose, few-flowered clusters in the junctions of the leaves; fruits yellow, green or brown.

        - (a) Fruits 5–7 cm (2–2.8 in) in diameter, smooth skinned **Sapote, p. 535**
        - (b) Fruits 2.5–3.2 cm (1–1.3 in) in diameter, rough skinned
          Sapodilla, p. 536

False Mastic

Willow Bustic

The Bumelia Genus

Bumelia Sw.

This is a small group of about 30 species of trees and shrubs ranging from southern North America to Brazil. Five species reach tree size in North America. The genus is of no economic importance and is apparently of limited value to wildlife. Bumelia has tiny flowers produced in clusters in the junctions of the leaves.

Members are shrubs or trees with spiny branches or branchlets. The deciduous to evergreen leaves are alternate, sometimes clustered near the tips of the branchlets, usually broadest above the middle and entire along the margin. The white flowers are bisexual, with a 5-lobed calyx, with 5 petals fused near their middle and each with a lobed appendage on each side, 5 fertile stamens (with pollen), 5 sterile stamens (without pollen), modified into petal-like structures, and a single pistil.

Key to Bumelia Species

A. Leaves densely hairy on lower surface, hairs rusty-brown, copper colored or silvery-white.

- **1.** Leaves with rust-brown and silvery-white hairs on the lower surface; small trees of the southeastern to southwestern U.S.
  Gum bumelia, p. 528
- **2.** Leaves with copper-colored to rust-colored hairs on the lower surface; small trees of the maritime forest of the Atlantic Coastal Plain
  Ironwood, p. 529

B. Leaves smooth to only sparsely hairy and pale green on the lower surface.

(Continued)

Gum Bumelia

Ironwood, Tough Bumelia

1. Leaves 7.5–15.3 cm (3–6 in) long, gradually falling in autumn; bright green above; trees of southeastern U.S. **Buckthorn bumelia, p. 530**
2. Leaves 2.5–4 cm (1–1.6 in) long, evergreen. pale blue or dull green above; trees of central and southern Florida and southern Texas **Saffron plum, p. 531**

Saffron Plum

Gum Bumelia

Bumelia lanuginosa (Michx.) Pers.

Gum bumelia is the largest-growing bumelia in North America. It occurs from the southeastern to southwestern U.S. and Mexico in open, sandy woods. This bumelia grows in dry, rocky soils and in lower, moist soils along the borders of swamps and streams. There are 3 varieties with different hair types on the leaves and branches, but the varieties are more easily distinguished by their range. Variety *lanuginosa* grows from northern Florida to Louisiana. Variety *albicans*, with leaves bearing silvery hairs on the lower surface, occurs from southern Illinois to Texas and Louisiana. The smallest and shrubbiest variety, variety *rigida*, is found from southern Oklahoma, Texas, New Mexico, Arizona, and Mexico.

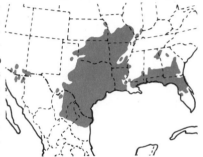

Gum Bumelia

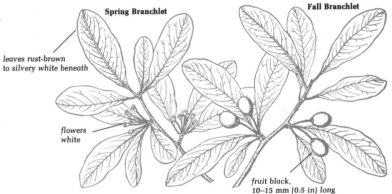

Spring Branchlet

Fall Branchlet

leaves rust-brown to silvery white beneath

flowers white

fruit black, 10–15 mm (0.5 in) long

The dense clusters of small white flowers open in summer, and the shiny black fruits ripen by the end of September. The fruits are eaten by quail, turkey, and other birds. Deer also consume the fruits and occasionally browse the leaves. Though the wood is close-grained and heavy, it is rather soft and weak and so is seldom used.

Appearance: small spiny tree or shrub from 6–12 m (20–40 ft) with a narrow, rounded crown; trunk straight, to 0.6 m (1.9 ft) in diameter. **Bark:** 1–1.4 cm (0.4–0.6 in) thick, deeply fissured and divided into narrow ridges and with thick, reddish-brown scales. **Branches:** short, thick, rigid, usually with stout, erect, slightly curved spines; branchlets slender, sometimes zigzaging, hairy at first, becoming nearly smooth and reddish-brown to ash-gray. **Winter buds:** 3–4 mm (0.1–0.2 in) long, broadest above the middle, blunt at the tip, covered with rusty scales. **Leaves:** simple, alternate, falling during the winter months, broadest above the middle, 2.5–6 cm (1–2.4 in) long, 0.8–2 cm (0.3–0.8 in) wide, rounded at the tip, tapering at the base, becoming thin, firm, dark green, and shiny above, *softly hairy below with rust-brown and silvery-white hairs;* the leafstalks slender, 3–15 mm (0.1–0.6 in) long, reddish-brown and sparsely hairy. **Flowers:** produced in 12- to 18-flowered clusters in the junctions of the upper leaves; each flower on a hairy stalk 3–4 mm (about 0.1–0.2 in) long, with a densely hairy, egg-shaped calyx, the 5 lobes broadest near the base, 2–4 mm (0.1–0.2 in) long, 5 petals fused into a tube slightly longer than the calyx lobes, with 5 fertile stamens (with pollen) and 5 sterile stamens (without pollen), and a single central, tiny pistil. **Fruits:** berry-like, 10–15 mm (0.5 in) long, broadest near the tip, black, fleshy, produced on a slender stalk; seeds about 6–8 mm (0.2–0.3 in) long.

Ironwood or Tough Bumelia *Bumelia tenax* (L.) Willd.

This small scrubby tree or shrub is native to the maritime woodlands of the outer Coastal Plain from South Carolina to southern Florida. Ironwood grows in the coastal dunes, in sand-pine evergreen forests, and with scrub oak. Both common names for the tree are appropriate because the young, flexible branches are difficult to break.

Flowering occurs from spring to early summer with the fruits maturing by autumn. The fruits and seeds are eaten by some birds and small mammals. The pale-brown wood is dense and hard, but is of no commercial value because of the plant's small size.

The trees grow to 8 m (30 ft) and have thick, fissured, reddish-brown bark and branches armed with stout spines. The simple, alternate *leaves* are 2–7 cm (0.8–2.8 in) long, broadest above the middle and *displaying silky-rust to coppery-gold hairs on the lower surface.* The tiny, whitish

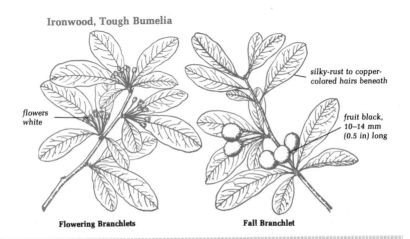

Ironwood, Tough Bumelia

silky-rust to copper-colored hairs beneath

flowers white

fruit black, 10–14 mm (0.5 in) long

Flowering Branchlets   **Fall Branchlet**

flowers grow in short clusters in the junctions of the leaves and the nearly globe-shaped, black, edible fruits are 10–14 mm (0.5 in) long.

Buckthorn Bumelia   *Bumelia lycioides* (L.) Pers.

Buckthorn bumelia is a small, slightly thorny tree or shrub that occurs in moist soils along streams or swamps in the Coastal Plain and Piedmont areas from Virginia to northern Florida, west to Texas, and north to Indiana. It is not common anywhere in its range and so is seldom noticed.

The dense flower clusters open in the summer followed by the development of the black fleshy fruits by autumn. Beyond identification features, very little is known about this plant. The light-brown or yellow wood is hard, but weak, and so is of no commercial value.

Appearance: tree to 9 m (30 ft), with an open, spreading crown; trunk short, to 15 cm (6 in) in diameter. **Bark:** thin, 8–12 mm (0.3–0.5 in) thick, smooth or developing thin, reddish-brown scales. **Branches:** stout, flexible, often with short, stout spines; branchlets short, thick, hairy when young, becoming smooth and light reddish-brown with age. **Winter buds:** tiny, 2–3 mm (0.1 in) long, blunt, covered with dark-brown scales. **Leaves:** simple, alternate, gradually falling in late autumn and winter, broadest at or above the middle, *7.5–15.3 cm (3–6 in) long, 1.2–5 cm (0.5–2 in) wide,* pointed at the tip, gradually tapering at the base, entire along the margin, with a thin, firm texture, bright green and smooth above, *light green and smooth beneath, sometimes hairy;* the leafstalks slender, 5–12 mm (0.2–0.5 in) long. **Flowers:** produced in dense, many-flowered clusters in the junctions of the leaves; each flower on a slender stalk 7–10 mm (0.3–0.4 in) long, with a 5-lobed, bell-shaped calyx 1–3 mm (0.1 in) long; with 5 fused petals 3–5 mm (0.1–0.2 in) long, with 5 fertile stamens and 5 petal-like sterile stamens, and a single, central pistil. **Fruits:** berry-like, egg-shaped to broadest at the middle, 1.5–2 cm (0.7 in) long, black, fleshy and containing a nearly globe-shape seed 6–8 mm (0.2–0.3 in) long.

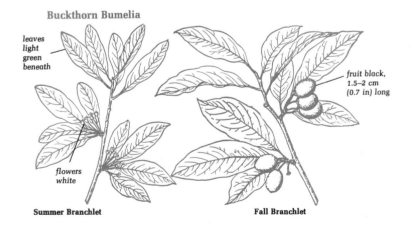

Buckthorn Bumelia

leaves
light
green
beneath

fruit black,
1.5–2 cm
(0.7 in) long

flowers
white

Summer Branchlet   **Fall Branchlet**

Saffron Plum

Bumelia celastrina H.B.K.
(synonym: *B. angustifolia* Nutt.)

The saffron plum, also known as tropical buckthorn and downward plum, is mostly confined to coastal hammocks and rocky shores from central Florida to the Keys and in southern Texas. It also occurs in the Bahama Islands, Cuba, and from northeastern Mexico, south to Colombia and Venezuela. A smaller and more narrow-leaved variety [*Bumelia celastrina* variety *angustifolia* (Nutt.) R. W. Long] can be found in the dry pinelands in the lower Florida Keys.

Tiny flowers are usually produced in autumn or early winter, although this plum also flowers earlier. The sweet, edible, black fruits develop a month or two later. They are eaten by wildlife, especially birds. The light-brown to orange wood is hard and heavy, but not very strong. Because of the small size of the trees, it is of no economic importance.

Saffron Plum

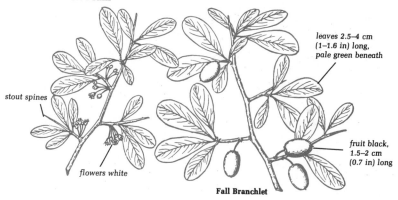

leaves 2.5–4 cm (1–1.6 in) long, pale green beneath

stout spines

fruit black, 1.5–2 cm (0.7 in) long

flowers white

Fall Branchlet

Appearance: small tree to 6 m (20 ft), with a dense, rounded crown; trunk short, to 20 cm (8 in) in diameter. **Bark:** thin, 8–12 mm (0.3–0.5 in) thick, deeply fissured into elongated or squarish plates, reddish-gray. **Branches:** slender, graceful, spreading; branchlets slender, with rigid, sharp-pointed spines to 2.5 cm (1 in) long, densely hairy when young, light reddish-brown or gray. **Winter buds:** small, egg-shaped, pointed at the tip, covered with stiff brown hairs. **Leaves:** simple, alternate to almost opposite, evergreen, *2.5–4 cm (1–1.6 in) long, 0.5–3 cm (0.2–1.2 in) wide,* broadest above the middle, rounded at the tip and tapering to a narrow wedge-shaped base, thicker and wavy along the margins, leathery, smooth, ***pale blue or dull green above, paler beneath;*** the leafstalks stout, 5–8 mm (0.2–0.3 in) long. **Flowers:** in few to many-flowered clusters; each flower consisting of a tiny, deeply lobed calyx 1.5–2 mm (less than 0.1 in) long; 5 small petals, each with a tiny, lobe-like appendage; 5 fertile stamens (with pollen) and 5 sterile stamens (without pollen), the stamens longer than the petals. **Fruits:** rounded or nearly so, 1.5–2 cm (0.7 in) long, black, on a slender, drooping stalk, containing a single seed 9–12 mm (0.3–0.5 in) long.

The Goldenleaf Genus   *Chrysophyllum* L.

Goldenleaf is a tropical genus of 75 to 80 species of trees and shrubs, mostly of the Americas, but also with a few species in Africa, Asia, Australia, and the Hawaiian Islands. Only 1 species, the satinleaf tree, is native to southern Florida. The West Indian star-apple (*Chrysophyllum cainito*) is cultivated in south Florida for its succulent edible purple or blue-green apple-like fruits. The light or reddish-brown wood is usually heavy, hard, strong, and durable and is used in the West Indies for construction, bridges, flooring, and as crossties.

Goldenleaf species are trees with simple, alternate, evergreen leaves that are usually silky hairy beneath. The dense flower clusters appear on short stalks along the branchlets. The flowers have a 5-parted calyx, 5 petals fused near the base into a bell-shape or nearly flat and circular-shape, white or greenish-white. The fruit is rounded to egg-shaped and contains a leathery, egg-shaped seed.

Satinleaf   *Chrysophyllum oliviforme* L.

Satinleaf is a handsome small tree found growing in rich hammocks of southern Florida including the Florida Keys. It also occurs in the West Indies. The leaves are striking in that the lower surface of the leaves is covered with reddish-brown or copper-colored hairs. The small, greenish-white flowers, produced in dense to loose clusters, appear throughout the year. These are soon followed by the dark purple, edible fruits, which are sometimes used to make jelly. This tree is cultivated in Florida as an ornamental for its brilliant silky leaves.

The trees are small and evergreen with thin reddish-brown, shallowly fissured bark and reddish-brown to light-gray branchlets. The *leaves* are *3–10 cm (1.2–4 in) long,* widest near the base, leathery, bright blue-green, shiny and smooth above, and *covered with bright shiny copper-colored hairs beneath.* The flowers are produced in few to many-flowered clusters in the junctions of the leaves. The tiny

Satinleaf

leaves with shiny,
copper-colored
hairs beneath

flowers
white

fruit dark
purple,
1.6–2.2 cm
(0.8 in) long

white flowers have 5 calyx lobes, 5 petals, 5 stamens, and a single pistil. The fruits, resembling an olive, are 1.6–2.2 cm (0.8 in) long, dark purple and contain a single large seed.

The Jungle Plum Genus   *Mastichodendron* H. J. Lam

This is a small genus of 7 species confined to tropical climates of the Americas. The one North American species, false mastic, has small yellow flowers with a strong, cheese-like smell. Some of the species, including the false mastic, produce handsome, durable wood used for construction, fence posts, cabinetwork, carving, and engraving. The fruits of several species are edible.

Jungle plums do not have spines on the branchlets, and their long-stalked, ever-green leaves have net-like veins beneath. The small flowers are produced in crowded clusters in the junctions of the leaves. Each flower is composed of a 5-parted calyx with the lobes 1–2 mm (less than 0.1 in) long, 5 to 6 petals fused near the middle, 5 fertile stamens (with pollen), and 5 sterile stamens (without pollen). The fruit is a dry berry, longer than wide, with a thin, leathery skin, and containing a single seed; the seed is broadest above the middle, light brown, and shiny.

False Mastic   *Mastichodendron foetidissimum* (Jacq.) H. J. Lam
(synonym: *Sideroxylon foetidissimum* Jacq.)

False mastic is a large evergreen tree occurring in rich hammocks in southern Florida and the Florida Keys, north along the eastern coast to Cape Kennedy. It also grows in the West Indies, Mexico, and Belize.

The small clusters of yellow flowers appear from early spring through autumn and have a disagreeably strong odor. The olive-shaped yellow fruits that ripen in March and April are edible, but the peppery taste and gumminess make it undesirable for human consumption. Some animals are known to eat the fruit, but its importance to wildlife is conjectural.

The wood of the false mastic is heavy, hard, strong, bright orange with thick yellow sapwood. It is valued in marine construction, ship and boatbuilding, furniture, and fence posts.

Appearance: tree to 25 (82 ft) with an irregular crown; trunk thick, straight, to 1.5 m (4.9 ft) in diameter. **Bark:** 8–10 mm (0.3–0.4 in) thick, dark gray to light red-brown, splitting into thick, flat scales and separated into thin layers. **Branches:** stout, upright; branchlets orange, slightly hairy at first but becoming smooth, brown tinged with red, marked with large round leaf scars. **Leaves:** alternate, simple, in clusters near the end of branches, 5–15 cm (2–6 in) long, broadest near the base to uniformly wide, pointed or rounded and slightly notched at the tip, tapering at the base, with thick margins slightly rolled inward, silky hairy beneath when unfolding, becoming thin and firm, smooth bright green above, *yellow-green and shiny beneath;* the leafstalks slender, 2.5–7 cm (1–2.8 in) long. **Flowers:** sometimes alone or in clusters in the junction of the leafstalk and branchlet, on stalks 1 cm (0.4 in) long or less, calyx green, bell-shaped with 5 to 6 rounded, yellow-green calyx lobes, about 2 mm (0.1 in) long, corolla 6–7 mm (0.2–0.3 in) across, green-yellow, 5 to 6 rounded lobes, *with 5 or 6 fertile stamens*

False Mastic

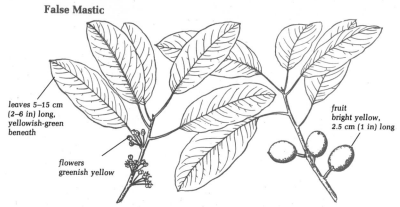

leaves 5–15 cm
(2–6 in) long,
yellowish-green
beneath

flowers
greenish yellow

fruit
bright yellow,
2.5 cm (1 in) long

(with pollen) and 5 or 6 sterile stamens (without pollen). **Fruits:** *berry,* olive-shaped, **about 2.5 cm (1 in) long, bright yellow** with a tough, smooth skin, and thin flesh; containing a single, large, brown seed, 1.2–1.7 cm (0.5–0.7 in) long, oblong to broadest above middle and rounded at the top, narrow at base, hard, shiny.

The Bustic Genus
Dipholis A. DC.

This is a small genus of perhaps 15 species of tropical America. A single species, the willow bustic, is native to southern Florida. Very little is known of their natural history and value to wildlife. Members of this genus are of limited economic importance; some yield good-quality lumber.

These trees and shrubs have alternate, evergreen leaves. The small flowers grow in clusters on club-shaped stalks produced in the junctions of the leafstalks and the branchlets. Individual flowers are composed of a 5-lobed calyx, the lobes almost equal, broadest near the base and rounded at the tip; a bell-shaped, 5-lobed white corolla; the spreading petals have a narrow or awl-shaped appendage on each side near the base. The fruit is a berry, egg-shaped to uniformly wide, with a thin dry flesh and containing an egg-shaped, leathery, shiny seed.

Willow Bustic
Dipholis salicifolia (L.) A. DC.

This evergreen tree is found in hammocks of southern Florida in the Everglade Keys and Florida Keys. It also occurs in the West Indies from the Bahama Islands southward and from southern Mexico to Guatemala and Belize. The **whitish-green flowers** are **borne in crowded clusters along the sides of the twigs** in the junctions of the leaves, and are followed by many black berries. Flowering is from January to May and the fruits mature in summer or autumn.

The reddish or dark-brown wood is hard, strong, heavy, tough, and of medium durability. It takes a fine polish but is not used to any extent in North America. In the West Indies, it is used mostly for posts and sometimes in heavy construction.

Willow Bustic

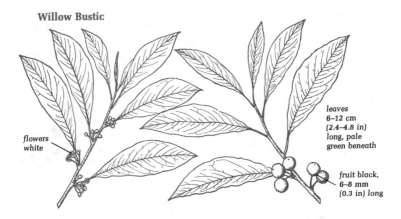

*leaves
6–12 cm
(2.4–4.8 in)
long, pale
green beneath*

*flowers
white*

*fruit black,
6–8 mm
(0.3 in) long*

Appearance: trees to 16 m (53 ft) with a rounded crown when grown in the open; trunk straight, to 50 cm (20 in) in diameter. **Bark:** 6–8 mm (0.2–0.3 in) thick, brown or reddish-gray, smooth and fissured, becoming rough and scaly or flaky. **Branches:** slender, curving upward; branchlets slender, brownish-green, rusty hairy but becoming smooth and gray to light reddish-brown. **Leaves:** simple, alternate, evergreen, broadest above the middle to uniformly wide, 6–12 cm (2.4–4.8 in) long, 2.5–4 cm (1–1.6 in) wide, sharp-pointed at the tip, tapering at the base, hairy when young, becoming dark green, smooth, and shiny above, paler and dull beneath. **Flowers:** *produced in clusters in the junctions of the leaves;* each flower with a reddish, silky hairy, bell-shaped calyx of 5 lobes, the lobes broadest near the base to uniformly wide, blunt at the tip, 1.2–1.8 mm (less than 0.1 in) long; a white, funnel-shaped *corolla of 5 petals, each with 2 small, basal lobes or appendages,* 5 fertile stamens opposite the lobes and alternating with 5 sterile stamens. **Fruits:** *a berry, nearly round to egg-shaped,* 6–8 mm (0.3 in) long, smooth, *black,* containing a single dark-brown, shiny seed.

The Sapote Genus   *Pouteria* Aubl.

This moderately large genus of perhaps 150 species occurs primarily in the tropical Americas. It is questionable if any species are native to North America. Yet the egg fruit tree (*Pouteria campechiana*) has been introduced in southern Florida where it now reproduces on its own. A second species, *P. dominigensis,* may also have naturalized, but it is rarely encountered.

Members of this genus are trees or shrubs with alternate, evergreen leaves. The flowers are produced in few-flowered clusters in the junctions of the leaves. Each flower has 4 to 6 free calyx lobes, 4 to 6 yellow, green, or white petals, 4 to 6 pollen-producing stamens, each alternating with a sterile stamen, and a single, central pistil. The fruit is a berry with 1 to several seeds.

Egg Fruit   *Pouteria campechiana* (HBK) Baehni

Egg fruit is a small to medium-size introduced tree that now reproduces on its own in some of the hammocks of southern Florida and the Keys. The common name is derived from the similarity of the pulp of the small fruit to that of a hard-boiled egg.

The trees grow to 25 m (82 ft) and bear simple, alternate, evergreen leaves. The *leaves* are *usually broadest above the middle* to widest at the middle, *10–22 cm (4–*

8.7 in) long, 5–10 cm (2–4 in) wide, pointed to somewhat rounded at the tip, tapering at the base, entire along the margin, and smooth. The tiny flowers are produced in few-flowered clusters in the junctions of the leaves. They are white and 7–10 mm (0.3–0.4 in) long. The nearly *globe-shaped berries* are *5–7 cm (2–2.8 in) in diameter, edible,* yellow, green, or brown, and *smooth skinned.*

The Sapodilla Genus   Manilkara Adans. (Achras L.)

(synonym: *Achras* L.)

This genus is made up of 30 to 40 species distributed in the tropics of the Northern and Southern Hemisphere, with a single species, wild dilly (*Manikara emarginata*) native to southern Florida. A second species, sapodilla, has been introduced into southern Florida and on occasion reproduces on its own in the woodland. These species are often cultivated for their edible fruits, or their valuable sweet, milky juices also used as food and for gum. Some species produce hard, strong, economically important timber.

Achras are trees, occasionally shrubs with stout, rounded branchlets, small naked buds, and sweet juice. The simple, alternate leaves are evergreen, leathery with slender indistinct, horizontal veins and tiny, netted veinlets, and usually in clusters at the end of branches. Flowers are produced singly or in small clusters in the junctions of the leaves. Individual flowers consist of a 6 to 8 lobed calyx, 6 petals, white, each a bit longer than the calyx, nearly circular, and furnished at the base with a pair of petal-like extensions, stamens as many as the corolla lobes, usually with 6 to 8 sterile stamens, and a single pistil. The fruit is round, 1- to 2-seeded, with an elongated point at the tip, and a hard, brittle skin enclosing a thick dry flesh. The seeds are oblong to egg-shaped, slightly flattened, hard, brittle, chestnut brown, and shiny.

Key to Sapodilla Species

A. Flowers pale yellow; leaves notched at the tip;
   trees of extreme southern Florida
      Wild dilly, p. 536
B. Flowers white; leaves usually sharp pointed at
   the tip; introduced trees of southern Florida
      Sapodilla, p. 538

Wild Dilly   Manilkara bahamensis (Baker) Lam & Meeuse
[synonym: *Achras emarginata* (L.) Little]

Wild dilly is a small tree that occurs occasionally in the Florida Keys and in hammocks at Cape Sable in southern Florida. It is also found on the Bahama Islands, Cuba, Hispaniola, and Puerto Rico. This species has long, thick, leathery leaves growing in clusters at the ends of twigs, forming an attractive, dense evergreen tree.

The flower clusters open in spring or autumn, with the fruits remaining until after the tree flowers the next year. The leaves are shed in their second year. The dark brown wood is hard, strong, and close-grained.

Appearance: a tree to 10 m (33 ft) tall with short, knotted trunk, 40 cm (16 in) in diameter with dense rounded crown usually smaller and shrubby. **Bark:** about 6 mm (0.2–0.3 in) thick, with rounded ridges breaking into small squarish gray or brown plates. **Branches:** thick, usually hollow and defective; branchlets in clusters at end of previous year's branches, covered at first with fine, soft dark brownish hairs becoming smooth and light orange-brown, and in the second year covered with thick ashy-gray or red-brown scaly bark. **Winter buds:** egg-shaped, sharp-pointed, covered with long curled rusty hairs. **Leaves:** in clusters at end of branchlets, 5–10 cm (2–4 in) long, oblong, broadest at middle, or occasionally broadest above middle, rounded or slightly notched at tip, with rounded or wedge-shaped base, margins slightly thick, wavy, evergreen, thick, leathery, bright red when unfolding and somewhat hairy on midrib beneath, becoming bright green and shiny, slightly covered above with whitish or bluish waxy material, with distinctly netted veins, midrib is smooth or covered with rusty hairs beneath; the leafstalks are slender, 12–25 mm (0.5–1 in) long, rusty hairy and grooved. **Flowers:** produced in hairy, *drooping clusters from junctions of new leaves,* or from those of leaves shed the previous year; each *flower 2–3 cm (0.8–1.2 in) long,* covered with long rusty hairs, with 6 calyx lobes, each 5–7 mm (0.2–0.3 in) long, lance-shaped and with the broadest part at base, pointed at tip, *light greenish-yellow* and covered with pale hairs; with 6 spreading *petals* 1.5–2 cm (0.6–0.8 in) across, *light greenish-yellow,* narrowly lance-shaped, sharp-pointed, entire or somewhat toothed, the extensions are slender petal-like but only half as long as corolla lobes, with 6 fertile stamens and 6 sterile stamens, all shorter than corolla. **Fruits:** berries on stout stalks about 2.5 cm (1 in) long, nearly round to somewhat broader above the middle, flattened at the tip, *2.5–3.2 cm (1–1.3 in) in diameter, brown and rough,* and tipped with long, spine-like projections, the flesh thick, spongy, and with milky juice; seeds usually about 12 mm (0.5 in) long, brown, smooth.

Wild Dilly

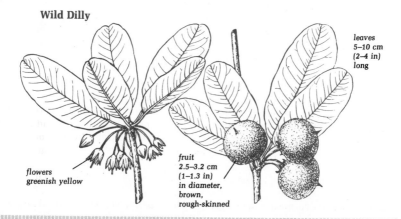

leaves
5–10 cm
(2–4 in)
long

flowers
greenish yellow

fruit
2.5–3.2 cm
(1–1.3 in)
in diameter,
brown,
rough-skinned

Sapodilla

Manilkara zapota (L.) Royen

(synonym: *Achras zapota* L.)

This handsome evergreen tree is native in southern Mexico and Central America south to Costa Rica. It has long been cultivated and has occasionally naturalized in southern Florida and Florida Keys. It was also introduced in the West Indies, Mexico, Central and South America, and tropical regions of the Eastern Hemisphere.

The light green bell or cup-shaped flowers and the brown rounded berries appear almost throughout the year. This is one of the most important commercial trees of tropical America because chicle, an important ingredient in chewing gum, is obtained from the milky sap. This species is extensively planted in tropical regions for its edible fruits as well as for shade and beauty. The dark red wood is very hard, heavy, strong, and durable. Where it is available, it is used in general and heavy construction, cabinetwork, furniture, crossties, tool handles, carts, rulers, and shuttles.

Appearance: evergreen tree 15 m (50 ft) tall and 50 cm (20 in) in diameter in cultivation, becoming over 30 m (100 ft) in forests with dense round crown. **Bark:** dark brown. **Branches:** spreading; branchlets stout, gray or brown, rough, widely forking. **Leaves:** usually in clusters near end of branchlets, alternate, 8–12 cm (3.2–4.8 in) long, broadest at middle, with ***sharp-pointed*** (rarely blunt) tip and narrow or wedge-shaped base, entire and somewhat thickened margins, smooth, shiny dark green above, dull and smooth beneath, the leafstalks slender, 0.5–2 cm (0.2–0.8 in) long, yellow-green covered with fine brown hairs. **Flowers:** produced singly in the junctions of leaves, on brown, finely hairy stalks, with 6 calyx lobes 4–6 mm (0.2 in) long, ***6 white petals 5–8 mm (0.2–0.3 in) long,*** 6 stamens opposite corolla lobes. **Fruits:** berry, rounded or egg-shaped, 3–8 cm (1.2–3.2 in) in diameter, fleshy with rough brown skin, sweet with milky juice; seeds 1 to several, flattened, broadest at base or at middle, shiny black or brown, about 1.5 cm (0.6 in) long, with whitish scar on inner edge.

The Ebony Family

Ebenaceae

There are approximately 275 species of trees and shrubs in the ebony family, mostly distributed in tropical regions of the world with only a few species extending into temperate zones. Of the 7 genera known in the family, only 1 reaches North America. Two species of the most important genus, known as persimmons or ebony in tropical countries, occur in North America.

This family is of economic importance for the valuable wood produced by many of the tropical species, and the large edible fruits produced by 2 of the temperate species. The dark-colored wood is hard and takes a high polish and is popular in cabinets and as decorative panels on interior furnishings. The delicious fruits are widely cultivated in the Orient and in California. The fruits also serve as a valuable food for many species of wildlife.

Members of this family are trees or shrubs with hard wood. The leaves are simple, alternate, deciduous to evergreen. Individual trees are usually either male or female. Flowers have a 3- to 7-lobed calyx that persists on the fruits, 3 to 7 petals that are fused except at the tips; in male flowers the stamens are usually 2 to 3 times as numerous as the petals; in female flowers a single pistil is present. The fruits are berries, usually fleshy, and contain 1 to several large, flattened seeds.

The Persimmon Genus

Diospyros L.

There are about 175 species in this genus widely distributed in the tropical and subtropical regions of the Americas, Africa, and especially Asia. Many of the species are valuable for their edible fruits, hard wood, or attractive appearance. The Kaki (*Diospyros kaki*), a persimmon from China and Japan, has a delicious fruit the size of an orange, which is sometimes sold in supermarkets. The Kaki are cultivated in California and thus are more commonly encountered on the West Coast. The two species native to North America are the common persimmon (*D. virginiana*), a tall tree with orange to purple fruits, and the Texas persimmon (*D. texana*), a smaller tree or shrub with black fruits.

The wood is dark colored, almost black in some tropical members, very hard and strong, and it can be finely polished. Since large persimmons are rare in North America, the commercial value is limited. Yet the wood is used for tool handles and turned wooden wares. Cabinets and furniture are made from some of the larger tropical members. Both North American species are important food sources for many kinds of wildlife.

Persimmons and other members of this genus are trees or large shrubs with deciduous or evergreen leaves. Buds at the ends of the branchlets are absent, but the lateral buds are broadest near the base and covered with 3 to 4 overlapping scales. The leaves are alternate, simple, and often leathery. Flowers are either male or female and are produced in the junctions of the leaves with the younger branchlets. Male flowers are produced in few-flowered clusters; calyx 4-lobed, petals 4-lobed, the lobes fused together to form a bell-shaped tube; stamens 8 to 16. Female flowers are produced singly in the leaf-and-branchlet junctions; with 4 calyx lobes, 4 fused petals, and a single pistil. The fruit is a large, juicy berry containing 1 to 10 flattened seeds.

Key to Persimmon Species

A. Leaves 7–13 cm (2.8–5.1 in) long, 3.5–8 cm (1.4–3.2 in) wide; fruits 2–6 cm (0.8–2.4 in) in diameter, orange to orange-purple; trees of eastern and southeastern U.S. **Common persimmon, p. 539**

B. Leaves 2–5 cm (0.8–2 in) long, 1–2.8 cm (0.4–1.1 in) wide; fruits 2–2.5 cm (0.8–1 in) in diameter, black; trees of Texas and northeastern Mexico **Texas persimmon, p. 541**

Common Persimmon

Common Persimmon   *Diospyros virginiana* L.

This tree is primarily a southern species but does occur as far north as southern New York and Connecticut. It is commonly seen growing along roadsides, fence rows, edges of fields, and on rocky hillsides. The best growth and largest persimmon trees are found in the Mississippi River Valley in rich bottomlands. The trees do not occur along the main range of the Appalachian Mountains. They grow in disturbed areas and in deciduous woodlands along with sycamore, red maple, sugar maple, cedar elm, yellow poplar, and several of the oaks and hickories.

These are slow-growing trees that produce small, but attractive bell-shaped flowers in spring. The large fleshy fruits mature by the end of the growing season. Persimmon fruits are a valuable food source to wildlife including whitetail deer, raccoons, foxes, skunks, many birds, and small rodents. People gather and eat the fruits after the skin has wrinkled and the pulp has become mushy, usually after the first frost. Otherwise, the fruit is so bitter that it causes a person's lips to pucker.

The dark-brown wood is very strong, very hard, and heavy. But it is not used commercially because it yields an inferior grade of lumber.

Appearance: large shrub, or small to medium-size tree 5–20 m (16–66 ft) tall, rarely

Common Persimmon

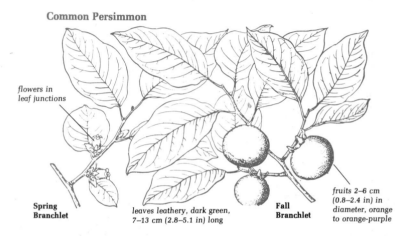

flowers in leaf junctions

Spring Branchlet

leaves leathery, dark green, 7–13 cm (2.8–5.1 in) long

Fall Branchlet

fruits 2–6 cm (0.8–2.4 in) in diameter, orange to orange-purple

taller, with a broad rounded crown; trunk usually straight, short, soon branching, to 0.8 m (2.6 ft) in diameter, rarely larger. **Bark:** moderately thick, 2–2.5 cm (0.8–1 in), developing short, thick, square blocks, dark gray to grayish-brown. **Branches:** stout, spreading; branchlets slender, light brown when young turning darker with age, smooth. **Winter buds:** terminal bud absent, lateral buds 2–4 mm (about 0.1–0.2 in) long, broadest near the base and tapering to a pointed tip, covered with 2 overlapping, dark reddish-brown scales. **Leaves:** alternate, deciduous, *7–13 cm (2.8–5.1 in) long, 3.5–8 cm (1.4–3.2 in) wide,* broadest near the base or near the middle, rounded at the base and abruptly pointed at the tip, the *margin entire, becoming leathery, dark green, shiny, and smooth above,* paler and smooth to slightly hairy on the lower surface; the leafstalks stout, 7–10 mm (0.3–0.4 in) long, usually hairy. **Flowers:** *male and female flowers on separate trees,* produced along the branchlets at the base of the leaves; male flowers 2 to 3 clustered, stalked, the corolla tubular, 1–1.4 cm (0.4–0.6 in) long, containing 8 stamens; *female flowers solitary, stalked, the corolla urn-shaped, 1.8–2.1 cm (0.7–0.9 in) long, greenish-yellow to cream-white,* with a single pistil inside the corolla. **Fruits:** *globe-shaped, 2–6 cm (0.8–2.4 in) in diameter, fleshy, orange to orange-purple,* the smooth skin becoming wrinkled at maturity, ripe at the end of first growing season, the fruit short-stalked and enclosed at the base by the persistent, thick, leathery calyx. **Seeds:** *flattened, uniformly wide along the sides and rounded at the ends, 1.2–2 cm (0.5–0.8 in) long,* reddish-brown.

Texas Persimmon

Diospyros texana Scheele

The Texas persimmon is also known as the capote or black persimmon. This scrubby tree grows mainly in central and Trans-Pecos Texas, south into northeastern Mexico. It occurs in the moist rich soils of river valleys and borders of prairies but sometimes can be found on dry rocky mesas and isolated canyons.

The small creamy white bell-shaped flowers bloom in spring on branches of the previous year when the leaves have grown about one-third of their length. The black sweet fruit ripens in August. A black dye can be obtained from the fruits. Despite its limited range, Texas persimmon is important to wildlife. Whitetail deer browse the leaves, while the ring-tailed cat, opossum, and the hog-nose skunk eat the fruits.

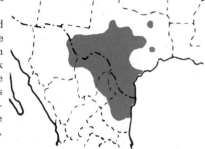

The heavy wood is black, sometimes streaked with yellow, and takes a handsome polish. It is used to make tool handles, engravers blocks, and small lathe work. Although the wood resembles that of tropical ebony trees, in the same genus, it is not as strong or as resilient.

Texas Persimmon

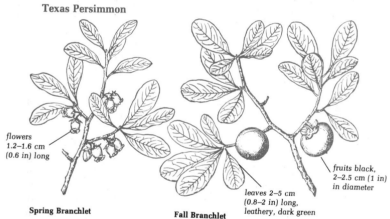

flowers
1.2–1.6 cm
(0.6 in) long

fruits black,
2–2.5 cm (1 in)
in diameter

leaves 2–5 cm
(0.8–2 in) long,
leathery, dark green

Spring Branchlet

Fall Branchlet

Appearance: small to medium-size tree 10–16 m (32–53 ft) tall, with a narrowly rounded crown; trunk usually straight, often soon branching, to 50 cm (20 in) in diameter. **Bark:** smooth, the outer layers peeling off to expose the smooth gray inner bark, light reddish gray. **Branches:** stout, erect, numerous; branchlets, slender, often crooked, hairy and ash gray when young, becoming smooth to lightly hairy by the end of the first season and eventually brown and marked with pale pores and leaf scars with age. **Winter buds:** blunt, 1–1.4 mm (less than 0.1 in) long, covered with rusty hairy scales. **Leaves:** alternate, *late deciduous to almost persistent, 2–5 cm (0.8–2 in) long, 1–2.8 cm (0.4–1.1 in) wide, usually broadest above the middle to uniformly wide,* abruptly tapering at the base, rounded, blunt or slightly notched at the tip, the margin entire, *leathery,* dark green, smooth to slightly hairy above, hairy beneath; the leafstalks short, thick, hairy. **Flowers:** male flowers in 1- to 3-flowered clusters on slender drooping hairy stems, the calyx 2–4 mm (0.1–0.2 in) long with 5 lobes, the lobes broadest at the base or lance-shaped, curved backward after the flower opens, petals much longer, creamy white, narrowed below the 5 short spreading lobes, each lobe with fringed margins; stamens 16, shorter than the petals and arranged in 2 rows; the female flowers occurring alone or in pairs on wider club-shaped stalks, calyx 6–8 mm (0.2–0.3 in) long, with silky, uniformly wide lobes, the petals twice as long, 9–12 mm (0.3–0.5 in) wide, with short spreading lobes, with a single pistil. **Fruits:** *a rounded berry, 2–2.5 cm (0.8–1 in) in diameter,* surrounded at the base with a large, thick, leathery calyx, *the outer skin of the fruit tough, black* at maturity, the inner fleshy part thin, sweet, and juicy; seeds 3 to 8 per fruit, triangular, 6–8 mm (0.2–0.3 in) long, somewhat flattened, with a bright red, shiny seed coat.

The Storax Family
Styracaceae

The storax family contains 6 genera and approximately 100 species mostly of tropical shrubs and trees. They are confined to North and South America, the Mediterranean region, eastern Asia, and the Malay Archipelago. Only 2 genera, the snowbells (*Styrax*) and the silverbells (*Halesia*), are native to North America.

Members of this family are of some economic importance because they produce a fragrant exudate known as balsams that are rich in benzoic acid (used as food preservative and in medicine) and storax, a liquid balsam (used as an expectorant and as an ingredient in perfume). These are obtained from the inner bark of species from the Mediterranean region and the Malay region. Many other species have attractive leaves and showy flowers. As a result, they are sometimes planted in gardens and parks. The trees are of little or no value to wildlife.

Most of the species of this family have reddish-brown bark and simple, alternate leaves that are usually covered with star-shaped hairs on the lower surface. The flowers are bisexual, showy, and produced singly or arranged in clusters. The calyx and corolla are usually 4- to 8-parted, stamens twice as many as the petals, and with a single pistil. The fruit is dry to fleshy, thick-walled, and with a 1-seeded, bony stone.

Key to Storax Genera

A. Flowers produced in short, hanging, few-flowered clusters along the branchlets; each flower generally with 5 calyx lobes and 5 petals; fruits long, 2 or 4 celled, winged
Silverbell, p. 542

Bigleaf Snowbell

B. Flowers produced in elongated clusters usually at the ends of the branchlets; each flower with 4 calyx lobes and 4 petals; fruits rounded, 1 celled
Snowbell, p. 546

The Silverbell Genus
Halesia L.

This small genus, along with many others, demonstrates the strong relationship between the trees and shrubs of North America and of China. There are 3 species in the eastern and southeastern U.S. and a single species in China. Because of their clusters of showy white flowers, they are sometimes planted as ornamentals. They are of little value for their wood, and they are of limited value to wildlife.

Silverbells are deciduous shrubs or trees usually with a scaly, reddish-brown bark. The branchlets and leaves are covered when young with star-shaped hairs. The leaves are alternate, large, toothed along the margin, and with a distinct stalk. The flowers are produced in hanging, few-flowered clusters along the branchlets. They are white, showy, bell-shaped, and with a 4- or 5-parted calyx and corolla. The fruits are dry, elongated, and with 2 or 4 lengthwise wings.

Key to Silverbell Species

A. Flowers with shallowly lobed petals (corolla), the lobes only one-fourth to one-third as long as the joined part of the petals; fruits with 4 lengthwise wings; trees of southeastern U.S.

Carolina Silverbell

    1. Fruits 3–5 cm (1.2–2 in) long, broadly winged; flower petals 1.5–2.5 cm (0.6–1 in) long; trees or shrubs of southeastern U.S.

                Carolina silverbell, p. 543

    2. Fruits 2–2.8 cm (0.8–1.1 in) long, narrowly winged; flower petals 1–1.5 cm (0.4–0.6 in) long; trees or shrubs of the southeastern U.S.

                Little silverbell, p. 544

B. Flowers with deeply lobed petals (corolla), the lobes as long or longer than the joined part of the petals; fruits with 2 lengthwise wings; trees of the Coastal Plain of the southeastern U.S.

                Two-winged silverbell, p. 545

Two-Winged Silverbell

Carolina Silverbell

Halesia carolina L.

This attractive shrub or small tree occurs on wooded slopes and along streambanks in the mountains from Virginia to Florida, west to Oklahoma. It grows in association with loblolly, shortleaf, and white pine, southern red oak, hickories, red maple, serviceberry, blackgum, and white oak. In the understory it is associated with American elder, sweetleaf, and hawthorn.

Carolina silverbell has a moderate rate of growth and lives about 100 years. It flowers in spring and bears handsome tan fruit in autumn that contrasts against the yellow leaves. There are 2 varieties of this species: the mountain silverbell (*Halesia carolina* variety *monticola*), which grows to 30 m (100 ft) tall bearing flowers that are 2.5 cm (1 in) long and a 4-winged fruit. The

Carolina Silverbell

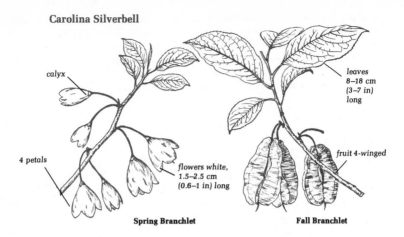

calyx

leaves
8–18 cm
(3–7 in)
long

4 petals

flowers white,
1.5–2.5 cm
(0.6–1 in) long

fruit 4-winged

Spring Branchlet

Fall Branchlet

typical carolina silverbell (*H. carolina* variety *carolina*) rarely grows over 10 m (33 ft) tall and is often shrubby, with smaller flowers and fruits. Carolina silverbell is not an important food source for wildlife, though the gray squirrel often dens in it.

The wood is soft, close-grained, and brown. Occasionally a tree will grow large enough for sawtimber, and is cut and used for paneling and cabinetwork. Since the trees are attractive, due to the showy flowers, they are often cultivated in the northern U.S. and Europe.

Appearance: wide-spreading shrub or small tree with rounded crown, rarely over 12 m (40 ft), except for variety *monticola*, which grows to 30 m (100 ft); trunk straight, 12–27 cm (5–11 in) in diameter, or in larger trees to 0.9 m (2.9 ft). **Bark:** thin, 8–12 mm (0.3–0.5 in) thick, separating into flat scales, slightly ridged, reddish-brown. **Branches:** stout, curving upwards; branchlets slender, thickly hairy at first, becoming smooth and grayish brown. **Winter buds:** 3–4 mm (0.1 in) long, egg-shaped, pointed at tip, covered with overlapping scales, dark red and hairy. **Leaves:** alternate, simple, deciduous, broadest at or above the middle, mostly 8–18 cm (3–7 in) long, 4–10 cm (1.6–4 in) wide, tapering to a pointed tip, rounded or gradually narrowed at the base, toothed along the margin, at first densely hairy above, becoming dark yellow-green and smooth, paler and smooth below, with a papery texture; leafstalks slender, 1–2 cm (0.4–0.8 in) long. **Flowers:** 2- to 5-flowered in slender, drooping clusters, each flower with a stalk 1–2 cm (0.4–0.8 in) long, hairy, calyx 5–6 mm (0.2 in) long with smooth, spreading, triangular, sharp-pointed lobes, *petals 1.5–2.5 cm (0.6–1 in) long, fused into a bell shape with short, smooth, rounded petals*, 10 to 16 stamens, and a single pistil, **Fruits:** oblong to broadest above the middle, longer than broad, *3–5 cm (1.2–2 in) long, 4-winged*, remaining on branches into the winter.

Little Silverbell   *Halesia parviflora* Michx.

Little silverbell is a small tree or shrub that is native to the Coastal Plain from southern South Carolina to northern Florida, Alabama, and eastern Mississippi.

It grows best on wooded slopes and floodplains, and also in dry, sandy soils. This silverbell flowers earlier than the other silverbells, beginning in March and continuing into April. The fruits mature by September or October. This species resembles the Carolina silverbell but can be distinguished by the narrower wings on the fruits.

Little silverbell is a small tree or shrub to 9 m (30 ft) and with thick, dark bark divided into deep furrows and roughened ridges. The simple leaves are usually broadest near the middle, 5–10 cm (2–4 in) long, 2.5–5 cm (1–2 in) wide, irregularly wavy and finely toothed along the margin. The small clusters of 2 or 3 drooping flowers are produced along the branchlets. Each flower is stalked, with a small green calyx, 4 *white petals fused into a bell shape, 1–1.5 cm (0.4–0.6 in) long.* The *narrowly 4-winged fruits are 2–2.8 cm (0.8–1.1 in) long.*

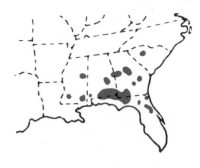

Little Silverbell

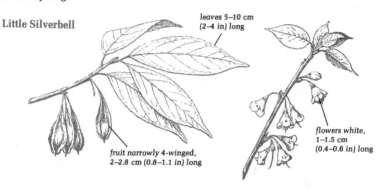

leaves 5–10 cm (2–4 in) long

fruit narrowly 4-winged, 2–2.8 cm (0.8–1.1 in) long

flowers white, 1–1.5 cm (0.4–0.6 in) long

Two-Winged Silverbell
Halesia diptera Ellis

Smaller than the Carolina silverbell, this tree or shrub grows in damp woods and swampy areas along the Coastal Plain from South Carolina to northwestern Florida and west to Texas.

The showy white clusters of flowers appear in spring and are followed by the distinctive 2-winged fruits in autumn. This species does not produce as many flowers as the other silverbell species, but is still an attractive ornamental. The wood is soft but strong, dense, and light brown and is not used commercially because of the tree's small size.

Two-winged silverbell grows to 10 m (33 ft) tall and has a thin bark that is ridged and peels off in thin, reddish-brown scales. The simple, alternate leaves are broad, widest at or above the middle, 6–12 cm (2.4–5 in) long, 4–10 cm (1.6–4 in) wide, irregularly toothed along the margins, and hairy when young but becoming smooth with age. The simple 3- to 6-flowered clusters of stalked flowers on a short axis are produced along the branchlets. Each *flower* has a small calyx, *large, white petals fused near the base into a bell shape.* The *broadly 2-winged fruit is 3.5–5 cm (1.4–2 in) long.* (See art on next page.)

Two-Winged Silverbell

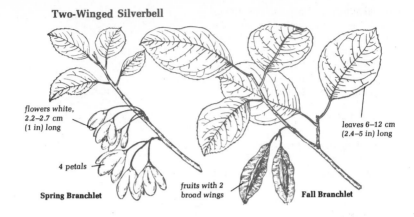

flowers white, 2.2–2.7 cm (1 in) long

leaves 6–12 cm (2.4–5 in) long

4 petals

Spring Branchlet

fruits with 2 broad wings

Fall Branchlet

The Snowbell Genus

Styrax L.

There are approximately 100 species of snowbells in tropical and warm temperate regions of Europe, Asia, and the Americas. The 4 North American species are shrubby, although 1 does reach tree size in the southeastern U.S. Several members of this genus have attractive flowers and are sometimes seen in parks and botanical gardens.

This genus is made up of trees or shrubs with alternate, simple, evergreen or deciduous leaves. The showy, white flowers are produced in unbranched, elongated spikes at the ends of the branchlets. Flowers consist of a 5-lobed calyx, 5 spreading petals (rarely more), 10 stamens (rarely more or less), and a single pistil. The fruits are almost rounded, dry to fleshy, irregularly splitting along 3 or 4 valves, 1 or 2 seeded.

Bigleaf Snowbell

Styrax grandifolia Ait.

This fragrant shrub or small tree is found in well-drained, rich woodlands or ravines and river bluffs along the Coastal Plain from Virginia to Florida and west to Texas. It has white flower clusters, hard, rounded, brown fruit in autumn, and large wide leaves (hence "bigleaf"). It is of little value to wildlife and is too small to be used for timber.

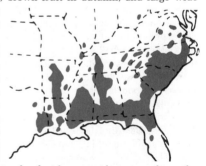

Appearance: shrub or tree to 12 m (40 ft) with a round-topped crown; trunk tall, straight to 2.4 m (7.8 ft) in diameter. **Bark:** thin, 0.8–1.3 cm (0.3–0.5 in) thick, close, smooth, dark red-brown. **Branches:** short, spreading; branchlets slender, yellowish, and densely hairy turning light or dark chestnut brown. **Winter buds:** tiny, 2–4 mm (0.1 in) long, pointed at the tip, 2–3 buds at the leaf scars. **Leaves:** alternate, simple, deciduous, widest at or above the middle, 6–18 cm (2.4–7 in) long, up to 12.7 cm (5 in) wide, pointed or rounded at the tip, narrowed toward base, finely toothed or nearly entire along the margin, dark green and smooth on the upper surface, pale green or grayish beneath, covered with star-shaped hairs; the leafstalks 4 mm (0.2 in) long, hairy. **Flowers:** fragrant, *in slender,*

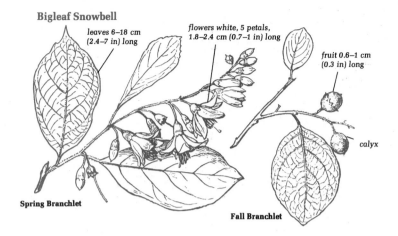

Bigleaf Snowbell

leaves 6–18 cm
(2.4–7 in) long

flowers white, 5 petals,
1.8–2.4 cm (0.7–1 in) long

fruit 0.6–1 cm
(0.3 in) long

calyx

Spring Branchlet

Fall Branchlet

sometimes leafy racemes 5–12 cm (2–4.8 in) long, *bearing up to 12 flowers,* each flower on a slender hairy stalk 4 mm (0.2 in) long with leaf-like bracts; *calyx is 5-lobed,* white petals with spreading narrow lobes 1.8–2.4 cm (0.7–1 in) long, when open about 2–2.5 cm (0.8–1 in) across; 10 stamens, as long as the petals, united near their bases; 1 pistil. **Fruits:** *rounded to broadest near the tip, 6–10 mm (0.3 in) long,* densely covered with short hairs, surrounded on the lower portion by the persistent calyx lobes; seed egg-shaped, dark orange-brown.

The Sweetleaf Family Symplocaceae

This family is composed of a single genus, the sweetleaf trees, with many species occurring in tropical regions of the Americas and Asia. Members of this family once grew in Europe.

The Sweetleaf Genus *Symplocos* Jacquin

This genus contains 275 to 300 species of trees and shrubs native to warmer regions of the Americas, Asia, and Australia. Only 1 species occurs in North America, the common sweetleaf of the southeastern U.S. The different sweetleafs are of little economic importance but have been used to produce a yellow dye. The bark and leaves were once used in medicines. The leaves are sweet tasting, making them attractive to browsing wildlife.

Members of this genus are trees or shrubs with alternate, simple, generally leathery, entire to toothed leaves. Flowers are yellow, usually bisexual or with male, female, and bisexual flowers. These flowers are produced in clusters at the tip or along the sides of the branchlets in the junctions of the leaves. Each flower has a bell-shaped calyx with 5 lobes, 5 petals joined near their bases, numerous stamens joined to the petals, and a single pistil. The fruit consists of an outer fleshy part surrounding a hard, bony, 1-seeded stone.

Common Sweetleaf *Symplocos tinctoria* (L.) L'Her.

The common sweetleaf is a small slender tree that occurs in moist rich soils, often in the shade of dense woods or along swamp borders. It grows from sea level to 1,200 m (4,000 ft) altitude along the Coastal Plain from Delaware to Florida, west to Texas and Oklahoma. In warmer areas, this species tends to be almost evergreen — its leaves from the previous season remaining through the spring flowering period and the unfolding of new leaves.

Though rarely planted as an ornamental, the common sweetleaf has attractive dense clusters of bright-yellow to creamy-yellow flowers in spring. The cylinder-shaped fruits mature in the summer or early autumn. The leaves are greedily consumed by cattle and horses and are browsed also by whitetail deer.

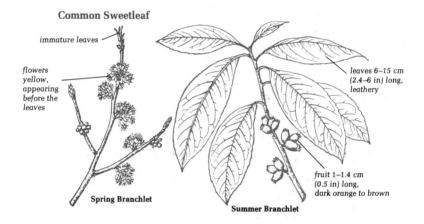

Common Sweetleaf

immature leaves

flowers yellow, appearing before the leaves

Spring Branchlet

leaves 6–15 cm (2.4–6 in) long, leathery

fruit 1–1.4 cm (0.5 in) long, dark orange to brown

Summer Branchlet

Appearance: shrub or small tree sometimes to 10 m (33 ft) with an open, spreading crown; trunk short, soon branching, to 30 cm (12 in) in diameter. **Bark:** 8–12 mm (0.3–0.5 in) thick, sometimes divided into narrow fissures and roughed by warty growths, gray to reddish-gray. **Branches:** slender, curving upward; branchlets slender, light green and hairy at first or smooth and covered with a few hairs, turning reddish-brown to reddish-gray, and becoming smooth and finally turning brown. **Winter buds:** 8–12 mm (0.4 in) long, broadest near the base, sharp-pointed at the tip, covered with overlapping light green, smooth or hairy scales that are fringed on their margins. **Leaves:** *alternate, simple, 6–15 cm (2.4–6 in) long, 2–6 cm (0.8–2.4 in) wide,* broadest near or above the middle, gradually tapering at the base, pointed to long-pointed at the tip, entire to shallowly and occasionally toothed along the margin, leathery, dark green and shiny above, paler and yellowish hairy beneath; the leafstalks stout, 8–12 mm (0.4 in) long. **Flowers:** produced in 6- to 12-flowered clusters, covered with orange to orange-brown scales, fragrant, appearing before the leaves appear; individual flowers bisexual, composed of 5 calyx lobes fused to form a cup, 2–2.5 mm (0.1 in) long, *5 petals, 6–8 mm (0.3 in) long, joined only at their bases, white;* stamens numerous, and a single pistil. **Fruits:** *egg-shaped, 10–14 mm (0.5 in) long, dark orange to brown,* with a thin fleshy outer part surrounding a 1-seeded stone.

The Joewood Family
Theophrastaceae

This is a small family of 5 genera and 70 species of the tropical regions of the Americas. Only 1 species grows in North America and that one, joewood (*Jaquinia keyensis*), occurs only in southern Florida. This joewood also is native to the West Indies. Other than those occasionally planted as ornamentals, most members of this family are of little natural or economic importance.

The trees and shrubs have watery juices and usually alternate, simple, leathery, evergreen leaves. The flowers are usually bisexual or with separate male and female flowers produced in branched clusters. Each flower has 5, almost free, calyx lobes; 5 petals united near the base to form an urn- to funnel-shaped flower, with 5 stamens and 5 sterile stamens, and a single pistil. The fruit is generally a berry.

The Jacquinia Genus
Jacquinia L.

This is a small genus of perhaps 25 species of trees and shrubs of tropical America and a single species, the joewood, in southern Florida. The common and scientific name of this genus honors the Austrian botanist, Nicholas Joseph Jacquin.

Jacquinias can be readily distinguished from other genera of this family by the opposite (rather than alternate) leaves. Entire along the margins, the leaves are thick, usually dotted with many tiny transparent glands. Flowers are produced in erect, branched clusters; each flower has 5 persistent calyx lobes, 5 petals, 5 stamens, and a tiny pistil. The fruits are rounded to egg-shaped berries.

Joewood
Jacquinia keyensis Mez

The joewood is limited to coastal hammocks in southern Florida southward over the Florida Keys to the Bahama Islands, Cuba, and Jamaica. The attractive yellowish-green leaves and small fragrant leaves make this species an attractive ornamental.

Flowering and fruiting occurs throughout most of the year. The rich brown wood is distinctively marked by darker rays extending across the trunk in cross section. This wood is hard, heavy, very close grained, but the trees are seldom large enough to be economically important.

Appearance: shrub or tree to 6 m (20 ft), with a dense, rounded crown; trunk straight, to 25 cm (10 in) in diameter. **Bark:** thin, smooth, blue-gray with pale patches. **Branches:** stout, rigid, spreading; branchlets slightly angled, hairy, and yellowish-green when young, becoming rounded, smooth, and reddish-brown or pale gray. **Winter buds:** small, nearly rounded. **Leaves:** *opposite,* alternate, or whorled in dense clusters near the ends of the branchlets, *3–7 cm (1.2–2.8 in) long, 1.5–3.5 cm (0.6–1.4 in) wide,* broadest above the middle to wedge-shaped, rounded or notched at the tip, tapering to the base, entire, *thick, leathery, gland-dotted,* yellowish-green; the leafstalks short, stout. **Flowers:** produced in erect clusters 5–7.5 cm (2–3 in) long at the ends of the branchlets; each *flower* with *5 rounded calyx lobes, 5 spreading pale-yellow petals, 5 stamens,* 5 sterile stamens, and a tiny, central pistil. **Fruits:** *berry, rounded, 8–10 mm (0.4 in) in diameter, orange-red,* with a leathery skin, and containing several light-brown seeds.

mm
cm 1 2 3 4 5 6 7 8 9 10 11
in 1 2 3 4

Joewood

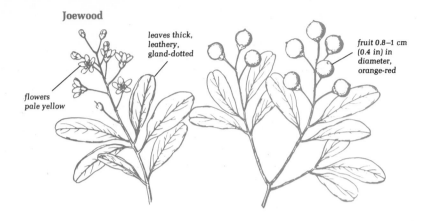

leaves thick,
leathery,
gland-dotted

fruit 0.8–1 cm
(0.4 in) in
diameter,
orange-red

flowers
pale yellow

The Myrsine Family

Myrsinaceae

This is a large family of over 1,000 species distributed among approximately 32 genera, most of tropical and subtropical regions of the Americas, Africa, Asia, Australia, and New Zealand. Two species in different genera reach into North America in southern and central Florida.

Members of this family are of little economic importance, although some produce edible fruits and others have ornamental value. A well-known introduced species is (*Ardisia crenata*) with attractive dark-green leaves and bright-red fruits. Cuttings of this bush or tree are often used for Christmas decorations.

These shrubs or trees have simple, largely alternate, leaves that are leathery, evergreen, and gland-dotted. Flowers may contain both sexes or be either male or female. They are small and produced in branched clusters. Each flower has 4 to 6 free or fused calyx lobes, 4 to 6 petals fused to form a trumpet-shaped flower, 4 to 6 stamens, and a single pistil. The fruits consist of a fleshy outer part surrounding a hard stony section that contains 1 to several seeds.

Key to Myrsine Genera

A. Flowers produced in many-flowered, branched clusters at the tips of the branchlets; or if in the junctions of the leaves, then long-stalked; trees of Florida **Ardisia, p. 551**

B. Flowers produced in dense, few-flowered branched clusters in the junctions of the leaves, the clusters on short stalks **Rapanea, p. 552**

The Ardisia Genus

Ardisia Sw.

This genus contains approximately 250 species distributed in tropical and subtropical regions of the world. Two species can be found in North America in southern Florida: the native marbleberry (*Ardisia escallonioides*) and a second species, *A. solanacea*, which was introduced from the East Indies. This species has the smaller flower clusters produced in the junctions of the leaves rather than at the tips of the branchlets. Ardisias are not of great economic importance, although some are used as ornamentals because of their attractive leaves and colorful fruits. Others produce edible fruits.

Members of this genus are shrubs or trees with alternate, evergreen leaves that are glandular-dotted on the lower surface. The small flowers are produced in branched, many-flowered clusters, usually at the ends of the branchlets. Each flower is composed of 5 (rarely 4) free calyx lobes; 5 (rarely 4 or 6) white to rose petals, 5 stamens, and a single pistil. The fruit is rounded, dry to slightly fleshy, with a central stony part that encloses a single seed.

Marbleberry *Ardisia escallonioides* Sch. & Dep. ex Schlect. & Cham.

Marbleberry is a well-known, common, small tree of coastal and inland hammocks and pinelands of southern Florida and the Florida Keys. It also occurs in the West Indies, Mexico, and Guatemala. Marbleberry is often found growing in the shade of tall trees, live oaks, and palmetto palms. The trees are either in flower or fruit most of the year. The branchlets usually bend downward under the weight of the large flower clusters or even heavier fruiting clusters. The rich dark wood is hard and heavy, but the trees are not large enough to yield commercial quantities of wood.

Appearance: large shrub or occasionally a small tree to 7.5 m (24.6 ft) tall with a narrow, rounded crown; trunk straight, to 15 cm (6 in) in diameter. **Bark:** thin, 3–4 mm (0.2 in) thick, scaly, light gray to nearly white. **Branches:** slender, upright;

Marbleberry

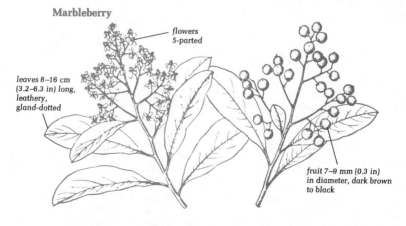

flowers 5-parted

leaves 8–16 cm (3.2–6.3 in) long, leathery, gland-dotted

fruit 7–9 mm (0.3 in) in diameter, dark brown to black

branchlets stout, slightly hairy and rusty brown turning dark brown or grayish-brown by the second year. **Winter buds:** small, 3–8 mm (0.2 in) long, slender, gradually tapering at the tip, reddish-brown. **Leaves:** simple, alternate, ***remaining on the branchlets until the following year, 8–16 cm (3.2–6.3 in) long, 3–5 cm (1.2–2 in) wide,*** narrow, broadest near the base, middle, or above, pointed to rounded at the tip, tapering to a wedge-shaped base, entire along the wavy margin, ***leathery, smooth, gland-dotted, yellow green above,*** paler beneath; the leafstalks stout, 6–12 mm (0.2–0.5 in) long, grooved. **Flowers:** produced in ***dense, many-flowered, terminal, branched clusters;*** each flower with a tiny 5-lobed calyx; 5 petals, white, rounded, fused near the base; 5 stamens, 1 tiny pistil. **Fruits:** rounded, ***7–9 mm (0.3 in) in diameter, dark brown turning shiny black at maturity,*** with a thin skin, a dry, thin fleshy part, and a central hard stone that contains the kidney-shaped seed.

The Rapanea Genus   *Rapanea* Aubl.

This genus contains approximately 160 species widely distributed in the tropical and subtropical regions of the Americas, Asia, and Africa. As with many other tropical groups, Rapanea has 1 species reaching North America and that in Florida.

Members of this genus are shrubs or trees with simple, alternate, evergreen, entire or rarely toothed leaves. The flowers are bisexual or the sexes occur in separate flowers on different trees and are produced in branched clusters in the junctions of the leaves. The small flowers are 4- or 5-parted and usually marked with glandular dots. The fruits are globe-shaped, dry or fleshy, and usually contain a single large seed.

Florida Rapanea   *Rapanea punctata* (Lam.) Lundell

This is a shrub, sometimes a small tree, that grows in hammocks and rivers of southern Florida, north along the eastern coast to central Florida, and in the Florida Keys. It also occurs in the Bahama Islands. Flowering is from winter through spring.

The small greenish flowers are produced along the branchlets in the junctions of the leaves. The fruits ripen during summer and fall. Little is known of its natural history or uses by wildlife. The wood is light brown, hard, and strong, but the trees are too small to be of commercial importance. It is sometimes used for posts.

Appearance: shrub or tree to 6 m (20 ft), with an open irregular crown; trunk short, sometimes crooked, to 15 cm (6 in) in diameter. **Bark:** thin, 2–4 mm (0.1 in) thick, light gray. **Branches:** slender, upright; branchlets slender, sparingly hairy and light reddish-brown. **Winter buds:** not known, probably similar to marbleberry. **Leaves:** simple, alternate, usually crowded near the ends of the branchlets, 6–10 cm (2.4–4 in) long, 1.2–4 cm (0.5–1.6 in) wide, uniformly wide to widest above the middle, rounded to notched at the tip, tapering at the base, ***entire, leathery,*** bright green and shiny above, paler beneath; the leafstalks stout, narrowly winged. **Flowers:** produced ***in short, densely flowered clusters in the junctions of the leaves;*** each ***flower small, 1.5–2.5 mm (to 0.1 in) long, white marked with purple,*** and composed of 5 tiny calyx lobes, fused mid-way; 5 petals, the lobes spreading; 5 stamens, 1 pistil. **Fruits:** in dense, crowded clusters, rounded, ***4–7 mm (0.1–0.3 in) in diameter, dark blue to nearly black,*** with a short, narrow tip, dryish, containing a single seed.

The Rose Family

Rosaceae

The rose family contains approximately 120 genera and 3,600 widely distributed species. They are especially abundant in North America, Europe, and Asia. Many are small herbaceous plants, but others are vines, shrubs, or trees. In our range, 74 species in 10 genera are trees. The exact number of species in this family is difficult to estimate because 2 genera, the hawthorns (*Crataegus*) and the brambles (*Rubus*) are highly variable, readily hybridize, and are difficult to distinguish with certainty.

It is an economically important family because it is a source of food, timber, and wood products. Members of this family are important to wildlife for food and cover. Apple, pears, plums, peaches, apricots, and cherries are some of the foods produced by members of this family. Furniture and cabinet makers value the hard, rich, reddish wood of certain cherry trees. Many species of cherries, crabapples, and plums have been selected and bred for their attractive flowers and are planted in parks, gardens, and along city streets. Several species have been introduced from Europe and Asia for this purpose.

The herbs, shrubs, or trees in this family have alternate, rarely opposite, simple or compound, deciduous to rarely evergreen leaves. The flowers are usually bisexual, with 5, often showy petals, white, pink, or red, numerous stamens, and with 1 or more pistils. Fruits may be dry or fleshy and often do not split open at maturity.

Key to Rose Genera

A. Flower parts (calyx, petals, and stamens) attached below the ovary or ovaries of the pistil; fruits dry or fleshy and cherry-like.

  1. Fruits 1–5, dry, splitting open at maturity.

    a. Leaves opposite, simple or irregularly feather-like compound (pinnate), 10–16 cm (4–6.3 in) long   **Lyontree, p. 554**

    b. Leaves alternate, simple, 4–8 cm (1.6–3.2 in) long   **Vauquelinia, p. 555**

  2. Fruits dry and nut-like or fleshy, not splitting open at maturity.

    a. Fruits dry, hard.

      (1) Leaves simple; petals absent; fruits with a long, feather-like extension   **Mountain mahoganies, p. 556**

      (2) Leaves usually 3- to 5-lobed; petals present, 6–8 mm (0.3 in) long, pale yellow to white; fruits 6–8 mm (0.3 in) long, without a long feather-like appendage   **Cliffrose, p. 560**

    b. Fruits fleshy, containing a hard or bony stone, each stone enclosing a seed   **Cherries, Plums, Peaches, p. 561**
    (Continued)

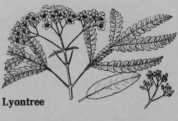

Lyontree

Torrey Vauquelinia

Curlleaf Mountain Mahogany

B. Flower parts (calyx, petals, and stamens) attached above the ovary or ovaries; fruits apple-like.

    1. Leaves compound and feather-like (pinnate)
                                Mountain-ashes, p. 587

    2. Leaves simple.

        a. Trees with deciduous, papery-textured leaves.

American Mountain-Ash

            (1) Flowers produced in once-branched, elongated clusters; ovary and fruits 10-celled in cross section
                                Serviceberries, p. 592

            (2) Flowers produced in rounded or flat topped clusters; ovary and fruits 2–5-celled in cross section.

                (a) Flowers with the styles united; fruits with a papery or leathery center   **Apples, Pears, p. 597**

Saskatoon Serviceberry

                (b) Flowers with the styles distinct; fruits with a bony center
                                Hawthorns, p. 605

        b. Trees with evergreen, thick, leathery leaves
                                  Photina, p. 620

Yellow Hawthorn

The Lyontree Genus   *Lyonothamnus* A. Gray

This consists of only 1 species native to North America on the California coastal islands. It was named for its discoverer, William S. Lyon. The description of the genus is the same as for the species.

Lyontree   *Lyonothamnus floribundus* A. Gray

The lyontree occurs on steep slopes of canyons from 150–600 m (490–2,000 ft) altitude on dry, rocky, and gravelly soils on the California coastal islands of Santa Catalina, San Clemente, Santa Cruz, and Santa Rosa. Lyontree usually grows in pure stands forming small groves.

    The dense flat-topped clusters of white flowers, its strangely varied leaves, and the bark hanging in shreds make this tree a distinctive one, but it is only occasionally planted as an ornamental because of the difficulty of growing it from seeds or cuttings. Lyontree is also known as the Catalina or Santa Cruz ironwood because of its heavy, hard, dense, close-grained wood, which is red with a yellowish-orange tint. This wood would be excellent for cabinets and woodwork if the tree grew more abundantly.

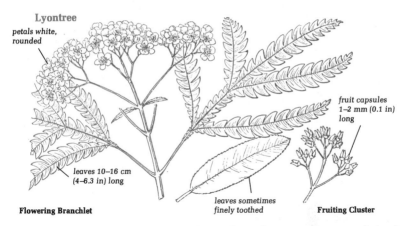

Lyontree

petals white, rounded

fruit capsules 1–2 mm (0.1 in) long

leaves 10–16 cm (4–6.3 in) long

leaves sometimes finely toothed

Flowering Branchlet

Fruiting Cluster

Lyontree is a bush or slender tree to 15 m (50 ft), with a narrow crown, and shredding, dark reddish-brown bark. The ***opposite leaves*** are ***lanced-shaped, 10–16 cm (4–6.3 in) long,*** to 1.7 cm (0.7 in) wide, long-pointed at the tip, entire, finely toothed, or lobed or ***irregularly feather-like, leathery, shiny green above,*** paler and sometimes hairy beneath. Flowers are produced in June or July in ***many-flowered, flat-topped clusters.*** Each flower has a 5-lobed, cup-shaped calyx, 5 rounded, white petals, 15 stamens, and 2 pistils. The fruits are egg-shaped ***capsules 1–2 mm (0.1 in) long.***

The Vauquelinia Genus   Vauquelinia Correa ex Humb. & Bonpl.

This is a small genus of 3 or 4 species native to Arizona and Mexico. Of the two species occurring in Arizona only the Torrey vauquelinia regularly reaches tree size. The few-flowered vauquelinia (V. *pauciflora*) is normally a shrub, but may rarely become a small tree in extreme southeastern Arizona.

Members of this genus are shrubs or trees with scaly bark. The alternate or rarely opposite leaves are toothed, leathery, and evergreen. Flowers are produced in branched clusters; each flower has a 5-parted calyx, 5 white petals, 15 to 25 stamens, and 5 pistils. The fruits are woody, 5-celled capsules.

Torrey Vauquelinia   Vauquelinia californica (Torr.) Sarg.

This species, named for California, actually occurs in southern Arizona, Baja California and Sonora, Mexico. It is usually a shrub, but at elevations near 1,500 m (4,900 ft), it grows to tree size. Torrey vauquelinia grows on grassy slopes or rocky ravines of mountain ranges.

The flowers are produced in spring and the woody fruits mature in autumn. This species is unimportant to wildlife. The hard, close-grained, dark brown wood is not used commercially.

It is a shrub or small tree to 6 m (20 ft) with a slender trunk and reddish-brown bark. The alternate ***leaves*** are simple, ***lance-shaped*** to uniformly wide, ***4–8 cm (1.6–3.2 in) long, 0.6–1.2 cm (0.4 in) wide,*** widely toothed on the margin, ***leathery,***

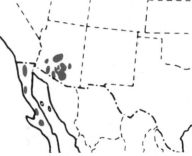

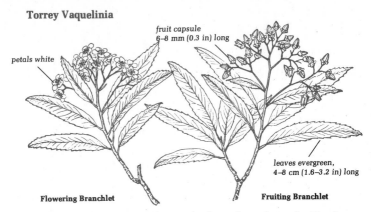

Torrey Vaquelinia

fruit capsule
6–8 mm (0.3 in) long

petals white

leaves evergreen,
4–8 cm (1.6–3.2 in) long

Flowering Branchlet

Fruiting Branchlet

evergreen, bright yellow-green and smooth above, hairy beneath. The flowers are produced in loose branching clusters 5–8 cm (2–3.2 in) across. Each flower has a short 5-lobed calyx, 5 white petals, 15 to 25 stamens, and 5 pistils. The woody, egg-shaped fruit *capsules* are *6–8 mm (0.3 in) long* and often persist until the spring of the following year.

The Mountain Mahogany Genus   Cercocarpus H.B.K.

This is a small group of perhaps 10 species, all native to western and southwestern North America. These thick-leaved, almost evergreen shrubs and trees occur in the dry mountain regions. Interestingly, the flowers always lack petals and the tiny fruits are tipped with a conspicuous tail that is much longer than the enclosed seed. This tail aids in spreading the seeds by wind. The scientific name *Cercocarpus* refers to the long-tailed fruits. The common name, mountain mahogany, is derived from the mahogany-colored, hard wood.

Mountain mahogany is of limited importance, but since it grows on dry, exposed mountain slopes it helps to minimize soil erosion. Antelope, mule deer, and black-tail deer often browse the twigs and leaves, and blue grouse eat the seeds and young leaves. The reddish-brown wood is hard, heavy, and occasionally is used in making small articles.

These shrubs or small trees have stiff branches and thick, almost evergreen leaves. The flowers are bisexual, and composed of a long calyx tube, no petals, 10 to 45 stamens, and a single pistil. The fruit is a narrow, hard nutlet, tipped with a long, hairy, feather-like projection. Each fruit contains a single seed.

Key to Mountain Mahogany Species

A. Leaves entire and with the margins curled under
  Curlleaf mountain mahogany, p. 556
B. Leaves toothed along the margin, or at least some teeth near the tip.

Curlleaf Mountain Mahogany

1. Leaves almost rounded, as wide as long, 3–6 cm (1.2–2.4 in) long, 2.5–5 cm (1–2.2 in) wide; trees of Santa Catalina Island, California
   Catalina mountain mahogany, p. 558

Catalina Mountain Mahogany

2. Leaves broadest above or near the middle, 1–4 cm (0.4–1.6 in) long, 0.5–1.2 cm (0.2–0.5 in) wide.

   a. Flowers 2–5 per cluster; calyx tube 7–10 mm (0.3–0.4 in) long; persistent feather-like style 4–9 cm (1.6–3.5 in) long on fruit; trees of Oregon, California, Arizona, and Baja California
      Birchleaf mountain mahogany, p. 559

Birchleaf Mountain Mahogany

   b. Flowers usually single, rarely in pairs or 3-flowered clusters; calyx tube 4–8 mm (0.1–0.4 in) long; persistent feather-like style 2.5–4 cm (1–1.6 in) long; trees of Texas, New Mexico, and Arizona
      Hairy mountain mahogany, p. 560

Hairy Mountain Mahogany

Curlleaf Mountain Mahogany   *Cercocarpus ledifolius* Nutt.

Curlleaf mountain mahogany ranges from northern Wyoming to southeastern Washington, south to southeastern California, northern Arizona, and western Colorado. It is also native to northern Baja California, Mexico. This species grows at altitudes of 1,500–2,700 m (4,900–8,900 ft) on dry, gravelly slopes and is associated with several oaks, pinyon, yellow, and lodgepole pine, aspen, and different spruces and firs. Pure stands sometimes occur.

This is a slow-growing shrub or twisted, small tree that provides both cover and browse for deer. The bright clear-red to dark-brown wood is extremely hard and so dense that it will not float in water. It makes excellent fuel, giving off intense heat while burning for a long time.

Appearance: shrub or small tree to 12 m (40 ft), with a compact, rounded crown; trunk short, straight or twisted, to 75 cm (30 in) in diameter. **Bark:** to 2.5 cm (1 in) thick, becoming deeply furrowed and scaly, reddish-brown. **Branches:** stout, spreading, twisted; branchlets stout, hairy when young, becoming smooth, often covered with whitish bloom, becoming silvery gray to dark brown with age. **Leaves:** alternate, simple, persisting until the second season, narrowly lance-shaped to uniformly wide, 1.5–3 cm (0.6–1.2 in) long, 8–17 mm (0.3–0.7 in) wide, pointed at the tip, wedge-shaped at the base, leathery, fragrant, ***entire and curled at the margin,*** dark green above, paler and hairy beneath; leafstalks short, 3–4 mm (0.2 in) long. **Flowers:** produced singly in the junctions of the leaves; each flower with a narrow calyx tube

Curlleaf Mountain Mahogany

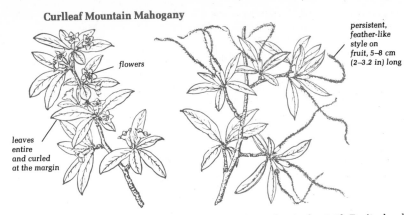

flowers

leaves
entire
and curled
at the margin

persistent,
feather-like
style on
fruit, 5–8 cm
(2–3.2 in) long

4–9 cm (1.6–3.6 in) long, no petals, 20 to 30 stamens, and a single pistil. **Fruits:** hard, narrow, rounded, 5–7 mm (0.3 in) long, tipped with the persistent, *feather-like style 5–8 cm (2–3.2 in) long.*

Catalina Mountain Mahogany   *Cercocarpus traskiae* Eastw.

This rare North American tree is native only to the steep mountain slopes of the Salte Verde Canyon on Santa Catalina Island. This species is in danger of becoming extinct because of its restricted range and because of the overbrowsing by goats that were in-

troduced to the island. It flowers in March and is followed by the development of the "long-tailed" fruits by summer.

Catalina mountain mahogany is a small tree to 7 m (23 ft) with a twisting trunk with wide-spreading branches. The alternate, simple *leaves are nearly circular to broadest above the middle, 3–6 cm (1.2–2.4 in) long, 2.5–5 cm (1–2.2 in) wide, coarsely toothed along the upper half of the margin,* leathery, dark green and hairy to almost smooth above, paler and hairy

Catalina Mountain Mahogany

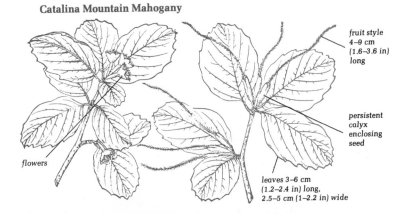

fruit style
4–9 cm
(1.6–3.6 in)
long

persistent
calyx
enclosing
seed

flowers

leaves 3–6 cm
(1.2–2.4 in) long,
2.5–5 cm (1–2.2 in) wide

beneath. The flowers are produced singly or in few-flowered clusters; each flower is 8–10 mm (0.4 in) long, petals absent, 10 to 30 stamens, and a single pistil. The fruits are small, narrow, cylinder-shaped, and tipped with a feather-like style 4–9 cm (1.6–3.6 in) long.

Birchleaf Mountain Mahogany *Cercocarpus betuloides* Nutt.

Birchleaf mountain mahogany is a highly variable species occurring from western Oregon south to Baja California, Mexico, and east to central Arizona. It usually occurs in dry, rocky slopes and washes from 1,200–3,000 m (4,000–9,900 ft) altitude. It is often found in chaparral vegetation growing with oaks. Varieties of this species are distinguished by leaf shape and teeth.

This is a slow-growing, long-lived tree that is able to survive both drought and fire. Flowering extends from March through May. Blacktail deer, mule deer, elk, and mountain sheep browse the young twigs and leaves. The reddish-brown, hard wood is of little commercial value; Indians once used it to make small implements and prayer sticks.

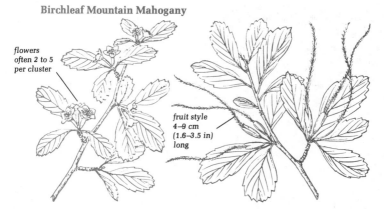

Birchleaf Mountain Mahogany

flowers often 2 to 5 per cluster

fruit style 4–9 cm (1.6–3.5 in) long

Appearance: shrubs or small trees to 8 m (26 ft) with an open crown; trunk single, straight. **Bark:** thin, smooth, becoming scaly and fissured on older trees, gray to brown. **Branches:** stiff, erect to spreading; branchlets slender but rigid, side branches often spine-like, reddish-brown, hairy becoming smooth with age. **Leaves:** alternate, simple, ***broadest above or near the middle, 1–3 cm (0.4–1.2 in) long, 0.5–1 cm (0.2–0.4 in) wide,*** pointed to rounded at the tip, tapering at the base, finely toothed above the middle, leathery, dark to gray green above, paler and smooth to hairy beneath; leafstalks 6–8 mm (0.3 in) long, stout, densely hairy, becoming smooth. **Flowers:** produced singly or in ***few-flowered clusters*** at the junction of the leaves and branchlets; each flower with a slender calyx tube 7–10 mm (0.3–0.4 in) long, covered with dense white hairs, petals absent, 15 to 25 stamens, and a single pistil. **Fruits:** hard, narrow, rounded, 4–7 mm (0.3 in) long, tipped with the persistent, ***feather-like style, 4–9 cm (1.6–3.5 in) long.***

Hairy Mountain Mahogany   *Cercocarpus breviflorus* A. Gray

Hairy mountain mahogany occurs from Trans Pecos Texas to northern New Mexico and Arizona south to northern Mexico. This species grows on dry rocky mountain ridges and slopes, usually from 1,500–3,000 m (4,900–9,900 ft) elevation. It is charac-terized by tiny flowers and small, narrow leaves with fine-toothed to entire margins.

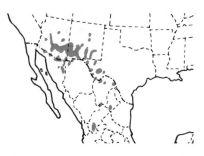

This cercocarpus is a small tree to 7 m (23 ft) with an open crown and a straight trunk covered with shallowly fissured, light reddish-brown scaly bark. The alter-nate, simple leaves are broadest near the tip, 1.2–2.5 cm (0.5–1 in) long, 0.6–1.2 cm (0.3–0.5 in) wide, the margins rolled back, shallowly toothed to entire, leathery, gray-green and hairy to smooth above, paler and hairy beneath. The ***flowers appear*** in spring, sometimes again in August, ***singly,*** in pairs, or rarely in 3-flowered clusters. Each flower consists of a narrow calyx tube 4–8 mm (0.1–0.4 in) long, no petals, 15–25 stamens, and a single pistil. The ***fruits*** are small, hard, 6–8 mm (0.2–0.3 in) long, and ***tipped with the persistent style 2.5–4 cm (1–1.6 in) long*** (resembling a narrow, deli-cate feather).

Hairy Mountain Mahogany

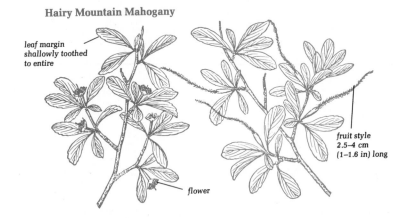

*leaf margin
shallowly toothed
to entire*

*fruit style
2.5–4 cm
(1–1.6 in) long*

flower

The Cliffrose Genus   *Cowania* D. Don

This is a small genus of 4 or 5 species of the dry regions of the southwestern U.S. and Mexico. Only 1, the cliffrose (*Cowania mexicana*), reaches tree size in North America. The wood and fibers of these plants were important to the Hopi Indians who had many practical and medicinal uses for them. Cliffroses are an important browse for mule deer.

Members of this genus are shrubs or small trees with scaly bark and rigid hairy branchlets. The leaves are alternate, simple, 3–5 lobed, leathery, gland-dotted on the upper surface, and almost evergreen to evergreen. The pale yellow to white flowers are produced singly and the fruits are 1-seeded, dry, hard, and produced in clusters.

Cliffrose
Cowania mexicana D. Don

This western member of the rose family is distributed from northern Utah to California and Colorado, south to central Mexico. It grows most abundantly on the southern rim of the Grand Canyon. It is found on rocky slopes and mesas, usually between 1,050–2,400 m (3,400–7,900 ft) in altitude.

Another local common name is quinine-bush, so called because of the bitter taste of the leaves.

The resinous and strongly fragrant flowers appear in early spring, while the silvery-haired fruits mature by October. Hopi Indians have used this species for medicines. They also made arrow shafts from the wood and made sandals, rope, and clothing from the fibers of the bark. Now it is occasionally cultivated in rock gardens. Mule deer and domestic stock browse the leaves.

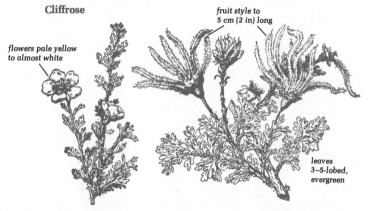

Cliffrose

flowers pale yellow to almost white

fruit style to 5 cm (2 in) long

leaves 3–5-lobed, evergreen

Appearance: shrub or small tree to 8 m (26 ft) with a narrow rounded crown; trunk short. **Bark:** scaly and shredding with age, gray. **Branches:** stiff, erect; branchlets slender, slightly spreading, red, hairy, and glandular, becoming gray or black and smooth with age. **Leaves:** alternate, simple, ***evergreen or nearly so,*** broadest above the middle, 6–15 mm (0.2–0.6 in) long, ***3- to 5-lobed along the margin,*** gland-dotted, leathery, dark green and smooth above, paler and white hairy beneath; leaves on some shoots and flower-bearing branchlets occasionally narrow and entire along the margin; leafstalks short. **Flowers:** produced singly at or near the tips of the branchlets, bisexual, occasionally with male flowers as well; each flower with a stalk 3–8 mm (0.1–0.3 in) long, calyx small, 5-lobed, hairy, 5 petals, broadest above the middle, 6–8 mm (0.2–0.3 in) long, cream, pale yellow to almost white; numerous stamens; 5 to 10 pistils. **Fruits:** maturing in October, 5 to 10 per flower, narrow, ***6–8 mm (0.2–0.3 in) long, leathery, smooth, each topped with a hairy, tail-like style to 5 cm (2 in) long.***

The Cherry, Plum, Peach Genus
Prunus L.

The 125 species of cherries and plums are native to temperate regions of Europe, Asia, and North America. Approximately 30 species are native to North America, of which 17 regularly reach tree size. Members of this genus are cultivated widely for their edible fruits. They are an important food source and provide cover for many species of wildlife. Some of the larger species produce excellent hardwood lumber.

These shrubs or trees have alternate, simple, usually deciduous leaves that are generally toothed along the margin and often with glands on the leafstalks. The attractive white or pink bisexual flowers are produced singly or in few-flowered clusters before or as the leaves are expanding. Each flower is composed of a 5-lobed, bell-, urn-, or tubular calyx, 5 rose to white, nearly rounded petals, 15 to 30 stamens, and a single pistil. The fruits are rounded to egg-shaped, with a thick, dry to juicy pulp that surrounds a hard, round to compressed stone. Inside the stone is the seed.

Key to Cherry, Plum, and Peach Specie

A. Flowers and fruits produced in several to many-flowered, elongated clusters.

   1. Leaves deciduous; flowers produced at the tips of the new shoots of the season.

      a. Leaves with sharp-pointed teeth along the margin; calyx lobes absent on the fruits; common, widespread trees
           Common chokecherry, p. 566

Common Chokecherry

      b. Leaves with blunt-pointed teeth along the margin; calyx lobes persisting on the fruits, common trees of eastern and southwestern North America   **Black cherry, p. 567**

   2. Leaves evergreen; flowers often produced in the junctions of leaf stems with branchlets.

      a. Trees of California and adjacent Mexico.

         (1) Leaves with many, coarse, spine-tipped teeth along the margin, 2.5–6 cm (1–2.4 in) long; trees of California and Baja California   **Hollyleaf cherry, p. 569**

Black Cherry

         (2) Leaves entire or with a few irregular teeth along the margin; trees of the Channel Islands and Baja California
             Catalina cherry, p. 570

      b. Trees of southeastern U.S.

         (1) Petals of the flower smaller than the calyx, creamy white; fruits egg-shaped to broadest at the middle, black; trees of southeastern Coastal Plain
           Carolina laurelcherry, p. 570

Hollyleaf Cherry

(2) Petals of the flower longer than the calyx, white, yellow on the inside; fruits rounded, orange-brown; trees of southern Florida
Myrtle laurelcherry, p. 571

B. Flowers and fruits produced singly or in round to flat-topped clusters (rarely slightly elongated).

Carolina Laurelcherry

1. Fruits with 2 opposite, lengthwise ridges or furrows, often with a bloom and sometimes hairy, stone usually compressed (plums, peaches).

a. Pistils and fruits smooth or nearly so.

(1) Flowers produced singly, occasionally in pairs, rarely in 3s.

(a) Branchlets spiny; leaves 3–5 cm (1.2–2 in) long, with a double row of teeth along the margin; fruits 10–12 mm (0.5 in) in diameter; introduced trees, naturalized in northeastern U.S.
Bullace plum, p. 572

Myrtle Laurelcherry

(b) Branchlets not spiny; leaves 5–10 cm (2–4 in) long, coarsely and irregularly toothed along the margin; introduced trees, widely naturalized **Garden plum, p. 572**

(2) Flowers produced in 3s or more per cluster, rarely less.

(a) Leafstalks commonly without round glands near the base of the leaf blade.

(a1) Fruits red to yellow, 1.8–3 cm (0.7–1.2 in) in diameter.

(a1a) Leaves almost round to broadest near the base, 2.5–7 cm (1–2.8 in) long, heart-shaped at the base; trees of California and Oregon
Klamath plum, p. 573

(a1b) Leaves broadest at or above the middle, 6–10 cm (2.4–4 in) long, rounded to gradually tapering at the base; common trees of eastern and midwestern North America
American plum, p. 574

Klamath Plum

(Continued)

(a2) Fruits dark reddish-purple to almost black, 1–2 cm (0.4–0.8 in) in diamter.

(a2a) Leaves broadest above or near the middle; rounded to heart-shaped at the base; trees of southeastern Coastal Plain and lower Piedmont **Flatwood plum, p. 575**

(a2b) Leaves lance-shaped to broadest near the middle, gradually tapering at the base; trees of Appalachian Mountains **Allegheny plum, p. 575**

(b) Leafstalks commonly with 2 or more (rarely 1) round, red to black glands near the base of the leaf blades.

(b1) Leaves with sharp-pointed teeth along the margin; trees of midwestern and southcentral U.S. **Mexican plum, p. 576**

(b2) Leaves with rounded or blunt teeth along the margin.

(b2a) Leaves dull dark green; trees of northern Midwest and northeastern North America **Canada plum, p. 577**

(b2b) Leaves shiny bright to dark green or yellowish-green.

Flowers 6–10 mm (0.2–0.4 in) in diameter, calyx lobes without tiny glands; leaves 3–8 cm (1.2–3.2 in) long; trees of southeastern and mid-southern U.S. **Chickasaw plum, p. 579**

**Flowers 12–15 mm (0.5–0.6 in) in diameter, calyx lobes*

American Plum

Flatwood Plum

Allegheny Plum

Mexican Plum

Canada Plum

Chickasaw Plum

with tiny glands; leaves 10–15 cm (4–6 in) long.

• Flowers produced on slender 1-year-old branchlets; leaves 10–15 cm (4–6 in) long, dark green; trees of southern Midwest and southwestern U.S. **Hortulan plum, p. 580**

•• Flowers produced on short spur shoots along the branchlets; leaves 6–10 cm (2.4–4 in) long, yellowish-green, trees of midwestern and south central U.S. **Wildgoose plum, p. 580**

Hortulan Plum

Wildgoose Plum

b. Pistils and fruits hairy.

(1) Leaves narrow, lance-shaped, 4–5 times longer than broad, long-pointed at the tip; fruits hairy at maturity.

(a) Fruits rounded, fleshy, not splitting open; leaves often exceeding 10 cm (4 in) in length; introduced trees, sometimes reproducing on their own **Peach, p. 581**

(b) Fruits compressed, dry, hard, splitting open to expose the stone; leaves usually less than 10 cm (4 in) long; introduced trees, sometimes reproducing on their own in California **Almond, p. 582**

(2) Leaves broad, almost round, broadest near the base or middle, short-pointed at the tips.

Desert Apricot

(a) Leaves 1.5–3.2 cm (0.6–1.3 in) long; branchlets often spine-tipped; flowers white; trees native to southern California
Desert apricot, p. 582

(b) Leaves 5–10 cm (2–4 in) long; branchlets not spine-tipped; flowers pinkish to white; introduced trees, reproducing on their own in California **Apricot, p. 583**
(Continued)

2. Fruits rounded or nearly so, without 1 or 2 ridges or furrows, lacking a bloom and always smooth, stone usually rounded (cherries).

a. Fruits with a persistent calyx at the base.

(1) Fruits 2–2.5 cm (0.8–1 in) across, yellow, dark red to almost black, sweet taste; introduced trees, reproducing on their own **Mazzard cherry, p. 583**

(2) Fruits 0.8–1.2 cm (0.3–0.5 in) across, red to reddish black, sour taste; introduced trees, reproducing on their own **Sour cherry, p. 584**

b. Fruits without a persistent calyx at the base.

(1) Leaves rounded or nearly so; introduced trees, reproducing on their own in northeastern North America **Mahaleb cherry, p. 584**

(2) Leaves lance-shaped to broadest near the middle, never more than half as wide as long.

(a) Leaves lance- or scythe-shaped, 8–15 cm (3–6 in) long, 2–3.2 cm (0.8–1.3 in) wide; trees of northern North America, extending southward in mountains **Pin cherry, p. 585**

(b) Leaves broadest near or above the middle, 3–8 cm (1.2–3.2 in) long, 0.8–3.8 cm (0.3–1.5 in) wide; trees of western North America **Bitter cherry, p. 586**

Mazzard Cherry

Mahaleb Cherry

Pin Cherry

Common Chokecherry　　　　　　　*Prunus virginiana* L.

Common chokecherry is widely distributed from Newfoundland, west to British Columbia and southern California, east to Maryland, and south in the mountains to Georgia. This cherry occurs in moist soils in open sites along roadsides, fencerows, and borders of woods. A pioneer species, among the first to establish itself on cutover land or old farmland, common chokecherry grows in association with pin cherry, aspens, paper birch, northern red oak, and red maple.

This is a fast-growing, short-lived tree that flowers in spring, and the fruits ripen in autumn. Grouse, prairie chicken, pheasant, and quail, along with over 25 species of songbirds, eat the fruits. Whitetail deer browse the young twigs and leaves. The fruits have been used in making tart jellies and preserves. The light brown wood is weak but hard, heavy, and close-grained. It is not valuable because of its small diameter and irregular shape.

Appearance: shrub or small tree to 8 m (26 ft), with an irregular rounded crown; trunk often crooked, to 20 cm (8 in) in diameter. **Bark:** 5–7 mm (0.2–0.3 in) thick, smooth to shallowly fissured, dark reddish-brown to grayish-brown. **Branches:** small erect to spreading; branchlets slender, reddish-brown to orange-brown and shiny, becoming dark reddish-brown. **Winter buds:** 3–4 mm (0.1–0.2 in) long, broadest near the base, rounded at the tip, covered with pale chestnut-brown scales. **Leaves:** alternate, simple, *deciduous*, broadest near the base to uniformly wide, 5–10 cm (2–4 in) long, 2.5–5 cm (1–2 in) wide, short-pointed at the tip, tapering to rounded at the base, *finely and sharply toothed along the margin*, dark green, shiny, and smooth above, light green beneath; leafstalks slender, 1–2 cm (0.4–0.8 in) long, with 2 glands near the base of the leaf. **Flowers:** *produced* in spring *in elongated clusters 8–15 cm (3.2–6 in) long;* each flower with a 5-lobed, cup-shaped calyx, 5 white, rounded petals, 15 to 20 stamens, and 1 pistil. **Fruits:** rounded or nearly so, 8–10 mm (0.4 in) in diameter, red, black, or yellow, shiny, thick-skinned, juicy, enclosing an egg-shaped stone.

Common Chokecherry

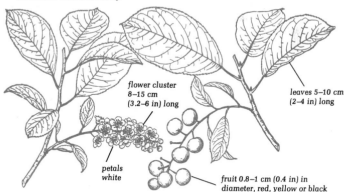

flower cluster
8–15 cm
(3.2–6 in) long

leaves 5–10 cm
(2–4 in) long

petals
white

fruit 0.8–1 cm (0.4 in) in
diameter, red, yellow or black

Black Cherry   *Prunus serotina* Ehrh.

This widely distributed tree grows from Nova Scotia to Minnesota, south to central Texas, and east to Florida. It also is native from southern New Mexico and western Arizona south to Guatemala. Black cherry thrives in a variety of soils but prefers moist, fertile conditions on north- or east-facing slopes and in protected coves. It occurs abundantly in pure stands or mixed forests of hardwoods and conifers. It grows in association with sugar maple, northern red oak, white pine, hemlock, beech, yellow birch, basswood, and white ash. It also grows among such smaller trees as flowering dogwood, redbud, mountain laurel, rhododendron, and witch hazel.

Black cherry grows rapidly, is moderately long-lived, and bears a large fruit crop every 3 or 4 years. Flowering is in spring as the leaves unfold. This species is important to man and wildlife. The leaves and inner bark contain the almond-flavored hydrocyanic acid, once used in cough medicine and tonics. Grouse, quail, prairie chicken, pheasant, and numerous songbirds, and small mammals eat the fruits. The cyanic acid in the wilted twigs and leaves in autumn may be dangerous to deer and cattle, though in spring whitetail deer can eat the fresh green leaves without ill effect.

The reddish-brown, close-grained wood is hard, takes a beautiful polish, and has been widely used in the manufacture of furniture, interior trim, veneers, tool handles, and small wooden wares. It ranks with walnut for cabinet wood and is similar to mahogany in color.

Appearance: tree to 30 m (100 ft), with a narrow to broadly rounded crown; trunk straight, to 1.5 m (4.9 ft) in diameter. **Bark:** moderately thick, 1.2–2 cm (0.5–0.8 in) thick, dark reddish-brown to nearly black (in the Gulf Coast, lighter to nearly white), smooth with horizontal pores when young, becoming fissured and scaly with age. **Branches:** slender, arching, often drooping at the ends; branchlets slender, smooth, pale green turning bright red to dark reddish-brown or gray-brown. **Winter buds:** 3–4 mm (0.1–0.2 in) long, broadest near the base, blunt to pointed at the tip, chestnut-brown. **Leaves:** alternate, simple, ***deciduous,*** broadest near the base, uniformly wide to lance-shaped, 5–15 cm (2–6 in) long, 2.5–4 cm (1–1.6 in) wide, pointed at the tip, tapering at the base and with 1 or more glands, ***finely and blunt toothed along the margin,*** texture papery but firm, dark green and shiny above, paler beneath; leafstalks slender, 1.2–2 cm (0.5–0.8 in) long. **Flowers:** stalked, many ***on a narrow, elongated inflorescence 10–15 cm (4–6 in) long;*** each flower with cup-shaped, 5-lobed calyx, 5 petals, white, broadest near tip; about 20 stamens; 1 pistil. **Fruits:** maturing from June to October, rounded, depressed at tip, 8–10 mm (0.3–0.4 in) in diameter, dark

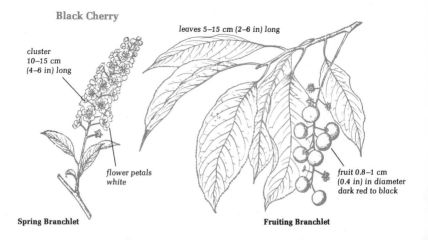

Black Cherry

cluster 10–15 cm (4–6 in) long

leaves 5–15 cm (2–6 in) long

flower petals white

fruit 0.8–1 cm (0.4 in) in diameter dark red to black

Spring Branchlet

Fruiting Branchlet

red to almost black at maturity, in long narrow clusters, thin-skinned, with dark-purple flesh, juicy, sometimes slightly bitter tasting, containing an egg-shaped stone 6–8 mm (0.2–0.3 in) long.

Hollyleaf Cherry   *Prunus ilicifolia* (Nutt.) D. Dietr.

The hollyleaf cherry grows along the Pacific coastal region from central California to northern Baja California. It occurs in moist, fertile valleys and from canyon bottoms to dry, rocky foothills but grows best in moist, sandy soils. This species can be found with several species of sumac and the California scrub oak. The characteristic evergreen, holly-like leaves give off a distinctive almond odor.

The trees grow rapidly when young but slower with age and often live more than 100 years. Large fruit crops are produced periodically, especially on trees growing in moist soils. The fruits attract birds and small mammals. Hollyleaf cherry is often cultivated as an ornamental in California and southern Europe. The pale, reddish-brown wood is hard, heavy, close-grained, but the trees are seldom large enough to be commercially important.

Appearance: shrub or small tree to 8 m (26 ft), with a dense, compact crown; trunk short, to 70 cm (27 in) in diameter, rarely larger. **Bark:** 6–14 mm (0.2–0.6 in) thick, with deep fissures separating the squarish plates, dark reddish-brown. **Branches:** slender, spreading; branchlets slender, smooth, light green turning to reddish-yellow and reddish-brown. **Leaves:** alternate, simple, ***evergreen,*** broadest near the base, ***2.5–6 cm (1–2.4 in) long,*** 2–4 cm (0.8–1.6 in) wide, pointed to rounded at the tip, tapering to rounded at the base, ***with coarse, spine-tipped teeth along the margin, thick, leathery,*** shiny and dark green above, paler beneath; leafstalks stout, 3–12 mm (0.1–0.5 in) long. **Flowers:** ***produced in many-flowered, elongated clusters 4–8 cm (1.6–3.2 in) long;*** each flower with a 5-lobed, cup-shaped calyx; 5 petals, white, broadest

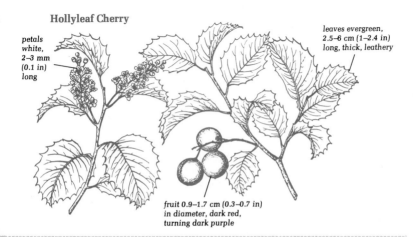

Hollyleaf Cherry

petals white, 2–3 mm (0.1 in) long

leaves evergreen, 2.5–6 cm (1–2.4 in) long, thick, leathery

fruit 0.9–1.7 cm (0.3–0.7 in) in diameter, dark red, turning dark purple

near the rounded tip, 2–3 mm (0.1 in) long; 15 to 20 stamens; 1 pistil. **Fruits:** rounded or nearly so, 9–17 mm (0.3–0.7 in) in diameter, dark red turning dark purple, fleshy thin, tart-tasting, enclosing a slightly flattened egg-shaped stone 7–15 mm (0.3–0.6 in) long.

Catalina Cherry   *Prunus lyonii* (Eastw.) Sarg.

The catalina cherry, a close relative of the hollyleaf cherry, is limited to the Channel Islands and northern Baja California. Catalina cherry differs from the hollyleaf cherry in having entire or irregularly toothed leaf margins and larger flowers and fruits. This

cherry is a shrubby tree to 9 m (30 ft) high with spreading branches and a broad, compact crown. The leathery, *evergreen leaves* are broadest near the base to lance-shaped, 5–8 cm (2–3.2 in) long, dark green and shiny, *entire or with a few irregular teeth along the thick and curled under margin.* The white *flowers* are *produced in elongated, dense-flowered clusters 7–10 cm (2.8–4 in) long.* The fruits are rounded, 2.5–3 cm (1–1.2 in) in diameter, dark purple to nearly black, with a thick, sweet, juicy flesh that encloses an egg-shaped stone.

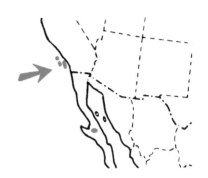

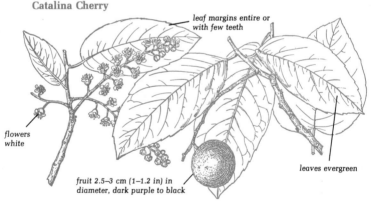

Catalina Cherry

leaf margins entire or with few teeth

flowers white

fruit 2.5–3 cm (1–1.2 in) in diameter, dark purple to black

leaves evergreen

Carolina Laurelcherry   *Prunus caroliniana* (Mill.) Ait.

Carolina laurelcherry ranges from the Coastal Plain from southeastern North Carolina to Florida and west to eastern Texas. It also occurs in Bermuda. This cherry grows in deep, well-drained, rich, moist bottomlands, bluffs, or stream banks.

This is a fast growing, short-lived tree that flowers in March or April. The black fruits ripen in autumn, often staying on the tree until the next flowering season. The fruits are slightly poisonous to humans, although birds can eat them. The reddish leaves of autumn or withered leaves contain hydrocyanic acid. When eaten, the hydrocyanic compounds react with stomach acids to release cyanide, which can be fatal to browsing mammals. The younger leaves can be eaten by whitetail deer with no ill effect. This species is often cultivated in the southern U.S. for hedges, screens, and for its attractive flowers. The light reddish-brown wood is hard and strong, but the trees are seldom large enough for commercial use.

Appearance: small to medium-size tree to 12 m (40 ft), with a broad to narrow crown; trunk straight, to 30 cm (12 in) in diameter. **Bark:** 3–4 mm (0.1–0.2 in) thick, smooth becoming roughened by shallow fissures, gray. **Branches:** slender, spreading to nearly upright; branchlets slender, smooth, turning reddish to light brown or

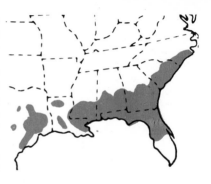

Carolina Laurelcherry

leaves evergreen

fruit 1–1.3 cm (0.5 in) long, shiny black

flower petals shorter than calyx lobes

Spring Branchlet

gray with age. **Winter buds:** 3–4 mm (0.1–0.2 in) long, broadest near the base and pointed at the tip, covered with overlapping, reddish-brown scales. **Leaves:** alternate, simple, *evergreen,* uniformly wide, 5–12 cm (2–4.8 in) long, 1.5–4 cm (0.6–1.6 in) wide, pointed at the tip, tapering at the base, entire or with a few sharp teeth along the margin, smooth, leathery, dark green and shiny above, paler and dull beneath; leafstalks stout, 4–9 mm (0.1–0.4 in) long. **Flowers:** *produced in many-flowered, elongated clusters* in junctions of the upper leaves, the clusters shorter than the leaves; each flower with a 5-lobed, narrowly bell-shaped calyx tube; *5 petals, creamy white, shorter than the calyx lobes;* boat-shaped; 15 to 30 stamens; 1 pistil. **Fruits:** uniformly wide, 1–1.3 cm (0.5 in) long, rounded at the tip and base, shiny, *black,* flesh thin, dry; enclosing an egg-shaped stone 0.9–1.2 cm (0.5 in) long.

Myrtle Laurelcherry   *Prunus myrtifolia* (L.) Urban

Myrtle laurelcherry is an evergreen tree native to hammocks, streams, and ponds of southern Florida. The flowers open in November, and the orange-brown fruits ripen in the spring or summer. The light reddish-brown wood is hard and close-grained but is not of commercial importance because of the tree's small size.

This is a small tree to 12 m (40 ft) with alternate, *evergreen* leaves that are broadest at the middle or near the base, 5–11 cm (2–4.4 in) long, 2.5–3.6 cm (1–1.4 in) wide, with entire, slightly thick, wavy margins, smooth, slightly leathery, shiny yellow-green above. The *flowers* are *produced in many-flowered, elongated clusters 3–7 cm (1.2–2.8 in) long;* each flower has a bright-orange calyx tube, *5 white petals, broadest near the tip,* yellow on the inside and toward the base. The fruits are produced in few-flowered clusters, each rounded or nearly so, 7–12 mm (0.4 in) in diameter, *orange-brown,* flesh thin, dry, and enclosing a thin-shelled stone.

Myrtle Laurelcherry

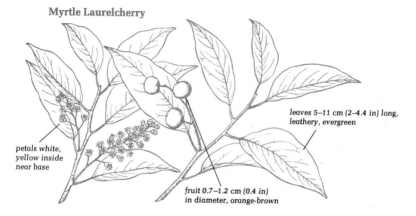

leaves 5–11 cm (2–4.4 in) long, leathery, evergreen

petals white, yellow inside near base

fruit 0.7–1.2 cm (0.4 in) in diameter, orange-brown

Bullace Plum
Prunus insititia L.

This native of western Asia and Europe was introduced in northeastern North America and now reproduces on its own. It can be found along roadsides, fencerows, and waste areas. It is occasionally planted as a hedge plant for its dense, spiny, branching system. Small clusters of white flowers appear in spring as the leaves are expanding. The dark-blue or nearly black fruits ripen by summer. They are very bitter but are eaten by birds and mammals. The reddish-brown wood is hard, heavy, and close-grained but is of little commercial value in North America, except for firewood.

Bullace plum is a bushy shrub or small tree to 6 m (20 ft) with a compact, rounded crown. The *spiny branches are short and stiff.* Alternate, deciduous leaves are broadest near or above the middle, 3–5 cm (1.2–2 in) long, pointed at the tip, gradually tapering at the base, with a double row of teeth along the margin. Flowers are produced singly or *in 2- or 3-flowered clusters* along the sides of twigs of the previous year. Each flower has a bell-shaped, 5-lobed calyx, and 5 broadly rounded petals. The *fruits* are *rounded, 10–12 mm (0.4–0.5 in) in diameter,* deep blue to black, with a thin, bitter flesh enclosing a flattened stone.

Garden Plum
Prunus domestica L.

The garden plum, native to Europe and Asia, was introduced into North America and now reproduces on its own in southeastern Canada and the northeastern U.S. to

Oregon. It is often found growing along roadsides and in old orchards, occasionally forming dense thickets. A cultivated variety with twice as many petals as the wild type is sometimes grown in parks and gardens. The wood is reddish-brown, hard, close-grained, takes an excellent polish, and has been used in Europe for cabinets and musical instruments.

Garden plum occurs as a shrub or short-trunked tree to 8 m (26 ft) with thin grayish to almost black bark. The alternate, deciduous leaves are broadest near or above the middle, 5–10 cm (2–4 in) long, pointed at the tip, tapering at the base, coarsely and somewhat irregularly toothed along the margin, dark green above, paler and hairy below. The white *flowers are produced singly or in clusters of 2 or 3.* Fruits are variable, but usually *egg-shaped, 2–3 cm (0.8–1.2 in) long, blue to bluish-black,* with a sweet flesh enclosing a large stone.

Klamath Plum   *Prunus subcordata* Benth.

The Klamath plum is native to western and southern Oregon and central California where it grows best on the eastern slopes of the coastal ranges and in dry valleys east of the Cascades. Klamath plum occurs in pure stands or with the western choke-cherry, Oregon crab, and Oregon white oak. The fruit is valuable. The wood is pinkish-brown, hard, and fine-grained, but the trees are too small to be commercially valuable.

Klamath plum occurs as a shrub or low branching tree to 8 m (26 ft), with a grayish-brown, ridged bark. The alternate, deciduous *leaves are broadest near the base to almost round, 2.5–7 cm (1–2.8 in) long, rounded at the tip, heart-shaped at the base,* doubly toothed along the margin, dark green and smooth above. White flowers are produced before the leaves appear in small, 2- to 4-flowered clusters. The *fruits are round, 2–3 cm (0.8–1.2 in) in diameter, dark red or yellow,* with a juicy flesh enclosing a flattened stone.

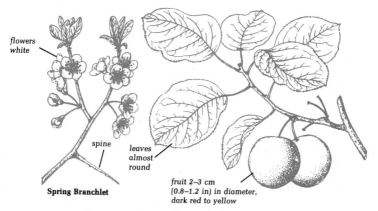

Klamath Plum

flowers white

spine

leaves almost round

fruit 2–3 cm (0.8–1.2 in) in diameter, dark red to yellow

Spring Branchlet

American Plum

Prunus americana Marsh.

American plum is a common tree widely distributed through eastern and midwestern North America and extends locally in the West. It grows in rocky or sandy soils along streams, woodlands, pastures, fencerows, and abandoned farmlands. In these areas

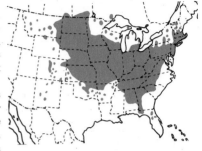

American plum grows with oaks, hackberry, holly, sumac, and hawthorns. Inch plum (*P. americana* variety *lanata*) is a variety of the American plum occurring in the Midwest and southcentral U.S. This variety has deep red fruits and leaves that are hairy on the lower surface.

This rapid-growing, short-lived tree has been cultivated in parks and orchards for its attractive, fragrant flowers and edible fruits. The fruits are used to make jellies, jams, preserves, and pies. American plum is valuable to whitetail deer, black bears, foxes, raccoons, squirrels, and many birds. The reddish-brown wood is hard and strong but is not used commercially because of the tree's small size.

Appearance: shrub or small spiny tree to 11 m (36 ft) with a broad, spreading crown; trunk straight, to 30 cm (12 in) in diameter. **Bark:** thin, to 1.5 cm (0.6 in) thick, smooth but breaking into thin plates with age, dark brown to reddish-brown. **Branches:** spreading; branchlets rigid, spreading, turning dark reddish-brown, with small spine-like side branchlets. **Winter buds:** 3–8 mm (0.1–0.3 in) long, broadest near the base and pointed at the tip, covered with chestnut-brown, overlapping scales. **Leaves:** alternate, deciduous, *broadest at or above the middle, 6–10 cm (2.4–4 in) long, 3.5–4.5 cm (1.4–1.8 in) wide,* sharp-pointed at the tip, *rounded to tapering at the base,* often with a double row of sharp-pointed teeth along the margin, dark green and smooth above, paler and smooth below; leafstalks slender, 1.5–2 cm (0.6–0.8 in) long, often with 2 large glands at the base of the leaf. **Flowers:** produced in 2- to 5-flowered clusters with or before the leaves develop, each flower on a slender stalk 8–15 mm (0.3–0.6 in) long, with a 5-lobed, bell-shaped calyx; 5 white, rounded petals 9–

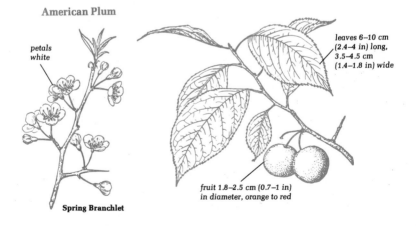

American Plum

petals
white

leaves 6–10 cm
(2.4–4 in) long,
3.5–4.5 cm
(1.4–1.8 in) wide

fruit 1.8–2.5 cm (0.7–1 in)
in diameter, orange to red

Spring Branchlet

12 mm (0.3–0.5 in) long, 20 to 30 stamens, and a single pistil. **Fruits:** produced singly or 2 to 4 per cluster, ***rounded to slightly elongated, 1.8–2.5 cm (0.7–1 in) long, orange to red,*** flesh bright yellow, juicy, enclosing a flattened stone.

Flatwood Plum   *Prunus umbellata* Ell.

A small spreading tree with little flowers and purple fruits, flatwood plum occurs from the Coastal Plain and lower Piedmont from southern North Carolina to central Florida and west to southern Arkansas and central Texas. It is usually found in river swamps and hammocks. The fruits are sometimes sold in southern markets and make excellent tart pies, jams, or jellies. The dark reddish-brown wood is hard, heavy, and close-grained but of little commercial value.

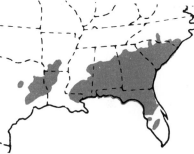

This is a small, often crooked tree to 6 m (20 ft) with alternate, deciduous leaves that are broadest at or above the middle, ***5–7 cm (2–2.8 in) long, 2.5–4 cm (1–1.6 in) wide, pointed at the tip, rounded to slightly heart-shaped at the base,*** with fine, sharp, incurved teeth, dark green and smooth above, paler and smooth to hairy beneath. The ***flowers*** appear before the leaves ***in 3- to 4-flowered clusters*** on slender stalks 1.5–2 cm (0.6–0.8 in) long. Each flower has a broadly bell-shaped calyx tube, 5 white petals, nearly rounded and narrowed at the base into a claw. The fruits mature from June to September and are rounded, 1.2–1.5 cm (0.5 in) in diameter, on slender stems 1.5–2.5 cm (0.6–1 in) long, covered with a tough, thick, ***nearly black,*** or ***dark red skin,*** the flesh is thick, sour, and encloses a round, flattened, thin-walled stone 9–12 mm (0.3–0.5 in) long.

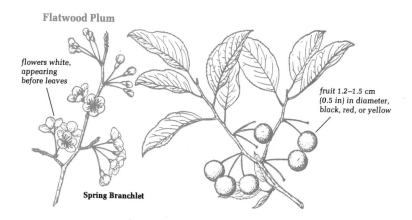

Flatwood Plum

flowers white, appearing before leaves

fruit 1.2–1.5 cm (0.5 in) in diameter, black, red, or yellow

Spring Branchlet

Allegheny Plum   *Prunus alleghaniensis* Porter

The Allegheny plum occurs from Connecticut to Pennsylvania south in the mountains to northeastern Tennessee. It grows best in rich soil along streams and wetlands. This species often forms pure thickets in openings or grows as individual trees in the

woods underneath larger trees. It grows
with oaks, hackberry, and holly.

This plum is rapid-growing, short-lived,
and characterized by white flowers fading
to pink, appearing before the leaves unfold, and purple fruit with a whitish or
bluish bloom. The fruits are edible and occasionally are used for pies and jellies.
They are eaten by whitetail deer, bears,
squirrels, foxes, other mammals, and songbirds. The trees provide good cover for

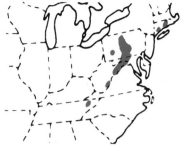

birds and smaller wildlife. The reddish-brown wood is hard and close-grained, but it
is not commercially important because of the small size of the trees.

Allegheny Plum

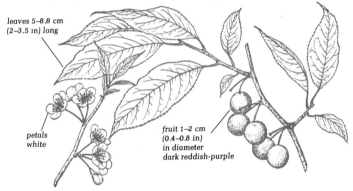

leaves 5–8.8 cm
(2–3.5 in) long

petals
white

fruit 1–2 cm
(0.4–0.8 in)
in diameter
dark reddish-purple

Appearance: small tree to 6 m (20 ft), with a narrow, rounded crown; trunk slender,
to 20 cm (8 in) in diameter. **Bark:** 6–8 mm (0.2–0.3 in) thick, fissured with thin, dark-
brown scales. **Branches:** rigid, upright, numerous; branchlets slender, covered with
pale hairs when young, becoming smooth, turning dark red and shiny to nearly black.
Winter buds: about 1 mm (less than 0.1 in) long, broadest near the base and tapering to
a pointed or rounded tip, covered with bright-red, overlapping scales. **Leaves:** alternate, simple, deciduous, broadest near the middle to lance-shaped, *5–8.8 cm (2–3.5
in) long, 1.7–3 cm (0.7–1.2 in) long, long-pointed at the tip, tapering at the base,*
finely and sharply toothed along the margin, dark green above, paler beneath, hairy
when young, becoming smooth; leafstalks slender, 1.5–2 cm (0.6–0.8 in) long, grooved
along the upper surface. **Flowers:** *produced in 2- to 5-flowered clusters,* each flower
on a slender stalk, with narrow, 5-lobed calyx lobes; 5 petals, white, rounded at the
tip; 15 to 20 stamens; 1 pistil. **Fruits:** *rounded to egg-shaped, 1–2 cm (0.4–0.8 in)
in diameter,* with a thick, tough, *dark reddish-purple skin* covered with a white or
bluish bloom, with a yellow, juicy, thick, mildly acid-tasting flesh, enclosing a thin-
walled stone 8–15 mm (0.3–0.6 in) long.

Mexican Plum   *Prunus mexicana* S. Wats.

This species is native to the Midwest and southcentral U.S. and also to northeastern
Mexico. Mexican plum occurs in open woods, rich woodlands, bottomlands, and in
rocky soils of prairie hillsides. It is often mistaken for the American plum but differs

in its hairy flower stalks, leafstalks, and flower parts. Also, the fruits are somewhat larger and purple with a whitish bloom.

Flowering occurs in spring before or as the leaves appear. Fruits mature in early autumn. The sweet, juicy edible fruits are purple when ripe and are eaten by many mammals and birds. The brown wood is hard and heavy but is seldom used commercially because of the tree's small size.

Appearance: shrub or small tree to 8 m (26 ft) with an open, irregular crown; trunk straight, to 25 cm (10 in) in diameter. **Bark:** 8–12 mm (0.3–0.5 in) thick, scaly on young branchlets, becoming rough and furrowed on older trunks, dark gray to almost black. **Branches:** stout; branchlets slender, smooth, shiny, light orange-brown turning grayish-brown with age. **Winter buds:** 3–4 mm (about 0.1–0.2 in) long, egg-shaped, pointed at the tip, covered with reddish-brown, finely hairy, overlapping scales. **Leaves:** alternate, simple, deciduous, broadest near the base or middle, *5–10 cm (2–4 in) long, 3–5 cm (1.2–2 in) wide,* with a long or short-pointed tip, rounded to wedge-shaped and often with glands at the base, *with a double row of fine teeth along the margin,* dark yellow-green, smooth, and shiny above, paler and hairy along the veins beneath; *leafstalks* 1–2 cm (0.4–0.8 in) long, stout, hairy, *often with 1 or more glands near the leaf blade.* **Flowers:** produced in 2- to 4-flowered clusters; each flower on a slender stalk, with a 5-lobed, narrowly bell-shaped calyx; 5 petals, white, almost round, 6.5–7.5 mm (0.3 in) long, often wavy on the margin; 20 to 30 stamens; 1 pistil. **Fruits:** produced singly or in small clusters, *rounded to slightly elongated, 2.5–3 cm (1–1.2 in) long, red turning purple,* with a thick, juicy flesh that encloses a nearly round stone 1.3–1.8 cm (0.5–0.7 in) long.

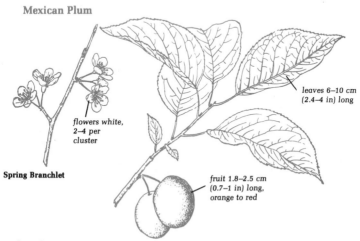

Mexican Plum

flowers white, 2–4 per cluster

Spring Branchlet

leaves 6–10 cm (2.4–4 in) long

fruit 1.8–2.5 cm (0.7–1 in) long, orange to red

Canada Plum   *Prunus nigra* Ait.

Canada plum is a small, straggly tree widely scattered in river valleys and limestone hillsides from New Brunswick to southern Manitoba and south to Iowa, Ohio, and Connecticut. It has been introduced in Nova Scotia. This plum grows in association with hawthorn, elder, smooth and shining sumac, sugar and red maples, ash, and yellow birch.

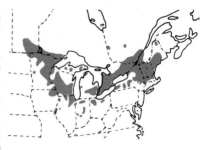

This plum has showy white flowers in spring with the orange-red to pink fruits maturing by autumn. Important to wildlife, the fruits are eaten by whitetail deer, bears, squirrels, raccoons, foxes, bobcats, and large birds. The ripe fruits are desirable for eating or cooking. Potatoes should not be planted near plum trees, because the trees often have aphids, which, though not harmful to the trees, do harm potatoes. The rich, reddish-brown wood is moderately heavy, hard, fine-grained but is not much used commercially.

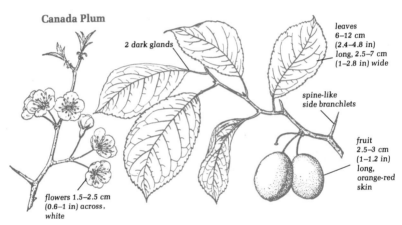

Canada Plum

2 dark glands

leaves 6–12 cm (2.4–4.8 in) long, 2.5–7 cm (1–2.8 in) wide

spine-like side branchlets

fruit 2.5–3 cm (1–1.2 in) long, orange-red skin

flowers 1.5–2.5 cm (0.6–1 in) across, white

Appearance: small crooked tree to 10 m (33 ft), with a narrow flat-topped, irregular crown; trunk short, to 30 cm (12 in) in diameter. **Bark:** 3–4 mm (0.1–0.2 in) thick, smooth with the outer layer splitting with age to expose the darker inner bark, light gray to brown or black. **Branches:** stout, crooked, upright; branchlets often zigzagging, with stout, spine-like side branchlets, bright green, hairy when young, becoming smooth, turning dark reddish-brown with age. **Winter buds:** 4–8 mm (0.1–0.4 in) long, pointed, covered with red to grayish-brown, triangular scales. **Leaves:** alternate, simple, deciduous, broadest at or near the base to broadest above the middle, *6–12 cm (2.4–4.8 in) long, 2.5–7 cm (1–2.8 in) wide,* narrowing abruptly to a long tapering tip, wedge-shaped to heart-shaped at the base, doubly toothed along the margin, reddish and hairy when unfolding, becoming thick, firm, *dull dark green above,* paler beneath; *leafstalks* stout, 1.2–2.5 cm (0.5–1 in) long, *with 2 large dark glands at the base of the blade.* **Flowers:** appearing with or before the leaves and produced in 3- to 5-flowered clusters on slender, smooth, dark red stalks; each flower 1.5–2.5 cm (0.6–1 in) across, the 5-lobed calyx tube broadly bell-shaped, the lobes narrow, pointed; 5 petals, broadest near the rounded tip, often irregular along the margin, narrowing to a claw-like base, white turning pink; 15 to 20 stamens, 1 pistil. **Fruits:** broadest near the middle to almost rounded, 2.5–3 cm (1–1.2 in) long, with a thick, orange-red skin, the flesh yellow, sour tasting, enclosing a flattened stone 2–2.5 cm (0.8–1 in) long.

Chickasaw Plum

Prunus angustifolia Marsh.

This plum is widely distributed throughout the southeastern and midsouthern U.S. It is most abundant in sandy soils and occurs along fencerows, pastures, fields, stream banks, sand dunes, and disturbed sites. It often forms dense thickets or can be found growing in association with pin cherry, red maple, ash, and birch.

Chickasaw plum is a fast-growing, short-lived tree that flowers in March or April, the fruits maturing by August. The thicket-forming nature of this plant renders it useful for erosion control. It serves as important cover and food for wildlife. The fruits are eaten by whitetail deer, bears, raccoons, squirrels, other mammals, and birds. And the reddish-brown wood is soft, weak, and of little commercial value.

Appearance: shrub or small tree to 8 m (26 ft) high, trunk rarely more than 20 cm (8 in) in diameter. **Bark:** 3–4 mm (0.1–0.2 in) thick, slightly furrowed with long thick scales, dark reddish-brown. **Branches:** slender, spreading; branchlets slender, bright red, shiny, smooth, becoming dull and reddish-brown. **Leaves:** alternate, simple, deciduous, lance-shaped or nearly so, *3–8 cm (1.2–3.2 in) long, 1–2.5 cm (0.4–1 in) wide,* pointed to long-pointed at the tip, tapering to rounded at the base, with many fine teeth along the margin, thin, smooth, *shiny, bright green above,* paler and dull beneath; *leafstalks* slender, 1–1.4 cm (0.4–0.6 in) long, smooth or hairy, *with 2 red*

Chickasaw Plum

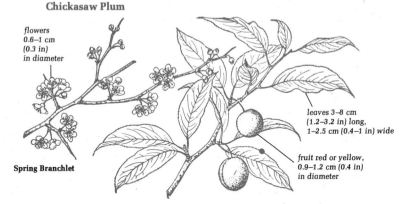

flowers
0.6–1 cm
(0.3 in)
in diameter

Spring Branchlet

leaves 3–8 cm
(1.2–3.2 in) long,
1–2.5 cm (0.4–1 in) wide

fruit red or yellow,
0.9–1.2 cm (0.4 in)
in diameter

glands near the base of the blade. **Flowers:** appearing before the leaves in 2- to 4-flowered clusters; *each flower 0.6–1 cm (0.3 in) in diameter,* with a 5-lobed, bell-shaped calyx; 5 white or creamy white petals, broadest at or near the rounded tip, narrowing at the base to a short claw; 15 to 20 stamens; 1 pistil. **Fruits:** rounded to egg-shaped, 0.9–1.2 cm (0.3–0.5 in) in diameter, bright red to yellow, shiny, flesh juicy, slightly acid-tasting, enclosing an egg-shaped stone 0.9–1.2 cm (0.3–0.5 in) long.

Hortulan Plum

Prunus hortulana Bailey

This small tree or shrub occurs in the southern Midwest. It grows on bottomlands, roadsides, and the margins of woodlands, where it sometimes forms thickets. Hortulan plum is similar in appearance to the wildgoose plum except that its dark green leaves are longer. Small mammals and many birds eat the fruits.

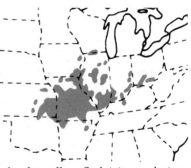

A large shrub or small tree with grayish-brown bark and reddish-brown branchlets, hortulan plum has alternate, deciduous *leaves* which are broadest near the base, *10–15 cm (4–6 in) long*, long-pointed at the tip, finely toothed along the margin, *dark green*, and with a slender leafstalk. The *flowers*, produced along slender branchlets, *are 1.2–1.6 cm (0.5–0.7 in)* across and white. The fruits are globe-shaped or nearly so, 2–3 cm (0.8–1.2 in) in diameter, dark red to yellow, flesh juicy, enclosing a thick-walled stone.

Hortulan Plum

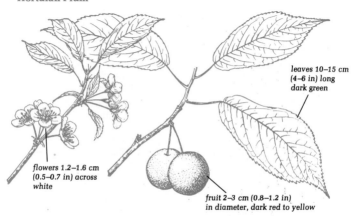

leaves 10–15 cm (4–6 in) long dark green

flowers 1.2–1.6 cm (0.5–0.7 in) across white

fruit 2–3 cm (0.8–1.2 in) in diameter, dark red to yellow

Wildgoose Plum *Prunus munsoniana* Wight & Hedrick

Wildgoose plum is a small tree, often forming thickets, of the midwestern and south-central U.S. It occurs in rich soils along streambanks, floodplains, pastures, roadsides, and the edges of woodlands. This plum frequently is found growing in association with chokecherries, pin cherries, elderberry, and wild rose.

This is a short-lived, fast-growing tree that can reach flowering and fruiting age in 3 years. The firm red fruits are tart and are sometimes used for jelly. Deer, bears, foxes, raccoons, and various game birds and songbirds eat the fruits. The densely growing trees provide excellent cover for smaller wildlife and good nesting sites for many birds. The pale reddish-brown wood is hard and heavy but of little commercial value because of its small size.

Wildgoose Plum

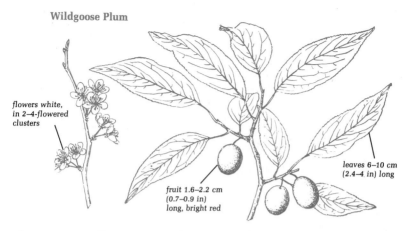

flowers white, in 2–4-flowered clusters

fruit 1.6–2.2 cm (0.7–0.9 in) long, bright red

leaves 6–10 cm (2.4–4 in) long

Appearance: small tree to 9 m (30 ft), open spreading, trunk usually straight, to 15 cm (6 in) in diameter. **Bark:** thin, to 10 mm (0.4 in) thick, smooth becoming scaly on old trunks, reddish-brown to gray-brown. **Branches:** spreading; branchlets upright to spreading, reddish-brown to gray. **Winter buds:** 2–4 mm (0.1 in) long, broadest near the base and rounded at the tip, covered with overlapping, chestnut-brown scales. **Leaves:** alternate, simple, deciduous, broadest at the middle to lance-shaped, *6–10 cm (2.4–4 in) long, 2–3.2 cm (0.8–1.3 in) wide,* short to long-pointed at the tip, rounded to wedge-shaped at the base, finely toothed along the margin, *yellowish-green,* shiny and smooth above, paler and slightly hairy beneath; leafstalks 1.5–2 cm (0.6–0.8 in) long, slender, sometimes bright red, usually with 2 glands near the base of the leaf blade. **Flowers:** *produced in 2- to 4-flowered clusters along the sides of the branchlets;* each flower on a stalk to 2.5 cm (1 in) long, with a 5-lobed, bell-shaped calyx; 5 white petals, 4–7 mm (0.1–0.3 in) long; 20 to 30 stamens; 1 pistil. **Fruits:** produced singly or in clusters of 2 to 3, rounded, 1.6–2.2 cm (0.7–0.9 in) long, bright red, rarely yellow, with a firm flesh enclosing a compressed stone.

Peach   Prunus persica Batsch

The edible peach is a native of China that has been widely planted throughout the world. In North America it occasionally naturalizes, reproducing on its own, and can be found along fencerows, roadsides, and abandoned farms from southern Ontario to Florida. Through selection and breeding, man has developed various forms, such as "free-stones" and "cling" peaches, with different colors and tastes. Double-flowering ornamental forms, with small or no fruits, are planted for their showy, pink, fragrant flowers.

Peaches are low trees to 7 m (23 ft) with broad, rounded crowns and thin, dark, reddish-brown bark that is smooth when young and becomes scaly with age. The alternate, deciduous *leaves* are usually *broadly lance-shaped, 8–15 cm (3–6 in) long, long-pointed at the tip,* rounded at the base, sharply toothed along the margin, light green and shiny above, paler and smooth beneath. The flowers appear before the leaves and are usually solitary along branchlets of the previous year. Each flower has a cup-shaped, 5-lobed calyx; 5 pink petals, 8–20 mm (0.3–0.8 in) long and rounded at the tip; 20 to 30 stamens, and a single pistil. Fruits are *nearly round, 4–10 cm (1.6–4 in) in diameter, grooved on 1 side, rose to reddish-pink, soft, hairy, with a sweet, juicy flesh* enclosing an egg-shaped stone.

Almond   *Prunus amygdalus* Batsch.

Almond, the source of the edible nut of the same name, is native to western Asia and northern Africa. It has been in cultivation for several thousand years and was introduced into California, where vast orchards produce almonds for use in cooking and eating. It occasionally reproduces on its own. Attractive double-flowering forms have been developed for use as showy ornamentals.

This is a small, spreading tree with alternate, deciduous *lance-shaped leaves 7–10 cm (2.8–4 in) long.* The leaves are long-pointed at the tip, rounded at the base, finely toothed along the margin and with a leafstalk to 2.6 cm (1 in) long. Flowers are produced singly or rarely in pairs. They are pink to white, 2.5–4 cm (1–1.6 in) across. The *fruits* are *4–5 cm (1.6–2 in) long, compressed, hairy* and with a *dry, hard flesh* that encloses a flattened, shallowly pitted stone.

Desert Apricot   *Prunus fremontii* S. Wats.

Desert apricot is a small tree that grows on rocky canyon slopes and desert mesas usually below 1,250 m (4,100 ft) elevation in southern California near Salton Sea Basin and in Baja California. It is named for General John Charles Fremont, an American explorer who collected one of the first specimens of this plant.

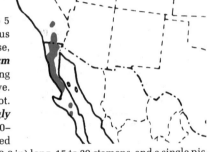

This species is a shrub or small tree to 5 m (17 ft) with alternate, simple, deciduous *leaves* that are broadest at or near the base, *1.5–3.2 cm (0.6–1.3 in) long, 1.5–2 cm (0.6–0.8 in) wide,* shallowly toothed along the margin, smooth and dark green above. The leaves resemble those of the apricot. The *flowers* are usually *produced singly or in clusters of 2 or 3.* Each flower is 10–13 mm (0.4–0.5 in) across, has a 5-lobed calyx tube, 5 white petals, each 4–6 mm (0.2 in) long, 15 to 20 stamens, and a single pistil. The fruit is unequally egg-shaped, 10–13 mm (0.4–0.5 in) long, yellowish, containing a thin-walled stone.

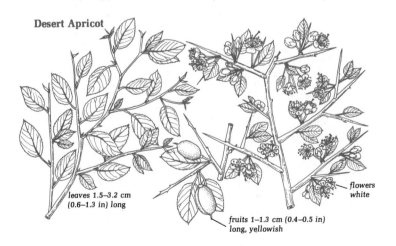

Desert Apricot

leaves 1.5–3.2 cm (0.6–1.3 in) long

flowers white

fruits 1–1.3 cm (0.4–0.5 in) long, yellowish

Apricot
Prunus armeniaca L.

The apricot, cultivated since ancient times, is native to China but was introduced long ago to western Asia. Apricots reached California in the 18th century and have been developed into a major crop. Although they are grown in many regions of North America, California is the primary producer of the apricots found in supermarkets. Birds and mammals sometimes spread the seeds along roadsides or waste areas where they develop into trees. These naturalized trees, reproducing on their own, are part of Californian plant communities.

This small tree has reddish bark and alternate, deciduous leaves. The leaves resemble those of desert apricot; they are ***broad, 5–10 cm (2–4 in) long,*** short-pointed at the tip, rounded at the base, closely toothed along the margin, and with a leafstalk 2–3 cm (0.8–1.2 in) long. The pinkish to white flowers are produced singly along the young branchlets. The ***fruits*** are ***round or nearly so, 2–3 cm (0.8–1.2 in) in diameter, orange to yellowish and smooth at maturity, fleshy, sweet,*** and enclosing a smooth stone.

Mazzard Cherry
Prunus avium (L.) L.

Mazzard cherry, also known as sweet cherry, has long been cultivated in Europe and North America for its commercially important, edible fruits. It reproduces on its own throughout eastern and midwestern North America, especially along fencerows, roadsides, and in open woods. This cherry is larger and has a longer life than many other cherries. Whitetail deer and rabbits feed on young twigs and leaves, while birds (ranging from grouse to robins, thrashers, and cedar waxwings) eat the fruits. The yellowish-red wood is strong and takes a fine polish. It is sometimes used to make furniture, musical instruments, and other small handcrafted articles.

This is a widespreading tree to 20 m (66 ft) high and with a smooth, gray to reddish-brown bark. The alternate, deciduous leaves are broadest at or near the base, 6–12 cm (2.4–4.7 in) long, short-pointed at the tip, tapering at the base, doubly toothed along the margin. The ***flowers*** are ***produced singly or in 3- to 5-flowered clusters*** along the sides of the branches. Each flower has a 5-lobed, urn-shaped calyx, 5 white, rounded petals, 15 to 25 stamens, and a single pistil. The ***fruits*** are ***rounded to heart-shaped, 2–2.5 cm (0.8–1 in) across, yellow, dark red to almost black, flesh sweet,*** juicy and enclosing a rounded to slightly flattened stone.

Mazzard Cherry

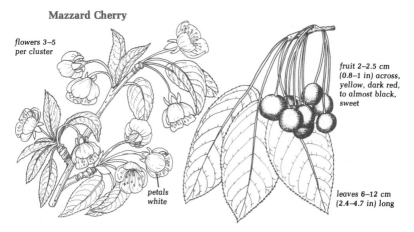

flowers 3–5 per cluster

petals white

fruit 2–2.5 cm (0.8–1 in) across, yellow, dark red, to almost black, sweet

leaves 6–12 cm (2.4–4.7 in) long

Sour Cherry
Prunus cerasus L.

Sour cherry, like the mazzard cherry, is native to southeastern Europe and Asia and was introduced into cultivation in North America. Birds, eating the fruits and passing the undigested stones, help in the reproduction of sour cherries along fences, roadsides, and the edges of woods. Sour cherry is more commonly encountered in eastern North America than in the West. It is cultivated for its fruits, which are used in pies, jams, jellies, and canning. Sour cherry differs from mazzard cherry in its hairy lower leaf surface and the usually smaller, sour fruits. Whitetail deer and rabbits feed on the young twigs and leaves, while raccoons, foxes, and many gamebirds and songbirds eat the fruits.

This is a short-trunked, spreading tree to 15 m (50 ft) with gray to brown, thinly scaled bark. The alternate, deciduous leaves are broadest at or above the middle, 5–10 cm (2–4 in) long, pointed at the tip, rounded at the base, doubly toothed along the margin, becoming dark green and smooth above, paler and hairy beneath. The white *flowers are produced in 2- to 5-flowered clusters* along the sides of the branches before or as the leaves unfold. Each flower has an urn-shaped, 5-lobed calyx, 5 white petals that are broadest near the rounded tip, 20 to 30 stamens, and a single pistil. The *fruits* are *rounded, 0.8–1.2 cm (0.3–0.5 in) in diameter, red to reddish-black, with a juicy, sour flesh* that encloses a small stone.

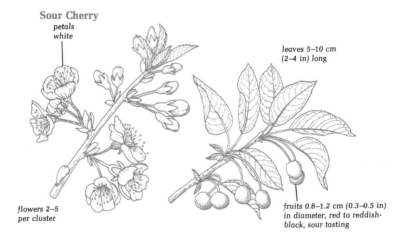

Sour Cherry
petals white

leaves 5–10 cm (2–4 in) long

flowers 2–5 per cluster

fruits 0.8–1.2 cm (0.3–0.5 in) in diameter, red to reddish-black, sour tasting

Mahaleb Cherry
Prunus mahaleb L.

This native of Europe and western Asia was introduced to North America as a stock plant for grafting garden cherries. It reproduces on its own in southeastern Canada and northeastern U.S. Mahaleb cherry is usually found along fencerows, roadsides, and abandoned home sites.

Mahaleb cherry is a shrub or small tree to 8 m (26 ft), with a broad, rounded crown, and thin, dark-gray bark. The alternate, deciduous *leaves are almost round in shape, 2.5–5 cm (1–2 in) long and wide,* short-pointed at the tip, heart-shaped at the base, finely toothed along the margin, and pale green on both sides. The white flowers are produced in 6- to 10-flowered, narrow, elongated clusters. The *fruits are round to egg-shaped, 5–7 mm (0.2–0.3 in) in diameter, reddish-black* and enclosing a small, rounded stone.

Mahaleb Cherry

petals
white

leaves 2.5–5 cm
(1–2 in) long

6–10 flowers
per cluster

fruits 5–7 mm (0.3 in)
in diameter

Pin Cherry

Prunus pensylvanica L. f.

This small, attractive tree inhabits most wooded areas of Canada from Newfoundland to British Columbia, south in the Rocky Mountains to Colorado, east to New York, and south in the Appalachian Mountains to Georgia. It grows singly or in pure stands along rivers in the western prairies. Its range overlaps with the bitter cherry (*Prunus emarginata*) and hybrids are frequently produced. Pin cherry is valuable as a reforesting agent after forest fires, forming pure stands that provide shade for seedlings of other tree species. The pin cherry soon dies off, making way for the new trees. Pin cherry grows in association with aspen, paper birch, red maple, northern red oak, yellow birch, mountain ash, mountain maple, red spruce, and Fraser fir.

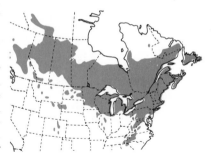

Flowering is in early spring when the leaves are half grown, and the bright red clusters of fruits mature in early autumn. Many birds are attracted to the fruits, including blue, ruffed, and sharp-tailed grouse, ring-necked pheasant, evening and rose-breasted grosbeak, robins, starlings, brown thrashers, thrushes, cedar waxwings, and the red-headed woodpecker. Small mammals such as foxes, rabbits, squirrels, and chipmunks eat the fruit. Mule deer, whitetail deer, and moose browse the young twigs and leaves. The light brown, soft, porous wood is not used commercially, except for firewood.

Appearance: low shrub or small tree to 12 m (40 ft), with a narrow, rounded crown; trunk straight, to 40 cm (16 in) in diameter. **Bark:** thin, 1–2 mm (less than 0.1 in) thick, peeling off in dark reddish-brown plates, marked by bands of widely spaced orange pores. **Branches:** slender, spreading; branchlets slender, light red, slightly hairy at first, becoming smooth, bright red, shiny, developing spine-like side branchlets. **Winter buds:** 1–2 mm (less than 0.1 in) long, egg-shaped to broadest at the middle, pointed, bright reddish-brown scales with tiny hairs along the margins. **Leaves:** alternate, simple, deciduous, *lance-shaped, sometimes scythe-shaped,* broadest at the base or the middle, *8–15 cm (3–6 in) long, 2–3.2 cm (0.8–1.3 in) wide,* tapering to a

Pin Cherry

petals
white

leaves 8–15 cm
(3–6 in) long
2–3.2 cm
(0.8–1.3 in) wide

fruit
bright red,
6–8 mm
(0.3 in) in
diameter

long-pointed tip, rounded at the base, with fine, sharp, often gland-tipped teeth, green or greenish-yellow, smooth, shiny above, paler beneath; leafstalks slender, 2–2.5 cm (0.8–1 in) long, smooth or slightly hairy, often with glands near the base of the leaf blade. **Flowers:** produced on short, slender stalks *in 4- to 5-flowered clusters;* each flower with a broadly urn-shaped calyx tube; 5 creamy white petals, 6–8 mm (0.2–0.3 in) long, rounded, narrowed to a claw at the base; 15 to 20 stamens; 1 pistil. **Fruits:** rounded, *6–8 mm (0.2–0.3 in) in diameter,* with thick, *bright red,* smooth *skin,* the flesh thin, sour, enclosing a thin-walled, slighty flattened stone.

Bitter Cherry　　　　　　　*Prunus emarginata* Dougl. ex Eaton

This species occurs from British Columbia to southern California, Arizona, and south-western New Mexico. It grows in moist, open woods, along streams, and in cut-over or burned-over areas from sea level to 2,400 m (7,900 ft) elevation. It grows best in full sun and cannot tolerate much shade from larger trees.

Bitter cherry is fast-growing and short-lived. Flowers appear from April to July when the leaves are nearly half grown, while the fruits mature in July or August. They are edible but bitter. Mule deer browse the young twigs and leaves. Black bears, rabbits, squirrels, and other small rodents eat the fruits. Blue grouse, ring-necked pheasant, thrushes, magpies, and other songbirds relish the fruits. The

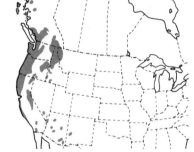

pinkish-brown wood is brittle, soft, and close-grained. It is sometimes used for furniture in the Northwest because it takes a high polish.

Appearance: shrub or small tree to 8 m (26 ft), sometimes taller, with a narrow, rounded crown; trunk to 25 cm (10 in) in diameter. **Bark:** 5–8 mm (0.2–0.3 in) thick, smooth, dark reddish-brown to dark brown, with large widely spaced, horizontal pores. **Branches:** slender, upright; branchlets slender, hairy when young becoming smooth, dark red to bright red, with short side branches. **Winter buds:** 3–4 mm (0.1–0.2 in) long, broadest near the base and pointed at the tip, covered with chestnut-brown overlapping scales. **Leaves:** alternate, simple, deciduous, *broadest near the*

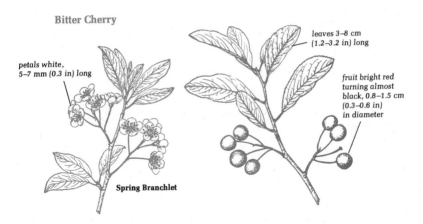

Bitter Cherry

petals white,
5–7 mm (0.3 in) long

leaves 3–8 cm
(1.2–3.2 in) long

fruit bright red
turning almost
black, 0.8–1.5 cm
(0.3–0.6 in)
in diameter

Spring Branchlet

middle to near the tip, 3–8 cm (1.2–3.2 in) long, 0.8–3.8 cm (0.3–1.5 in) wide, rounded to pointed at the tip, tapering and with 1 to 4 dark glands at the base, short, irregularly toothed along the margin, thin, hairy when young, becoming smooth, dark yellow-green above, paler and smooth or softly hairy beneath; leafstalks stout, 3–7 mm (0.1–0.3 in) long. **Flowers:** produced in 5- to 12-flowered spreading clusters in the junctions of the upper leaves, each flower 9–12 mm (0.5 in) across, on a slender stalk, with a 5-lobed, cup-shaped calyx; 5 petals, white to greenish-white, broadest above the middle and rounded at the tip, 5–7 mm (0.3 in) long; 15 to 20 stamens; 1 pistil. **Fruits:** *rounded, 8–15 mm (0.3–0.6 in) in diameter, bright red turning almost black at maturity,* flesh bitter, enclosing an egg-shaped stone 3–4 mm (0.2 in) long.

The Mountain-Ash Genus   Sorbus L.

There are about 75 species of mountain-ash distributed throughout the northern and higher elevations in North America, Europe, and Asia. The trees do best in cool, moist habitats, along swamp borders and wooded hillsides. They also grow in poor soils and become established on exposed, broken ground. Three species are native to North America, 2 in the eastern half and the other in the Northwest. The common European mountain-ash has been introduced as an ornamental along with several hybrids and selections of this species. It occasionally reproduces on its own in disturbed sites.

The mountain-ash's economic importance centers on the decorative qualities of its handsome leaves, showy flowers, and bright red fruits. The trees are often planted in parks and gardens. Members of this genus are valuable to wildlife because the fruits persist on the trees into winter, providing food when other foods are scarce. Moose often browse the twigs and leaves. Grouse and many other birds, squirrels, and other rodents feed on the fruits. The wood is moderately light with little strength and is of no commercial value.

These shrubs or small round-topped trees have thin, smooth to slightly scaly, fragrant, light-gray bark. The branchlets have large, pointed, often gummy winter buds. Leaves are alternate, simple or feather-like (pinnately compound). The bisexual white flowers are produced in broad clusters at the ends of the branchlets. Each flower has a tiny calyx, 5 petals, many stamens, and a single pistil. The fruits are rounded or nearly so, berry-like, orange to red, and bitter tasting. They contain 1 or 2 chestnut-brown, shiny seeds.

Key to Mountain-Ash Species

A. Leaflets rounded to almost squared at the tip, coarsely toothed, usually along the upper half to one-fourth of leaf margin; trees of Northwest
Sitka mountain-ash, p. 588

B. Leaflets sharp pointed, occasionally rounded at the tip, finely toothed along the margin; trees of eastern North America or introduced trees.

1. Leaflets smooth on the upper surface; winter buds gummy, with a few hairs or smooth.

a. Leaflets dull green, 3–8 cm (1.2–3.2 in) long; fruits orange-red, 4–8 mm (0.1–0.3 in) in diameter
American mountain-ash, p. 589

b. Leaflets bluish to gray-green, 5–8 cm (2–3.2 in) long; fruits red, 6–10 mm (0.2–0.4 in) in diameter **Showy mountain-ash, p. 590**

2. Leaflets hairy on both surfaces at maturity; winter buds densely hairy, but not gummy; introduced trees from Europe
European mountain-ash, p. 591

American Mountain-Ash

European Mountain-Ash

Sitka Mountain-Ash

Sorbus sitchensis Roem.

This mountain-ash derived its common name from Sitka, Alaska, where it was discovered. It ranges south from Alaska to central California, east to northern Idaho and northwestern Montana. Sitka mountain-ash prefers moist, rich soils along stream borders or rocky hillsides. It grows mostly in association with conifers.

This graceful tree is slow growing but produces abundant seed crops each year. It is often cultivated in parks and gardens for the masses of white flowers and bright red fruits. Richardson's grouse, several thrushes, and robins are attracted to the fruits.

Appearance: shrub or small tree to 9 m (30 ft), with a rounded, open crown; trunk straight, to 30 cm (12 in) in diameter. **Bark:** thin, 2–4 mm (about 0.1 in) thick, smooth to scaly with age, light gray, inner bark with a pleasant odor. **Branches:** slender, spreading; branchlets slender, reddish-brown and hairy, turning dark brown and smooth with age, marked with prominent leaf scars. **Winter buds:** 6–15 mm (0.2–0.6 in) long, cone-shaped, sharp-pointed at the tip, gummy, covered with several overlapping, dark-red scales. **Leaves:** alternate, deciduous, feather-like (pinnately compound), 10–15 cm (4–6 in) long, with 7 to 11 leaflets, each leaflet broadest near the base to almost uniformly wide, 2–6 cm (0.8–2.4 in) long, **rounded to almost squared at the tip, coarsely toothed usually on the upper 1/2 to 1/4 of leaf margin,** dark green and smooth above, paler beneath, often hairy; leafstalks

Sitka Mountain Ash

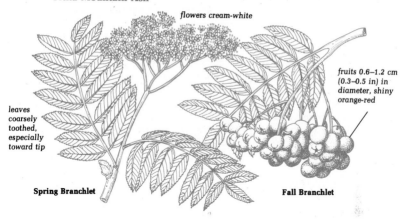

flowers cream-white

fruits 0.6–1.2 cm (0.3–0.5 in) in diameter, shiny orange-red

leaves coarsely toothed, especially toward tip

Spring Branchlet

Fall Branchlet

stout, 3.5–5 cm (1.4–2 in) long, red. **Flowers:** produced in dense, many-flowered, flat-topped clusters 7–10 cm (2.8–4 in) across, each flower with a tiny, urn-shaped, 5-lobed calyx, 5 petals, creamy white, almost rounded, 6–8 mm (0.3 in) long, 20 stamens, 1 pistil. **Fruits:** produced in clusters, each fruit rounded, 0.6–1.2 cm (0.3–0.5 in) in diameter, shiny orange-red, containing 1 or 2 brown, egg-shaped seeds 3–4 mm (0.2 in) long.

American Mountain-Ash · *Sorbus americana* Marsh.

American mountain-ash occurs in eastern North America from Newfoundland to southeastern Manitoba to northern Illinois and south into the Appalachian Mountains to Georgia. This species grows at higher elevations on rocky sites, most slopes, and in seepage areas. It is a small tree, usually growing under taller ones. Trees often growing in association with the mountain-ash include yellow birch, paper birch, red spruce, Fraser fir, balsam fir, northern red oak, red maple, and yellow buckeye.

This is a slow-growing and relatively short-lived tree. It is occasionally planted as an ornamental for its handsome leaves and brightly colored fruits. The small clusters of flowers appear in spring, and the fruits mature by August. Squirrels, ruffed

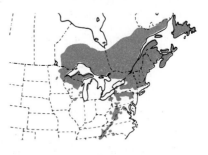

and sharp-tailed grouse, and many songbirds eat the fruits. In the northern part of the tree's range, moose browse the young twigs and leaves. The raw fruits are not palatable but can be made into jelly. The wood is brown, close-grained, soft and weak, and commercially unimportant.

Appearance: shrub or small tree to 9 m (30 ft), with an open, rounded crown; trunk straight, to 50 cm (20 in) in diameter. **Bark:** thin, 2–4 mm (0.1 in) thick, smooth, gradually breaking into small scales, light gray. **Branches:** slender, spreading; branchlets slender, spreading, hairy when young becoming smooth, dark reddish-brown to gray.

Winter buds: 11–13 mm (0.5 in) long, cone-shaped, often curved at the sharp-pointed tip, covered with several, overlapping, *gummy,* dark red *scales.* **Leaves:** alternate, deciduous, feather-like (pinnately compound), 12–25 cm (5–10 in) long, with 9–17 opposing leaflets, each leaflet lance-shaped to uniformly wide, 3–8 cm (1.2–3.2 in) long, *gradually tapering to a sharp point,* rounded to wedge-shaped at the base, *finely sharp-toothed along the margin,* thin, *dull green,* paler and hairy to smooth beneath; leafstalks slender, 5–7.5 cm (2–3 in) long, grooved, dark green to reddish. **Flowers:** produced in dense, many-flowered, flat-topped clusters 8–15 cm (3.2–6 in) across, at the tips of the branchlets; each flower with tiny, broad, bell-shaped, 5-lobed calyx, 5 petals, white, nearly circular, 2–4 mm (0.1 in) long, with many stamens and a single pistil. **Fruits:** produced in dense clusters, each *fruit rounded or pear-shaped, 4–8 mm (0.2 in) in diameter,* shiny, *bright orange-red,* slightly fleshy, containing 1 or 2 dark, angled seeds 2–3 mm (0.1 in) long.

American Mountain-Ash

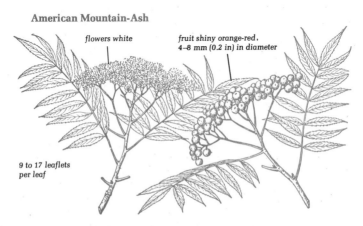

flowers white

fruit shiny orange-red, 4–8 mm (0.2 in) in diameter

9 to 17 leaflets per leaf

Showy Mountain-Ash — *Sorbus decora* (Sarg.) Schneid.

This handsome tree grows in southern Greenland, Labrador, and Newfoundland, to Quebec, south to Iowa, and eastward to New York and Maine. It adapts to many different kinds of soils and conditions but it is particularly common through the Acadian Forest Region. It often grows in association with the American mountain-ash. The *flowers of showy mountain-ash are larger and appear about 10 to 12 days later than those of the American mountain-ash.*

This attractive bushy tree has no commercial importance but it is often planted as an ornamental. Its value to wildlife is similar to that of the American mountain-ash. The wood is brown, close-grained, soft, and weak.

Appearance: small bushy tree to 20 m (66 ft), with a rounded crown; trunk to 30 cm (12 in) in diameter. **Bark:** thin, 2–5 mm (0.1–0.2 in) thick, smooth, becoming scaly, gray-green. **Branches:** stout, spreading; branchlets slender, reddish-brown to gray, smooth. **Winter buds:** 10–14 mm (0.4–0.6 in) long, cone-shaped, sharp-pointed at the

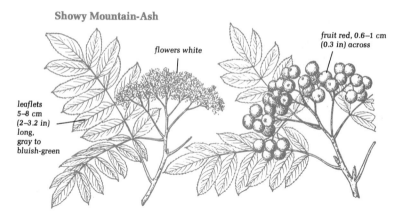

Showy Mountain-Ash

flowers white

fruit red, 0.6–1 cm
(0.3 in) across

leaflets
5–8 cm
(2–3.2 in)
long,
gray to
bluish-green

tip, shiny, covered with several overlapping, dark reddish-brown, *gummy scales.*
Leaves: alternate, deciduous, feather-like (pinnately compound), to 25 cm (10 in)
long, with 11 to 15 leaflets, each leaflet broadest near the base or the middle, *5–8 cm (2–3.2 in) long,* sharp pointed at the tip, finely toothed along the margin, entire toward
the base, *bluish to gray-green,* paler beneath, hairy when young *becoming smooth at maturity;* leafstalks slender, 6–8 cm (2.4–3.2 in) long, grooved. **Flowers:** produced in
dense, many-flowered clusters 6–12 cm (2.4–4.8 in) across, each flower with a tiny, 5-lobed calyx, 5 white petals, each nearly circular, 3–5 mm (0.1–0.2 in) long, many
stamens, and a single pistil. **Fruits:** produced in dense clusters, each *fruit* rounded,
0.6–1 cm (0.2–0.4 in) across, shiny, *red,* containing 1 or 2 dark, angled seeds 3–4 mm
(0.1–0.2 in) long.

European Mountain-Ash   *Sorbus aucuparia* L.

This native of Europe, widely planted in North America, reproduces on its own from
Newfoundland and Labrador to British Columbia and southwestern Alaska, south
into the northern U.S. In addition to being planted in parks and gardens, European
mountain-ash is found along fences, bogs, and the edges of swamps and streams.
Unlike the American mountain-ash, the winter buds are not gummy but are covered
with dense white to gray hairs.

This rapid-growing tree is cultivated in North America for its attractive leaves and
bright-red fruits. Folklore contains reference to these trees, which were considered
protection from evil spirits. The large showy flower clusters vary from hairy to almost
smooth. The *leaves are smaller than the American species.* The fruits persist on the
trees into winter but are eventually consumed by birds. The light brown wood is hard,
fine-grained, and occasionally used for making tool handles and other wooden wares.

Appearance: small tree to 18 m (60 ft), with an open rounded crown; trunk short to
80 cm (31 in) in diameter. **Bark:** thin, 3–6 mm (0.1–0.2 in) thick, smooth becoming
scaly with age, gray. **Branches:** stout, spreading; branchlets slender, smooth, shiny,
gray. **Winter buds:** stout, 9–12 mm (about 0.3–0.5 in) long, broadly cone-shaped, *not gummy,* covered with several, densely hairy, overlapping scales. **Leaves:** alternate,
deciduous, feather-like (pinnately compound), *12–25 cm (5–10 in) long,* with 9 to 15
leaflets per leaf, each leaflet lance-shaped to uniformly wide, 2.5–7.5 cm (1–3 in) long,
blunt to sharp-pointed at the tip, sharply toothed along the margin, green above, paler
beneath, *hairy on both sides;* leafstalks slender, short. **Flowers:** produced in dense,
many-flowered flat-topped clusters 10–15 cm (4–6 in) across, each flower with a tiny

European Mountain-Ash

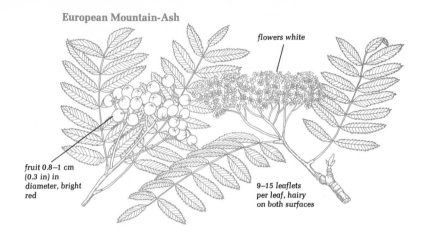

flowers white

*fruit 0.8–1 cm
(0.3 in) in
diameter, bright
red*

*9–15 leaflets
per leaf, hairy
on both surfaces*

5-lobed calyx, 5 petals, white, nearly circular, 4–5 mm (about 0.2 in) long; many stamens, 1 pistil. **Fruits:** produced in clusters, each *fruit rounded, 0.8–1 cm (0.3 in) in diameter, bright red,* fleshy, with 1 or 2 dark-brown seeds 3–4 mm (0.2 in) long.

The Serviceberry Genus   Amelanchier Medic.

Serviceberries comprise a small genus of about 25 species of trees and shrubs native to North America, Europe, Northern Africa, and Asia. In North America, they occur throughout the north temperate forests and mountain regions. They grow in a variety of soils and may occur anywhere from swamps to dry, rocky hillsides. Other common names are juneberry, shadblow, and shadbush, the last 2 originating from the fact that the tree blossoms when the shad are migrating up the rivers.

The delicate, white flowers blossom in early spring before the leaves appear, and the fruits mature in early summer. Mule deer and whitetail deer relish the young twigs and leaves. Squirrels, chipmunks, and many songbirds consume the fruits. Occasionally bear do also. Because of their attractive early spring flowers and songbird-attracting fruits, serviceberries are commonly planted in gardens and parks. The wood is hard and heavy, but the trees are seldom large enough to be commercially important.

Members of this genus are shrubs or small trees with smooth, sometimes scaly, gray bark. The alternate, simple, deciduous leaves are generally widest at or below the middle, and entire to toothed along the margins. The white flowers are produced in elongated clusters at or near the ends of the branches in spring. Each flower is bisexual, with a 5-lobed bell-shaped calyx, 5 narrow, strap-shaped petals, usually with 20 stamens, and a 5-parted pistil. The fruits are round to pear-shaped, red to purple, fleshy to dry, sweet, and containing 5 to 10 chestnut-brown seeds.

Key to Serviceberry Species

A. Leaves coarsely toothed, with 3–6 teeth per cm,
the leaf margins often entire near the base.

1. Leaves nearly rounded, 0.5–3 cm (0.2–1.2 in) long, 0.5–2.5 cm (0.2–1 in) wide, hairy at maturity; trees of western U.S.
     Utah serviceberry, p. 593
2. Leaves broadest near the base to uniformly wide, 2–6 cm (0.8–2.4 in) long, 2–4 cm (0.8–1.6 in) wide, smooth above at maturity.

   a. Leaves pale to dark green; petals of the flowers 0.9–1.5 cm (0.3–0.6 in) long; fruits reddish-purple to black; trees of northwestern North America
       Saskatoon serviceberry, p. 594
   b. Leaves bright green; petals of the flowers 7–10 mm (0.3–0.4 in) long; fruits dark purple to nearly black; trees of northern Midwest to northeastern North America
       Roundleaf serviceberry, p. 595

B. Leaves finely toothed, with 5–10 teeth per cm, the leaf margins toothed from base to tip.

   1. Flower petals 10–14 mm (0.4–0.6 in) long; fruits red to dark purple; straggling shrub or small tree of midwestern and eastern North America   **Downy serviceberry, p. 596**
   2. Flower petals 8–13 mm (0.3–0.5 in) long; fruits purplish-black; usually trees of Minnesota, Wisconsin, Iowa, and northern Illinois   **Inland serviceberry, p. 597**

Utah Serviceberry

Saskatoon Serviceberry

Downy Serviceberry

Utah Serviceberry   *Amelanchier utahensis* Koehne

The Utah serviceberry occurs in scattered locations throughout the western U.S. and northern Baja California. It is found from southeastern Oregon, south to southern California, New Mexico, and Trans Pecos Texas. This species grows in dry canyons, rocky slopes, and mountain sides at altitudes of 1,200–2,400 m (3,900–7,900 ft).

Utah serviceberry produces white or pink clusters of flowers in the spring and dark bluish-purple fruits in the fall. The fruits were eaten raw by Indians and sometimes made into bread or mixed with other foods by the pioneers. Ground squirrels and many types of birds eat much of the fruit before it fully matures. Blacktail deer, and sheep, goats, and cattle browse the leaves and young twigs. The wood is heavy, hard, and strong but the trees are seldom large enough for commercial use.

Appearance: spreading shrub or small, many-branched tree to 8 m (26 ft), with an open, rounded crown. **Bark:** thin, 4–6 mm (0.2 in) thick, smooth to shallowly fur-

Utah Serviceberry

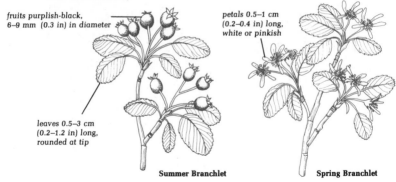

fruits purplish-black,
6–9 mm (0.3 in) in diameter

petals 0.5–1 cm
(0.2–0.4 in) long,
white or pinkish

leaves 0.5–3 cm
(0.2–1.2 in) long,
rounded at tip

Summer Branchlet   **Spring Branchlet**

rowed with age, ash–gray. **Branches:** slender, irregular; branchlets slender stiff, reddish-brown to gray, densely hairy when young, becoming smooth. **Winter buds:** similar to Saskatoon serviceberry. **Leaves:** alternate, simple, deciduous, *0.5–3 cm (0.2–1.2 in) long, 0.5–2.5 cm (0.2–1 in) wide, broadest above or at the middle, nearly rounded, rounded at the tip*, rounded, squared, or heart-shaped at the base, the **margin toothed above the middle,** leathery, yellowish-green, *hairy on both surfaces,* sometimes becoming smooth; leafstalks slender, 6–15 mm (0.2–0.6 in) long, hairy to smooth. **Flowers:** produced in 3- to 12-flowered, elongated clusters at the tips of the branchlets; each flower with green, 5-lobed calyx 2.2–3.6 mm (0.1 in) long; 5 petals, white or pinkish, 5–10 mm (0.2–0.4 in) long, strap-shaped, rounded at the tip; 10 to 15 stamens; pistil with 4 styles. **Fruits:** produced in clusters 5–7.5 cm (2–3 in) long, each rounded to egg-shaped, 6–9 mm (0.3 in) in diameter, fleshy at first, light brown, turning purplish-black at maturity, containing several small brown seeds 3–8 mm (0.1–0.3 in) long.

Saskatoon Serviceberry   *Amelanchier alnifolia* (Nutt.) Nutt.

(synonym: *A. florida* Lindl.)

This variable species occurs from Alaska to northern California, east to Wisconsin and scattered to southwestern Ontario. It grows on moist stream or lake banks, hillsides, prairies, and dry mountain slopes. At higher elevations, this serviceberry forms short dense thickets that prevent erosion.

Flowering is in early spring followed soon by numerous fleshy fruits. These were gathered by Indians and settlers as food and are still used in making jam. The fruits, ripening over several weeks, are important to wildlife. Mule deer, whitetail deer, and moose browse the young twigs and leaves. Beaver and marmot eat the bark. The northwest chipmunk, red squirrel, black bear, and many birds feed on the fruits.

Appearance: thicket-forming shrub or small tree to 12 m (40 ft), with an upright, open, rounded crown. **Bark:** thin, 3–4 mm (0.1–0.2 in) thick, smooth or finely furrowed, brown and tinged with red to gray. **Branches:** slender, erect to sometimes

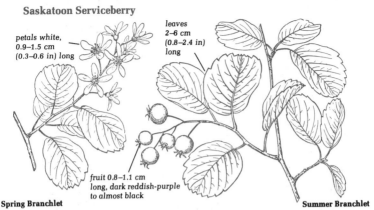

Saskatoon Serviceberry

petals white,
0.9–1.5 cm
(0.3–0.6 in) long

leaves
2–6 cm
(0.8–2.4 in)
long

fruit 0.8–1.1 cm
long, dark reddish-purple
to almost black

Spring Branchlet

Summer Branchlet

drooping near the tip; branchlets slender, sparsely covered with white hairs, becoming smooth with age, red to red-brown to dark grayish-brown. **Winter buds:** 2–8 mm (0.1–0.3 in) long, egg-shaped to broadest near the middle, pointed at the tip and covered with russet to chestnut-brown scales. **Leaves:** alternate, simple, deciduous, *2–6 cm (0.8–2.4 in) long, 2.5–4 cm (1–1.6 in) wide, broadest near the base to uniformly wide,* rounded to slightly indented at the tip, rounded to heart-shaped at the base, *entire near the base, sharply and coarsely toothed along the upper margin,* with a papery to leathery texture, pale to dark green above, paler beneath, hairy when young, becoming smooth with age; leafstalks slender, 12–25 mm (0.5–1 in) long, hairy or smooth. **Flowers:** produced in 3- to 20-flowered short, branched clusters, usually at or near the tips of the branchlets; each flower bisexual, with a 5-lobed, green, bell-shaped calyx, *5 white petals, each 0.9–1.5 cm (0.3–0.6 in) long, strap-shaped,* rounded at the tips; usually 20 stamens; 1 pistil. **Fruits:** produced in clusters 3–5 cm (1.2–2 in) long, each fruit rounded to egg-shaped, 6–11 mm (0.2–0.4 in) long, *dark reddish-purple to near black,* fleshy, sweet-tasting, containing 5 to 10 reddish-brown seeds.

Roundleaf Serviceberry   *Amelanchier sanguinea* (Pursh) DC.

Roundleaf serviceberry occurs in woods and thickets from Maine west to Minnesota, south to Iowa, east to New Jersey, and extends in scattered locations along the Appalachian Mountains to western North Carolina. It grows best in well-drained soils. The scientific name *sanguinea* is derived from the blood-red twigs.

This is a shrub or small tree to 6 m (20 ft) high, with reddish-brown bark, and slender, spreading, red to wine red, smooth branches and branchlets. The simple, alternate leaves are *3–6 cm (1.2–2.4 in) long, 2–4 cm (0.8–1.6 in) wide, broadest near the base,* variably and *coarsely toothed along the margin,* bright green and hairy when young. Flowers, produced in clusters, have a green, 5-parted calyx, *5 white, strap-shaped petals 7–10 mm (0.3–0.4 in) long,* and 20 stamens. The fruits are produced in drooping clusters, each *fruit rounded, 9–11 mm (0.4 in) in diameter, dark purple to nearly black,* containing several seeds 2.5–3.5 mm (0.1 in) long.

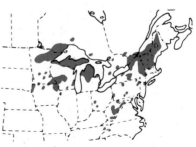

Downy Serviceberry

Amelanchier arborea (Michx. f.) Fern.
(synonym: *A. laevis* Wieg.)

Downy serviceberry is named for its densely silver-haired leaves. Also known as shadblow and serviceberry, this species ranges from New Brunswick to eastern Minnesota, south to eastern Texas and Florida. It occurs in woods, along river banks, swamps, and rocky slopes. This is a small tree found growing in association with several oaks, yellow poplar, hickories, sweet birch, loblolly and shortleaf pines.

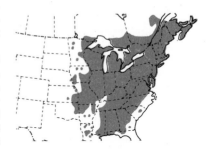

The drooping clusters of showy white fragrant flowers appear in early spring and stand out against the often leafless trees. The juicy fruits can be used in pies, puddings, and muffins, but the long ripening time and the fact that the birds eat them make it difficult to gather many at one time. During the summer, thrushes, songbirds, squirrels, other rodents, and even bears feed on the fruits. Whitetail deer browse the leaves and young twigs.

The hard, brown wood is as heavy as persimmon wood, but the small size of the tree makes it unsuitable for anything but tool handles or other small articles. The trees are occasionally planted for their attractive flowers.

Downy Serviceberry

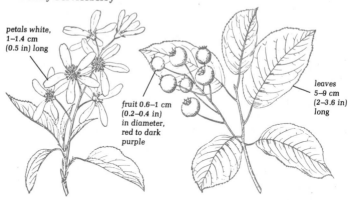

petals white, 1–1.4 cm (0.5 in) long

fruit 0.6–1 cm (0.2–0.4 in) in diameter, red to dark purple

leaves 5–9 cm (2–3.6 in) long

Appearance: shrub or small tree to 12 m (40 ft), with a narrow, rounded crown and a single trunk to 70 cm (28 in) in diameter. **Bark:** 5–12 mm (0.2–0.5 in) thick, smooth when young, becoming slightly ridged and furrowed, ash-gray to almost black. **Branches:** slender, erect to spreading; branchlets slender, flexible, reddish-brown to gray-brown, smooth to slightly hairy. **Winter buds:** 10–12 mm (0.4–0.5 in) long, tapering to a pointed tip, covered with overlapping reddish-brown to yellowish-green scales. **Leaves:** alternate, simple, deciduous, 5–9 cm (2–3.6 in) long, 2.5–3.5 cm (1–1.4 in) wide, broadest at or near the middle, tapering to an abrupt point at the tip, rounded or slightly heart-shaped at the base, *finely toothed along the margin,* dark green above, sparsely hairy but becoming smooth, paler beneath and densely hairy; leafstalks slender, 1–25 cm (0.4–1 in) long, smooth. **Flowers:** produced in 3- to 15-flowered clusters at or near the tips of the branchlets; each flower bisexual with a cone-shaped, 5-lobed calyx; *5 petals, strap-shaped, 1–1.4 cm (0.4–0.6 in) long,* straight or twisted; 20 stamens, 1 pistil. **Fruits:** produced in open clusters, each fruit rounded, 6–10 mm (0.2–0.4 in) in diameter, ***red to dark purple,*** fleshy, containing 5 to 8 black seeds, each 3.5–4 mm (0.2 in) long.

Inland Serviceberry

Amelanchier interior Nielsen

This serviceberry is native to Minnesota, Wisconsin, western Iowa, northern Illinois, and northern Michigan where it grows in dry woods along bluffs or slopes. The flowers appear in May or June, and the fruits, which are eaten by birds and small mammals, mature by July or August. Inland serviceberry is *similar in appearance to the downy serviceberry but can be distinguished by its smaller flowers in short clusters and its smaller size.*

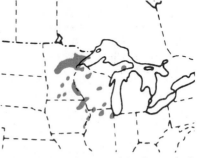

Inland serviceberry is a straggling shrub or small tree to 8 m (26 ft) with reddish-brown winter buds that are 7–13 mm (0.3–0.5 in) long and pointed at the tip. The alternate, simple leaves are deciduous, broadest at or below the middle, 3–7 cm (1.2–2.8 in) long, 2–5 cm (0.8–2 in) wide, pointed at the tip, rounded to almost heart-shaped at the base, and finely toothed along the margin. Flowers are produced in 6- to 12-flowered elongated clusters; each flower with *5 white petals 8–13 mm (0.3–0.5 in) long,* 15 to 20 stamens, and a 5-parted pistil. The fruits are rounded, 6–8 mm (0.3 in) in diameter, ***purplish-black,*** juicy, edible, containing several smooth, brown seeds.

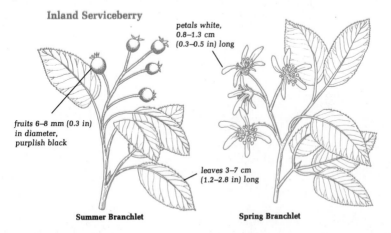

Inland Serviceberry

petals white,
0.8–1.3 cm
(0.3–0.5 in) long

fruits 6–8 mm (0.3 in)
in diameter,
purplish black

leaves 3–7 cm
(1.2–2.8 in) long

Summer Branchlet

Spring Branchlet

The Pear, Apple Genus

(synonym: *Malus* Mill.)

This genus of about 55 species is native to North America, southern Europe, western Asia, and northern Africa. Pears and apples are sometimes classed in separate genera because the pear genus has pear-shaped fruits containing gritty stone cells, and the apple genus has rounded fruits lacking stone cells. But the flowers and leaves are virtually the same.

Fossils indicate that the fruits of these trees were eaten by prehistoric man and cultivated for more than 2,000 years. Europeans brought them to North America where many escaped cultivation and grew wild. John Smith used the term "crabapple" in describing native species growing in Virginia. Probably sweet crabapple and southern crabapple, with bitter fruit and beautiful spring flowers, are the native species he saw. The Siberian crabapple was introduced early in the history of America along with European species. Indians and early traders, as well as an eccentric missionary named Johnny "Appleseed" Chapman, carried seeds and seedlings to all parts of North America. The common edible pear (*Pyrus communis*) is the best known and most widely cultivated of the pears. Animals spread the seeds of the edible pear, allowing it on occasion to become established in fields or edges of woodlands. The Bradford Callary pear (*P. calleryana*), a selection of another species, is frequently planted as a street tree in cities, especially in the eastern U.S.

Apple and pear trees are popular for many reasons. Beauty in bud, as well as attractive flowers and varieties of form, make them useful in garden plantings. Fruits are often commercially or locally made into pies, cider, sauces, jams, and jellies. The fruits also attract many kinds of wildlife, mainly ring-necked pheasant, ruffed grouse, several kinds of songbirds, bears, foxes, small mammals, and whitetail deer. The close-grained, heavy wood is of little importance commercially, though it is used to some extent for tool handles and wooden ware. It makes excellent fuel.

Members of this genus have scaly, thin, gray to red-brown bark and slender branches marked with circular bud scars and narrow horizontal leaf scars. The branches form a narrow to broad, round open crown. Leaves are simple, alternate, and deciduous, with entire, toothed, or lobed margins and slender stalks. The attractive white to rose-colored, fragrant, bisexual flowers grow in clusters at ends of short, spur-like branches. The calyx tube is urn- or bell-shaped with 5 lobes. The 5 petals are rounded at the tip, narrow and claw-shaped at the base. Twenty to 30 stamens in 3 rows are joined to petals at the base by a disk. The drooping fruit is usually rounded or pear-shaped, depressed at the base, with thick, firm, juicy flesh, and containing shiny, brown, pointed seeds.

Key to Pear and Apple Species

A. Fruits pear-shaped, containing microscopic stone cells in the flesh to give a gritty taste; introduced trees **Common pear, p. 599**

B. Fruit rounded or "apple-shaped," flesh not gritty.

    1. Fruits rounded, 2.5–8 cm (1–3.2 in) in diameter, often as wide as long, with a waxy coating.

        a. Mature leaves hairy on the lower surface.

        (1) Leaves coarsely toothed and somewhat lobed along the margin; fruits 2.5–4 cm

(1–1.6 in) in diameter, sour to tart taste; trees of midwestern U.S.
        Prairie crabapple, p. 600
(2) Leaves with regular, fine teeth along the margin; fruits 2–8 cm (0.8–3.2 in) in diameter, sweet taste; introduced and widely cultivated   **Apple, p. 601**

b. Mature leaves smooth on the lower surface.

(1) Leaves lance-shaped, 2½–3 times as long as broad, often rounded at the tip; trees of southeastern U.S.
        Southern crabapple, p. 602
(2) Leaves broadest near the base or the middle, up to 2 times as long as broad, short to long-pointed at the tip; trees of eastern North America
        Sweet crabapple, p. 603

2. Fruits uniformly wide, about twice as long as wide, 1.2–2 cm (0.5–0.8 in) long, lacking a waxy coating; trees of Pacific Coastal Region
        Oregon crabapple, p. 604

Prairie Crabapple

Oregon Crabapple

Common Pear   *Pyrus communis* L.

The common pear, widely cultivated in North America, can be found growing wild along fencerows, old fields, and secondary woodlands from Maine to Missouri, south to Texas and Florida. Under cultivation the trees are heavily pruned for greater production and ease of harvesting, so they seldom reach full size.

Flowering is in early spring, with the fruits ripening by early fall. A season of heavy fruit production usually is followed by a light crop the next year. The fallen fruits attract deer and cattle in autumn. Small mammals will sometimes feed on developing

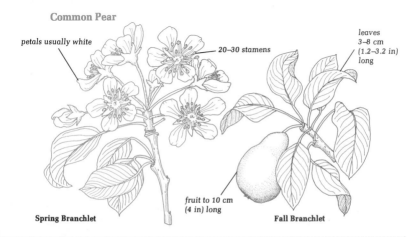

Common Pear

petals usually white

20–30 stamens

leaves
3–8 cm
(1.2–3.2 in)
long

fruit to 10 cm
(4 in) long

Spring Branchlet   **Fall Branchlet**

fruits. The hard, fine-grained reddish-brown wood is of excellent quality and can be employed in carvings, rules, and drawing instruments.

Appearance: small trees to 20 m (66 ft), with a rounded or cone-shaped crown; trunk straight, to 30 cm (12 in) in diameter, rarely larger. **Bark:** 5–8 mm (0.2–0.3 in) thick, scaly with shallow fissures, dark brown to gray. **Branches:** short, stout, upright; branchlets stout, smooth, reddish-brown and often with small, yellow dots. **Winter buds:** 3–6 mm (0.1–0.2 in) long, egg-shaped, blunt and hairy at tip, usually with 2 side buds. **Leaves:** alternate, simple, deciduous, 3–8 cm (1.2–3.2 in) long, broadest below, at, or above the middle, narrowing to a sharp-pointed tip, rounded at the base, fine-toothed or entire along the margin, thick, leathery, hairy when young, becoming dark, shiny green above, paler and smooth or slightly hairy beneath; leafstalk slender, as long as or longer than the blade. **Flowers:** produced in few to many-flowered clusters on spur-like branchlets of the previous year's growth; each flower on slender, often hairy stems 1.5–5 cm (0.6–2 in) long, with a green, 5-lobed, urn-shaped, hairy calyx, 5 white or pink petals, rounded, narrowing at the base; 20 to 30 stamens, pistil with 4 or 5 branches. **Fruits:** *pear-shaped, to 10 cm (4 in) long, hard, becoming fleshy* at maturity, the *flesh containing gritty stone cells,* and with a leathery core containing several large, brown seeds.

Prairie Crabapple

Pyrus ioensis (Wood) Bailey
[synonym: *Malus ioensis* (Wood) Britton]

Prairie crab is a small tree, similar to other crabapples but located in the Midwest. It occurs from Indiana to southwestern Minnesota south to central Texas and Louisiana. This tree grows in prairies, woodland openings, pastures, and bottomlands and is associated with oaks, cottonwood, shell-bark hickory, and hawthorn. *Its most distinguishing characteristic is the dense hairiness of new growth in summer. The leaves are shorter and oval in shape with deep irregular teeth.* This species is slow-growing and short-lived and has no serious enemies except fire.

The prairie crabapple is a handsome tree occasionally cultivated for ornamental use, especially Bechtels crabapple, a double-flowering form often found in parks and gardens. The heavy wood has little commercial use, though the hard bitter fruit makes excellent jellies and cider. Prairie crabapple fruit is an important source of food for more than 20 species of songbirds, pheasant, grouse, turkey, and quail, along with squirrels and other rodents. Whitetail deer eat the fruit and forage the twigs and foliage. Songbirds and grouse use the dense crabapple thickets for cover.

Appearance: small tree to 6 m (20 ft) with open, rounded crown, often forming dense thickets, trunk to 45 cm (18 in) in diameter. **Bark:** 6–9 mm (0.2–0.3 in) thick, with lengthwise furrows and ridges of reddish-brown scales. **Branches:** stout, spreading; branchlets slender, some with sharp spines on the short side shoots, covered with dense white hairs when young, becoming smooth, dark gray to reddish-brown. **Winter buds:** 2–4 mm (0.1 in) long, egg-shaped, hairy, covered with overlapping reddish-brown scales. **Leaves:** alternate, deciduous, broadest at or near the base to uniformly wide, 5.5–11 cm (2.2–4.4 in) long, 2.5–4 cm (1–1.6 in) wide, rounded or pointed at the tip, tapering to rounded at the base, *coarsely toothed and somewhat lobed on the*

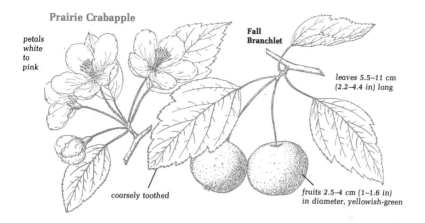

Prairie Crabapple

petals
white
to
pink

Fall
Branchlet

leaves 5.5–11 cm
(2.2–4.4 in) long

coarsely toothed

fruits 2.5–4 cm (1–1.6 in)
in diameter, yellowish-green

margin, covered with dense hairs when young, dark green and shiny above, paler and hairy beneath; leafstalks stout, 2–5 cm (0.8–2 in) long, hairy. **Flowers:** produced in 3- to 7-flowered clusters on short side shoots, each flower 3–5 cm (1.2–2 in) across, white to pink, stalked, with a densely hairy, 5-lobed, bell-shaped calyx, 5 petals, broadest near the rounded tip, numerous stamens, 1 pistil. **Fruits:** 1 to several on stalks to 2.5 cm (1 in) long, *rounded, 2.5–4 cm (1–1.6 in) in diameter,* depressed at the tip and base, yellowish-green; seeds slightly flattened, 6–8 mm (0.3 in) long, dark brown.

Apple
Pyrus malus L.

[synonyms: *Malus pumila* Mill., *M. sylvestris* (L.) Mill.]
This species, also known as wild or common apple, is native to Asia and Europe but is cultivated and also grows wild from Nova Scotia to southern Ontario and other parts of Canada, southward and west, locally in eastern Washington and northern Idaho. This is the apple of ancient history with more than 3,000 varieties developed by accident, as well as by cultivation, since colonial times. Seedling plants have often been mistaken for native crabapples but can be *easily recognized by the hairy outer surface of the calyx and leafstalks, as well as the absence of spines.*

It is widely grown as a fruit and ornamental tree; some dwarf and double-flowered varieties are occasionally seen in gardens and public parks. Good fruit crops appear every other year or more. Fruit on wild trees is usually coarse and sour. Wildlife depends heavily on this tree for food, nesting, and protection. Gamebirds, such as grouse and ring-necked pheasant, and songbirds, such as purple finch, flicker, robin, cedar waxwing, and woodpecker, eat the fruits, seeds, and buds. Black bears, foxes, marmots, rabbits, raccoons, red squirrels, and other small rodents consume the fruit and bark, while whitetail deer browse twigs, foliage, and fruit. The red-brown wood is hard, close-grained, and is used in making tools, bowls, and decorative carving.

Appearance: medium-size tree to 12 m (40 ft), with a broad, rounded crown; trunk short, to 90 cm (35 in) in diameter. **Bark:** 8–10 mm (0.3–0.4 in) thick, dark brown-gray, broken into irregular flaky plates. **Branches:** stout, spreading; branchlets stout, densely hairy, light green becoming purplish or reddish-brown, then smooth and dark gray-brown. **Winter buds:** 2–4 mm (0.1 in) long, blunt, hairy. **Leaves:** alternate, deciduous, 4–10 cm (1.6–4 in) long, 3–5.5 cm (1.2–2.2 in) wide, broadest at base or toward the

Apple

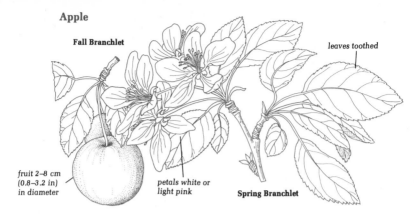

Fall Branchlet

leaves toothed

fruit 2–8 cm (0.8–3.2 in) in diameter

petals white or light pink

Spring Branchlet

middle, narrowing to a blunt or short-pointed tip, rounded or heart-shaped at the base, ***toothed or nearly entire along the margin,*** thick, dark green, smooth above, ***lightly to very densely hairy beneath;*** leafstalks stout, 1.5–3 cm (0.6–1.2 in) long, hairy. **Flowers:** produced in few-flowered clusters; each flower 3–8 cm (1.2–3.2 in) across, on stout, hairy stalks 2–5 cm (0.8–2 in) long, with an urn-shaped calyx, petals broadest above middle, white or light pink, rounded at tip and usually without teeth; numerous stamens, 1 pistil. **Fruits:** *(an apple), rounded, 2–8 cm (0.8–3.2 in) in diameter,* green, yellow, red, sometimes elongated, indented at both ends, with a semi-hard, juicy flesh surrounding several small brown to black seeds.

Southern Crabapple

Pyrus angustifolia Ait.

[synonym: *Malus angustifolia* (Ait.) Michx.]

This small tree, also called narrowleaf crabapple, occurs along the Coastal Plain from Maryland to northwestern Florida, west to Louisiana and Texas. It grows in woods and thickets, especially along riverbanks, and often is found with sweetgum, red maple, tulip tree, southern red oak, long-leaf and loblolly pines.

Southern crabapple is a short-lived tree that has been planted as an ornamental for many years. It was a favorite of George Washington, who enjoyed the tart fragrance of the flowers in spring. The sour fruit is used to make jelly, preserves, and cider. Whitetail deer, foxes, raccoons, skunks, squirrels, quail, turkeys, and many smaller birds eat the fruits. The hard, light reddish-brown wood is commercially un-

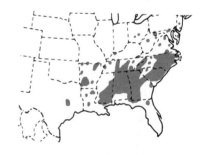

important but has been used in making tool handles, levers, and small wooden ware objects.

Appearance: small tree, often forming thickets, to 9 m (30 ft), with a broad, rounded crown; trunk to 30 cm (12 in) in diameter. **Bark:** thin, 4–8 mm (0.1–0.3 in) thick, scaly and narrowly ridged, reddish-brown. **Branches:** stout, spreading; branchlets stiff, spreading, hairy when young, becoming smooth, brown. **Winter buds:** 1.5–3 mm (0.1 in) long, blunt, covered with overlapping, chestnut-brown scales. **Leaves:** alternate, deciduous, *2–4 cm (0.8–1.6 in) long, 0.8–1.5 cm (0.3–0.6 in) wide, broadest near the*

Southern Crabapple

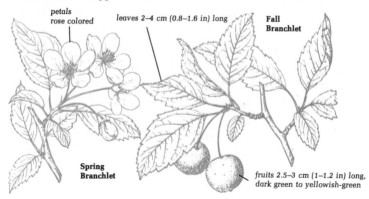

petals
rose colored

leaves 2–4 cm (0.8–1.6 in) long

Fall Branchlet

Spring Branchlet

fruits 2.5–3 cm (1–1.2 in) long, dark green to yellowish-green

base to broadly lance-shaped, rounded to pointed at the tip, tapering at the base, entire or finely toothed along the margin, thick, leathery, shiny dark green above, paler beneath, **hairy when young, becoming smooth with age;** leafstalk slender, 2–2.5 cm (0.8–1 in) long. **Flowers:** produced in few-flowered clusters on short lateral shoots, each flower 2–2.5 cm (0.8–1 in) across, rose-colored, stalked, fragrant, with a 5-lobed, urn-shaped calyx; 5 petals, broadest at the tip; numerous stamens; 1 pistil. **Fruits:** rounded, 2.5–3 cm (1–1.2 in) in diameter, skin dark green to pale yellow-green, with a hard flesh; seeds slightly flattened, dark brown.

Sweet Crabapple   *Pyrus coronaria* L.

[synonym: *Malus coronaria* (L.) Mill., *M. glabrata* Rehd.]

Sweet crabapple is a small tree that occurs from central New York to eastern Kansas and across the southern states to western South Carolina. It grows best in upland woods in moist, rich soil. These trees have sharp spines on the twigs, and the flowers appear later than those of cultivated varieties. Their leaves are smooth at maturity and half as broad as they are long, often triangular in shape with a rounded base.

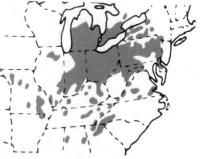

The sweet crabapple is slow-growing and short-lived, with fragrant flowers appearing in May or June when the leaves have unfolded. The fruit matures in late autumn. It is cultivated as an ornamental for its attractive blossoms, dense form, and spicy odor. The fruits are used to make cider and tart jelly. Grosbeaks and whitetail deer eat the fruits, and songbirds favor the tree for nesting and protection. The wood is heavier than the southern crabapple and is used for tools, small domestic articles, and as firewood.

Appearance: short bushy tree to 9 m (30 ft), with a broad, rounded crown; trunk straight, to 35 cm (14 in) in diameter. **Bark:** 6–10 mm (0.2–0.4 in) thick, with lengthwise furrows and ridges that separate in long scales, reddish-brown. **Branches:** slender, spreading, often angular in cross section; branchlets slender, with spine-like lat-

Sweet Crabapple

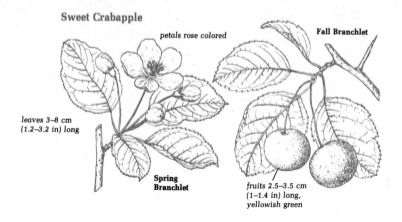

petals rose colored

Fall Branchlet

leaves 3–8 cm
(1.2–3.2 in) long

Spring
Branchlet

fruits 2.5–3.5 cm
(1–1.4 in) long,
yellowish green

eral spurs, covered with dense hairs when young, becoming smooth and reddish-brown to light brown. **Winter buds:** 2–4 mm (0.1 in) long, rounded at the tip, covered with overlapping red scales. **Leaves:** alternate, deciduous, ***broadest near the base or middle, 3–8 cm (1.2–3.2 in) long, 1.5–4 cm (0.6–1.6 in) wide, short to long-pointed at the tip,*** rounded to heart-shaped at the base, coarsely toothed along the margin, hairy when young, becoming smooth at maturity, bright green above, paler beneath; leaf-stalks stout, 4–5 cm (1.6–2 in) long. **Flowers:** produced in few-flowered clusters on short, lateral spur shoots; each flower 1.8–3.8 cm (0.7–1.5 in) across, rose-colored, on slender stalks 1.2–2.5 cm (0.5–1 in) long, calyx 5-lobed, urn-shaped, hairy; 5 petals, broadest near the rounded tip; numerous stamens, 1 pistil. **Fruits:** rounded to globe-shaped, usually wider than long, 2.5–3.5 cm (1–1.4 in) long, yellowish-green when mature, with a waxy covering, flesh firm, bitter-tasting; seeds slightly flattened, dark brown.

Oregon Crabapple

Pyrus fusca Raf.

[synonym: *Malus diversifolia* (Bong.) Roem, *M. fusca* (Raf.) Schneid.] This species occurs in moist rich soils along streams and low river bottoms in the Pacific Coast region from southern Alaska to northwestern California. A lowland tree, this crabapple grows up to 800 m (2,600 ft) elevation on the western slopes of the Cascade Mountains. It usually occurs in dense pure thickets but also grows in association with red alder, willow, broadleaf maple, and western dogwood. Fruits vary from yellow to red in color.

This slow-growing species is planted occasionally as an ornamental. Its fruits were once an important food for Indians who dried them for winter. It is still an important food for such wildlife as deer, small mammals, and many birds which feed on the fruits. The trees, especially the thickets, provide excellent cover and nesting sites for some of the songbirds. The wood is fine-grained, hard, light reddish-brown, suitable for mallets, tool handles, and small turnery.

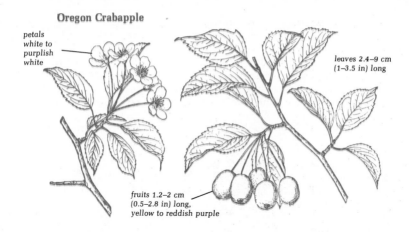

Oregon Crabapple

petals
white to
purplish
white

leaves 2.4–9 cm
(1–3.5 in) long

fruits 1.2–2 cm
(0.5–2.8 in) long,
yellow to reddish purple

Appearance: large shrub or small tree to 12 m (40 ft), with a spreading, rounded crown; trunk to 45 cm (18 in) in diameter. **Bark:** 4–6 mm (0.2 in) thick, with large flattened scales, reddish-brown. **Branches:** slender, spreading; branchlets slender, hairy when young becoming smooth, shiny and turning dark brown. **Winter buds:** 1.5–3 mm (0.1 in) long, rounded at the tip, covered with overlapping, reddish-brown scales. **Leaves:** alternate, deciduous, lance-shaped to broadest near the middle, *2.4–9 cm (1–3.5 in) long, 1.2–4 cm (0.5–1.6 in) wide,* pointed to long-pointed at the tip, tapering to rounded at the base, *often shallowly 3-lobed,* sharply toothed along the margin, thick, dark-green and smooth above, paler and sometimes slightly hairy beneath; leafstalks stout, 2.5–4 cm (1–1.6 in) long, hairy. **Flowers:** 5 to 12 per cluster at the tips of the short side shoots; each flower 1.6–2.2 cm (0.5–0.9 in) across, white to pinkish-white, with a 5-lobed, bell-shaped calyx, 5 petals, broadest near the rounded tip; numerous stamens, 1 pistil. **Fruits:** *uniformly wide to broadest near the tip, 1.2–2 cm (0.5–0.8 in) long, half as wide, yellow to reddish-purple at maturity,* flesh thin, dry, sour-tasting; seeds slightly flattened, brown.

The Hawthorn Genus

Crataegus L.

This is a large genus of shrubs and small to medium-size trees, primarily of North America but also of Mexico, South America, Europe, and Asia. They commonly occur on disturbed sites, along the margins of woodlands, along streams, and in abandoned fields. As a genus hawthorns are easy to identify. But the identification of individual species is extremely difficult, so difficult that even botanists do not agree precisely how many are present in the U.S. and Canada. The identification problems arise from the widespread hybridization and genetic changes in which the characteristics on an individual tree or population of trees may show greater variation than exist between known species. Over 700 species have been described worldwide. Current estimates for valid species in North America range from 26 to 150. *The discussion here will be a conservative one, focusing on the 26 most commonly encountered and distinguishable hawthorns.* Most other species for North America could be considered hybrids.

Because of their dense branching system and leaves, hawthorns provide excellent cover and nesting sites for many smaller birds. The small fruits are eaten by many birds, especially cedar waxwings, fox sparrows, and ruffed grouse. They are also eaten by rodents and small birds. Whitetail deer and mule deer browse the young twigs and leaves.

Hawthorns usually have spreading spiny branches and rounded, dark-brown winter buds. The alternate, deciduous leaves are simple, toothed, and shallowly to deeply lobed. Flowers are bisexual, produced singly or more often in clusters, with a 5-lobed calyx; 5 petals, white, rarely pink or red; 5–25 stamens; 1 pistil. Fruits are rounded, pear-shaped or egg-shaped, usually red but sometimes yellow, green, or almost black, with a thin to thick (often hard) flesh, and containing 1–5 nut-like units, each with 1 seed.

Key to Hawthorn Species

A. Veins of the leaves extending to the tips of the lobes only, not to the sinuses.

  1. Fruits bluish-black, black, or very dark red.

Black Hawthorn

    a. Branches with thorns 1–2 cm (0.4–0.8 in) long; fruits bluish-black; widespread northern trees   **Black hawthorn, p. 610**

    b. Branches with thorns 4–7 cm (1.6–2.8 in) long; fruits dark red; trees of northwestern North America

        Columbia hawthorn, p. 610

Fleshy Hawthorn

  2. Fruits red, orange, yellow, or green at maturity.

    a. Nutlets (within the fruits) with lengthwise cavities or deep pits on their inner surface.

      (1) Leaves dark green and shiny; wide-ranging trees **Fleshy hawthorn, p. 610**

      (2) Leaves dull yellow-green; trees of eastern North America

          Pear hawthorn, p. 611

    b. Nutlets not pitted on inner surface.

      (1) Flowers produced singly, rarely in 2s or 3s; calyx lobes leaf-like; trees of eastern U.S. **One-flowered hawthorn, p. 611**

      (2) Flowers produced in few to many-flowered clusters; calyx lobes not leaf-like.

        (a) Leaves, flowers, and flower-cluster stalks with tiny glands; flowers in few-flowered clusters.

(a1) Leaves broadest above the middle, with 1–3 shallow lobes; trees of southeastern U.S. **Yellow hawthorn, p. 611**

(a2) Leaves broadest at or below the middle, with 3–5 pairs of shallow lobes; trees of eastern North America
Entangled hawthorn, p. 612

(b) Leaves, flowers, and flower-cluster stalks without tiny glands; flowers in few- to many-flowered clusters.

(b1) Leaves broadest above the middle to uniformly wide.

(b1a) Leaves thin, leafstalks slender; fruits 4–10 mm (0.2–0.4 in) in diameter.

Branches mainly without spines; leaves yellow-green and shallowly 3-lobed; trees of southeastern and southern midwestern U.S.
Green hawthorn, p. 612

**Branches spiny; leaves dark green and rarely lobed; trees of outer Coastal Plain of southeastern U.S.*
May hawthorn, p. 613

(b1b) Leaves firm to leathery, leafstalks stout; fruits 7–15 mm (0.3–0.6 in) in diameter.

Leaves unlobed or rarely shallowly lobed on nonflowering branchlets.

• Leaves thick, leathery, dark green and shiny above; trees of eastern North America
Cockspur hawthorn, p. 614

• • Leaves firm but not leathery nor shiny above, yellowish-green.

Leaves hairy beneath at maturity; trees of Arkansas and Louisiana.
Barberryleaf hawthorn, p. 614

Yellow Hawthorn

Green Hawthorn

May Hawthorn

Cockspur Hawthorn

(Continued)

Leaves smooth beneath at maturity; trees of Trans-Pecos Texas
Tracy hawthorn, p. 614

**_Leaves lobed on flowering branchlets, deeply lobed on non-flowering shoots; trees of eastern North America_
Dotted hawthorn, p. 614

Dotted Hawthorn

(b2) Leaves broadest near the base, sometimes near the middle.

Round-Leaved Hawthorn

(b2a) Leaves of flowering branchlets tapering to a narrow base.

*_Leaves almost round, widest above the middle; widely distributed northern trees_
Round-Leaved hawthorn, p. 615
**_Leaves broadest near the base or middle, pointed to abruptly short-pointed at the tip._

• Trees of eastern U.S.; leaves 3.5–7 cm (1.4–2.8 in) long
Brainerd hawthorn, p. 615
•• Trees of western U.S.; leaves 3–4 cm (1.2–1.6 in) long
Cerro hawthorn, p. 616

(b2b) Leaves of flowering branchlets broadly rounded to squared-off at the base.

*_Young leaves rough to touch due to short, stiff hairs; fruits with a persistent calyx; trees of eastern North America_
Fanleaf hawthorn, p. 616
**_Young leaves hairy or smooth, but not rough to touch._

• Flower stalks and leaves with dense, long hairs; leafstalks stout
Downy hawthorn, p. 616
•• Flower stalks and leaves

Downy Hawthorn

smooth or with short hairs; leafstalks slender.

Leaves on flowering branches uniformly wide to slightly widest near the base; trees of Northeast
Scarlet hawthorn, p. 617

Scarlet Hawthorn

Leaves on flowering branches broadest near the base to triangular shaped.

Fruits with a thin, dry, often hard flesh; trees of eastern North America
Frosted hawthorn, p. 618
Fruits with a thick soft flesh; of southern Midwest

Kansas hawthorn, p. 618

Frosted Hawthorn

B. Veins of the leaves extending to the tips of the lobes and to the sinuses.

  1. Fruits with 3–5 nutlets per fruit, each containing a seed.

    a. Fruits depressed at stem, globe-shaped, red.

      (1) Leaves pointed to long pointed at the tip; calyx not persisting on the fruits; trees of eastern North America
        Washington hawthorn, p. 619
      (2) Leaves rounded to pointed at the tip; calyx persisting on the fruits.

Washington Hawthorn

        (a) Leaves hairy; flower clusters hairy; trees of southeastern Coastal Plain and southern Midwest
          Parsley hawthorn, p. 619
        (b) Leaves smooth at maturity; flower clusters smooth; trees of southern U.S. **Littlehip hawthorn, p. 619**

    b. Fruits globe-shaped, bluish-black; trees of Colorado **Willow hawthorn, p. 619**

  2. Fruits with 1 nutlet containing 1 seed; introduced trees now growing wild
        English hawthorn, p. 620

Willow Hawthorn

Black Hawthorn

Crataegus douglasii Lindl.

This ranges from southwestern Ontario to the Pacific Coast and occurs throughout the Rocky Mountains. It is a shrub or small tree to 12 m (40 ft) with shallowly and *often irregularly lobed leaves* that are broadest above or near the middle, 2–4.2 cm (0.8–1.7 in) long, 1.4–2.8 cm (0.6–1.1 in) wide, dark green, shiny, and smooth. Small clusters of 5 to 12 flowers are produced in spring followed in autumn by nearly globe-shaped, *dark reddish-purple to black fruit 0.8–1 cm (0.3–0.4 in) in diameter.*

Black Hawthorn

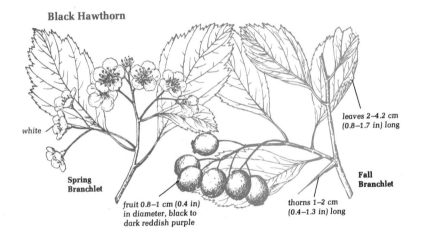

white

Spring
Branchlet

fruit 0.8–1 cm (0.4 in)
in diameter, black to
dark reddish purple

leaves 2–4.2 cm
(0.8–1.7 in) long

Fall
Branchlet

thorns 1–2 cm
(0.4–1.3 in) long

Columbia Hawthorn

Crataegus columbiana Howell

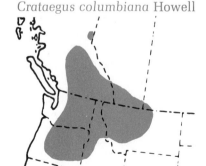

A straggling shrub or small tree, Columbia hawthorn ranges from British Columbia to northeastern California, eastern Oregon, and Idaho. The short-stalked leaves are broadest near the base to above the middle, 3–7 cm (1.2–2.8 in) long, only *shallowly lobed,* singly or doubly toothed along the margin, and hairy on both surfaces. White flowers are produced in 3–8-flowered clusters. Fruits are nearly globe-shaped, *8–11 cm (3.2–4.4 in) in diameter, dark red,* and hairy to smooth.

Fleshy Hawthorn

Crataegus succulenta Schrad.

Fleshy hawthorn is a wide-ranging species extending from Nova Scotia and Maine west to Montana, Utah, and Colorado, and south to Tennessee and North Carolina. It is a tree to 8 m (26 ft) with branches armed with long spines 3–4.5 cm (1.2–1.8 in) long. **Leaves** are broadest below or above the middle, 3–7 cm (1.2–2.8 in) long, 2–5.2 cm (0.8–2.1 in) wide, shallowly lobed near the tip, **dark green, shiny** and smooth. Flowers are produced in several-flowered clusters. The **fruits** are borne on slender stalks and are **globe-shaped, 0.8–1.6 cm (0.3–0.7 in) in diameter, and bright red.**

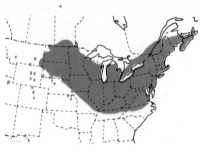

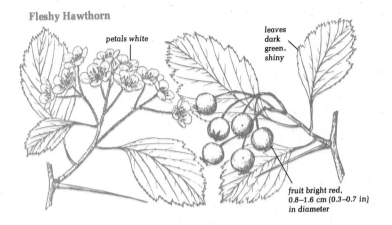

Fleshy Hawthorn

petals white

leaves dark green, shiny

fruit bright red, 0.8–1.6 cm (0.3–0.7 in) in diameter

Pear Hawthorn *Crataegus calpodendron* (Ehrh.) Medic.

Pear hawthorn is an eastern North American tree related to fleshy hawthorn; it differs by having dull yellow-green and thinner leaves, and more elongated fruits.

One-Flowered Hawthorn *Crataegus uniflora* Muenchh.

This ranges from New York to northern Florida, and west to eastern Texas and Oklahoma. It is a shrub, rarely a tree, with leaves widest near the tip, 1.5–3 cm (0.6–1.2 in) long, 0.7–2 cm (0.3–0.8 in) wide, sometimes shallowly lobed near the tip, and hairy. The white **flowers** are **produced singly** or rarely in 2s or 3s. Fruits are almost globe-shaped, 8–12 mm (0.3–0.5 in) in diameter, dull red or yellowish-green.

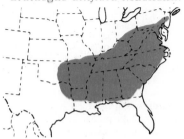

Yellow Hawthorn *Crataegus flava* Ait.

A shrub or small tree of the southeastern U.S., yellow hawthorn grows to 5 m (16 ft) and the branches are armed with spines to 6 cm (2.4 in) long. **Leaves** are **widest** *above the middle,* 2–5 cm (0.8–2 in) long, 1–3 cm (0.4–1.2 in) wide, *shallowly lobed,* and hairy. White *flowers* are produced *in 3–5-flowered clusters.* Fruits are globe-shaped, 0.8–1.6 cm (0.3–0.7 in) in diameter, and red.

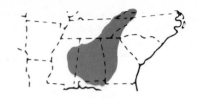

Yellow Hawthorn

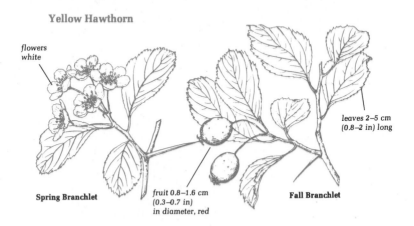

flowers white

leaves 2–5 cm (0.8–2 in) long

Spring Branchlet

fruit 0.8–1.6 cm (0.3–0.7 in) in diameter, red

Fall Branchlet

Entangled Hawthorn

Crataegus intricata Lange

(synonyms: *C. biltmoreana* Beadle, *C. boyntonii* Beadle, *C. rubella* Beadle)

This is a large shrub or small tree of eastern North America. *Leaves* are variable in shape, generally *broadest at or below the middle,* 2.8–5.5 cm (1.1–2.2 in) long, 1.5–5 cm (0.6–2 in) wide, with 3–5 pairs of shallow lobes. The leaves are dark green and smooth to hairy. White *flowers are produced in several-flowered clusters.* Fruits are broadest above the middle, 8–14 mm (0.3–0.6 in) in diameter, and red, orange, yellow, or green.

Green Hawthorn

Crataegus viridis L.

This is a largely *spineless tree* of the southeast and southern Midwest. Leaves are variable, but *usually broadest above the middle,* 3–6 cm (1.2–2.4 in) long, 1.5–3 cm (0.6–1.2 in) wide, shallowly 3-lobed near the tip, *yellowish-green* and largely smooth. The clusters of white flowers are followed in autumn by globe-shaped *fruits 4–7 mm (0.1–0.3 in) in diameter,* and *bright red to orange.*

Green Hawthorn

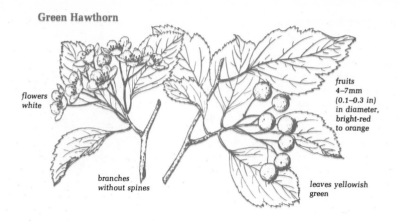

flowers
white

fruits
4–7mm
(0.1–0.3 in)
in diameter,
bright-red
to orange

branches
without spines

leaves yellowish
green

May Hawthorn — *Crataegus aestivalis* (Walt.) Torr. & Gray

May hawthorn is a tree of the outer Coastal Plain from North Carolina to Mississippi. This **spiny tree** has narrow **leaves** that are **broadest near or above the middle,** 3–6 cm (1.2–2.4 in) long, 1–3.6 cm (0.4–1.5 in) wide, coarsely toothed and rarely lobed, smooth, **dark and shiny.** Flowers are produced singly or in 2- or 3-flowered clusters. Fruits are longer than wide to globe-shaped, 8–10 mm (0.3–0.4 in) in diameter, and red in color.

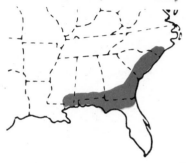

May Hawthorn

leaves dark-green,
shiny

flowers
white

fruits
bright red,
0.8–1 cm
(0.4 in) in
diameter

Cockspur Hawthorn
Crataegus crus-galli L.

(synonyms: C. acutifolia Sarg., C. canbyi Sarg., C. hannibalensis Palmer, C. pyracanthoides Beadle, C. regalis Beadle)

This is a small tree ranging from southern Quebec and Ontario to northern Louisiana, Alabama, and northwestern Georgia, and west to eastern Kansas. **Leaves** are broadest above or near the middle, 2–6 cm (0.8–2.4 in) long, 1–3.2 cm (0.4–1.3 in) wide, **usually not lobed,** smooth. White to red flowers are produced in many-flowered clusters and the **fruits** are broadest above the middle, **0.7–1 cm (0.3–0.4 in) in diameter,** dull red or green.

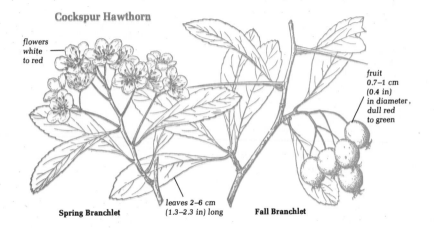

Cockspur Hawthorn

flowers white to red

fruit 0.7–1 cm (0.4 in) in diameter, dull red to green

leaves 2–6 cm (1.3–2.3 in) long

Spring Branchlet   **Fall Branchlet**

Barberryleaf Hawthorn
Crataegus berberifolia Torr. & Gray

This hawthorn is native to Arkansas and Louisiana and is related to cockspur hawthorn. Its leaves resemble those of the bayberry genus (*Myrica*).

Tracy Hawthorn
Crataegus tracyi Ashe ex Eggl.

Normally a shrub, Tracy hawthorn occurs in the Trans-Pecos region of Texas from the Edwards Plateau westward. It is similar to the cockspur hawthorn but has **more coarsely toothed leaf margins.**

Dotted Hawthorn
Crataegus punctata Jacq.

(synonyms: C. collina Chapm., C. peoriensis Sarg., C. suborbiculata Sarg., C. verruculosa Sarg.)

Dotted hawthorn extends from Quebec to Georgia, and west to Minnesota and Oklahoma. It is a shrub or small tree with slender spines to 6 cm (2.4 in) long. The thick leaves are broadest above the middle, 2.8–5.8 cm (1.6–2.3 in) long, 1.6–4.2 cm

(0.6–1.7 in) wide, often doubly toothed along the margin, with 1 or 2 deep lobes, gray-green and hairy to smooth. White flowers are produced in many-flowered clusters. Fruits are globe-shaped, 1–1.5 cm (0.4–0.6 in) in diameter, and red to yellow.

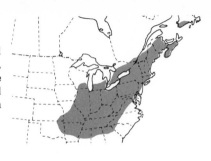

Dotted Hawthorn

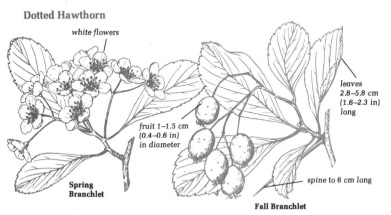

white flowers

fruit 1–1.5 cm (0.4–0.6 in) in diameter

Spring Branchlet

leaves 2.8–5.8 cm (1.6–2.3 in) long

spine to 6 cm long

Fall Branchlet

Round-Leaved Hawthorn

Crataegus chrysocarpa Ashe
(synonyms: *C. dodgei* Ashe, *C. irrasa* Sarg., *C. jonesae* Sarg., *C. margaretta* Ashe)

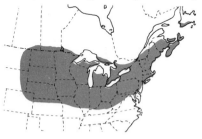

This is a large shrub or small tree ranging from Newfoundland to Pennsylvania and westward to the Rocky Mountains. The smooth to hairy *leaves are very broad, widest at or above the middle, 2–10 cm (0.8–4 in) long, 1.6–7 cm (0.6–2.8 in) wide,* usually with several shallow lobes, often dull but sometimes shiny. Flowers are produced in several-flowered clusters, and the nearly rounded fruits are 7–10 mm (0.3–0.4 in) in diameter, bright red or rarely yellow.

Brainerd Hawthorn

Crataegus brainerdii Sarg.
(synonym: *C. coleae* Sarg.)

Brainerd hawthorn is native to Quebec and New England to North Carolina, and west to Michigan. This is a *spiny shrub or tree* with *shallowly lobed leaves that are broadest near the base.* It is more closely related to the fanleaf hawthorn than other hawthorns.

Cerro Hawthorn

Crataegus erythropoda Ashe

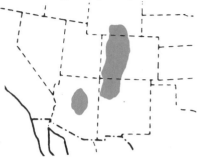

This is a shrub or small tree native from Washington to Wyoming, and south to Arizona and New Mexico. The **leaves are broadest near the base or middle, 3–4 cm (1.2–1.6 in) long, 1.5–3.5 cm (0.6–1.4 in) wide,** occasionally shallowly lobed, dark green and smooth at maturity. The white flowers are produced in 5–10-flowered clusters. Fruits are longer than wide, 8–12 mm (0.3–0.5 in) in diameter, and bright red to almost black.

Fanleaf Hawthorn

Crataegus flabellata (Bosc.) K. Koch
(synonyms: *C. beata* Sarg., *C. brumalis* Ashe,
C. brazoria Sarg., *C. compta* Sarg., *C. filipes* Ashe,
C. gravis Ashe, *C. macrosperma* Ashe, *C. populnea* Ashe)

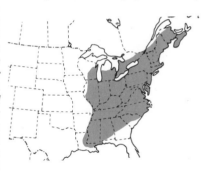

This shrub or small tree is native to northeastern North America and extends to South Carolina and Louisiana. Spines 3–4 cm (1.2–1.6 in) long occur along the branchlets. **Leaves are broad near the base to the middle, sometimes triangular shaped,** 2.6–6 cm (1–2.4 in) long, 2–5 cm (0.8–2 in) wide, shallowly lobed, **covered with rough hairs when young,** usually smooth at maturity. Flowers 3 to 15 per cluster while the fruits are globe-shaped to broadest above the middle, 8–15 mm (0.3–0.6 in) in diameter, bright red and with a juicy flesh.

Downy Hawthorn

Crataegus mollis Scheele
(synonyms: *C. arnoldiana* Sarg.,
C. canadensis Sarg., *C. submollis* Sarg.)

This species is a spreading tree to 12 m (40 ft) occurring from southern Ontario to Alabama, and west to Oklahoma. It is frequently found in limestone soils. Branches are almost thornless. The **leaves** usually are broadest near the base, **3.5–10 cm (1.4–5 in) long, 3–8 cm (1.2–3.2 in) wide,** lobed, often deeply so, **dark yellowish-green** and smooth above and **hairy beneath.** Flowers are produced in many-flowered, spreading clusters. Fruits are on short stalks, almost globe-shaped, 9–16 mm (0.3–0.7 in) in diameter, red, and with a thick flesh.

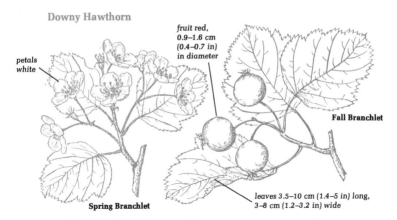

Downy Hawthorn

petals
white

fruit red,
0.9–1.6 cm
(0.4–0.7 in)
in diameter

Fall Branchlet

leaves 3.5–10 cm (1.4–5 in) long,
3–8 cm (1.2–3.2 in) wide

Spring Branchlet

Scarlet Hawthorn

Crataegus coccinea L.
(synonyms: *C. pedicellata* Sarg.,
C. pennsylvanica Ashe. *C. pringlei* Sarg.)

This shrub or small tree ranges from north-eastern North America to Minnesota and Illinois, and south to Kentucky. The branches are armed with spines 2–4 cm (0.8–1.6 in) long. Leaves are broadest near the base to almost rounded, 3–7 cm (1.2–2.8 in) long, 2.6–6.2 cm (1–2.5 in) wide, often shallowly lobed on the upper half, coarsely toothed, ***dark green and smooth except for some hairs on the veins.*** Flowers are produced on long slender stalks in many-flowered clusters. Fruits are nearly globe-shaped, usually longer than round, 0.8–1.4 cm (0.3–0.6 in) in diameter, bright red, with a thick flesh.

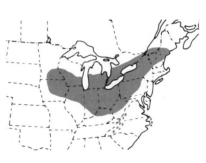

Scarlet Hawthorn

petals white

spines 2–4 cm
(0.8–1.6 in) long

leaves 3–7 cm
(1.2–2.8 in)
long, 2.6–6.2 cm
(1–2.5 in) wide

fruit
0.8–1.4 cm
(0.3–0.6 in)
in diameter,
bright red

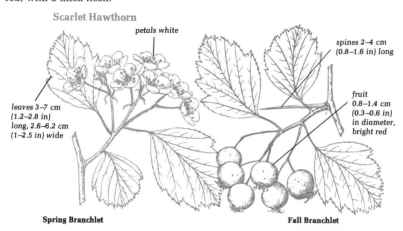

Spring Branchlet

Fall Branchlet

Frosted Hawthorn

Crataegus pruinosa (Wendl.) K. Koch

(synonyms: *C. disjuncta* Sarg.,
C. gattingeri Ashe, *C. leiophylla* Sarg., *C. mackenzii* Sarg.)

This is a widespread small tree from Newfoundland to North Carolina and west to Wisconsin and Oklahoma. Branches are armed with sharp spines 2–4 cm (0.8–1.6 in) long. *Leaves are* broad, especially near the base, *2.6–6 cm (1–2.4 in) long, 2–5 cm (0.8–2 in) wide,* shallowly lobed, dark green, covered with a waxy bloom, and smooth. Flowers are produced in few-flowered clusters followed by the globe-shaped fruits that are 1–1.6 cm (0.5 in) in diameter, dark red to green, and *with a thin flesh.*

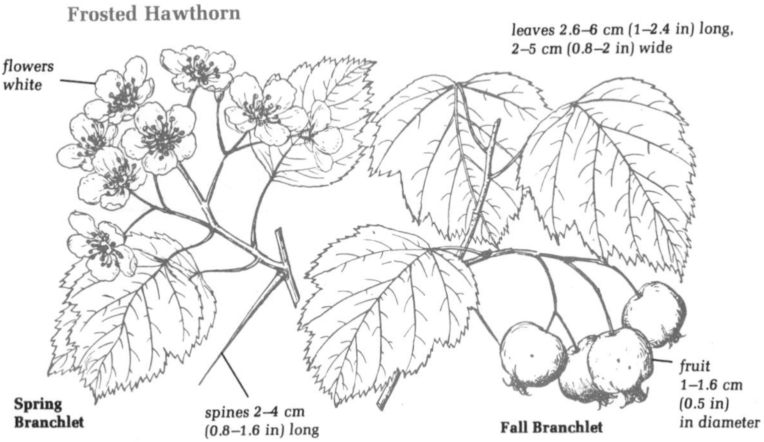

Frosted Hawthorn

flowers white

leaves 2.6–6 cm (1–2.4 in) long, 2–5 cm (0.8–2 in) wide

Spring Branchlet

spines 2–4 cm (0.8–1.6 in) long

Fall Branchlet

fruit 1–1.6 cm (0.5 in) in diameter

Kansas Hawthorn

Crataegus coccinioides Ashe

Kansas hawthorn extends from southern Illinois and Missouri to eastern Kansas, Oklahoma, and Arkansas. The branches are armed with stout, dark spines 3–5 cm (1.2–2 in) long. *Leaves* are *broadest near the base, 3.5–6 cm (1.4–2.4 in) long, 3–5 cm (1.2–2 in) wide,* with 4 to 5 pairs of lobes, yellow-green and smooth. White flowers are produced in 5- to 7-flowered clusters. Fruits are nearly globe-shaped, 1.2–1.7 cm (0.5–0.7 in) in diameter, bright red.

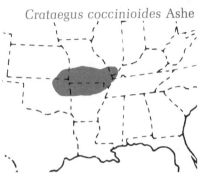

Washington Hawthorn   *Crataegus phaenopyrum* (L. f.) Medic.

This hawthorn is native to the eastern and midwestern U.S. Because of its attractive flowers, bright orange to scarlet autumn leaves, and bright red fruits persisting on the trees until winter, Washington hawthorn has been widely planted in parks and gardens throughout North America and Europe. It grows to 12 m (40 ft) with slender spines 3–5 cm (1.2–2 in) long on the branches. *Leaves* are broadest near the base, *2–6 cm (0.8–2.4 in) long, 2–5 cm (0.8–2 in) wide, with 1–4 pairs of shallow lobes,* dark green and shiny above, and usually smooth. White flowers are produced in many-flowered clusters along the branchlets. Fruits are *globe-shaped, 5–8 mm (0.3 in) in diameter,* and bright red.

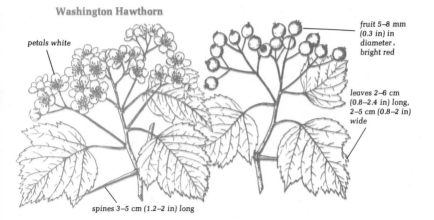

Washington Hawthorn

petals white

fruit 5–8 mm (0.3 in) in diameter, bright red

leaves 2–6 cm (0.8–2.4 in) long, 2–5 cm (0.8–2 in) wide

spines 3–5 cm (1.2–2 in) long

Parsley Hawthorn   *Crataegus marshallii* Eggl.

This hawthorn of the southeastern Coastal Plain and southern Midwest is similar to the Washington hawthorn, but the *fruits are much smaller.*

Littlehip Hawthorn   *Crataegus spathulata* Michx.

Littlehip hawthorn is a southern tree apparently related to parsley and Washington hawthorns. *It differs in having smaller, narrower, often unlobed leaves that gradually taper at the base.*

Willow Hawthorn   *Crataegus saligna* Greene

This is a Colorado species with *narrow leaves* and *small bluish-black fruits that are 5–8 mm (0.2–0.3 in) in diameter.* (See art on next page.)

Willow Hawthorn

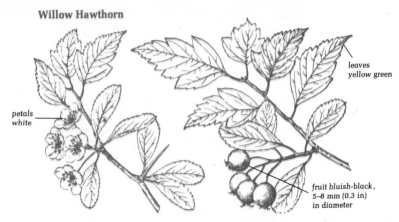

leaves
yellow green

petals
white

fruit bluish-black,
5–8 mm (0.3 in)
in diameter

English Hawthorn *Crataegus monogyna* Jacq,

This is native to Europe and western Asia, and was introduced into North America for its attractive flowers. It has escaped from cultivation and is often found growing wild along roadways, vacant lots, fields, and the margins of woodlands. English hawthorn is a tree to 12 m (40 ft) with stout branches and sharp spines to 2 cm (0.8 in) long. Leaves are broadest near the base or above the middle, 1.5–4 cm (0.6–1.6 in) wide, with 3 to 7 lobes, dark green and smooth. Flowers are produced in many-flowered clusters. ***Fruits are nearly globe-shaped, 6–10 mm (0.2–0.4 in) in diameter, and red.***

The Photina Genus *Heteromeles* M. Roem.

(synonym: Photina Lindl.)

This is a small genus of about 40 species of trees and shrubs native to Asia and with a single species native to western North America. This species, the Christmasberry, occurs in California and Baja California, Mexico.

Members of this genus are deciduous or evergreen shrubs with alternate simple leaves that are finely toothed along the margin. The bisexual, white flowers are produced in many-flowered, branched clusters. The small, red fruits contain only a few seeds.

Christmasberry *Heteromeles arbutifolia* M. Roem,

(synonym: Photina arbutifolia Lindl.)

This shrub or small tree is also known as California holly, hollyberry, and toyon. Its range is limited to the coastal mountains and the foothills of the Sierra Nevada from northern California south into Baja California, Mexico. It is found principally on the lower mountain slopes and foothills.

Because of the attractive leaves and bright-red fruit appearing from October to December, this tree is extensively cultivated in California. Small mammals, songbirds, and the banded-tailed pigeon eat the fruits. The leaves of the christmas-berry resemble those of the madrone tree, hence the scientific name *arbutifolia* or "leaves like arbutus," the technical name for madrone.

Christmasberry is a large **evergreen** shrub or small tree to 6 m (20 ft). The leaves are alternate, **simple, thick, and leathery,** uniformly wide or broadest at the middle, 5–10 cm (2–4 in) long, 2.5–3 cm (1–1.2 in) wide, prominently toothed along the margin, smooth, dark green, shiny above and paler beneath. The white flowers are produced in clusters 1–1.5 cm (0.4–0.6 in) across; each flower has a short, 5-lobed calyx, 5 petals, each 3–4.5 mm (0.1–0.2 in) long, and 10 stamens. The **fruit** is somewhat **pear-shaped to egg-shaped,** bright or pale scarlet, rarely yellow, **7–8 mm (0.3 in) long**, and contains several brown, flattened seeds 2.5–3 mm (0.1 in) long.

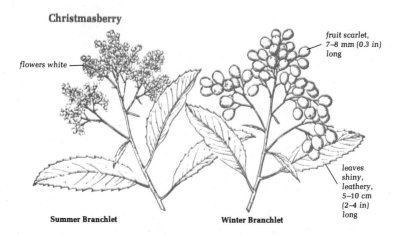

Christmasberry

flowers white

fruit scarlet,
7–8 mm (0.3 in)
long

leaves
shiny,
leathery,
5–10 cm
(2–4 in)
long

Summer Branchlet   **Winter Branchlet**

The Coco-Plum Family   Chrysobalanaceae

This is a family of 17 genera and 420 species of lowland tropical Asia, Africa, and the Americas. Members of this family were once classed within the rose family (Rosaceae), but recent studies have shown them to be distinct. This family is of limited economic importance; some members produce edible fruits. Two genera are native to North America, but only one, coco-plum, is a tree or shrub. The other genus and species, gopher apple (*Licania michauxii*), is a low woody herb or shrub to 40 cm (16 in) tall and occurs in the pine barrens, sand dunes, and oak scrublands of the southeastern U.S.

Members of this family are woody herbs, shrubs, or trees with alternate, simple, entire, usually leathery leaves. The leafstalks often have a pair of glands. Flowers are produced in elongated to flat-topped, branched or unbranched clusters. Each flower has a 5-lobed calyx, 5 petals (sometimes 4 or absent, often unequal), 2 to 100 stamens, rarely more, and a single pistil. Fruit dry to fleshy, variable in shape, often egg-shaped.

mm
cm   1   2   3   4   5   6   7   8   9   10   11
in   1   2   3   4

Coco-Plum

Chrysobalanus icaco L.

In the U.S. coco-plum occurs on sandy beaches, river banks, low hammocks, and swamps of southern Florida and the Florida Keys. The leathery, evergreen leaves, juicy, fragrant white to pink fruits, and the blunt-ridged seeds are the distinguishing features. Coco-plum is occasionally planted for its attractive shape, evergreen leaves, and tiny white flowers that appear continuously throughout spring and summer. The fruits, resembling small plums, have a sweet flesh and are commonly made into jellies and preserves. The wood is light brown, hard, heavy, and is occasionally used in carpentry.

This shrub or tree grows to 5 m (17 ft) tall, with a dense, rounded crown. The *alternate, evergreen leaves* are broadest near the middle to *almost rounded, 2–8 cm (0.8–3.2 in) long,* 1.2–6 cm (0.5–2.4 in) broad, smooth, leathery, dark green and shiny above, and light yellowish-green below. Flower clusters are 2.5–5 cm (1–2 in) long. Each flower is 5–7 mm (0.2–0.3 in) long, with a bell-shaped calyx, *5 white petals,* 12–26 stamens, and a pistil. The fruits are *1.8–5 cm (0.7–2 in) long, egg-shaped to broadest near the tip,* bright pink, yellow, or creamy white.

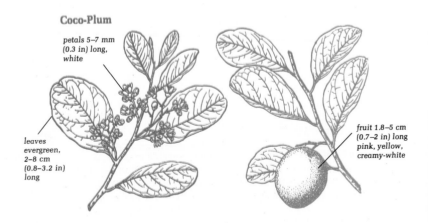

Coco-Plum

petals 5–7 mm (0.3 in) long, white

leaves evergreen, 2–8 cm (0.8–3.2 in) long

fruit 1.8–5 cm (0.7–2 in) long pink, yellow, creamy-white

The Legume Family

Leguminosae

This is one of the largest families of flowering plants, containing approximately 550 genera and 14,000 species. Legumes are present on every continent but are especially abundant in warmer to tropical climates. Most of the North American species, such as clover, are not woody, but there are at least 43 native species of trees. Three genera and 4 species of introduced trees are also included in this book since they have escaped from cultivation and reproduce on their own. Many other foreign legumes have been introduced, especially in southern Florida and California, but have not naturalized and are thus not included in this book.

The legume family is divided into 3 natural subdivisions or subfamilies: the Mimosoideae (including the mimosa tree and mesquite), Caesalpinioideae (including redbud and honeylocust), and the Papilionoideae (including black locust and yellowwood). The Mimosoideae species have regular, or symmetrical, flower parts, with the petals and calyx lobes folded in bud like an accordian. The Papilionioideae species have typical pea- or bean-shaped flowers and the calyx and petals overlapping in bud. The third subfamily, Caesalpinioideae, has regular to irregular flowers with 5 distinct petals, and the calyx and petals also overlapping in bud.

Legumes are among the economically most important families of flowering plants. Peas, beans, peanuts, clovers, and alfalfa are but a few of the many food or fodder crops obtained from legumes. Many of them are soil builders because they have small, bacteria-containing nodules on their roots, which can convert atmospheric nitrogen (N_2) into a form (NO_3) in the soil that can be used by other plants. Beautiful, exotic timbers such as rosewood, vermilion, and African zebrawood are sought for cabinetwork and hand-turning. Dyes, stains, oils, and balsams are also extracted from members of this family. Many species (redbud, brooms, lupines, and wisteria, for example) are grown for their attractive flowers in landscape plantings. They are very important to wildlife. Leaves, buds, flowers, fruits, and seeds serve to support a host of animals ranging from deer to small birds and rodents.

Members of this family are deciduous or evergreen trees, shrubs, vines, and herbs with mostly alternate, usually compound (with feather-like, hand-shaped, or with 3-leaflet) leaves. Flowers are male or female or else bisexual, symmetrical to irregular, and normally have 5 sepals (calyx) and 5 petals. Stamens may be 5, 10, or many, sometimes united on the lower half, and with a single pistil. The fruits are usually a pod (bean or pea-like), rarely segmented, flattened to rounded, soft, leathery or becoming woody at maturity, often but not always splitting open along 2 valves, and enclosing 1 to several hard seeds.

Key to the Subfamilies of Legumes

A. Flowers regular, small, arranged in densely flowered heads or spikes; 10 or more stamens, extending beyond the petals; calyx lobes and petals folded in bud   **Mimosoideae, p. 624**
                 (Continued)

Glandular Mesquite

Sweet Acacia

B. Flowers slightly to strongly irregular (asymmetrical); stamens 10 or fewer, rarely extending beyond the petals; calyx lobes and petals overlapping in bud.

    1. Flowers slightly to strongly irregular, but not pea-like, the single uppermost petal inside the 2 side or wing petals; stamens usually free
        Caesalpinioideae, p. 644

Eastern Redbud

Yellow Paloverde

Honeylocust

    2. Flower pea-like, with a single, large upright petal outside of and overlapping the 2 side or wing petals, and the 2 bottom-most petals forming a V-shaped keel; stamens commonly united into a tube   **Papilionoideae, p. 658**

Texas Sophora

Desert Ironwood

Black Locust

Key to Genera in Legume Subfamily Mimosoideae

A. Flower with numerous stamens, more than 10 per flower.

    1. Trees with short to long, stout, paired spines at the base of the leaves (Guadeloupe blackbead rarely armed); fruits often thick to nearly rounded in cross section, sometimes flattened.

Sweet Acacia

   a. Stamens free or only slightly united at the base; fruits straight or slightly twisting, the seeds not attached to the mature pods by a thread-like appendage   **Acacia, p. 625**

   b. Stamens united into a tube at or below the middle; fruits twisting when splitting open and the seeds attached by a thread-like appendage   **Blackbead, p. 632**

Ebony Blackbead

2. Trees without paired spines at the base of the leaves; fruits always flattened, dry.

   a. Fruits splitting open at maturity, the valves of the fruit separating from the persistent margins   **Lysiloma, p. 635**

   b. Fruits not splitting open or opening very late and only partially, the valves of the fruits not separating from the marginal ribs; includes mimosa tree   **Albizia, p. 637**

B. Flowers with 10 stamens per flower.

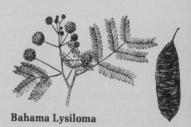

1. Flowers produced in cylinder-shaped spikes; fruits cylinder-shaped, thick, almost rounded, do not split open at maturity   **Mesquite, p. 639**

2. Flowers produced in rounded heads; fruits flattened, splitting open along 2 valves at maturity   **Leadtree, p. 641**

Bahama Lysiloma

Glandular Mesquite

Mimosa Tree

The Acacia Genus

Acacia Mill.

The acacias with over 1,000 species comprise one of the largest genera in the legume family. These plants, mostly trees, are found in virtually all tropical and subtropical regions of the world. They are particularly numerous in Australia. The North American species are poorly known and in need of study. Fifteen species are estimated as native to North America — 6 are usually trees but occasionally with shrubby members,

4 are usually shrubs but occasionally reach tree size, and the remaining ones are always shrubby.

The 4 species that may become trees are Berland's acacia (*Acacia berlandleri* Benth.), Roemeria's acacia (*A. roemeriana* Scheele), constricted acacia (*A. constricta* Benth.), and pineland acacia (*A. pinetorum* F. J. Hermann). Pineland acacia occurs in pinelands and on shell mounds in southern Florida; the others are southwestern species. Roemeria's acacia has tiny branches with 1–3 pairs of side branches (pinnae) per leaf. Constricted acacia also have spiny branches but usually with 4–6 pairs of side branches per leaf and with fruits that are strongly constricted between the seeds. Berland's acacia is not spiny and have 6–11 pairs of side branches per leaf.

There are more cultivated species of acacias in North America than native ones. Most occur in California where they have easily adapted to the periodic dry conditions. There are too many introduced species to be enumerated in this book; however, 5 species should be mentioned as they are naturalizing in either Florida or California. They are all native to Australia and instead of having the twice-compound and feather-like (bipinnate) leaves, the trees (except the seedling stage) have only modified leafstalks that become leaf-like and are called phyllodes. The side branches and true leaflets have been lost. This is possibly an adaptation to the arid climates of Australia.

The ear-leaf acacia (*Acacia auriculiformis* A, Cunn. ex Benth.) is a shrub or small tree with a rounded crown, drooping branches, and narrow, willow-like leaves up to 15 cm (6 in) long. This species is increasingly to be found in the pine-palmetto palm woodland in southern Florida. The silver wattle (*A. dealbata* Link.) is a handsome ornamental reaching nearly 30 m (100 ft) in Australia and to 15 m (50 ft) in North America. It has silvery-gray, fine leaves and slender spikes of yellow flower heads. Another species, the blueleaf acacia (*A. cyanophylla* Lindley) has escaped from cultivation and grows wild in California and Florida. It has flattened or flanged branchlets, slightly broader leaves that vary in shape, straight or twisted, leathery, and olive-gray in color. The short golden wattle [*A. longifolia* (Andrews) Willd.], perhaps the most common acacia in California, has broad leaves with conspicuous veins. Its golden flowers bloom in late winter and are produced in short, cylinder-shaped spikes. This acacia is often used for highway and hedge plantings. The blackwood acacia (*A. melanoxylon* R. Brown) is one of the largest of the introduced acacias growing to approximately 20 m (66 ft) high. It has leaves that are broadest near the base, up to 15 cm (6 in) long, and the creamy yellow flowers are produced in heads 5–8 cm (2–3.2 in) wide.

Acacias have many economic uses besides horticultural ones. They are the source of valuable dyes, gums, and tannins. Their wood goes into everything from fine furniture to fence posts to tobacco pipes. The shrubs and trees are important in erosion control. Besides, acacias provide food and shelter for many species of wildlife. Deer, horses, and cattle eat the bark, leaves, and fruits.

Acacias are trees or shrubs with hard, often irregularly grained wood and usually paired spines at the base of the leaves. The North American acacias have twice compound and feather-like (bipinnate) leaves with 1 to several pairs of side branches, each having many leaflets. The flowers are mostly bisexual and produced in densely flowered, yellow to yellowish-white heads, spikes, or once-branched, elongated clusters. The tiny, bell-shaped calyx is shorter than the tube or funnel-shaped, fused petals. There are many stamens and a single pistil. The fruits are variable, usually long, narrow, flattened to almost rounded in cross section, straight or curved, often dry, leathery to woody, and often constricted between the seeds.

Key to Acacia Species

A. Flowers in densely flowered, rounded heads.

   1. Leaves with 2–8 pairs of side branchlets (pinnae) per leaf.

     a. Leaves 4–8 pairs of side branchlets per leaf, rarely less; trees of Florida, but also in Louisiana and California.

       (1) Leafstalk 1.5–4 cm (0.6–1.6 in) long, with a small, circular gland; trees of southern Florida, but planted elsewhere   **Sweet acacia, p. 627**

       (2) Leafstalks 0.2–0.6 cm (0.1–0.3 in) long, with an elongated gland; trees of southern Florida   **Twisted acacia, p. 628**

     b. Leaves 2–4 pairs of side branchlets per leaf.

       (1) Leaflets hairy; trees of South and Southwest   **Small's acacia, p. 629**

       (2) Leaflets smooth; trees of southern Florida, but planted elsewhere   **Sweet acacia, p. 627**

   2. Leaves with 10–22 pairs of side branchlets per leaf; southern Florida   **Steel acacia, p. 629**

B. Flowers produced in densely flowered spikes.

   1. Leaflets 4–7 mm (about 0.2 in) long; fruits leathery, often twisting at maturity; trees of southwestern deserts   **Catclaw acacia, p. 630**

   2. Leaflets 5–10 mm (0.2–0.4 in) long; fruits papery, not twisting at maturity; trees of southwestern Texas and Mexico   **Wright's acacia, p. 631**

Sweet Acacia

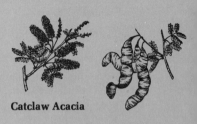
Catclaw Acacia

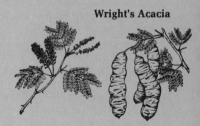
Wright's Acacia

Sweet Acacia

Acacia farnesiana (L.) Willd.

The sweet acacia is a highly variable, thorny shrub or small tree of the American tropics and subtropics. In North America it is native to southern Florida but is cultivated in northern Florida, west to Louisiana, and also locally in California. This acacia was introduced into Europe in the early 17th century and into tropical regions of Africa and Asia. In Florida, it is found growing in dry, sandy soils in pinelands, hammocks, and disturbed areas.

   Flowering usually occurs in February

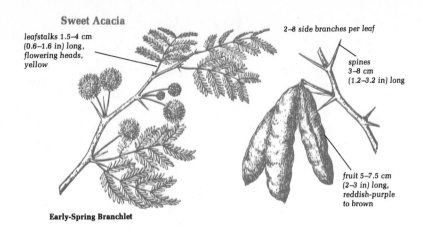

Sweet Acacia

leafstalks 1.5–4 cm (0.6–1.6 in) long, flowering heads, yellow

2–8 side branches per leaf

spines 3–8 cm (1.2–3.2 in) long

fruit 5–7.5 cm (2–3 in) long, reddish-purple to brown

Early-Spring Branchlet

and March when bright-yellow, fragrant heads of flowers appear. The fruits persist on the tree and ripen throughout the year. These trees are valuable as a food source and cover for wildlife. Larger birds eat the seeds.

The reddish-brown wood is hard, close-grained, and durable. It has been used for fence posts, some farm tools, and smaller wooden wares. The gummy sap can be used to manufacture mucilage. In France, large plantations of sweet acacia are raised for their fragrant blossoms, which are used in the perfume industry.

Appearance: shrub or tree to 10 m (33 ft) with a spreading, flattened or rounded crown; trunk often straight, to 45 cm (18 in) in diameter. **Bark:** thin, with narrow furrows and ridges, becoming shaggy with age, reddish-brown. **Branches:** irregular, spreading; branchlets slender, sometimes zigzag, hairy when young, becoming smooth with age, armed with a pair of stiff spines 3–8 cm (1.2–3.2 in) long at the base of each leaf. **Leaves:** alternate, deciduous, *twice compound* and feather-like (bipinnate), 2.5–10 cm (1–4 in) long, composed of *2–8 pairs of side branches (pinnae),* each with *10–25 pairs of leaflets,* each leaflet 3–6 mm (0.1–0.2 in) long, narrow, unequal at the base, bright green; *leafstalks 1.5–4 cm (0.6–1.6 in) long.* **Flowers:** produced in *densely flowered, fragrant, yellow, rounded, stalked heads,* often in clusters of 1–5 heads, the heads 1.4–1.8 cm (0.7 in) wide; each flower with a tiny tubular calyx, a small tubular corolla (petals), with about 20 yellow stamens, and a single pistil. **Fruits:** cylinder-shaped pods 5–7.5 cm (2–3 in) long, becoming woody, dark reddish-purple or brown, containing several thick, shiny seeds 6–8 mm (0.2–0.3 in) long.

Twisted Acacia
Acacia tortuosa (L.) Willd.

Twisted acacia is a spiny shrub or small tree of shell mounds and roadsides of southern Florida. This acacia was once thought to occur in southwestern Texas, but those populations are better referred to as the shrubby Schaffner's acacia, *Acacia schaffneri.* Flowering can occur any time of the year but occurs mostly from March through June. It is of no value to man and of little value to wildlife.

The trees have irregular, spreading crowns, with alternate, feather-like, pinnately compound leaves, and paired spines along the branchlets at the base of each leaf. Each leaf has **4–8 pairs of side branches** (pinnae) and each of those have 15–20 pairs of tiny, narrow leaflets 3–4 mm (0.2 in) long; **leafstalks 2–6 mm (0.1–0.3 in) long.** The tiny, fragrant, yellow **flowers** are produced **in densely flowered heads** 6–12 mm (0.2–0.5 in) across. The pods are narrowly cylinder-shaped, 8–10 cm (3.2–4 in) long, slightly constricted between the seeds, reddish-brown, woody.

Twisted Acacia

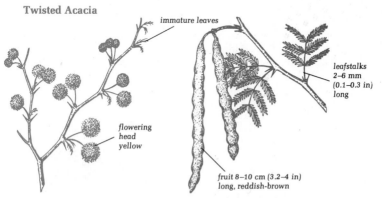

immature leaves

leafstalks
2–6 mm
(0.1–0.3 in)
long

flowering
head
yellow

fruit 8–10 cm (3.2–4 in)
long, reddish-brown

Small's Acacia

Acacia smallii Isely

This species ranges basically from Louisiana to Texas but also occurs in southern California and Arizona. It is found along the margins of woodlands, along roads, and in disturbed sites. The dense clusters of yellow flowers appear in early spring.

Small's acacia is a shrub or small, spreading tree to 5 m (17 ft). Branches are armed with paired spines at the base of each leaf. The alternate **leaves** are twice pinnately (feather-like) compound, **with 2–4** (rarely more) **pairs of side branchlets** (pinnae), each with 9–17 pairs of leaflets. The **leaflets** are 2.5–4 mm (0.1 in) long, and uniformly long to widest near the middle and **hairy.** The tiny **flowers** are produced **in densely flowered heads.** Fruits are 3–10 cm (1.2–4 in) long, 7–10 mm (0.3–0.4 in) in diameter, almost rounded in cross section, straight to slightly twisted, becoming woody and dark brown to black at maturity.

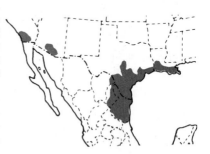

Steel Acacia

Acacia macracantha H & B ex Willd.

This acacia is native to the hammocks of south Florida and the West Indies. It is similar to the twisted acacia but has more pairs of side branches (pinnae) per leaf.

Steel acacia is a small tree with spreading branches armed with stout, paired spines at the base of the leaves. The twice-compound and feather-like (pinnate) **leaves** have **10–22 pairs of side branchlets,** each with 12–20 pairs of tiny, uniformly wide leaflets. A small, cup-shaped gland is present on the upper part of the leafstalk. The small, yellowish flowers are produced in **densely flowered heads.** Fruits are 6–14 cm (2.4–5.5 in) long, 6–10 mm (0.2–0.4 in) wide, narrow, somewhat compressed, becoming woody and black at maturity.

Acacia greggii A. Gray

Catclaw Acacia

This small acacia occurs in the vast expanses of the southwestern deserts from southern Nevada and Utah to Mexico. It has characteristic curved spines along the branchlets and is found in dry, sandy or gravelly soils from sea level to 1,500 m (5,000 ft) in elevation. It usually occurs as a large shrub along washes, on mesas, canyon slopes, and banks of arroyos in the desert and desert grasslands. It often forms dense thickets but also grows in association with mesquite and blue paloverde.

Catclaw acacia is slow growing and has a long flowering period, usually from April to October when the creamy yellow flowers appear in profusion. The fruits mature by July but remain on the trees through winter. This species is of considerable importance to wildlife. The dense thickets provide excellent cover for mammals and birds. The seeds are the main food source of scaled quails. Jackrabbits and livestock browse the leaves if other forage is in short supply.

The hard, heavy, close-grained wood is used for fuel and occasionally for trinkets. The Pima and Papago Indians made a meal, called *pinole*, from the pods, which was prepared as a mush. Also, the light golden honey produced from the flowers is considered to be one of the best produced from desert flowers.

Appearance: shrubs or small trees to 7 m (23 ft), often forming thickets, with an irregular crown; trunk short, straight, to 30 cm (12 in) in diameter. **Bark:** thin, furrowed

Catclaw Acacia

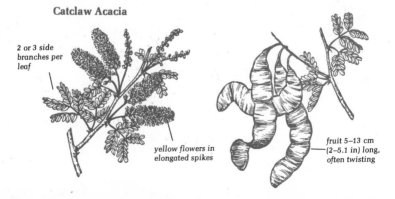

2 or 3 side branches per leaf

yellow flowers in elongated spikes

fruit 5–13 cm (2–5.1 in) long, often twisting

and scaly on older trunks, grayish-black. **Branches:** slender, spreading; branchlets armed with claw-like spines, lightly hairy to smooth, pale brown. **Leaves:** alternate, deciduous, twice compound and feather-like (bipinnate), 2.5–7.5 cm (1–3 in) long, with 2 or 3 pairs of side branches (pinnae), each with 4–6 pairs of leaflets, each *leaflet 4–7 mm (about 0.2 in) long,* broadest above the middle, short-stalked. **Flowers:** *produced in densely flowered, elongated spikes* 3–6.2 cm (1.2–2.5 in) long, fragrant, creamy yellow, in the junction of the leaves and branchlets; each flower with a tiny 5-parted calyx 1–3 mm (0.1 in) long, 5 fused petals 2–6 mm (0.1–0.2 in) long, stamens numerous, and a single pistil. **Fruits:** *pods, 5–13 cm (2–5.1 in) long, flattened, often twisting,* constricted between the seeds; seeds 6–8 mm (0.3 in) long.

Wright's Acacia   *Acacia wrightii* Benth.

This is a spiny shrub or small tree that occurs in central to southwestern Texas and into northern Mexico. It forms thickets in the dry, rocky limestone soils of prairies, flood plains, and washes between sea level and 900 m (3,000 ft) in elevation. In the northern part of its range, this species appears to hybridize with catclaw acacia (*Acacia greggii*).

The thickets formed by this acacia provide shelter for small animals and many birds. Quail, doves, and rodents eat the seeds. A good-quality honey can be made from the yellow flowers. Wright's acacia has been used as an ornamental because of its ability to tolerate dry climates. It is also used for fence posts and as firewood.

Like the catclaw acacia, Wright's acacia has claw-like spines along the branchlets and between the points of attachment of the alternate leaves. The twice compound and feather-like (bipinnate) leaves have 1 or 2 pairs of side branches (pinnae), each with 2–6 pairs of leaflets 5–10 mm (0.2–0.4 in) long. The *leaflets are larger than those of the catclaw acacia.* The tiny creamish-yellow *flowers are clustered on an elongated spike* 4–6 cm (1.6–2.4 in) long. The pods are 5–15 cm (2–6 in) long, 1.5–2.5 cm (0.6–1 in) wide, flattened, straight to slightly curved, light brown, with thick but somewhat papery walls.

Wright's Acacia

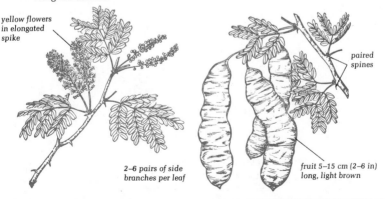

yellow flowers in elongated spike

paired spines

2–6 pairs of side branches per leaf

fruit 5–15 cm (2–6 in) long, light brown

The Blackbead Genus
Pithecellobium Mart.

This genus includes about 90 species of tropical and subtropical plants. It occurs from southern North America to South America, and in tropical Asia, Malaysia, and Australia. Four of the 5 species reaching into the southern U.S. are trees; of these, 2 occur in Texas, while the other 2 are native to Florida.

Members of the genus are generally found on the edges of forests, on waterways, or in developing young forests. Those species that grow in open areas have their fruit and seeds dispersed by birds, while the forest-dwelling trees have somewhat fleshy fruits that are dispersed by mammals. The wood is hard, heavy, but brittle; little of the timber is suitable for uses other than fence posts and fuel. The bark contains a yellow dye, used in tropical America for tanning animal hides.

Blackbead trees or shrubs are either unarmed or armed with spines at the base of the leaves. The compound leaves have a double-feather-like arrangement (bipinnate or sometimes just pinnate) with few to many leaflets that sit opposite one another on the leafstalk or sometimes alternately at the base. The flowers appear in broad, rounded, or spike-like clusters. Each flower usually contains both sexes. Flowers have a bell-shaped calyx, tubular corolla, many stamens, and a single pistil. The fruiting pods are straight or curved, flattened or round, with 2 halves enclosing several oblong seeds that sit side by side in the pod.

Key to Blackbead Species

A. Leaves twice compound and feather-like (bipinnate), with 3–20 pairs of leaflets per side branch, the leaflets tiny, 3–12 mm (0.1–0.5 in) long; pods straight or nearly so, becoming woody; trees of southwestern U.S.

   1. Flowers in elongated clusters 1.6–3.8 cm (0.6–1.5 in) long; leaflets 3–6 pairs per side branch of the leaves   **Ebony blackbead, p. 633**

   2. Flowers in dense clusters in nearly rounded heads; leaflets 8–20 pairs per side branch of the leaves   **Huajillo, p. 633**

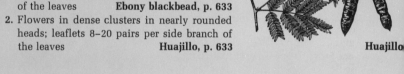

Huajillo

B. Leaves bipinnate, with just 2 pairs of leaflets per side branch, the leaflets large, 2.5–5 cm (1–2 in) long; pods curving or twisting at maturity, leathery; trees of south Florida.

   1. Branchlets smooth, rarely with spines; leaflets leathery   **Guadeloupe blackbead, p. 634**

   2. Branchlets regularly armed with paired sharp spines at the base of each leaf; leaflets with a papery to nearly leathery texture   **Catclaw blackbead, p. 635**

Catclaw Blackbead

Ebony Blackbead   *Pithecellobium flexicaule* (Benth.) Coult.

The ebony blackbead is a small evergreen member of the legume family from Texas and Mexico. It is also seen as a cultivated tree in southern Florida, sometimes known as Texas ebony. This tree occurs in a variety of soils from sandy silts to clay loams. It is common as a scrubby thorn bush along Texas roadsides or as a medium-size yard tree. Along the Rio Grande, ebony black-bead reaches its maximum size in a few scattered wooded areas, up to 10 m (33 ft) tall and a trunk to 1 m (3.3 ft) in width. It grows in association with mesquite and cacti.

The wood is heavy, close-grained, and handsomely red and yellow colored. These features make it a sought-after material in cabinet work. It is also excellent for fence

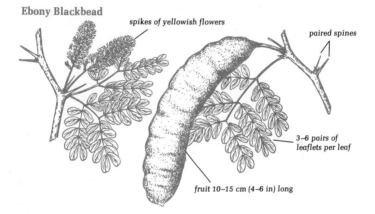

Ebony Blackbead

spikes of yellowish flowers

paired spines

3–6 pairs of leaflets per leaf

fruit 10–15 cm (4–6 in) long

posts or as fuel wood. The seeds are edible and nutritious. Mexicans roast them and use their pods for a coffee substitute.

Ebony blackbead is a small tree with a large, rounded crown. The branches are heavy, zigzag, and **armed with paired spines** at the base of the leaves. The twice-compound and feather-like (bipinnate) compound leaves are 3.8–5 cm (1.5–2 in) long, and composed of 2 or 3 pairs of side branches, each bearing **3–6 opposing pairs of small, leathery leaflets.** The leaflets are 6–9 mm (0.2–0.3 in) long and rounded at the tips. From June to August fragrant spikes, 1.6–3.8 cm (0.6–1.5 in) long, of yellowish flowers bloom from short spurs along the branchlets. The fruiting **pods** are **10–15 cm (4–6 in) long,** 2.5–3.1 cm (1–1.2 in) wide, thick, **straight or slightly curved,** and containing reddish-brown seeds. The pods mature in the fall but can remain on the tree until the following summer.

Huajillo   *Pithecellobium pallens* (Benth.) Standl.

The huajillo, or ape's earring as it is sometimes referred to, is really a Mexican species that extends just north over the border into Texas. This small-growing tree occurs more often as a low clump-forming shrub in Texas, but reaches 9–10 m (up to 33 ft) in

Mexico. It is found on sandy or clay river soils, on riverbanks and bluffs, and occasionally in moist rich soils of lagoons or in mesquite brushland. The flowers are sought by bees. Sheep and goats browse the leaves in winter. The dark, hard, and heavy wood is sometimes made into wooden ware.

The yellowish-white *flowers* appear from May to August *in dense, many-flowered, nearly rounded, clusters* that sit on erect, or nearly upright, stalks. The

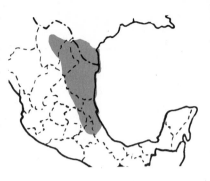

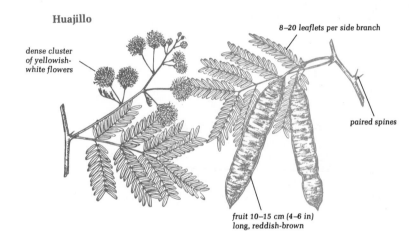

Huajillo

dense cluster of yellowish-white flowers

8–20 leaflets per side branch

paired spines

fruit 10–15 cm (4–6 in) long, reddish-brown

leaves are arranged alternately on the branchlets. The leaf bases are armed with paired spines and the leaves are twice compound and feather-like (bipinnate) with *8–20 tiny, opposing leaflets.* The pods ripen by midsummer, but may remain on the trees even after opening for almost a year. They are 10–15 cm (4–6 in) long, 1.6–1.8 cm (0.7 in) wide, reddish-brown with thick margins outside, yellowish within and contain compressed, somewhat rounded, shiny, dark brown seeds, 0.6–0.8 cm (0.3 in) long.

Guadeloupe Blackbead   *Pithecellobium guadelupense* (Pers.)
Chapm. (synonym: *P. keyense* Britton)
Guadeloupe blackbead is a shrub or small evergreen tree from southern Florida including the Keys. It is also widely distributed in the Bahamas, the West Indies, and on the Yucatan Peninsula. It occurs in rocky or sandy soils in pine woods and scrub hammocks as well as on open sand dunes near the shore.

This blackbead grows to 6 m (20 ft) in southern Florida. The branchlets *rarely have paired spines* at the base of the leaves, as often seen in other members of the genus. The twice compound and feather-like (bipinnate) *leaves have a pair* of side branches, each bearing **2 broad, to almost rounded, leathery leaflets 2.5–5 cm (1–2 in) long** and 1.2–4 cm (0.5–1.6 in) broad. Flowers are produced in dense, round heads that are borne in branched clusters at the tips of the branchlets. The pods are 5–15 cm (2–6 in) long, 7–10 mm (0.3–0.4 in) wide, and contain the shiny, black seeds.

Catclaw Blackbead   *Pithecellobium unguis-cati* (L.) Benth.

This small evergreen tree forms dense, spiny thickets in coastal southwestern Florida and the Florida Keys. The native range extends through the West Indies and into Mexico and northern South America. It grows in sandy or coral-laden soils in wooded scrublands, dunes, hammocks, and along roadsides. In nutrient-poor coral soils, catclaw blackbead is usually a shrub, but in richer soils it reaches tree size. The bark has astringent properties and was once widely used as a medicine.

Like Guadelupe blackbead, the leaves of this species consist of **2 pairs of leaflets** although the stalks of the leaflets are shorter than the stalks of the leaves, which helps to distinguish the two. The **branchlets** are **regularly armed with a pair of spines at the base of each leaf.** The flowers occur in dense rounded clusters about 2.5 cm (1 in) in diameter, and receive a purplish tinge from the brightly colored filaments. The flat, bright red-brown fruit pods are distinctively coiled (which remind some people of a cat's claw). The seeds are shiny, nearly black, beadlike, and have red appendages.

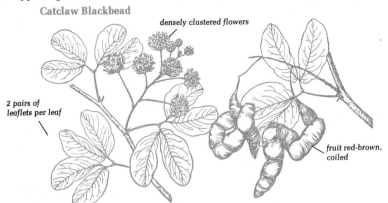

Catclaw Blackbead

densely clustered flowers

2 pairs of leaflets per leaf

fruit red-brown, coiled

The Lysiloma Genus   *Lysiloma* Benth.

Lysiloma is a small genus of about 35 species distributed in tropical America. Three species exist in the U.S., of which only the Bahama lysiloma *(Lysiloma latisiliquum)* attains tree size. Lysiloma species are of limited economic value for they are neither abundant nor well-formed. However, the durable wood is easily worked and can be used in furniture or interior trim. Some species are planted in the Southwest for erosion control and roadside ornamentation.

These are shrubs or moderate to large smooth-barked trees. The deciduous leaves are compound and feather-like (pinnate) with 2 to many pairs of secondary branches bearing numerous tiny leaflets or sometimes a few large leaflets. The flowers are clustered into round heads or cylindrical spikes. They are mostly 5-parted, white, and bisexual, although male flowers are sometimes found at the bottom of a flower cluster. The fruits are papery pods (legumes) usually 8- to 12-seeded; flattened and enclose the shiny, hard seeds.

Bahama Lysiloma

Lysiloma latisiliquum (L.) Benth.
(synonym: *L. bahamense* Benth.)

The Bahama lysiloma is a small to medium-size tree, reaching perhaps 20 m (66 ft) in height. It is basically a West Indian species whose natural range reaches southernmost Florida. This species, common on some of the upper Keys as well as on the tip of the Florida peninsula, grows in sandy soils in hammocks and is considered to be one of the more characteristic trees in the Pineland Ridge. Bahama lysiloma invades the pinelands around hammocks until fire sweeps through, killing the lysilomas but leaving the pines unharmed.

The trees are not very important commercially and are of limited value to wildlife. The wood is hard and durable and is sometimes used in the West Indies in general construction.

Members of this species are shrubs or trees to 20 m (66 ft), with a spreading crown, and unarmed branches and branchlets. The alternate, deciduous leaves are twice compound and feather-like (bipinnate). Each **leaf** is 10–18 cm (4–7 in) long, **contains 4–8 side branches** (pinnae), **each with 8–15 pairs of leaflets** 0.8–1.5 cm (0.3–0.6 in) long. The **flowers** are **in** several to **many rounded heads.** Each flower has a short calyx 1.5–3 mm (0.1 in) long, a greenish-white corolla (fused petals) 4–5 mm (0.2 in) long,

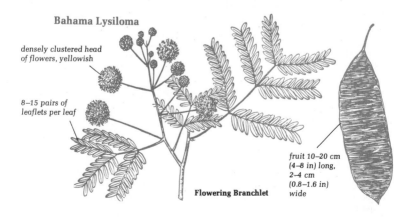

Bahama Lysiloma

densely clustered head of flowers, yellowish

8–15 pairs of leaflets per leaf

Flowering Branchlet

fruit 10–20 cm (4–8 in) long, 2–4 cm (0.8–1.6 in) wide

numerous *yellowish stamens,* and a single pistil. The thin, *flattened pods* are *10–20 cm (4–8 in) long,* 2–4 cm *(0.8–1.6 in) wide,* and contain several hard, flattened seeds.

The Albizia Genus

Albizia Durazz.

Albizia is a moderately large genus of trees and shrubs, largely of tropical and subtropical regions of the Americas, Australia, Africa, and Asia. Two species have been introduced into North America, the well-known mimosa or silk tree (*Albizia julibrissin*), common in the midwestern and southeastern U.S., and the woman's tongue tree (*A. lebbeck*) of south Florida.

These are fast-growing trees that can begin to flower and fruit in only 3 or 4 years. In general, species of albizia are used as shade or ornamental trees, although some produce wood that is used for furniture, paneling, fence posts, and as fuel. The bark has been used in tanning leather and for medicinal purposes.

Members of this genus are small- to medium-size trees and shrubs with alternate, deciduous, twice compound and feather-like (bipinnate) with numerous small leaflets. The flowers are grouped in heads or slightly elongated clusters, each flower is usually bisexual, generally 5-parted, the calyx lobes fused into a tube, the petals fused into a narrow trumpet-shape, 20–50 stamens, united into a tube, and with a single pistil. The fruits are straight, flattened dry pods containing several hard seeds.

Key to Albizia Species

Woman's Tongue

A. Flowers yellow to whitish-yellow; leaflets 2–4.5 cm (0.8–1.8 in) long, 1–1.7 cm (0.4–0.7 in) wide; introduced trees of southern Florida
Woman's tongue tree, p. 637
B. Flowers light pink (due to stamens); leaflets 8–15 mm (0.3–0.6 in) long, 3–5 mm (0.2 in) wide; introduced trees of the southeastern and midwestern U.S. **Mimosa tree, p. 638**

Woman's Tongue, Lebbeck's Albizia   *Albizia lebbeck* (L.) Benth.

This albizia is indigenous to warmer, drier parts of Indo-Malaysia but is now grown in northern Africa, Australia, South and Central America, the West Indies, and southern Florida. In Florida, this tree will grow to 15 m (50 ft) in height but in its native range it will grow twice as high. The wood resembles that of walnut and thus is a prime choice for cabinet work.

Woman's tongue has a spreading crown and large, twice compound and feather-like (bipinnate) leaves. The numerous tiny *leaflets* are narrow, *2–4.5 cm (0.8–1.8 in) long, 1–1.7 cm (0.4–0.7 in) wide. Flowers* are *yellow to whitish-yellow* and clustered in many-flowered heads. Fruits are large, flattened pods 14–20 cm (5.5–8 in) long and remaining on the trees for some time after reaching maturity. As the pods dry out the seeds loosen and rattle every time a wind blows, thus leading to the common name the West Indians gave to this tree, woman's tongue.   *(See art on next page.)*

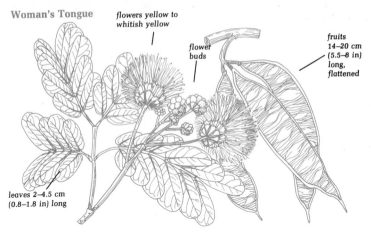

Woman's Tongue

flowers yellow to whitish yellow

flower buds

fruits 14–20 cm (5.5–8 in) long, flattened

leaves 2–4.5 cm (0.8–1.8 in) long

Mimosa Tree, Silk Tree   *Albizia julibrissin* Durazz.

This small, attractive tree is native to subtropical and temperate Asia from Iran to China and Japan. It has been in cultivation in other countries for over 100 years, first in England and Europe, then in North America. It is widely planted and grows wild from Washington, D.C., to Florida, west to Texas, and even in California. Besides parks and yards, mimosa trees can be seen along roadsides, abandoned sites, clearings, and along the edge of forests. The wide-spreading crown, graceful leaves, and showy flower clusters make this a popular flowering tree, especially in the southeastern U.S.

They are small trees to 15 m (50 ft) tall and with large **twice-compound and feather-like (bipinnate) leaves.** Each leaf consists of a central stalk, 6–16 side branches, each with 18–30 pairs of small, narrow leaflets. The flowers are clustered together in **fluffy pink heads,** usually the central flower is much larger than the others. Each flower has a tubular, 5-parted calyx and corolla, and numerous stamens fused into a tube around the central pistil. The fruits are **thin, flat, 8–20 cm (3.2–8 in) long, 2–3.5 cm (0.8–1.4 in) broad** and contain several, hard, flattened seeds.

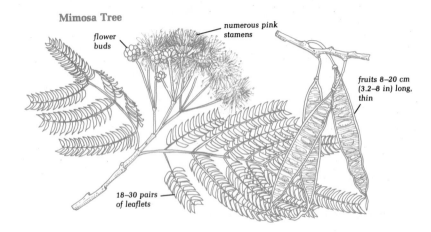

Mimosa Tree

flower buds

numerous pink stamens

fruits 8–20 cm (3.2–8 in) long, thin

18–30 pairs of leaflets

The Mesquite Genus

Prosopis L.

The mesquites are a small group of approximately 30 species of spiny trees or shrubs. They are distributed principally in warmer regions of the Americas, although a few species are present in Asia and Africa. There are 5 species in North America, 3 of which reach tree size. All are native to the Southwest and adjacent Mexico.

Mesquites are characteristic of desert and dry prairie landscapes. The leaves and fruits are edible and are vital to the existence of many species of wildlife, especially deer, peccary, rabbits, and rodents. The trees are seldom large enough to yield lumber, even though the wood is hard, durable, and takes an attractive finish.

Members of this genus are shrubs or trees, generally with rounded spreading crowns and spiny branches. The deciduous leaves are twice-compound and feather-like (bipinnate), usually with 1 or 2 pairs of side branches (pinnae), each with 5–21 pairs of leaflets. The small yellow to cream flowers are produced in many-flowered spikes or heads. Each flower has a tiny, 5-lobed calyx, 5 petals, almost free, 10 stamens, and a single pistil. The fruits are narrow, cylinder-shaped, sometimes tightly coiled, almost rounded, sometimes constricted between the seeds, and do not split open at maturity.

Key to Mesquite Species

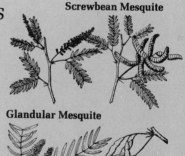

Screwbean Mesquite

Glandular Mesquite

A. Fruits tightly coiled, resembling a screw; leaves with 5–8 pairs of leaflets per side branchlet (pinnae); trees of Southwest

   Screwbean mesquite, p. 639

B. Fruits straight or slightly twisted; leaves with 7–20 pairs of leaflets per side branchlet (pinnae).

 1. Leaflets hairy, 6–12 mm (0.2–0.5 in) long; trees primarily of southwestern deserts

   Mesquite, p. 640

 2. Leaflets smooth, 1–5 cm (0.4–2 in) long; trees of southwestern U.S.

   Glandular mesquite, p. 641

Screwbean Mesquite

Prosopis pubescens Benth.

Screwbean mesquite is a small, thorny shrub or tree. It occurs from southern Nevada south into Mexico in dry sandy or rocky soils from 30–1,200 m (100–4,000 ft) in elevation. Like other mesquites, screwbean can survive in the open desert but is more abundant along creeks and riverbottoms, floodplains, irrigation ditches, and washes. It reaches its greatest height along the banks of the Gila River in Arizona.

Unlike the straight fruits of other mesquites, screwbeans have tightly coiled pods that resemble the threads on a screw. When young, the pods are tender and sweet and are popular raw or cooked. The tough wood is extremely durable and well suited for fence posts, tool handles, and firewood. Roadrunners and quail eat the seeds. Jackrabbits, cottontail rabbits, rats, and deer browse the leaves.

This shrub or small tree reaches 10 m (33 ft) and has slender, reddish-brown branchlets armed with paired, white, sharp-pointed spines at the base of each leaf. The deciduous *leaves* are twice compound and feather-like (bipinnate) with 1 or 2 pairs of side branches (pinnae), each 3.8–5 cm (1.5–2 in) long and *containing 5–8 pairs of small leaflets.* The greenish-white flowers are produced in elongated cylinder-shaped spikes 5–7.5 cm (2–3 in) long. Individual flowers are only 3–4 mm (0.2 in) long. The *spiral pods are 3–5 cm (1.2–2 in) long,* straight, brown, hairy when young, smooth and becoming woody at maturity.

Screwbean Mesquite

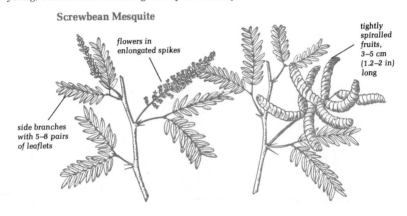

flowers in enlongated spikes

tightly spiralled fruits, 3–5 cm (1.2–2 in) long

side branches with 5–8 pairs of leaflets

Mesquite   *Prosopis velutina* Wooton

This shrub or small tree is native to southern Arizona, southern California, and Mexico. It grows in sandy, rocky soils in canyons, on bottomland, and along washes up to 1,750 m (5,800 ft) elevation and is a common element of the Arizona deserts.

In spring these desert trees are covered with bright-green leaves and clusters of greenish-yellow flowers. The fragrant flowers attract bees, and result in an excellent honey. The ripe fruits are eaten by deer, livestock, and peccaries. Indians grind the fruits to make a meal that is used in foods or drinks. The dense, hard wood is the best firewood in the desert Southwest. It has also been used to build corrals and make small utensils.

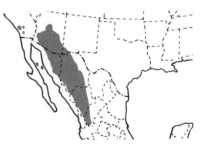

Appearance: shrubs or small trees to 10 m (33 ft) with a slightly spreading, rounded crown; trunk short, soon branching, to 60 cm (24 in) in diameter, rarely larger. **Bark:** thin, rough, separating into thin scales, reddish-brown. **Branches:** slender, spreading, often crooked, armed with straight spines to 5 cm (2 in) long, hairy, brown. **Leaves:** alternate, deciduous, often crowded on short spur shoots, twice compound and feather-like (bipinnate), with 1 or 2, rarely 3, side branches (pinnae), **each with 15–20 pairs of crowded leaflets,** each leaflet broadest at the middle, 6–12 mm (0.2–0.5 in) long, 3–6 mm (0.1–0.2 in) wide, hairy, short-stalked. **Flowers:** produced in many-flowered, yellowish-green spikes, 3.8–8 cm (1.5–3.2 in) long; each flower with a tiny 5-parted calyx, 5 narrow petals, 10 stamens, and a single pistil. **Fruits: *pods 10–18 cm (4–7 in) long, straight,*** narrow, slightly constricted between the seeds.

Glandular Mesquite *Prosopis glandulosa* Torrey

This species of mesquite ranges from southern Kansas to western Louisiana and California south through Mexico. It grows in dry valleys and uplands where it proliferates and degrades the quality of grazing land. Glandular mesquite is **similar to mesquite, but can be distinguished by its smooth leaflets; mesquite has hairy leaflets.** Wildlife uses are the same as for mesquite.

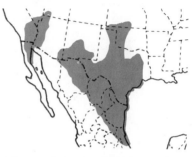

Glandular mesquites may be spiny shrubs or small trees, often forming thickets, with a broad spreading crown. Leaves have 1 pair of side branches (pinnae), each with 7–18 pairs of leaflets, the **leaflets** uniformly wide, **1–5 cm (0.4–2 in) long**, 2–4 cm (0.8–1.6 in) wide, and **smooth.** The yellow flowers are produced in many-flowered spikes. Fruits are **long,** narrow, **straight,** rounded, **10–25 cm (4–10 in) long,** 6–9 mm (0.2–0.3 in) in diameter, and slightly constricted between the seeds.

Glandular Mesquite

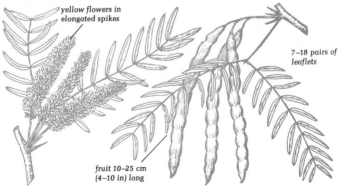

yellow flowers in elongated spikes

7–18 pairs of leaflets

fruit 10–25 cm (4–10 in) long

The Leadtree Genus *Leucaena* Benth.

There are approximately 40–50 species of leadtree occurring primarily in Central and South America and the West Indies. Three species barely extend into North America, 1 in south Florida and the others in the extreme Southwest. Little is known about the species' importance to wildlife. For man, the trees provide fodder for livestock, green fertilizer, shade and ornamentation, fencing, and some lumber.

These are trees or shrubs, normally without spines, with alternate, twice-compound and feather-like (bipinnate) leaves. Each leaf consists of a central stalk and few to many side branches (pinnae), each containing the few to many, usually small leaflets. The white to yellow flowers are bisexual and densely clustered in rounded heads. Each flower consists of a small tubular calyx with 5 lobes, 5 petals, 10 stamens, and a single pistil. The pods are straight to slightly curved, flattened, and open along both margins at maturity to expose the small, flattened, shiny seeds.

Key to Leadtree Species

A. Compound leaves with 2–5 side branches (pinnae) each with 3–20 pairs of leaflets, 0.8–2.5 cm (0.3–1 in) long.

 1. Each side branch of compound leaf with 3–8 pairs of leaflets; flowering heads 2–3 cm (0.8–1.2 in) in diameter, yellowish; trees of Texas, New Mexico, and Mexico
 Littleleaf leadtree, p. 642

 2. Each side branch of compound leaf with 10–20 pairs of leaflets; flowering heads 1.5–2 cm (0.6–0.8 in) in diameter, white; trees of south Florida, introduced in Texas and California
 Leadtree, p. 643

B. Compound leaves with 14–20 pairs of side branches (pinnae), each with 15–40 pairs of leaflets, the leaflets 3–8 mm (0.1–0.3 in) long, trees of southern Texas and Mexico
 Great leadtree, p. 643

Great Leadtree

Littleleaf Leadtree

Leucaena retusa Benth.

This attractive small tree or shrub occurs primarily in central and Trans-Pecos Texas, New Mexico, and northern Mexico. Littleleaf, sometimes referred to as Wahoo, occurs on dry, well-drained, rocky limestone soils. Because of overbrowsing by cattle, it is not common on open hillsides but is now found in live oak groves from 450–1,650 m (1,400–5,500 ft) elevation.

Littleleaf leadtree grows to 8 m (26 ft) with light gray to brown bark. The *leaves* are alternate, *twice compound and feather-like (bipinnate),* 7.5–20 cm (3–8 in) long, *composed of 2–5 side branches* (pinnae), *each with 3–8 pairs of opposing leaflets* 0.8–2.5 cm (0.3–1 in) long. The small yellow flowers are densely clustered in globe-shaped heads 2–3 cm (0.8–1.2 in) in diameter. Flowering extends from April to October. The pods are flattened,

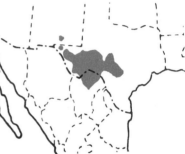

7.5–25 cm (3–10 in) long, 0.8–1.2 cm (0.3–0.5 in) wide, thin and papery, containing many small, hard, shiny seeds.

Leadtree

Leucaena leucocephala (Lam.) DeWit
[synonym: *L. glauca* (L.) Benth.]

Leadtree is a small, spreading tree of tropical America. It occurs naturally from southern Florida, through the West Indies to South America. It has also been introduced into southern Texas and California. It grows in sandy soils and is found in

pine-palmetto woodlands, disturbed sites, hammocks, and in coastal woodlands. The leaves are high in protein and when dried and milled are used as a substitute for alfalfa to feed cattle. The seeds are used in jewelry; and in the West Indies, they are eaten with rice. Leadtrees are used as shade trees for the smaller coffee plants, as hedges or windrows, or as ornamental shade trees.

   This is a shrub or small tree growing to 10 m (33 ft) and with unarmed branchlets and alternate, twice compound and feather-like (bipinnate) leaves. Each leaf is 10–30 cm (4–12 in) long, **has 2–4 pairs of side branches** (pinnae), **each with 10–20 pairs of small leaflets** 8–15 mm (0.3–0.6 in) long. The flowers are in dense, many-flowered heads 1.5–2 cm (0.6–0.8 in) in diameter. Each flower has a short calyx 1–2 mm (less than 0.1 in) long, 5 petals, 10 long stamens, and a single pistil. The pods are long, flattened, 8–15 cm (3.2–6 in) long, 2–4 cm (0.8–1.6 in) wide, thickened at the margins, and containing several, flattened, shiny seeds.

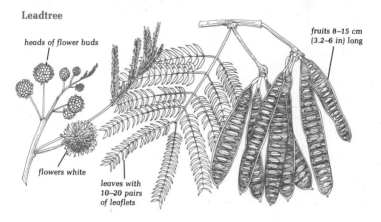

Leadtree

heads of flower buds

fruits 8–15 cm
(3.2–6 in) long

flowers white

leaves with
10–20 pairs
of leaflets

Great Leadtree

Leucaena pulverulenta (Schlecht.) Benth.

Great leadtree is a medium-size tree in its native range of southern Texas and adjacent Mexico. It grows along streams, in thickets and woods, and on limestone bluffs. This is an attractive tree because of its spreading branches and large, lacy leaves. It is used as a street tree or shade tree in southern Texas.

This species is a tree to 15 m (50 ft) or a large shrub with a broad, rounded crown. The alternate leaves are twice-compound and feather-like (bipinnate), 10–25 cm (4–10 in) long, with **14–20 pairs of side branches** (pinnae), each with 15–40 pairs of opposing **tiny leaflets 3–8 mm (0.1–0.3 in) long.** The tiny white flowers are clustered together in round heads at the tips of the branchlets. The flattened, thin, straight pods are 10–30 cm (4–12 in) long, 1.7– 2 cm (0.7–0.8 in) wide, with thickened margins and containing several, shiny, hard seeds.

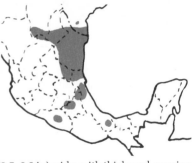

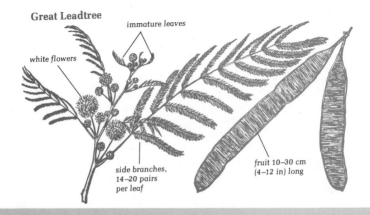

Great Leadtree

immature leaves

white flowers

side branches, 14–20 pairs per leaf

fruit 10–30 cm (4–12 in) long

Key to Genera in the Legume Subfamily Caesalpinioideae

A. Leaves simple; flowers irregular, approaching a pea-like flower **Redbud, p. 645**

B. Leaves feather-like (pinnate) or twice-compound and feather-like (bipinnate).

    1. Leaves feather-like (pinnate).

        a. Flowers usually male or female, sometimes bisexual, small, each flower less than 1 cm (0.4 in) across, greenish-white, calyx lobes and petals similar **Honeylocust, p. 648**

        b. Flowers bisexual, 2.2–2.6 cm (1 in) wide, yellow **Tamarind, p. 650**

    2. Leaves twice-compound and feather-like (bipinnate).

Eastern Redbud

Honeylocust

a. Flowers unisexual, calyx lobes and petals similar.

  (1) Leaves always twice-compound and feather-like (bipinnate); flowers with 5 petals, 10 stamens; fruits thick and woody at maturity **Coffee tree, p. 651**

  (2) Leaves twice-compound and feather-like (bipinnate) and feather-like (pinnate); flowers with 3–5 petals, 3–5 stamens; fruits flattened and leathery
          Honeylocust, p. 648

b. Flowers bisexual, calyx lobes and petals distinct.

  (1) Leaves with 2 or 4 long, narrow, flattened, strap-shaped side branches, the leaflets reduced, soon falling away
          Parkinsonia, p. 652

  (2) Leaves with 1–20 pairs of side branches, not flattened or strap-shaped, the leaves small to large, deciduous

    (a) Leaves with 1 pair of side branches per leaf   **Paloverde, p. 653**

    (b) Leaves with 2–20 pairs of side branches per leaf.

      (b1) Side branches 2–12 per leaf, leaflets usually less than 5 mm (0.2 in) long, rarely to 7 mm (0.3 in); petals yellow to orange, sometimes with red spots **Poinciana, p. 656**

      (b2) Side branches 11–22 per leaf; leaflets 5–10 mm (0.2–0.4 in) long; flowers with 5 petals, 4 orange-red to scarlet, 1 whitish streaked with red
          Flamboyant, p. 658

Kentucky Coffee Tree

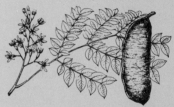

Jerusalem-Thorn

Yellow Paloverde

Flowerfence Poinciana

The Redbud Genus   Cercis L.

This is a small genus of 8 species, of which 5 occur in China, 1 in southern Europe and western Asia, and 2 in North America. Redbuds may have originated in China and migrated elsewhere. The fossil record suggests that the genus once had a much wider range than at present, but this range was greatly reduced by glaciers during the Ice Age, 50 to 70 million years ago.

  Because of their small size, attractive leaves, and flowers, redbuds are widely used as ornamentals. The eastern redbud (*Cercis canadensis*) is the most popular species for this purpose. In recent years, a white-flowered form of the eastern redbud has been introduced into the nursery trade. The Chinese redbud (*C. chinensis*), similar to the eastern redbud but more shrubby, is sometimes seen in parks and botanical gardens.

Redbuds are of limited economic importance. They are too small for the strong durable wood to be of use commercially. And they are of little value to wildlife.

Members of this genus are shrubs or trees with alternate, simple, deciduous, heart-shaped leaves. The flowers, appearing in early spring before or with the leaves, are produced on the older branchlets in few-flowered clusters. They are small, pink to rose colored, and shaped like a pea flower. The fruit is a small, flattened, dry pod that contains several hard, shiny seeds.

Key to Redbud Species

A. Leaves with a papery texture, the leafstalks 4–10 cm (1.6–4 in) long; trees of the eastern, midwestern, and southeastern woodlands

Eastern redbud, p. 646

B. Leaves with a somewhat leathery texture, the leafstalks 1–3 cm (0.4–1.2 in) long; trees of western and southwestern U.S.

California redbud, p. 647

Eastern Redbud

Cercis canadensis L.

This small attractive tree is a welcome sight in spring, for its clusters of dark-pink flowers appear before many trees have produced their mature leaves. From southern Ontario to Texas and Florida, eastern redbud occurs on rich, moist sites, preferring river bottoms and stream banks. It often forms a distinct understory in the woods, along with dogwood. Eastern redbud grows in association with oak, hickory, pine, yellow poplar, dogwood, and hawthorn. The Texas redbud is a variety of the eastern redbud [*Cercis canadensis* variety *texensis*] and is limited to Texas and Oklahoma. The leaf base of the Texas variety is more deeply lobed and kidney shaped.

Redbud trees are short-lived and grow rapidly in favorable sites. They flower in April and May, and the pods, fully grown in the South by June, fall in late autumn. The trees are of insignificant value to wildlife.

Appearance: short trees to 8 m (26 ft), rarely taller, with a low, spreading, flat to rounded crown; trunk short, straight, to 30 cm (12 in) in diameter. **Bark:** 1–1.4 cm (0.4–0.6 in) thick, scaly, sometimes divided into narrow, scaly ridges. **Branches:** stout, spreading; branchlets slender, slightly angled, smooth, brown. **Winter buds:** tiny, rounded, covered with overlapping, chestnut-brown scales. **Leaves:** alternate, simple, deciduous, ***broadly heart-shaped, 7.5–12.5 cm (3–5 in) long*** and wide, short-pointed at the tip, entire along the margins, with a ***papery texture,*** smooth and dark blue-green above, slightly hairy and paler below; the leafstalk 4–10 cm (1.6–4 in) long, slender. **Flowers:** in tight to loose ***clusters of 4–8 flowers along the older branchlets*** only; each flower 1.1–1.3 cm (0.5 in) long, like a pea flower, light to dark pink, on

Eastern Redbud

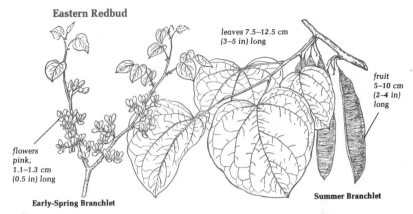

leaves 7.5–12.5 cm
(3–5 in) long

fruit
5–10 cm
(2–4 in)
long

flowers
pink,
1.1–1.3 cm
(0.5 in) long

Early-Spring Branchlet

Summer Branchlet

stalks 8–12 mm (0.3–0.5 in) long. **Fruits:** pods 5–10 cm (2–4 in) long, hanging, often in clusters, flat, containing several seeds, the seeds 6–8 mm (0.2–0.3 in) long, flattened.

California Redbud

Cercis occidentalis Torr. ex Gray

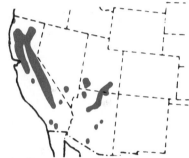

California redbud is a large, rounded shrub or small tree up to 7 m (23 ft) in height. It is native from California to southern Arizona and can grow in dry, gravelly or moist soils from 150 m (500 ft) elevation on the coastal side of the mountains to 1,800 m (6,000 ft) in desert areas. It occurs along mountain streams, dry hillsides, or within canyons, including the Grand Canyon. California redbud is characteristic of chaparral and oak woodlands. The *leaves* are *rounded to kidney shaped,* 3–9 cm (1.2–3.6 in) long and broad, *somewhat leathery,* and with *leafstalks 1–3 cm (0.4–1.2 in) long.* The reddish-purple flowers are 8–12 mm (0.3–0.5 in) long and produced along the older branchlets. The flattened pods are 4–9 cm (1.6–3.6 in) long.

California Redbud

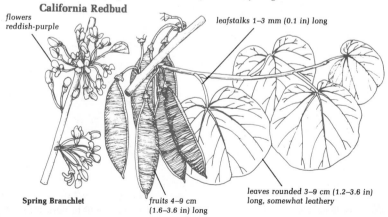

flowers
reddish-purple

leafstalks 1–3 mm (0.1 in) long

Spring Branchlet

fruits 4–9 cm
(1.6–3.6 in) long

leaves rounded 3–9 cm (1.2–3.6 in)
long, somewhat leathery

The Honeylocust Genus   *Gleditsia* L.

This is a small genus of approximately 12 tree species scattered in warm temperate, subtropical, and tropical regions of the Americas, Asia, and western Africa. There are 2 species in North America, the waterlocust (*Gleditsia aquatica*) of the southeastern U.S. and the honeylocust (*G. triacanthos*) of the eastcentral states. A hybrid between these two is often referred to as the Texas honeylocust.

Honeylocust obtains its name from the sweet-tasting pulp inside the pods. Many wild animals, including deer, rabbits, and squirrels, eat the fruits. The trees are sometimes used for hedgerows, windbreaks, and fuel.

They are tall trees with large spines along the trunk and main branches. The alternate, deciduous leaves are once or twice compound and feather-like. Flowers are either male or female, sometimes bisexual and are produced in simple greenish-white clusters. The pods are long and flattened.

Key to Honeylocust Species

A. Pods long, narrow, 15–45 cm (6–18 in) long, many-seeded; trees of eastcentral U.S.
                          Honeylocust, p. 648

B. Pods short, 2.5–5 cm (1–2 in) long; trees of southeastern Coastal Plain   **Waterlocust, p. 649**

Water Locust

Honeylocust   *Gleditsia triacanthos* L.

Honeylocust is a medium-size to large tree, common on the floodplains of major rivers and on limestone soils of the midwestern and southcentral U.S. It is tolerant to droughts and salt. This is generally a lowland species but can be found up to 1,500 m (5,000 ft) elevation. Common trees growing in association with honeylocust include red maple, persimmon, black gum, box elder, black water, ashes, and some oaks. The Texas honeylocust (*Gleditsia* X *texana* Sarg.) is a hybrid of honeylocust and waterlocust. These hybrids range from Mississippi to Texas and in the Mississippi River Valley to Arkansas, the area where the two species overlap. The hybrids have orange-red male flower clusters in April. The fruits are intermediate in size and shape between the fruits of the parent species.

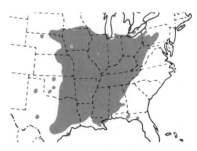

Honeylocusts are moderately fast-growing trees that can live over 120 years. Flowering and fruiting can begin at 5 years of age. The flowers appear in May or June, and the fruits ripen by autumn but many remain on the trees into winter. Whitetail

Honeylocust

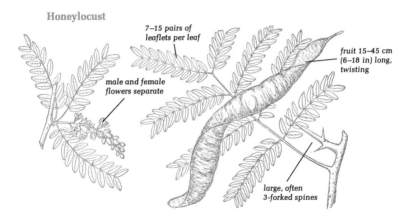

7–15 pairs of leaflets per leaf

fruit 15–45 cm (6–18 in) long, twisting

male and female flowers separate

large, often 3-forked spines

deer, cattle, rabbits, gray and fox squirrels, and quail will eat the seeds and parts of the pods. Grazing animals also eat the young seedlings and saplings.

A thornless selection with a straight trunk and attractive spreading shape is widely used as a street and shade tree in cities and villages. The tough, hard but somewhat brittle wood is not widely used for lumber.

Appearance: medium to tall tree to 30 m (100 ft), rarely taller, with a broad, open crown; trunk short 60–90 cm (24–35 in) in diameter, rarely larger. **Bark:** 1.2–2 cm (0.5–0.8 in) thick, developing deep lengthwise fissures and narrow rough ridges. **Branches:** slender, spreading, sometimes even drooping; *branchlets* slender, greenish-red turning brown and *armed with long-pointed, often 3-forked spines,* the spines occurring singly or in clusters. **Winter buds:** terminal bud lacking, lateral ones minute. **Leaves:** alternate, deciduous, *once or twice compound and feather-like, 15–20 cm (6–8 in) long,* with *4–7 pairs of side branches, each with 7–15 pairs of opposing leaflets, the leaflets broadest near the base,* 2.5–5 cm (1–2 in) long, 1.2–2.1 cm (0.5–0.9 in) wide, pointed to blunt at the tip, dark green and shiny above, paler below. **Flowers:** *male and female flowers separate,* the male flowers in short, many-flowered elongated clusters 5–7 cm (2–2.8 in) long, the pistillate flowers in slender few-flowered clusters 7–9 cm (2.8–3.6 in) long. **Fruits:** *long, narrow, flattened, 15–45 cm (6–18 in) long, many-seeded,* dark brown, twisting at maturity.

Waterlocust   *Gleditsia aquatica* Marshall

Waterlocust is a medium-size tree of the southeastern Coastal Plain ranging from North Carolina to southcentral Florida to east Texas. It grows in rich bottomlands subject to periodic flooding. Trees that grow in association include cypress, sycamore, sweetgum, blackgum, and swamp cottonwood. The wood is extremely durable and is used primarily for fence posts.

The tree is similar in appearance to honeylocust, but the waterlocust has less rough bark and often has smaller leaves and leaflets. The green-white flowers appear after the leaves in spring. The *fruiting pods are much smaller, 2.5–5 cm (1–2 in) long,* thin and flattened, and *contain 1–3 round, orange-brown seeds.*

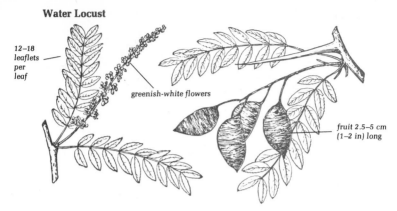

Water Locust

12–18 leaflets per leaf

greenish-white flowers

fruit 2.5–5 cm (1–2 in) long

The Tamarind Genus

Tamarindus L.

Since this genus contains only 1 species, the information given below for the species is the same as for the genus.

Tamarind

Tamarindus indicus L.

This handsome, medium-size tree probably originated in Africa or Asia, although no one is certain. Tamarind has been cultivated in India for centuries and was introduced very early in the tropical Americas. Today, it can be found in cultivation and growing wild from Florida to Brazil. It is found along roadsides, yards, streets, and low hills, especially near the coast.

The fleshy pods have many uses. They contain large amounts of sugar and are used in candies, jellies, sauces, and beverages. The juice has been used as a laxative. The flowers, seeds, bark, and young leaves were also used medicinally. The wood burns with an intense heat and has been used in construction and for tool handles and furniture. Bees make an excellent honey from the flowers.

Tamarind is a slow-growing, long-lived tree with a rounded crown and a massive trunk to 1.5 m (4.9 ft) in diameter. The leaves are alternate and feather-like (pinnate),

Tamarind

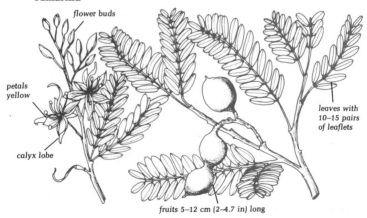

flower buds

petals yellow

leaves with 10–15 pairs of leaflets

calyx lobe

fruits 5–12 cm (2–4.7 in) long

each side branch bearing 10–15 pairs of small leaflets 16–20 mm (0.6–0.8 in) long. The pale *yellow flowers* are 2.2–2.6 cm (about 1 in) wide and consist of 4 petal-like calyx lobes 8–10 mm (0.3–0.4 in) long, *3 petals* with pink to red veins, *3 stamens,* and a single pistil. The brown pods are 5–12 cm (2–4.7 in) long, *thick, brittle and hard on the outside, containing a fleshy pulp inside* that surrounds the 3 or 4 flattened seeds.

The Coffee Tree Genus *Gymnocladus* Lam.

There are only 2 species remaining in this genus, but the geological record suggests that it was once more extensive. Fossil leaves, 50 to 70 million years old, have been found in Europe, although the genus is extinct there today. Only 1 species exists in China (*Gymnocladus chinensis*) and 1 in North America (*G. dioicus*). Both species have handsome wood that is hard, durable, and finishes to a high luster. The wood has been used in cabinetwork. The mature seeds are hard and do not serve as a food source to wildlife.

Members of this genus are medium-size trees with deciduous, twice-compound feather-like (bipinnate) leaves. The white to purplish-white flowers are produced in large clusters. The flowers and the trees are either male or female. The large fruiting pods are hard and woody at maturity and contain several large seeds embedded in a sweet pulp.

Kentucky Coffee Tree *Gymnocladus dioicus* (L.) K. Koch.

This tree is widely distributed in midwestern and eastern North America. From Wisconsin to northern Louisiana, the Kentucky coffee tree grows in deep, rich soils in bottomlands, deep ravines, and moist lower slopes in the Appalachian Mountains. It can be found with many other forest trees, such as sweetgum and tupelo in the South or oaks and hickories in the North.

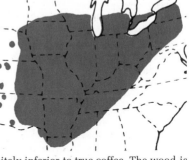

Kentucky coffee trees grow at a moderate rate and live less than 100 years. In May or June, the flowers appear for 7–10 days. The male flower clusters are half as long as female ones. The large, thick pods mature by fall but often remain on the tree well into late winter. The sticky pulp inside the fruit seems to be of low appeal to wildlife.

Early pioneers made a coffee substitute from the roasted seeds, although it was definitely inferior to true coffee. The wood is used in cabinets or for railroad ties, fence posts, and general construction, though the trees are never abundant in any location.

Appearance: medium-size tree to 30 m (100 ft) with a narrow shape and rounded crown; trunk straight, to 90 cm (35 in) in diameter. **Bark:** 1.8–2.5 cm (0.7–1 in) thick, deeply fissured and scaly, dark gray. **Branches:** stout, spreading; branchlets stout, covered with dense short hairs when young, reddish-brown. **Winter buds:** 6–9 mm (0.2–0.3 in) long, blunt, covered with dark-brown bud scales. **Leaves:** alternate, deciduous, *twice compound and feather-like (bipinnate), 30–90 cm (12–35 in) long, 45–60 cm (17–24 in) broad,* composed of 5–9 branches, each branch bearing 4–7 pairs of opposing leaflets, the leaflets broadest near the base, 5–6.2 cm (2–2.5 in) long, 2.2–2.8 cm (1 in) wide, pointed at the tip, light green, hairy when young, becoming smooth with age. **Flowers:** *male and female flowers on separate trees;* the male flowers in branched, elongated clusters 7.5–10 cm (3–4 in) long; the female flowers in branched, elongated

Kentucky Coffee Tree

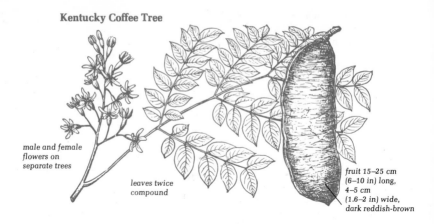

male and female flowers on separate trees

leaves twice compound

fruit 15–25 cm (6–10 in) long, 4–5 cm (1.6–2 in) wide, dark reddish-brown

clusters 25–30 cm (10–12 in) long, each flowered with a 5-lobed calyx 1.5–1.9 cm (0.6–0.8 in) long, 5 petals, keeled, 10 stamens in male flowers or a single pistil in female flowers. **Fruits:** *tough, hard pod, uniformly wide, 15–25 cm (6–10 in) long, 4–5 cm (1.6–2 in) wide, dark reddish-brown,* with a thick, dark pulp inside surrounding the large nearly rounded seeds.

The Parkinsonia Genus
Parkinsonia L.

This is a small genus of perhaps 4 species confined to warmer regions of America and southern Africa. Only 1 of these, the Jerusalem thorn, reaches tree size and is native to the southwestern U.S. Parkinsonias have been widely cultivated throughout the tropical regions of the world. *Members of this genus are easily distinguished because the leaves look like long, narrow streamers.* The branches and branchlets are green and photosynthetic; they produce food for the tree just as the leaves do.

Jerusalem Thorn or Paloverde
Parkinsonia aculeata L.

This green-barked, thorny shrub or small tree is native from southern Texas, New Mexico, and Arizona through Mexico to South America. They have been introduced in California, Florida, and the West Indies and now reproduce on their own there.

Jerusalem thorn grows in desert grasslands and canyons and does best in moist sandy or gravelly soils from 900–1,350 m (2,900–4,500 ft) elevation. They are usually found growing in association with mesquite and blue paloverde. The hard, heavy wood is occasionally used for fuel.

Appearance: spiny shrub or small tree to 12 m (40 ft), with an open, spreading head; short trunk. **Bark:** thin, smooth, green turning brown or reddish brown on older trunks. **Branches:** slender, spreading, green; *branchlets* slender, *green, with paired sharp spines* where the leaves are attached. **Leaves:** alternate, twice-compound and feather-like (bipinnate) but *modified into 2 or 4 long, narrow, flattened yellowish-green, strap-like strips 20–40 cm (8–16*

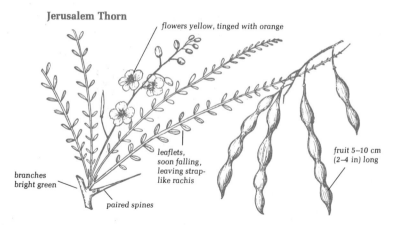

Jerusalem Thorn

flowers yellow, tinged with orange

leaflets,
soon falling,
leaving strap-
like rachis

branches
bright green

paired spines

fruit 5–10 cm
(2–4 in) long

in) long, each with 22–30 pairs of opposing tiny leaflets 7–9 mm (about 0.3 in) long, the ***leaflets soon falling leaving the persistent strap-like strips;*** the leafstalks short. **Flowers:** the pea-like flowers are produced on short stalks and loosely clustered on an elongated spike. Each flower has 5 short calyx lobes, ***5 petals, almost rounded, yellow tinged with orange, 8–13 mm (0.3–0.5 in) long,*** 10 stamens, and a single pistil. **Fruits:** pods 5–10 cm (2–4 in) long, thickened and leathery, constricted between the seeds, brown; seeds 1–1.2 cm (0.5 in) long.

The Paloverde Genus
Cercidium Tulasne

The paloverdes make up a small genus of 10 species limited to the warmer, usually drier regions, of the southwestern U.S., Mexico, and Central and South America. Three paloverdes reach tree size in North America — the blue, border, and yellow paloverdes. These are small trees and shrubs with green branches that are armed with a pair of spines at the base of the leaves. The twice-compound and feather-like (bipinnate) leaves have only 1 pair of side branches (pinnae) that bear 1–7 pairs of opposing leaflets. The flowers are clustered in many-flowered heads. Fruits are somewhat flattened, slightly constricted between the few seeds.

Key to Paloverde Species

A. Leaves and leaflets yellowish-green, 4–10 pairs
of leaflets per side branch (pinnae)
Yellow paloverde, p. 654

B. Leaves and leaflets dark green to bluish-green, 1–
4 pairs of leaflets per side branch (pinnae).

    1. Leaves and leaflets bluish-green; flowers yel-
low, the largest petal all yellow
Blue paloverde, p. 654

    2. Leaves and leaflets dark green; flowers yellow,
the largest petal yellow spotted with red
Border paloverde, p. 655

Blue Paloverde

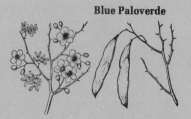

Yellow Paloverde *Cercidium microphyllum* (Torr.) Rose & Johnst.

The yellow paloverde is a common shrub or small tree on desert plains and foothills from 150–1,000 m (500–3,300 ft) elevation in southern California, Arizona, and north-western Mexico. It is more tolerant of dry conditions than blue paloverde and thus

occupies many more sites. This is a charac-teristic species of the Arizona desert, along with the desert ironwood, saguaros, chol-las, prickly pear, and hedgehog cacti. Yel-low paloverde are important browse for small desert mammals, especially the jackrabbit. It is browsed by livestock only when other food is scarce.

This spiny shrub or tree grows to 6 m (20 ft), has yellowish-green bark and branches. The alternate *leaves* are *twice-compound and feather-like (bipinnate)*, each of the *2 side branches with 4–10 pairs of opposing yellow-green leaflets.* The flowers are in short, few-flowered clusters, each pale yellow, 1–1.3 cm (0.5 in) in diameter. Fruiting pods are 4–10 cm (1.6–4 in) long, 8–12 mm (0.3–0.5 in) wide, thickened, and contain-ing 1 to 5 rounded, shiny seeds.

Yellow Paloverde

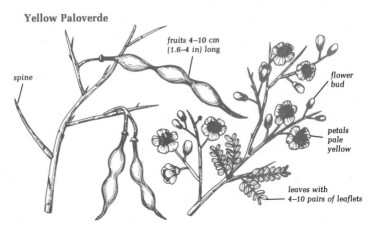

fruits 4–10 cm (1.6–4 in) long

spine

flower bud

petals pale yellow

leaves with 4–10 pairs of leaflets

Blue Paloverde *Cercidium floridum* Benth. ex Gray

Blue paloverde is native from Texas to the desert regions of southeastern California and into northwestern Mexico. It grows in sandy soils from sea level to 1,200 m (4,000 ft) in desert scrubland, canyons, oc-casional hillsides, and desert grasslands. It commonly grows in association with mes-quites, catclaw blackbead, and yellow palo-verde. This species has distinctive blue-green branches and leaves.

This is an especially attractive tree when

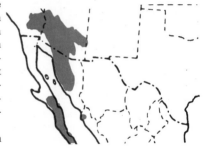

the bright yellow flowers appear in great masses in March or April. Mountain sheep and burro deer browse the twigs and leaves. Smaller mammals eat the seeds in summer and fall. Pima and Papago Indians in Arizona cook the young pods and seeds like lima beans, or grind the ripe seeds for gruel.

Appearance: short tree to 10 m (33 ft), with a low spreading crown; trunk crooked, usually 15 to 25 cm (6–10 in) in diameter. **Bark:** thin, smooth, pale green, turning reddish-brown at the base of older trunks. **Branches:** stout, spreading, blue-green; branchlets slender, armed with paired sharp spines 5–7 cm (2–2.8 in) long. **Leaves:** al-

Blue Paloverde

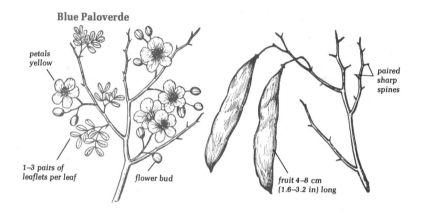

petals yellow

1–3 pairs of leaflets per leaf

flower bud

paired sharp spines

fruit 4–8 cm (1.6–3.2 in) long

ternate, early deciduous, twice-compound and feather-like (bipinnate), ***with 1 pair of side branches, each with 1–9 pairs of blue-green leaflets,*** the leaflets 5–8 mm (0.2–0.3 in) long. **Flowers:** produced in few-flowered elongated clusters, each flower 1.2–2 cm (0.5–0.8 in) across, composed of 5 small calyx lobes, ***5 yellow petals,*** 10 stamens, and a single pistil. **Fruits:** pods 4–8 cm (1.6–3.2 in) long, 9–15 mm (0.3–0.6 in) wide, somewhat flattened, containing 1–4 seeds.

Border Paloverde   *Cercidium macrum* Johnst.

This close relative of blue paloverde inhabits southern Texas and northeastern Mexico, living up to its name as a border species. It occurs in sandy loam or clay soils at relatively low elevations and grows to 8 m (26 ft) with green bark and green, spiny, crooked branches and often zigzagging branchlets. The ***leaves*** are ***2–2.6 cm (0.8–1.1 in) long,*** twice compound and feather-like, ***with 2 side branches, each with 2 pairs of dark-green*** leaflets. Flowers are produced in few-flowered, elongated clusters; each ***flower is yellow but the largest petal is red-spotted.*** The fruiting pods are 2.5–6.5 cm (1–2.6 in) long, 7–12 mm (0.3–0.5 in) wide, flattened and contain 1–5 dark, shiny flattened seeds.

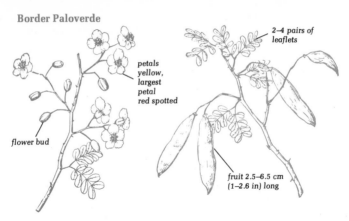

Border Paloverde

2–4 pairs of leaflets

petals yellow, largest petal red spotted

flower bud

fruit 2.5–6.5 cm (1–2.6 in) long

The Poinciana Genus

Caesalpinia L.
(synonym: *Poinciana* L.)

This is a large genus of about 200 species widely distributed in tropical and sub-tropical regions of the world. Some authorities prefer to split this genus into several smaller ones; but for this book, it is sufficient to consider the many species in one large genus. Several native North American members are vines or shrubs, while many tree species have been introduced in gardens in Florida and California. But only 3 are common enough or reproduce on their own and thus warrant inclusion here.

Members of the genus are trees, shrubs, vines, or herbs, often with spines, with alternate, twice-compound and feather-like (bipinnate) leaves. The flowers are produced in elongated, often branched clusters. Each flower has a 5-lobed calyx, 5 petals, yellow to orange or sometimes with red spots, 10 stamens, and a single pistil. Fruits are flattened dry pods, almost rounded to uniformly wide, sometimes splitting open at maturity.

Key to Poinciana Species

A. Each side branch (pinnae) of the compound leaf with 3–5 pairs of leaflets; trees of southern Texas and northern Mexico
  Mexican poinciana, p. 657

B. Each side branch (pinnae) of the compound leaf with 6–12 pairs of leaflets.

  1. Leaves with 5–10 pairs of side branches per leaf; flower and flower cluster stalks smooth or hairy but not covered with sticky hairs; trees of southern Florida, extreme Southwest, and California **Flowerfence poinciana, p. 657**

  2. Leaves with 6–12 pairs of side branches per leaf; flower and flower cluster stalks covered with sticky hairs; trees of southern Texas to southern California
  Paradise poinciana, p. 658

Mexican Poinciana
Caesalpinia mexicana Gray
(synonym: *Poinciana mexicana* (Gray) Rose)

This shrub or small tree is native to northern Mexico and southern Texas where it is also cultivated for its attractive, golden-yellow flowers. It grows best on light, sandy soils. Mexican poinciana may reach 10 m (33 ft) in height. It has branches without spines, and alternate, twice-compound and feather-like (bipinnate) leaves. A ***leaf is composed of 2–4 pairs of side branches*** (pinnae) plus a single terminal one. Each of these has 3–5 pairs of leaflets, the leaflets are broadest near or just below the middle, 0.8–2.2 cm (0.3–0.9 in) long. The fragrant, golden-yellow flowers are produced in elongated, branched clusters. The fruiting pods are almost uniformly wide, 4–7 cm (1.6–2.8 in) long, flattened, and split open with force at maturity.

Flowerfence Poinciana
Caesalpinia pulcherrima (L.) Swartz
(synonym: *Poinciana pulcherrima* L.)

This attractive tropical shrub or small tree was introduced as a popular garden plant in frost-free areas of North America. It is especially common in southern Florida but can also be seen in the southwestern U.S., including southern California. Flowerfence poinciana is widely planted throughout tropical cities, towns, and outposts of the world. It grows best in well-drained, sandy soils.

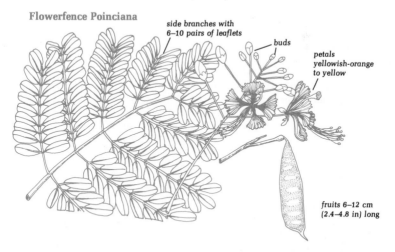

Flowerfence Poinciana

side branches with 6–10 pairs of leaflets

buds

petals yellowish-orange to yellow

fruits 6–12 cm (2.4–4.8 in) long

These small trees have alternate, twice-compound and feather-like (bipinnate) ***leaves, each with 5–10 pairs of side branches,*** each bearing 6–10 pairs of leaflets. The leaflets are broadest near the middle to the base, 1–2.5 cm (0.4–1 in) long. The yellowish-orange to yellow flowers are produced in elongated clusters. The fruits or pods are uniformly wide, 6–12 cm (2.4–4.8 in) long, 1.5–2 cm (0.6–0.8 in) wide, flattened, and splitting open suddenly at maturity.

Paradise Poinciana　　　　　　*Caesalpinia gilliesii* (Wall.) Dietr.

(synonym: *Poinciana gilliesii* Wall. ex Hook.)

This small tree is native to Argentina and Chile. It has escaped from cultivation and is often found along roadsides and disturbed sites from Texas to California. Paradise poinciana is frequently planted because of its ability to survive dry conditions and its attractive bright yellow and orange flowers.

It is a shrub or small tree to 5 m (17 ft) with alternate, twice-compound and feather-like (bipinnate) leaves. ***Each leaf is composed of 6–12 pairs of side branches*** (pinnae). The side branches have 7–11 pairs of leaflets, each leaflet broadest near the middle, 3–7 mm (0.1–0.3 in) long and 1.8–2.4 cm (0.7–1 in) wide. The flowers are produced in elongated clusters at the tips of the branchlets. The ***branches of the flower clusters and the flower stalks are covered with sticky hairs.*** Fruits are uniformly wide, 6–12 cm (2.4–4.8 in) long, 1.4–2 cm (0.6–0.8 in) wide, flattened, gland-dotted, splitting open at maturity with an explosive force scattering the seeds.

The Flamboyant Genus　　　　　　　　　　*Delonix* Raf.

This is a small African genus of 3 species. Attractive trees with showy flowers, they are often planted as street trees in tropical climates. One species, the flamboyant tree, has been introduced in southern California and southern Florida. Members of this genus have alternate, twice-compound and feather-like (bipinnate) leaves with many side branches (pinnae) and leaflets. The flowers are produced in large clusters. Each flower is bisexual, large, showy, and contains 10 stamens. The fruits are long, narrow, and flattened but somewhat thick, and woody.

Flamboyant Tree　　　　　　　　　*Delonix regia* (Bojer) Raf.

This native of the Malagasy Republic in Africa is one of the showiest of the flowering trees. It is widely cultivated in most warm regions of the world. In North America, it is found in southern California and southern Florida, including the Keys. It is closely related to poinciana trees.

A tree to 15 m (50 ft) with a wide-spreading crown, the flamboyant has large, delicate, twice-compound and feather-like (bipinnate) leaves. ***Large clusters of firy red, orange, or yellow and red flowers*** seem to set the trees ablaze at flowering time. ***Each flower is 7–10 cm (2.8–4 in) in length,*** with a 5-parted calyx, ***5 large, showy, unequal, spoon-shaped petals, 4 petals orange-red to scarlet, 1 whitish streaked with red,*** 10 stamens, slender and red, 1 pistil. The fruiting pods are 15–60 cm (6–24 in) long, 5–6 cm (2–2.4 in) wide, flattened, 6–9 mm (0.2–0.3 in) thick, hard, splitting lengthwise into 2 sections, and containing numerous narrow, mottled seeds.

Key to Genera in the Legume Subfamily Papilionoideae

Yellowwood

A. Flowers with the 10 stamens free.

　　1. Flowers white, produced in large, twice-branched, elongated clusters (panicles)
　　　　　　　　　　　　Yellowwood, p. 659

2. Flowers bluish-purple to rosy-white, produced in elongated unbranched clusters (racemes), each flower stalked **Sophora, p. 661**

B. Flowers with 9 stamens fused into a tube plus 1 free for most of its length.

Texas Sophora

1. Flowers in elongated, unbranched clusters (racemes), each flower stalked.

  a. Leaves with tiny glands on the surface.

    (1) Branches without spines; leaves with 10–22 pairs of leaflets; flowers white **Kidneywood, p. 663**

    (2) Branches with paired spines at the base of the leaves; leaves with 2–5 pairs of leaflets, falling away very early; flowers purple; includes desert smoketree **Dalea, p. 663**

Desert Smoketree

  b. Leaves without tiny glands.

    (1) Leaves consisting of 3 leaflets (trifoliolate); flowers red to orange-red **Coral bean, p. 664**

    (2) Leaves feather-like (pinnate); flowers white, pink, or rose-purple.

      (a) Side branches of the leaves with a single leaflet at the tip (odd pinnate); fruits flattened, thin, papery **Locust, p. 666**

      (b) Side branches of the leaves without a single leaflet at the tip (even pinnate); fruits thick, almost round in cross section **Desert ironwood, p. 670**

Black Locust

2. Flowers in elongated, branched clusters (panicles), each flower stalked.

  a. Flowers purplish-blue; fruits 7.5–10 cm (3–4 in) long, with 4 papery, wavy-margined wings **Fish poison tree, p. 671**

  b. Flowers pink; fruits 2.5–3.5 cm (1–1.4 in) long, thick, egg-shaped, unwinged **Angelins, p. 671**

Florida Fish Poison Tree

The Yellowwood Genus   *Cladrastis* Raf.

This is a small genus of 4 or 5 species. A single species occurs in the hardwood forest of the southeastern and lower midwestern U.S. The remaining species are native to

China and Japan. Members of this genus are deciduous trees with compound, feather-like leaves with a single leaflet at the tip (odd-pinnate). The flowers are produced in long, hanging clusters. The fruits are flattened, dry pods.

Yellowwood
Cladrastis kentukea (Dum.-Cours.) Rudd

[synonym: *C. lutea* (Michx. f.) K. Koch]

This small tree, named for its attractive wood, has been a rare species in the East even from the time it was discovered by the French botanist, Michaux, in 1796. Its natural range is limited to the Appalachian Mountains in western North Carolina and eastern Tennessee, and also in Arkansas and Missouri. Found mostly in rich, well-drained, limestone soils, yellowwood occurs in river valleys, slopes, and ridges, and along streams. It is found growing in association with yellow birch, beech, basswood, and black cherry.

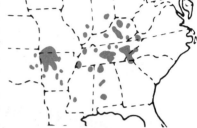

Yellowwood is a slow-growing, moderately long-lived tree that produces loose clusters of delicate white flowers around mid-June. The fruits mature by August or September. The wood is durable, medium weight, and takes a beautiful finish. It is a favored wood for gunstocks, when available. Because of the attractive flowers, the trees are occasionally planted in gardens and parks.

Yellowwood

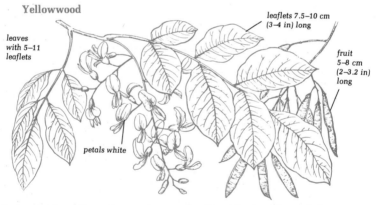

leaves with 5–11 leaflets

leaflets 7.5–10 cm (3–4 in) long

fruit 5–8 cm (2–3.2 in) long

petals white

Appearance: medium-size tree to 18 m (60 ft), with a broad rounded crown; trunk straight, to 60 cm (24 in) in diameter. **Bark:** thin, silvery gray, the lighter colored inner bark sometimes showing through cracks in the outer bark. **Branches:** stout, spreading; branchlets slender, zigzag, brittle. **Winter buds:** tiny, hidden by the leaves or ringed by the leaf scars. **Leaves:** alternate, deciduous, feather-like and compound (bipinnate), 20–30 cm (8–12 in) long, with 5–11 leaflets, the leaflets 7.5–10 cm (3–4 in) long, broadest near the middle. **Flowers:** produced in *elongated, hanging clusters 30–35 cm (12–14 in) long;* each flower with a short bell-shaped calyx, 5 *petals, white,* shaped like a pea flower, the upper one circular, the 2 wing petals straight, the remaining 2 forming a nearly straight keel; *10 stamens, free,* 1 pistil. **Fruits:** *pods 5–8 cm (2–3.2 in) long, thin, flattened,* smooth, dry, papery, and containing 4–6 small, compressed seeds.

The Sophora Genus

Sophora L.

Sophora, a genus of roughly 50 evergreen and deciduous trees, shrubs, and perennials, is widely scattered throughout warmer regions of the world. All of the trees are noted for their handsome flowers and leaves, including the 2 American tree species — coralbean (*Sophora secundiflora*) and Texas sophora (*S. affinis*). Some of the species have been introduced and cultivated as ornamentals. The hardiest of these is the Japanese pagoda tree, which is native to China and Korea. Members of this genus have smooth, unarmed branches with alternate leaves that are feather-like with one terminal leaflet (odd pinnate). The leaves may have a few to many leaflets. The flowers are in large, hanging clusters. Each flower has a bell-shaped calyx, pea-flower shaped petals, 10 stamens, and a single pistil. The pods are long, narrow, fleshy to leathery, constricted between the seeds, and usually do not split open at maturity.

Key to Sophora Species

Coralbean

A. Leaves with 5–9 leaflets; flowers bluish-purple; pods 2.5–13 cm (1–5.2 in) long, slightly constricted between the seeds; trees of Texas, New Mexico, and Mexico   **Coralbean, p. 661**

B. Leaves with 13–15 leaflets; flowers rosy-white; pods 1.2–7.5 cm (0.5–3 in) long, tightly constricted between the seeds; trees of Arkansas, Louisiana, Texas, and Oklahoma

       Texas sophora, p. 662

Coralbean, Mescalbean

Sophora secundiflora (Ortega) Lag.

This small, evergreen tree or shrub is found in moist limestone soils in southwestern Texas, New Mexico, and Mexico. It often forms dense thickets or small groves along streams, the seashore, or in mountains up to 1,500 m (5,000 ft).

Coralbean grows slowly and flowers in early spring as the leaves are appearing. The fruits mature by early fall. The red seeds contain poisonous alkaloids and are avoided by wildlife. Indians once exploited these narcotic properties for ceremonies. In this case, tiny amounts of groundup seed were added to a drink to induce an excited or delirious state, followed by a deep sleep. The orange-red wood is hard, heavy, and close-grained, but has no commercial uses.

Appearance: small trees to 12 m (36 ft) with a narrow crown; trunk straight, to 25 cm (10 in) in diameter. **Bark:** thin, shallowly fissured with thin, flattened ridges, dark gray to almost black. **Branches:** stout, upright; branchlets hairy, green to orange-brown. **Leaves:** alternate, compound and feather-like with a single terminal leaflet (odd pinnate), 10–15 cm (4–6 in) long, with usually **5–9 leaflets**, the leaflets broadest near the middle, 2.5–6 cm (1–2.4 in) long, 1.2–4 cm (0.5–1.6 in) wide, leathery, shiny.

Coralbean

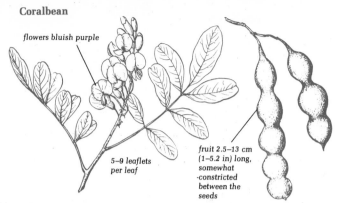

flowers bluish purple

5–9 leaflets per leaf

fruit 2.5–13 cm (1–5.2 in) long, somewhat -constricted between the seeds

Flowers: fragrant, produced in dense, elongated spikes 5–13 cm (2–5.2 in) long; each flower stalked, with a short, bell-shaped calyx, ***petals 5,*** pea-flower shaped, ***bluish-purple,*** 1.4–1.7 cm (0.7 in) long, 10 stamens, 1 pistil. **Fruits:** pods on stalks 6–25 mm (0.2–1 in) long, ***2.5–13 cm (1–5.2 in) long,*** woody, hard, ***somewhat constricted between the seeds,*** not splitting open at maturity; seeds red, almost globe-shaped, 1–1.4 cm (0.4–0.6 in) long, hard.

Texas Sophora

Sophora affinis Torr. & Gray

Texas sophora is native from southwestern Arkansas and northwestern Louisiana to southern Oklahoma and central Texas. Like the coralbean, this species grows on limestone hills, streambanks, and ravines where it may form small thickets. A small tree, it has a rounded crown and stout, spreading branches. The feather-like compound ***leaves*** are somewhat longer than coralbean leaves, and ***usually have 13–15 leaflets.*** The ***flowers*** are a ***rosy-white*** and appear from April to June in drooping clusters. The ***pods*** are ***1.2–7.5 cm (0.5–3 in) long,*** black, 4–8-seeded, tightly constricted between the seeds to appear as separate beads on a string.

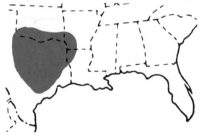

Texas Sophora

flowers rose white

13 to 15 leaflets per leaf

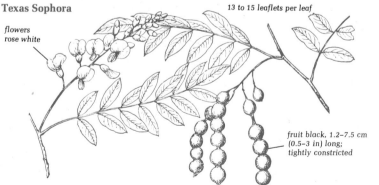

fruit black, 1.2–7.5 cm (0.5–3 in) long; tightly constricted

The Kidneywood Genus *Eysenhardtia* H.B.K.

This is a small genus of only 4 or 5 species confined to tropical and subtropical regions of the Americas. Just 1 tree species occurs in North America, the kidneywood (*Eysenhardtia polystachya*) of the Southwest. Another species, the Texas kidneywood (*E. texana*), is a small shrub that grows to less than 2 m (6.6 ft) in height. Members of this genus have alternate, compound and feather-like (pinnate) leaves. The flowers are produced on long spikes, usually at the ends of the branchlets. Each flower has a bell-shaped calyx with 5 lobes, 5 petals, 10 stamens, united for more than half their length into a tube, and a single pistil. The fruiting pods are small but usually numerous.

Kidneywood *Eysenhardtia polystachya* (Ort.) Sarg.

Kidneywood is a shrub or small tree native to southern Arizona, New Mexico, and Mexico. It grows in dry soils along ridges and slopes of the upper desert grassland and the lower oak woodland at 1,200–1,500 m (3,900–5,000 ft) elevation. A yellow to orange dye can be obtained from the wood. Deer and livestock browse the leaves.

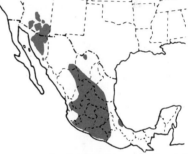

This is a multistemmed shrub or small tree to 7 m (23 ft). The branches and branchlets are slender and unarmed. Leaves are alternate, **compound and feather-like (pinnate),** 10–13 cm (4–5.2 in) long, **with 10–22 pairs of leaflets,** each 4–20 mm (0.2–0.8 in) long. The **leaves and flowers are gland-dotted,** giving the plant a distinctive odor. The white flowers appear on spikes 7.5–15 cm (3–6 in) long in April or May. The fruiting **pods** are **stalked, 1–1.4 cm (0.5 in) long, 3–4 mm (0.2 in) wide,** thin, flattened and contain 1 or 2 flattened, reddish-brown seeds.

Kidneywood

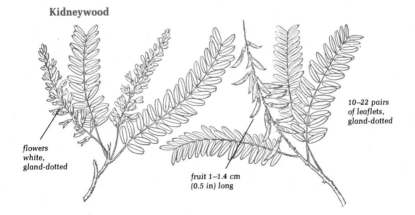

flowers
white,
gland-dotted

fruit 1–1.4 cm
(0.5 in) long

10–22 pairs
of leaflets,
gland-dotted

The Dalea Genus *Dalea* L.

Dalea, with approximately 150 species of tropical trees, shrubs, and herbs, is confined to the Americas. Although a dozen species occur in the warmer parts of the U.S., only

1, the desert smoketree (*Dalea spinosa*), ever attains tree size. It is similar in appearance to the kidneywood, even to the extent of having glandular hairs on the leaves, except that dalea have distinctly irregular, pea-like, purple flowers. The tree species have simple leaves that fall away early in autumn. The 1-seeded pods are small.

Desert Smoketree   *Dalea spinosa* A. Gray

The common name comes from the smoky or silvery-gray appearance of the short spiny tree. It grows to a maximum of 8 m (26 ft) in eastern California and extends into the low desert lands of western Mexico. It is often found growing in gravelly or sandy washes.

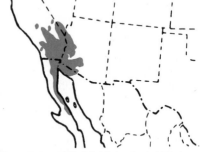

Smoketrees are leafless most of the year. Yet their branches appear to be clothed because the **branchlets** and **young branches** are **densely covered by gray hairs** and are armed with sharp, paired spines. The **few** simple **leaves** are scattered near the bases of the branchlets and **remain on the trees only a few weeks.** The flowers bloom in early June in few-flowered clusters. Each flower has a short calyx 4–5 mm (to 0.2 in) long, covered with reddish sunken glands. The thin **pods are 5–7 mm (0.3 in) long,** broadest near the base, and covered with amber-colored glands.

Desert Smoketree

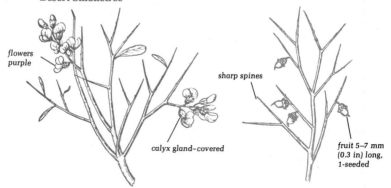

flowers
purple

sharp spines

calyx gland–covered

fruit 5–7 mm
(0.3 in) long,
1-seeded

The Coral Bean Genus   *Erythrina* L.

This is a medium-size genus of approximately 100 species of trees, shrubs, and a few herbs widely distributed in tropical and subtropical regions of the world. Many of the species are cultivated for their attractive, brightly colored flowers. Only 2 species ever reach tree size in North America: the eastern coral bean and the southwestern coral bean. Members of this genus have been used as ornamentals, in medicines, and in making dyes, fibers, and lacquers. The seeds are highly poisonous. They are of limited value to wildlife.

Coral beans are spiny small trees or shrubs with alternate, 3-leaflet leaves (trifoliolate). Flowers are often produced in showy elongated clusters. Each flower has a short 5-lobed calyx, elongated; pea-flower shaped, red to orange petals, 10 stamens (9 united into a tube, 1 free), and a single pistil. The long, narrow pod, usually is constricted between the red and black kidney-shaped seeds.

Key to Coral Bean Species

Eastern Coral Bean

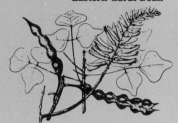

A. Leaves broadly triangular and gradually tapering to a tip; pods 10–25 cm (4–10 in) long; trees of southwestern U.S. and Mexico
   Southwestern coral bean, p. 665
B. Leaves spear-shaped, almost 2-lobed, broad at the base and abruptly tapering to a long tip; pods 5–10 cm (2–4 in) long; trees of southeastern Coastal Plain   **Eastern coral bean, p. 665**

Southwestern Coral Bean

Erythrina flabelliformis Kearney

This large, spiny shrub sometimes reaches tree size in its native range in Arizona, New Mexico, and Mexico. It grows on dry, rocky canyon slopes, washes of the higher desert mountains, desert grasslands, or even in oak woodlands, at 1,000–1,500 m (3,200–5,000 ft) elevation. The light wood is sometimes used for making corks, and the red seeds, or beans, are used for necklaces. All parts of the plant, particularly the seeds, contain poisonous alkaloids.

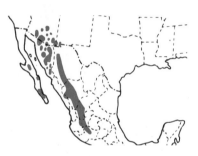

Southwestern coral beans are without leaves most of the year, including spring when the flowers are in blossom. The alternate *leaves* have 3 leaflets, the leaves 2.5–7.5 cm (1–3 in) long, 4–8.7 cm (1.5–3.5 in) wide, *broadly triangular and gradually tapering to a point.* The *flowers,* produced in long, upright spikes, have a short calyx 7–9 mm (0.3 in) long; narrow, *red petals (corolla)* 2.5–5 cm (1–2 in) long; 10 stamens, and a single pistil. The *pods* are *10–25 cm (4–10 in) long,* 1.2–2 cm (0.5–0.8 in) wide, rounded, leathery, constricted between the seeds; the seeds are bright red, bean-shaped, and poisonous.

Eastern Coral Bean

Erythrina herbacea L.

This small tree occurs in sandy soils in hammocks, Coastal Plain, and pinelands from North Carolina to Texas. Eastern coral bean grows to tree size only in the southern end of its range; further north it is shrubby and even dies back each winter. The brittle branches are easily broken by tropical storms, resulting in many deformed or unusual shapes. The tree is used as an ornamental because of its large,

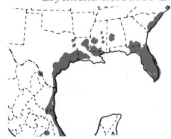

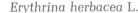

showy, scarlet flowers. Other economic uses are minor; it is of little value to wildlife.

Eastern coral bean occurs as a shrub or small tree with paired spines along the branchlets and 3-leaflet leaves. The leaves are 15–20 cm (6–8 in) long, 2.6–6 cm (1–2.4 in) wide, the leaflets are *spear-shaped, almost 2-lobed, broad near the base and abruptly tapering to a long tip,* dull green to yellowish green. The flowers, produced in large, upright spikes, bloom in April to June and have a short, 7–9 mm (0.3 in) long calyx; showy, tubular, scarlet petals (corolla), 4–5.6 cm (1.6–2.2 in) long; 10 stamens, and a single pistil. The *pods* are long and narrow, *5–10 cm (2–4 in) long,* leathery, and strongly constricted between the seeds.

Eastern Coral Bean

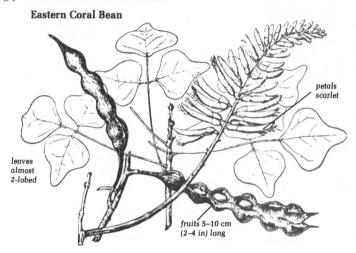

petals
scarlet

leaves
almost
2-lobed

fruits 5–10 cm
(2–4 in) long

The Locust Genus   *Robinia* L.

This is a small genus of about 15 species of trees and shrubs. Most are native to the Southeast, but others occur in the Southwest and Mexico. Three species regularly reach tree size in North America – the black locust and clammy locust of the eastern U.S., and the New Mexican locust of the Southwest. A fourth species, the little known Kelsey locust (*Robinia kelseyi*), is a shrub or small tree of the Smoky Mountains. It has smooth twigs and rosy blossoms. The pods are densely covered with purple hairs.

Locusts are of some importance as timber trees, although they are most commonly used as fence posts because the wood is highly durable in contact with the soil. Locusts are also used to prevent soil erosion and to reclaim abandoned sites with poor soil. They are of limited value to wildlife; the leaves are browsed by larger mammals, and the seeds are eaten by rodents and larger birds.

Members of this genus are shrubs or trees with pairs of sharp spines along the branchlets where the leaves are attached. The leaves are feather-like with a single leaflet at the end (odd-pinnate). The pea-shaped flowers are produced in elongated branched clusters; each flower consists of a bell-shaped calyx; 5 white or pink petals; 10 stamens (9 united into a tube and a free tenth one), and a single bent pistil. The long, narrow pods are thin, papery, and contain several to many hard seeds.

Key to Locust Species

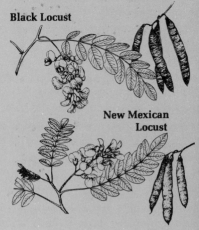

Black Locust

A. Flowers white; fruits smooth, without hairs at maturity; branchlets smooth, reddish-brown
Black locust, p. 667

B. Flowers rose-colored; fruits covered with gland-tipped hairs; branchlets covered with glandular hairs, reddish-brown.

New Mexican Locust

    1. Branchlets, flower stalks, and fruits not sticky but covered with glandular hairs; small trees of southwestern U.S.
        New Mexican locust, p. 668

    2. Branchlets, flower stalks, and fruits sticky due to secreting glandular hairs; small trees of eastern U.S.   **Clammy locust, p. 669**

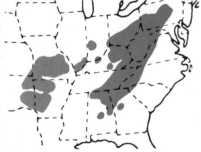

Black Locust   *Robinia pseudoacacia* L.

The natural range of this medium-size tree is the central Appalachian and Ozark mountains but it has been cultivated widely and now reproduces on its own throughout eastern North America and parts of the West. Black locust grows best in moist limestone soils from sea level to about 1,350 m (4,500 ft) elevation. It can be found in moist woodlands, farm lots, along fences and roads, and in urban environments. Many hardwoods grow in association with black locust, including oaks, hickories, tulip trees, maples, and some of the hard pines.

Black locust grows rapidly and can begin to flower at 6 years of age, although 10–12 years is normal. The flowers appear in May and June, and the pods mature by early fall. Whitetail deer browse the foliage, and quail and squirrel eat the seeds. Bees produce a good honey from the floral nectar.

The wood is hard, heavy, and durable. It was widely sought for use in shipbuilding and was exported to 19th-century England for that purpose. It is used today mainly for fence posts, railroad ties, fuel, and craft items. Most black locust are attacked by the locust borer beetle which can ruin the timber.

Appearance: medium-size tree to 18 m (60 ft), with an open, irregular crown; trunk straight to irregular, to 1.2 m (3.9 ft) in diameter. **Bark:** thick, to 4 cm (1.6 in), deeply furrowed and scaly, dark brown. **Branches:** short, upright, brittle; ***branchlets*** slender, brittle, ***smooth*** and ***reddish-brown*** at the end of the first year, armed with a pair of small spines where the leaves are attached. **Winter buds:** tiny, usually 3- or 4-clustered, covered with overlapping scales. **Leaves:** alternate, deciduous, compound and feather-like (pinnate), 20–35 cm (8–14 in) long, with 7–19 leaflets, each leaflet 3.8–5 cm (1.5–2 in) long, 1.2–1.8 cm (0.5–0.8 in) wide, broadest near the middle to uniformly wide, dull dark green. **Flowers:** produced in loose, hanging clusters 10–14 cm (4–5.5 in) long, very fragrant; each flower with a 5-lobed green calyx; 5 petals, pea-

Black Locust

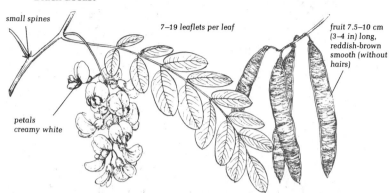

small spines

7–19 leaflets per leaf

fruit 7.5–10 cm (3–4 in) long, reddish-brown smooth (without hairs)

petals creamy white

flowered shaped, ***creamy white*** with a yellow blotch on the uppermost petals; 10 stamens, and a single bent pistil. **Fruits:** flattened pods 7.5–10 cm (3–4 in) long, 1.1–1.3 cm (0.5 in) broad, ***smooth***, reddish-brown, containing 4–8 dark, spotted seeds.

New Mexican Locust   *Robinia neomexicana* A. Gray

This locust is found on moist sites along mountain streams from Trans-Pecos Texas, through New Mexico, and into Utah and Nevada. It grows from 1,200–2,500 m (3,900–8,200 ft) elevation in the conifer belt together with pinyon, juniper, and yellow pine, and the Gambel oak.

New Mexican locust is important as browse for goats, mountain sheep, mule deer, blacktail deer, and porcupine. Small mammals, such as chipmunks, and larger birds, such as Gambel's quail, eat the seeds. Several Indian tribes once gathered the pods in the fall and ate them fresh, or else stored and cooked the dried beans. Today, this locust is valued as an erosion-control plant because it grows fast and tends to form thickets.

New Mexican Locust

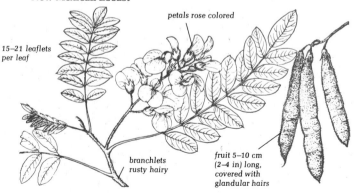

petals rose colored

15–21 leaflets per leaf

branchlets rusty hairy

fruit 5–10 cm (2–4 in) long, covered with glandular hairs

Appearance: small trees to 8 m (26 ft), often forming dense thickets; trunk straight to crooked, to 20 cm (8 in) in diameter. **Bark:** thin, less than 1 cm (0.4 in) thick, slightly furrowed, light brown. **Branches:** short, brittle; ***branchlets rusty hairy*** and reddish-brown, armed with a pair of curved spines where the leaves are attached. **Winter buds:** as in black locust, but hairy. **Leaves:** alternate, compound and feather-like (pinnate), 15–30 cm (6–12 in) long, with 15–21 short-stalked leaflets, the leaflets 3.5–4.5 cm (1.4–1.8 in) long, 2.2–2.8 cm (about 1 in) broad, broadest near the middle, blue-green. **Flowers:** produced in ***short, compact, many-flowered, elongated, showy clusters;*** the cluster and flowers covered with numerous, gland-tipped hairs, each flower with a short 5-lobed bell-shaped calyx; ***5 rose-colored petals 2–2.5 cm (to 1 in) long,*** pea-flower shaped; 10 stamens, and a single pistil. **Fruits:** pods 5–10 cm (2–4 in) long, 6–10 mm (0.2–0.4 in) wide, flattened, thin, covered with glandular hairs, containing 3–8 dark-brown, spotted seeds.

Clammy Locust   *Robinia viscosa* Vent.

Clammy locust is native to the bases of mountains from Pennsylvania to Alabama. It is planted and reproduces on its own throughout the eastern U.S., including New England. This locust grows on drier sites and ridge tops up to 1,200 m (4,000 ft) altitude. This fast-growing, short-lived tree grows underneath the taller-growing scarlet oak, black tupelo, sourwood, and white pine.

It is an attractive tree that is sometimes planted as an ornamental because of its pretty rose-colored flowers. Clammy locust is also used to prevent soil erosion. It is of limited value to wildlife.

This is a shrub or small tree to 10 m (33 ft) with dark reddish-brown ***branches and branchlets, sticky*** because of the conspicuous, long, glandular hairs. The alternate, compound and feather-like (pinnate) leaves are 18–30 cm (7–12 in) long, composed of 13–21 leaflets, the leaflets widest below the middle, dark green. The flowers are pea-shaped, 1.7–2 cm (0.7–0.8 in) long, pale to deep rose-colored and on slender, hairy stalks. The ***pods*** are ***slender, 5–8.8 cm (2–3.5 in) long, sticky because of the erect, glandular hairs.***

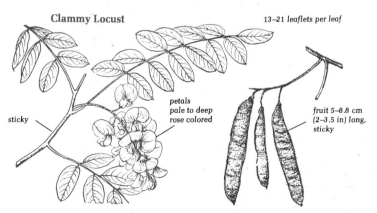

Clammy Locust

13–21 leaflets per leaf

petals
pale to deep
rose colored

sticky

fruit 5–8.8 cm
(2–3.5 in) long,
sticky

The Desert Ironwood Genus

Olneya A. Gray

There is only 1 species in this genus, and it is native to southwestern North America. Since there is only 1 species, the information given for the species, below, is the same as for the genus.

Desert Ironwood

Olneya tesota A. Gray

The desert ironwood occurs on sandy or gravelly slopes, along low hillsides, and on mesas in the Arizona and Colorado deserts, and from southwestern California to Sonora, Mexico. Because of its similarity in climate requirements to those of citrus plants, ironwood is a good indicator of proper climatic conditions for citrus planting.

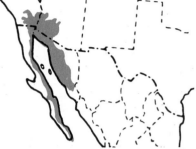

The wood of this tree is so heavy it will sink in water. It can easily dull saws and axes, yet Indians managed to work arrowheads and tool handles out of it. The color and appearance are similar to mahogany.

Desert ironwoods are small trees with stringy, gray bark, spiny branchlets, and **gray** to **bluish-green feather-like (pinnate) leaves.** The flowers appear in late spring in few-flowered clusters. They are pea-flower shaped and pale rose-purple. The **pods** are **4–6 cm (1.6–2.4 in) long, thick-walled,** covered with glandular hairs, and contain a few black seeds, each 8–10 mm (0.3–0.4 in) long.

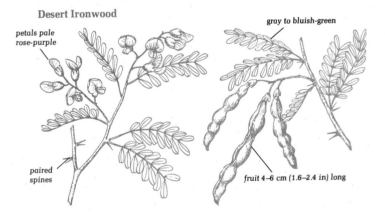

Desert Ironwood

petals pale rose-purple

gray to bluish-green

paired spines

fruit 4–6 cm (1.6–2.4 in) long

The Fish Poison Tree Genus

Piscidia L.

This small genus is composed of approximately 10 species of trees and shrubs of southern Florida, the West Indies, Mexico, and Central America. In North America, it is represented by a single species, the Florida fish poison tree. The common and Latin names of the genus refer to the use of the bark and leaves of 1 species by Caribbean people to poison fish.

Members of this genus have stout branches with alternate, feather-like leaves with a single leaflet at the end (odd-pinnate). The pea-shaped, white and red-tipped flowers occur in elongated clusters along the branchlets before the leaves appear. The elongated pods are distinctly 4-winged and slightly constricted between the seeds.

Florida Fish Poison Tree   *Piscidia piscipula* (L.) Sarg.

This species occurs commonly along the shores of Biscayne Bay to the southern Keys in Florida. It also occurs in the West Indies and southern Mexico. Little is known about its natural history or importance to wildlife. The hard, heavy, yellow-brown wood is extremely durable and has been used for boat construction, fuel, and in the making of charcoal. In the West Indies, the bark, roots, young branchlets, and leaves were ground to a fine powder and thrown into waters containing fish. This stunned the fish, making harvest easier.

The trees are small to 15 m (50 ft) with irregular crowns, twisted branches, and thin, gray, mottled bark. The evergreen leaves are alternate, feather-like with a single leaflet at the tip (odd-pinnate), 10–23 cm (4–9.1 in) long and bearing 5–11 dark green leaflets. Flowering occurs in spring before the leaves appear in dense clusters of 3 to 12 blossoms. Each flower is 1.6–2 cm (0.7–0.8 in) long, long stalked, and with ***purplish-blue petals.*** The ***pods*** ripen by late summer and are ***7.5–10 cm (3–4 in) long,*** 2.5–3.7 cm (1–1.5 in) wide, light brown, and ***with 4 papery, wavy-margined wings.***

Florida Fish Poison Tree

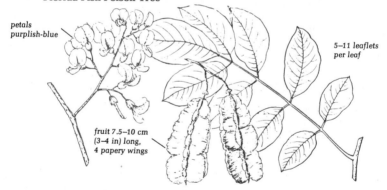

petals
purplish-blue

5–11 leaflets
per leaf

fruit 7.5–10 cm
(3–4 in) long,
4 papery wings

The Angelin Genus   *Andira* Lam.

This is a small genus of about 25 species distributed in tropical regions of the Americas and Africa. A single species occurs naturally in North America, only in southern Florida. Members of the genus are trees with alternate, feather-like (pinnate) leaves. Pink to purple pea-like flowers are produced in many-flowered, branched clusters at the tips of the branchlets. The fruits are dry, woody, and 1-seeded.

Cabbage Angelin   *Andira inermis* (W. Wright) D.C.

This attractive tree is native to northern South America, Central America, Mexico, the West Indies, possibly the Florida Keys, and western tropical Africa. It has been introduced as an ornamental tree in southern Florida. The bark and seeds are poisonous. In the West Indies, the wood is used in making high-quality cabinets and furniture.

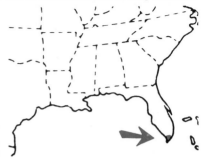

A spreading tree to 10 m (33 ft), cabbage angelin has rough gray bark that emits an unpleasant odor when cut. The leaves are alternate, feather-like (pinnate), with 7–13 smooth, green leaflets, each 5–13 cm (2–5.1 in) long, and 2.5–5 cm (1–2 in) broad. The broad, branched flower clusters bear numerous *pink, pea-like blossoms* in both summer and winter. The fruiting *pods* are *thick, egg-shaped, 2.5–3.5 cm (1–1.4 in) long,* and contain a single large seed.

The Loose Strife Family   Lythraceae

This is a moderate-size family of 22 genera and about 450 species of the Americas, Africa, Europe, Asia, Australia, and the South Pacific. Most members are herbs, but a few are shrubs or small trees. One of these, the crape myrtle, has been introduced into the southern U.S. The family is of minor economic importance. Some species are grown as ornamentals because of their attractive flowers and others, such as henna, yield dyes.

Members of this family are herbs, shrubs, or (rarely) trees, with simple leaves that are either opposite on the branchlets or whorled. Flowers are bisexual and produced in flat-topped or elongated, branched or unbranched clusters. Each flower typically has 4 or 6 calyx lobes and petals, 8 or 12 stamens, and a single pistil. Fruits are dry capsules which may or may not split open at maturity.

The Crape Myrtle Genus   *Lagerstroemia* L.

This small south and east Asian genus of perhaps 30 species has become widely known throughout the warm temperate and subtropical regions of the world for their beautiful flowers.

Crape Myrtle   *Lagerstroemia indica* L.

This handsome shrub or small tree has been extensively planted, often along streets, throughout the South and is most abundant in the Southeast. Crape myrtle occasionally escapes from cultivation and grows wild in the countryside or on vacant lots. The species is winter hardy as far north as Baltimore, Maryland. Flower colors range from white to pink to red to violet.

Crape myrtle is a shrub or small tree to 7 m (23 ft), with simple, entire, deciduous leaves that are opposite on the branchlets (sometimes alternate on the upper branchlets). The leaves are broadest near the middle or above, 3–7 cm (1.2–2.8 in) long, 1.5–3.5 cm (0.6–1.4 in) wide, pointed to rounded at the tip, and tapering to rounded at the base. Flowers are produced in *erect, elongated and branched, many-flowered clusters.* Each flower consists of a 6- to 9-lobed calyx, *usually 6 pink petals, each with a long slender claw, often fringed,* many stamens, and a single ovary. The fruits are capsules, broadly egg-shaped, 1–1.5 cm (0.4–0.6 in) long.

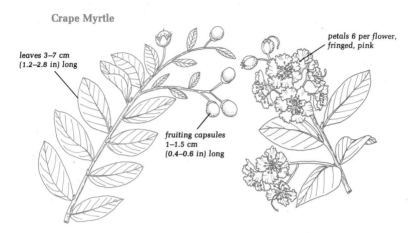

Crape Myrtle

leaves 3–7 cm
(1.2–2.8 in) long

petals 6 per flower,
fringed, pink

fruiting capsules
1–1.5 cm
(0.4–0.6 in) long

The Myrtle Family

Myrtaceae

This large family of approximately 100 genera and 3,000 species is widely distributed in tropical and subtropical regions of the world, but is especially abundant in Australia and Central and South America. The 4 genera native to North America occur only in southern Florida. Many nonnative species, chiefly Australian, have been introduced for their ornamental value or to serve as windbreaks. Among the more commonly encountered of the introduced trees are several species of Australian gum trees (*Eucalyptus*) and cajete trees (*Melaleuca*). The Myrtle family is important because many species yield edible fruits, cloves and allspice, and lumber.

Members of this family are shrubs to large trees with opposite, or (less frequently) alternate, leathery, evergreen leaves which are dotted with numerous, tiny glands. Flowers are bisexual, symmetrical, and are normally produced in clusters. Generally, there are 4 or 5 sepals, 4 or 5 petals, many stamens, and a single pistil.

Key to Myrtle Genera

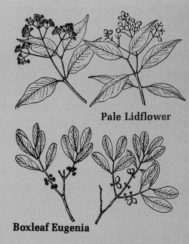

A. Leaves opposite.

   1. Flowers without petals; calyx forming a small lid over the flower, falling away when flowers open   **Lidflower, p. 674**

   2. Flowers with petals; calyx persisting when flowers open.

      a. Floral cup splitting irregularly between the calyx lobes   **Guava, p. 675**
      b. Floral cup not splitting between the calyx lobes.

         (1) Flowers solitary, clustered, or densely clustered on an unbranched stalk   **Eugenia, p. 677**
         (Continued)

Pale Lidflower

Boxleaf Eugenia

(2) Flowers produced in few to many-flowered, branched clusters; includes twinberry eugenia **Nakedwood, p. 681**

B. Leaves alternate.

    1. Flowers very showy, produced in dense clusters around the branchlets, giving a bottle-brush appearance   **Cajeput tree, p. 682**

    2. Flowers not showy or only moderately so, solitary, in flat-topped clusters, or in branched clusters   **Gum tree, p. 682**

Twinberry Eugenia

Blue Gum

The Lidflower Genus   *Calyptranthes* Sw.

This genus contains about 80 species limited to tropical America, 2 of them native to Florida. They are often shrubs or small trees of lower elevations. Because of their aromatic and astringent nature the flower buds and fruits are used as spices.

    Members of this genus are shrubs or trees with a rounded crown and leaves that are opposite on the branchlets. The bisexual flowers are small and produced in many-flowered clusters. Each flower has a tiny, 4- or 5-lobed top-shaped calyx; 2 to 5 petals (sometimes absent); numerous stamens, and a single pistil. Fruits are 1- to 4-seeded berries.

Key to Lidflower Species

A. Leaves long-pointed at the tip, finely hairy beneath   **Pale lidflower, p. 674**

B. Leaves abruptly pointed at the tip, smooth beneath   **Myrtle-of-the-River, p. 675**

Pale Lidflower   *Calyptranthes pallens* Griseb.

Pale lidflower is a shrub or small tree that occurs in the hammocks of coastal southern Florida, the Florida Keys, and the West Indies. Flowering and fruiting can occur anytime during the year. The wood, not used commercially, is brown to reddish-brown, hard, strong, and close-grained.

    The trees grow to 8 m (26 ft), with a narrow, rounded crown and thin, gray-to-almost-white bark. The **opposite, evergreen leaves** are uniformly wide to broadest near the base, 3–8 cm (1.2–3.2 in) long, 1.2–2.2 cm (0.5–0.9 in) wide, tapering to a **long-pointed tip,** leathery, covered with tiny glands, dark green and shiny above, **finely hairy beneath.** Flowers are 3–4 mm (0.1 in) long and produced in stalked, many-flowered clusters, Each

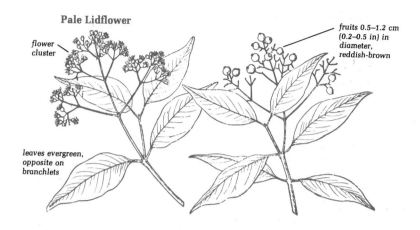

Pale Lidflower

flower cluster

fruits 0.5–1.2 cm (0.2–0.5 in) in diameter, reddish-brown

leaves evergreen, opposite on branchlets

flower is composed of a hairy, 4–5 lobed calyx, no petals, with many stamens in several rows, and a single pistil. Fruits are berries, 0.5–1.2 cm (0.2–0.5 in) in diameter, rounded or nearly so, reddish-brown, with a thin dry flesh and enclosing several small seeds.

Myrtle-of-the-River   *Calyptranthes zuzygium* (L.) Sw.

This species is a rare tree native to southern Florida, Key Largo, and the West Indies. The small, whitish flower clusters appear in spring followed by red berries in the summer. The light brown wood is hard and strong, but the trees are too scarce and small to yield wood commercially.

The trees are small to 12 m (40 ft), with a rounded crown, and smooth, pale-gray bark. The *opposite, evergreen leaves* are broadest near the middle, 3.5–6 cm (1.4–2.4 in) long, 1.8–3.8 cm (0.7–1.5 in) wide, *tapering to an abrupt point at the tip,* wedge-shaped at the base, covered with many tiny transparent dots, *smooth,* shiny, and dark yellow-green above, paler and smooth beneath. Flowers are produced in small few-flowered clusters in the junctions of the leaves and branchlets. Each *flower* is composed of a tiny, 4–5 lobed calyx, *no petals,* many stamens, and a single pistil. Fruits are berries, rounded, 4–6 cm (1.6–2.4 in) in diameter, reddish, enclosing 1 to 4 shiny, brown seeds.

The Guava Genus   *Psidium* L.

This genus contains approximately 150 species of trees and shrubs widely distributed in tropical America. Only 1 species, the long-stalk stopper, is native to North America, and that is only in southern Florida. The common or edible guava is cultivated in Florida and to a lesser extent in southern California.

Members of this genus have entire, even leaves that occur opposite on the branchlets. The bisexual flowers are produced singly or in few-flowered clusters at the junctions of the upper leaves and the branchlets. Flowers have a small, 4- or 5-lobed calyx, 4 or 5 white petals, many stamens, and a single pistil. The fruits are berries.

Key to Guava Species

A. Leaves 3–5 cm (1.2–2 in) long; calyx lobes 2–3 mm (0.1 in) long; petals 2–3 mm (0.1 in) long; fruit 6–10 mm (0.2–0.4 in) in diameter; small trees of southern Florida

Long-stalk stopper, p. 676

B. Leaves 4–8 cm (1.6–3.2 in) long; calyx lobes 5–8 mm (0.2–0.3 in) long; petals 1–1.7 cm (0.4–0.7 in) long; fruit 3–6 cm (1.2–2.4 in) in diameter; cultivated or wild trees of southern Florida and California **Common guava, p. 676**

Long-Stalk Stopper
Psidium longipes (Berg) McVaugh

(synonyms: *Eugenia longipes* Berg, *Eugenia bahamensis* Kiaerskou)
This is a small tree of the hammocks of southern Florida, the Florida Keys, and the Bahamas. It is a rare plant and is seldom seen. Flowering and fruiting may occur any month of the year.

Long-stalk stoppers are shrubs or small trees with spreading to upright branches. The simple, *opposite, evergreen leaves* are broadest near the middle or the base to nearly round, 3–5 cm (1.2–2 in) long, entire along the margin, gland-dotted, shiny green above, and paler beneath. *Flowers* are *produced singly on a long, slender stalk;* each flower with a 4-lobed calyx 2–3 mm (0.1 in) long; 4 white, spreading petals, each 2–3 mm (0.1 in) long; many stamens, and a single pistil. Fruits are berries, nearly round, 6–10 mm (0.2–0.4 in) in diameter, and black.

Common Guava
Psidium guajava L.

This species is widely cultivated throughout much of the tropical and subtropical world. It was introduced into southern Florida from South America and now also grows wild along roadsides, old fields, and in hammocks. Flowers occur in spring, but may extend into summer, and are followed by yellow edible fruits. The fruits, rich in vitamin C, are used in making jelly, preserves, paste, and fruit drinks.

Common guava is a shrub or tree to 10 m (33 ft), with thin, smooth, reddish-brown to gray bark. The opposite, evergreen leaves are uniformly long, 4–8 cm (1.6–3.2 in) long, rounded to pointed at the tip, rounded at the base, entire along the margin, dark green and smooth above, paler and slightly hairy beneath. *Flowers are produced singly.* Each flower has a 4- or 5-lobed calyx 5–8 mm (0.2–0.3 in) long; 4 or 5 *white petals 1–*

1.7 cm (0.4–0.7 in) long; many stamens, and a single pistil. ***Fruits*** are **berries,** rounded or nearly so, *3–6 cm (1.2–2.4 in) across,* fleshy, with a fragrant, sour pulp.

The Eugenia, or Stopper, Genus Eugenia L.

This is a large genus of about 500 species of trees and shrubs of the tropics. They are often difficult to identify and resemble species in other genera of this family. Five species are native to North America and these all occur in central to southern Florida. Economically, this genus is of some importance. Cloves are the dried flower buds of a species native to the Molucca Islands. The rose apple (*Eugenia jambos*) is often grown for shade and for its aromatic fruits.

Members of this genus are shrubs or trees, with scaly bark and simple, opposite, evergreen leaves. The leaves are entire and have tiny glands on one or both surfaces. White flowers are produced singly or in clusters from the junction of the leaves. Each flower has a floral cup topped with a 4-lobed calyx, 4 petals, many stamens, and a single pistil. Fruits are berries, fleshy, dry or leathery, and contain 1 to 4 rounded to flattened seeds.

Key to Eugenia Species

A. Flowers short-stalked and densely clustered on a short elongated spike.

1. Leaves rounded at the tip, usually broadest above the middle; fruits 5–8 mm (0.2–0.3 in) in diameter; trees of southern Florida
Boxleaf eugenia, p. 677

2. Leaves short, broad-pointed at the tip, usually broadest near the base; fruits 10–12 mm (0.4–0.5 in) in diameter; trees of southern Florida
White stopper eugenia, p. 678

B. Flowers 1 to several, long stalked, each coming from the junction of a leaf and branchlet, not clustered on a central stalk.

1. Leaves long-pointed at the tip; berries bright red at maturity; trees of coastal hammocks, southern Florida and the Keys
Redberry eugenia, p. 679

2. Leaves rounded at the tip; berries black at maturity; trees of hammocks of lower Florida Keys **Spiceberry eugenia, p. 680**

Boxleaf Eugenia

Redberry Eugenia

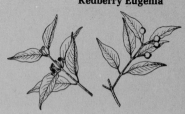

Boxleaf Eugenia *Eugenia foetida* Pers.

[synonyms: *E. myrtoides* Poir., *E. buxifolia* (Sw.) Willd.]

This is a shrub or small tree widely distributed from Cape Kennedy through southern Florida, the Florida Keys, and the West Indies. *It is the dominant shrub in some of the Florida Keys.* Small white flowers appear from mid-summer to early autumn

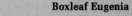

followed by black to dark-brown fruits, which serve as a good food source for many birds. The leaves give off an unpleasant, skunklike odor. The wood, sometimes used for fuel, is dark reddish-brown, hard, and very heavy.

Appearance: small shrubby tree to 6 m (20 ft), with a rounded crown; trunk short, branching close to the ground, to 30 cm (12 in) in diameter. **Bark:** thin, 2–4 mm (0.1 in) thick, becoming scaly, light reddish-brown. **Branches:** mostly upright; branchlets slender, hairy at first becoming gray to reddish-gray with age. **Leaves:** simple, opposite, *evergreen,* broadest above the middle, 3–6 cm (1.2–2.4 in) long, 1.5–4 cm (0.6–1.6 in) wide, *with a rounded tip,* tapering at the base, entire, leathery, dark green above, yellowish-green and *gland-dotted beneath;* leafstalks short, stout, or absent. **Flowers:** produced in 6- to 12-flowered, elongated, unbranched clusters in the junction of the leaves and branchlets; each flower with a tiny, hairy, gland-dotted, 4-lobed calyx, 4 white rounded petals, many stamens, and a single pistil. **Fruits:** berries, globe-shaped, *5–8 mm (0.2–0.3 in)* in diameter, black, rough on the surface, yellowish-orange turning *black or dark brown with age,* and containing a single seed. **Seeds:** 2–3 mm (0.1 in) in diameter, pale shiny brown.

Boxleaf Eugenia

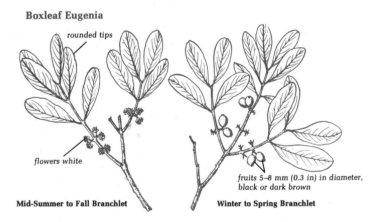

rounded tips

flowers white

Mid-Summer to Fall Branchlet

fruits 5–8 mm (0.3 in) in diameter, black or dark brown

Winter to Spring Branchlet

White Stopper Eugenia *Eugenia axillaris* (Sw.) Willd.

This species of shrubs or small trees grows in sandy or rocky soils in hammocks of central and southern Florida, the Florida Keys, and in Bermuda and the West Indies. The small white flowers usually occur in summer and autumn, but may be found throughout the year. Edible black fruits are evident from November to April. The leaves give off an unpleasant odor when crushed. Occasionally used for firewood, the reddish-tinged brown wood is hard, heavy, and close-grained.

White stopper eugenia grows to 8 m (26 ft) and has a thin, shallowly fissured, scaly brown bark. The opposite. simple, *evergreen leaves* are broadest near the base, 3–7 cm (1.2–2.8 in) long, 1.5–4 cm (0.6–1.6 in) wide, with a short, broad-pointed tip, rounded at the base, entire, leathery, dark green above, paler and **with tiny black dots beneath.** Small bisexual flowers are produced in short, few-flowered clusters in the junction of the upper leaves. Each flower consists of a 4-lobed, hairy, gland-covered calyx, 4 white petals, many stamens, and a single pistil. Fruits are rounded berries, **1–1.2 cm (0.4– 0.5 in) in diameter, bluish-black,** gland-dotted, juicy, sweet, and enclosing several rounded seeds.

White Stopper Eugenia

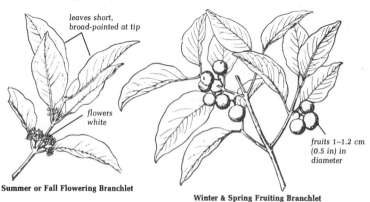

leaves short, broad-pointed at tip

flowers white

fruits 1–1.2 cm (0.5 in) in diameter

Summer or Fall Flowering Branchlet

Winter & Spring Fruiting Branchlet

Redberry Eugenia   *Eugenia confusa* DC.

This is the most common of our native eugenia species. It occurs in coastal hammocks of southern Florida, the Florida Keys, and the West Indies. Redberry eugenia is sometimes cultivated for its shiny leaves and white flowers. Flowering is in autumn, and fruits ripen the following spring. The light brown wood is hard, heavy, and durable and is sometimes used for posts or fuel.

Appearance: small trees to 18 m (59 ft), with a narrow, rounded crown; trunk straight, to 40 cm (16 in) in diameter. **Bark:** thin, 3–5 mm (0.1–0.2 in) thick, scaly, reddish-brown. **Branches:** stout, erect; branchlets slender, gray. **Leaves:** simple, **opposite, evergreen,** uniformly wide to broadest near the base, 3–7 cm (1.2–2.8 in) long, 2–4 cm (0.8–1.6 in) wide, **with a long narrow pointed tip,** rounded to wedge-shaped at the base, entire, dark green and very shiny above, paler and **black dotted beneath;** leafstalks 5–7 mm (0.2–0.3 in) long. **Flowers:** produced in several- to many-flowered clusters; each flower with a glandular, 4-lobed calyx, 4 white rounded petals, many stamens, and a single pistil. **Fruits:** *ber-*

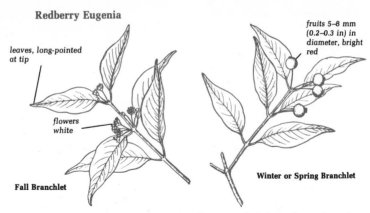

Redberry Eugenia

leaves, long-pointed at tip

flowers white

Fall Branchlet

fruits 5–8 mm (0.2–0.3 in) in diameter, bright red

Winter or Spring Branchlet

ries, globe-shaped, *5–8 mm (0.2–0.3 in) in diameter, bright red,* rough to the touch because of numerous glands, flesh thin, dry, and containing 1 rounded, light brown, shiny seed.

Spiceberry Eugenia   Eugenia rhombea (Berg) Krug & Urban

Spiceberry eugenia is an attractive evergreen tree native to the hammocks of the lower Florida Keys and the West Indies. Small white flowers are produced in spring and are followed by bright red to black berries in fall and early winter. These are eaten by

birds and small mammals. The light-brown wood is hard and heavy but is of little commercial value.

These are small trees to 8 m (26 ft), with a rounded crown and thin, smooth gray or reddish gray flaking bark. The simple, *opposite, evergreen leaves* are broadest near the base, 3–6 cm (1.2–2.4 in) long, 1.5–4 cm (0.6–1.6 in) wide, rounded at the tip, tapering to a wedge-shaped base, entire, leathery, *with many tiny black glands,* dull olive-green above and paler beneath.

Spiceberry Eugenia

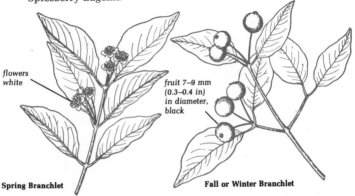

flowers white

fruit 7–9 mm (0.3–0.4 in) in diameter, black

Spring Branchlet

Fall or Winter Branchlet

Flowers are produced in small, few-flowered clusters in the junctions of the upper leaves. Each flower has a 4-lobed calyx, 4 white petals, many stamens, and a single pistil. **Fruits: *berries,*** globe-shaped, ***7–9 mm (0.3–0.4 in)*** in diameter, ***black*** and covered with many glands.

The Nakedwood Genus   *Myrcianthes* Berg.

This small to moderate size genus of about 40 species is native to tropical America. One species, twinberry eugenia, extends into North America only in southern Florida.

Members of this genus are shrubs to tall trees with evergreen leaves that are opposite or in groups of 3. The leaves have many tiny glands on both surfaces. Bisexual flowers are produced in spreading, branched clusters from the junctions of the upper leaves and the branchlets. Individual flowers are small, with a floral cup topped with a 4- or rarely 5-lobed calyx, 4 white petals, many stamens, and a single pistil. Fruits are 1- to 2-seeded berries.

Twinberry Eugenia   *Myrcianthes fragans* (Sw.) McVaugh
(synonym: *Eugenia dicrana* Berg.)

Twinberry eugenia is a shrub or small tree native to southern Florida from Cape Kennedy to Key West, and to the West Indies. It grows in rocky or sandy soils and is often found in hammocks. The wood is light brown and hard, but of little commercial value because of the tree's small size. A variety of twinberry eugenia (*Myrcianthes fragans* variety *simpsonii*), has been recognized with more flowers per cluster and larger petals than the typical variety. This variety occurs in hammocks in Dade County, southern Florida.

The trees grow to 8 m (26 ft), and have a smooth, thin, red or reddish-brown, scaly bark. The leaves are ***opposite, evergreen,*** broadest above the middle to near the middle, 2–6 cm (0.8–2.4 in) long, 0.8–4 cm (0.4–1.6 in) wide, pointed to rounded at the tip, wedge-shaped at the base, ***entire,*** leathery, ***covered with numerous, small black dots,*** pale green and smooth above,

Twinberry Eugenia

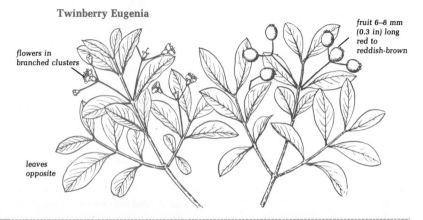

flowers in branched clusters

fruit 6–8 mm (0.3 in) long red to reddish-brown

leaves opposite

paler beneath. ***Flowers in 3- to 15-flowered, spreading clusters.*** Each flower is 6–8 mm (0.2–0.3 in) in diameter, with a tiny 4-lobed calyx, 4 petals 8–12 mm (0.3–0.5 in) long, many stamens, and a single pistil. Fruits are rounded to egg-shaped berries, 6–8 mm (0.2–0.3 in) long, red to reddish-brown, rough on the surface due to many glands, and enclosing 1 or 2 light brown seeds.

The Melaleuca Genus   Melaleuca L.

This is a small Australian genus of 6 species. These are attractive trees that have been planted throughout tropical and subtropical regions of the world. Several species have been introduced into cultivation, but the cajeput tree (*Melaleuca quinquenervia*) is the one most commonly encountered. It is cultivated in southern California and Florida.

Members of this genus are trees with alternate, leathery leaves. Bisexual flowers are produced singly or in short to long spikes. Each flower has 5 calyx lobes, 5 petals, many stamens, and a 3-parted ovary. Fruits are capsules that split open at maturity.

Cajeput Tree   *Melaleuca quinquenervia* (Cav.) S. T. Blake

Cajeput tree has been planted in southern Florida and California. In Florida, it has escaped from cultivation and grows wild in low wet areas and cypress swamps. In California, the trees grow well along the coast and can tolerate poor soils. This is an attractive tree due to the arrangement of the flowers and long stamens around the branchlets giving a bottle-brush appearance.

These trees grow to 15 m (48 ft), with hanging branches and bark shedding in thin strips exposing a reddish inner bark. The simple, alternate leaves are broadest near the middle, 5–10 cm (2–4 in) long, 1.8–2.5 cm (0.7–1 in) wide, gradually tapering at the tip and base, entire, leathery to stiff, aromatic when crushed because of the numerous tiny glands on both surfaces, and gray-green. ***Showy white flowers are produced around the branchlets giving a bottle-brush appearance.*** Fruits are small, rounded to almost square capsules, woody, 3–5 mm (0.1–0.2 in) in diameter, and splitting open to shed the very small seeds.

The Gum Tree Genus   Eucalyptus L'Her.

This is a large genus of trees native to Australia with many species widely planted in tropical and subtropical regions of the world. The trees grow rapidly and some thrive even in nutrient-poor desert soils. They are used for windbreaks, soil stabilization, fuel, and for their attractive leaves and bark. Many species have been introduced into North America, especially California and Florida. In addition to the blue gum, several others occur frequently. The river red gum (*Eucalyptus camaldulensis*) with shorter, narrower leaves than the blue gum, is common in the Sacramento and San Joaquin Valleys of California. Forest red gum (*E. tereticornis*), also planted in California, has stalked flowers produced in flat-topped clusters. Often used as an ornamental, round-leaf eucalyptus (*E. polyanthemos*) has almost rounded leaves and flowers produced in elongate, branched clusters. Manna gum (*E. viminalis*) is cultivated for its smooth white bark and long ribbon-like leaves.

Members of this genus are trees, often very tall, with alternate, stiff leaves (leaves of young shoots may be opposite). Flowers are produced singly, in heads, in unbranched or branched clusters. Flowers often are top- or bell-shaped, with 4 sepals and petals fused to form a cap which is present in bud and falls away as the flowers open, many stamens, and a single pistil with an inferior ovary. Fruits are capsules splitting along 3 to 6 valves.

Blue Gum   *Eucalyptus globulus* Labill.

Blue gum is the most common of all the *Eucalyptus* species introduced from Australia. It is widely planted along the California coast. Because of its rapid growth, blue gum is often used as a windbreak. The wood is used in fireplaces and woodstoves. These trees cannot survive prolonged temperatures of −6 C (20 F).

Blue gum is a large tree that grows to 80 m (263 ft), with a narrow rounded crown, and bark which shreds in long thin strips to expose the tan and green trunk. The **alternate, evergreen, hanging leaves** are **sickle-shaped, 12–18 cm (4.7–7.1 in) long**, gradually tapering to a long point, tapering to unequally rounded at the base, entire, dark green, and smooth. Flowers are produced singly in the junction of the upper leaves; flower buds are 4-sided with a rounded cap on top that falls away when the flowers open; each flower has 4 calyx lobes, **4 petals fused to form the cap on top of the bud**, numerous stamens, and a single pistil. Fruits are woody capsules, 4-parted, opening along 4 valves to release the black seeds.

Blue Gum

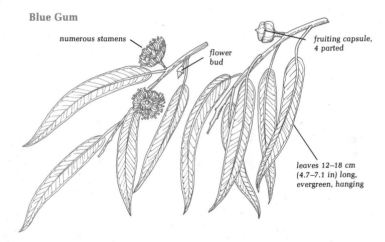

numerous stamens

flower bud

fruiting capsule, 4 parted

leaves 12–18 cm (4.7–7.1 in) long, evergreen, hanging

The Pomegranate Family   Punicaceae

This family contains only 1 genus and only 2 species. Members are shrubs or small trees native to the region from the Mediterranean to the Himalayas. Since this is such a small family, the description of the species will also describe the genus and the family.

Pomegranate   *Punica granatum* L.

This historically important shrub or small tree has been in cultivation for over 5,000 years. There are ancient paintings of it in Egyptian temples and on stone reliefs in Armenia. It is cultivated for its attractive flowers — and less so for its fruit — in southern Florida, southern California, and the frost-free areas of the Southwest, but apparently it does not grow wild in these regions. The large red fruits are sometimes available in supermarkets, especially before Christmas. The sweet, juicy seeds are eaten, and the remainder of the fruit is discarded.

Pomegranate are large, open, spreading shrubs or small trees to 15 m (49 ft), with slender, sometimes spiny branches. The deciduous, simple leaves are opposite or nearly so, or clustered together, lance-shaped to widest near or above the middle, 2–8 cm (0.8–3.2 in) long, entire along the margin, and shiny green above. Large, **showy, red to orange,** bisexual **flowers** are produced in clusters of 1 to 5. Each flower contains a bell-shaped calyx, 5 to 7 petals, **many free stamens,** and a single pistil. **Fruits** are **large, round, 5–10 cm (2–4 in) in diameter, with a thick, leathery skin covering juicy red seeds.**

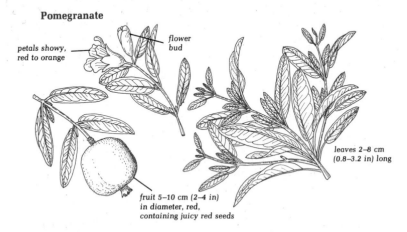

Pomegranate

petals showy,
red to orange

flower
bud

leaves 2–8 cm
(0.8–3.2 in) long

fruit 5–10 cm (2–4 in)
in diameter, red,
containing juicy red seeds

The Melastome Family   Melastomataceae

This is a large family of roughly 4,000 species of herbs, vines, shrubs, and, infrequently, trees of tropical regions of the world, especially South America. Although several species are native and several others cultivated, only 1 tree, the Florida tetrazygia, is native to North America.

Members of this family have opposite or whorled leaves with 3 to 9 very distinctive, lengthwise veins joining at the tip and entire along the margin. The bisexual flowers are often showy, usually with a bell-shaped calyx, 4 or 5 free petals, stamens equal to or twice as many as petals, and a single pistil. Fruits are berry-like or capsules which split open at maturity.

The Tetrazygia Genus   *Tetrazygia* L.C. Rich.

This small genus of approximately 15 species is native to the West Indies, with 1 species reaching southern Florida. The generic name, *Tetrazygia*, refers to the 4-parted (tetra) flowers.

Members of the genus are trees or shrubs with opposite, evergreen leaves with 3 to 5 main veins. Flowers are produced in showy, many-flowered clusters; each flower has a rounded to urn-shaped calyx, 4 to 6 petals, twice as many stamens as petals, and a single pistil. The 3- or 4-celled berry is topped by the remains of the calyx.

Florida Tetrazygia   *Tetrazygia bicolor* (Mill.) Cogn.

This species, named for its leaves which are dark green above and silvery white beneath, is native to hammocks and sandy pine woods in Dade County, Florida. Grown as an ornamental, it flowers in late spring and summer, with the black fruits maturing later in summer or fall.

This is a shrub or tree to 9 m (30 ft), with opposite, evergreen leaves lance-shaped or nearly so, **7.5–12 cm (3–4.7 in) long, 2.5–4 cm (1–1.6 in) wide, with 3 main, lengthwise veins,** and the margin entire and somewhat rolled under. The flowers are produced in elongated, branched clusters; each flower has a 4- or 5-lobed, urn-shaped calyx, and 4 or 5 white petals. The fruit is 4- or 5-parted, berry-like, black, rounded to slightly longer than round, 8–10 mm (0.3–0.4 in) long.

Florida Tetrazygia

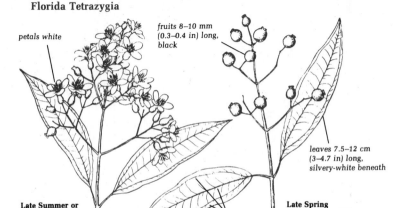

petals white

fruits 8–10 mm (0.3–0.4 in) long, black

leaves 7.5–12 cm (3–4.7 in) long, silvery-white beneath

Late Summer or Fall Branchlet

Late Spring Summer Branchlet

3 main veins

The Combretum Family   Combretaceae

This is a family of tropical trees, shrubs, and vines native to Central and South America, Africa, Asia, and Australia. Only a few of the approximately 475 species occur in subtropical regions. Some of the tropical members are important timber sources; others have showy flowers and are used as ornamentals.

Four species are treated in this book. The white and the button mangrove are native to coastal areas of southern Florida. The Indian almond, widely planted in other countries for its edible kernels, has been introduced into Florida. The oxhorn bucida was carried to southern Florida from the West Indies.

Members of this family are tall trees, vines, or less frequently shrubs with alternate or opposite, simple, entire, evergreen leaves. The small flowers are generally bisexual, 5-parted, and are produced in rounded to elongated clusters. Fruits are various; some are winged and lightweight; others are hard, heavy, or even fleshy.

Key to Combretum Genera

Button Mangrove

A. Leaves alternately arranged on the branchlets.

    1. Flowers and fruits in dense, rounded heads; trees or shrubs of brackish coastal areas of Florida   **Button mangrove, p. 686**

    2. Flowers produced singly along a narrow, unbranched spike; trees or shrubs of pinelands or hammocks of Florida.

        a. Leaves 10–30 cm (4–12 in) long; flowering spikes with male flowers near the tip and bisexual or female flowers near the base; fruits egg-shaped, 4–8 cm (1.6–3.2 in) long; introduced tree in Florida   **Terminalia, p. 687**

Oxhorn Bucida

        b. Leaves 3–9 cm (1.2–3.5 in) long; flowering spikes with all bisexual flowers; fruits egg-shaped, 7–9 mm (0.3–0.4 in) long; introduced tree in southern Florida   **Bucida, p. 688**

White Mangrove

B. Leaves oppositely arranged on the branchlets; trees of coastal regions of Florida   **White mangrove, p. 689**

The Button Mangrove Genus   *Conocarpus* L.

This is a small genus of 2 species native to swamps in tropical and subtropical America and West Africa. The button mangrove is native to southern Florida. The genus name *Conocarpus* refers to the cone-like fruits. The species description will also serve for the genus.

Button Mangrove   *Conocarpus erectus* L.

This mangrove occurs in brackish waters of muddy tidal lagoons and bays from southern Florida and the Keys to Bermuda, the West Indies, Central and South America, and western Africa. The plants form dense thickets or groves. Away from the coastal shores, button mangrove will break from its normal shrubby appearance and become a tree.

    Dense, rounded flower heads and fruits are produced throughout the year. The wood is very hard, strong, and very heavy and is an excellent fuel because it burns slowly and gives off considerable BTUs of heat. The trees seldom grow large enough to yield construction lumber. The silver button mangrove (*C. erectus* variety *sericea*) is sometimes cultivated for its densely silky, hairy leaves.

Button Mangrove

flowers in dense heads

fruits 2–2.8 cm (0.8–1.1 in) in diameter

leaves evergreen, 2–10 cm (0.8–4 in) long

Appearance: spreading shrub or tree to 20 m (66 ft), with a narrow, rounded crown; trunk straight to 75 cm (29.5 in) in diameter, rarely larger. **Bark:** 4–8 mm (0.2–0.3 in) thick, developing broad, flat ridges composed of thin scales, gray to dark brown. **Branches:** short, stout, usually spreading; branchlets slender, often narrowly winged, yellowish-green turning gray to brown with age, smooth or finely hairy. **Leaves: *alternate,*** simple, variable in shape, broadest at the base, the middle, or above the middle, *2–10 cm (0.8–4 in) long, 1.2–4 cm (0.5–1.6 in) wide,* pointed at the tip, tapering, with 2 glands at the base, entire, leathery, evergreen, dark shiny green to light green above, paler beneath, smooth to silky hairy; leafstalks stout, 9–12 mm (0.4 in) long. **Flowers: *produced in dense, rounded, many-flowered heads,*** several heads aggregated together in an elongated, branched cluster; each flower ***tiny, green,*** with a 5-parted calyx, ***petals absent,*** 5 to 8 stamens, and a single pistil. **Fruits:** cone-like, rounded to egg-shaped, 2–2.8 cm (0.8–1.1 in) in diameter, purplish-green, containing small flattened, reddish-brown seeds.

The Terminalia Genus

Terminalia L.

This is a large tropical genus of roughly 200 species distributed in the Americas, Africa, Asia, and Australia. Although no species are native to North America, the Indian almond has been introduced into Florida, the West Indies, and other parts of the American tropics.

Members of this genus are trees with leaves crowded together, alternate or nearly opposite, at the ends of the branchlets. The small, bisexual flowers are produced in spikes, and the fruits are dry and drupe-like.

Indian Almond

Terminalia catappa L.

Indian almond was introduced into southern Florida for use as a shade tree and to investigate its potential as a nut producer. It now grows wild there and extends through the Florida Keys. It is salt tolerant and does well in sandy soils, and along beaches. The small greenish to white flowers can be seen throughout the year, especially in spring. Fruits mature in late summer or early autumn. All parts of the tree are astringent and have been employed in tropical medicines.

This is a medium to large tree to 24 m (79 ft), with a straight trunk, sometimes spreading at the base, and with dark, scaly bark (smooth and gray when young). The alternate, entire *leaves* are broadest near the rounded tips, *10–30 cm (4–12 in) long,* and narrowing at the base, thick, leathery, and dark green. *Flowers are produced in narrow, elongated spikes 9–15 cm (3.5–5.9 in) long. The flowering spike often has male flowers near the tip and female and/or bisexual flowers near the base.* Each flower has a tiny, 5-lobed, green calyx, no petals, 10 stamens, and a single pistil. The dry, almost woody fruits are 4–8 cm (1.6–3.2 in) long, egg-shaped, with an outer leathery layer surrounding a light brown stone. The stone contains a single, edible, oily nut.

The Bucida Genus

Bucida L.

This small genus of 3 or 4 species is represented in North America by the oxhorn bucida. A second West Indian species, the spiny bucida (*Bucida spinosa* Jennings), has been reported in southern Dade County but is apparently not well enough established to be included here. Bucidas are spine-bearing trees with alternate leaves often crowded near the tips of the branchlets. Flowers are produced in narrow, elongated spikes. Fruits are rounded to egg-shaped, leathery, and do not split open at maturity.

Oxhorn Bucida

Bucida buceras L.

Oxhorn bucida, a native of the West Indies, has been widely planted as a shade and ornamental tree in south Florida. It grows wild in hammocks there and in the Keys. The small greenish-white flowers are produced in late spring, and the dry fruits mature in mid to late summer. Since they are tolerant of salt sprays, the trees can be grown near beaches.

This is a tree to 25 m (82 ft), with a straight trunk, thick, fissured, rough or scaly, dark brown bark, and a broad, rounded crown. The simple, alternate leaves are broadest above the middle to near the middle, 3–9 cm (1.2–3.6 in) long. The small *flowers* are *borne on slender spikes to 10 cm (4 in) long;* each flower with a 5-lobed, bowl-shaped calyx, petals

Oxhorn Bucida

cluster of
bisexual flowers

fruits 7–9 mm
(0.4 in) long

leaves 3–9 cm
(1.2–3.6 in) long

absent, 10 stamens, and a single pistil. Fruits are ***egg-shaped, 7–9 mm (0.4 in) long,*** dry, leathery and reddish-brown.

The White Mangrove Genus   *Laguncularia* Gaertn. f.

This small genus of 2 species occurs in tropical America and Africa. The white mangrove is native to North America only along the coast of central and southern Florida. The species description will also serve for the genus.

White Mangrove   *Laguncularia racemosa* (L.) Gaertn. f.

White mangrove grows in muddy tidal shores, bays, and lagoons in Florida, the West Indies, and Central and South America. This species generally occurs on higher ground than the red and button mangroves. It is shrubby, sometimes tree size, and often forms dense thickets or grooves. A characteristic feature is the development of specialized roots (pneumatophores) that grow above the water or oxygen-deficient muddy soils and are exposed to air, thus permitting the root system of the plant to breathe.

This is a fast-growing tree and is known to produce flowers and fruits when only 1 year old. Flowering and fruiting occur throughout most of the year. The fruits are buoyant and spread to new growing sites by water. The yellowish-brown wood is hard, strong, not very durable, and is used for fuel, posts, or small tool handles. Bees make a good honey from the flowers.

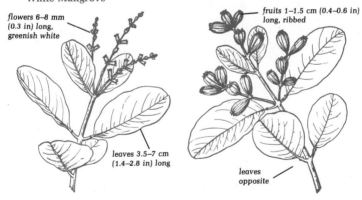

White Mangrove

flowers 6–8 mm (0.3 in) long, greenish white

fruits 1–1.5 cm (0.4–0.6 in) long, ribbed

leaves 3.5–7 cm (1.4–2.8 in) long

leaves opposite

Appearance: low shrub or tree to 18 m (59 ft), with a narrow rounded crown; trunk short, often crooked, rarely to 40 cm (16 in) in diameter. **Bark:** thin, 3–4 mm (0.1 in) thick, forming long, narrow, scaly ridges, reddish-brown. **Branches:** stout, spreading; branchlets slender, smooth, becoming reddish-brown with age. **Winter buds:** naked, lacking scales. **Leaves:** ***opposite,*** simple, broadest near the base to uniformly wide, ***3.5–7 cm (1.4–2.8 in) long, 2.5–3 cm (1–1.2 in) wide,*** rounded to slightly notched at the tip, gradually tapering at the base, entire, thick, leathery, smooth, dark green above, lighter beneath; leafstalks 9–12 mm (0.4 in) long, reddish, often with 2 glands at the base of the blade. **Flowers:** *produced on hairy spikes from the junctions of the new leaves and stems;* each flower small, greenish-white, 6–8 mm (0.2–0.3 in) long, with a 5-lobed calyx; 5 round, whitish petals; 10 stamens, and a 1-celled ovary. **Fruits:** *dry, leathery, broadest above the middle, 1–1.5 cm (0.4–0.6 in) long, tipped with the remnants of the calyx, with 10 narrow, lengthwise ribs,* reddish, enclosing a brittle stone which contains a thin, leathery, dark red seed.

The Oleaster Family   Elaeagnaceae

This small family of 3 genera and about 50 species is native to North America, Europe, southern Asia, and Australia. One species of oleaster and 3 species of buffaloberries are native to North America, but only 1 of the buffaloberries is a tree. A distinctive feature of this family is the silvery to brown, scaly (peltate) hairs that cover the stems and leaves. Oleasters, which have limited economic importance, have been introduced into North America as windbreaks and ornamentals.

Members of this family are shrubs or small trees with alternate, opposite, or whorled leaves. The leaves are simple, entire, and leathery. Flowers are bisexual or male and female, produced singly or in clusters. Fruits are dry and hard or fleshy and contain a single seed.

Key to Oleaster Genera

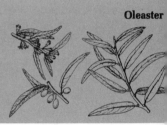

Oleaster

A. Leaves opposite, male and female flowers on separate plants **Buffaloberry, p. 690**
B. Leaves alternate, flowers bisexual or male or female both occurring on same plant **Oleaster, p. 691**

The Buffaloberry Genus   *Shepherdia* Nutt.

This North American genus contains 3 species: 2 that are shrubs and 1 that reaches tree size. They are sometimes cultivated for their attractive leaves and fruits which are a food source for birds and other wildlife.

Buffaloberries are shrubs or small trees with opposite, simple leaves which are silvery beneath. Male and female flowers are produced in small clusters on the branchlets of the previous season. The nearly rounded to egg-shaped fruits are fleshy and 1-seeded.

Silver Buffaloberry   *Shepherdia argentea* (Pursh) Nutt.

Silver Buffaloberry occurs in sandy soils of the plains and canyons of the West but is centered in the northern Great Plains region of Manitoba, Saskatchewan, Alberta, the Dakotas, and Montana. It is tolerant of very cold temperatures and can survive droughts.

Flowering is in spring with abundant fruit produced by summer. Black bears, small mammals, quail, thrashers, and other birds eat the fruit. The dark brown wood is soft, weak, and of no commercial value. It is sometimes planted as a windbreak and for erosion control.

Appearance: spreading shrub occasionally forming dense thickets or small trees to 5 m (16 ft); trunk short, branching close to the ground. **Bark:** thin, smooth when young, becoming somewhat ridged and shredding into long strips, dull gray. **Branches:** short, stout; ***branchlets*** stout, ***covered with dense, silvery-white scales.*** **Winter buds:** 2–4 mm (0.1 in) long, narrow, blunt at the tip, covered with silvery and

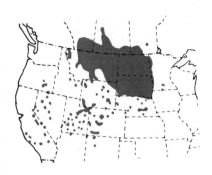

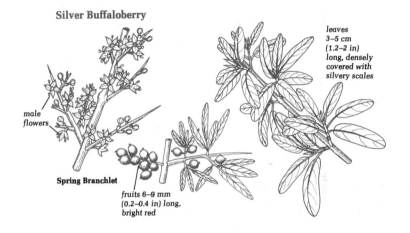

Silver Buffaloberry

male flowers

Spring Branchlet

fruits 6–9 mm (0.2–0.4 in) long, bright red

leaves 3–5 cm (1.2–2 in) long, densely covered with silvery scales

reddish scales. **Leaves:** opposite, simple, widest near the middle to uniformly wide, ***3–5 cm (1.2–2 in) long, 7–10 mm (0.3–0.4 in) wide,*** rounded at the tip, rounded at the base, entire, leathery, ***covered on both sides with dense silvery scales;*** leafstalks stout, 4–6 mm (0.2 in) long. **Flowers:** ***male and female flowers on separate trees; male flowers*** produced in small clusters near the tips of the branchlets, each ***with*** a broadly bell-shaped, ***4-lobed calyx, no petals, and 8 stamens;*** female flowers produced on short stalks near the tips of the branchlets, each with a bell-shaped calyx, and an 8-lobed nectary surrounding the single pistil. **Fruits:** produced singly or in clusters, rounded, 6–9 mm (0.2–0.4 in) long, somewhat fleshy, smooth, bright red and enclosing an egg-shaped, flattened seed 3–4 mm (0.1 in) long.

The Oleaster Genus

Elaeagnus L.

This is a genus of perhaps 45 species, primarily of southern Europe and Asia, with 1 shrubby species, the silverberry (*Elaeagnus commutata*), which is native to Alaska, western Canada, and the northern Great Plains. Of the several European and Asian species introduced into North America, 2 are often encountered. Chinese oleaster (*E. umbellata*), which is a native of China, is a large, spreading shrub often planted along fence rows and to attract birds. Oleaster, or Russian olive, is widely planted and grows wild in many areas.

Members of this genus are shrubs or trees, often spiny with alternate, entire, deciduous to evergreen leaves which are covered with silvery to brown scales. Flowers are produced singly or in clusters. Fruits are small, fleshy to leathery, and contain a hard stone.

Oleaster, Russian Olive   *Elaeagnus angustifolia* L.

This attractive tree is native to southern Europe and central Asia and was introduced into North America during colonial times. Because of its dense branches, extreme hardiness, and resistance to drought, it has been extensively planted as a windbreak in the prairie states and provinces. On windy days, the silvery lower leaf surfaces make this an especially attractive tree. Many species of birds nest in oleaster and feed on the fruits.

Oleaster is a shrub or small tree to 8 m (26 ft). The **leaves** are **alternate,** narrow, widest near the base, 4–9 cm (1.6–3.6 in) long, 1.2–2.4 cm (0.5–1 in) wide, pointed at the tip, entire, dark green above, and **covered** with **silvery white scales beneath.** Flowers appear in spring in clusters of 1 to 3 at the base of the current year's leaves, each with 4 calyx lobes, petals absent, 4 stamens, and a single pistil. Fruits mature in early fall and are egg-shaped, 1–1.5 cm (0.4–0.6 in) long, densely covered with silvery scales, with a pithy flesh enclosing a hard stone 8–11 mm (0.3–0.4 in) long.

Oleaster or Russian Olive

flowers with 4-lobed calyx, petals absent

fruit 1–1.5 cm (0.4–0.6 in) long

leaves 4–9 cm (1.6–3.6 in) long, silvery-white scales beneath

The Protea Family   Proteaceae

The protea family is one of the largest plant groups in the dry climates of the Southern Hemisphere. It includes about 55 genera and over 1,200 species. Roughly 15 genera and 475 species occur in South Africa alone, and another 700 species are native to Australia, where the seasons are long and dry. Members of this family are adapted to conserve water during dry seasons and have long, deep-growing root systems. The only species in the Northern Hemisphere, those with large attractive flowers, were introduced for ornamental purposes. Over 100 species from 20 genera are used as ornamentals.

The Queensland or Macadamia nut, whose edible seeds are considered a delicacy, is a commercially important member of this family in Hawaii. Silk oak is the sole tree-size representative of this family in North America.

Protea family members usually have alternate, simple or compound leaves, though some species have opposite or whorled (3 or more leaves originating from the same position on the stem) arrangements. The floral parts (calyx and corolla are indistinguishable) are 4-parted, free above the base, opposite each other, and fused to the 4 stamens; the pistil has a 1-celled ovary and simple style. The flowers are often clustered into heads or spikes that are covered by densely hairy bracts. The fruit is a capsule, somewhat fleshy on the outside with a hard central seed, nut, or dry pod that opens on one side.

The Silk Oak Genus   *Grevillea* R. Br.

This large genus includes about 190 species of trees and shrubs native to most of Oceania and eastern Malaysia. Members of this genus, adapted to prolonged dry seasons, grow in arid soils under a variety of conditions. In North America, 1 species, the silk oak, grows wild in the warmer parts of the U.S.

Silk oaks are trees or shrubs that have evergreen leaves. Large, showy flower clusters are usually produced at the ends of branches. The flowers contain both male and female parts, and are symmetrical about any line which splits them into halves. The calyx lobes and petals are fused at the base, and usually long styles of pistil project from the flower's center.

In America, silk oak is grown as an ornamental. In its native Australia, it and several other species are prized for their handsomely grained wood, which is used extensively in cabinetwork and furniture. Bees also make honey from the flowers of some species.

Silk Oak   *Grevillea robusta* A. Cunn.

The silk oak is a medium-size to large tree that is native to Australia, but has been introduced to and naturalized in many tropical and subtropical areas, particularly in South and Central America. It has been established in southern Florida and is under cultivation in southern California and Arizona. This hardy, drought-resistant species, which may be found growing along highways, prefer well-drained, sandy soils.

Rapid and extensive growth and plentiful annual seed crops are characteristic of silk oaks. These trees produce deep-yellow flowers in feather-like clusters, which appear at leaf bases, on branchlets, or on the trunk itself. Flowers and the pod-like fruits have been observed growing side by side; presumably both may be present throughout the year. The flowers are a valuable source of nectar for both birds and bees, and the species is classified as a honey tree. Unfortunately, silk oak is greatly troubled by scale insects.

Like several close relatives, silk oak is valued for its wood, whose grain is marked by rays or lines reminiscent of oak. Durability and luster make it a valued material in cabinetwork, paneling, interior finishes, and furniture. Silk oak is also used as a shade or ornamental tree. In some countries it is planted to shade coffee bushes from too much direct sunlight. In temperate North America, young trees are potted as houseplants.

Appearance: tree to 20 m (66 ft) in North America but to 50 m (164 ft) in Australia, with a round-topped crown resembling an oak; trunk straight, to 0.9 m (3 ft) in diameter. **Bark:** becoming rough and deeply furrowed, gray. **Branches:** numerous, breaking easily; branchlets stout, silky hairy when young, becoming smooth with age. **Leaves:**

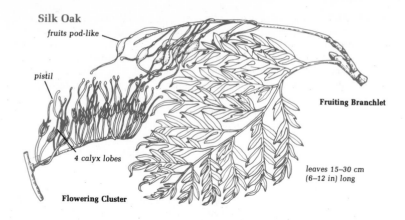

Silk Oak
fruits pod-like
pistil
4 calyx lobes
Flowering Cluster
Fruiting Branchlet
leaves 15–30 cm
(6–12 in) long

alternate, *evergreen, deeply lobed and pinnately compound, resembling a fern leaf, 15–30 cm (6–12 in) long,* the leaflet pairs narrow, deeply lobed, smooth, light green above, paler and with silky brown hairs beneath; leafstalks stout, 5–7.5 cm (2–3 in) long, widening suddenly at the base. **Flowers: *produced in narrow, elongated, many-flowered, unbranched clusters (racemes) 10–20 cm (4–8 in) long, golden yellow,*** showy; each flower on a slender stalk 0.9–1.8 cm (0.4–0.7 in) long; with a 4-lobed calyx, the lobes narrow, 1.1–1.3 cm (0.4–0.5 in) long, yellow, curling downward; petals lacking; 4 stamens opposite the sepals; and a single pistil. **Fruit: *pod-like, 2–3 cm (0.8–1.3 in) long,*** slightly flattened on one side, ***opening on one side;*** containing 1 or 2 ellipse-shaped, flattened, winged, brown seeds about 0.7–0.9 cm (0.3–0.4 in) long.

The Mangrove Family   Rhizophoraceae

This is a small family of 16 genera and about 120 species of trees, shrubs, and vines of the tropics. They are more abundant in Africa, Asia, and Australia than in the Americas. The red mangrove is the sole member of the family occurring naturally in North America, where it is restricted to southern Florida. Some of the Asian and African species are valuable sources of timber, while others serve as fuel.

Members of this family are woody, have astringent bark and opposite, simple, entire leaves. They normally produce bisexual flowers in elongated, branched, or un-branched clusters. Each flower has from 3 to 16 calyx lobes which persist into fruiting, an equal number of petals, and 2 to 4 times as many stamens as petals. Fruits may be berry-like or dry and do not split open at maturity, or, rarely, a capsule which splits open.

The Mangrove Genus   Rhizophora L.

There are 3 species in this genus that are widely distributed along tropical seashores of the world. Only 1, the red mangrove, is native to Florida. The other 2 species occur along coastal Africa, the East Indies, and Australia. All 3 have root systems, adapted to growth in salt water, that allow greater exchange of air. The species description below approximates that of the genus.

Red Mangrove

Rhizophora mangle L.

Red mangrove is common on large, muddy flats of coastal southern Florida, including the Keys. It sometimes occurs inland along riverbanks. This species is widespread throughout coastal regions of tropical America. Two other native species of mangrove, the button and white mangroves, belong to the combretum family (see page 686).

The pale yellow flowers and the fruits can be seen most months of the year. This mangrove has precocious seeds; that is, they germinate and develop into an elongated, unbranched seedling while still on the parent tree. They then fall off, float away, or become lodged in mud where they continue to grow, forming a new plant. The dark reddish-brown wood is used for posts, fuel, and, in some cases, cabinetwork and shipbuilding in the West Indies. The tannin-rich bark has been used for leather tanning, dyes, and medicines.

Red Mangrove

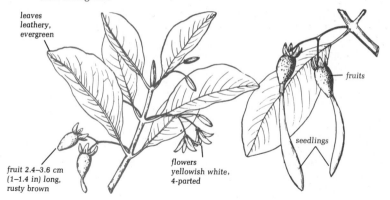

leaves leathery, evergreen

fruits

seedlings

fruit 2.4–3.6 cm (1–1.4 in) long, rusty brown

flowers yellowish white, 4-parted

Appearance: shrubs or small trees to 25 m (82 ft), usually with a rounded or flat-topped crown; trunk often short, to 1 m (3.3 ft), rarely larger. **Bark:** 8–12 mm (0.3–0.5 in) thick, thin and smooth on younger trees, developing lengthwise furrows and scaly ridges, gray, reddish on the inside. **Branches:** stout, spreading, often with hanging aerial roots; branchlets stout, smooth, reddish-brown turning gray with age. **Winter buds:** 2.5–5 cm (1–2 in) long, covered with 2 green scales. **Leaves:** *opposite*, simple, broadest near the base to the middle, 5–15 cm (2–6 in) long, 2.5–5 cm (1–2 in) wide, rounded to pointed at the tip, tapering at the base, *entire, leathery, evergreen*, dark green and shiny above, paler beneath; leafstalks stout, 1.3–4 cm (0.5–1.6 in) long. **Flowers:** *produced in clusters of 2 or 3* from the junctions of the young leaves and the stems; each flower 2–2.6 cm (0.8–1 in) in diameter, stalked, with 4 sharp-pointed calyx lobes, 4 narrow, yellowish-white petals, the *petals hairy on the inner surface*, 8 stamens, and 1 pistil. **Fruits:** broadest near the base and egg-shaped, 2.4–3.6 cm (1–1.4 in) long, dry, hard, rusty brown; the *seed germinates while the fruits are still on the tree and forms a torpedo-shaped seedling*, sometimes to 30 cm (12 in) long.

The Silktassel Family

Garryaceae

This small North American family consists of 1 genus, containing about 16 species of evergreen shrubs or occasionally small trees. They occur in California, southwestern U.S., Mexico, Guatemala, and the West Indies. All American species are shrubs; however, the wavyleaf silktassel does attain tree size. This genus was once included in the dogwood family, but most authorities now consider it to be distinct.

Members of this family are shrubs or trees with opposite, simple, entire, evergreen leaves. Flowers are either male or female and are produced on separate plants in hanging, catkin-like clusters. Fruits are a rounded, dry, 1- or 2-seeded berry.

The Silktassel Genus

Garrya Dougl.

Since the silktassel family contains only 1 genus, the description of the family applies here. The genus was named in honor of Nicholas Garry of the Hudson Bay Company who aided David Douglas in his travels to the Northwest.

Wavyleaf Silktassel

Garrya elliptica Dougl.

This is a small evergreen shrub or tree native to the chaparral and mixed evergreen forest of the coastal ranges from Oregon to central California. It grows to 3 m (10 ft) tall on dry, gravelly or rocky slopes, but in the richer, sandy soils of the more northern climates, it develops into a short-trunked tree. Because of its bitter bark, leaves, and fruit, this species is also known as quinine bush. Wavy silktassel commonly grows in association with ponderosa pine, manzanita, ceanothus, and other shrubs.

Flowers appear from December through February. Male trees, with their attractive flowering tassels, are occasionally cultivated as ornamentals along the Pacific Coast. It is not an important food source to wildlife, although mule deer have been

Wavyleaf Silktassel

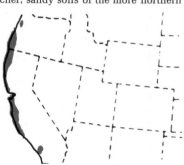

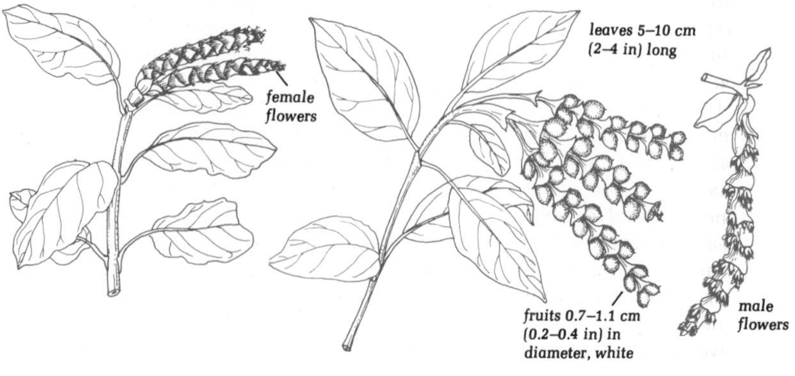

leaves 5–10 cm
(2–4 in) long

female
flowers

fruits 0.7–1.1 cm
(0.2–0.4 in) in
diameter, white

male
flowers

known to browse the leaves. The hard, close-grained, grayish-brown wood has been used for fine cabinetwork, though its rarity has limited its use commercially.

Appearance: low shrub or small tree to 6 m (20 ft), with a rounded crown; trunk short, branching close to the ground. **Bark:** thin, smooth or nearly so, green turning dark brown. **Branches:** stout, 4-angled, young branchlets densely hairy, turning gray or dark brown. **Leaves:** *opposite,* simple, *evergreen,* broadest near or just below the middle, 5–10 cm (2–4 in) long, 2.2–5 cm (0.9–2 in) wide, rounded to pointed at the tip, tapering to rounded at the base, wavy along the margin, leathery, dark green and smooth above, densely wooly beneath; leafstalks stout, 6–12 mm (0.2–0.5 in) long. **Flowers:** *male and female flowers on separate trees; male flowers produced in a drooping, catkin-like tassel 5–12 cm (2–5 in) long,* each flower has a 4-lobed calyx, no petals, and 4 stamens; female flowers produced in stouter catkin-like tassels 4–8 cm (1.6–3.2 in) long. **Fruits:** produced in dense, elongated clusters, each fruit rounded, 7–11 mm (0.2–0.4 in) in diameter, white, hairy, less so with age, and enclosing 1 or 2 seeds.

The Dogwood Family Cornaceae

This is a small family of about 18 genera and 110 species distributed mainly in the temperate regions of North America, Europe, and Asia. A few species are native to tropical and subtropical regions of Africa and South America. Dogwood (*Cornus*) is the only genus native to North America. Many of the species are showy and are grown as ornamentals throughout the world. In North America the trees are not large enough to yield commercial quantities of lumber.

Members of this family are trees or shrubs, rarely herbs, with opposite or rarely alternate, simple, usually deciduous leaves. The flowers are typically produced in branched, round to flat-topped clusters, sometimes surrounded by large, showy bracts. Flowers are small, bisexual, or male or female in some non-North American species, in which case the sexes occur on separate plants. Each flower has a 4- or 5-lobed calyx, 4 or 5 free petals, 4 or 5 stamens, and a single pistil. Fruit is a berry or drupe containing 1 or 2 stones.

The Dogwood Genus Cornus L.

The 40 or 45 species of dogwood are native to temperate regions of the Northern Hemisphere of North America, Europe, Asia, and Africa, with 1 exception in Peru. Seven species reach tree size in North America, while 6 other species are shrubs. Two additional species are small herbs native to the colder regions of the U.S., Canada, and Alaska. They are common in open woods, and along fence rows, streams, and roadsides. Dogwoods grow best in moist, fertile soils.

Several dogwoods have been introduced into cultivation in North America. The more commonly encountered of these are the Japanese dogwood (*Cornus kousa*) and also the Cornelian cherry (*Cornus mas*). The Japanese dogwood resembles the American flowering dogwood, except that it flowers about 2 or 3 weeks later, and the petal-like structures enclosing the flowers are pointed at the tip. The Cornelian cherry, native to southern Europe and western Asia, is one of the earliest of the flowering trees to bloom. It produces profuse, striking clusters of small, yellow flowers along its branchlets before the leaves appear.

Dogwoods are grown for their attractive stems, flowers, and fruits in parks, gardens, and yards. One explanation for the name "dogwood" has it that an astringent tonic made from the bark was formerly used to wash mangy dogs. A more likely derivation is from "daggerwood," sticks once used to skewer meats. The fruits are a valuable source of food for wildlife, especially birds in the Northeast. Wild turkey, bobwhite quail, ruffed grouse, wood duck, and other gamebirds feed on the fruits. Whitetail and mule deer browse the twigs and leaves.

Dogwoods are small trees or shrubs with simple, opposite or, rarely, alternate, deciduous leaves. The veins of the leaves characteristically curve toward the tip of the leaf. The small, 4-parted flowers are bisexual and grow in clusters along the side or at the tips of branchlets. The flower clusters are sometimes surrounded by 4 to 8 distinct, white, petal-like bracts. The small, often rounded, fruits are red, white, blue, or green and have a thin pulp surrounding 1 or 2 hard stones.

Key to Dogwood Species

A. Leaves opposite.

  1. Flowers greenish-yellow, produced in dense clusters, surrounded by 4–6 large, showy, white, sometimes pink, petal-like structures.

Flowering Dogwood

    a. Four petal-like structures enclosing the flowers, very broad near the tip, almost as broad as long, rounded or notched at the tip; trees of eastern North America
Flowering dogwood, p. 699

    b. Six, sometimes 4, petal-like structures enclosing the flowers, longer than broad, pointed at the tip; trees of coastal western North America **Pacific dogwood, p. 700**

Pacific Dogwood

  2. Flowers white or cream, produced in branched, many-flowered clusters, not enclosed by large, showy, petal-like structures.

    a. Leaves with stiff hairs on upper surface, rough to touch; trees of midwestern and southern U.S. **Roughleaf dogwood, p 701**

    b. Leaves smooth or with sparse soft hairs above.

      (1) Leaves usually 5 cm (2 in) long or less, with 3 or 4 pairs of main lateral veins per leaf; shrubs or trees of California and Oregon **Brown dogwood, p. 702**

      (2) Leaves usually longer than 5 cm (2 in), with 4–8 pairs of main lateral veins per leaf.

(a) Fruits pale blue; branches and branchlets turning brown or gray; trees of low wetlands of southeastern U.S.
   Stiffcornel dogwood, p. 702

(b) Fruits dull white; branches and branchlets turning red or reddish-purple; widespread northern tree or shrub **Red-osier dogwood, p. 703**

Red-Osier Dogwood

B. Leaves alternate; trees of eastern North America
   Alternate-leaf dogwood, p. 704

Flowering Dogwood   *Cornus florida* L.

The small and graceful flowering dogwood grows from extreme southwestern Maine to eastern Kansas south to eastern Texas and Florida in a variety of soils from well-drained, light upland soils to deep, moist soils along streams and lower slopes. This

tree grows near or under many taller trees including some of the hickories, the oaks (chestnut, white, scarlet, and black), tulip tree, several pines, red maple and the American beech. It also occurs with smaller trees and shrubs such as redbud and hawthorns. There are several varieties of flowering dogwood, including variety *rubra*, with pink bracts surrounding the flowers.

   This fast growing, short-lived tree bears clusters of showy, white to pinkish-white flowers appearing before leaves unfold, followed by red, berry-like fruits. This tree is popular as a flowering ornamental and for the many species of songbirds and small mammals attracted to the fruits in autumn. Squirrels and raccoons also consume the fruit. Whitetail deer browse the leaves and twigs, especially enjoying new sprout growth. The fruit is poisonous for humans. The bark has been used instead of quinine as a remedy for fevers. Flowering dogwood is also useful for its rapid decomposition, contributing calcium and other minerals important to soil enrichment. The shining red-brown wood is hard, tough, close-grained, and good for making tool handles. It was formerly used for shuttles, machinery parts, hubs of small wheels, barrel hoops, and occasionally engravers' blocks.

   Appearance: small tree with bushy, pyramidal or rounded crown; growing to 15 m (49 ft); trunk straight or crooked, to 50 cm (20 in) in diameter. **Bark:** rough, 6–8 mm (0.2–0.3 in) thick, fissured into small, thin, angular scales, grayish-brown to nearly black. **Branches:** stout, spreading or upright; branchlets slender, smooth or nearly smooth, pale green or reddish, becoming reddish-gray or light brown with many leaf scars. **Winter buds:** 2 types formed in mid-summer, leaf and flower; leaf buds narrow, cone-shaped, covered with 2 opposite scales; flower buds at end of new growth, nearly rounded to biscuit-shaped, covered with 4 scales. **Leaves:** opposite, deciduous, simple, broadest near base to broadest at middle, 6–15 cm (2.4–6 in) long, 3.7–5.2 cm

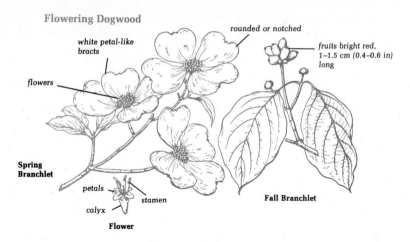

Flowering Dogwood

white petal-like bracts

rounded or notched

fruits bright red, 1–1.5 cm (0.4–0.6 in) long

flowers

Spring Branchlet

petals

stamen

calyx

Fall Branchlet

Flower

(1.5–2.1 in) wide, pointed at the tip, rounded or narrowed at base, margins with shallow teeth or entire, firm, thick, bright green and slightly hairy above, paler and hairy beneath; turning scarlet in autumn; leafstalks 1.2–2 cm (0.5–0.8 in) long, grooved. **Flowers: tiny,** produced **in dense, crowded heads** and **surrounded by 4 large white,** occasionally pink, **petal-like structures;** each flower with a narrowly funnel-shaped, 4-lobed calyx, 4 strap-shaped, green with yellow-tipped petals; 4 stamens, and a single pistil. **Fruit:** clusters of bright **scarlet red,** oblong **berries, 1–1.5 cm (0.4–0.6 in) long,** tipped with remains of calyx; thin, mealy, bitter flesh, enclosing a stone.

Pacific Dogwood   *Cornus nuttallii* Audubon

Also known by the common names of flowering dogwood, western flowering dogwood, and mountain dogwood, this species occurs in coniferous forests of southwestern British Columbia, south through the mountains to southern California, with local populations in Idaho. This tree is common in bottomlands, moist river soils, and along stream banks at altitudes of 750–1,950 m (2,460–6,398 ft). The largest trees occur near Puget Sound and in redwood forests of northern California. Pacific dogwood grows in association with Douglas fir, western hemlock, maples, Nuttall willow, red and white alders, and pine.

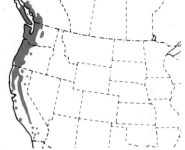

It is **similar to** its eastern counterpart, the **flowering dogwood, but the flowers of Pacific dogwood are surrounded by 4 to 6 (usually 5) bracts rather than only 4.** The tree itself is often cultivated as an ornamental in northwestern states for its profusion of star-like flowers throughout spring and large, bright red or orange clusters of fruits in autumn.

Bandtailed pigeons, along with quail and grosbeaks, hermit thrushes, vireos, and waxwings consume these fruits as an important part of their diet. Black bears and beavers feast on fruits, wood, and foliage. Blacktail and mule deer browse the twigs and foliage. The light, reddish-brown, fine-grained, heavy wood is extremely hard and

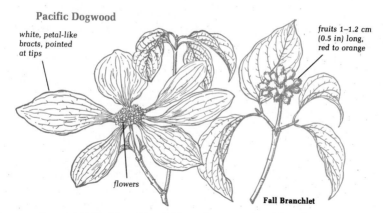

Pacific Dogwood

white, petal-like
bracts, pointed
at tips

fruits 1–1.2 cm
(0.5 in) long,
red to orange

flowers

Fall Branchlet

strong and occasionally is used in making cabinets and tool handles.

   Appearance: handsome tree, even more magnificent than its eastern relative, sometimes to 30 m (98 ft), with a rounded or pyramid-shaped crown; trunk straight, to 60
cm (24 in) in diameter. **Bark:** 6–8 mm (0.2–0.3 in) thick, broken into small, thin scales,
reddish-brown. **Branches:** spreading, horizontal, branchlets slender, hairy, light green
becoming smooth, dark reddish-purple, marked by prominent leaf scars. **Winter buds:**
2 types formed in mid-summer, leaf buds narrow, 0.8–1.2 cm (0.3–0.5 in) long, covered with 2 opposite scales; flower buds rounded or nearly so. **Leaves:** clustered at the
end of branches, opposite, deciduous, simple, broadest at or near base or above
middle, 8–15 cm (3–6 in) long, 3.5–9 cm (1.4–3.5 in) wide, tapered to a short, sharp-
pointed tip, tapered at the base, wavy-toothed along the margin, bright green and
slightly hairy above, paler and covered with white hairs beneath; leafstalks short,
stout, hairy, grooved. **Flowers:** tiny, produced *in dense, crowded heads* and *surrounded by 4 to 6 showy, white* or rarely pale pink, *petal-like structures;* each flower
with a yellowish-green, 4-lobed calyx, 4 yellowish-green petals, 4 stamens, and a
single pistil. **Fruit:** *berry-like* and produced *in dense rounded heads of 30 to 40;
each 1–1.2 cm (0.4–0.5 in) long,* flattened egg-shaped, *bright red or orange,* flesh
thin, mealy, enclosing a blunt-pointed stone, grooved.

Roughleaf Dogwood

Cornus drummondii C.A. Meyer

The hardy roughleaf dogwood is a shrub or small tree found in extreme southern Ontario west to Nebraska, south to Texas, and north to Ohio. Thickets are usually found
along roadsides, fencerows, pastures, and margins of woods in rocky or clay soils and
sometimes in moist soils of stream banks.
Roughleaf dogwood grows in association
with overcup and cherrybark oaks, American elm, sycamore, water hickory, and several willows.

   This species is fast growing and relatively long-lived. It produces flowers at the
ends of new growth in spring, and it bears
mature fruit in autumn. It will withstand
extreme cold and very dry spells. Whitetail
deer often browse the twigs and foliage,
while songbirds, as well as turkey, quail,

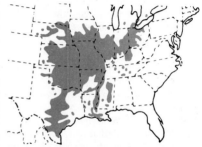

and small mammals, consume the berry-like fruits. It is a favorite nesting place for many birds, especially Bell's vireo. The greenish wood is hard and close-grained and sometimes used in lathe work. The roughleaf dogwood is not economically valuable, although its spreading underground stems are effective in controlling soil erosion.

Appearance: thicket-forming shrub to 4 m (13 ft), sometimes a narrow tree to 10 m (32 ft) with open, irregular crown; trunk short, to 30 cm (12 in) in diameter. **Bark:** 2–4 mm (0.1 in) thick, shallowly fissured, scaly, dark reddish to gray-brown. **Branches:** thin, upright, stiff; branchlets slender, brown to reddish-gray, often red when young, hairy. **Winter buds:** end bud egg-shaped, 4–5 mm (0.2 in) long, pointed at the tip, hairy, side buds smaller. **Leaves:** simple, opposite, deciduous, broadest at or near the base or broadest at middle, *4–9 cm (1.6–3.5 in) long, 3–4.5 cm (1.2–1.8 in) wide,* pointed at the tip, rounded at the base, thickened and wavy along the margins, covered with silvery hairs when unfolding, becoming *dull yellow-green* and *rough, with short, stiff white hairs above,* paler and densely hairy beneath; leafstalk 0.5–1 cm (0.2–0.4 in) long, stout, hairy, grooved. **Flowers:** produced in many-flowered, flat to slightly round-topped, spreading clusters at the tips of the branchlets, hairy; each flower with a 4-lobed, hairy calyx, 4 narrow, short, white petals, 4 stamens, and a single pistil. **Fruit:** produced in flat or round-topped clusters with green or red branches and stalks, fruit white, rounded, 6–8 mm (0.2–0.3 in) in diameter, covered with tiny hairs, pulp thin, enclosing 1 or 2 smooth, rounded seeds.

Brown Dogwood *Cornus glabrata* Benth.

Brown dogwood is a shrub or small tree native to California and Oregon. It grows in moist sites on lower mountain slopes to 1,750 m (5,741 ft) elevation. Dense thickets are often produced, especially along streams. Flowering is in May or June.

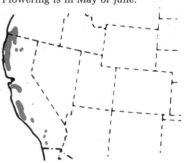

More often a shrub, this dogwood grows to 6 m (20 ft) with reddish-purple to brown, smooth branchlets. The opposite leaves are widest near the base or the middle, *2.5–5.5 cm (1–2.2 in) long, 1.5–2.6 cm (0.6–1 in) wide,* pointed at the tip, and *gray-green* and *almost smooth above.* The small flowers are produced in branched, round to nearly flat-topped clusters. Fruits are almost round, 8–10 mm (0.3–0.4 in) in diameter, white to bluish, with a thin flesh enclosing a hard stone.

Stiffcornel Dogwood *Cornus stricta* Lam.

Named for its stiff, upright branches, the stiffcornel dogwood is a small tree primarily of the Coastal Plain from eastern Virginia to central Florida, west to Louisiana, and north to southeastern Missouri. It generally grows in swampy, low wetlands and along streams and riverbanks. This species is distinguished from other dogwoods by its loose, open flower clusters without showy bracts and open clusters of blue fruits.

Attractive enough to have been cultivated for ornament since 1758, the stiffcornel dogwood has little other commercial value. Several species of birds, including quail, catbirds, mockingbirds, robins, and brown thrashers are attracted to the fruits. The whitish wood is hard and fine-grained but is not used for lumber because of its small size.

Appearance: shrub or small tree to 4.5 m (15 ft), with a flat-topped crown; trunk branching close to the ground, to 10 cm (4 in) in diameter. **Bark:** 2–4 mm (0.1 in) thick, smooth, becoming furrowed with shallow ridges exposing inner brown bark, gray. **Branches:** slender, upright, smooth, slightly hairy toward the tips, turning greenish to **brown** or **gray**. **Winter buds:** 3–4 mm (0.1 in) long, egg-shaped, sharp-pointed, covered with hairy, overlapping, reddish-brown scales. **Leaves:** opposite, simple, lance-shaped to egg-shaped, **4–10 cm (1.6–4 in) long, 1.5–4 cm (0.6–1.6 in) wide,** tapering to a pointed tip, rounded or broadly tapered at the base, margin entire, **dark green and smooth above,** whitish green and smooth to slightly hairy below. **Flowers:** produced in many-flowered, rounded or flat-topped, open clusters 3–5 cm (1.2–2 in) across; each flower with 4 tiny calyx lobes, 4 small, white, spreading petals, 4 stamens, and a single pistil. **Fruits:** small, rounded, 5–8 mm (0.2–0.3 in) in diameter, **pale blue,** flesh thin, enclosing a hard, furrowed stone.

Red-Osier Dogwood   *Cornus stolonifera* Michx.

This species—also known as American dogwood, kinnikinnik, or squawbush—is distributed widely from Newfoundland across Canada to the Yukon and central Alaska, south in the U. S. to California, east to Nebraska and to New York. It is also located in northern Mexico. The red-osier dogwood usually occurs along streams, rivers, and moist sites at altitudes of 450–2,700 m (1,476–8,858 ft). It often grows in association with willows and alders. The western dogwood, *Cornus occidentalis*, is treated here as a variety of red-osier dogwood. The variety *occidentalis* differs by having lengthwise grooves on the stones and slightly longer petals.

Red-osier dogwood resembles roughleaf dogwood with the exception of its reddish twigs. Clusters of white flowers are produced from May to August, with white to lead-colored, or sometimes bluish, fruits maturing by mid-summer to autumn. The bright red twigs, especially obvious during the leafless winter months, make this dogwood a popular ornamental. Fruits are eaten by many birds, including ruffed grouse, sharptail grouse, bobwhite quail, and Hungarian partridge. Whitetail deer, mule deer, cottontail, snowshoe hare, moose, and elk browse the twigs and foliage.

Appearance: thicket-forming shrub or small tree to 5 m (16 ft) tall; seldom with a single trunk. **Bark:** thin, 1–3 mm (0.1 in) thick, red, occasionally greenish, smooth but with prominent lenticels. **Branches:** rising, spreading, or bending downward along the ground, **reddish** or purplish, smooth, slender; **branchlets red to reddish purple,** with flattened or spreading hairs. **Winter buds:** 3–6 mm (0.1–0.2 in) long, egg-shaped, with long tapered points, leaf buds smaller than flower buds. **Leaves:** opposite, simple, deciduous, broadest near the base, **6–9 cm (2.4–3.6 in) long, 2–4 cm (0.8–1.6 in) wide,** tapering to a pointed tip, rounded at the base, entire along the margins, dark green and smooth above at maturity, covered with a whitish bloom and soft white

Red-Osier Dogwood

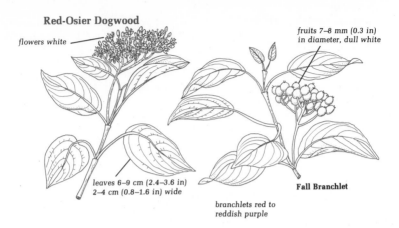

flowers white

fruits 7–8 mm (0.3 in)
in diameter, dull white

leaves 6–9 cm (2.4–3.6 in)
2–4 cm (0.8–1.6 in) wide

Fall Branchlet

branchlets red to
reddish purple

hairs when young, becoming smooth beneath; leafstalks 1–1.5 cm (0.4–0.6 in) long, with flattened or spreading hairs, red, flattened above. **Flowers:** produced in many-flowered, flat-topped clusters 3–6 cm (1.2–2.4 in) across; each flower with a 4-lobed, hairy calyx, 4 dull white, narrow petals, 4 stamens, and a single pistil. **Fruits:** produced in round-topped clusters of 10 to 30 fruits, each *rounded, 7–8 mm (0.3 in) in diameter, dull white,* flesh thin, enclosing an egg-shaped, furrowed stone.

Alternate-Leaf Dogwood   *Cornus alternifolia* L.f.

This alternate-leaved species, distinctive because other dogwoods have opposite leaves, grows in Newfoundland and eastern Quebec, west to southeastern Manitoba, south to northern Arkansas, and northwest Florida and Georgia. This modest-size tree prefers moist, rich soils along borders of streams and ponds. Often called blue pagoda, umbrella dogwood, or pigeon-berry, it is subtly attractive in spring with small cream-colored flowers and more striking in autumn with bright foliage and blue fruit on red stalks. It grows in associa-tion with tulip tree, several oaks, white pine, basswood, American elm, white ash, red maple, flowering dogwood, elder, redbud, and sassafras. It is rapid-growing and short-lived. The pagoda-like

shape is formed by horizontal branches in progressively smaller tiers. A profusion of flowers and the autumn color make this a desirable ornamental. Thin bark makes this dogwood vulnerable to fire. It is sometimes damaged by dogwood borer and several pest insects, but is not prone to any serious diseases. Many species of songbirds, grouse, pheasant, prairie chicken, and turkey eat the fruits. Squirrels and small mam-mals consume the fruits and leaves, while whitetail deer browse the twigs and foliage. The reddish-brown wood is heavy, hard, and close-grained and not used commer-cially.

Appearance: many-stemmed shrub or small tree to 9 m (30 ft) high, with a broad, flat-topped crown having storied appearance due to whorls of long, slender branches radiating out in horizontal planes; trunk short to 20 ᴄm (8 in) in diameter. **Branches:**

Alternate-Leaf Dogwood

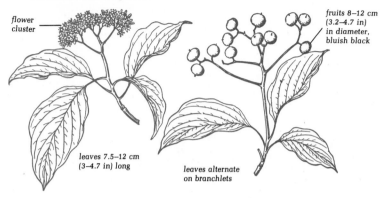

flower cluster

fruits 8–12 cm (3.2–4.7 in) in diameter, bluish black

leaves 7.5–12 cm (3–4.7 in) long

leaves alternate on branchlets

slender, smooth, greenish-yellow to brown. **Bark:** 3–4 mm (0.1 in) thick, smooth or divided with shallow fissures, dark reddish-brown. **Winter buds:** alternate or almost opposite, oval, sharp-pointed, covered with shiny, chestnut brown scales. **Leaves:** *alternate* or nearly opposite, simple, deciduous, clustered near the end of branches, broadest near the base, 7.5–12 cm (3–4.7 in) long, 5–8.5 cm (2–3.4 in) wide, pointed at the tip, heart-shaped or rounded at the base, slightly toothed, wavy or entire along the margin, yellowish-green and smooth or slightly hairy above, paler and hairy beneath; leafstalk slender, 3–5 cm (1.2–2 in) long, grooved. **Flowers:** produced in *many-flowered, flat-topped, branched clusters* at the ends of the stems; each flower with a narrow cup-shaped, 4-lobed calyx, 4 cream-white, narrow petals, 4 stamens, and a single pistil. **Fruits:** *rounded, 8–12 cm (3.2–4.7 in) in diameter, bluish-black,* flesh dry and bitter to taste, enclosing 1 or 2 egg-shaped, many-grooved stones.

The Tupelo Tree Family   Nyssaceae

This small family of 3 genera and 8 species of shrubs and trees is native to eastern North America and China, including Tibet. Only the tupelos (*Nyssa*) are native to North America. Members of this family were formerly included in the dogwood family; however, recent studies show sufficient differences to warrant a family designation of their own.

Members are trees or shrubs with alternate, simple, entire or slightly toothed, deciduous leaves. Flowers are male, female, or bisexual with both types occurring on a single tree. Male flowers are produced in heads, elongated or flat-topped clusters; female and bisexual flowers occur singly or in small heads. Fruits are rounded, somewhat fleshy, enclosing a hard stone, or dry and winged.

The Tupelo Genus   Nyssa L.

This is a small genus of 5 species, 2 in eastern Asia and the remaining 3 in eastern North America. Fossil records of preglacial species indicate that tupelos were once more widely distributed across Europe, Asia, and North America.

These deciduous trees are excellent for shade or ornamental plantings. In autumn the leaves turn a brilliant scarlet. The black tupelo is important to wildlife. Whitetail deer browse the leaves, while small mammals, gamebirds, and songbirds feed on the fruits. The trees are harvested for lumber, veneer, or woodpulp.

Tupelos are trees or shrubs with alternate, simple, deciduous, entire or slightly toothed leaves. The flowers are male or female, or bisexual; the male flowers clustered in many-flowered heads; the female or bisexual flowers are produced singly or in small clusters. Fruits are berry-like, with a thin, fleshy outer part enclosing a hard stone.

Key to Tupelo Species

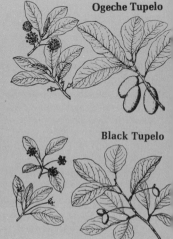

Ogeche Tupelo

A. Female flowers solitary at or near the ends of the branchlets; fruits generally 2.5 cm (1 in) long or longer.

   1. Leaves pointed at the tip; fruits dark purple; trees of southeastern Coastal Plain and lower Mississippi River Valley **Water tupelo, p. 706**
   2. Leaves rounded at the tip; fruits bright red; trees of southeastern Coastal Plain
            Ogeche tupelo, p. 707

Black Tupelo

B. Female flowers in 2- to 5-flowered clusters at or near the ends of the branchlets; fruits 1–1.5 cm (0.4–0.6 in) long; trees of eastern North America **Black tupelo, p. 708**

Water Tupelo
Nyssa aquatica L.

This species, also called sour gum or swamp tupelo, occurs on the Coastal Plain from southeastern Virginia to north Florida, to southeastern Texas, and north in the Mississippi Valley to western Tennessee and southern Illinois. It is found in cypress and other swamps, bottomlands, or sites periodically under water in soils ranging from clays to rich silt. Water tupelo occurs in almost pure stands or mixed with bald cypress, sometimes overcup and water oaks, black willow, swamp cottonwood, red maple, sweetgum, and slash pine. In spring a white, cottony down appears on new growth throughout the treetop and is shed as leaves mature.

These trees are fast growing in well-drained bottomlands but slower growing in swampy sites. They are long lived and begin flowering and fruiting when the trees are about 30 years old. Every year water tupelos produce heavy seed crops, mostly distributed by water. Turkeys and woodchucks, plus many species of songbirds, including robins, mockingbirds, thrushes, thrashers, and starlings consume the fruit. White-tail deer browse twigs and foliage. The soft, light brown wood is close-grained and weak and used for paneling, woodenware, packing boxes, and crates. A good mature stand will produce commercially important timber. Tupelo honey is popular in specialty stores.

Water Tupelo

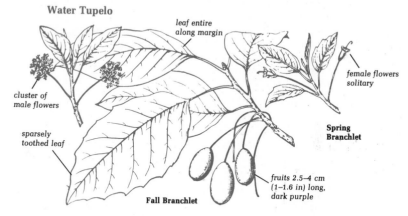

leaf entire along margin

cluster of male flowers

female flowers solitary

sparsely toothed leaf

Spring Branchlet

Fall Branchlet

fruits 2.5–4 cm (1–1.6 in) long, dark purple

Appearance: medium-size tree to 35 m (115 ft), with a narrow, rounded or cone-shaped crown; trunk straight, often spreading at the base, to 1.5 m (5 ft) in diameter. **Bark:** 6–10 mm (0.2–0.4 in) thick, developing lengthwise furrows and ridges composed of small scales, dark brown. **Branches:** short, stout, spreading; branchlets stout, dark red and finely hairy when young, becoming smooth and brown with age. **Winter buds:** large, 2–2.5 cm (0.8–1 in) long, nearly globe-shaped, covered with light, reddish-brown scales. **Leaves:** alternate, simple, deciduous, widest near the base to almost uniformly wide, *10–22 cm (4–8.7 in) long,* 5–12 cm (2–4.7 in) wide, *pointed at the tip,* tapering, rounded, or slightly heart-shaped at the base, entire or irregularly and sparsely toothed along the margin, leathery, dark green, shiny, and nearly smooth above, paler and finely hairy beneath; leafstalks stout, 2–5 cm (0.8–2 in) long, grooved, hairy. **Flowers:** both male and female flowers produced on same tree; *male flowers clustered together in dense, many-flowered heads* 1–1.5 cm (0.4–0.6 in) in diameter, the heads on slender hair stalks; *female flowers solitary.* **Fruit:** produced on a slender stalk, uniformly wide to widest near the tip, *2.5–4 cm (1–1.6 in) long, dark purple,* with a thin flesh enclosing a hard, ridged stone.

Ogeche Tupelo   *Nyssa ogeche* Bartr. ex Marsh.

This shrub or small tree is restricted to the stream banks and river swamps of the Coastal Plain of southeastern South Carolina, Georgia, and northern Florida. Permanently wet sites or soils flooded for long periods are best conditions for growth and regeneration. This species occurs in association with slash pine, pondcypress, bald cypress, water tupelo, sweetbay, swamp tupelo and red maple.

Flowering occurs from January to May. The fruits ripen by summer but remain on the tree until after the leaves fall. As a result of its rarity, this species is not economically important. The white wood is coarse-grained and tough but weak and difficult to split. The ripe fruit is made into preserves. Its acidic juice can be used as a substitute for limes. Some birds and small animals eat the fruit.

This is a many-stemmed shrub to medium-sized tree to 18 m (59 ft), with a narrow, rounded crown and scaly, dark brown bark 4–6 mm (0.1–0.2 in) thick. The leaves are alternate, simple, deciduous, variable in shape but usually broadest at or above the middle, *8–16 cm (3.2–6.3 in) long,* 5–8 cm (2–3.2 in) wide, *rounded at the tip,* entire or sparsely and irregularly toothed along the margin, dark green and smooth above, paler and hairy beneath. Flowers appear from January to May, male flowers in

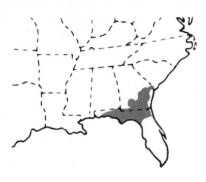

Ogeche Tupelo

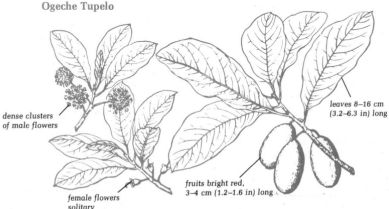

dense clusters
of male flowers

female flowers
solitary

fruits bright red,
3–4 cm (1.2–1.6 in) long

leaves 8–16 cm
(3.2–6.3 in) long

dense rounded heads 1–1.5 cm (0.4–0.6 in) in diameter on slender stalks 1–25 cm (0.4–9.8 in) long; *female flowers solitary on stout hairy stalks,* about 1–1.5 cm (0.4–0.6 in) long. Fruits are uniformly wide and rounded at the tip, *3–4 cm (1.2–1.6 in) long,* smooth, *bright red;* flesh thick, juicy, sour, and enclosing a flattened, 10 to 12 narrowly winged stone.

Black Tupelo   *Nyssa sylvatica* Marsh.

Black tupelo is a lowland tree widely distributed throughout eastern North America. Authorities recognize 2 varieties based primarily on habitat. Typical black tupelo (*N. sylvatica* variety *sylvatica*) occurs in uplands and stream bottoms in cooler climates and light textured soils from southwestern Maine to New York and extreme southern Ontario south to eastern Texas, northern Florida and disjunctly in central and southern Mexico. Swamp tupelo [*N. sylvatica* variety *biflora* (Walt.) Sarg.] occurs almost exclusively in heavy organic or clay soils of wet bottomlands, ponds, and sloughs of the Coastal Plain from Delaware south to Florida and eastern Texas. Swamp tupelo also has narrower leaves.

These trees have moderate growth rate

and longevity. Flowers appear in spring when leaves are nearly grown; while the fruits mature in autumn. The small greenish flowers are an excellent source of nectar for bees. Black bears and foxes frequently eat the fruit, while whitetail deer and beavers browse the twigs and foliage. Black tupelo is a food source for wood ducks, wild turkeys, robins, pileated woodpeckers, mockingbirds, brown thrashers, thrushes, flickers, and starlings. Brilliant autumn coloring and abundant blue fruit make these trees excellent for shade and ornamental planting. The wood is soft, tough, yellowish-white, and has been used where a light, nonsplitting wood is required, such as in docks and wharves.

Black Tupelo

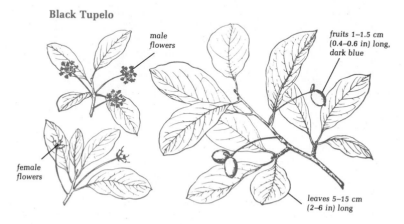

male flowers

fruits 1–1.5 cm (0.4–0.6 in) long, dark blue

female flowers

leaves 5–15 cm (2–6 in) long

Appearance: medium-size tree to 40 m (131 ft), rarely taller, with a rounded crown; trunk straight, to 2 m (6.6 ft) in diameter; trunk of swamp tupelo spreading at the base, often with upright roots rising above the surface of the water. **Bark:** 2–4 cm (0.8–1.6 in) thick, becoming deeply furrowed and with scaly longitudinal ridges, light brown. **Branches:** slender, spreading or drooping; branchlets slender, reddish-brown, slightly hairy at first, becoming smooth. **Winter buds:** 3–6 mm (0.1–0.2 in) long, blunt or rounded at the tip, covered with overlapping, dark brown scales. **Leaves:** alternate, often crowded near the tips of the branchlets, simple, deciduous, broadest near the base to near the tip, *5–15 cm (2–6 in) long, 2.5–10 cm (1–4 in) wide,* blunt or short broad-pointed at the tip, rounded to tapering at the base, entire, wavy, and rarely with coarse irregular teeth along the margin, dark green and shiny above, paler and often hairy below; leafstalks 1–2.5 cm (0.4–1 in) long. **Flowers:** male flowers in dense, many-flowered heads, the heads on slender, hairy stalks; *female flowers produced in 2 to several flowers per cluster.* **Fruits:** often in 2s or 3s, egg-shaped to broadest near the middle, *1–1.5 cm (0.4–0.6 in) long,* rounded at the ends, *dark blue,* with a thin, bitter-tasting flesh surrounding a hard stone, 10- to 12-ribbed in swamp tupelo.

The Olax Family   Olacaceae

This is a small family of 25 genera and about 125 species of tropical plants, most of which are found in Africa and Asia. Members include trees, shrubs, and woody vines. They are recognized by their simple, alternately-placed leaves with smooth margins, their small flowers in sideways-extending clusters. Each flower has 4 to 6 petals and sepals, 4 to 12 stamens opposite the petals, and a 5-celled pistil; and a 1-seeded, hanging stone-fruit or berry. Some genera have large thorns or spikes on their branchlets. Two genera, each with a single species, occur in North America.

Key to Olax Genera

Gulf Graytwig

A. Branches and branchlets armed with unbranched sharp-pointed spines; petals free, not united into a tube **Tallowwood, p. 710**

B. Branches and branchlets unarmed; petals united into a tube with only the tips free **Graytwig, p. 711**

The Tallowwood Genus
Ximenia L.

Tallowwood, with 5 distinctive species, is widely distributed around the globe. The genus was named after Francisco Ximenes, a 16th-century Dominican priest who, in 1615, published a book on the plants and animals of Mexico. The tallowwood (*Ximenia americana* L.) is the lone North American species.

This small group of trees and shrubs are parasitic on the roots of other trees. The branches and branchlets are armed with sharp unbranched spines. Leaves are evergreen, entire, broadest near the base or the middle and pointed at the tip. Flowers are arranged in small clusters and have 4 or 5 petals and 8 or 10 stamens. The fruit is like a small plum with a fleshy outer part and a hard stony center.

Tallowwood, Hog Plum
Ximenia americana L.

Tallowwood, a shrub or short tree, is known in tropical regions around the world. In North America, its range covers peninsular Florida and the Keys; it also occurs south to Brazil, on Africa's west coast, the Indian peninsula, and many islands in Oceania and the South Pacific. It is common in arid soils, along shores down to the high-tide mark, and in dry forest regions at elevations up to 150 m (492 ft). It also occurs in coastal hammocks and along roadsides and trails in Florida, but is most frequently encountered in the peninsular scrubland as a low, spiny shrub with vine-like branches. Its tree-form resembles members of the citrus family. This small tree often grows as a parasite on the roots of other trees.

Both the flowers and fruit are present throughout the year. The yellow flowers are produced in small clusters on delicate stalks at or near the leaf bases; the fruits are yellow and plum-like, sour-sweet, and edible, though not delectible. Hydrocyanic acid can be extracted from the plant; eating too many fruits can bring about toxic aftereffects.

The wood is very heavy, tough, close-grained, brownish-red, with lighter-colored sapwood. Tallowwood is easily workable and is quite handsome when polished. It is sometimes used as a substitute for sandalwood, hence the common name of false sandalwood. The bark is very acidic and is occasionally employed as a tanning agent.

Tallowwood

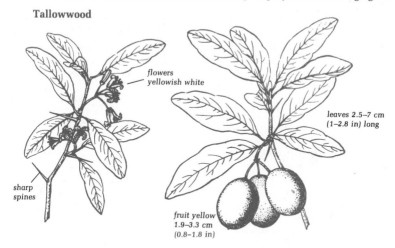

flowers yellowish white

leaves 2.5–7 cm (1–2.8 in) long

sharp spines

fruit yellow 1.9–3.3 cm (0.8–1.8 in)

Appearance: *low shrub* or *short tree*, growing to 9 m (30 ft), with a narrow *irregular crown* and *twisted form;* trunk crooked and narrow, generally 8–12 cm, rarely to 25 (3.2–4.7 in, rarely to 9.8) in diameter. **Bark:** thin and smooth, red-brown, very astringent. **Branchlets:** spreading, crooked or twisted, *armed with stout, straight spines* 0.8–2.5 cm (0.3–1 in) long, located singly at joints on the branchlets; reddish-brown when new becoming gray with age; angled, smooth, sometimes thickly covered with lenticels. **Leaves:** alternate, evergreen, simple, broadest at the middle, 2.5–7 cm (1–2.8 in) long, 1.2–2.5 cm (0.5–1 in) wide; rounded, notched, or pointed at the tip, gradually tapering to a wedge-shaped base; slightly thick and leather-textured, margins smooth and slightly curled under; upper surface bright shiny green; paler below; leafstalk slender, 0.5–1 cm (0.2–0.4 in) long. **Flowers:** in short-stalked clusters of 2 to 4, fragrant, *yellowish-white,* emerging from the leaf junctions, to 1.2 cm (0.5 in) in width, with 4 petals very hairy on the inner surfaces, curled and narrow; 8 erect stamens borne at the base of the ovary; pistil oblong and green. **Fruits:** *plum-like yellow, plum-shaped* to round, *1.9–3.3 cm (0.8–1.8 in) long, 1.6–2.5 cm (0.7–1 in) wide,* with a *single, light-red pit.*

The Graytwig Genus

Schoepfia Schreb.

The 12 or 14 species comprising this genus have managed to spread out over an impressive range. In the Americas, the graytwig genus extends from the southernmost parts of Florida and California to Brazil and Peru. It also occurs from southern Japan and southern and western China to the East Indies and the eastern Himalayas. The genus is named in honor of a German physician and botanist, Johann David Schoepf, who traveled in North America and the West Indies during the 18th century. A single species, Gulf graytwig (*S. chrysophylloides*), occurs in North America.

Members are trees or shrubs with slender, unarmed (thornless) branchlets; the alternate, simple leaves are entire, leathery, and have short stems. The bell-shaped flowers bloom at the leaf bases, either singly or in pairs, with 4 to 6 outward curling petals that are united at the base. The fruits are nearly enclosed in a large floral disk, and the stone is papery or brittle-textured.

Gulf Graytwig, Whitewood

Schoepfia chrysophylloides (A. Rich.) Planch.

The Gulf graytwig is a short, tropical tree ranging from Miami southward to Venezuela. It occurs in sandy or coral-based soils, from sea level to 150 m (492 ft) in elevation, in hammocks and in drier seasonal forests. These uncommon trees are commercially unimportant and little is known about their natural history. Flowers and fruits are produced throughout the year.

The tree is short to 10 m (33 ft), and erect, with a narrow irregular crown composed of upraised, slender but crooked branches, and zigzag, smooth, gray branchlets. The trunk may reach a diameter of 45 cm (18 in), but is usually much smaller. The thin, gray-brown bark is close and deeply furrowed. The simple leaves are 3–7.5 cm (1.2–3 in) long, 1.9–3.2 cm (0.8–1.8 in) wide, blunt or sharply pointed at the tip, and often asymmetrically wedge-shaped at the base. The pink or red flowers are produced in groups of 1 to 3 in the junctions of the leaves; each flower has short stalk, a shallowly 4-lobed calyx, and **4 petals fused to form a tube 2–4 mm (0.1 in) long.** The stone fruit is olive-shaped and scarlet red, 1–1.2 cm (0.4–0.5 in) long, and contains up to 3 seeds.

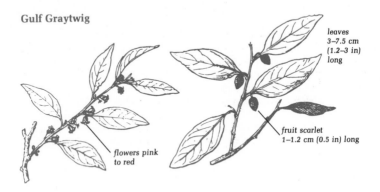

Gulf Graytwig

leaves
3–7.5 cm
(1.2–3 in)
long

fruit scarlet
1–1.2 cm (0.5 in) long

flowers pink
to red

The Spindle Tree Family

Celastraceae

This is a large family of 55 genera and 850 species, occurring primarily in tropical and subtropical regions of the world, but also in temperate regions of North America, Europe, and Asia. Six genera containing 7 species are native to North America. Four of them are tropical and occur only in southern Florida; another is native to the Southwest. Members of this family are of limited economic importance. Some yield oils used in cooking or making soap, yellow dye, fine-grained wood for small objects, and extracts used in medicines.

Members are trees and shrubs that are rarely viny, with opposite (rarely alternate) simple leaves. Flowers are small, bisexual or male or female; each flower has 3 to 5 sepals, 3 to 5 free petals, 5 stamens, and a single pistil. Fruits are capsules, berries, berry-like, or dry and winged.

Key to Spindle Tree Genera

A. Trees with distinct evergreen or deciduous leaves.

   1. Leaves alternate.

      a. Leaves 2.5–4 cm (1–1.6 in) long, grayish-green; fruits 3- or 4-angled capsules; trees of southern Florida   **Mayten, p. 713**

      b. Leaves 4–6.8 cm (1.6–2.7 in) long, yellowish-green; fruits berry-like, rounded; trees of the Florida Keys
                    Schaefferia, p. 714

Eastern Wahoo

Falsebox

   2. Leaves opposite.

      a. Leaves sharply toothed along the margin; trees of temperate regions; includes wahoos   **Euonymus, p. 715**

      b. Leaves entire or with a few rounded teeth; trees of tropical regions of Florida.

         (1) Flowers bisexual; fruits red; trees of southern Florida
                      Crossopetalum, p. 717

         (2) Flowers male or female, occurring on separate trees; fruits dark blue to black; trees of southern Florida
                      Falsebox, p. 717

B. Tree leafless most of year; branches dense, very spiny   **Canotia, p. 718**

Canotia

The Mayten Genus   *Maytenus* Molina

This is a medium-size genus of about 200 species distributed throughout most of tropical and subtropical America. One species, the Florida mayten, occurs in southern Florida. Some species are attractive and are grown in subtropical areas as ornamentals. Members of this genus are shrubs or small trees with simple, alternate, evergreen

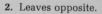

leaves. Flowers are bisexual, sometimes with male and female flowers as well, and produced singly or in clusters. Floral parts are in 5s. Fruits are small, 2- or 4-parted capsules.

Florida Mayten
Maytenus phyllanthoides Benth.

Florida mayten grows in scattered coastal areas of western Florida, extreme southern Florida, and the Keys. It is found in hammocks and sandy dunes but is also native to Mexico and Central America. Small white flowers are produced in spring or summer, with the red fruits maturing by winter. Birds eat the fleshy covering of the seeds and in the process disperse the seeds.

Florida mayten is usually a shrub or small tree to 6 m (20 ft), with a short trunk, and thin, smooth, pale gray bark. The simple, *alternate, evergreen* leaves are widest near the tip, *2.5–4 cm (1–1.6 in) long,* 1.2–2 cm (0.5–0.8 in) wide, rounded or notched at the tip, entire and sometimes wavy along the margin, leathery, and *grayish-green.* Flowers are solitary or in small clusters in the junction of the leaves, with a tiny 5-lobed calyx, 5 white, rounded petals, 5 stamens (sometimes absent), and a single pistil. *Fruits are 3- or 4-angled capsules,* broadest near the rounded tip, 6–12 mm (0.2–0.5 in) long, short-stalked, splitting open to expose 2 to 4 small seeds.

The Schaefferia Genus
Schaefferia Jacq.

This is a small genus of 5 species of subtropical and tropical regions of the Americas. One species, yellowwood, is native to the U.S. only in southern Florida. The species are of little economic value; fuel and limited amounts of lumber are used in the West Indies.

Members of this genus are shrubs or trees with simple, alternate, evergreen leaves. Flowers are either male or female and they occur on separate trees. Floral parts are in 4s. Fruits are small, berry-like, and fleshy.

Yellowwood
Schaefferia frutescens Jacq.

This rare North American tree is found only on some of the Florida Keys where it occurs in hammocks. Yellowwood also is native to the Bahamas, the West Indies, Mexico, and northern South America. Flowering is in spring with the bright-red fruits maturing in late fall. The bright-yellow wood is hard and heavy but not used commercially because the trees are too small.

Yellowwoods are trees to 12 m (40 ft), with upright branches forming a narrow rounded crown, and thin, pale brown bark. The *alternate, evergreen leaves* are broadest above or near the middle, *4–6.8 cm (1.6–2.7 in) long,* 1.2–2.5 cm (0.5–1 in) wide, pointed to rounded at the tip, entire and usually rolled under along the margins, **yellowish-green** and smooth. Tiny male and female flowers occur in separate small clusters in the junctions of the leaves. Fruits are **berry-like,** globe-shaped, 5–8 mm (0.2–0.3 in) in diameter, bright red, and containing 2 seeds.

The Euonymus Genus

Euonymus L.

This is a large genus of about 175 species of trees and shrubs of temperate and subtropical regions of the world, occurring mostly from the Himalaya Mountains to China and Japan. There are 4 species native to North America, 2 of which are trees. In addition, several species have been introduced into cultivation in North America. The most widely cultivated is winged euonymus *(Euonymus alatus)*, a shrub with conspicuous and distinctive corky wings on the branchlets.

Members of this genus are shrubs or trees with 4-angled branchlets and opposite (rarely alternate and whorled) evergreen or deciduous, leaves. Flowers are usually bisexual, solitary or in small clusters in the junction of the leaves. Floral parts are usually in 4s or 5s. Fruits are capsules, usually 4- or 5-celled, each cell containing 1 or 2 seeds.

Key to Euonymus Species

Eastern Wahoo

A. Flowers with 4 calyx lobes, 4 petals, and 4 stamens; fruits usually deeply 4-lobed; trees of eastern and midwestern U.S. and southern Canada
Eastern wahoo, p. 715

B. Flowers with 5 calyx lobes, 5 petals, and 5 stamens; fruits usually deeply 3-lobed; trees of western Washington, Oregon, and California
Western wahoo, p. 716

Eastern Wahoo

Euonymus atropurpureus Jacq.

This is a common shrub or small tree of eastern North America, including the Midwest. It usually occurs in open woodlands, thickets, woodland borders, hillsides, and ravines. The largest trees are found in deep, rich humus soils. They grow in association with many other trees including dogwood, eastern redbud, hawthorn, sycamore, white oak, and northern red oak.

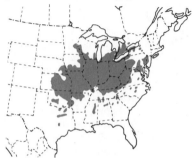

Eastern wahoo is a relatively fast-growing, short-lived tree. The dark-purple flowers appear in spring with fruits maturing in fall but often persisting on the branchlets into winter. The seeds are eaten by many species of birds. Whitetail deer eat the young branchlets and leaves. The nearly white wood is dense and hard, but the trees are too small to be commercially valuable. The trees are sometimes planted for their attractive red leaves in autumn and persistent fruits.

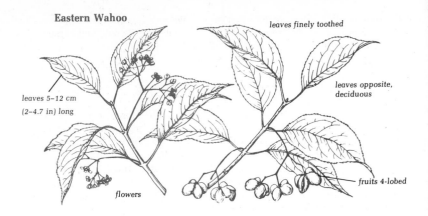

Eastern Wahoo

leaves finely toothed

leaves opposite, deciduous

leaves 5–12 cm (2–4.7 in) long

fruits 4-lobed

flowers

Appearance: small shrub or tree to 8 m (26.3 ft), with a rounded crown; trunk straight; branching close to the ground, to 18 cm (7.1 in) in diameter. **Bark:** thin, 2–4 mm (0.1 in) thick, smooth or with thin scales, ash gray. **Branches:** stout, spreading; branchlets often 4-angled when young, green turning brown with age. **Winter buds:** 2–4 mm (0.1 in) long, broadest near the base and pointed at the tip, covered with narrow, overlapping scales. **Leaves:** simple, *opposite, deciduous,* broadest near the base to near the middle, 5–12 cm (2–4.7 in) long, 2.5–5 cm (1–2 in) wide, long-pointed at the tip, broadly narrowing to rounded at the base, *finely toothed along the margin,* light green and smooth above, paler and often sparsely hairy beneath; leafstalks slender, 1–1.5 cm (0.4–0.6 in) long. **Flowers:** produced in 6- to 18-flowered, branched clusters on slender stalks 2.5–5 cm (1–2 in) long, in the junction of the leaves; each flower with a small, *4-lobed calyx, 4 rounded petals, 4 stamens,* and a single pistil. **Fruit:** a deeply, *4-lobed capsule,* 10–14 mm (0.4–0.6 in) in diameter, reddish-purple to purplish, splitting open to expose the seeds.

Western Wahoo   *Euonymus occidentalis* Nutt. ex Torr.

This small tree is native to southern Washington, western Oregon, and coastal regions of central and northern California. It also occurs in southern California. Western Wahoo grows on moist wooded slopes and in canyons in mixed coniferous and hardwood forests and with coastal red-woods. A tree of lower elevations, it is seldom found above 1,800 m (5,906 ft). Flowering is from April to June with the fruits maturing in autumn.

Western wahoo is a shrub or tree to 6 m (20 ft), with an open, irregular crown. The *opposite, deciduous leaves* are broadest near the base, 3–9 cm (1.2–3.5 in) long, 1.5–5 cm (0.6–2 in) wide, short pointed at the tip, tapering at the base, finely toothed along the margin. Flowers in 1- to 5-

flowered stalked clusters in the junction of the leaves; each **flower** with a **5-lobed calyx, 5 rounded, brownish-purple petals, 5 stamens,** and a single pistil. Fruits are deeply **3-lobed capsules,** rounded and depressed at the tip, splitting open to release the small seeds.

The Crossopetalum Genus Crossopetalum P. Browne

This small genus of about 18 species is confined to tropical regions of the Americas. Two species are native to North America, only in southern Florida. Christmas berry (Crossopetalum ilicifolium) is a low shrub with spiny leaf margins and often grows in pine woods. Florida crossopetalum is a shrub or small tree with entire or rounded-toothed margins.

    Members of this genus are shrubs or trees with opposite, leathery, evergreen leaves. Small flowers are produced singly or in clusters and consist of a 4- or 5-lobed calyx, 4 or 5 petals, 5 stamens, and a single pistil. Fruits are small, berry-like, fleshy or dry.

Florida Crossopetalum Crossopetalum rhacoma Crantz

This species is native to southern Florida, including the Keys, but also occurs in the West Indies, Mexico, and northern South America. In Florida, it grows in hammocks and in pine dominated woodlands. Red to purplish flowers and small dark fruits occur throughout the year.

    Florida crossopetalum is a shrub or tree to 6 m (20 ft), with a short trunk and slender branchlets. The simple, **opposite,** or in 3s, **evergreen leaves** are widest at the middle or near the base, 1–4 cm (0.4–1.6 in) long, 0.5–2 cm (0.2–0.8 in) wide, rounded to pointed at the tip, tapering to a narrow base, **entire or with shallow, rounded teeth,** leathery, yellowish-green, and smooth above. **Flowers** are tiny, **bisexual,** and produced in long-stalked clusters in the junction of the leaves. Each flower has a 4-lobed calyx, 4 petals, 4 stamens, and a single pistil. **Fruits** are **berry-like,** egg-shaped, 5–7 mm (0.2–0.3 in) long, red, fleshy, stalked, and containing 1 or 2 seeds.

The Falsebox Genus Gyminda (Griseb.) Sarg.

This small genus contains 2 species native to tropical America. One of them, the false-box, just reaches North America in southern Florida. Both species are seldom seen because they are uncommon and don't attract the eye. They are of no economic importance, though the fruits are thought to be a minor food source to birds.

    Members of this genus are shrubs or trees with 4-angled branchlets and simple, opposite, evergreen leaves. The tiny flowers are male or female and occur on separate trees. Fruits are small, berry-like, and usually 1- to 2-seeded.

Falsebox Gyminda latifolia (Sw.) Urban

This species is rare in southern Florida, and in the Keys where it grows in hammocks. It is native also to the West Indies and Mexico. Falsebox is largely restricted to lower elevation coastal regions of limestone soils.

Falsebox are shrubs or trees to 8 m (26 ft), with a short trunk, and thin, reddish-brown bark. Branchlets are usually 4-angled. The *opposite, evergreen leaves* are widest near the middle to near the tip, 3.8–5 cm (1.5–2 in) long, 2–2.8 cm (0.8–1.1 in) wide, usually rounded at the tip, tapering at the base, *entire to sparsely rounded-toothed along the margin,* light green to yellow-green and smooth above. Flowers are *male or female,* produced in few-flowered, short, branched clusters in

the junction of the leaves. Fruits are rounded to egg-shaped, 5–8 mm (0.2–0.3 in) in diameter, fleshy, *dark blue to black,* and contain 1 or 2 seeds.

The Canotia Genus

Canotia Torrey

This genus contains a single species, the canotia, of southwestern U.S. and Mexico. So the information given for the species is the same for the genus.

Canotia

Canotia holacantha Torr.

This interesting species is native to central and western Arizona, southern Utah, and adjacent northern Mexico. It is sometimes common on the drier slopes and hillsides in shrub dominated vegetation and desert from 650 to 1,600 m (2,133–5,249 ft) elevation. Unlike most North American trees and shrubs, canotia is leafless most of the year. *Canotia resembles the paloverde but is more densely branched and upright.* The trees are moderately long-lived, living over

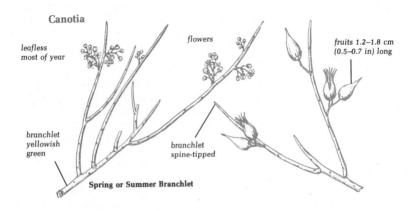

Canotia

leafless most of year

flowers

fruits 1.2–1.8 cm (0.5–0.7 in) long

branchlet yellowish green

branchlet spine-tipped

Spring or Summer Branchlet

100 years. Greenish-white flowers are produced from May to August with the small fruits maturing in fall. They are of little value to wildlife aside from providing cover for small birds.

Canotia is a shrub or tree to 6 m (20 ft), with a dense, irregularly rounded crown, a short trunk, and deeply furrowed light brown bark. The branches and branchlets are erect, **yellowish-green, densely clustered, and spine-tipped.** The leaves are **small, scale-like, and early deciduous.** Flowers are produced in tiny 3- to 8-flowered clusters along the branchlets. The flowers consist of a 5-lobed calyx, 5 petals, 5 short stamens, and a single pistil. Fruits are dry capsules, egg-shaped, 1.2–1.8 cm (0.5–0.7 in) long, with a beak 6–8 mm (0.2–0.3 in) long, splitting open to release the 1 or 2 flattened, winged seeds.

The Holly Family   Aquifoliaceae

There are only 3 genera in this family but about 400 species. Only 1 genus, the hollies, occurs in North America, and it contains about 380 species. Family members are widely distributed in tropical and temperate regions of the Americas, Europe, Africa, Asia, and Australia. The family is of limited commercial value. Some species yield a hard, white wood; others are valuable as decorative plants because of the evergreen leaves and berries.

The description of family characteristics will be omitted since only the holly genus occurs in North America.

The Holly Genus   *Ilex* L.

Hollies comprise a large genus of perhaps 380 species of tropical, subtropical, and temperate regions of the Americas, Europe, Africa, and Asia. There are 11 species reaching tree size in North America, although there are other totally shrubby species. The native species occur only in the eastern, southeastern, or southcentral regions of the U.S. Many foreign species have been introduced, but none are as well known as the English holly *(Ilex aquifolium)*. English holly was introduced into North America in colonial days and, like the American holly, has dense, spiny, evergreen leaves and bright red berries on the female trees. Its flowers and fruits are produced on the previous year's branchlets, while in the American holly they are borne on the current year's branchlets.

The trees are spring flowering with the fruits maturing by fall. Fruits are only produced on trees bearing female flowers. Trees producing male flowers supply the pollen, but the flowers do not develop into the berry-like fruits. The fruits are an important food source to game and songbirds. The wood is light colored, tough, not very strong, and of very little economic value.

Members of this genus are trees or shrubs with alternate, simple, evergreen or deciduous leaves. Flowers are tiny, white to greenish-white, and usually male or female. Each flower is generally composed of a 4- to 6-lobed calyx, 4 to 6 free to partly fused petals, 4 to 6 stamens (in male flowers), and a single pistil with a superior, 4- to 8-celled ovary.

Key to Holly Species

A. Leaves evergreen.

    1. Leaves regularly or irregularly toothed, the teeth and leaf spine-tipped.

American Holly

        a. Leaves stiff, leathery, with large, coarse, spine-tipped teeth; fruits bright red to orange, rarely yellow; trees of eastern, southeastern, and southcentral U.S.
                    American holly, p. 723

        b. Leaves leathery, but not stiff, with remote shallow teeth; fruits black, trees of southeastern Coastal Plain
                    Large gallberry, p. 724

    2. Leaves entire or toothed, the teeth rounded to sharp-pointed, but the teeth and tip not spine-tipped.

        a. Leaves entire along the margin.

            (1) Leaves narrow, uniformly wide, 1–4 cm (0.4–1.6 in) long, 2–7 mm (0.1–0.3 in) wide; trees of southeastern Coastal Plain   **Myrtle dahoon, p. 725**

            (2) Leaves broadest near the middle or just below, 4–7.5 cm (1.6–3 in) long, 2.5–4 cm (1–1.6 in) wide; trees of southern Florida   **Tawnyberry holly, p. 725**

Dahoon

        b. Leaves with rounded or sharp-pointed teeth along the margin, at least the upper half.

            (1) Leaves 3–10 cm (1.2–4 in) long, with sharp-pointed teeth on the upper half; trees of southeastern Coastal Plain
                    Dahoon, p. 725

            (2) Leaves 1–4.2 cm (0.4–1.7 in) long, with rounded teeth along the margin; trees of southeastern U.S.   **Yaupon, p. 726**

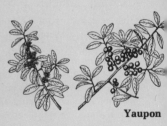

Yaupon

B. Leaves deciduous, falling away in autumn.

    1. Trees in fruit.

        a. Seeds smooth on the back, usually with more than 5 seeds per fruit.

            (1) Leaves usually hairy beneath; sepals at base of fruit smooth; trees of eastern North America
            Common winterberry, p. 727

Common Winterberry

(2) Leaves smooth beneath; sepals at base of fruit hairy; trees of northeastern coastal U.S.**Smooth winterberry, p. 728**

b. Seeds regularly or irregularly furrowed on the back, usually with 5 or fewer seeds per fruit.

(1) Leaves with rounded teeth; trees of southern U.S.   **Possum haw, p. 729**

(2) Leaves with sharp-pointed teeth or entire.

(a) Leaves rounded or nearly so at the base; finely hairy beneath; leaves appearing wrinkled due to slightly sunken veins; trees of southeastern Coastal Plain   **Sarvis holly, p. 730**

(b) Leaves usually tapering to a narrow base, occasionally rounded; usually smooth beneath; leaves not appearing wrinkled.

(b1) Leaves 6–16 cm (2.4–6.3 in) long, pointed at the tip; trees of eastern U.S.
Mountain winterberry, p. 730

(b2) Leaves 4–8 cm (1.6–3.2 in) long, the tip usually contracted to a narrow point; trees of southeastern Coastal Plain   **Carolina holly, p. 731**

2. Trees in flower.

a. Trees with male flowers.

(1) Flowers in branched clusters.

(a) Leaves gradually tapering to a narrow base.

(a1) Leaves usually hairy beneath; calyx lobes hairy on the margins; trees of eastern North America
Common winterberry, p. 727

(a2) Leaves smooth beneath, except for a few hairs on the veins; trees of northeastern coastal areas
Smooth winterberry, p. 728

(b) Leaves rounded or nearly so at the
(Continued)

Possum Haw

Mountain Winterberry

Common Winterberry

base; rare trees of southeastern Coastal Plain **Sarvis holly, p. 730**

(2) Flowers stalked, several present but not on branched clusters.

(a) Leaves with rounded teeth; flowers with 4 sepals, 4 petals, and 4 stamens **Possum haw, p. 729**

(b) Leaves with sharp-pointed teeth; flowers usually with 5 sepals, 5 petals, and 5 stamens.

(b1) Leaves 6–16 cm (2.4–6.3 in) long, tip pointed; trees of eastern U.S.
Mountain winterberry, p. 730

(b2) Leaves 4–8 cm (1.6–3.2 in) long; the tip usually contracted to a narrow point; trees of southeastern Coastal Plain **Carolina holly, p. 731**

b. Trees with female flowers.

(1) Flowers or immature fruits with a long stalk, 7 mm (0.3 in) long or more.

(a) Leaves gradually tapering to a long narrow base; trees of southeastern and southcentral U.S.
Possum haw, p. 729

(b) Leaves rounded or nearly so at the base; trees of southeastern Coastal Plain **Sarvis holly, p. 730**

(2) Flowers or immature fruits short-stalked, 6 mm (0.2 in) long or less.

(a) Flowers with hairy calyx lobes.

(a1) Leaves smooth beneath.

(a1a) Leaves 6–16 cm (2.4–6.3 in) long; pointed at the tip; trees of eastern U.S.
Mountain winterberry, p. 730

(a1b) Leaves 4–8 cm (1.6–3.2 in) long; the tip usually contracted into a narrow point; trees of southeastern Coastal Plain **Carolina holly, p. 731**

(a2) Leaves usually hairy beneath; trees of eastern North

Possum Haw

Mountain Winterberry

America
Common winterberry, p. 727

Common Winterberry

(b) Flowers with smooth calyx lobes.

(b1) Leaves with rounded teeth; trees of southern U.S.
Possum haw, p. 729

(b2) Leaves with sharp-pointed teeth.

(b2a) Flowers principally on long branchlets of the current year; trees of northeastern U.S.
Smooth winterberry, p. 728

(b2b) Flowers principally produced on short, spur shoots.

* *Leaves 6–16 cm (2.4–6.3 in) long, pointed at the tip; trees of eastern U.S.*
Mountain winterberry, p. 730

* *Leaves 4–8 cm (1.6–3.2 in) long; the tip usually constricted to a narrow point; trees of southeastern Coastal Plain* **Carolina holly, p. 731**

American Holly

Ilex opaca Ait.

This attractive tree is native to the eastern, southeastern, and southcentral regions of the U.S. It grows in several soil types, but is generally found in deep, moist bottomlands. American holly often grows in association with sweet gum, red maple, hackberry, southern red oak, and southern magnolia.

This is a slow-growing, long-lived species, especially popular in fall and near Christmas. Of all the native hollies, this is the most sought-after because of the evergreen, spiny leaves, and bright red berries. It is grown as an ornamental. There are over 300 varieties or cultivated forms. The fruits are eaten by over 20 species of songbirds and gamebirds including thrushes, mockingbirds, robins, catbirds, grouse, quail, and turkey.

The nearly white wood is tough, dense, and turns brown with age and exposure to air. The trees are generally too small to yield commercial quantities of wood. It has been used in making small wooden wares.

Appearance: tree to 15 m (49 ft), rarely taller, with a pyramid-shaped crown; trunk straight, short, to 60 cm (23.6 in) in diameter, rarely larger. **Bark:** thin to moderately

American Holly

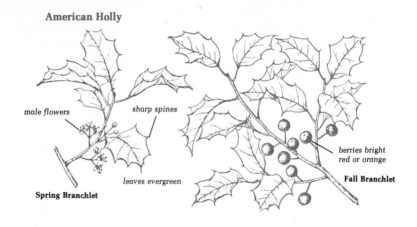

male flowers   sharp spines

berries bright
red or orange

leaves evergreen   **Fall Branchlet**

Spring Branchlet

thick, to 12 mm (0.5 in) thick, rough due to wart-like processes, light gray. **Branches:** short, slender; branchlets stout, covered with fine, rust-colored hairs, becoming smooth and pale brown with age. **Winter buds:** 3–8 mm (0.1–0.3 in) long, pointed or rounded at the tip, covered with narrow, overlapping scales. **Leaves:** alternate, simple, **evergreen,** broadest near the base or near the middle, 4–10 cm (1.6–4 in) long, 2–4.8 cm (0.8–1.9 in) wide, pointed at the tip, rounded at the base, **almost entire to coarsely toothed, the teeth ending in sharp spines, stiff, leathery,** dark green to dull yellow-green and smooth above, paler beneath; leafstalks short, stout, grooved. **Flowers:** male and female flowers on separate trees; male flowers in 3- to 12-flowered clusters in the junction of the leaves; female flowers solitary or in 2s or 3s in the junction of the leaves. **Fruits:** berry-like, rounded to egg-shaped, 8–12 mm (0.3–0.5 in) in diameter, **bright red or orange, rarely yellow,** containing 4 irregularly grooved seeds.

Large Gallberry   *Ilex coriacea* (Pursh) Chapm.

This small evergreen holly is native to the southeastern Coastal Plain from Virginia to Florida, and west to Texas. It grows in low, wet areas such as swamps, bays, river floodplains, and along streams and ponds. Large gallberry is one of the few native hollies with black fruits. Flowers appear in April and May, while the fruits mature in September or October. The fruits do not stay on the branchlets into winter or spring as with most other species.

Large gallberry is a shrub or tree to 6 m (20 ft), with finely hairy young branchlets which are often sticky. The alternate, simple, **evergreen leaves** are broadest near or above the middle, 3.6–6.8 cm (1.5–2.7 in) long, 1.5–4 cm (0.6–1.6 in) wide, pointed at the tip, with **irregular and remotely spaced spine-tipped teeth,** dark green and smooth above. Male and female flowers are on separate trees, flowers produced in few to many-flowered (male flowers only) clusters in the junction of the leaves. **Fruits** are **berry-like,** rounded or nearly so, 7–10 mm (0.3–0.4 in) in diameter, **black,** and enclosing several small seeds.

Myrtle Dahoon

Ilex myrtifolia Walt.

This small tree or more often a shrub is native to the southeastern Coastal Plain from North Carolina to central Florida, and west to Louisiana. It grows in low, wet woodlands, swamps, or along streams and ponds. This species is **closely related to the dahoon** and is **distinguished from it by its smaller, narrower leaves.** As in other southeastern species, flowering is in spring with the red fruits maturing in late fall.

Myrtle dahoon is an open shrub or small tree to 8 m (26 ft), with a dense, compacted crown. The alternate simple leaves are **evergreen, narrow and uniformly wide, 1–4 cm (0.4–1.6 in) long, 2–7 mm (0.1–0.3 in) wide,** bristle-tipped, tapering at the base, **entire along the margin,** dark green and smooth above. Male and female flowers occur on separate trees, with flowers produced singly or in few-flowered clusters in the junction of the leaves. Fruits are berry-like, rounded, 6–8 mm (0.2–0.3 in) in diameter, red, and containing several ribbed seeds.

Tawnyberry Holly

Ilex krugiana Loes.

This West Indian holly is restricted in North America to extreme southern Florida. It grows in pinewoods and hammocks. Flowering is in winter with the black fruits maturing in summer. Tawnyberry holly differs from other native hollies by its long-pointed leaf tips.

This is a shrub or small tree to 10 m (33 ft), with an irregular, open crown. The simple, alternate, **evergreen leaves** are **broadest below or near the middle, 4–7.5 cm (1.6–3 in) long, 2.5–4 cm (1–1.6 in) wide,** long pointed at the tip, rounded to broadly tapering at the base, **entire.** Male and female flowers occur on separate trees, produced in short, dense clusters in the junction of the leaves. Fruits are berries, rounded, 5–7 mm (0.2–0.3 in) in diameter, black, containing 3 or 4 smooth seeds.

Dahoon

Ilex cassine L.

This species is native to the southeastern Coastal Plain from Virginia to southern Florida, and west to southeastern Texas. It occurs at lower elevations in moist woods, swamps, and along streams, and grows in association with southern red oak, Nuttall oak, sweet gum, pond pine, willows, and sugarberry. Dahoon is sometimes grown as an ornamental in the southeastern U.S. for its attractive red berries and dense, evergreen leaves.

The trees are slow growing and generally short lived. White flowers are produced in May or June and the red fruits mature in October or November but persist on the branchlets well into winter or spring. The fruits are a valuable food for many species of overwintering songbirds. Turkey, grouse, quail, and small mammals also feed on them. Whitetail deer will browse the young growth. The pale brown wood is soft, light, and of no commercial importance.

Appearance: shrub or small tree to 8 m (26 ft), with a rounded crown, trunk short, branching close to the ground. **Bark:** thin, 2–4 mm (0.1–0.2 in) thick, becoming rough, dark gray. **Branches:** dense, slender, spreading to erect; branchlets finely hairy for 2 or 3 years, turning dark brown with age. **Winter buds:** tiny, 1–2 mm (0.1 in) long, pointed

Dahoon

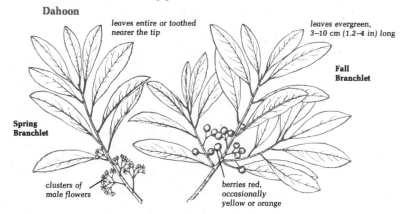

leaves entire or toothed nearer the tip

leaves evergreen, 3–10 cm (1.2–4 in) long

Fall Branchlet

Spring Branchlet

clusters of male flowers

berries red, occasionally yellow or orange

at the tips, hairy. **Leaves:** alternate, simple, *evergreen*, lance-shaped, uniformly wide, or broadest above the middle, 3–10 cm (1.2–4 in) long, 0.5–3 cm (0.2–1.2 in) wide, pointed at the tip, rarely rounded, tapering at the base, *entire or sharply toothed above the middle*, dark shiny green and smooth above on mature leaves, paler beneath; leafstalks 5–10 mm (0.2–0.4 in) long, grooved, hairy to smooth. **Flowers:** unisexual, trees either male or female with a 4-lobed calyx, and 4 white petals; male flowers in short, branched, round-topped clusters in the junctions of the leaves; female flowers solitary or 2- or 3-flowered clusters in the junctions of the leaves. **Fruits:** berry-like, rounded, 6–8 mm (0.2–0.3 in) in diameter, red, occasionally yellow or orange, and containing 4 irregularly grooved seeds.

Yaupon, Cassina   *Ilex vomitoria* Aiton

Yaupon is an evergreen shrub or small tree ranging along the Coastal Plain from Virginia to Florida, and west to Texas and Arkansas. It often forms dense thickets along stream and pond margins and shallow swamp lands. Yaupon is often found growing with slash pine, pond pine, black gum, swamp tupelo, and red maple.

This is a slow-growing species that often multiplies by sending new sprouts up from the roots. Flowering ranges from March to May and fruiting from October through November. The red fruits serve as a food source for wild turkey, quail, and many songbirds. Whitetail deer browse the young twigs and leaves. The almost white wood is hard and durable but the trees are too small for the wood to be of economic value.

Appearance: dense, many-branched shrub or small tree to 8 m (26 ft), with a spreading, rounded crown; trunk short, branching close to the ground. **Bark:** thin, 1–3 mm (0.1 in) thick, light reddish-brown. **Branches:** slender; branchlets stiff, wide spreading, finely hairy when young, turning light gray. **Winter buds:** tiny, 1–2 mm (0.1 in) long, rounded or blunt at the tip, covered with dark brown to nearly black scales. **Leaves:** alternate, simple, *evergreen,* broadest at the middle to uni-

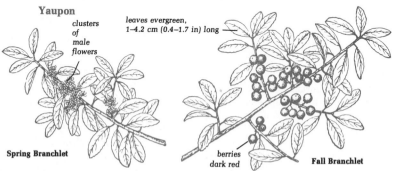

Yaupon

clusters of male flowers

leaves evergreen, 1–4.2 cm (0.4–1.7 in) long

Spring Branchlet

berries dark red

Fall Branchlet

formly wide, 1–4.2 cm (0.4–1.7 in) long, 0.7–1.8 cm (0.3–0.7 in) wide, pointed to nearly rounded at the tip, tapering to a narrow base, ***with rounded teeth along the margin,*** leathery, dark shiny green above and paler beneath. **Flowers:** unisexual, trees either male or female; male flowers in dense, stalked clusters in the junction of the leaves; female flowers solitary or in few-flowered clusters in the junction of the upper leaves. **Fruits:** berry-like, rounded, 5–8 mm (0.2–0.3 in) in diameter, dark red, and containing several grooved seeds.

Common Winterberry

Ilex verticillata (L.) A. Gray

This common plant is native to swamps, bogs, streams, and wet areas ranging from Newfoundland and Quebec, Canada, to Florida and Louisiana. It can be found growing in association with alders, sycamore, maples, sweet gum, sugarberry, and many other lowland trees. Winter branches with the persistent bright red berries are sometimes gathered for use in Christmas decorations.

Like other hollies, common winterberry is slow growing. Flowering is in spring, April to July depending on the latitude, and the fruits mature in late fall. The fruits are eaten by many birds in late winter or early spring. This includes the brown thrasher, robin, mockingbird, catbird, and bluebirds. The twigs, leaves, and fruits

Common Winterberry

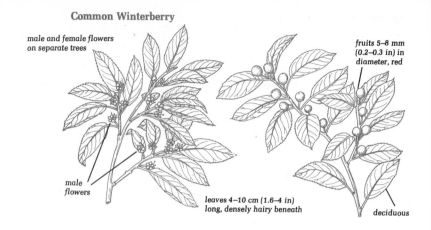

male and female flowers
on separate trees

fruits 5–8 mm
(0.2–0.3 in) in
diameter, red

male
flowers

leaves 4–10 cm (1.6–4 in)
long, densely hairy beneath

deciduous

are of minor importance to mammals, including whitetail deer. The trees never grow large enough to be of commercial value, even for firewood.

Appearance: commonly a shrub or small tree to 8 m (26 ft), with a rounded crown; trunk short, branching close to the ground. **Bark:** thin, 1–2 mm (0.1 in) thick, smooth, brown to dark gray. **Branches:** stout, erect to spreading; branchlets slender, smooth to hairy, turning dark brown with age. **Winter buds:** small, 2–3 mm (0.1 in) long, nearly rounded, covered with overlapping scales. **Leaves:** alternate, simple, *deciduous,* broadest near the base, the middle, or above the middle, 4–10 cm (1.6–4 in) long, 1.5–4.8 cm (0.6–1.9 in) wide, pointed at the tip, *tapering to a narrow base,* sharply toothed along the margin, light to dark green and smooth to sparsely hairy above, *densely hairy beneath;* leafstalks slender, 5–10 mm (0.2–0.4 in) long. **Flowers:** either male or female and on separate trees, with a 4-parted calyx and 4 petals; male flowers in few to many-flowered, short, branched clusters in the junction of the leaves; female flowers solitary or in 3-flowered clusters in the junction of the leaves. **Fruits:** berry-like, rounded, 5–8 mm (0.2–0.3 in) in diameter, red, with 5 to 10 smooth seeds.

Smooth Winterberry   *Ilex laevigata* (Pursh) A. Gray

This species is native to the northeastern U.S., but does extend as far south as South Carolina. It grows at lower elevations, generally in swamps, wet woodlands, and along streams and ponds. Flowering is in spring with red to orange fruits maturing by autumn and persisting into winter, thus making it a popular element in Christmas decorations.

Smooth winterberry is typically a shrub or small tree to 6 m (20 ft), with alternate, simple, *deciduous* leaves. The *leaves* are lance-shaped to broadest near the middle, 4–9 cm (1.6–3.5 in) long, 1.4–3 cm (0.6–1.2 in) wide, pointed at the tip, *tapering to a narrow base,* shallowly toothed along the margin, light to dark shiny green and smooth above, smooth beneath except for some hairs on the main vein. Male and female flowers occur on separate trees. Male flowers are produced in branched clusters in the junction of the leaves. Female flowers are produced singly or in pairs in the junction of the leaves. Fruits are berry-like, rounded, 8–10 mm (0.3–0.4 in) in diameter, orange to red, ***containing several smooth seeds.***

Possum Haw

Ilex decidua Walt.
(synonym: *I. longipes* Chapm.)

This small southern holly extends from Maryland to Florida and west to Missouri and Texas. It grows in such lowland sites as hammocks, stream and pond borders, and floodplains. Possum haw can usually be found growing in association with several

oaks, sweet gum, sycamore, buttonbush, and the American elm. Winter branchlets bearing orange to scarlet berries are gathered for use in Christmas decorations.

It is a relatively fast-growing and short-lived holly. Flowering is in April or May with the fruits maturing in late fall and persisting on the branchlets into winter and early spring. The fruits are eaten by turkey, quail, and numerous songbirds. Whitetail deer will browse the young new growth. The yellowish-white wood is hard

and dense but the trees are too small to be of commercial value.

Possum Haw

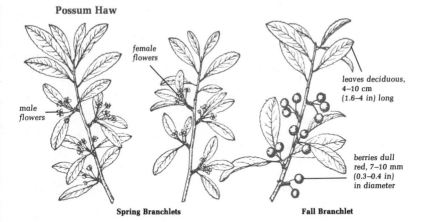

male flowers

female flowers

leaves deciduous, 4–10 cm (1.6–4 in) long

berries dull red, 7–10 mm (0.3–0.4 in) in diameter

Spring Branchlets　　　　　**Fall Branchlet**

Appearance: shrub or small tree to 10 m (33 ft), with an open, spreading crown; trunk short, branching close to the ground, to 20 cm (7.9 in) in diameter. **Bark:** 2–4 mm (0.1–0.2 in) thick, becoming rough with age, light brown. **Branches:** stout, spreading to upright; branchlets slender, smooth, light to silvery gray. **Winter buds:** tiny, 1–3 mm (0.1 in) long, nearly rounded, blunt at the tip, covered with light gray scales. **Leaves:** alternate, simple, ***deciduous,*** broadest near or above the middle, 4–10 cm (1.6–4 in) long, 0.8–3 cm (0.4–1.2 in) wide, rounded to notched at the tip, ***tapering to a narrow base, with shallow rounded teeth along the margin,*** light to dark green and smooth above, paler beneath; leafstalks slender, 0.5–1.5 cm (0.2–0.6 in) long, grooved. **Flowers:** male and female flowers on separate trees; male flowers on slender-stalk, occurring in the junction of the leaves; female flowers short-stalked and produced singly or in pairs in the junction of the leaves. **Fruits:** berry-like, rounded, sometimes depressed on top, 0.7–1 cm (0.3–0.4 in) in diameter, orange or red, containing several, irregularly grooved seeds.

Sarvis Holly

Ilex amelanchier M. A. Curtis

This is the rarest of our native hollies, occurring in widely scattered populations from North Carolina to southern Alabama and Louisiana. It grows in sandhills and in woodlands bordering streams and ponds. Flowering is in April or May with the fruits maturing by October or November.

Sarvis holly is a large shrub or small tree to 5 m (16 ft), with an open, rounded crown. The alternate, simple, *deciduous* leaves are widest near or below the middle, 4–10 cm (1.6–4 in) long, 1.5–4.5 cm (0.6–1.8 in) wide, pointed at the tip, *rounded or nearly so at the base,* entire to finely toothed along the margin, dull green and smooth above, *finely hairy beneath.* Male and female flowers are produced on separate trees in the junction of the leaves. Fruits are berry-like, rounded or nearly so, 7–10 mm (0.3–0.4 in) in diameter, dull red, containing several seeds, each with 2 deep furrows on the back.

Mountain Winterberry

Ilex montana Torr. & Gray

(synonym: *I. monticola* A. Gray)

This species is restricted largely to rich woodlands and mountain slopes from New York and Massachusetts through the southeast to Louisiana. It occurs up to 1,700 m (5,577 ft) in elevation and grows in mixed forest underneath larger trees. Mountain

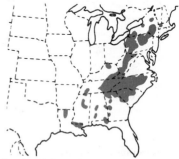

winterberry is occasionally grown for its bright scarlet berries, which persist on the branches long after the leaves have fallen.

The small, white flowers are produced from May to August with the fruits maturing in late fall. The fruits are an important food for many birds including the bluebird, catbird, mockingbird, robin, and hermit thrush. They are eaten to a lesser extent by squirrels, raccoons, and rodents. Whitetail deer browse the young branchlets and leaves, but this holly is not a preferred deer food. The almost white wood is hard and dense but of no commercial value because of the small size of the trees.

Appearance: shrub or small tree to 12 m (39 ft), with an open, often pyramid-shaped crown; trunk short, branching close to the ground, to 20 cm (7.9 in) in diameter, rarely larger. **Bark:** thin, 1–3 mm (0.1 in) thick, becoming warty, light brown. **Branches:** slender, spreading; branchlets slender, often zigzagging, smooth, pale reddish-brown to dark gray. **Winter buds:** 3–4 mm (0.1 in) long, egg-shaped to nearly

Mountain Winterberry

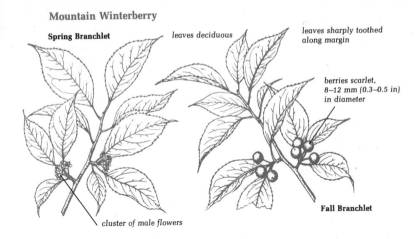

Spring Branchlet   *leaves deciduous*   *leaves sharply toothed along margin*

berries scarlet, 8–12 mm (0.3–0.5 in) in diameter

cluster of male flowers   **Fall Branchlet**

round, covered with slightly overlapping, light brown scales. **Leaves:** alternate, simple, *deciduous,* lance-shaped to broadest near the base, *6–16 cm (2.4–6.3 in)* long, 2.5–6 cm (1–2.4 in) wide, long-pointed at the tip, rounded to tapering at the base, *sharply toothed along the margin,* light to dark green and smooth above, paler and smooth beneath; leafstalks slender, 8–12 mm (0.3–0.5 in) long. **Flowers:** unisexual, the trees either male or female; male flowers 1 to 3 on slender stalks to 12 mm (0.5 in) long and produced in the junctions of the leaves, with a short, 4- or 5-lobed calyx, 4 or 5 broad, white petals 6–8 mm (0.2–0.3 in) across, and 4 or 5 stamens; female flowers on short stalks in the junction of the leaves, similar to male flowers except stamens are absent and a single pistil is present. **Fruits:** berry-like, rounded, 8–12 mm (0.3–0.5 in) in diameter, scarlet, and containing conspicuously ribbed seeds.

Carolina Holly   *Ilex ambigua* (Michx.) Torr.

This is another of the deciduous-leaved species of holly in the southeastern U.S. Unlike most other hollies, this one is native to drier upland woods and rich woodlands, mainly in the Piedmont, but also extending into the Coastal Plain. Flowering is from April to June with the red berries maturing in August or September.

Carolina holly is generally a shrub or less frequently a small tree to 6 m (20 ft), with a broad, rounded crown. *Leaves* are alternate, simple, *deciduous,* lance-shaped to broadest at or above the middle, usually *4–8 cm (1.6–3.2 in) long,* 1.5–3 cm (0.6–1.2 in) wide, pointed at the tip, tapering or rounded at the base, *finely to coarsely toothed,* and usually smooth. Male and female flowers occur on separate trees, male

flowers in clusters, female flowers usually solitary in the junction of the upper leaves. *Fruits* are *berry-like,* rounded, 5–9 mm (0.2–0.4 in) in diameter, red, and *containing* 4, *deeply furrowed seeds.*

The Spurge Family

Euphorbiaceae

This is a very large family of about 300 genera and over 5,000 species. Members occur primarily in tropical regions of the world, but are also represented in the temperate regions of North America, Europe, and Asia. The family is composed of herbs, shrubs, or trees, including some of great economic importance. Rubber, castor and tung oil, tapioca, vegetable tallow, dyes, timber, and the decorative poinsettia are some of the valuable products obtained.

Among the many native species, 7 are large enough to be considered as trees. Two of the introduced species grow wild.

Leaves of members of this family are alternate (rarely opposite), simple (rarely hand-shaped, palmately compound). Flowers are regular, either male or female, and occur on the same plant or different plants. Each flower usually has 5 fused or free calyx lobes, 5 petals (sometimes absent), 1 to many stamens in male flowers, and a single pistil with a usually 3-lobed, superior ovary. Fruits are capsule-like and split open at maturity or berry-like.

Key to Spurge Genera

A. Fruits dry to fleshy capsules, usually 2- or 3-parted, splitting open at maturity.

  1. Branchlets deciduous; leaves appearing to be feather-like compound on the branchlets, entire   **Phyllanthus, p. 733**

  2. Branchlets persistent, leaves simple, entire or toothed.

Sapium

    a. Flowers produced in elongate, slender, un-branched spikes.

      (1) Leaves, flowers, fruits with very milky sap; fruits 2- or 3-parted capsules, 1–1.8 cm (0.4–0.7 in) wide   **Sapium, p. 733**

      (2) Leaves, flowers, fruits not or only slightly milky; fruits 3-parted capsules, 6–9 mm (0.2–0.4 in) wide   **Oysterwood, p. 735**

Oysterwood

    b. Flowers produced singly or in short, dense clusters in the junction of the leaves   **Maidenbush, p. 736**

B. Fruits berry-like or resembling a small apple, fleshy.

  1. Fruits berry-like, ivory white or red; male flowers in short, densely-flowered clusters   **Milkbark, Whitewood, p. 737**

  2. Fruits apple-like, yellowish-green to red; male flowers in slender, unbranched spikes   **Manchineel, p. 738**

Milkbark, Whitewood

The Phyllanthus Genus

Phyllanthus L.

This is a large genus of the tropical regions of the world, especially Africa and Asia. The species are often difficult to identify since the differences between the species are slight. One species, the gooseberry tree, has been introduced into southern Florida.

Members of this genus are herbs, shrubs, or trees with alternate, simple, entire leaves. Flowers are unisexual with male and female flowers on the same plant or on separate plants. Flowers are small, with 4 to 6 sepals, without petals, 3 to 5 stamens (in male flowers), and a single ovary (in female flowers). Fruits are 3-parted capsules.

Gooseberry Tree

Phyllanthus acidus (L.) Skeels

This native of tropical Asia is widely cultivated in tropical regions of the world, including southern Florida. It has escaped from cultivation, reproducing on its own in vacant lots and other disturbed sites.

Gooseberry is a shrub or tree to 10 m (33 ft), with rough, gray bark. The **alternate leaves are spirally arranged and hang along slender branchlets to give the appearance of feather-like (pinnate) compound leaves,** the leaves are broadest near the base, 2.5–7.5 cm (1–3 in) long, 2–4 cm (0.8–1.6 in) wide, entire, and pointed at the tips. Flowers are produced in elongated, slender, branched clusters, the clusters containing both male and female flowers. They are tiny and red to pink. **Fruits are fleshy capsules,** broadest near the flattened tip, greenish-yellow to white, and containing 6 small, brown, flattened seeds.

The Sapium Genus

Sapium P. Br.

This medium-size genus consists of about 100 species of tropical, subtropical, and warm temperate regions. Only 1 species is native to North America. Two others, the Chinese tallowtree and the Brazil sapium, have been introduced and are thought to grow wild. The willow-like Brazil sapium [*Sapium glandulosum* (L.) Morong] has reportedly escaped from cultivation in northwestern Florida. The Chinese tallowtree is more widespread in the southeastern U.S. and is described later in more detail.

Members of this genus are trees or shrubs with milky sap and alternate or opposite, evergreen leaves. The flowers, produced in unbranched spikes, are male or female, occurring on the same tree, or the trees may be either male or female. Male flowers have a 2- or 3-parted calyx, no petals, 2 or 3 stamens; female flowers with a 2- or 3-parted calyx, no petals, stamens absent, and a single pistil with a 2- or 3-parted ovary. Fruits are a 2- or 3-lobed capsule, each segment containing a seed.

Key to Sapium Species

A. Leaves lance-shaped to uniformly wide, finely toothed; fruit a 2-lobed capsule; trees of southern Arizona and northwestern Mexico
  Jumping bean sapium, p. 734
B. Leaves very broad near the base and tapering to a long pointed tip; fruits a 3-lobed capsule; introduced tree, naturalized from South Carolina to Texas **Chinese tallow tree, p. 734**

Jumping Bean Sapium

Jumping Bean Sapium　　　　　　*Sapium biloculare* (S. Wats.) Pax

This is native to southern Arizona and northwestern Mexico where it grows in rocky or gravelly soils along streams and rivers, and in the desert. It normally grows between 300 and 750 m (984–2,461 ft) elevation. The milky sap is poisonous and will cause a

painful swelling if it comes into contact with eyes, nose, or taken internally. The seeds are one of the sources of Mexican jumping beans. The seeds move or jump because of internal movements of the larva of a moth *(Carpcapsa saltitans)*, which infects and inhabits the seeds. The larva slowly consumes the center of the seed and kills it.

Jumping bean sapium is a shrub or small tree to 6 m (20 ft), and with alternate, simple, deciduous *leaves.* They are *lance-shaped to narrow and uniformly wide,* 2–6 cm (0.8–2.4 in) long, and *finely toothed along the margin.* The tiny male or female flowers are produced along a slender spike to 6 cm (2.4 in) in length, entirely with male flowers or with males on the upper half and females on the lower half. *Fruits are 2-lobed capsules,* widest near the tip, 1–1.4 cm (0.4–0.6 in) wide, each lobe containing a rounded, mottled brown seed 10–14 mm (0.4–0.6 in) long.

Jumping Bean Sapium

flowering spike

fruits 2-lobed capsules

leaves 2–6 cm (0.8–2.4 in) long

Chinese Tallow Tree　　　　　　*Sapium sebiferum* (L.) Roxb.

This species, native to China and Japan, was introduced as an ornamental or shade tree. It now grows wild in the Coastal Plain from South Carolina to Texas and Oklahoma. Chinese tallow tree is fast growing and has adapted to a wide range of soils. All parts contain a poisonous, milky juice. Flowering is in spring with the fruits and seeds maturing by fall. The waxy coating on the seeds is used by the Chinese for making soap and candles. In autumn, the trees are especially attractive because the red leaves contrast sharply with the white, waxy seeds.

Chinese tallow tree is a medium-size spreading tree to 15 m (49 ft), with smooth (widely fissured on older trees) reddish-brown bark. The alternate, simple *leaves* (resembling poplar leaves) are *widest near the base,* 4–8 cm (1.6–3.2 in) long, tapering to a long pointed tip, ***entire but wavy along the margin,*** and with 2 glands at the base of the blade. Flowers are produced in long, slender spikes to 10 cm (4 in) long, male flowers above, female flowers near the the base. ***Fruits are rounded, 3-lobed capsules 1.2–1.8 cm (0.5–0.7 in) in diameter,*** the outer falling away at maturity leaving the large white, waxy seeds.

The Oysterwood Genus

Gymnanthes Sw.

This is a small genus of perhaps 12 species distributed in tropical regions of the Americas. One species, the oysterwood, is native to North America in southern Florida. None of the species is of economic importance.

Members of this genus are trees or shrubs with alternate, simple, evergreen leaves. Flowers are tiny, male or female, but produced on the same trees, the males on elongated spikes, the females at the base of the spikes. Fruits are 3-lobed capsules.

Oysterwood

Gymnanthes lucida Sw.

Oysterwood is common in hammocks, low woods, and coastal areas of southern Florida, the Keys, the West Indies, and Mexico. Small green flowers are produced in spring with the fruiting capsules maturing by autumn. The dark brown, yellow-streaked wood is very hard, heavy, durable, and is used in making small wooden objects.

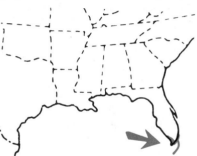

Oysterwoods are trees or shrubs to 10 m (33 ft), with a narrow crown, and smooth to fissured, reddish-brown to gray bark. The alternate, ***simple, evergreen*** leaves are broadest near the base, 6–14 cm (2.4–5.5 in) long, entire to remotely toothed, dark green and shiny above. ***Male flowers occur in dense, elongated spikes 2–5 cm*** (0.8–2 in) ***long; female flowers 2 or 3, each long-stalked and produced at the base of the male spikes.*** Fruits are 3-lobed capsules broadest above the middle to rounded, depressed on top, 6–9 mm (0.2–0.4 in) in diameter, dark brown, long-stalked, the stalk to 3 cm (1.2 in) long, and containing 2 or 3 rounded, shiny brown seeds.

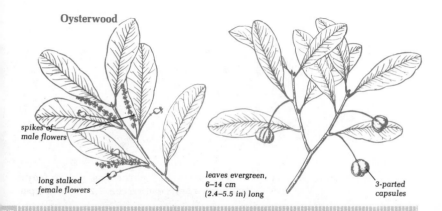

Oysterwood

spikes of male flowers

long stalked female flowers

leaves evergreen, 6–14 cm (2.4–5.5 in) long

3-parted capsules

The Maidenbush Genus

Savia Willd.

This is a small genus of 20 tree and shrub species of tropical and subtropical climates. One species, the Bahama maidenbush, reaches North America in the lower Florida Keys.

Members of this genus are woody, with alternate, simple leaves. Trees are either male or female. Male flowers are in short, dense clusters, while the female flowers are produced singly or in few-flowered clusters. Fruits are a 1-seeded capsule.

Bahama Maidenbush

Savia bahamensis Britton

This species is usually a shrub, but occasionally reaches tree size and occurs only in hammocks of the lower Florida Keys and the Bahama Islands. Flowering is in spring with the small, dry fruits maturing by summer. The species is of no commercial value and of limited use to wildlife.

Maidenbush is a shrub or tree to 3 m (9.8 ft), with smooth, thin, gray or whitish bark. The alternate, evergreen **leaves** are produced in 1 plane, broadest at or above the middle, 2–5 cm (0.8–2 in) long, 1.5–3.8 cm (0.6–1.5 in) wide, **entire,** leathery and dark shiny green. **Male flowers** are tiny, produced **in short, dense clusters in the junction of the upper leaves; female flowers are** produced singly or in **few-flowered clusters also in leaf junctions. Fruits** are **dry, globe-shaped capsules, 5–7 mm (0.2–0.3 in) long,** and **splitting into 3 sections at maturity.**

The Milkbark or Whitewood Genus

Drypetes Vahl.

This is a small to medium-size genus of tropical evergreen trees or shrubs. The two species that occur in North America are confined to southern Florida. They are not economically important, although in other countries they are occasionally used for posts, fuel, or in construction.

Members of this genus are trees or shrubs with milky juice and alternate, simple, evergreen leaves. Flowers are unisexual, the plants either male or female, with a 4- or 5-parted calyx, no petals, 3 to 12 or more stamens (absent in female flowers), and a single pistil (aborted in male flowers). Fruits are berry-like and globe-shaped.

Key to Milkbark or Whitewood Species

A. Bark milky white; berries smooth, 1.5–2.5 cm (0.6–1 in) in diameter, ivory white
Milkbark or Whitewood, p. 737

B. Bark light brown and reddish-tinged; berries hairy, 7–10 mm (0.3–0.4 in) in diameter, bright red **Guiana plum, p. 737**

Guiana Plum

Milkbark, Whitewood · *Drypetes diversifolia* Krug & Urban

This tree is sparsely distributed throughout the Florida Keys where it grows in rocky or sandy soils. It is rather conspicuous and easily spotted because of its milk-white bark. It flowers in spring with the white fruits maturing by fall. The brown, yellow-streaked wood is dense, hard, but weak and brittle and thus is commercially unimportant.

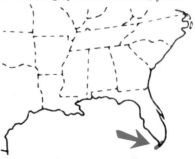

Milkbark is a shrub or tree to 12 m (39 ft), with a **smooth, milky white bark,** sometimes mottled with gray or brown patches. The alternate, simple leaves are broadest near the base to uniformly wide, 8–12 cm (3.2–4.7 in) long, 2.5–5 cm (1–2 in) wide, entire, leathery, dark green and shiny above, and paler beneath. Male flowers, tiny, greenish-white, are produced in short dense clusters in the junction of the leaves; female flowers are produced singly or in 2- or 3-flowered clusters. **Fruits** are **berry-like, globe to egg-shaped, 1.5–2.5 cm (0.6–1 in) long, ivory white,** and enclosing a single hard stone.

Milkbark, Whitewood

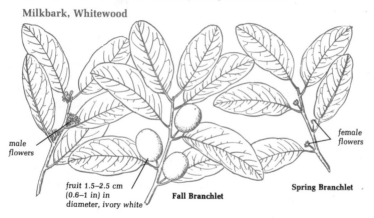

male flowers

female flowers

fruit 1.5–2.5 cm (0.6–1 in) in diameter, ivory white

Fall Branchlet

Spring Branchlet

Guiana Plum · *Drypetes lateriflora* (Sw.) Krug & Urban

Guiana plum occurs in coastal hammocks on the east coast of Florida, extreme southern Florida, the Keys, and the West Indies. Unlike its close relative, the milkbark tree, this species flowers in the fall and winter with the hairy red fruits maturing in spring or summer.

Guiana plum is a shrub or tree to 10 m (33 ft), with **smooth, thin, light brown** and reddish-tinged bark, developing thin scales with age. The alternate, simple leaves are uniformly wide, 8–10 cm (3.2–4

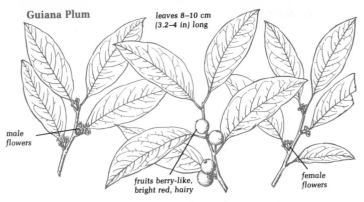

Guiana Plum

leaves 8–10 cm (3.2–4 in) long

male flowers

fruits berry-like, bright red, hairy

female flowers

in) long, entire, almost leathery, dark green and shiny. Male flowers, tiny, greenish white, are produced in short, densely flowered clusters in the junctions of the upper leaves; female flowers are produced singly or in few-flowered clusters. **Fruits are berry-like, globe-shaped,** 7–10 mm (0.3–0.4 in) in diameter, **bright red** and covered **with soft hairs,** and enclosing a single, thin-walled stone.

The Manchineel Genus — Hippomane L.

This is a small genus of 2 or 3 species of tropical regions of the Americas. The northern most extension of 1 species, the manchineel, reaches southern Florida. All the species have a poisonous, milky latex. Members of the genus are shrubs or low trees, with leaves alternate, simple, entire, or toothed along the margin, and bearing 1 or 2 glands on the leafstalk. Flowers are male or female, occurring on the same tree or separate trees. Fruits resemble small apples.

Manchineel — *Hippomane mancinella* L.

This tree occurs along beaches and low areas near the coast from Cape Sable, Florida, to the Keys, the West Indies, and Central and South America. An eradication program has reduced the number of these trees, especially along swimming beaches. The poisonous milky sap in all plant parts can cause severe skin inflammations and if swallowed can be fatal. Unknowing swimmers sometimes hang their towels on the trees and later after drying themselves develop serious skin problems from the sap. The dark brown wood is soft and light, and has limited use because of the sap.

Manchineel are small trees to 12 m (39 ft), with milky sap, a spreading, rounded crown, and a thin warty, fissured gray to dark brown bark. The alternate, nearly evergreen, simple leaves are broadest near the base, 4–10 cm (1.6–4 in) long, pointed at the tip, wavy or finely toothed along the margin, dark yellowish-green and shiny. Manchineel **flowers** in spring on long, **slender, unbranched spikes** 6–15 cm (2.4–6 in) long; tiny yellowish-green male flowers are produced on the upper three-fourths of the spike and a few female flowers are produced at the base. Fruits are **rounded** to

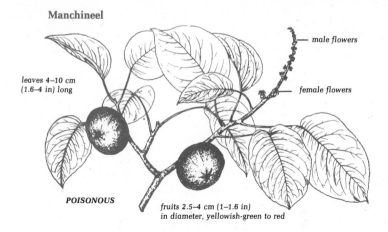

Manchineel

leaves 4–10 cm
(1.6–4 in) long

— *male flowers*

— *female flowers*

POISONOUS

fruits 2.5–4 cm (1–1.6 in)
in diameter, yellowish-green to red

depressed rounded, apple-like, poisonous, 2.5–4 cm (1–1.6 in) in diameter, with 6 to 8 slight lobes, light *yellow-green to red,* with a greenish white flesh and containing 6 to 8 seeds.

The Buckthorn Family   Rhamnaceae

This moderate-size family of 58 genera and about 900 species is widely distributed throughout temperate, subtropical, and tropical regions of the world. Twelve of the approximately 75 native North American species are trees. Many other species have been introduced from Europe or Asia. The most noteworthy of these are 2 species of buckthorns, covered later, and the jujube. Jujube (*Ziziphus jujube*), a native of Asia, was introduced into the southeastern U.S. for its edible fruits. It now reproduces on its own from Alabama to Louisiana.

Several members of this family are economically important. Green and yellow dyes are obtained from buckthorns. Extracts from the bark and leaves of selected species are used medicinally for their purgative properties or as a stimulant. Many species of ceanothus are showy and cultivated in gardens and parks. This family is of considerable value to wildlife because of prolific crops of fruits produced each year. Young twigs and leaves of some species are browsed by all North American deer.

Members of this family are trees, shrubs, or vines, sometimes spiny. The leaves are simple, alternate or opposite, deciduous or evergreen, and with stipules. Flowers are small, usually bisexual, with 4 or 5 sepals, 4 or 5 small petals (sometimes absent), 4 or 5 stamens, and a single pistil with a superior ovary. Fruits are usually berry-like, nuts, or capsules.

Key to Buckthorn Genera

A. Fruits a dry capsule, splitting into 3 sections at maturity.

   1. Flowers with showy blue, purple, pink, or

Soldierwood

white petals, the petal claw-shaped; fruits many per cluster **Ceanothus, p. 740**

2. Flowers with small, nonshowy yellow or white petals; fruits few per cluster, usually 3 or less **Nakedwood, p. 743**

B. Fruits fleshy, rounded or nearly so, not splitting open at maturity.

1. Fruits with 2 or 4 seeds
Buckthorn, p. 746

2. Fruits with single seed enclosed in a stone.

a. Leaves alternate; branchlets ending in sharp spines **Condalia, p. 752**
b. Leaves opposite, rarely alternate, branchlets not spine-tipped.

(1) Flowers with uncrested calyx lobes
Darling plum, p. 754
(2) Flowers with the calyx lobes crested on the inner surface **Leadwood, p. 755**

Carolina Buckthorn

Bluewood

The Ceanothus Genus

Ceanothus L.

Ceanothus is a genus of perhaps 55 species occurring in the temperate and warm temperate regions of North America. The vast majority of the species are native to the western regions and especially abundant in California. Most are shrubs of varying heights, but 3 species regularly grow to small trees.

Many of the species are of value as ornamental plants because of the cluster of attractive blue, purple, pink, or white flowers and often evergreen leaves. In addition, they serve as an important food source to some wildlife, especially mule deer. The plants are too small for the wood to be used commercially.

Members of this genus are shrubs or small trees with spreading, occasionally spiny branchlets. The simple leaves are alternate or opposite, deciduous or evergreen, usually toothed, and with 3 main veins. Flowers are white, blue, purple, or pink, bisexual, produced in many-flowered, branched, elongate to spreading clusters. Each flower consists of an urn-shaped, deeply 5-lobed calyx; 5 free, hooded, clawed petals; 5 stamens opposite the petals, and a single pistil. Fruits are 3-lobed capsules.

Key to Ceanothus Species

Feltleaf Ceanothus

A. Branchlets slender, flexible, not spine-tipped.

1. Branchlets angled; leaves smooth beneath or with a few hairs along the veins; trees of coastal Oregon and California
Blueblossom, p. 741
2. Branchlets rounded; leaves usually hairy be-

neath; trees of Santa Rosa, Santa Cruz, and
Santa Catalina Island, California
Feltleaf ceanothus, p. 742

Spiny Ceanothus

B. Branchlets rigid, wide-spreading, ending in a
sharp spine; leaves entire or nearly so; trees of
southwestern California and Baja California,
Mexico   **Spiny ceanothus, p. 742**

Blueblossom

Ceanothus thyrsiflorus Eschsch.

Blueblossom is native to the Pacific Coast of the U.S., ranging from southwestern
Oregon to central California. It grows in canyons and on shaded hillsides and slopes,
usually at low elevations but up to 700 m (2,297 ft) elevation. It occurs in redwood
forests, mixed coniferous forests, and
scrubby brushlands.

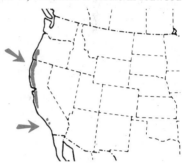

In spring the numerous clusters of blue
flowers add considerable color along the
coastal hillsides and highways. The plants
are of no commercial importance, but the
young twigs and leaves are an important
food for mule deer. The light-brown wood
is soft, not strong, and not used.

Appearance: large shrub or small tree to
6 m (20 ft), with a narrow, open crown;
trunk short, branching close to the ground.

Blueblossom

flowers
light to
deep blue

fruits 3-lobed,
sticky, almost black

branchlet angled

leaves 2–5 cm (0.8–2 in) long,
smooth, hairy on veins
of lower surface

Bark: thin, 1–3 mm (0.1 in) thick, smooth becoming roughened with thin scales,
reddish-brown. **Branches:** slender, upright; ***branchlets*** slender, spreading; ***angled,***
green and slightly hairy when young, becoming smooth and reddish-brown with age.
Winter buds: small, covered with scales. **Leaves:** simple, alternate, ***evergreen,***
broadest near the middle or base to uniformly wide, ***2–5 cm (0.8–2 in) long,*** 1.2–2.6
cm (0.5–1.1 in) wide, round to pointed at the tip, rounded to tapering at the base,

finely gland-toothed along the margin, with 3 conspicuous main veins, dark green and smooth above, paler beneath; leafstalks stout, 8–12 mm (0.3–0.5 in) long. **Flowers:** light to deep blue, rarely white, bisexual, produced in many-flowered, branched clusters 3–8 cm (1.2–3.2 in) long, at the tips of the branchlets or in the junction of the upper leaves. **Fruits:** capsules, 3-lobed, nearly globe-shaped, 3–4 mm (0.1–0.2 in) across, sticky, almost black, splitting open to release the smooth tiny seeds.

Feltleaf Ceanothus *Ceanothus arboreus* Greene

Feltleaf ceanothus is restricted to Santa Rosa, Santa Cruz, and Santa Catalina Islands off the coast of southern California. It grows in the shrubby vegetation on slopes. The pale blue flowers appear from February through May with the fruits maturing in summer or early fall.

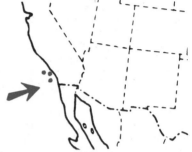

This ceanothus is a large shrub or small tree to 7 m (23 ft), with flexible, soft hairy *rounded branchlets.* The simple, alternate, *evergreen leaves* are very broad, especially near the base or middle, 3–9 cm (1.2–3.5 in) long, 2–6 cm (0.8–2.4 in) wide, pointed to rounded at the tip, rounded at the base, *toothed along the margins,* dull green and with fine short hairs above, paler and *very hairy beneath,* some plants with almost smooth leaves. Flowers, pale blue, are produced in many-flowered, branched, elongated clusters. Fruits are triangle-shaped capsules, 6–9 mm (0.2–0.4 in) across, becoming black at maturity.

Feltleaf Ceanothus

*flowers
pale blue*

*leaves toothed,
hairy beneath*

*fruits 6–9 mm
(0.2–0.4 in)
across, black*

Spiny Ceanothus *Ceanothus spinosus* Nutt.

Spiny ceanothus naturally occurs in southwestern California and adjacent Baja California, Mexico. It grows on dry slopes and hillsides of coastal scrub and chaparral vegetation, at usually less than 950 m (3,117 ft) elevation. This species is the only tree size ceanothus with rigid, spine-tipped branchlets. Large clusters of pale blue to almost white flowers can appear from February to May.

This species is a large shrub or small tree to 6 m (20 ft), with **stiff, widespreading, spine-tipped branchlets.** The simple, **alternate, evergreen leaves** are uniformly wide to widest at the middle, 1.4–3 cm (0.6–1.2 in) long, 0.7–1.4 cm (0.3–0.6 in) wide, rounded at the tip, tapering at the base, entire or with a few, irregular teeth, leathery, bright green above, paler beneath. Flowers are pale blue to almost white, produced in many-flowered, branched, elongate clusters. Fruits are globe-shaped capsules 4–6 mm (0.1–0.2 in) across, sticky, black.

Spiny Ceanothus

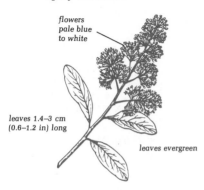

flowers pale blue to white

leaves 1.4–3 cm (0.6–1.2 in) long

leaves evergreen

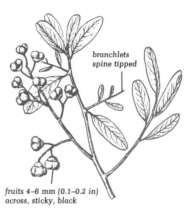

branchlets spine tipped

fruits 4–6 mm (0.1–0.2 in) across, sticky, black

The Nakedwood Genus

Colubrina Brong.

This is a small genus of about 25 species distributed in tropical and subtropical regions of the Americas, Asia, Madagascar, and the South Pacific. Four species are native to North America, 3 are small trees, and the remaining 1 is always a shrub. In our range, they are restricted to southern Florida. They are of limited economic importance and minor value to wildlife.

Members of the genus are shrubs or small trees with simple, alternate, evergreen leaves. Flowers are tiny, produced in short, branched, few-flowered clusters in the junction of the leaves. Each flower is bisexual, with a 5-lobed calyx, 5 yellow or white petals, 5 stamens, and a single pistil. Fruits are 3-lobed, capsule-like, globe-shaped or nearly so, splitting open at maturity.

Key to Nakedwood Species

A. Leaves thin, papery; trees of upper Florida Keys
Soldierwood, p. 744

B. Leaves leathery.

(Continued)

1. Leaves hairy on the upper surface and densely rusty hairy on the lower surface; trees of southern Florida   **Cuban colubrina, p. 744**
2. Leaves smooth on the upper surface and slightly hairy, mainly on the veins, below; trees of southern Florida

    Coffee colubrina, p. 745

Soldierwood   *Colubrina elliptica* (Sw.) Briz. & Stern.

This small tree grows in hammocks in the upper Florida Keys. It is also native to the Bahamas, the West Indies, southern Mexico, and Guatemala. Flowering and fruiting may occur throughout the year. The dark brown yellow-tinged wood is hard, heavy, and strong. It is occasionally used as fence posts in the West Indies.

Soldierwood is a shrub or small tree to 8 m (26 ft), rarely taller, with thin orangish-brown scaly bark which peels off in thin pieces. The simple, alternate ***evergreen leaves*** are broadest near the base or the middle, 4–12 cm (1.6–4.7 in) long, 4–6 cm (1.6–2.4 in) wide, pointed to blunt at the tip, usually rounded at the base, entire, ***thin, dark green*** and ***shiny above***, and rusty hairy beneath. Small bisexual flowers are produced in short, branched clusters in the junction of the upper leaves. Fruits are a 3-lobed capsule, almost globe-shaped, 6–9 mm (0.2–0.4 in) in diameter, splitting into 3 sections at maturity to release the seeds.

Soldierwood

leaves thin, papery, 4–12 cm (1.6–4.7 in) long

fruits 3-lobed, 6–9 mm (0.2–0.4 in) in diameter

bisexual flowers

Cuban Colubrina   *Colubrina cubensis* (Jacq.) Brongn.

Cuban colubrina is found in hammocks and pinelands in southern Florida. It is also native to the Bahamas, Cuba, and Hispaniola. Like soldierwood, this species can be found in flower or fruit almost any month of the year. The trees are too small to be of value as a source of lumber.

This is a shrub or small tree to 9 m (30 ft), with hairy branchlets. The simple, alternate, *evergreen leaves* are widest near the middle or just below the middle, 5–10 cm (2–4 in) long, 1.5–4 cm (0.6–1.6 in) wide, rounded to pointed at the tip, rounded to tapering at the base, with a few, shallow, rounded teeth along the margin, *leathery, dark green and hairy above,* paler and *densely hairy beneath.* Flowers, tiny, are produced in branched spreading

clusters in the junction of the upper leaves. Fruits are 3-lobed capsules, globe-shaped or nearly so, 6–9 mm (0.2–0.4 in) in diameter.

Coffee Colubrina
Colubrina arborescens Sarg.

This small tree is native to southern Florida, the West Indies, Mexico, and Central America. In Florida, it grows in hammocks, especially in the Keys. Flowering and fruiting occurs irregularly throughout the year. Coffee colubrina is not presently of any economic importance nor of much value to wildlife.

Coffee colubrina is a shrub or small tree to 8 m (26 ft), with hairy young branchlets. The simple, alternate, *evergreen leaves* are broadest near the middle or just below, 5–14 cm (2–5.5 in) long, 2.8–6.5 cm (1.1–2.6 in) wide, pointed to blunt at the tip, rounded to tapering at the base, entire, *leathery, dark green and smooth above,* paler and *with rusty hairs on the lower surface.* Flowers are tiny and produced in

short, branched clusters in the junction of the leaves. Fruits are 3-parted capsules, rounded or nearly so, 6–10 mm (0.2–0.4 in) in diameter, almost black, splitting open at maturity.

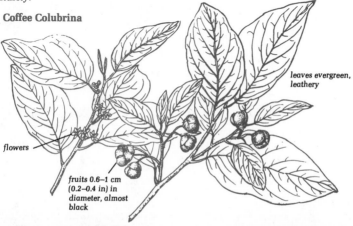

Coffee Colubrina

leaves evergreen, leathery

flowers

fruits 0.6–1 cm (0.2–0.4 in) in diameter, almost black

The Buckthorn Genus

Rhamnus L.

This is a relatively large genus of about 100 species of trees and shrubs distributed in temperate and tropical regions of the world. Five of our native species reach tree size. Two European species, the European buckthorn and glossy buckthorn, have been introduced and are reproducing and spreading on their own. Both of these species were introduced as ornamentals, primarily for use as hedges. Extracts from the bark of some species have been used in medicines. The fruits are a valuable food to many birds.

Members of this genus are small trees or shrubs sometimes with rigid, spine-tipped branches. Leaves are simple, alternate, evergreen to deciduous, and entire to variously toothed along the margins. Flowers are bisexual or bisexual and unisexual on the same tree. The flowers are 4 or 5 parted and produced in the junction of the leaves. Fruits are berry-like, fleshy, and contain from 2 to 4 seeds.

Key to Buckthorn Species

A. Trees with male or female flowers only or with bisexual and male or female flowers; seeds usually grooved on the back; winter buds covered with scales.

European Buckthorn

  1. Leaves alternate.

   a. Leaves evergreen, 5–15 mm (0.2–0.6 in) wide; branchlets rigid, often spine-tipped; trees of California and Arizona
   Hollyleaf buckthorn, p. 747

   b. Leaves deciduous, 2.5–4 cm (1–1.6 in) wide; branchlets slender, usually not spine-tipped; trees of southwestern U.S. and Mexico   **Birchleaf buckthorn, p. 748**

Cascara Buckthorn

  2. Leaves opposite; introduced trees, especially of eastern North America
   European buckthorn, p. 748

B. Trees with bisexual flowers; seeds smooth on the back; winter buds without scales, covered with dense hairs.

  1. Leaves evergreen; trees of California, southern Nevada, Arizona, and New Mexico
   California buckthorn, p. 749

  2. Leaves deciduous.

   a. Flowers clustered, arising from a single stalk in the junction of the leaves (cymose); leaves 4–16 cm (1.6–6.3 in) long.

Carolina Buckthorn

    (1) Leafstalks 1.2–2.4 cm (0.5–1 in) long; flowers arising on a long stalk, longer than the leafstalks; trees of northwestern North America
    Cascara buckthorn, p. 750

(2) Leafstalks 0.8–1.8 cm (0.4–0.8 in) long; flowers arising from a short stalk, shorter than the leafstalks; trees of southern U.S. and Mexico
Carolina buckthorn, p. 751

b. Flowers solitary or clustered, not on a central stalk, each flower on a stalk in the junction of the leaves; leaves 3–7 cm (1.2–2.8 in) long; introduced trees, primarily of eastern North America
Glossy buckthorn, p. 752

Glossy Buckthorn

Hollyleaf Buckthorn

Rhamnus crocea Nutt.

This evergreen buckthorn is usually a straggly shrub, but in protected sites it reaches tree size. It grows in canyons, ravines, and dry washes of lower mountain slopes from northern California to Arizona and adjacent Mexico. Hollyleaf buckthorn occurs from sea level to 1,000 m (3,281 ft), elevation in scrub woodland, chaparral, or mixed hardwood and coniferous forests. Several varieties are known. Variety *pirifolia* C. B. Wolf is usually a tree with entire to round-toothed leaves. Variety *ilicifolia* is more often a shrub with sharp-toothed leaves.

Flowers occur from March to April with the fruits maturing by summer or early fall. These are eaten by birds or small mammals. Hollyleaf buckthorn is sometimes planted in gardens and parks in California. The plant is too small for its wood to be of any value.

Appearance: usually a shrub or small tree to 8 m (26 ft); with a spreading, open

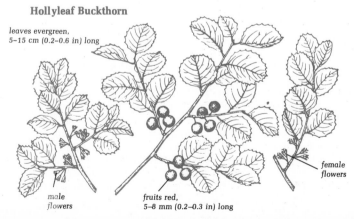

Hollyleaf Buckthorn

leaves evergreen, 5–15 cm (0.2–0.6 in) long

male flowers

fruits red, 5–8 mm (0.2–0.3 in) long

female flowers

crown; trunk short, branching close to the ground. **Bark:** thin, 1–4 mm (0.1–0.2 in) thick, smooth becoming rough with age, dark gray. **Branches:** slender, spreading to upright; branches slender, *rigid, often spine-tipped.* **Winter buds:** 1–2 mm (0.1 in) long, rounded, covered with tiny scales. **Leaves:** simple, *alternate, evergreen,* broadest near the base to *almost round, 5–15 mm (0.2–0.6 in) long, 3–12 mm (0.1–0.5 in) wide,* rounded to short-pointed at the tip, rounded at the base, usually with gland-tipped teeth along the margin, leathery, yellowish-green and shiny above, paler beneath; leafstalks 1–4 mm (0.1–0.2 in) long, stout. **Flowers:** bisexual and male or female flowers on same plant; produced in short stalked clusters in the junction of the upper leaves; each flower has a tiny 4-lobed calyx, no petals, 4 stamens (absent in female flowers), and a single pistil (aborted in male flowers). **Fruits:** berry-like, egg-shaped, 5–8 mm (0.2–0.3 in) long, red, slightly fleshy, containing 1 to 3 seeds.

Birchleaf Buckthorn *Rhamnus betulifolia* Greene

This southwestern species occurs from southern Utah and Nevada southward into northern and central Mexico. They grow along streams and moist canyons from 1,700 to 2,350 m (5,557–7,710 ft) elevation. Birchleaf buckthorn is usually found growing in association with oaks and ponderosa pine. Flowering is in May and June with the juicy berries maturing in summer to early fall. These are eaten by many species of birds. Mule deer will browse the young twigs and leaves.

Birchleaf buckthorn is a shrub or tree to 6 m (20 ft), with a rounded crown. The simple, *alternate, deciduous leaves* are uniformly wide to widest near the middle, 5–15 cm (2–6 in) long, 2.5–4 cm (1–1.6 in) wide, rounded to pointed at the tip, usu- · ally rounded or nearly so at the base, with fine sharp teeth along the margin, bright green and shiny above. Flowers are in small, few-flowered clusters in the junction of the upper leaves; each flower with a tiny, 4-lobed calyx, 4 or 5 small, greenish petals, sometimes falling away early, 4 or 5 stamens, and a single pistil. Fruits are rounded or nearly so, 4–9 mm (0.1–0.4 in) in diameter, black to dark purple, shiny, juicy, and containing 3 seeds.

European Buckthorn *Rhamnus cathartica* L.

This European native has escaped from cultivation and naturalized throughout eastern North America. Generally, it is found along fencerows, fields, vacant lots, and open woods. It is distinguished from most of our native species by its spine-tipped branchlets and sharply toothed leaves. European buckthorn is very hardy, resistant to insect attack, and makes a good hedge plant because it responds well to pruning. The black fruits will cause nausea in people but are readily eaten by many birds.

This is a shrub or small tree to 8 m (26 ft), with slender, rather rigid, usually spine-tipped branches. The simple, *opposite, deciduous leaves* are broadest at or above the middle, 3–7 cm (1.2–2.8 in) long, 2.5–5.5 cm (1–2.2 in) wide, rounded to sharp pointed at the tip, rounded to tapering at the base, toothed along the margin with gland-tipped teeth, dark green and smooth above. Bisexual and sometimes male and female flowers occur in few-flowered clusters in the junction of the leaves; floral

European Buckthorn

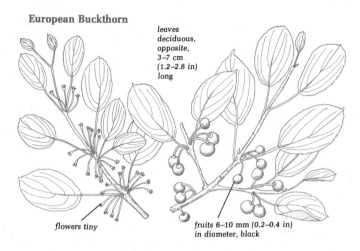

leaves deciduous, opposite, 3–7 cm (1.2–2.8 in) long

flowers tiny

fruits 6–10 mm (0.2–0.4 in) in diameter, black

parts in 4s. Fruits solitary or 2- to 5-clustered, berry-like, rounded, 6–10 mm (0.2–0.4 in) in diameter, black, juicy, and containing 3 or 4 seeds which are plump and grooved.

California Buckthorn

Rhamnus californica Eschsch.

California buckthorn is native to California, extreme southern Nevada, Arizona, southwestern New Mexico, and adjacent Mexico. In California, it can be found growing along the coast, on hillsides, and in ravines; while in Arizona it is commonly seen in canyons and protected ravines, usually from 1,250–2,300 m (4,101–7,546 ft) elevation. It occurs in a variety of forest types ranging from scrub woodlands to redwood forests.

The small greenish flowers are produced in spring, with the black fruits maturing from early summer into fall. The fruits are eaten by mule deer, black bear, and several species of birds, including the band-tailed pigeon. Mule deer also browse the young twigs and foliage. The trees are too small for the wood to be of any value.

Appearance: shrub or tree to 6 m (20 ft), with a spreading, open crown, trunk short, branching close to the ground, to 15 cm (6 in) in diameter. **Bark:** thin, 2–4 mm (0.1–0.2 in) thick, smooth becoming roughened with age, usually reddish-brown. **Branches:** slender, spreading to upright; branchlets slender, hairy when young, becoming smooth. **Winter buds:** *tiny,* 1–2 mm (0.1 in) long, without scales, rounded. **Leaves:** simple, alternate, *evergreen* or nearly so, uniformly wide to widest near the middle, 2.5–8 cm (1–3.2 in) long, 1.2–3 cm (0.5–1.2 in) wide, pointed to rounded at the tip, rounded at the base, entire to finely toothed along the margin, dark shiny green and smooth above, paler and sometimes hairy beneath; leafstalks slender, 0.6–1.4 cm (0.3–0.6 in) long, smooth to hairy. **Flowers:** small, bisexual, stalked, produced in few to many-flowered small clusters in the junction of the leaves; each flower with a 4-lobed calyx, 4 or 5 tiny petals, sometimes absent, 4 or 5 stamens, and a single pistil. **Fruits:** berries, rounded or nearly so, 6–14 mm (0.2–0.6 in) in diameter, green, red, usually turning black at maturity, slightly juicy, containing 2 or 3 *smooth seeds.*

Cascara Buckthorn   *Rhamnus purshiana* DC.

Cascara buckthorn is native to southern and southwestern British Columbia, south to western Oregon and northern California. It grows in bottomlands, canyons, and lower mountain slopes to 900 m (2,953 ft) elevation. This buckthorn can also be found along

fencerows and roadsides. It rarely forms large pure stands but most often grows in association with other trees including Douglas fir, western redcedar, hemlock, and several maples. *This is the only native species of deciduous trees on the northwest coast whose winter buds are scaleless and protected only by dense hairs.*

Small flowers are produced in May or June and the fruits mature in autumn. The fruits are an important food source for wildlife, especially the band-tailed pigeon, catbird, mockingbird, thrushes, and many small mammals. Blacktailed and mule deer together with bighorn sheep browse the young twigs and leaves. The yellowish-brown wood is hard and heavy but of no commercial value because the trees are too small. Cascara buckthorn is sometimes used as an ornamental hedge or shrub.

Cascara Buckthorn

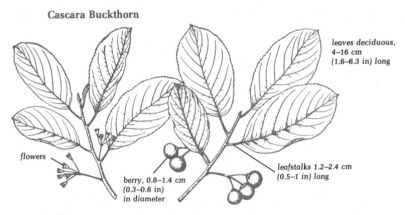

leaves deciduous, 4–16 cm (1.6–6.3 in) long

flowers

leafstalks 1.2–2.4 cm (0.5–1 in) long

berry, 0.8–1.4 cm (0.3–0.6 in) in diameter

Appearance: shrub or small tree to 12 m (39 ft), with a narrow, rounded crown; trunk straight, to 40 cm (15.8 in) in diameter. **Bark:** moderately thin, 5–8 mm (0.2–0.3 in) thick, smooth, developing thin scales, dark brown to gray. **Branches:** slender, spreading to upright; branchlets slender, finely hairy and yellowish-green when young, becoming smooth and reddish-brown with age. **Winter buds:** *tiny, naked, covered with rusty brown hairs.* **Leaves:** simple, alternate, *deciduous,* uniformly wide to widest above the middle, 4–16 cm (1.6–6.3 in) long, 1.8–6 cm (0.8–2.4 in) wide, rounded to short-pointed at the tip, rounded at the base, finely toothed to almost entire, dark green and usually smooth above, paler and smooth to hairy beneath; *leaf-stalks stout, 1.2–2.4 cm (0.5–1 in) long.* **Flowers:** *bisexual,* stalked, produced in dense, few to many-flowered clusters in the junction of the leaves; each flower with a 5-lobed calyx, 5 tiny petals folded around the 5 stamens, and a single pistil. **Fruits:** berry-like, globe-shaped or nearly so, *0.8–1.4 cm (0.3–0.6 in) in diameter, black,* slightly fleshy, containing 2 or 3 smooth seeds.

Carolina Buckthorn
Rhamnus caroliniana Walt.

This small tree is native to the southern U.S. and adjacent northeastern Mexico. It grows in open woods, on hillsides, and along streams and does best in rich, moist limestone soils. This species is found growing in association with many other trees including blackgum, pin oak, eastern red-cedar, beech, sycamore, southern magnolia, dogwood, and hawthorns.

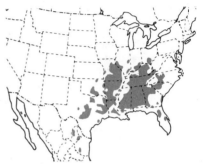

Carolina buckthorn is a slow growing, usually short-lived plant which produces tiny greenish-yellow flowers in May or June. The sweet, edible fruits mature by September or October. Many birds feed on them including the pileated woodpecker. Whitetail deer browse the young twigs and leaves. The light brown wood is hard, brittle, and of no value commercially because of the small size of the trees.

Carolina Buckthorn

leaves deciduous,
5–12 cm
(2–4.7 in) long

leafstalks
0.8–1.8 cm
(0.3–0.7 in)
long

bisexual flowers

fruits black,
0.7–1 cm
(0.3–0.4 in)
in diameter

Appearance: shrub or small tree to 12 m (39 ft), with open, rounded crown; trunk straight, branching close to the ground, to 20 cm (7.9 in) in diameter. **Bark:** thin, 2–4 mm (0.1–0.2 in) thick, smooth to slightly furrowed, light gray. **Branches:** slender, spreading; branchlets slender, reddish-brown and hairy when young, becoming smooth and gray with age. **Winter buds:** tiny, about *1 mm (0.04 in) long, hairy.* **Leaves:** simple, alternate, deciduous, broadest near the middle, 5–12 cm (2–4.7 in) long, 2.5–5 cm (1–2 in) wide, pointed at the tip, tapering to slightly rounded at the base, remotely toothed, sometimes with rounded teeth along the margin, dark yellow-green and smooth at maturity, paler and smooth to hairy beneath; *leafstalks slender, 0.8–1.8 cm (0.3–0.7 in) long,* hairy. **Flowers:** bisexual, produced in few-flowered, short-stalked clusters in the junction of the leaves or along the branchlets; each flower with a tiny, 5-lobed calyx, 5 small, broad petals, folded around the 5 short stamens, and a single pistil. **Fruits:** berries, rounded or nearly so, *0.7– 1 cm (0.3–0.4 in) in diameter, black,* slightly fleshy, containing 2 to 4 small seeds.

Glossy Buckthorn
Rhamnus frangula L.

This species was introduced from Europe, has escaped from cultivation, and is rapidly spreading across eastern North America. It grows along fencerows, edges of woodlands, and old fields. The small, pale yellow flowers appear in spring with the fruits maturing in late summer and early fall. Birds consume the fruits, digesting the fleshy pulp and dispersing the small, hard seeds in the process. Glossy buckthorn is sometimes planted as hedge.

This is a shrub or small tree to 6 m (20 ft), with simple, alternate, *deciduous* leaves. The leaves are broadest near the base, middle, or near the tip, 3–7 cm (1.2–2.8 in) long, 1.6–4 cm (0.7–1.6 in) wide, pointed at the tip, entire or with a few, small glandular teeth near the tip, dark green and smooth above, paler and slightly hairy beneath. Flowers are *bisexual,* produced in stalked clusters of 2 to 10 in the junction of the leaves. Fruits are berry-like, rounded, 4–8 cm (1.6–3.2 in) in diameter, red turning almost black, containing 2 or 3 smooth seeds.

Glossy Buckthorn

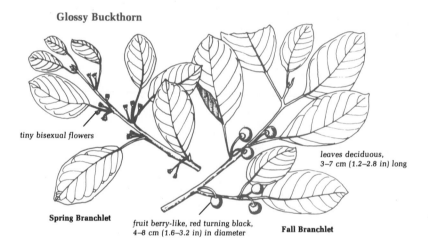

tiny bisexual flowers

leaves deciduous,
3–7 cm (1.2–2.8 in) long

Spring Branchlet

fruit berry-like, red turning black,
4–8 cm (1.6–3.2 in) in diameter

Fall Branchlet

The Condalia Genus
Condalia Cav.

This is a small genus of about 15 species of spiny trees and shrubs of the southwestern U.S., Mexico, and southern South America. At least 8 species are native to the U.S., but only 2, the bluewood and bitter condalia, on occasion reach tree size. They are of limited value except as excellent firewood and as a food source for many birds and mammals.

Members of this genus have spiny branches and simple, alternate, leaves. The tiny white flowers are produced singly or in small clusters in the junction of the leaves. Each flower has 5 sepals, no petals, 5 stamens inserted on the margin of a disk, and a single pistil. Fruits are berry-like and contain a single seed.

Key to Condalia Species

A. Leaves 1.2–4 cm (0.5–1.6 in) long, mature leaves smooth; fruits 6–9 mm (0.2–0.4 in) in diameter, sweet tasting; trees of southern Texas and Mexico   **Bluewood, p. 753**

B. Leaves 5–14 mm (0.2–0.6 in) long, mature leaves densely hairy; fruits 4–6 mm (0.2 in) in diameter, bitter tasting; trees of southwestern Arizona and southeastern California   **Bitter condalia, p. 754**

Bluewood

Condalia hookeri M.C. Johnst.
(synonym: *C. obovata* Hook.)

This species is limited to the drier regions of southern Texas and northeastern Mexico. It is more often shrubby than tree size and regularly forms dense thickets which are difficult to penetrate.

Bluewood flowers in spring with the shiny black fruits maturing irregularly throughout the summer. The fruits are sweet and make a good jelly, but the thorny branches deter collectors. Many birds, including mockingbirds, white-necked raven, and golden-fronted woodpecker, along with the ringtailed cat, eat the fruits. The light-red wood is very hard, heavy, and dense but is of little value except for firewood. Because of the density of the wood, it gives off considerable Btu units of heat.

Appearance: shrub or small tree to 9 m (30 ft), with an irregular, spreading crown; trunk short, branching close to the ground. **Bark:** thin, 3–5 mm (0.1–0.2 in) thick, smooth, becoming furrowed and scaly with age, pale gray to brown. **Branches:** rigid,

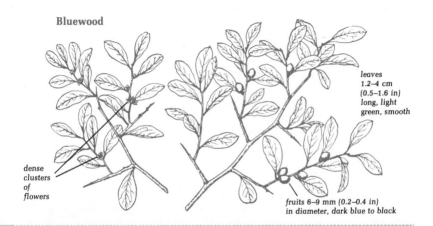

Bluewood

leaves
1.2–4 cm
(0.5–1.6 in)
long, light
green, smooth

dense
clusters
of
flowers

fruits 6–9 mm (0.2–0.4 in)
in diameter, dark blue to black

wide spreading; branchlets stout, ending in sharp spines, velvety hairy and green when young, becoming smooth and brown with age. **Leaves:** simple, alternate, often on short lateral shoots, broadest above the middle, *1.2–4 cm (0.5–1.6 in) long,* 8–14 mm (0.3–0.6 in) wide, rounded and sometimes notched at the tip, tapering at the base, entire, leathery, *light green and shiny;* leafstalks short. **Flowers:** short-stalked, 2 to 4 in the junction of the upper leaves; each flower with 5 tiny sepals, petals absent, 5 stamens, and a single pistil. **Fruits:** berry-like, rounded or nearly so, 6–9 mm (0.2–0.4 in) in diameter, dark blue to black, fleshy, sweet, enclosing a single flattened seed.

Bitter Condalia

Condalia globosa Johnst.

Bitter condalia is native to southwestern Arizona, southeastern California, and northwestern Mexico. It grows along washes and sandy plains to 800 m (2,625 ft) elevation in the desert and scrub vegetation dominated by the creosote bush. Flowering is in March or April with the fruits maturing by mid summer.

This is a large shrub or small tree to 6 m (20 ft), with a spreading, rounded crown, and stiff branches and branchlets ending in spines. *Leaves* are simple, alternate, narrow and broadest near the tip, 5–14 mm (0.2–0.6 in) long, 2–5 mm (0.1–0.2 in) wide, rounded at the tip, tapering to a narrow base, entire along the margin, and *densely covered with fine hairs.* Flowers are produced singly or in pairs in the junction of the leaves; each flower with 5 tiny sepals, no petals, 5 stamens, and a single pistil. Fruits are berry-like, rounded to egg-shaped, 4–6 mm (0.2 in) in diameter, black, juicy, *bitter tasting,* and containing a single seed.

The Darling Plum Genus

Reynosia Griseb.

This is a small genus of about 15 species centered in the West Indies and with 1 species extending into southern Florida. Fruits of many of the species are edible and used locally to make jellies, preserves, and beverages.

Members of this genus are trees or shrubs, without spines, and with simple, generally opposite, leathery, evergreen leaves. The tiny, stalked, bisexual flowers are produced in small, flat-topped, branched clusters in the junction of the leaves. Fruits are berry-like, slightly fleshy, containing a stone which encloses the seed.

Darling Plum

Reynosia septentrionalis Urban

Darling plum is common in extreme southern Florida, especially along the Florida Keys. It also occurs in the Bahama Islands. This species grows in hammocks and near mangrove. The small fruits are edible and serve as a good food for many birds. The exceptionally hard and dense dark-brown wood will barely float in water.

This is a shrub or tree to 10 m (33 ft), with reddish-brown bark which develops large, plate-like scales with age. The *op-*

Darling Plum

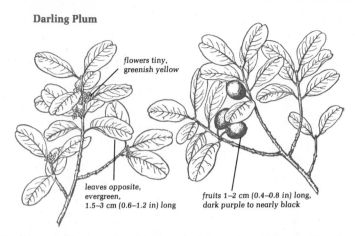

flowers tiny,
greenish yellow

leaves opposite,
evergreen,
1.5–3 cm (0.6–1.2 in) long

fruits 1–2 cm (0.4–0.8 in) long,
dark purple to nearly black

posite evergreen leaves are broadest near the base or the middle to uniformly wide, 1.5–3 cm (0.6–1.2 in) long, 7–15 mm (0.3–0.6 in) wide, rounded and often notched at the tip, tapering at the base, entire, leathery, and dark green. The tiny yellow-green flowers are produced in dense, short clusters in the junction of the leaves; each flower has a 5-lobed calyx, no petals, 5 stamens, and a single pistil. Fruits are egg-shaped or nearly so, 1–2 cm (0.4–0.8 in) long, dark purple to nearly black, edible, and enclosing a single stone.

The Leadwood Genus   *Krugiodendron* Urban

This genus contains only 1 species, the leadwood tree, of southern Florida, the Bahama Islands, the West Indies, Mexico, and Central America. Information concerning the genus is the same as for the species.

Leadwood   *Krugiodendron ferreum* (Vahl) Urban

Leadwood is a common tree along the eastern coast of southern Florida where it grows in hammocks and in scrubby oak woodlands. The small greenish flowers are produced in late spring, with the black fruits ripening by summer. This species is appropriately named, for the reddish-brown wood is so dense it is one of the heaviest of all North American woods and will sink in water.

Leadwoods are shrubs or trees to 9 m (30 ft), with a thin, roughened to scaly, light gray bark. The simple, *opposite*, rarely alternate, *evergreen leaves* are broadest near the base, 2.5–4 cm (1–1.6 in) long, 2–2.6 cm (0.8–1.1 in) wide, rounded and notched at the tip, rounded at the base, entire, leathery, and bright shiny green above. Flowers are produced in few-flowered clusters in the junction of the leaves; each flower consisting of a 5-lobed *calyx,* the *lobes crested on the inner surface,* no petals, 5 stamens, and a single pistil. Fruits are egg-shaped to nearly rounded, 7–10 mm (0.3–0.4 in) in diameter, slightly fleshy, black, containing a single-seeded stone.

Leadwood

flowers
greenish

fruits 7–10 mm
(0.3–0.4 in) in
diameter, black

leaves opposite,
evergreen

Spring Branchlet

Summer Branchlet

The Bladdernut Family

Staphyleaceae

This family is composed of 6 genera with about 25 species of trees and shrubs occurring in both temperate and subtropical regions of Europe, Asia, and North America. Only 1 of these genera, the bladdernuts (*Staphylea*), is native to North America. The common name of this family is derived from the unusual fruits, which are inflated, bladder-like capsules. This family is of little economic importance, although they are sometimes cultivated for their handsome bright green leaves, white flowers, and interesting fruits.

Members of this family have opposite, deciduous, feather-like (pinnate) compound leaves or leaves composed of 3 leaflets (trifoliolate). The bisexual flowers are produced in slightly elongated, modestly branched, hanging clusters. Individual flowers have 5 calyx lobes, 5 petals, 5 stamens, and a single pistil. The fruits are a 3-parted, thin-walled, inflated capsule.

The Bladdernut Genus

Staphylea L.

This small genus of about 15 species of shrubs and small trees is native to temperate regions of North America, Europe, and across Asia to China and Japan. They are typically found as understory trees in deciduous, hardwood forests. Two species are native, 1 in eastern North America and the other in the mountains of California. The trees are of little value to wildlife.

Bladdernut trees are shrubs or small trees with opposite, compound leaves composed of 3 leaflets, 2 lateral ones and 1 terminal one. The flowers are grouped in elongated, branched clusters in the junction of the leaves along the younger branchlets; individual flowers are white to greenish-white, on jointed stalks, bisexual, with 5 calyx lobes, the lobes fused at the base, 5 petals, the lobes slightly longer than the calyx, 5 stamens, and 3 pistils. Fruits are an inflated or bladder-like capsule, 3 parted and 3-lobed at the tip; seeds small, globe-shaped.

Key to Bladdernut Species

A. Individual leaflets of the 3-parted leaf 5–10 cm (2–4 in) long; bladder-like fruits 4–6 cm (1.6–2.4 in) long; trees of eastern North America
         American bladdernut, p. 757

B. Individual leaflets of the 3-parted leaf 2.4–5.8 cm (1–2.3 in) long; bladder-like fruits 2.5–5 cm (1–2 in) long; trees of Sierra Nevada in California
         Sierra bladdernut, p. 758

American Bladdernut

American Bladdernut   *Staphylea trifolia* L.

This small shrub or tree is usually found in woodland thickets from Quebec to Georgia and as far west as Kansas and Nebraska. It occurs in rich, moist sites along streams and rivers. The American bladdernut does not grow in pure stands, but is found with northern red oak, hemlock, white pine, basswood, yellow birch, and yellow poplar. It is also found growing in association with other trees its size including hawthorn, dogwood, redbud, and sumac.

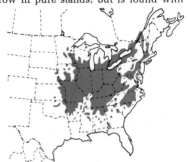

   This is a fast growing but short-lived tree. It flowers in spring and the fruits mature and shed the seeds in the autumn of the same year. Often planted for its ornamental value, it also has some value as an erosion control plant because of its dense underground root system. It is of no value to wildlife except as occasional nesting sites for songbirds.

   Appearance: shrubs or small trees to 8 m (26 ft), with an open, spreading crown;

American Bladdernut

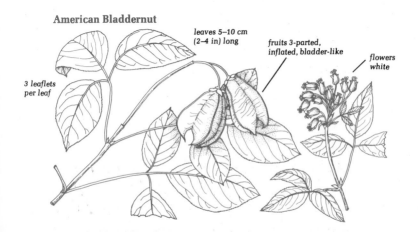

leaves 5–10 cm
(2–4 in) long

fruits 3-parted,
inflated, bladder-like

flowers
white

3 leaflets
per leaf

trunk short, branching close to the ground, to 15 cm (6 in) in diameter. **Bark:** thin, smooth, with green or white stripes. **Branches:** slender, light green and shiny but becoming dark brown with age. **Winter buds:** 2–4 mm (0.1–0.2 in) long, broadest near the base and tapering to a pointed tip, covered with broad scales. **Leaves:** opposite, *compound, composed of 3 leaflets, the leaflets 5–10 cm (2–4 in) long, 2.5–7 cm (1– 2.8 in) wide,* broadest below, at, or above the middle, pointed at the tip, fine-toothed along the margin, rounded at the base, the side leaflets unequally rounded at the base, hairy when young, becoming smooth with age, bright green above, paler and slightly hairy beneath; flowers produced in drooping clusters 5–10 cm (2–4 in) long, rather showy; each flower white, produced on a jointed stalk 8–12 mm (0.3–0.5 in) long, with 5 calyx lobes 7–10 mm (0.3–0.4 in) long, blunt at the tips, 5 spoon-shaped petals, the petals slightly longer than the calyx lobes, 5 stamens, and with 3 pistils. **Fruits:** *dry, inflated, 3-parted, bladder-like capsules, 4–6 cm (1.6–2.4 in) long,* egg-shaped, broadest at the base, 3-lobed at the tip; seeds few, 2–4 mm (0.1–0.2 in) long, egg-shaped, light brown, shiny.

Sierra Bladdernut
Staphylea bolanderi A. Gray

More often a shrub than a tree, the Sierra bladdernut grows in the chaparral and woodlands of the foothills of the Sierra Nevada in northern to central California. It is not abundant anywhere in its range and is usually found between 300 and 1,500 m (984–4,921 ft) in elevation. The attractive white flowers appear in April and May.

The trees grow to 6 m (20 ft) high with an open spreading crown. The *3 individual leaflets* of the leaves are broadest near the base to almost round, *2.4–5.8 cm (1– 2.3 in) long,* pointed at the tip, finely toothed along the margin, and smooth. The flowers are composed of 5 white calyx lobes, each 8–10 mm (0.3–0.4 in) long, 5 white petals, each 9–12 mm (0.4–0.5 in) long, and with 3 central pistils. The *fruits are bladder-like capsules 2.5–5 cm (1–2 in) long,* 3-parted; seeds light brown, 4–7 mm (0.2–0.3 in) long, egg-shaped.

The Soapberry Family
Sapindaceae

This is a large family of about 150 genera and 2,000 species widely distributed throughout tropical and subtropical regions of the world. Although most species are trees or shrubs, many are large vines. Six genera containing 7 species are represented in the North American tree flora. Several others have been introduced. However, only 1 of them, the goldenrain tree, is widely cultivated and is occasionally encountered in the wild. The soapberry family is of some economic importance for its edible fruits (litchi, akee) and ornamentals (goldenrain tree).

Members of this family are trees, shrubs, or vines with alternate, simple or compound leaves. Flowers are regular or irregular, often male or female, and produced in branched clusters. The flowers are usually 5 free or fused sepals, 5 free petals, 8 to 10 stamens, and a single pistil with a superior ovary. Fruits may be nuts, capsules, berries or berry-like or winged, fleshy or dry.

Key to Soapberry Genera

A. Leaves compound, deciduous or evergreen, not sticky.

   1. Leaves feather-like (pinnate or bipinnate) compound.

      a. Fruits 3-parted capsule, leathery or papery, splitting open at maturity.

         (1) Leaves usually twice feather-like (bipinnate) compound; flowers yellow
            Goldenrain tree, p. 759

         (2) Leaves feather-like (pinnate); flowers white or rose to pink.

            (a) Leaflets 5–15 per leaf, uniformly wide to broadest above the middle; flowers white
                Cupania, p. 760

            (b) Leaflets 5–7 per leaf, lance-shaped; flowers rose to pink
                Mexican buckeye, p. 761

      b. Fruits berries or berry-like, fleshy.

         (1) Leaves with 6–19 leaflets per leaf; leaflets pointed at the tip
                Soapberry, p. 762

         (2) Leaves with 2–6, usually 4 leaflets per leaf; leaflets blunt or notched at the tip
                Inkwood, p. 764

   2. Leaves of 3 leaflets (trifoliolate) all arising from same point
            White ironwood, p. 765

B. Leaves simple, evergreen, usually sticky
            Hopbush, p. 766

Goldenrain Tree

Mexican Buckeye

Western Soapberry

Inkwood

The Goldenrain Tree Genus   *Koelreuteria* Laxm.

This small genus of about 6 species is native to Asia, mainly China, Japan, and Korea. They are attractive trees with deciduous, compound leaves and attractive clusters of yellow flowers. One species, the goldenrain tree, has been widely planted in North America.

    Members of this genus are deciduous trees with feather-like (pinnate) or twice feather-like (bipinnate) leaves. Flowers are produced in terminal clusters, each flower with 5 calyx lobes, 4 petals, 8 stamens, and a single pistil. Fruits are papery capsules.

Goldenrain Tree

Koelreuteria paniculata Laxm.

Goldenrain tree was first introduced in 1763. Fast growing, it is an attractive ornamental and one of the few North American trees with yellow flowers in early summer. It is planted along streets in the eastern U.S.

This is a small tree to 15 m (49 ft), with a rounded crown and alternate, deciduous, feather-like (pinnate) or *twice feather-like* (bipinnate) *leaves.* Each leaf has 7 to 17 leaflets, the leaflets broadest near the base, 3–8 cm (1.2–3.2 in) long, and irregularly lobed or toothed. Bisexual flowers are produced in large, hanging, elongated, branched clusters; each *flower* irregular, *yellow,* 8–21 mm (0.3–0.8 in) wide. *Fruits* are *3-parted, bladder-like, papery capsules* 2.5–5 cm (1–2 in) long.

Goldenrain Tree

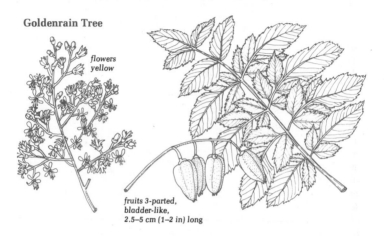

flowers
yellow

fruits 3-parted,
bladder-like,
2.5–5 cm (1–2 in) long

The Cupania Genus

Cupania L.

This is a small genus of perhaps 40 species of trees and shrubs native to tropical America. Only 1 species reaches North America and this is restricted to southern Florida. Members of this genus have unequal, feather-like (pinnate), alternate, evergreen leaves. The trees may be male or female, or have male, female, and bisexual flowers on the same trees. Small flowers are produced in branched or unbranched clusters, each flower with 5 free sepals, 5 petals (sometimes absent), 8 stamens (aborted in female flowers), and a single pistil. Fruits are 3-lobed, stalked capsules.

The Florida Cupania

Cupania glabra Sw.

Florida cupania is a rare shrub or small tree in hammocks of southern Florida and the Florida Keys. It is more common in the West Indies where it grows much larger. Flowering is in early spring with the fruits maturing by summer.

They grow to 15 m (49 ft), and have alternate, *feather-like* (pinnate) *leaves,* each *with 5 to 15 leaflets.* The leaflets are uniformly wide to broadest above the middle, 6–18 cm (2.4–7.1 in) long, 2.5–8 cm (1–3.2

in) wide, shallowly and irregularly toothed, rounded or notched at the tip, dark green and shiny above. Flowers are produced in elongated, branched clusters; each ***flower*** has 5 sepals, 5 rounded ***white petals,*** and a single pistil with a 3-parted, superior ovary. Fruits are ***3-lobed, stalked capsules,*** 1.2–1.8 cm (0.5–0.8 in) long, ***leathery,*** each segment with a large seed.

The Mexican Buckeye Genus

Ungnadia Endl.

This is a genus of just 1 species native to southwestern U.S. and adjacent northern Mexico. Information concerning the genus is the same as for the species.

Mexican Buckeye

Ungnadia speciosa Endl.

Mexican buckeye occurs in limestone soils along stream banks, canyons, and bluffs in Texas, New Mexico, and Mexico. Attractive pink flowers are produced in the spring, with the fruits maturing in September or October. The seeds are mildly poisonous and are not commonly eaten by birds or mammals.

They are shrubs or small trees to 9 m (30 ft), with thin, smooth (shallowly fissured on older trees), light gray to brown bark. The deciduous ***leaves*** are alternate, feather-like (pinnate) compound, and ***composed of 5 to 7 leaflets;*** the leaflets opposite, ***lance-shaped,*** 7–12 cm (2.8–4.7 in) long, 3.5–5 cm (1.4–2 in) wide, toothed along the margin, dark shiny green above, paler beneath. Flowers are produced in short clusters on young branchlets before or as the leaves are expanding. Flowers may be bisexual or male or female, irregular, fragrant, with a 5-lobed calyx, 4 or 5 ***petals, rose to pink,*** widest near the tip and claw-shaped, 7 to 10 stamens, and a single pistil

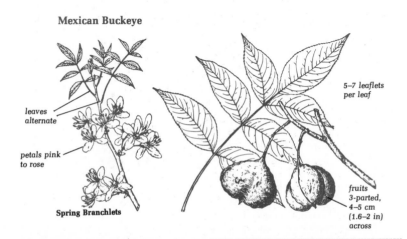

Mexican Buckeye

leaves alternate

petals pink to rose

Spring Branchlets

5–7 leaflets per leaf

fruits 3-parted, 4–5 cm (1.6–2 in) across

with a superior, 3-celled ovary. Fruits are stalked capsules, 3-parted, 4–5 cm (1.6–2 in) across, leathery, splitting open to release the large seeds; seeds round, 1–1.4 cm (0.4–0.6 in) in diameter, smooth, shiny black to brown.

The Soapberry Genus

Sapindus L.

Soapberries are a medium-size genus of approximately 40 species of trees and shrubs. Members are widely distributed throughout tropical regions of the globe, particularly in Asia. In North America 2 species are found, both of them in the southern U.S. These are western and wingleaf soapberries.

Soapberries are shrubs or trees with large feather-like (pinnate) compound leaves and berry-like, dark-orange to yellow fruits. These berries, when rubbed in water, will produce a lather and can be used as a substitute for soap. Flowers are usually either male or female, minute, and produced in large clusters in the junction of the leaves or at the end of the branchlets. Each flower has 4 or 5 calyx lobes, 4 or 5 petals, 8 to 10 stamens, and a single pistil. Fruits are berry-like and contain a single seed.

Key to Soapberry Species

A. Leaves with 7–19 leaflets, with a single end leaflet; leaflets 3.7–10 cm (1.5–4 in) long; trees of southcentral and southwestern U.S.
  Western soapberry, p. 762
B. Leaves with 6–12 leaflets, without a single end leaflet; leaflets 8–18 cm (3.2–7.1 in) long; trees of Florida **Wingleaf soapberry, p. 763**

Wingleaf Soapberry

Western Soapberry

Sapindus drummondii Hook & Arn.

The western soapberry is a small to medium-size tree of the western U.S. and Mexico. Ranging from southern Kansas to northern Mexico, these trees grow on moist clay or limestone upland sites, to elevations of 750–1,900 m (2,461–6,234 ft) above sea level.

They may be found along rivers and sides of canyons in the upper desert, desert grasslands, and oak-dominated woodlands. In Mexico the trees seek the cooler mountain reaches.

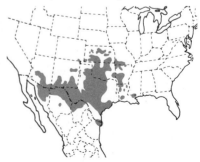

Western soapberry is moderately slow-growing. Large, showy clusters of tiny flowers are produced from May through June. The fruits mature in September or October. Wildlife seldom use this tree. The berry-like fruits have a leathery coat that contains the poisonous substance saponin,

Western Soapberry

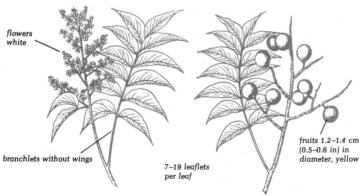

flowers white

branchlets without wings

7–19 leaflets per leaf

fruits 1.2–1.4 cm (0.5–0.6 in) in diameter, yellow

which produces a good, soapy lather. The dense, hard, light-brown wood is mostly used for fuel or in basketry.

Appearance: tree, reaching 15 m (49 ft), with a rounded crown, or a large shrub; trunk to 60 cm (23.6 in) in diameter. **Bark:** gray to reddish, divided into narrow scaly plates. **Branches:** erect, branchlets yellow-green, later pale gray, finely hairy to smooth, are marked with small lenticels. **Winter buds:** small and rounded, in pairs at the bases of the leaves. **Leaves:** alternate, deciduous, feather-like (pinnate) compound up to 45 cm (17.7 in) long, *composed of 7 to 19 leaflets* arranged alternately on the central stalk; *leaflets* lance-shaped, *3.7–10 cm (1.5–4 in) long,* 1.2–1.8 cm (0.5–0.8 in) broad, unequal-sided, long pointed at the tip, pale yellow-green, smooth above, short-haired below, leathery, terminal leaflet smaller. **Flowers:** produced in elongate, branched clusters, 15–23 cm (6–9 in) long; each flower small with 5 sepals, much smaller than the 5 round-tipped, white petals, which contract at the base into a hairy claw-like shape, 8 to 10 stamens, and a single pistil. **Fruits:** smooth, berry-like, yellow, 1.2–1.4 cm (0.5–0.6 in) in diameter, leathery, black, 1-seeded.

Wingleaf Soapberry

Sapindus saponaria L.
(synonym: *S. marginatus* Willd.)

Wingleaf soapberry is widespread in the American tropics and is relatively common in coastal hammocks of southern Florida and the Keys. It is less common in central and northern Florida and has even been reported in coastal regions of Georgia. White flowers are produced in May and June. Like other soapberries, this species contains saponins in the fruits, which make a good substitute for soap.

The trees grow to 15 m (49 ft), with a broad rounded crown, and pale gray, scaly bark. The alternate, deciduous, feather-like (pinnate compound *leaves have 3 to 6 pairs of leaflets; leaflets 8–18 cm (3.2–7.1 in) long,* and narrowly lance-shaped. The tiny usually male or female white flowers are produced in elongate, many-

Wingleaf Soapberry

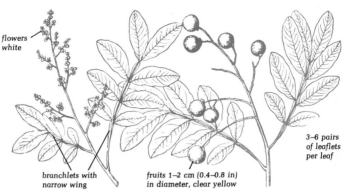

flowers
white

3–6 pairs
of leaflets
per leaf

branchlets with
narrow wing

fruits 1–2 cm (0.4–0.8 in)
in diameter, clear yellow

branched clusters. Fruits are globe-shaped, 1–2 cm (0.4–0.8 in) in diameter, fleshy, clear yellow, containing a single, poisonous seed.

The Inkwood Genus

Exothea Macfadyen

This small genus of 3 species is confined to tropical America, with 1 species in southern Florida. Members are shrubs or trees with alternate, evergreen, feather-like (pinnate) compound leaves. Flowers are either male, female, or bisexual and occur on the same or separate plants. Each flower is composed of a persistent, 5-parted calyx, 5 petals, 7 to 10 stamens (in male flowers), and a single ovary. Fruits are 1-seeded berries.

Inkwood

Exothea paniculata (Juss.) Radlk

Inkwood is an uncommon tree of the eastern coast of southern Florida, the Florida Keys, and much of the West Indies. It grows in hammocks, shell mounds, and chalky soils where it is fairly slow growing. Birds eat the fleshy berries. The reddish-brown wood is hard, heavy, durable and has been used for posts and pilings and for tools.

The trees are small to medium-size, to 15 m (49 ft), with bright red bark which separates into large scales. The alternate, evergreen, feather-like (pinnate) compound *leaves* have **2 to 6 (usually 4) leaflets** which are opposite each other. Leaflets are broadest at the middle, 5–12.5 cm (2–5 in) long, **blunt or notched at the tip,** tapering to an unequal base, entire, shiny dark green and smooth on both surfaces. Flow-

ers are produced in elongated, branched clusters at the tips of the branchlets. The flowers may be male, female, or bisexual on the same or different trees. Each flower is composed of 5 sepals, 5 whitish petals, 8 stamens, and a single pistil. **Fruits are berry-like, 8–12 mm (0.3–0.5 in) in diameter,** fleshy, orange, and 1-seeded.

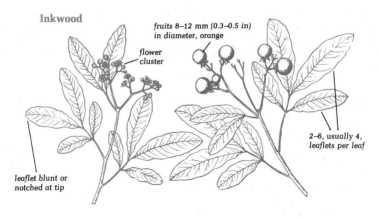

Inkwood

fruits 8–12 mm (0.3–0.5 in)
in diameter, orange

flower
cluster

2–6, usually 4,
leaflets per leaf

leaflet blunt or
notched at tip

The White Ironwood Genus

Hypelate P. Browne

This genus contains only 1 species, the white ironwood of southern Florida. Because there is only 1 species, the description of the genus is the same as for the species.

White Ironwood

Hypelate trifoliata Sw.

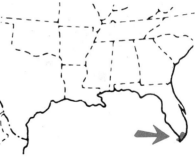

This species is rare, occurring sparingly in hammocks or pinelands of the lower Florida Keys. It is also native to the West Indies. The small white flowers are usually produced in spring or summer. The rich, dark-brown wood is hard, heavy, and was once used for tools and construction, but is seldom used today because of its scarcity.

White ironwoods are shrubs or trees to 13 m (43 ft), with a thin, smooth, reddish-gray bark. Leaves are alternate, evergreen, **each leaf composed of 3 leaflets,** all aris-

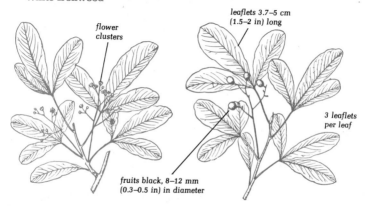

White Ironwood

flower
clusters

leaflets 3.7–5 cm
(1.5–2 in) long

3 leaflets
per leaf

fruits black, 8–12 mm
(0.3–0.5 in) in diameter

ing from the same point. The leaflets are broadest above the middle, 3.7–5 cm (1.5–2 in) long, 1.8–3.2 cm (0.8–1.3 in) wide, blunt or notched at the tip, tapering at the base, entire, leathery, dark shiny green above, bright green beneath. Male and female flowers are produced in separate clusters in the junctions of the upper leaves on the same tree. Each flower has a 5-lobed calyx, 5 short, rounded, white petals, 8 stamens, and a single pistil. *Fruits* are almost *globe-shaped to egg-shaped,* 8–12 mm (0.3–0.5 in) in diameter, *black, fleshy,* and containing a large seed.

The Hopbush Genus   *Dodonaea* Mill.

This is a medium-size genus of about 50 species, primarily Australian, but with a few species elsewhere. There is only 1 which reaches tree size in North America, the Florida hopbush.

Members of this genus are shrubs or trees with alternate, usually evergreen, sticky leaves. Flowers are small and produced in elongated, branched clusters. Each flower is composed of a tiny 3- to 7-lobed calyx, no petals, 6 to 10 stamens, and a single pistil with a 2- to 4-celled, superior ovary.

Florida Hopbush   *Dodonaea viscosa* (L.) Jacq.

(synonym: *D. microcarya* Small)

This is a small tree native to the lower Florida Keys where it grows in hammocks and pinelands. It is also widely distributed in tropical regions of the world. Flowering and fruiting is irregular and may occur throughout the year. The leaves and bark have been used in folk medicines, although ill-advisedly because of the poisonous saponins in these and all soapberry plants.

Florida hopbush is a shrub or small tree to 3 m (10 ft), with alternate, *simple, evergreen* to deciduous leaves that are narrow spatula-like, broadest near the tip, 2.5–5 cm (1–2 in) long, 0.5–1 cm (0.2–0.4 in) wide, entire, *yellowish-green and sticky.* The yellowish-green flowers are produced in small clusters in the junctions of the leaves and branchlets. Each flower is composed of usually 4 sepals, no petals, 5 to 8 stamens, and a single pistil. Sometimes the flowers may be just male or female. *Fruits are capsules 0.6–1.2 cm (0.3–0.5 in) long, 3-parted* and *3-winged,* and notched at both ends.

The Horsechestnut Family   Hippocastanaceae

This is a small family of 2 genera and 15 species. The horsechestnut genus (*Aesculus*) of North America, Europe, and Asia contains 13 species of deciduous trees or shrubs, while the Mexican and South American genus (*Billia*) has 2 evergreen species. Members of this family are widely used as ornamentals and shade trees because of their handsome spreading shape and attractive clusters of flowers. Some species are important timber trees. Extracts from the leaves, fruits, and seeds have been used in medicines and as poisons.

Members of this family are trees or shrubs with large winter buds covered with overlapping, often sticky scales. The opposite, hand-shaped and compound leaves are deciduous or evergreen, entire or toothed. Flowers are produced in branched clusters with upper male flowers and lower bisexual ones. They are irregular, with 5 sepals, 5 petals of various colors, 5 to 8 stamens, and a single pistil with a superior ovary. Fruits are leathery, 3-valved capsules containing 1 to 3 large seeds.

The Buckeye Genus

Aesculus L.

This is a small genus, containing 13 species of trees and shrubs of the north temperate regions around the world. Five species of trees are native to moist woodlands in North America. The rest occur in southeastern Europe, India to China, and Japan. Horsechestnut is native to the Balkans in Greece, but has been extensively planted in the U.S., southern Canada, and Europe for its showy foliage and flowers.

Although the genus has many distinctive characteristics, such as the compound leaves, the ***fruit is one of the most easily recognizable features.*** This is a large, brown, satin-shiny nut, which is enclosed alone or in pairs in a leathery, greenish capsule that splits open when the buckeye is ripe. Although it resembles the edible seed of the chestnut tree, wild-food gatherers should be wary of the buckeye. It contains the poison aesculin, which can induce vomiting, stupor, twitching, and even paralysis. For this reason, these trees are largely shunned by wildlife. Two of the species, Ohio and yellow buckeyes, are valuable as timber trees. All the species, as well as their numerous hybrids, have been extremely popular shade trees and ornamentals.

Buckeyes are small to medium-size trees or shrubs. The bark is gray to brown-gray, becomes scaly or cracked with age, and has an unpleasant odor. The leaves are opposite, deciduous, 5 to 7 leaflets in hand-like arrangement (palmately compound), each with saw-tooth margins, and with very long leafstalks. Winter buds are occasionally sticky, and covered with many, overlapping scales. Flowers are borne in large clusters at the ends of branches in spring after the leaves have appeared. Many flowers are male or female; bisexual ones occur at the base of the clusters. Each flower has a tubular or bell-shaped, 5-lobed calyx, 4 or 5 petals, unequal in size, resembling a claw, 8 or 10 stamens with long slender stalks, and a single pistil. Fruits are capsules, smooth to spiny, and splitting open to shed the 1 to 3 large brown seeds.

Key to Horsechestnut Species

A. Winter buds not sticky; flowers with the claw part of the petals longer than the calyx.

   1. Flowers with a bell-shaped calyx; petals pale yellow-green, yellow, or yellowish-white.

Ohio Buckeye

      a. Flower petals almost equal in length; fruits covered with blunt spines; trees of east central U.S.   **Ohio buckeye, p. 768**

      b. Flower petals very unequal in length; fruits not spiny; trees of eastern and southeastern U.S.   **Yellow buckeye, p. 769**

   2. Flowers with a tubular calyx; petals scarlet, cream, or yellowish-green.   (Continued)

Yellow Buckeye

a. Petals scarlet; fruits 3.8–5.8 cm (1.5–2.3 in) thick; trees of southeastern U.S.
   Red buckeye, p. 771

b. Petals pink, cream, or yellowish-green; fruits 2.2–4.1 cm (0.9–1.6 in) thick, trees of southeastern U.S. **Painted buckeye, p. 772**

B. Winter buds sticky; flower with the claw part of the petals shorter than the calyx.

1. Leaflets stalked; flowers with 4 petals; trees of California **California buckeye, p. 773**

2. Leaflets without a stalk (sessile); flowers with 5 petals; introduced trees, commonly cultivated **Horsechestnut, p. 774**

Red Buckeye

Horsechestnut

Ohio Buckeye, Fetid Buckeye — *Aesculus glabra* Willd.

The Ohio buckeye is a medium-size tree of the eastcentral U.S. It ranges from lowlands to the western slopes of the Allegheny Mountains to the southern shores of Lake Erie and to southcentral Texas. This buckeye prefers moist sites such as river

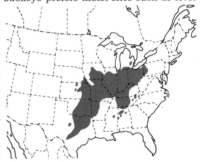

bottoms and streambank soils. It some-times grows on drier sites, such as those which support hickory and oak, and in clay soils, but growth is slower then and these trees are not attractive. Ohio buckeye is typical of mixed tree stands, and is found as a minor component in at least 2 forest types in the beech-sugar maple-basswood forest and with northern red oak and other oaks, white ash, several hick-ories, and black walnut. It is not found on open sites. The Texas buckeye, *Aesculus glabra* variety *arguta*, occurs in parts of Oklahoma, Kansas, and Texas. This variety has 7 leaflets per leaf while the typical form has 5 leaflets.

Growth and life-span are both moderate with most trees living to 80 to 100 years. The tree produces clusters of pale yellow-green flowers from March to May, and the fruits and seeds mature from September to mid-October. Buckeyes seem relatively disease and pest-free. The tree is little used by wildlife, although squirrels sometimes eat the soft young nuts. Both nuts and leaves have a poisonous alkaloid.

This tree well deserves the nickname "Fetid Buckeye." The twigs, bark, flowers, and leaves all produce an offensive odor when crushed. Despite this property, Ohio, the Buckeye State, selected this species as its state tree. The wood is white, close-grained, and light. It is easy to carve, and resists splitting. It is ideal to use in the man-ufacture of artificial limbs. The wood has been employed in many other ways, as paper pulp, in woodenware, and as troughs for catching maple sap in the spring. Despite the many uses found, buckeye is of minor commercial importance, because of its increasing rarity.

Appearance: medium-size tree, normally 9–15 m, rarely to 25 (30–49 ft, rarely to

Ohio Buckeye

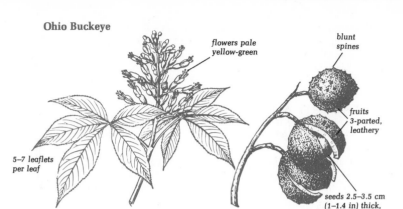

flowers pale yellow-green

blunt spines

fruits 3-parted, leathery

5–7 leaflets per leaf

seeds 2.5–3.5 cm (1–1.4 in) thick, dark reddish-brown

82), with a broad, open, rounded crown; trunk straight, to 80 cm (32 in) in diameter. **Bark:** 1.7–2 cm (0.7–0.8 in) thick on old trees, dark brown, deeply furrowed, broken into thick, scaly plates. **Branches:** small and spreading; branchlets orange-to-reddish-brown, covered with orange-colored pores, drooping with upcurved ends. **Winter buds:** 1.5–1.7 cm (0.6–0.7 in) long, widest at the middle, pointed at the tip, with many red-tinted, nearly triangular scales; enlarging to 3.8–5 cm (1.5–2 in) long in spring, yellow. **Leaves:** opposite, deciduous, hand-shaped; with 5 or 7 oval-oblong leaflets, 10–15 cm (4–6 in) long, 3.5–6 cm (1.4–2.4 in) wide, narrowly tapered at both tip and base, margins finely but irregularly toothed, yellow-green and smooth above, paler beneath, yellow in fall; *leafstalks generally as long as the leaves, enlarged at the base and leaving a horseshoe-shaped scar on the twig.* **Flowers:** male and female and bisexual in erect clusters, 12.5–15 cm (5–6 in) long, on the same tree; each flower 1.2–3.8 cm (0.5–1.5 in) long, pale yellow-green, with a 5-lobed, bell-shaped calyx, 2 pairs of nearly equal petals, the upper pair sometimes marked with red stripes, 7 stamens, on long, curved filaments with orange anthers. **Fruits:** a leathery capsule, 3-parted, 2.5–5 cm (1–2 in) long, the husk covered with blunt spines, containing 1, 2, or 3 seeds, the seeds dark reddish-brown, shiny, 2.5–3.5 cm (1–1.4 in) thick.

Yellow Buckeye, Sweet Buckeye   *Aesculus octandra* Marsh.

Yellow buckeye is a large-size tree of the American southeast. It ranges from the mountains of southwestern Pennsylvania to northern Alabama and Georgia, as well as west to Texas. This buckeye therefore encounters a fairly wide range of climatic varia-

tion, and occurs to an elevation of 1,860 m (6,070 ft), in the Great Smoky Mountains in North Carolina. As with all buckeyes, the yellow buckeye is a moist-site tree, but requires good drainage. Best growth occurs in river bottoms and along streambanks in deep, dark humus soils. It is not a pioneer species, so it is not seen in old fields or other open land. It is a minor component of at least 6 forest types, where it is associated with sugar maple, beech, yellow birch, black cherry, red spruce, Fraser fir,

northern red oak, and basswood, among many other hardwood species.

Seedling development is fast in the yellow buckeye, and the tree is moderately long-lived, reaching maturity in 60 to 80 years. The tree survives competition with other forest members fairly well, and is tolerant of shading by bigger trees. The yellow or yellowish-white flower clusters appear in April and May, when the leaves are half-grown. The fruit is a leathery and spiny capsule containing 1 or 2 brown, shiny, large seeds which ripen in September. The plant is generally unpalatable to wildlife. Livestock is attracted to the young shoots and sweet seeds and becomes poisoned by them. The Indians found a way to remove the poison, called aesculin, by roasting the seeds among stones to loosen the shells, then peeling, mashing, and leaching them in water for several days. A tasty, nutritious flour was produced.

Its shape and foliage make the buckeye an attractive shade tree. It is frequently encountered in yards and along streets in rural towns. The softest of American hardwoods, it is at the bottom of the list of the 35 leading timbers of the U.S. It makes poor lumber.

Yellow Buckeye

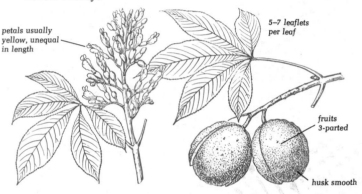

petals usually yellow, unequal in length

5–7 leaflets per leaf

fruits 3-parted

husk smooth

Appearance: medium to tall tree, to 26 m (85 ft) in height, with a small, long, well-rounded crown made up of hanging branches; trunk straight, thick, to 1 m (3.3 ft) in diameter. **Bark:** 1.7–2 cm (0.7–0.8 in) thick, dark brown and scaly, the outer layer often covered with a whitish bloom, the inner bright yellow or scarlet. **Branches:** opposite, hanging, tapering into stout branchlets, at first orange-brown and smooth, becoming darker. **Winter buds:** 1.6–1.8 cm (0.7–0.8 in) long, *not sticky,* covered with broad, slightly fuzzy pale brown scales that are rounded on the back; the inner scales growing up to 5 cm (2 in) long by spring, bright yellow or sometimes red. **Leaves:** opposite, deciduous, hand-shaped, with 5 to 7 leaflets; the central leaflet is largest, 10–15 cm (4–6 in) long and 3.8–6.4 cm (1.5–2.5 in) across; leaflets broadest near or just above the middle, abruptly sharp-pointed at the tip, gradually narrowed to a wedge-shaped base, with sharp teeth along the margins, dark yellow-green, smooth at maturity, turning a clear yellow in the fall; leafstalks slender, 10–15 cm (4–6 in) long, slightly hairy. **Flowers:** produced in large, branched, loosely flowered clusters; each flower with a *bell-shaped calyx; 4 petals, yellow,* in some varieties red, pink, or creamy, very unequal, the upper pair erect, the lower pair larger, with shorter claws; stamens usually 7, shorter than the petals, and a single pistil. **Fruits:** a *leathery, 3-parted capsule,* 5–7.5 cm (2–3 in) long, the *husk thin, smooth* brownish, and pitted; seeds large, 2 per capsule, brown, with a conspicuous, pale scar.

Red Buckeye

Aesculus pavia L.

(synonym: *A. discolor* Pursh)

The red buckeye is a short tree or shrub of the southeastern U.S. It grows in rich, moist soil, in woods and along streambanks at low elevations from Virginia to northern Florida, and west to Louisiana. Because it grows beneath most other trees, this buckeye is referred to as an understory tree. It grows under river birch, loblolly pine, yellow buckeye, and many oaks.

Growth is rapid, although the red buckeye is short lived. It may begin to bloom early in life, when it is less than a meter (3.3 ft) tall. Flowering occurs in the different parts of its range throughout the spring months, with displays of large clusters of showy red flowers. As with other buckeyes, the fruit is a pod containing 1 or 2 chestnut-brown seeds that contain a distasteful and poisonous juice. Most wildlife avoid this tree and other buckeyes, although squirrels may eat the nuts when they have just fallen.

The red buckeye seldom if ever reaches sufficient height to be of economic value as a timber tree. However, its short stature makes it a popular ornamental shrub. A successful ornamental hybrid, *Aesculus* X *carnea*, has been created by crossing red buckeye with the European horsechestnut (*A. hippocastanum*). It has the showy flowers of the red buckeye, combined with the handsome foliage of the latter.

Red Buckeye

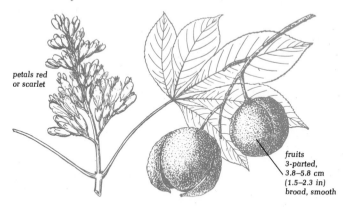

petals red or scarlet

fruits 3-parted, 3.8–5.8 cm (1.5–2.3 in) broad, smooth

Appearance: short tree, to 6 m (20 ft), but more often a shrub to 4 m (13 ft), with an open crown; trunk slender, to 10–12 cm (4–4.7 in) in diameter. **Bark:** smooth, dark gray or brown. **Branches:** large and erect; young branchlets smooth or covered with fine hairs, gray or brown, round. **Winter buds:** *not sticky,* covered with overlapping scales. **Leaves:** opposite, deciduous, *hand-shaped,* 18.5–32 cm (7.3–12.6 in) long, *with 5 to 7 stalked leaflets,* the center one the largest; leaflets are 5–15 cm (2–6 in) long, oblong and broadest at the middle or just above, tapering and pointed at the tips, wedge-shaped at the base, finely toothed along the margin, papery thin in texture, dark green and shiny above, paler below. **Flowers:** produced in clusters 10–20 cm (4–

7.9 in) long, each flower with a scarlet ***tubular calyx,*** 8–16 mm (0.3–0.6 in) long, with 5 short, blunt lobes; ***petals*** 4 or 5, ***red,*** 2.5–4 cm (1–1.6 in) long, with hairy claws; stamens 6 to 8, slightly longer than the petals. **Fruits:** a capsule, 3.8–5.8 cm (1.5–2.3 in) broad, ***spherical, smooth, leathery, containing 1 or 2 large shiny, poisonous brown seeds.***

Painted Buckeye, Dwarf Buckeye

Aesculus sylvatica Bartr.
(synonym: *A. georgiana* Sarg.)

The painted, or dwarf buckeye is a short tree or shrub of the southeastern U.S. It grows on moist sites in woodlands, often along streams, from southern Virginia to northern Florida, and up to elevations of 1,000 m (3,281 ft), in the Blue Ridge Mountains. Among its forest associates are several species of oak, sycamore, willow, cottonwood, and river birch.

Like most of the smaller members of the buckeye group, this is a fast-growing, short-lived tree. The yellow or yellow-red flowers are produced in showy clusters that open in April to May, after the leaves have emerged; the familiar buckeye fruit matures by the fall. Wildlife use this tree very little if at all, since the leaves and fruits are toxic. The tree is too small to be of economic value as a source of lumber.

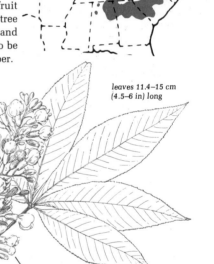

Painted Buckeye

leaves 11.4–15 cm (4.5–6 in) long

fruit 2.2–4.1 cm (0.9–1.6 in) thick

seed

petals pink, cream, or yellowish green

Appearance: short tree, to 10 m (33 ft) tall, with an open, rounded crown; trunk slender, to 25 cm (9.8 in) in diameter. **Bark:** thin, dark brown, surface broken into small, thin scales. **Branches:** slender, erect, and spreading; branchlets stout, smooth, orange-green and marked at first with pale lenticels, later turning red-brown. **Winter buds:** 7–9 mm (0.3–0.4 in) long, covered with light reddish-brown scales, which are narrowed, rounded, and pointed at the tip. **Leaves:** opposite, deciduous, hand-shaped, with 5 leaflets, 11.4–15 cm (4.5–6 in) long, 3.8–6.4 cm (1.5–2.5 in) wide, broadest around the middle, tapering at the tip and base, finely and often doubly-toothed along the margin, slightly hairy early in season, yellow-green above, green, smooth or hairy below. **Flowers:** bisexual or male, in the same cluster, the clusters 10–20 cm (4–7.9 in) long, with the bisexual flowers near the base; calyx 5-lobed, 6–14 mm (0.2–0.6 in) long, downy, red above, pale yellow on the lower side; ***corolla*** of **4** hairy ***petals, yellowish-green, pink, or cream,*** the upper pair 2.4–3.6 cm (1–1.5 in) long, broadest near the tip; the lower or lateral pair 2–3 cm (0.8–1.2 in) long, broadest near the tip; stamens usually 7, long, slender. **Fruits:** a leathery, 3-parted ***capsule, 2.2–4.1 cm (0.9–1.6 in) thick,*** containing 1 to 3 large, dark-brown, shiny seeds.

California Buckeye *Aesculus californica* (Spach) Nutt.

California buckeye is a low, handsome tree, or more often a shrub, occurring exclusively in California. There, it grows in the humid coastal belt, eastward to the streams of the Sacramento Valley, and south to northern Los Angeles county, at elevations ranging from 150–1,250 m (492–4,101 ft).

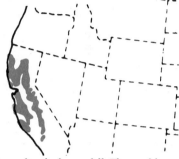

This buckeye grows on moist stream borders, as well as in dry, gravelly soils on sides of canyons. Best growth occurs in the coastal range canyons, north of San Francisco. The tree is a member of the western chaparral forest type, and is associated with live oak, redbud, digger pine, and manzanita, among others.

A moderately fast-growing, long-lived tree, the California buckeye produces in May showy erect clusters of white or pale pink flowers that are quite hairy. The seeds mature after the leaves fall. The seed-bearing husks persist for a while after the leaves have fallen. There is little known wildlife use of this species except as protective cover.

The pale yellow or white wood is soft, light, and close-grained and has no value as lumber. The trees are used as attractive ornamentals in parks in California and Europe. Indians once added the ground nuts to small ponds and streams to stupefy fish.

California Buckeye

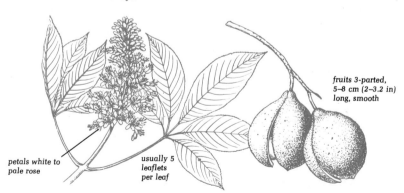

petals white to pale rose

usually 5 leaflets per leaf

fruits 3-parted, 5–8 cm (2–3.2 in) long, smooth

Appearance: a short tree or large shrub, rarely reaching 9 m (30 ft) in height, with a flat-topped, open crown; trunk short, often enlarged at the base, 10–12.5 cm (4–5 in) in diameter. **Bark:** 8–10 mm (0.3–0.4 in) thick, nearly smooth, light to pale gray.

Branches: stout, wide-spreading; branchlets stout, reddish to gray-brown when young, darkening with age, smooth. **Winter buds: *very sticky;*** cone-shaped, pointed at the tip, covered with narrow, pointed, overlapping dark brown scales. **Leaves:** opposite, deciduous, hand-shaped, with a conspicuously larger middle leaflet, 4 to 7, usually 5 leaflets, 10–15 cm (4–6 in) long, 3.8–5 cm (1.5–2 in) broad, widest at the middle, pointed at the tip and base, with fine sharp teeth along the margins, dark green and shiny above, paler below; leafstalks slender, 7.5–10 cm (3–4 in) long, grooved. **Flowers:** produced in long-stalked, erect clusters, many-flowered, 10–20 cm (4–7.9 in) long; each flower 2.5–2.9 cm (1–1.2 in) long, calyx 2-lobed, slightly toothed, narrowly bell-shaped, densely hairy; ***petals*** narrow, 1.2–1.6 cm (0.5–0.7 in) long, ***white to pale rose;*** stamens 5 to 7, with long, slender filaments and bright orange anthers; pistil 1, with a densely hairy ovary. **Fruits: *capsule, nearly pear-shaped, 5–8 cm (2–3.2 in) long,*** smooth, short-stalked, containing 1 to 2 seeds per fruit, the seeds pale orange-brown, 3.8–5 cm (1.5–2 in) wide.

Horsechestnut   *Aesculus hippocastanum* L.

The horsechestnut is native to Europe where it has been widely planted as a street and park tree. It was introduced into North America during colonial days and widely planted for its flowers and attractive leaves. It grows into a large, spreading tree requiring ample space.

Horsechestnut is fast growing and reaches heights of up to 25 m (82 ft). The compound ***leaves*** are opposite, deciduous, 10–25 cm (4–9.8 in) long and ***have 5 to 7 leaflets*** arranged like the fingers of a hand (palmate); the leaflets are broadest above the middle and doubly toothed along the margins. ***White flowers*** are produced in large clusters on sweeping branches that give the tree the appearance of an enormous candelabra. Fruits are spiny, leathery, green capsules that contain 1 or 2 shiny, dark-brown seeds that mature in autumn.

Horsechestnut

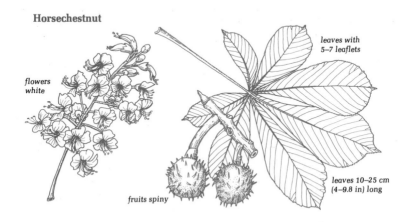

flowers
white

leaves with
5–7 leaflets

leaves 10–25 cm
(4–9.8 in) long

fruits spiny

The Maple Family   Aceraceae

This is a small family of only 2 genera and about 125 species. The genus *Dipteronia* contains 2 species native to central and southern China. The remainder of the species belong to the widespread genus of maples, *Acer*. China contains about two-thirds of the different species of maples, and the rest occur in North America, Europe, Asia Minor, and Japan. Thirteen species are native to North America, 9 to the eastern U.S. and Canada, and 4 to the western states and provinces. Of the many species introduced from Europe and Asia, only 2 are commonly encountered: the Norway maple and sycamore maple.

Members of this family are trees, occasionally shrubs, with opposite, deciduous, rarely evergreen leaves. The leaves are simple or compound, entire or variously lobed, and often toothed. Male and bisexual flowers occur on the same or on separate plants, or male and female flowers occur on separate plants. The flowers have 5 sepals, 5 or 0 petals, 4 to 10 stamens, and a single pistil. ***Fruits are always paired, each with a conspicuous wing.***

The Maple Genus

Acer L.

This genus contains many well-known and economically important species of trees. Maples are a major component of the extensive deciduous, hardwood forest covering vast areas of North America. Canada has chosen the maple as its national tree. The excellent hard, strong wood is used to make furniture, flooring, veneer, cabinets, and for many other goods. Maple syrup is obtained principally from sugar maple. Many native species and several introduced ones are grown as shade or ornamental trees. The Japanese maple (*Acer palmatum*) is an attractive shrub or small tree with deeply lobed, almost star-shaped leaves. There are many cultivated selections of this maple including those with finely dissected leaves and others with deep purple to dark red leaves.

The family description will serve for that of the genus.

Key to Maple Species

A. Leaves simple.

    1. Flowers and fruits produced in elongate, stalked, narrow to spreading, branched or unbranched clusters; the flowers with petals.

        a. Flowers and fruits in long, narrow unbranched or only slightly branched clusters (racemes or slender panicles).

            (1) Flower clusters upright; trees of northeastern North America, central Canada, and Appalachian Mountains
                Mountain maple, p. 777

            (2) Flower clusters hanging.

                (a) Leaves deeply 5-lobed, 14–30 cm (5.5–11.8 in) long; 2-winged fruits 3–4 cm (1.2–1.6 in) long; trees of west coastal North America
                Bigleaf maple, p. 778
                (Continued)

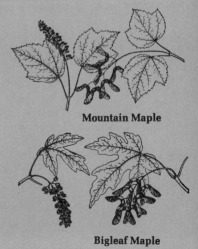

Mountain Maple

Bigleaf Maple

(b) Leaves shallowly 3-lobed, 8–16 cm (3.2–6.3 in) long; 2-winged fruits 1.8–2.4 cm (0.8–1 in) long; trees of northeastern North America, including Appalachian Mountains
Striped maple, p. 779

Striped Maple

b. Flowers and fruits in branched, elongate and spreading near the base or middle, or spreading clusters.

(1) Flowering clusters upright; leafstalks with milky sap; introduced trees, widely planted, especially in cities
Norway maple, p. 780

(2) Flowering clusters hanging; leafstalks with clear sap.

Norway Maple

(a) Leaves 3–5-lobed, 7.5–16 cm (3–6.3 in) long.

(a1) Leaves 3–5-lobed, sharply double toothed along the margins; fruits 1.8–2.2 cm (0.8–1 in) long, the wings with an acute 45° or less spread; trees of western North America
Rocky Mountain maple, p. 781

Rocky Mountain Maple

(a2) Leaves 5-lobed, coarsely toothed along the margins; fruits 3–5 cm (1.2–2 in) long, the wings spreading at an angle of 90° or less; introduced trees
Sycamore maple, p. 782

Sycamore Maple

(b) Leaves 7–9 lobed, 3–10 cm (1.2–4 in) long, trees of coastal regions of Pacific Northwest
Vine maple, p. 783

Vine Maple

2. Flowers and fruits produced in stalkless or nearly so clusters; each flower and fruit stalked, stalks arising or appearing to arise from one location; the flowers usually lacking petals or the petals soon falling away.

a. Flowers appearing long before the leaves develop; the 2-winged fruits forming a V-shaped sinus.

(1) Leaves 3–5-lobed, pale green to whitish beneath, flowers with petals; fruits 1.2–

Red Maple

2.6 cm (0.5–1.1 in) long, trees of eastern North America **Red maple, p. 783**

(2) Leaves deeply 5-lobed, white to silvery beneath; flowers without petals; fruits 4–7.5 cm (1.6–3 in) long; trees of eastern and midwestern North America **Silver maple, p. 785**

b. Flowers appearing as the leaves are expanding or after; 2-winged fruits forming a U-shaped sinus.

(1) Leaves finely or softly hairy beneath when mature.

(a) Leaves dark green; bark dark brown, gray to nearly black.

(a1) Leaves 3–5-lobed, 12–15 cm (4.7–5.9 in) long at maturity; trees of eastern North America **Black maple, p. 786**

(a2) Leaves 3-lobed, 5–12 cm (2–4.7 in) long at maturity; trees of southern Rocky Mountains and Mexico **Bigtooth maple, p. 787**

(b) Leaves dark yellow-green; bark almost white; trees of southeastern U.S. **Chalk maple, p. 788**

(2) Leaves smooth beneath or with a few hairs on the veins.

(a) Leaves 7.5–20 cm (3–8 in) long; bark dark gray to grayish-brown; fruits 3–3.5 cm (1.2–1.4 in) long; common trees of eastern North America **Sugar maple, p. 789**

(b) Leaves 3.8–9 cm (1.5–3.5 in) long; bark whitish; fruits 1.6–3 cm (0.7–1.2 in) long; trees of southeastern U.S. **Florida maple, p. 790**

B. Leaves feather-like (pinnate) compound, with 3, rarely 5, leaflets per leaf; widespread trees of North America **Boxelder, p. 791**

Silver Maple

Black Maple

Bigtooth Maple

Sugar Maple

Boxelder

Mountain Maple

Acer spicatum Lam.

Mountain maple is primarily a northern tree extending from Saskatchewan to Labrador, south to Wisconsin and extending along the higher elevations of the Appalachian Mountains to northern Georgia. It grows in cool habitats such as the edges of mountain streams, ravines, or in woodlands in deep, rich, moist soils. This maple often grows in the shade of many other trees including sugar maple, eastern hemlock, beech, yellow birch, red fir, balsam fir, and tulip tree. Flowering is in late spring with the hanging winged fruits maturing in July. Whitetail deer and moose browse saplings, young twigs, and leaves.

This is a shrub or small tree to 30 m (98 ft), with an irregular, uneven, rounded crown, and often with more than 1 main trunk. The simple, opposite, deciduous leaves have *3 shallow lobes, 8–12 cm (3.2–4.7 in) long and wide,* the lobes pointed at the tips, *with coarse, sharp-pointed teeth along the margin,* yellowish-green above, paler and softly hairy beneath. *Flowers* are pale yellow and produced *in slender, narrow, upright clusters* after the leaves are fully developed. Fruits are dry, 2-winged, 1.2–2 cm (0.5–0.8 in) long, the wings spreading at an angle of 90° or less.

Mountain Maple

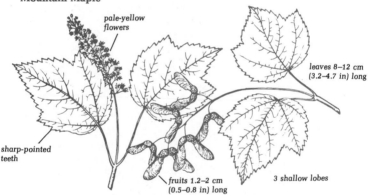

pale-yellow flowers

leaves 8–12 cm (3.2–4.7 in) long

sharp-pointed teeth

fruits 1.2–2 cm (0.5–0.8 in) long

3 shallow lobes

Bigleaf Maple

Acer macrophyllum Pursh

Bigleaf maple is the only maple species in the Pacific Northwest that becomes a medium- to large-size tree. Its range extends from southwestern British Columbia to southern California. Due to the effects of the Ice Ages on the distribution of plants, this species is more closely related to some of the European maples than to North American species. It grows in a variety of soil types from sea level to 1,000 m (3,280 ft), in the northern part of its range and to nearly 2,000 m (6,560 ft) in California. Best growth occurs in deep, rich soils. This species may form dense pure stands, al-

though it is more commonly found in association with Douglas fir, western hemlock, vine maple, redwoods, willows, and live oak.

Growth is rapid for the first 40 or 50 years, then slows as these trees approach a maximum age of 275 years. Flowering is in April or May with the winged fruits maturing by autumn. Seed production is often heavy, especially in open-grown trees. Squirrels, chipmunks, mice, evening grosbeaks, and many other birds eat the seeds. Blacktail deer, mule deer, and elk feed on saplings, young twigs, and leaves.

Bigleaf maples are an important source of hardwood lumber in the Northwest. The light-brown wood is hard but not very strong, and is used for furniture, paneling, cabinets, musical instruments, and veneer. Older trees frequently produce knobby outgrowths or burls that give the wood an interesting configuration prized in veneer work. These trees are often planted for shade in cities.

Bigleaf Maple

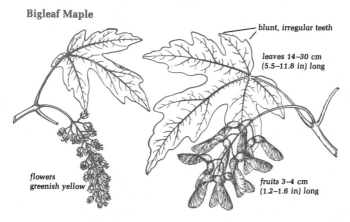

blunt, irregular teeth

leaves 14–30 cm (5.5–11.8 in) long

flowers greenish yellow

fruits 3–4 cm (1.2–1.6 in) long

Appearance: medium to large trees to 30 m (98 ft), with a narrow or broad, rounded crown; trunk straight, to 1 m (3.3 ft) in diameter, rarely larger. **Bark:** 1.2–2 cm (0.5–0.8 in) thick, becoming deeply furrowed with small, flattened plates, gray to reddish-brown. **Branches:** stout, spreading, sometimes drooping; branchlets stout, green turning dark red to gray. **Winter buds:** 6–9 mm (0.2–0.4 in) long, rounded at the tip, covered with overlapping, broad, rounded, reddish-brown scales. **Leaves:** simple, opposite, deciduous, large, *14–30 cm (5.5–11.8 in) long and wide,* usually slightly wider than long, deeply 5-lobed, pointed at the tips, heart-shaped or nearly so at the base, with *a few blunt irregular teeth* along the margin, almost leathery, dark shiny green and smooth above, paler and usually smooth beneath; leafstalks stout, 20–30 cm (7.9–11.8 in) long, with a milky sap when broken. **Flowers:** male and female flowers produced in the same, many-flowered, hanging, elongated clusters, 10–15 cm (4–6 in) long; the flowers greenish-yellow, fragrant, with usually 5 small sepals and petals, 4 to 6 stamens in male flowers, and a single pistil in the female flowers. **Fruits:** 2-winged, *3–4 cm (1.2–1.6 in) long,* 1.1–1.4 cm (0.5–0.6 in) wide, hairy over the seed, the wings slightly spreading, usually at an angle of 60° or less.

Striped Maple, Moose Wood   *Acer pensylvanicum* L.

This often shrubby maple is native to northeastern North America and extends southward in the higher elevations of the Appalachian Mountains to northern Georgia. It grows in moist, rich woodlands from sea level to 1,000 m (3,280 ft) elevation in the southern portion of its range. Striped maple grows in association with sugar maple, beech, yellow birch, eastern hemlock, and balsam fir. Flowering is in early spring, with the fruits maturing in late spring. Grouse, rodents, and songbirds eat the fruits, and whitetail deer and moose browse the young twigs and leaves. The bright green bark with **conspicuous white, lengthwise stripes readily distinguishes young striped maples from other species.**

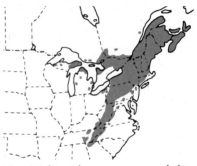

Striped maple is a shrub or small tree to 12 m (39 ft), with an uneven rounded to flat-topped crown, with thin, **smooth greenish-brown bark marked with long thin**

Striped Maple

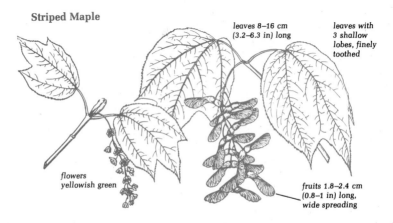

leaves 8–16 cm (3.2–6.3 in) long

leaves with 3 shallow lobes, finely toothed

flowers yellowish green

fruits 1.8–2.4 cm (0.8–1 in) long, wide spreading

white stripes. The simple, opposite, deciduous leaves have **3 shallow lobes near the tip,** occasionally without lobes, as wide or slightly wider than long, 8–16 cm (3.2–6.3 in) long, 10–18 cm (4–7.1 in) wide, with **many fine teeth along the margin,** pale yellowish-green and smooth. Flowers are produced in long, narrow, hanging, many-flowered clusters at the ends of the branchlets. Fruits are dry, 2-winged, 1.8–2.4 cm (0.8–1 in) long, the wings wide spreading, between 90° and 140°.

Norway Maple   *Acer platanoides* L.

Norway maple was imported from Europe and has become one of the most popular and widely planted trees in North America. It is often the most commonly encountered street tree in cities and towns. It grows well in a variety of soils, even in nutrient-poor, compacted soils in cities. It is more tolerant of dust, smoke, and air pollutants than native species. Many varieties have been selected or developed for their shape, leaf form, color, or suitability for the urban environment. Best known among these are Crimson King and Summershade.

The trees reach 30 m (98 ft), usually with a dense, rounded crown. The simple, opposite, deciduous leaves are 5-, occasionally 7-lobed, 8–16 cm (3.2–6.3 in) long, 10–18 cm (4–7.1 in) wide, the lobes pointed, with remote, pointed teeth along the margin, bright green and shiny, **leafstalks with a milky sap** when broken. Flowers are bisex-

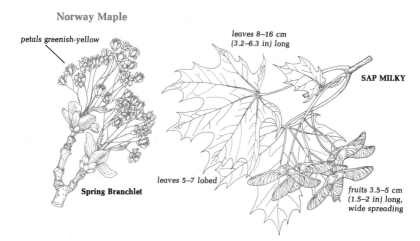

Norway Maple

petals greenish-yellow

leaves 8–16 cm
(3.2–6.3 in) long

SAP MILKY

leaves 5–7 lobed

Spring Branchlet

fruits 3.5–5 cm
(1.5–2 in) long,
wide spreading

ual or male and produced in an erect, few to many-flowered, branched cluster. *Fruits are dry, hanging, 2-winged, 3.5–5 cm (1.5–2 in) long, the wings widely spreading, almost at 180°.*

Rocky Mountain Maple   *Acer glabrum* Torr.

This is a small tree widely scattered throughout western and Pacific northwestern regions of North America. Its range extends from southern Alaska to the Sonoran Desert in New Mexico. It grows in wet sites usually at elevations of 1,200–1,800 m (3,900–5,900 ft), but reaches 2,700 m (8,860 ft) in the southern end of its range. It grows in sheltered canyons, ravines, along streams, and on moist slopes. Several species of trees can be found growing in association, including pinyon pine, yellow pine, and spruce. The leaves vary from one part of its range to another. The Douglas maple (*Acer glabrum* variety *douglasii*) occurs in the northern part of the range and differs by having 3 to 5 shallowly lobed leaves and fruits with a narrower angle of spread between the wings.

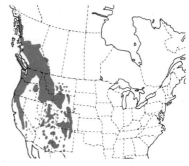

The greenish-yellow flowers are produced in May (Arizona, New Mexico) to July (Alaska, Canada) and the winged fruits mature in August or September. The seeds are eaten by rodents and birds. Whitetail and mule deer browse the twigs and leaves. The light-brown wood is hard and heavy but not commercially important because the trees are too small. It is excellent for campfires and wood stoves.

Appearance: shrub or small tree to 9 m (29.5 ft), with an irregular, often rounded crown; trunk short, branching close to the ground, to 25 cm (9.8 in) in diameter. **Bark:** thin, 2–6 mm (0.1–0.2 in) thick, smooth, reddish-brown to gray. **Branches:** few, slender, spreading to upright; branchlets slender, pale green and smooth turning reddish-brown with age. **Winter buds:** 2–5 mm (0.1–0.2 in) long, pointed at the tip, covered with overlapping, bright red scales. **Leaves:** simple, opposite, deciduous, almost rounded in outline, *7.5–14 cm (3–5.5 in) long, 3- to 5-lobed, rarely with 3 leaflets,*

Rocky Mountain Maple

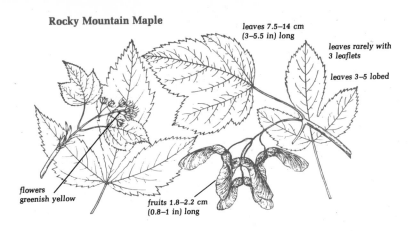

leaves 7.5–14 cm
(3–5.5 in) long

leaves rarely with
3 leaflets

leaves 3–5 lobed

flowers
greenish yellow

fruits 1.8–2.2 cm
(0.8–1 in) long

pointed at the tips, rounded to slightly heart-shaped at the base, **sharply double toothed** along the margins, papery, dark green and shiny above, paler and smooth beneath; leafstalks stout, 2.5–12 cm (1–4.7 in) long. **Flowers:** male and female flowers normally on separate trees, the flowers produced in slender, branched, hanging, few-flowered clusters at the ends of the branchlets; each flower with a tubular 5-lobed calyx, petals usually 5, yellowish-green, 6 to 8 stamens in male flowers, and a single pistil in the female flowers. **Fruits:** 2-winged, dry at maturity, **1.8–2.2 cm (0.8–1 in) long,** with a **small angle of spread between the wings,** usually 45° or less.

Sycamore Maple   *Acer pseudoplatanus* L.

Sycamore maple, a native of Europe and western Asia, has been cultivated in North America since colonial days. It has been widely planted in cities but is not as common as the Norway maple; neither is it as hardy, being more susceptible to insects and disease. One of the few maples that can be tolerant of salt spray, it is often planted near seashores.

Sycamore Maple

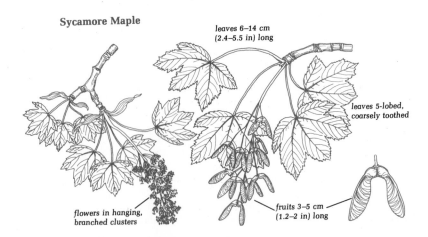

leaves 6–14 cm
(2.4–5.5 in) long

leaves 5-lobed,
coarsely toothed

flowers in hanging,
branched clusters

fruits 3–5 cm
(1.2–2 in) long

It is a small to medium-size tree to 30 m (98 ft), with a dense, broadly rounded crown, and an unusually short trunk branching close to the ground. The simple, opposite, deciduous *leaves are 5-lobed,* as broad or slightly broader than long, *6–14 cm (2.4–5.5 in) long,* 8–16 cm (3.2–6.3 in) wide, the lobes pointed at the tips, *coarsely toothed* along the margins, dark green and smooth above. Flowers are yellow, produced in narrow, hanging, many-flowered clusters 8–14 cm (3.2–5.5 in) long. Fruits are dry, 2-winged, *3–5 cm (1.2–2 in) long,* the wings spreading at a narrow angle, usually less than 90°.

Vine Maple   *Acer circinatum* Pursh

This small maple is one of the few deciduous trees in the coastal, largely evergreen forests of the Pacific Northwest. It grows in bottomlands and wet, west-facing slopes from sea level to 1,400 m (4,590 ft) elevation. Trees growing in association include coastal redwood, sitka spruce, Douglas fir, western redcedar, and bigleaf maple. Vine maple occasionally is gnarled and twisted and trails along the ground, hence its common name. It is not commercially important, but is sometimes used for firewood or as an ornamental.

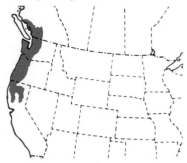

Vine maple is a shrub or small tree to 15 m (49 ft), rarely taller, with an irregular, broadly rounded crown and a short, often crooked trunk. The simple, opposite, *deciduous leaves,* are nearly circular in

Vine Maple

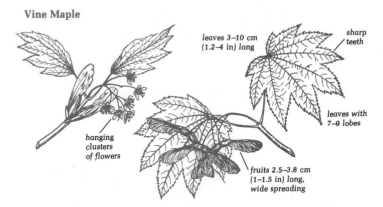

leaves 3–10 cm (1.2–4 in) long

sharp teeth

leaves with 7–9 lobes

hanging clusters of flowers

fruits 2.5–3.8 cm (1–1.5 in) long, wide spreading

outline, *3–10 cm (1.2–4 in) long,* usually wider, *7- to 9-lobed,* the lobes pointed at the tip, *sharply toothed* along the margins, bright yellowish-green above, paler beneath. Flowers are produced in loose, hanging clusters from the ends of the branchlets. *Fruits* are 2-winged, *2.5–3.8 cm (1–1.5 in) long,* with *wide spreading wings* at angles of 140° to 180°.

Red Maple   *Acer rubrum* L.

This is one of the most common tree species in eastern North America. It occurs from Quebec, Canada, south to southern Florida, west to eastern Texas, and north to Min-

nesota and southern Ontario. It grows from sea level to 1,400 m (4,590 ft) elevation in
a variety of soil and forest types. It grows
equally well along the borders of swamps
as it does in dry upland sites. Best growth
is attained in the moist, deep, rich soils of
ravines and coves. Red maple is a major element of many forest types. In the northern
portion of its range, it grows in association
with gray, yellow, and paper birch, sugar
maple, American beech, and white pine. In
the South, associated trees include sweetbay, blackgum, green ash, pin and southern red oak, and slash and loblolly pines.

This maple can successfully establish itself in recently cleared areas and partially
open woodlands.

Red maple grows rapidly for 20 to 30 years and may live 75 to 100 years. The flowers appear in early spring, long before the leaves. In the North, they open in April or
May, while in the South they blossom in December or January. The fruits mature 4 to 6
weeks later. Rodents are the largest consumers of the fruits. Whitetail deer and rabbits
eat the young shoots and leaves.

This maple is often planted as a shade tree along streets and in yards. Cultivated
forms have been selected for their ability to grow in urban environments and for their
attractive red and orange fall foliage. Maple syrup can be made from the sap, but the
sap contains less sugar than that from sugar maple. The light-brown wood is heavy but
not as hard as that of sugar maple. It is used in furniture, flooring, cabinets, veneer,
and for small wooden objects.

Appearance: medium to tall tree to 28 m (92 ft), rarely taller, with a narrow to
broadly rounded crown; trunk straight, to 1.5 m (5 ft) in diameter. **Bark:** thin to 1.4 cm
(0.6 in) thick, smooth but developing shallow ridges with flat scaly plates, dark gray.
Branches: stout to slender, upright to spreading; branchlets slender, smooth, green
turning red to reddish-brown with age. **Winter buds:** 3–4 mm (0.1–0.2 in) long,
broadest near the base and rounded at the tip, covered with overlapping, dark red
scales. **Leaves:** simple, opposite, deciduous, broadest near the base, 5–15 cm (2–6 in)

Red Maple

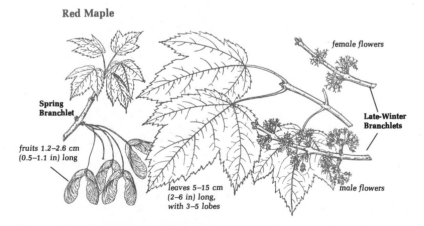

Spring
Branchlet

fruits 1.2–2.6 cm
(0.5–1.1 in) long

female flowers

Late-Winter
Branchlets

leaves 5–15 cm
(2–6 in) long,
with 3–5 lobes

male flowers

long, 3.5–10 cm (1.4–4 in) wide, ***3- to 5-lobed,*** the lobes pointed at the tip, ***singly or doubly toothed along the margin,*** usually rounded at the base, papery, light green and smooth above, ***paler and often whitish beneath;*** leafstalks slender, 5–10 cm (2–4 in) long, smooth to slightly hairy. **Flowers:** bisexual, or often male and female in separate clusters on the same or different trees, produced in few to many-flowered clusters along the upper part of the young branchlets; each flower on a slender stalk, with a short 5-lobed calyx, 5 short, inconspicuous petals, 5 to 8 stamens (absent in female flowers), and a tiny single pistil (aborted in male flowers). **Fruits:** hanging on a slender stalk, 2-winged, dry, ***1.2–2.6 cm (0.5–1.1 in) long,*** 6–12 mm (0.2–0.5 in) wide, the wing red, reddish-brown, or yellow, the wings at a 50° to 60° angle of spread.

Silver Maple   *Acer saccharinum* L.

This common maple occurs from New Brunswick, Canada, to Florida, west to Oklahoma, Kansas, and Nebraska. The largest silver maples occur where they grow in abundance in the lower Ohio River Valley. This lowland species usually grows in wet,

poorly drained, mucky or peaty soils of floodplains, stream and river bottoms, and along ponds and lakes. It grows in association with many other trees including the American elm, red maple, basswood, river birch, swamp white oak, and slippery elm.

As in other maples, growth is rapid for the first 25 to 30 years, with the trees reaching full size at 90 to 110 years. Silver maples seldom live more than 125 to 140 years. They can withstand short periods of flooding but are very susceptible to fire. Flowering is in late winter or early spring before the leaves expand, with the fruits ripening in April or May. Large seed crops are produced almost every year. ***The winged seeds are the largest produced by any native maple.*** Rodents, mainly fox, gray, and red squirrels, and birds, especially pine and evening grosbeaks, feed on the seeds. Whitetail deer browse the young twigs and foliage. The larger branches and the trunk, hollowed by heart-rot, provide excellent dens for squirrels or raccoons.

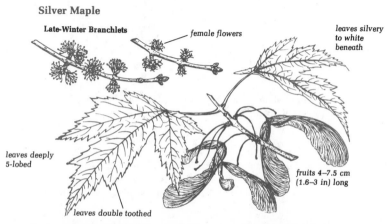

Silver Maple

Late-Winter Branchlets — *female flowers*

leaves silvery to white beneath

leaves deeply 5-lobed

fruits 4–7.5 cm (1.6–3 in) long

leaves double toothed

The pale-brown wood—hard, strong, but brittle—is inferior to that of sugar or red maple. It is sometimes used for inexpensive furniture and for crates and veneer. While it is an attractive tree, it is subject to damage by pests, high winds, and heavy, wet spring snows which cause the brittle wood to split. It was popular as a street tree in the early 1900s, but is not today because of its tendency to split.

Appearance: medium to tall tree to 30 m (98 ft), rarely taller, with a large, spreading, round-topped crown, trunk short, thick, straight, to 90 cm (35.4 in) in diameter, rarely larger. **Bark:** thin to 2 cm (0.8 in) thick on older trees, smooth, developing shallow furrows and large flat thin scales, sometimes free at the ends giving a somewhat shaggy appearance, gray to brownish-gray. **Branches:** stout, spreading to nearly upright; branchlets slender, sometimes hanging, brittle, green turning bright reddish-brown with age. **Winter buds:** 6–8 mm (0.2–0.3 in) long, broadest near the middle or base, rounded or nearly so at the tip, covered with overlapping, red to reddish-brown scales. **Leaves:** simple, opposite, deciduous, broadest near the base to near the middle, *14–20 cm (5.5–7.9 in) long, 10–18 cm (4–7.1 in) wide, deeply 5-lobed, with narrow sinuses,* the *margins irregularly double toothed,* pointed at the tips, square to heart-shaped at the base, papery, bright green and smooth above, *paler* and *white to silvery beneath;* leafstalks slender, 7.5–10 cm (3–4 in) long, often reddish. **Flowers:** small, greenish-yellow, male and female flowers in separate clusters on the same tree or different trees; each flower with a short, 5-lobed calyx, no petals, 3 to 7 stamens in male flowers, and a single hairy pistil in the female flowers. **Fruits:** 2-winged, on slender stalks, 4–7.5 cm (1.6–3 in) long, 1–1.8 cm (0.4–0.8 in) wide, prominently veined, the wings spreading at an approximate angle of 90°.

Black Maple   *Acer nigrum* Michx.

Black maple is native to parts of eastern North America and the Midwest. It has been considered by some to be a variety of sugar maple, but the two species are sufficiently different to be distinguished. It grows in a variety of soil types and generally occupies the area covered by ice during the last glacial period. A lowland species, it occurs near streams, rivers, and in rich woodlands, usually at less than 750 m (2,461 ft) elevation, but up to 1,650 m (5,413 ft) in the southern Appalachian Mountains. It often grows in association with sugar maple, gray birch, yellow birch, red maple, beech, white oak, and white pine.

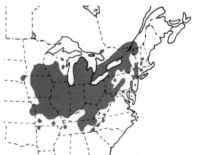

The tree grows rapidly for the first 25 or so years and then slowly, sometimes living over 200 years. Flowering is in April or May before or as the new leaves are expanding. The winged fruits mature by late summer or early fall. Grouse eat the buds, while whitetail deer browse the young growth. Black maple wood is cut and sold as sugar maple. It is used in flooring, furniture, cabinets, veneer, plywood, and cutting blocks. Black maple can also be tapped in late winter for the sugary sap, which can be boiled down to yield maple syrup.

Appearance: medium to large tree to 25 m (82 ft), rarely taller, with an open, flat to round-topped crown; trunk straight, to 1.2 m (3.9 ft) in diameter. **Bark:** thin on young trees to 2 cm (0.8 in) thick on older ones, becoming deeply furrowed, with long narrow, irregular ridges, gray to almost black. **Branches:** stout, spreading to upright;

Black Maple

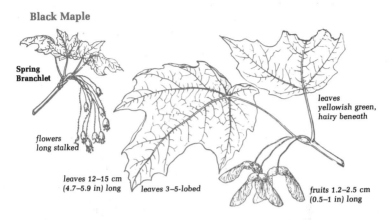

Spring
Branchlet

*flowers
long stalked*

*leaves 12–15 cm
(4.7–5.9 in) long*   *leaves 3–5-lobed*

*leaves
yellowish green,
hairy beneath*

*fruits 1.2–2.5 cm
(0.5–1 in) long*

branchlets stout, reddish-brown and hairy at first, becoming grayish-brown and smooth with age. **Winter buds:** 3–5 mm (0.1–0.2 in) long, egg-shaped and pointed at the tip, covered with overlapping, hairy, reddish-brown scales. **Leaves:** simple, opposite, deciduous, *3- to 5-lobed,* about as long as wide, 12–15 cm (4.7–5.9 in) long, short-pointed at the tip, with a few coarse teeth along the margin, rounded to heart-shaped at the base, dark green above, *yellowish-green* and *usually hairy beneath;* leafstalks stout, 7.5–12.5 cm (3–5 in) long, usually hairy, drooping with age. **Flowers:** male and female flowers in separate clusters or in the same cluster, produced in few to many-flowered clusters at the base of the newly emerging leaves; each flower yellow, with a broad, 5-lobed calyx, no petals, 6 to 8 stamens in the male flowers, and a single pistil in female flowers. **Fruits:** 2-winged, dry at maturity, *1.2–2.5 cm (0.5–1 in) long,* with a narrow to wide angle between the wings.

Bigtooth Maple   *Acer grandidentatum* Nutt.

This maple is native to higher elevations of the central and southern Rocky Mountains and into Texas and northern Mexico. It grows in moist sites such as wet canyons, valleys, and along stream banks at elevations of 1,200 to 2,100 m (3,940–6,890 ft). It is usually found with ponderosa pine, velvet ash, and in Arizona with Arizona sycamore. There are two varieties, based on leaf shape and lobing.

Flowering is in April or May as the leaves are expanding. The winged fruits do not mature until late August or September. Birds and rodents feed on the fruits. White-tail and mule deer browse the young twigs and leaves. The light-brown wood is hard and heavy and burns well in wood-stoves. It is not used commercially, however, because of the tree's small size.

Appearance: shrub or small tree to 15 m (49 ft), with an open, rounded crown; trunk straight, short, branching close to the ground, to 24 cm (9.5 in) in diameter. **Bark:** thin, to 6 mm (0.2 in) thick, developing plate-like scales with age, dark brown. **Branches:**

Bigtooth Maple

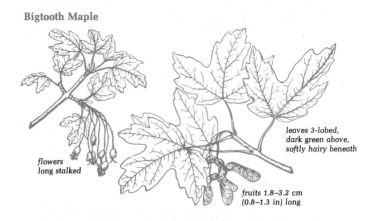

leaves 3-lobed,
dark green above,
softly hairy beneath

flowers
long stalked

fruits 1.8–3.2 cm
(0.8–1.3 in) long

stout, usually upright; branchlets slender, bright red and smooth turning reddish-brown to gray with age. **Winter buds:** 1–2 mm (0.1 in) long, pointed at the tip, covered with overlapping, bright red, hairy scales. **Leaves:** simple, opposite, deciduous, *3-lobed* with broad, shallow spaces between, 5–12 cm (2–4.7 in) long and wide, pointed at the tips, flattened to heart-shaped at the base, with a few large blunt teeth along the margins; *dark green* and shiny above, paler *usually softly hairy beneath;* leafstalks, 2.5–5 cm (1–2 in) long, smooth. **Flowers:** male and female flowers on the same tree, produced in few to many-flowered, long-stalked clusters at the base of the newly emerging leaves; each flower with a 5-lobed bell-shaped calyx, no petals, 6 to 8 stamens in the male flowers, and a single pistil in the female flowers. **Fruits:** 2-winged, dry at maturity, *1.8–3.2 cm (0.8–1.3 in) long,* the wings spreading at an angle of 60° to 90°.

Chalk Maple   Acer leucoderme Small

The chalk or white-barked maple is the rarest and smallest of the maples native to eastern North America. It is found in scattered locations throughout the southeastern U.S. It grows in moist woodlands, mainly along streams or river banks and in ravines.

Flowering is in March or April and the fruits mature in May or June and sometimes persist on the trees into summer.

This is a small tree to 12 m (39 ft), with a compact, rounded crown, and thin, smooth, pale, almost *white bark.* The simple, opposite, deciduous leaves are 3- to 5-lobed, 5–8.2 cm (2–3.3 in) long, with a few coarse, sometimes rounded teeth along the margin, papery, dark yellow-green above, *bright yellow-green* and *finely hairy* beneath. Tiny flowers are borne on long, slender, hanging stalks. Fruits are on long slender stalks, 2-winged, 1.2–2 cm (0.5–0.8 in) long, 5–8 mm (0.2–0.3 in) wide, the wings widely spreading.

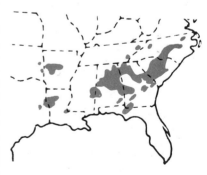

Chalk Maple

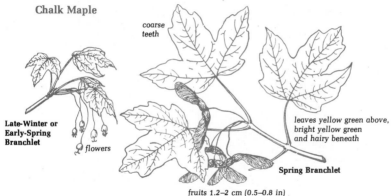

coarse teeth

Late-Winter or Early-Spring Branchlet

♀ flowers

leaves yellow green above, bright yellow green and hairy beneath

Spring Branchlet

fruits 1.2–2 cm (0.5–0.8 in) long, wings wide spreading

Sugar Maple

Acer saccharum Marsh

This tall, handsome tree is among the best known trees in eastern North America. Sugar maples are native from Nova Scotia south to northern Georgia and west to eastern Texas and Minnesota. They grow in a variety of soil types, but do best in deep, rich, well-drained soils. They are lowland trees (though not found in swamps) occurring to 1,600 m (5,250 ft) elevation. Sugar maples are a main component of the eastern deciduous forest, growing in association with American beech, yellow birch, black cherry, red oak, white oak, white pine, white spruce, and eastern hemlock. The young trees or seedlings prefer shaded conditions.

These trees grow rapidly for the first 35 to 40 years and usually reach maximum height at 125 to 150 years of age. In best sites, the trees may live for 250 years. Flowering is in early spring with the 2-winged fruits maturing by late spring or early summer. These trees are valuable to wildlife. Birds and small mammals eat the seeds, while whitetail deer feed on young twigs, buds, and leaves. Gray squirrels and porcupines eat branchlet tips, and strip the bark, sometimes girdling the trees, causing death.

Sugar maples have been planted as shade trees along streets and in parks. Dense, upright forms are planted where space is limited. Indians taught maple-syrup making to the early pioneers. The technique has been passed down, improved, and perfected by each generation. Today sugar maple syrup has grown into a multimillion dollar industry. In late winter, the sap is collected, boiled, and concentrated into a delicious syrup. The sap contains from 2–6 percent sugar; thus 32 gallons (121 liters) are needed to make 1 gallon (4 liters) of syrup.

The light-brown wood is very hard, close-grained, durable, shock resistant, and takes a beautiful polish. It is used to make furniture, veneer, cabinets, musical instruments, and a host of smaller items.

Appearance: medium to tall trees to 30 m (98 ft), with a uniform, full, round-topped

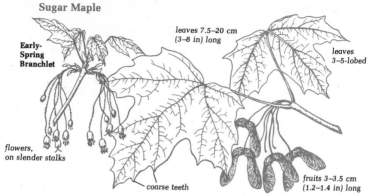

Sugar Maple

Early-Spring Branchlet

flowers, on slender stalks

coarse teeth

leaves 7.5–20 cm (3–8 in) long

leaves 3–5-lobed

fruits 3–3.5 cm (1.2–1.4 in) long

crown; trunk stout, straight, to a maximum of 1.8 m (6 ft) in diameter. **Bark:** thin to 2 cm (0.8 in) thick on older trees, smooth becoming slightly fissured to deeply furrowed with age, dark gray to grayish-brown. **Branches:** stout, upright to spreading, often short; branchlets slender, smooth, green turning orange to reddish-brown with age. **Winter buds:** 6–12 mm (0.2–0.5 in) long, cone-shaped and pointed at the tip, covered with 4 to 8 pairs of reddish-brown, slightly hairy, overlapping scales, lateral buds smaller. **Leaves:** simple, opposite, deciduous, broadest near the base, *7.5–20 cm (3–8 in) long and broad, 3- to 5-lobed,* the lobes pointed at the tip, *with a few coarse teeth along the margin,* broadly squared to heart-shaped at the base, papery, bright green, and smooth above, paler and *smooth below* (sometimes with a few hairs on the veins), leafstalks slender, 4–8 cm (1.6–3.2 in) long. **Flowers:** small, bisexual and male or female flowers on the same tree, produced in slender, few-flowered clusters just below the newly emerging leaves; each flower *hanging on a long, slender stalk 1.8–7.5 cm (0.8–3 in) long,* with a 5-lobed calyx, no petals, 7 or 8 stamens (absent in female flowers), and a single pistil. **Fruits:** 2-winged, *3–3.5 cm (1.2–1.4 in) long,* the wings at about a 60° angle of spread.

Florida Maple

Acer barbatum Michx.

Florida maple is a small to medium-size tree of the southeastern U.S. It is closely related to the sugar maple and occurs from Virginia to Florida and west to Texas and Oklahoma. This maple grows in moist, rich soils along river or stream banks and in low, wet woodlands. Flowering is in April or May with the fruits maturing in June or July and sometimes persisting into early fall. This maple is sometimes planted for shade in the South.

This is a tree to 18 m (59 ft), with a usually dense, rounded crown and *nearly whitish bark.* The simple, opposite, deciduous leaves, almost circular on outline, are *3.8–9 cm (1.5–3.5 in) long,* slightly wider, *3- or 5-lobed,* entire to coarsely and irregularly toothed along the margin. Flowers are similar to those of the sugar maple but smaller in size. Fruits are 2-winged, *1.6–3 cm (0.7–1.2 in) long,* 4–8 mm (0.2–0.3 in) wide, the wings at a 60° to 70° angle.

Florida Maple

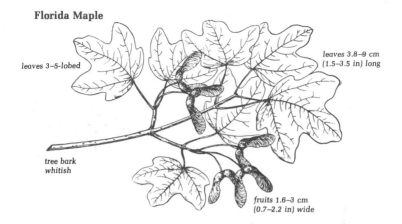

leaves 3–5-lobed

leaves 3.8–9 cm
(1.5–3.5 in) long

tree bark
whitish

fruits 1.6–3 cm
(0.7–2.2 in) wide

Boxelder

Acer negundo L.

The leaves of the wide-ranging boxelder resemble those of an ash — so much so that it is commonly called the ash-leaf maple. But its flowers and fruits are typically maple. It occurs from Canada to Florida and from the east to the west coast of North America.

It grows in a variety of soil types, but does best in lowland sites along rivers, streams, ponds, or seasonally flooded flats. It often grows with cottonwood, willows, silver maple, sycamore, and black tupelo.

Boxelder grows rapidly for the first 15 or 20 years, then slowly living 75 to 100 years. Flowering is in early spring with the clusters of hanging fruits maturing by autumn. The seeds are eaten by squirrels, mice, and various birds including the grosbeak. Whitetail deer browse the young twigs and leaves. This species was once planted as a street tree, but the weak wood and the abundant fruits render it undesirable in street-side situations. It was in-

Boxelder

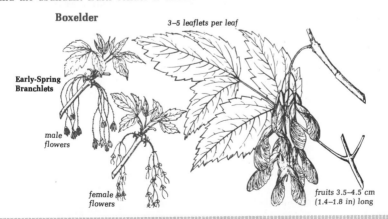

3–5 leaflets per leaf

Early-Spring
Branchlets

male
flowers

female
flowers

fruits 3.5–4.5 cm
(1.4–1.8 in) long

troduced into Europe where it now grows wild, rapidly spreading, often along rivers or streams.

The cream-white wood is soft, weak, and lightweight and of little value. It has been used for making crates, boxes, paper pulp, and for firewood.

Appearance: small to medium-size tree to 20 m (65.6 ft), rarely taller, often with an irregular shape and an uneven, broad crown; trunk straight to crooked, branching close to the ground, to 1.2 m (3.9 ft) in diameter. **Bark:** thin, to 1.2 cm (0.5 in) thick on older trees, with deep furrows and broad rounded ridges separating in thick scales, light brown to gray. **Branches:** stout, wide spreading to upright; branchlets slender, green and smooth turning gray to brown with age. **Winter buds:** 3–8 mm (0.1–0.3 in) long, pointed at the tip, covered with overlapping, orangish-brown scales. **Leaves:** opposite, deciduous, *feather-like* (pinnate) compound, *with 3*, rarely 5, *leaflets per leaf,* the leaflets broadest near the base, middle, or the tip, 5–12 cm (2–4.8 in) long, 3.2–7 cm (1.3–2.8 in) wide, pointed to long pointed at the tip, rounded to tapering at the often uneven base, with irregular and coarse teeth along the margin, papery, light green and smooth above, paler and usually hairy beneath; leaflet stalks slender, short. **Flowers:** small, yellowish-green, male and female flowers in separate trees; each flower on a slender stalk, with a 5-lobed calyx (smaller in female flowers), petals absent, 4 to 6 functional stamens (in male flowers), and a single pistil in the female flowers. **Fruits:** often in hanging clusters, stalked, *2-winged, 3.5–4.5 cm (1.4–1.8 in) long,* 5–10 mm (0.2–0.4 in) wide, the wings at a narrow angle of spread, *less than 45°.*

The Torchwood Family Burseraceae

This exotic family contains 18 genera and about 500 species widely distributed within the tropical regions of the world, especially the Americas, Africa, and Malaysia. A single genus, *Bursera*, occurs in the U.S. It is represented by 3 species, 2 in the Southwest, and 1 in southern Florida.

Nearly all members of the torchwood family have an aromatic, gummy sap, which has been used for medicine, in the arts, and in the religious rites of primitive societies. Myrrh and frankincense oils from 2 species were used in biblical times for incense, tonics, and stimulants. Today they are used in perfumes and incense. Resins from other species have been used in the manufacture of gum bases, plasters, glue, varnish, and incense. The wood has been used in building and for small wood products such as matchsticks and toothpicks.

These are small trees or shrubs with resinous, dark wood. The leaves are alternate, deciduous, and feather-like (pinnate) and compound, with small leaflets. Flowers are produced in long, branched clusters. The small, symmetrical flowers are male or female, or bisexual, with a 3- to 5-lobed calyx, 4 or 5 free petals, stamens equal to the number of petals or twice as many, and a single pistil. The fleshy, berry-like fruit dries and splits as it matures, exposing the seeds.

The Torchwood Genus *Bursera* Jacq. ex L.

This genus of perhaps 100 resin-bearing species is native to tropical regions of the Americas. Only 3 species are native to North America, 2 in the Southwest, and 1 in southern Florida. The trees are of some economic importance for their lumber and resins.

Members of this genus are trees or shrubs, with thin, peeling bark and scented, resinous sap. The alternate feather-like (pinnate) compound, deciduous leaves have 3 to 9 leaflets per leaf. Flowers are tiny, white, bisexual or male or female, with a 3- to 5-lobed calyx, 3 to 5 petals, 6 to 10 stamens, and a single pistil. Fruits are egg-shaped to rounded, 3-parted, fleshy, splitting open at maturity.

Key to Torchwood Species

A. Leaves with 10–20 pairs of leaflets, the leaflets 5–7 mm (0.2–0.3 in) long; trees of southwestern U.S. and Mexico **Elephant tree, p. 793**

B. Leaves with 3–11 pairs of leaflets, the leaflets 1.5–20 cm (0.6–7.9 in) long.

Elephant Tree

   1. Leaves with 3–7 pairs of leaflets, the leaflets 6–7.5 cm (2.4–3 in) long; trees of southern Florida **Gumbo-limbo, p. 794**

   2. Leaves with 5–11 pairs of leaflets, the leaflets 1.5–4 cm (0.6–1.6 in) long; trees of southern Arizona **Fragrant bursera, p. 795**

Gumbo-Limbo

Elephant Tree
                           Bursera microphylla A. Gray

The elephant tree is a short and squat, seldom-seen tree of the southwestern U.S., and Mexico, where it is more common. Found on rocky, desert slopes at 300–600 m (980–1,970 ft) elevation, this northern-most member of the genus is characteristic of ex-tremely dry regions, where it grows in association with many kinds of shrubby trees and cacti.

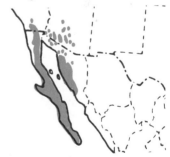

    Flowering is in June before the leaves appear, and the fruits ripen by the end of October. There is little published information on the ecology and natural history of the elephant tree. In the U.S., botanists hadn't verified the presence of the ele-phant tree until 1937. Mysterious tales of a tree with elephant trunks for branches, which bled blood (reddish sap) when it was cut, spurred on venturesome naturalists into the California desert. Finally, an ex-pedition of scientists and foresters verified its presence and mapped its range.

    The tree is economically important in Mexico, where the resinous gum is extracted and used as a varnish base, wood preservative, adhesive, and even as a remedy for venereal disease. The leaves and wood yield an aromatic oil, called copal, which has been used by Mexican and American Indians in religious ceremonies.

    Appearance: small tree *3–5 m (9.8–16.4 ft) in height,* attaining greatest growth in Arizona; with a wide, open-topped crown; *trunk is disproportionately massive, ir-regular and short to 0.7 m (2.3 ft) across at the base.* **Bark:** 1.1–1.3 cm (0.5–0.6 in) thick, composed *of an outer, middle, and inner bark, each of which is separable into several layers;* the outer bark white or pale yellow, membrane-like, peeling off in

Elephant Tree

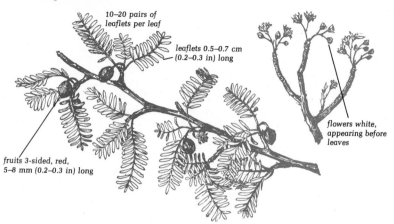

10–20 pairs of leaflets per leaf

leaflets 0.5–0.7 cm (0.2–0.3 in) long

flowers white, appearing before leaves

fruits 3-sided, red, 5–8 mm (0.2–0.3 in) long

thin sheets like birchbark; middle layers green and thin; the inner thick and corky, red or reddish-brown, exuding a red gum when cut. **Branches:** stout, erect, and spreading, sharply tapering into slender, red, zigzag branchlets which are roughened after the first year by numerous leaf scars. **Leaves:** alternate, deciduous, feather-like (pinnate) compound, 2.5–2.9 cm (1–1.2 in) long, with usually *10 to 20 pairs of tiny leaflets,* the leaflets elongate, *0.5–0.7 cm (0.2–0.3 in) long,* 0.1–0.3 cm (0.1 in) wide, rounded at the tip, narrowly wedge-shaped at the base; leafstalks absent. **Flowers:** small, some male or female, most bisexual, 0.4–0.6 cm (0.2–0.3 in) long, mostly in 3-flowered clusters on slender stalks, with a minute 5-lobed calyx, 5 narrow white petals, 10 stamens, short. **Fruits:** produced singly, *3-sided, 5–8 mm (0.2–0.3 in) long,* hanging on a thickened stalk, *skin red,* splitting into 3 sections, each containing a narrow, triangular, gray seed.

Gumbo-Limbo
Bursera simarouba (L.) Sarg.

This medium-size tree ranges from Cape Kennedy to the southern Florida Keys. A truly tropical tree, gumbo-limbo also is native to the West Indies, tropical Mexico, Guatemala, and northern South America. It grows in limestone soils of coastal hammocks or in mixed forests. It is readily recognized by its reddish-brown, smooth, oily-looking bark, which peels off in sheets like the yellow birch to reveal a greenish-brown layer beneath. A grayish resin in the bark, twigs, and leaves tastes and looks like turpentine.

The tree grows rapidly, and can be propagated by placing young green sprouts into the ground. It flowers in late winter or spring, prior to or with the unfolding of the leaves. The dark red, almost football-shaped fruits ripen in the summertime. Little is known about the value of gumbo-limbo to wildlife. But it is susceptible to attack by dry-wood termites and other insects.

The gumbo-limbo has been planted as an ornamental and a shade tree. Its most important economic feature has been its resin, which is known as Chibou, Cachibou, or gomart resin in the West Indies. It has been used to make glue, varnish, coating for canoes, and incense and has been used medicinally to treat gout. The cream-colored to light-brown wood is light, soft, and weak. It is suited to boxes and crates, interior carpentry, and fenceposts, firewood, charcoal, and a variety of small wood products such as matchsticks and toothpicks.

Appearance: medium-size tree to 20 m (65 ft), with a spreading, round-topped crown; trunk short and thick, to 0.9 m (2.9 ft) in diameter. **Bark:** *1.1–1.8 cm (0.5–0.8 in) thick, reddish-brown to green, smooth, inner bark whitish or reddish; outer bark is resinous, with an odor of turpentine.* **Branches:** few, massive, crooked, and

Gumbo-Limbo

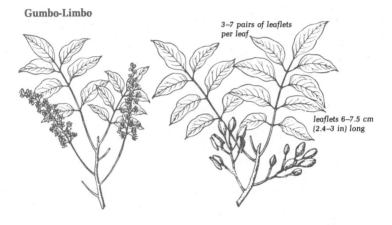

3–7 pairs of leaflets per leaf

leaflets 6–7.5 cm (2.4–3 in) long

horizontal, sometimes growing close to the ground; branchlets stout, reddish-brown, crooked smooth-barked, marked with lenticels and large, elevated, vaguely heart-shaped, yellow leaf scars. **Winter Buds:** short and rounded, blunt at the tip, with three broad, more-or-less short pointed scales. **Leaves:** alternate, deciduous in early winter or sometimes remaining until the following spring, *feather-like* (pinnate) *compound, 15–20 cm (6–7.9 in) long, 10–15 cm (4–6 in) broad, with 3 to 7 leaflets,* opposite in pairs except for the terminal leaflet, the leaflets 6–7.5 cm (2.4–3 in) long, 3.5–5 cm (1.4–2 in) wide, broadest near the base, with a pointed tip and blunt base, entire, dark green, smooth and shiny above, paler beneath. **Flowers:** minute, 4–6 mm (0.1–0.2 in) across, borne in many-flowered clusters or in unbranched spikes 5–10 cm (2–4 in) long; male and female flowers usually separate but on the same tree; calyx lobes and petals 5, green; stamens are as long as the petals in the male flowers, and much shorter in the female. **Fruits:** in short clusters, *diamond-shaped, slightly three-angled,* pointed at both ends, 1.1–1.3 cm (0.5–0.6 in) long and 0.8–1 cm (0.4 in) wide, red, *splitting into 3 parts, revealing 1 or 2 triangular, whitish seeds.*

Fragrant Bursera *Bursera fagaroides* (H.B.K.) Engler

Fragrant bursera is rare in the U.S. where it is found only at the western base of the Baboquivari Mountains in Pima County, Arizona. It is native also to western Mexico. It usually grows on dry, limestone slopes or cliffs from 1,200–1,400 m (3,940–4,590 ft) elevation. This bursera occurs at a higher elevation than the elephant tree, the other southwestern species of *Bursera*.

This species is a resinous shrub or small tree to 5 m (16 ft), with alternate, feather-like (pinnate) compound leaves. There are **5 to 11 leaflets per leaf, lance-shaped, 1.5–4 cm (0.6–1.6 in) long,** entire, and with a distinct citrus odor when crushed. Flowers are produced in few to several flowered clusters on a short side twig just below the new leaves. Fruits are 3-angled, 8–10 mm (0.3–0.4 in) long, gray, splitting open at maturity to expose a single seed.

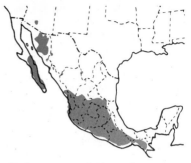

The Cashew Family

Anacardiaceae

This medium-size family contains 77 genera and about 600 species distributed mainly in tropical and subtropical regions of the world. A small number of species extend into temperate regions of North America, Europe, and Asia. Five genera are native to the U.S. and Canada. Many others have been introduced, especially in Florida and California. Two of these, the mango (*Mangifera*) and the pepper tree genus (*Schinus*), have introduced species that now grow wild in parts of the South.

Some members of this family have resinous secretions which can cause severe skin irritation. These include poison ivy, poison oak, poison sumac, and the Florida poison tree. Other species are commercially valuable for their fruits and nuts. These include cashew, pistachio, mango, and hog plum. Many species are important food sources for birds and mammals. Resins, lacquers, and varnishes are made from the resinous gums of several species.

Members of this family are vines, shrubs, or trees with resinous, sometimes poisonous, oils or gums. The leaves are opposite, usually feather-like (pinnate) compound, and occasionally simple, deciduous or evergreen. Flowers are regular, usually bisexual, rarely male and female, generally with 5 sepals, 5 free petals, 5 to 10 stamens, and a single pistil. Fruits are typically berry-like with a single seed.

Key to Cashew Genera

A. Leaves simple.

    1. Leaves deciduous; flowers produced in large, open airy, few-flowered clusters
                        Smoke tree, p. 797

    2. Leaves evergreen; flowers produced in large, dense, many-flowered clusters.

        a. Leaves small, 2–10 cm (0.8–4 in) long; fruits small, 3–10 mm (0.1–0.4 in) long
                        Sumac, p. 799

        b. Leaves large, 10–20 cm (4–7.9 in) long;

American Smoke Tree

Lemonade Sumac

fruits large, fleshy, usually 10 cm (4 in) or
more in length   **Mango, p. 807**

B. Leaves feather-like (pinnate) compound or 3 leaflets per leaf.

    1. Leaves deciduous.

        a. Leaves with 7–13 leaflets; fruits ivory to
grayish-white   **Poison sumac, p. 807**
        b. Leaves with 9–31 leaflets; fruits dark red to
reddish-brown   **Sumac, p. 799**

    2. Leaves evergreen.

        a. Leaves with 3–7 leaflets.

            (1) Leaflets rounded at the tip; fruits uni-
formly wide, 1–1.5 cm (0.4–0.6 in)
long, yellowish-orange
Poison tree, p. 809
            (2) Leaflets pointed at the tip; fruits round-
ed, 6–8 mm (0.2–0.3 in) in diameter,
red or reddish-brown
Sumac, p. 799

        b. Leaves with 9–41 leaflets.

            (1) Leaves with 9–19 leaflets, the leaflets 2
to 3 times as long as wide; fruits
reddish-brown   **Pistache, p. 810**
            (2) Leaves with 19–41 leaflets, the leaflets
3 to 4 times as long as wide; fruits pink
Pepper tree, p. 810

Poison Sumac

Staghorn Sumac

Florida Poison Tree

The Smoke Tree Genus   *Cotinus* Mill.

This genus contains 2 species, 1 in North America and the other, the European smoke
tree (*Cotinus coggygria*), widely distributed throughout southern Europe to the Hima-
layan Mountains. The European smoke tree has been planted in the eastern U.S. for its
large feathery masses of flowers and attractive fall foliage. The American smoke tree
occurs only in scattered parts of the South.

    Members of this genus are shrubs or small trees with yellowish wood. The leaves
are simple, alternate, deciduous, and entire along the margins. Flowers are bisexual
and male or female on the same plant or male or female on separate plants, the flowers
produced in large, loose, elongated clusters. The fruits are small, rounded to uniformly long, and dry.

American Smoke Tree   *Continus obovatus* Raf.
(synonym: *C. americanus* Nutt.)

The American smoke tree is rare in the mountains of Tennessee, Alabama, Missouri,
and Oklahoma, but commonly occurs as a low shrub in the Edwards Plateau region of

Texas. It grows generally in limestone soils of dry, rocky slopes or in Texas in mountain canyons and on high hills. It is found at elevations up to 1,000 m (3,281 ft).

This is a fast-growing tree that has the ability to sprout from the root system if the trunk is cut. Its reproductive capacity is usually low because many of its flower clusters are sterile. Flowers are produced in April and May, with the fruits maturing by late summer or early fall. The small dry fruits are of limited value to wildlife. But they are eaten by some birds.

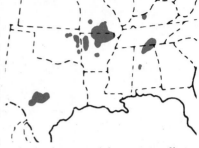

The yellow to orangish-yellow wood is soft though durable, but of no economic value today because of the tree's small size and scarcity. A yellow dye used during the Civil War was made from the wood.

American Smoke Tree

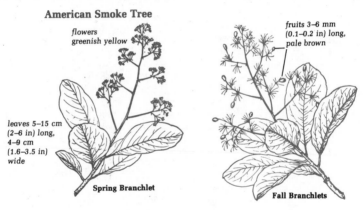

flowers greenish yellow

leaves 5–15 cm (2–6 in) long, 4–9 cm (1.6–3.5 in) wide

Spring Branchlet

fruits 3–6 mm (0.1–0.2 in) long, pale brown

Fall Branchlets

Appearance: low shrub or short tree to 12 m (39 ft), with an open rounded crown; trunk straight, to 35 cm (13.8 in) in diameter. **Bark:** to 4 mm (0.2 in) thick, furrowed and broken on the surface into thin, oblong scales, gray to black. **Branches:** spreading; branchlets slender, often drooping, purple, turning green then reddish-brown or gray with age, smooth. **Winter buds:** 3–4 mm (0.1–0.2 in) long, pointed at the tip, covered with thin, hairy, reddish-brown scales. **Leaves:** *simple,* alternate, ***deciduous,*** broadest near the base to above the middle, 5–15 cm (2–6 in) long, 4–9 cm (1.6–3.5 in) wide, rounded to slightly notched at the tip, rounded to narrowing at the base, entire to slightly wavy along the margin, papery, light purple and hairy when young, turning dark olive-green above, paler and finely hairy beneath; leafstalks 0.6–5 cm (0.5–2 in) long, slender, smooth or hairy. **Flowers:** male and female flowers usually on different trees, greenish-yellow, ***produced in large, open, airy clusters but with few flowers;*** each flower with a 5-lobed calyx, 5 petals, 5 stamens in male flowers, and a single pistil in female flowers. **Fruits:** small, kidney-shaped, 3–6 mm (0.1–0.2 in) long, pale brown, produced on slender, hairy stalks, 3.5–5 cm (1.4–2 in) long and enclosing a bony structure which contains the seeds.

The Sumac Genus   Rhus L.

This is a moderately large genus of about 120 species, mainly of southern Africa, but also of subtropical and temperate regions of North America, Europe, and Asia. There are about 15 species that are native to North America, 9 of them growing large enough to be considered trees. The remainder are low shrubs. One of these, the littleleaf sumac (*Rhus microphylla*) of Texas, New Mexico, and Arizona, may on rare occasions reach tree size. It has the smallest leaflets of any of our sumacs, ranging from 0.6 to 1.4 cm (0.2–0.6 in) long.

Sumacs are fast growing, usually short-lived plants that are important to wildlife. Their thicket-forming growth provides excellent cover for birds, and small and large animals. The fruits, produced in large quantities each year, are eaten by over 30 species of birds, as well as by rodents, and small mammals. The twigs and leaves are browsed by mule and whitetail deer, moose, and mountain sheep. The wood is soft, weak, and of no commercial value.

Members of this genus are shrubs, vines, or trees with alternate, simple or feather-like (pinnate) compound, deciduous or evergreen leaves. Winter buds are tiny, naked (without scales), and covered with dense hairs. Flowers are small, usually with male or female flowers in separate clusters or with bisexual and male and female flowers together on the same plant. Fruits are berry-like, small, rounded to egg-shaped, containing a stone and seed.

Key to Sumac Species

A. Leaves simple, not compound.

   1. Leaves pointed at the tip.

Lemonade Sumac

      a. Leaves dark yellowish-green, flat, margins entire or with a few sharp teeth; trees of coastal southern California
          Lemonade sumac, p. 800

      b. Leaves dark green, the margins rolled under, always entire; trees of southwestern Arizona and Baja California, Mexico
          Kearney sumac, p. 801

   2. Leaves rounded at the tip.

      a. Fruits red, covered with sticky glandular hairs, 6–8 mm (0.2–0.3 in) in diameter; trees of southern Arizona and southwestern California
          Sugar sumac, p. 801

      b. Fruits white, smooth, 3–5 mm (0.1–0.2 in) in diameter; trees of coastal regions of southern California
          Laurel sumac, p. 802

B. Leaves feather-like (pinnate) compound or 3 leaflets per leaf.

            (Continued)

1. Leaves with 9–31 leaflets per leaf, feather-like compound, deciduous.

    a. Leaflets sharply toothed along the margins, the stalk bearing the leaflets not winged.

        (1) Branches and branchlets densely covered with thick, long, soft brown hairs; trees of eastern and central North America **Staghorn sumac, p. 802**

        (2) Branches and branchlets smooth or with some fine hairs when young; widespread North American trees **Smooth sumac, p. 803**

    b. Leaflets entire or with a few coarse teeth along the margin, the stalk bearing the leaflets winged.

        (1) Leaflets 1.8–2.4 cm (0.8–1 in) wide; trees of eastern U.S. **Shining sumac, p. 804**

        (2) Leaflets 0.6–1.2 cm (0.3–0.5 in) wide; trees of Texas, Oklahoma, New Mexico, and Mexico **Prairie sumac, p. 806**

2. Leaves with 3 or 5, rarely 7 leaflets per leaf, evergreen; trees of southwestern U.S. and northwestern Mexico **Mearns sumac, p. 806**

Staghorn Sumac

Smooth Sumac

Shining Sumac

Lemonade Sumac

Rhus integrifolia (Nutt.) Benth. & Hook. f. ex Brewer & Wats.

This small tree or bush grows in dry canyons and on ocean bluffs below 800 m (2,600 ft) elevation along the southern California coast and adjacent Channel Islands. The plants often grow in sandy beach soils and form thickets on the sea-facing bluffs. In sheltered ravines, lemonade sumac grows to tree size. The plants can be found in flower anytime from March through May with the fruits maturing in late summer. The thickets provide excellent cover for many birds and small mammals, which also feed on the ripened fruits. The fruits have been used to make a lemon-like drink.

These sumacs are thicket-forming shrubs or small trees to 8 m (26 ft), with stout, reddish, finely hairy branchlets. The alternate, *simple, evergreen leaves* are *broadest near the base to uniformly wide, 2.2–4.8 cm (0.9–1.9 in) long, 1.8–2.8 cm (0.8–1.2 in) wide,* usually rounded at the tip and base, entire or with a few sharp teeth along the margin, leathery, dark yellowish-green and smooth above, and paler below. The tiny white to rose flowers are produced in dense, many-flowered, branched, elongated clusters, 2.5–8 cm (1–3.2 in) long, at

Lemonade Sumac

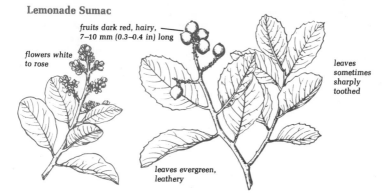

flowers white
to rose

fruits dark red, hairy, —
7–10 mm (0.3–0.4 in) long

leaves
sometimes
sharply
toothed

leaves evergreen,
leathery

the tips of the branchlets. Fruits are clustered, each berry-like, egg-shaped, 7–10 mm (0.3–0.4 in) long, flattened, sticky, dark red, hairy, and enclosing a flattened stone and seed.

Kearney Sumac

Rhus kearneyi Barkley

Kearney sumac is a large shrub or small tree found on dry desert slopes at 300–450 m (980–1,470 ft) elevation in Yuma County, Arizona. It also occurs in scattered localities in northern and central Baja California, Mexico. This is one of the sumac species with simple leaves rather than the feather-like compound leaves.

The plants grow to 5 m (16 ft), with an open, often irregular, spreading crown. The alternate, **evergreen, simple leaves** are broadest below the middle to uniformly wide, 2.5–5.5 cm (1–2.2 in) long, 1.2–3 cm (0.5–1.2 in) wide, usually rounded at the tip, and base, the **margins entire but rolled under,** leathery, dark green, and smooth. The small white flowers are produced in short, crowded clus-

ters at the tips of the branchlets. Fruits are produced in crowded clusters, each berry-like, uniformly wide to egg-shaped, 8–10 mm (0.3–0.4 in) long, somewhat flattened, reddish, and covered with hairs.

Sugar Sumac

Rhus ovata S. Wats.

Sugar sumac is generally a shrub native to the central Arizona mountains, southern California, and Baja California, Mexico. It grows in dry, rocky soils on hillsides and ridges and is usually associated with open scrubby vegetation. This sumac is one of the species often planted in poor dry soils to prevent erosion. The seeds are eaten by many birds.

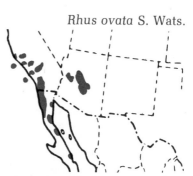

This species is a shrub or small tree to 8 m (26 ft), with a rounded, irregular crown.

The trunk is short, branching near to the ground, and covered with a thin, smooth, grayish-brown bark. The alternate, ***simple, evergreen leaves*** are broadest near the base, 4–8.5 cm (1.6–3.4 in) long, 2–4.8 cm (0.8–1.9 in) wide, short pointed at the tip, rounded at the base, entire along the margins, leathery, shiny yellow-green, and smooth. The tiny flowers are produced in tight, dense, upright, elongated clusters at the tips of the branchlets. Fruits are produced in dense clusters, each fruit berry-like rounded or nearly so, ***6–8 mm (0.2–0.3 in) in diameter, reddish, sticky*** with glandular hairs, slightly acid to sweet tasting, containing a flattened stone and seed.

Laurel Sumac *Rhus laurina* Nutt.

This shrub or small tree grows on the dry slopes of shrubby woodlands and coastal scrub forests of southern California including Santa Catalina Island. It grows from sea level to about 1,000 m (3,281 ft) elevation. Flowering is in June or July with the small,

whitish fruits maturing by autumn. The fruits are eaten by many small birds including the California thrasher and the Audubon warbler.

This species grows to 5 m (16 ft), with a large, spreading, rounded crown and reddish, finely hairy branchlets. The alternate, ***simple, evergreen leaves*** are lance-shaped, ***4.5–10 cm (1.8–4 in) long, 2.2–4 cm (0.9–1.6 in) wide,*** pointed at the tip, usually rounded at the base, entire along the margin, dark shiny green above, and paler beneath. Flowers produced in dense, slender branched, elongate, upright clusters to 15 cm (6 in) long at the ends of the branchlets. ***Fruits*** produced in dense clusters, each berry-like, rounded, ***3–5 mm (0.1–0.2 in) in diameter, whitish, smooth,*** containing a small flattened stone and seed.

Staghorn Sumac *Rhus typhina* L.

Staghorn sumac is a common tree or shrub of eastern and central North America, ranging from New Brunswick, Canada, to the southern Appalachian Mountains, and west to Iowa. It usually grows in upland sites in rich soils, but also occurs in gravel and

sandy, nutrient-poor soils. This species occurs along streams, near swamps, roadsides, railroad embankments, and the margins of woodlands. It gets its name from the young branchlets, which are densely covered with long hairs and resemble the velvet-covered horns of a buck deer in early autumn.

This sumac is moderately fast growing and short-lived. In addition to spreading via seeds, it often spreads by sprouts from the older clumps. Flowering is in early summer and the fruits ripen by August but remain on the trees throughout autumn. Many gamebirds and songbirds eat the fruits. Cottontail rabbits eat the bark and leaves when in reach. Whitetail deer and moose browse the twigs and leaves, and also use

Staghorn Sumac

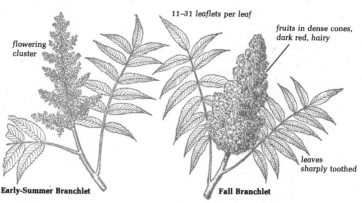

flowering cluster

11–31 leaflets per leaf

fruits in dense cones, dark red, hairy

leaves sharply toothed

Early-Summer Branchlet

Fall Branchlet

the dense stands as cover. A sour lemon-like tea can be made by boiling the fruits. This species is sometimes planted as a border tree or as "edge" for wildlife.

Appearance: shrub or short tree to 10 m (33 ft), with a flat, open crown; trunk slender, often several present, leaning or crooked, up to 20 cm (7.9 in) in diameter, rarely larger. **Bark:** thin, to 4 mm (0.2 in) thick, smooth, developing small scales with age, dark brown to yellowish-brown. **Branches:** stout, upright to spreading; *branchlets thick, densely covered with long, soft brown hairs,* becoming smooth in 3 or 4 years, with a milky resinous sap drying black when exposed to air. **Winter buds:** 5–7 mm (0.2–0.3 in) long, cone shaped, covered with long, silky, pale brown hairs. **Leaves:** alternate, *deciduous,* feather-like (pinnate) compound leaves, 40–60 cm (15.8–23.6 in) long, *with 11 to 31 leaflets,* the leaflets lance-shaped to almost uniformly wide, curved, 5–12 cm (2–4.7 in) long, 2–4 cm (0.8–1.6 in) wide, long pointed at the tip, rounded to slightly heart-shaped at the base, *sharply toothed along the margins,* dark green and smooth above at maturity, paler, usually hairy and often whitish beneath, turning brilliant red or orange in autumn. **Flowers:** tiny, male and female flowers in separate clusters on different trees or with bisexual and male or female flowers on the same tree, produced in dense, branched, elongate, cone-shaped clusters at the tips of the branchlets, clusters of male flowers often 25–30 cm (9.8–11.8 in) long, the female clusters shorter. **Fruits:** *produced in dense, upright, cone-shaped clusters,* each fruit berry-like, rounded, 3–5 mm (0.1–0.2 in) in diameter, covered with dark reddish hairs, enclosing a small stone and seed.

Smooth Sumac

Rhus glabra L.

This common sumac is widespread throughout much of North America but is especially abundant in the eastern and midwestern U.S. It grows in a variety of sites and soil conditions, but the largest specimens occur in moist, rich, lowlands. Smooth sumac is often found near rivers or streams, along margins of woodlands, and especially on abandoned farmlands. It is a pioneer species that can quickly establish itself in open, sunny locations. Often it

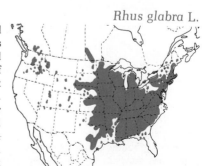

grows near staghorn sumac. Other trees that grow in association include red maple, sweetgum, southern red and willow oaks, and sycamore.

Smooth sumac is a fast-growing, short-lived shrub or tree. The numerous flowers are produced from June through August, with the fruits ripening in September and October. Since male and female flowers are on separate trees, *only* those *trees with female flowers bear fruit.* Over 30 species of birds feed on the fruits including the grouse, pheasant, wild turkey, and many songbirds. Whitetail deer browse the twigs and leaves, and use sumac thickets for cover. Rabbits eat the bark and young twigs. This species is sometimes planted to stabilize steep banks and prevent erosion. *Autumn leaves are a bright red to orange.*

Appearance: shrub or small tree to 7 m (23 ft), with an irregular, rounded, open crown; trunk short, branching close to the ground, to 10 cm (4 in) in diameter. **Bark:** thin, to 4 mm (0.2 in) thick, smooth developing slight ridges with age, gray. **Branches:** stout, short, spreading to upright; *branchlets* stout, *smooth.* **Winter buds:** 3–4 mm (0.1–0.2 in) long, rounded, covered with thick, whitish hairs. **Leaves:** alternate, *deciduous,* feather-like (pinnate) compound, large, with *11 to 31 leaflets,* the leaflets lance-shaped to almost uniformly wide, 5–9.5 cm (2–3.8 in) long, 1.2–3 cm (0.5–1.2 in) wide, long pointed at the tip, rounded at the base, *sharply toothed along the margin,* papery, dark green, shiny and smooth above, paler, finely hairy and often with a whitish cast beneath; leafstalk smooth. **Flowers:** male and female flowers in separate clusters on different trees; male flowers in many-flowered, loose, branched, elongated clusters, 15–25 cm (6–9.8 in) high at the ends of the branchlets; female flowers in dense, many-flowered branched, elongated clusters 10–15 cm (4–6 in) high at the ends of the branchlets. Each flower with 5 sepals, 5 yellowish-green petals, 5 stamens in male flowers, and a single pistil in female flowers. **Fruits:** produced in large pyramid-shaped clusters to 15 cm (6 in) long, each fruit berry-like, rounded, 3–5 mm (0.1–0.2 in) in diameter, dark red, hairy, and containing a flattened stone and seed.

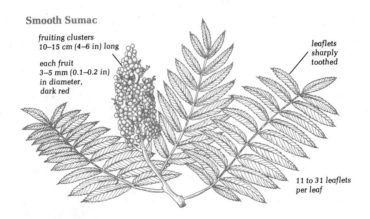

Smooth Sumac

fruiting clusters 10–15 cm (4–6 in) long

each fruit 3–5 mm (0.1–0.2 in) in diameter, dark red

leaflets sharply toothed

11 to 31 leaflets per leaf

Shining Sumac
Rhus copallina L.

Shining sumac is a shrub or small tree native to eastern North America from southeastern Maine to southern Florida, west to eastern Texas, Oklahoma, and eastern Kansas. It generally grows in dry soils on hillsides, along margins of woodlands, roads, and right-of-ways, and in abandoned fields. Along the edges of a deciduous forest, it grows under sugar maple and northern red, white, and post oaks.

This is a fast-growing but short-lived tree. The greenish-yellow flowers are produced from June to August, depending upon latitude. The fruits mature in late summer to autumn but often remain on the tree into winter. The fruits are eaten by grouse, quail, wild turkey, pheasant, and a host of songbirds. Young twigs and leaves are a favored food of the whitetail deer. Rabbits eat the bark and young branchlets. This species is planted to attract birds and other wildlife and for its brilliant red and orange-red autumn foliage.

Shining Sumac

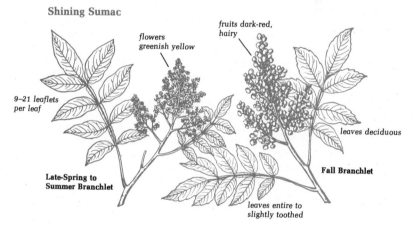

flowers greenish yellow

fruits dark-red, hairy

9–21 leaflets per leaf

leaves deciduous

Late-Spring to Summer Branchlet

Fall Branchlet

leaves entire to slightly toothed

Appearance: slender shrub or small tree to 8 m (26 ft), with a rounded crown; trunk short, slender, to 15 cm (6 in) in diameter. **Bark:** 6–12 mm (0.2–0.5 in) thick, smooth when young becoming roughened and developing large thin scales with age, light brown. **Branches:** slender, upright to spreading; branchlets green and usually densely hairy when young, turning reddish-brown and sparsely hairy with age. **Winter buds:** tiny, 2–4 mm (0.1–0.2 in) long, rounded, covered with dense, reddish-brown hairs. **Leaves:** alternate, *deciduous,* feather-like (pinnate) compound, 12–24 cm (4.7–9.5 in) long, *with 9 to 21 leaflets,* the leaflets broadest below the middle to uniformly wide, 3.7–6.2 cm (1.5–2.5 in) long, *1.8–2.4 cm (0.8–1 in) wide,* long pointed at the tip, rounded and often unequal at the base, *entire or slightly toothed along the margin,* dark green, shiny and smooth above, paler and hairy beneath, the winged stalk bearing the leaflets. **Flowers:** male and female flowers in separate clusters on different plants; the flowers tiny, greenish-yellow, produced in many-flowered, dense, upright, branched, pyramid-shaped clusters at the ends of the branchlets; each flower with 5 sepals, 5 small petals, 5 stamens, and a single pistil. **Fruits:** produced in dense clusters, each fruit berry-like, egg-shaped, and slightly flattened, 3–5 mm (0.1–0.2 in) long, dark red, covered with fine, glandular hairs, enclosing a stone and seed.

Prairie Sumac *Rhus lanceolata* (A. Gray) Britton

This species is native from southern Oklahoma and eastern Texas to southern New Mexico, and adjacent Mexico. It grows in dry, rocky soils and is more commonly encountered on the Edwards Plateau in Texas than any other region of the U.S. In the

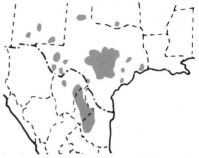

past, botanists considered prairie sumac only a variety of shining sumac (*Rhus copallina*), but its larger clusters of fruits and narrower leaflets warrant species status.

Flowers are produced in July or August, with the fruits maturing in September or October. They are of considerable importance to wildlife, especially quail, grouse, and prairie chickens. Whitetail deer browse the young twigs and leaves. Like other species of sumac, the fruits of prairie sumac can be used to make a tart-tasting beverage. A black dye can be made from the fruits. Prairie sumac is occasionally planted for erosion control and for its bright red or orange autumn leaves.

Appearance: thicket-forming shrub or small tree to 10 m (33 ft), with a rounded crown; trunk short, branching close to the ground, to 20 cm (7.9 in) in diameter. **Bark:** thin, to 4 mm (0.2 in) thick, smooth, becoming scaly with age, light brown. **Branches:** stout, spreading to upright; branchlets slender, greenish to red, hairy when young, becoming smooth and gray with age. **Winter buds:** tiny, 2–3 mm (0.1 in) long, rounded, covered with dense hairs. **Leaves:** alternate, *deciduous,* feather-like (pinnate) compound, 12–24 cm (4.7–9.5 in) long, *composed of 9 to 21 leaflets,* the leaflets linear to lance-shaped, 2.5–7.5 cm (1–3 in) long, *0.6–1.2 cm (0.3–0.5 in) wide,* often curved, long pointed at the tip, rounded to tapering at the base, *entire or with a few coarse teeth along the margin,* papery, dark green and shiny above, paler and slightly hairy below. **Flowers:** male and female flowers in separate clusters on different plants; the flowers yellowish-green to white, produced in dense, branched, upright, many-flowered clusters at the ends of the branchlets. Each flower with 5 sepals, 5 tiny petals, 5 stamens, and a single pistil. **Fruits:** produced in dense, cone-shaped clusters; each fruit berry-like, rounded or nearly so to somewhat flattened, *dark red, covered with glandular hairs,* enclosing a small, flattened stone and seed.

Mearns Sumac *Rhus choriophylla* Woot. & Standl.

Mearns sumac, generally a shrub, becomes a small tree in Arizona. Its range extends

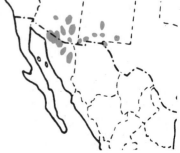

from Trans-Pecos Texas to southern Arizona, and Sonora, Mexico. It is closely related to the evergreen sumac (*Rhus sempervirens*), and apparently hybridizes with it. Flowering extends from July to August with the fruits maturing in autumn. The fruits are eaten by several species of birds.

Members of this species are shrubs or short trees to 5 m (16 ft), with an open, irregular crown. The alternate, *evergreen, feather-like (pinnate) compound leaves* have *3 to 5, rarely 7, leaflets* which are broadest near the base, 2.5–5 cm (1–2 in) long, 1.2–2.5 cm (0.5–1 in) wide, pointed at the tip, usually rounded and uneven at the base, entire on the margins, dull dark green above, and paler and slightly hairy beneath. Flowers are tiny, produced in many-flowered, elongated but spreading, branched clusters 5–6 cm (2–2.4 in) long and wide. Fruits are produced in elongated clusters, each fruit berry-like, rounded or nearly so, 6–8 mm (0.2–0.3 in) in diameter, covered with red or brown hairs, and enclosing a small stone and flattened seed.

The Mango Genus   Mangifera L.

This is a medium-size genus of about 40 species of trees, all native to tropical Asia. One species, the mango, bears large edible fruits and has been introduced into tropical regions throughout the world. It is cultivated in the West Indies and Central and South America. In southern Florida it has escaped from cultivation and now grows wild in hammocks.

Members of this genus are trees with simple, alternate, evergreen leaves. Flowers are bisexual and male or female on the same tree or different trees. The flowers are produced in large, branched, elongated clusters. Fruits are often large, fleshy, usually rounded to egg-shaped, and often with a turpentine odor.

Mango   Mangifera indica L.

This medium-size to large tree is native to India, and has been used since prehistoric times. Mangos are one of the sacred trees of Buddhists and Hindus. Orchards of mango trees are grown in southern Florida for their delicious fruits. They may be eaten fresh, or used to make jam or mango pickles. Dozens of varieties of mangos have been developed to improve the size, flavor, and fragrance of the fruits, to increase productivity, and to strengthen resistance to diseases and pests.

In Florida, mango is a tree to 15 m (49 ft), with a wide spreading crown and thick, gray, corky bark. The leaves are **simple, alternate, evergreen,** but crowded together to almost form a whorl, lance-shaped to narrow and broadest near the middle, **10–20 cm (4–7.9 in) long,** pointed to long pointed at the tip, tapering at the base, leathery, dark green, shiny, and smooth. The yellowish-green to greenish-white, rarely pink, very fragrant flowers are produced in large, branched, elongate, many-flowered clusters; each flower with a 4- or 5-lobed calyx 2–3 mm (0.1 in) long, 4 or 5 petals, 4–5 mm (0.1–0.2 in) long, with 1 or 2 fertile stamens, and 3 or 4 sterile ones, and with a single pistil. Fruits are **large, rounded to egg-shaped,** variable in size, may weigh up **to 2 kg (4.4 lbs),** red or pink tinged with yellow or green, with a thin skin covering a sweet to acid, orange pulp, the pulp surrounding a single, large stone that contains the seed.

The Poison Sumac Genus   Toxicodendron Mill.

This is a small genus of about 22 species of North American and Asian trees, shrubs, and vines. Three North American species are among the most unpopular plants: poison sumac (*Toxicodendron vernix*), poison oak (*T. quercifolium*), and poison ivy (*T. radicans*). Only poison sumac grows to tree size in North America. All of these plants release oils when the leaves, stems, roots, flowers, or fruits are touched. The oils cause a skin rash, sometimes quite severe and painful. Some of the worst cases of poisoning occur when the plants are burned and the smoke contacts skin and mucus linings of the mouth, throat, and nose.

Members of the genus are woody with feather-like (pinnate) compound leaves or with 3 leaflets per leaf. The bisexual or male and female flowers are produced in elongate, branched, many-flowered clusters. Individual flowers have a 5-parted calyx, 5 petals, 5 or 10 stamens, and a single pistil. Fruits are small, berry-like, dry to slightly fleshy.

Poison Sumac   *Toxicodendron vernix* (L.) Kuntze

Poison sumac is a small tree of the eastern lowlands, ranging from southern Quebec to central Florida, and west to Texas. It grows along streams, floodplains, and swampy woodlands and occurs in association with red maple, American elm, black ash, sweet-bay, and tupelo.

It is one of the better-known members of the cashew family and is actually more closely related to poison ivy and poison oak than to sumacs. Similar appearance led botanists to once place poison sumac in the same genus as the sumacs. The white waxy fruits make poison sumac easy to distinguish from the true sumacs.

They are a fast growing, short-lived tree that produces separate clusters of male and female flowers at the base of the leaves in early summer. The fruits ripen in early fall but may persist on the trees throughout the winter. Grouse, turkey, pheasant, quail, and many songbirds feed on the fruits. The oils in all parts of the plant can cause a severe dermatitis, comparable to the rashes caused by poison ivy.

Appearance: shrub or occasionally a small tree to 7 m (23 ft), with a narrow, rounded crown; trunk slender, to 15 cm (6 ft) in diameter. **Bark:** thin, 2–4 mm (0.1–0.2 in) thick, smooth, light gray. **Branches:** slender, drooping; branchlets slender, dark green and usually finely hairy when young, becoming gray and smooth with age. **Winter buds:** 3–19 mm (0.1–0.8 in) long, broadest near the base and pointed at the tip, covered with overlapping, dark purple scales. **Leaves:** alternate, ***deciduous, feather-like (pinnate) compound,*** 18–35 cm (7.1–13.8 in) long, with ***7 to 13 leaflets,*** the leaf-lets broadest near the base, the middle, or above the middle, 3.5–6.5 cm (1.4–2.6 in) long, 1.2–2.4 cm (0.5–1 in) wide, pointed at the tip, tapering at the base, entire along

Poison Sumac *POISONOUS!*

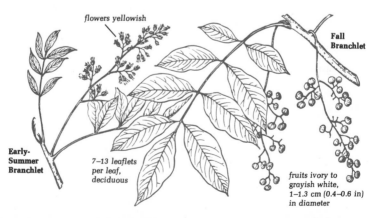

flowers yellowish

Fall
Branchlet

Early-
Summer
Branchlet

7–13 leaflets
per leaf,
deciduous

fruits ivory to
grayish white,
1–1.3 cm (0.4–0.6 in)
in diameter

the margin, dark shiny green and smooth at maturity; leafstalks slender. **Flowers:** tiny, yellowish, male and female flowers on separate plants, produced in large, branched, elongate clusters (panicles) in the junctions of the upper leaves. **Fruits:** produced in large branched clusters, each ***fruit berry-like, rounded, 1–1.3 cm (0.4–0.6 in) in diameter, ivory to grayish-white,*** sometimes tinged with yellow, and containing a single stone which encloses the seed.

The Poison Tree Genus
Metopium P. Br.

This is a small genus of 2 or 3 species of southern Florida, the West Indies, Mexico, and Central America. Only 1 of them, the Florida poison tree, is native to North America. The sap from any part of the plant including the wood can cause a severe skin rash comparable to that caused by poison ivy.

Members of this genus are shrubs or trees with leathery, evergreen, feather-like (pinnate) compound leaves. The yellow-green flowers are male or female and produced in upright clusters on separate trees. Floral parts are in 5s. The fruit is egg-shaped to uniformly wide, the outer coat thick and resinous, containing a brittle stone.

Florida Poison Tree
Metopium toxiferum (L.) Krug & Urban

Like its relatives, poison sumac and poison oak, Florida poison tree is very poisonous and contact with it should be avoided. The sap is caustic and people can develop serious skin and mucus irritation from handling the leaves, flowers, fruits, bark, and wood. It is native to southern Florida, the Bahamas, and the West Indies. In Florida, it grows in hammocks, pine woodlands, and on sandy dunes. Flowering is usually from early to late spring, but can occur any month of the year.

It is a shrub or tree to 12 m (39 ft), with a short trunk, reddish-brown, scaly bark, and stout branches that form a low, broad crown. The feather-like (pinnate) compound ***leaves*** are ***evergreen,*** and composed of ***3 to 7 leaflets,*** the leaflets broadest

Florida Poison Tree *SAP POISONOUS!*

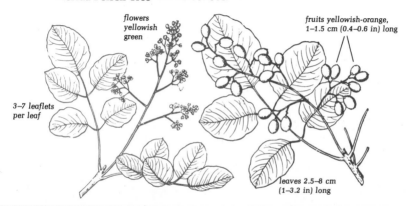

flowers yellowish green

fruits yellowish-orange, 1–1.5 cm (0.4–0.6 in) long

3–7 leaflets per leaf

leaves 2.5–8 cm (1–3.2 in) long

near the base or middle, 2.5–8 cm (1–3.2 in) long, **rounded** and **often notched at the tip,** entire, leathery, dark green, and shiny. The tiny, yellowish-green flowers are produced in elongate, branched clusters in the junction of the upper leaves. Each flower is composed of a 5-lobed calyx, 5 small petals, 5 stamens in male flowers, and a single pistil in female flowers. **Fruits** are **uniformly long, 1–1.5 cm (0.4–0.6 in) long,** rounded at the tip, **yellowish-orange,** shiny, not splitting open at maturity, and enclosing a bony stone.

The Pistache Genus   *Pistacia* L.

The 8 or 9 species of this genus are native to the warmer regions of the world, including the lower Rio Grande in North America. They also occur in southern Mexico, the Canary Islands, China, and the Mediterranean countries. Only 1 species, the Texas pistache is native to North America.

The genus includes both trees and shrubs with deciduous or evergreen leaves. The leaves are feather-like (pinnate) compound or 3-parted. The small flowers are produced in clusters with the male and female flowers occurring on separate trees. Each flower has a small, usually lobed calyx, no petals, 3 to 5 stamens in the male flowers, and a single pistil in the female flowers. The fruit is fleshy, uniformly long, and contains a single stone that encloses the seed.

Texas Pistache   *Pistacia texana* Swingle

This species is native to the lower Rio Grande Valley in Texas and northeastern Mexico. It grows in rocky limestone soils along streambanks, on cliffs, and especially near the junction of the Pecos and Rio Grande rivers. It is of no commercial use and probably of limited value to wildlife.

The plants are shrubs or small multi-trunked trees to 10 m (33 ft), with evergreen to tardily deciduous **leaves** that are feather-like (pinnately) compound and **contain 9 to 19 dark green leaflets.** The leaflets are 0.8–2.5 cm (0.4–1 in) long, 7–9 mm (0.3–0.4 in) wide, and lance-shaped to broadly rounded and entire along the margin. The flowers appear before or as the leaves unfold, male flowers in densely flowered, elongate clusters 1.9–3.7 cm (0.8–1.5 in) long, female flowers in loosely flowered elongate clusters 4–7 cm (1.6–2.8 in) long. The **fruits** are borne in elongated clusters, each fruit **egg-shaped or nearly so, 6–8 mm (0.2–0.3 in) long, 4–5 mm (0.1–0.2 in) wide, reddish-brown.**

The Pepper Tree Genus   *Schinus* L.

This is a small genus of about 20 species of trees and shrubs, mostly of South America. One species, the pepper tree, was introduced into the southwestern U.S. from Peru. Many of the species have a gummy resin that is used in medicinal preparations to treat cataracts, and especially venereal and urinary diseases.

Members of this genus are trees with alternate, evergreen feather-like (pinnate) compound leaves. The small, whitish flowers are either male or female and produced in large, upright, many-flowered, branched, elongate clusters. Fruits are rounded, berry-like, leathery to slightly fleshy, not splitting open at maturity, and containing a hard stone.

Pepper Tree   *Schinus molle* L.

These graceful, attractive evergreen trees are planted as shade trees from southern Texas to southern California. They occasionally spread on their own and become naturalized in dry, sandy soils. The small fragrant seeds have been used in some countries as an adulterant in black pepper. A resinous gum made from the bark that dries bluish-white has been used in folk medicine to treat digestive disorders.

Pepper trees grow to 15 m (49 ft), with a spreading, rounded crown, and graceful, hanging branches and branchlets. The alternate, evergreen, feather-like **leaves** are **composed of 19 to 41 leaflets,** the leaflets **linear to lance-shaped, 1–6 cm (0.4–2.4 in) long,** and entire to obscurely toothed along the margin. Male and female flowers occur on separate trees. The flowers are tiny, yellowish-white, numerous, and produced in large, branched, elongate clusters. **Fruits** are **rounded, 5–9 mm (0.2–0.4 in) in diameter, pink,** leathery, resinous, containing a bony stone that encloses a single seed.

The **Quassia** Family   Simaroubaceae

The quassia family, consisting of approximately 20 genera and 120 species of trees, shrubs, and a few herbs, is well known in the tropics and subtropics of the Northern Hemisphere. Six genera, each containing a single species, are found in North America. Crucifixion thorn is a spiny shrub or tree of the American southwest, while bitterbush, paradise tree, Mexican Alvaradoa, and baycedar are natives of Florida. The tree of heaven, an introduced species, grows wild in many parts of the country.

Most members of the Quassia family contain a bitter, usually milky sap, which is water soluble. In South America, the bark or wood of many species is used as a bitter tonic to treat fevers. Best known of these is bitterwood (*Quassia amara*), a tree of northeastern South America. Its wood was often cut into chips and sold to be mixed with water. Sometimes cups were fashioned of the wood, which imparted its remedial properties to the water poured into it. It is still used in some medicines today.

The trees and shrubs have alternate, feather-like compound, rarely simple leaves. Their small numerous, symmetrical flowers are either male or female or bisexual, appearing in clusters either at the bases of leaves or at the ends of the branchlets. The flowers consist of 3 to 5 sepals and petals, up to 10 stamens, and 2 to 5 more or less joined pistils. The fruit may be a stonefruit (drupe), berry, capsule, or winged seed.

Key to Quassia Genera

A. Trees with leaves throughout most of the year, or at least during the summer months; trees lacking spines.

    1. Leaves feather-like (pinnate) compound leaves.

        a. Leaflets 1.2–1.8 cm (0.5–0.8 in) long, leaves

(Continued)

with 21–41 leaflets per leaf; fruits dry, hairy 2- or 3-winged capsules; trees of south Florida and Mexico

Alvaradoa, p. 812

b. Leaflets 4–15 cm (1.6–6 in) long, leaves with 5–41 leaflets per leaf; fruits fleshy stone fruits, berries, or dry and 1-winged.

(1) Leaves 30–90 cm (11.8–35.4 in) long, with 11–41 leaflets per leaf; fruits dry, winged; introduced tree; tree of heaven

Ailanthus, p. 813

(2) Leaves 15–36 cm (6–14.2 in) long, with 10–18 leaflets per leaf; fruits fleshy berries, not winged.

(a) Flowers with 10 stamens; leaves lacking a single leaflet at the tip; trees of south Florida; includes paradise tree **Simarouba, p. 815**

(b) Flowers with 5 stamens; leaves with a single leaflet at the tip; trees of south Florida **Picramnia, p. 816**

2. Leaves simple, 2.5–3.8 cm (1–1.5 in) long, evergreen; trees of central and southern Florida **Baycedar, p. 816**

B. Trees leafless most of the year; twigs ending in stout, sharp spines; trees of Arizona, southeastern California, and Mexico

Crucifixion thorn, p. 817

Tree of Heaven

Paradise Tree

The Alvaradoa Genus

Alvaradoa Liebm.

This is a small genus of about 6 species centered in the West Indies. Most of the species occur only in Cuba or Jamaica, but 1 species, the Mexican alvaradoa, is widespread in tropical America. This tree also is native to south Florida. Alvaradoa trees contain very bitter-tasting chemical compounds, especially in the bark.

Members of this genus are shrubs or small trees with bitter tasting bark and alternate, deciduous, feather-like compound leaves. The tiny flowers are either male or female and produced in large branched clusters. Male flowers have 5 calyx lobes, 5 petals, and 5 stamens; female flowers have 5 calyx lobes, no petals, no stamens, and 3 pistils. The fruits are 2- or 3-winged capsules.

Mexican Alvaradoa

Alvaradoa amorphoides Liebm.

Like so many other members of the Ailanthus family, Mexican alvaradoa is a shrub or short, evergreen tree with a bitter juice in the leaves, twigs, and bark. This plant occurs in hammocks from Florida to Mexico, and south into Central America. Little has been published on its growth characteristics and use by wildlife. It has no commercial value.

Mexican alvaradoa may attain a height of 15 m (49 ft), with a trunk diameter of about 15–20 cm (6–7.9 in). The young branchlets are covered with velvety hair, but later become smooth, dull red-brown, and covered with lenticels and leaf scars. The alternate, **evergreen leaves** are **feather-like compound,** 10–30 cm (4–11.8 in) long, and crowded at the ends of the branchlets. They are composed of **21 to 41 long, narrow leaflets, 1.2–1.8 cm (0.5–0.8 in) long,** 0.5–0.7 cm (0.2–0.3 in) wide, with rounded tips and narrow bases, which sit

directly on the main leafstalk with a smooth margin. The flowers are male or female and are borne separately in long, profuse clusters at the ends of the branchlets; the male clusters grow up to 40 cm (15.8 in) long, though the female ones are shorter. The calyx is 0.2–0.3 cm (0.1 in) long, deeply 5-lobed, and bell-shaped; petals are lacking. The **fruits** are densely hairy, **2- or 3-winged capsules,** approximately 1.7–1.9 cm (0.7–0.8 in) long, and light tinged with red; seeds are pale yellow, 0.7–0.9 cm (0.3–0.4 in) long, and pointed at both ends.

The Ailanthus Genus *Ailanthus* Desf.

This is a small genus of about 10 species of trees native to Asia and northern Australia. The tree of heaven (*Ailanthus altissima*) was brought from northern China to England in the mid-18th century. From there, it was introduced into the U.S. in 1874 as an urban ornamental.

Members of this genus are trees with large alternate, deciduous, feather-like compound leaves having 13 to 41 leaflets per leaf, each with a few large teeth on the margin near the base of the leaf. Each tooth has a large, round gland on the lower surface. Individual trees bear male or female and/or bisexual flowers. The small flowers are produced in large branched clusters at the tips of the branchlets. Each flower is composed of 5 tiny, partly fused calyx lobes, 5 or 6 narrow petals, 10 stamens, and 5 to 6 pistils; in male flowers the pistils are absent. Fruits are winged and consist of a small flattened seed in the middle of a large narrow wing.

Tree of Heaven, Ailanthus *Ailanthus altissima* (Mill.) Swingle

Of all the trees that have been used in cities for ornamentation, none can match the hardiness of the tree of heaven. It is a short to medium-size tree that is cultivated and grows wild from Massachusetts and Ontario, south through the eastern U.S., and to a lesser degree from the southern Rocky Mountains to California. It resembles the sumac tree, but large teeth on the bases of its leaflets help to distinguish it from the sumac. It grows at low elevations in a wide variety of soils, including the very poorest and driest. A frequent companion of city street lamps, the tree of heaven also grows in nonclimax, mixed deciduous woods, clearings, vacant lots, yards, and along the edges of woodlands. Often it will completely take over a clearing and rapidly become a thick, impassible stand.

The tree of heaven is extremely fast growing, up to 3 m (9.8 ft), in a single season, and is short-lived. It was originally selected as an urban tree because of its rapid growth rate and ability to withstand the stresses of cities. However, once it becomes established, this tree is very difficult to rout, and as a consequence many people regard it as a pest. Another unpopular feature is the unpleasant odor sent out by the male flowers. The flowers bloom after the leaves appear, usually in late June. The winged seeds are produced in large clusters that mature in late summer, but may remain on the tree through winter.

The tree is of little value to wildlife, but is used as an ornamental. The wood is too soft and weak to use in manufacturing; even moderately heavy storms may bring down dozens of trees, as will snow and strong winds.

Yet, despite its faults and unpleasantnesses, this little tree graces and keeps green even the most blighted urban areas. It manages to thrive in smoggy air, and like all trees produces oxygen. This is the tree in Betty Smith's *A Tree Grows in Brooklyn*, a novel about a young girl who was inspired by a tree of heaven's determination to survive.

Tree of Heaven

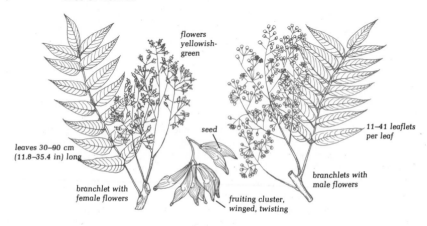

flowers yellowish-green

seed

11–41 leaflets per leaf

leaves 30–90 cm (11.8–35.4 in) long

branchlet with male flowers

branchlet with female flowers

fruiting cluster, winged, twisting

Appearance: a short to medium-size tree, growing to a maximum of 25 m (82 ft), with a loose, open crown, well-rounded even when young; trunk slender, up to 1 m (3.3 ft) in diameter; often many small trees found growing together in clumps. **Bark:** thin, gray, slightly rough; smooth and green on new growth. **Branches:** loose, spreading, the lower ones tending to droop; weak and breakable; branchlets are coarse, yellowish to red-brown, velvety-downy; with heart-shaped leaf scars and lenticels. **Winter buds:** solitary, relatively small and half-spherical, with 2 or 4 exposed scales, brownish, downy; terminal bud absent. **Leaves:** alternate, deciduous, *feather-like (pinnately) compound, 30–90 cm (11.8–35.4 in) long; with 11 to 41 leaflets in pairs along a central stalk,* with a single, terminal leaflet; leaflets 5–15 cm (2–6 in) long, about one-third as wide; narrowly pointed at the tip, broadest near the base and blunt; margin entire except for *2 or more coarse, glandular teeth near the base;* smooth-textured, dark green above, paler below; leafstalks smooth, round, and swollen at the base. **Flowers:** *male and female flowers on separate trees,* or male and female parts in same flower; small, yellowish-green, in clusters 15–30 cm (6–11.8 in) in length; calyx 5-lobed; corolla of 5 greenish, hairy petals; stamens usually 10; male flowers ill-smelling. **Fruits:** *1 seed in the center of a long wing, spirally twisted,* reddish or yellowish-brown; in dense clusters on the tree.

The Simarouba Genus

Simarouba Aubl.

The simarouba genus is small, comprising 4 species of trees that occur only in tropical America, from southern Florida to Brazil. Plants in this genus contain a resin that is a volatile oil, as well as the bitter ingredient quasin, which is said to have medicinal properties. A single species, the paradise tree (*Simarouba glauca*), is native to North America.

These trees have evergreen leaves which are feather-like (pinnately) compound, with long leafstalks. The flowers are in long and widely branched clusters (panicles) at the ends of branches or at the bases of leaves. The flowers are small, usually with a 5-lobed calyx, 5 petals, usually 10 stamens, and 5 carpels in the pistil, which is inserted in a floral disk. The fruit is a cluster of 1 to 5 slightly fleshy stone-fruits (drupes).

Paradise Tree

Simarouba glauca D.C.

This small tree occurs in south Florida and on the Florida Keys, as well as in Cuba, Jamaica, Nicaragua, and Brazil. It grows at low elevations in coastal hammocks with species such as magnolias, baytrees, live oaks, and other Quassia family members.

The paradise tree is not particularly fast-growing. Its flowers appear in early spring in long clusters (panicles), and the fruits develop shortly thereafter. The fruits mature by early May when they become bright red or purplish. Little is known about its use by wildlife, nor is this plant used by man.

Paradise trees occasionally reach heights of 15 m (49 ft); the crown is rounded, and the straight trunk 45–50 cm (17.7–19.7 in) in diameter. The branchlets are pale green at first, but darken with age and become marked by large, oval leaf scars. The feather-like compound leaves are 15–25 cm (6–9.8 in) long, with usually **6 to 8 pairs of opposite or alternate,** egg-shaped **leaflets,** which are 4–8 cm (1.6–3.2 in) long, dark red

Paradise Tree

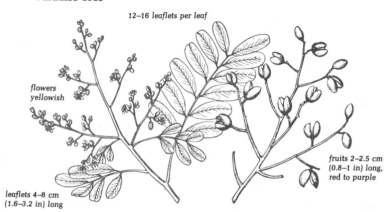

12–16 leaflets per leaf

flowers yellowish

fruits 2–2.5 cm (0.8–1 in) long, red to purple

leaflets 4–8 cm (1.6–3.2 in) long

when they unfold but soon become dark green, shiny, and leathery. The small, yellowish flowers are produced on short bluish stems. The **fruits** are **fleshy, berry-like, 2–2.5 cm (0.8–1 in) in length, red to purple,** and occur in groups of up to 5. Each fruit contains an orange-brown seed that is about two-thirds the length of the fruit.

The Picramnia Genus

Picramnia Sw.

This is a small genus of about 30 species of trees and shrubs of the tropical regions of North, Central, and South America. Only 1 species, bitterbush (*Picramnia pentandra*), is native to North America, along the coast of southern Florida. The generic name comes from the ancient Greek words for *bitter* and *bush,* referring to the bitter ingredient in the bark and twigs.

Members of this genus have unequally feather-like (pinnately) compound leaves and thick, nearly leathery leaflets. The flowers are either male or female and borne in branched or unbranched elongated clusters. Each flower is composed of 3 to 5 calyx lobes, 3 to 5 white to greenish petals or the petals absent, in the male flowers 3 to 5 stamens, in the female flowers a single 3- to 5-celled pistil. The fruits are small berries.

Bitterbush

Picramnia pentandra Sw.

Bitterbush grows on the southern shores of Florida in sandy soils at or near sea level. In Florida, it is rarely a tree, but in the West Indies and Central and South America, it grows to a short, slender tree. It may be mistaken for young plants of the paradise tree (*Simarouba glauca*).

The wood is white, hard, and heavy, but is of little use because the trees are small in size and scarce. Cubans have used the bark and leaves to combat fevers. The trees are also raised as ornamentals in Florida, and they are used as honey trees.

Bitterbush is a shrub or small tree with a narrow crown, slender trunk, and **smooth, thin, bitter** bark. The branchlets are pale brown or yellowish-green, and covered with short hairs. The **leaves** are alternate, **evergreen, feather-like compound** with a single terminal leaflet (odd pinnate), **20–36 cm (7.9–14.2 in) long,** and composed of **5 to 9 leaflets;** the leaflets slightly alternate. Leaflets are broadest at the middle, 5–10 cm (2–4 in) long, tapering to rounded at the base, tapering to long pointed at the tip, dark green and shiny above, paler beneath. Male and female flowers are produced in clusters on separate plants and appear in late winter to early spring. The oblong fleshy berries are 1–1.5 cm (0.4–0.6 in) long, red turning black, and contain 1 to 3 seeds.

The Baycedar Genus

Suriana L.

This genus contains a single species, the baycedar. Botanists placed it in its own family, the surianaceae, for many years. It is now considered to be a member of the quassia family. Information given for the species is the same as for the genus.

Baycedar, Suriana

Suriana maritima L.

Baycedar is common in scattered localities along sandy beaches and dry coasts in central and southern Florida, including the Florida Keys. Its range extends southward into the Caribbean, covering much of the Atlantic shore of tropical America. Baycedar is recognized by its dense masses of grayish green, narrow, succulent foliage, and by the few small, yellow flowers that grow in clusters at the ends of the branchlets.

This species flowers and produces fruits and seeds throughout the year. The fruit is dry, hard, and contains a single seed. The wood is red-brown in the center, and lighter on the outer part. It is heavy, hard, and durable, but the plants are usually too small and too few in number to be useful for construction. However, the stress-resisting qualities of this wood help the tree survive the high winds and storms of the tropics.

Appearance: a shrub or small tree, up to 5 m (16 ft) high, with a cone-shaped crown and a short trunk, 12–13 cm (4.7–5.1 in) in diameter; commonly found in small, rounded clumps, 1–2.5 m (3.3–8.2 ft) in diameter. **Bark:** dark gray or brown, becoming thick, cracked, or *shaggy, peeling off in flexible, ragged strips to reveal the light yellow inner bark.* **Branches:** numerous, erect, slender, dense; branchlets at first green, turning brown, stout, and flexible, hairy. **Leaves:** alternate, *evergreen, simple,* numerous, *2.5–3.8 cm (1–1.5 in) long,* narrow, broadening from a narrow base upward, rounded at the tip, green, grayish-downy on both sides, margins entire, with a slightly salty taste. **Flowers:** *bisexual, 1.1–1.3 cm (0.5–0.6 in) in diameter,* either solitary or in few-flowered clusters in the dense clumps of leaves, on pale yellow stalks; *sepals 5, large, pointed, hairy; petals 5, rounded, shorter than the sepals; 10 stamens; 5 separate pistils.* Fruits: *each flower produces 5 small, dry, nut-like fruits, each containing 1 seed.*

The Crucifixion Thorn Genus   *Holacantha* Gray

This is one of the 3 unrelated genera that have been given the name of crucifixion thorn. It contains several species of shrubs and 1 tree species, which occur over the drier parts of the Sonoran Desert region. These plants are recognized by the absence of leaves, the large clusters of fruits that remain on the plants for several years, and especially by their large, rigid, spiny branches.

Crucifixion Thorn, Holacantha   *Holacantha emoryi* A. Gray

This is a small tree of southern Arizona, southeastern California, and Sonora, Mexico; it is one of 3 crucifixion thorns that are native to the Sonoran Desert. It grows in fine-textured, poorly drained river soils at about 150–600 m (490–1,970 ft) elevation. Normally occurring in low-lying desert valleys and alluvial bottomlands in drier regions, the species can often be found on un-stabilized sand dunes. Crucifixion thorns are characteristic of desert areas receiving somewhat above-average rainfall, where the desert takes on a woodland aspect.

Other species found here may include the giant saguaro cactus, the palo verdes, and desert ironwood, as well as many other cacti and shrubs of the legume and sunflower families. As with other desert plants, leaves of this tree are small and soon fall away to prevent excess evaporation.

Holacantha grows about 2–4 m (6.6–13.1 ft) high, and has a scruffy form with a dense crown. The ***branches*** and ***twigs*** are **stout, ending in sharp spines,** and at first are densely and finely hairy. The ***scale-like leaves fall off quickly.*** The flowers bloom in dense clusters during the rainy season; male and female flowers appear on separate plants. Each flower has 5 to 8 hairy, reddish-purple sepals and petals, from 12 to 16 stamens, and 5 to 10 carpels. ***Fruits*** consist of ***a ring of 5 to 10 flattened, 1-seeded segments,*** each 2–4 mm (0.1–0.2 in) long, and remaining on the branches for several years.

The Citrus Family Rutaceae

This is a large family of about 150 genera and 1,000 species of trees, shrubs, and some herbs. They are widely distributed in the tropical, subtropical, and to a lesser extent in the temperate regions of the world. Five genera are native to North America. One of these contains a species, the Berlandier esenbeckia (*Esenbeckia berlandieri*), of northern Mexico that just extends north of the border near Los Fresnos, Texas. Since only 4 trees of this species grow in the U.S., it is mentioned here and not discussed later. Species of 2 introduced genera, citrus and the trifoliate orange, have been introduced, are commonly encountered in some regions, and have become established as part of our tree flora.

This is an economically important family. It contains the orange, lemon, lime, and grapefruit trees as well as other important but less-known citrus fruits. Bitter, aromatic oils are obtained from several of the tropical members. They are used as flavorings, spices, incense, and in perfumes.

Members of this family are trees, shrubs, or herbs with alternate or opposite, deciduous or evergreen, usually feather-like (pinnate) compound or simple gland-dotted leaves. Flowers are bisexual or male and female and produced in dense, short to long, loose clusters. Fruits can be a dry capsule, a berry or berry-like, or dry, flattened and winged.

Key to Citrus Genera

A. Leaves opposite.

    1. Fruits rounded, berry-like; trees of southern Florida   **Torchwood, p. 819**

Torchwood

    2. Fruits flattened, dry, winged; trees of southern Texas   **Baretta, p. 821**

Baretta

B. Leaves alternate.

    1. Leaves simple or appearing simple, evergreen; leafstalks often winged   **Citrus, p. 822**

    2. Leaves feather-like (pinnate) compound or with 3 leaflets per leaf, deciduous to nearly evergreen.

Lime

        a. Fruits dry, flattened, circular in outline, broadly winged   **Hoptree, p. 826**

        b. Fruits leathery to fleshy, rounded to egg-shaped, not winged.

Common Hoptree

            (1) Leaves feather-like (pinnate) compound, with 5–11, rarely 3, leaflets per leaf; flowers tiny in many-flowered branched clusters; fruiting capsules splitting open at maturity

                    Prickly ash, p. 828

Hercules Club

            (2) Leaves with 3 leaflets; flowers showy, solitary, or in few-flowered clusters; fruits rounded, not splitting open, like a miniature orange

                Trifoliate orange, p. 834

Trifoliate Orange

The Torchwood Genus   *Amyris* L.

This is a small genus of about 20 species of trees and shrubs of tropical regions of the Americas. Two species range northward only into southern Florida. The plants abound in fragrant oils and resins that occur in all parts of the trees, including the wood. These have been used as incense and in folk medicines. The light yellow wood is very hard and fragrant, and takes an excellent polish but has limited use because the trees are usually too small for timber.

    Members of this genus are shrubs or trees with opposite or alternate, usually evergreen, compound leaves. The leaves have 3 to 5 leaflets or rarely a single leaflet, conspicuously gland-dotted. Flowers are white, often bisexual, sometimes also with male or female flowers, produced in elongate, branched, many-flowered clusters. Each flower has a 4-lobed, gland-dotted calyx, 4 white petals, 8 stamens, and a single pistil. Fruits are berry-like, often mealy, resinous, and contain a single seed.

Key to Torchwood Species

A. Fruits rounded, 5–9 mm (0.2–0.4 in) in diameter; leaflets 2.5–7.5 cm (1–3 in) long; trees of coastal eastern Florida and the Keys **Torchwood, p. 820**

B. Fruits broadest near the tip, 7–14 mm (2.8–5.5 in) long; leaflets 6–12 cm (2.4–4.7 in) long; rare trees of extreme southern Florida

Balsam torchwood, p. 821

Torchwood   *Amyris elemifera* L.

This slender evergreen shrub grows in moist, low-lying coastal hammocks from mid-Florida to the lower Keys, where it attains its greatest size. It is also native to the Bahamas, the West Indies, and Central America. Flowering can extend from August to

December with the fruits ripening the following spring. Birds feed on the pulpy fruits, although it is not a preferred food. People have valued the hard, close-grained wood but the trees are too small and scarce to be of much commercial importance. The twigs are sometimes burned as incense and were once used for torches in the West Indies. The bark, wood, leaves, twigs, flowers, and fruits all contain oils that give off a pungent odor when crushed.

The plants are shrubs or trees to 5 m (16

Torchwood

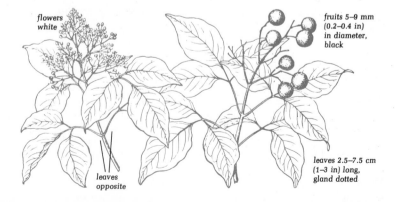

flowers white

fruits 5–9 mm (0.2–0.4 in) in diameter, black

leaves opposite

leaves 2.5–7.5 cm (1–3 in) long, gland dotted

ft), rarely taller, with a small, rounded crown. The *opposite, evergreen leaves* are compound and consist of *3, occasionally 5 leaflets,* the leaflets broadest near the base, 2.5–7.5 cm (1–3 in) long, pointed to long pointed at the tip, rounded to widely tapering at the base, entire, slightly leathery, shiny yellow-green and gland-dotted. The tiny flowers are produced in branched, elongated clusters to 5 cm (2 in) long. The *fruits* are also produced in clusters, each *rounded, 5–9 mm (0.2–0.4 in) in diameter,* black, smooth but gland-dotted, and containing a single, brown seed.

Balsam Torchwood *Amyris balsamifera* L.

The balsam torchwood, or balsam amyris, is rare in North America. It is found only in a few hammocks of southern Florida. There it grows in sandy or rocky soils. This species is also native to the West Indies and Central and South America. It resembles

its relative, the torchwood, but can be distinguished by the fruits, which are broadest near the tip instead of rounded, and by the larger leaflets.

The plants are shrubs or small trees to 10 m (33 ft), with *opposite, evergreen* compound *leaves* that consist of *3 to 5 leaflets.* The leaflets are lance-shaped to broadest near the base, 6–12 cm (2.4–4.7 in) long, pointed to long-pointed at the tip, usually rounded at the base, entire, *yellow green and dull beneath,* gland-dotted. The tiny white flowers are produced in many-flowered, branched, elongate clusters at or near the ends of the branchlets. Fruits are in clusters, each *broadest near the rounded tip, 7–14 mm (0.3–0.6 in) long,* black, gland-dotted.

The Baretta Genus *Helietta* Tulasne

This is a small genus of about 6 species, all native to the tropical and subtropical regions of the Americas, from Brazil to North America. Only 1 species, the baretta, is native to North America and that is restricted to extreme southern Texas. Like other members of this family, all species of this genus have resinous leaves that give off a pleasant but slightly pungent odor. They are of little economic importance, but are used for firewood.

Members are shrubs or trees with opposite compound leaves composed of 3 leaflets, the leaflets gland-dotted. Flowers are small, usually bisexual, and produced in branched, elongate clusters. Fruits are dry, winged on one side and uniformly wide, and usually produced in clusters of 1 to 4.

Baretta *Helietta parvifolia* (A. Gray) Benth.

Baretta is a slender, evergreen shrub or small tree native to extreme southern Texas and northeastern Mexico. It forms large thickets on the dry soils near the Rio Grande, but the best growth is obtained on the limestone ridges of the Sierra Madre in Mexico. Flowering is in April or May, with the small winged fruits maturing in September or October.

These trees may reach 7 m (23 ft) in height with a small, irregular crown, a short trunk, and slender branchlets. The *opposite, evergreen leaves* consist of 3 leaflets per leaf, the leaflets widest near or above the middle, 1.2–5 cm (0.5–2 in) long,

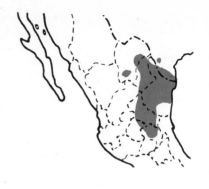

1–1.4 cm (0.4–0.6 in) wide, rounded and sometimes notched at the tip, long tapering at the base, entire, gland-dotted, and strongly aromatic when crushed, shiny yellow-green and smooth above, paler beneath. The tiny, greenish-white, bisexual flowers are produced in elongate, branched, many-flowered clusters, 2.5–6.5 cm (1–2.6 in) long, usually in the junctions of the upper leaves. *Fruits* occur usually in clusters of 3 or 4, *dry, winged, almost uniformly wide, 8–12 mm (0.3–0.5 in) long,* 4–7 mm (0.2–0.3 in) wide, rigid, and resinous.

Baretta

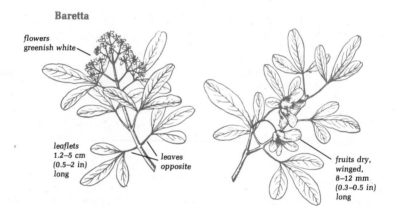

flowers greenish white

leaflets 1.2–5 cm (0.5–2 in) long

leaves opposite

fruits dry, winged, 8–12 mm (0.3–0.5 in) long

The Citrus Genus

Citrus L.

This is a small genus of about 16 species of shrubs or small trees native to southern and southeastern Asia and Malaysia but widely cultivated in tropical, subtropical, and warm temperate regions of the world. Species of this genus are particularly valuable for their delicious edible fruits (oranges, lemons, grapefruits, limes, and others), and their oils used in flavoring and as a source of citric acid. Many of the species and cultivated selections of these species are grown in Florida and California.

The most commonly encountered species are the sweet orange, sour orange, lemon, and lime. Other species cultivated in North America include tangerines (*Citrus reticulata*), grapefruits (*C. paradisi*), and citrons (*C. medica*).

Members of this genus are shrubs or small trees usually armed with sharp spines along the branchlets. The alternate, evergreen leaves are simple, entire to sharply toothed, gland-dotted, and aromatic when crushed. Flowers are produced singly or in pairs, normally bisexual, white to pink, with a 4- to 5-lobed calyx, usually 5 petals, 20 to 60 stamens, and a single pistil. Fruits are rounded to pear-shaped, with a leathery, resinous skin covering, a sour to sweet-tasting pulp divided into many segments, and containing several seeds.

Key to Citrus Species

A. Leafstalks broadly winged, the wing 5–15 mm (0.2–0.6 in) wide, broadest near the tip.

    1. Branchlets armed with many stout spines; the winged leafstalks 5–9 mm (0.2–0.4 in) wide; fruits longer than wide, broadest near the middle, green to yellow; cultivated trees of subtropical climates   **Lime, p. 823**

    2. Branchlets unarmed or only sparsely armed with short spines; the winged leafstalks 10–15 mm (0.4–0.6 in) wide; fruits rounded, orange to red; cultivated trees of subtropical climates   **Sour orange, p. 824**

B. Leafstalks narrowly winged, the wing 1–4 mm (0.1–0.2 in) wide.

    1. Mature fruits rounded, flattened or depressed near the tip, yellowish-green to orange, the skin separating from the sweet tasting pulp; branchlets usually with a few short spines; cultivated trees of Florida, California, Texas, and Arizona   **Sweet orange, p. 825**

    2. Mature fruits longer than wide, broadest near the base, green to yellow, the skin not separating easily from the very sour tasting pulp; branchlets armed with numerous spines; cultivated trees of subtropical climates   **Lemon, p. 825**

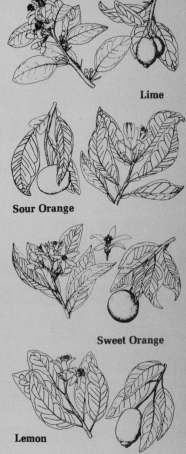

Lime

Sour Orange

Sweet Orange

Lemon

Lime   *Citrus aurantifolia* (Christm.) Swingle

Limes were first introduced into North America by Columbus in 1493. They are extensively cultivated through Latin America and in southern Florida. Birds and small mammals have spread the seeds so the tree now grows wild in some of the coastal hammocks. Unlike oranges, limes are picked green. In south Florida, they are used to make the delicious, tart-tasting key lime pie, a specialty of the region.

Limes are shrubs or trees to 8 m (26 ft), with stout branchlets *armed with green spines 5–14 mm (0.2–0.6 in) long.* The alternate, evergreen, simple leaves are broadest near the base or middle, 4–8 cm (1.6–3.2 in) long, 2–4 cm (0.8–1.6 in) wide, pointed at the tip, rounded at the base, round-toothed along the margin, dark green and shiny; the *leafstalks* articulated just below the blade, *winged, the wing 5–9 mm (0.2–0.4 in) wide.* Flowers are white, produced singly or in pairs in the junction of the leaves, with a 4- or 5-lobed calyx, 4 or 5 narrow petals, 20 to 25 stamens, and a single pistil. Fruits are longer than wide, broadest at the middle, 3.4–6 cm (1.4–2.4 in) in diameter,

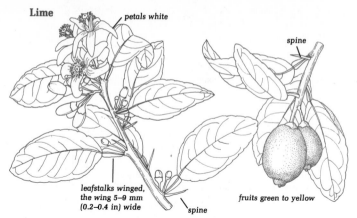

Lime

petals white

spine

leafstalks winged,
the wing 5–9 mm
(0.2–0.4 in) wide

fruits green to yellow

spine

depressed at the tip, bumpy on the surface, **green to yellow thin skin,** not separating easily from the very sour-tasting pulp.

Sour Orange

Citrus aurantium L.

This orange is believed native to southwestern China, Burma, and Assam. It has been cultivated for several hundred years and was introduced into Florida in the mid-1500s. Sour orange has escaped from cultivation and grows wild in coastal hammocks of southern Florida. The lower trunk and roots of young plants are widely used to graft the upper trunk and branches of the sweet orange. The grafted trees are much more successful than those on their own root stock.

These are small trees to 6 m (20 ft), with branchlets unarmed or **only sparsely armed with short spines.** The alternate, evergreen, simple leaves are broadest near the middle or above, 5.6–11 cm (2.2–4.3 in) long, 3.5–7.5 cm (1.4–3 in) wide, pointed at the tip, tapering at the base, entire to small rounded teeth along the margin, shiny dark green, very aromatic when crushed; the **leafstalks** articulated just below the blade, 1.4–2.5 cm (0.6–1 in) long, **broadly winged, the wing 10–15 mm (0.4–0.6**

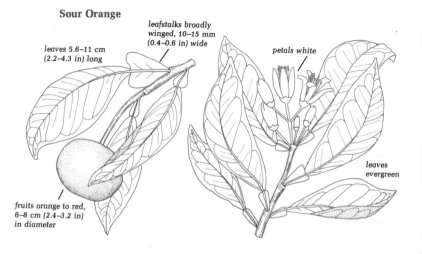

Sour Orange

leaves 5.6–11 cm
(2.2–4.3 in) long

leafstalks broadly
winged, 10–15 mm
(0.4–0.6 in) wide

petals white

leaves
evergreen

fruits orange to red,
6–8 cm (2.4–3.2 in)
in diameter

in) wide. Flowers are produced singly along the branchlets, with a 5-lobed calyx, 5 white petals, 20 to 25 stamens, and a single pistil. Fruits are **rounded,** often depressed at the tip at maturity, 6–8 cm (2.4–3.2 in) in diameter, with a **leathery orange to red skin,** enclosing a bitter-tasting pulp.

Sweet Orange   *Citrus sinensis* (L.) Osbeck

Sweet orange is one of the most popular fruits in the world and is cultivated in all countries with a tropical or subtropical climate. It is native from southeastern China to Bangladesh and was introduced into tropical America by Columbus in 1493. It is grown commercially in Florida, California, Texas, and Arizona. When Florida became a state in 1821, orange growing was actively encouraged. Existing sour orange trees were grafted with buds from sweet orange trees. This resulted in the gradual production of sweet oranges from the sour orange tree.

These are shrubs or small trees to 8 m (26 ft), with a rounded crown and branchlets armed with a few to many slender, flexible short spines. The alternate, evergreen, simple leaves are broadest near the base, or the middle, 5–9.5 cm (2–3.8 in) long, 2.2–5 cm (0.9–2 in) wide, pointed to rounded at the tip, tapering at the base, entire or with a few small rounded teeth along the margin, dark shiny green above, very aromatic when crushed; the **leafstalks stout,** 6–12 mm (0.2–0.5 in) long, **narrowly winged, the wing 2–4 mm (0.1–0.2 in) wide.** Flowers solitary or in few-flowered clusters in the junctions of the leaves, each flower with a 5-lobed calyx, 5 white petals, 20 to 25 stamens, and a single pistil. Fruits are **rounded, often flattened or depressed at the tip,** 5–12 cm (2–4.7 in) in diameter, covered with a thick, leathery, **yellowish-green to orange rind,** enclosing a sweet tasting pulp divided into many segments, not separating easily.

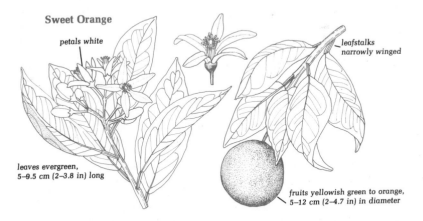

Sweet Orange

petals white

leafstalks
narrowly winged

leaves evergreen,
5–9.5 cm (2–3.8 in) long

fruits yellowish green to orange,
5–12 cm (2–4.7 in) in diameter

Lemon   *Citrus limon* (L.) Burm. f.

Lemons were probably introduced into Florida by Indians or Spanish explorers long before active settlements were established. They now grow naturally in many of the coastal hammocks in southern Florida, the Keys, and tropical America. Like their relatives, the oranges, lemons originate in southern Asia. Lemons are grown commercially in Florida, California, and to a lesser extent in Arizona and Texas. They are normally picked green and treated with a gas or chemicals to bring out the bright-yellow "supermarket" color.

These are small trees with an open crown and short, spreading branches and branchlets usually armed with numerous, stout spines 0.5–2.5 cm (0.3–1 in) long. The alternate, evergreen simple leaves are broadest near the base to the middle, 4.5–10 cm (1.8–4 in) long, 1.5–5.5 cm (0.6–2.2 in) wide, usually pointed but sometimes rounded at the tip, widely tapering at the base, with shallow teeth along the margin, light green and shiny, aromatic when crushed; the *leafstalks short, stout, narrowly winged, the wing 1–2 mm (0.1 in) wide.* Flowers are solitary or in pairs in the junctions of the upper leaves, each with a 4- to 5-lobed calyx, 4 or 5 petals, white within and above, reddish-purple below, 20 to 40 stamens, and a single pistil. Fruits are *longer than wide, broadest near the base,* 5–10 cm (2–4 in) long, rounded at the end, covered with a thin to somewhat thick *yellow skin,* not separating easily from the juicy, sour-tasting pulp.

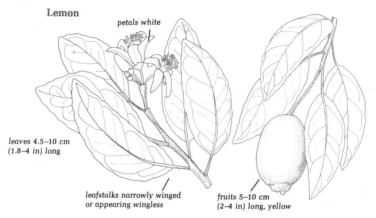

Lemon

petals white

leaves 4.5–10 cm
(1.8–4 in) long

leafstalks narrowly winged
or appearing wingless

fruits 5–10 cm
(2–4 in) long, yellow

The Hoptree Genus

Ptelea L.

The hoptrees are a small group of about 10 species of trees and shrubs native to the U.S. and Mexico. Two species, the common hoptree and the California hoptree, reach tree size in North America. The trees are of little economic value and of limited benefit to wildlife. When the botanist Linnaeus first described this genus, he noted that the fruits resembled those of certain ash trees and thus adopted the Greek word for ash, *ptelea,* as the scientific name.

Members of this genus are small trees or shrubs with usually alternate, rarely opposite, compound leaves, the leaves composed of 3 to 5 leaflets. The flowers are small, bisexual or with male or female flowers together in branched, spreading clusters generally at the ends of the branchlets. Each flower has a 4- or 5-parted calyx, 4 or 5 petals, 4 or 5 stamens in male flowers, and single pistil in female flowers. Fruits are flattened, broadly winged, the wing forming a circle around the 1 to 3 central seeds.

Key to Hoptree Species

A. Leaflets 10–15 cm (4–6 in) long, 5–8 cm (2–3.2 in) broad, pointed at the tip; fruits 2.2–2.8 cm (0.9–1.2 in) in diameter **Common hoptree, p. 827**

B. Leaflets 2–7.2 cm (0.8–2.9 in) long, 1–3 cm (0.4–
1.2 in) broad, rounded or blunt at the tip; fruits
1.2–2 cm (0.5–0.8 in) in diameter
California hoptree, p. 828

Common Hoptree

Ptelea trifoliata L.
(synonym: *Ptelea angustifolia* Benth.)

The common hoptree has a wide though scattered range extending from southern Ontario to Mexico, and from New York to California. It grows primarily on gravelly or rocky slopes along the edges of woodlands, and can tolerate quite heavy shading by other trees. It is often found growing near dogwood, hawthorn, wild plum, sassafras, and eastern redcedar.

The hoptree is both slow growing and short lived. In the spring, clusters of small, greenish-white, foul-smelling flowers appear, which are pollinated by carrion flies. The thin, nearly round, winged seeds hang in dense, drooping clusters that remain on the trees throughout most of the winter. They are of limited value to wildlife, except where thickets occur, which provide songbirds and gamebirds with nesting sites and shelter from predators.

In the past, the seeds were used in beer-making as a substitute for hops flavoring, hence the common name. In the days when it was thought that anything that tasted bad was good for you, a tonic made from the juice of hoptree was substituted for quinine to treat a number of ailments. The bright, shiny foliage and buff-colored seeds make this an attractive ornamental hedge plant. The wood is hard, heavy, close-grained, yellowish-brown, and satiny, although the tree does not grow large enough for commercial use.

Common Hoptree

*flowers
greenish
white*

*fruits flattened, winged,
2.2–2.8 cm (0.9–1.2 in)
in diameter*

*leaves pointed
at the tip*

*leaflets 10–15 cm
(4–6 in) long*

Spring Branchlet

Appearance: low, spreading shrub, or a short tree, to 7.5 m (24.6 ft), with a broad, round-topped crown; trunk slender, short, straight or crooked, to 20 cm (7.9 in) in diameter. **Bark:** 2–4 mm (0.1–0.2 in) thick, smooth, gray, with an unpleasant odor. **Branches:** short, twisted, often interwoven, upright; branchlets slender, dark reddish-brown, smooth or hairy. **Winter buds:** tiny, rounded, wooly, pale yellow, partly sunk into the bark and invisible until the leaves drop. **Leaves:** *alternate, deciduous,* compound, *usually with 3 leaflets,* the middle leaflet usually larger, the leaflets broadest near the base or uniformly wide, 10–15 cm (4–6 in) long, 5–8 cm (2–3.2 in) broad, pointed at the tip, tapering at the base, finely toothed along the margin, shiny dark green above, paler and slightly hairy below, and gland-dotted. **Flowers:** bisexual and male or female flowers in the same clusters, produced in widely branching, round-headed, many-flowered clusters usually at the ends of the branchlets; each flower with a 4- or 5-parted calyx, 4 or 5 petals, 3 or 4 stamens, and a single pistil. **Fruits:** *flattened, broadly winged,* with 2 or 3 seeds in the center, *circular, 2.2–2.8 cm (0.9–1.2 in) in diameter,* leathery.

California Hoptree

Ptelea crenulata Greene

California hoptree is a shrub or small tree of the coastal mountains and western foothills of the Sierra Nevada in California. It is usually found growing in canyons and flats below 625 m (2,000 ft) elevation. The small greenish flowers are produced in April or May with the fruits maturing in late summer or early autumn.

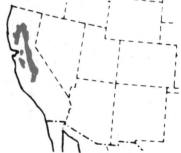

The plants are shrubs or small trees to 5 m (16 ft), with alternate, deciduous compound leaves composed of 3 leaflets. The *leaflets* are broadest near the base, the middle, or the tip, *2–7.2 cm (0.8–2.9 in) long,* 1–3 cm (0.4–1.2 in) wide, *blunt or rounded at the tip,* tapering to uneven at the base, with small rounded teeth along the margin, gland-dotted, bright green and smooth above. The flowers are produced in spreading, branched clusters usually at the ends of the branchlets. *Fruits* are flattened, winged all around, *almost circular, 1.2–2 cm (0.5–0.8 in) in diameter,* produced in clusters.

The Prickly Ash Genus

Zanthoxylum L.

This is a large genus of over 200 species, primarily of tropical regions of the world, but extending in temperate regions in North America and eastern Asia. Six species reach tree size in North America, all in the southern or southwestern states. All the species have spicy, bitter tasting oils in the bark, leaves, and fruits, which have been used in the preparation of medicines. The wood is of no commercial value and the trees are of little benefit to wildlife.

Members of this genus are usually shrubs or trees with aromatic bark and trunks and branches often armed with stout spines. The alternate, deciduous to evergreen leaves are usually feather-like (pinnate) compound. Flowers are small, mostly male or female and occur on different plants, rarely on the same plant. Fruits are usually clustered, each leathery to fleshy, 2-valved, splitting open at maturity to release the single seed.

Key to Prickly Ash Species

A. Leaves with many pointed to rounded teeth along the margin.

    1. Flowering clusters large, wide branching, elongate, produced at the ends of branchlets.

        a. Leaves with 7–9 leaflets, the leaflets 2.5–6.2 cm (1–2.5 in) long, smooth on the surface; trees of southeastern U.S.
        Hercules club, p. 829

        b. Leaves with 5, sometimes 3 or 7 leaflets, the leaflets 1.2–4 cm (0.5–1.6 in) long, crinkled on the surface; trees of central west Texas   **Texas hercules club, p. 830**

    2. Flowering clusters, short, dense, produced in the junction of leaves and at tips of previous year's branchlets   **Lime prickly ash, p. 831**

Hercules Club

B. Leaves entire or rarely with a few scattered teeth along the margin.

    1. Leaves with an odd number of leaflets, 5–11.

        a. Branches and branchlets armed with curved or straight spines; leaves deciduous; trees of eastern North America
        Common prickly ash, p. 831

        b. Branches and branchlets without spines; leaves evergreen; trees of lower Florida Keys   **Yellowheart, p. 832**

    2. Leaves with an even number of leaflets, 4–12, leathery, evergreen; trees of southern Florida
    Biscayne prickly ash, p. 833

Yellowheart

Hercules Club

Hercules club is a small tree of the southeastern U.S. It occurs from southern Virginia to mid-Florida, and west to eastern Texas. It is not abundant, but grows as scattered trees near the coast in light, sandy soil, often on bluffs of islands, riverbanks, or dunes. Best growth is reached near streams in moist, rich soils with good drainage. Hercules club is an understory forest component that occurs with several varieties of pine, sweetgum, and southern red, blackjack, and bluejack oaks.

Zanthoxylum clava-herculis L.

Small, greenish-yellow flowers are produced in April and May, before the leaves. The dense clusters of small, red pods mature throughout the summer. Some birds feed on the seeds.

The light-brown wood is soft, weak, and has no economic value. The leaves and bark, on the other hand, have found their place in American folk medicine. The oil derived from them is used as a drug to treat toothaches. The chewed parts at first have a pleasant flavor, which soon becomes a stinging or numbing sensation. In the past, the bark was so widely collected that the trees became scarce along the southeastern coast.

Hercules Club

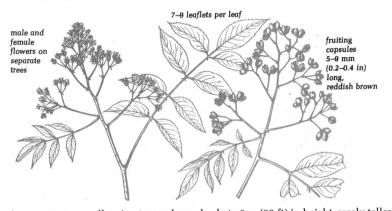

7–9 leaflets per leaf

male and female flowers on separate trees

fruiting capsules 5–9 mm (0.2–0.4 in) long, reddish brown

Appearance: a small, spiny tree or large shrub, to 9 m (30 ft) in height, rarely taller, with a round-topped crown; trunk short, to 50 cm (19.7 in) in diameter, often forming dense clumps. **Bark:** thin, 1–4 mm (0.1–0.2 in) thick, light gray, with many pyramid-shaped, corky, spine-tipped outgrowths on the trunk and branches, eventually losing the spines with age. **Branches:** stout, wide spreading, spiny; branchlets stout, hairy when young, gland-dotted, with large, raised, nearly heart-shaped leaf scars, also with stout spines to 1.5 cm (0.6 in) long. **Winter buds:** short, 3–5 mm (0.1–0.2 in) long, blunt, dark brown to nearly black. **Leaves:** alternate, nearly evergreen, often remaining on the trees until new *leaves* appear, feather-like (pinnate) compound, 12.5–20 cm (5–7.9 in) long, *with 7 to 9 leaflets,* the leaflets broadest near the base, *2.5–6.2 cm (1–2.5 in) long,* pointed at the tip, rounded to widely tapering at the base, *rounded to pointed teeth along the margin,* leathery, shiny green above, paler beneath; leafstalks stout, spiny. **Flowers:** male and female *flowers* on separate trees, *produced in many-flowered, wide branching, elongated clusters;* each flower with 5 minute sepals, 5 tiny petals, 5 stamens in male flowers, and 3 pistils in female flowers. **Fruits:** produced in dense clusters, each a leathery pod 5–9 mm (0.2–0.4 in) long, reddish-brown, splitting open at maturity with the single pitted seed hanging from the capsule.

Texas Hercules Club   *Zanthoxylum hirsutum* Buckl.

This species is native to central west Texas where it grows in dry sandy or gravelly soils. It was for many years considered to be a variety of hercules club (*Zanthoxylum clava-herculis*), but is now considered to represent a distinct species. It is normally a shrub, but occasionally reaches tree size.

Texas hercules club is a shrub or small tree to 5 m (16 ft), armed with stout curved spines on the branches and branchlets. The alternate, nearly evergreen *leaves* are feather-like (pinnate) compound, 4–8 cm (1.6–3.2 in) long, rarely longer, **with 5, sometimes 3 or 7, leaflets;** the leaflets broadest near the middle, **1.2–4 cm (0.5– 1.6 in) long,** rounded at the tip, tapering at the base, **round-toothed along the margin, leathery,** gland-dotted and aromatic, **crinkled,** dark shiny green. Male and female flowers occur on separate trees in branched, elongate, many-flowered clusters before the leaves expand. Fruits are in clusters, each fruit almost rounded, 7–12 mm (0.3–0.5 in) in diameter, glandular dotted and fragrant if squeezed, green turning reddish-brown, splitting open at maturity to release the shiny black seed.

Lime Prickly Ash

Zanthoxylum fagara (L.) Sarg.

The lime prickly ash is usually a shrub but sometimes becomes a small, evergreen tree in southern Florida. It also occurs along the coast and lower Rio Grande valley in Texas. It ranges throughout the West Indies to Central and South America. In Florida, it normally grows in the rich soils of hammocks.

This species flowers from April until June when the short clusters of yellowish-green flowers are produced at the tips of the previous year's branchlets. The fruits mature in August or September but they are of little value to wildlife. In fact, the bark, leaves, flowers, and fruit contain spicy-smelling, bitter-tasting oils that seem to deter most wildlife. The reddish-brown wood is very hard and heavy, but of no economic value because of the small size of the trees.

Appearance: shrub or small tree to 9 m (30 ft), with a narrow rounded crown; trunk slender, often bent, to 35 cm (13.8 in) in diameter. **Bark:** 2–4 mm (0.1–0.2 in) thick, smooth, developing small scales or corky protuberances, gray. **Branches:** stout, upright, armed with hooked spines; branchlets slender, zigzag, gray, armed with hooked spines. **Winter buds:** tiny, 2–4 mm (0.1–0.2 in) long, rounded, hairy. **Leaves:** alternate, evergreen, feather-like (pinnate) compound, 7.5–10 cm (3–4 in) long, with 7 to 9 **leaflets,** broadest above the middle, **1–3 cm (0.4–1.2 in) long,** 5–14 mm (0.2–0.6 in) wide, rounded and often notched at the tip, tapering at the base, **with many small, rounded teeth along the upper margins of the leaflets,** leathery, bright green and shiny; leafstalks broadly winged. **Flowers:** tiny, yellowish-green, male and female flowers on separate trees; each flower with 4 tiny sepals, 4 petals, 4 stamens in male flowers, 2 pistils in female flowers. **Fruits: produced in short clusters,** each broadest near the tip, 3–6 mm (0.1–0.2 in) long, reddish-brown, splitting open at maturity to release a shiny, dark seed.

Common Prickly Ash

Zanthoxylum americanum Mill.

Common prickly ash is usually a shrub but occasionally reaches tree size. It occurs from southern Quebec to Georgia, and west to the Central Plains states. This tree

grows on both upland rocky hillsides and on moist, lowlying ground, in open woods,
on bluffs, or in thickets. It is fairly sensi-
tive to shading and does not grow in dense,
mature forests. This species is often found
beneath such species as beech, red oak,
hemlock, silver maple, and black willow.

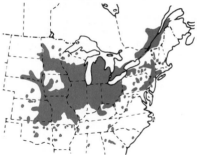

It is a fast growing plant often sending
up shoots from underground spreading
stems, and often forming thickets. The
small, greenish-yellow flowers appear in
April and May before the leaves emerge.
The fruits form dense, nearly spherical,
clusters which ripen in late July. No parts
of the tree attract wildlife. But the orange larvae of the giant swallowtail butterfly
(*Papilio* species) in the South is often found on the twigs.

This tree is well known as a folk-cure for toothaches and rheumatism. All parts of
the plant contain xanthoxylin, an aromatic, bitter oil that is used in some medical preparations. The oil is especially concentrated in the bark and roots, which are sought
commercially. The soft, light-brown wood is of little use.

Appearance: small, spiny tree or shrub, occasionally to 10 m (33 ft), with a rounded
crown; trunk short. **Bark:** thin, smooth, becoming furrowed with age, gray or brown,
with light blotches. **Branches:** slender, numerous, dark brown; branchlets rigid, covered *with many flat-based, curved or straight spines,* usually in pairs at the crescent-
shaped leaf scars. **Winter buds:** small, 4–6 mm (0.1–0.2 in) long, rounded, covered
with red, wooly hairs. **Leaves:** alternate, deciduous, feather-like (pinnate) compound,
15–20 cm (6–7.9 in) long, *with 5 to 11 leaflets,* the *leaflets* broadest near the base, *3–6
cm (1.2–2.4 in) long,* 1.5–2 cm (0.6–0.8 in) wide, pointed at the tips, rounded at the
base, *entire or with a few teeth along the margin,* dark green, slightly wrinkled
above, paler beneath, hairy when young; leafstalks stout, 2–4 cm (0.8–1.6 in) long,
rusty hairy. **Flowers:** male and female flowers on separate plants and appearing before
the leaves; male and female flowers in short clusters of 2 to 10 on short shoots from
previous year's buds; each flower without a calyx, 5 or 6 green but red-tipped petals, 5
to 6 stamens in male flowers and 2 to 5 pistils per female flower. **Fruits:** produced in
dense clusters on last year's growth, the fruits small, rounded capsules, 4–5 mm (0.1–
0.2 in) in diameter, reddish-brown, pitted on the surface, spice-scented, containing a
tiny, shiny, black, pitted seed.

Yellowheart

Zanthoxylum flavum Vahl.

Yellowheart is a rare tree found only in
North America in the lower Florida Keys.
It also occurs in the Bahamas, and the West
Indies. This species was once fairly abundant, but has been so exploited for its
beautiful wood that it is now also rare in
the West Indies. The wood is yellow to
light orange. It is hard, fine-grained,
strong, and takes a satiny polish. It has
been used for cabinets, paneling, inlay
work, and small wooden crafts. It is
planted in the West Indies as a shade tree.

These are trees to 10 m (33 ft), with a rounded crown and smooth to lightly fissured, light gray bark. The stout **branchlets** are **not armed with spines.** The **leaves** are alternate, evergreen or nearly so, feather-like (pinnate) compound, 10–25 cm (4–9.8 in) long, **with 5 to 9 leaflets;** the **leaflets** broadest near the middle or base to almost uniformly wide, **2.5–7.5 cm (1–3 in) long,** 1.2–3.7 cm (0.5–1.5 in) wide, pointed at the tip, rounded to tapering at the base, **entire,** shiny green and smooth to sparsely hairy at maturity. Male and female flowers in separate delicate clusters at the bases of the upper leaves. Fruits are produced in small clusters, each an egg-shaped capsule 6–9 mm (0.2–0.4 in) long, dark reddish-brown, splitting open at maturity to release the single, shiny black seed.

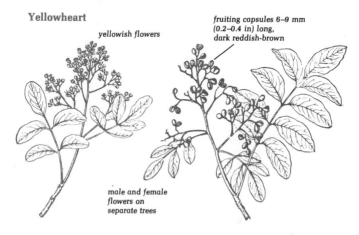

Yellowheart

yellowish flowers

fruiting capsules 6–9 mm (0.2–0.4 in) long, dark reddish-brown

male and female flowers on separate trees

Biscayne Prickly Ash

Zanthoxylum coriaceum A. Rich.

The Biscayne prickly ash is a small tree or shrub of coastal hammocks of southern Florida, including the Florida Keys. It is also native to the West Indies. Often the branches are armed with curved spines. Flowering usually extends from spring into early summer with the fruits maturing by late summer or early autumn.

The plants may grow to 7 m (23 ft), with a short, fluted trunk covered with thin, smooth gray mottled bark. The stout branches are armed or unarmed with curved spines and are reddish-brown. The alternate, **evergreen,** feather-like (pinnate) compound **leaves** are 10–20 cm (4–7.9 in) long, **composed of 2 to 6 pairs of leaflets.** Leaflets are broadest above the middle, 2.5–6 cm (1–2.4 in) long, 1.4–2.2 cm (0.6–0.9 in) wide, rounded at the tip, tapering at the base, entire, **leathery,** dark yellowish-green, and shiny. Small, yellow flowers are produced in many-flowered, elongate, branched clusters. Fruits are egg-shaped capsules 4–6 mm (0.1–0.2 in) long, brown, splitting open at maturity to release a shiny, black seed.

Biscayne Prickly Ash

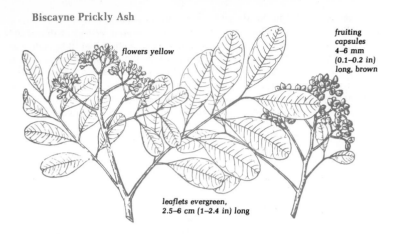

flowers yellow

fruiting
capsules
4–6 mm
(0.1–0.2 in)
long, brown

leaflets evergreen,
2.5–6 cm (1–2.4 in) long

The Trifoliate Orange Genus   *Poncirus* Raf.

This genus contains a single species, the trifoliate orange (*Poncirus trifoliata*). It is native to northern China and Korea and has been cultivated in Japan, Europe, and North America for many years. The description of the genus is the same as for the species.

Trifoliate Orange   *Poncirus trifoliata* (L.) Raf.

The trifoliate orange is a small tree introduced to the U.S. from northern China in 1850. It was, and still is, widely cultivated in the South as an ornamental tree. In protected areas, it can grow as far north as Boston. It tolerates poor acid soils and can be grown where many other trees will not survive. White, fragrant flowers are produced in spring on the older, bare, spiny branches. The fruits resemble miniature oranges and ripen in early fall, but they are too sour to eat. The trees are often planted as a hedge because of their dense branching pattern and thorns.

Trifoliate Orange

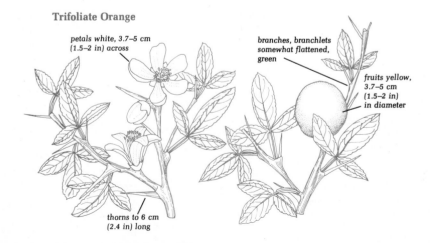

petals white, 3.7–5 cm
(1.5–2 in) across

branches, branchlets
somewhat flattened,
green

fruits yellow,
3.7–5 cm
(1.5–2 in)
in diameter

thorns to 6 cm
(2.4 in) long

They are shrubs or small trees to 7 m (23 ft), with an irregular crown. **Branches** and **branchlets** are **stiff, somewhat flattened, green, and armed with stout thorns** up to 6 cm (2.4 in) long. The alternate, **deciduous leaves are 3-parted** with the center leaflet markedly larger, the leaflets broadest near the middle, to 8.5 cm (3.4 in) long, aromatic, rounded to notched at the tip, tapering and the 2 lateral leaflets uneven at the base, with small, rounded teeth along the margin, almost leathery, dark green and smooth. Flowers are white, 3.7–5 cm (1.5–2 in) across, with 5 small green calyx lobes, 5 thin, narrow petals, 8 to 10 stamens, and a single pistil. Fruits are **rounded, 3.7–5 cm (1.5–2 in) across, yellow**, with a thin skin and sour pulp and many large, white to brown seeds.

The Mahogany Family
Meliaceae

The mahogany family is composed of about 50 genera and approximately 500 species. Almost all are tropical and occur in the Americas, Africa, Asia, and Australia. Only 1 genus, mahogany (*Swietenia*), is native to North America. The imported Chinaberry (*Melia azedarach*) grows wild in the warmer regions of North America.

This family is best known for its highly prized wood, which serves man in a variety of ways and produces a beautiful finish. Another member of the family, called Spanish cedar, produces the wood used in cigar boxes. The bark of many species is used medicinally, although only that of the Chinaberry has become economically important in European and American medicine.

Members of this family include both trees and shrubs. They have alternate, feather-like (pinnately) compound leaves, rarely simple or twice feather-like (bipinnate), which lack stipules. Flowers are in loose, erect clusters on slender stalks, and are usually bisexual or occasionally male and female. Each flower has 3 to 5 fused or free sepals, 3 to 5 free petals, and 5 to 10 stamens whose stalks are joined to form a tube; and a single pistil. Fruits are a stone fruit (drupe), capsule, or berry.

Key to Mahogany Genera

A. Leaves feather-like (pinnate); flowers with white or yellow petals; fruits are 5-celled capsules splitting open at maturity; seeds winged
Mahogany, p. 836

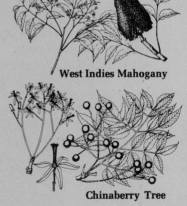

West Indies Mahogany

B. Leaves twice feather-like (bipinnate); flowers with purple petals; fruits fleshy, not splitting open at maturity, seeds not winged
Chinaberry, p. 837

Chinaberry Tree

The Mahogany Genus

Swietenia Jacq.

Named for the eminent Dutch botanist and physician, Baron von Swieten, the genus contains 5 species of mahogany that are limited to tropical America, from southern Florida to Venezuela, western and southwestern Mexico, and the eastern coast of Central America. Only 1 species, the West Indies mahogany, occurs in the U.S.

All are tree species, with heavy, dark red wood that has considerable commercial value. The leaves are abruptly feather-like (pinnate), with long stalks, smooth, and remain on the tree throughout the year. The leaflets are opposite, pointed at the tip, and blunt at the base. Bisexual flowers are produced in long-stemmed branched clusters. The fruit is a distinctive, 5-celled, 5-parted capsule that opens from the base, looking when mature like a soggy umbrella. The winged seeds are suspended within the capsule near the top, and flutter away when released.

West Indies Mahogany

Swietenia mahagoni (L.) Jacq.

This small tree of southern tropical Florida and the Keys was the first discovered and is the most highly prized species of mahogany. It has served from the days of the Spanish Conquistadores to the present as one of the loveliest woods. It occurs natu-

rally in many of the West Indies and the Bahama Islands, and is commonly planted in Puerto Rico and the Virgin Islands. West Indies mahogany is the national emblem of the Dominican Republic. Mahogany grows in thick stands in the hammocks along the shores of the Florida Keys. Moreover, it is often planted as a street and shade tree because of its dense, attractive crown.

Mahogany is a fast-growing, relatively long-lived tree, although few old specimens may be found since so many were cut. Flowers are produced in July and August on slender, slightly fuzzy stalks, while the fruits ripen in the fall or early winter. They are of little value as a food source to wildlife.

The sapwood is whitish or yellowish, while the heartwood is red or yellow when first cut, darkening with time to a rich, reddish-brown. The wood is moderately hard, heavy, and strong, and is easily worked. It resists both dry rot and termites.

Mahogany is one of the most valuable of all tropical woods. A cathedral built in

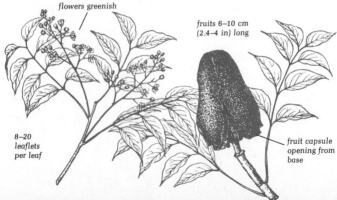

West Indies Mahogany

flowers greenish

fruits 6–10 cm (2.4–4 in) long

8–20 leaflets per leaf

fruit capsule opening from base

Santo Domingo in 1514 is the oldest example of carved mahogany in the Americas. Today, the wood is used in fine furniture, cabinet-making, interior finishes, and veneers.

Appearance: tree, to 15 m (49 ft) in height, with a large, round crown; trunk short, straight, to 0.6 m (2 ft) in diameter, the larger specimens being massively buttressed at the base. **Bark:** 1.5–1.7 cm (0.6–0.7 in) thick, on small trees smooth, gray, slightly cracked, becoming red and rough with age; inner bark pink and bitter. **Branches:** large, spreading, ending in angular branchlets which are reddish-brown their first year, becoming increasingly gray. **Winter buds:** 0.2–0.4 cm (0.1–0.2 in) long, with broad, oval, loosely overlapping, light-red scales. **Leaves:** alternate, evergreen, *feather-like* (pinnate) *compound*, 10–18.5 cm (4–7.3 in) long, with 4 to 10 pairs of shiny green leaflets, the leaflets egg- to lance-shaped, 2.5–6 cm (1–2.4 in) long and 1.2–2.2 cm (0.5–0.9 in) wide, long-pointed, uneven at the base, leathery, entire, dark green above, yellowish to reddish-brown beneath. **Flowers:** small, produced in slender short-branched clusters in the junction of the leaves; each flower 5–7 mm (0.2–0.3 in) across, with 5 tiny sepals and 5 *white or yellow petals,* 10 stamens fused in a short tube, and a pistil with a 5-celled ovary. **Fruits:** *capsule,* egg-shaped or pear-shaped, *6–10 cm (2.4–4 in) long* and 3–5 cm (1.2–2 in) broad, hard and thick-walled, *splitting from the base into 5 parts* and releasing many flat, long-winged seeds.

The Chinaberry Genus   *Melia* L.

This is a small genus of about 25 species of trees or shrubs. All are native to southern Asia and Australia. One species, the Chinaberry tree, has been introduced throughout the southern U.S.

Members of this genus have evergreen to nearly deciduous, alternate leaves that are feather-like (pinnate) or twice feather-like (bipinnate) with many small leaflets. The bisexual flowers are produced in elongate, branched clusters. The fragrant, white to purple flowers have a 4 or 5 lobed, deeply parted calyx, 5 or 6 free petals, 10 to 12 stamens, their stalks fused into a tube, and a single ovary. Fruits are usually rounded, fleshy, and containing a stone.

Chinaberry Tree   *Melia azedarach* L.

Also known as the China tree or the Pride of India, this species is native to the Himalaya Mountains and eastern Asia. It was widely planted in the southern U.S. for its attractive flowers and shade. Chinaberry is found throughout the South and Southeast, where it has escaped from parks and yards, and grows in thickets, old fields, and on disturbed sites. It is readily recognized by its twice feather-like (bipinnate) foliage, as well as by the clusters of yellow, nearly round fruit.

Chinaberry is both fast-growing and short-lived. It is susceptible to fire, but will sprout back rapidly from the roots. Masses of purplish flowers appear in spring. Fruits ripen in the fall and are poisonous. The fruits are eaten by catbirds, robins, and mockingbirds, and cause a mild intoxication and temporary paralysis if the birds consume too many. The tree itself is usually pest free.

Besides its horticultural value, the fruit and bark of the Chinaberry have been used medicinally for their narcotic and vermin-killing properties. The sapwood is yellowish-white, and the heartwood attractive light- to reddish-brown. The wood is soft, weak, and brittle, and susceptible to attack from termites. It has been used for firewood, tool handles, cabinets, furniture, and cigar boxes.

Appearance: small, wide-branching tree to 15 m (49 ft), with a round, or nearly rounded crown; trunk straight, to 60 cm (23.6 in) in diameter. **Bark:** thin, becoming

Chinaberry

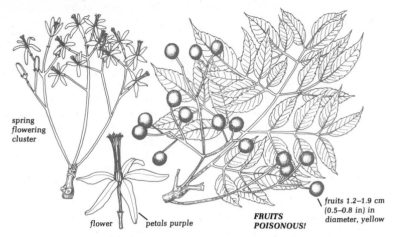

spring
flowering
cluster

flower | petals purple

*FRUITS
POISONOUS!*

fruits 1.2–1.9 cm
(0.5–0.8 in) in
diameter, yellow

furrowed when older, dark or reddish brown, inner bark is whitish, slightly bitter or astringent. **Branches:** crowded, spreading, ending in greenish, smooth branchlets. **Leaves:** alternate, deciduous, ***twice feather-like*** (bipinnately) compound, 20–41 cm (7.9–16.1 in) long, with many leaflets, the leaflets broadest near the base, 2.5–7 cm (1–2.8 in) long, 0.9–1.8 cm (0.4–0.8 in) wide, pointed at the tip, sharply toothed, smooth, thin, bright green. **Flowers:** produced in many-flowered branched clusters (panicles) 10–25 cm (4–9.8 in) long; the numerous, attractive, fragrant flowers are 7–9 mm (0.3–0.4 in) long and 1.6–1.9 cm (0.7–0.8 in) across, with 5 greenish sepals, 1–2 mm (0.1 in) long, ***5 purplish petals,*** narrow and slightly curled back, 8–10 mm (0.3–0.4 in) long; usually 10 stamens, and a pale-green pistil. **Fruits:** ***rounded, 1.2–1.9 cm (0.5–0.8 in) in diameter, yellow,*** flesh is bitter and poisonous, and containing a stone enclosing up to 5 narrow, dark brown seeds.

The Caltrop Family
Zygophyllaceae

This family includes about 25 genera and 250 species of largely tropical and subtropical trees, shrubs, and herbs. Of these, only the lignumvitae genus, with 2 species occurs in North America. Many of the species are economically important in the American tropics. Several of the lignumvitaes yield a heavy, durable, split-resistant wood.

Members of this family have branches that are sometimes jointed where leaves are attached. The flowers are bisexual, stalked, generally with 5 sepals, 5 petals, 10 stamens, and a single pistil. Fruits are dry capsules which split open at maturity, rarely a berry.

The Lignumvitae Genus
Guaiacum L.

This is a small genus of 7 or 8 species of trees and shrubs of the West Indies, Mexico, and Central and South America. Two species, the holywood lignumvitae of southern Florida, including the Keys, and the Texas lignumvitae of Texas and Mexico, are native to North America. Their dense, hard wood is valuable.

Trees have scaly bark, stout branchlets, and opposite, feather-like (pinnate) compound leaves. The bisexual flowers are produced singly or in few-flowered clusters at the ends of the branchlets. The fruits are angled or winged capsules which split open at maturity.

Key to Lignumvitae Species

A. Leaves with 3–4 pairs of leaflets, the leaflets 2.5–3 cm (1–1.2 in) long, 1.2–1.8 cm (0.5–0.8 in) wide; flowers bright blue; trees of southern Florida and tropical America
Holywood lignumvitae, p. 839

B. Leaves with 4–8 pairs of leaflets, the leaflets 1.2–1.8 cm (0.5–0.8 in) long, 2–5 mm (0.2 in) wide; flowers purple; trees of southcentral Texas and northern Mexico **Texas lignumvitae, p. 840**

Holywood Lignumvitae

The holywood lignumvitae was once more abundant than it is today in southern Florida and the Keys. So many trees have been cut that only a few large specimens remain. The tree is also native to the Bahamas and the West Indies. Flowering occurs in late spring with the fruits maturing by summer. Used as an ornamental in southern Florida, this tree is one of the few North American plants with truly blue flowers. The yellow to greenish wood is hard, heavy, and so dense it will sink in water.

Guaiacum sanctum L.

Holywood Lignumvitae

petals blue

capsules bright orange, 1.4–2 cm (0.6–0.8 in) long

3–4 pairs of leaflets per leaf

These are short trees to 10 m (33 ft), with a rounded crown, irregular spreading to drooping branchlets, a short, stout, gnarled trunk, and chalk white bark. The opposite, largely evergreen *leaves* are feather-like (pinnate) compound *with 3 or 4 pairs of leaflets.* The leaflets are *broadest near the tip, 2.5–3 cm (1–1.2 in) long, 1.2–1.8 cm (0.5–0.8 in) wide,* rounded at the tip, unequal at the tapering base (resembling pairs of butterfly wings), and dark shiny green. The flowers are produced in clusters, stalked, 1.5–1.8 cm (0.6–0.8 in) across, with 5 short sepals, and 5 attractive, *very blue petals.* Fruits are bright-orange capsules, 1.4–2 cm (0.6–0.8 in) long, strongly angled, which split open to reveal the *black seeds* covered with a red fleshy skin.

Texas Lignumvitae

Guaiacum angustifolium Engelm.
[synonym: *Porliera angustifolia* (Engelm.) Gray]

This scrubby shrub or small tree is native to central, western, and southwestern Texas, and northeastern Mexico. It grows in open scrub vegetation and deserts. The purple flowers appear in spring, with the capsules maturing in summer. Texas lignumvitae is of little value to wildlife. The wood is very hard and heavy but of limited value because of the tree's small size and low growing branches.

Texas lignumvitae is a clump forming shrub or small tree to 6 m (20 ft), with short, thick, irregular branches and branchlets. The opposite, evergreen leaves are feather-like (pinnate) compound, with *4 to 8 pairs of leaflets,* the leaflets, *lance-shaped to narrow but uniformly wide, 1.2–1.8 cm (0.5–0.8 in) long, 2–5 mm (0.2 in) wide,* often curving, pointed at the tip, unequal at the base, leathery, and dark shiny green. The flowers are solitary or in few-flowered clusters at the ends of the short branchlets, each flower 0.8–2 cm (0.4–0.8 in) across, with 5 sepals, 5 rounded, *purple petals,* 10 stamens, and a single pistil. Fruits are *heart-shaped, 2- or rarely 4-lobed capsules,* 0.8–1.6 cm (0.4–0.7 in) across, enclosing 1 to 3 shiny, *red, orange or yellow* seeds.

The Malpighia Family

Malpighiaceae

This is a moderate size family of 60 genera and about 800 species of trees, shrubs, or vines. The plants are native to tropical regions of southeastern Asia, Africa, and especially Central and South America where they are most abundant. The flowers and fruits of many species are often showy and are cultivated as ornamentals in tropical climates and in greenhouses farther north. Some of the tropical species produce an excellent hard lumber used in furniture.

Members of this family have opposite, simple, evergreen leaves that are entire along the margin. The stalked flowers are produced in racemes. Each flower is bisexual, rarely male or female, with 5 sepals, each with a pair of glands on the outer surface, 5 usually clawed petals, 10 stamens, their stalks often fused near the base, and a single pistil with a superior ovary. Fruits are berry-like and somewhat fleshy or dry and winged.

The Byrsonima Genus

Byrsonima Rich.

This is a medium-size genus containing about 100 tree and shrub species of the tropical regions of Central and South America. Only 1 species, the Key byrsonima, reaches tree size in North America and then only in southern Florida. Members of this genus are of limited economic importance. The wood is often used for fuel.

Species are trees or shrubs with simple, opposite, evergreen leaves that are entire along the margin. Flowers are produced in narrow, elongated clusters; each flower is stalked, bisexual, with 5 sepals, each with a pair of glands on the outer surface, 5 petals, red, purple, yellow, or white, usually 10 stamens, and a single pistil with a superior ovary.

Key Byrsonima

Byrsonima lucida DC.

Key byrsonima is a large, tropical shrub or small tree native to southern Florida, the Bahamas, and the West Indies. In Florida, it is usually found in pine woodlands with limestone soils. It is an attractive plant with shiny evergreen leaves and bright showy clusters of flowers in spring and early summer. It is grown in southern Florida and elsewhere as an ornamental.

The plants are multi-trunked shrubs or small trees to 6 m (20 ft), with an irregular, often flat-topped crown and thin, smooth, pale brown bark. The ***opposite, simple, evergreen leaves*** are uniformly wide to broadest near the tip, ***2–5 cm (0.8–2 in) long***, 0.6–2 cm (0.3–0.8 in) wide, pointed to rounded at the tip, tapering at the base, ***entire, leathery***, dark shiny green above, and paler beneath. Flowers are produced in narrow, elongate, upright clusters of 5 to 12; each flower is long-stalked, with a 5-lobed calyx, 5 petals, white turning yellow or

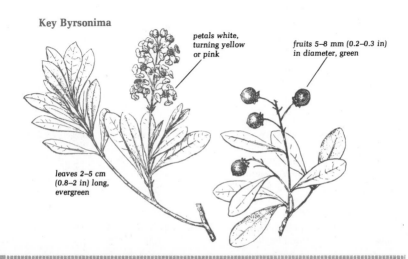

Key Byrsonima

petals white, turning yellow or pink

fruits 5–8 mm (0.2–0.3 in) in diameter, green

leaves 2–5 cm (0.8–2 in) long, evergreen

pink, 10 stamens, and a 3-celled pistil. ***Fruits are berry-like,*** rounded, ***5–8 mm (0.2–0.3 in) in diameter,*** green, with a thin, dry flesh surrounding a single hard stone and seed.

The Ginseng Family Araliaceae

This medium-size family of about 55 genera and 700 species occurs in both tropical and temperate regions of the world. There are several genera and species native to North America, but only 1 species reaches tree size, the devil's walking stick. This family is well known for the ginseng root (widely used for medicinal purposes), ivies (extensively cultivated as ornamental vines), rice paper, and several other species used for landscape plantings.

Members of this family are trees, shrubs, or vines, rarely herbs, with alternate, simple or compound leaves. Flowers are small, often green or white, and produced in branched, flat-topped clusters. The flowers are bisexual or male or female, the plants sometimes male or female, and composed of 4 or 5 calyx lobes, usually 5 petals, 5 free stamens, and a usually 5-celled pistil. Fruits are small, rounded, fleshy, and contain up to 5 seeds.

The Aralia Genus *Aralia* L.

This is a small genus of about 30 species, most of which are shrubs or herbs, occurring principally in North America and Asia. The Japanese angelica tree (*Aralia elata*) is sometimes grown as an ornamental and is often preferred to our North America tree species because it is hardy. Otherwise, it is of little economic value and of limited use to wildlife.

Aralias are trees, shrubs, or herbs, sometimes climbing, and often armed with spines. The alternate, entire leaves are lobed or compound (twice feather-like, bipinnate) and deciduous. The bisexual flowers, sometimes male or female, are produced in large, flat-topped clusters. The small fleshy fruits contain 2 to 5 flattened seeds.

Devil's Walking Stick *Aralia spinosa* L.

This species, primarily of the southeastern U.S., can be found as far north as New Jersey and west to Missouri and Texas. It grows in low hammocks, along streams, and in moist, well-drained, rich woodland soils. The streams along which it grows bring it into association with other trees including willows, willow and live oaks, sweet gum, and the American elm.

Devil's walking stick is a fast growing, short-lived tree that often spreads by underground runners. Flowering is in mid summer with the juicy black fruits maturing in autumn. Chipmunks, fox, skunks, and other small mammals eat the fruits; many birds feed on them too, including sparrows and thrushes. The brown, yellow-streaked wood is soft, weak, and brit-

tle, and of little economic value. The bark, roots, and berries have been used in home remedies as stimulants.

Devil's Walking Stick

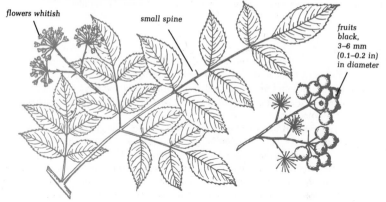

flowers whitish

small spine

fruits black, 3–6 mm (0.1–0.2 in) in diameter

Appearance: shrub or small tree to 7 m (23 ft), with an open, irregular crown; trunk short, branching close to the ground, to 20 cm (7.9 in) in diameter, rarely larger. **Bark:** thin, 2–4 mm (0.1–0.2 in) thick, shallowly furrowed and with wide irregular ridges light to dark brown. **Branches:** stout, wide spreading, ***armed with short, stout spines;*** branchlets stout, spiny, light orange turning light brown. **Winter buds:** 9–24 mm (0.3–0.9 in) long, cone-shaped, blunt at the tip, covered with reddish-brown scales. **Leaves:** alternate, deciduous, ***double feather-like (bipinnate),*** 40–80 cm (15.8–31.5 in) long, ***side branches*** (pinnae) ***unequal, armed with small spines,*** each side branch usually with 5 or 6 pairs of leaflets; each leaflet broadest near the base, 5–8 cm (2–3.2 in) long, 3.5–4.5 cm (1.4–1.8 in) wide, pointed at the tip, rounded to wedge-shaped at the base, with many sharp teeth along the margin, dark green and smooth above, paler beneath. **Flowers:** tiny, produced in densely branched clusters; each flower whitish. **Fruits:** fleshy berry, 3- to 5-sided to rounded, 3–6 mm (0.1–0.2 in) in diameter, black, juicy.

The Dogbane Family   Apocynaceae

This large family contains about 180 genera and 1,500 species of trees, shrubs, vines, or herbs. They are common in tropical regions of the world but are also well represented in North America, Europe, and in temperate Asia. All of the species native to North America are herbs or vines. One tree species, oleander, has been introduced and widely cultivated in Florida and the southwestern U.S. This family is best known in North America for the periwinkle, commonly used as ground cover.

Members of this family have milky sap, and alternate, opposite, or whorled, simple, entire leaves. The regular, bisexual flowers are usually large, showy, fragrant, and produced in a branched cluster. The flowers have a tubular, 5-lobed calyx, 5 petals usually fused below, 5 stamens, and a single pistil. Fruits are in pairs, dry and splitting open or fleshy and not splitting open.

The Oleander Genus   Nerium L.

This is a small genus of 3 species native to a region extending from Japan to the Mediterranean. Oleander (*Nerium oleander*) is a well-known flowering tree in tropical and subtropical climates and is often seen in large display greenhouses. Since the genus is so small, the species description below serves for the genus as well.

Oleander   *Nerium oleander* L.

Oleander is a well-known flowering tree in tropical and subtropical climates. It is also frequently seen in conservatories and large display greenhouses, and is occasionally planted near homes and along roadsides. Several cultivated forms have been developed for their size and the color of their flowers. The milky sap in the leaves and branchlets is poisonous.

It is a shrub or small tree to 10 m (33 ft), with slender, upright branches, light green branchlets, and milky sap. The *simple, opposite leaves* are lance-shaped to broadest near the middle, *5.5–12 cm (2.2–4.8 in) long, 0.8–2 cm (0.4–0.8 in) wide,* pointed to long pointed at the tip, tapering at the base, *entire, leathery,* dark shiny green. Flowers are produced in several-flowered, spreading clusters; each flower has a tubular, 5-lobed, green calyx, *5 showy petals, white to purple, fused below,* free and spreading above, 5 stamens, and a single pistil. *Fruits are paired, leathery pods 7–15 cm (2.8–6 in) long* which split open at maturity to release the small, flattened seeds, each seed with a long tuft of soft hair.

The Nightshade Family   Solanaceae

This large family consists of about 90 genera and 2,500 species that are mainly herbs, although some are trees and shrubs. Although many species are native to North America, only 1, the mullein nightshade, becomes a small tree. The tree tobacco (*Nicotina glauca*), a native of Argentina and Chile, has been introduced into the warmer regions of North America. It now grows wild along roads and in disturbed sites from Florida and Texas to California.

The potato family is economically very important for the many foods and drugs obtained from its species. The more commonly known fruits are eggplant, potatoes, peppers, and tomatoes; valuable drugs produced by other species include belladonna and stramonium. The fruits of some species, for example, deadly nightshade, are poisonous.

Members of this family are usually herbs, vines, or occasionally trees and shrubs with alternate, rarely opposite, entire or divided leaves. The bisexual flowers are produced in branched, few to many-flowered clusters. Each flower has a 4- to 6-lobed calyx, 5 petals variously fused and shaped like a wheel or ball, 5 stamens, and a single pistil with a superior ovary. Fruits are many-seeded berries.

The Nightshade Genus   *Solanum* L.

This is a large genus of roughly 1,700 species mainly of tropical regions of the world, but with a few species extending well into North America, where only 1 of them reaches tree size. The nightshade genus is valuable because potatoes, eggplant, and tomatoes are obtained from certain species.

Members of this genus are herbs, vines, shrubs, or rarely trees covered with minute star-shaped hairs. The leaves are alternate, simple, entire to variously lobed or parted. Bisexual flowers are white, yellow, blue, or purple and shaped like a wheel. Fruits are rounded to almost rounded berries.

Mullein Nightshade

Solanum erianthum D. Don
(synonym: *S. verbascifolium* Jacq.)

Mullein nightshade is native to southern Florida including the Keys but grows mainly along the eastern coast. It also grows in coastal hammocks and disturbed sites in extreme southern Texas, the West Indies, and Central and South America. The large clusters of white flowers followed by yellow berries may be seen throughout the year. Some birds and small mammals feed on the fruits.

Appearance: shrub or small tree to 5 m (16 ft), rarely taller, with a low, flat crown; trunk straight, short, to 8 cm (3.2 in) in diameter. **Bark:** thin, 1–2 mm (less than 0.1 in) thick, becoming roughened by wartlike projections, light green to grayish-brown. **Branches:** spreading; branchlets stout, without spines, ***densely hairy,*** becoming smooth and grayish-brown with age. **Leaves:** alternate, simple, evergreen, broadest near the base to near the middle, ***10–30 cm (4–11.8 in) long, 4–14 cm (1.6–5.5 in) wide,*** long-pointed at the tip, rounded to tapering at the base, entire to wavy along the margins, ***yellowish-green and hairy above, paler and densely hairy on the lower surface;*** leafstalks slender, 2–3 cm (0.8–1.2 in) long, hairy. **Flowers:** produced in broad, branched, many-flowered, round-topped clusters; each flower with a hairy, 5-lobed calyx, 6–12 mm (0.2–0.5 in) long; ***5 white petals, spreading to form a starshape,*** 2–2.6 cm (0.8–1.1 in) across; with 5 stamens, the yellow pollen sacs touching each other, and a single pistil. **Fruits:** ***rounded, 1.2–2 cm (0.5–0.8 in) in diameter, yellow, juicy,*** containing numerous, small, brown seeds.

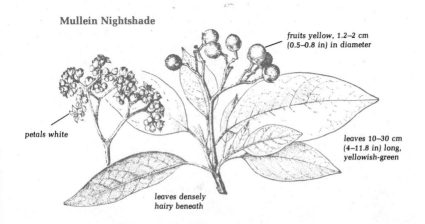

Mullein Nightshade

fruits yellow, 1.2–2 cm
(0.5–0.8 in) in diameter

petals white

leaves 10–30 cm
(4–11.8 in) long,
yellowish-green

leaves densely
hairy beneath

The Borage Family   Boraginaceae

This is a moderately large family of about 100 genera and 2,000 species. The plants are widely distributed throughout the temperate, subtropical, and tropical regions of the world, with the greatest concentration of species in the Mediterranean region. Although many genera are native to North America, only 3 contain species that reach tree size. The family is best known for the cultivated or ornamental herbs including Virginia bluebells, forget-me-nots, and heliotrope.

Members of this family are mostly herbs, but with some trees and shrubs often with dense rough hairs. Leaves are alternate, rarely opposite, simple, and deciduous or evergreen. Flowers are bisexual and produced in branched clusters, often coiling at the ends. Flower parts are in 5s except for the single pistil. Fruits are rounded, berry-like but usually dry, and enclosing 2 to 4 seeds.

Key to Borage Genera

Bahama Strongbark

A. Fruits partly or totally enclosed by the persistent, large calyx; includes geiger tree   **Cordia, p. 846**
B. Fruits not enclosed by the calyx, the calyx small.

1. Fruits consisting of 4 stone-like parts, each containing a single seed; trees of southern Florida   **Strongbark, p. 848**
2. Fruits consisting of 2 stones, each containing 2 seeds; trees of southern Texas; includes anaqua   **Ehretia, p. 850**

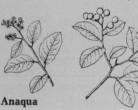

Anaqua

The Cordia Genus   *Cordia* L.

This is a large genus of over 200 species of tropical and subtropical regions, but is especially abundant in Central and South America. Two species are native to North America, the geiger tree of southern Florida and the anacahuita of extreme southern Texas. Members of this genus are of some economic importance. A few species yield valuable timber which is used in shipbuilding, and for furniture and interior trim. Other species are cultivated as shade trees or for their attractive flowers.

Members are trees or shrubs with alternate, simple, evergreen entire leaves. The regular, bisexual flowers are produced in few to many-flowered, branched clusters, the branches of the cluster laxly coiling. Each flower has a tubular or bell-shaped calyx, 5 petals, fused and funnel-shaped, 5 stamens, fused to the inner surface of the fused petals, and a single pistil containing a 4-lobed ovary.

Key to Cordia Species

A. Petals orange to orangish-red; fruits enclosed by a smooth, ivory white calyx; trees of southern Florida   **Geiger tree, p. 847**

B. Petals white with a yellow center; fruits partly or entirely enclosed by a conspicuously ribbed calyx; trees of extreme southern Texas

Anacahuite, p. 848

Anacahuita

Geiger Tree

Cordia sebestena L.

This species is native to extreme southern Florida and the Florida Keys, the West Indies, southern Mexico, and Central and South America. It grows in sandy, nutrient-poor soils of hammocks and tolerates salt spray. The bright orange clusters of flowers are produced throughout the year. As a result, the geiger trees are sometimes planted as ornamentals. The dark-brown wood is heavy, hard, close-grained, and has been used in Latin America to make cabinets and furniture. It is too scarce in North America to be of value as lumber.

Appearance: small shrubs or trees to 9 m (30 ft), with a rounded crown; trunk straight, tall, to 15 cm (6 in) in diameter. **Bark:** thin, 10–18 mm (0.4–0.7 in) thick, irregularly furrowed with narrow ridges composed of thick scales, dark brown to nearly black. **Branches:** slender, upright; branchlets stout, dark green and hairy when young, turning ash-gray with age. **Leaves:** alternate, simple, evergreen, broadest near the base, 10–15 cm (4–6 in) long, 5–10 cm (2–4 in) wide, short pointed to rounded at the tip, usually rounded to slightly heart-shaped at the base, entire to remotely and shallowly toothed along the margin, dark green and rough to the touch above, paler and often smooth beneath; leafstalks stout, 2.5–5 cm (1–2 in) long, hairy. **Flowers:** produced in branched, spreading, flat-topped clusters; each flower with a tubular calyx 9–15 mm (0.3–0.6 in) long, *5 orange to orangish-red petals,* fused below the spreading lobes, 2.5–4 cm (1–1.6 in) across, 5

Geiger Tree

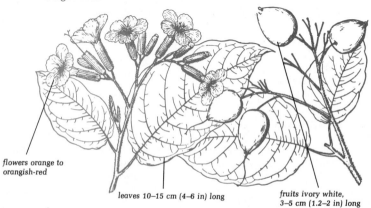

flowers orange to orangish-red

leaves 10–15 cm (4–6 in) long

fruits ivory white, 3–5 cm (1.2–2 in) long

stamens, and a single pistil. **Fruits: *enclosed by the persistent, ivory white calyx,*** broadest near the base and abruptly tapering to a pointed tip, 3–5 cm (1.2–2 in) long, berry-like but with a thin flesh covering a thick-walled stone and seed.

Anacahuite
Cordia boissieri A. DC.

This is a rare tree of extreme southern Texas and northeastern Mexico. It grows on dry limestone ridges and dry arid depressions. The white flowers are produced from September to June, followed by the light reddish-brown fruits. The dark-brown wood is light, soft, and of no commercial value.

These are small trees to 8 m (26 ft), with a rounded crown. The alternate, simple leaves are broadest near the base to nearly uniformly wide, 10–14 cm (4–5.5 in) long, 6–10 cm (2.4–4 in) wide, pointed or rounded at the tip, rounded to heart-shaped at the base, entire or with a few rounded teeth along the margin, dark green and somewhat rough to the touch on the upper surface. ***Flowers are white with a yellow center*** and produced in spreading clusters, the open flower 2–2.5 cm (0.8–1 in) across. **Fruits** are **partly or totally enclosed by a ribbed, orange-brown persistent calyx,** the *fruit* egg-shaped, broadest near the base, 2.2–3 cm (0.9–1.2 in) long, **bright reddish-brown,** and containing a single stone and seed.

Anacahuite

flowers white with yellow center

ribbed persistent calyx

fruits bright reddish-brown, 2.2–3 cm (0.9–1.2 in) long

leaves 10–14 cm (4–5.5 in) long

The Strongbark Genus
Bourreria P. Br.

This is a small genus of about 25 species of trees and shrubs of tropical America, especially abundant in the West Indies. Two tree-size species are native to southern Florida, the Bahama strongbark and the rough strongbark.

Members of this genus are trees or shrubs with alternate, simple, evergreen leaves. The bisexual flowers are produced in branched, many-flowered, flat to round-topped clusters. Each flower has a bell-shaped, 2- to 5-lobed calyx, 5 petals, fused below to form a funnel-shaped tube, 5 stamens, and a single pistil. Fruits are berry-like, rounded, with an outer fleshy layer enclosing 4 seeds.

Key to Strongbark Species

A. Leaves 6–12 cm (2.4–4.7 in) long, 4–8 cm (1.6–3.2 in) wide, smooth on the upper surface; trees of southern Florida and the Keys

Bahama strongbark, p. 849

B. Leaves 2.5–6.5 cm (1–2.6 in) long, 1.2–3.5 cm (0.5–1.4 in) wide, rough to touch on upper surface; trees of lower Florida Keys

Rough strongbark, p. 850

Bahama Strongbark

Bourreria ovata Miers

This West Indian species of strongbark also occurs naturally in extreme southern Florida and the Keys. Flowering is in spring or autumn, although flowers occur throughout most of the year. The tree is of little importance to wildlife. The orange-streaked brown wood is hard, strong, and sometimes used as fuel.

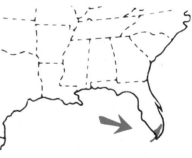

These are bushy shrubs or trees to 12 m (39 ft), with slender, hairy spreading branchlets, and thin, scaly reddish-brown bark. The alternate, simple, evergreen leaves are broadest near or above the middle, **6–12 cm (2.4–4.7 in) long,** 4–8 cm (1.6–3.2 in) wide, rounded to pointed at the tip, tapering at the base, entire, **dark yellowish-green and smooth.** The flowers are produced in branched, open clusters,

Bahama Strongbark

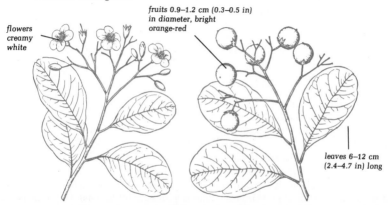

flowers creamy white

fruits 0.9–1.2 cm (0.3–0.5 in) in diameter, bright orange-red

leaves 6–12 cm (2.4–4.7 in) long

each flower long stalked, creamy-white. Fruits are rounded, 9–12 mm (0.3–0.5 in) in diameter, bright orange-red, with a thin dry flesh covering 4 stones, each containing 1 seed.

Rough Strongbark

Bourreria radula (Poir.) D. Don

Rough strongbark is a rare tree restricted in North America to the pinelands and hammocks of the lower Florida Keys. It also occurs in the West Indies. The small white flowers are produced throughout the year.

These plants are shrubs or small trees to 12 m (39 ft), with slender, sparsely hairy branchlets and thin, scaly reddish-brown bark. The alternate, simple, evergreen leaves are *2.5–6.5 cm (1–2.6 in) long, 1.2– 3.5 cm (0.5–1.4 in) wide,* rounded and usually notched at the tip, tapering to a narrow base, entire, *dark green and rough above.* The small white flowers are produced in branched, few-flowered clusters. Fruits are rounded, 9–14 mm (0.3–0.6 in) in diameter, orange, with a thin flesh covering 2 to 4 stones, each containing 1 seed.

The Ehretia Genus

Ehretia P. Br.

This is a small genus of about 40 species, mainly of tropical regions, but also extending into warm temperate areas. In North America, the only native species of this genus, the anaqua is found in southern Texas and northeastern Mexico.

Members of this genus are shrubs or trees with alternate, simple, deciduous to nearly evergreen leaves. The small flowers are produced in branched clusters, the branches somewhat coiled. Each flower consists of a 5-lobed calyx, 5 petals fused at the base to form a short tube, 5 stamens, and a single pistil. Fruits are berry-like, rounded, fleshy, and containing a small stone.

Anaqua

Ehretia anacua (Teran & Berland.) Johnst.

This shrub or small tree grows in poor, dry soils of central and southern Texas and adjacent northeastern Mexico. Tree-size members of this species usually occur in higher river valley soils. Clusters of white flowers normally are produced from March to April, although some are occasionally produced in autumn after the rains. The light-brown wood is hard and heavy and is used to make fence posts and tool handles. The trees are planted for shade in northern Mexico and southern Texas.

Appearance: shrub or small tree to 15 m (49 ft), with a rounded crown; trunk straight, to 10 cm (4 in) in diameter. **Bark:** moderately thick, 1–2.5 cm (0.4–1 in) thick, developing thick scales and becoming furrowed on older trees, gray to reddish-brown. **Branches:** stout, upright to spreading; branchlets slender, often crooked, covered with numerous stiff hairs, turning light brown. **Winter buds:** end

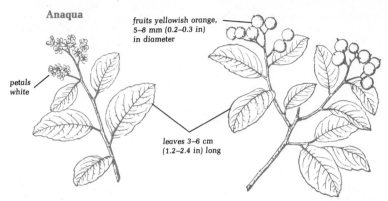

Anaqua

fruits yellowish orange,
5–8 mm (0.2–0.3 in)
in diameter

petals
white

leaves 3–6 cm
(1.2–2.4 in) long

bud absent, side buds very small, 1–2 mm (less than 0.1 in) long, covered with 2 pairs of overlapping, reddish-brown scales. **Leaves:** alternate, simple, nearly evergreen, broadest near the middle to uniformly wide, *3–6 cm (1.2–2.4 in) long,* 1.2–2.8 cm (0.5–1.1 in) wide, rounded to pointed at the tip, rounded to broadly tapering at the base, entire or irregularly toothed along the margin, shiny light to dark green and rough above, paler and hairy beneath; leafstalks stout, 3–8 mm (0.1–0.3 in) long. **Flowers:** produced in elongate, branched, densely-flowered clusters; each flower with a small, deeply divided calyx, *5 white petals,* shallowly tubular, 5 stamens, and a single pistil. **Fruits:** produced in clusters, each berry-like, rounded, 5–8 mm (0.2–0.3 in) in diameter, *yellow-orange,* containing 2 stones, each with 2 seeds.

The Verbena Family

Verbenaceae

This medium-size family of about 75 genera and 3,200 species is distributed largely in tropical and subtropical regions of the world, with some members extending into temperate regions of North America, Europe, and Asia. Most of the native North American species are herbs or shrubs, but 2 of the genera each have a species reaching tree size.

The verbena family contains many species of economic importance. Some, including teak and zither wood, yield valuable lumber. Others contain oil-bearing glands that are used in scenting or flavoring teas and other foods. Many species are grown for their showy flowers.

Members of this family are herbs, vines, shrubs, or trees with opposite, rarely alternate, entire or lobed leaves. Flowers are bisexual, often asymmetrical, and produced in elongate, unbranched clusters (racemes), or branched, spreading, round-topped clusters. Each flower has a 4- or 5-lobed calyx, tubular 4- or 5-lobed corolla, usually 4 stamens, and a single pistil. Fruits are berry-like or less commonly capsules.

Key to Verbena Genera

A. Fruits berry-like, usually rounded, light reddish-brown, containing 4 seeds; flowers in un-

Florida Fiddlewood

branched, elongate clusters (racemes)
Fiddlewood, p. 852
B. Fruits capsules, egg-shaped with uneven sides, green, containing 1 large seed; flowers in dense heads **Black mangrove, p. 853**

Black Mangrove

The Fiddlewood Genus

Citharexylon L.

This is a medium-size genus of 50 to 75 species of trees and shrubs, largely of tropical America. Most species are slow growing trees with very hard, dense wood. Only 1 species, the Florida fiddlewood, is native to North America.

Members are trees or shrubs with simple, opposite, leathery, evergreen leaves. The small bisexual flowers are produced in narrow, unbranched, elongated clusters (racemes). Fruits are berry-like, containing 2 stones, each with 2 seeds.

Florida Fiddlewood

Citharexylon fruticosum L.

Florida fiddlewood extends from coastal central Florida south to the Keys, and also occurs in the West Indies. It grows mainly in coastal hammocks and pinelands but is especially abundant near Florida's Biscayne Bay.

The drooping clusters of fragrant flowers occur year-round and are followed by black, sweet, edible fruits. The fruits are a food source for birds and small mammals. This is a slow growing tree with bright red to reddish-brown wood which is very hard, heavy, and strong, and has been used to make musical instruments and furniture, and as fence posts in the West Indies. Florida fiddlewood is often planted as an ornamental in yards, and along streets and highways.

Florida Fiddlewood

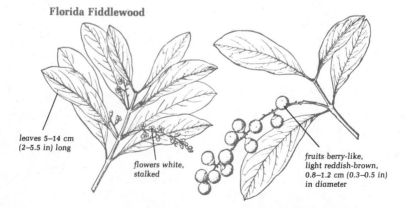

leaves 5–14 cm (2–5.5 in) long

flowers white, stalked

fruits berry-like, light reddish-brown, 0.8–1.2 cm (0.3–0.5 in) in diameter

Appearance: shrub or small tree to 12 m (39 ft), with a narrow irregular crown; trunk straight, usually short, to 30 cm (11.8 in) in diameter. **Bark:** 1–4 mm (less than 0.2 in) thick, smooth when young, developing small scales with age, reddish-brown to gray. **Branches:** slender, upright; branchlets slender, slightly angled, yellowish and hairy becoming gray to grayish-brown and smooth with age. **Leaves:** *opposite, evergreen,* simple, uniformly wide to widest near or above the middle, *5–14 cm (2– 5.5 in) long, 2.5–3.8 cm (1–1.5 in) wide,* pointed to rounded at the tip, tapering to a narrow base, entire, shiny yellow green and smooth to hairy, paler beneath; leafstalks stout, 1.5–2 cm (0.6–0.8 in) long. **Flowers:** stalked flowers produced in narrow, elongate, unbranched, many-flowered clusters, 5–30 cm (2–11.8 in) long; each flower 9–12 mm (0.3–0.5 in) long, with a 5-lobed calyx, 5 white, finely hairy petals, 4 fertile stamens, and a single pistil. **Fruits:** produced in drooping clusters, *rounded to egg-shaped, 8–12 mm (0.3–0.5 in) in diameter, light reddish-brown, with a thin fleshy pulp surrounding 2 nutlets, each containing 2 seeds.*

The Black Mangrove Genus — *Avicennia* L.

This is a small genus of about 15 species widely distributed throughout tropical regions of the world. The species are largely restricted to coastal tidal areas. Only 1 species, the black mangrove, is native to North America.

Members of this genus are trees or shrubs with opposite, simple, evergreen, entire leaves. The flowers are bisexual and produced in heads or elongate, unbranched clusters. Each flower consists of 5 sepals, 4 petals, fused below, 4 stamens, and a single pistil. Fruits are usually large 1-seeded capsules.

Black Mangrove — *Avicennia germinans* (L.) L.

(synonym: *A. nitida* Jacq.)

Black mangrove is a common evergreen tree native to the coastal regions of tropical and subtropical America and Africa. This species often forms dense thickets in sandy tidal flats and lagoons. In North America, it is found along the East and West coasts

from northern to southern Florida, and in scattered populations in southern Louisiana and southern Texas.

Groves of black mangrove are virtually impenetrable because of the dense branches. The trees produce many upright, unbranched roots above water and around the edges of the trees to provide the extensive root system with air. These also trap debris and detritus brought in by tides.

White flowers are usually produced in June or July but can occur throughout the year. They are rich in nectar and make an excellent honey. The dark-brown to nearly black wood is very hard, heavy, and strong, and has been used for posts, in marine construction, and for fuel.

Appearance: bushy shrub or tree to 12 m (39 ft), with a dense, rounded crown; trunk short, usually branching close to the ground, to 30 cm (11.8 in) in diameter, rarely larger. **Bark:** 6–12 mm (0.2–0.5 in) thick, smooth when young, developing irregular scales with age, dark gray to dark brown. **Branches:** stout, spreading; branchlets stout, slightly angled, gray to brown and finely hairy, becoming darker, smooth with

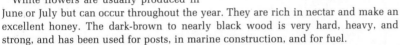

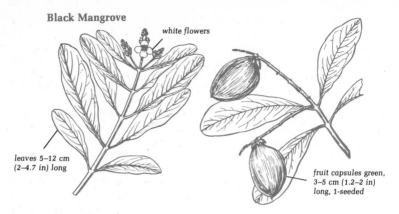

Black Mangrove

white flowers

leaves 5–12 cm
(2–4.7 in) long

fruit capsules green,
3–5 cm (1.2–2 in)
long, 1-seeded

age. **Leaves: *opposite*,** simple, ***evergreen,*** uniformly wide to widest near or below the middle, ***5–12 cm (2–4.7 in) long, 2–4 cm (0.8–1.6 in) wide,*** rounded to pointed at the tip, tapering at the base, entire and often slightly rolled back at the margins, leathery, yellowish-green to dark green and shiny above, paler and hairy beneath; leafstalks stout, 3–12 mm (0.1–0.5 in) long, grooved. **Flowers: *produced in dense, several-flowered, cone-shaped heads*** 2–5 cm (0.8–2 in) long; each flower with a 5-lobed calyx, 4 petals, white, rounded at the tip, fused below to form a bell-shaped tube, 4 stamens, and a single pistil. **Fruits:** a ***capsule, egg-shaped, 3–5 cm (1.2–2 in) long, green, with unequal sides,*** sometimes curbed at the tip, ***containing a single large seed, the seed often germinating and splitting open the fruit while still on the parent tree.***

The Olive Family

Oleaceae

This is a medium-size family of 29 genera and about 600 species of trees and shrubs. They are widespread in both tropical and temperate regions, but are most abundant in southeastern Asia and Australasia. Economically important members of this family include the edible olive, ashes (for lumber), and forsythia, gardenia, and privet (as ornamentals).

Members are woody plants with leaves that are opposite, simple, feather-like (pinnate) compound, or with 3 leaflets per leaf. Flowers are produced in elongate, branched or unbranched clusters or clustered in the junction of the leaves. They may be bisexual or male and female on separate plants. Flower parts are commonly in 4s with the petals frequently absent. Fruits may be capsules, berries or berry-like, nuts, or dry and winged.

Key to Olive Genera

A. Leaves simple and fruits berry-like.

    1. Flowers with petals.

        a. Flowers in dense, many-flowered clusters;

Devilwood

each flower small, 10 mm (0.4 in) long or less.

(1) Flowers produced in short, branched clusters in the junction of the leaves; leaves 10–14 cm (4–5.5 in) long; includes devilwood **Osmanthus, p. 855**

(2) Flowers produced in elongated, branched clusters at the tips of the branchlets; leaves 3–6 cm (1.2–2.4 in) long **Privet, p. 856**

b. Flowers in large, open, airy clusters; each flower 1.4–2.8 cm (0.6–1.2 in) long **Fringetree, p. 857**

2. Flowers without petals **Forestiera, p. 858**

B. Leaves feather-like (pinnate) compound or rarely simple; fruits dry, flattened, winged **Ash, p. 861**

Narrow-Leafed Forestiera

Green Ash

The Osmanthus Genus

Osmanthus Lour.

This small genus of about 15 species is native to North America, eastern Asia, Japan, and the South Pacific. Only 1 species, the devilwood, occurs in North America. A chinese species, *Osmanthus fragrans*, is sometimes cultivated for its small, fragrant cream to yellow flowers.

Members are trees or shrubs with opposite, simple, evergreen, entire or toothed leaves. The bisexual or male or female flowers are produced in elongate to round-topped, branched clusters. Each flower has a 4-lobed calyx, 4 petals fused part way to form a tube; 2, rarely 4, stamens, and a single pistil.

Devilwood *Osmanthus americanus* (L.) Benth. & Hook. f. ex Gray

Devilwood is a small evergreen tree or shrub of the southeastern Coastal Plain, extending from southeastern Virginia to southeastern Louisiana. It usually grows in rich woodlands, along rivers and streams, and in hammocks.

Flowering is in April or May with the blue stone fruits maturing from August through October. The fruits are eaten by birds and small mammals. The dark-brown wood is hard, heavy, and very difficult to split, but it is of little economic value because of the small size of the trees.

Appearance: shrub or small tree to 15 m (49 ft); trunk is short, soon branching, growing to 25 cm (9.8 in) in diameter.
Bark: thin, 2–4 mm (less than 0.2 in) thick, becoming roughened and developing thin

scales with age, dark gray to reddish-gray. **Branches:** slender; branchlets slender, slightly angled, light reddish brown turning gray with age. **Winter buds:** 9–12 mm (0.4–0.5 in) long, narrowly lance-shaped, covered with 2 thick, narrow, reddish-

Devilwood

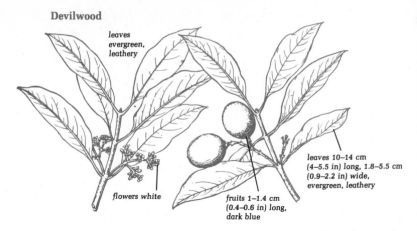

leaves evergreen, leathery

leaves 10–14 cm (4–5.5 in) long, 1.8–5.5 cm (0.9–2.2 in) wide, evergreen, leathery

flowers white

fruits 1–1.4 cm (0.4–0.6 in) long, dark blue

brown, hairy scales. **Leaves:** opposite, simple, evergreen, uniformly wide to widest above the middle, 10–14 cm (4–5.5 in) long, 1.8–5.5 cm (0.8–2.2 in) wide, pointed, rarely rounded, at the tip, tapering at the base, entire but rolled under at the margins, leathery, bright shiny green and smooth above, paler beneath; leafstalks stout, 1.6–2 cm (0.7–0.8 in) long. **Flowers:** *produced in short, branched clusters in the junction of the leaves,* with bisexual, male or female flowers, *each flower with* a short, 4-lobed calyx, *4 white petals* fused into a tube 3–5 mm (0.1–0.2 in) long, with 2 stamens in male flowers, and a single pistil in female flowers. **Fruits:** *stone fruits,* uniformly wide to widest above the middle, *1–1.4 cm (0.4–0.6 in) long, dark blue,* with a thin flesh surrounding a thin-walled stone.

The Privet Genus   *Ligustrum* L.

This is a medium-size genus of about 50 species of trees and shrubs of eastern Asia, Malaysia, and Australia, with 1 species in Europe and North Africa. Of the several species introduced into North America, only 2 are commonly encountered: the Japanese privet and the California privet. California privet is a shrub or small tree growing wild in some of the southern states. Japanese privet *(Ligustrum japonicum)* also has naturalized from cultivated plants but is primarily a large shrub.

Members of this genus are woody plants with opposite, simple, evergreen or deciduous leaves. The bisexual, white flowers are produced in elongate, branched clusters (panicles). Each flower has a 4-lobed calyx, 4 petals fused to form a tube, 2 stamens, and a single pistil. Fruits are 1- to 4-seeded, berry-like stone fruits.

California Privet   *Ligustrum ovalifolium* Hassk.

This species is native to Japan and was introduced into North America in 1847. It has been widely planted as a hedge, especially in the southern states. The cream-white flowers are produced in June, with the black berries maturing in summer. The glossy green leaves are distinctive.

This is a shrub or small tree to 5 m (16 ft), with a rounded crown. The opposite, simple, late deciduous to nearly evergreen leaves are broadest at or just below the middle, 3–6 cm (1.2–2.4 in) long, 1.2–2.8 cm (0.5–1.2 in) wide, pointed at the tip, entire, dark shiny green above, and yellowish-green beneath. The *flowers are produced in elongated branched clusters 5–10 cm (2–4 in) long, each flower cream-white, 6–*

10 mm (0.2–0.4 in) long. Fruits are round, berry-like, 6–9 mm (0.2–0.4 in) in diameter, black.

The Fringetree Genus

Chionanthus L.

This small genus contains 2 species, 1 in the southeastern U.S. and a related species in China. Both have been introduced into cultivation and are widely planted for their light, airy clusters of white flowers. The leaves of the Chinese species *(Chionanthus retusus)* are smaller and widest near the base or middle rather than uniformly wide as found in our native species.

Members of this genus are shrubs or small trees with opposite, simple, entire, deciduous leaves. Male and female flowers are produced on separate trees or the flowers are bisexual, in large, loose, branched clusters (panicles). Each flower has a 4-parted calyx, 4 petals, 2 stamens in bisexual and male flowers, and a single pistil in female flowers. Fruits are 1-seeded stone fruits.

Fringetree

Chionanthus virginicus L.

This attractive tree occurs from New Jersey south to Florida, and west to Missouri, Oklahoma, and Texas. It grows along moist stream banks, ridges, and hillsides in sandy to deep-rich soils. Fringetree is usually found with red oak, tulip tree, basswood, tupelo, several species of hickories, dogwood, and hawthorns.

This is a fast growing, short-lived tree that is remarkably free of harmful insects or diseases. Profuse clusters of fragrant flowers are produced in spring, with the dark fruits maturing by late summer. The fruits are eaten by many species of wildlife including whitetail deer, quail, turkey, and many songbirds. The light-brown wood is hard and heavy but is of no timber value because of the small size of the trees. Fringetree does make an excellent ornamental.

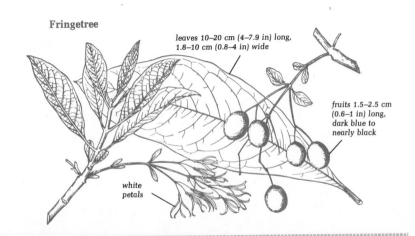

Fringetree

leaves 10–20 cm (4–7.9 in) long,
1.8–10 cm (0.8–4 in) wide

fruits 1.5–2.5 cm
(0.6–1 in) long,
dark blue to
nearly black

white
petals

Appearance: shrub or small tree to 10 m (33 ft), with a dense, rounded crown; trunk short, branching close to the ground, to 20 cm (7.9 in) in diameter. **Bark:** 6–12 mm (0.2–0.5 in) thick, developing small, flattened scales, reddish-brown. **Branches:** stout; branchlets stout, light green and smooth or hairy when young, turning ash-gray with age. **Winter buds:** 3–4 mm (0.1–0.2 in) long, broadly egg-shaped, pointed at the tip, covered with 5 pairs of light brown, overlapping scales. **Leaves:** opposite, simple, deciduous, usually uniformly wide, *10–20 cm (4–7.9 in) long, 1.8–10 cm (0.8–4 in) wide*, pointed to long-pointed at the tip, tapering at the base, entire along the wavy margin, dark green above, paler and hairy beneath; leaflets stout, 1.7–2.5 cm (0.7–1 in) long. **Flowers:** *produced in large, loose, airy clusters 10–15 cm (4–6 in) long;* each flower bisexual, with 4 sepals, 4 white petals 1.4–2.8 cm (0.6–1.2 in) long, and a single pistil. **Fruits:** *stone fruits*, egg-shaped, *1.5–2.5 cm (0.6–1 in) long, dark blue to nearly black*, containing a single seed.

The Forestiera Genus

Forestiera Poir.

This is a small genus of about 20 species of small trees or shrubs of North America, the West Indies, Mexico, and Central and South America. The 4 species of trees native to North America are restricted largely to the southern states. They are of little value as ornamentals and no value for wood. The fruits are eaten by birds and small mammals.

Members of this genus are woody plants with thin bark. The opposite, simple, evergreen-to-deciduous leaves are entire or toothed. The small flowers are bisexual or male or female. Each flower has 4 to 6 unequal sepals, no petals, 2 to 4 stamens in male and bisexual flowers, and a single pistil in female and bisexual flowers. Fruits are a 1- or rarely 2-seeded, small stone fruit.

Key to Forestiera Species

A. Leaves 6–12 cm (2.4–4.7 in) long, 2.5–3.5 cm (1–1.4 in) wide, sparsely toothed above the middle; trees of southern and southeastern U.S.
>> **Swamp privet, p. 859**

B. Leaves 1.2–5 cm (0.5–2 in) long, 0.3–2 cm (0.2–0.8 in) wide, entire along the margin.

1. Leaves lance-shaped or narrow but widest near the tip, 1.2–3 cm (0.5–1.2 in) long, 3–7 mm (0.1–0.3 in) wide.

Narrow-Leafed Forestier

  a. Leaves hairy above and below; trees of southern Arizona
>> **Desert olive forestiera, p. 859**
  b. Leaves smooth; trees of southern and southwestern Texas
>> **Narrow-leafed forestiera, p. 860**

2. Leaves broadest near or above the middle, 2–5 cm (0.8–2 in) long, 1.2–2 cm (0.5–0.8 in) wide; trees of Georgia and Florida
>> **Florida privet, p. 860**

Swamp Privet   *Forestiera acuminata* (Michx.) Poir.

Swamp privet is centered in the central and southern Mississippi River Valley, but also occurs in the Coastal Plain to South Carolina, and in Kansas, Oklahoma, and Texas. It grows primarily along river and stream banks, floodplains and flatlands in association with sycamore, sweet gum, and slippery elm.

Flowering is in early spring before the leaves appear, and the small, purple stone fruits fall soon after ripening in June or July. They are eaten by mallards, wood ducks, and quail. Whitetail deer browse the young twigs and leaves. The yellowish-brown wood is soft, light, and weak, and of no commercial importance.

Appearance: shrub or small tree to 10 m (33 ft), with an irregular crown; trunk short. **Bark:** 2–4 mm (less than 0.2 in) thick, becoming roughened and slightly furrowed with age, dark brown. **Branches:** slender, spreading; branchlets slender, light yellowish-brown and smooth, turning darker with age. **Winter buds:** 1–2 mm (less than 0.1 in) long, egg-shaped, broadest near the base and pointed at the tip, covered with several overlapping scales. **Leaves:** opposite, simple, deciduous, broadest near the middle, *6–12 cm (2.4–4.7 in) long, 2.5–3.5 cm (1–1.4 in) wide,* pointed at the tip, tapering at the base, *sparsely toothed above the middle,* yellowish-green above, paler beneath; leafstalks slender, 6–12 mm (0.2–0.5 in) long. **Flowers:** *male and female flowers on separate trees or with some bisexual flowers;* male flowers in dense many-flowered clusters along the branchlets, *each flower with no petals and 4 stamens;* female flowers in several-flowered clusters, each with a slender stalk, with 4 usually sterile stamens, and a single pistil. **Fruits:** *stone fruits,* uniformly wide to broadest above the middle, *2.5–3 cm (1–1.2 in) long,* slightly compressed, with a thin dry flesh surrounding a 1-seeded stone.

Desert Olive Forestiera   *Forestiera phillyreoides* (Benth.) Torr.

Native to southern Arizona and adjacent Mexico, desert olive forestiera is usually a shrub, but occasionally a small tree. It grows in canyons and on dry rocky slopes, normally between 750–1,400 m (2,500–4,600 ft) elevation. Flowering occurs early in the year, from January through March. The small stone fruits mature by summer.

The plants are densely branched shrubs or trees to 8 m (26 ft), with opposite, simple, nearly *evergreen leaves.* They are *lance-shaped to broadest near the tip, 1.6–2.5 cm (0.7–1 in) long, 3–6 mm (0.1–0.2 in) wide,* green and hairy above and beneath. Tiny male and female flowers are produced on different trees in small clusters in the junction of the leaves. The fruits are egg-shaped, 6–10 mm (0.2–0.4 in) long, with a thin flesh covering a single, 1-seeded stone.

Narrow-Leafed Forestiera

Forestiera angustifolia Torr.

This stiff-looking shrub or small tree is native to southern and southwestern Texas and adjacent Mexico. It grows in dry rocky soils in canyons and along hillsides. The tiny leaves and stiff, spreading branches and branchlets serve as good field features that distinguish this privet from the other native ones.

These grow to 7 m (23 ft), and have a short, crooked trunk with smooth gray bark. The opposite, often clustered, simple *evergreen leaves* are *linear to narrow and widest near the tip, 1.2–3 cm (0.5–1.2 in) long, 4–7 mm (0.2–0.3 in) wide*, leathery, smooth, and light green. Flowers are bisexual or male and female, tiny, greenish yellow, and produced in clusters usually on short shoots. Egg-shaped stone fruits are 0.6–1.2 cm (0.2–0.5 in) long, black, slightly curved, and 1-seeded.

Narrow-Leafed Forestiera

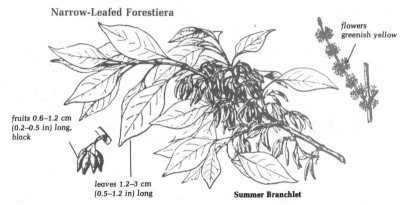

flowers greenish yellow

fruits 0.6–1.2 cm (0.2–0.5 in) long, black

leaves 1.2–3 cm (0.5–1.2 in) long

Summer Branchlet

Florida Privet

Forestiera segregata (Jacq.) Krug & Urban

This species of privet is native to coastal regions from southwestern Georgia to southern Florida and the West Indies. Male and female flowers are produced on separate trees in spring with the bluish-black fruits produced throughout the summer and into autumn.

Florida privet is a densely branched shrub or tree with opposite, simple, *evergreen leaves* that are *broadest near or above the middle, 2–5 cm (0.8–2 in) long, 1.2–2 cm (0.5–0.8 in) wide*, rounded at the tip, tapering at the base, entire, dark green above and paler beneath. Tiny male or female flowers are produced in dense, short, 3- or 4-flowered clusters in the junctions of the leaves. The egg-shaped stone fruits are 6–9 mm (0.2–0.4 in) long with a thin flesh covering a large hard stone which encloses the single seed.

The Ash Genus

Fraxinus L.

This is a medium-size genus of about 70 species of trees or shrubs, mainly of north temperate regions of the world. In North America, 16 species reach tree size. A few more species occur in Mexico and Central America. Others are native to Europe and Asia. Although ashes grow in a variety of sites, they are mainly trees of lowlands. Some of the species are important timber trees, while others are valuable for their shade and as ornamentals.

Members of this genus are trees or shrubs with large opposite, usually deciduous, feather-like (pinnate) compound leaves composed of from 1 to 11 leaflets. The flowers are bisexual or more commonly male and female and then on separate trees. The flowers have a small calyx, usually without petals, 2 or 4 stamens in male and bisexual flowers, and a long, narrow pistil in female and bisexual flowers. Fruits are dry, flattened, and winged.

Key to Ash Species

A. Branchlets 4-sided or strongly angled.

1. Leaves composed of 5–11 leaflets; trees of midwestern U.S. and Canada **Blue ash, p. 863**

2. Leaves composed of a single leaflet (simple) or rarely with 3 leaflets per leaf; trees of southwestern U.S. **Singleleaf ash, p. 864**

Blue Ash

B. Branchlets rounded, not winged.

1. Trees of eastern North America, including eastern Texas.

   a. Fruits with a distinct rounded, swollen basal part (seed) and a long flattened wing extending to or near the top of the seed.

Singleleaf Ash

     (1) Leafletstalks, at least the lower ones, narrowly winged, short, usually 5 mm (0.2 in) long or less; widespread trees of eastern and mid North America **Green ash, p. 865**

     (2) Leafletstalks without a wing, usually 4–15 mm (0.2–0.6 in) long.

       (a) Leaflets 6–15 cm (2.4–6 in) long, often whitish beneath; fruits 2.5–
(Continued)

Green Ash

6.5 cm (1–2.6 in) long; trees of eastern North America

White ash, p. 866

(b) Leaflets 12–25 cm (4.7–9.8 in) long, pale green to yellowish-green beneath; fruits 5–8 cm (2–3.2 in) long; trees of southeastern Coastal Plain

Pumpkin ash, p. 868

b. Fruits flattened, the wing extending to the base of the seed.

(1) Leaflets with a distinct stalk; fruits with a small cup-shaped, persistent calyx at the base; trees of southeastern U.S.

Carolina ash, p. 868

(2) Leaflets lacking a distinct stalk; fruits without a small persistent calyx; trees of northeastern North America

Black ash, p. 869

2. Trees of western North America, including central and southwestern Texas.

a. Flowers with petals.

(1) Flowers with 4 petals, fragrant; leaves 12–18 cm (4.7–7.1 in) long; fruits 1.2–2.5 cm (0.5–1 in) long; trees of southwestern U.S. and Mexico

Fragrant ash, p. 871

(2) Flowers with 2 petals, not fragrant; leaves to 12 cm (4.7 in) long; fruits 2–3 cm (0.8–1.2 in) long; trees of California

Two-petal ash, p. 871

b. Flowers without petals.

(1) Leaflets of a leaf with distinct stalks, to 4 cm (1.6 in) long.

(a) Leaflets from 2/3 to 3/4 as wide as long, leafletstalks 8–40 mm (0.3–1.6 in) long; trees of Oklahoma and Texas **Texas ash, p. 872**

(b) Leaflets 1/4 to 1/2 as wide as long, leafletstalks 2–5 mm (less than 0.2 in) long.

(b1) Leaflets 2.5–4 cm (1–1.6 in) long, shallowly round-toothed above the middle, densely hairy beneath; trees of Texas, Nevada, and

White Ash

Pumpkin Ash

Carolina Ash

Black Ash

Fragrant Ash

Texas Ash

California **Velvet ash, p. 873**

(b2) Leaflets 7.5–10 cm (3–4 in) long, entire or with widely spaced, sharp pointed teeth along the margin, smooth or with a few tufts of hairs beneath; trees of southern Texas and Mexico
Berlandier ash, p. 873

Velvet Ash

Berlandier Ash

(2) Leaflets of a leaf lacking distinct stalks or if present then 2 mm (less than 0.1 in) long or less.

(a) Leaflets 3–10 cm (1.2–4 in) long, 1–4 cm (0.4–1.6 in) wide.

(a1) Leaves 12–35 cm (4.7–13.8 in) long, with 5 to 7, rarely 3 leaflets, the leaflets hairy beneath; trees of coastal Washington, Oregon, and California **Oregon ash, p. 874**

Oregon Ash

(a2) Leaves 8–15 cm (3.2–6 in) long, with 7 to 9 leaflets, the leaflets slightly bumpy and smooth to sometimes hairy; trees of Arizona, New Mexico, and Texas
Chihuahua ash, p. 875

(b) Leaflets 0.8–2.5 cm (0.4–1 in) long, 0.3–1.2 cm (0.2–0.5 in) wide.

(b1) Leaves with 3, sometimes 5 to 7 leaflets, the leaflets broadest near the tip or middle, 3 times longer than broad; trees of southwestern Texas and Mexico **Gregg ash, p. 876**

(b2) Leaves with 5 to 9 leaflets, the leaflets broadest near the middle, twice as long as wide or wider; trees of southern Arizona **Goodding ash, p. 876**

Gregg Ash

Blue Ash   *Fraxinus quadrangulata* Michx.

This midwestern ash extends as far north as southern Ontario, Canada, and south to Alabama and Arkansas. It usually occurs in limestone soils of dry uplands, hillsides, and even bottomlands. Blue ash is commonly found growing in association with several oaks, mockernut hickory, sweet gum, black tupelo, American elm, hawthorn, redbud, and flowering dogwood.

This is a fast-growing species that may live 125 to 150 years. Flowering clusters appear before the leaves have expanded in spring. The winged fruits mature in autumn, and are a moderately valuable source of food to woodducks, quail, turkey, and many songbirds. Whitetail deer eat the young twigs and leaves. The yellowish-brown, hard, heavy, and durable,

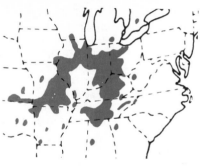

but somewhat brittle, wood is used for flooring and interior finishes. Blue ash is usually sold as white ash to mills. It is sometimes planted in parks and gardens as an ornamental and for shade.

Blue Ash

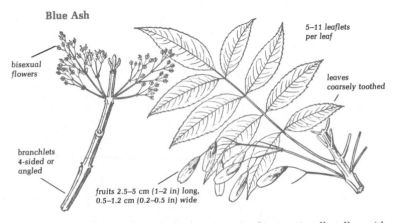

bisexual flowers

5–11 leaflets per leaf

leaves coarsely toothed

branchlets 4-sided or angled

fruits 2.5–5 cm (1–2 in) long, 0.5–1.2 cm (0.2–0.5 in) wide

Appearance: small to medium-size tree to 20 m (66 ft), occasionally taller, with a slender, rounded crown; trunk straight, to 90 cm (35.4 in) in diameter. **Bark:** 8–12 mm (0.3–0.5 in) thick, irregularly fissured and developing scaly, irregular plates, gray to light reddish-gray. **Branches:** stout, spreading; *branchlets stout, angled to 4-sided,* developing slight wings where the leaves are attached. **Winter buds:** 6–8 mm (0.2–0.3 in) long, broadest near the base, pointed at the tip, covered with 3 pairs of dark reddish-brown, overlapping scales. **Leaves:** opposite, deciduous, feather-like (pinnate) compound, 20–30 cm (7.9–11.8 in) long, *composed of 5 to 11 leaflets,* the leaflets lance-shaped, broadest near the base or uniformly wide, *8–13 cm (3.2–5.1 in) long, 2.5–5 cm (1–2 in) wide,* long pointed at the tip, unevenly rounded at the base, *coarsely toothed along the margins,* yellowish-green and smooth above, paler and smooth to hairy beneath; leafstalks slender. **Flowers:** usually bisexual and produced in elongate, many-flowered clusters; each flower with a minute calyx, no petals, 2 stamens, and a narrow pistil. **Fruits:** produced in clusters, each dry, flattened, winged, uniformly wide to broadest near the tip, 2.5–5 cm (1–2 in) long, 5–12 mm (0.2–0.5 in) wide, rounded and often notched at the tip.

Singleleaf Ash   *Fraxinus anomala* Torr.

This southwestern ash is found primarily along streams and gulches from 625–1,875 m (2,000–6,100 ft) elevation. Flowering occurs in April or May with the winged fruits maturing 4 to 6 weeks later. The fruits are of limited value to wildlife. The light-brown wood is hard and heavy, but of no timber value because of the small size of the trees.

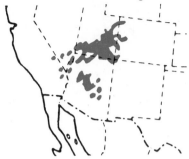

Singleleaf ash are shrubs to spreading trees to 8 m (26 ft), and with rounded crowns. The *leaves are usually simple or with 2 or 3 leaflets per leaf.* They are *almost circular* to broadest near the base, *4–5 cm (1.6–2 in) long, 2.5–5 cm (1–2 in) wide,* rounded to pointed at the tip, entire or with some rounded to pointed teeth along the margins, dark green and smooth at maturity. Flowers are produced in dense, elongate, many-flowered, male or female, sometimes bisexual flower clusters. Fruits are dry, flattened, winged, broadest near the tip, 1.2–2 cm (0.5–0.8 in) long, and rounded at the tip.

Singleleaf Ash

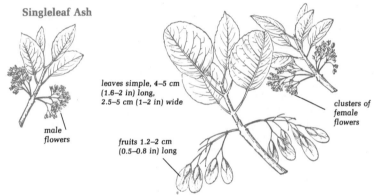

leaves simple, 4–5 cm (1.6–2 in) long, 2.5–5 cm (1–2 in) wide

clusters of female flowers

male flowers

fruits 1.2–2 cm (0.5–0.8 in) long

Green Ash   *Fraxinus pennsylvanica* Marsh.

Green ash is the most widely distributed of all native American ashes. It extends from Cape Breton Island and Nova Scotia to Alberta, Canada, and south to Texas and northern Florida. This ash is usually found along stream banks, floodplains, wet

upland sites and is most common along the Mississippi River Valley. It may form almost pure stands or grow in association with many other trees including boxelder, red maple, pecan, sugarberry, sweet gum, American elm, sycamore, willow oak, and black willow.

Green ash is a relatively fast growing tree. Flowers are produced in early spring with the clusters of winged fruits maturing

Green Ash

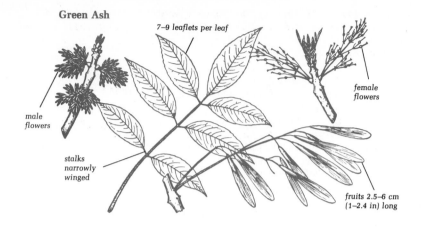

7–9 leaflets per leaf

female flowers

male flowers

stalks narrowly winged

fruits 2.5–6 cm (1–2.4 in) long

in autumn. The large seed crops, produced almost every year, are important as food for woodducks, quail, turkey, cardinals, finches, and squirrels and other rodents. Whitetail and mule deer along with moose browse the young twigs and leaves. The light-brown wood is hard, heavy, and moderately strong, and is used for tool handles, oars, paddles, baseball bats, snowshoes, tennis rackets, and frames. Green ash has been widely planted as a shade and street tree.

Appearance: small to medium-size tree to 20 m (66 ft), with a round-topped crown; trunk tall, slender, to 50 cm (19.7 in) in diameter, rarely larger. **Bark:** 8–12 mm (0.3–0.5 in) thick, slightly furrowed with flat, scaly ridges, brown to grayish-brown, sometimes tinged with red. **Branches:** stout, upright to spreading; branchlets slender, round, green and smooth to hairy when young, becoming smooth and turning ash-gray with age, marked with half circular leaf scars. **Winter buds:** 3–5 mm (0.1–0.2 in) long, broadest near the base, usually rounded at the tip, covered with 3 pairs of rust colored, overlapping scales. **Leaves:** opposite, deciduous, feather-like (pinnate) compound, 25–30 cm (9.8–11.8 in) long, *composed of 7 to 9 leaflets,* the leaflets lance-shaped to uniformly broad, 10–15 cm (4–6 in) long, 1.2–3 cm (0.5–1.2 in) wide, long pointed at the tip, tapering at the base, *faintly toothed above the middle, entire below,* bright green to yellowish-green above, paler and smooth to hairy beneath; leafstalks stout, hairy; *leafletstalks narrowly winged.* **Flowers:** male and female flowers produced in separate clusters on different trees; male flowers with a tiny, cup-shaped calyx, no petals, and 2 stamens; female flowers with a deeply lobed calyx, no petals or stamens, and a long, narrow pistil. **Fruits:** produced in clusters, each dry, flattened, winged, broadest at or above the middle, *2.5–6 cm (1–2.4 in) long, 6–9 mm (0.2–0.4 in) wide,* rounded and usually notched at the tip.

White Ash   *Fraxinus americana* L.

White ash is the most common native ash. It extends from Cape Breton Island and Nova Scotia to southern Ontario, south to northern Florida and eastern Texas. It grows in deep, rich, and moist — but well-drained — soils and is often found along streams and lower slopes of hills and mountains. White ash occurs from sea level to 1,050 m (3,500 ft) in the Cumberland Mountains and grows in association with many other trees including tulip tree, black cherry, American beech, sweet gum, red maple, willows, oaks, and hickories.

Growth is slow during the sapling stage, but increases over the next 50 years. The trees are either male or female. The male trees usually flower each year, while the female trees flower heavily every 2 or 3 years. Flowering is in April or May. Whitetail deer browse the young twigs and leaves. Woodducks, quail, turkey, grouse, finches, grosbeaks, cardinals and other songbirds eat the winged seeds. This is the most valuable species of ash for timber production. The light-brown wood is strong, tough, and rather lightweight. It is used to make tool handles, furniture, veneer, paneling, and baseball bats.

White Ash

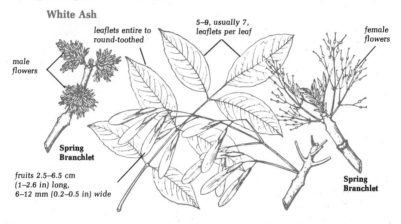

leaflets entire to round-toothed

5–9, usually 7, leaflets per leaf

male flowers

female flowers

Spring Branchlet

fruits 2.5–6.5 cm (1–2.6 in) long, 6–12 mm (0.2–0.5 in) wide

Spring Branchlet

Appearance: medium-size tree to 25 m, rarely to 35 (82 ft, rarely to 115), with a narrow to broadly rounded or pyramid shaped crown; trunk straight, tall, to 1.5 m, rarely to 2 (5 ft, rarely to 6.6) in diameter. **Bark:** becoming thick, 2.5–8 cm (1–3.2 in) thick, deeply fissured with broad, flat, scaly ridges, dark brown to gray. **Branches:** stout, upright to spreading; branchlets thick, stout, dark green and slightly hairy when young, becoming light orange to eventually gray and smooth with age. **Winter buds:** 10–14 mm (0.4–0.6 in) long, broadly egg-shaped, blunt at the tip, and covered with overlapping, rusty hairy scales. **Leaves:** opposite, deciduous, feather-like (pinnate) compound, 20–30 cm (7.9–11.8 in) long, ***composed of 5 to 9, usually 7, leaflets,*** the leaflets broadest near the base or middle, ***6–15 cm (2.4–6 in) long, 3.7–7.5 cm (1.5–3 in) wide,*** pointed at the tip, wedge-shaped to rounded at the base, ***nearly entire to round-toothed along the margin,*** papery, dark green and smooth above, paler and smooth to slightly hairy beneath; leafstalks stout, grooved, the leaflet stalks 5–15 mm (0.2–0.6 in) long. **Flowers:** male and female flowers in separate clusters on different trees; male flowers in dense clusters, each flower with a slightly 4-lobed calyx, no petals, and 2 or 3 stamens; female flowers in elongate, many-flowered clusters, each flower with a deeply lobed calyx and a single, long-stalked pistil. **Fruits:** produced in dense clusters to 20 cm (7.9 in) long, each dry, flattened, winged, broadest near the tip, ***2.5–6.5 cm (1–2.6 in) long, 6–12 mm (0.2–0.5 in) wide,*** and pointed or notched at the tip.

Pumpkin Ash

Fraxinus profunda (Bush) Bush

(synonym: *F. tomentosa* Michx. f.)

Pumpkin ash is a tree primarily of the southeastern Coastal Plain, but is also present in the mid-Mississippi and Ohio River valleys. It grows in river bottoms, swamps, and low wet sites, and often occurs in association with bald cypress, water tupelo, swamp

cottonwood, willows, and water locust. Flowering is in April or May with the fruits maturing from August to October. The fruits are eaten by woodducks and many other birds. Whitetail deer browse the young twigs and leaves.

Pumpkin ashes are trees to 30 m (98 ft), with a narrow, open crown. The opposite, deciduous, feather-like (pinnate) leaves are 20–45 cm (7.9–17.7 in) long, and composed of 7 to 9 leaflets; the *leaflets* are lance-shaped to broadest near the middle, *12–25 cm (4.7–9.8 in) long, 3–12 cm (1.2–4.7 in) wide,* pointed to long pointed at the tip, tapering to rounded at the base, *entire to slightly toothed, dark yellow-green* and smooth above, paler and softly hairy beneath. Male and female flowers are in separate clusters on different trees. **Fruits** are dry, flattened, winged, broadest at or above the middle, *5–8 cm (2–3.2 in) long, 8–12 mm (0.3–0.5 in) wide,* rounded or notched at the tip.

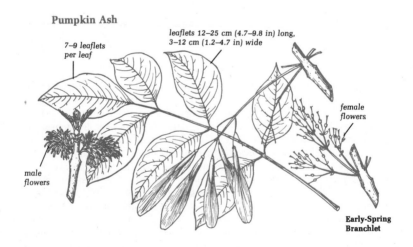

Pumpkin Ash

7–9 leaflets per leaf

leaflets 12–25 cm (4.7–9.8 in) long, 3–12 cm (1.2–4.7 in) wide

female flowers

male flowers

Early-Spring Branchlet

Carolina Ash

Fraxinus caroliniana Mill.

Carolina ash is a small tree of the southeastern Coastal Plain from southeastern Virginia to Florida, and west to eastern Texas. It normally grows along lagoons, and in swamps and other lowland sites. This ash often grows in association with hollies, sweet gum, southern red oak, sugarberry, and willows.

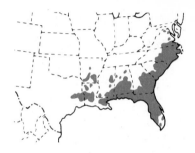

The trees are generally male or female with the yellowish-green flowers appearing in early spring and the fruits maturing in summer or autumn. The light-colored wood is soft, weak, and inferior to that from other ashes, and is of no value as timber.

Appearance: small tree to 12 m (39 ft), with an open, rounded crown; trunk often short, to 30 cm (11.8 in) in diameter. **Bark:** 1–4 mm (less than 0.2 in) thick, separating into small, flattened scales, light gray and often blotched. **Branches:** slender, short; branchlets slender, green, and smooth to hairy when young, turning gray with age, marked with large, rounded leaf scars. **Winter buds:** 3–4 mm (0.1–0.2 in) long, broadest near the base and pointed at the tip, covered with 3 pairs of overlapping, reddish-brown scales. **Leaves:** opposite, deciduous, feather-like (pinnate) compound, 16–30 cm (6.3–11.8 in) long, *composed of 5 to 7 leaflets,* the *leaflets* broadest near the base to uniformly wide, *8–15 cm (3.2–6 in) long, 5–8 cm (2–3.2 in) wide,* pointed to long pointed at the tip, tapering to rounded at the base, *usually sharply toothed along the margin,* dark green and smooth above at maturity, paler and smooth to softly hairy beneath. **Flowers:** male and female flowers in separate clusters on different trees; male flowers in dense, elongate clusters, each flower with a minute calyx, no petals, 2 or 4 stamens, and no pistil; female flowers in elongate, many flowered clusters, *each flower with a deeply divided, cup-shaped calyx,* no petals, no stamens, and a long narrow pistil. **Fruits:** several to many per cluster, each dry, flattened, winged, broadest near or above the middle, *3–5.5 cm (1.2–2.2 in) long, 1–2 cm (0.4–0.8 in) wide,* rounded or notched at the tip.

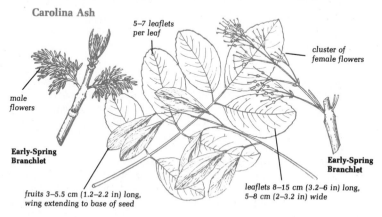

Carolina Ash

5–7 leaflets per leaf

cluster of female flowers

male flowers

Early-Spring Branchlet

Early-Spring Branchlet

fruits 3–5.5 cm (1.2–2.2 in) long, wing extending to base of seed

leaflets 8–15 cm (3.2–6 in) long, 5–8 cm (2–3.2 in) wide

Black Ash

Fraxinus nigra Marsh.

Black ash is native to northeastern North America and is the only ash that grows in Newfoundland. It is found in swamps, along banks of streams and lakes, and in bogs. Black ash can tolerate some standing water. Pure stands sometimes occur, but usually this ash grows in association with black spruce, balsam fir, white cedar, eastern hemlock, yellow birch, paper birch, and tamarack.

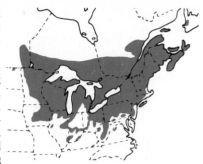

This is a moderate to slow growing species, depending upon location. Flowering is in early spring before the leaves appear, with the fruits ripening by late summer. The fruits are an important food for wood-ducks, grouse, turkey, many songbirds, and small mammals. Whitetail deer and moose heavily browse the twigs and young leaves. The dark-brown wood is heavy, tough, and durable, and is used for interior trim, cabinets, furniture, and veneer.

Black Ash

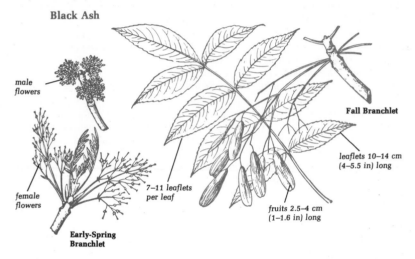

male flowers

female flowers

Early-Spring Branchlet

7–11 leaflets per leaf

Fall Branchlet

leaflets 10–14 cm (4–5.5 in) long

fruits 2.5–4 cm (1–1.6 in) long

Appearance: medium-size trees to 20 m (66 ft), with a narrow, open crown; trunk slender, sometimes leaning, to 50 cm (19.7 in) in diameter, rarely larger. **Bark:** 5–12 mm (0.2–0.5 in) thick, furrowed and with large, irregular, scaly ridges, gray, sometimes with a slight reddish tinge. **Branches:** stout; branchlets stout, dark green and slightly hairy when young, becoming gray with age and marked by large, rounded leaf scars. **Winter buds:** 4–7 mm (0.2–0.3 in) long, broadest near the base and pointed at the tip, covered with 3 pairs of overlapping, dark-brown scales. **Leaves:** opposite, deciduous, feather-like (pinnate) compound, 25–40 cm (9.8–15.8 in) long, composed of 7 to 11 leaflets, the leaflets broadest near the base, 10–14 cm (4–5.5 in) long, 3–6 cm (1.2–2.4 in) wide, long pointed at the tip, tapering to rounded at the base, sharply toothed along the margin, dark green above, paler and with tufts of hairs beneath; leaf-stalks stout. **Flowers:** male and female flowers occur separate or with bisexual flowers on the same tree or different trees; male flowers with a tiny, cup-shaped calyx, no petals, and 2 stamens; female flowers with a tiny but lobed calyx, no petals or stamens, and a long narrow pistil. **Fruits:** produced in clusters, each fruit dry, flattened, winged, uniformly long to broadest above the middle, 2.5–4 cm (1–1.6 in) long, 4–6 mm (0.2 in) wide, rounded and sometimes notched at the tip.

Fragrant Ash

Fraxinus cuspidata Torr.

This attractive shrub or tree is native to the southwestern U.S. from Arizona to southwestern Texas and adjacent Mexico. There it grows in dry, well-drained soils of rocky slopes and ridges, or in canyons, usually from 1,050–1,700 m (3,500–5,600 ft) eleva-

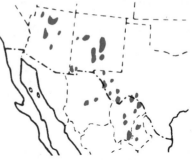

tion. It is of no importance for lumber. Deer sometimes browse the leaves and young twigs. This is the only native species of ash with petals and a strong fragrance when in flower.

It is a shrub, rarely a tree to 8 m (26 ft), with smooth gray bark. The opposite, deciduous **leaves** are feather-like (pinnate) compound, **12–18 cm (4.7–7.1 in) long,** composed of 3, 5, or 7 leaflets, the leaflets **lance-shaped, 3.5–7 cm (1.4–2.8 in) long,** long pointed at the tip, sharply and sparsely toothed along the margin, dark green and smooth. The bisexual flowers are produced in large, open-branched clusters; each flower with a 4-lobed, cup-shaped calyx, **4 long, narrow, white petals 1.2–1.6 cm (0.5–0.7 in) long,** 2 stamens, and a single pistil. Fruits are dry, winged, broadest near the tip, **1.2–2.5 cm (0.5–1 in) long,** rounded at the tip, and pale green.

Fragrant Ash

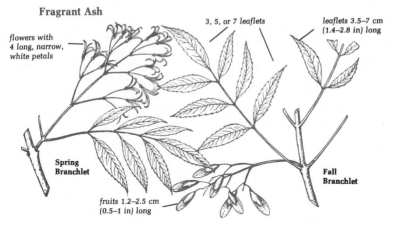

flowers with 4 long, narrow, white petals

3, 5, or 7 leaflets

leaflets 3.5–7 cm (1.4–2.8 in) long

Spring Branchlet

Fall Branchlet

fruits 1.2–2.5 cm (0.5–1 in) long

Two-Petal Ash

Fraxinus dipetala Hook. & Arn.

Two-petal ash is usually a shrub, though sometimes a small tree, that grows on dry slopes and foothills of the coastal mountain ranges and the Sierra Nevada of California. It is more common along streams and rivers below 1,050 m (3,500 ft) elevation. Flowering is in spring with the clusters of winged fruits maturing in late summer. Two-petal ash is of limited importance to wildlife and of no value as timber.

Members are shrubs or small trees to 7 m

(23 ft), with opposite, deciduous, feather-like (pinnate) compound *leaves to 12 cm (4.7 in) long.* They are *composed of 3 to 7, rarely 9, leaflets;* the leaflets broadest near the base or tip, 2–5 cm (0.8–2 in) long, 0.5–2.5 cm (0.3–1 in) wide, sharply toothed along the margin, dark green and smooth. Flowers are bisexual or male or female, produced in elongate, branched clusters (panicles), *each flower with 2 white petals.* Fruits are dry, flattened, winged, uniformly wide to broadest above the middle, *2–3 cm (0.8–1.2 in) long,* 5–8 mm (0.2–0.3 in) wide, and rounded at the tip.

Texas Ash
Fraxinus texensis (Gray) Sarg.

This ash is restricted to southern Oklahoma, and central and southern Texas where it grows in limestone soils of hillsides and bluffs. Male and female flowers are produced on separate trees in early spring as the leaves are unfolding. Texas ash looks much like white ash except that it usually has 5 leaflets per leaf, the leaflets rounded or pointed at the tip. The light-brown wood is strong, heavy, and hard, and has been used in construction, but the trees are not abundant enough to be of importance as timber.

Texas ashes are trees to 16 m (53 ft), with dark gray, deeply furrowed bark. The opposite, deciduous feather-like (pinnate) compound leaves are 12–20 cm (4.7–7.9 in) long and composed of *usually 5,* rarely 7 *leaflets;* the leaflets are broadest below or above the middle, *2.5–8 cm (1–3.2 in) long, 2–5 cm (0.8–2 in) wide, rounded or pointed at the tip,* coarsely round-toothed along the margin, becoming leathery, dark green and smooth above. Male and female flowers are produced in separate, branched clusters on different trees; male flowers with a tiny, 4-lobed calyx, no petals, 2 stamens; female flowers with a cup-shaped 4-lobed calyx, and a single pistil. Fruits are produced in short clusters, dry, flattened, winged, broadest near the tip, *1.7–2.5 cm (0.7–1 in) long, 3–8 mm (0.1–0.3 in) wide,* rounded at the tip, and light green.

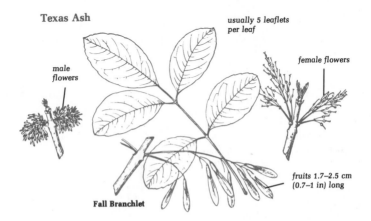

Texas Ash

usually 5 leaflets per leaf

female flowers

male flowers

fruits 1.7–2.5 cm (0.7–1 in) long

Fall Branchlet

Velvet Ash — *Fraxinus velutina* Torr.

Velvet ash is a southwestern tree extending from southwestern Texas to Nevada and southern California. It grows along streams, rivers, and moist washes generally in canyons up to 2,000 m (6.600 ft) elevation. It occurs with cottonwoods and pines, and sometimes forms almost pure stands. The shape and size of the leaflets and the amount of hairiness varies greatly. Flowering is in early spring, with the fruits ripening in September. The fruits are of little value to wildlife. The trees are attractive and are commonly planted for shade.

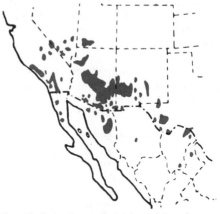

These are trees to 12 m (39 ft), with a rounded, spreading crown. The opposite, deciduous, feather-like (pinnate) leaves are 10–15 cm (4–6 in) long and composed of 3 to 5 leaflets. The **leaflets** are broadest near the base, middle, or tip, **2.5–4 cm (1–1.6 in) long, 2–2.5 cm (0.8–1 in) wide,** pointed at the tip, tapering to rounded at the base, shallowly round toothed above the middle, pale green and smooth above, **densely hairy beneath.** Male and female flowers are produced in separate clusters on different trees. Fruits are dry, flattened, winged, broadest at or above the middle, **1.5–2.2 cm (0.6–0.9 in) long,** 4–6 mm (0.2 in) wide, rounded or notched at the tip.

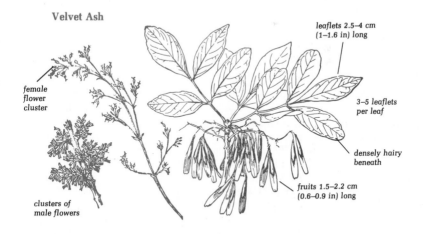

Velvet Ash

female flower cluster

clusters of male flowers

leaflets 2.5–4 cm (1–1.6 in) long

3–5 leaflets per leaf

densely hairy beneath

fruits 1.5–2.2 cm (0.6–0.9 in) long

Berlandier Ash — *Fraxinus berlandierana* A. DC.

This ash is native to southern Texas and adjacent Mexico. It grows along stream banks and in moist canyons. Flowering is in early spring with the fruits maturing in May. This ash is of limited value as timber but is planted as a shade and ornamental tree.

The Berlandier ashes are small trees with a rounded crown and opposite, deciduous, feather-like (pinnate) compound leaves. The leaves consist of *3 to 5 leaflets* which are lance-shaped to broadest near or above the middle, *7.5–10 cm (3–4 in) long*, 1.2–4 cm (0.5–1.6 in) wide, pointed at the tip, entire or with *widely spaced, sharp-pointed teeth,* dark green, shiny, and smooth. Greenish male or female flowers, similar to those of white ash, are produced on separate trees. *Fruits* are dry, flattened, winged, broadest near the tip, *3–4 cm (1.2–1.6 in) long,* 5–8 mm (0.2–0.3 in) wide, and blunt to pointed at the tip.

Berlandier Ash

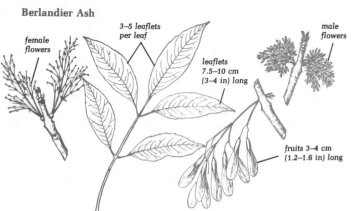

female flowers

3–5 leaflets per leaf

leaflets 7.5–10 cm (3–4 in) long

male flowers

fruits 3–4 cm (1.2–1.6 in) long

Oregon Ash

Fraxinus latifolia Benth.
(synonym: *F. oregona* Nutt.)

Oregon ash is native to the Pacific Coast from western Washington to central California. Here the trees grow in moist rich soils along streams and rivers, and in canyons to 500 m (1,600 ft) elevation. They may be encountered in almost pure stands, but usually grow in association with red alder, broadleaf maple, California laurel, and grand fir. This is the only western species of ash that is commercially valuable as a timber.

This is a fast-growing tree for the first 75 years and then grows slowly, reaching a maximum age of 250 years. Flowering is in spring with the clusters of fruits maturing in early autumn. The seeds are a minor food source to pine grosbeaks, Douglas chickarees, and other birds. The yellowish-brown wood is hard but relatively lightweight and is used to manufacture furniture and interior trim. Oregon ash is sometimes planted as a shade tree.

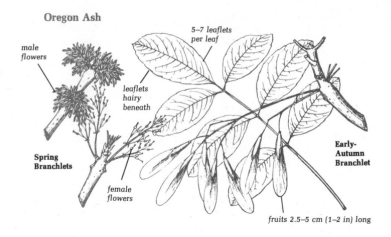

Oregon Ash

male flowers

5–7 leaflets per leaf

leaflets hairy beneath

Spring Branchlets

female flowers

Early-Autumn Branchlet

fruits 2.5–5 cm (1–2 in) long

Appearance: medium-size to tall trees to 25 m (82 ft), with a narrow to broad, spreading crown; trunk straight, tall, to 1.2 m (4 ft) in diameter. **Bark:** 2–4 cm (0.8–1.6 in) thick, developing deep fissures and broad flat ridges, reddish-brown to dark gray. **Branches:** stout, usually upright; branchlets stout, densely hairy the first year, turning reddish-brown to gray with age, marked by large, crescent-shaped leaf scars. **Winter buds:** 3–8 mm (0.1–0.3 in) long, broadest near the base and pointed at the tip, covered with 4 pairs of overlapping, hairy scales. **Leaves:** opposite, deciduous, feather-like (pinnate) compound, *12–35 cm (4.7–13.8 in) long, composed of 5 to 7, rarely 3, leaflets,* the leaflets broadest near the base or middle, *4–10 cm (1.6–4 in) long, 2–4 cm (0.8–1.6 in) wide,* with a short, broad point at the tip, tapering at the base, *entire to remotely and shallowly toothed along the margin,* light green above, *paler and hairy beneath;* leafstalks long, stout. **Flowers:** male and female flowers are produced in separate clusters; male flowers with a minute calyx, no petals, and 2 stamens; female flowers with a tiny but deeply lobed calyx, no stamens, and a long, narrow pistil. **Fruits:** produced in dense clusters; each dry, flattened, winged, uniformly wide to broadest above the middle, *2.5–5 cm (1–2 in) long,* 5–9 mm (0.2–0.4 in) wide, rounded and sometimes notched at the tip.

Chihuahua Ash

Fraxinus papillosa Lingel.

This Mexican species of ash extends into North America in southeastern Arizona, southwestern New Mexico, and the Trans-Pecos region of Texas. Chihuahua ash differs from other ashes in its small broad, stalkless leaflets.

This is a shrub or small tree with opposite, feather-like (pinnate) compound *leaves 8–15 cm (3.2–6 in) long.* The *leaves* are *composed of 7 to 9 leaflets,* the leaflets broadest near the middle, 3–6 cm (1.2–2.4 in) long, 1–2.5 cm (0.4–1 in) wide, dark

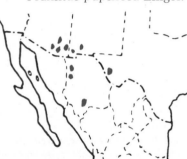

green and smooth above, paler, **slightly bumpy** and sometimes hairy **beneath.** Flowers are similar to those of white ash only smaller. Fruits are dry, flattened, winged, usually broadest above the middle, **2.5–3.8 cm (1–1.5 in) long,** 3–8 mm (0.1–0.3 in) wide, and rounded at the tip.

Gregg Ash   *Fraxinus greggii* A. Gray

Gregg ash is found in the U.S. only in the Trans-Pecos region of southwestern Texas and northern Mexico. It grows in dry rocky soils on hillsides and in canyons, but the best growth occurs along stream or river beds. Flowering is in March or April with the

fruits maturing 8 to 12 weeks later. The leaves are eaten by deer, rabbits, ground squirrels, and small rodents. Birds feed on the seeds. The brown wood is hard and heavy, and is used for fuel.

This is a shrub or small tree to 8 m (26 ft), with dark gray to almost black bark. The opposite, deciduous leaves are feather-like (pinnate) compound, 2–6 cm (0.8–2.4 in) long, **composed of usually 3,** sometimes 5 to 7 **leaflets,** the leaflets broadest near the tip to the middle, **0.8–2.5 cm (0.4–1 in) long, 3–7 mm (0.1–0.3 in) wide,** pointed or rounded at the tip, entire or sparingly round-toothed along the margin, leathery, dark green and usually smooth. Bisexual and male or female flowers are produced in short, branched clusters to 2.5 cm (1 in) long; each flower with a cup-shaped, 4-lobed calyx, petals absent, 1 or 2 stamens, and a single pistil. **Fruits** are dry, winged, broadest near or above the middle, **1.5–2 cm (0.6–0.8 in) long,** 3–8 mm (0.1–0.3 in) wide, rounded at the tip, and pale green.

Gregg Ash

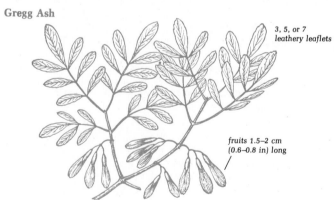

3, 5, or 7
leathery leaflets

fruits 1.5–2 cm
(0.6–0.8 in) long

Goodding Ash   *Fraxinus gooddingii* Little

Goodding ash is restricted to the southern border of Arizona and adjacent northeastern Sonora, Mexico. It grows in dry, rocky soils of desert grassland or scrub vegetation. **It**

is similar to Gregg ash, but this species typically has 5 to 9 leaflets rather than 3, and they are wider.

These are shrubs or small trees with opposite, evergreen or nearly so, feather-like (pinnate) compound leaves which are 4–8 cm (1.6–3.2 in) long; the leaflets are broadest near the middle, 1–2.5 cm (0.4–1 in) long, leathery, dark green. Flowers are produced in short, few-flowered, branched clusters, generally less than 3 cm (1.2 in) long. Fruits are dry, flattened, winged, broadest near or above the middle, 1.2–2 cm (0.5–0.8 in) long, rounded at the tip.

The Foxglove Family · Scrophulariaceae

This is a large family of about 220 genera and 3,000 species widespread throughout the world, but with the greatest number of species in temperate North America, Europe, and Asia. Most members are herbs. No native trees of North America belong to this family. One member introduced to North America, the Chinese royal paulownia, is an attractive tree that is widely cultivated.

Members of this family are herbs, vines, shrubs, or rarely trees with simple, alternate or opposite, entire or lobed leaves. Flowers are bisexual and usually asymmetrical, with a 5-lobed calyx, 5 fused petals, 4 stamens, and a single pistil. Fruits are dry capsules which split open at maturity.

The Paulownia Genus · *Paulownia* Sieb. & Zucc.

There are perhaps 12 to 14 species of paulownias native to Asia, but primarily China. This genus of deciduous trees has also been placed in the bignonia family (Bignoniaceae) which is very closely related to the foxglove family. Paulownias have characteristics that are intermediate between the two. Only the royal paulownia is commonly encountered in North America.

Royal Paulownia · *Paulownia tomentosa* (Thumb.) Sieb. & Zucc.

Royal paulownia is native to China, but has been in cultivation in Japan and Europe for several hundred years. It was introduced to North America in 1834 as an ornamental tree for its large upright clusters of purple flowers. This species is often encountered in the southern states near homes, parks, or vacant lots where it has reproduced on its own. It is hardy as far north as Boston.

The trees are fast growing, to 15 m (49 ft), with a round crown, spreading branches, and rough, dark-brown bark. Leaves are simple, opposite, deciduous, broadest near the base, ***14–30 cm (5.5–11.8 in) long, 8–20 cm (3.2–7.9 in) wide, long-pointed at the tip, heart-shaped at the base,*** entire or shallowly 3-lobed, hairy above and densely so beneath. The ***flowers*** are produced ***in branched, pyramid-shaped clusters to 35 cm (13.8 in) long;*** each flower 4–6 cm (1.6–2.4 in) long and with a funnel to bell-shaped, purple corolla (the fused petals). ***Fruits are leathery capsules 4–8 cm (1.6–3.2 in) long,*** egg-shaped, densely glandular hairy, brown, splitting open at maturity to release the winged seeds.

The Bignonia Family

This is a moderate-size family of about 120 genera and 650 species. Members are mainly tropical, but some genera extend into temperate regions of North America and Asia. There are 4 genera that contain trees in North America. Although this family is of limited economic importance, some members yield useful timber, and many are planted for their showy, spectacular flowers.

Members of this family are trees, shrubs, or vines, rarely herbs, with usually opposite, compound or occasionally simple, evergreen to deciduous leaves. The often showy bisexual flowers are produced in branched clusters or singly. Each flower has a 5-lobed calyx, 5 petals fused to form a bell or funnel-shaped corolla, 4 stamens, and a single pistil.

Key to Bignonia Genera

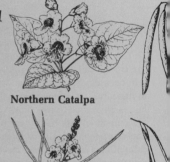

A. Leaves deciduous, usually with a papery texture; fruits long, narrow, cylinder-shaped.

    1. Leaves opposite, very broad, wider near the base, 8–18 cm (3.2–7.1 in) wide; flowers with 2 fertile stamens   **Catalpa, p. 878**

Northern Catalpa

    2. Leaves alternate, narrow, linear to lance-shaped, 2–5 mm (0.1–0.2 in) wide; flowers with 4 fertile stamens   **Desert willow, p. 881**

B. Leaves persistent, leathery; fruits rounded or nearly so.

    1. Leaves usually clustered on short side shoots, 5–15 cm (2–6 in) long, 2–5 cm (0.8–2 in) wide   **Calabash, p. 882**

Desert Willow

    2. Leaves alternate, not clustered on short side shoots, 12–20 cm (4.7–7.9 in) long, 3.5–10 cm (1.4–4 in) wide   **Black calabash, p. 883**

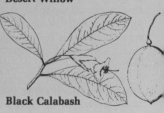

Black Calabash

The Catalpa Genus

This small genus of 12 species of attractive trees is native to North America, the West Indies, and Asia. Two species are native to North America, the northern catalpa in the midwestern states and the southern catalpa in the southeastern U.S. The trees are often planted along streets and in yards for shade, but especially for their large showy clusters of flowers. The West Indian species are the only evergreen members of this genus.

Members are shrubs or trees with opposite, simple leaves which are entire to shallowly lobed. The bisexual flowers are produced in branched, elongated clusters; each flower with a calyx splitting irregularly or 2-lipped, 5 petals fused with 3 larger lobes below and 2 larger ones above, 2 fertile stamens, and a single pistil. Fruits are long, narrow, cylinder-shaped capsules splitting open to release the papery-winged seeds.

Key to Catalpa Species

A. Flower clusters with many flowers, each flower 3–5 cm (1.2–2 in) across; leaves short-pointed at the tip; trees largely of eastern U.S.
Southern catalpa, p. 879
B. Flower clusters with few flowers, each flower 6–7 cm (2.4–2.8 in) across; leaves long-pointed at the tip; trees largely of eastern U.S.
Northern catalpa, p. 880

Southern Catalpa

Southern Catalpa   *Catalpa bignonioides* Walt.

This handsome tree can be seen from southern New England throughout the southeastern states to Texas. Its native range from western Florida to Louisiana has been obscured by its widespread planting and naturalization in the eastern U.S. It grows in the rich, moist soils found along stream and river banks and, in its native range, occurs with southern magnolia, live oak, and slash and longleaf pines.

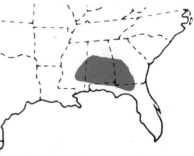

Southern catalpa is a fast-growing tree that begins to produce flowers at 6 to 8 years old. The showy white flowers appear from May to July with the fruits ripening by autumn. The fruits are of little value to wildlife. The light-brown wood is coarse-grained and weak, and is used for posts, inexpensive interior trim, and furniture.

Appearance: tree to 15 m (49 ft), rarely taller, with a broad spreading, rounded crown; trunk straight, soon branching, growing eventually to 1 m (3.3 ft) in diameter. **Bark:** 3–9 cm (1.2–3.5 in) thick, smooth when young, separating into large, irregular scales, light brown to reddish-brown. **Branches:** stout, often spreading, brittle; branchlets stout, green to purplish and hairy when young, becoming light orange or brown and smooth with age. **Winter buds:** end bud absent, side buds 2–5 mm (0.1–0.2 in) long, rounded, covered by overlapping, reddish-brown scales. **Leaves:** *opposite*, simple, deciduous, *very broad, widest near the base, 10–26 cm (4–10.2 in) long, 8–16 cm (3.2–6.3 in) wide,* short pointed to rounded at the tip, *rounded to heart-shaped at the base,* entire or shallowly 3-lobed, papery, light green and smooth above, paler and often hairy beneath; leafstalks stout, 10–15 cm (4–6 in) long. **Flowers:** produced in *branched, pyramid-shaped, many-flowered clusters* at the ends of the branchlets; each flower with an irregularly lobed calyx 7–12 mm (0.3–0.5 in) long, 4 or 5 petals fused to form a bell shape, 4–5 cm (1.6–2 in) long, white, the upper lobes with yellow spots, the lower one with purple spots, with 2 fertile stamens, and a single pistil.

Southern Catalpa

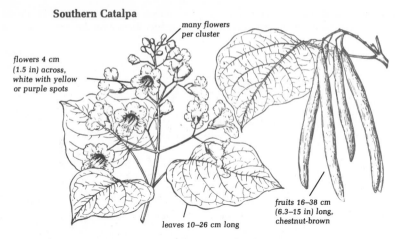

*many flowers
per cluster*

*flowers 4 cm
(1.5 in) across,
white with yellow
or purple spots*

*fruits 16–38 cm
(6.3–15 in) long,
chestnut-brown*

leaves 10–26 cm long

Fruits: produced in clusters, each a long, narrow pod 16–38 cm (6.3–15 in) long, chestnut brown, splitting open to release the flattened seeds, the seeds with a tuft of white hairs at the ends.

Northern Catalpa   *Catalpa speciosa* Warder

This large tree is native from southwestern Indiana and southern Illinois to Tennessee and Arkansas. It has been widely planted, especially in the eastern U.S. where it occasionally escapes and becomes established along roads, fields, or the margins of woodlands. Native trees are found in moist, rich soils along streams and lakes. Northern catalpa often grows in association with white oak, white ash, American and slippery elms, basswood, and mockernut hickory.

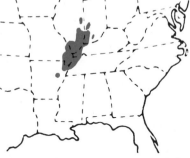

These are fast-growing trees that begin to produce flowers and fruits when about 15 years old, with large crops of pods produced every 2 or 3 years. Showy flowers are produced in early summer with the fruits maturing in autumn. The wood is weak which often results in branches breaking or splitting during storms. The light-brown wood is soft and coarse-grained, and is used for fence posts, telephone poles, and inexpensive furniture. Northern catalpa is often planted as an ornamental tree.

Appearance: medium to large trees to 30 m (98 ft), rarely taller, with a narrow to broad rounded crown; trunk straight, tall, to 1 m (3.3 ft) in diameter, rarely larger. **Bark:** 1.6–2.6 cm (0.7–1.1 in) thick, developing irregular shallow fissures and thick scales, reddish-brown. **Branches:** stout, upright to spreading; branchlets slender, light green and hairy when young, becoming orange to reddish-brown with age. **Winter buds:** end bud lacking, side buds 2–5 mm (0.1–0.2 in) long, rounded, covered with about 6 reddish-brown overlapping scales. **Leaves:** *opposite,* simple, deciduous, *very broad, widest near the base, 10–30 cm (4–11.8 in) long, 8–18 cm (3.2–7.1 in) wide,* long pointed at the tip, *rounded to heart-shaped at the base,* entire, occasionally with 1 to 3 irregular teeth along the margin, heavy papery to almost leathery, dark green and smooth above, paler and softly hairy beneath; leafstalks stout 10–16 cm (4–6.3 in) long. **Flowers:** produced in ***open, few-flowered, branched clusters*** at the ends of the branchlets; each flower with a greenish-purple, irregularly lobed calyx 6–12 mm (0.2–0.5 in) long, 5 white petals, fused to form a bell-shape, with yellow spots on the inner surface, the lower lobe with purple spots, with 2 fertile stamens, and a single pistil. **Fruits:** narrow, cylinder-shaped pods 25–60 cm (9.8–23.6 in) long, to 2 cm (0.8 in) in diameter, dark brown, splitting into 2 halves at maturity to release the flattened, winged light-brown seeds.

Northern Catalpa

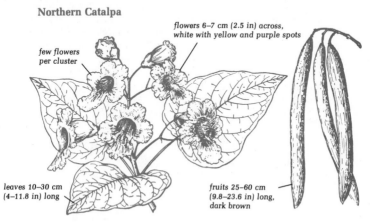

flowers 6–7 cm (2.5 in) across, white with yellow and purple spots

few flowers per cluster

leaves 10–30 cm (4–11.8 in) long

fruits 25–60 cm (9.8–23.6 in) long, dark brown

The Desert Willow Genus

Chilopsis D. Don

This genus contains only 1 species, the desert willow, of the southwestern U.S. and adjacent Mexico. The description of the genus is the same as for the species.

Desert Willow

Chilopsis linearis (Cav.) Sweet

Desert willow ranges from central and southern Texas to southeastern California and Mexico. It is usually found in desert washes and desert grasslands from 400–1,600 m (1,300–5,300 ft) elevation growing in gravelly or rocky soils. This species is most com-

mon and reaches its largest size along streams and low places. It grows in association with creosote bush, joshua tree, and paloverdes.

The showy fragrant flowers can be seen from April through August, with the long thin fruits maturing by September or October and remaining on the tree during the winter. The dark-brown wood is soft and weak, and is used locally for posts or as fuel. Desert willow is widely planted in the Southwest for its delicate willowy leaves and attractive flowers.

Appearance: shrub or small tree to 10 m (33 ft), with a narrow crown; trunk short, often twisted, to 25 cm (9.8 in) in diameter, rarely larger. **Bark:** 3–8 mm (0.1–0.3 in) thick, splitting into broad scaly ridges, dark brown. **Branches:** slender, upright; branchlets slender, light reddish-brown and smooth to hairy, becoming darker with age. **Winter buds:** tiny, 2–4 mm (0.1–0.2 in) long, flattened, hairy, covered with overlapping scales. **Leaves:** *alternate,* simple, deciduous, *linear to narrowly lance-shaped, 8–16 cm (3.2–6.3 in) long, 2–5 mm (0.1–0.2 in) wide, somewhat curved,* long pointed at the tip, tapering at the base, entire, light green and smooth; leafstalks very short. **Flowers:** stalked, produced along an unbranched, many-flowered, hairy, elongate cluster (raceme) to 6 cm (2.4 in) long; each flower with a cup-shaped calyx splitting into 2 broad lobes, 5 *pink, white, or purple petals fused to a funnel shape,* 2.5–3.5 cm (1–1.4 in) long, with 2 upper lobes and 3 lower ones, the lobes spreading, yellow or purple lines on the inner surface, *with 2 pairs of stamens,* and a single pistil. **Fruits:** long, narrow, cylinder-shaped capsules 10–30 cm (4–11.8 in) long, brown at maturity, splitting open along 2 valves at maturity to release the flattened, narrow seeds, each winged, with long hairs at the ends.

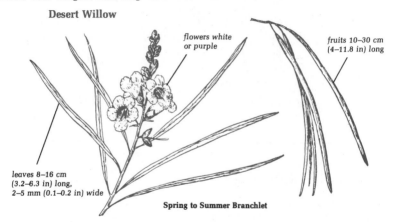

Desert Willow

flowers white or purple

fruits 10–30 cm (4–11.8 in) long

leaves 8–16 cm (3.2–6.3 in) long, 2–5 mm (0.1–0.2 in) wide

Spring to Summer Branchlet

The Calabash Tree Genus   *Crescentia* L.

This is a small tropical American genus of about 6 species that are centered in the West Indies but also occur in Central and South America. One species occurs in southern Florida, either native or introduced long ago by Indians.

Members of this genus are trees or shrubs with simple, alternate, entire, evergreen leaves. The large bisexual flowers are produced singly or in few-flowered clusters along the older branchlets. Fruits are large, rounded to football-shaped, with a hard shell enclosing a thick spongy pulp and many flattened seeds.

Common Calabash Tree   *Crescentia cujete* L.

Common calabash tree occurs in the Florida Keys, the West Indies, southern Mexico, and Central and South America. This tree had been widely planted throughout Latin America and Florida. The large hard shells of the fruits have been used for bowls, cups, water containers, and musical instruments. The trees may produce flowers and fruits any month of the year.

These are small trees to 10 m (33 ft), with spreading, long branches forming an open, irregular crown. The alternate, simple, ***evergreen leaves are often clustered on short side branches,*** lance-shaped to broadest near the tip, ***5–15 cm (2–6 in) long, 2–5 cm (0.8–2 in) wide,*** rounded at the tip, entire, bright green, and smooth. Flowers are 1.2–2 cm (0.5–0.8 in) long, with a cup-shaped calyx 2–3 cm (0.8–1.2 in) long, 5 petals, fused in a funnel shape, 5–6.5 cm (2–2.6 in) long, light green and purple streaked, with 5 wavy lobes, 3–4 cm (1.2–1.6 in) across, 4 stamens, and a single pistil. ***Fruits are rounded or nearly so, 15–30 cm (6–11.8 in) in diameter, with a hard shell,*** enclosing a whitish pulp and thin, flattened, dark-brown seeds.

The Black Calabash Genus

Amphitecna Miers

(synonym: *Enallagma* Baill.)

This is a small genus of 3 or 4 species of trees, all native to tropical regions of the Americas. One species, the black calabash, is native to southern Florida.

Members are shrubs or trees with alternate, simple, entire, evergreen leaves. Large bisexual flowers are produced singly or in few-flowered clusters. Each flower has an unevenly lobed calyx, 5 fused petals to form a tubular flower, 4 stamens, and 1 pistil.

Black Calabash

Amphitecna latifolia (Mill.) A.H. Gentry

[synonym: *Enallagma latifolia* (Mill.) Small]

This small tropical American tree grows in hammocks from northern South America to Central America, the West Indies, and extreme southeastern Florida. The purplish-white flowers are produced in spring, with the fruits maturing by late summer or fall.

The trees are sometimes cultivated for their interesting fruits.

Black calabash are trees to 6 m (20 ft), with long slender, spreading and often drooping branches. The ***alternate,*** evergreen, simple ***leaves*** are usually broadest above the middle, ***12–20 cm (4.7–7.9 in) long, 3.5–10 cm (1.4–4 in) wide,*** pointed, rarely rounded at the tip, tapering to a narrow base, entire, ***leathery,*** dark green and shiny above. The flowers are solitary on long stalks 3.5–5 cm (1.4–2 in) long, each flower with a small green calyx, the thick, leathery petals fused into a tube 4–5 cm (1.6–2 in) long, ***dull purplish-white, bad smelling. Fruits*** are ***egg-shaped, 7–12 cm (2.8–4.7 in) long, 4–8 cm (1.6–3.2 in) wide,*** dark green, at maturity with a thin hard shell enclosing a pulp mass and many small, flattened seeds.

(See drawing on next page.)

Black Calabash

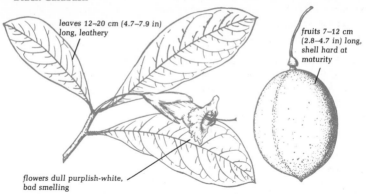

leaves 12–20 cm (4.7–7.9 in) long, leathery

fruits 7–12 cm (2.8–4.7 in) long, shell hard at maturity

flowers dull purplish-white, bad smelling

The Madder Family   Rubiaceae

This is one of the larger families of flowering plants, with approximately 500 genera and 7,000 species. Members are primarily tropical but many also occur in temperate and cold regions. Most North American species are herbs, but 7 genera contain species that are trees. The Madder family is economically important because of the food, drug, and ornamental products obtained from it. Coffee and gardenias are among them.

Members of this family are usually herbs, occasionally shrubs or trees, with opposite or whorled, simple, entire leaves, with stipules present. Bisexual flowers are produced in branched clusters or dense heads, usually with 4 or 5 calyx lobes and fused petals, 4 or 5 stamens, and a single pistil. Fruits are capsules, berries or berry-like, fleshy to dry.

Key to Madder Genera

Button Bush

A. Flowers and fruits produced in dense, rounded heads   **Button bush, p. 885**

B. Flowers and fruits produced singly or in branched clusters.

    1. Fruits dry capsules, splitting into 2 sections at maturity.

        a. Flowers white, 3–4 cm (1.2–1.6 in) long, the lobes linear; capsules longer than wide, 8–12 mm (0.3–0.5 in) long
            Caribbean princewood, p. 886

        b. Flowers yellowish-green, 1.4–2.6 cm (0.6–1.1 in) long, the lobes broadest near the base; 1 or 2 calyx lobes greatly enlarged and petal-like, pink to cream **Pinckneya, p. 887**

Caribbean Princewood

Pinckneya

2. Fruits fleshy, berries or berry-like.

    a. Flowers white to yellowish-white.

        (1) Fruits large, 6–10 cm (2.4–4 in) long; flowers in dense, short, branched clusters   **Genipa, p. 888**

        (2) Fruits small, 4–10 mm (0.2–0.4 in) long; flowers in stalked, open, branched clusters.

            (a) Leaves hairy beneath; flowers with a 4-lobed calyx and 4 fused petals   **Velvetseed, p. 889**

            (b) Leaves usually smooth beneath; flowers normally with a 5-, sometimes 4-lobed, calyx and 5, rarely 4, fused petals   **Balsamo, p. 891**

    b. Flowers orange-red to scarlet   **Hamelia, p. 891**

Everglades Velvetseed

The Button Bush Genus   *Cephalanthus* L.

This small genus of 7 or 8 species is widespread in the Americas, Asia, and Africa. One species, the button bush, is a common shrub or small tree of eastern North America. They are attractive plants, sometimes grown for their heads of white flowers, but otherwise are of no economic importance.

These are woody plants with opposite, simple, entire, evergreen to deciduous leaves. The tiny bisexual flowers are produced in dense, rounded, many-flowered heads. Each flower has a 4-lobed calyx and corolla. Fruits develop at maturity into 2 1-seeded nutlets.

Button Bush   *Cephalanthus occidentalis* L.

Button bush ranges in North America from Nova Scotia to Florida, west to Minnesota and through the Southwest to California. This is a lowland species commonly growing along streams, rivers, lakes, swamps, and wet floodplains. It grows in association with other lowland trees including cottonwoods, willows, swamp and water tupelos, and overcup, cherrybark, nuttall, live, and willow oaks. Dense pure stands of button bush often develop along lake shores.

This is a fast growing, short-lived species. Flowering is from May to August; the southern button bushes bloom earlier than the northern, which flower by mid to late summer. The fruits mature in autumn. Ducks, especially mallards, feed on the

Button Bush

fruiting heads

leaves 6–18 cm (2.4–7.1 in) long

dense heads of white flowers, 2.5–5 cm (1–2 in) in diameter

seeds. Whitetail deer sometimes browse the leaves and young twigs. The dense thickets serve as excellent cover and nesting sites for many birds and the light-brown wood is light but tough, though of no commercial value.

Appearance: shrub or tree to 15 m (49 ft), with a rounded, spreading crown; trunk straight to crooked, usually branching close to the ground, to 25 cm (9.8 in) in diameter. **Bark:** 3–5 mm (0.1–0.2 in) thick, becoming fissured with broad, flat, scaly ridges, dark grayish-brown to almost black. **Branches:** slender, upright to spreading, crooked; branchlets light green, smooth, turning dark brown with age. **Winter buds:** end buds usually absent, side buds, tiny, almost submerged in the bark. **Leaves:** opposite or whorled, deciduous, lance-shaped, uniformly wide to broadest near the middle, 6–18 cm (2.4–7.1 in) long, 1.4–8 cm (0.6–3.2 in) wide, pointed at the tip, tapering to rounded at the base, entire, papery, dark green and smooth above, paler and slightly hairy beneath; leafstalks stout, 5–15 mm (0.2–0.6 in) long, grooved, smooth. **Flowers:** *produced in dense, rounded, many-flowered heads* 2.5–5 cm (1–2 in) in diameter; each flower with a 4-lobed calyx 1–2 mm (less than 0.1 in) long, *4 white petals fused to form a funnel-shaped corolla* 0.5–1 cm (0.3–0.4 in) long, 4 stamens, and a single pistil. **Fruits:** *produced in dense, rounded heads,* each uniformly wide to narrowly pyramid-shaped, 6–10 mm (0.2–0.4 in) long, splitting in 2 with small, flattened seeds.

The Caribbean Princewood Genus   Exostema (Pers.) Rich.

This is a small genus of about 25 species, all native to tropical America, but most abundant in the West Indies. Only 1 species occurs in North America – that in the Florida Keys.

Members of this genus are shrubs or trees with simple, opposite, entire, evergreen leaves. The bisexual flowers are produced singly or in few-flowered clusters in the junction of the leaves. Each flower has a 5-lobed calyx, and 5 white petals fused to form a narrow tube, spreading at the lobes. Fruits are 2-celled capsules containing many seeds.

Caribbean Princewood   Exostema caribaeum (Jacq.) Roem. & Schult.

Caribbean princewood occurs in hammocks and pine dominated woodlands of the

Florida Keys. It also occurs in the West Indies, Mexico, and Central and South America. This species is commonly found in open sites, clearings, and the margins of woodlands. The large, fragrant white to yellow flowers are produced in spring or summer. The trees are of little value to wildlife and are of no commercial use.

These are shrubs or small trees to 8 m (26 ft), with a narrow crown. The simple, opposite, evergreen leaves are broadest near the base or middle, 4–8 cm (1.6–3.2 in) long, 1.2–3 cm (0.5–1.2 in) wide, short pointed at the tip, tapering to a narrowed base, entire, leathery, dark green above, yellowish-green below. Bisexual flowers are produced singly in the junction of the leaves; each flower has a cup-shaped calyx 1–2 mm (less than 0.1 in) long, *5 petals fused into a narrow tube 3–4 cm (1.2–1.6 in) long,* the lobes spreading, 5 stamens, and a single pistil. *Fruits are capsules 8–12 mm (0.3–0.5 in) long,* dark brown, *splitting into 2 parts at maturity* to release the small flattened seeds.

Caribbean Princewood

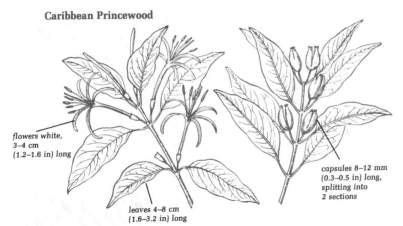

flowers white, 3–4 cm (1.2–1.6 in) long

leaves 4–8 cm (1.6–3.2 in) long

capsules 8–12 mm (0.3–0.5 in) long, splitting into 2 sections

The Pinckneya Genus   Pinckneya Michx.

The genus contains only 1 species restricted to the southeastern U.S. The description of the genus is the same as for the species.

Pinckneya   *Pinckneya pubens* Michx.

Pinckneya is a rare plant of the Coastal Plain from southern South Carolina to northern Florida. It is a lowland tree or shrub growing in sandy soils along streams or in swamps. The attractive flowers are produced in May, and the fruiting capsules mature in late summer.

These are mainly shrubs or small trees to 8 m (26 ft), with opposite, simple, decid-uous leaves broadest near or below the middle, 8–20 cm (3.2–7.9 in) long, 4–10 cm (1.6–4 in) wide, pointed at the tip, tapering to a narrow base, entire, dark green and hairy above, paler and hairy be-neath. Bisexual flowers are produced in open, few-flowered clusters near the ends of the branchlets. Each flower has a **5-lobed, bell-shaped calyx, usually with 1 or 2 lobes enlarging and becoming petal-like, 3.6–8 cm (1.5–3.2 in) long, pink to cream, 5 petals fused into a narrow tube 1.4–2.6 cm (0.6–1.1 in) long, yellowish-green with purple lines,** the small narrow lobes spreading, 5 stamens, and a single pistil. Fruits are **capsules, rounded, 2–3 cm (0.8–1.2 in) long, splitting into 2 parts at maturity** to release the flattened seeds.

Pinckneya

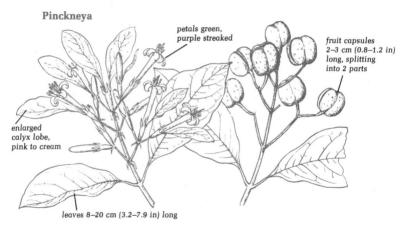

petals green, purple streaked

fruit capsules 2–3 cm (0.8–1.2 in) long, splitting into 2 parts

enlarged calyx lobe, pink to cream

leaves 8–20 cm (3.2–7.9 in) long

The Genipa Genus

Genipa L.

This small genus of 8 to 10 species is restricted to the tropical regions of America, but chiefly to the West Indies. One species, the seven-year apple, is also native to southern and southwestern Florida. Some species produce edible fruits that are some-times used for marmalade. Others are used by Indians in decoration and folk medi-cine.

These are trees or shrubs with simple, opposite, evergreen leaves. Bisexual flowers are clustered in the junction of the leaves. Each flower has a 5- to 6-lobed calyx, 5 white petals fused to form a bell-shaped corolla, 5 or 6 stamens, and a single pistil. Fruits are large fleshy berries containing many flattened seeds.

Seven-Year Apple

Genipa clusiifolia (Jacq.) Griseb.

This evergreen species grows in sandy or rocky soils of coastal hammocks of southern Florida. It is also native to the West Indies. Clusters of white flowers can be found throughout most of the year. Thus, the fruits are usually seen in various stages of maturity. The fruits are eaten by large birds and mammals but are barely palatable to people.

Seven-year apple is a tree or shrub to 4 m (13 ft), with a dense, rounded head. The opposite, simple, evergreen leaves are broadest above the middle, 5–15 cm (2–6 in) long, 2.5–7.5 cm (1–3 in) wide, broadly rounded at the tip, tapering to a narrow base, entire, leathery, shiny green and smooth above. *Flowers occur in dense, short, branched clusters in the junction of the leaves;* each flower with a 5-lobed calyx to 10 mm (0.4 in) long, 5 or 6 petals, white to yellow, fused to form a funnel-shape corolla, 5 or 6 stamens, and a single pistil. *Fruits are large berries,* often broadest near the tip, *6–10 cm (2.4–4 in) long,* thick skinned, containing a pulp and numerous flattened seeds.

The Velvetseed Genus

Guettarda L.

This is a medium-size genus of approximately 80 species of trees and shrubs of tropical and subtropical climates. Two species are native to southern Florida, the only representatives in North America. Members of this genus are of no economic importance and are of limited value to wildlife.

Members are woody plants with opposite or whorled, simple evergreen leaves. Bisexual or both bisexual and male or female flowers occur in short, branched clusters in the junction of the leaves. The petals are fused to form a trumpet-shaped flower. Fruits are large berries with many seeds.

Key to Velvetseed Species

A. Flowers 1.2–2.8 cm (0.5–1.1 in) long; leaves 6–15 cm (2.4–6 in) long, 2.5–5 cm (1–2 in) wide, rough-to-the-touch above; trees of southern Florida **Roughleaf velvetseed, p. 889**

B. Flowers 1 cm (0.4 in) long or less; leaves 2.2–6.4 cm (0.9–2.5 in) long, 1.2–2.8 cm (0.5–1.1 in) wide, hairy to smooth above, not rough; trees of southern Florida **Everglades velvetseed, p. 890**

Everglades Velvetseed

Roughleaf Velvetseed

Guettarda scabra (L.) Vent.

This species occurs in hammocks and pine woodlands in southern Florida. Roughleaf velvetseed also ranges through the West Indies to Central and South America. The small yellowish-white flowers are produced in summer, and the fruits mature in late fall or winter. This can be **distinguished from the everglades velvetseed by its larger broader leaves, which are rough to the touch.**

Roughleaf velvetseed is a shrub or small tree to 10 m (33 ft), with an open, irregular crown. The opposite, simple, evergreen **leaves** are **6–15 cm (2.4–6 in) long, 2.5–5 cm (1–2 in) wide,** rounded to pointed at the tip, tapering at the base, entire, **dark green and rough-to-the-touch** above, paler and densely hairy beneath. Flowers are

produced in slender, long-stalked, few-flowered clusters. Each flower has a small 4-lobed, cup-shaped calyx 2–4 mm (0.1 in) long, **4 petals fused to form a narrow tubular corolla 1.2–2.8 cm (0.5–1.1 in) long,** 4 stamens, and a single pistil. **Fruits** are **berry-like, rounded, 6–10 mm (0.2–0.4 in) in diameter, red,** hairy, with 2 to 4 seeds.

Everglades Velvetseed   *Guettarda elliptica* Sw.

This tropical American species occurs naturally in hammocks and pine dominated woodlands in southern Florida. It also is native to Mexico, the West Indies, and northern South America. Everglades velvetseed is often overlooked because its flowers and fruits are not conspicuous. Flowers are produced in May or June with the fruits maturing by late autumn.

Members are trees or shrubs to 6 m (20 ft), with an open irregular crown. The opposite, simple, evergreen **leaves** are broadest near the middle, **2.2–6.4 cm (0.9–2.5 in) long, 1.2–2.8 cm (0.5–1.1 in) wide,** pointed to rounded at the tip, tapering at the base, entire, **dark green and hairy to smooth above,** paler and hairy beneath. Flowers are produced in long-stalked, few-flowered, slender clusters, often at the base of the current year's branchlets. Each flower has a cup-shaped, 4-lobed calyx, 2–4 mm (0.1 in) long, **4 petals fused to form a**

Everglades Velvetseed

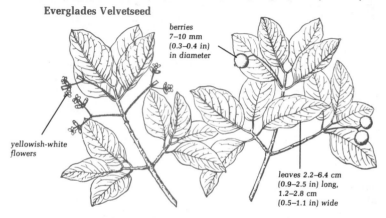

berries
7–10 mm
(0.3–0.4 in)
in diameter

yellowish-white
flowers

leaves 2.2–6.4 cm
(0.9–2.5 in) long,
1.2–2.8 cm
(0.5–1.1 in) wide

tubular corolla to 1 cm (0.4 in) long, yellowish-white, 4 stamens, and a single pistil. *Fruits are berries, rounded, 7–10 mm (0.3–0.4 in) in diameter, dark purple,* hairy, enclosing 2 to 4 seeds.

The Balsamo Genus — *Psychotria* L.

This is a large tropical American genus of about 750 species that are primarily lowland trees, shrubs, or herbs. Four species extend into North America in southern Florida, but only 1 of those, Seminole balsamo, becomes a small tree. The Bahama balsamo (*Psychotria ligustrifolia*) may on rare occasions grow large enough to be considered a tree; however, it is normally a shrub.

Members of this genus are usually woody plants with opposite, simple, evergreen, entire leaves with small leaf-like appendages (stipules) at the base of the leafstalk. Flowers are produced in branched, few to many-flowered clusters in the junction of the leaves or at the ends of the branchlets. Each flower has a 4- or 5-lobed calyx, a funnel-shaped corolla with 4 or 5 lobes, 4 or 5 stamens, and a single pistil. Fruits are berry-like.

Seminole Balsamo — *Psychotria nervosa* Sw.
(synonym: *P. undata* Jacq.)

Seminole balsamo grows along the eastern coast of Florida from St. Johns County south to the Florida Keys. It also is native to the West Indies, Mexico, and Central America. The flat-topped clusters of small white flowers are produced in spring or summer with the red fruits maturing in late summer or fall. The fruits are eaten by many species of birds.

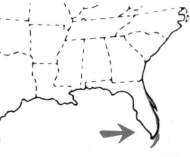

These are shrubs or small trees to 5 m (16 ft), with opposite, entire, evergreen *leaves* which are broadest near the middle to lance-shaped, *6–15 cm (2.4–6 in) long,* pointed at the tip, tapering at the base, entire, *dark green, shiny,* and *smooth.* The bisexual flowers are produced in open, flat-topped clusters. Each flower has a short, 5-lobed calyx; tubular, white corolla with 5 lobes, 5 stamens, and a single pistil. *Fruits are berry-like, red, rounded to slightly longer than wide, 4–7 mm (0.2–0.3 in) long,* with 1 or 2 seeds.

The Hamelia Genus — *Hamelia* Jacq.

This is a small tropical American genus of 16 species of shrubs or small trees. The largest number of species is in the West Indies and Central America. One species, the scarletbush, extends northward into southern Florida.

These are shrubs or trees with simple, opposite or whorled leaves. The flowers are produced in branched clusters. Each flower is bisexual, with a short calyx, a tubular red or yellow corolla with 5 lobes, 5 stamens, and a single pistil. Fruits are rounded to elongate berries.

Scarletbush — *Hamelia patens* Jacq.

Scarletbush is usually a shrub or sometimes a small tree in southern Florida. It is also native to Mexico, the West Indies, and Central and South America. The plants quickly become established in disturbed sites, along roads, in clearings and hammocks. Flowers and fruits can be found throughout the year. The juicy fruits are readily eaten by many birds. The tiny, hard seeds pass through the birds unharmed and are thus dispersed.

These are shrubs, occasionally trees, to 5 m (16 ft), with a rounded crown and slender, often multiple trunks. The simple, opposite or whorled leaves are broadest near the middle, 5–15 cm (2–6 in) long, 2.5–7.5 cm (1–3 in) wide, short pointed at the tip, tapering to a narrow base, entire, dark green and usually red-veined above, smooth to slightly hairy. Flowers are bisexual, *produced in branched clusters, the flowers 1-ranked.* Each flower has a small 5-lobed calyx, petals fused to form a narrow tube, the *tube 1.5–2.2 cm (0.6–0.9 in) long, orange-red to scarlet,* 5-lobed at the tip, 5 stamens, and a single pistil. *Fruits are berries,* rounded to longer than wide, *5–10 mm (0.2–0.4 in) long, dark red turning black, juicy,* containing numerous, tiny seeds.

The Honeysuckle Family   Caprifoliaceae

This family contains 18 genera and approximately 450 species, mainly small trees, shrubs, or vines. They occur throughout the world, both tropical and temperate, but have the greatest concentration of species in eastern North America and eastern Asia. Two North American genera, the elders (*Sambucus*) and the viburnums (*Viburnum*), have 5 species each that reach tree size.

Many of the viburnums are cultivated and grown as ornamentals for their beautiful flowers and attractive fruits. The elders are occasionally cultivated. The fruits are edible and used to make wine, jams, or jellies. Species in both genera are important to wildlife. Whitetail deer, mule deer, and elk browse the leaves and young twigs. Grouse, jays, grosbeaks, and thrushes are among the many birds that eat the fruit. The wood is of no commercial value.

Members of this family are trees, shrubs, vines, and rarely herbs with opposite, simple or compound leaves. Bisexual, often showy, flowers are produced in branched, rounded to flat-topped clusters. Each flower consists of a 4- or 5-lobed calyx, 5 fused petals, 4 or 5 stamens, and a single pistil with an inferior ovary. Fruits are typically berries.

Key to Honeysuckle Genera

A. Leaves feather-like (pinnate) compound, composed of 3–9 leaflets; fruits with 2–5 seeds
Elders, p. 893

B. Leaves simple; fruits containing a single stone and seed; includes nannyberry
Viburnums, p. 897   **Nannyberry**

The Elder Genus

Sambucus L.

The elders are a small genus of about 30 species of shrubs or small trees of the Americas, Europe, and Asia. They are primarily temperate plants with a few species occurring in subtropical climates. Seven species are native to North America; 5 reach tree size; and the remaining 2 are always shrubs. The species are of limited economic importance, but serve as a valuable food source to wildlife.

Members of this genus are woody plants with stout but soft, pithy branches and large, opposite deciduous to almost evergreen, feather-like compound leaves. Small, bisexual, white, yellow, or pinkish flowers are produced in large, spreading, round to flat-topped clusters. Each flower has a 3- to 5-lobed calyx, 3 to 5 petals fused near the base, 5 stamens, and a single pistil. The juicy berry-like stone fruits contain 3 to 5 seeds.

Key to Elder Species

A. Fruits dark blue, purple, or nearly black; flowers in rounded to flat-topped clusters.

American Elder

  1. Leaves with 5–9 leaflets, the leaflets 5–15 cm (2–6 in) long.

    a. Leaves with 5–7 leaflets, the leaflets broadest near the base to uniformly wide, finely and sharply toothed along the margin; shrubs or trees of eastern North America **American elder, p. 894**

    b. Leaves with 5–9 leaflets, the leaflets broadest near the middle to uniformly wide, coarsely toothed; trees of western North America **Blue elder, p. 895**

Blue Elder

  2. Leaves with 3–5 leaflets, the leaflets 1.5–6 cm (0.6–2.4 in) long.

    a. Leaflets smooth or nearly so; fruits almost black, lacking a conspicuous bloom; trees of southwestern U.S. **Mexican elder, p. 896**

    b. Leaflets hairy, especially beneath; fruits black to dark blue with a heavy, waxy coating; trees of Sierra Nevada, California **Velvet elder, p. 896**

B. Fruits bright red to scarlet; flowers in elongated clusters; trees of coastal region of Pacific Northwest **Pacific red elder, p. 897**

Mexican Elder

American Elder

Sambucus canadensis L.

This common elder occurs throughout eastern North America from Nova Scotia to Florida, west to Texas and Minnesota. Typically, it is found in rich moist soils along streams and rivers, margins of woodlands, fence rows, and railroad right-of-ways.

Like other elders, American elder is more abundant in disturbed sites than in forests. The Florida elder is no longer recognized as a distinct species, but is now classified as a variety (*Sambucus canadensis* variety *laciniata*) of American elder.

These fast growing, short-lived trees or shrubs occasionally form thickets due to the production of new shoots from the root system. Flowering varies from spring to summer depending upon location. The fruits ripen in mid to late summer and are used to make jelly, jam, pies, and alcoholic and other beverages. Quail, pheasant, and grouse are among the more than 45 species of birds that feed on the fruits, which are a food source as well to whitetail deer, squirrels, and other rodents.

American Elder

flowers white

leaves with 5–7 leaflets, sharply toothed

fruits dark purple, 4–6 mm (0.2 in) in diameter

Appearance: shrub or in the southern part of its range a small tree to 6 m (20 ft), with a round crown; trunk short, to 25 cm (9.8 in) in diameter. **Bark:** 2–5 mm (0.1–0.2 in) thick, becoming roughened and furrowed with age, yellowish-brown to brown. **Branches:** stout, upright to slightly spreading; branchlets stout, rigid, smooth, light brown to grayish-brown, marked with conspicuous shield-shaped leaf scars. **Winter buds:** small, 1.5–3 mm (0.1 in) long, broadest near the base and pointed at the tip, covered with overlapping, reddish-brown scales. **Leaves:** opposite, deciduous, feather-like (pinnate) compound, 15–25 cm (6–9.8 in) long, ***composed of 5 to 7 leaflets, the leaflets broadest near the base to uniformly wide,*** 6–12 cm (2.4–4.7 in) long, 2–4 cm (0.8–1.6 in) wide, long-pointed at the tip, rounded at the slightly unequal base, ***sharply toothed along the margin,*** dark green shiny, and smooth above, paler and smooth to slightly hairy beneath; leafstalks stout, 5–8 cm (2–3.2 in) long; leafletstalks 3–6 mm (0.1–0.2 in) long. **Flowers:** produced in large, branched, round or flat-topped, many-flowered clusters to 18 cm (7.1 in) across; each flower bisexual, with a tiny 5-lobed calyx, 5 white petals, 5 stamens, and a single pistil. **Fruits:** produced in large clusters, each berry-like, rounded, 4–6 mm (0.2 in) in diameter, deep purple, juicy, containing 3 to 4 yellow seeds.

Blue Elder

Sambucus cerulea Raf.
(synonym: *S. glauca* Nutt.)

Blue elder is a handsome tree, occurring from western Montana to southern British Columbia, south to southern California, New Mexico, Trans-Pecos Texas, and Mexico. Often a spreading shrub, it grows best along banks and washes of streams, fencerows, edges of fields, and in rocky pastures. It is basically not a forest tree.

Blue elder is a fast-growing, short-lived tree. Flowering is in late spring to early summer with the fruits maturing in late summer or autumn. It is extremely important to wildlife because of its widespread occurrence. Songbirds such as the black-headed grosbeak, steller jay, crested mynah, brown thrasher, and russet-backed thrush eat the fruits. Rabbits, squirrels, and other small mammals eat the fruit and bark. The twigs and foliage are browsed by blacktail deer, mule deer, and elk. The fruit is often used for pies, jelly, and wine. Indians called this tree "the tree of music" and used the pithy stems to make flutes. The wood is soft, weak, coarsely grained, dark yellowish-brown, and of no economic value.

Blue Elder

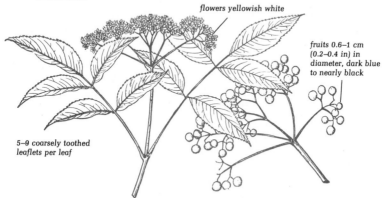

flowers yellowish white

fruits 0.6–1 cm (0.2–0.4 in) in diameter, dark blue to nearly black

5–9 coarsely toothed leaflets per leaf

Appearance: shrub or small tree to 15 m (49 ft), with a broad, rounded crown; trunk straight, to 40 cm (15.8 in) in diameter. **Bark:** 2–4 mm (0.1 in) thick, irregularly ridged and furrowed, sometimes scaly, dark brown to reddish-brown. **Branches:** stout, spreading; branchlets stout, green, and hairy when young, becoming light brown and smooth with age, with large, triangular leaf scars and a thick white pith. **Winter buds:** often in pairs or even clustered, the largest one 10–20 mm (0.4–0.8 in) long, broadest at the base, tapering at the point, covered with 4 to 6 chestnut-brown, overlapping scales. **Leaves:** opposite, deciduous, feather-like (pinnate) compound, 12–18 cm (4.7–7.1 in) long, *composed of 5 to 9 leaflets, the leaflets broadest at the middle to uniformly wide,* the lower leaflets sometimes 3-parted, 5–15 cm (2–6 in) long, 1.2–5 cm (0.5–2 in) wide, long-pointed at the tip, rounded to tapering at the base, *coarsely toothed,* hairy when young, becoming smooth, bright green above, paler below; leaf-stalk stout, 3–5 cm (1.2–2 in) long, leafletstalks slender, 6–12 mm (0.2–0.5 in) long. **Flowers:** produced in broad, spreading, many-flowered, flat-topped clusters; each flower with a 3- to 5-parted calyx, 4 to 6 yellowish-white petals, 4 to 6 stamens, and a single pistil. **Fruits:** berry-like stone fruit, rounded, *6–10 mm (0.2–0.4 in) in diameter, dark blue to nearly black,* covered with a wax-like coating, juicy, with 3 to 5 seeds.

Mexican Elder · *Sambucus mexicana* Presl

This elder is widespread in Mexico and extends into North America in New Mexico, Arizona, California, and Nevada. It is a low-elevation species growing to 1,200 m (3,900 ft). Typical habitat includes ditches, stream and river banks, seepage areas, and low wet spots in the desert grasslands. The fruits are an important food to many birds. Mule deer eat leaves and young twigs. The velvet elder is closely related to this species and is considered by some authorities to be the same species.

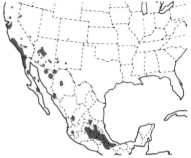

Mexican elder is a shrub or small tree to 10 m (33 ft), with opposite, deciduous to almost evergreen, feather-like (pinnate) compound leaves. The *leaves consist of 3 to 5 leaflets, the leaflets* nearly round to broadest near the base, *1.5–6 cm (0.6–2.4 in) long,* finely toothed. Bisexual white flowers are produced in wide spreading, branched, many-flowered, flat-topped clusters to 20 cm (7.9 in) across. Berry-like stone fruits are rounded, *5–7 mm (0.2–0.3 in) in diameter, almost black,* juicy, without a waxy coating, containing 1 to 3 seeds.

Mexican Elder

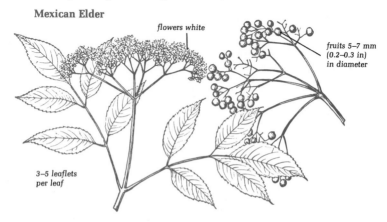

flowers white

fruits 5–7 mm (0.2–0.3 in) in diameter

3–5 leaflets per leaf

Velvet Elder · *Sambucus velutina* Dur. & Hilg.

This elder is native to the Sierra Nevada of California and extreme western Nevada. It grows in moist sites along streams and rivers and in canyons, often from 600–2.500 m (2,000–8,200 ft) elevation. The fast-growing plants flower in spring or early summer and usually produce abundant fruit by fall. These are eaten by quail, grouse, and many songbirds. Mule deer browse the leaves and young twigs.

Velvet elder is commonly a shrub or small tree to 10 m (33 ft), with a broad, rounded crown. The opposite, deciduous leaves are feather-like (pinnate) compound, generally with 3 to 5 leaflets; the *leaflets* are broadest near the base or middle, *1.6–5.5 cm (0.7–2.2 in) long, hairy*, finely toothed. Bisexual, white flowers are produced in spreading, branched, flat-topped clusters to 24 cm (9.5 in) across. *Fruits are berries*, rounded, *4–6 mm (0.2 in) in diameter, black to dark blue*, covered with a heavy, waxy covering.

Pacific Red Elder *Sambucus callicarpa* Greene

Pacific red elder is a coastal species extending from Alaska to British Columbia, Washington, Oregon, and northern California. It occurs at lower elevations and is commonly found growing in coastal scrub forest or with redwoods, Douglas fir, and spruce. Flowering extends from March to July with the fruits maturing in late summer or early fall. The fruits are an important food to birds. This elder is considered by some to be a variety of the European elder and is referred to as *Sambucus racemosa* variety *arborescens*.

This is a large shrub or small tree to 6 m (20 ft), with opposite, deciduous, feather-like (pinnate) compound leaves. The *leaves consist of 5 to 7 leaflets,* the *leaflets lance-shaped*, 6–16 cm (2.4–6.3 in) long, long pointed at the tips, sharply toothed along the margins, with stiff hairs, especially along the veins. Bisexual *white flowers* are produced in *branched, many-flowered, elongated clusters* to 10 cm (4 in) across. The *berry-like stone fruits* are rounded, 4–6 mm (0.2 in) in diameter, *bright red to scarlet.*

The Viburnum Genus Viburnum L.

This is a large genus of approximately 150 species of trees and shrubs widespread in temperate and subtropical regions of the world. Of the 15 species native to North America, 5 become small trees. One species, the American cranberry bush (*Viburnum trilobum*), is a shrub that rarely becomes a small tree so it is omitted in this book. Many species are cultivated for their attractive, showy clusters of flowers.

Members of this genus are small trees or shrubs with opposite, simple, entire, toothed or lobed, deciduous or evergreen leaves. Bisexual flowers are produced in large, branched, spreading, usually round to flat-topped clusters. Each flower has a 5-lobed calyx, 5 small petals, 5 stamens, and a single pistil. Berry-like fruits enclose a single-seeded stone.

Key to Viburnum Species

A. Leaves entire, wavy, or with a few blunt teeth along the margin.

    1. Clusters of flowers on a long stalk; leaves 10–15 cm (4–6 in) long, deciduous; trees of southeastern Coastal Plain   **Possumhaw, p. 898**

    2. Clusters of flowers on a very short stalk; leaves 2–6 cm (0.8–2.4 in) long, evergreen; trees of coastal swamps in extreme southeastern U. S.   **Walter viburnum, p. 899**

B. Leaves finely to coarsely toothed along the margin.

    1. Leafstalks and lower leaf surfaces covered with dense rusty hairs; trees of southeastern U.S.   **Rusty blackhaw, p. 899**

    2. Leafstalks and lower leaf surfaces smooth to sparsely hairy.

        a. Leaves short to long-pointed at the tip, with tiny dark glands on the lower surface; trees of midwestern and northeastern U.S. and Canada   **Nannyberry, p. 900**

        b. Leaves blunt or with only some leaves pointed, without tiny glands on the lower surface; trees of midwestern and eastern U.S.   **Blackhaw, p. 901**

Rusty Blackhaw

Nannyberry

Blackhaw

Possumhaw Viburnum

Viburnum nudum L.

Possumhaw viburnum is native to the eastern Coastal Plain where it extends from Connecticut to Florida and west to Texas. It usually grows along swamps or streams or low hillsides. These spring flowering shrubs or small trees often produce abundant fruit in autumn. Ruffed grouse, brown thrasher, cedar waxwing, squirrels, and other rodents eat the fruits.

These are woody plants to 6 m (20 ft), with a spreading, rounded crown. The simple, opposite, deciduous leaves are usually broadest near or above the middle, 10–15 cm (4–6 in) long, 3.8–5 cm (1.5–2 in) wide, *entire or slightly wavy along the margin,* dark green and shiny above. Bisexual white flowers are produced in *spreading, branched, flattened to slightly*

round-topped clusters. The rounded berry-like fruits are pink or red turning deep blue, 6–8 mm (0.2–0.3 in) in diameter, and enclosing a single-seeded stone.

Walter Viburnum — *Viburnum obovatum* Walter

This viburnum is a common small tree in coastal swamps, hammocks, and low wet woods in the Coastal Plain from South Carolina to Florida and extreme southeastern Alabama. It grows in association with hawthorns, hollies, and many other lowland species. Walter viburnum is a fast-growing species that flowers in spring, with bright red to black fruits maturing during the summer. These are eaten by many birds.

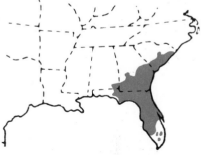

This is a shrub or small tree to 9 m (30 ft), with a broad, spreading crown. The opposite, simple, *evergreen leaves* are broadest above or near the middle, *2–6 cm (0.8–2.4 in) long,* 0.6–3.8 cm (0.3–1.5 in) wide, rounded at the tip, *entire or with a few blunt teeth along the margin,* leathery, dark shiny green above, paler and gland-dotted beneath. Small, bisexual, white *flowers are produced in small, flat-topped clusters* to 6 cm (2.4 in) across. Berry-like fruits are broadest near the middle and longer than wide, 5–8 mm (0.2–0.3 in) long, bright red to black and enclosing a stone and seed.

Rusty Blackhaw — *Viburnum rufidulum* Raf.

Rusty blackhaw is widespread throughout the southeastern U.S. ranging from Virginia to Florida, west to Texas, Oklahoma, and eastern Kansas. It typically occurs along streams, hillsides, roads, woodland margins, and clearings. This viburnum often grows in association with sweet gum, cedar elm, dogwood, several oaks, and loblolly, shortleaf, and Virginia pines.

It is a fast growing, short-lived species that produces clusters of white flowers in the spring. The berry-like fruits mature in autumn. These are sweet and edible, and are eaten by turkey, grouse, quail, many songbirds, squirrels, and other small rodents. Whitetail deer also eat the fruits and browse the twigs and leaves. The reddish-brown wood is hard and heavy, but is of no commercial value because of the small size of the trees.

Appearance: shrub or small tree to 9 m (30 ft), with an open, irregular crown; trunk slender, branching close to the ground, to 40 cm (15.8 in) in diameter. **Bark:** 3–6 mm (0.1–0.2 in) thick, developing shallow furrows and small, blocky plates, gray, reddish-brown to almost black. **Branches:** stout, spreading; branchlets often rigid, light brown and hairy when young, becoming darker and smooth with age. **Winter buds:** flower buds 8–12 mm (0.3–0.5 in) long, leaf buds 4–7 mm (0.2–0.3 in) long, broadest near the base, pointed at the tip, covered with 2 reddish-brown, hairy scales. **Leaves:** opposite, simple, deciduous, usually broadest at or above the middle, *4–8 cm (1.6–3.2 in) long, 3–6 cm (1.2–2.4 in) wide, pointed at the tip,* tapering to rounded at the base, finely toothed along the margin, shiny dark green above, paler and *rusty hairy below,* especially when young; *leafstalks* 5–12 mm (0.2–0.5 in) long, *densely hairy.* **Flowers:** produced in spreading, branched, many-flowered, flat- or round-topped clusters;

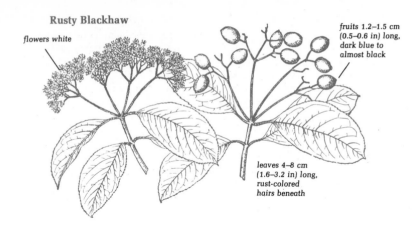

Rusty Blackhaw

flowers white

fruits 1.2–1.5 cm (0.5–0.6 in) long, dark blue to almost black

leaves 4–8 cm (1.6–3.2 in) long, rust-colored hairs beneath

each flower bisexual, with a narrow, 5-lobed calyx, 5 white petals 3–4 mm (0.1–0.2 in) long, 5 stamens, and a single pistil. **Fruits:** produced in dense clusters, each a berry-like stone fruit, broadest near the middle, rounded at the tip, 1.2–1.5 cm (0.5–0.6 in) long, red turning dark blue to black at maturity, enclosing a single-seeded stone.

Nannyberry   *Viburnum lentago* L.

This attractive small tree is native to midwestern and northeastern U.S. and adjacent Canada. It grows on rocky hillsides, along edges of woodlands, stream banks, and swamps from sea level to 800 m (2,600 ft) elevation. Nannyberries usually grow in association with sweet gum, river birch, basswood, tulip tree, white, red, and black oaks, and white pine and hemlock.

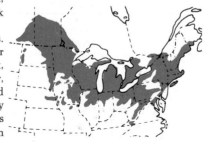

These are fast growing, short-lived trees. Attractive white clusters of flowers appear in spring with the often abundant sweet, edible fruits maturing in late summer, which are eaten by turkey, ruffed and sharp-tailed grouse, pheasant, and many songbirds. Whitetail deer browse the twigs and leaves. The orange to reddish-brown wood is hard and strong, but of no commercial value because of the small size of the trees. The trees are often planted as ornamentals for their flowers, fruits, and bright red branchlets.

Appearance: shrub or bushy small tree to 10 m (33 ft), with a rounded crown; trunk short, branching close to the ground, to 20 cm (7.9 in) in diameter. **Bark:** 4–6 mm (0.2 in) thick, developing irregular, broken plates, dark reddish-brown, with a foul odor when broken. **Branches:** stout, tough; branchlets slender, light green and slightly hairy, turning dark reddish-brown and smooth with age. **Winter buds:** leaf buds 4–6 cm (1.6–2.4 in) long, flower buds 5–10 cm (2–4 in) long, covered with 2 large scales. **Leaves:** opposite, simple, deciduous, broadest near base or middle to rounded, *5–10 cm (2–4 in) long,* 2.5–3.8 cm (1–1.5 in) wide, *usually short to long pointed at the tip,* rounded at the base, *sharply toothed along the margin,* papery, *bright shiny green and smooth above,* yellowish-green beneath; leafstalks 2.5–3.8 cm (1–1.5 in) long, slender. **Flowers:** produced in dense, many-flowered, rounded heads to 12 cm (4.7 in)

Nannyberry

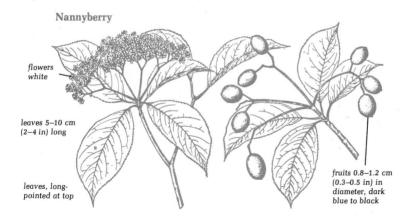

flowers white

leaves 5–10 cm (2–4 in) long

leaves, long-pointed at top

fruits 0.8–1.2 cm (0.3–0.5 in) in diameter, dark blue to black

in diameter; each flower bisexual, with a tiny 5-lobed calyx, 5 white to cream petals, 5 stamens, and a single pistil. **Fruits:** in dense clusters, each rounded, 8–12 mm (0.3–0.5 in) in diameter, dark blue to black, sweet, juicy, containing a single-seeded stone.

Blackhaw
Viburnum prunifolium L.

This is a common species of the eastern and midwestern U.S. It grows in a variety of soils and usually is found on hillsides, and along the margins of woodlands, clearings, and stream banks. American elm, white pine, pitch pine, sweet gum, dogwood, and hawthorn commonly grow in association with blackhaw.

Clusters of white flowers are produced in spring, with the dark edible fruits maturing in autumn. Grouse, turkey, quail, many songbirds, and small mammals eat the fruits. Whitetail deer browse the young twigs and leaves. The reddish-brown wood is hard and strong but of no commercial importance because of the small size of the trees. Blackhaw is occasionally planted as an ornamental, but is not as popular as the nannyberry.

Appearance: large shrub or small tree to 10 m (33 ft), with a compact crown; trunk short, crooked, branching close to the ground, to 25 cm (9.8 in) in diameter. **Bark:** 6–9 mm (0.2–0.4 in) thick, shallowly furrowed and developing flat, irregular plates, reddish-brown. **Branches:** stout, spreading; branchlets slender, spine-like, light brown and hairy when young, becoming grayish-brown and smooth with age. **Winter buds:** leaf buds 5–7 mm (0.2–0.3 in) long, flower buds 12–14 mm (0.5–0.6 in) long, broadest near the base and pointed at the tip, covered by 2 scales. **Leaves:** opposite, simple, deciduous, broadest at or above the middle, to almost rounded, ***4–8 cm (0.2–0.3 in) long,*** 2.5–4.5 cm (1–1.8 in) wide, ***pointed to blunt at the tip,*** rounded to tapering at the base, ***finely toothed along the margin,*** papery, ***dark yellowish-green above,*** paler beneath, leafstalks short, slender. **Flowers:** produced in branched, many-flowered, round-topped clusters; each flower bisexual, with a short, 5-lobed calyx, 5

Blackhaw

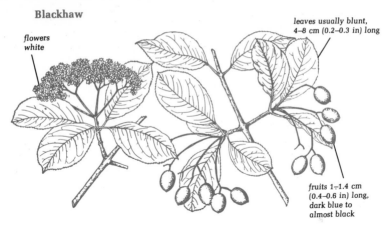

flowers white

leaves usually blunt, 4–8 cm (0.2–0.3 in) long

fruits 1–1.4 cm (0.4–0.6 in) long, dark blue to almost black

white, fused petals 2–3 mm (0.1 in) long, 5 stamens, and a single pistil. **Fruits:** berry-like stone fruits, broadest near the middle and rounded near the tip and base, 1–1.4 cm (0.4–0.6 in) long, dark blue to almost black, with a mealy flesh enclosing the single-seeded stone.

The Sunflower Family Compositae

The sunflower family is one of the largest families of flowering plants, with approximately 1,100 genera and 25,000 species. The plants are widely distributed throughout the world from cold northern climates to hot tropical forests. There are several hundred species in North America, nearly all herbs, with a few shrubs, and a single tree species, big sagebrush. The eastern baccharis (*Baccharis halimifolia*), of the eastern and southern Coastal Plain, is a shrub that may on rare occasions approach tree size.

Economically, this family is extremely important. Foods obtained from this family include lettuce, endive, artichoke, sunflower, and safflower. Many species serve as a major food source to wildlife. Many are cultivated for their attractive flowers, including marigolds, asters, daisies, dahlias, cinerarias, and chrysanthemums. Others are weeds such as cockleburs, thistles, and dandelions.

Members of the sunflower family are herbs, or small shrubs (rarely trees) with alternate or opposite, simple leaves which are usually lobed or toothed. Flowers are produced in head-like clusters that are surrounded by a series of leaf-like bracts; thus the head of flowers is usually mistaken for a single flower, such as those of the daisy or sunflower. Such heads have showy sterile flowers on the margins and fertile bisexual ones in the center-disk. Each flower has the calyx modified into hairs or scales, 5 petals fused to form a tube, 5 stamens, and a single pistil. Fruits are 1-seeded, dry, variously shaped, usually small, and not splitting open.

The Sagebrush Genus Artemisia L.

This is a large genus of about 300 species of herbs, shrubs, or rarely trees, mostly of temperate and cold temperate regions of the world. They emit an aromatic, almost pungent odor when handled. Only 1 species, the big sagebrush, ever reaches tree size in North America. Species of sagebrush often are the dominant plant in arid and semi-arid regions. The plants are an important source of food to browsing animals.

Members of this genus have alternate leaves which are entire, toothed, or variously dissected. Flowers are produced in heads on elongate, branched or unbranched clusters. The heads are small, inconspicuous, greenish-yellow, yellow or white, containing many bisexual flowers. Fruits are small, hard, dry, 1-seeded, not splitting open.

Big Sagebrush   *Artemisia tridentata* Nutt.

Big sagebrush is the most widely distributed shrub of the western U.S. It grows in dry gravelly or rocky soils from British Columbia to Baja California, Mexico, and extends eastward to western Nebraska. This species is common in the Great Basin region and

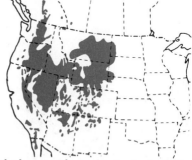

can be found on plains, deserts, hills, and lower mountain slopes. The plants can even thrive in alkaline or basic soils.

These fast-growing plants normally flower in September or October with the fruits maturing soon afterwards. Big sagebrush is extremely important as a food source and for cover to many species of wildlife. The leaves, flowers, and fruits are the main diet of the sage grouse. The sharptailed and dusky grouse also utilize this plant, but to a lesser degree. Antelope, mule deer, elk, and mountain sheep browse the leaves and young twigs. Jack rabbits, ground squirrels, and smaller rodents eat the leaves and seeds. The light-brown wood is hard and dense, and is used for firewood.

Big Sagebrush

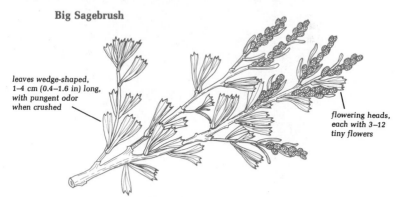

leaves wedge-shaped, 1–4 cm (0.4–1.6 in) long, with pungent odor when crushed

flowering heads, each with 3–12 tiny flowers

Appearance: shrub, occasionally a small tree to 6 m (20 ft), with a rounded crown; trunk short, branching close to the ground, to 30 cm (11.8 in) in diameter. **Bark:** thin, shredding into long, flat, thin strips, grayish-brown. **Branches:** stout, upright to spreading; branchlets stout, stiff, green and densely hairy turning brown and becoming smooth with age. **Winter buds:** tiny, 1–2 mm (less than 0.1 in) long, blunt, densely hairy. **Leaves:** alternate, simple, evergreen to late deciduous, *wedge-shaped, 1–4 cm (0.4–1.6 in) long,* 3–14 mm (0.1–0.6 in) wide, *usually with 3 blunt teeth,* occasionally 4- to 9-toothed, *covered with dense gray to silvery-white hairs on both surfaces,* giving off a *pungent odor when crushed;* leafstalks largely absent. **Flowers:** produced in heads on narrow, elongate, branched clusters at the ends of the branchlets, surrounded by leaf-like bracts near the base, becoming smaller toward the tip; *heads small, containing 3 to 12 tiny flowers,* the flowers tube-shaped, 2.5–3.5 mm (1–1.4 in) long. **Fruits:** dry, hard, flattened, broadest near the tip, 2–2.5 mm (0.8–1 in) long, brown.

MONOCOTS

As explained in more detail on pages 27 and 163, this book divides trees into two main groups: conifers (gymnosperms) and flowering trees (angiosperms). The flowering trees are classified either as dicots (including the hardwoods) or monocots (including the yuccas and palms). Following is a discussion of the monocots.

Key to Yuccas and Palms (Monocots)

A. Leaves long, narrow, bayonet-like; flowers large, showy; fruits a 3-celled leathery or fleshy, elongated capsule containing many seeds; trees are yuccas   **Lily family, p. 904**

B. Leaves very large, fan-shaped or feather-shaped; flowers small, numerous, inconspicuous and sometimes hardly noticeable; fruits 1-celled, usually fleshy and globe-shaped, 1-seeded, rarely 2- or 3-seeded; trees are palms and palmettos   **Palm family, p. 916**

Aloe Yucca

Saw Palmetto

Florida Cherry Palm

The Lily Family   Liliaceae

This is a large family of perhaps 240 genera and over 4,000 species of plants widely distributed throughout the world. Members of the family are especially common in warm temperate and tropical regions. Although there are over 150 species in more than 35 genera in North America, nearly all of these are herbs or vines. Three genera, primarily in the Southwest, are large enough to be considered shrubs and a third, the yuccas (*Yucca*), has 11 members that reach tree size. Two other southwestern species are occasionally large enough to be considered small trees and may be confused with the yuccas. The Biglow nolina (*Nolina bigelovii*) is a large, coarse, grass-like plant of rocky or gravelly hillsides at 150–1,150 m (490–3,800 ft) elevation in desert areas of the Mohave Desert, Baja California, and Sonora, Mexico. Normally, this plant has a short stem about 1 m (3.2 ft) high, but a few plants have been seen with trunks 3 m (9.9 ft) high. The desert spoon (*Dasylirion wheeleri*) is another large, coarse, yucca-like plant but is usually stemless. The conspicuous stout prickles on its leaves and the male and female flowers produced on separate plants readily distinguish it from the others.

This family is of high economic importance because of the ornamental value of many members such as tulips, crocuses, scillas, lilies, and because of the food value of asparagus and onions. The family is of moderate importance to wildlife, with some members providing cover and fleshy berries or seeds.

Members of this family are mainly herbs, occasionally woody, often with erect stems with alternate or clustered leaves. The flowers usually are bisexual, and the parts are generally large and showy in an inner and outer series of 3 petal-like segments. The fruits are a fleshy to leathery capsule or berry often with numerous large seeds.

The Yucca Genus *Yucca* L.

This is a medium-size genus consisting of perhaps 40 species of yuccas, all occurring in the New World in the warmer parts of North America, the West Indies, and Mexico. Yuccas are adapted particularly to dry or desert areas. They may or may not have a conspicuous stem; thus some reach the size of small trees, while others form large clumps of tightly clustered leaves. There are approximately 35 species in North America, with 11 of them exceeding 3.5 m (11.5 ft) in height and thus being considered trees. Two occur in the southeastern U.S. on the Coastal Plain; the remaining species are native to the southwestern or western U.S.

Because of their unusual shapes and attractive flowers, yuccas are cultivated as ornamentals in dry, semi-desert or desert areas. The tough fibers in the leaves can be used to make baskets, mats, or a poor quality rope. Yuccas are a minor source of food and cover for wildlife.

Yuccas are evergreen bushes or small trees with a rind-like bark and, when present, short stout branches. The long, bayonet-like leaves are evergreen and persist for several years, often covering the branches and trunk. The flowers usually are densely clustered on a short to very long, erect stalk that is usually branched. Individual flowers are showy, often globe-shaped, and composed of 6 petal-like segments that are cream-white to white and may or may not be fused near the base into a short tube. Both sexes are present on each flower. There are 6 stamens and a single 6-sided pistil in the center of the flower. The fruits are cylindrical, rounded or 6-sided, leathery or fleshy capsules that do not split open to release the numerous flattened seeds.

Key to Yucca Species

A. Plants of the southeastern U.S., Coastal Plain.

  1. Leaf margin with numerous small teeth; seeds thick, 1.5–2 mm (0.1 in)   **Aloe yucca, p. 907**

  2. Leaf margin smooth, without teeth; seeds thin, 1.2–1.5 mm (less than 0.1 in)

          Moundlily yucca, p. 908

B. Plants of western or southwestern U.S., arid and desert areas.

(Continued)

1. Stalk of the flower cluster very long, 1–2 m (3.2–6.6 ft) high; fruit upright
Soaptree yucca, p. 909

2. Stalk of the flower cluster short, usually less than 1 m (3.3 ft) in height; fruits spreading or hanging.

a. Leaves with numerous, small, sharp-pointed teeth along the margin; the wall of the fruit thin, dry; trees from Utah to Arizona **Joshua tree, p. 910**

b. Leaves smooth or fibrous along the margin, rarely with minute teeth; the wall of the fruit thick, fleshy.

(1) Mature leaves 20–60 cm (8–24 in) long, usually less than 0.5 m (1.6 ft).

(a) Leaves bayonet-like, widest near the middle, 5–8.2 cm (2–3.2 in) wide, dark green, semi-flexible; fruits 7.5–10 cm (3–4 in) long and tapering to a short-pointed tip; trees of Mohave Desert and vicinity
Mohave yucca, p. 911

(b) Leaves spine-like, only 1–1.2 cm (0.4–0.5 in) wide, yellowish-green, very stiff; fruits 5–8.2 cm (2–3.2 in) long and tapering at the tip into 3 pointed beaks; trees of southwestern Texas and Mexico
Beaked yucca, p. 912

(2) Mature leaves 60–150 cm (23–60 in) long, usually from ⅔–1½ m (2.2–4.9 ft).

(a) Flowers small, 2.5–5 cm (1–2 in) long, the individual segments of the flower free of each other.

(a1) Flowering stalk and its branches densely hairy, flowering July through September; leaves gray to yellowish-green; trees of Arizona, New Mexico, and Sonora, Mexico
Schott yucca, p. 913

(a2) Flowering stalk and its branches smooth, without hairs, flowering from December to April; leaves

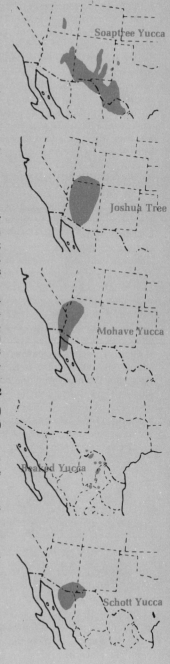

bluish-green; trees of southern Texas and adjacent Mexico **Trecul yucca, p. 913**

(b) Flowers large, 5–10 cm (2–4 in) long, the individual segments of the flower united near the base or forming a short tube.

(b1) Flowers numerous, in a dense, almost ball-shaped cluster, about as wide as tall; trees of extreme southwestern Texas and adjacent Mexico **Carneros yucca, p. 914**

(b2) Flowers numerous, in an elongated cluster, taller than broad.

(b2a) Leaves dark green; flower segments united into a distinct short tube; fruits 7.6–10 cm (3–4 in) long; trees of western Texas and adjacent Mexico **Faxon yucca, p. 915**
(b2b) Leaves dark yellowish-green; flower segments fused only at the base, not forming a distinct tube; fruits 10–14 cm (3.9–5.5 in) long; trees of southwestern Texas, southeastern New Mexico, and Mexico **Torry yucca, p. 915**

Aloe Yucca, Spanish Bayonet

Yucca aloifolia L.

The aloe yucca is a distinctive small tree of the Coastal Plain from North Carolina to central Florida and along the Gulf Coastal Plain to Louisiana. It also occurs in the West Indies and southeastern Mexico. This yucca is restricted largely to sand dunes and margins of brackish marshes but may be found growing on the edges of some coastal pine woods. The only other tree this can be confused with is the moundlily yucca, which grows in the same general region. The aloe yucca's numerous tiny teeth along the margin of the leaves distinguish it from the moundlily yucca's smooth leaf margin.

This tree usually flowers in June, July, or August, with the flowers opening only at night. As with other yuccas, the flowers of this species are pollinated principally by the yucca moth, which is active only at night. The fruits resemble tiny bananas but are bitter-tasting and are not favored by wildlife. Aloe yuccas are grown commonly as ornamental trees near homes or at resort areas along the beaches. Some cultivars have yellow or white striped leaves.

Aloe Yucca, Spanish Bayonet

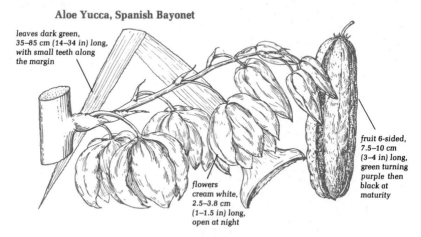

leaves dark green, 35–85 cm (14–34 in) long, with small teeth along the margin

flowers cream white, 2.5–3.8 cm (1–1.5 in) long, open at night

fruit 6-sided, 7.5–10 cm (3–4 in) long, green turning purple then black at maturity

Appearance: small tree, usually 2–5 m (6.5–16.4 ft), with a narrow cylinder-shape; trunk single or occasionally with a few branches, to 15 cm (5.9 in) in diameter, erect to inclining, slightly swollen at the base. **Bark:** thin, to 8–10 mm (0.3–0.4 in), dark brown, rough, with conspicuous scars left by the fallen leaves. **Branches:** short, stout, upright, covered with the numerous, closely arranged leaves. **Leaves:** evergreen and persisting for several years, *35–85 cm (14–34 in) long,* 3–6.5 cm (1.2–2.6 in) wide, very narrow lance-shaped, widest near the middle, flaring at the base to form a short broad base, with a stiff, brown to reddish-brown tip, *with numerous small teeth along the margin,* dark green and smooth. **Flowers:** conspicuous and numerous in a tight, branched, upright flower cluster 30–80 cm (11.8–31.5 in) tall; individual flowers bisexual produced on stalks 2.5–5 cm (1–2 in) long, night flowering, the petal-like structures 2.5–3.8 cm (1–1.5 in) long, often broadest near the middle, rounded to pointed at the tip, creamy white, sometimes streaked with green or purple, stamens 6, pistil 1, usually 3-parted near the base. **Fruits:** elongated, 6-sided, slightly widest near the middle, 7.5–10 cm (3–4 in) long, 3–4 cm (1.2–1.6 in) thick, hanging on short stalks, light green and smooth, turning dark purple then black at maturity, drying and shedding seeds while still on tree. **Seeds:** *rounded, 6–8 mm (0.2–0.3 in) long, flattened, 1.5–2 mm (0.1 in) thick, with a narrow rim on the side,* black, shiny.

Moundlily Yucca   *Yucca gloriosa* L.

The moundlily yucca is the second yucca species in the coastal regions of the southeastern U.S. that often grows large enough to be considered a tree. It occurs on sand dunes and along the borders of seacoast beaches and the emerging woodlands. On the Atlantic Coast, the plants seldom exceed 1 m (3.3 ft) in height; however, in the Gulf Coastal region, they may reach 3–5 m (9.8–16.4 ft) in height. This yucca is encountered rarely in the wild but is commonly planted along beaches. The flower cluster is larger and more attractive than that of the related aloe yucca. Flowering begins in late summer, and the fruits mature in the late fall. The tree is of little or no value to wildlife.

Appearance: small trees 1–3 m (3.2– 9.8 ft), rarely taller, with a narrow cylinder shape; trunk short, stout, usually straight and unbranched or with a few branches, 8–

Moundlily Yucca

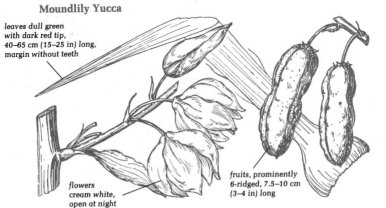

leaves dull green with dark red tip, 40–65 cm (15–25 in) long, margin without teeth

flowers cream white, open at night

fruits, prominently 6-ridged, 7.5–10 cm (3–4 in) long

15 cm (3.2–5.9 in) in diameter, often growing in clumps of several trunks. **Bark:** thin, 4–8 mm (0.2–0.3 in), smooth, light gray, seldom seen, usually covered by the persistent leaves. **Branches:** usually absent; when present, short, stout, erect, covered with leaves. **Leaves:** evergreen and persisting for several years, *40–65 cm (15–25 in) long,* 2.5–6 cm (1–2.4 in) wide, long, narrow, lance-shaped, broadest near the middle, with a short broadened base and a stiff, dark red tip, *the margin entire (without teeth),* upper surface dull green and usually rough, lower surface paler and smooth. **Flowers:** conspicuous, produced in a large, branched, upright flower cluster 60–120 cm (23–47 in) high, the flower cluster stalked, the stalk 80–120 cm (31–47 in) high; individual flowers bisexual, produced on stalks 2.5–5 cm (1–2 in) long, spreading or hanging, night flowering, the petal-like structures 4–5 cm (1.6–2 in) long, usually broadest near the base and tapering to a pointed tip, thin, the segments fused at the base, cream-white and sometimes streaked with purple or green, stamens 6, pistil 1, 3-lobed at the base. **Fruits:** elongated, prominently 6-ridged, rounded at the base and sharp-pointed at the tip, 7.5–10 cm (3–4 in) long, 2.2–2.6 cm (0.9–1 in) thick, leathery, usually hanging, green turning reddish-brown at maturity. **Seeds:** nearly rounded, 6–8 mm (0.2–0.3 in) long, *flattened, 1.2–1.5 mm (0.1 in) thick,* black, shiny.

Soaptree Yucca

Yucca elata Engelm.

The soaptree yucca is a distinctive yucca and is common in southern Arizona and New Mexico but also occurs in southwestern Texas and adjacent Mexico. It grows on mesas, in washes, on plains and desert grasslands, and in deserts, normally at 500–2,000 m (1,640–6,600 ft) elevation. In desert grasslands, the soaptree yucca may be the principal tree species. The long and extremely narrow leaves and the very long-stalked flowers are the most obvious identifiers.

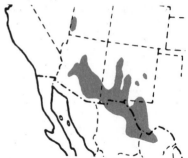

Growth is slow, and some of the existing taller trees may be 250 to 300 years old. Flowering occurs in late spring or early summer, and the fruits mature in late summer to early fall. The trunk is composed of yellowish-brown wood that is soft, spongy, and valueless. It does contain a slick, soap-like fluid that has been used as a substitute for soap. The young flower stalks are edible and can be used as an emergency food source. The leaves contain tough fibers that can be used in making baskets or low-quality twine or rope.

Appearance: small tree, usually 2–5 m (6.5–16.4 ft), occasionally to 10 m (33 ft), with a narrow cylinder shape; trunk single, or with a few branches, 15–22 cm (5.9–8.7 in) in diameter, covered with dead hanging leaves on the upper half, bare below. **Bark:** thin, 4–8 mm (0.2–0.3 in), smooth but with shallow irregular furrows, gray to brown. **Branches:** few, often less than 5, short, stout, with a dense cluster of leaves at the tip. **Leaves:** evergreen and persisting for many years, *25–75 cm (10–30 in) long, 0.3–1.2 cm (0.1–0.5 in) wide, very narrow, linear, rapier-like,* flaring at the short, broadened base, usually straight, flattened, and with a light brown, sharp-pointed tip, the margin thin, papery, and with occasional white threads or fibers attached to the margin, pale yellowish-green and smooth. **Flowers:** *conspicuous, produced at the end of a long, upright stalk, 1–2 m (3.2–6.6 ft) high* and branched near the tip; flowers numerous in large branched clusters, bisexual, the petal-like segments 3–5 cm (1.2–2 in) long, broadest near the base or the middle and tapering to a point, white to greenish-white; stamens 6, pistil 1. **Fruits:** a dry capsule, broadly cylinder-shaped, sometimes widest near the base, rounded to short-pointed at the tip, 3.6–5 cm (1.4–2 in) long, 2.5–3.6 cm (1–1.4 in) thick, splitting open lengthwise in 3 parts from the tip to the base, green, turning brown at maturity. **Seeds:** numerous, rounded, 7–9 mm (0.3–0.4 in) across, very thin, with a thin wing on the margin, black at maturity.

Joshua Tree

Yucca brevifolia Engelm.
[synonym: *Y. arborescens* (Torr.) Trel.]

Because of its branching pattern, the small Joshua tree is unusually striking. It is native to arid mesas and mountain slopes, usually at 650–2,200 m (2,100–7,300 ft) elevation, and is distributed widely in the Mohave Desert from southwestern Utah to western Arizona. In some areas within its range, the Joshua tree forms scattered groves. The tree consists of a single upright trunk until it flowers for the first time, and then it develops lateral branches.

The Joshua tree flowers in early spring,

and its fruits mature by early summer. Both the cactus woodpecker and the redshafted flicker make holes in the stem or branches for their nests. Owls sometimes occupy these trees, and wrens often use nests that have been abandoned by the original occupants. Other than as nesting sites, the trees are of minor importance to wildlife.

Joshua Tree

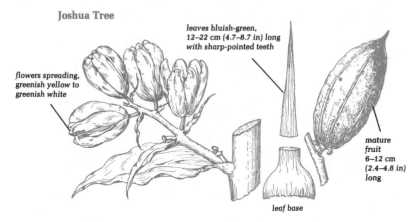

flowers spreading,
greenish yellow to
greenish white

leaves bluish-green,
12–22 cm (4.7–8.7 in) long
with sharp-pointed teeth

mature
fruit
6–12 cm
(2.4–4.8 in)
long

leaf base

Appearance: small to medium-size trees to 15 m (50 ft) with an overall rounded to narrowly rounded shape; trunk single, stout, straight, to 0.8 m (2.6 ft) in diameter, rarely larger. **Bark:** moderately thick, 2–3 cm (0.8–1.2 in), rough, composed of deep furrows forming narrow oblong plates, gray to reddish-brown. **Branches:** stout, spreading, often at right angles. **Leaves:** evergreen, persisting for several years and clustered near the tips of the branches, *12–22 cm (4.7–8.7 in) long, bayonet-like,* broadest near the base and tapering to a long, hard, dark tip, *the margin covered with numerous, tiny sharp teeth,* bluish-green, smooth. **Flowers:** conspicuous, produced in a dense, upright and branched, many-flowered cluster 15–22 cm (5.9–8.7 in) high; individual flowers bisexual, short-stalked, *spreading,* night-flowering, the petal-like structures 2.5–6 cm (1–2.4 in) long, broad to narrow, waxy, united near the base but free for most of their length, stamens 6, pistil 1. **Fruits:** elongated, slightly *3-angled, 6–12 cm (2.4–4.8 in) long, 4–6 cm (1.6–2.4 in) thick, spreading,* light red to yellowish-brown, becoming darker at maturity. **Seeds:** almost rounded, 1–1.3 cm (0.4–0.5 in) across, flattened, and with a narrow margin, black.

Mohave Yucca

Yucca mohavensis Sarg.

The Mohave yucca is a small upright tree, primarily of the Mohave Desert of southeastern California, but also extending into northern Arizona, southern Nevada, and northern Baja California. It grows in the desert, on plateaus, and no nountain slopes at altitudes up to 1,350 m (4,500 ft). This species is closely related to the Torrey yucca of western Texas and eastern Arizona. But the Mohave yucca has shorter leaves and has a different range.

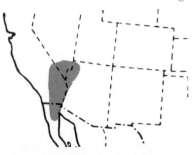

Flowering is in March through May, and the fruits mature in August or September. The light-brown wood is soft and spongy and of no economic use. The long leaves have tough fibers, which were used by Indians to make baskets, blankets, and some cordage.

Mohave Yucca

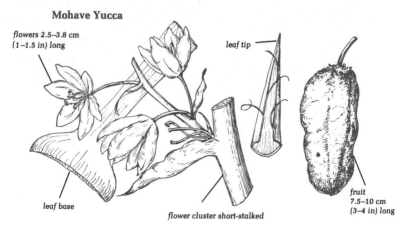

flowers 2.5–3.8 cm (1–1.5 in) long

leaf tip

leaf base

flower cluster short-stalked

fruit 7.5–10 cm (3–4 in) long

Appearance: small tree to 6 m (20 ft), usually smaller, usually with a single erect trunk or with a few short, stout branches; the branches spreading, to 15–20 cm (5.9–7.9 in) in diameter; the trunk and branches often covered with the persistent leaves. **Bark:** thin, 8–12 mm (0.3–0.5 in), becoming rough and scaly, dark brown. **Leaves:** evergreen and persisting for several years, *40–60 cm (15–24 in) long* (about 0.5 m or 1.6 ft), 5–8.2 cm (2–3.2 in) wide, bayonet-like, widest at the middle, flaring abruptly at the base, tapering to a stiff, sharp-pointed tip, smooth, reddish, and becoming fibrous on the margin, otherwise dark green and smooth. **Flowers:** conspicuous and numerous in an *upright-branched flower cluster 30–45 cm (11.8–17.7 in) high;* individual flowers bisexual, produced on slender stalks 2.5–3.8 cm (1–1.5 in) long, petal-like parts 2.5–3.8 cm (1–1.5 in) long, broadest near the middle, united at the base into a short tube, pointed at the tip, cream white, sometimes purple-streaked on the outer parts, stamens 6, pistil 1. **Fruits:** a fleshy to *leathery capsule 7.5–10 cm (3–4 in) long,* 3.5–4 cm (1.4–1.6 in) thick, rounded, widest below the middle, *with a short-pointed tip,* turning dark brown to almost black at maturity. **Seeds:** almost rounded, 7–9 mm (0.3–0.4 in) across, flattened, 2–4 mm (0.1–0.2 in) thick, turning black.

Beaked Yucca

The beaked yucca, a small, rarely encountered tree, is found in North America only in Brewster County in extreme southwestern Texas and in Coahuila and Chihuahua, Mexico. It usually grows to 3 or 4 m (9.8–13 ft) and has a single upright trunk, which occasionally has a few short branches. The *narrow, spine-like leaves* radiate in a dense cluster at the tips of the branches. They are yellowish-green turning light brown, *stiff,* 20–60 cm (8–24 in) long, *only*

Yucca rostrata Engelm. ex Trel.

1–1.2 cm (0.4–0.5 in) wide, and tipped with a long, hard, needle-like point. The large white flowers are 5–6.6 cm (2–2.6 in) long and produced in dense clusters on a short, 0.3–1.3 m (1–4.3 ft) high, smooth, branched stalk. The distinctive **fruits** or capsules are upright, persistent, **5–8.2 cm (2–3.2 in) long** and 1.2–2.5 cm (0.5–1 in) broad, widest near the base and **tapering at the tip into 3 pointed beaks.** The small black seeds are numerous, flattened, and smooth. This is a poorly known species of yucca but is distinguished from other yuccas by its narrow, short leaves and beaked fruits.

Schott Yucca

Yucca schottii Engelm.

The Schott yucca is confined to dry slopes, plains, and grasslands on mountain ranges from 1,350–2,350 m (4,400–7,700 ft) in southern Arizona, southwestern New Mexico, and into adjacent Sonora, Mexico. It is a small upright tree 2–7 m (6.5–23 ft) high, with a single unbranched stem or with a few short, stout branches. The evergreen **leaves,** which are densely clustered near the tips of the branches, are lance-shaped but broadest near the middle, 0.3–1 m (1–3.3 ft) long, 3–5 cm (1.2–2 in) wide, flattened, with a long, stout, sharp tip, and **gray to yellowish-green.** Flowering usually occurs from July through September with numerous, stalked, white, globe-shaped **flowers 2.5–5 cm (1–2 in) long clustered on a large, densely hairy, upright stalk** 0.3–1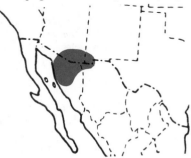
m (1–3.3 ft) high. The fleshy capsules, which mature from October to December, are cylinder-shaped, 7.5–14 cm (3–5.5 in) long, 2.5–3.2 cm (1–1.3 in) in diameter, green turning dark brown to black at maturity. The hairy flower stalks readily distinguish this yucca from others.

Schott Yucca

leaves gray to yellowish green

leaf tip

flowering Jul–Sep

flowers white, 2.5–5 cm (1–2 in) long

flower stalk hairy

leaf base

fruit 7.5–14 cm (3–5.5 in) long, Oct to Dec

Trecul Yucca

Yucca treculeana Carr.

The Trecul yucca is a small tree of southcentral and southern Texas and adjacent Mexico, where it grows on hillsides or open flatlands, or in chaparral regions. It can reach 8 m (26.3 ft) in height with its single trunk or with a few stout, spreading branches near the top. The large, narrow, evergreen *leaves* are 0.8–1.3 m (2.6–4.3 ft) long, 2.5–8 cm (1–3.2 in) wide, and *bluish-green* in color. Flowering may begin as early as December or as late as April, and the creamy-white, globe-shaped *flowers* are 2.5–5 cm (1–2 in) long and *produced in large, dense, many-flowered, branched clusters 0.6–1.5 m* (1.9–4.9 ft) high. The fruits are leathery capsules that are cyl-inder-shaped, 5–11 cm (2–4.3 in) long, 2–3 cm (0.8–1.2 in) thick, and reddish-brown

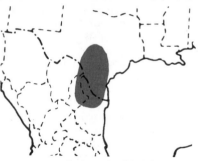

to black. The thin flattened seeds are 3–6 mm (0.1–1.2 in) thick, and reddish-brown to black. The thin flattened seeds are 3–6 mm (0.1–0.2 in) in diameter. The Trecul yucca is similar to the Faxon yucca, but can be distinguished by its concave rather than flat-tened leaves.

Trecul Yucca

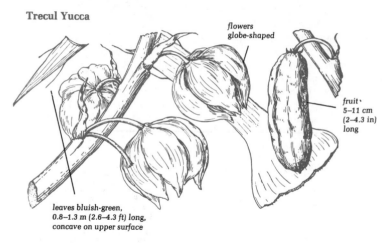

flowers
globe-shaped

fruit,
5–11 cm
(2–4.3 in)
long

leaves bluish-green,
0.8–1.3 m (2.6–4.3 ft) long,
concave on upper surface

Carneros Yucca

Yucca carnerosana (Trel.) McKelvey

The carneros yucca is restricted to Brewster County, Texas, and adjacent northeastern Mexico. It grows in limestone foothills at elevations of 900–2,100 m (2,900–6,900 ft). It is a small tree to 6 m (20 ft) and usually with a straight unbranched trunk. The evergreen leaves are persistent, lance-shaped, 90–130 cm (35–51 in) long, 5–7.5 cm (2–3 in) across, and tipped with a stiff spine. The stalk bearing the flower cluster is 1.5–2 m (5–7 ft) tall, and the *flowers are tightly grouped in a branched, ball-shaped cluster.* The individual *flowers are 5–8.2 cm (2–3.2 in)* long and similar to

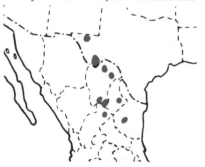

other species of yucca. The fruits are leathery capsules, often broadest near the base, and tipped with an abrupt point, 7.5–11.5 cm (3–4.5 in) long, turning reddish-brown at maturity.

Faxon Yucca
Yucca faxoniana Sarg.

Faxon yucca is confined to the high desert plateau of western Texas and to the state of Chihuahua in Mexico. It is a medium-size yucca growing to a height of 15 m (50 ft). The trees may be unbranched or with a few short branches that will be covered with 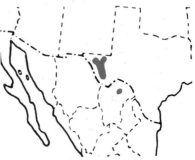 the persistent, hanging dead leaves. The evergreen *leaves* are 0.7–1.5 m (2.3–4.9 ft) long, 6–7.8 cm (2.4–3.1 in) wide, widest above the middle, with a short dark tip, the margins smooth and breaking apart to form loose spreading fibers or threads, *dark green* and smooth. The *flowers are produced in* spring in a *many-flowered, branched cluster 1–1.3 m (3.2–4.3 ft) high.* Individual *flowers* are white to greenish-*white, 5.5–7 cm (2.2–2.8 in)* long, and hang by a slender stalk. The brown to black fruits are 7.6–10 cm (3–4 in) long and mature by early summer. The segments of the flowers united into a narrow tube distinguish this yucca from other species that have the segments free of one another.

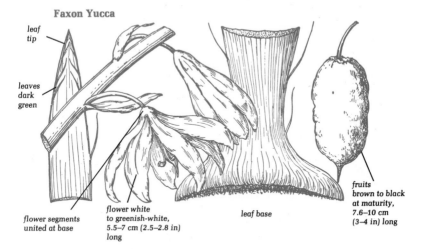

Faxon Yucca

leaf tip

leaves dark green

flower segments united at base

flower white to greenish-white, 5.5–7 cm (2.5–2.8 in) long

leaf base

fruits brown to black at maturity, 7.6–10 cm (3–4 in) long

Torrey Yucca
Yucca torreyi Shafer
(synonym: *Y. macrocarpa* Cov.)

The Torrey yucca is a small tree found only in southwestern Texas, extreme southeastern New Mexico, and extending into Mexico. It grows mainly on the dry plains and is an unbranched or few-branched plant 1–8 m (3.2–26.3 ft) high. The branches usually are

covered with the persistent evergreen
leaves, which are 0.6–1.5 m (1.9–4.9 ft)
long, bayonet-like, concave, and **dark yellowish-green.** The flowers are produced in
March through April on densely flowered,
upright stalks 1–1.2 m (3.2–3.9 ft) high. Individual flowers are 5–10 cm (2–4 in) long;
the individual segments are cream-white.
Fruits are leathery **capsules 10–14 cm
(3.9–5.5 in) long,** 3.1–5 cm (1.2–2 in)
across, rounded, often broadest near the
base, tapering to a pointed tip and turning
dark brown to black at maturity. This species can be distinguished from the Mohave
yucca by its range, fruits, and flowers.

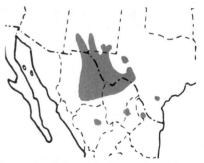

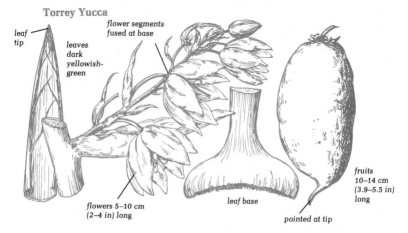

Torrey Yucca

leaf tip

flower segments fused at base

leaves dark yellowish-green

flowers 5–10 cm (2–4 in) long

leaf base

pointed at tip

fruits 10–14 cm (3.9–5.5 in) long

The Palm Family

Palmae

The palm family is a large tropical to subtropical family of approximately 4,000
species throughout the world. Of the 9 genera of palms native to North America, 8
have members that are trees. All are native to Florida and the southern Coastal Plain
except for the California washingtonia, which is native to the southwestern U.S. Two
other introduced genera, the date palms and the coconut palm, are included because
of their importance. Many other genera and species have been introduced into North
America, primarily in Florida and in the extreme southwestern U.S., including
southern California. Among the more commonly encountered, introduced palms are
the fishtail palms, the queen palms, the manila or veitchia palms, and the Madagascar palms. The fishtail palms *(Caryota)* are natives of southeastern Asia and are readily distinguished from the native species by their twice-branched leaves composed of
many fan-shaped leaflets. The clumping fishtail palm *(Caryota mitis)* forms large,
many-stemmed clumps, while another fishtail palm *(C. urens)* is a tall, single-trunked
tree. The queen palm *(Arecastrum romanzoffianum)* is a medium-size, column-
shaped tree to 15 m (50 ft) and with a broad rounded crown of feather-like leaves, each
one growing to 4 or 5 m (13–16.4 ft) in length. The manila palm *(Veitchia merrillii)* is

another column-shaped tree with feather-like leaves, and it resembles a small royal palm. It is used to line avenues and has attractive red fruits that enhance its ornamental qualities. The small to medium-size, clump-forming Madagascar palm (*Chrysalidocarpus lutescens*), with gracefully curved stems that are conspicuously ringed, is a favorite landscaping plant for homes. This palm has attractive, fine-textured, yellowish-green, spreading to slightly drooping leaves.

North Americans often overlook the economic importance of this family. Palms provide food, shelter, and commercial products for millions of people worldwide. Coconut, copra, oils, dates, carnauba wax, and coarse fibers are among the more important products. Palms provide cover for nesting birds and for small animals. They are not an important food source for wildlife, although the smaller fleshy fruits are eaten by birds and mammals.

Members of this family are woody vines, shrubs, or trees with largely unbranched, column-shaped trunks that may be very short or long. The leaves are usually simple and fan-shaped or compound and feather-like and clustered in a large head or scattered and alternating on climbing or shrubby species. The leaves have a conspicuous stalk with a base that often persists on the trunk. Flowers are usually produced in large, many-flowered, branched, elongated clusters. Individual flowers are small, often white and fragrant, bisexual, or else the sexes are in separate flowers. There are commonly 6 sepals, petals, and stamens per flower along with a single pistil that is 3-celled at the base. The fruits are usually a berry or leathery, dry, and berry-like, small to large, generally with 1 large seed per fruit.

Key to Palm Genera

A. Leaves large, feather-like (pinnate), several times longer than broad.

  1. Trees with smooth trunks but often with conspicuous horizontal rings (leaf scars); individual trees containing both sexes.

  a. Fruits small, 1–2 cm (0.4–0.8 in) long, black, bluish-purple, or orange-scarlet at maturity; leaves with a plain base, sometimes extending down the trunk as a sheath.

  (1) Column-shaped trees to 40 m (132 ft), the trunk with a bulge above the middle and cement gray; with conspicuous bright green leaf bases encircling top of trunk 1.5–2 m (4.9–6.6 ft) long; fruits globe-shaped, 1–1.4 cm (0.4–0.6 in) in diameter, black to bluish-purple; trees native to southern Florida
  Royal palm, p. 919

  (2) Column-shaped trees to 8 m (26.2 ft), the trunk straight, uniform, grayish-
  (Continued)

Florida Royal Palm

green; fruits globe-shaped, 1.6–2 cm
(0.6–0.8 in) in diameter, orange-scarlet;
trees of southern Florida

Cherry palm, p. 921

Florida Cherry Palm

Coconut Palm

b. Fruits large, 12–35 cm (4.7–13.8 in) long,
hard, green, yellow, or light brown and
containing a single large seed 6–25 cm
(2.4–9.9 in) long; leaves with a conspicuous, coarse, cloth-like webbing at the base;
introduced and naturalized trees of southern Florida **Coconut palm, p. 922**

2. Trees with the trunk covered with the persistent bases of the dead leaves; individual trees
either male or female; cultivated trees primarily in California **Date palm, p. 923**

B. Leaves fan-like, circular or nearly so in outline,
never several times longer than broad.

1. Leaves with stout spines along the margins of
the leaf bases.

a. Column-shaped tree to 15 m (50 ft) with a
straight, erect, unbranched trunk; leaves 1–
1.5 m (3.2–4.9 ft) long; trees native to
southwestern U.S.

Washingtonia palm, p. 924

Date Palm

California Washingtonia

b. Small trees or shrubs to 8 m (26.3 ft), often
with horizontal or creeping trunks, sometimes branched or forming a clump of several trunks, leaves 0.6–1 m (1.9–3.3 ft) long;
trees of southeastern U.S.

shrub
form

tree
form

(1) Trunk usually creeping, sometimes
branched; leafstalks armed with small
spines along the margins; fruits 1.5–2
cm (0.6–0.8 in) in diameter, fleshy and
juicy; trees of southern Florida

Saw Palmetto

Saw palmetto palm, p. 925

(2) Trunks upright, forming multi-
stemmed clumps; leafstalks armed with
stout, hooked, orange spines along the
margin; fruits 5–8 mm (0.2–0.3 in) in
diameter, dry, leathery, bluish-black at
maturity; trees of southern Florida

Everglades palm, p. 926

Everglades Palm

2. Leaves smooth or with fibrous threads along the margins of the leaf bases.

  a. Leafstalks extending part way into the leaf blades; trees of southern Coastal Plain, including Florida   **Palmetto palm, p. 927**

  b. Leafstalks ending at the junction of the stalk and the blade.

    (1) Leafstalks forked at the base near the attachment to the trunk; leaves pale green to silvery-white on the lower surface; fruits small, dry, ivory-white at maturity; trees of southern Florida

                Thatch palm, p. 929

    (2) Leakstalks unbranched at the base; leaves bright silvery-white on the lower surface; fruits small, fleshy, purple to black at maturity; trees of southern Florida   **Silver thatch palm, p. 931**

Cabbage Palmetto

Bush Palmetto

Brittle Thatch Palm

Florida Thatch Palm

Florida Silver Palm

The Royal Palm Genus   *Roystonea* O.F. Cook

The royal palm genus consists of a small group of about 16 species in tropical regions of the Americas from northern South America throughout the Caribbean and with 1 species native to southern Florida. They are attractive trees that do best in rich soil and full sunlight. Royal palms are the palms most frequently used as street or avenue trees, for landscaping buildings, and for planting wherever a formal avenue effect is desired. The Cuban royal palm (*Roystonea regia*) is the most commonly encountered royal palm in southern Florida. This palm typically has red to purple fruits that are longer than broad. The Puerto Rican royal palm (*R. borinquena*), with its crowded flower clusters and yellowish-brown fruits, is encountered occasionally. The Palmiste cabbage palm (*R. oleracea*), native to the West Indies, has also been introduced in southern Florida. This palm has a tall straight trunk and lacks the royal palm's characteristic bulge at or above the middle of the trunk.

  Royal palms are medium-size to tall, unarmed trees with tall, column-shaped trunks, sometimes with a bulge at or above the middle and a broad, round-topped crown. The feather-like leaves are long, large, and spreading. The bases of the leaves are tightly pressed together to form a bright green cylinder (crownshaft) just below the leaf blades. Individual trees produce male and female flowers. The flowers are in densely branched, hanging clusters that are produced at the base of the crownshaft. Male flowers are small and contain 6 to 12 stamens; while the female flowers contain a single pistil and aborted stamens. The fruits are small, globe to egg-shaped, leathery, and they mature in summer. There is a single, light-brown seed per fruit.

Florida Royal Palm   *Roystonea elata* (Bartr.) F. Harper

The Florida royal palm is an attractive tree native to southern Florida, except for the Keys. It occurs in rich, moist hammocks and can be observed in the Everglades National Park. The occasional bulge in the trunk, the long, feather-like leaves, and the conspicuous, bright green crownshaft readily distinguish it from other native palms. In spite of these distinguishing features, separating this palm from other royal palms is difficult for most people. (See Key.) The fragrant white flowers appear in spring, and the fruits mature in the summer. It is of no importance to wildlife and is valued solely as an ornamental.

Appearance: medium to ***tall column-shaped tree*** to 40 m (132 ft), with a broad spreading crown; trunk straight, unbranched, to 0.6 m (1.9 ft) in diameter. **Bark:** a smooth tough rind, ***cement gray,*** usually with conspicuous ringed scars (from the fallen leaves). **Leaves: *large, feather-like,*** spreading, to 4 m (13.1 ft) long, composed

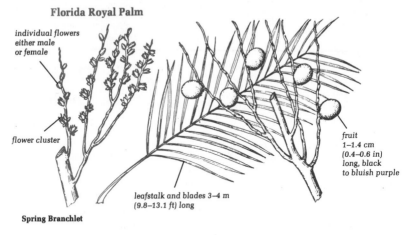

Florida Royal Palm

individual flowers either male or female

flower cluster

Spring Branchlet

leafstalk and blades 3–4 m (9.8–13.1 ft) long

fruit 1–1.4 cm (0.4–0.6 in) long, black to bluish purple

of numerous, strap-shaped leaflets, dark green; the leafstalks stiff, 3–4 m (9.8–13.1 ft) long, almost rounded, becoming flattened at the long, green, sheathing base, unarmed; ***crownshaft (below leaf blades) 1.5–2 m (4.9–6.6 ft) long, bright green.*** **Flowers:** produced in spring in dense, branched, hanging clusters to 0.6 m (1.9 ft) long; the individual ***flowers either male or female,*** white, fragrant, small, 5–8 mm (0.2–0.3 in) in diameter. **Fruits:** numerous, leathery, globe-shaped to broadest near the base, 1–1.4 cm (0.4–0.6 in) long, smooth, turning ***black to bluish-purple at maturity.*** **Seeds:** 1 per fruit, light brown.

The Cherry Palm Genus   *Pseudophoenix* H. Wendl.

The cherry palms are a small genus of perhaps 4 species in the Caribbean region and with 1 species native to North America. This small group of palms resembles young royal palms, but the cherry palms produce the new elongated clusters of flowers at the top of the crownshaft (below leaf blades). But the royal palms always produce them at the base of the crownshaft.

They are small trees with a single, erect, unarmed trunk and large, spreading, feather-like leaves. The leaves are composed of numerous small, lateral leaflets, and the central stalk is channeled on the upper surface. The flowers contain both sexes and are produced on elongated branched clusters. The fruits are small, leathery, and globe-shaped, and are often 2- or 3-lobed.

Florida Cherry Palm   *Pseudophoenix sargentii* H. Wendl.

The Florida cherry palm is found in North America only in the upper Florida Keys but also is native to the Bahamas, Cuba, and Hispaniola. Many of the original sites and trees have been destroyed due to developments and road constructions. Yet the attractiveness of this palm led to its introduction in south Florida as an ornamental.

Appearance: small tree to 8 m (26.2 ft) high with a broad, spreading, round-topped crown; trunk straight, erect, unbranched, 20–30 cm (7.9–11.8 in) in diameter. **Bark:** a smooth rind, grayish-green when young, banded with light-brown ring scars. **Leaves:** large, feather-like, spreading, to 3 m (9.8 ft) long, composed of 160 to 180 leaflets per leaf, dark yellow-green; the leafstalks slender, short, to 0.6 m (2 ft) long, *channeled on the upper surface,* unarmed. **Flowers:** produced on many-flowered, elongated, branched clusters, to 1 m (3.3 ft) in length; the immature flowers (buds) enclosed in a narrow, boat-shaped bract; the individual *flowers bisexual, yellowish,* small; the sepals consisting of a mere rim, the petals often persisting on the fruit. **Fruits:** numerous, berry-like, short-stalked, globe-shaped, *1.6–2 cm (0.6–0.8 in) in diameter,* 1-, 2-, or 3-lobed, *turning orange-scarlet at maturity.* **Seeds:** 1, 2, or 3 per fruit, globe-shaped, light reddish-brown.

Florida Cherry Palm

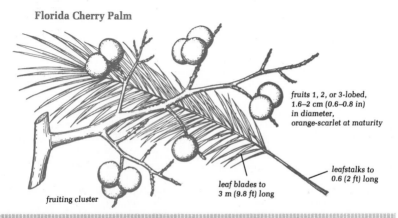

fruits 1, 2, or 3-lobed,
1.6–2 cm (0.6–0.8 in)
in diameter,
orange-scarlet at maturity

leafstalks to
0.6 (2 ft) long

leaf blades to
3 m (9.8 ft) long

fruiting cluster

The Coconut Palm Genus

Cocos L.

Most authorities recognize only 1 species in this genus, the coconut palm. This palm is widespread in tropical regions of the world and must be considered as one of the most economically valuable species of trees worldwide.

Coconut Palm

Cocos nucifera L.

The coconut is without question the most familiar palm in the world and is often called man's most useful tree. In North America, the coconut occurs along coastal areas of southern Florida and the Keys. It has not grown successfully in southern California. It occurs along coastlines throughout tropical regions of the world, having spread from its probable native range in southeast Asia. The characteristic trunk, leaves, and fruits easily separate this palm from all others.

In North America, the economic value and importance of this tree is seldom recognized. It is an important food source in tropical countries. The large seed contains a rich and nutritious milk and a thick lining of solid meat. The dried meat is the source of palm oil, which is consumed locally and exported for use in soaps, margarines, lubricants, cosmetics, and fuels. The dried meat is nutritious. It is shredded and sold as a flavoring for cakes, candies, and other confections.

A serious virulent disease, known as lethal yellowing, has been responsible for the death of thousands of coconut palms in Florida and threatens the future of the tree.

Appearance: medium-size trees to 20 m (66 ft), occasionally taller, with a large rounded crown; ***trunk usually inclined,*** unbranched, 30–50 cm (12–20 in) in diameter, usually enlarged at the base and narrowing above, ***marked with rough, crescent-shaped scars*** (from the fallen leaves). **Bark:** a tough, light gray rind. **Leaves:** large, feather-like, spreading and arching, 2–5 m (6.5–16.4 ft) long, to 5 m (16.4 ft) wide, composed of numerous lateral, narrow leaflets, shiny green above, paler beneath; the leafstalks short, stout, unarmed, grooved above, with a coarse, cloth-like webbing at the base. **Flowers:** produced on ***short, once-branched, elongated clusters 0.6–1.3 m***

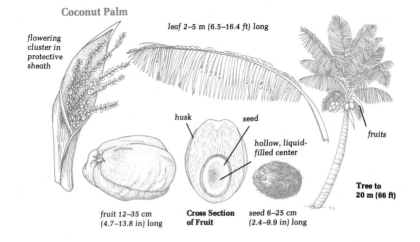

Coconut Palm

leaf 2–5 m (6.5–16.4 ft) long

flowering cluster in protective sheath

husk *seed*

hollow, liquid-filled center

fruits

Tree to 20 m (66 ft)

fruit 12–35 cm (4.7–13.8 in) long **Cross Section of Fruit** *seed 6–25 cm (2.4–9.9 in) long*

(1.9–4.3 ft) long; the individual flowers are either functionally male or female, but both are present in the same flower cluster; the male flowers small, scattered; the female flowers larger, few, located near the base of the flower cluster. **Fruits:** 1 to several clustered, *large, 12–35 cm (4.7–13.8 in) long, often roughly 3-sided to broadest near the base* and tapering toward the tip, the thick husk green, yellow, or light brown. **Seeds:** *large, usually 6–25 cm (2.4–9.9 in) long,* globe-shaped to egg-shaped, *with 3 "eyes,"* dark brown, with a *hard outer shell enclosing a hollow, liquid-filled center.*

The Date Palm Genus   Phoenix L.

Date palms are a small genus of perhaps 18 species of palms native to tropical Asia and Africa. Several species have been introduced into southern Florida, California, southern Arizona, and Texas. Two of these are either well known or relatively common: the date palm and the Canary Island date palm. The Canary Island date palm (*Phoenix canariensis*) was introduced more than 100 years ago and is one of the best palms for planting along avenues. It is a stocky, single-trunked tree to 20 m (66 ft) high with large, yellow-green, feather-like leaves growing to 7 m (23 ft) long. In addition to these, the Senegal and the pygmy date palms have been introduced into tropical regions of North America and are encountered occasionally. The Senegal date palm (*Phoenix reclinata*) is a fast-growing, multi-stemmed tree to 14 m (46 ft) high with bright green, feather-like leaves. The pygmy date palm (*Phoenix roebelenii*) is a small, single-trunked tree growing to only 3.5 m (11.5 ft) high at maturity and with dark green, shiny leaves.

The different species of date palms hybridize readily, and this causes some difficulty in distinguishing the species. They are an economically important group of trees because of their ornamental value and as an important food source.

Date palm trunks are covered with the persistent bases of the fallen leaves. The leaves are large, feather-like, short-stalked, and clustered in a dense rounded crown. Individual trees are either male or female. The flowers are produced in large, many-branched, elongated clusters, and the individual male flowers are white and fragrant, with cup-like sepals, free petals, and 6 stamens. The female flowers have similar sepals and petals but have 3 pistils instead of the pollen-bearing stamens. The fruits are a rounded to slightly elongated, 1-seeded berry.

Date Palm   *Phoenix dactylifera* L.

The date palm, a native of northern Africa and Arabia, has been introduced into south Florida, California, Arizona, and Texas. It is doubtful that the date palm has naturalized anywhere in North America. The date palm occurs in southern Florida, but is not common. When encountered, it is usually near buildings. This economically important palm is cultivated extensively in southern California and in parts of southern Arizona for its nutritious, edible fruits. Attempts to establish a date industry in Florida were unsuccessful because these palms require dry hot summers for good fruit development.

The date palm is a stout tree growing to 10 m (33 ft) high, usually with a single trunk covered with persistent leaf bases and topped with *15 to 20 large feather-like leaves,* which are gray-green and stiff and may be *up to 6 m (20 ft) long. Individual trees produce only male or female flowers,* and only the female trees can produce fruits.

The tiny white flowers are very abundant in dense, branched, long-stalked clusters. The fruits are berries 3–4 cm (1.2–1.6 in) long and produced abundantly in large hanging clusters. A single tree is capable of producing over 100 k (220 pounds) of fruit annually.

The Washingtonia Palm Genus   *Washingtonia* Wendl.

The Washingtonia fan palms are the only genus of palms native to the southwestern U.S. Only 1 species, the California washingtonia, is native in North America. This small genus was named to honor George Washington. A second species, the Mexican washingtonia (*Washingtonia robusta*) has been introduced into subtropical regions of North America, especially in California, Arizona, Texas, and southern Florida. It can be distinguished from the native species by its taller, narrower trunk; its leaves are not as deeply split and lack the thread-like fibers, and the tips of the leaves hang.

Although of minor importance to wildlife, these palms are of considerable importance as ornamentals and are widely cultivated in desert, subtropical, and tropical areas. The persistent dried leaves provide cover and nesting sites for some birds and small mammals.

Washingtonia palms are column-shaped trees with a broad rounded crown of fan-shaped leaves. The leaves are circular in outline and composed of a many-folded blade that often splits to or below the middle. The long stalks are armed with stout spines along the margins. The flowers are produced in many-flowered, elongated, branched clusters that develop near the bases of the leaves. Individual flowers are bisexual, white, 6-parted; the single pistil is 3-parted at the base. The fruits are berries that turn black at maturity and contain a single seed.

California Washingtonia   *Washingtonia filifera* (Linden) H. Wendl.

This attractive, well-known, but rare palm is native to southwestern Arizona, southeastern California, and northern Baja California. It grows in a few isolated and scattered groves, usually along streams or in canyons with higher levels of soil moisture than in the adjacent desert areas. The California washingtonia normally is found at 150–1,000 m (490–3,300 ft) elevation. The persistent dead leaves often hide the trunk; although in many cities the leaves are removed because they are fire hazards and become breeding sites for rats.

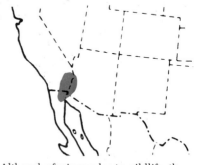

One of the largest and most extensive stands of this palm is near Palm Springs, California. These trees are planted frequently along avenues and streets in the Southwest, southern Florida, and other tropical or subtropical regions of the world. Although of minor value to wildlife, these palms do serve as nesting sites for some wrens and orioles. Indians once gathered the seeds and ground them into flour, and they used the leaves as thatch.

Appearance: small- to medium-size, column-shaped trees to 15 m (50 ft), rarely taller, with a broad rounded crown; trunk tall, straight, unbranched, often spreading at the base, 0.3–1.3 m (1–4.3 ft) in diameter. **Bark:** a scaly rind, thick, becoming shallowly furrowed with age, gray to reddish-brown, often covered with persistent, hanging, dead leaves. **Leaves:** *fan-shaped,* the *blades 1–1.5 m (3.2–4.9 ft) in diame-*

California Washingtonia Palm

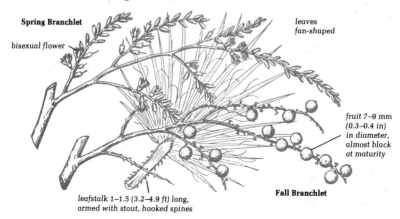

Spring Branchlet

bisexual flower

leaves fan-shaped

fruit 7–9 mm (0.3–0.4 in) in diameter, almost black at maturity

leafstalk 1–1.5 (3.2–4.9 ft) long, armed with stout, hooked spines

Fall Branchlet

ter, circular in outline, consisting of 40 to 60 folds, usually torn between the folds to near the middle and with thread-like fibers between the lobes, light green; the **leafstalks stout, 1–1.5 m (3.2–4.9 ft) long,** 4–7 cm (1.6–2.8 in) broad, spreading some at the base, **armed with stout, hooked spines along part or all of the margins. Flowers:** produced in many-flowered, elongated, branched, drooping clusters 2–5 m (6.5–16.4 ft) long; the immature flowers or buds enclosed in a narrow, boat-shaped bract (spathe) 35–60 cm (13–24 in) long, yellowish; the individual flowers bisexual, white, small, slightly fragrant. **Fruits: numerous, berry-like, usually** broadest near the middle to almost round, rounded at the tip, **7–9 mm (0.3–0.4 in) long, almost black at maturity. Seeds:** 1 per fruit, broadest near the middle, 5–7 mm (0.2–0.3 in) long, tan to brown.

The Saw Palmetto Palm Genus
Serenoa Hook. F.

There is only 1 species of saw palmetto, and that is restricted to coastal areas of the southeastern Coastal Plain. This is the only native species of palm that branches. Because there is just a single species, the description of the genus is the same as that of the species.

Saw Palmetto
Serenoa repens (Bartr.) Small

The saw palmetto occurs along the Coastal Plain from South Carolina to southern Florida and west to southeastern Louisiana. The typical saw palmetto is a sprawling or creeping palm with horizontal stems that occasionally are upright and tree-like. This is a common palm in scrub land through much of Florida. It is of little economic value. The fruits are an important late-fall and early-winter food for whitetail deer in Florida. Other mammals, such as raccoons, also feed on the ripe fruits.

Appearance: small trees or shrubs to 7 m

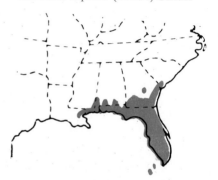

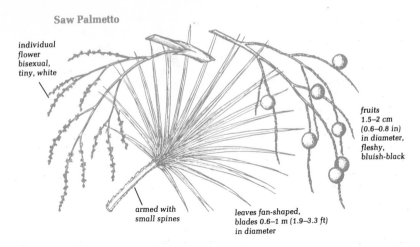

Saw Palmetto

individual
flower
bisexual,
tiny, white

fruits
1.5–2 cm
(0.6–0.8 in)
in diameter,
fleshy,
bluish-black

armed with
small spines

leaves fan-shaped,
blades 0.6–1 m (1.9–3.3 ft)
in diameter

(23 ft) high with a broad, rounded, sometimes open crown; **trunk usually horizontal and creeping, occasionally upright,** unbranched or **branched. Bark:** the trunk usually covered with the persistent, reddish-brown leaf bases. **Leaves:** *fan-shaped,* the blades 0.6–1 m (1.9–3.3 ft) in diameter, circular in outline, divided, sometimes to the middle, yellowish-green, blue-green, or rarely silvery-white; the *leafstalks* stout to slender, 3-sided, to 1.5 m (4.9 ft) long, *armed with small spines along the margin.* **Flowers:** produced on a branched, elongated cluster to 1 m (3.3 ft) in length; individual flowers bisexual, white, small, the sepals small, 1–2 mm (0.1 in) long, petals 3–6 mm (0.1–0.2 in) long, with 6 stamens and a single pistil. **Fruits:** *berry-like,* nearly globe-shaped to egg-shaped, *1.5–2 cm (0.6–0.8 in) in diameter, fleshy and juicy, turning bluish-black at maturity.* **Seeds:** 1 per fruit, longer than broad, grooved.

The Everglades Palm Genus   Acoelorraphe H. Wendl.

(synonym: *Paurotis* O. F. Cook)

This genus consists of a single species native to southern Florida, the West Indies, and parts of the Caribbean coast of Central America. The information and description of the genus are the same as for the species.

Everglades Palm   Acoelorraphe wrightii

(Griseb. & H. Wendl.) H. Wendl. ex Becc.

This small, clump-forming palm occurs naturally in brackish swamps. But it thrives in cultivation in rich soils on upland or drier sites. Because it grows in colonies or large clumps, the outermost trees may lean outward. Characters to look for include the fan-shaped leaves with the leafstalks armed with stout curved spines; the trunk covered with a fibrous matting; and thin, narrow, persistent bases of the dead leaves.

Appearance: small tree to 8 m (26 ft) tall, forming *large clusters* or clumps due to a

common spreading root system and with a rounded crown; trunk slender, upright, unbranched, to 15 cm (6 in) in diameter, usually *covered with the narrow persistent bases of the dead leaves* and a fibrous matting. **Bark:** a thin rind, usually covered. **Leaves:** *fan-shaped*, the blades 0.6–1 m (1.9–3.3 ft) long, almost circular in outline, usually deeply divided, light green above, becoming silvery beneath; the leafstalks slender, 20–60 cm (8–24 in) long, rust-colored hairs at the base, *armed with orange, stout, hooked spines, with a webby fibrous sheath at the base.* **Flowers:** produced on an elongated branched cluster 60–90 cm (23–35 in) long; individual *flowers* bisexual, *greenish-yellow*, 2–3 mm (0.1 in) wide; the sepals 3, short, broad; the petals 3, united near the base, longer than broad and pointed at the tip; stamens 6, pistil 1. **Fruits:** numerous, *rounded or nearly so, 5–8 mm (0.2–0.3 in) in diameter,* outer skin leathery, *bluish-black to black.* **Seeds:** 1 per fruit, rounded to almost globe-shaped, 4–6 mm (0.2 in) in diameter, hard, light chestnut brown.

The Palmetto Palm Genus

Sabal Adans.

There are perhaps 25 species of palmetto palms, all found in warm regions of the Western Hemisphere, primarily in the Caribbean and adjacent coastal areas of North, Central, and South America. Six species occur in southern North America; 3 are shrubs and 3 are trees. Palmettos occur commonly along the southern Coastal Plain and in Florida. Even though some species are suitable for planting along streets or avenues, they are of minor economic importance.

They are shrubs or trees with solitary, usually stout, trunks that are topped with a dense rounded crown of fan-shaped leaves. The long-stalked leaves are nearly rounded in outline, tough, leathery, many-folded, and divided into many narrow, long-pointed segments. The flowers are produced in a many-flowered, elongated, branched cluster that is produced at the base of the leaves. Individual flowers are bisexual, white, 3-parted with 6 stamens and a single pistil that is 3-parted at the base. The fruits are small dry berries with a thin sweet flesh, usually globe-shaped and occasionally 2- or 3-lobed.

Key to Palmetto Palm Species

Cabbage Palmetto

Bush Palmetto

Texas Palmetto

A. Trees of southeastern Coastal Plain; fruits 1-lobed, almost globe-shaped.

    1. Medium to tall trees to 25 m (82 ft); leaves dark green, the leafstalk 2–2.3 m (6.5–7.5 ft) long; trees of Atlantic Coastal Plain and Florida   **Cabbage palmetto, p. 928**

    2. Bush often with no trunk but can be small tree, 2–3 m (6.5–10 ft), leaves bluish-green, the leafstalk 1–1.5 m (3.2–4.9 ft) long; trees of Gulf Coastal Plain   **Bush palmetto, p. 928**

B. Trees of southern Texas; fruits often 2- or 3-lobed   **Texas palmetto, p. 929**

Cabbage Palmetto *Sabal palmetto* (Walt.) Lodd. ex Schult. & Schult.

The cabbage palmetto is a slender tree that ranges from the Florida Keys north throughout Florida to southeastern Georgia and North Carolina. Its native habitat is along the Coastal Plain in brackish marshes, seacoast woodlands, or hammocks and sandy soils near the coast. This is the most common tree-size palm in Florida and has been designated as the state tree there. It is often cultivated and is an excellent avenue tree. Tolerant of a variety of soils, the cabbage palmetto will also grow in either sun or shade. Flowering is in spring, and the fruits mature in the fall of the same year.

Appearance: *medium to tall tree to 25 m (82 ft),* rarely taller, with a tight rounded crown; trunk straight, erect, unbranched,

Cabbage Palmetto

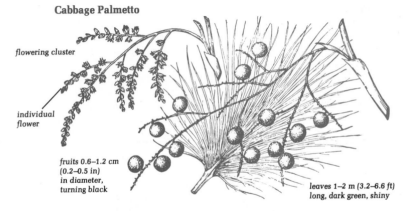

flowering cluster

individual flower

fruits 0.6–1.2 cm (0.2–0.5 in) in diameter, turning black

leaves 1–2 m (3.2–6.6 ft) long, dark green, shiny

to 48 cm (19 in) in diameter, with shallow incomplete rings (leaf scars). **Bark:** tough brown to gray rind, often covered with the persistent, dead leaf bases. **Leaves: *fan-shaped,*** large, the ***blades 1–2 m (3.2–6.6 ft) long,*** rarely larger, almost circular in outline ***but wider than long,*** divided into numerous hanging segments, ***dark green and shiny above,*** paler beneath; the ***leafstalks stiff, 2–2.3 m (6.5–7.5 ft) long,*** flattened above, ***unarmed.*** **Flowers:** produced in large, broad, branched, hanging clusters to 2 m (6.6 ft) long; individual flowers bisexual, white to yellowish-white, 5–6 mm (0.2 in) across; the sepals short, 1.5–2 mm (0.1 in) long, broadest at the base and pointed at the tip; the petals 3–4 mm (0.1–0.2 in) long, united at the base; stamens 6, pistil 1. **Fruits:** numerous, almost globe-shaped to broadest above the middle, ***0.6–1.2 cm (0.2–0.5 in) in diameter,*** dry, smooth, ***turning almost black at maturity.*** **Seeds:** 1 per fruit, shiny, brown.

Bush Palmetto *Sabal minor* (Jacq.) Persoon

This small palmetto is native to the Coastal Plain from South Carolina to southeastern Texas and north along the Mississippi Valley to southeastern Arkansas. In its eastern range, it is usually a bush and develops no trunk above ground. In its western range it may become a small tree. It normally occurs on alluvial soils of floodplains and on sandy soils including pinelands. Flowering is in June or early July, and the fruits ripen in October or November. Although the dried leaves are used occasionally for thatch roofs for huts, this tree is of no economic value and of limited use to wildlife.

Appearance: bush or small tree to 2 or 3 m (6.5–10 ft) with a rounded crown; trunk straight, short, stout, unbranched, to 30 cm (12 in) in diameter. **Bark:** a tough, grayish-brown, rough rind. **Leaves:** fan-shaped, large, the **blade 1–1.5 m (3.2–4.9 ft) long,** almost circular in outline, divided to or below the middle into numerous segments, **bluish-green,** paler beneath; the **leafstalks stout, 1–1.5 m (3.2–4.9 ft) long, concave** on the upper surface, unarmed. **Flowers:** produced in large, branched, elongated clusters to 1 m (3.3 ft) long; individual flowers bisexual, white, 5–7 mm (0.2–0.3 in) across; the 3 sepals only 1.5–2 mm (0.1 in) long, broadest at the base; the petals 3–4 mm (0.1–0.2 in) long; the 6 stamens united with the petals; pistil 1. **Fruits:** numerous, nearly globe-shaped, **8–10 mm (0.3–0.4 in) in diameter, dry, turning brown to black at maturity.** **Seeds:** 1 per fruit, reddish-brown.

Texas Palmetto

Sabal texana (C.F. Cook) Becc.

The Texas palmetto is restricted to the lower Rio Grande Valley in extreme southern Texas and in northeastern Mexico. This medium-size tree is used occasionally as a street tree in southern Texas. The leaves can be used for baskets, chair seats, or thatch. This palm grows **to 15 m (50 ft) high** with a stout, column-shaped trunk and a dense rounded crown of fan-shaped leaves. The persistent **yellow-green leaves reach 2 m (6.6 ft) long;** they are divided to or below the middle, and they have stout leafstalks as long as the blades. The flowers are

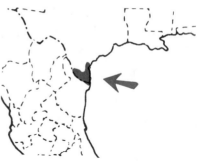

produced in large, branched—somewhat flattened—clusters to 2.5 m (8.2 ft) long. Individual flowers are bisexual, small, white, fragrant, and the fruits are **small, globe-shaped or nearly so, usually 2- or 3-lobed, 2–2.5 cm (0.8–1 in) in diameter, dry,** sweet, turning black at maturity.

The Thatch Palm Genus

Thrinax Sw.

The thatch palms are a small genus of trees native to the West Indies, adjacent Central America, and extreme southern Florida. There are 2 species in North America, and both of these are confined to southern Florida and the Keys. They are attractive small trees that are related to the silver thatch palm (*Coccothrinax*) but can be distinguished from it by their forked or split leaf bases. These palms are of limited economic importance and of little value to wildlife.

Thatch palms are small slender trees without spines and with almost rounded, fan-shaped leaves. The leaves consist of a many-folded blade that is usually split to past the middle of the leaf. The leafstalks are long, slender, often drooping, and split to form a forked base. The bisexual flowers are produced on large, elongated, branched flower clusters. Flowering is in spring (May and June), and the individual flowers are white; sepal and petals are 6-parted, with 6 stamens and a single pistil. The fruits are small, berry-like, ivory-white, bitter, and contain a single seed.

Key to Thatch Palm Species

A. Leaves pale green above and silvery white beneath; flowers and fruits without a stalk
   Brittle thatch palm, p. 930
B. Leaves shiny green above and pale green beneath; flowers and fruits stalked
   Florida thatch palm, p. 931

Brittle Thatch Palm
Florida Thatch Palm

Brittle Thatch Palm
Thrinax morrisii H. Wendl.
(synonyms: *Thrinax microcarpa* Sarg., *T. keyensis* Sarg.)

The brittle thatch palm is a small tree native to southern Florida, including the Keys, and the larger West Indian islands. It grows in dry coral soils or pineland sand, often in hammocks and along coastal shores. Sometimes the trees are planted as ornamentals, but they are of little importance. In the West Indies, the dried leaves are used occasionally for brooms or roof thatch.

Brittle Thatch Palm

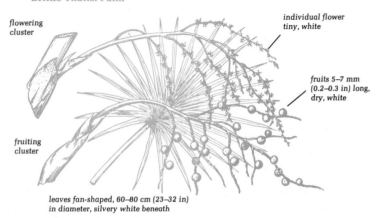

flowering cluster

individual flower tiny, white

fruits 5–7 mm (0.2–0.3 in) long, dry, white

fruiting cluster

leaves fan-shaped, 60–80 cm (23–32 in) in diameter, silvery white beneath

Appearance: small tree to 12 m (40 ft), slender, column-shaped, with a small, rounded, open crown; trunk unbranched, narrow, to 25 cm (10 in) in diameter. **Bark:** a thin gray to brownish-gray, smooth rind, younger trees often covered with rough matted fibers from the bases of the leaves. **Leaves: *fan-shaped,*** the **blades 60–80 cm (23–32 in) in diameter,** circular in outline, ***divided nearly to the base,*** pale green above, ***silvery white beneath;*** the leafstalks stiff, 0.6–1 m (1.9–3.3 ft) long, flattened on the upper surface, unarmed. **Flowers:** produced on many-flowered, elongated, branched clusters 1–2 m (3.2–6.6 ft) long; the immature flowers enclosed in a narrow, boat-shaped sheath; the individual flowers bisexual, ivory-white, fragrant, the sepals and petals forming a small tubular flower with 6 stamens and a single pistil. **Fruits:** numerous, ***rounded, 5–7 mm (0.2–0.3 in) long,*** without a stalk, ***dry, white at maturity.*** **Seeds:** 1 per fruit, smooth, rounded, 4–6 mm (0.1–0.2 in) in diameter, chestnut brown.

Florida Thatch Palm   *Thrinax radiata* Lodd. ex Schult. & Schult.

(synonyms: *Thrinax parviflora* Sw.,
T. floridana Sarg., *T. wendlandiana* Becc.)

The Florida thatch palm is a small tree native to southern Florida, the Keys, the West Indies, Yucatan, and Belize. It is found mainly in hammocks and along rocky shores. Its distinguishing features are the large, fan-like leaves that are pale green beneath; long branched flower clusters; and small whitish, dry fruits.

Appearance: small slender tree to 10 m (33 ft), column-shaped, with a small rounded crown; trunk unbranched, narrow, to 15 cm (6 in) in diameter. **Bark:** a gray rind, often with the persistent dead leaf base on the upper half. **Leaves: *fan-shaped,*** the **blades 0.8–1.2 m (2.6–3.9 ft) in diameter,** circular in outline, ***divided to the middle into numerous stiff segments,***

yellowish-green and shiny above, pale green beneath; the leafstalks stout, 1–1.5 m (3.2–4.9 ft) long, flattened on the upper surface, unarmed. **Flowers:** produced on many-flowered, long, narrow, branched clusters 1–1.3 m (3.2–4.3 ft) long; the immature flowers enclosed in a narrow, boat-shaped sheath; the individual flowers bisexual, white, fragrant, ***short-stalked,*** the sepals and petals forming a very small cup-shaped flower with 6 stamens and a single pistil. **Fruits:** numerous, almost rounded, 1–1.4 cm (0.4–0.6 in) in diameter, ***short-stalked,*** smooth, dry, white at maturity. **Seeds:** 1 per fruit, rounded, 9–12 mm (0.4–0.5 in) in diameter, dark brown.

The Silver Thatch Palm Genus   *Coccothrinax* Sarg.

The silver thatch palms are a small genus with all members occurring in the Western Hemisphere tropics and with a single species, the Florida silver palm, in southern Florida. These palms grow in limestone soils and do well in partial shade. They are similar to the thatch palms except that they have dark purple fruits and unforked leaf bases. They are of little economic importance; the leaves are used occasionally for making baskets or hats.

These palms are small unarmed (without spikes) trees with slender trunks and rounded, fan-shaped leaves. The leaves consist of a multi-folded blade that is deeply split and silvery white on the underside. The leafstalks are long, slender, and unbranched but are often covered with a sheath of coarse fibers at the base. The flowers, which contain both sexes, are produced on elongated, slender, hanging, branched clusters. Individual flowers are small and white; the sepals and petals are united into a cup-shaped structure, with 6 to 12 stamens and a single pistil. The fruits are small, nearly globe-shaped berries that are purple to black.

Florida Silver Palm   *Coccothrinax argentata* (Jacq.) Bailey

The Florida silver palm is a small tree native to pinelands and sandy flats in southern Florida (including the Keys), the Bahamas, and the West Indies. It usually is found growing in limestone soils. The deep silver cast on the lower surface, together with the unarmed, fan-shaped leaves, readily separates this palm from all other native palms. In some of the West Indian Islands, the leaves are used for making mats, baskets, or hats.

Appearance: small column-shaped tree to 8 m (27 ft) high, with a rounded crown; trunk straight, unbranched, to 15 cm (6 in) in diameter. **Bark:** a smooth rind, light gray. **Leaves:** *fan-shaped,* the blades *45–60 cm (17–24 in) in diameter, circular in*

Florida Silver Palm

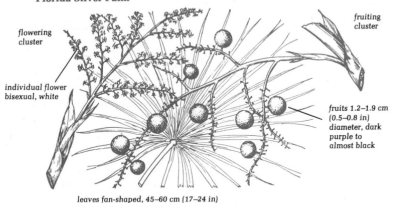

flowering cluster

individual flower bisexual, white

fruiting cluster

fruits 1.2–1.9 cm (0.5–0.8 in) diameter, dark purple to almost black

leaves fan-shaped, 45–60 cm (17–24 in)
in diameter, bright silvery white beneath

outline, divided below the middle, pale yellow-green and shiny above, *bright silvery-white beneath;* the leafstalks slender, 0.7–1 m (2.3–3.3 ft) long, unarmed. **Flowers:** produced on many-flowered, elongated, branched clusters 2.4–3 m (7.9–9.8 ft) long; the immature flowers (buds) enclosed in a narrow, boat-shaped bract; the individual flowers bisexual, white, small; the sepals and petals united into a cup-shaped structure with 6 to 12 stamens and a single pistil. **Fruits:** numerous, *berry-like, globe-shaped, 1.2–1.9 cm (0.5–0.8 in) in diameter, fleshy, turning dark purple to almost black at maturity.* **Seeds:** 1 per fruit, globe-shaped, light brown.

Trees in Winter

To survive, trees must adapt to seasons and climates. In North America maximum growth of branchlets and the production of new leaves — and usually flowers — occur during warm spring days. Summer growth continues at a slower pace. This is especially so in some species because energy is diverted into fruit production.

In autumn, colder temperatures and shorter days trigger a remarkable phenomenon in most hardwoods and in the few deciduous conifers. The leaves stop producing food and instead form a seal (abscission layer) at the point where the leafstalk is attached to the branchlets, causing the leaf and stalk to fall away. The trees then become dormant. By then most of the sap has descended, and the metabolic functions have slowed almost to a standstill. This makes the tree relatively resistant to damage from freezing temperatures.

By winter's onset, the twigs have buds that house the embryonic stems, leaves, and — sometimes — flowers of the next season. The types and configurations of buds and leaf scars, as well as other twig features, aid in the identification of genus and, often, species.

The Winter Key. The following key offers contrasting pairs of descriptions with illustrations to help you identify the more commonly encountered deciduous trees, primarily of the eastern and midwestern U.S. In most cases, the key shows species that are representative of all or part of their genus. In larger genera, such as oaks, the large number of species with closely similar features makes identification of species difficult and beyond the scope of this key. Yet in the case of oaks and other genera, you can consult the appropriate genus sections earlier in the book to help determine the species or at least narrow down the possibilities.

All evergreen species of conifers and hardwoods are omitted from this key because they are fully described in keys that occur earlier in the book. Also omitted are rare genera and species occurring only in small regions.

How to identify trees in winter. You will find it helpful to use a sharp knife or razor blade and a 10× hand magnifier. Here are suggested steps:

1. Remove an end portion of a branchlet (about 12 cm; 5 in), checking to be sure it is not dead or damaged, or deformed by insects or browsing animals.

2. Observe! Are the leaf scars and side buds opposite each other or alternate along the twigs? Note any spines or thorns, especially near the leaf scars. Is an end, or terminal, bud present or absent? If present, is it covered by a single cone-shaped scale, 2 scales, or 3 or more overlapping scales? Occasionally, the embryonic leaves will be without scales (naked).

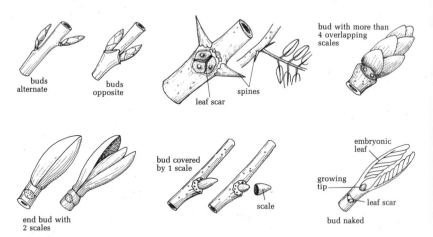

3. Examine the leaf scars with your hand magnifier to observe the sealed ends (bundle traces) of the vascular tissues that once supplied the leaf with water and nutrients. The common number of traces is 3, although 1, 5, 7, and 9 occur too. Infrequently, there will be many traces scattered in no discernable pattern, as in the magnolias.

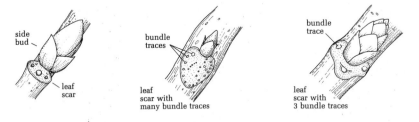

4. Cut lengthwise halfway through the twig to expose a section of the central pith. Is the pith chambered or diaphragmed? If not, the pith is called continuous.

5. Note whether the freshly cut twigs have a distinctive odor or fragrance.
6. Proceed to the brief key that follows on the major groups of trees.

Winter Key to Hardwoods

(groups in leafless condition)

A. Winter branchlets with opposite leaf scars   **Group 1, p. 935**
B. Winter branchlets with alternate leaf scars.
  1. Branchlets with spines (armed), thorns or tiny scales   **Group 2, p. 936**
  2. Branchlets without spines (unarmed).
    a. Branchlets with a spicy, wintergreen, or pungent odor when crushed or broken   **Group 3, p. 936**
    b. Branchlets without a distinct odor when broken or crushed.
      (1) Branchlets with chambered or diaphragmed pith, sometimes only near leaf scars   **Group 4, p. 936**
      (2) Branchlets with continuous pith.
        (a) Winter buds covered with a single scale or naked or indistinctly scaly   **Group 5, p. 937**
        (b) Winter buds covered with 2 to many scales.
          (b1) Leaf scars with 1 bundle-trace scar, sometimes U-shaped   **Group 6, p. 937**
          (b2) Leaf scars with 3 to many bundle-trace scars.
            (b2a) End (terminal) buds present   **Group 7, p. 938**
            (b2b) End buds absent   **Group 8, p. 938**

Group 1: Winter branchlets with opposite leaf scars.
A. Winter buds covered with 2 scales

Flowering dogwood
Dogwood Genus, p. 697

Silver buffaloberry
Buffaloberry Genus, p. 690

Nannyberry, p. 900
Viburnum Genus in part, p. 897 *
(see also B2 below)

Striped maple, p. 779
Maple Genus in part, p. 775 *
(see also B2 below)

B. Winter buds covered with 4, 6, or more scales
  1. End (terminal) buds absent

Common elderberry
Elder Genus, p. 893

Northern catalpa
Catalpa Genus, p. 878

Button bush
Button Bush Genus, p. 885

American bladdernut
Bladdernut Genus, p. 756

  2. End buds present

Red maple, p. 784

Horsechestnut
Buckeye Genus, p. 767

Fringetree
Fringetree Genus, p. 857

Sugar maple, p. 789

Black ash
Ash Genus, p. 861

Wahoo
Euonymus Genus, p. 715

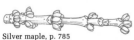

Silver maple, p. 785
Maple Genus in part, p. 775 *
(see also A above)

European buckthorn
Buckthorn Genus, p. 746

Viburnums, pp. 897–901
Viburnum Genus in part, p. 897 *
(see also A above)

California Privet
Privet Genus, p. 856

---

*Consult the page noted in the species label. The "in part" page reference in the genus label reminds you that the genus is represented by another twig or twigs elsewhere in these keys.

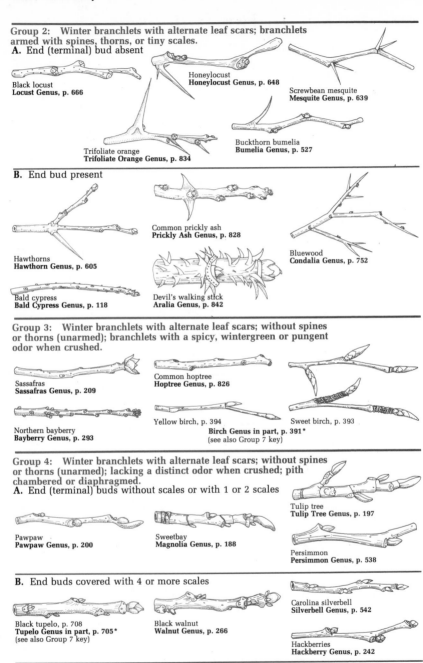

Group 2: Winter branchlets with alternate leaf scars; branchlets armed with spines, thorns, or tiny scales.

A. End (terminal) bud absent

Black locust
Locust Genus, p. 666

Honeylocust
Honeylocust Genus, p. 648

Screwbean mesquite
Mesquite Genus, p. 639

Trifoliate orange
Trifoliate Orange Genus, p. 834

Buckthorn bumelia
Bumelia Genus, p. 527

B. End bud present

Common prickly ash
Prickly Ash Genus, p. 828

Hawthorns
Hawthorn Genus, p. 605

Bluewood
Condalia Genus, p. 752

Bald cypress
Bald Cypress Genus, p. 118

Devil's walking stick
Aralia Genus, p. 842

Group 3: Winter branchlets with alternate leaf scars; without spines or thorns (unarmed); branchlets with a spicy, wintergreen or pungent odor when crushed.

Sassafras
Sassafras Genus, p. 209

Common hoptree
Hoptree Genus, p. 826

Yellow birch, p. 394
Birch Genus in part, p. 391*
(see also Group 7 key)

Sweet birch, p. 393

Northern bayberry
Bayberry Genus, p. 293

Group 4: Winter branchlets with alternate leaf scars; without spines or thorns (unarmed); lacking a distinct odor when crushed; pith chambered or diaphragmed.

A. End (terminal) buds without scales or with 1 or 2 scales

Tulip tree
Tulip Tree Genus, p. 197

Pawpaw
Pawpaw Genus, p. 200

Sweetbay
Magnolia Genus, p. 188

Persimmon
Persimmon Genus, p. 538

B. End buds covered with 4 or more scales

Carolina silverbell
Silverbell Genus, p. 542

Black tupelo, p. 708
Tupelo Genus in part, p. 705*
(see also Group 7 key)

Black walnut
Walnut Genus, p. 266

Hackberries
Hackberry Genus, p. 242

---

*Consult the page noted in the species label. The "in part" page reference in the genus label reminds you that the genus is represented by another twig or twigs elsewhere in these keys.

Group 5: Winter branchlets with alternate leaf scars; without spines or thorns (unarmed); lacking a distinct odor when crushed; pith continuous; winter buds covered with a single scale, or naked or indistinctly scaly.

A. End (terminal) bud present

  1. Buds covered with 1 scale

Weeping willow
Willow Genus, p. 472

Paper mulberry
Paper Mulberry Genus, p. 263

American sycamore
Sycamore Genus, p. 219

  2. Buds naked, lacking scales

Witch hazel
Witch Hazel Genus, p. 226

B. End bud absent

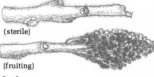

(sterile)

(fruiting)

Yellowwood
Yellowwood Genus, p. 659

Kentucky coffee tree
Coffee Tree Genus, p. 651

Staghorn sumac
Sumac Genus, p. 799

Group 6: Winter branchlets with alternate leaf scars; without spines or thorns (unarmed); without a distinct odor when crushed; pith continuous; buds covered with 2 scales; leaf scars with 1 bundle trace, sometimes U-shaped.

A. Winter buds covered with only 2, rarely 3, scales

Sweet pepperbush
Pepperbush Genus, p. 509

Crape myrtle
Crape Myrtle Genus, p. 672

Cliffrose
Cliffrose Genus, p. 560

B. Winter buds covered with 4 to many scales

Common winterberry
Holly Genus, p. 719

Oleaster
Oleaster Genus, p. 691

European larch
Larch Genus, p. 76

Sourwood
Sourwood Genus, p. 513

*Consult the page noted in the species label. The "in part" page reference in the genus label reminds you that the genus is represented by another twig or twigs elsewhere in these keys.

Group 7: Winter branchlets with alternate leaf scars; without spines or thorns (unarmed); without a distinct odor when crushed; pith continuous; buds with 2 to many scales; leaf scars with 3, 5, 7, 9 or many traces; end buds present.

A. Winter buds covered with usually 2 or occasionally 3 scales

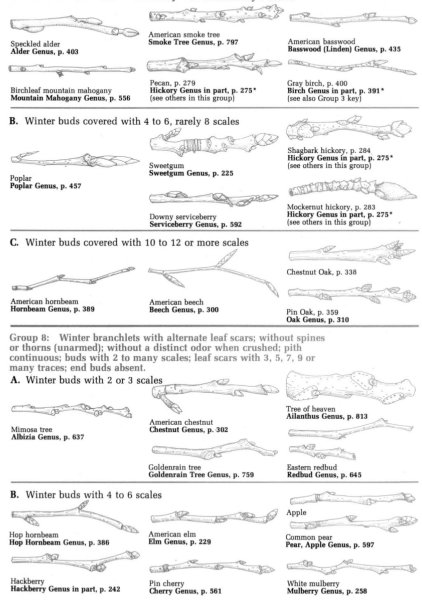

Speckled alder
Alder Genus, p. 403

American smoke tree
Smoke Tree Genus, p. 797

American basswood
Basswood (Linden) Genus, p. 435

Birchleaf mountain mahogany
Mountain Mahogany Genus, p. 556

Pecan, p. 279
Hickory Genus in part, p. 275*
(see others in this group)

Gray birch, p. 400
Birch Genus in part, p. 391*
(see also Group 3 key)

B. Winter buds covered with 4 to 6, rarely 8 scales

Poplar
Poplar Genus, p. 457

Sweetgum
Sweetgum Genus, p. 225

Shagbark hickory, p. 284
Hickory Genus in part, p. 275*
(see others in this group)

Downy serviceberry
Serviceberry Genus, p. 592

Mockernut hickory, p. 283
Hickory Genus in part, p. 275*
(see others in this group)

C. Winter buds covered with 10 to 12 or more scales

American hornbeam
Hornbeam Genus, p. 389

American beech
Beech Genus, p. 300

Chestnut Oak, p. 338

Pin Oak, p. 359
Oak Genus, p. 310

Group 8: Winter branchlets with alternate leaf scars; without spines or thorns (unarmed); without a distinct odor when crushed; pith continuous; buds with 2 to many scales; leaf scars with 3, 5, 7, 9 or many traces; end buds absent.

A. Winter buds with 2 or 3 scales

Mimosa tree
Albizia Genus, p. 637

American chestnut
Chestnut Genus, p. 302

Tree of heaven
Ailanthus Genus, p. 813

Goldenrain tree
Goldenrain Tree Genus, p. 759

Eastern redbud
Redbud Genus, p. 645

B. Winter buds with 4 to 6 scales

Hop hornbeam
Hop Hornbeam Genus, p. 386

American elm
Elm Genus, p. 229

Apple

Common pear
Pear, Apple Genus, p. 597

Hackberry
Hackberry Genus in part, p. 242

Pin cherry
Cherry Genus, p. 561

White mulberry
Mulberry Genus, p. 258

*Consult the page noted in the species label. The "in part" page reference in the genus label reminds you that the genus is represented by another twig or twigs elsewhere in these keys.

Index